OXFORD MEDIEVAL TEXTS

General Editors
D. E. GREENWAY   B. F. HARVEY
M. LAPIDGE

THE CHRONICLE OF JOHN OF WORCESTER

THE CHRONICLE OF JOHN OF WORCESTER

VOLUME II

THE ANNALS FROM 450 TO 1066

EDITED BY

R. R. DARLINGTON†
AND
P. McGURK

TRANSLATED BY

JENNIFER BRAY†
AND
P. McGURK

CLARENDON PRESS · OXFORD
1995

Oxford University Press, Walton Street, Oxford OX2 6DP

Oxford New York

Athens Auckland Bangkok Bombay
Calcutta Cape Town Dar es Salaam Delhi
Florence Hong Kong Istanbul Karachi
Kuala Lumpur Madras Madrid Melbourne
Mexico City Nairobi Paris Singapore
Taipei Tokyo Toronto

and associated companies in
Berlin Ibadan

Oxford is a trade mark of Oxford University Press

Published in the United States
by Oxford University Press Inc., New York

British Library Cataloguing in Publication Data
Data available

Library of Congress Cataloging in Publication Data
Data applied for
ISBN 0–19–822261–0

1 3 5 7 9 10 8 6 4 2

Typeset by Hope Services (Abingdon) Ltd.
Printed in Great Britain on acid-free paper by
Biddles Ltd., Guildford & King's Lynn

PREFACE

On his death in 1977, R. R. Darlington left behind a draft text of the annals for 450 to 1066 of the chronicle of John of Worcester with a full critical apparatus and detailed historical notes for the annals to 901. I prepared Darlington's text to meet the conventions of the Oxford Medieval Texts, completed and revised his historical notes, and contributed the appendices on the Abingdon and Bury interpolations (Appendices A and B); I am also responsible for the introduction and for the palaeographical judgements on which it and much of the critical apparatus are based. A preliminary draft of half the translation was prepared by the late Jennifer Bray.

The chronicle will be published in three volumes. The present vol. ii covers the annals for 450 to 1066. Vol. iii will appear next and will give the annals for 1067 to 1140. Vol. i will be published last. It will provide a general introduction, an edition of the episcopal lists, of the royal genealogies and accounts, and some indication of the contents of the chronicle before 450 and of the earlier books in the Marianus world history on which the chronicle of John of Worcester is largely based. The introduction will examine the sources used by John, consider his method and the value of his work, and assess its reception in the twelfth and thirteenth centuries. The supplementary annals prepared by John for the self-styled *chronicula* (Dublin, Trinity College MS 503), which is itself closely related to his main chronicle, will be edited separately in an appendix to vol. i.

Darlington would have wished to acknowledge a debt to Dorothy Whitelock, who read and commented upon the annals to 901. I have incurred many more obligations. Over the years both staff and students of the History Department at Birkbeck College have offered stimulus and support. Christopher Brooke first suggested the chronicle's inclusion in this series, and encouraged its progress with much kindness and patience. David Dumville has assisted in many ways: it was characteristic of him (in response to

a tentative enquiry) to send, by return of post, full print-outs of all the Asser transcripts. Diana Greenway, Barbara Harvey and Michael Lapidge have been vigilant editors, and an enormous debt is owed Michael Lapidge in the final preparation of the text for the press. Among others who have helped in particular ways I might mention Bruce Barker-Benfield, Arno Borst, Paul Fouracre, Simon Keynes, Bernard Meehan, Pamela Selwyn, Colin Tite, and Tessa Webber. Librarians and staff of Corpus Christi College, Oxford, Corpus Christi College, Cambridge, Trinity College, Dublin, Lambeth Palace Library, the British Library and the Bodleian Library have been unfailingly helpful in making possible the examination of their John of Worcester and Marianus manuscripts. Anne Gelling has been courteously efficient in seeing the book through the press. The main debt has been to Martin Brett. He has been firmly and continuously helpful, and without him the enterprise would have proceeded even more slowly and much more uncertainly. At a later stage Leofranc Holford-Strevens improved every part of this volume, removing innumerable errors, offering many helpful suggestions, and making changes of substance. To all I should like to express my warmest thanks. I can only hope that the edition is worthy of the scholar who sadly did not live to complete it.

P. McGURK

26 September 1991

CONTENTS

LIST OF PLATES

ABBREVIATIONS

AC	*Historiæ Anglicanæ circa tempus conquestus Angliæ a Guilielmo Notho, Normannorum duce, Selecta Monumenta: excerpta ex magno uolumine, cui titulus est 'Historiæ Normannorum Scriptores Antiqui', a doctissimo uiro Andrea Duchesne . . . , ed.* Franciscus Maseres (London, 1807), pp. 355–66
ADL	*Annales Domitiani Latini,* ed. F. P. Magoun, Jr, 'Annales Domitiani Latini: an edition', *Mediaeval Studies,* ix (1947), 235–95
AG	*Les Annales de l'Abbaye Saint-Pierre de Jumièges, chronique universelle des origines au XIIIᵉ siècle,* ed. Jean Laporte ([Rouen], 1954).
AMSM	*Chronique de Robert de Torigni, abbé du Mont-Saint-Michel, suivie de divers opuscules historiques de cet auteur et de plusieurs religieux de la même abbaye,* ed. Léopold Delisle, (2 vols., Rouen, 1872–3), ii. 207–30
AS	*Acta Sanctorum,* ed. J. Bollandus *et al.* (Brussels, 1643 ff.)
ASC	Anglo-Saxon Chronicle
ASE	*Anglo-Saxon England*
ASN	D. N. Dumville and M. Lapidge, *The Annals of St Neots with Vita Prima Sancti Neoti,* in Dumville-Keynes, *ASC* xvii (Cambridge, 1984), pp. 1–107
AU	'Annales Uticenses', ed. Léopold Delisle, in *Orderici Vitalis Angligenæ, coenobii Uticensis monachi, Historiæ Ecclesiasticæ Libri Tredecim,* ed. A. Le Prévost (5 vols., Paris, 1835–55), v. 139–73

Anglia Sacra	H. Wharton, *Anglia Sacra* (2 vols., London, 1691)
Anon. hist. abbat.	*Historia Abbatum auctore anonymo* in Plummer, *Bede*, i. 388–404
Anon. uita Cuthberti	*Two Lives of Saint Cuthbert. A Life by an Anonymous Monk of Lindisfarne and Bede's Prose Life*, ed. and trans. B. Colgrave (Cambridge, 1940), pp. 59–139
Asser	*Asser's Life of King Alfred together with the Annals of Saint Neots erroneously ascribed to Asser*, ed. W. H. Stevenson (Oxford, 1904, rev. edn. 1959), pp. 1–96
Bately, *MS A*	*MS A*, ed. J. Bately in Dumville-Keynes, *ASC* iii (Cambridge, 1986)
BCS	W. de Gray Birch, *Cartularium Saxonicum* (3 vols. and index, London, 1885–99)
BHL	[Bollandists], *Bibliotheca Hagiographica Latina*, (2 vols., Brussels, 1899–1901), with suppl. by H. Fros (1986)
Bede, *De temporum ratione, Chronicon*	Bedae, *Chronica Maiora*, in *Chronica Minora*, ed. Theodor Mommsen, (*MGH, Auctores Antiquissimi*, ix, xi, xiii, 3 vols.; Berlin, 1892–8; iii. 246–327
Bede, *Hist. abbat.*	*Historia Abbatum auctore Baeda*, in Plummer, *Bede*, i. 364–87
Bede, *Vita Cuthberti*	*Two Lives of Saint Cuthbert: A Life by an Anonymous Monk of Lindisfarne and Bede's Prose Life*, ed. and trans. B. Colgrave (Cambridge, 1940), pp. 142–307
Brett, 'John of Worcester'	M. Brett, 'John of Worcester and his contemporaries', *The Writing of History in the Middle Ages: Essays presented to Richard William Southern*, ed. R. H. C. Davis and J. M. Wallace–Hadrill (Oxford, 1981), pp. 101–26
Brooks, *Canterbury*	N. Brooks, *The Early History of the Church of Canterbury: Christ Church from 597 to 1066* (Leicester, 1984)
Chronicon de Abingdon	*Chronicon monasterii de Abingdon*, ed. J. Stevenson (2 vols., RS ii; London, 1858), i

Chronicula	*Chronicula* of John of Worcester, in Dublin, Trinity College MS 503
Cont. Bede	*Continuatio Baedae* in *HE*, pp. 572–7
Dialogues	Grégoire le Grand, *Dialogues*, ed. A. de Vogüé (Sources Chrétiennes, cclx, cclxv; 2 vols., Paris, 1979–80)
Die Heiligen Englands	*Die Heiligen Englands*, ed. F. Liebermann (Hanover, 1889)
Dugdale, *Monasticon*	W. Dugdale, *Monasticon Anglicanum*, ed. J. Caley, H. Ellis, and B. Bandinel (6 vols. in 8, London, 1817–30)
Dumville–Keynes, *ASC*	*The Anglo-Saxon Chronicle: A Collaborative Edition*, ed. D. N. Dumville and S. D. Keynes (Cambridge, 1983–)
EHR	*English Historical Review*
Encomium Emmae	*Encomium Emmae Reginae*, ed. A. Campbell (Royal Historical Society, Camden 3rd ser., lxxii; London, 1949)
Epistola Cuthberti	Cuthbert, *Epistola de Obitu Bedae*, in *HE*, pp. 579–87
Felix, *Vita Guthlaci*	*Felix's Life of Saint Guthlac*, ed. and trans. B. Colgrave (Cambridge, 1956)
Flodoard	*Les Annales de Flodoard*, ed. P. Lauer (Paris, 1905)
Freeman, *NC*	E. A. Freeman, *The Norman Conquest*, (3rd edn., 6 vols.; Oxford, 1867–79)
GP	*Willelmi Malmesbiriensis monachi de gestis pontificum Anglorum libri quinque*, ed. N. E. S. A. Hamilton (RS lii; London, 1870)
GR	*Willelmi Malmesbiriensis monachi de gestis regum Anglorum libri quinque*, ed. W. Stubbs (RS xc; 2 vols., London, 1887–9)
HDE	*Historia Dunelmensis Ecclesiae* in *Symeonis monachi opera*, i. 3–160
HE	*Bede's Ecclesiastical History of the English People*, ed. B. Colgrave and R. A. B. Mynors (OMT, Oxford, 1969; rev. edn. 1990)
HR i	*Historia Regum* in *Symeonis monachi opera*, ii. 3–91

HR ii	*Historia Regum* in *Symeonis monachi opera*, ii. 91–5
HR iii	*Historia Regum* in *Symeonis monachi opera*, ii. 98–283
Haddan and Stubbs, *Councils*	A. W. Haddan and W. Stubbs, *Councils and Ecclesiastical Documents relating to Great Britain and Ireland* (3 vols.; Oxford, 1869–78), iii
Handbook of British Chronology	*Handbook of British Chronology*, ed. E. B. Fryde, D. E. Greenway, S. Porter, and I. Roy (3rd edn., London, 1986)
Harmer, *Writs*	F. E. Harmer, *Anglo-Saxon Writs* (Manchester, 1952)
Harrison, *Framework*	K. Harrison, *The Framework of Anglo-Saxon History to A.D. 900* (Cambridge, 1976)
Heads of Religious Houses	*The Heads of Religious Houses: England and Wales 940–1216*, ed. D. Knowles, C. N. L. Brooke and Vera London (Cambridge, 1972)
Hemming	*Hemingi Chartularium Ecclesiae Wigornensis*, ed. T. Hearne (2 vols., Oxford, 1723)
HH, *HA*	*Henrici archidiaconi Huntendunensis historia Anglorum*, ed. T. Arnold (RS lxxiv; London, 1879)
Hincmar, *Vita Remigii*	*Vita Remigii episcopi Remensis auctore Hincmaro*, ed. B. Krusch (*MGH SrM*, iii), pp. 239–341
Historians of the Church of York	*Historians of the Church of York and of its Archbishops*, ed. J. Raine (3 vols., RS lxxi; London, 1879–94)
Hugh of Fleury	*Hugonis Floriacensis monachi Benedictini Chronicon*, ed. B. Rottendorf (Münster, 1638)
JW	John of Worcester
JW *Epis. Lists*	The episcopal lists preceding the chronicle of John of Worcester (to be published in vol. i)
JW *Accounts*	The accounts of the various English kingdoms attached to the genealogical trees, preceding the chronicle of John of Worcester (to be published in vol. i); the numbers refer to the paragraphs in these accounts

JW *Gen.*	The genealogical trees preceding the chronicle of John of Worcester (to be published in vol. i)
JW *Notes*	The notes on particular kings placed around the trees (to be published in vol. i)
K	J. M. Kemble, *Codex Diplomaticus Aevi Saxonici* (6 vols., London, 1839–48)
Keynes, *Diplomas*	S. Keynes, *The Diplomas of King Æthelred 'the Unready' 978–1016* (Cambridge, 1980)
Keynes-Lapidge *Alfred*	S. Keynes and M. Lapidge, *Alfred the Great: Asser's Life of King Alfred and Other Contemporary Sources* (Harmondsworth, 1983)
Lapidge–Winterbottom, *Life*	*Wulfstan of Winchester. The Life of St Æthelwold*, ed. M. Lapidge and M. Winterbottom (OMT, 1991)
LP	*Liber Pontificalis*, ed. L. Duchesne (2 vols., 2nd edn., Paris 1955; 3rd vol. with Duchesne's additions published by C. Vogel, Paris, 1957)
Levison, *England and the Continent*	W. Levison, *England and the Continent in the Eighth Century* (Oxford, 1946)
Liber Eliensis	*Liber Eliensis*, ed. E. O. Blake (Royal Historical Society, Camden 3rd ser., xcii; London, 1962)
MGH	*Monumenta Germaniae Historica*:
Epp.	*Epistolae*
PLAC	*Poetae Latini Aevi Carolini*
SrM	*Scriptores rerum Merowingicarum*
SS	*Scriptores*
Mar.	Marianus Scottus, *Chronicon*; bk. iii was printed by G. Waitz, *MGH SS* v (1844), 481–562
Memorials Dunstan	*Memorials of St Dunstan, Archbishop of Canterbury*, ed. W. Stubbs (RS lxiii; London, 1874)
Memorials St Edmund's	*Memorials of St Edmund's Abbey*, ed. T. Arnold (3 vols., RS xcvi; London, 1890–6), i

O'Donovan, i.	M. A. O'Donovan, 'An Interim Revision of Episcopal Dates for the Province of Canterbury, 850–950: part i', *ASE* i (1972), 23–44
O'Donovan, ii.	M. A. O'Donovan, 'An Interim Revision of Episcopal Dates for the Province of Canterbury, 850–950: part ii', *ASE* ii (1973), 91–113
PL	*Patrologia Latina*, ed. J.-P. Migne (221 vols.; Paris, 1844–64)
Plummer, *Bede*	C. Plummer, *Venerabilis Baedae Opera Historica* (2 vols., Oxford, 1896)
Plummer, *Chronicle*	C. Plummer and J. Earle, *Two of the Saxon Chronicles Parallel* (2 vols., Oxford, 1892–9, repr. 1952)
Poole, *Studies*	R. L. Poole, *Studies in Chronology and History* (Oxford, 1934)
Robertson, *Charters*	A. J. Robertson, *Anglo-Saxon Charters* (2nd edn., Cambridge, 1956)
Robinson, *Worcester*	J. A. Robinson, *St Oswald and the Church of Worcester* (British Academy, Supplemental Papers, v; London, 1919)
Robinson, *Wells*	J. A. Robinson, *The Saxon Bishops of Wells* (British Academy, Supplemental Papers, iv; London, 1918)
Roger of Wendover	*Rogeri de Wendover Chronicon sive Flores Historiarum*, ed. H. G. Coxe (3 vols., London, 1849)
RS	Rolls Series
S	P. H. Sawyer, *Anglo-Saxon Charters: An Annotated List and Bibliography* (London, 1968)
Scharer	A. Scharer, *Die angelsächsische Königsurkunde im 7. und 8. Jahrhundert* (Vienna, 1982)
Stenton	F. M. Stenton, *Anglo-Saxon England* (3rd edn., Oxford, 1971)
Stephanus, *Vita Wilfridi*	*Vita Wilfridi I episcopi Eboracensis auctore Stephano*, ed. W. Levison in *Passiones*, ed. B. Krusch and W. Levison (*MGH SrM*, vi), pp. 163–263

Stevenson, *Asser*	W. H. Stevenson, *Asser's Life of King Alfred together with the Annals of Saint Neots erroneously ascribed to Asser* (Oxford, 1904; rev. D. Whitelock, 1959)
Symeonis monachi opera	*Symeonis monachi opera omnia*, ed. T. Arnold (2 vols., RS lxxv; London, 1888)
Thorpe	*Florentii Wigorniensis monachi Chronicon ex Chronicis*, ed. B. Thorpe (English Historical Society; 2 vols., London, 1848–9)
Vita Wulfstani	*The Vita Wulfstani of William of Malmesbury*, ed. R. R. Darlington (Royal Historical Society, Camden 3rd ser., xl; London, 1928)
WM	William of Malmesbury
Weaver, *Chronicle of John of Worcester*	*The Chronicle of John of Worcester 1118–40*, ed. J. R. H. Weaver (Anecdota Oxoniensia, 4th ser., xiii; Oxford, 1908)
Whitelock, *ASC*	*The Anglo-Saxon Chronicle: A Revised Translation*, ed. D. Whitelock with David C. Douglas and Susie L. Tucker (London, 1961)
Whitelock, *EHD*	D. Whitelock, *English Historical Documents, c. 500–1042* (2nd edn., London and New York, 1979)
Whitelock, Brett, and Brooke, *Councils*	D. Whitelock, M. Brett, and C. N. L. Brooke, *Councils and Synods with other Documents relating to the English Church, i: A. D. 871–1204* (2 parts, Oxford, 1981)
Winterbottom, *Lives*	*Three Lives of English Saints*, ed. M. Winterbottom (Toronto, 1972)

INTRODUCTION

IF the author of the annals edited in these volumes never expressed the pious hope (as William of Malmesbury did for the biography of Wulfstan of Worcester) that an audience would exist as long as the pole turned the stars and literature survived, his chronicle none the less achieved a tolerable renown.[1] It was well known and frequently used in the twelfth and thirteenth centuries; and it has long been regarded by modern scholars as of value for our knowledge of the Anglo-Saxon period, of the later eleventh century, and of the first forty years of the twelfth. The shortcomings of the only accessible modern text of this chronicle are the justification for a new edition.

The chronicle used to go under the name of Florence of Worcester. It is a world history extending from the beginning of mankind to 1140, the year of the imperfect ending of the main manuscript, Oxford, Corpus Christi College MS 157. If it covers the history of the world, its focus from 450 onwards is English history. Compiled at Worcester in the first half of the twelfth century, its traditional attribution to the monk Florence rests on the laudatory description of him under the annal for 1118 which records his death: 'Non. Iulii obiit Florentius Wigornensis. Huius subtili scientia et studiosi laboris industria preeminet cunctis haec chronicarum chronica.' This attribution to Florence has been questioned for four reasons. First, as has just been seen, the chronicle extends beyond the year of Florence's death (1118) to 1140, and there seems no break in style or approach after 1118. Second, the annals from 1102 incorporate passages from the Canterbury historian Eadmer's *Historia Novorum*, which could not have been inserted before 1122, the year in which that work was completed. Third, Orderic Vitalis, on his visit to Worcester not

---

[1] 'Est enim ex habundanti argumenta querere; ubi et ad credendum fides excitat, et ad legendum materia inuitat. Qua de causa pio patri lectores non defuturos arbitror; dum polus rotabit sidera; dum ulla in mundo erit littera': *Vita Wulfstani*, p. 3, see also p. v.

later than 1124, described a chronicle clearly identical with ours which a monk named John was writing.[2] Finally, in the chief manuscript of the chronicle, this John identifies himself as author in a hexameter ('corrigat ista legens offendit si qua Iohannes') under the annal for 1138. The hand which wrote this annal wrote the annals from 1128 (from the words 'de iuramento') to 1140, and clearly corrected and annotated this principal manuscript. It is therefore reasonable to suppose that this chief manuscript was a fair copy prepared for John, and to assign him a major role in the chronicle's compilation; the part played by Florence remains elusive.[3]

The chronicle survives in five copies and in a single leaf from a sixth, which will all be described below. The chief manuscript, the already mentioned Oxford Corpus manuscript, is a working copy on which, directly or indirectly, the other copies depend, and the transmission of the text, as Dr Brett showed in his pioneering study, can be followed through a close examination of the five copies.[4] Brett distinguished at least three stages in the development of the text, the first two extending to 1131, represented by four derivative chronicle manuscripts, the third extending to at least 1140, witnessed by the present revised state of the Oxford Corpus manuscript.

On his visit to Worcester, Orderic Vitalis said that John was continuing the world chronicle of Marianus Scotus on the orders of Bishop Wulfstan of Worcester, who died in 1095. This world chronicle was the work of the Irish anchorite at Mainz, Marianus, who probably completed it in 1076. It gave (in its original recension) a history of the world from the creation of man to 1076.[5]

[2] *The Ecclesiastical History of Orderic Vitalis*, ed. Marjorie Chibnall, ii (OMT, 1969), 186-8.

[3] Assessments of John's role and of Wulfstan's inspiration were made by R.R. Darlington, *Vita Wulfstani*, pp. xvii f.; id., *Anglo-Norman Historians* (London, 1947), pp. 14-15; Antonia Gransden, 'Cultural transformation at Worcester in the Anglo-Norman period', *British Archaeological Association Conference Transactions*, i: *Medieval Art and Architecture at Worcester Cathedral* (Leeds, 1978), pp. 1-14, at 7; Brett, 'John of Worcester'. [4] Brett, 'John of Worcester'.

[5] The preface and colophon of the Vatican Marianus (MS Pal. lat. 830), suggest a recension in 1076, though the MS apparently transcribed in 1076 seems to copy a draft, of which part at least was written in 1073. The best account of the palaeography of the Vatican MS is still B. Güterbock, 'Aus irischen Handschriften in Turin und Rom', *Zeitschrift für vergleichende Sprachforschung*, xxxiii (1895), 86-105, at pp. 89-100. The recension used by John of Worcester is represented by London, BL Cotton Nero C. V (see p. LXV below); it extended to 1087.

For this it relied on a variety of early Christian and early medieval sources, providing in addition useful and contemporary information on the eleventh-century history of the East Franks and of those Irish who settled among them at that time. Marianus, who argued that the Dionysian era for the Incarnation had been dated twenty-two years too late, dated events after the Christian era by two dates, his own, and the Dionysian. A copy of Marianus' chronicle was brought to England, William of Malmesbury tells us, by Bishop Wulfstan's colleague, Robert of Lorraine, bishop of Hereford, and it was presumably through Hereford that John of Worcester obtained his copy of the Marianan chronicle which provided him with the bulk of his history.[6] It is possible that Wulfstan ordered both the transcription of the world chronicle of Marianus and (as Orderic states) the grafting on to it of an English chronicle. Thus the enterprise apparently started on Wulfstan's orders may have begun before his death in 1095 and continued until at least 1140, the year of the imperfect ending of the Oxford Corpus copy of the chronicle.

If John did add to the Marianan account of world events by occasionally supplementing or correcting Marianus, the main interest of his chronicle is his account of events in England. His chief source till the early twelfth century is the Anglo-Saxon Chronicle.[7] The introduction to vol. i will discuss which versions were used and whether a different or specially confected version lay behind his account, but that his chronicle is never too far from the Anglo-Saxon enterprise a glance at the notes of this edition will show. The only other source identified by John is Bede,

---

[6] GP iv. 164 (p. 300 f). For Robert of Hereford, Marianus, and the chronicle of John, see W. H. Stevenson, 'A contemporary description of the Domesday Survey' EHR, xxii (1907), 73–84. Robert also wrote a chronological treatise, for which see A. Cordoliani, 'L'activité computistique de Robert, évêque de Hereford', Mélanges offerts à René Crozet, ed. Pierre Galais and Yves-Jean Riou (Poitiers, 1966), i. 333–40. Eight copies of this treatise survive. Two were known to Stevenson: Oxford, Bodleian Library, Auct. F.3.14 (Malmesbury) and F.5.19. The six others are Oxford, Bodleian Library, Auct. F.1.9 (in which John of Worcester's hand appears); Cambridge, Trinity College O.7.41; Durham, Dean and Chapter Library, Hunter 100 (excerpted); Glasgow, Hunterian Museum T.4.2; London, BL Cotton Tiberius E. IV; and Egerton 3088. This treatise was sometimes accompanied by Marianus' decennovenal cycles. Though based on Marianus, the treatise is not (as is sometimes implied) an excerpt of his chronicle or of his chronological arguments.

[7] For some discussion, see R. R. Darlington and P. McGurk, 'The "Chronicon ex Chronicis" of "Florence" of Worcester and its use of sources for English history before 1066', Anglo-Norman Studies, v (1982), 185–96.

whose *Historia Ecclesiastica* is the basis of the text in the annals to 731, sometimes supplementing, and sometimes correcting, the Anglo-Saxon Chronicle; on occasion, discrepancies between the two are openly recorded (e.g. 672). Bede's *Historia Abbatum* and *Vita Cuthberti*, as well as the anonymous *Historia Abbatum* and Felix's *Vita Guthlaci*, were also known and used by John. For the years from 847 to 887 Asser's *Vita Ælfredi* was John's main source. As is well known, the only surviving Anglo-Saxon manuscript of Asser's life was lost in the Cotton fire of 1731, and John is an important witness to its text and a crucial aid in any attempted reconstruction. For much of the tenth century and in the early eleventh century, the chronicle is supplemented and stylistically transformed by saints' lives: the lives of Dunstan by B, Adelard, and Osbern, the life of Oswald by Byrhtferth, and the life of Ælfheah by Osbern. These are the main sources for John before 1066, but he makes occasional and fitful use of other texts: for instance, episcopal successions, *passiones* of Æthelbert of Hereford and Kenelm, locally based and probably now lost sources, sources common to him and to other historians like William of Malmesbury, and Coleman's lost life of Bishop Wulfstan. Possibly because of some of these lost sources, from the early eleventh century John gives much supplementary information, whose value has long been acknowledged. After 1066 John continues to attend to the Anglo-Saxon Chronicle, though there are increasing divergences and much additional information.

These then are the main ingredients in the compilation of the first stage of the chronicle. The later stages have been examined by Dr Brett, and will be considered further in this introduction. They are marked by further recourse to sources already used or to the mining of new ones: among others, to some northern annals from 778 to 803, to Hugh of Fleury's *Historia Ecclesiastica*, to some Norman annals, to the *Historia Dunelmensis Ecclesie*, to William of Malmesbury's *Gesta Pontificum*, and to Eadmer's *Historia Novorum*. This recourse can be studied in detail in this edition and will be considered further in the introduction to vol. i.

I. THE MANUSCRIPTS USED IN THIS EDITION

The composition of John of Worcester's chronicle is most profitably approached through the twelfth-century witnesses already mentioned: there are five complete copies, and a single leaf from a sixth. John himself composed and partly transcribed an abbreviated *chronicula*, as he termed it, based on the larger work, which he called the *chronica chronicarum*; this manuscript will be described and its evidence occasionally used in the critical apparatus. A description of the Marianus manuscript, London, British Library, Cotton Nero C. V, which is known to have been at Worcester, though it may not have been John of Worcester's exemplar, is also included. A description of these manuscripts follows, preceded in each case by a brief assessment of the manuscript's chief features.

1. Manuscripts of the Chronicle

The chronicle being a long work, all the manuscripts with the exception of Dublin, Trinity College MS 502, are substantial folio volumes.

C= Oxford, Corpus Christi College 157

This is the chief manuscript of the chronicle; from it were derived, directly or indirectly, the other five witnesses. It was the only one to extend to 1140 where it now ends imperfectly, and to contain revised annals for 1128 to 1131. It was written at Worcester by three scribes, C^1, C^2 and C^3, all three of whom corrected and added to the text, and transformed a fair copy into a working one. The third scribe has been plausibly identified with John of Worcester; the date of his final writing was presumably in or shortly after 1140.

Physical description

329 × 250 (243 × 182). In the chronicle 42 long lines to a page, but two (occasionally three) columns on pp. 77*c*–147, 153–201, 248 ll. 34–251. The preliminary apparatus is normally on 42 lines but varies from long lines to two or many more columns. The scribe who either erased or added whole pages wrote on a varying number of lines, from 38 on p. 76 to 51 on p. 72.

Two flyleaves + 402 pages, which are paginated save for the first two leaves, which are foliated. There are three pp. 77 (77*a–c*); an unnumbered page after p. 189; no p. 266; and an unnumbered leaf after p. 396.

Collation. 1⁴ (lacks 1): fos. 1–2, and pp. 3–4. 2⁸: pp. 5–20. 3⁸: pp. 21–40, though pp. 31–4 form a bifolium inserted later. 4⁶ (lacks 4–6), pp. 41–6 are three single leaves. 5⁴: pp. 47–54. 6⁸: pp. 55–70. 7² (lacks 2): pp. 71–2 is a single leaf. 8⁴: pp. 73–6 (an added bifolium). 9² (lacks 2): pp. 77*a–b* is a single added leaf. 10¹⁰: pp. 77*c*–96. 11–13⁸: pp. 97–144. 14⁴: pp. 145–52. 15–16⁸: pp. 153–84. 17¹⁰: pp. 185–203 (the page after p. 189 is unnumbered). 18⁸ (lacks 1–2): pp. 204–15. 19–20⁸: pp. 216–47. 21¹⁰ (lacks 2, 7, 8): pp. 248–61. 22–3⁸: pp. 262–94 (no p. 266). 24¹⁰ (lacks 1): pp. 295–310. 25⁶: pp. 311–22. 26–7⁸: pp. 323–54. 28¹⁰ (lacks 4, 8): pp. 355–70. 29⁶: pp. 371–82. 30⁶: pp. 383–[98] (leaf after p. 396 is unnumbered; it is not certain that it is conjugate with pp. 383–4).

Contents

fo. 1–p. 3   'De pontificali sede quomodo primitus statuta sit Wigorne et de possessionibus que a regibus subregulis, et a bone recordationis uiris date sunt Wigornensi ecclesie. Egregio Merciorum regi Wlfario qui regum totius Mercie . . . sed eam successor illius Samson episcopus abstulit' (Dugdale, *Monasticon* i. 607–9).

p. 4ᵃ   'Genealogia regum Francorum. Ex genere Priami fuit Meroueus . . . Philippus genuit Lodowicum qui nunc regnat' (VI: 1108–37).

p. 4ᵃ–4ᵇ: 'Genealogia ducum Normannie. Anno ab incarnatione Domini. DCCCLXXVI. Rollo cum suis Normanniam penetrauit. XV. kal. Decembris, et regnauit annis .LIII. . . . huic successit Rotbertus filius eius maior, quo uiuente, adhuc successerat in ducatum frater eius rex Anglorum, Willelmus et eo mortuo rex Heinricus.'

pp. 5–29, l. 16   Consular tables, which are largely based on those at the opening of Marianus' Chronicle; a second set entitled 'alia secundo uestigio emendatio' (according to Jerome) starts at p. 21, l. 13, and

the third ('tertia emendatio secundum Martirologium et passiones paparum et decretales epistolas eorum') on p. 23. The marginal annals are extended and include Worcester entries. The last annal is for 1100, the death of William II.

p. 29, l. 17–34[a] List of popes added by C[3] (on pp. 29–30 over erasure, pp. 31–4 being an inserted bifolium). 'i. Petrus sedit annos .xxv., menses .ii., dies .viii. et passus cum Paulo [?*corr.* from Paulus] .iii. kal. Iul. feria .ii. luna .xxiii.' Paler ink used from '.cli. Siluester Sabiniensis episcopus diebus .lv.' (III: 1045) to '.clxvii. Honorius Ostiensis episcopus' (II: 1124–30). There are traces below the rewriting on pp. 29, 30 of arcades and of columns with papal names arranged in a more congested manner than those erased names which are still visible on p. 35.

p. 35 Framed, erased (but still visible) list of popes, giving names only, and by scribe C[1], end with John XII (955–64).

pp. 36–7[a] Disciples of Christ. 'Nomina .lxx. discipulorum Christi. i. Iacobus iustus . . . lxxii. Philemon. ⟨H⟩i sunt qui electi fuerunt ab apostolis in ordine pro quibus qui recesserant.' This list and those which follow are enclosed in multi–coloured frames; those on p. 45 are different, are only in red, and have arcades.

pp. 37[b]–8 'Nomina Hebreorum pontificum usque ad Salomonis imperium secundum Iosephum hystoriographum', continuing with the bishops of Jerusalem to '.xxviii. Cirillus' (*c.* 349–86).

p. 39 At the top, inscribed in arches over the appropriate columns: 'Cantia', 'East Saxonia', 'East Anglia', 'Suth Saxonia'.

1. 'Nomina archiepiscoporum Dorubernensis ecclesie' to '.xxxiv. Anselmus' (1093–1109) with '.xxxv. Radulfus' (1114–22), added subsequently by scribe C[1], and an unnumbered '⟨W⟩illelmus' (1123–36) added by ?C[3].

2. 'Nomina episcoporum Hrofensis ecclesie' to '.xxii. Radulfus' (1108–14). 'Hic post Anselmum Dorubernie suscepit archipresulatum.' An unnumbered '⟨A⟩rnulfus' (1115–24) added probably by C¹, followed by '⟨I⟩ohannes' (1125–37) added by ?C³.

3. 'Nomina episcoporum Lundoniensis ecclesie' to '.xxxv. Ricardus' (1108–27). An unnumbered '⟨G⟩ilebertus' (1128–34) in capitals, added by ?C³ (apparently over erasure).

4. Note on the coming of Christianity to East Anglia followed by 'Nomina episcoporum East Anglorum' (like some of the others this list has notes on the history of bishoprics and bishops interspersed with the lists) to '.xxv. Herebertus' (1091–1119) followed by an unnumbered '⟨E⟩overardus' (1121–45), in capitals, added (possibly by C³).

5. (a) 'Nomina episcoporum Australium Saxonum. .i. Wilfridus' (d. c.709) (b) 'Nomina episcoporum Sealesiensis ecclesie' to '.xix. Heca' (1047–57). (c) 'Nomina episcoporum Cicestrensis ecclesie' to '.xxii. Radulfus' (1091–1123) followed by an unnumbered '⟨S⟩igefridus' (I: 1125–45) partly in capitals, added by ?C³.)

p. 41   West Saxon bishops. 'Westsaxonia' inscribed at top, and above this, within arcs, 'Suthregia', 'Barrocia', 'Suthamtonia', 'Wilsetania', 'Dorsetania', 'Sumorsetania', 'Domnania'.

1. 'Nomina presulum Dorcestrensis ecclesie' to '.ii. Aegelbrihtus' (c. 660).

2. 'Nomina presulum Wentane civitatis' to '.xxxi. Willelmus' (1107–29), followed by an unnumbered '⟨H⟩einricus' (1129–71) in capitals, added (possibly by C³).

3. 'Nomina episcoporum Sunnungnensis ecclesie' to '.xi. Rogerius' (1107–39).

4. 'Nomina presulum Scireburnensis ecclesie' to '.xxiv. Aluuoldus' (1045–58).

5. 'Nomina presulum Fontaniensis ecclesie' to '.xv. Iohannes' (1088–1122), followed by an unnumbered '⟨G⟩odefridus' (1123–35) partly in capitals, added by ?C³.

6. 'Nomina presulum Cridiatunensis ecclesie' to '.xii. Willelmus' (1107–37).

p. 43 At top are inscribed 'Hecana', 'Hwiccia', 'Mercia', 'Middanglia', 'Lindissis', 'Suthanglia'.

1. 'Nomina praesulum Magesetensium' to '.xxx. Reignelmus' (1107–15) extended to an unnumbered 'Ricardus' (1121–7) by C³, and by another later hand to 'Gilebertus' (1148–63).

2. 'Nomina presulum Huuicciorum' to '.xxvi. Teoulfus' (1115–23), followed by an unnumbered 'Simon' (1125–50), in capitals, added possibly by C¹, 'Iohannes' (1151–7) and 'Aluredus' (1158–60) by another hand, and 'Rogerus' (1164–80) and 'Baldewinus' (1180–4) by yet another.

3. List of four first Mercian bishops to '.iv. Gearoman' (?662–7).

4. 'Nomina episcoporum Licetfeldensium' to '.xxiii. Rotbertus' (1086–1117).

5. 'Nomina episcoporum Leogerensium' (ending with Lincoln bishops after the bishops of Dorchester) to '.xviii. Rotbertus' (1094–1123). '⟨A⟩lexander' (1123–48) is added by C³, and '⟨R⟩otbertus' (1148–66) added by another hand.

6. 'Nomina episcoporum Lindisfarorum' to '.ix. Brihtredus' (836×839–862×866?).

7. 'Nomina episcoporum Dorcestrensium. Aetla.'

p. 45 Right quarter of page has texts mostly taken from Bede on Paulinus, Aidan, and Chad. Remainder of page is divided into five arcaded columns, above which are inscribed in the first line 'Deira', 'Bernicia', and 'Terra Pictorum', and in the second 'Nomina archiepiscoporum et episcoporum Northhumbrane gentis'. (There seems to be an attempt to synchronize the columns.)

1. 'Nomina archiepiscoporum Eboracensium' to '.xxv. Thomas' (1109–14), followed by an unnumbered '⟨T⟩urstinus' (1119–40) in capitals, added by C³.

2. 'Nomina episcoporum Rypensium. .i. Eathed.' (c. 678).

3. 'Nomina episcoporum Hagustaldensium' to '.xiv. Tidferthus' (813).

4. 'Nomina episcoporum Lindisfarnensium' to '.xiv.

Cutheard' (899–*c*.915), followed by list opening with 'Wilredus' and ending with '⟨R⟩annulfus' (1099–1128) added by ?C³ (fourteen names in all, of which the first ten are over erasure with erased red numerals and initial letters just visible).

5. 'Nomina episcoporum Candide Case' to '.vii. Heathoredus' (803×?).

p. 47 Genealogical tree from Adam to the sons of Woden, six of whom are named as ancestors of the royal dynasties of Kent, East Anglia, Mercia, Deira, Wessex (with Bernicia), and Lindsey.

p. 48 Kentish genealogical tree from Wehta to Baldred, and appropriate accounts.

p. 49 Genealogical trees and accounts for the East Anglians (Woden to 'Eadmund') and East Saxons ('Seaxnete' to 'Sigeraed').

p. 50 Mercian genealogical tree from Woden to Ceolwulf and accounts.

p. 51 Lindsey genealogy.

Accounts of the Northumbrian kings, and genealogical tree from Woden to the ancestors of the Deiran, Bernician, and West Saxon kings.

p. 52 Northumbrian genealogical tree from Yffi and Ida to Osbyrht and 'Aelle' and notes on 'Ælle', Edwin, Oswald, Osuuine, Ceolwulf, Eadberht, and Ælfwald (I).

p. 53 West Saxon genealogical tree from Cerdic to 'Aedward' (II) and accounts.

p. 54 Names set out in genealogical form but without the connecting links for (i) the house of Goduuine to Harold (II); (ii) the Norman rulers from Willelm (I) to Heinric (I) and Mathildis with Atheleidis shown as their offspring. By the side, an account of royal succession after the death of Edward the Confessor, ending with Henry I.

p. 55 Short computistical texts, written in two stages, the first group being rubricated, and in a smaller script than the second. An exercise in the first group gives the *annus presens* as the forty-seventh year of the Emperor Henry (IV) and as 1125 (in the Marianus reckoning), and another in the second refers to the first year of the Emperor Charles (possibly Henry V) with the world-year of 5311 (?1106)

pp. 56–69   Nineteen-year tables for 532 years with three cycles of annals entered in the margins, many of which are based on those in Marianus, the last of those added dating 1100.

pp. 70–1   Comparative tables of years from the beginning of the world ('secundum Hebraicam ueritatem, Septuaginta interpretes, Grecorum supputationem et chronicam Eusebii') and from the Incarnation ('secundum Hebraicam ueritatem, Grecorum editionem, cronicam Eusebii quam transtulit Ieronimus, cronicam Eusebii uel sancti Bede, secundum abbatem Dionisium'), and finally two columns, 'anni ab origine mundi rationabiliter probati', and 'anni ab Incarnatione Domini nostri secundum euuangelium'.

p. 71   Table for the day of the week of 1 January for 532 years, arranged in 28 cycles of 19 years each.

pp. 72–7a   Bede, *De locis sanctis*. 'Incipit opusculum Bedae presbiteri impense docti de locis sanctis et de situ Ierusalem. Situs urbis Ierusalem pene . . . studio tibi temperare satagas. De situ terre promissionis Bede presbiteri opusculum explicit feliciter.'

p. 77b   (On the significance of the measurements of the Cross.) '⟨A⟩postolicam sententiam in qua dicitur . . . qua ad caelum ascendamus preparauit Iesus Christus Dominus noster qui cum patre et spiritu sancti uiuat et regnat Deus per omnia saecula saeculorum. amen.'

   Drawing of Crucifixion (which preceded the writing of the text) with a woman on left holding crossed sticks (interpreted as the widow of Sarepta) and a man on the right standing on a large fish (see C. M. Kauffmann, *Romanesque Manuscripts 1066–1190* (London, 1975), no. 55).

pp. 77c–396   Chronicle.

pp. 77c–9   Prologue. 'Incipit inquisitio ubi primum pasca constiterit id est quotis kalendis Christus resurrexit. Diuino informamur precepto . . . ad incarnationem iuxta hystoriam sacri evangelii. Finit prologus.'

pp. 79–86   Chapter-list. 'Incipiunt hic Mariani Scotti cronica

clara . . . ⟨.xcii.⟩ ⟨D⟩e Heinrico pio imperatore.' The list is incomplete, and does not extend as far as that in Marianus. Perhaps the difficulties of deciding on suitable chapter headings for the bulky English material caused the list's temporary abandonment.

p. 89   'Primus liber incipit ab Adam usque ad Christum. Incipit epistola Dionisii Exigui ad Patronium episcopum de ratione pascali. Domino beatissimo et nimium desiderantissimo patri Petronio episcopus.'

p. 396   ends (1140) 'ut si Rotbertus renueret sponte reddere castellum, suspenderetur.'

On pp. 382–3 are the representations of the visions of Henry I and of the storm in which the king was nearly overwhelmed, in which script and pictures are integrated, and which preceded the text (reproduced by J. Weaver, *Chronicle of John of Worcester*, pls. 1–2).

History, script, and date

The history of the manuscript is intermittently recorded on the flyleaves.

fo. iʳ   'Liber Collegii Corpus Christi Oxon ex dono Mri. Henrici Parey art. mag. et eiusdem Coll. socii Julii 8° 1618'. *Trilinguis bibliothecae spectaculum: Some Manuscripts of Corpus Christi College, Oxford Displayed to the Double Crown Club* (Oxford, 1978) identifies him as Henry Parry the Younger (b. ?1594), fellow of Corpus, and an important source of monastic manuscripts generally from the West Country. He was probably the son of the bishop of Worcester of the same name.

(s. xv²): 'memorandum quod frater Thomas S⟨tray⟩nsham deliberauit istum librum fratri Thome Powycke monacho maioris Maluernie. Et ipse deliberauit predicto Thome Straynsham librum uocatum Guido de Bello Troiano anno Domini millesimo .cccc. octogesimo'. Thomas Straynsham was chamberlain of Worcester priory 1482–3.

fo. iʳ   (s.xiv) list of contents.

(s. xvi²) expanded and given folio- and page-references.

(s. xvii, several hands) notes concerning the Bodley witness of Marianus Scotus (MS Bodley 297), and on Bale's consideration of the chronological errors of Marianus

Scotus. On the left is written in pencil, the earlier Corpus shelf mark: 'D.4.5'.

fo. i^v   'no. 1624. 157–D.4.5'.

fo. ii^r   (s. xiv²) notes on episcopal succession at Worcester, and on the translation of the relics of Oswald.

(s. xvii) verses; (s. ?) pencilled note: 'ii + 398 pages'.

Offsets of paste-downs are seen in the inner boards. They are the impressions of two leaves from a fourteenth-century manuscript (a commentary on Aristotle's *Physics*), which are now kept as Corpus MS 490, fo. 17. The same manuscript provided paste-downs for MSS 83, 188, and possibly 59.

There were three main scribes. C¹ wrote most of the codex from p. 5 to p. 363 with the exception of those leaves added or rewritten by C³. C² wrote pp. 364–79, l. 35 ('fere promisit'). C³ wrote p. 379, l. 36 ('De iuramento')–p. 396; p. 4; pp. 29 l. 17 ('Petrus sedit annos')–34; 72–7*b*. All three are responsible for corrections in the text, and marginal additions and emendations, C³ for the greatest number. C³ seems responsible for most of the usually unerased scribbles in the upper margins which indicated the text to be inserted or erased, a practice to which he is unusually prone in his other manuscripts. The opening pages, that is fos. 1–2. pp. 3–4, are written by two other scribes, C⁴ (fos. 1^{r–va} l. 39 ('et liberauit'), 2^v–p. 3) and C⁵ (fos. 1va l. 40 ('Prefatus')–2^r). A few marginal additions were added by single scribes, who are identified in the critical apparatus. C⁶ contributed some marginal notes in the pre-450 section of the chronicle.

The scribe who rewrote the annals for 1128 (from l. 35 'De iuramento')–1131 and continued the chronicle to 1140 has been plausibly identified with the author, John of Worcester, partly because of the hexameter under the annal for 1138. The very informal hand in which these later annals are written is found in two other Worcester manuscripts, Oxford, Bodleian Library, MS Auct. F.1.9 (fos. 2^v–4ra; 4rb l. 18 ('sit pascha')–39^v; 18^r–23^v l. 41 ('luna'); and 25^r–26^r), and Cambridge, University Library, MS Kk.4.6 (fos. 17^{*r}–223^v). This hand shares features with the more formal hand which rewrote some entries, contributed many marginal additions and corrections, and added some texts (e.g. genealogies of the French kings and of the Norman dukes on p. 4, and fuller papal lists on pp. 30–4), and it is reasonable to assume that these were also the work of John. This more formal hand

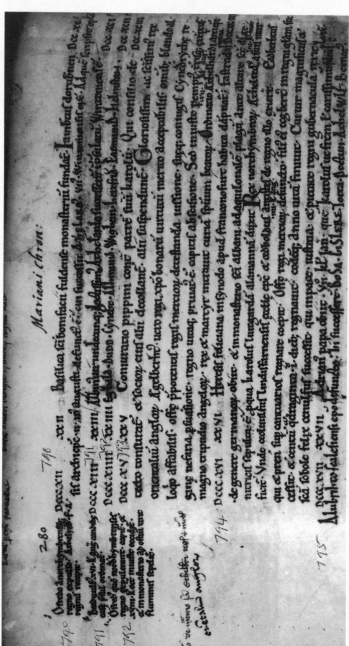

Pl. 1. Oxford. Corpus Christi College MS 157, p. 280 (upper half): annals for 790–5. Scale 1:1.84. Scribe C¹ wrote the annals and the left-hand marginal additions, scribe C³ was responsible for the rewriting under annals 790–2 and 795 and the scribbles in the upper margin indicating the text to be erased under 790–2. The illustrations from the Corpus manuscript are reproduced by kind permission of the President and Fellows of Corpus Christi College, Oxford.

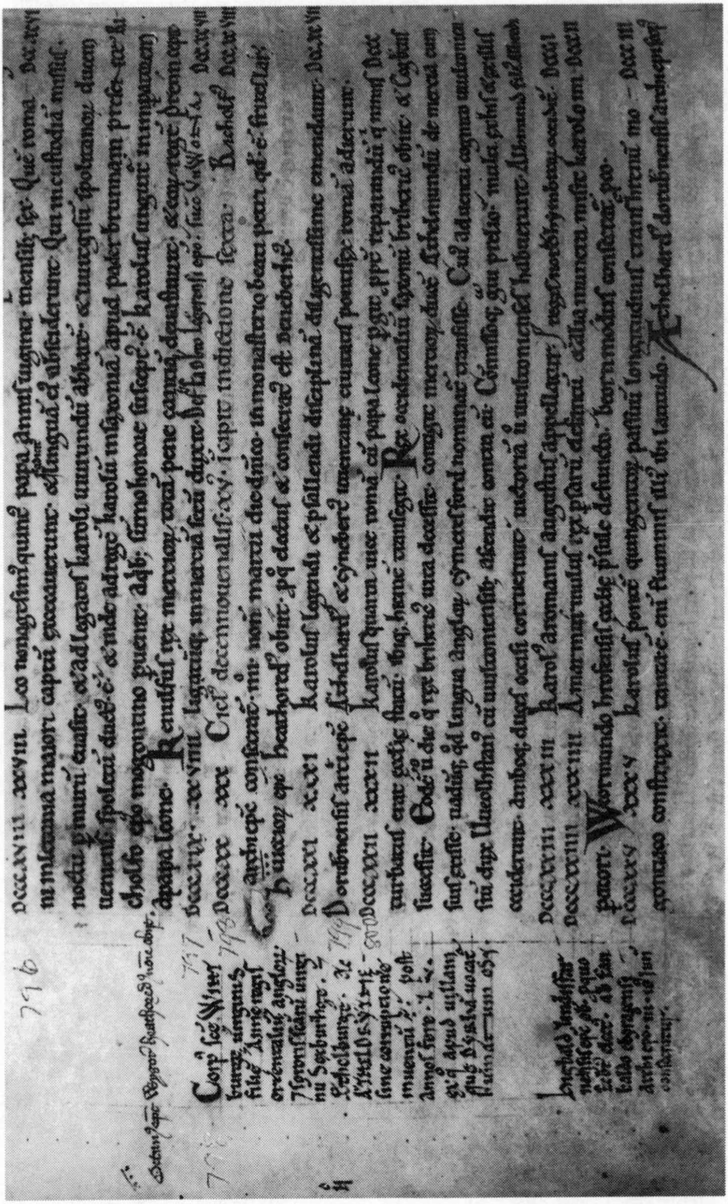

Pl. 2. Oxford. Corpus Christi College MS 157, p. 280 (lower half): annals for 796–803. Scale 1:2.27. Scribe C¹ wrote the annals, scribe C² the lower left marginal addition, scribe C³ the marginal addition above it and the entry on Leicester episcopal succession at the end of 796.

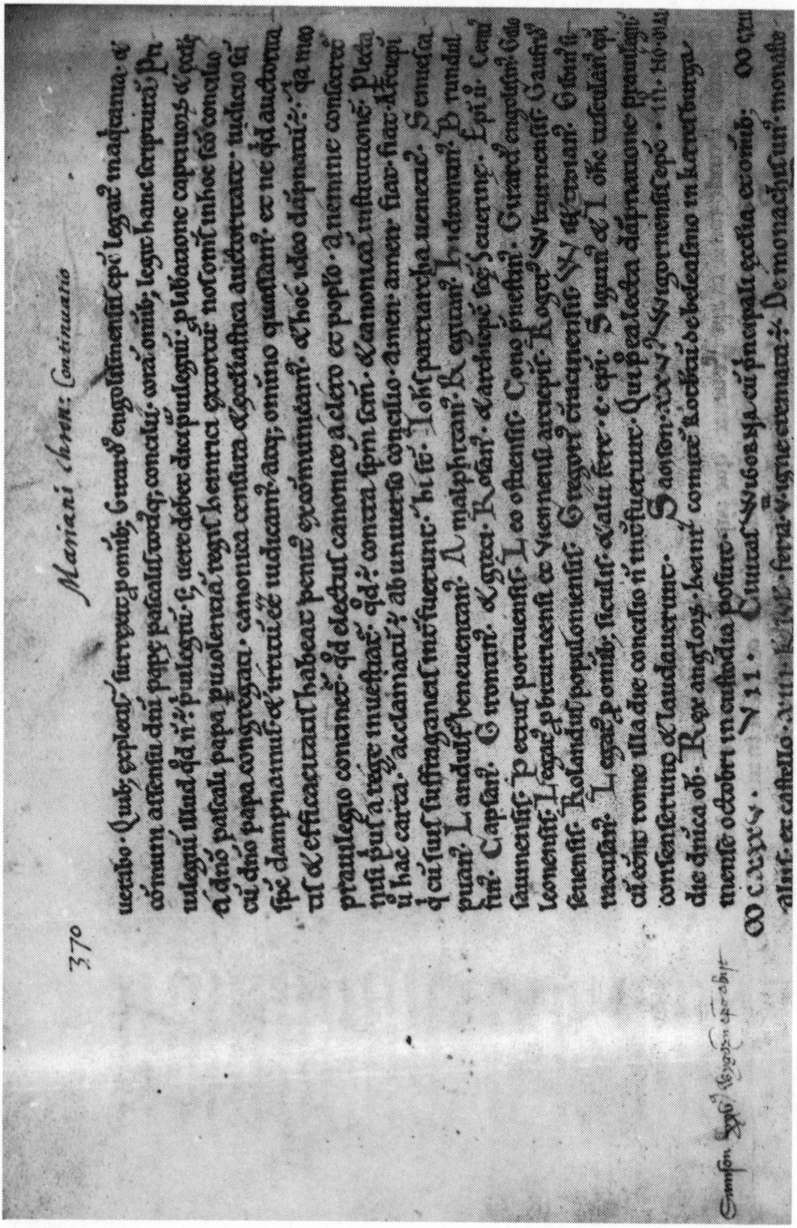

Pl. 3. Oxford. Corpus Christi College MS 157, p. 370 (upper half): part of the annal for 1112. Scale 1:2.1. Scribe C² wrote the text.

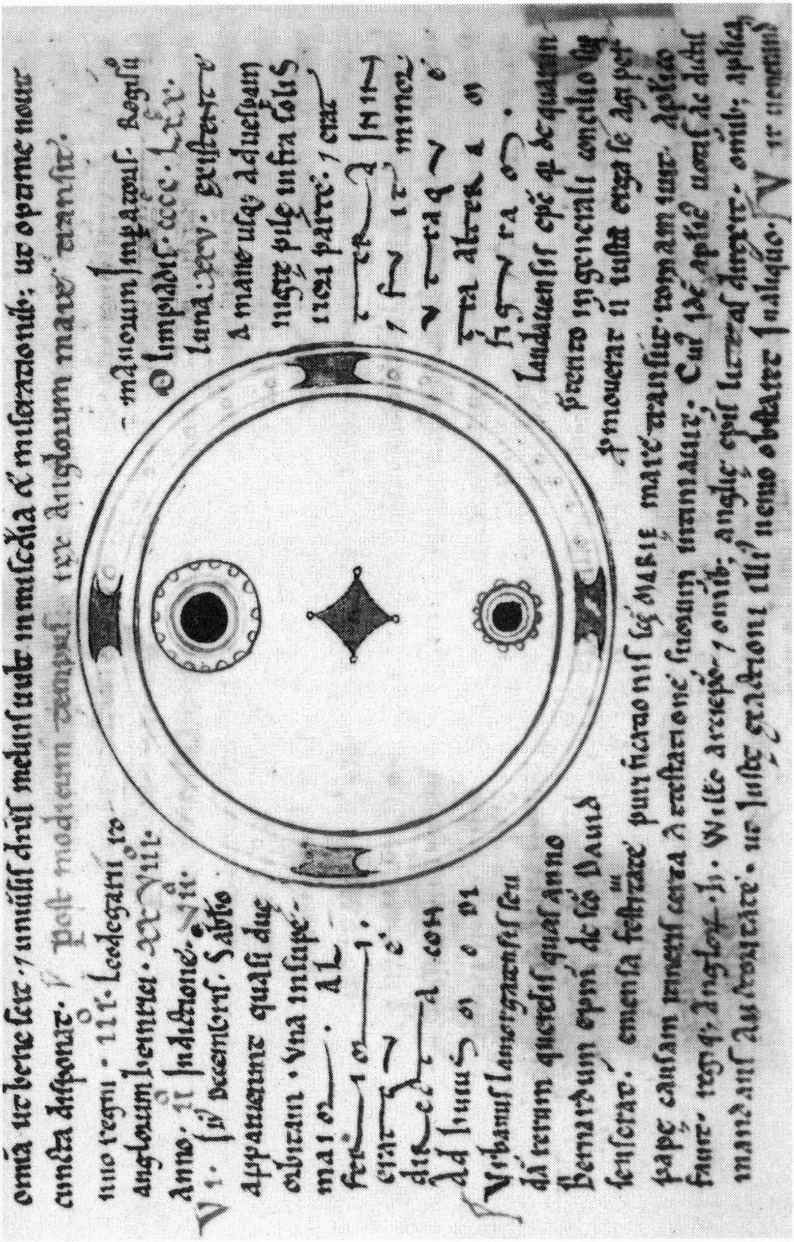

Pl. 4. Oxford. Corpus Christi College MS 157, p. 380 (lower half): part of the annal for 1128. Scale 1:1.38. Scribe C³ wrote the text, which is illustrated by a diagram of sun-spots.

wrote the major part of the *chronicula* (Dublin, Trinity College Library MS 503) and appeared in the two manuscripts already mentioned, as well as probably in the Worcester Passional, London, British Library, MS Cotton Nero E. I, Part I, fos. 53^v–54^v Part II, fos. 156^r–165^r, 174^v–176^v, 187^r–188^v, and many corrections in Part II. In the *Liber Pontificalis* section of Cambridge, Univ. Library, MS Kk.4.6, this scribe exercised a supervisory and correcting role as he came to do in the main chronicle manuscript, collaborating with a scribe with whom he also worked in copying the treatises of Robert of Hereford and of Gerland in the earlier leaves of Bodleian MS Auct. F.1.9. He shared the writing of most of the latter manuscript with C^2, from whom he is not always easily distinguishable.[8]

On pp. 382–3 script and picture seem well integrated, and it is therefore possible that C^3 (or John) was an artist.[9] The style of the Crucifixion on p. 77*b* is very different, and though the text above on the same page seems to be C^3's more formal hand, it would seem unlikely that he drew the scene.

The annals down to 1128 are written by C^1 (Pls. 1–2) and C^2 (Pl. 3); C^3 (Pl. 4) wrote the remainder from early in 1128 (the oath, p. 379, l. 35 'De iuramento') to 1140, the earlier part of C^3's contribution being over erasures. Other John of Worcester manuscripts testify to a version of the annals for 1128–31 which is not now in C, and this version must have lain underneath the erasures of C^3. It is therefore possible that the main body of C was written in 1131, or, alternatively, in the course of 1128–31, there being no strong evidence that the text before 1128 was written gradually, year by year or period by period.[10] Episcopal lists are an uncertain guide to the dating of manuscripts, but the list of contents above shows that the latest bishops in the original were Ralph, archbishop of Canterbury, who was translated from Rochester in 1114, and Theulf of Worcester, appointed in 1113 and consecrated in

---

[8] Elizabeth A. McIntyre, 'Early Twelfth-Century Worcester Cathedral Priory, with Special Reference to the Manuscripts Written there', D. Phil. thesis (Oxford, 1978) discusses the scribes and manuscripts of the period, though the views taken above differ in some respects.

[9] See M. Camille, 'Seeing and reading: some visual implications of medieval literacy and illiteracy', *Art History*, viii (1985), 26–49, at pp. 27–8.

[10] It has been suggested that some of the 12th-c. annals look as if they had been written year by year. The annals for 1100–28 (to 'promisit') were in fact written by the second main scribe, C^2, whose script and layout were untidier than scribe C^1's, and might give the impression of a desultory approach.

1115. The lists were therefore either drafted in 1114 or possibly written shortly after that year. The lists were patchily updated to 1129, the year when Henry of Blois was appointed to Winchester, and these updated lists are, with one exception, reproduced by witness B.

C³'s annals for 1128–40 must obviously have been begun after 1131. The reference under 1134 (p. 385) to Henry of Blois, bishop of Winchester, as 'non tunc, sed nunc Romane ecclesie legatus' indicates a *terminus post quem* of 1139 for that annal. As Henry's legation lapsed in 1143 on the death of Pope Innocent II, C³ could have completed his annals for 1128–40 (and presumably his revision of the main text) by that date.

Pls. 1–2 show writing by all three main scribes. The text on both is written by scribe C¹, as are the first three marginal entries (Northern) on the left of Pl. 1. Scribe C² wrote the last marginal entry on the left on the succession at Lindisfarne of Pl. 2, and scribe C³ seems responsible for the remaining marginal entry on the invention of Wihtburg's body (Pl. 2), the rewriting under annals 790–2, 795, and 797, and the upper marginal scribbles indicating the text to be erased under 790–2.[11]

E= Evesham, Almonry Museum s.n.

This is a single leaf from a Worcester copy of witness C, written in a hand very close to that of the chief scribe in C. It seems to have been the exemplar of the two copies of the chronicle to be described next, Dublin, Trinity College 502, and London, Lambeth Palace Library 42.

One binding leaf from a Psalter contains the last few words of annal 531 ('a mortuis resurrexit anno .xviii. Tiberii Cesaris iuxta hystoriam') to 532 ('Archadius in anno centesimo .xvi. Dioclitiani incipiens, regnauit an⟨nis .xiiii.⟩').

375 × 280 ⟨270 × 180⟩; 2 cols.; 39 lines. Those parts of the recto which had been wrapped against the Psalter are dark and some of the writing has been lost.

Written presumably at Worcester in a hand very close to the main hand in C, and of the same date. The Psalter was described

---

[11] For other reproductions of the scripts in C, see *New Palaeographical Society*, Series II. i (London 1913–30), Pls. 86–7 (reproducing pp. 355, and 77b) and C.R. Hart, 'The early section of the *Worcester Chronicle*', *Journal of Medieval History*, ix (1983), 251–315, where figs. 1–7 reproduce pp. 314, 304, 282, 43, 50, 52, and 47.

by N. R. Ker.[12] He dated it to the first half of the fourteenth century and described it as written for use in the abbey of Evesham.

H= Dublin, Trinity College 502

This is the only chronicle manuscript of relatively small format. It was written in a single hand probably at Coventry towards the middle of the twelfth century. It omits from the Marianus text used by John the preface and chapter-list to the whole work, the *recapitulatio* at the end of bk. i, and all of bk. ii. It was used by Howard in his edition of 'Florence' of Worcester. It was copied, as Dr Brett showed, from a copy of C, in all probability E.

Physical description

(i +) 266 folios originally in two volumes. 135 × 195 ⟨80 × 140: 40 × 140⟩. A varying no. of cols. on fos. 1^r–16^v. 2 cols. on fos. 25^r–67^r, and on fo. 72^v (the last page of a quire with letters well spaced out). Long lines on fos. 17^r–24^r; 30 lines save for fos. 10^r–16^v, where up to 42 lines are used for the genealogies and accounts. Continuous foliation in pencil done in July 1961 has replaced an imperfect pencil numeration, possibly by William Howard, which ran from 1 to 107 (with two '39's) for vol. 1, and from 1 to 154 for vol. 2 (with unnumbered leaves between fos. 8 and 9, 56 and 57, and 100 and 101; nos. 49 and 89 missing; no. 154 used twice; and the present fo. 266 a loose unnumbered leaf). The manuscript was rebacked in 1988, and the original folios 266, 265 were renumbered 265, 266, which is their correct order.

Collation. Fos. 1–257: all of 8. Fo. 210 is an inserted slip with a stub appearing between fos. 216 and 217. Fos. 258–65 form a quire of 10 lacking 9 and 10, and fo. 266 is a singleton. The quires of the Marianus–John chronicle are numbered by a contemporary hand from fo. 17^r (the opening of the chronicle), 1–12 in Roman numerals (I–XII), 13–31 in Greek numerals (Π–Λ), quire 28 being unnumbered and quires 29–31 numbered '28–30'.

---

[12] N. R. Ker, *Medieval Manuscripts in British Libraries*, ii: *Abbotsford–Keele* (Oxford, 1977), p. 709.

Contents

fo. 7ʳ 'Hecana Huuiccia' written above:
1. 'Presulum Magesetensium' to 'Rodbertus' (1131–48).
2. 'Presulum Wicciorum' to 'Symund' (1125–50), extended by a later hand to 'Iohannes' (1151–7).

fo. 7ᵛ 'Mercia' written above:
1. 'Nomina episcoporum Licetfeldensium' (unnumbered after the first seven) to 'Petrus' (1072–85).
2. 'Nomina episcoporum Couentrensium: i. Rodbertus de Linisig' (1086–1117) to '.iii. Rogerus de Clintun' (1129–48), extended by one hand to '.iv. Walterus' (1149–59), and by a much later one to 'Gaffridus de Muscham' (1198–1208).

fo. 8ʳ 'Mid Anglia' written above: 'Nomina presulum Leogerensium' (Leicester-Dorchester-Lincoln) to '.xxii. Alexander' (1123–48), extended to 'Rodbertus' (1148–66).

fo. 8ᵛ 1. 'Lindissis' written above (the hand responsible for the addition in fo. 6ᵛ wrote here: 'Lincoln and Lindsey'): 'Presulum Lindisfarorum' (unnumbered) to 'Brihtredus' (836×839–862×866?).
2. 'Suthanglia' written above 'Dorkecetrensium. Ættla.'

fo. 9ʳ 'Deira' written above:
1. 'Nomina archiepiscoporum et episcoporum Northumbrane gentis' to '.xxvi. Turstanus' (1119–40).
2. 'Ripensium: Eathed' (c. 679).
3. 'Agustaldensium' to '.xiv. Tidferthus' (813–21).

fo. 9ᵛ 1. 'Bernicia' written above: 'Nomina episcoporum Lindisfarnensium' to '.xxiv. Randulfus' (1099–1128), which a much later (fourteenth-century) hand completed by inserting in the left margin the names of 'Milredus, Wigredus, Uhtredus, Sexhelmus', which were missing both here and originally in C.
2. 'Terra Pictorum' above: 'Presulum Candidae Case' to '.vii. Heathoredus' (803×?).

fo. 10ʳ Genealogy from Adam to the sons of Woden.
fo. 10ᵛ Kentish genealogical tree and accounts.
fo. 11ʳ East Anglian genealogical tree and accounts.
fo. 11ᵛ East Saxon genealogical tree and accounts.

fos. 12^{r-v} Mercian genealogical tree and accounts.

fo. 12^v Lindsey genealogical tree.

fos. 13^{r-v} Northumbrian accounts.

fo. 13^v Genealogy from Woden to the direct ancestors of the Deiran, Bernician, and West Saxon royal houses.

fo. 14^r Deiran and Bernician genealogical trees with notes on some kings.

fo. 14^v West Saxon genealogical tree and notes on some kings.

fos. 15^{r-v} West Saxon accounts, and account of post-Conquest kings to Henry I's accession, as in C.

fos. 16^{r-v} ('De partitione regnorum, et pagis et episcopatibus Angliae') = GR i. 99–105 (i. 100–1). These are added in an early thirteenth-century hand. 'De regno Cantuariorum. ⟨R⟩eges Cantuariorum dominabantur . . . uel pro ignauia amitterent.'

fo. 16^v 'De archiepiscopatibus Cantuariensibus et Eboracensibus' = GR, iii. 300 (ii. 352–3). '⟨H⟩abebat autem ex antiquo Cantuariensis . . . et nuper Wellensis in Bathoniam.'

fos. 16^{r-v} 'De sedibus episcoporum in concilio' = GR, iii. 301 (ii. 353). '⟨C⟩antuarie archiepiscopus, concilio . . . secundum tempora ordinationum sedilia sua agnoscant.'

fo. 17^r (Marianus Scotus–John of Worcester Chronicle.) Omitted are the preface and chapter-list, the *recapitulatio* at the end of bk. i, and bk. ii. (H starts bk. i at c. 11 on fo. 25^r, and in consequence cc. 1–10 on fos. 17^r–24^v form an unidentified group of chronological texts with no apparent connection with the following chapters of bk. i.) 'Incipit epistola Dionisii Exigui ad Patronum episcopum de ratione paschali. Domino beatissimo et nimium desiderantissimo patri Petronio.'

fo. 260^r Main hand ends: 'et Cirencestrensi ecclesie abbatis iure praeficitur. Venerandi abbates Reignaldus Ramesiensis .xiii. Kl. Iun. et Willelmus Glaornensis Herueus prius Bancornensis post modum Eliensis primus episcopus .iii. Kl. Sept. obiit.' A later hand adds some annals for 1132–8 which are slightly abbreviated versions of the continuation of John's chronicle in MS C by scribe C^3: 'Stella cometis .viii. Id. Oct. per .vii. dies apparuit. Maxima pars Lundonie ciuitatis in ebdomada pentecostes

igne combusta est. Anno .xxxiii. ex quo rex Anglorum
Henricus regnare cepit.' In the margin the years
.MCLIII. MCXXXII.

fo. 264ʳ (.MCXXXVIII.) ends: 'in Northhymbria in manu ualida
illo proficiscitur'.

History, script, and date

Written by one hand towards the middle of the twelfth century,
save for fo. 16 (*Gesta Regum* extracts), which is in an early thirteenth-century hand, and the extension of the chronicle to 1138 on
fo. 260ʳ, l. 22–fo. 264ʳ, which is by two different hands, the second slightly later than the main scribe. Rewriting by another
scribe over erasure on fo. 239, l. 26 'Hoc anno'–30.

William Howard signs on fo. 1ʳ and elsewhere, adds notes on
fos. 10ʳ (here completing an entry), 133ᵛ and possibly 2ʳ, where
two names missing from the list of disciples are supplied from the
named William Lambard codex G (Dublin, Trinity College 503).
The lion sketched on fos. 1ʳ and 266ᵛ is found in other Howard
manuscripts. Ussher's notes on fos. 160ᵛ and 253ᵛ. A fourteenth-
century hand has written on fos. 264ᵛ and 265ʳ notes on local earls
of Coventry, Warwick, and Chester from the eighth to the early
thirteenth century, and another hand of the same date has added
at the foot of fo. 265ʳ some random notes on the Statute of
Mortmain, on the expulsion of the Jews, and on the extent of the
Northumbrian kingdom and on its bishoprics. A fourteenth-century hand (rather like that which wrote on fos. 264ʳ and 265ʳ)
indicates on fo. 204ʳ a source for completing the gap in the annal
for 1016, and on fo. 264ʳ suggests that the continuation from the
reign of Stephen in the 'Coventry' manuscript of Marianus–
Florence may have been by Henry of Huntingdon. On fo. 1ʳ the
call-mark '27' is struck through, then different hands have entered
'.O. O.5' (Ussher) 'J.33' (struck through), and 'G.46' (Foley).

The listing of four Coventry bishops with the accompanying
rubric (on fo. 7ᵛ), which is not found in other JW manuscripts,
and the writing in capitals of the name Leofric on fos. 212ᵛ, 216ᵛ,
and 219ᵛ might indicate the manuscript's Coventry provenance,
argued by Dr Brett from the twelfth-century marginal note under
1070 ('in hoc concilio degradatus est de sede episcopali abbas
Leofwinus et reuersus ad abbatiam suam, scilicet Covintr'. unde
prius assumptus fuerat'), the much later *notae* signs pointing to

Leofric's name (fos. 212^v, 214^r, 215^v, and 216^v), and the late marginal reference to him as 'huius ecclesie fundator' on fo. 219^v;[13] to these signs could be added the thirteenth-century marginal entry s.a. 1102 on fo. 245^v ('in hoc anno .xiiii. Kl. Maii indictione .x. pontificatus autem domini Paschalis II pape anno tertio translata est sedis episcopalis de Cestria apud Couentreiam'), and the faded fifteenth-century note next to Pope Benedict V on fo. 1^v ('tempore istius Papae Leofricus factus est dux Merciorum'). The entries in the episcopal lists by the original main hand do not point to later than 1131 and the consecration of Robert de Bethune, bishop of Hereford, but the first updating of these lists (probably not all that much later than the main hand) brings this down to the consecration of John of Pagham, bishop of Worcester in 1151.[14]

L= London, Lambeth Palace 42

This was written at Abingdon by a late twelfth-century hand. It was copied from a copy of C, in all probability from E. It omits the preface and chapter-list to the whole work as well as cc. 70–83 of bk. ii. It had some Abingdon interpolations which are printed below in Appendix A.

Physical description

fos. i + 154. 368 × 270 ⟨275–80 × 173–85⟩

Collation. 1$^{?8}$: fos. 1–7. 2$^{?8}$ (lacks 6): fos. 8–14. 3–19^8: fos. 15–150. 20^6 (lacks 4 and 6): fos. 151–4.

Contents

fo. 1^r	Genealogical tree from Adam to Woden.
fo. 1^v	Kentish genealogical tree and accounts.
fo. 2^r	East Anglian genealogical tree and accounts.
fo. 2^v	East Saxon genealogical tree and accounts.

---

[13] Brett, 'John of Worcester', p. 106 n. 1.

[14] I am grateful to Mrs Pamela Selwyn for drawing my attention to London, BL Harley 247, a collection of historical papers in the hands of John Stow and others, where fos. 37–8 and 42–4 contain translations, possibly in Holinshed's hand, of selective 'Florence' annals 779–850, 992–3, 1101–3. The text here appears to be of the H-type.

fos. 3^{r-v}	Mercian genealogical tree and accounts.
fo. 3^{v}	Lindsey genealogical tree.
fos. 3^{v}–4^{r}	Deiran and Bernician accounts.
fo. 4^{r}	Genealogy from Woden to the direct ancestors of the Deiran, Bernician, and West Saxon royal houses.
fo. 4^{v}	Deiran and Bernician genealogical trees with notes on some Northumbrian kings.
fo. 5^{r}	West Saxon genealogical tree with notes on some West Saxon kings.
fos. 6^{r-va} l. 31	Accounts of West Saxon kings and of post-Conquest kings corresponding to those in C.
fos. 6va l. 31–7ra l. 4	Extended account of kings to the accession of Henry II.
fo. 8^{r}	'Nomina .lxx. duorum discipulorum Christi.'
fos. 8^{r-v}	'Nomina Hebreorum pontificum' continuing with the bishops of Jerusalem.
fo. 9^{r}	'Nomina Romanorum Pontificum' to 'Alexander' (III: 1159–81) extended by a late twelfth-century hand to 'Clemens' (III: 1187–91). A fifteenth-century hand adds many names, which had been omitted from the defective list, ending with 'Benedictus' (IX: 1032–44).
fo. 9^{v}	(Throughout the episcopal lists, C's notes on bishoprics and bishops are spasmodically copied, though laid out on the page differently.) 'Cantia' written across two-thirds of the page above:

1. 'Nomina archiepiscoporum Dorobernensis ecclesie' to 'Thomas' (Becket: 1162–70), extended by one hand to 'Stephanus' (Langton: 1207–28), and by a second to 'Bonefacius' (of Savoy: 1248–70).
2. 'Nomina episcoporum Rofensis' to 'Arnulfus' (1115–24).

'East Anglia' written above: 'Nomina episcoporum Lundoniensis ecclesie' to 'Ricardus' (1108–27).

fo. 10^{r}	1. 'East' written above 'Nomina episcoporum East Anglorum' to 'Eouerardus' (1121–45).

2. 'Suthsaxonia' written above 'Nomina episcoporum Australium Saxonum' to 'Heca' (1047–54).

'Nomina presulum Cicestrensis ecclesie' to 'Saffredus' (1125–45).

fos. 10ᵛ–11ʳ 'West Saxonia, Suthreia, Barrochia, Suthamnia (*sic*), Wilsetonia, Dorsetonia, Sumersetania, Domnania' written above:

1. 'Nomina presulum Dorcestrensis' to 'Egelbertus' (*c*.650–*c*.660).
2. 'Nomina presulum Wentane ciuitatis' to 'Henricus' (1129–71).
3. 'West Saxonum. Nomina presulum Sunnugnensis ecclesie' to 'Gocelinus' (1142–84).
4. 'West Saxonia. Nomina presulum Scireburnensis ecclesie' to 'Alfwoldus' (1045–58).
5. 'Nomina presulum Fontaniensis' to 'Godefridus' (1123–35).
6. 'Nomina episcoporum Cridiatunensis ecclesie' to 'Willelmus' (1107–37).

fos. 11ʳ⁻ᵛ 'Mertia' written above:

1. List of first four Mercian bishops to 'Gearoman' (?662–7).
2. 'Nomina episcoporum Liccesfeldensium' to 'Rotbertus' (Peche: 1121–6).
3. 'Hecana' written above: 'Nomina presulum Magesetensium' to 'Ricardus' (1121–7).
4. 'Wictia' written above: 'Nomina presulum Wicciorum' to 'Symundus' (1125–50).
5. 'Id est Anglia. Lindissis. Nomina episcoporum Lindisfarorum' to 'Brihtredus' (836×839–862× 866?).
6. 'Nomina episcoporum Loegerensium' to 'Rotbertus' (1148–66).

fo. 12ʳ 'Deira' and 'Bernitia' written above 'Nomina archiepiscoporum et episcoporum Northumbrane gentis'

1. 'Eboracensium' to 'Turstanus' (1119–40).
2. 'Ripensium: Cathed' (*c*. 679).
3. 'Agustaldensium' to 'Tidferthus' (813–21).
4. 'Lindisfarnensium episcoporum' to 'Randulfus' (1099–1128). L includes the four bishops originally missing from H, and probably originally from C

(before these were replaced by C³'s rewriting of the list).

5. 'Terra Pictorum' written above: 'Presulum Candide Case' to 'Aeathoredus' (791×803?).

fo. 12ᵛ   ('De partitione regnorum, et pagis et episcopatibus Angliae') = *GR* i. 99–105 (i. 100–1). 'De regno Cantuariorum. ⟨R⟩eges Cantuariorum dominabantur proprie in Cantia in quo sunt hii . . . uel per ignauia amitterentur.'

'De archiepiscopatibus Cantuariensis et Eboracensis' = *GR* iii. 300 (ii. 352–3). '⟨H⟩abebat autem ex antiquo Cantuariensis archiepiscopatus . . . et nuper Wellensis in Bathoniam.'

'De sedibus episcoporum in concilio' = *GR* iii. 301 (ii. 353). 'Cantuarie archiepiscopus concilio . . . secundum tempora ordinationum sedilia sua agnoscant.'

fos. 13–14   Blank.

fo. 15ʳ   Marianus Scotus–John of Worcester Chronicle. (The preface, chapter-list, and ii. 70–83 are omitted.) 'Primus liber incipit ab Adam usque ad Christum. Incipit epistola Dionisii Exigui ad Patronum episcopum. De ratione paschali. Domino beatissimo et nimium desiderantissimo patri Petronio . . .' (L omits [bk. ii] 'cap. .lxviiii. Post ascensionem Domini saluatoris-cap. .lxxxiii.').

fo. 153ʳ   (1131) 'et Cirecscestrensis ecclesie abbatis iure preficitur.'

History, script, and date

Written by one hand of the later twelfth century.

fos. 6ʳ, 15ʳ   (s. xiv², xv¹ respectively) 'Iste liber est ecclesie sancte Marie Abendonensis. Quicumque ipsum alienauerit, celauerit uel aliquo modo defraudauerit anathema sit ei amen' ('fiat fiat' adds on fo. 15ʳ) 'amen'.

fo. 1ʳ   (s. xv) 'Iste est liber .lxxxviii. in inuentorio almoriali claustri'; (s. xvi¹?) 'iste liber pertinet ad me Edouardum Jones(?) presbiterum'. Top left corner: '# E. d. 2. fol vol. 221'.

fo. 1ʳ,   'Lumley' (at foot of page).

fo. 14ᵛ   (s. xvi) text identified as Marianus Scotus and atten-

tion drawn to two other exemplars in the Bodleian
and in Corpus Christi, Oxford. Above, (s. xvii¹?)
statement corrected with suggestion that the text is
not all Marianus, but may be the 'chronicon Mariani
Scoti defloratum a Roberto Herefordensi episcopo'.

fo. 62ᵛ (s. xii, contemporary) note on Marianus: '⟨T⟩empo-
ribus Henrici imperatoris floruit Marianus Scottus . . .
nullos sententie sue sectatores habuit'.

fo. 1ᵛ (ss. xvi, xvii) notes listing the contents, identifying
the chronicle as that of Marianus Scotus, and referring to excerpts made by Robert of Hereford, to the
printed text by Trithemius on the 'De concordia
evangelistarum', and to the other copies in the
Bodleian.

There are marginal notes on the Abingdon entries in fifteenth-
century hands. The Abingdon interpolations (those for 688–1065
are printed in appendix A) indicate L's origins. The latest names
by the original hand in the papal and episcopal lists are Alexander
III and Becket, and date the manuscript to at least after 1162. The
Abingdon additions are very closely related to the first Abingdon
chronicle, London, BL Cotton, Claudius C. IX, the compilation of
which was dated by Stenton to before 1170.[15] It is very likely that
the same scribe wrote both L and the Cotton manuscript. The two
must be dated on palaeographical grounds to the late twelfth century, and this late date stands in the way of any attempt at identifying the scribe of the two manuscripts with the compiler of the
Abingdon chronicle and L's Abingdon entries. It is possible,
though, that in the course of writing L, this scribe himself composed its Abingdon entries, extracting extensively from the first
Abingdon chronicle (which he may already have transcribed) and
(under 948) from Wulfstan's *Vita S. Æthelwoldi*. L's annal for 948,
with its summary of the history of Abingdon, reads like a new
composition, however much it may have borrowed and rearranged
its two sources: suffice it to cite 'post cuius discessum quid huic
loco contigerit usque ad gloriosi principis Æthelstani imperium
quia nusquam certi quicquam addiscere potui, suo meus stilus
caruit officio.'[16]

[15] F. M. Stenton, *The Early History of the Abbey of Abingdon* (Oxford, 1915), p. 5.
[16] London, BL Add. 43705, made by Laurence Nowell in 1566, was largely confined
to selected (abbreviated and occasionally paraphrased) entries of English interest from

B= Oxford, Bodleian Library, Bodley 297

This is a Bury manuscript copied directly from C by two scribes (who at first sought to reproduce their exemplar page by page) before its final revision by John, and probably before 1143. It has numerous additions in the margins, some of which show close connections with the Annals of St Neots, and numerous interpolations, some with Bury connections. Both are printed in Appendix B.

Physical description

382 × 285. ⟨285 × 208⟩. 42 lines to p. 280, 44 thereafter. Normally two cols. Long lines in the Chronicle on pp. 201–50 l. 32; 254 l. 27–265; 345–6. In initial pages and in bk. i more columns (up to 10) are used.

1 paper flyleaf. ii + 427 pages.

Collation. 1–4⁸: pp. 1–64. 5⁴: pp. 65–72. 6–27⁸: pp. 73–424; p. 425 single. Two series of quire-marks consisting of roman numerals, most of them lost through binder's clipping:
(i) on the last page of a quire, starting with the chronicle proper (quire 6 being marked .i. on p. 88); (ii) on the first page of a quire, starting with quire 1.

Contents

pp. 1–25   Consular tables. 'Alia secundo uestigio emendatio' on
            p. 17 and 'tertia emendatio' on p. 19.

743 to 1101, apparently taken from a MS held by the administrators of the estate of a Dr Wotton, probably Nicholas Wotton, dean of Canterbury (d. 1567); its Abingdon entries suggest connections with an L-like witness. In turn this was copied (by five later 16th-c. scribes) in London, BL Harley 556, itself then expanded and amplified. A translation of Harley 556 was made by Holinshed in 1572, and copied by John Stowe in the same year on fos. 51–119ᵛ of the volume of transcripts in his hand, Harley 563. Some of the marginal or interlinear additions to Harley 556 are added in translation to Harley 563, thus suggesting that the two paper volumes remained together for the additions to be made. The two Harley MSS passed into D'Ewes's hands; (see A. G. Watson, *The Library of Sir Simonds D'Ewes* (London, 1966), pp. 296–7 on B. 146, p. 311 on M. 34). Harley 556 was borrowed by Ussher. Harley 1757 (fos. 7–78, fos. 7 and 41 transposed), a late 16th-c. transcript of all Marianus–John from 742 to 1131, also seems related to an L-like witness; it came to the Harley collection by way of Robert Glover and Humphrey Wanley; see C. E. Wright, *Fontes Harleiani* (London, 1972), pp. 166, 343. The most distinctive misreading shared with L by all these transcripts and translations is the rendering of the bishop of Sherborne's name at the opening of 958 as '.Lsi. . . .', corresponding to the gaps before and after these letters in the Abingdon MS.

p. 25, l.
20–p. 30 List of popes to 'Honorius Ostiensis episcopus' (II: 1124–30). Another hand or hands, not unlike that of the second main scribe of the codex, has written the length of Honorius' pontificate, and extended the list to 'Eugenius III monachus Clarisualliensis' (III: 1145–53). The length of this pope's rule is given, and the list is extended by a late thirteenth-century hand to '⟨G⟩regorius' (IX: 1227–41).

p. 31 'Nomina .lxxii. discipulorum Christi.'

pp. 31–2 'Nomina Hebreorum Pontificum' extended to the bishops of Jerusalem.

p. 33 'Cantia' written above:

1. 'Nomina archiepiscoporum Dorubernensis ecclesie' to '.xxxvi. Willelmus' (1123–36), the only pontiff the length of whose pontificate is not given.
2. 'Nomina episcoporum Hrofensis ecclesie' to '.xxiiii. Iohannes' (1125–37).

'East Saxonia' written above:

3. 'Nomina episcoporum Lundoniensis ecclesie' to '.xxxvi. Gilebertus' (1128–34).

'East Anglia' written above:

4. 'Nomina episcoporum Eastanglorum' to '.xxvi. Euerardus' (1121–45).

'Suthsaxonia' written above:

5. 'Nomina episcoporum Australium Saxonum. .i. Wilfridus' (d. c. 709).
6. 'Nomina episcoporum Sealesiensis ecclesie' to '.xix. Heca' (1047–57).
7. 'Nomina episcoporum Cicestrensis ecclesie' to '.xxiii. Sigefridus' (I: 1125–45).

Throughout the episcopal lists, notes on bishoprics and bishops are interspersed, exactly as in C.

p. 35 'Suthregia, Barrocia, Suthamtonia, Willsetania, Dorsetania, Sumorsetania, Domnania' written above another heading 'West Saxonia', which in turn is above:

1. 'Nomina presulum Dorcestrensis ecclesie' to '.ii. Aegelbrihtus' (c. 660).
2. 'Nomina presulum Wentane ciuitatis' to '.xxxii. Heinricus' (1129–71).

3. 'Nomina episcoporum Sunnungnensis ecclesie' to '.xi. Rogerius' (1107–39).

4. 'Nomina presulum Scireburnensis ecclesie' to '.xxiv. Aluuoldus' (1045–58).

5. 'Nomina presulum Fontaniensis ecclesie' to '.xvi. Godefridus' (1123–35).

6. 'Nomina presulum Cridiatunensis ecclesie' to '.xii. Willelmus' (1107–37).

p. 37 'Hecana Hwiccia' written above:

1. 'Nomina presulum Magesetensium' to '.xxxii. Ricardus' (1121–7).

2. 'Nomina presulum Huuicciorum' to '.xxvii. Simon' (1125–50).

'Mercia' written above the first four Mercian bishops to '.iiii. Gearoman' (? 662–? 667), and:

3. 'Nomina episcoporum Licetfeldensium' to '.xxiii. Rotbertus' (1086–1117).

'Middanglia, Lindissis, Suthanglia' written above:

4. 'Nomina episcoporum Leogerensium' (Leicester–Dorchester–Lincoln) to '.xix. Alexander' (1123–48).

5. 'Nomina episcoporum Lindisfarorum' to '.ix. Brihtredus' (836×839–862×866), extended to '.xii. Æscuuius' (975×979–1002).

6. 'Nomina episcoporum Dorcestrensium: Aetla.'

7. A list, added by the hand responsible for extending the Lindsey list: 'Nomina episcoporum Elgensium' to '.ii. Nigellus' (1133–69), extended to '.v. ⟨E⟩ustachius' (1198–1215). A different and a thirteenth-century hand extended the list to 'Galfridus de Burgo' (1226–8).

p. 39 'Deira, Bernicia' written above:
'Nomina archiepiscoporum et episcoporum Northumbrane gentis.'

1. 'Nomina archiepiscoporum Eboracensium' to '.xxvi. Turstanus' (1119–40).

2. 'Nomina episcoporum Rypensium. i. Eathed' (c. 678).

3. 'Nomina episcoporum Hagustaldensium' to '.xiiii. Tidferthus' (813–21).

4. 'Nomina episcoporum Lindisfarnensium' to '.xxix. Gaufridus' (1133–41), the list corresponding to that revised by C³.

'Terra Pictorum' written above:

5. 'Nomina episcoporum Candide Case' to '.vii. Heathoredus' (803×?).

p. 40   Genealogical tree from Adam to the sons of Woden, six of whom are named as the ancestors of the royal dynasties of Kent, East Anglia, Mercia, Deira, Wessex (with Bernicia), and Lindsey.

p. 41   Kentish genealogy and accounts.

p. 42   1. East Anglian genealogical tree and accounts.
        2. East Saxon genealogical tree and accounts.

p. 43   Mercian genealogical tree and accounts.

p. 44   Lindsey genealogical tree. Northumbrian accounts.
Genealogical tree from the sons of Woden to the direct ancestors of the Deiran, Bernician, and West Saxon royal houses.

p. 45   Deiran and Bernician genealogical trees and notes on some kings.

p. 46   West Saxon genealogical tree and notes on some kings.

p. 47   West Saxon accounts, and account of post-Conquest kings ending as C did originally with the words 'Heinricus successit', but continued by a later hand to the accession of Stephen. Names set out in genealogical form as in C without connecting lines: (i) the house of Godwine to Harold (II); (ii) Norman rulers from 'Willelmus' (I) to 'Heinricus' (I) and 'Mathildis'. A later hand added the names of William I's two sons Robert and Richard, of Henry I's second wife Adela, and of Henry I's son William and daughter Maud.

p. 48   Thirteenth-century hand adds genealogical trees (i) from Charlemagne to Louis IX (1226–70); (ii) from Rollo and Alfred to the children of Henry III, to whom a later hand has added the children of Edward I.

p. 49   Computistical tracts (as in C).

pp. 50–6   532-year cycle, where the latest marginal annal is, like C's, for 1100, with three thirteenth-century annals added at a later date.

pp. 64–5   Table (as in C) of world and incarnation years according to various computations.

pp. 66–70   'Incipit opusculum Bede presbiteri impense docti de locis sanctis et de situ Ierusalem. Situs urbis Ierusalem . . . sed lectionis orationisque studio tibi temperare satagas.'

p. 71   (Text on the significance of the measurements of the cross). 'Apostolorum sententiam in qua dicitur . . . qui cum patre et sancto uiuit et regnat per omnia secula seculorum. Amen.'

Drawing of Crucifixion with an iconography different from C's: a chalice below the cross and a woman on the left with outstretched hands. Reproduced in O. Pächt and J. J. G. Alexander, *Illuminated Manuscripts in the Bodleian Library, Oxford*, iii; *British School* (Oxford, 1972), no. 167, pl. 17.

p. 72   1. Genealogy of French kings to '⟨P⟩hilippus genuit Ludouuicum' (VI: 1108-37).

2. Genealogy of Norman dukes and kings to 'Willelmus et, eo mortuo, rex Heinricus'.

pp. 72–3   Three hands have added a text (on the kings of Wessex and England, and the main events in the history of Bury St Edmunds resembling occasionally the *Annales S. Edmundi*) entitled: 'De regibus Anglorum post sanctum Ædmundum quot annos quique regnauerunt. Anno ab incarnatione Domini .DCCCLVI. sanctus rex et martyr Ædmundus . . . Hardecanutus frater eius similiter .iii. annos regnauit. Huius priuilegium libertatis quod dedit ecclesie sancti Ædmundi ibidem adhuc' *[continuing from the lower margin of p. 72 to the lower margin of p. 73]* . . . 'Iste post octauum annum supradicte abbatie et post primum annum Henrici .ii. decessit cui domnus Hugo successit.'

p. 73–423ᵃ   (Chronicle of Marianus Scotus–John of Worcester.)

pp. 73–5   'Incipit inquisitio ubi primum pasce constiterit id est quotis kalendis Christus resurrexerit. Diuino informamur precepto ut quod nobis ad aliis fieri uolumus' . . . (p. 75) 'iuxta historiam sacri euangelii. Finit prologus.'

pp. 75–82   'Incipit hic Mariani Scotti Cronica clara. Incipiunt capitula primi libri. i. De disputatione Dionisii Exigui super passionem et resurrectionem

Christi . . . (p. 82) ⟨.xcii.⟩. 'De Heinrico Pio imperatore', followed by four blank lines.

pp. 82–423ᵃ   'Primus liber incipit ab Adam usque ad Christum. Incipit epistola Dionisii Exigui ad Patronium episcopum de ratione pascali. 1. Domino beatissimo et nimium desiderantissimo patri Petronio' . . . (p. 423ᵃ) (1131) 'Herueus prius Bancornensis postmodum Eliensis primus episcopus .iii. Kl. Sept. obiit, indictione ix.'

pp. 423ᵇ–424   (*The Chronicle of Jocelin of Brakelond*, ed. H. E. Butler (NMT, 1949), pp. 106–9). 'Miraculum de cipho sancti Ædmundi. Anno gratie .MC. nonagesimo .VIII. uoluit. Gloriosus martyr Eadmundus . . . postmodum ueritatem opstructum est os loquencium iniqua.'

pp. 424–5   (*The Chronicle of Jocelin of Brakelond*, pp. 111–16.) 'Qualiter Abbas Samson uidit corpus sancti Ædmundi. Audite celi que loquar audiat terra facta Samsonis . . . iuxta dictum sapientis felix quem faciunt aliena pericula cautum.'

History, script, and date

In the binding are paste-downs: (i) a flyleaf of an early fourteenth-century canon-law manuscript; (ii) fragments of a thirteenth-century treatise on Roman law; and (iii) a small piece of a fourteenth-century gradual.

p. 1   (s. xii) 'Liber sancti Ædmundi regis et martyris'; (s. xiv²) the Bury press-mark 'C. 53'. Sir John Prise's hand occurs *passim*.

fo. 1ʳ (paper flyleaf)   (printed) 'Marianus Scotus. Ex dono Georgii Broome de Holton in comitatu Oxon armigeri.' The list of acquisitions based on the Register of Benefactors (printed in *Summary Catalogue of Western Manuscripts*, i (Oxford, 1953), p. 96) shows that it was acquired in 1608. (above) '(2468)/Bodl. 297', and '63/155'; (below) 'Jur. V. 37'.

fo. 1ᵛ   'F.105 (2468)/Bodl. 297'. followed by 'i. b. I/Jur. V. 37'.

Written by two scribes: B^1 pp. 1–344, B^2 pp. 345–423^a, the former being responsible for most of the additions and interlineations (including those in the part of the manuscript written by B^2), the latter for some of the additions in the lower margins. Various hands contribute marginal and interlineated additions, of which B^3, B^4, B^5, B^6 each contribute more than one addition. Probably another eight contributed one each. The two extracts from the chronicle of Jocelin of Brakelond (pp. 423^b–425) are in an early thirteenth-century hand.

The manuscript's origin is established by the many additions and interpolations relating to Bury St Edmunds, both in the preliminary matter and in the chronicle proper, contributed by scribe B^1.[17]

MacIntyre showed that B's layout matched exactly that of C before C^3 added the closely written lists of popes, French kings, and Norman dukes.[18] That B^1 and B^2 were copying simultaneously is suggested by the extravagantly spaced-out writing and one blank column at the end of the last quire written by B^1 (pp. 327–44), which must have been written after the following quire (pp. 345–60, the first stint by B^2) had been begun. This suggests that B's exemplar was unbound when it was being copied. Brett has persuasively argued that the writing of many of the Bury additions by the main scribe in B indicates that C was taken to B for copying.[19] B copied C before its final annals (1128–31) had been rewritten, before they had been extended to 1140 (when C ends imperfectly at present) or beyond, and before 1143 (for Henry of Blois, referred to as legate, must have relinquished his legateship on the death of Innocent II). That is to say, B must be dated before 1143; in consequence, the extension by a hand or hands

[17] T. A. M. Bishop's assertion (cit. Whitelock ap. Stevenson, *Asser*, p. cxli n. 2) that the second scribe of the Annals of St Neots (pp. 19–74) wrote BL Cotton Charter XXI. 6, dated 1138, and added the genealogy of Norman dukes and French kings on p. 72 of B—accepted by E. P. McLachlan, 'The scriptorium of Bury St. Edmunds in the third and fourth decades of the twelfth century: books in three related hands and their decoration', *Mediaeval Studies*, xl (1978), 333–4, who discussed this composite hand together with a larger group of contemporary Bury books, but called into question by R. M. Thomson, 'The library of Bury St. Edmunds Abbey in the eleventh and twelfth centuries', *Speculum*, xlvii (1972), 642 n. 150—is based on the false premise that p. 72 is in a different hand from the other preliminary matter.

[18] Brett, 'John of Worcester', p. 107 and n. 2, noting Dr McIntyre's recognition of the coincidence of format between C and B.

[19] Brett, 'John of Worcester', pp. 107–8.

resembling scribe B²'s of the papal lists taken from C, which there ended with Honorius II (1124–30), down to Eugenius III (1145–53) occurred after the copying of the chronicle. That this took place after 1133 is suggested by the episcopal lists, which, having copied C (updated to 1129) almost exactly, continue with Geoffrey Rufus (1133–41). B seems therefore to have been written between 1133 and 1143.

P = Cambridge, Corpus Christi College 92

This manuscript contains three chronicles, the chronicle of John to 1131, the 'Intermediate Compilation' (1132–54), and the Bury Chronicle in the Peterborough version from 1152 to 1295. At its opening it is strikingly close to L, and this closeness is confirmed by the incorporation or marginal addition of many of L's Abingdon interpolations, as can be seen from Appendix A. But it has the Marianus chapters (70–83) from bk. ii omitted by L, and its probably indirect connections with C are demonstrated by its occasional mindless copying of readings that represent two stages of the Worcester compilation. The chronicle of John and nearly all the 'Intermediate Compilation' were written by three late twelfth-century hands, but this compilation was completed, and the Bury–Peterborough chronicle written, by one from the late thirteenth century. It is argued below that the first three scribes worked at Abingdon, and the fourth probably wrote at or for Peterborough.

Physical description

Three flyleaves, two at the opening, one at the end, from a large missal of the fourteenth century, containing part of the Office for Palm Sunday. A fourth flyleaf at the end (fo. 204) has figures scribbled on the recto, and notes in pencil, now partly erased, on events down to Edward I.

378 × 252 ⟨280 × 190; 280 × 77⟩. 2 cols. normally of 44 lines, though 42 (to fo. 39ʳ) and 43 (fos. 80-8) are found.

Collation. 2 flyleaves. 1⁸ (lacks 1): fos. 1–7. 2 (difficult to reconstruct, a stub found after fo. 13): fos. 8–13. 3¹⁰: fos. 14–23. 4–16⁸: fos. 24–127. 17¹⁰ (lacks 8): fos. 128–36. 18–21⁸: fos. 137–68. 22⁸ (lacks 7 and 8): fos. 169–74. 23¹²: fos. 175–86. 24¹²: fos. 187–98. 25⁶ (lacks 6): fos. 199–203. 2 flyleaves.

Contents

1. 'Nomina archiepiscoporum Dororernensis [*sic*] ecclesie' to 'Ricardus' (1174–84), extended by one hand to 'Stephanus' (1207–28), and by a second to '⟨B⟩onifacius' (1245–70).

2. 'Nomina episcoporum Rofensis' to 'Arnulfus' (1114 ×1115–1124), extended to 'Gilebertus' (1185–1214).

'East Anglia' in capitals at top of page above:

3. 'Nomina episcoporum Lundoniensis ecclesie' to 'Gilebertus' (1128–46) extended to 'Willelmus' (1198×1199–1221).

Notes on bishoprics and bishops are interspersed throughout the lists. These are exactly like those in L,

both in their selection of those from C and in their arrangement on the page.

fo. 10ʳ   'East Saxonum' written in capitals at top above:

1. 'Nomina episcoporum East Anglorum' to 'Eouerardus' (1121–45) extended to 'Iohannes' (1200–14).

'Suthsaxonia' above:

2. 'Nomina episcoporum Australium Saxonum' to 'Heca' (1047–57).

3. 'Nomina presulum Cicestrensis ecclesie' to 'Saffredus' (I: 1125–45), extended to 'Symon' (1204–7).

fos. 10ᵛ–11ʳ   'West Saxonia, Iuthreia' (*sic*, corrected much later to 'Suthreia'), 'Barrochia, Suthamnia' (*sic*, see L), 'Wilsetonia, Dorsetonia, Sumersetania, Domnania' above:

1. 'Nomina presulum Dorcestrensis' to 'Egelbrihtus' (*c*. 660).

2. 'Nomina presulum Wentane civitatis' to 'Henricus' (1129–71), extended to 'Petrus' (1205× 1206–1238).

3. 'West Saxonum. Nomina presulum Sunnugnensis [*sic*] ecclesie' to 'Gocelinus' (1142–84), extended to 'Herebertus' (1194–1217).

4. 'West Saxonia. Nomina presulum Scireburnensis ecclesie' to 'Alfuuoldus' (1045–58).

5. 'Nomina presulum Fontaniensis' to 'Godefridus' (1123–35), extended to 'Iocelinus' (1206–42).

6. 'Nomina episcoporum Cridiatunensis ecclesie' to 'Willelmus' (1107–37), extended to 'Henricus' (1194–1206).

fos. 11ʳ⁻ᵛ   1. 'Mertia' written above list of first four Mercian bishops to 'Gearoman' (?662–7).

2. 'Nomina episcoporum Liccesfeldensium' to 'Rotbertus' (Peche, 1121–6), extended to 'Galfridus' (1198–1208).

3. '⟨H⟩ecana' above 'Nomina presulum Magesetensium' to 'Ricardus' (1121–7), extended to 'Egidius' (1200–15).

4. 'Wictia' above 'Nomina presulum Wicciorum' to

'Theouulfus' (1115–23), extended to '⟨M⟩augerus' (1199×1200–1213).

5. 'Id est Anglia. Lindissis. Nomina episcoporum Lindisfarorum' to 'Brihtredus' (836×839–862× 866?).

6. 'Nomina episcoporum Loegerensium' (ends with Lincoln bishops after some of Dorchester) to 'Rotbertus' (1148–66), extended to '⟨H⟩ugo' (1213–35).

fo. 12ʳ   'Deira' and 'Bernitia' are the headings above:

1. 'Nomina archiepiscoporum et episcoporum Northumbrane gentis Eboracensium' to 'Turstanus' (1119–50), extended to '⟨G⟩alfridus' (1191–1212).

2. 'Ripensium. Cathed' (c. 679).

3. 'Agustaldensium' to 'Tidferthus' (813–21).

4. 'Lindisfarnensium episcoporum' to 'Randulfus' (1099–1128), extended to '⟨P⟩hilippus' (1197–1208).

5. 'Terra Pictorum. Presulum Candide Case' to 'Aeathoredus' (803×?).

fo. 12ᵛ   ('De partitione regnorum, et pagis et episcopatibus Angliae') = *GR* i. 99–105 (i. 100–1). 'De regno Cantuariorum. Reges Cantuariorum dominabantur . . . uel pro ignauia amitterent.'

'De archiepiscopis Cantuariensis et Eboracensis' = *GR* iii. 300 (ii. 352–3). 'Habebat autem ex antiquo Cantuariensis archiepiscopus . . . et nuper Wellensis in Bathoniam.'

'De sedibus episcoporum in concilio' = *GR* iii. 301 (ii. 353). 'Cantuarie archiepiscopus concilio . . . ceteri secundum ordinationum sedilia sua agnoscant.'

fo. 15ʳ   (Marianus Scotus–John of Worcester Chronicle. Like HL P omits the preface and chapter list but, unlike them, its bks i–ii are complete.) 'Primus liber incipit ab Adam usque ad Christum. Incipit epistola Dionisii Exigui ad Petronium episcopum de ratione paschali. Domino beatissimo et nimium desiderantissimo . . . .'.

fo. 167ᵛ   Annal for 1131 (and with it the Chronicle of John of Worcester) ends: 'Herueus prius Bancornensis postmodum Eliensis primus episcopus .iii. Kl. Septembris obiit.'

'Intermediate Compilation' (1132–54) = *Memoriale fratris Walteri de Coventria*, ed. W. Stubbs (RS lviii; London, 1872), pp. 153–83. (1132) 'Anno sequenti fuit rex Henricus ad natale apud Dunstaple, ad pascha apud Wdestoch . . .'.

fo. 175^{va}15   'benedictus est et in thronum regni splendidissime collocatus.' Bury Chronicle in the Peterborough version 1152–1295, printed Thorpe, ii. 136–279 (but see comments by A. Gransden in *The Chronicle of Bury St Edmunds* (NMT, 1964), pp. xvii, xliv: (1152) 'Conrado imperatore successit Frederico imperator. Celebrata est diuorcium . . .'.

fo. 203^{r} Annal (for 1295) ends 'uersus Scotiam ad debellandum inimicos suos'.

History, script, and date

fo. 1^{r} 'Liber Abbatie et conuentus de Burgo sancti Petri'. Archbishop Parker has written below in red: 'hic liber olim cenobii S Edmundi.'

Four scribes. Three of the later twelfth century: P^1 (fos. 1–23). P^2 (fos. 24–83vb l. 38 'coequatur'). P^3 (fos. 83vb l. 38 'Tibianus'–174). One of the end of the thirteenth century: P^4 (fos. 175–202va l. 38 'finiuit ad placitum'. Another scribe *c.* 1300 completed the Peterborough Chronicle (fos. 202va l. 38 'qui apud'–203). P^3 was responsible for most marginal additions, but at least one more scribe of the later twelfth century, P^5, contributed others.

The annals in Marianus were not always clearly laid out; when the text of one year ran over into the next, it might be uncertain where the subsequent annal started or even whether it had any entries of its own. This uncertainty, which was transmitted to the JW manuscript C, was made worse by P's occasional practice of arranging year-numbers, consuls, and annals, in separate groups of three or four, thus making it often almost impossible to assign an entry to a particular year in a consolidated group.

Down to fo. 64rb l. 22 (Marianus ii, 69: 'formam domini'), P follows L very closely, copying exactly the genealogies and lists at the opening, reproducing precisely their layout column by column, sharing errors in the papal lists and elsewhere, and never extending the bishops' lists, except in the case of Canterbury. L, or

a faithful copy of L, must have been its exemplar. After fo. 64[r], particular readings and the incorporation in the text, or the later addition in the margin, of some Abingdon entries demonstrate P's continued use of L or of L's replica.[20] Since L did not have bk. ii. 70–83, P supplied them from another source. That this source was very like C after revision by C[3] is suggested by the copying of many of C[3]'s revised entries, and by P's placing in the margin of those marginal entries in C for which no location in the text was clearly marked; Dr Brett has shown that P used a version of C after it had been copied by B.[21] There are many places where P combines readings from two stages of C, thus demonstrating continued use of L: a simple example is 911, where P gives the Marianus entry twice, once, like C, at the opening, and a second time, like HL, at the end; and another is the muddled and unintelligible combination under 790–2 of entries from the revised C and from the earlier stage of C as represented by HL. There is every sign that P used a remarkably faithful version of C. P's annals for 1128–31, on the other hand, like B's, are those in C which JW erased, and which are preserved in HL. P could have copied them from L, but, as one or two readings (to be evidenced in the critical apparatus) argue against this, P probably derived them from a version of C that despite having many of C[3]'s textual and marginal changes kept (like B) C's earlier version of the annals for 1128–31. The greater part of P (to fo. 174[va] l. 15, that is, nearly to the end of the 'Intermediate Compilation' under 1154) was written by three contemporary scribes.[22] That they worked in the second half of the twelfth century might be confirmed by the lists of popes and archbishops of Canterbury, which have been extended by P[1] beyond those in its exemplar L, to Alexander III (1159–81) and Richard of Dover (1174–84) respectively. An Abingdon connection and origin are suggested both by the closeness of P to L, and by its interest, both in text and margin, in

[20] Its use of Abingdon interpolations is inconsistent. A few (e.g. 948, 963) are incorporated in the text, some (e.g. 977, 1044) are ignored, and yet others (e.g. 984, 1048) are added in the margin by scribe P[5].

[21] Brett, 'John of Worcester', pp. 108, 109.

[22] For the 'Intermediate Compilation' see *Memoriale fratris Walteri de Coventria*, ed. W. Stubbs (RS lviii; London, 1872), i, pp. xxxv–xlvii, Antonia Gransden, *Historical Writing in England* (2 vols., London, 1974–82), i. 139–40, and for some comments on P, see Diana Greenway, 'Henry of Huntingdon and the manuscripts of his *Historia Anglorum*', *Anglo-Norman Studies*, ix (1986), 103–26 at p. 121, App.2.

many of L's Abingdon entries in the chronicle of John of Worcester. As almost all the text which immediately follows the John of Worcester chronicle in P, the 'Intermediate Compilation' (to 1152, or fo. 174^v and the end of a quire), was copied by the main hand of the Worcester annals, this must also have been written at Abingdon. The later scribe P^4 completed the 'Intermediate Compilation' on the first leaf and a quarter of a new quire (possibly replacing a single leaf originally written by P^3) and copied the Bury chronicle either for or at Peterborough.[23]

2. The John of Worcester Chronicula

G= Dublin, Trinity College 503

This manuscript of small format describes itself as a *chronicula* based on the larger *chronica chronicarum*. It is in part an abbreviation of the larger work and in part an expansion through the use of sources unknown to, or not fully exploited by, the compiler of the main chronicle. The greater part of the *chronicula* (to 1123) is written in John of Worcester's hand, but the annals were extended to 1141 and have Gloucester interpolations. This continuation shows knowledge of the finally revised text of C, and the chronicle was probably completed at Gloucester towards the middle of the twelfth century.

Physical description

fos. 151. 90 × 120. ⟨65 × 105⟩.

Collation. 1$^{?12}$: fos. 1–12. 2^{14} (lacks 5 and 11): fos. 13–24. 3$^{?12}$: fos. 25–36. 4^6: fos. 37–42. 5^8: fos. 43–50. 6^{12} (lacks 1, 5, and 7): fos. 51–9. 7^{10} (lacks 4 and 5): fos. 60–7. 8–11^8: fos. 68–99. 12^{10} (lacks 3 and 7): fos. 100–7. 13^{10} (lacks 3 and 9): fos. 108–15. 14^{12}: fos. 116–27. 15^{14} (lacks 4 and 12): fos. 128–39. 16$^{?12}$: fos. 140–51.

---

[23] *The Chronicle of Bury St. Edmunds*, ed. Antonia Gransden (NMT, 1964), p. xliv states that P copied the Bury MS of the Bury Chronicle (London, College of Arms, Arundel 30). London, BL Add. 35168, a late 13th-c. MS from Crowland, has a text of Marianus and John of Worcester on fos. 3^r–157^v exactly like that of P, reproducing its errors, being misled by its marginal additions, and taking at least two marginal instructions very literally. As in P, Marianus–John is followed by the 'Intermediate Compilation' on fos. 157^v–164^v. It looks like a direct copy of P. However, it had access to the general preface and chapter-lists of Marianus, which are omitted from P, and did not reproduce the preliminary tables shared by L and P.

Contents

1. 'Nomina episcoporum Australium Saxonum. Wilfridus' (d. *c.* 709).
2. 'Nomina episcoporum Sealesiensis ecclesie' to '.xix. Heca' (1047–54).
3. 'Nomina episcoporum Cicestrensis(?) ecclesie' to '.xxiii. Sigefridus' (I: 1125–45).

fos. 31ᵛ–33ᵛ   'Suthregia, Barrocia, Suthamtonia, Wilsetonia, Dorsetania, Sumersetania, Domnania' written above 'Westsaxonia', which is in turn written above (across five pages):
1. 'Nomina presulum Dorcestrensis ecclesie' 'to '.ii. Aegelbrihtus' (*c.* 660).
2. 'Nomina presulum Wentane ciuitatis' to '.xxxii. Henricus' (1129–71).
3. 'Nomina episcoporum Sunnungnensis ecclesie' to '.xi. Rogerius' (1107–39).
4. 'Nomina presulum Scireburnensis ecclesie' to '.xxiv. Ælwoldus' (1045–58).
5. 'Nomina presulum Fontaniensis ecclesie' to '.xvii. Rodbertus' (1136–66).
6. 'Nomina presulum Cridiatunensis ecclesie' to '.xii. Willelmus' (1107–37).

fo. 34ʳ   'Hecana' written above: 'Nomina presulum Magesetensium' to '.xxxiii. Rodbertus' (1131–48).

fo. 34ᵛ   'Huuiccia' written above an untitled list of Worcester bishops to '.xxvii. Simon' (1125–50), extended by one hand to '.xxxv. Iohannes de Const.' (1196–8), and by another to '.xxxvi. Malgerus' (1200–12), though the numeral before the latter seems to have been written by the scribe who contributed the first additional Worcester bishops.

fos. 35ʳ⁻ᵛ   'Mercia, Midd Anglia, Lindissis' written across the opening above:
1. The first four bishops of Mercia to 'Iearomon' (?662–7).
2. 'Nomina episcoporum Licetfeldensium' to '.xxiii. Rodbertus' (1086–1117).
3. 'Nomina episcoporum Leogerensium' (Leicester–Dorchester–Lincoln) to '.xix. Alexander' (1123–48).

4. 'Nomina episcoporum Lindisfarorum' to '.ix. Brihtredus' (836×839–862×866?).

fo. 36ʳ 'Deira' written above:
1. 'Nomina archiepiscoporum Eboracensium' to 'xxvi. Turstinus' (1119–40).
2. 'Nomina episcoporum Rypensium: Eathed' (c. 678).

fos. 36ʳ⁻ᵛ 'Bernicia' written above:
1. 'Hagustaldensium' to '.xiv. Tidferthus' (813–21).
2. 'Nomina episcoporum Lindisfarnensium' to '.xxviii. Rannulfus' (1099–1128).
3. 'Terra Pictorum gentis. Nomina episcoporum Candide Case' to '.vii. Heathoredus' (791×803).

fo. 37ʳ *Chronicula* opens: 'Brytannia insula habet in longitudine . . .' (text based on the Anglo-Saxon Chronicle and on Bede).

fo. 113ᵛ The section written by C³ ends (1123): 'Anselmo quoque abbate de sancto Eammundo pro petendo pallio Romam iuit'.

fo. 151ᵛ (1141) ends: 'pauperum, cedibus hominum uiolationibus ecclesiarum crudeliter'.

History, script, and date

A note on the front inner binding states: 'rebacked Oct. 1951'; one on the end flyleaf reads: 'foliation corrected July 1961 151 folios'.

On fo. 1ʳ changes of owner are recorded: 'Gulielmo Howard dedit Gulielmus Lambard 30 die Novemb. 1594' in Howard's hand; 'Guilielmo Lamb[a]r[de] uendidit Io[hann]aes' [Stowe?] Idus Feb. 1573' in Lambard's hand. 'Wm. Lambarde 1573' on fos. 25ʳ, 37ʳ, and (rather faded) at the top of fo. 1ᵛ. Annotations elsewhere, e.g. fos. 54ʳ, 68ʳ, may be by the same hand.

There are shelf-marks on fo. 1ʳ: 'A. 41' (Foley) in the margin between Lambard's and Howard's entries; also 'A.21', below this 'G.5.114' (struck through), 'GGG 5,' (Ussher), and at the bottom below, a pencil entry which has been rubbed out, 'E. 6. 4' (Lyon).

In the episcopal lists, there are notes in two fifteenth-century hands on bishoprics. One of these contributed a note on fo. 37ʳ: 'Cronica de cronicis Ffloriacensis / monaci / ecclesie / [.. ...] / Wyrgc/estri*ensis* / ciuitatis / [.. ...] / qui floruit annis .xv. [.] / 1115'.

Four scribes: (1) G¹, the hand plausibly identified as that of

John of Worcester from fo. 37^r (beginning of the chronicle)–113^v l. 23 (1123: 'pro petendo pallio Romam iuit'); (2) G^2 on fos. 1^v–36^v, 113^v l. 24 (1123: 'Alexander rex Scottorum' . . .)–115^r l. 24 (1125: 'sui abbates'), 116^v l. 17 (1126: 'sicut intrare' . . .)–151^v (1141); (3) G^3 on fo. 115^v; (4) G^4 on fos. 116^r (opening of 1126)–116^v l. 17 (1126: 'per uices suas').

If John was the principal author of the main chronicle, then there is enough internal evidence to suggest that he compiled this self-styled *chronicula* from its opening to 1123 (fos. 37^r–113^v l. 23); the evidence G gives of both John's sources and methods will be examined in the introduction to vol. i of this edition.[24] Fos. 37^r–113^v l. 23 appear to be in John's more formal hand, but another hand wrote nearly all the rest of G (fos. 113^v l. 24–115^r and fos. 116^v l. 17–151^v), and prefixed the preliminary genealogies and episcopal lists on fos. 1^v–36^r.[25] Weaver pointed to the internal evidence which suggested that the text from 1123 had Gloucester connections. At the very least, G^2 was copying a compilation based on the chronicle of John of Worcester but with a number of Gloucester interpolations.[26] The Gloucester compilation was chronologically confused; in Weaver's view G's numerous grammatical and other errors suggested that it was copied by an unintelligent and inferior scribe. The confusion can be seen in the annals for 1128–31. G gives first the version more or less as in the earlier stage of C as preserved in B down to 1131, and then backtracks without warning with texts from C^3: that is, the account of the Great Council of London (1128), which G says took place, not in the twenty-eighth (as in C^3), but in the twenty-seventh year of Henry I (1127–8); the remarkable sunspots of 1128; and the visions of Henry I, assigned to 1130 by C^3. The Gloucester compiler used, then, two versions of C for these years (1128–31). In a similar way his annals from 1123–8 show an affinity with those in HL, and those for 1132–40 inevitably represent the continuation as in C^3. Some of the annals for 1131–40 in C^3 are confusingly dated, and G seems to have inherited these confusions. This compiler or the scribe G^2 prefixed the genealogies and lists, which

---

[24] It is hoped to publish the distinctive annals of G in an appendix to vol. i.

[25] See J. H. Harvey, 'The fire of York', *Yorkshire Archaeological Journal*, xli (1966), 365–7, at p. 367 n. 1, where are recorded the opinions of Darlington and Wormald that fos. 1^v–36^r and 123^v–151^v are by the same hand.

[26] Weaver, *Chronicle of John of Worcester*, pp. 4–7.

give a *terminus post quem* of 1146×47 (William of Norwich), and which copied the revised papal list inserted over erasures by John in C.[27] In G a largely worthless new text entitled 'regalis prosapia Anglorum descendens de Adam', which introduced these lists, may perhaps be assigned to the Gloucester compiler on the grounds of shared incompetence. It is possible that John of Worcester parted with, or surrendered, the unfinished *chronicula*, and that a Gloucester compiler continued the text to 1141, combining rather unsuccessfully under 1128–31 two versions of the main chronicle, and confusingly interpolating Gloucester and other entries in the last decade covered by C³. It is also just possible that G² was this Gloucester compiler. The preliminary matter could have been added at the same time. As the continuation to 1141 has Gloucester matter, it is probable that both the preliminaries and the continuation were written there.[28]

3. A Marianus Scotus Manuscript

This large substantial manuscript was written by three hands of the early twelfth century. It was probably at Worcester in the twelfth century.

JW used the recension of Marianus Scotus' chronicle of which London, British Library, Cotton Nero C. V is a representative. Even though it is not certain that he used this manuscript as his exemplar of the second recension, it has been thought useful to give its readings.[29]

---

[27] Harvey, 'The fire of York', records Darlington's opinion that the episcopal lists were written between 1146 and 1150. These limits were presumably provided by the succession of William of Norwich (1146), and by the absence of successors to Simon of Worcester and Robert de Sigillo of London, who both died in 1150.

[28] Stowe is known to have transcribed an extremely selective translation (with its focus on English events) of G by Holinshed, London, BL Harley 563, fos. 1–49. A complete transcription of G in later 16th-c. hands is found in London, BL Harley 67 (to 1052) and Harley 357, fos. 1–17 (from 1052). These two paper transcripts, though separately bound and written in different hands, complete each other. Both belonged to the library of D'Ewes: Watson, *Library of Sir Simonds D'Ewes*, p. 57 (A.443) and p. 327 (X.75). The transcript of G by John Joscelin, Archbishop Parker's secretary, is very selective and starts in 1130 (London, BL Cotton Caligula A. VI, fos. 230–5).

[29] G. Waitz, *Chronicon Mariani Scotti* (*MGH SS* v), 481–2. Valerie I. J. Flint, 'The date of the chronicle of "Florence" of Worcester', *Revue bénédictine*, lxxxvi (1976), 115–19, was the first to draw attention to the differences between C and its supposed exemplar N. Some of the differences between the two reflect, not a different exemplar, but C's editing: e.g. s.a. 688, the pope's death is recorded before, not after, the Kilian

N= London, British Library Cotton Nero C. V

Contents

Brief description

c.318 × c.230 ⟨235 × 165⟩. Long lines and two columns of 40 lines. Three hands of the early twelfth century: (1) N¹ on fos. 5–26, and probably the last added annals on fo. 158ᵛ (annals 1083–7); (2) N² on fos. 27–48, 65–158; (3) N³ fos. 49–64. A twelfth-century hand has added 'Ordinatio Wlstani episcopi' under 1062, and 'Ob. Wlstanus et Rodbertus episcopi' under 1095. The origin of the codex is not known. It might be the codex used by Robert of Hereford.

II. THE ORDER OF THE PRELIMINARY MATTER

Orderic Vitalis describes the names of judges, kings, and priests of the Hebrews, of consuls, dictators, emperors, and Roman pontiffs,

entry, probably in conformity with John's practice of placing papal matters at the opening of an annal; and s.a. 596 John substituted a text from Bede's *Historia Ecclesiastica* on the Gregorian mission for Marianus' account. In the earlier centuries, John sometimes supplements Marianus (thus s.a. 299 extracts from Bede on the martyrdoms of Alban, Aaron, and Julius are added) or fills in a gap (thus the blank between 125 and 136 in consuls is plugged, presumably by recourse to the consular tables).

and of English kings and bishops, which were certainly to be
found in the chronicle of John.[30] Marianus had prefixed his chronicle with three items: (i) consular tables according to three
different systems with occasional annals; (ii) a list of popes; and
(iii) twenty-eight tables of nineteen–year cycles with marginal
annals.[31] The descriptions above show that these were retained by
the Worcester chronicler in C. He added annals in the margins of
the nineteen-year tables, and expanded the preliminaries with lists
of Hebrew judges, priests, and kings, of genealogies of English
kings (going back to Adam through Woden), and of English bishops, the kings and bishops being accompanied by accounts of the
dynasties and bishoprics. Table 1 sets out the order of preliminaries in each witness, excluding what is not chronological in C and
B.

Two pairs of manuscripts stand out. B is closest to C, and this
closeness extends to an exact reproduction of a significant part of
C, the only differences within the scope of Table 1 being the
different location of the lists of French kings and Norman dukes.[32]
P is very close to L in the range and order of its preliminaries; it
displays a like fidelity to the layout of L's preliminary pages.
Unlike B, HLP have brief texts on the English bishoprics and
councils, which appear also in the *Gesta Regum*: by omitting the
substantial Marianan consular tables and nineteen-year cycles, they
reduce the non-English scope of these preliminaries. G stands
apart from the rest: it omits the genealogical trees from the
accounts of the kingdoms (6*), and has a unique text (10) 'regalis
prosapia' at its beginning.

---

[30] *Ecclesiastical History of Orderic Vitalis*, ii. 188–9.

[31] The possibly autograph MS of Marianus has two computistical tables before the
consular tables at the opening of the codex, and a list of Irish kings before the papal,
but these were not carried over into the recension represented by Cotton Nero C. V,
and are therefore omitted from Table 1. G. Waitz, *Chronicon Mariani Scotti*, pp. 485–9
lists the contents of the Vatican MS.

[32] In C, scribe C³ added these at the beginning of the codex, immediately after texts
on the Mercian diocese and on Worcester estates. B omitted the Worcester texts (presumably as not relevant to Bury), and placed the French and Norman lists at a more
appropriate point after the lists of English kings.

TABLE I. *Order of preliminary matter*

N	C	B	H	L	P	G
	7					
	8					
I	I	I				
2a	2b	2b				
						10
	4	4		6	6	6*
						7
						8
			2a			2b
	5	5	4	4	4	4
				2a	2a	
	6	6	5	5	5	5
			6			
			9	9	9	
		7				
		8				
3	3	3				

1. Consular tables.
2a. List of popes as in Marianus.
2b. List of popes rewritten by scribe C³.
3. Nineteen-year cycles.
4. Lists of Hebrew prophets, kings, and bishops.
5. Lists of English bishops with some notes.
6. Genealogies of English kings from Adam, through Woden, with accounts of the kingdoms and notes on some kings.
6*. Accounts of kingdoms without genealogies.
7. List of French kings added to C by scribe C³.
8. List of Norman dukes added to C by scribe C³.
9. Short texts on bishoprics and councils, also found in *GR*.
10. Short text entitled 'regalis prosapia' (found only in G).

III. THE COMPOSITION OF THE CHRONICLE

1. The Stages in the Writing of the Chronicle

The table of preliminaries illustrates some of the differences between the witnesses, which were examined in Martin Brett's

fundamental article.[33] C has long been recognized as the archetype of the chronicle, an archetype subject to changes and revisions. Brett's view that H and L are closely related, and represent an early stage of revision, is confirmed by this edition. His suggestion that HL derived from a copy of C, and not from C itself, is triumphantly confirmed by collation of the single leaf E, which is in a presumably Worcester hand very close to the main hand of C, and which stands revealed, so far as the evidence of its two pages permits, as their postulated exemplar.[34] This early stage of C, to which HL testify, included most of the alterations and additions made by the first two main scribes (designated C^1 and C^2 in the apparatus), and a few made by the third (designated C^3, who is assumed to be John of Worcester). B, C's faithful copy, represents a later stage in the chronicle, and incorporates many of the other changes in C, which were mostly made by C^3. P is hybrid: it is very close to L, as the above table and descriptions indicate, but it also reflects changes made at a stage later than HL, sometimes combining unhappily the two stages in the same annal.[35]

As it stands now, C is the sole witness to John of Worcester's final revisions; although a later hand of H and the 'Gloucester' hand of G certainly had access to some of C's annals for 1128 (from 'De iuramento') to 1140, neither made a complete copy. The most significant changes of this final revision were the rewriting (with substantial additions) of the annals 1128 (from 'De iuramento') to 1131, and the continuation to 1140, for, as the above descriptions show, HLBP testify to a version of the chronicle ending in 1131 with different and briefer annals for 1128–31. Very few of C's marginal additions are absent from B. These few could have been part of the final revisions of the chronicle: these include C^3's addition of the legend of Hermannus Contractus (C, pp. 325–7), and the marginal reference (by a hand possibly later

---

[33] Brett, 'John of Worcester'.

[34] Table 1, however, shows the differences between H and L, which particular readings confirm; and the relationship between the preliminaries of the two will be considered in vol. i. Two examples of differences in the episcopal lists are: (i) H appears to preserve C's originally defective Durham list, and (ii) the seventh bishop of Elmham is (erroneously) Hunferth (over an erasure) in C, Hunuerth in H, and Hlh (? for Alheard) in L. Differences between H and L in the body of the chronicle such as L's occasional chapter-rubrication (e.g. 813 n. j, 855 p. 274 n. f), absent both from C and H, could be accounted for by L's initiative.

[35] e.g. annals 790–2, 911.

than C³) to celestial phenomena under 1117.[36] This final stage cannot be firmly dated. The annals for 1128–31 must have been rewritten in or after 1131, the reference (in these rewritten entries) to Stephen 'qui nunc imperat' under 1130 indicates a date after 1135 for that annal, and, as Davis observed, the reference under 1134 to Henry of Blois, bishop of Winchester, as 'non tunc, sed nunc Romane ecclesie legatus' indicates a date (at least for that annal) after 1139 and before Henry's legation lapsed on the death of Innocent II in 1143.[37] There is no sign that the annals were written year by year or episode by episode; it is certainly possible that the annals for 1128 (from 'De iuramento') to 1140 were recorded in 1140 or in the year (up to 1143) when the chronicle ended.[38]

C's penultimate stage is represented by B and P, and to some extent by G. P is later than B, but the evidence of script and of episcopal lists suggests a date between 1133 and 1143 for B.[39] To the chronicle were added at this stage many passages from the *Gesta Pontificum*, a large number of mostly misplaced passages on episcopal successions, and some other alterations and changes (e.g. David entries under 463, 542, and 605, the *Visio Eucherii* under 741, and the spurious *Hadrianum* under 773);[40] and to the preliminary matter, lists of French kings and Norman dukes, and a substituted revised papal list. Nearly all the additions and alterations are in John's hand (C³), some of them being guided by

[36] It is of course possible that B ignored or deliberately omitted these additions.

[37] See Weaver, *Chronicle of John of Worcester*, p. 10 for the references to Stephen and Henry of Blois. As H. W. C. Davis pointed out (ibid., 10–11), John was in exile about the year 1134 at Winchcombe abbey, and it was there that he learned the anecdotes about the dreams of Henry I which he records under 1130. As Gransden, 'Cultural transition at Worcester', (see above, p. xviii n. 3) p. 7, has remarked, John must have been back in Worcester by 1139 when Matilda's forces entered and sacked the city.

[38] These annals are laid out on the page in John's characteristic and uneven manner (Pl. 4), but there are no signs of long pauses or breaks in the campaign. There were second thoughts as in the poorly spaced rewriting in the middle of p. 381 under annal 1130, dealing with the episode of ordeal at Worcester (and guided by repeated scribbles in the upper margin), or in the addition of the death of Abbot Guy of Pershore under 1136.

[39] The episcopal and papal lists in B exactly reproduced those in C, as revised in or after 1129 (to include the succession of Henry of Blois at Winchester), and their sole extension (by one of B's two main scribes) was the inclusion of Geoffrey Rufus under Durham (succeeded 1133). The additions of the length of Honorius II's pontificate, and of the popes to Eugenius III (1145–53) are later.

[40] These passages are easily recognized in the edition by being placed in a right-hand column.

his characteristic unerased scribbles in the upper margins.[41] If the episcopal successions provided new misplaced dates, many of the additions from the *Gesta Pontificum* simply gave more information about the location or history of monasteries or places, and did not advance the normally terse narrative of the chronicle.[42] The self-styled *chronicula*, G, stands apart from the other witnesses, as reference to the above description will show, but at the least, the section written by John to annal 1123 (which includes additions incorporated by B) testifies to the penultimate stage of the chronicle.

The previous stage is revealed by HL. E, the apparently fair copy of this stage of revision that they used, is written by a hand very close to the main scribe of C, and could conceivably have been written as soon after the completion of this stage of the chronicle, in or after 1131, as the resources of the Worcester scriptorium permitted.[43] Whereas B was written in or after 1133, E must have been written before that date. HL preserve C's original readings when these made way for revisions at the penultimate stage. In the chronicle, this HL stage included: (i) marginal additions like the Northern (e.g. 778, 791, 803) or Norman (e.g. 897, 914, 942) annals; (ii) entries from Hugh of Fleury's *Historia Ecclesiastica* (e.g. 577, 674, 840); (iii) Durham matters based on, or borrowed from, the *Historia Dunelmensis Ecclesiae* (e.g. 651, 845, 928, 1020); (iv) one or two items from the *Gesta Pontificum* (e.g. 620, 626, 636, 879). In the preliminary matter, the three short texts on bishoprics and councils (also found in the *Gesta Regum*, but neither in C nor in B), were added, but Marianus' consular-tables and nineteen-year cycles dropped.[44] Whereas nearly all the

---

[41] See e.g. the upper marginal scribble in C on pp. 288 and 303: the first shows what is to be deleted s.a. 863, and the second what is to be inserted s.a. 897.

[42] Three examples of misplaced episcopal successions can be seen in C on p. 288 s.aa. 857, 859, and 860. Examples of additions from *GP* are found on p. 263 s.a. 666, the descriptions of Lichfield, Leicester, and Dorchester, or on p. 274 s.a. 726, where the episcopal succession at Rochester from Aldwulf to Siward is listed. Sometimes, the additions from *GP* were inaccurate (e.g. s.a. 659, where Trumhere is made to succeed on Ceollach's death, and not on his resignation, or s.a. 795 with its inaccuracies in the list of Selsey bishops) or confusing (e.g. where the marginal addition near annal 882 describes the foundation of Athelney which had already been entered in the chronicle s.a. 887).

[43] The speed at which E was written would have depended on the number of scribes employed. A single scribe could have taken many months to copy a text as substantial as Marianus–John of Worcester.

[44] That the three short texts were written by a different and later hand in H does not affect the case for their presence in the exemplar of HL. For the location of these texts in HLP, see above Table I.

changes at the penultimate stage were made in John's hand, all three main scribes contributed to this previous one, the main scribe (C¹), for instance, wrote the Northern and Norman annals, the second (C²) all but one of the borrowings from the *Historia Dunelmensis Ecclesie*,[45] and John (C³), among a few other additions, the *Gesta Pontificum* entries. It is interesting that the *Gesta Pontificum* was used at this stage before the much more extensive plunderings at the penultimate one. The earliest possible date for this stage is 1125, the year of the first edition of the *Gesta Pontificum*. The three short texts dealing with bishoprics, archbishoprics, and councils added to the preliminary matter are shared with the *Gesta Regum*, though the first of these texts is missing in the first version of Malmesbury's history as preserved in the Troyes version.[46] Since the second version of the *Gesta Regum* can be dated to 1124–5, the texts could have been borrowed from that source; however, their bald, factual character makes it possible that they were borrowed (and very lightly adapted) by William of Malmesbury from Worcester.[47] The only other possible guide to the date of the HL stage is the Durham *Historia Regum*, which will now be considered.

The third set of annals in the Durham *Historia Regum* from 849–1129 depends to a great extent on John of Worcester. The printed version in the Rolls Series is based on the sole complete copy, Cambridge, Corpus Christi College 139, and is a revised text. Parts of an earlier stage may be seen in a version extending to 1119 (found in an abbreviation, Liège, Bibliothèque Universitaire 369C), and in the version to 1121 preserved in Howden's *Chronica*.[48] Up to 1119, John of Worcester is the *Historia Regum*'s main source, though it also looks elsewhere: from 849 to 888, to

---

[45] C³ does contribute one entry from *Historia Dunelmensis Ecclesie* under 1070. This is wrongly placed, and, given the original entry under 1071, unnecessary and misleading.

[46] Troyes, Bibliothèque Municipale MS 294bis. The second passage in the *GR* iii. 300 (ii. 342) apparently refers to the first text ('sicut in libro primo duxisse me memini') even though the text is missing from the Troyes manuscript. For a discussion of the Troyes version, see Brett, 'John of Worcester', pp. 114–15.

[47] In his prologue (*GR* i. 2), William explains that he will deal briefly with the East Saxons and the East Anglians: 'et nostra cura et posterorum memoria putamus indigna'.

[48] See discussion in Brett, 'John of Worcester', pp. 119–22, and the description of the Liège abbreviation (which effectively starts in 1069) in B. Meehan, 'Geoffrey of Monmouth, *Prophecies of Merlin*: new manuscript evidence', *Bulletin of the Board of Celtic Studies*, xxviii (1978), 37–46.

the annals associated with Byrhtferth of Ramsey, which are like John dependent on Asser, and which are the first set of annals in the *Historia Regum* manuscript; in the late eleventh and early twelfth centuries, to Eadmer's *Historia Novorum*, which the *Historia Regum* also knew through John; to miscellaneous northern and Durham annals sometimes of great importance; and to a set of Norman annals. It was selective in its use of John, omitting for the most part Continental annals which John had taken from Marianus, abbreviating elsewhere, and frequently dropping items of local, non-northern interest (e.g. the death of Florence of Worcester). This means that its omission of C's marginal annals could be deliberate. It certainly omits all the additions found in B, and not in HL; it has readings found in HL, and erased in C; and it seems to ignore most of the additions (except those from Eadmer) found in HL. It is possible, though incapable of proof, that its use of Norman annals and some Durham sources was triggered by marginal additions in C of Norman annals and of entries based on the Durham *Historia Dunelmensis Ecclesie*. Clearly some changes made to C were in the *Historia Regum*'s exemplar: the rewritten entries for the children of Edward the Elder (901), for instance, the introduction of monks at Worcester (969), Edgar's coronation at Bath (973), and the translation of Cuthbert (1104). Clearly too the *Historia Regum* used a version of C which did not have some changes found in HL: the antipope Gregory VIII appears as 'Mauricio' in C over an erasure s.a. 1118 and in HL, but as 'Burdino' in the *Historia Regum*; the words 'ex respectu diuino et sapientia', s.a. 959, which seem required by the sense, were omitted by HL, but are retained in the *Historia Regum*; the text of annal 1115, altered in HL, retains its original form in the *Historia Regum*. On the other hand, the *Historia Regum* would insert some marginal additions at different points from HL. Its annal for 1108 was clearly different from that in C and its copies, and seems close to the E version of the Anglo-Saxon Chronicle; it could just conceivably be further evidence of different annals for particular years at Worcester. All the above details point to the *Historia Regum*'s access to a version of the chronicle earlier, though not necessarily very much earlier, than HL's exemplar. The *Historia Regum* was dated plausibly by Brett between 1122, the date of Eadmer's completed *Historia Novorum*, and 1135, the latest possible date for its earliest abbreviation.[49] In C some of Eadmer's

[49] Brett, 'John of Worcester', pp. 120-1.

additions are marginal whereas in the *Historia Regum* they are incorporated in the text. It is possible, though rather unlikely, that C was the exemplar used by the *Historia Regum*. If it was not, then this exemplar must have incorporated C's Eadmer marginalia in its text. It must have been later than C, which (in its original version extending to 1131) was written either between 1128 and 1131 or in or after 1131. Why the *Historia Regum* stopped using John after its annal for 1120,[50] and why its fullest, though revised, version ended in 1129 and its earlier ones in 1119 and 1121, are not easy to explain, but whatever the explanations, the exemplar of John used by the *Historia Regum* need not have been earlier than 1128–31, and only slightly earlier than that used by HL. Brett's suggestion that the *Historia Dunelmensis Ecclesie* was exchanged for a copy of John in a single transaction remains the most economical hypothesis. It is also possible that the exchange was staggered, so that a copy of the *Historia Dunelmensis Ecclesie* reached Worcester first before a copy of John embellished, among other things, with Durham ecclesiastical material was sent in exchange. Worcester could have made two copies of the chronicle quite soon after 1128–31, one for Durham, and the second, E, HL's exemplar.[51] B's fidelity to C is most reasonably explained, as Brett has suggested, by its being taken to Bury some time between 1133 and 1143.[52]

Three layers of C can thus be tentatively dated: the latest between 1140 and 1143; the B layer between 1133 and 1143; and the HL layer at or before 1131. It remains to consider the light thrown on the composition of the chronicle by the Eadmer additions and by the relationship between the preliminary matter and the chronicle.

2. *The Additions from Eadmer's* Historia Novorum

Over sixty years ago, Darlington remarked that the annals of John between 1091 and 1121, which either add in the margin or

---

[50] The *Historia Regum*'s substantial borrowings from John end with the annal for 1119, but Brett, 'John of Worcester', p. 120 n. 2 draws attention to a 'last clear echo of John' under 1120.

[51] Producing two copies of a substantial text from a single exemplar would have taken time even if many scribes were employed, though it is true that the *Historia Regum*'s use of John is confined to a relatively short part of his chronicle.

[52] Brett, 'John of Worcester', p. 107: 'Since many of the Bury additions [to the chronicle of John in B] were made *currente calamo* by the main scribe, it seems to follow that C was taken to Bury for copying. . . .'

incorporate passages from Eadmer, could not have been written before that work's completion.[53] The last two books of the *Historia Novorum* continue the narrative from the death of Anselm in 1109 to that of Archbishop Ralph in October 1122; an autograph copy of this complete work survives. Brett has shown that John used a slightly earlier copy of the six-book text, and hence is unlikely to have written this part before 1123.[54] Three palaeographical points can be made here. There are no Eadmer passages incorporated in the text written by the main scribe (C^1). His Eadmer additions are marginal (1091, 1098, 1099, 1108), and are, apart from the last, 'Continental' in content. Conversely, the second scribe (C^2) either incorporates Eadmer passages of largely English concerns within his annals 1102–21, or, at a later stage, rewrites his text, and one annal (1095) of his colleague's, to incorporate Eadmer's words or sentences. Third, the one Eadmer contribution that may have been made by the third main scribe (John or C^3), the rewriting of 1115, may have been later than the others, since it was not picked up by HL or the *Historia Regum*. This alteration may have been part of John's editing and tidying-up, continuing a process which he may have initiated earlier for execution by others. Eadmer was added by scribe C^2 in two stages, but by scribe C^1 only after he had completed his main scribal stint. This could illustrate the gradualness of changed plans in the compilation of the chronicle. C is the surviving fair copy: the decision to use Eadmer (who ends in 1122, and could have reached Worcester by 1123) could have been made when C's exemplar was written, some time after 1122, and further additions from Eadmer were made during or after the writing of C; or this incorporation of Eadmer could have been made first when C was being written, and C's exemplar could have been either written before 1122 or ignorant of Eadmer or both.

3. The Preliminaries Dealing with English Bishops and Kings

Among their preliminary texts all the John of Worcester manuscripts include lists of English bishops, and genealogical trees of

---

[53] *Vita Wulfstani*, pp. xvi f. Darlington considered that the last part of Eadmer (bks. v–vi), the annals as 1114–22, 'cannot have been available at Worcester until 1121, and was probably not circulated until the summer of 1124'.

[54] M. Brett, 'A note on the *Historia Novorum* of Eadmer', *Scriptorium*, xxxii (1979), 56–8; id. 'John of Worcester', pp. 111–12.

the English dynasties extending back to Adam through Woden. Into the lists of English bishops are dovetailed notes on individual bishops, and on the creation and division of bishoprics; accompanying the English dynastic genealogies there are accounts of the generations between Adam and Noah, histories of different kingdoms, and, in the cases of Wessex and Northumbria, a few notes on holy kings. If the lists of bishops are the English counterpart to Marianus' papal list, the genealogical trees and accounts, in their detail and scope, go far beyond the consular tables of Marianus and his nineteen-year cycles with their marginal annals, and testify to a living English tradition of genealogies, regnal lengths, and annals. On the page, the accounts are written around the trees, which were set down first, and with which they were closely related. It is reasonable to suppose that the preparation of these lists and accounts preceded the chronicle; their terminal dates seem to confirm this assumption. The updated marginal annals in the Easter cycles, the dynastic accounts, and the trees do not go beyond 1100.[55] The episcopal lists did not originally go beyond 1114, and the reference to the translation in that year of Ralph from Rochester to Canterbury. The narratives in the episcopal lists, in the dynastic accounts, and in the notes on holy kings show striking parallels with the text of the annals, though their compiler did also look elsewhere. Darlington's discovery that the text of the dynastic accounts shared the same mix of Asser and of Latin rendering of the chronicle narrative with some annals led him to reverse the plausible priority of preliminaries over annals in the John of Worcester enterprise.[56] As the accounts do not seem to show independent knowledge of Asser, he argued that their source must have been the completed chronicle. One entry in the chronicle, however, might argue against Darlington's view; the marginal

---

[55] On p. 55 of C, there is a set of chronological exercises written by the main hand in two stages. The references to the 47th year of Henry IV and to 1103 in the first group (Weaver, *Chronicle of John of Worcester*, p. 8 and n. 1), and to the first year of the Emperor Charles (possibly Henry V, that is, 1106) in the second, indicate a German context for these exercises, as Brett has pointed out ('John of Worcester', p. 104 n. 4). These exercises are not in the two Marianus MSS (Vat. Pal. lat. 830 and Cotton, Nero C. V); C may have taken them from another source. If they were in C's Marianus, then the *terminus post quem* for each is 1103 and ?1106. It might be noted that the last emperor to succeed in the Marianus decennovenal annals is Henry IV (1056), and the last pope, Clement III (1084).

[56] Darlington-McGurk, '"Chronicon ex Chronicis" of "Florence" of Worcester', *Anglo-Norman Studies*, v (1982), 188 n. 14.

addition (by the main hand next to the 849 annal) in the chronicle witness C of a Wigstan text, which is an integral part of the Mercian dynastic accounts. If this addition to the chronicle was not the correction of an omission, but an afterthought (as were most of the main hand's marginal additions), then the chronicle would seem here to have borrowed from the accounts. Here at least the compiler of the accounts must have borrowed his text from outside the chronicle, probably from a Wigstan *passio*, and its use there could have prompted its addition to the chronicle. A solution to this possible obstacle to Darlington's view might be to regard the composition of both chronicle and preliminary accounts as evolving over some years when mutual borrowing could have taken place. The accounts could well have borrowed their Asser and their Latin rendering of the Anglo-Saxon Chronicle from an earlier stage of John of Worcester's annals, and the annals in turn could well have borrowed an entry like the Wigstan addition from the dynastic accounts.

The close parallels between the dynastic accounts (particularly for the East Saxons and the East Anglians) and William of Malmesbury's *Gesta Regum* have long been recognized. The hypothesis of a gradual evolution of the Worcester accounts could well affect views of the relationship between the two. If the accounts were composed after the chronicle, then they should be dated after 1131, and are therefore likely to have borrowed from Malmesbury since the probable date for the composition of the second version of the *Gesta Regum* was 1124–5. But if the compilation of the accounts cannot be firmly dated—their internal dating limit is 1100 and the accession of Henry I—then William could well have borrowed from them, or both could have borrowed from a common source.

4. The Marginal Annals in the Nineteen-Year Cycles

A similar interdependence may be seen when comparing the marginal annals added by the Worcester compiler to the nineteen-year cycles with those in the chronicle.[57] In his possibly autograph manuscript (Vat. Pal. lat. 830), Marianus added in the margins of the nineteen-year cycles various annals. Among these were: the

[57] To be published in vol. i of this edition.

succession and regnal lengths of emperors and popes; some Irish entries (e.g. two for Patrick s.aa. 425 and 433, and the death of Kilian, abbot of the Irish, at Cologne s.a. 1003); and a few others (e.g. the Council of Nicaea s.a. 315 [*sic*], the births of Jerome s.a. 330 and Augustine of Hippo s.a. 354). These were for the most part kept and slightly extended in the English representative of the second recension, BL Cotton MS Nero C. V.[58] The apparent additions made to the marginal annals in witness C include an updating to 1100 and the death of William II (as has already been noted); episcopal succession at Worcester from Bosel to Samson;[59] references to the coming of Augustine to England, and to his death; a note on the beginning of the *regnum Francorum* (425); the martyrdom of St Edmund (? 867); the arrival of the Normans under Rollo in Normandy (877); an attempted filling of a gap left by Marianus in these decennovenal cycles in the popes after John XII; and references to the deaths of the Virgin (14), and of St Ambrose (397), and to the birth of St Martin of Tours (315). With the exception of the death of St Ambrose, these entries are found in the chronicle annals, and could have been taken thence. There are sometimes verbal echoes, an exact correspondence being the Norman annal used for the arrival of Rollo (877). As many of these supplementary entries in the nineteen-year cycles were among John's additions to Marianus' chronicle, it is obviously difficult to say whether they were added to the chronicle first, or, in a trial run, to the nineteen-year cycles. John, though, clearly borrowed one batch of supplementary entries in his nineteen-year cycles from the main Marianus chronicle, and that is the unfortunate filling of the gap in popes (in Marianus' decennovenal annals) between John XII (955–64) and the death of Benedict VIII (1024). In the margins of the chronicle in the Vatican Marianus manuscript, a confused series of papal successions had been added to plug the gap; these marginal additions were incorporated in the chronicle texts of the Cotton Marianus manuscript and in the JW

---

[58] Entries added include the ordination of Wulfstan s.a. 1062 and the deaths of Wulfstan and Robert of Hereford s.a. 1095.

[59] Among these additions, the death of Oswald is celebrated under annal 992 with a couplet: 'Aula Dei patuit Oswaldo pridie martis / Pontifici summo celsa petendo poli.' This couplet is found in the 10th-c. metrical calendar from Ramsey published by M. Lapidge, 'A tenth-century metrical calendar from Ramsey', *Revue bénédictine*, xciv (1984), 327–69, at pp. 352, 361. The Ramsey second line reads 'Pontifici summo alta . . .' whereas a 12th-c. Winchcombe versifier recast it as 'Summo pontifici celsa . . .'

witness C. John transferred these popes in all their confusions to the margins of his nineteen-year cycles.[60] The supplementary reference to Mary's death (14) in John's decennovenal cycles could also have been taken from Marianus' chronicle, though here another possible source might have been the consular tables which preceded the nineteen-year cycles. Recourse to sources other than the chronicle can be seen in the addition by John (to his cycle annals) of the regnal lengths of Pope Evaristus and Pope Lucius, which were neither in Marianus' cycles nor in his chronicle, and which John may have taken from Marianus' list of popes. Evidence does therefore suggest that John took some at least of his supplementary entries in the nineteen-year cycles from his chronicle or from other sources.[61] But the births of Martin of Tours (315), Jerome (330) and Augustine (354) raise other problems and could suggest a two-way traffic between chronicle and marginal entries in the nineteen-year cycles. Martin's birth was recorded in Marianus' annals but not in his nineteen-year cycles, those of Jerome and Augustine in the latter but not in the former. John first omitted (whether inadvertently or deliberately) all three births from his chronicle, but in the cycles he added the birth of Martin, substituting it for Marianus' notice of the Council of Nicaea, and conceivably borrowing it from Marianus' annal for 315. But probably at an early stage scribe C¹ added all three births in the appropriate margins in his chronicle, very probably taking them from his own decennovenal annals. This does not necessarily prove that most of the annals in the margins of the nineteen-year cycles were

[60] The gap is filled by John XIII (965–72) correctly under 965; two unidentifiable Stephens under 973 and 981 (given the sequence of popes who follow, the second Stephen may be Stephen VIII (IX) 939–42); Marinus under 989 (presumably Marinus II 942–6); Agapitus under 998 (? Agapitus II 946–55); Octavian under 1003 (? John XII 955–64); Leo under 1009 (? Leo VIII 963–65); and Benedict under 1017 (? Benedict V 964). The papal list in HL which extends beyond John XII (the last pope in Marianus' original list as in that originally in C) includes these confusing additions. Engagingly, the Vatican Marianus manuscript has a later marginal note near the first of these popes: 'de his papis dubitamus'.

[61] Under 78, Marianus gave the length of Pope Evaristus' pontificate as 10 years, and John's as 13 years, 7 months, and 2 days. Under 244, the periods for Pope Lucius I are 5 months, and 3 years, 3 months, and 3 days, respectively. In neither case did Marianus' regnal length correspond to the interval before the next pope in the marginal annals, and John probably looked here to Marianus' list of popes. The death of Mary is added to the 19-year cycle in C under the year 14. It was not in Marianus' cycle at this point, though he included it at the appropriate year in both the consular tables and the annals. It is impossible to decide how many of John's differences from Marianus came from his exemplar.

added before the compilation of the chronicle. There could have been, as has been postulated in the case of the Wigstan entry, a continued interdependence of chronicle and preliminaries, and the compilation of both could have proceeded intermittently and sometimes simultaneously.

5. A Postulated Early Eleventh-Century Stage in the Chronicle

The Durham *Historia Regum*, Eadmer, and the John of Worcester preliminaries do not date very precisely the composition of the chronicle. The most that the *Historia Regum* shows is the availability of a John chronicle text down to 1120 at Durham by 1131. The Eadmer borrowings indicate a stage after 1122 when they were added. The dynastic accounts seem to point to a stage in the composition of the chronicle, into which Asser had been integrated, *c*.1100. The annals added to the decennovenal cycles might suggest a continuing interdependence of preliminaries and chronicle.

In 1983 a paper by Dr C. R. Hart on the early section of the chronicle of John of Worcester concluded that much of the chronicle to the end of 1017 had been compiled at Ramsey during the last two decades of the reign of Æthelred 'the Unready'.[62] Dr Hart identified for the first time some of the chronicle's sources and described the ways the chronicler interwove them, but much of his study turns on assumptions, not generally accepted, about the Ramsey origins *c*.1000 of the Annals of St Neots and of the B version of the Anglo-Saxon Chronicle, and is concerned with wide-ranging and speculative discussions of the ABC versions of the Anglo-Saxon Chronicle. The relationship between the Anglo-Saxon Chronicle and John of Worcester will be considered in the introduction to vol. i of this edition. Hart's strongest arguments for the Ramsey origin of the pre-1018 John of Worcester annals are stylistic, and are not all convincing. The frequent use of superlatives, for instance, is not the exclusive mark of Byrhtferth or of Ramsey, as annals 709 and 714 (based on Bede and Felix respectively) show. A glance at the annals before 1016 in this edition reveals them as largely a careful patchwork of existing texts, either in their original or in translation; in consequence, there are

---

[62] C. R. Hart, 'The early section of the *Worcester Chronicle*', *Journal of Medieval History*, ix (1983), 251–315.

clear stylistic differences between the annal for 668, which is based on Bede, and that for 959, which derives from lives of tenth-century saints. The differences extend to those phrases or passages whose source cannot be identified: the description of Edgar's coronation and his naval progress under 969, and the panegyric of him under 975, read quite differently from the accounts of St Werburg under 675 and of Bede's death under 734. The differences might be explained by still unidentified sources, or reflect a chameleon-like adaptability of the chronicler, but this is not a noted characteristic of Byrhtferth's writing. Two of Hart's arguments must be faced. The exclamation under 897 in the midst of a sober rendering of the Anglo-Saxon chronicle ('O quam crebris uexationibus, quam grauibus laboribus, quam duris lamentabilibus, non solum a Danis qui partes Anglie tunc temporis occupauerant, uerum etiam ab his Satane filiis tota uexata est Anglia!') is unexplained, and unexpected, and is reminiscent, if more restrained, of some of Byrhtferth's outbursts, but it is a unique example, and could have been derived from a lost source. The annal for 1016 is unparalleled in its use of Sallust and Bede for stylistic, and not informative, reasons, but it is by no means certain that a Ramsey origin would explain the annal's heterogeneity. There are throughout the chronicle, from its renderings and improvements of Marianus (both before and after 450) to well into the eleventh century, a careful attention to detail, a willingness to infer and deduce, a habit of rearranging narrative or texts for clarity or in chronological order, which suggest a single enterprise. The use of Osbern's *Vita Dunstani* and *Vita Elphegi* in 958, 959, 986, 1008, 1011, and 1012 might be regarded as decisive for a twelfth-century date for these annals. If Osbern used a Ramsey version of John of Worcester to 1018, as Hart has suggested, it can be asked why he was so selective. The occasionally fleeting appearances, in the chronicle, of a phrase or two apparently from Osbern is on the other hand quite typical of the Worcester compiler's method. Another of Hart's postulated Ramsey compilations of c.1000, the Annals of St Neots, has been shown in a recent edition to date from the twelfth century.[63]

The chronicle must therefore continue to be recognized as a Worcester enterprise commissioned by Wulfstan of Worcester. Its

[63] *ASN*, pp. xlv n. 49, lxiv f.

compilation may have extended from 1095 to 1143. If the absence of Eadmer's history from the main text (as opposed to its marginal addition) by the main scribe in witness C is significant, then a pre-Eadmer phase can be recognized. If the dynastic accounts were compiled after the chronicle, and the updating of the episcopal lists to 1114 occurred later than this, then it could be argued that a chronicle up to at least 1100 already existed by that year. On the other hand, if the computistical exercises in the archetype manuscript (on p. 55) belonged to the Marianus exemplar used by John, the enterprise could not have commenced before 1103× 1106. The terminal dates for the enterprise are therefore 1095× 1106–1140×1143.

Within these limits, the 1120s and the very early 1130s seem crucial. This is suggested by the evidence of the many revisions of witness C, apparently in progress c.1128, and before 1133; by Orderic Vitalis' testimony that, on his visit to Worcester before 1124, John was working on the chronicle; and by the chronicle's use of Eadmer in or after 1123. John must have been responsible for this final period. His continued interest in the writing of annals is demonstrated both by his apparently final revision of C (1140×1143), and by his compiling, and writing, the self-styled *chronicula* (G), a work clearly later than the penultimate stage of C. The discarding of this work, and its completion at Gloucester at a later date, may indicate the end of John's concern with the writing of annals. If the end of the Worcester chronicle enterprise can be fixed in the 1140s, its beginnings, its elaboration and form before the 1120s, and the role of Florence in this earlier stage, cannot be established.

IV. EDITIONS AND TRANSLATIONS OF JOHN OF WORCESTER'S CHRONICLE

Lord William Howard's edition of 1592, *Chronicon ex Chronicis ab initio mundi usque ad annum Domini 1118 deductum, auctore Florentio Wigorniensi monacho. Accessit etiam continuatio usque ad annum Christi 1141 per quendam eiusdem coenobii eruditum. Nunquam antehac in lucem editum* (London, 1592), was based on H, which he possessed. As the preface to his edition indicates, he was able to supplement that incomplete manuscript by recourse to G,

which William Lambard placed at his disposal, and subsequently
gave him in 1594. H was selective in its use of Marianus, omitting
the prologue and chapter-list and the whole of bk. ii. These omissions handicapped Howard in his editing of the text, causing bk.
iii to be numbered ii, and creating some difficulties with
chapter-numbers. Omitting the earliest part of bk. i (c. 1–10), he
started with c. 11 (H, fo. 25ʳ), and discreetly edited the text,
introducing new headings and some dates. As Florence died in
1118, Howard divided the chronicle at that year into the works of
Florence and his continuator. His recourse to G was limited: not
at all in the chronicle before 1125; occasionally in the annals
1125–35, though H remains the base MS; much more for 1136;
and completely after the opening of annal 1137 to the end of G in
1141, even ignoring H's annal for 1138. From the body of G, he
extracted, for use as a preface to the Worcester episcopal lists, the
text on the original division of the Mercian diocese.[64] He ended
his edition of the preliminaries with the texts common to witnesses HLP of John's chronicle and to William of Malmesbury's
Gesta Regum.[65] He entitled the genealogical trees and accounts of
the dynasties 'regalis prosapia', the heading given by G to its
largely worthless preliminary account of English royal descent,
which Howard with good judgement omitted. He used G's episcopal lists to correct and complete H, though on occasion he preserved H's additions when they were not in G. Howard's text was
faultily reprinted at Frankfurt in 1601 (*Matthai Westmonasteriensis
Flores Historiarum et Chronicon ex Chronicis auctore Florentio
Wigorniensi*, Frankfurt, 1601); the Frankfurt text was excerpted in
M. Bouquet's *Recueil des historiens des Gaules et de la France*, xiii
(Paris, 1786), 67–78. H. Petrie's edition, *Monumenta Historica
Britannica* (London, 1848), pp. 522–644, differed from Howard's
both in its scope and in the witnesses used. Covering the years
450–1066, though concerned only with English matters before
1000,[66] it relied on two witnesses not known to Howard (C and L,
called respectively A and B), and used both Howard's edition and
the witnesses B and P. It also collated the Marianus text against

---

[64] This is found in G s.a. 678 and on fos. 51ᵛ–52ᵛ. It was taken by G from C fo. 1ʳ.

[65] Howard's edn., pp. 581–4. See the descriptions of HLP above, pp. xxxix, xliv, lvi.

[66] Anomalous is Petrie's (and following Petrie, Thorpe's), inclusion of the comet of
868, which is neither in the Anglo-Saxon Chronicle nor in Asser, but is taken from
Marianus.

that in London, British Library, Cotton Nero MS C. V. It identified in its marginal references and footnotes many of the chronicle's sources. Using both C and L, it normally sided with L where they differed. Thus only those marginal and textual changes in C which L adopted were printed in the text, though others were intermittently shown in the critical apparatus. The resulting text was closer to L than to C³'s. Petrie printed the episcopal lists and the royal genealogies and accounts, expanding considerably the apparatus for the former, and borrowing from Howard the title 'regalis prosapia' for the latter. Like Howard, Petrie printed the texts on the divisions of the early kingdoms and bishoprics also found in *Gesta Regum*, though he unaccountably gave C, which lacks them, as one of the two witnesses.

The editorial practice of Benjamin Thorpe's edition, *Florentii Wigorniensis Monachi Chronicon ex Chronicis* (English Historical Society; 2 vols., London, 1848–9), was shifting: its two consistent principles, characteristically abandoned on occasion, were its exclusion of Marianus, and its inclusion of L's Abingdon entries in the footnotes. The footnotes suggest recourse to C and L, but up to 1066, Thorpe resolutely follows Petrie's text, though in many ways his is less useful. Very occasionally it shows independent use of the witnesses, but more often than not it drops information of value in Petrie. From 1066 to 1127 it follows C more consistently with occasional recourse to Howard and to L. Its annals for 1128–41 are maddeningly unsteady, looking principally to Howard, though also from time to time to C. The end of 1140, and the annal for 1141, which are not in C, are taken from Howard, and therefore ultimately from G. The arbitrary inclusion of G's Gloucester entries to 1141 was matched in the annals for 1152–96, which have nothing to do with Worcester and represent the Peterborough version of the Bury Chronicle, derived from witness P. In the episcopal lists and genealogies and accounts, he kept the title 'regalis prosapia', the appropriated text on the division of the Mercian diocese, and the short texts also found in the *Gesta Regum* on the early kingdoms and bishoprics.

The first scholarly edition of the chronicle was confined to the annals for 1118–40.[67] The editor, J. R. H. Weaver, disentangled the confusions of earlier editions, and, in using witnesses CHG,

---

[67] Weaver, *Chronicle of John of Worcester.*

rightly insisted on C's primacy, clearly evaluated the role of John in the writing and completion of the annals after the death of Florence, and correctly assessed the complications of G.

A few years after Thorpe's edition, two translations were published. The first, in 1853, was by Joseph Stevenson, and was based on Petrie's edition down to 1066, and on Thorpe's for 1066–1141, including the English episcopal lists, royal genealogies, accounts of English kingdoms, and the texts common to the John of Worcester witnesses HLP and William of Malmesbury's *Gesta Regum*.[68] The latter were also translated in the second translation, by Thomas Forester, which was, however, based entirely on Thorpe, translating the so-called second continuation to 1296.[69]

V. THIS EDITION

1. Reproduction of the Layout of C

Examples of C's layout may be seen in Pls. 1–2. A new annal begins with a Marianan year on the left of a line, followed immediately by an imperial year, with the Dionysian year on the right.[70] Within each year an English annal is usually distinguished from Marianus' by a large initial. There are differences in scribal practice: C^3 omits the imperial years (C^2 only omitting its very last one s.a. 1128 on p. 379), and C^2 does not leave enough space within the text block for the large initial R (which announces a new Roman emperor) which consequently encroaches on the margin.

In this edition, at the beginning of each annal, Dionysian, imperial, and Marianan years are placed in that order (thus reversing that of the manuscripts), and Marianan and English annals, and Roman imperial successions are given separate paragraphs.

In the possibly autograph manuscript Vat. Pal. lat. 830, Marianus often allowed one line for each annal; as a result fuller

---

[68] *The Church Historians of England*, ii. 1; *Containing the Anglo-Saxon Chronicle. The Chronicle of Florence of Worcester*, ed. and in part trans. by J. Stevenson (London, 1853), pp. 171–404.

[69] *The Chronicle of Florence of Worcester with the Continuation*, trans. T. Forester (London, 1854).

[70] The plate does not show that the Marianan year is in red, and that down to p. 271 a yellow line frames the Dionysian.

years were short of space, and were either wrapped around above
in runovers, or were continued below in the lines assigned to
leaner or blank annals. That could lead to unsettled dates for some
events, particularly when this spilling-over was combined with the
many marginal accretions characteristic of Marianus' working copy.
This uncertainty in dating is reflected in the English copy of
Marianus (London, BL Cotton MS Nero C. V) and in MS C of
John of Worcester. It is sometimes therefore difficult to assign an
event to a particular year; this edition notes the spilling-over of
annals from one year to the next one or two, and a possible uncertainty of date (e.g. 507 n. c, 620 nn. i and 1 (p. 84), 628 nn. a and
4). This uncertainty is more obvious when Marianus' text is fuller,
in the earlier rather than in the later annals printed in this volume.

It has not been possible to reproduce the different scribal practices (such as C^2 and C^3's tendency to write the names of persons,
and sometimes places, in capitals), or the overlay of alterations and
additions which sometimes transformed a very fair copy into a
messy working text, but two of the stages in the evolution of the
chronicle are shown by two parallel columns of text (e.g. 959).

Interlineations and marginal additions in MS C later than the
twelfth century have normally been ignored.

2. Other Conventions

Material from identified sources is in italics, but four points
should be noted. First, the text of Asser. Since the text in
Stevenson's edition is a reconstruction partly based on John of
Worcester's extensive excerpts, it is clearly difficult to know what
of John of Worcester's text should be in italics. Here the
sixteenth-century transcripts of Asser, and some relevant passages
in the Annals of St Neots and in the first section of the Durham
Historia Regum have been used and presented; those passages and
words have accordingly been put in italics where there is reasonable supporting evidence, though no pretence is made at establishing a definitive Asser text. Second, some texts do not survive in
satisfactory editions (e.g. Hugh of Fleury's *Historia Ecclesiastica* or
Osbern's *Vita Elphegi*); recourse is sometimes had to manuscript
evidence, particularly if this has Worcester connections. Third, the
Anglo-Saxon Chronicle. John's use of this chronicle is a central
issue which will be considered in the introduction to vol. i. His

text is a translation, and consequently is not shown in italics, but the historical notes show the more important agreements and disagreements with the witnesses of the Anglo-Saxon Chronicle. When years are not shown in these notes for the Anglo-Saxon Chronicle (or, for that matter, for the Annals of St Neots or, in Appendix B, for Flodoard), the year is as in John. The evidence presented of the Anglo-Saxon Chronicle witnesses A, B, and G is based on the recent editions of Bately, Taylor, and Lutz, that of witness E on the facsimile, and that of witnesses C, D, F, and of *ADL* on an examination of the manuscripts in the British Library.[71] Fourth, John of Worcester's entries on the beginnings of the solar cycles (e.g. s.aa. 644, 672). These can be regarded as John's contributions even though in the pre-450 annals, and very occasionally in those in this volume, Marianus had drawn fitful attention to them. They are not therefore shown in italics. The historical commentary concentrates on the English material assembled by JW. There will be some comment on the value and unreliability of Marianus in vol. i.

The selective critical apparatus shows the main differences between the different recensions, and also gives some evidence for identifying particular witnesses. Variants in the spelling of names have for the most part been ignored.

Names of English bishops and rulers in the translation and commentary have normally been spelt as in the *Handbook of British Chronology*.

Anglo-Saxon Æ æ and Ð ð or Þ þ are printed as they appear in John of Worcester's text.

E *caudata* (ę) has been rendered as *e*.

Capital U and V are printed as V, Uu as W, and lower case u and v as u.

⟨ ⟩ indicate an editorial addition to the base MS C; to the base MS H, in the case of the recension preserved by HL; and to L and B in Appendices A and B respectively.

---

[71] Bately, *MS A*; *MS B*, ed. Simon Taylor (= Dumville-Keynes, *ASC* iv (Cambridge, 1983); Angelika Lutz, *Die Version G der Angelsächsischen Chronik* (Munich, 1981); *The Peterborough Chronicle*, ed. D. Whitelock (Early English Manuscripts in Facsimile, iv; Copenhagen, 1954). A is Cambridge, Corpus Christi College 173, D is Oxford, Bodleian Laud. Misc. 636 and the remaining five are in the BL Cotton Collection: B, Tiberius A. VI; C, Tiberius B. I; F (which is bilingual and contains *ADL*), Domitian VIII; and G, Otto B. XI.

THE CHRONICLE OF
JOHN OF WORCESTER
450-1066

SIGLA

John of Worcester

C   Oxford, Corpus Christi College 157
E   Evesham, Almonry Museum s.n.
H   Dublin, Trinity College 502
L   London, Lambeth Palace Library 42
B   Oxford, Bodleian Library, Bodley 297
P   Cambridge, Corpus Christi College 92

G   Dublin, Trinity College 503

JW   agreement of all witnesses

C^1 C^2 C^3 indicate the first, second, and third scribes; and similarly for the scribes of the other witnesses. The page-numbers of C are indicated in the left-hand margin.

Marianus Scotus

N   London, BL Cotton Nero C. V
Mar.   Vat. Pal. lat. 830 and N; or Vat. Pal. lat. 830 when N's reading is given

Asser (annals 849–88)

As   Stevenson, *Asser* (when used without other Asserian sigla, signifies agreement of all witnesses with Stevenson's text)

(As)   Stevenson, *Asser* when Stevenson's text is not supported by all witnesses

Ac   Cambridge, Corpus Christi College 100, from Acott for Archbishop Parker

Acott   London, BL Cotton Otho A. XII. Largely destroyed by fire

Ao   London, BL Cotton Otho A. XII* (s. xvi), from Acott after some interpolations had been made for Archbishop Parker

Au   Cambridge, University Library, Add. 3825 (s. xvi^ex), possibly a fair copy of a proof of Parker's edition of 1574

Aw   *Asserius de rebus gestis Ælfredi*, ed. F. Wise (Oxford, 1722)

Norman Annals

AU   *Annales Uticenses* (Annals of Saint-Évroul).
AG   *Annales Gemmeticenses* (Annals of Jumièges).
AC   *Annales Cadomenses* (Annals of Caen).
AMSM   Annals of Mont Saint-Michel

Visio Eucherii (annal 741)

These *sigla* are those used for the decree-text in *MGH Capitularia Regum Francorum* ii. 2. 432–3.

1   Sirmondi (J. Sirmond, *Capitula Caroli Calvi et successorum* (Paris, 1623), pp. 181–2)
2   Paris, BN lat. 5095
3   Vatican, Bibl. Apost., lat. 4982.
4   Rome, Bibl. Vallicelliana, C. 16.
5   Baronius (C. Baronius, *Annales Ecclesiastici ad A. 858* (12 vols., Mainz, 1601–8), x. 177)
6   Vatican, Bibl. Apost., Reg. lat. 291 (part only)
7   Copenhagen, Royal Library, Gl. kgl. S. 166
8   Paris, BN lat. 4628a

p. 242   **[450]** (xxvii) 472 *Valentinianus. Auienus.*[1] Angli Saxones, *Martiani*[2] *principis tempore, Beda teste, Brittanniam tribus longis nauibus adue*cti sunt, qui *de tribus Germanie populis fortioribus, id est Saxonibus, Anglis et Iutis aduenerant. De Iutarum origine sunt Cantuarii et Vectuarii, de Saxonibus Orientales Saxones, Meridiani Saxones, Occidui Saxones, de Anglis* uero *hoc est de illa patria que Angulus dicitur, Orientales Angli, Mediterranei Angli, Merci, tota Northanhymbrorum progenies, ceterique Anglorum populi sunt* exorti. Quorum *primi duces fuisse perhibentur duo fratres Hengst et Hors. Erant autem isti filii Wictgisli, cuius pater Witta, cuius pater Wecta, cuius pater*[a] *Woden, de cuius stirpe multarum prouinciarum regium genus originem duxit.*[3]

    Concilium in Epheso contra Euticen presbiterum, qui Constantinopoli monasterio celeberrimo presidebat, dicens Deum[b] *tantum esse Christum, non hominem. In quo Hilarius diaconus cum Iulio episcopo Puteolano uice pape Leonis missi fuerunt. Qui diaconus quia pro uiolata fide illic clamauit pro anima sua latenter fugit ad Romam. Theodosius imperator cum magna pompa a Placidia et Leone*[4] *et omni senatu deductus* ⟨*est*⟩, *et in mausoleo ad apostolum Petrum depositus. Huius Theodosii tempore, concilio apud Kartaginem ab impiissimo Honorico Wandalorum rege habito, beatus Theonestus, cum alii sedibus quoque suis episcopi pellerentur, a Philippis sedis sue urbe depulsus, cum discipulis suis peregrinationis causa seu consolationis percipiende gratia Romam sub tempore Leonis pape uenit. A quo fauorabiliter susceptus, et aliquandiu ibi commoratus, inde ad beatum Ambrosium Mediolanensem episcopum contendit. Ab ipso quoque caritatiue susceptus, Theodosio principi tunc ibi degenti per ipsum est presentatus, et ab utrisque postremo in pace*

p. 243   *dimissus. Inde* | *aduenit Vindelicam primam Tracie*[5] *urbem augustam, ubi et passus est unus ex discipulis eius Vrsus. Discedens ergo inde, uenit ad Sigismundum regem Allobrogum et ab eo dirigitur ad Treuirensem Paulinum, indeque nauigio urbem adiit Mogontiacum. Vbi, contra hereticos fortissime sana dimicantem doctrina, secundum*

---

    [a] *interlin.* C[1]   [b] Deum *JW (N)*, Dominum *Mar.*

---

    [1] Mar.
    [2] Marcian (450–7). Bede (*HE* i. 15, v. 24) assigned the coming of the English, not to 450, but to the reigns of Marcian and Valentinian III. JW's omission of the reference to Valentinian as emperor and his 450 must be influenced by Marianus, who assigns the opening of Marcian's reign to that year and mentions Valentinian not as emperor but as consul.

[**450**] Valentinianus. Avienus.[1] In the time of the Emperor Marcian,[2] as Bede testifies, the Anglo-Saxons came to Britain in three warships. They came from three very powerful Germanic tribes, namely, the Saxons, the Angles, and the Jutes. Of Jutish origin are the peoples of Kent and of the Isle of Wight. From the Saxons come the East Saxons, the South Saxons, and the West Saxons. From the Angles, that is, those from the country that is called Angeln, are descended the East Angles, the Middle Angles, the Mercians, the whole race of the Northumbrians, and the other Anglian peoples. Their first leaders are said to have been two brothers, Hengest and Horsa. They were the sons of Wihtgils, son of Witta, son of Wecta, son of Woden, from whose stock the royal houses of many kingdoms derived their descent.[3]

A council was held at Ephesus against the priest Eutyches, who ruled a most renowned monastery in Constantinople, and who affirmed that Christ is only God, not man. To this council Hilarus the deacon, and Julius, bishop of Pozzuoli, were sent on Pope Leo's behalf. The deacon fled for his life in secret to Rome after protesting against the injury done to the Faith. The body of the Emperor Theodosius was borne with great pomp by Placidia and Leo[4] and the whole senate and placed in a mausoleum at St Peter's. In the time of this Theodosius a council was held by the most impious Hunneric, king of the Vandals, at Carthage. When the other bishops were driven from their sees, the blessed Theomnestus was also expelled from his see at Philippi, and came to Rome (in Pope Leo's time) with his four disciples, both as a pilgrim and for comfort. He was received favourably by Pope Leo and stayed there some time. Then he went eagerly to St Ambrose, bishop of Milan, by whom also he was lovingly received. By him he was also presented to the Emperor Theodosius, who was then staying at Milan, and was finally sent away by both in peace. From there he went to Augsburg, the first imperial city of Thrace,[5] where one of his disciples, Ursus, suffered martyrdom. Leaving accordingly, he came to Sigismund, king of the *Allobroges* [Burgundians], and was sent by him to Paulinus of Trier. From there he made his way by boat to the city of Mainz. There he left a second disciple, Alban, who, striving most valiantly with sound teaching against the

---

[3] *HE* i. 15.   [4] Pope Leo I (440–61).
[5] Marianus has the correct *Rhaetia*.

*reliquit discipulum Albanum, martirio uerissime[a] super niuem dealba-
tum.*

   *Romanorum quinquagesimus .iii. Martianus secundum alios regnauit
annis .vii., iuxta autem eum qui tunc historiam conscripsit[1] annis .viii.,
secundum historiam Romanam[2] annis .vii., mensibus duobus, hoc est
quasi usque kalend. Iulii in anno quadringentesimo quadragesimo
quinto post passionem.[3]*

[451] (i) 473 *Martianus. Adelfius.[4]* Childericus filius Merouei
regum Francorum quartus.[5] *Pugna facta[b] in Galliis inter Ethium et
Attalam Hunorum regem cum utriusque populi cede Attala fugatur in
Gallias superiores.[6]*

[452] (ii) 474 *Herculianus. Asporatius.[c] Iohannes baptista duobus
monachis caput suum iuxta Herodis habitaculum reuelat, quod
E⟨me⟩ssam[d] Fenicis urbem cum magno honore perlatum est.[7]*

[453] (iii) 475 *Opilio. Vincomalus. Sinodus Calcidonensis facta, ubi
Eutices et Dioscorus dampnati sunt. Sanctus Leo papa sic: 'de pascali
obseruantia sancte memorie Theophilus ad Theodosium Augustum
seniorem scribens, per .c. annos a primo predicti principis consulatu
digessit ordinem diei festi. Cuius instructionis .lxxiv. annus nunc
euoluitur, quo Opilione consule pridie idus Aprilis celebrata est sacra
solennitas, unde sequenti anno .ii.[e] non. Aprilis consequitur' et reliqua.
Sed annus, qui erit .lxxvi., discordat, ut uidetur, siquidem .viii. kalend.
Maii pasca constituit⟨ur⟩[f] cum .xv. kalend. Maii, ut uidetur, deberet
fieri.[8]*

[454] (iiii) 476 *Ethius. Studius. Episcopus Deogratias ordinatur in
basilica Fausti die dominica .viii. kalendas Nouembris.[9]*

[455] (v) 477 *Valentius.[g] Antemius. Valentinianus[10] Augustus .xi.
kalend. Octobris Ethium patricium et Boetium Kartagine occidit.
Valentinianus autem ab amicis Ethii .xiii. kalend. Aprilis in campo
Martio occiditur. Maximus[11] uero, uir, gemini consulatus et patricie*

---

[a] uerisi *erased before* uerissime *C*   [b] facta est *HL*   [c] *erasure after second* a,
and tius *interlin. C*[1]   [d] Emessam *Mar.*, Edissam *JW (N)*   [e] *interlin. C*[1], *om.*
Mar.   [f] constituitur *Mar.*, constituit *JW (N)*   [g] Valentius *JW*, Valent. .vii. *(N)*

---

[1] Prosper of Aquitaine.   [2] The *Historia Romana* of Paul the Deacon.

heretics, was made most truly white, exceeding snow, by martyr-dom.

Marcian, the fifty-third Roman emperor, according to some ruled seven years, according to the author of the contemporary history,[1] eight years, according to the *Roman History*,[2] seven years, two months, that is up to 1 July in the year 445 after the Passion.[3]

[451] Marcian. Adelphius.[4] Childeric, son of Merovech, became the fourth of the Frankish kings.[5] A battle took place in Gaul between Aetius and Attila, king of the Huns, in which there was slaughter on both sides; Attila fled into Gallia Superior.[6]

[452] Herculanus. Sporachius. John the Baptist revealed his head to two monks next to Herod's dwelling, and it was taken to the city of Emesa in Phoenicia with great honour.[7]

[453] Opilio. Vincomalus. A synod was held at Chalcedon at which Eutyches and Dioscorus were condemned. The holy Pope Leo spoke thus: 'Theophilus of holy memory, writing to the Emperor Theodosius the elder about the observance of Easter, laid down the date of the feast-day for a hundred years from the first consulship of the abovementioned emperor. The seventy-fourth year of his cycle is now unrolling, in which, Opilio being consul, the sacred solemnity was celebrated on 12 April, in the following year it falls on 4 April,' and so on. But the year that will be seventy-sixth seems not to be right since Easter falls on 24 April, whereas it should be, it seems, on 17 April.[8]

[454] Aetius. Studius. Bishop Deogratias was ordained in the basilica of Faustus on Sunday, 25 October.[9]

[455] Valens. Anthemius. The Emperor Valentinian[10] slew the patrician Aetius and Boethius at Carthage on 21 September. Valentinian, however, was slain by friends of Aetius in the Campus Martius on 20 March. But Maximus,[11] the holder of two

---

[3] Mar.   [4] Mar.
[5] Norman Annals. *AU, AG, ASN* (all 450) record Childeric's succession.
[6] Mar.
[7] Mar.   [8] Mar.   [9] Mar.
[10] Valentinian III 425-55.   [11] Petronius Maximus 455.

dignitatis, alia die .xii. kalend. Aprilis Rome sumpsit imperium. Post mensem autem alterum, nuntiato ei ex Affrica Giserici regis aduentu, multisque nobilibus popularibus ex urbe fugientibus, cum Maximus, data abeundi cunctis licentia, trepidus uellet abscedere, septuagesimo .vii. adepti imperii die a famulis Valentiniani dilaniatus est, et menbratim in Tiberim proiectus, sepultura quoque caruit. Post hec consecuta est multis digna lacrimis Romana captiuitas, cum enim urbem omni presidio uacuam Gisericus obtinuit, .iiii. idus Iulii, feria .iiii., occurrens sibi sanctus papa Leo extra portas, ita eum sua supplicatione Deo agente[a] *liniuit, ut cum omnia potestati eius essent contradita,*[b] *ciuitati tamen ab igne et cede et supplicio parceret. Roma uero per .xiiii. dies secura et libera scrutatione omnibus opibus suis euacuata est, multaque milia captiuorum prout cuique etate uel arte placuerat, cum regina et filiabus eius Kartaginem sunt adducta. Hoc anno, hoc est quadringentesimo quinquagesimo quinto incarnationis iuxta Dionisium, pasca dominicum .viii. kalend. Maii recte celebratum est, ordinatione sancti Theophili, quod sanctus papa Leo .xv. kalend. Maii potius obseruandum protestabatur.*[1]

Hengst et Hors cum Wyrtgeorno Brytonum rege in loco qui dicitur Ægelesthrep pugnauere, et, licet in ea pugna Hors occisus esset, Hengst tamen [2]uictoriam habuit[2] et post hec cum filio suo Æsc regnare coepit.[3]

[456] (vi) 478 *Varan. Iohannes.* Ciclus .xxv. decennouenalis incipit indictione .ix. *Post Maximum in Galliis Auitus*[4] *sumpsit imperium.*[5]

[457] (vii) 479 *Constantinus. Rufus. Auitus Placentie deposuit imperium.* [c]*Martiano defuncto apud Constantinopolim,*[d] *Leo*[6] *orientis, Maiorianus*[7] *Italie suscepit imperium. Hucusque in cronica Eusebii in cuius fine hec habentur. Post consulatum Theodosii .xvii. et Festi, Gisericus*[8] *Wandalorum rex Kartaginem ingressus est .xiiii. kalend. Nouembris, in qua regnauit annis .xxvii., mensibus .iii., diebus .vi. Post hunc regnauit Hunerix,*[9] [e]*id est Honoricus,*[e] *filius eius annis .vii.,*

---

[a] *interlin.* C[1]   [b] *con interlin.* C[1]   [c] Ardabures et Maximinianus *appear here after a gap left for a new year Mar.*   [d] *partly over erasure* C   [e-e] id est Honoricus *written above* Hunerix C[1]L[1] *(N*[2]*?), om.* HP, *uel* Onoricus *written above* Hunericus B[1]?

---

[1] Mar.   [2-2] No equivalent in ASC.   [3] ASC.   [4] Avitus 455-6.

consulships and a man of patrician status, seized imperial power at Rome the next day, 21 March. However, two months later news was received of King Gaiseric's arrival from Africa, and many of the nobles and common people fled from the city, since a fearful Maximus wished to escape, and gave permission to all to leave. On the seventy-seventh day from his assumption of power he was torn to pieces by Valentinian's retainers, and the pieces thrown into the Tiber. He had no tomb. After this there followed Rome's captivity, worthy of many lamentations, for Gaiseric took a quite undefended city on Tuesday, 12 July. The holy Pope Leo met him outside the gates and, with God's help, so persuaded him that, although everything was entirely in his power, he yet spared the city fire and slaughter and punishment. But in fourteen days Rome, after an assured and unmolested search, was emptied of all her treasures, and many thousands of captives (suitable because of their age or skill) were taken off to Carthage with the queen and her daughters. In this year, the 455th of the Lord's incarnation in Dionysius' reckoning, the Lord's Easter was, according to the calculation of the blessed Theophilus, correctly celebrated on 24 April, but the holy Pope Leo argued that it should be observed instead on 17 April.[1]

Hengest and Horsa fought Vortigern, king of the Britons, in a place called *Ægelesthrep* and, although Horsa was killed in that battle, Hengest [2]was victorious,[2] and after that began to reign with his son Æsc.[3]

[456] Varanes. John. The twenty-fifth cycle of nineteen years began in the ninth indiction. Avitus[4] assumed power in Gaul after Maximus.[5]

[457] Constantinus. Rufus. Avitus laid down the imperial power at Piacenza. After Marcian's death at Constantinople, Leo[6] became emperor in the East, Majorian[7] in Italy. Up to this point, these events are recorded at the end of the chronicle of Eusebius. On 19 October, after the seventeenth consulship of Theodosius and of Festus, Gaiseric,[8] king of the Vandals, entered Carthage on 19 October, where he reigned for twenty-seven years, three months, and six days. After him, Hunneric,[9] that is Honoric, his son, ruled

---

[5] Mar.   [6] Leo I 457-74.   [7] Majorian 457-61.   [8] Gaiseric 439-77.
[9] Hunneric 477-84.

mensibus .x., diebus .xxviii., qui in fine anni septimi regni sui catholice ecclesie persecutionem mouit, omnesque ecclesias clausit et cunctos Domini catholicos sacerdotes cum Eugenio Kartaginensi episcopo exilio religauit ipseque Dei iudicio scatens uermibus uitam finiuit. Post eum regnauit Guntamundus,[1] Gentuni eiusdem Honorici fratris filius, annis .xi., mensibus .ix., diebus .xi. Qui .iii. anno regni sui cimiterium sancti martyris Agilei apud Kartaginem catholicis dari precepit, Eugenio Kartaginensi episcopo ab eodem de exilio iam reuocato. Decimo autem anno regni sui ecclesias catholicorum aperuit, et omnes Dei sacerdotes petente Eugenio Kartaginensi episcopo de exilio reuocauit. Que ecclesie fuerunt clause annis decem, | mensibus .vi., diebus .v. Hoc est ab .viii. anno Honorici, id est ex die .vii. idus Februarii usque in decimum^a annum regis Guntamundi die .iiii. idus Augusti in quo completi sunt supradicti anni .x., menses .vi., dies .v. Qui memoratus Guntamundus rex postmodum uixit annos duos, mensem unum. Post quem regnauit Trasamundus,[2] Gentunis filius, annis .xxvi., mensibus .viii., diebus .iiii. Ab exordio ergo imperii Auiti usque annum .xxvi. Trasamundi, a .xiiii. autem anno imperii et morte Valentis usque in annum .xxvi. Trasamundi anni sunt ⟨. . .⟩^b Post quem regnauit Hildericus,[3] filius Honorici, annos .viii., dies .viii. Qui in exordio regni sui Bonifacium episcopum apud Kartaginem in ecclesia sancti Agilei ordinari precepit et omnibus catholicis libertatem restituit. Quo regnante assumpta tyrannide Geilemar[4] regnum eius inuasit, in quo fecit annos tres et totidem menses, qui tanta homicidia scelestus commisit ut nec parentibus parceret. Fiunt ergo ab exordio regni Giserici regis usque ad exitium Wandalorum anni ⟨. . .⟩^b Ab interitu ergo Valentis quod erat in .xiiii. anno regni eius usque ad supradictum tempus sunt anni ⟨. . .⟩^b Collecta ergo omnium summa annorum ab Adam usque ad Wandalorum perditionem fiunt .v. milia .dccxxxiii.[5]

Hengst et Æsc in loco qui dicitur Creccanford cum Brytonibus proelium commisere et ex eis .iiii. milia uirorum[6] in ore gladii peremere, reliqui Cantiam penitus dimisere et cum magno metu ad Lundoniam fugere.[7]

Romanorum quinquagesimus quartus Leo secundum omnes regnauit

---

^a .xi. HL   ^b space left blank JW(N)

---

[1] Gunthamund 484–96.   [2] Thrasamund 496–523.   [3] Hildric 496–523.
[4] Gelimer 531–4.   [5] Mar.   [6] ASC EFG have 'four troops'.
[7] ASC A (457) (B) CEF (much shorter, omits conquests) (456).

p. 244

for seven years, ten months, and twenty-eight days. At the end of the seventh year of his reign, he set afoot the persecution of the Catholic church, and closed all churches and sent all Catholic priests of the Lord, together with Eugenius bishop of Carthage, into exile, and he himself, by the judgement of God, ended his life infested with worms. Gunthamund,[1] son of that same Honoric's brother, Gentunnus, reigned after him for eleven years, nine months and eleven days. He, in the third year of his reign, ordered that the cemetery of the holy martyr Agylleus at Carthage be given to the Catholics. He had already recalled Eugenius bishop of Carthage from exile. In the tenth year of his reign he opened up the Catholic churches and, at the request of Eugenius bishop of Carthage recalled all God's priests from exile. These churches were closed for ten years, six months, and five days, that is, from 7 February, in Hunneric's eighth year, until 10 August in King Gunthamund's tenth year, in which period were completed the ten years, six months, and five days mentioned above. This king Gunthamund, already mentioned, then lived two years and one month. Thrasamund,[2] Gentunus' son, reigned after him for twenty-six years, eight months, and four days. From the beginning of Avitus' reign to the twenty-sixth year of Thrasamund, there are . . . years, but from the fourteenth regnal year and death of Valens to the twenty-sixth year of Thrasamund there are . . . years. After Thrasamund, Hilderic,[3] son of Hunneric, reigned for eight years and eight days. At the beginning of his reign he ordered that Boniface be ordained bishop of Carthage in the church of St Agylleus, and he restored the freedom of all Catholics. In his reign Gelimer,[4] who had usurped power, invaded his kingdom, over which he ruled three years and as many months; this wicked man committed so many murders that he did not spare even his kinsmen. Thus from the beginning of the rule of King Gaiseric to the destruction of the Vandals were . . . years, and from the death of Valens, which was in the fourteenth year of his reign, to the time mentioned are . . . years. Therefore, the complete total of all the years from Adam to the destruction of the Vandals was 5733.[5]

Hengest and Æsc joined battle with the Britons at a place called *Creacanford* and slew 4,000 men[6] with the edge of the sword. The rest entirely abandoned Kent and fled to London in great fear.[7]

Leo, the fifty-fourth emperor of the Romans, according to all

annis decem et septem, et hoc est usque kalendas Iulii in anno quadrin-
gentesimo sexagesimo primo post passionem.[1]

[458] (i) 480 *Leo Augustus. Maiorianus Augustus.[a] Maiorianus[b] in*
Affricam mouit procinctum.[2]

[459] (ii) 481 *Ricimer. Patricius. Alexandria et Egiptus errore*
Dioscori heretici languescit.[3]

[460] (iii) 482 *Magnus. Apollonius. Heresis Acephalorum, Calcido-*
nense concilium impugnantium, apparuit. Acephali autem dicuntur[c] sine
capite, quia auctor eorum non apparet.[4]

[461] (iiii) 483 *Seuerinus. Dagalaiphus. Maiorianus iuxta Dertonam*
ciuitatem .viii. idus Augusti occiditur, immissione Ricimeris, cui
Seuerum,[5] *natione Lucanum, Rauenne succedere fecit in regnum. Leo*
papa obiit .iiii. kalend. Iulii.[6]

[462] (v) 484 *Leo Augustus. Seuerus Augustus,[d] Hilarius[7] quadra-*
gesimus quintus papa consecratur .ii. idus Nouembris, qui sedit annis
septem, mensibus .vi.[8]

[463] (vi) 485 *Basilius. Viuianus. [e]Theodorus episcopus ciuitatis, que*
Cyria dicitur, eo quod a Cyro rege Persarum sit condita, scribit de
uera incarnatione dominica[f] contra Euticen et Dioscorum qui negant
humanam carnem in Christo.[e][9]

[C³BP]
[g]Dauid qui et Dewi ex patre
rege Sancto nomine et Nonna
matre nascitur.[g][10]

[464] (vii) 486 *Rusticus. Olibrius. Beorgor rex Alanorum apud*
Pergamum a patricio Ricimere peremptus est.[11]

---

[a] interlin. C¹B¹, om. HL   *[b] Augustus add. HL*   *[c] id est add. (N)*
[d] interlin. C¹B¹   *[e–e] Theodorus . . . Christo] over erasure C³*   *[f] dominica HL,*
Domini *C³BP*   *[g–g] Dauid . . . nascitur] add. at line-end, extending into mg. C³, om.*
HL

---

[1] Mar.   [2] Mar.   [3] Mar.   [4] Mar.
[5] Libius Severus 451–5.   [6] Mar.   [7] Hilarus 461–8.

the authorities, ruled seventeen years, and that is up to 1 July in the 461st year after the Passion.[1]

[458] Leo Augustus. Majorian Augustus. Majorian prepared an expedition against Africa.[2]

[459] Ricimer. Patricius. Alexandria and Egypt languished in the error of the heretic Dioscorus.[3]

[460] Magnus. Apollonius. The heresy of the Acephali who opposed the Council of Chalcedon was made manifest. The Acephali are so called because their author is not to be seen.[4]

[461] Severinus. Dagalaiphus. Majorian was killed near the city of Dertona on 6 August at the instigation of Ricimer. He made Severus[5] the Lucanian the successor to the Empire at Ravenna. Pope Leo died on 28 June.[6]

[462] Leo Augustus. Severus Augustus. Hilarus[7] was consecrated the forty-fifth pope on 12 November; he reigned seven years and six months.[8]

[463] Basilius. Vivianus. Theodoret, bishop of the city called Cyrrhus because it was founded by Cyrus, king of the Persians, wrote about the true incarnation of the Lord to refute Eutyches and Dioscorus, who denied Christ's humanity.[9]

> David or Dewi was born to his father, King Sanctus by name, and his mother Nonna.[10]

[464] Rusticus. Olybrius. Beorgor, king of the Alans, was slain by the patrician Ricimer at Pergamum.[11]

---

[8] Mar.   [9] Mar.
[10] The *Annales Cambriae* assign David's death to 601, and Rhigyfarch in his *Vita* of David gives him a life-span of 147 years. Some discussion of David's dates in M. Miller, 'Date-guessing and Dyfed', *Studia Celtica*, xii–xiii (1977–8), 33–60.
[11] Mar.

[465] (viii) 487 *Arminericus. Basiliscus. Seuerus Rome in palatio fraude Ricimeris ueneno perimitur.*[1]
Hengst et Æsc cum Brytonibus prope Wippidesfleote, [2]id est Wippidi tranatorium,[2] pugnauerunt, et .xii. duces exercitus [2]cum multis aliis[2] occiderunt, cum unus tantum[3] miles[4] cui nomen Wipped erat ex suis in acie corruit.[5]

[466] (ix) 488 *Leo. iii.* v.c.c.[6] *Theodorus predictus episcopus Cirie scribit historiam ecclesiasticam, que Tripertita dicitur, a fine librorum Eusebii, id est ab anno .xx. Constantini magni usque ad tempus huius Leonis imperatoris, quo et ipse episcopus obiit.*[7]

[467] (x) 489 *Puseus. Iohannes. Anthemius*[8] *a Leone imperatore ad Italiam mittitur, qui tertio ab urbe miliario in loco Brontotas suscepit imperium.*[9]

[468] (xi) 490 *Anthemius Augustus. Marcellinus occiditur in Sicilia. Victorius iubente papa Hilario scripsit pascalem circulum quingentorum triginta duorum annorum.*[10]

[469] (xii) 491 *Martianus. Zeno. Arabundus imperium temptans, iussus Anthemii exilio deportatur.*[11]

[470] (xiii) 492 *Seuerus. Iordanes. Romanus patricius, affectans imperium, capite truncatur. Hilarius papa obiit .x. kalend. Martii. Simplicius*[12] *papa .xlvi. sedit annis .xv.*[13]

[471] (xiiii) 493 *Leo Augustus .iiii.*[a] *Probianus. Aspar affectans tyrannidem Constantinopoli a Leone imperatore occiditur.*[14]

[472] (xv) 494 *Festus. Martianus. Ricimer patricius, Rome facto imperatore Olibrio,*[15] *Anthemium, contra reuerentiam principis et ius affinitatis, cum graui clade ciuitatis extinguit, qui .xl. die glorie sue defunctus est. Olibrius autem mense .vii. imperii uitam exiuit.*[b16]

---

[a] *interlin. C¹B¹, om. HL*   [b] finiuit *LP*

[1] Mar.   [2–2] No equivalent in ASC.   [3] Not in ASC.
[4] ASC BC omit 'þegn' accidentally.   [5] ASC AE (465) BC (461) F (455, *sic*).
[6] 'v.c.c.', and in later annals 'v.c.' and 'c.c.', presumably derive from misunderstanding of v.c.(*Vir clarissimus*). and its plural vv.cc. (*uiri clarissimi*).
[7] Mar.   [8] Anthemius 455–6.   [9] Mar.

[465] Herminericus. Basiliscus. Severus was poisoned in the palace at Rome through the treachery of Ricimer.[1]

Hengest and Æsc fought the Britons near *Wippidesfleote*, [2]that is the estuary of the Wipped,[2] and killed twelve of the army's leaders [2]and many others.[2] Only one of their own men, an outstanding[3] warrior[4] called Wipped, fell in the battle.[5]

[466] Leo for the third time v.c.c.[6] The abovementioned Theodoret, bishop of Cyrrhus, wrote the church history that is called the *Tripertita*, a continuation of Eusebius' books, that is from the twentieth year of Constantine the Great to the time of the Emperor Leo under whom the bishop himself died.[7]

[467] Pusaeus. John. Anthemius[8] was sent to Italy by the Emperor Leo and became emperor three miles from the city, in the place called *Brontotas*.[9]

[468] Anthemius Augustus. Marcellinus was slain in Sicily. Victor, at the request of Pope Hilarus, drew up the Easter cycle for 532 years.[10]

[469] Marcianus. Zeno. Arvandus, who attempted to seize the imperial power, was sent into exile at Anthemius' command.[11]

[470] Severus. Jordanes. The patrician Romanus, aspiring to imperial power, was beheaded. Pope Hilarus died on 20 February. Simplicius,[12] the forty-sixth pope, ruled for fifteen years.[13]

[471] Leo Augustus for the fourth time. Probianus. Aspar, attempting usurpation, was killed by the Emperor Leo at Constantinople.[14]

[472] Festus. Marcian. At Rome the patrician Ricimer, after making Olybrius[15] emperor, slew Anthemius, with considerable slaughter in the city, an offence against the reverence due to emperors and to the bond of kinship, and he died on the fortieth day from his achievement. Olybrius, however, departed this life in the seventh month of his reign.[16]

---

[10] Mar.   [11] Mar.   [12] Simplicius 468–83.   [13] Mar.
[14] Mar.   [15] Olybrius 472.   [16] Mar.

[473] (xvi) 495 *Leo Augustus* v.c. *Gundibaldo hortante, Glicerius*[1]
Rauenne sumpsit imperium. Eodem anno Leo nepotem suum Leonem
consortem facit imperium.[2]

Hengst et Æsc[3] quarta uice[3] cum Brytonibus pugnauere et,
[3]potita uictoria,[3] innumerabilia spolia tulere, in qua pugna Brytones Anglos sicut ignem[.4] fugerunt.[5]

[474] (xvii) 496 *Leo Augustus* *ᵃiunior c.ᵃ Nepos*[6] *Rome Glicerio suc-*
p. 245 *cessit in regnum. Leo imperator hoc anno obiit.* | *Hec Cassiodorus.*
Iordanis episcopus sic in cronica ab eo hoc tempore composita, sic
quoque: 'Leo Leonem iuniorem ex Ariagne filia nepotem suum in impe-
rio ordinans orientali, anno .xvi. imperii sui obiit'.[7] Francorum rex
Childericus hoc anno uita decessit et regni heredem suum filium
Clodoueum reliquit.[8] Hic *.x. anno regni sui usque Sequanam,*
sequenti tempore usque Ligerim, regnum suum dilatauit.[9] *.xv.* autem
Alamannos, rege eorumᵇ occiso, *cepit* et *tributarios constituit*[10] et
primus regum Francorumᶜ a sancto Remigio die pasce, cum *.iii.*
*milia uirorum de exercitu suo, sororibusque*ᵈ duabus *Alboflede et Lan-*
deilde,[11] regenerationis lauacrum suscepit. *Processu uero temporis*
per consilium regine sue Christianissime *Rothildis, ecclesiam in hon-*
ore apostolorum Petri et Pauli in Parisius ciuitate fecit, et *post contra*
Alaricum Arrianum hostiliter *pergens, a sancto Remigio benedictionem*
petiit. Cui et benedictionem dedit et uictoriam in uerbo Christi spopon-
*dit, flaxonem*que *uino a se benedicto plenum dedit, precipiens ut tam*
longe ad bellum procederet quandiu illi et suis illud uinum non defi-
ceret. Bibit inde rex ac regalis familia et numerosa turba populi et *uas*
uini detrimentum non patitur, sed more fontis inundatione repletur.
Mouit igitur rex exercitum suum uersus Parisius[12] *ciuitatem,* et *.x.*
miliario ab ea regem *Gothorum Alaricum interfecit* et *post uictoriam,*
multis ciuitatibus sue dicioni subiugatis, usque Tolosam perrexit et post
cum gloriosa uictoria ad propria rediit.[13] *Per idem tempus imperator*

ᵃ⁻ᵃ iunior c.] v.c.c *H*, iunior consul *interlin. above* v.c. *L*   ᵇ *over erasure C*
ᶜ tempore Leonis iunioris *add. LP*   ᵈ sororibus *HL*

---

[1] Glycerius 473.   [2] Mar.   [3-3] No equivalent in ASC.
[4] ASC E has 'very grievously' for 'as if from fire'.   [5] ASC.
[6] Julius Nepos 473-5.   [7] Mar.
[8] Norman Annals. *AG* (472), *AU* and *ASN* (473) record the succession of Clovis
(481-511), which succeeds, in the first two Norman annals, the death of Childeric.
[9] Hincmar, *Vita Remigii,* c. 12. This life is in the Worcester Passional, Cambridge,
Corpus Christi College MS 9, pp. 62-136, which was just possibly the source.

[473] Leo Augustus v.c. With the encouragement of Gundobad, Glycerius[1] seized power at Ravenna. In the same year Leo made his grandson Leo co-emperor.[2]

Hengest and Æsc fought [3]a fourth time[3] with the Britons and, [3]having gained the victory, [3]carried off incalculable spoil. In that battle the British fled from the Angles as if from fire.[4,5]

[474] Leo Augustus the Younger consul. Nepos[6] succeeded Glycerius at Rome as emperor. The emperor Leo died in this year. Thus Cassiodorus, concerning him. And Bishop Jordanes, in the chronicle he composed at this time, also wrote that Leo died in the sixteenth year of his reign, appointing Leo the Younger, his grandson by his daughter Ariadne, emperor.[7] Childeric, king of the Franks, died this year and left his son Clovis heir to the realm.[8] He extended his kingdom, in the tenth year of his reign, as far as the Seine, and later the Loire.[9] In the fifteenth year, he conquered the Alamanni, killing their king, and made them tributary.[10] He was the first of the Frankish kings to receive the baptism of regeneration from St Remigius on Easter Day with 3,000 men of his army and his two sisters, Albofled and Lanthechild.[11] Indeed, in the course of time, on the advice of his most Christian queen Clothild, he built a church dedicated to the Apostles Peter and Paul in the city of Paris, and afterwards, setting off to make war on Alaric the Arian, he sought St Remigius' blessing. The saint not only gave Clovis his blessing but promised victory in the Word of Christ. He gave him a flask full of wine which he had blessed and instructing him to prosecute the war so long as the wine did not fail him and his men. Then the king, the royal household, and a great crowd of people drank and the flask of wine suffered no diminution, but was filled to overflowing like a fountain. Therefore the king advanced with his army towards the city of Paris,[12] and ten miles from it he killed Alaric, king of the Goths, and when, after his victory, he had subdued many cities to his rule, he penetrated as far as Toulouse and afterwards he returned home, after a glorious victory.[13] At the same time the

---

[10] Ibid., c. 13.   [11] Ibid., c. 15.

[12] This error for Poitiers is not found in any printed witness. It could have been caused by the scribe's (or compiler's) eye momentarily resting on the words 'Parisius ciuitate' above in the same chapter.

[13] Hincmar, Vita Remigii, c. 19.

Anastasius illi coronam auream gemmis ornatam et *tunicam* ac baltheum*ᵃ misit, et ab ea die consul et augustus est appellatus.* Deinceps *coronam auream cum gemmis que regnum appellari solet,* sancto Petro, beato Remigio suggerente, *direxit. Post hec omnia in pace* uitam finiuit, *et in ecclesia sancti Petri apostoli quam ipse et regina sua edificauerunt* honorifice *sepultus est.*¹

Romanorum .lv. Leo² iunior mox paucis mensibus cum puerile, ordinante tamen patre,³ rexisset imperium, manu sua generum Zenonem coronans imperatoremque constituens, rebus humanis excessit. Zenon⁴ autem natione Isaurus, gener Leonis imperatoris, regnauit annis .xvii. Hec Iordanis episcopus, et hoc est iuxta historiam Romanam quod Leo regnauerit annis .xvi. ac mensibus .vi., hoc est usque kalend. Ianuarii. In eodem .xvi. quo Leo obiit ᵇTheodoricus rex Romam optinuit,ᵇ ᶜtempore Leonis iunioris.ᶜ

*Romanorum quinquagesimus .vi. Zenon regnauit secundum omnes annis .xvii., hoc est usque kalend. Ianuarii, in anno quadringentesimo septuagesimo nono post passionem.*⁵

[475] (i) 497   *Proconsulatus Leonis Augusti iunioris. Ciclus decennouenalis .xxvi. incipit indictione .xiii. Orestes, Nepote in Dalmatias fugato, filio Augustulo⁶ dedit imperium.*⁷

[476] (ii) 498   *Basiliscus .ii.ᵈ Armatus.* Ciclus solis incipit .iiii. concurrentibus bissextilibus. *Ab Odouacre Orestes et frater eius Paulus occisi sunt, nomenque regis Odouacer⁸ assumpsit sine purpura et regalibus insignibus.*⁹

[477] (iii) 499   *Proconsulatus Basilisci. Armati. Iste Zenon Leonem Augusti filium interficere quesiuit, sed mater eius pro eo alium forma similem optulit. Leonem uero occulte clericum fecit quique in clericatu usque ad Iustini tempora uixit.*¹⁰

Ælle et eius tres filii Cymen, Plencing et Cissa cum tribus nauibus in Britaniam uenere, et in loco qui uocatur Cymenesora

---

ᵃ blatteam Hincmar, *Vita Remigii*, baltteam *over erasure* Cambridge, Corpus Christi College MS 9   ᵇ⁻ᵇ Theodoricus . . . optinuit] *expunctuated* C, *om.* HLBP ᶜ⁻ᶜ tempore Leonis iunioris] *om.* L   ᵈ *om.* HL (N)

---

¹ Hincmar, *Vita Remigii*, c. 20.   ² Leo II 474.
³ As Marianus had correctly stated at the opening of this annal, Leo II was in fact the grandson of Leo I, by his daughter Ariadne and Zeno.

Emperor Anastasius sent him a golden crown adorned with gems
and a tunic and baldric and from that day he was called consul
and emperor. Afterwards, at St Remigius' instance, he sent the
golden crown with gems, which was by custom called his royalty,
to St Peter. After these events, he ended his life, and was buried
with honour in the church of St Peter the apostle, which he and
his queen had built.[1]

Leo the Younger,[2] fifty-fifth emperor of the Romans, when he
had ruled the empire as a boy for a few months although by his
father's appointment,[3] crowned his son-in-law Zeno, made him
emperor, and departed human affairs. But Zeno,[4] by race an
Isaurian, father of the Emperor Leo, ruled seventeen years. Thus
says Bishop Jordanes. According to the Roman History, Leo
reigned sixteen years and six months, that is, until 1 January. In
that sixteenth year in which Leo died, in the time of Leo the
Younger, King Theodoric gained Rome.

Zeno, fifty-sixth emperor of the Romans, reigned seventeen
years, according to all, that is until 1 January in the 479th year
after the Passion.[5]

[475] The proconsulship of Leo the Younger Augustus. The
twenty-sixth cycle of nineteen years began in the thirteenth indiction. Orestes gave the empire to his son Augustulus[6] after driving
Nepos in exile to Dalmatia.[7]

[476] Basiliscus II. Armatus. The solar cycle begins with four concurrents in a bissextile year. Orestes and his brother Paul were
killed by Odoacer; Odoacer[8] assumed the name of king without
the purple and the royal insignia.[9]

[477] The proconsulship of Basiliscus and Armatus. Zeno sought
to kill Leo, the emperor's son, but his mother brought forward in
his place someone who looked like him. She made Leo take holy
orders secretly and he lived as a cleric until the time of Justin.[10]

Ælle and his three sons Cymen, Wlencing, and Cissa came to
Britain with three ships, beached their ships at a place called

[4] Zeno 474-91.   [5] Mar.   [6] Romulus 475-6.   [7] Mar.
[8] Odoacer 476-93.   [9] Mar.   [10] Mar.

suas naues appulere, ibique Brytones multos occidere et ceteros in siluam que Andredesleage nominatur fugauere.[1]

[478] (iiii) 500   *Ellius v.c.c.*[2]

[479] (v) 501   *Zenon augustus.*[3]

[480] (vi) 502   *Basilius iunior.*[4]

[481] (vii) 503   *Placidius v.c.c. Odouacer in Dalmatiis Oduiam et perimit.*[5]

[C³BP⁵]
ªRegnante Zenone imperatore, facta est inuentio cripte *sancti Michaelis* archangeli *in Gargano monte.*[ª6]

[482] (viii) 504   *Seuerinus v.c.c. Simplicius papa Acatium Constantinopolitanum et Petrum Alexandrinum episcopum Euticianos dampnat.*[7]

[483] (ix) 505   *Faustus v.c.c. Corpus Barnabe apostoli et euangelium Mathei eius stilo scriptumᵇ reperitur, ipso reuelante.*[8]

[484] (x) 506   *Teodericus. Venantius. Apostolicus papa Simplicius obiit .vi. non. Martii. Felix⁹ papa .xlvii. qui sedit annis .viii.*[10]

[485] (xi) 507   *Simmachus v.c.c. Honoricus rex Wandalorum Arrianus in Affrica, exiliatis defugatisque plusquam .cccxxxiiii. episcopis catholicis, ecclesias clausit, plebem uariis affecit suppliciis, et quidem innumeris manus abscidens et linguas precidit, nec tamen loquelam catholice confessionis eripere potuit.*[11]

Ælle cum Brytonibus prope Mearcredesburnan, [12]hoc est riuum Mearcredi,[12] pugnans [12]multos ex eis occidit et ceteros fugauit.[12,13]

ª⁻ª Regnante . . . monte] *mg. alongside 481–3 C³, alongside 482–4 P⁵, om. HL, incorporated under Zeno (474–91) G*   ᵇ *interlin.* C¹

---

[1] ASC. F lacks the reference to the flight of the Britons.   [2] Mar.
[3] Mar.   [4] Mar.   [5] Mar.

Cymenesora, and there slew many Britons and put the others to flight in a wood called *Andredeslea*.[1]

[478] Illus v.c.c.[2]

[479] Zeno Augustus.[3]

[480] Basilius the Younger.[4]

[481] Placidius v.c.c. Odoacer defeated and slew Oduia in Dalmatia.[5]

> In the reign of the Emperor Zeno the crypt of St Michael the Archangel was discovered on Monte Gargano.[6]

[482] Severinus v.c.c. Pope Simplicius condemned as Eutychians the bishops Acacius of Constantinople and Peter of Alexandria.[7]

[483] Faustus v.c.c. The body of the apostle Barnabas and the Gospel of St Matthew, written by his own pen, were discovered through Matthew's own revelation.[8]

[484] Theodoric. Venantius. The apostolic Pope Simplicius died on 2 March. Felix[9] was elected forty-seventh pope, and reigned eight years.[10]

[485] Symmachus v.c.c. Hunneric, the Arian king of the Vandals in Africa, exiled or chased out more than 334 Catholic bishops, closed churches, afflicted the common people with various punishments, cutting off innumerable people's hands, and cutting out tongues, but he could not silence the voice of Catholic faith.[11]

Ælle, fighting the Britons near *Mearcredesburna*, [12]that is Mearcred's Brook, slew many of them and put the rest to flight.[12,13]

---

[6] Hugh of Fleury, p. 130 (with date).   [7] Mar.   [8] Mar.
[9] Felix III (II) 483–92.   [10] Mar.   [11] Mar.
[12-12] No equivalent in ASC.   [13] ASC. Not F (erasure under present annal).

Acatium et Petrum episcopos Euticianos.[1]

[487] (xiii) 509   *Boetius v.c.c. Odouacer Feba rege Rugorum uicto captoque regno potitus est.*[2]

[488] (xiiii) 510   *Dinamius. Sifidius. Theodoricus*[3] *rex intrauit Italiam, his consulibus, teste Cassiodoro. Cui Odouacer | ad Isontium pug-*
p. 246   *nam parans, uictus cum tota gente fugatus est. Iterum eodem anno Verone in pugna uincitur Odouacer.*[a][4]
Hengst,[b] postquam regnum Cantuuariorum .xxxiiii. annis strenuissime rexisset, uite finem fecit, [c]cui filius suus Æsc in regnum successit[c] et .xxiiii. annis regnauit.[5]

[489] (xv) 511   *Probinus. Eusebius.*[6]

[490] (xvi) 512   *Faustus iunior c.c. Theodoricus ad Ducam fluuium Odouacrem uincit et Rauennam fugiens obsidetur.*[7] [d]Hoc anno beatus Mamertus Viennensis episcopus sollennes letanias instituit, id est rogationum.[d][8]

[491] (xvii) 513   *Olibrius iunior c.c. Odouacer cum Rugis egressus Rauenna*[e] *nocte, ad pontem Candidia⟨ni⟩*[f] *a Theodorico rege memorabili certamine superatur. Tunc Wandali pace suppliciter postulata, a Sicilie solita depredatione cessarunt. Eodem anno Zeno imperator obiit. Sanctus Patricius Hibernie arciepiscopus annorum .cxxii. beatissima fine obiit.*[9]
Ælle et Cissa [10]filius suus[10] Andredesceaster post longam obsessionem fregerunt et eius habitatores a paruo usque ad minimum peremerunt.[11]
Romanorum quinquagesimus .vii. Anastasius[12] *secundum omnes regnauit annis uiginti septem, hoc est usque kalend. Maii in anno quingentesimo sexto post passionem.*[13]
[492] (i) 514   *Anastasius augustus.*[a] *Rufus. Hic duas naturas, id est*

---

[a] over erasure C   [b] runs on to 489 C   [c–c] cui . . . successit] cui successit in regnum Æsc filius suus (eius L) HL   [d–d] Hoc anno . . . rogationum] mg. alongside 490–1 C¹B¹, mg. alongside 489–91 P³   [e] Ravennam LB   [f] Candidiam JW

---

[1] Mar.   [2] Mar.   [3] Theoderic 490–526.   [4] Mar.
[5] ASC. Not F (erasure under present annal). ASC mentions neither the death of Hengest nor the length of his reign. ASC E gives 34 years for Æsc.

[**486**] Decius. Longinus. Pope Felix also condemned the Eutychian bishops Acacius and Peter.[1]

[**487**] Boethius v.c.c. Odoacer, having conquered and captured Feletheus, king of the Rugi, obtained his kingdom.[2]

[**488**] Dynamius. Sividius. During their consulships, according to Cassiodorus, King Theoderic[3] entered Italy. He overcame Odoacer as he was preparing for battle by the Isonzo, and put him to flight with all his people. Again in the same year, Odoacer was defeated in battle at Verona.[4]

When Hengest had ruled the kingdom of Kent most vigorously for thirty-four years, he came to the end of his life. His son Æsc succeeded him to the throne and reigned for twenty-four years.[5]

[**489**] Probinus. Eusebius.[6]

[**490**] Faustus the Younger c.c. Theoderic defeated Odoacer at the river *Duca* and Odoacer fled to Ravenna where he was besieged.[7] In this year the blessed Mamertus, bishop of Vienne, instituted solemn litanies, namely Rogations.[8]

[**491**] Olybrius the Younger c.c. Odoacer left Ravenna by night with the Rugi, and was defeated at the Bridge of Candidianus by King Theoderic in a historic battle. Then the Vandals begged for peace, and gave up their customary plundering in Sicily. In the same year the Emperor Zeno died. St Patrick, archbishop of Ireland, made a most blessed end at the age of 122.[9]

Ælle and Cissa, [10]his son,[10] broke into *Andredesceaster* after a long siege, and slew the inhabitants right down to the very least.[11]

Anastasius,[12] the fifty-seventh Roman emperor, reigned, according to all, for twenty-seven years, that is, until 1 May in the year 506 after the Passion.[13]

---

[6] Mar.   [7] Mar.
[8] Norman Annals. *AU* (490), *AG* (488).   [9] Mar.   [10–10] Not in ASC.
[11] ASC ABCE (491) F (490).   [12] Anastasius 491–518.   [13] Mar.

[492] (i) 514 *Anastasius augustus.*^a *Rufus. Hic duas naturas, id est humanitatis et diuinitatis, secundum Euticium negauit in Christo.*[1]

[493] (ii) 515 *Albinus v.c.c. Gelasius*[2] *papa quadragesimus octauus sedit annis .iiii. et mensibus .x.*[3] Sextus regum Francorum Thedericus.^b [4]

[494] (iii) 516 *Asterius. Presidius.* Ciclus decennouenalis .xxvii. incipit indictione .ii. *Theodericus rex Rauennam ingressus, Odouacrem molientem sibi insidias occidit.*[5]

[495] (iiii) 517 *Victor v.c.c. Gelasius papa Nemesium episcopum a Felice papa dampnatum ecclesie sue restituit.*[6]

Hoc in anno duces duo Cerdic scilicet et suus filius Cynric .v. nauibus in Brytanniam sunt aduecti, et in loco qui Cerdicesora nominatur appellentes eodem die cum Brytonibus dimicauerunt ⁷illosque uictos fugere compulerunt.[7,8]

[496] (v) 518 *Paulus v.c.c. Gelasius papa* librum^c *contra Euticen et Nestorium componit et obiit .xiii. kalend. Decembris.*[9]

[497] (vi) 519 *Anastasius Augustus c.c. Anastasius imperator nullius inimicorum suorum meruit uindictam audire sicut nec ipse ecclesie iura seruauit. Anastasius*[10] *papa quadragesimus .ix. post Petrum sedit anno uno et mensibus .vi.*[11]

[498] (vii) 520 *Paulinus. Iohannes. Trasamundus Wandalorum rex catholicas clausit ecclesias, et ducentos uiginti .v. episcopos in exilium in Sardiniam misit. Anastasius papa uoluit occulte reuocare Acatium Constantinopolitanum episcopum dampnatum, et non potuit, qui etiam diuino nutu percussus est. Anastasius papa obiit .v. kalend. Iunii. Simmachus*[12] *papa quinquagesimus annis quindecim.*[13]

[499] (viii) 521 *Iohannes v.c.c. Propter electionem Simmachi pape et Laurentii Festus exconsul nobilissimus et exconsul Probinus ex parte*

---

^a *interlin.* C¹B¹   ^b Thedericus CB, Theodoricus H, Theodericus cuius mater erat Ebroinus L, Thedericus *corrected to* Theodericus P¹   ^c libro (N)

---

[1] Mar.   [2] Gelasius I 491–6.   [3] Mar.

[492] Anastasius Augustus. Rufus. Anastasius, following Eutyches, denied the two natures, that is the human and the divine, in Christ.[1]

[493] Albinus v.c.c. Gelasius,[2] the forty-eighth pope, reigned four years and ten months.[3] Theuderic the sixth king of the Franks.[4]

[494] Asterius. Presidius. The twenty-seventh cycle of nineteen years began in the second indiction. King Theoderic entered Ravenna, and killed Odoacer, who was plotting against him.[5]

[495] Viator v.c.c. Pope Gelasius restored Bishop Nemesius, condemned by Pope Felix, to his church.[6]
   In this year two leaders, namely Cerdic and his son Cynric, came to Britain in five ships, and, landing at a place called *Cerdicesora*, they fought the Britons on the same day [7]and, having defeated them, forced them to flee.[7,8]

[496] Paulus v.c.c. Pope Gelasius wrote a book against Eutyches and Nestorius and died on 19 November.[9]

[497] Anastasius Augustus c.c. The Emperor Anastasius was never rewarded with the news that any of his foes had been punished, since he did not himself observe the laws of the church. Anastasius,[10] the forty-ninth pope after Peter, reigned one year and six months.[11]

[498] Paulinus. John. Thrasamund, king of the Vandals, closed the Catholic churches and sent 225 bishops into exile in Sardinia. Pope Anastasius wished to restore Acacius, the condemned bishop of Constantinople, in secret, but could not, and was struck down by divine command. Pope Anastasius died on 28 May. Symmachus[12] was the fiftieth pope, and ruled for fifteen years.[13]

[499] John v.c.c. As a result of the election of Pope Symmachus and of Laurentius, the most noble ex-consul Festus and the

---

[4] Norman Annals. *AU, AG, ASN* record Theuderic's succession under 492. Theuderic 511-34.
   [5] Mar.   [6] Mar.   [7-7] No equivalent in ASC.   [8] ASC.
   [9] Mar.   [10] Anastasius II 496-8.   [11] Mar.
   [12] Symmachus 486-514.   [13] Mar.

Laurentii aduersus F⟨au⟩stum^a exconsulem ceterosque ex Simmachi parte in medio urbis cedes et homicidia fecerunt clericosque multos occiderunt. Vnde etiam sanctus Pascasius diaconus post mortem suam in pena positus erat, quia contra populum in electione Laurentii usque in finem uite sue permansit sicut in Dialogo legitur.¹ Et hoc fuit peccatum minimum, id est culpa ignorantie, quia ipse putauit rectius ᵇesse coram Deo quod fecit quam aliter.ᵇ²

[500] (ix) 522   *Patricius. Hipatius. Rex Theodericus Romam uenit et senatum affabiliter tractat.³*

[501] (x) 523   *Auienus. Pompeius. Theodericus rex Romane plebi donauit annonas.⁴*
   Port et duo filii sui Byda^c et Meagla cum duabus nauibus in Brytanniam uenere in loco qui dicitur Portesmutha et iuuenem quendam Brytonum nobilissimum ⁵cum multis aliis⁵ occiderunt.⁶

[502] (xi) 524   *Auienus iunior. Probus. Rex Theodericus aquam Rauennam perduxit, cuius formam sumptu proprio instaurauit, que longis ante fuerat ad solum redacta temporibus.⁷*

[503] (xii) 525   *Cetheus v.c.c. Virtute regis Theoderici, uictis Vulgaribus, Sirmium recepit Italia.⁸*

[504] (xiii) 526   *Theodorus. Sabinianus. ᵈCiclus solis incipit .iiii. concurrentibus bissextilibus.ᵈ Simmachus papa multa ecclesiarum opera a fundamentis fecit uel prisca renouauit. Ad beatum Petrum et Paulum et sanctum Laurentium pauperibus habitacula construxit, et omni anno per Affricam uel Sardiniam episcopis qui ᵉin exilio erantᵉ pecuniam et uestes ministrabat.ᶠ⁹*

[505] (xiiii) 527   *Messala. Ariobinna.ᵍ¹⁰*

ᵃ Faustum *Mar.*, Festum *JW (N)*   ᵇ⁻ᵇ esse . . . aliter] *extends into mg.* C   ᶜ uel Be *interlin. above* Byda C¹   ᵈ⁻ᵈ Ciclus . . . bissextilibus] *om.* H   ᵉ⁻ᵉ in . . . erant] erant in exilio H   ᶠ *504 annal runs on to 505 and 506* CB, *507 n.* b *placed here* H   ᵍ *last two letters* -na *interlin.* C¹, Ariobina HL

---

¹ *Dialogues*, iv. 42   ² Mar.   ³ Mar.   ⁴ Mar.
⁵⁻⁵ No equivalent in ASC.

ex-consul Probinus on Laurentius' side committed slaughter and murder in the middle of the city against the ex-consul Faustus and others of Symmachus' party, and killed many clerics. And so even the holy Paschasius the Deacon suffered after his death, since, as can be read in the *Dialogues*,[1] he persevered in opposition to the people until the end of his life in the choice of Laurentius. And this was the least of sins, that is, the fault of ignorance, because he thought that what he did was more virtuous before God than any other course of action.[2]

[**500**] Patricius. Hypatius. King Theoderic came to Rome, and dealt amicably with the senate.[3]

[**501**] Avienus. Pompeius. King Theoderic gave grain to the Roman people.[4]

Port and his two sons Bieda and Mægla came to Britain in two ships to a place called Portsmouth and killed a very noble young Briton [5]together with many others.[5,6]

[**502**] Avienus the Younger. Probus. King Theoderic brought water to Ravenna, rebuilding at his own expense the aqueduct which long before had been razed to the ground.[7]

[**503**] Cethius v.c.c. Through King Theoderic's resolution, Italy regained Sirmium after the defeat of the Bulgarians.[8]

[**504**] Theodorus. Sabinianus. The solar cycle begins with four concurrents in a bissextile year. Pope Symmachus built many churches from the foundations and restored old ones. He built dwellings for the poor near S. Pietro, S. Paolo (fuori le mura), and S. Lorenzo (fuori le mura), and each year he distributed money and clothing to the bishops who were in exile throughout Africa and Sardinia.[9]

[**505**] Messala. Ariobindus.[10]

---

[6] ASC ABCEF (add. to F with year not clear, and omission of killing of Britons). BC do not describe the British noble as young.
[7] Mar.   [8] Mar.   [9] Mar.   [10] Mar.

[506] (xv) 528 *Anastasius augustus .iii.*^{a1}

[507] (xvi) 529 *Venantius iunior. Celer.* ^b*Theodericus contra Francos misit exercitum suum. Qui Gallias Francorum depredatione confusas, uictis hostibus ac fugatis, suo acquisiuit imperio.*^{b,c2}

[508] (xvii) 530 *Importunus v.c.c.*³
Cerdic et suus filius Cynric regem Brytonum Natanleod et .v.
p. 247 milia uirorum in ore gladii peremerunt. | A cuius nomine illa
regio usque ad Cerdicesford Natanleod^{d4} traxit uocabulum.^{e5}

[509] (xviii) 531 *Boetius v.c.c. Apud Kartaginem Olimpius quidam Arrianus in balneis sanctam Trinitatem blasphemauit, statimque ignis iaculo imminente uisibiliter combustus est.*^{f6}

[510] (xix) 532 *Felix. Secundinus. Barnabas quoque quidam Arrianus episcopus dum contra regulam fidei quendam baptizans dixisset: 'Baptizo te, Barnabas, in nomine patris per filium in spiritu sancto.' Statim aqua, que fuerat ad baptizandum deportata, nusquam comparuit. Quod aspiciens qui baptizandus erat, confestim ad ecclesiam catholicam abiit, et baptismum Cristi suscepit.*^{g7}

[511] (xx) 533 *Paulus. Muscianus.*⁸

[512] (xxi) 534 *Probus. Clementinus. Fulgentius in confessione fidei et scientia floruit.*⁹

[C³? BP]
^hEt sanctus Leonardus claruit.^h

[513] (xxii) 535 *Senator v.c.c.* Ciclus decennouenalis .xxviii.
incipit indictione .vi. *Simmachus papa obiit .xiiii. kalend. Augusti.
Hormisda*¹⁰ *papa quinquagesimus primus sedit annis .viii.*¹¹

---

^a *om. HL*   ^{b–b} Theodericus . . . imperio] *under 504* H   ^c *507 annal runs on to 508* CBP, *507 annal runs together with 504–6 (see 504 n. f)* H, *507 annal under 508* L   ^d *corrected to* Natanleage *B*⁵   ^e *508 annal starts under 508 but after the end of 507, which extends well on to 508* CLB   ^f *509 annal runs on to 510* CB, *merges with 510–11* P   ^g *510 annal starts under 511* CB, *merges with 509 and 511* P   ^{h–h} et . . . claruit] *add. at end of annal* C³?, *om. HL*

---

¹ Mar.   ² Mar.   ³ Mar.

[506] Anastasius Augustus, consul for the third time.[1]

[507] Venantius the Younger. Celer. Theoderic sent his army against the Franks. When he had defeated the enemy, and had put the Franks to flight, he gained for his empire the Gallic territories thrown into confusion by the depredations of the Franks.[2]

[508] Importunus v.c.c.[3]
Cerdic and his son Cynric slew Natanleod, king of the Britons, and 5,000 men with the edge of the sword. The area *Natanleod*,[4] right up to Charford, derives its name from him.[5]

[509] Boethius v.c.c. At Carthage, a certain Arian, Olympius, blasphemed against the Holy Trinity in the baths and at once, struck by a fiery dart, was burnt to death for all to see.[6]

[510] Felix. Secundinus. Also one Barnabas, an Arian bishop, said, while performing a baptism, contrary to the law of the Faith: 'I, Barnabas, baptize you in the name of the Father, by the Son, in the Holy Spirit.' The water which had been brought in for baptism at once disappeared. When the man to be baptized saw that, he immediately went to a Catholic church and received the baptism of Christ.[7]

[511] Paulus. Muscianus.[8]

[512] Probus. Clementinus. Fulgentius flourished in the confession of the Faith and in learning.[9]
St Leonard shone forth.

[513] Senator v.c.c. The twenty-eighth cycle of nineteen years began in the sixth indiction. Pope Symmachus died on 19 July. Hormisdas,[10] the fifty-first pope, reigned eight years.[11]

---

[4] 'Natanleod' is erroneously repeated here for 'Natanleaga' (Netley, Hants.).
[5] ASC   [6] Mar.   [7] Mar.   [8] Mar.   [9] Mar.
[10] Hormisdas 514–23.   [11] Mar.

[514] (xxiii) 536 *Cassiodorus consul sic: 'me etiam consule, in uestrorum laude temporum adunato clero uel populo Romano, ecclesie rediit optata concordia.'*[1] Occidentales Saxones in Brytanniam cum tribus nauibus uenientes in loco qui*[a]* Cerdicesora uocatur appulerunt. Quorum primates Stuf et Wihtgar, Cerdici nepotes,[2] extiterunt. Ii*[b]* mox[3] pugnam cum Brytonibus ineuntes [4]quosdam ex eis occiderunt[4] quosdam uero fugauerunt.[5]

[515] (xxiiii) 537 *Florentius. Anthemius. Theodericus rex filiam suam Amalsuindam Eutharico uiro glorioso copulauit.*[6] .vii. rex Francorum Teodebertus.[7]

[516] (xxv) 538 *Petrus v.c.c. Eutharicus Cillica*[c] *a senatu et plebe exceptus est ad consulatum.*[8] *[d]⟨San⟩ctus Maurus duodennis beato Benedicto a parentibus traditur.[d]*[9]

[517] (xxvi) 539 *Eutaricus [e]scilicet Cillica.[e] Iustinus* Augustus. *Hormisda papa composuit clerum psalmisque erudiuit.*[f][10]

[518] (xxvii) 540 *Anastasius imperator .iiii.*[g] *Hormisda papa misit Ennodium Ticinensem episcopum aliosque ad Anastasium imperatorem docendum. Anastasius uero spernens et heresi fauens Euticetis, catholicos persecutus, et diuersis partibus inimicorum uallatus agminibus, sepe congemens diuino fulmine periit. Iordanis episcopus historiam tunc ita scripsit: 'Anastasius imperator merens et furens, maior octogenario regni .xxviii., rebus humanis excessit.'*

Romanorum quinquagesimus octauus Iustinus[11] *senior secundum historiam Romanam et Iordanem episcopum qui tunc cronicam composuit et uixit, imperauit annis .ix., iuxta Bedam tantum annis .viii., hoc est usque kalend. Ianuarii.*[12]

---

[a] dicitur *erased after* qui *C*   *[b]* Hii *LP*   *[c]* Cillia *LP*   *[d–d]* Sanctus . . . traditur] *mg. alongside 517–18 (515–18 P) C³P³, om. L, at 517 n. f. B, under Anastasius (491–518) G*   *[e–e]* scilicet Cillica] *interlin. C¹H¹, om. LP, scilicet Scilica interlin. B¹?*   *[f]* 516 n. d. incorporated here B*   *[g]* interlin. C¹L¹B¹P³, om. H*

---

[1] Mar.

[2] The identification of Stuf and Wihtgar as 'Cerdici nepotes' comes from ASC 534's 'nefum', which can mean both 'grandsons' and 'nephews'.

[514] Thus the Consul Cassiodorus: 'In my consulship too, to the glory of your reign, the desired peace returned to the church when the clergy and the Roman people were united.'[1] The West Saxons came to Britain with three ships and landed at a place called *Cerdicesora*. Their leaders were Stuf and Wihtgar, nephews of Cerdic.[2] They soon[3] joined battle with the Britons, [4]some of whom they slew,[4] some they put to flight.[5]

[515] Florentius. Anthemius. King Theoderic married his daughter Amalaswintha to Eutharic, an illustrious man.[6] Theudebert the seventh king of the Franks.[7]

[516] Peter v.c.c. Eutharic Cillica was admitted to the consulship by the senate and the people.[8] At the age of twelve St Maur was entrusted to St Benedict by his parents.[9]

[517] Eutharic, that is Cillica. Justin Augustus. Pope Hormisdas set the clergy in order, and taught them the psalms.[10]

[518] Anastasius Augustus, consul for the fourth time. Pope Hormisdas sent Ennodius, bishop of Pavia, and others to instruct the Emperor Anastasius. Anastasius, however, rejecting them, and favouring the Eutychian heresy, persecuted Catholics. Surrounded on opposite sides by throngs of enemies, with frequent lamentation he perished by a divine thunderbolt. Bishop Jordanes then wrote thus in his history: 'The Emperor Anastasius, over eighty, and after a reign of twenty-eight years, in grief and in rage, departed from human affairs.'

Justin the Elder,[11] the fifty-eighth emperor, according to the Roman history and to Bishop Jordanes (who lived and composed his chronicle then), reigned nine years; eight years, however, according to Bede, that is until 1 January.[12]

---

[3] Not in ASC.   [4-4] No equivalent in ASC.   [5] ASC.
[6] Mar.
[7] Norman Annals. *AG, AU* record Theudebert's succession under 514. Theudebert I 534-48.
[8] Mar.   [9] Hugh of Fleury, p. 138.   [10] Mar.
[11] Justin I 518-27.   [12] Mar.

[519] (i) 541   *Rusticus. Vitalis. Iustinus nomen hereticorum cepit extinguere eorum ubique ecclesias catholice consecrare.*[1]

Cerdic et Cynric regnare ceperunt et eodem anno cum Brytonibus in loco qui nominatur Cerdicesford pugnauerunt [2]et uictores extiterunt.[2,3]

[520] (ii) 542   *Valerius. Iustinianus. Iustinus Amantium prepositum palatii et Andream cubicularium occidit. Misalem et Ardaburem cubicularios Sardicam in exilium misit.*[4]

[521] (iii) 543   *Simmachus. Boetius. Hormisda papa obiit .viii. Idus Augusti. Sancta Brigida Scotta uirgo in Hibernia obiit.*[5]

[522] (iiii) 544   *Maximus v.c.c. Iohannes*[6] *papa quinquagesimus secundus annis duobus, mensibus decem sedit.*[7]

[523] (v) 545   *Opilio. Iustinus Augustus. Theodericus autem, Arrianus imperator Italie, Iohannem papam et Theodorum et Agapitum consulares uiros et Agapitum patricium ad Iustinum imperatorem Constantinopolim misit, interminans, nisi dimitterentur heretici in pace degere, ipse etiam omnes catholicos Italie occideret. Iohannes uero papa, Constantinopolim ueniens, ad portam que uocatur auream, populorum turbis ei occurrentibus in conspectu omnium roganti ceco lumen reddidit. Iustinus autem imperator, fletibus legatorum pro certo imminente cede catholicorum populorum motus, hereticos dimittere cessit; Iohannes uero papa, cum rediens Rauennam uenisset, Theodericus eum cum comitibus*[a] *carceris afflictione peremit, inuidia ductus quia catholice*[b] *defensor pietatis Iustinus eum honorifice suscepit.*[8] [c]*Theodericus imperator Symmachum patricium interfecit sed et Boetium consularem uirum summe prudentie, qui dialecticam, arithmeticam atque musicam suo sermone nobilitauerat*[d] *et alios libellos elegantissime composuerat, idem tyrannus exilii pena dampnauit et in territorio Mediolanensi iugulari fecit.*[c9]

---

a runs on to 524 B   b runs on to 524 C (N)   c–c Theodericus . . . fecit] mg. alongside 523–4 C³, alongside 522–3 P³, at foot of page with sign pointing to 523 B⁴, under Justin I (518–28) G   d altered from nobilitauitrat C³, nobilitauit erat H, nobilitauerat L, nobilitarat B, nobilitauit rat P, nobilitauit G, nobilitauat (with suspension sign over -uat) Hugh of Fleury witness Cambridge, Corpus Christi College MS 265, p. 521

---

[1] Mar.   [2–2] No equivalent in ASC.

[519] Rusticus. Vitalis. Justin began to wipe out the race of heretics, and to consecrate their churches everywhere according to Catholic practice.[1]

Cerdic and Cynric began to rule, and in the same year they fought the Britons in a place called Charford, [2]and were victorious.[2,3]

[520] Valerius. Justinian. Justin killed Amantius, the prefect of the palace, and Andreas, the *cubicularius*. He sent the *cubicularii* Misalis and Ardaburis into exile to Sardica.[4]

[521] Symmachus. Boethius. Pope Hormisdas died on 6 August. St Bridget, the Irish virgin, died in Ireland.[5]

[522] Maximus v.c.c. John, the fifty-second pope,[6] ruled for two years and ten months.[7]

[523] Opilio. Justin Augustus. Theoderic, the Arian emperor of Italy, sent Pope John and Theodore and Agapitus, men of consular rank, and the patrician Agapitus, to the Emperor Justin at Constantinople, threatening that unless heretics were permitted to live in peace, he for his part would kill all the Catholics in Italy. But Pope John, arriving at the gate called the Golden at Constantinople, as crowds of people came to meet him, restored sight to a blind man who pleaded with him in the full view of all. The Emperor Justin, moved by the lamentations of the legates and by the threatened slaughter of the Catholic people, gave up the persecution of the heretics. But, when on his return, Pope John came to Ravenna, Theoderic killed him and his companions with the rigours of imprisonment, driven by envy because Justin, the defender of Catholic piety, received him with honour.[8] The Emperor Theoderic killed the patrician Symmachus, and the same tyrant condemned to the punishment of exile, and had murdered in the region of Milan, Boethius, of consular rank, a man of the greatest wisdom, who ennobled Dialectic, Arithmetic, and Music by his writing, and composed other books of great elegance.[9]

---

[3] ASC. E and additions to A identify the kingdom and speak of West Saxon princes ruling thereafter.

[4] Mar.   [5] Mar.   [6] John I 523–6.   [7] Mar.   [8] Mar.

[9] Hugh of Fleury, pp. 132–3. Hugh associates these executions with Pope John's imprisonment, which Marianus assigns to this year.

[524] (vi) 546 *Probus iunior. Filoxenus. Quo anno, id est consulatu Probi iunioris, etiam Simmachum patricium Rauenne occidit. Iohannes papa obiit .xv. kalend. Iunii. Cuius corpus translatum est et sepultum in basilica sancti Petri apostoli. Huius Iohannis sanctus Gregorius meminit in libro Dialogorum.*[1] *Theodericus autem anno sequenti subita morte Rauenne periit.*[a2]

[525] (vii) 547 *Olibrius v.c.c. Gothi autem Athalaricum,*[3] *ex Theoderico rege natum, cum matre eius sibi preficiunt. Hildericus Wandalorum rex episcopos ab exilio reuerti et ecclesias instaurari precepit, post annos septuaginta quattuor heretice profanationis. Post Trasimundum enim Hildericus, ex Valentiniani imperatoris captiua filia genitus, Wandalorum suscepit imperium. Qui sacramento a*
p. 248 *Trasamundo | astrictus, ne catholicis in regno suo consuleret, antequam regnum susciperet, episcopos ab exilio reuerti iussit, eisque*[b] *ecclesias reformari precepit. Felix*[4] *papa .liii. sedit annis .iiii., mensibus duobus. Acephalorum heresis abdicatur, qui dicunt Paulum apostolum in epistolis suis precepisse feminas diaconas debere fieri, quia eas commemorat post diaconos.*[5]

[526] (viii) 548 *Maburtius v.c.*[c] *Hoc anno, Dionisius computum*[d] *suum incepit, ita dicens inter cetera: 'presentis anni monstremus exemplum, indictio quippe .iiii. est et lunaris ciclus .xi. et decennouenalis .xiiii., et quia endecadis .vi. est annus eum embolismum esse necesse est. A .xv. itaque luna preteriti festi usque ad quartamdecimam presentis, quot dies sint diligentius inquiramus et inueniemus procul dubio quando pasca celebrare debemus. Transacto anno per indictionem .iii. pasce quartamdecimam lunam nono die kalend. Aprilis, id est .xxiiii. die mensis Martii fuisse, quis dubitat?' et reliqua. Et paulo ante dicit: 'Hoc monemus quod ciclus iste nonaginta quinque annorum, quem fecimus, non per omnia in se ipsum reuertitur, et ideo post expletionem .xcv. annorum, non ad quintum ciclum sancti Cirilli, qui incepit ciclos suos ab anno centesimo .liii. Dioclitiani, quorum .v. ciclum nobis necessario preposuimus, sed ad nostrum primum ciclum, quem nos ab anno*

---

[a] *runs on to* 525 C (N)   [b] *que interlin.* C[1]   [c] v.c.c. HL   [d] compotum HL

[524] Probus the Younger. Philoxenus. In that year, that is in the consulship of Probus the Younger, Theoderic also killed the patrician Symmachus at Ravenna. Pope John died on 18 May. His body was translated and buried in the church of St Peter the Apostle. St Gregory mentioned this John in the book of the Dialogues.[1] However, Theoderic died suddenly at Ravenna in the following year.[2]

[525] Olybrius v.c.c. The Goths took as their ruler Athalaric,[3] son of King Theoderic, in association with his mother. Hilderic, king of the Vandals, ordered the bishops to return from exile and their churches to be restored after seventy-four years of defilement by heretics. Hilderic, son of the captive daughter of the Emperor Valentinian, became the ruler of the Vandals after Thrasamund. Although Thrasamund had bound him by an oath, before becoming ruler, not to look after the Catholics in his kingdom, he ordered the bishops to return from exile, and he commanded them to re-establish their churches. Felix,[4] the fifty-third pope, ruled four years and two months. The heresy of the Acephali was abandoned. They said that Paul the Apostle had commanded in his epistles that women should be ordained deacons, because he mentioned them after deacons.[5]

[526] Mavortius v.c. In this year Dionisius began his computation, saying thus, among other things: 'let us take the present year as an example. It is in fact the fourth indiction, and the eleventh year of the lunar cycle, and the fourteenth year of the nineteen-year cycle, and because it is the sixth year of the series of eleven, it must be intercalary. And so, from the fifteenth lune of the aforementioned feast to the fourteenth of the present, let us carefully inquire how many days there are and we shall undoubtedly discover when we ought to celebrate Easter. Who doubts that in the year now past, in the third indiction, the fourteenth lune of Easter was on the ninth day of the kalends of April, that is 24 March?' and so on. And a little earlier he says: 'We give this warning because the cycle of ninety-five years which we have computed does not return completely to its starting-point, and so, after the completion of the ninety-five years the reader does not come to the fifth cycle of St Cyril, who began his cycles in the 153rd year of Diocletian, the fifth cycle of which we have of necessity before us, but to the first

[1] Dialogues, iii. 2, iv. 31.   [2] Mar.   [3] Athalaric 526-34.
[4] Felix IV (III) 526-30.   [5] Mar.

ducentesimo .xlviii. eiusdem Dioclitiani, incepimus lector accurrat' et reliqua. **Sanctus Benedictus abbas uirtutum gloria claruit quas sanctus Gregorius in Dialogo conscripsit.** *Iustinus Constantinopoli Iustinianum sororis sue filium ante .iiii. mensem obitus sui imperatorem faciens obiit. Romanorum .lix. Iustinianus[1] omni teste hystorico regnauit annis .xxxviii., hoc est usque kalend. Ianuarias in anno quingentesimo .lii. post passionem.[a2]*

[527] (i) 549   *Iustinianus Augustus v.c. Bilisarius patricius de Persis mirabiliter triumphauit.[3]*

Cerdic et Cynric [4]quarta uice[4] in loco qui dicitur Cerdicesleage pugnauerunt cum Brytonibus.[5]

[528] (ii) 550   *Decius v.c.c. Bilisarius, a Iustiniano in Affricam missus, Wandalorum gentem deleuit.[6]* Teodebaldus rex Francorum .viii. regnauit anno uno.[7]

[529] (iii) 551   *Lampadius. Orestes. His consulibus Felix papa obiit .iiii. idus Octobris. Bonifacius[8] papa quinquagesimus quartus annis duobus.[9]*

[530] (iiii) 552   *[b]Proconsulatus[c] Lampadii et Orestis.[b] Corpus sancti Antonii monachi a Deo reuelatum Alexandriam defertur, et in ecclesia beati Iohannis baptiste humatur.[10]*

Cerdic et Cynric Vectam [d]uel Wihtam[d] insulam ceperunt et [11]illam suis nepotibus Stuue et Wihtgaro dederunt[11] paucosque[12] homines in Wihgarabyrig peremerunt.[13]

[531] (v) 553   *Item [e]proconsulatus Lampadii et Orestis.[e] His consulibus Bonifacius papa obiit .xvii. die mensis Octobris. Mercurius[14] papa quinquagesimus quintus [f]post Petrum presedit ecclesie[f] annis*

---

[a] Rex Francorum Sigebertus regnauit annis xiiii et occisus est insidiis Fredegundi *add. L, add. upper mg. without any signe de renvoi* P³   [b-b] Proconsulatus . . . Orestis] *over erasure* C¹   [c] *proconsules* HL   [d-d] uel Wihtam *interlin.* C¹P³, *om.* HL, uel Wictam *interlin.* B¹   [e-e] proconsulatus . . . Orestis] proconsules Lampadius et Orestes HL   [f-f] post . . . ecclesie *om.* L

---

[1] Justinian 527–65.   [2] Mar.   [3] Mar.   [4-4] Not in ASC.
[5] ASC. Not in F (erasure under modern entry).   [6] Mar.

cycle, which we began in the 248th year of same Diocletian', and so on. The abbot St Benedict was renowned for the miracles which St Gregory described in the *Dialogues*. Justin died at Constantinople, making Justinian, his sister's son, emperor four months before his death.

Justinian,[1] the fifty-ninth emperor, according to every historical witness, reigned thirty-eight years, that is until 1 January in the 552nd year after the Passion.[2]

[527] Justinian Augustus v.c. The patrician Belisarius triumphed wonderfully over the Persians.[3]

Cerdic and Cynric fought the Britons [4]for a fourth time[4] in a place called *Cerdicesleag*.[5]

[528] Decius v.c.c. Belisarius, sent to Africa by Justinian, destroyed the race of the Vandals.[6] Theudebald, eighth king of the Franks, reigned one year.[7]

[529] Lampadius. Orestes. During their consulship, Pope Felix died on 12 October. Boniface[8] was the fifty-fourth pope, and reigned for two years.[9]

[530] The proconsulship of Lampadius and Orestes. The body of St Anthony the Monk, divinely revealed, was borne to Alexandria and buried in the church of St John the Baptist.[10]

Cerdic and Cynric took the Isle of Vecta (or Wight) [11]and gave it to their nephews Stuf and Wihtgar,[11] and they slew a few men[12] in *Wihtgarabyrig*.[13]

[531] A further proconsulship of Lampadius and Orestes. In their consulship Pope Boniface died on 17 October. Mercurius,[14] the fifty-fifth pope after Peter, ruled the church for two years. This is

---

[7] Norman Annals. *AU, AG, ASN* record the succession of Theudebald and the length of his reign under 527. The further succession of Chlothar and of his four sons recorded by these annals is counted in JW's numbering of later Frankish kings. Theudebald 548–55.

[8] Boniface II 530–2.   [9] Mar.   [10] Mar.

[11–11] Not in ASC under this year, but under 534.

[12] 'paucosque' translates 'fea' of ASC A (original form) BC, whereas A (?scribe 8) E reads 'feala'.

[13] ASC. F omits the slaying at *Wihtgarabyrig*.   [14] John II 533–5.

annorum protenditur, in cuius anno .xiii. Dominus noster Iesus Christus passus est .viii. die kalendarum Aprilis, luna .xv. atque .vi. kalend. Aprilis, luna .xvii., ^aa mortuis resurrexit anno .xviii. Tiberii Cesaris iuxta hystoriam sacri *euuangelii.*[1]

[532] (vi) 554 *Iustinianus Augustus. Cyclus magnus paschalis* hic incipit indictione decima. *Iustinianus leges Romanorum multis libris nimis prolixe et inutili dissonantia conscriptas, intra duodecim libros coartauit in unum, quem librum codicem Iustinianum*[2] *nominari precepit. Sanctus Beda sic:* ^b'*Dionisius pascales scribit circulos incipiens ab anno dominice incarnationis* ^c*quingentesimo tricesimo secundo,*^c *qui est annus ducentesimus quadragesimus octauus Dioclitiani post consulatum Lampadii et Orestis quo anno Iustinianus codex orbi promulgatus est.' Hec Beda. Cum ergo supputando a Dioclitiano usque ad ciclum Dionisii dicit Beda primum annum cicli Dionisii ipsum fuisse annum ducentesimum quadragesimum octauum Dioclitiani post consulatum Lampadii et Orestis, satis quod uerum est ostendit, annum primum cicli Dionisii sextum* ⟨esse⟩^d *Iustiniani. Ex ipso itaque primo anno cicli Dionisii, id est .vi. anno Iustiniani, numerando supra uersus usque ad Dioclitianum iuxta chronicam Eusebii uel Bede supputemus, atque inde iterum usque ad ciclum Dionisii secundum scripturam diuinam apostolicosque uiros, qui tunc temporibus ipsis | etiam de ipsis annis bene disputauerunt, non*

p. 249   *tantum ut ostendamus mendacium chronicarum, sed ut defendamus sacratissimam ueritatem euangelicam uirosque catholicos ecclesie, qui post euangelium perhibent Dominum nostrum Iesum Christum .vi. kalend. Aprilis, luna .xvii., a mortuis resurrexisse id est Ieronimum et Augustinum. Victorius etiam ad Hilarium papam sic: 'primo uero azimorum die, Dominus noster Iesus Christus cenans cum suis discipulis postquam sui corporis et sanguinis sacramenta patefecit, ad montem Oliueti, sicut euangelia sancta testantur, progressus, ibique detentus est a Iudeis tradente discipulo. De hinc .vi. feria subsequente, id est .viii. die kalend. Aprilis crucifixus est et sepultus, tertio die, hoc est .vi. kalend. Aprilis, dominico die resurrexit a mortuis' et reliqua. Cassiodorus quoque senator expositorque sacri*^a *psalterii in sua chronica*

---

^a E starts here   ^b CB *switch to two columns at this point*   ^{c–c} quingentesimo
. . . secundo] *appropriate numerals interlin. above words* C (N)   ^d esse L *Mar.,* est
CHBP, *mutilated* E

---

[1] Mar.
[2] The single code of law prepared on Justinian's orders and published on 16

the term of the great Easter cycle of 532 years, in whose thirteenth year Our Lord Jesus Christ suffered on 25 March, on the
fifteenth lune, and rose from the dead on 27 March, on the seventeenth lune, in the eighteenth year of Tiberius Caesar, according
to the account of the Holy Gospel.[1]

[532] Justinian Augustus. The great Paschal cycle began here in
the tenth indiction. The laws of Rome, written with excessive pro-
lixity and profitless contradiction in many volumes, Justinian con-
densed into twelve books in one work which he ordered to be
called the *Codex Justinianus.*[2] The holy Bede says this: 'Dionysius
drew up the Easter cycles beginning with the 532nd year of the
Lord's incarnation, which is the 248th year of Diocletian, after the
consulships of Lampadius and Orestes, in which year the *Codex
Justinianus* was published throughout the world'. Thus Bede.
When, therefore, by reckoning from Diocletian to the cycle of
Dionysius, Bede says that the first year of the Dionysian cycle was
itself the 248th year of Diocletian after the consulship of Lampadius and Orestes, he states the truth clearly enough, that the first
year of the Dionysian cycle is the sixth of Justinian. And so from
that first year of the Dionysian cycle—that is, the sixth year of
Justinian—let us calculate by reckoning back to Diocletian, in
accordance with the chronicles of Eusebius and Bede, and from
Diocletian forward again to the cycle of Dionysius, in accordance
with Holy Scripture and those apostolic men, who, in those very
times, also discussed those very years thoroughly, not only that we
may show the falsehoods of the chronicles, but that we may
defend the most holy truth of the Gospel and the Catholic
churchmen, that is Jerome and Augustine, who following the
Gospel declared that Our Lord Jesus Christ rose from the dead on
27 March on the seventeenth lune. Also, Victor to Pope Hilarus
thus: 'But on the first day of the Passover Our Lord Jesus Christ,
taking supper with his disciples, after revealing the sacrament of
His Body and Blood, went to the Mount of Olives, as the Holy
Gospels bear witness, and there was held by the Jews, being
betrayed by a disciple. Then, on the following Friday, that is 25
March, he was crucified and was buried; on the third day, that is
Sunday, 27 March, he rose from the dead', and so on. Thus also

Nov. 534. It included laws still valid from earlier codes and subsequent novels, and
omitted or brought up to date all obsolete laws.

*Cassiodorus quoque senator expositorque sacri^a psalterii in sua chronica
sic: 'his consulibus Dominus noster Iesus Christus passus est .viii. die
kalend. Aprilis, et defectio solis facta est qualis antea uel postmodum
nunquam fuit,' et reliqua. Ab ipso ergo primo anno cicli Dionisii, regnauit Iustinianus annis quinque usque in annum quingentesimum uicesimum .vii. incarnationis secundum Dionisium. (.xiii.).^{b1} Inde Iustinus
senior regnauit annis octo usque in annum quingentesimum nonum decimum secundum Dionisium. (.xl.). Inde Anastasius regnauit annis uiginti septem usque in annum quadringentesimum nonagesimum secundum
incarnationis secundum Dionisium. (.lvii.).^c Inde Zeno regnauit annis
decem et septem usque in annum quadringentesimum septuagesimum
quintum incarnationis secundum Dionisium. (.lxxiiii.).^d Inde Leo regnauit annis decem et septem usque in annum quadringentesimum quinquagesimum octauum incarnationis secundum Dionisium. (.lxxxi.).
Inde Martianus regnauit annis septem usque in annum quadringentesimum quinquagesimum primum incarnationis secundum Dionisium.
(.cviii.). Inde Theodosius regnauit annis uiginti septem usque in annum
quadringentesimum uigesimum quartum incarnationis secundum Dionisium. (.cxxiii.). Inde Honorius regnauit annis quindecim usque in
annum quadringentesimum nonum incarnationis secundum Dionisium.
(.cxxxvi.). Inde Archadius regnauit annis tredecim usque in annum
trecentesimum nonagesimum sextum incarnationis secundum Dionisium.
(.cxlvii.). Inde Theodosius regnauit annis undecim usque in annum
trecentesimum octogesimum quintum incarnationis secundum Dionisium.
(.cliii.). Gratianus annis sex usque in annum trecentesimum septuagesimum nonum incarnationis secundum Dionisium. (.clvii.). Inde Valens
annis quattuor usque in annum trecentesimum septuagesimum quintum
incarnationis secundum Dionisium. (.clxviii.) Inde Valentinianus annis
undecim usque in annum trecentesimum sexagesimum quartum incarnationis secundum Dionisium. (.clxix.). Inde Iouianus^e regnauit mensibus
.viii. usque in annum trecentesimum sexagesimum tertium incarnationis
secundum Dionisium. (.clxxi.). Inde Iulianus regnauit annis duobus
mensibusque .viii. usque in annum ^fincarnationis trecentesimum sexagesimum primum^f secundum Dionisium. (.cxcv.). Inde Constantius regnauit annis uiginti quattuor usque in annum trecentesimum tricesimum
septimum incarnationis secundum Dionisium. (.ccxxvi.). Inde Constantinus magnus regnauit annis .xxx. et .i. usque in annum trecentesimum*

^a om. EHL   ^b these numerals here and subsequently are in the text in CELBP, first
few numerals in mg. in H   ^c corrected to .lxvii. C¹?, .vii. (after correction) B

Cassiodorus Senator, the commentator on the Holy Psalms, in his chronicle: 'Under these consuls, Our Lord Jesus Christ suffered on 25 March and an eclipse of the sun occurred, the like of which there never was before or afterwards;' and so on. Therefore, from that first year of the Dionysian cycle, Justinian's reign went back five years to the 527th year of the Incarnation, according to Dionysius. (13).[1] Thence Justin the Elder's reign went back eight years to the 519th year of the Incarnation, according to Dionysius. (40). Then Anastasius' reign went back twenty-seven years to the 492nd year of the Incarnation, according to Dionysius. (57). Thence Zeno's reign went back seventeen years to the 475th year of the Incarnation, according to Dionysius. (74). Then Leo's reign went back seventeen years to the 458th year of the Incarnation, according to Dionysius. (81). Thence Marcian's reign went back seven years to the 451st year of the Incarnation, according to Dionysius. (108). Thence Theodosius' reign went back twenty-seven years to the 424th year of the Incarnation, according to Dionysius. (123). Thence Honorius' reign went back fifteen years to the 409th year of the Incarnation, according to Dionysius. (136). Thence Arcadius' reign went back thirteen years to the 396th year of the Incarnation, according to Dionysius. (147). Thence Theodosius' reign went back eleven years to the 385th year of the Incarnation, according to Dionysius. (153). Gratian's six years to the 379th year of the Incarnation, according to Dionysius. (157). Thence Valens' four years to the 375th year of the Incarnation, according to Dionysius. (168). Thence Valentinian's eleven years to the 364th year of the Incarnation, according to Dionysius. (169). Thence Jovian's reign went back eight months to the 363rd year of the Incarnation, according to Dionysius. (171). Thence Julian's reign went back two years eight months to the 361st year of the Incarnation according to Dionysius. (195). Thence Constantius' reign went back twenty-four years to the 337th year of the Incarnation, according to Dionysius. (226). Thence Constantine the Great's went back thirty-one years to the

---

^d *corrected to* .lxxxiii. C^t?   ^e Iouinianus *EHL*, Iouianus *corrected to* Iouinianus *P*³
^{f-f} incarnationis . . . primum] .ccclxi. incarnationis *HL*

---

[1] The parenthetic numerals in this annal record the cumulative total of regnal lengths to be deducted from 532.

sextum incarnationis secundum Dionisium. (.ccxxvii.). Ab anno uero persecutionis .iiii. Constantinus regnare incepit iuxta chronicam Eusebii uel Bede. Tunc annum tertium persecutionis que in anno nono decimo Dioclitiani incepta est nulli deputant. Quem Isidorus episcopus cum multis aliis etiam cum anno altero Galerio Maximiano conscripsit. (.ccxlvii.).ᵃ Inde Dioclitianus regnauit annis .xx. usque in annum ducentesimum octogesimum quintum incarnationis secundum Dionisium; usque autem in annum ducentesimum octogesimum nonum incarnationis iuxta chronicam Eusebii uel Bede, quiᵇ de annis incarnationis contradicunt sancto euuangelio. Inter Dioclitianum autem atque ciclum Dionisii per ciclos .xiii. decennouenales desunt .vii. anni, quos sic iuxta diuinam scripturam bene possumus inuestigare. Dioclitianus enim, in anno ducentesimo septuagesimo .viii. incarnationis secundum Dionisium incipiens, regnauit annis .xx. In cuius anno .xix., id est in anno ducentesimo nonagesimo septimo incarnationis iuxta Dionisium, in quo .v. kalend. Aprilis pasca contigit conuenit hoc quod Eusebius in cronica |

p. 250 sua ita dicit: 'Anno .xix. Dioclitiani mense Martio in diebus pasce ecclesie subuerse sunt.' Quarto autem persecutionis anno Constantinus regnare orsus est. Secundo persecutionis anno Dioclitianus Nicomedie, Maximianus Mediolani purpuram deposuerunt. Apparet ergo quod unus annus erat inter Dioclitianum et Constantinum, duo autem anni secundum multos, quibus Galerius gener Dioclitiani regnauit. Galerius ergo regit tertium persecutionis annum, incipiens in anno nono decimo Dioclitiani, et terminans in anno primo Constantini, id est in anno .ccxcix. incarnationis secundum Dionisium. Constantinus, itaque in anno quarto persecutionis incipiens, regnauit triginta annis, mensibus .x. usque in annum .cccxxx. incarnationis secundum Dionisium in quo indictione .iii. obiit .xxv. die mensis Maii. Inde Constantius, teste Orosio, regnauit annis .xxvii. usque in annum .ccclvii. incarnationis secundum Dionisium. In decretali epistola sancti Iulii pape apostolice sedis tunc ita ueritas intimatur: 'In nomine Domini Dei et Saluatoris nostri Iesu Christi, imperantibus quoque Constantio et Constante Augustis, anno .iiii. sub die .viii. kalend. Octobris indictione .vi. et reliqua, sicut supra. Constantius uero obiit .iii. die mensis Nouembris sicut in Tripartita Ecclesiastica Historia[1] legitur. Si autem Constantius regnauit

---

ᵃ .ccxlvii. CBP Mar., .ccxlii. EHL   ᵇ interlin. Cᵗ

---

[1] Compiled by Cassiodorus Senator from Epiphanius Scholasticus' Latin version of the ecclesiastical histories of Socrates, Sozomen, and Theodoret.

306th year of the Incarnation, according to Dionysius. (227). But Constantine began to reign in the fourth year of the Persecution, according to the chronicles of Eusebius and Bede. Then no one counted the third year of the Persecution, which began in the nineteenth year of Diocletian. Bishop Isidore, with many others as well, assigned it, with a second year, to Galerius Maximinianus. (247). From then Diocletian's reign went back twenty years to the 285th year of the Incarnation, according to Dionysius; but to the 289th year of the Incarnation, according to the chronicles of Eusebius and Bede, which in computing the years from the Incarnation disagree with the Holy Gospel. But between Diocletian and the cycle of Dionysius seven years are missing in the thirteen nineteen-year cycles which we thus, following holy writings, are able to examine thoroughly. Diocletian, beginning in the 278th year of the Incarnation, according to Dionysius, reigned twenty years. In his nineteenth year, that is in the 297th year of the Incarnation, according to Dionysius, Easter fell on 28 March, which is in accord with what Eusebius said in his chronicle: 'In the nineteenth year of Diocletian, in March, in the Easter period, the churches were destroyed.' However, in the fourth year of the Persecution, Constantine began to reign. In the second year of the Persecution, Diocletian at Nicomedia, and Maximian at Milan, laid aside the purple. Therefore it is clear that there was one year between Diocletian and Constantine, but according to many there were two years during which Galerius, son-in-law of Diocletian, reigned. Galerius, therefore, reigned in the third year of the Persecution, beginning in the nineteenth year of Diocletian, and ending in the first year of Constantine, that is, in the 299th year of the Incarnation, according to Dionysius. And so Constantine, beginning in the fourth year of the Persecution, reigned thirty years ten months to the 330th year of the Incarnation, according to Dionysius, when, in the third indiction, he died on 25 May. Orosius bears witness that Constantius reigned then twenty-seven years to the 357th year of the Incarnation, according to Dionysius. The truth is made clear in this way, in the decretal of St Julius pope of the apostolic see: 'In the name of the Lord God and of Our Saviour Jesus Christ, in the fourth year of the reign of the emperors Constantius and Constans, on 24 September, in the sixth indiction', and so on, as above. But Constantius died on 3 November, as is to be read in the *Tripartite History of the Church*.[1] Whether

.xxvii. annis secundum Orosium, aut si Valentinianus et Valens annis .xvii. et Gratianus .vii. uel Archadius annis .xiii. regnauerunt, sicut in chronica Isidori episcopi uel in expositione Melliti habetur, non certum secundum diuinam scripturam inuenitur. Quia autem annus quartus Constantini et Constantis, qui est trecentesimus .xxxiii. incarnationis secundum Dionisium, erat indictione .vi. atque annus nonus Honorii consulatus sui undecies, et Constantii secundo, quem finiuit in anno .ccccxvii. incarnationis secundum Dionisium, indictione .xv. erat, secundum scripturam dubitandum non est. Intra quos duos annos per .iiii. decennouenales ciclos .iiii. anni in chronicis desunt. Iulianus igitur, in anno .lxxx. Dioclitiani incipiens, regnauit annis duobus, mensibus .viii. obiitque .vi. kalend. Iulii in anno trecentesimo sexagesimo incarnationis secundum Dionisium. Iouianus,[a] in anno octogesimo tertio Dioclitiani incipiens, regnauit mensibus .viii. et obiit .xiiii. kalend. Martii in anno trecentesimo .lxi. incarnationis secundum Dionisium. Valentinianus, in anno .lxxxiiii. Dioclitiani incipiens, regnauit annis .xi., mensibus quinque et obiit .xvii. die mensis Septembris in anno .ccclxxii. incarnationis secundum Dionisium. Valens, in anno .xcv. Dioclitiani incipiens, regnauit annis .iiii. usque in annum .ccclxxvi. incarnationis secundum Dionisium. Gratianus, in anno nonagesimo .ix. Dioclitiani incipiens, regnauit annis sex usque in annum .ccclxxxii. incarnationis secundum Dionisium. Theodosius, in anno. .cv. Dioclitiani incipiens, regnauit annis .xi. et obiit die .xvii.[b] mensis Ianuarii in anno .cccxciii. incarnationis secundum Dionisium. Archadius, in anno centesimo .xvi. Dioclitiani incipiens, regnauit annis[c] .xiiii., mensibus .iiii. et obiit kalend. Maii in anno .ccccviii. incarnationis secundum Dionisium. Honorius, in anno .c⟨xxx⟩i.[d] Dioclitiani incipiens, regnauit annis .xv. usque in annum .ccccxxiiii. incarnationis secundum Dionisium. Huius anno .ix. quem finiuit .ccccxvii. incarnationis secundum Dionisium cum .x. kalend. Maii deberet pasca celebrari, celebratum est .viii. kalend. Aprilis, sed hora baptizandi aqua non uenit in baptisterium, ideoque baptisma non actum erat ipsa nocte. Illa autem nocte que lucebat in diem dominicum .x. kalend. Maii fons sacer ex sese repletus est hora baptizandi. Hoc autem actum in fine anni .ix. Honorii. Theodosius, in anno .cxlvi. Dioclitiani incipiens, regnauit annis .xxvii. usque in

---

[a] Iouinianus *EHL*, Iouianus *changed to* Iouinianus *P*³   [b] x *interlin.* C¹   [c] E *ends here*   [d] .cxxxi. Mar.

Constantius reigned twenty-seven years, according to Orosius, or Valentinian and Valens reigned seventeen years and Gratian seven, or Arcadius thirteen years, as is maintained in the chronicle of Bishop Isidore and in the exposition of Mellitus, is not to be found clearly in holy texts. However, that the fourth year of Constantine and Constans, which is the 333rd year of the Incarnation, according to Dionysius, was in the sixth indiction, and that the ninth year of Honorius—his eleventh consulship, and Constantine's second—which he ended in the 417th year of the Incarnation according to Dionysius, was in the fifteenth indiction, is not to be doubted according to those texts. Between those two years, during the four cycles of nineteen years, four years are missing in the chronicles. Thus Julian, beginning in the eightieth year of Diocletian, reigned two years eight months and died on 26 June in the 360th year of the Incarnation, according to Dionysius. Jovian, beginning in the eighty-third year of Diocletian, reigned eight months and died on 16 February in the 361st year of the Incarnation, according to Dionysius. Valentinian, beginning in the eighty-fourth year of Diocletian, reigned eleven years, five months, and died on 17 September in the 372nd year of the Incarnation, according to Dionysius. Valens, beginning in the ninety-fifth year of Diocletian, reigned four years to the 376th year of the Incarnation, according to Dionysius. Gratian, beginning in the ninety-ninth year of Diocletian, reigned six years up to the 382nd year of the Incarnation, according to Dionysius. Theodosius, beginning in the 105th year of Diocletian, reigned eleven years, and died on 17 January in the 393rd year of the Incarnation, according to Dionysius. Arcadius, beginning in the 116th year of Diocletian, reigned fourteen years, four months, and died on 1 May in the 408th year of the Incarnation, according to Dionysius. Honorius, beginning in the 131st year of Diocletian, reigned fifteen years, up to the 424th year of the Incarnation, according to Dionysius. In his ninth year, completed in the 417th year of the Incarnation, according to Dionysius, when Easter should have been celebrated on 22 April, it was celebrated on 25 March, but, at the time of baptism, the water did not come into the font and so the baptism was not performed that night. However, on the eve of Sunday, 22 April, the holy font filled of its own accord at the hour of baptism. This occurred at the end of the ninth year of Honorius. Theodosius, beginning in the 146th year of Diocletian,

*annum .ccccl. incarnationis secundum Dionisium. Ita in libris legitur,
testificante Prospero, qui in ipso etiam tempore partem ad chronicam
Eusebii addidit: 'Hoc anno, id est uigesimo primo anno Theodosii,
pasca celebratum est .ix. kalend. Maii, ut supradictum est. De hoc
quoque, id est ipso anno, Pascasinus episcopus scribit ad papam Leonem
ut supra.' Ipse autem est annus .viii. decennouenalis cicli, qui est
.ccccxliiii. annus incarnationis iuxta Dionisium, in quo finitus est annus
.xxi. Theodosii. Martianus, in anno .cxxiii. Dioclitiani incipiens, regnauit annis .vii., mensibus .ii. secundum historiam Romanam hoc est
usque kalend. Iulii in anno .cccclvii. incarnationis secundum Dionisium. Prosper ita iterum: 'anno .v. Martiani capta est Roma .iiii. idus*

p. 251 *Iulii eodemque anno pasca celebratum est | .viii. kalend. Maii, ordi-
nante episcopo Alexandrino Theophilo' et reliqua. 'Quod pasca sanctus
papa Leo .xv. kalend. Maii celebrandum potius protestabatur' et
reliqua. Sanctus autem Theophilus pasca .viii. kalend. Maii in anno
.cccclv. incarnationis secundum Dionisium recte constituit, cum nec in
anno tricesimo antea neque in anno .x. postea celebratum est pasca .xv.
kalend. Maii. Nouissimus itaque cicli decennouenalis est annus .ix.
Honorii et .v. Martiani. Leo, in anno .clxxx. Dioclitiani incipiens,
regnauit annis .xvii. usque kalend. Iul. in anno .cccclxxiiii. incarnationis secundum Dionisium. Leo iunior regnauit mensibus .vi., hoc est
usque kalend. Ianuarii in eodem anno obitus Leonis senioris. Zeno, in
anno .cxcviii. Dioclitiani incipiens, regnauit annis .xvii. usque ad
annum .ccccxcii. incarnationis secundum Dionisium. Anastasius, in
anno .ccxv. Dioclitiani incipiens, regnauit annis .xxvii. usque ad
annum quingentesimum octauum decimum incarnationis secundum
Dionisium. Iustinus senior, in anno .ccxlii. Dioclitiani incipiens, regnauit annis .vii. usque ad annum quingentesimum .xxvi. incarnationis
secundum Dionisium. Iustinianus, in anno .ccl. Dioclitiani incipiens,
regnauit annis .v. usque ad primum annum ciclorum Dionisii, qui est
annus ducentesimus quinquagesimus quintus Dioclitiani iuxta predictam
rationem sanctorum uirorum, non annus ducentesimus .xlviii. secundum
chronicas iniquas. Certum est enim annum .iiii. Constantini et Constantis qui est annus .cccxxxiii. incarnationis secundum Dionisium
indictione .vi. constitisse, teste sancto Iulio papa, etiam tunc ipsam
rem scribente. Annum etiam nonum Honorii, qui est annus .ccccxvii.*

reigned twenty-seven years, until the 450th year of the Incarnation, according to Dionysius. This is to be read in the texts, according to Prosper's testimony, who added a section to the chronicle of Eusebius at this very time: 'In this year, that is in the twenty-first year of Theodosius, Easter was celebrated on 23 April, as is mentioned above. Bishop Paschasinus wrote to Pope Leo about it also, that is about this very year, as above.' For it is the eighth year of the nineteen-year cycle which is the 444th year of the Incarnation, according to Dionysius, when the twenty-first year of Theodosius was completed. Marcian, beginning in the 173rd year of Diocletian, reigned seven years, two months, according to the *Roman History*, that is until 1 July in the 457th year of the Incarnation, according to Dionysius. Again, thus Prosper: 'In the fifth year of Marcian, Rome was taken on 12 July, and in the same year Easter was celebrated on 24 April, as Theophilus, bishop of Alexandria, prescribed', and so on. 'Pope St Leo declared that Easter should rather be on 17 April', and so on. However St Theophilus correctly established Easter on 24 April in the 455th year of the Incarnation, according to Dionysius, since neither in the thirtieth year before nor in the 10th year afterwards, was Easter celebrated on 17th April. Thus the ninth year of Honorius and the fifth of Marcian were the last years of nineteen-year cycles. Leo, beginning in the 180th year of Diocletian, reigned seventeen years to 1 July in the 474th year of the Incarnation, according to Dionysius. Leo the Younger reigned six months, that is until 1 January in the same year in which Leo the Elder died. Zeno, beginning in the 198th year of Diocletian, reigned seventeen years, until the 492nd year of the Incarnation, according to Dionysius. Anastasius, beginning in the 215th year of Diocletian, reigned twenty-seven years, until the 518th year of the Incarnation, according to Dionysius. Justin the Elder, beginning in the 242nd year of Diocletian, reigned seven years, to the 526th year of the Incarnation, according to Dionysius. Justinian, beginning in the 250th year of Diocletian, reigned five years, until the first year of the cycle of Dionysius, which is the 255th year of Diocletian, according to the aforementioned calculations of holy men, not the 248th year of the erring chroniclers. For it is certain that the fourth year of Constantine and Constans, which is the 333rd year of the Incarnation, according to Dionysius, was in the sixth indiction, as witnessed by Pope St Julius, also writing on that very

incarnationis secundum Dionisium, indictione quintadecima, consulatu Honorii undecies et Constantii secundo, teste sancto Pascasino episcopo cum sancto Leone papa. Annum item .xxi. Theodosii, qui est annus quadringentesimus quadragesimus quartus incarnationis secundum Dionisium, indictione .xii., teste eodem episcopo Pascasino cum sancto Leone papa. Annum quoque quintum Martiani indictione .viii. qui est annus .cccc. quinquagesimus quintus incarnationis secundum Dionisium teste etiam sancto Leone papa. Annus itaque quartus Constantii et Constantis sexta erat indictione, scribente sancto Iulio papa. In anno nono Honorii, pasca erat .x. kalend. Maii, teste episcopo Pascasino cum sancto Leone papa. In anno uicesimo primo, Theodosii pasca erat .ix. kalend. Maii eisdem testibus. In anno quinto Martiani pasca erat .viii. kalend. Maii. A nullo uero papa uel episcopo mittitur epistola uel scribitur decretalis epistola nisi ipse sciat quid in ea scribit uel mittit.[1]

[533] (vii) 555 *Mercurius qui et Iohannes papa obiit .vi. kalend. Iunii, Agapitus*[2] *papa quinquagesimus sextus post Petrum. Interea Athalaricus rex Gothorum octo annis imperans obiit. Cuius mater Amalsuuinda*[3] *Theodatum*[4] *sociauit sibi in regnum quam Theodatus post dies aliquantos* ᵃ*strangulari in balneo*ᵃ *precepit. Quia uero ipsa uiuens se suumque filium Iustiniano imperatori commendauit, ideo Iustinianus Theodato iratus est. Theodatus autem, ut imperator hoc ei dimitteret, misit ad eum Constantinopolim papam Agapitum. Agapitus uero imperatorem in heresim Euticetis corruentem, conuertit ad fidem. Anthimium quoque Constantinopolitanum episcopum, prefate heresis defensorem, duas naturas in Christo negantem, in exilium coegit, et Mennam in loco eius episcopum consecrauit. Agapitus uero papa ibi Constantinopoli obiit .x. kalend. Maii et sepultus est Rome .xii. kalendas Octobris.*[5]

ᵃ⁻ᵃ (strangu)lari . . . bal(neo)] *mg.* C

---

[1] Mar. The beginning of the second great Paschal cycle is Marianus' excuse for this laboured and confused disquisition, where his own chronology (always based on 'evangelical truth') is contrasted favourably with that of the 'erroneous' chroniclers. In this annal the supposed errors of the chroniclers include dating the accession of Diocletian at 289, and not 285, and assigning 248 years, not 255, to the period between the resignation of Diocletian and 532. These mutually exclusive errors have little to do with Marianus' redating of the year of the Incarnation. For the latter, see H. Petrie, *Monumenta Historica Britannica* (London, 1848), pp. 123-5.

matter; that the ninth year of Honorius, which is the 417th year of
the Incarnation according to Dionysius, was in the fifteenth indiction, in the eleventh consulship of Honorius and the second of
Constantius, on the testimony of St Paschasinus the bishop and St
Leo the pope; and that the 21st year of Theodosius, which is in
the 444th year of the Incarnation, according to Dionysius, was in
the twelfth indiction, on the testimony of the same Bishop
Paschasinus and St Leo the pope; also, that the fifth year of Marcian was in the eighth indiction, which is the 455th year of the
Incarnation, according to Dionysius, is also on the testimony of St
Leo the pope. And so the fourth year of Constantius and Constans
was in the sixth indiction, as St Julius the pope wrote. In the
ninth year of Honorius Easter was on 22 April, as Bishop Paschasinus and St Leo the pope bear witness. In the twenty-first year of
Theodosius Easter was on 23 April, according to the same witnesses. In the fifth year of Marcian Easter was on 24 April. Certainly no pope or bishop sends a letter or writes a decretal without
knowing what he writes or what he sends.[1]

[533] Pope Mercurius, also known as John, died on 27 May. Agapitus[2] was the fifty-sixth pope after Peter. Meanwhile, Athalaric,
king of the Goths, died after ruling for eight years. His mother
Amalaswintha[3] made Theodahad[4] joint ruler with herself, and
Theodahad, some days later, ordered her to be strangled in her
bath. But because she, during her lifetime, commended her son to
the emperor, Justinian was angry with Theodahad. But Theodahad
sent Pope Agapitus to him at Constantinople so that the emperor
might absolve him of this crime. Agapitus converted the emperor,
who was falling into the heresy of Eutyches, back to the faith; he
also drove into exile Anthemius, bishop of Constantinople, a
defender of the aforementioned heresy, and denier of the two
natures in Christ, and consecrated Mennas bishop in his place.
Pope Agapitus died there in Constantinople on 22 April, and was
buried at Rome on 20 September.[5]

[2] Agapitus I 535-6.   [3] Amalaswintha 534-5.
[4] Theodahad 534-6.   [5] Mar.

[534] (viii) 556 *Siluerius*[1] *papa quinquagesimus .vii. post Petrum anno uno mensibus duobus.*[a] *Interea ad Affricam, quam multis annis Wandali possidebant, a Iustiniano cum exercitu Bilisarius patricius missus est, et Wandalorum gentem deleuit. Kartago quoque anno excessionis sue .xcvi. recepta est, pulsis deuictisque Wandalis*[b] *et rege eorum Gelemaro prelio uicto et capto Constantinopolim misso. Kartago uero recessit anno .cccc. tricesimo nono incarnationis iuxta Dionisium, Theodosii iunioris .xvi. Agapito uero papa*[c] *mortuo, misit Iustinianus imperator Bilisarium contra Theodatum. Qui cum moras apud Siciliam fecisset, Theodatus obiit. Cui Wintigis*[d2] *successit. Bilisarius uero uidens sibi incongruum tempus bellandi intra urbem Romam se muniuit. Wintigis*[d] *autem cum Gothis per annum Romam obsidet, et Romanorum omnia etiam reliquias sanctorum ita diripuit, ut matres menbra natorum suorum eo anno pre fame comederent.*[3]

Primus rex[e] Occidentalium Saxonum[4] Cerdic hac uita decessit et filius suus Cynric solus post illum .xxvi. annis[5] regnauit.[f6] |

[535] (ix) 557 *Tunc statim precepto Theodore auguste, consentiente Iustiniano imperatore, papam Siluerium, quia Anthimium hereticum Constantinopolitanum episcopum, ab Agapito papa expulsum, noluit reuocare, Bilisarius, licet nolens, expulit ad Pontianam insulam in qua obiit .xii. kalend. Iulii.*[7]

[536] (x) 558 *Vigilius*[8] *papa quinquagesimus .viii. post Petrum annis .xviii., mensibus .vi.*[9] *[g]Sanctus Benedictus migrauit ad Dominum.*[g10]

[537] (xi) 559 *Bilisarius Wintigisum bello*[h] *captum Constantinopolim secum perduxit ad imperatorem Iustinianum.*[11]

[538] (xii) 560 Eclipsis solis facta est .xiiii. kalend. Martii ab hora prima usque ad tertiam.[12]

---

[a] *541 n . a placed here* L   [b] *B reverts to long lines*   [c] *interlin.* C¹   [d] Witigis *from* Wintigis C   [e] *om.* HL   [f] *C reverts to long lines after this*   [g–g] Sanctus . . . Dominum] *mg. near 536* C³ *(initial S reworked)* B¹, *line struck through this* L, *mg. with line pointing to 548* P³, *under Justinian (527–65)* G   [h] bellum *(N)*

---

[1] Silverius 536–7.   [2] Vitigis 536–40.   [3] Mar.
[4] ASC F alone describes Cerdic as first king of the West Saxons.
[5] ASC AE give 26 years, the other versions 27. ASC have under this year JW's 530 n. 11 (p. 37).

[534] Silverius,[1] fifty-seventh pope since Peter, reigned one year, two months. Meanwhile the patrician Belisarius was sent with an army by Justinian to Africa, which the Vandals had held for many years, and he destroyed the Vandal people. Furthermore, ninety-six years after its loss, Carthage was recaptured, the Vandals driven back and defeated, and their king, Gelimer, defeated and captured in battle, and sent to Constantinople. Carthage was lost in the 439th year of the Incarnation, according to Dionysius, in the sixteenth of Theodosius the Younger. After the death of Pope Agapitus, the Emperor Justinian sent Belisarius against Theodahad. When Belisarius had passed some time in Sicily, Theodahad died. Vitigis[2] succeeded him. Belisarius, seeing that the time was unsuitable for war, took up a defensive position within the city of Rome. But Vitigis with his Goths besieged Rome for a year and plundered all that the Romans possessed, even the relics of the saints, so that in that year mothers ate their children's limbs from hunger.[3]

Cerdic, the first king of the West Saxons,[4] departed this life and his son Cynric reigned alone after him for twenty-six years.[5,6]

[535] Then at once, at the command of the Empress Theodora, and with the agreement of the Emperor Justinian, Belisarius, although unwilling, expelled Pope Silverius to the island of Ponza, where he died on 20 June, because he would not recall Anthemius, the heretical bishop of Constantinople, expelled by Pope Agapitus.[7]

[536] Vigilius[8] the fifty-eighth pope after Peter, reigned eighteen years and six months.[9] St Benedict passed to the Lord.[10]

[537] Belisarius took Vitigis a prisoner of war with him to the Emperor Justinian at Constantinople.[11]

[538] A solar eclipse took place from the first to the third hour on 16 February.[12]

---

[6] ASC.   [7] Mar.   [8] Vigilius 537–55.   [9] Mar.
[10] Hugh of Fleury, p. 138, who gives the year of Benedict's death.
[11] Mar.   [12] ASC.

[539] (xiii) 561   *Bilisarius iterum ad Affricam uenit.*[1]

[540] (xiiii) 562   *Bilisarius Guntarium regem Wandalorum occidit.*[2] Eclipsis solis facta est .xii. kalend. Iulii et apparuerunt stelle hora pene dimidia ab hora diei .iii.[3]

[54I] (xv) 563   *ᵃ⟨F⟩acta est Bizantiumᵇ mortalitas magna. Qua de causa, eodem anno cepit celebrari solennitas sancte Dei genitricis Marie purificationis* ipsiusᶜ *et cessauit mortalitas illa.ᵃ*[4] *Bilisarius Wandalos rei publice substrauit.*[5]

[542] (xvi) 564   *ᵈEtᵉ Romam ueniens, crucem auream librarum centum et gemmis pretiosissimis ornatam suis uictoriis inscriptam beato Petro per manus Vigilii pape optulit.ᵈ*[6]

[543] (xvii) 565   [C³BP]
                                      ᶠDauid qui et Dewi Mene-
                                      wensem presulatum in Walia
                                      suscepit.ᶠ[7]

[544] (xviii) 566   *Anno .xiii. magni cicli pascalis, id est octauo decimo Iustiniani, annus dominice passionis secundo continetur, non antea, id est anno passionis primo et modo secundo. A passione igitur Christi usque in predictum annum habetur ciclus magnus pascalis quingentorum triginta duorum annorum.*[8]

Wihtgar [9]nepos Cerdici regis Occidentalium Saxonum[9] mortem obiit, et in Wihtgarabyrig, [9]id est in ciuitate Wihtgari,[9] tumulatus fuit.[10]

ᵍCapto Wintigiso, Gothiʰ trans Padum Hiltebaldum[11] *sibi regem constituunt eodemque anno occiditur. Cui Erarius*[12] *successit, et ante annum occisus est. His temporibus, factum est illud quod sanctus Gregorius in Dialogo suo*[13] *retulit de episcopis qui ob catholicam fidem*

ᵃ⁻ᵃ (F)acta . . . illa] *mg. alongside 541-4 C³B¹, inserted 534 n. a. L, mg. near 550 P³*, Anno .xvi. regni Iustiniani G   ᵇ Bizantii *Hugh of Fleury, though the Cambridge Corpus MS 265 p. 525 has* Bizantium   ᶜ *om. Hugh of Fleury,* ipsius *from* illius *Cambridge Corpus MS 265 p. 525*   ᵈ⁻ᵈ Et . . . optulit] *rewritten partly over erasure, presumably to accommodate 543 n. f, and made to start under 541 where there was no erasure C³, starts under 541 B, under consolidated 536-44 P*   ᵉ Bilisarius HL *(N)*   ᶠ⁻ᶠ Dauid . . . suscepit] *add. partly over erasure C, om. HL,*   ᵍ *under 548-50 (N)*   ʰ *interlin.* C¹

[539] Belisarius went again to Africa.[1]

[540] Belisarius killed Guntarius, king of the Vandals.[2]
A solar eclipse took place on 20 June and the stars were visible for almost half an hour from the third hour of the day.[3]

[541] A great plague broke out in Byzantium. In consequence the feast of the Purification of the Holy Mother of God began to be celebrated in this year and the plague stopped.[4] Belisarius subjected the Vandals to the state.[5]

[542] Coming to Rome, Belisarius gave the blessed St Peter by the hands of Pope Vigilius a gold cross of 100 lb., adorned with most precious stones, and inscribed with his triumphs.[6]

[543]   David, also known as Dewi, received the bishopric of Menevia in Wales.[7]

[544] In the thirteenth year of the great Easter cycle, that is the eighteenth year of Justinian, and no earlier, the year of the Lord's Passion was encompassed for the second time; that is, in the first Passion year and then the second. That is to say, the great Easter cycle of 532 years ran from Christ's Passion to the abovementioned year.[8]
Wihtgar, [9]nephew of Cerdic, king of the West Saxons,[9] died and was buried in *Wihtgarabyrig*, [9]that is in the city of Wihtgar.[9,10]
After the capture of Vitigis the Goths across the Po made Hildebad[11] their king; he was killed in the same year. Eraric[12] succeeded him and was killed within a year. In these times occurred the incident that St Gregory recounted in his *Dialogues*,[13] of the bishops who spoke when their tongues had been

---

[1] Mar.   [2] Mar.   [3] ASC.
[4] Hugh of Fleury, p. 138. Here two readings in Cambridge, Corpus Christi College MS 265, p. 525 are, as the apparatus shows, closer to JW than those in the printed text. Hugh assigns this plague to the 15th year of Justinian.
[5] Mar.   [6] Mar.
[7] The source for this date is not known. Tradition, as related by Rhigyfarch, assumes that David was bishop by the time of the synod of Brefi, dated by the *Annales Cambriae* to 569.
[8] Mar.   [9–9] This identification is not in ASC at this point.
[10] ASC.   [11] Hildebad 540–1.   [12] Eraric 541.   [13] *Dialogues*, iii. 32.

truncatis linguis loquebantur, quorum unus, propter luxuriam in quam postea cecidit, hoc miraculo priuatus est.[1]

[547] (xxi) 569 *^a*In prouincia Berniciorum Ida regnum suscepit et .xii. annis regnauit. Hic ex reginis sex filios, Addam, Bælricum, Theodricum, Æthelricum, Theodherum, Osmærum, et sex habuit ex pelicibus, Occ, Alricum, Eccam, Osuuold, Sogor, Sogetherum.[2] Ex quibus regalis Northanhymbrorum prosapia fuit propagata. Ida fuit filius Eoppe, qui fuit Ese, qui fuit Ingui, qui fuit Angenuuit, qui fuit Aloc, qui fuit Benoc, qui fuit Brand, qui fuit Bealdeag, qui fuit Woden, qui fuit Frythelaf, *^b*qui fuit Frithulf,*^b* qui fuit Finn, qui fuit Godulf, qui fuit Geate.[3]

[551] (xxv) 573 *Ciclus decennouenalis secundus incipit indictione quarta decima.*[4]

[552] (xxvi) 574 *Baduuilla*[5] *qui et Totila Erario successit.*[6]
Kynric *⁷*rex Occidentalium Saxonum,[7] in loco qui Searesbyrig*^c* nominatur, cum Brytonibus dimicauit eosque fugauit. Cuius pater Cerdic, qui fuit Elese, *^d*qui fuit Esle,*^d* qui fuit Geuuis, qui fuit Wig, qui fuit Fræuuine, qui fuit Freoðegar, qui fuit Brand, qui fuit Bealdeag, qui fuit Woden.[8]

[553] (xxvii) 575 *Vigilius papa ob eandem causam, qua et decessor eius Siluerius indignatione Auguste per Antimum scribonem Constantinopolim perductus, indeque ⟨in⟩^e exilium actus, deinde reuocatus ad Romam, ueniensque Siciliam in ciuitate Siracusa obiit et sepultus est Rome uia Salaria iuxta Marcellum. Iste est Vigilius cui Arator librum suum optulit cuius etiam in eiusdem libri prologo meminit ita:*

> *Publica libertas sanctissime papa Vigili.*
> *Aduenis incluso soluere uincla gregi.*[9]

---

^a runs on to 548-50 C, starts under 548 and runs on to 549 B   ^{b–b} qui fuit Frithulf] om. HL   ^c possibly over erasure C   ^{d–d} qui ... Esle] om. H   ^e om. JW

---

¹ Mar.
² Ida's sons (who are not in ASC, though an interlineation in F refers to his Northumbrian succession) and the length of his reign are found in JW *Northum. Accounts* 1. ASC A (addition by ?scribe 8) EF record his 12-year reign, but also mention the building of Bamburgh which is not in JW.

cut out because of their Catholic faith. One of them was deprived of this miraculous gift because of the excesses into which he later fell.[1]

[547] In Bernicia Ida took control and reigned twelve years. By his queens he had six sons: Adda, Bælric, Theodric, Æthelric, Theodhere, Osmær; and by his concubines six: Ogg, Alric, Ecca, Oswald, Sogor, Sogetherf.[2] From them descended the royal line of Northumbria. Ida was the son of Eoppa, son of Esa, son of Ingui, son of Angenwit, son of Aloc, son of Benoc, son of Brand, son of Bældæg, son of Woden, son of Freotholaf, son of Freothowulf, son of Finn, son of Godwulf, son of Geata.[3]

[551] The second cycle of nineteen years began in the fourteenth indiction.[4]

[552] Badwilla,[5] also known as Totila, succeeded Eraric.[6]
   Cynric, [7]king of the West Saxons,[7] fought the Britons in a place called Salisbury, and put them to flight. He was son of Cerdic, son of Elesa, son of Esla, son of Gewis, son of Wig, son of Fræwine, son of Freothegar, son of Brand, son of Bældæg, son of Woden.[8]

[553] Pope Vigilius incurred the empress's anger for the same reason as his precedessor Silverius, and was taken to Constantinople by the *scribo* Anthinus, and thence sent into exile. Then he was recalled to Rome, and, reaching Sicily, he died in the city of Syracuse, and was buried at Rome in the church of St Marcellus on the Via Salaria. He was the Vigilius to whom Arator offered his book, and who is also mentioned in the prologue of the same book, thus:

   Public freedom, most holy Pope Vigilius,
   You come to loose the bonds of your imprisoned flock.[9]

---

[3] ASC. Ida's genealogy is given in ASC A (erased but partly recovered from G) BC but not in EF.
   [4] Mar.   [5] Totila 541-53.   [6] Mar.   [7-7] Not in ASC.
   [8] ASC. ABCEF record the Salisbury victory but EF omit the genealogy. F refers to Æthelberht and his reign.
   [9] Mar.

56 CHRONICON IOHANNIS WIGORNENSIS [554–5]

[554] (xxviii) 576 Pelagius[1] quinquagesimus .ix. papa annis .xi., mensibus .xi.[2]

[555] (xxix) 577 Totila cum Gothis totam Italiam inuadit. Exinde per Campaniam uirique Dei Benedicti abbatis cenobium iter faciens, Romam obsidionibus circumcludit. Et tunc fames pene similis precedenti contigit. Fessis autem et non ualentibus Romanis | menia tueri, Totila porta Hostiensi urbem intrat. Qui nocte capiens urbem, ut parceret Romanis, tubas sonari precepit ut Romani uel paululum inimicorum rabiem deuitarent et aliquantum temporis cum eis quasi pater cum filiis habitauit. Hanc illi, ut datur conici, animi benignitatem, qui nimie ante crudelitatis fuit, beati patris Benedicti, quem cum modo Romam uenire uellet, audierat monita contulerit, quando Totilam increpauit et de sua morte sibi predixit post .ix. annos.[3] [a]Regnante Francorum rege Dagoberto,[4] qui quartus erat a Clodoueo, qui primus Christianitatem a sancto suscepit Remigio, comes palatinus Badefridus uocabulo ex uxore Framehilde sanctam genuit Austrobertam. Que processu temporis, a sancto Audomaro Taruernensi episcopo sacro uelamine consecrata. Post in cenobio Portus nominato sub spirituali matri nomine Burgofledis sanctimonialibus est aggregata. Cuius monasterii erat consuetudo ut uicissim a sororibus coquerentur panes. Sed cum hec Christi famula die quadam in ordine uicis sue hoc in opere laboraret, habebat secum unam tantum adolescentulam que apud eam fuerat educata. Cumque clibanus fuisset igne succensus et panes in promptu ad coquendum parati, cum post igne abstracto, a fauillis uel prunis que remanserant debuisset mundari, fasciculus qui erat in summitate ligni colligatus, casu igne adustus est totus. Quod ubi famula Dei aduertit, conlidens manus una ad alteram altiusque ingemiscens ait: 'Ve nobis, quid acture sumus? panes peribunt. Opus enim hoc recuperari modo non potest. Et currens festina obserauit ostium domus. Deinde signo crucis munita, medium inter ignium uapores clibanum sola ingreditur, arreptisque manicis, quibus utebatur in brachiis, clibanum omnem mundauit. Egressa demum, diligenter officium compleuit, et nec unum

p. 253

---

[a] Regnante . . . gloriosa (p. 58)] mg. alongside 555–69 C (a minute hand sloping to left, and different from others), lower mg. below 627 B[3], mg. alongside 552–6, with sign pointing to 556 or just possibly end of 555 P[3], under Justin II (565–78) G

---

[1] Pelagius I 556–61.   [2] Mar.   [3] Mar.   [4] Dagobert I 629–38.

[554] Pelagius,[1] the fifty-ninth pope, reigned eleven years, eleven months.[2]

[555] Totila and the Goths invaded the whole of Italy. From there he marched through Campania to the monastery of Abbot Benedict, the man of God, and besieged Rome. And then a famine almost like the earlier one seized Rome. When the Romans were exhausted and not able to defend the walls, Totila entered the city through the Ostian gate. He took the city by night, and, to spare the Romans, ordered the trumpets to be sounded so that the Romans might escape, if only for a little while, the ferocity of their enemies and, for a short time, he lived with them as a father with his sons. It is possible to speculate that this kindliness of spirit, in one who had before been extremely cruel, was brought about by the admonitions of the blessed father Benedict, whom he had heard as he was on the point of going to Rome, when he rebuked Totila, and spoke prophetically to him about his death nine years later.[3] In the reign of the Frankish king, Dagobert,[4] who was the fourth after Clovis (who first received Christianity from St Remigius), the count of the palace, Badefrid by name, begot St Austroberta on his wife Framehild. She, in due course, was consecrated with the holy veil by St Omer, bishop of Thérouanne. Afterwards, in the convent called *Portus* (Abbeville), under a spiritual mother, Burgofled by name, she joined the nuns. It was the custom of that convent that the loaves be baked by the sisters in turn. But one day, when Christ's handmaiden was taking her turn at that task, she had with her only a young girl who had been brought up with her. When the oven had been heated up by the fire and the loaves were prepared and ready to be baked, and when afterwards, the fire had been taken away and the oven was due to be cleared of the embers and live coals which remained, a bundle of twigs which had been placed on top of the wood was completely burnt by accident. When God's handmaiden observed that, wringing her hands and groaning very loudly, she said: 'Alas for us! What shall we do? The loaves will be ruined: our work simply cannot be rescued.' In great haste, she locked the doors of the building. Then, strengthened by the sign of the cross, she went into the middle of the oven alone, among the smoke of the fires, and grasping the sleeves she wore on her arms, she cleaned the whole oven. Finally, when she came out, she diligently

quidem capillum capitis nec denique fimbriam uestimenti eius non est ausus ignis attingere. Precepit tum *puelle ut patefaceret ostium domus, multisque eam contestata est sermonibus, ne cuiquam quod uiderat indicaret.* Hac uirtute multisque aliis uirtutibus adornata *in eodem monasterio .iiii. iduum Februarium die transiuit* ad Dominum *uirgo gloriosa.*[a]1

[556] (xxx) 578   Kynric et Ceaulin apud Beranbyrig Brytonibus bellum intulerunt et illos fugauerunt.[2]

[557] (xxxi) 579   Sigebertus[3] .xiii. rex Francorum occisus est fraude Hilperici germani sui cum quo bellum inierat, regnumque eius[b] Childebertus filius eius adhuc puerulus cum Brunicilde matre regendum suscepit.[4]

[558] (xxxii) 580   *Pelagius papa ecclesiam beatorum apostolorum Philippi et Iacobi incepit construere.*[5]

[559][f] (xxxiii) 581   *Rome Cassiodorus prius consul inde senator postea monachus clarus habetur.*[6]

Ælle in[d] prouincia Deirorum regnum suscepit et ferme .xxx. annis illud strenuissime rexit.[7] *Ad* cuius[e] *nomen beatus Gregorius cum Angligenos pueros in foro Romano uenales inuenerit positos alludens ait: Alleluia laudem Dei creatoris illis in partibus oportet cantari.*[8] Interim super Bernicios regnauerunt Adda primogenitus Ide .vii. annis, Clappa .v., Theodwlf .i., Freothulf .vii., Theodric .vii., Æthelric duobus uiuente Ælle. Quo mortuo et filio eius Eduuino regno expulso super ambas prouincias .v. annis regnauit.[9] Ælle fuit filius Yffe, [f]cuius pater Wuscfrea, cuius pater Wilgels, cuius pater Westoruualena, cuius pater Seomel, cuius pater Suuearta, cuis pater Seafugel, cuius pater Seabald, cuius pater

---

[a] *see above p. 56 n. a*   [b] *om.* HL   [c] 558 C   [d] *mg.* C[1]   [e] cuius G *and from* cui B, cui C, cui, *but with abbreviation sign (possibly in error) below* i H
[f] cuius . . . Woden *(p. 60)] possibly rewriting over erasure* C

---

[1] *Vitae Austrobertae, Acta SS* Feb. ii. 419-23.
[2] ASC. A West Saxon victory is probably inferred by JW. (ASC F has an erasure here).
[3] Sigebert I 561-75.

completed her task, and the fire dared not touch one hair of her head or, indeed, the hem of her garment. Then she ordered the girl to open the door of the building, and adjured her with many words not to disclose what she had seen. Adorned with this miracle and many others, the glorious virgin passed to the Lord in the same monastery on 10 February.[1]

[556] Cynric and Ceawlin did battle with the Britons at Barbury and put them to flight.[2]

[557] Sigebert,[3] the thirteenth king of the Franks, was killed by the treachery of his brother Chilperic whom he had engaged in war, and his son Childebert, still a child, received the kingdom with his mother Brunhild.[4]

[558] Pope Pelagius began to build the church of the blessed apostles Philip and James.[5]

[559] At Rome, Cassiodorus, first consul, then senator, became a famous monk.[6]

Ælle became king of Deira and ruled most vigorously for almost thirty years.[7] St Gregory, when he found English youths put up for sale in the Roman market-place, said, making a play on Ælle's name: 'Alleluia, the praise of God the Creator ought to be sung in those parts.'[8] Meanwhile, Bernicia was ruled by Adda, Ida's eldest son, for seven years; Clappa for five; Theodwulf for one; Freothulf for seven; Theoderic for seven; Æthelric for two, in Ælle's lifetime. When, after Ælle's death, his son Edwin had been driven from his kingdom, Æthelric ruled both provinces for five years.[9] Ælle was the son of Yffe, son of Wuscfrea, son of Wilgils, son of Westerfalca, son of Seomel, son of Swearta, son of Sæfugel, son of

---

[4] Norman Annals. *AU, AG* (556), *ASN* (534).   [5] Mar.   [6] Mar.

[7] The length of Ælle's reign is given in ASC A (as recovered from G) BCEF (in ASC his kingdom is described as 'of the Northumbrians') and in JW *Northum. Accounts* 2, though the date of his accession is 560 in all ASC versions (F not quite clear). 'Ferme''s equivalent is not in ASC.

[8] *HE* ii. 1.

[9] This regnal list agrees, in its detail and in some phrases, with that in JW *Northum. Accounts* 2.

Siggeot, cuius pater Suueabdeag, cuius pater Siggar, cuius pater Weagdeag, cuius pater Woden.*a1*

[560] (xxxiiii) 582   Ciclus solis incipit .iiii. concurrentibus bissextilibus.

Ceaulin filius Cynrici regimen regni Occidentalium Saxonum suscipiens triginta tribus annis regnauit.*b2*

[561] (xxxv) 583   *Victor Capuanus episcopus librum de Pasca scribens Victorii arguit errores.*3 Æthelbryht rex Cantuuariorum regnare cepit et .lvi. annis, teste Beda, regnauit.4

[562] (xxxvi) 584   *Vir sanctissimus Herculanus nutritor beati Gregorii, ipso in Dialogo suo*c5* hoc referente, Perusine ciuitatis episcopus fuit. Qui precepto Totile regis Gothorum super murum sue ciuitatis capite truncatus est. His quoque temporibus, beatus pater Benedictus magnis uite meritis et apostolicis uirtutibus fulsit. Quod autem sanctus Gregorius his temporibus fuerit ipse in libro Dialogi sui ita probat.*6 *d**Vir quoque uite uenerabilis Cherbonius Populonii episcopus magnam in diebus nostris sanctitatis sue probationem dedit.*d7*

[564] (xxxviii) 586   *Priscianus grammaticus apud Constantinopolim clarus habetur. Pelagius papa obiit .vi. nonas Martii.*
   *Romanorum sexagesimus Iustinus minor*8* regnauit annis undecim, hoc est quasi usque*e* kalendas Ianuarii.*9

[565] (i) 587   *Iohannes*10* papa sexagesimus annis .xiii.*11
   Columba presbiter et abbas de Scottia12 *Brytan*niam *uenit, et, regnante Pictis Bridio rege potentissimo,* septentrionales Pictos *ad fidem*

---

    a *see above p. 58 n. f*   *b* et usque ad Norðhimbros regnum dilatauit *interlin.* B5
    c suae *(N)*   *d–d* Vir . . . dedit] *runs on to 563 CHB, under 563 L*   *e* om.
HL

    1 ASC. A (as recovered from G) BC give the genealogy of Ælle, but omit Seomel and Swearta who appear in JW *Northum. Gen.*
    2 ASC. A (as recovered from G) BCEF (year not clear in F) give Ceawlin's reign as 30 years. The 33 years here agree with JW *West Saxon Accounts* 3, and might just be reconciled with ASC's dates of 560 for the accession, and 592 for the expulsion, of Ceawlin.

Sæbald, son of Sigegeat, son of Swefdæg, son of Sigegar, son of Wægdæg, son of Woden.[1]

[560] The solar cycle begins with four concurrents in a bissextile year.

Ceawlin, son of Cynric, received the government of the kingdom of the West Saxons and reigned thirty-three years.[2]

[561] Victor, bishop of Capua, writing a treatise on Easter, confuted the errors of Victorius.[3]

Æthelberht, king of Kent, began to rule, and reigned fifty-six years, as Bede testifies.[4]

[562] The most holy man Herculanus, who fostered St Gregory, as he himself mentions in his *Dialogues*,[5] was bishop of the city of Perugia. He was beheaded at the command of Totila, king of the Goths, on the wall of his own city. Also in these times the blessed father Benedict shone brightly in the great merits of his life and in the apostolic virtues. That St Gregory himself lived in these times he himself demonstrates in the book of his *Dialogues*.[6] Cherbonius, also a man of admirable life, and bishop of Populonia, gave striking proof in our time of his sanctity.[7]

[564] Priscian, the famous grammarian, was renowned at Constantinople. Pope Pelagius died on 2 March.

Justin the Less,[8] sixtieth emperor of the Romans, reigned eleven years, that is almost until 1 January.[9]

[565] John,[10] the sixtieth pope, reigned thirteen years.[11]

Columba, priest and abbot, came to Britain from Ireland,[12] and, in the reign of Brude, the most powerful king of the Picts, converted

---

[3] Mar.
[4] JW's date for Æthelberht's accession was calculated from Bede. ASC A (?scribe 8) EF date his accession to 565 and give his reign's length as 53 years under 565, and as 56 (E) and 53 (F) under 616.
[5] *Dialogues*, iii. 13.   [6] *Dialogues*, iii. 11.   [7] Mar.
[8] Justin II 656–78.   [9] Mar.
[10] John III 561–74.   [11] Mar.
[12] 'de Scottia' for Bede's 'de Hibernia' could possibly be explained by 'of Scottum' in ASC A (as recovered from G) BC.

Christi conuertit. Vnde insulam Hii *ab eis in possessionem monasterii* construendi *accepit.*[1]

[566] (ii) 588   *Narsis patricius* missus[a] *ad Italiam, Totilam occidit, totamque Italiam ad rem publicam reduxit. Qui deinde per inuidiam Romanorum pro quibus multa contra Gothos laborauit, accusatus apud Iustinum et coniugem eius Sophiam quod seruitio premeret Italiam recessit Neapolim Campanie et Longobardos [b]introduxit in Italiam.[b2]*

[568] (iiii) 590   *Leuigildus[3] rex Gothorum quasdam Hispanie regiones sibi rebelles in potestatem regni sui superando redigit.[4]*

Æthelbryht rex Cantuariorum,[5] dum regi Occidentalium Saxonum[5] Ceaulino et Cuthe eius filio[6] bellum intulerit, ab eis in Cantiam est fugatus duobus eius ducibus Oslauo et Cnebbano in Wibbandune trucidatis.[7]

[569] (v) 591   *Iohannes papa ecclesiam sanctorum apostolorum[c] Philippi et Iacobi, quam predecessor eius Pelagius ceperat, perficiens dedicauit.[8]* |

p. 254   [570] (vi) 592   *Ciclus [d].iii. decennouenalis[d] incipit indictione .iii.[9]*

[571] (vii) 593   *Germanus Parisiorum episcopus obiit.[10]*

Regis Ceaulini frater Cuthulf,[11] in loco qui dicitur Bedanforda, cum Brytonibus dimicauit et, [12]uictor existens[12] quattuor regias[e] uillas eis abstulit, scilicet Liganburh, Eglesburh, Bensingtun et Egnesham, et eodem anno uitam decessit.[13]

[572] (viii) 594   *Fortunatus poeta in Galliis clarus habetur.[14]*

[573] (ix) 595   *Armenii fidem Christi suscipiunt.[15]*

---

[a] *interlin.* C[1]   [b–b] (intro)duxit in Italiam] *written in mg.* C *(apparent erasure at the beginning of a blank annal (567) on next line)*   [c] *om.* HL   [d–d] .iii. decennouenalis] decennouenalis .iii. HL   [e] *interlin.* C[1]

---

[1] *HE* iii. 4.   [2] Mar.   [3] Leovigild 569–86.   [4] Mar.
[5] Æthelberht and Ceawlin are not described as kings here in ASC.

the northern Picts to the Christian faith. After that he received from them the island of Iona to build a monastery.[1]

[566] The patrician Narses was sent to Italy, killed Totila, and restored all Italy to the empire. Then he was accused, through the envy of the Romans for whom he had striven much against the Goths, before Justin and his wife Sophia of oppressing Italy with servitude; he retired to Naples in Campania, and introduced the Lombards into Italy.[2]

[568] Leovigild,[3] king of the Goths, brought under his control by conquest certain areas of Spain in rebellion against him.[4]

Æthelberht, king of Kent[5] when he made war on Ceawlin, king of the West Saxons,[5] and on his son Cutha,[6] was put to flight by them after two of his ealdormen, Oslaf and Cnebban, were cut down at *Wibbandun*.[7]

[569] Pope John completed and dedicated the church of the holy Apostles Philip and James which his predecessor Pelagius had begun.[8]

[570] The third cycle of nineteen years begins in the third indiction.[9]

[571] Germanus, bishop of Paris, died.[10]

Cuthwulf, brother of King Ceawlin,[11] fought the Britons in a place called *Biedcanford* and, [12]emerging victorious,[12] took from them four royal townships, namely Limbury, Aylesbury, Bensington, and Eynsham, and in the same year he departed this life.[13]

[572] The poet Fortunatus was renowned in Gaul.[14]

[573] The Armenians received the Christian faith.[15]

---

[6] ASC F (in an interlineation) alone indicates the relationship of Ceawlin and Cutha and calls them brothers.
[7] ASC. BC omit 'cut down'.   [8] Mar.   [9] Mar.   [10] Mar.
[11] E alone of the ASC versions calls Cutha (presumably Cuthwulf) the brother of Ceawlin.
[12-12] Probably inferred by JW.   [13] ASC.   [14] Mar.   [15] Mar.

[574] (x) 596   *Redemptus Ferentine*[1] *ciuitatis episcopus clarus ut legitur in Dialogo*[2] *habetur.*[3]

[575] (xi) 597   *Iustinus imperator amentia obiit.*

Romanorum sexagesimus primus Tiberius Constantinus[4] *regnauit annis septem usque in annum quingentesimum septuagesimum primum post passionem Domini.*[5]

[576] (i) 598   *Gregorius tunc apocrisiarius in Constantinopoli et post papa in Iob·expositionem condit. Iohannes papa obiit .iii. idus Iulii.*[6]

[577] (ii) 599   *Benedictus*[7] *papa sexagesimus primus annis .iiii., mensibus duobus.*[8] *ᵃSanctus Maurus .lxxii.* annorum migrauit ad Dominum.*ᵃ*[9]

[10]Rex Occidentalium Saxonum[10] Ceaulin et [10]filius suus[10] Cuthuuine[11] in loco qui uocatur Deorham cum Brytonibus pugnauere et eorum tres reges Commeail, Condidan et Farinmæil [10]cum multis aliis[10] trucidauere, illisque tres ciuitates uidelicet Glauueceaster, Cirenceaster, Bathanceaster abstulere.[12]

[578] (iii) 600   *Gregorius Euticium Constantinopolitanum episcopum, Tiberio presente, conuicit ita ut Tiberius librum Euticii de resurrectione destruens, suis catholicis allegationibus deliberaret flammis cremandum. Scribebat autem Euticius corpus nostrum in resurrectione inpalpabile et uentis aerique subtilius esse futurum contra illud dominicum: 'palpate et uidete quia spiritus carnem et ossa non habet sicut me uidetis habere.'* [13,14]

[579] (iiii) 601   *Gens Longobardorum, rege Albuuino, comitante fame et mortalitate, omnem repente inuadit Italiam, ipsamque uastatura Romanam obsidet urbem. Denique cum uastantibus omnia per circuitum Longobardis fames abundaret, multa milia frumenti nauibus Benedictus papa ab Egipto dirigens Romam sub studio misericordie releuauit.*[15]

ᵃ⁻ᵃ Sanctus . . . Dominum] *mg. near 577 C³L¹B¹P⁵, under Tiberius 578-82 G*

---

[1] Near Viterbo.   [2] *Dialogues,* iii. 38.   [3] Mar.
[4] Tiberius Constantine 578-82.   [5] Mar.
[6] Mar.   [7] Benedict I 575-9.   [8] Mar.
[9] Hugh of Fleury, p. 138 says that Maurus died, at the age of 72, 41 years after the death of Benedict.

[574] Redemptus was the illustrious bishop of *Ferentis*,[1] as is to be read in the *Dialogues*.[2,3]

[575] The Emperor Justin died insane.

Tiberius Constantine,[4] sixty-first emperor of the Romans, reigned seven years up to the 571st year after the Lord's Passion.[5]

[576] Gregory, then *apocrisiarius* in Constantinople and afterwards pope, composed his commentary on Job. Pope John died on 13 July.[6]

[577] Benedict,[7] the sixty-first pope, reigned four years, two months.[8] St Maurus, at 72, passed over to the Lord.[9]

Ceawlin, [10]king of the West Saxons, and his son[10] Cuthwine[11] fought the Britons in a place called Dyrham and slew their three kings, Conmail, Condidan, and Farinmail, [10]with many others[10] and took from them three cities, namely, Gloucester, Cirencester, and Bath.[12]

[578] Gregory confuted Eutyches, bishop of Constantinople, in the presence of Tiberius, so that Tiberius, rejecting Eutyches' book about the Resurrection, decided, on the promptings of his Catholic subjects, that it should be consigned to the flames, for Eutyches wrote that our bodies will be impalpable and more delicate than wind or air at the resurrection, contrary to the Lord's words: 'Touch and see, for a spirit hath not flesh and bones, as you see me to have.'[13,14]

[579] The Lombards, under King Alboin, attended by hunger and death, suddenly invaded all Italy and besieged the very city of Rome in order to lay it waste. At last, when hunger was widespread through the Lombards' destruction of everything in the vicinity, Pope Benedict in his zealous charity relieved it by bringing a very great amount of grain from Egypt in ships.[15]

[10-10] Not in ASC.
[11] In ASC Cuthwine (who is mentioned before Ceawlin), is not described as Ceawlin's son, as he is here and in JW *West Saxon Gen.*
[12] ASC.   [13] Luke 24: 39.   [14] Mar.   [15] Mar.

[580] (v) 602   Chilpericus*a* rex Francorum quintus decimus.[1]

[581] (vi) 603   *Gothi per Erminigildum, Leuigildi filium, bifarie diuisi mutua cede uastantur.*[2]

[582] (vii) 604   *Pelagius*[3] *sexagesimus secundus papa annis decem, mensibus duobus. Benedictus papa obiit .ii. kalend. Augusti. Hoc anno factum est quod sanctus Gregorius scribit in Dialogo*[4] *de monacho Gerontio.*

Romanorum sexagesimus secundus Mauricius[5] *regnauit annis uiginti uno, mensibus quattuor usque kalend. Maii in anno quingentesimo nonagesimo secundo post passionem.*[6]

[583] (i) 605   *Pelagius papa sine iussione Mauricii ordinatus est, eo quod Longobardi Romam per circuitum obsiderent ita ut nullus foras progredi posset.*[7]

[584] (ii) 606   *b*In loco qui uocatur Fethanleah, Ceaulin rex Occidentalium Saxonum et filius eius Cutha[8] cum Brytonibus certauere. In quo certamine inter confertissimos Cutha fortiter dimicans ruit. Rex tamen Ceaulin uictoriam habuit, eisque multa spolia detraxit et uillas quam plures abstraxit.[9]

[585] (iii) 607   *Erminigildus, Leuigildi Gothorum regis filius, ob fidei catholice confessionem inexpugnabilem a patre Arriano regno priuatus, in uincula et in carcerem missus est. Ad extremum nocte sancta dominice resurrectionis securi in capite percussus, regnum celeste pro terreno rex et martir possidere promeruit. Cuius frater Recaredus*c*[10] mox ut regnum post patrem suscepit, omnem Gothorum cui preerat gentem, instante Leandro Hispanitano episcopo qui et Erminigildum docuerat, catholicam conuertit ad fidem.*[11]

---

a Gilpericus *JW*   *b* has here Sauci *(om. (N), though has a blank space)*, a Leuigildo rege obtentis Gothis subieciuntur *Mar.*   *c* from Ricardus *C*t

[1] Norman Annals. *AU, AG, ASN* (579). ?Chilperic I 561–84.
[2] Mar.   [3] Pelagius II 579–90.   [4] *Dialogues*, iv. 27.
[5] Maurice 582–602.   [6] Mar.
[7] Mar. JW could have deliberately ignored the entry in ASC A (addition by hand 8) EF for the accession of Maurice under this year as he had already followed Marianus in dating it to 582.

[580] Chilperic was the fifteenth king of the Franks.[1]

[581] The Goths, divided into two parties by Hermenigild, son of Leovigild, were destroyed by mutual slaughter.[2]

[582] Pelagius,[3] the sixty-second pope, reigned ten years, two months. Pope Benedict died on 31 July. In this year there took place what St Gregory wrote in his *Dialogues*[4] about the monk Gerontius.

Maurice,[5] the sixty-second Roman emperor, reigned twenty-one years, four months, up to 1 May in the 592nd year after the Passion.[6]

[583] Pope Pelagius was ordained without Maurice's mandate because the Lombards besieged Rome on all sides so that no one could go out.[7]

[584] Ceawlin, king of the West Saxons, and his son Cutha[8] fought with the Britons in a place called *Fethanleag*. In that battle fell Cutha, fighting bravely where the crush was greatest. But King Ceawlin was victorious and seized from them great booty, and took very many townships.[9]

[585] Hermenigild, son of Leovigild, king of the Goths, because of his unconquerable belief in the Catholic faith, was deprived of rule by his Arian father, chained, and imprisoned. Finally, on the night of Easter Sunday, he was struck on the head with an axe, winning possession, as king and martyr, of a heavenly kingdom in place of an earthly one. His brother, Reccared,[10] as soon as he inherited the kingdom after his father, converted the whole race of Goths, whose ruler he was, to the Catholic faith at the urging of Leander, bishop of Seville, who had also instructed Hermenigild.[11]

---

[8] The identification of Ceawlin as king of the West Saxons and of Cutha as his son are not in ASC here, though the genealogy in ASC ABC (685) and in JW *West Saxon Gen.* gives Ceawlin a son Cutha.

[9] ASC ABCE. The apparent additions here 'inter confertissimos', 'fortiter dimicans', and 'rex tamen Ceawlin uictoriam habuit' could account for the omission of ASC's 'in anger returned to his land' (not E).

[10] Reccared 586–601.   [11] Mar.

[586] (iiii) 608   Childebertus Francorum rex sextus decimus.[1]

[588] (vi) 610   Ciclus solis incipit .iiii. concurrentibus bissex-
p. 255   tilibus. *Pelagius papa Helie Aquiliensi episcopo no|lenti .iii.
capitula Calcidonensis sinodi suscipere epistolam satis utilem misit, quam sanctus
Gregorius adhuc diaconus compleuit.*[2] *"Sanctus Audoenus nascitur."*[a3]
Ælle rex Deirorum .xxx. anno regni sui[4] decessit et Æthelric
Ide filius[5] post illum super ambas prouincias .v. annis regnauit.[6,7]

[589] (vii) 611   Ciclus decennouenalis .iiii. incipit indictione .vii.
*Sanctus pater Columbanus ex Hibernia, insula sanctorum, cum sancto
Gallo aliisque probatis discipulis uenit in Burgundiam, ibique, permit-
tente Theodorico rege, monasterium quod Luxouium dicitur edificauit.
Exinde a Brunihilda fugatus, Alamanniam ingreditur ubi sanctum
Gallum reliquit. Ipse uero in Italiam transiens, monasterium quod
Bouium dicitur edificauit, ubi pater multorum monachorum extitit.*[b8]

[590] (viii) 612   *'Septimus decimus rex Francorum Lotharius.'*[c9]

[591] (ix) 613   Ceol[10] filius Cuthuulfi fratris regis Ceaulini[11] regnare cepit et .v. annis[12] Occidentalium Saxonum rector extitit.[13]

[592] (x) 614   *Hoc tempore, .xvi. kalend. Nouembris diluuium factum est ut flumen Tiberis super muros urbis Rome influeret, et per
alueum eiusdem fluminis cum magna serpentium multitudine draco mire
magnitudinis usque ad mare descendit. Quam inundationem pestilentia
que dicitur inguinaria statim secuta est, ut pauci de multis remanerent,
in qua primus papa Pelagius obiit .viii. idus Febr.* [d]*Gregorius*[14] *sexa-*

[a-a] Sanctus . . . nascitur] *mg. near* 588 *C'B'*, *mg. alongside* 587-8 *with possible
sign pointing to* 587 *P³, under Maurice (582-602) G*   [b] *runs on to* 590 *CHB*
[c-c] Septimus . . . Lotharius] *under* 590, *but continues from* 589 *which has run over on to*
590, *and therefore just possibly meant for* 589 *CB,* Lotharius rex Francorum .xvii. *H,* Rex
Francorum Lotharius .xvii. *L*   [d] 593 *starts here Mar.*

---

[1] Norman Annals. *AU* (585), *ASN* (apparently 579, but *recte* 585). *AG* records the
death of Childeric in error under 585. Childebert II 575-592×595.
[2] Mar.   [3] Norman Annals. *AU, AG.*
[4] The length of Ælle's reign is not given here but under 560 in ASC A (original
form) BCE, and under an indeterminate year in F.
[5] The relationship of Ida to Æthelric is not in ASC.
[6] For the view that a scribal misunderstanding lay behind the extension of Æthelric's
rule over Deira (which is recorded neither in ASC nor in JW *Northum. Accounts*), see

[586] Childebert was the sixteenth king of the Franks.[1]

[588] The solar cycle begins with four concurrents and a bissextile year. Pope Pelagius sent a most beneficial letter (which St Gregory, still a deacon, completed) to Elias, bishop of Aquileia, who was unwilling to accept the three chapters of the Council of Chalcedon.[2] St Ouen was born.[3]

Ælle, king of Deira, died in the thirtieth year[4] of his reign, and Æthelric, son of Ida,[5] ruled both provinces after him for five years.[6,7]

[589] The fourth cycle of nineteen years begins in the seventh indiction. The holy father Columbanus went from Ireland, the island of saints, with St Gallus, and other proven disciples, into Burgundy, and there with the permission of King Theuderic he built the monastery called Luxeuil. Then, chased out by Brunhild, he entered Alemannia, where he left St Gallus. But he himself crossed into Italy and built the monastery which is called Bobbio, where he was called father to many monks.[8]

[590] Chlothar was the seventeenth king of the Franks.[9]

[591] Ceola,[10] son of Cuthwulf, King Ceawlin's brother,[11] began his reign and was ruler of the West Saxons for five years.[12,13]

[592] At this time, on 17 October, there was a flood which made the river Tiber flow over the walls of the city of Rome, and a dragon of amazing size, with a great multitude of serpents, passed down the channel of the same river to the sea. That flood was followed at once by the so-called 'bubonic plague', so that few survived out of many, and Pope Pelagius was among the first to die of it on 6 February. Gregory,[14] the sixty-third pope, reigned

---

M. Miller, 'The dates of Deira', *ASE* viii (1979), 49. ASC F does not give the succession of Æthelric.

[7] ASC.   [8] Mar.
[9] Norman Annals. *AU, AG, ?ASN* (all 588). Chlothar II 584–629.
[10] ASC A (correction by hand 8) E have Ceolric, A (originally) BC Ceol.
[11] The relationship of Ceola to Ceawlin is not given here in ASC, but under 611, where ASC calls Ceola's father Cutha.
[12] ASC A (originally) BC 5 years, A (addition) E 6.   [13] ASC.
[14] Gregory I 590–604.

*gesimus tertius papa annis tredecim mensibus sex. Qui in hac tribula-
tione a cunctis electus, cum letaniam septiformem ordinasset, dum
Deum deprecarentur subito .lxxx. homines obierunt. Septiformis autem
letania ideo dicitur, quia in .vii. ordinibus populus erat constitutus,
primo ordine clerus, secundo abbates cum monachis, tertio abbatisse cum
suis, quarto infantes, quinto omnes laici, sexto uidue, septimo
coniugate.*[1]

Pugnatum est in loco qui dicitur Wodnesbeorh, [2]id est mons
Wodenis,[2] et strage non modica facta rex Ceaulin anno imperii sui
.xxxiii. expulsus est regno.[3]

[593] (xi) 615   Ceaulin, Cuuichelm et Crida perierunt.[4] Æthelric
rex Northanhymbrorum obiit. Æðelfrið uero filius eius gubernacula regni suscepit et .xxiiii. annis tenuit.[5] Cui sunt geniti .vii. filii,
Eanfrith, sanctus[a] Oswald, Oslaf, sanctus[b] Osuuiu, Offa, Osuudu,
Oslac et una filia sancta[b] Æbbe nomine.[6]

[594] (xii) 616   *Auares contra Romanos dimicantes auro magis quam
armis pelluntur. Sanctus Gregorius in Dialogo suo*[7] *ita dicit: 'ante hoc
triennium in meo monasterio monachus nomine Iustus medicus ante obitum suum suo germano Copioso, sibi in infirmitate seruienti, .iii. aureos
occulte se habere innotuit quos super eum in sterquilinio sepeliri feci.
Eodem anno monachus alius cum a nobis fuisset sepultus, remanentem
ibi unum de fratribus Iohannem nomine uocauit, qui nobis hoc pallens
et tremens indicauit et post dies .x. obiit.'*[8]

[595] (xiii) 617   *Biennio ante scriptum Dialogum, ecclesia Arriano-
rum iuxta Romam in loco nomine Subura cum catholice consecraretur,
et introducte essent in eam sancti Sebastiani et sancte Agathe martyrum reliquie, diabolus in figura porci per populum transiens exiuit.
Post paucos autem dies nubes celitus descendens, totam miro odore
repleuit ecclesiam.*[9] *Gregorius papa anno imperii Mauricii, .xiii. indic-*

---

[a] *interlin. C[1]B[1]P[1], om. HL*   [b] *interlin. C[1]B[1], om. HLP*

---

[1] Mar.   [2-2] Not in ASC.
[3] ASC ABCE. The length of Ceawlin's reign is not given here in ASC (see above,
p. 60 n. 2). The statement in JW *West Saxon Accounts* 4 that Ceola had undeservedly
rebelled against Ceawlin is neither here nor in ASC.
[4] ASC ABCE.
[5] ASC ABCE record the accession of Æthelfrith but neither the length of his reign
(which is given in JW *Northum. Accounts* 5) nor the death of Æthelric.

thirteen years and six months. Chosen by all in this tribulation, he drew up the sevenfold litany. While they were calling on God, eighty people died suddenly. The sevenfold litany is so called because the people were grouped in seven orders: in the first order the clergy; in the second the abbots with their monks; in the third the abbesses with their nuns; in the fourth the children; in the fifth the laity at large; in the sixth the widows; in the seventh the married women.[1]

A battle was fought in a place called *Wodensbeorh*, [2]that is Woden's Mount,[2] and after no little slaughter King Ceawlin was driven out of his kingdom in the thirty-third year of his reign.[3]

[593] Ceawlin, Cwichelm, and Creoda died.[4] Æthelric, king of the Northumbrians, died, but Æthelfrith, his son, undertook the governance of the realm, and held it for twenty-four years.[5] To him were born seven sons: Eanfrith, St Oswald, Oslaf, St Oswiu, Offa, Oswudu, Oslac, and a daughter called St Æbbe.[6]

[594] The Avars, fighting against Rome, were driven off by gold rather than by arms. St Gregory said thus in his *Dialogues*:[7] 'Three years before this, in my monastery, a monk and physician, Justus by name, before his death informed his brother Copiosus, who was caring for him in his sickness, that he had three gold coins hidden. I had these buried above him in the dung pit. In the same year another monk, having been buried by us, called on one of the brothers remaining there, John by name. Pale and trembling, John told us this and ten days later he died.'[8]

[595] Two years before the *Dialogues* were written, when the Arian church near Rome, in a place called Suburra, was consecrated according to Catholic rites, and the relics of the holy martyrs Sebastian and Agatha were placed in it, the devil departed in the likeness of a pig, passing through the congregation. A few days later a heavenly cloud descended, filling the whole church with a wonderful odour.[9] Pope Gregory, in the thirteenth year of the

---

[6] The children of Æthelfrith are in the order neither of JW *Northum. Accounts* 3 nor of *De primo Saxonun aduentu* (*Symeonis monachi opera*, ii. 374). For the view that Æbbe was full sister to Oswiu, see Miller, 'Dates of Deira', *ASE* viii (1979), 43. Sanctity is not ascribed to Oswiu in JW *Northum. Accounts*.

[7] *Dialogues*, iv. 57.   [8] Mar.   [9] *Dialogues*, iii. 30.

tione, .xiii. sinodum episcoporum .xxiiii. ad corpus beati Petri apostoli congregans, de necessariis ecclesie decernit inter que etiam hec. 'In sancta Romana ecclesia, cui diuina dispensatio preesse me uoluit, dudum consuetudo est ualde reprehensibilis exorta ut quidam ad sacri altaris ministerium cantores eligantur et in diaconatus ordine constituti modulationi uocis inseruiant quos ad predicationis officium elemosi-narumque studium uacare congruebat. Vnde fit plerumque ut ad sacrum ministerium dum blanda uox queritur, queri congrua uita negligatur. Et cantor minister Domini moribus stimulet, cum populum uocibus delectat. Qua de re, presenti decreto constituo ut in sede hac sacri altaris ministri cantare non debeant, solumque euuangelice lectionis officium inter missarum sollennia ex⟨s⟩oluant.ᵃ Psalmos uero ac reliquas lectiones censeo per subdiaconos uel si necessitas exigit per minores ordines exhiberi. Si quis autem contra hoc decretum meum uenire temp-tauerit anathema sit. Et responderunt omnes: Anathema sit.'¹*

[596] (xiiii) 618 *Cenobium sancti Benedicti abbatis a Longobardis* p. 256   *noctu inuaditur. Monachi autem Romam | petierunt, codicem sancte regule et pondus panis ac mensuram uini secum deferentes.²*

Gregorius papa, *diuino admonitus instinctu, anno aduentus Anglo-rum in Brytan*nia *centesimo* quadragesimo septimo,³ *misit seruum Dei Agustinum et alios plures cum eo monachos* Deum *timentes predi-care uerbum Dei genti Anglorum,* indictione .xiiii.⁴

[597] (xv) 619 *Gregorius adiecit in missa* 'diesque nostros *in tua* pace disponas, atque ab eterna dampnatione nos eripi et in electo-rum tuorum iubeas *grege numerari*.'⁵

Prefati doctores hoc anno, Beda teste, Brytanniam uenere et regem Cantuuariorum Æthelbryhtum imperii sui anno tricesimo quinto ad fidem Christi conuertere. ᵇNec distulit rex *quin doctor*i suo ᶜAugustino *sed*em episcopalem *in Doruuerni*ᶜ metropoli sua *donaret.*⁶ ᵈQui *regio fultus adminiculo ecclesiam inibi antiquo Romanorum fidelium opere factam recuperauit, et in nomine sancti*

ᵃ exoluant C, exoluant *from* exsoluant B   ᵇ *runs on to 598 and 599 CB, and on to* 598 L   ᶜ⁻ᶜ Augustino . . . Doruuerni] *possibly over erasure* C   ᵈ *598 from this point* H

¹ Mar.   ² Mar.
³ By substituting the 147th year for Bede's 150th, JW dates the coming of the Eng-lish to 450.   ⁴ HE i. 23.   ⁵ Mar.   ⁶ HE i. 26.

reign of Maurice, in the thirteenth indiction, assembling a synod of twenty-four bishops at the tomb of St Peter the Apostle, made decrees about the requirements of the Church, among them these: 'In the Holy Roman Church, over which divine dispensation has pleased to place me, the extremely reprehensible custom has arisen of choosing some cantors for the service of the holy altar. Made deacons, they serve the beauty of the voices who ought to be free to perform the duty of preaching and the business of giving alms. From this it very often happens that while an agreeable voice is sought for the holy office an appropriate life is regarded of no consequence. The cantor, as a minister of the Lord, should inspire by his conduct, whereas he delights the people with his singing. Concerning this matter I rule in the present decretal that, in this see, ministers at the holy altar ought not to sing and may discharge only the office of reading of the Gospel in the course of the solemnities of the mass. I decree that the psalms and other readings be delivered by subdeacons or, if need be, by members of minor orders. If anyone attempts to oppose this my decree, may he be excommunicate.' And all replied: 'May he be excommunicate.'[1]

[596] The monastery of the abbot St Benedict was invaded at night by the Lombards. The monks went to Rome, taking with them the codex of the holy rule, the correct weight of bread, and the measure of wine.[2]

In the 147th year[3] after the arrival of the Angles in Britain, in the fourteenth indiction, Pope Gregory, urged on by divine inspiration, sent Augustine, the servant of God, and many God-fearing monks with him to preach the word of God to the English people.[4]

[597] Gregory added to the mass 'dispose our days, in thy peace and command that we be snatched from eternal damnation and numbered in the flock of thine elect'.[5]

The aforementioned teachers came to Britain this year, according to Bede, and converted Æthelberht, king of Kent, to the Christian faith in the thirty-fifth year of his reign. Nor did the king delay in giving his teacher Augustine an episcopal see in Canterbury, his capital.[6] He, aided by royal support, restored the church built there of old by the labour of the Roman believers, and

saluatoris sacrauit.[1] *a*Ceoluulf, filius Cuthe fratris regis Ceaulini,[2] sceptra regni Occidentalium Saxonum suscipiens, .xiiii. annis[3] tenuit, et uel Anglis aut Brytonibus uel Pictis aut Scottis bellum semper intulit. Qui fuit Cuthe, qui fuit Cynric, qui fuit Cerdic.[4]

[600] (xviii) 622   Teodebertus rex Francorum .xviii. et Theoderi-cus cum Lothario patruele suo bellum gesserunt et afflixerunt nimis.[5] *b*⟨D⟩*octor apostolicus et ueri solis nuntius Yuo presul inclitus migrauit ad Dominum. Qui in Perside ut orientale sidus ortus finibus occiduis Brytannie a Domino est destinatus.*[b6]

[601] (xix) 623   *Gregorius, nonodecimo[c] anno Mauricii, indictione .iiii., scribens Agustino[d] eodem modo Lundonie quoque et Eboraci epis-copis accepto a sede apostolica pallio metropolitanos esse debere decer-nit.* *e*In uita Gregorii sic: 'apostolos ad missam nicil aliud cantasse legimus nisi tantum[f] orationem dominicam.'*[7]

[603] (xxi) 625   *Mauricius imperator cum filiis suis Theodosio, Tiberio et Constantino a Foca,*[8] *qui fuit strator Prisci patricii, occidi-tur. Si sanctus pater abbas Benedictus, sicut sui scribunt, .xii. kal. Aprilis, sabbato sancto Pasce, obiit, in hoc anno uidetur obisse. Nisi enim in anno nonagesimo sexto, qui est ante istum nunc inceptum ciclum, obisset, quod incredibile est quia forsitan uix tunc natus fuit, aliter obitus eius in hoc termino, scilicet .xii. kal. Aprilis, inueniri non posset quia nec pascalis festiuitas ex tunc nunc usque .xi. kal. Aprilis celebrata est. In hoc autem anno plus minusue etatis sue nonagesimo possibile est credere eum obisse.*[9]

Rex fortissimus et glorie cupidissimus, Æthelfryð plus omnibus Anglorum primatibus gentem Brytonum uastauit, pluresque terras eorum, exterminatis uel subiugatis indigenis, aut tributarias genti

---

a runs on to 599 *CB*   *b–b* ⟨D⟩octor . . . destinatus] *mg. alongside 600–3 C*[3], *mg. alongside 599–602 P*[3], *under Maurice 582–602 G*   *c* nono *over erasure C*[1], octauodecimo *Mar.*   *d* Augustino *HLBP*   *e* runs on to 602 *CHB, under 602 L*   *f* interlin. *C*[1]

---

[1] *HE* i. 33.

[2] Ceolwulf's relationship to Ceawlin is not stated here in ASC, though it might pos-sibly have been inferred from the genealogies in ASC ABC. It is made plain in JW *West Saxon Gen.*

[3] The length of Ceolwulf's reign (which is mentioned in JW *West Saxon Accounts* 5, but not in ASC), could have been inferred from the dates for his accession (597) and

dedicated it in the name of the holy Saviour.[1] Ceolwulf, son of
Cutha, King Ceawlin's brother,[2] became king of the West Saxons,
and reigned for fourteen years[3] and made war continuously on the
Angles, or the Britons, or the Picts, or the Scots. He was the son
of Cutha, son of Cynric, son of Cerdic.[4]

[600] Theudebert, eighteenth king of the Franks, and Theuderic
waged war on their cousin Chlothar and they caused severe damage.[5] The apostolic teacher and herald of the true sun, the celebrated Bishop Ives, passed to the Lord; having risen like an
eastern star in Persia, he was directed by the Lord for the western
land of Britain.[6]

[601] Gregory, in the nineteenth year of Maurice and in the
fourth indiction, writing to Augustine, and after the same fashion
to the bishops of London and of York, decreed that they should
be metropolitans upon receipt of the pallium from the apostolic
see. In the life of Pope Gregory thus: 'We read that the apostles
sang nothing at mass other than the Lord's prayer.'[7]

[603] The Emperor Maurice, with his sons Theodosius, Tiberius,
and Constantine, was killed by Phocas,[8] who was the groom of the
patrician Priscus. If, as his followers write, the holy father, Abbot
Benedict died on Holy Saturday, 21 March, it would seem that he
died this year. For, unless he died in the ninety-sixth year, which
is before this cycle which has now begun (which is incredible
because he may have been only just born then) his death on this
date, that is 21 March, cannot be found in any other year because
the Easter feast was not celebrated on 22 March between that
ninety-sixth year and now. But it is possible to believe that he
died when he was about ninety years old.[9]

Æthelfrith, the most vigorous of kings and the most desirous of
glory, more than any other English ruler ravaged the race of
Britons, and made more of their lands tributary to, or ready for

death (611). ASC ABC take the genealogy (which E omits) beyond Cerdic and back to
Woden.
    [4] ASC.
    [5] Norman Annals. *AU* (598), *AG* (599). Theudebert II 595–612. Theuderic II
595–612×613.
    [6] *Vita Yvonis Goscelini, PL* clv. 82–3.   [7] Mar.
    [8] Phocas 602–10.   [9] Mar.

Anglorum, aut habitabiles fecit. Vnde motus profectibus eius, Aedan rex Scottorum cum immenso exercitu contra illum *uenit, sed cum paucis uictus aufugit.* Quod bellum *in loco qui dicitur Degsastan, anno regni sui .xi.,* Focatis uero imperatoris *primo, Æthelfriđ perfecit.*[1] Is etiam longo post tempore[2] *collecto exercitu ad ciuitatem Legionum, que a Brytonibus Carlegion appellatur, diuino agente iudicio,* ᵃut beatus predixerat Agustinusᵃᵇ archiepiscopus, ex Brytonum *sacerdo*tibus *qui ad exorandum Deum pro milite bellum agente mille .cc.* prius extincxit, *et sic ceteras nefande militie copias deleuit.*[3]

Romanorum sexagesimus tertius Focas regnauit annis octo usque kal. Maii in anno sexcentesimo post passionem.[4]

[604] (i) 626   *Imago Foce .vii. kal. Maii, indictione .vii., Romam delata est, sicut in uita sancti Gregorii legitur, et postquam a clero et senatu acclamatum est ei in basilica Iulii, iussu sancti Gregorii, in basilica sancti Cesarii Lateranensi palatio constituta* est.[5]

Augustinus Mellitum et Iustum ordinauit episcopos, Mellitum ad predicandum prouincie Orientalium Saxonum qui ut *uerbum ueritatis* cum rege suoᶜ Sæberhto, regis Æthelberhti nepote, *predicante Mel*lito, accepere. *In Lundonia* sua metropoli *rex* ipse Æthelberht *fecit ecclesiam sancti Pauli apostoli. Iustum uero in ciuitate Dorubreui, quam gens Anglorum Hroueceaster cognominat, Augustinus episcopum ordinauit.* Laurentium quoque presbiterum ordinans archiepiscopum pro se, paruo post tempore ad regnum migrauit celeste ᵈ*.vii. kalend Iunii, feria .iii.*ᵈ⁶

[605] (ii) 627   Anglorum apostolus, Romanorum decus, *beatus papa Gregorius*ᵉ *postquam sedem Romane et apostolice ecclesie .xiii. annos, menses .vi. et dies decem gloriosissime rexit, .iiii. idus Marti*i, feria *.vi., ad eternam regni celestis sedem translatus est.*ᶠ⁷

ᵃ⁻ᵃ ut . . . Agustinus] ut praedixerat beatus Augustinus *HL*   ᵇ Augustinus *HLBP*   ᶜ *interlin. H, om. L*   ᵈ⁻ᵈ .vii. . . . feria .iii.] *interlin.* Cᵗ   ᵉ patre Gordiano *interlin.* B⁵   ᶠ Hic papa gloriosus ante decem an(nos) sui obitus Augustinum cum Christianit(at)e Ang(liam) destina(uit) *interlin.* B⁵

settlement by, the English when he had exterminated or subjugated the inhabitants. Thence, disturbed by his successes, Aedan, king of the Irish [of Dál Riada], marched against him with a huge army, but fled, defeated, with a handful of men. Æthelfrith accomplished this battle in a place called *Degsastan*, in the eleventh year of his reign and in the first of the Emperor Phocas.[1] He also, much later,[2] assembled an army at the city of Chester, which is called Caerllion by the Britons, and through the execution of divine judgement, as the blessed Archbishop Augustine had foretold, he first slew 1,200 of the British priests who had gathered to pray to God for the army fighting the battle, and thus he destroyed the other troops of the impious army.[3]

Phocas, sixty-third emperor of the Romans, reigned eight years to 1 May in the 600th year after the Passion.[4]

[604] The statue of Phocas was taken to Rome on 25 April in the seventh indiction, as is to be read in the life of St Gregory, and when it had been acclaimed by clergy and senate in the basilica of Julius, it was set up on St Gregory's orders in the basilica of St Caesarius in the Lateran palace.[5]

Augustine ordained Mellitus and Justus as bishops, Mellitus to preach in the kingdom of the East Saxons so that they, with their king, Sæberht (the nephew of King Æthelberht), received the word of truth from Mellitus' preaching. King Æthelberht himself built the church of St Paul the Apostle in London, his metropolis. Augustine ordained Justus bishop of the city of Dorubrevium, which the English call Rochester. He also ordained the priest Lawrence archbishop in his place, and, a little while later, on Tuesday, 26 May, he passed to the heavenly kingdom.[6]

[605] The apostle of the English, the honour of the Romans, the blessed Pope Gregory, after ruling the see of Rome and the apostolic church most gloriously for thirteen years, six months, and ten days, was translated to the eternal see of the kingdom of heaven on Friday, 12 March.[7]

---

[1] *HE* i. 34.
[2] The battle of Chester is not dated by Bede, but ASC EF date it to 605.
[3] *HE* ii. 2.   [4] Mar.   [5] Mar.   [6] *HE* ii. 3.   [7] *HE* ii. 1.

[C³BP⁵]

*ᵃSanctus Dauid, qui et Dewi,
Menewensis episcopus in Walia
migrauit ad Dominum.ᵃ¹*

[606] (iii) 628 *Sabinianus² sexagesimus quartus papa anno uno,
mensibus decem.³*

[607] (iiii) 629 *Preterini et Benedicti per orientem uel Egiptum ciuile
bellum faciunt ac sese mutua | cede prosternunt.⁴*
⟨C⟩eoluulf ⁵rex Occidentalium Saxonum⁵ Australibus bellum
intulit Saxonibus.⁶

p. 257

[608] (v) 630 *Ciclus decennouenalis .v. incipit indictione .xi. Sabinianus papa obiit .vi. kal. Martii. Bonifacius⁷ sexagesimus quintus papa
mensibus .x., obiit .iii. idus Decembris. Hic impetrauit a Foca ut sedes
apostolica caput esset ecclesie cum antea Constantinopolis primam se
omnium scriberet. Ipse quoque constituit in ecclesia beati Petri cum
episcopis .lxx. duobus, presbiteris .xxxiii., diaconibus et omni clero, sub
anathemate, ut nullus pontifice uiuente aut episcopo ciuitatis sue presumat loqui aut partes sibi de episcopatu facere, sed tertio die depositionis eius, adunato clero et filiis ecclesie, tunc electio fiat.⁸*

[609] (vi) 631 *Bonifacius⁹ sexagesimus sextus papa annis sex, mensibus .ix. ᵇIste obtinuit a Foca ut in ueteri fano quod Pantheon uoca-
batur et a Domitiano imperatore constructum erat ecclesia in honore
omnium sanctorum consecraretur ubi dudum omnium idolorum cultus
agebatur.¹⁰*

[611] (vii) 633 *Perse contra rem publicam grauissima bella gerentes,
multas Romanorum prouincias et ipsam Ierosolimam auferunt, et,
destruentes ecclesias, sancta quoque prophanantes, inter ornamenta
sanctorum uel communium locorum etiam uexillum dominice crucis
abducunt. Heraclius¹¹ qui Affricam regebat, Focam occidit.¹²*

ᵃ⁻ᵃ Sanctus . . . Dominum] *add. at end of annal* C³, *om.* HL, *add. upper mg. with sign
pointing to 611ᵃ* P⁵   ᵇ *this sentence runs on to 610 CHLB, under 610* P

---

¹ For this date, which is not recorded elsewhere, see above, p. 12 n. 2.
² Sabinian 604–6.   ³ Mar.   ⁴ Mar.   ⁵⁻⁵ Not in ASC.
⁶ ASC ABCE.   ⁷ Boniface III 607.   ⁸ Mar.

> St David, also known as Dewi,
> bishop of Menevia in Wales,
> passed over to the Lord.[1]

[606] Sabinian,[2] the sixty-fourth pope, reigned for one year and ten months.[3]

[607] The Preterini and the Benedicti made civil war throughout the East and Egypt, and destroyed each other with mutual slaughter.[4]

Ceolwulf, [5]king of the West Saxons,[5] waged war on the South Saxons.[6]

[608] The fifth cycle of nineteen years began in the eleventh indiction. Pope Sabinian died on 24 February. Boniface,[7] the sixty-fifth pope, reigned ten months, and died on 11 December. He succeeded in his request to Phocas that the apostolic see should be the head of the Church, whereas before Constantinople used to describe herself as the first of all the churches. He also decreed, in the church of St Peter, with seventy-two bishops, thirty-three priests, the deacons, and all the clergy, that, on pain of excommunication, no one in the lifetime of the pontiff or bishop of a city should discuss or seek support for himself in the succession to a bishopric. But on the third day after the pontiff's burial, an election should be held when the clergy and sons of the church were assembled.[8]

[609] Boniface,[9] the sixty-sixth pope, reigned six years, nine months. He succeeded in his request to Phocas that a church should be consecrated in honour of all the saints in the old temple, called the Pantheon and built by the Emperor Domitian, where formerly the cult of all the idols was practised.[10]

[611] The Persians, waging very severe war against the empire, took many Roman provinces and Jerusalem itself, and, destroying churches and profaning what was holy, they even carried off, among the ornaments of holy and public places, the relic of the Lord's cross. Heraclius,[11] who ruled Africa, slew Phocas.[12]

---

[9] Boniface IV 608–15.   [10] Mar.   [11] Heraclius 610–41.
[12] Mar.

Ceoluulf rex obiit cui fratris sui Ceoli filius Cynegils successit et
.xxxii. annis regnauit.¹ Qui fuit Ceol, qui fuit Cutha, qui fuit
Cerdic.^{a2,3}
*Romanorum sexagesimus quartus Heraclius regnauit annis .xxvii.
usque kal. Maii in anno sexcentesimo uigesimo septimo post passionem
Domini.*⁴

[612] (i) 634 *Anastasius Persa monachus nobiliter pro Christo passus. Qui natus in Perside magicam a patre artem puer^b didicit, sed ubi
a captiuis Christianis nomen Christi accepit, in eum mox toto animo
conuersus est. Bonifacius papa obiit .viii. kalendas Iunii.*⁵

[614] (iii) 636 Kynegils et filius suus Cuichelm⁶ in Beandune
contra Brytones aciem direxere et pugnantes duo milia quadraginta
sex⁷ ex eis interemere.⁸

[615] (v) 637 *Deusdedit,⁹ qui et Theodatus, sexagesimus septimus
papa annis .iiii. Anastasius supradictus, relicta Perside, Calcedoniam
Ierapolimque Christum querens pertransiit, ac deinde Ierosolimam
petiit, ubi baptizatus .iiii. ab eadem urbe miliario, monasterium abbatis
Anastasii intrauit, in quo .vii. annis regulariter uixit. Qui cum
Cesaream Palestine orationis gratia uenisset captus a Persis, et multa
diu uerbera inter carceres et uincula a Marzabana duce perpessus est.
Deusdedit papa constituit secundam missam in clero. Eodem tempore
factus est terre motus magnus mense Augusto, indictione .vi. Post hec
secuta est clades in populo, id est percussio scabiarum, ita ut nullus
posset mortuum suum agnoscere.^{c10}*

[616] (v) 638 ^{d}*Ciclus solis incipit .iiii. concurrentibus bissextilibus.*^{d}

---

^{a} 605 *n.* a (p. 78) upper mg. with sign pointing here P⁵ ^{b} interlin. C¹
^{c} cognoscere *Mar.* $^{d-d}$ Ciclus ... bissextilibus] mg. alongside with signe de renvoi C¹

---

¹ ASC ABCE do not record the death of Ceolwulf in this year, nor do they describe
the family relationship of Ceola and Ceolwulf, which is specified in JW *West Saxon
Accounts* 6, but is different in *West Saxon Gen.* Cynegils is given a reign of 31 years by
ASC ABCE and by JW *West Saxon Accounts* 11.
² This genealogy appears in ASC A (original annal; largely recovered from G) BC.
JW has wrongly substituted Cerdic for Cynric as Cutha's father. Under 591 JW
describes Ceola as son of Cuthwulf. Cutha and Cuthwulf could be the same person
though in JW *West Saxon Gen.* and *Accounts* 4 and 5 they are distinguished.

King Ceolwulf died; Cynegils, son of his brother Ceola, succeeded him, and reigned thirty-two years.[1] He was the son of
Ceola, son of Cutha, son of Cerdic.[2,3]

Heraclius, the sixty-fourth emperor of the Romans, reigned
twenty-seven years, to 1 May in the 627th year after the Lord's
Passion.[4]

[612] The monk Anastasius suffered nobly for Christ in Persia. A
native of Persia, he learnt magical arts in his boyhood from his
father, but when he heard the name of Christ from Christian captives he was at once converted to Him with his whole heart. Pope
Boniface died on 25 May.[5]

[614] Cynegils and his son Cwichelm[6] drew up their battle-line
against the Britons at *Beandun*, and in the battle they also slew
2,046[7] of them.[8]

[615] Deusdedit,[9] also known as Adeodatus, the sixty-seventh
pope, reigned four years. The abovementioned Anastasius left Persia, and in his search for Christ passed through Chalcedon and
Hierapolis, and then went to Jerusalem, where he was baptized.
There, four miles from the same city, he entered the monastery of
Abbot Anastasius, where he lived seven years according to the
rule. When he went to Caesarea in Palestine in order to pray, he
was taken by the Persians, and for a long time endured many
blows in prison and in chains from the commander, Marzabanes.
Pope Deusdedit established a second office for the clergy. At the
same time there was a great earthquake in August in the sixth
indiction. After this there followed a disaster for the people, that
is an outbreak of scabies, which was such that no one could recog-
nize his own dead.[10]

[616] The solar cycle begins here with four concurrents in a bissextile year.

---

[3] ASC.   [4] Mar.   [5] Mar.
[6] ASC describes Cwichelm as son of Cynegils under 648 but not under this annal.
[7] ASC A (as recovered from G) agrees with JW's figure of men slain; A (present
form) and E have 2,065; and BC 2,045.
[8] ASC.   [9] Deusdedit (later Adeodatus I) 615–18.   [10] Mar.

*Rex Cantuariorum Æthelber*htus, *filius Irmenrici, cuius pater Octa, cuius pater Oric cognomento Oisc, cuius pater Hengst, quinquage*simo *sex*to imperii sui, *uicesimo primo anno accepte fidei, die uicesima quarta mensis Februarii* conscendit *regni celestis gaudia.* Cui *Ædbold*us suus *filius* successit. Verum *fidem Christi non solum recipere nolu*it, *sed et patris* ^a*uxorem* sibi in matrimonium sociauit.[1] Rex Orientalium Anglorum Reduuald *Athelfrithum* Deirorum Berniciorumque regem, *occidit* in bello iuxta *amn*em, *qui uocatur Idle.* Cui *Eduuin*e, *iuxta oraculum quod acceperat, successit*[2] et septem filios Athelfrithi[a] expulit.[3] *Sæber*ht *rex Orientalium Saxonum, regna petens perennia, tres filios suos, qui pagani perdurauerant, regni temporalis heredes reliquit,* qui *mox idolatrie palam seruire* cepere et Mellitum episcopum Lundonie *de suo regno expulere.* Ipse uero *Cantiam uenit,* et, habito *consilio cum Laurentio* arciepiscopo, *ad partes* Gallie cum Iusto Hrofensi episcopo *secess*it. *Sed non multo tempore reges, qui a se ueritatis preconem expuler*e, *demonicis cultibus impune seruier*e. *Nam egressi contra gentem Geuuissorum in prelium, omnes pariter cum sua militia* ^b*corruer*e.[1] *Cum uero et Laurentius Mellitum Iustumque*[c] *esset secuturus, ipsa nocte apparuit ei princeps apostolorum* Petrus *illum*que *flagellis aff*ecit *artioribus.* ^d*Mane* autem^d *facto, ad regem* Eadbaldum *uenit et quantis uerberibus esset laceratus ostendit.* Quod ut uidit *multum extimuit,* omn*em idolatrie*[e] *cult*um anathematizauit, *conub*ium *non legitim*um *abdica*uit, *fidem Christi suscepit, Galliam*[f] *misit, Mellitum* et[b] *Iustum reuocauit.*[4]

[619] (viii) 641 ^g*Deusdedit papa obiit .vi. idus Nouembris.*[g][5] |

p. 258 [620] (ix) 642 *Bonifacius*[6] *sexagesimus octauus papa annis .v.* ^hHic *constituit ut nullus trahatur de ecclesia.*[h] ⁱ*Predictus sanctus Anastasius tandem mittitur Persidem ad regem eorum Chosroen. A quo tertio per interualla temporis uerberatus, ad extremum occisus est cum aliis multis. Mox tunica eius indutus quidam demoniacus curatus est.*[j][7]

---

^{a–a} uxorem . . . Athelfrithi] *written over erasure* C¹   ^{b–b} (corru)ere. Cum . . . Mellitum et] *rewritten in paler ink and in a compressed hand extending into mg. on one line* C   ^c et Iustum HL   ^{d–d} (Ma)ne autem] *darker ink and larger hand* C   ^e *darker ink and larger hand* C   ^f *in* Galliam HL   ^{g–g} Deusdedit . . . Nouembris] *placed with Deusdedit entry under 615 Mar.*   ^{h–h} Hic . . . ecclesia] *placed after* papa *in 620 n. d (p. 82) (N)*   ⁱ *runs on to 621–2 CB, all consolidated under 620–4 P*   ^j *see App. B for mg. addition near 620–1 B¹*

Æthelberht, king of Kent, son of Eormenric, whose father was
Octa, whose father was Oeric, surnamed Oisc, son of Hengest,
ascended to the joys of the heavenly kingdom on 24 February, in
the fifty-sixth year of his rule, the twenty-first after he received
the Faith. His son Eadbald succeeded him; he not only refused to
accept the faith of Christ, but even took to wife his father's
widow.[1] Rædwald, king of the East Angles, killed Æthelfrith, king
of Deira and Bernicia, in battle near the river called the Idle.
Edwin succeeded him, in accordance with the prophecy he had
received,[2] and drove out the seven sons of Æthelfrith.[3] Sæberht,
king of the East Saxons, went to the eternal kingdom, leaving as
heirs of his temporal kingdom his three sons who had remained
pagan, and who soon began to practise idolatry openly, and
expelled Mellitus, bishop of London, from their kingdom. He
went to Kent, and when he had taken counsel with Archbishop
Lawrence, retired to Gallic territory with Justus, bishop of
Rochester. But the kings who had driven out the herald of the
truth from their presence did not long serve the cult of demons
with impunity. For all alike fell, with their army, when they went
out to do battle with the people of the Gewisse.[1] On that very
night, when Lawrence was on the point of following Mellitus and
Justus, Peter, the prince of the Apostles, appeared to him and
scourged him severely. When morning came, he went to King
Eadbald and showed him the number of blows with which he was
scarred. When Eadbald saw that, he was filled with fear, cursed
the whole cult of idolatry, left his unlawful marriage, received the
Christian faith, sent to Gaul, and recalled Mellitus and Justus.[4]

[619] Pope Deusdedit died on 8 November.[5]

[620] Boniface,[6] the sixty-eighth pope, reigned five years. He
decreed that no one should be forcibly removed from a church.
The aforementioned St Anastasius was at length sent to Persia to
their King Chosroes. He was scourged by him three separate
times, and at last killed, with many others. At once a possessed
man, clad in Anastasius' tunic, was cured.[7]

---

[1] *HE* ii. 5.   [2] *HE* ii. 12.   [3] ASC E.   [4] *HE* ii. 6.
[5] Mar.   [6] Boniface V 619–25.   [7] Mar.

Beatus Laurentius archiepiscopus, regnante Eadboldo *rege, .iiii. die[a]*
nonarum Februariarum[b] transiuit ad Dominum. *Post quem Mellitus,*
qui erat episcopus Lundonie tertius ab Agustino,[c] sedem suscepit Doru-
uernensis ecclesie.[1]

[d]*Bonifacius papa obiit .viii. kalendas Nouembris.*[d2]

[e]Mellito successit Cedd frater Ceadde ad Lundonie presulatum.[e3]

[625] (xiiii) 647   *Honorius*[4] *sexagesimus nonus papa annis .xii. Supe-*
rueniens Heraclius imperator *cum exercitu, superatis Persis, Chris-*
tianos qui erant captiuitati reduxit.[5]

Mellitus archiepiscopus *postquam ecclesiam rexit annis .v., .viii.*
kalendarum Maiarum die, ad celos migrauit, Eadboldo regnante.[6] *Cui*
successit Iustus Hrofensis ecclesie episcopus et pro se Romanum [f]conse-
crauit antistitem.[f7]

[626] (xv) 648   *Vir Deo dilectus Paulinus*[8] [g]*a beato Gregorio cum*
ceteris predicandi gratia *in Angliam missus,* tertius processu temporis Hrofensis episcopus[g9] *a Iusto archiepiscopo* Norðhumbrane genti
pontifex *ordinatus, ad Eduuinum* eiusdem gentis *regem cum* illius
sponsa, *regis* Eathelberhti *filia, a*b Eadboldo rege uirginis eiusdem
missus est *fratre.*[10]

[627] (xvi) 649   [h]*Reliquie beati martiris Anastasii, primo monas-*
terium suum, deinde Romam aduecte, uenerantur in monasterio beati
Pauli apostoli quod dicitur ad Aquas Saluias.[h11]

Quidam sicarius Eomer uocabulo missus est *a rege* Westsaxonum
Cuichelmo, qui[i] *ad regem* Eduuinum *primo die pasce uenit, et euagi-*
nata sub ueste[j] sica [k]impetum in illum *fecit.[k] Verum Lilla, minister*
regi amicissimus, mox ante ictum pungentis suum interposuit corpus, sed
tanta ui ferrum infixit hostis ut etiam regem uulneraret per corpus

---

[a] *interlin.* C'   [b] Februarium HL   [c] Augustino HLP   [d-d] Bonifacius
. . . Nouembris] *placed at end of annal after* 620 *n. e HL*   [e-e] Mellito . . . presula-
tum] *add. at line end* C³, *placed before* 620 *n. d HL*   [f-f] consecrauit antistitem] *add.*
at line end in mg. C³   [g-g] a beato . . . episcopus] *add. mg. with signe de renvoi* C³
[h-h] Reliquie . . . Saluias] *at end of* 626 *(N)*   [i] *interlin.* C¹   [j] ueste sua HLP
[k-k] impetum . . . fecit] impetum illum fecit H, in illum impetum fecit L

---

[1] *HE* ii. 7. Bede seems to start the pontificate of Mellitus in 619, giving him an
episcopacy of 5 years ending on 24 April 624. Since Marianus assigned 619 to Boniface
V's accession, with which JW connected the death of Lawrence and the succession of
Mellitus, and since the annals for 619–23 are written in a block in the Vatican and
Nero Marianus manuscripts, it is possible that the scribe of JW C made a mistake in

The blessed Archbishop Lawrence passed to the Lord on 2 February, in the reign of King Eadbald. Mellitus, who was the third bishop of London after Augustine, received the see of Canterbury after him.[1]

Pope Boniface died on 25 October.[2]

Cedd, brother of Chad, succeeded Mellitus to the bishopric of London.[3]

[625] Honorius,[4] the sixty-ninth pope, reigned twelve years. The Emperor Heraclius intervened with his army, defeated the Persians and brought home the Christians who had been captured.[5]

Archbishop Mellitus, after ruling the Church for five years, went to heaven on 24 April in Eadbald's reign.[6] Justus, bishop of Rochester, succeeded him, and consecrated Romanus bishop in his place.[7]

[626] Paulinus, a man beloved of God,[8] was sent to England with others by the blessed Gregory in order to preach. Later he was to be the third bishop of Rochester.[9] He was ordained bishop of the Northumbrian people by Archbishop Justus, and sent to Edwin, king of that same people, with Edwin's bride (King Æthelberht's daughter), by King Eadbald, that maiden's brother.[10]

[627] The relics of the blessed martyr Anastasius, brought first to his own monastery, and then to Rome, were venerated in the monastery of the blessed Apostle Paul [alle Tre Fontane] which is called *Aquae Salviae*.[11]

An assassin called Eomer was sent by Cwichelm, king of the West Saxons, and he came to King Edwin on Easter Sunday and, unsheathing his dagger beneath his tunic, attacked him. Lilla, the king's most trusted thegn, at once threw himself before the attacker's blow, but the enemy thrust in his weapon with such

assigning the opening of this annal to 620 and that the original JW text might have correctly dated these events to 619.

[2] Mar.

[3] The erroneous succession of Cedd to Mellitus at London (presumably soon after 620) probably follows *GP* ii. 73 (p. 142).

[4] Honorius I 625–38.   [5] Mar.   [6] *HE* ii. 7.

[7] *HE* ii. 8. JW's date is, as under 620, a year too late possibly for the same reasons.

[8] *HE* ii. 9.   [9] *GP* ii. 73 (p. 134).

[10] *HE* ii. 9. The year of Paulinus' consecration is 625 in Bede and ASC. For a possible explanation for JW's date see above, n. 1.

[11] Mar.

occisi militis. Eadem autem nocte pasce dominici peperit regina filiam regi, que die pentecostes de Norðanhymbrorum gente prima a Paulino episcopo baptizata Eanfled est uocata.[1] Quinquagesimo etatis sue anno Penda regnum Merciorum suscepit et .xxx. annis tenuit,[2] qui fuit Pybbe, qui fuit Cride, qui fuit Cineuuald, qui fuit Cnebbe, qui fuit Iceli, qui fuit Eomeri, qui fuit Angengeat, qui fuit Offe, qui fuit Wermund, qui fuit Wihtlenge, qui fuit Wage, qui fuit Wothelgeat, qui fuit Woden.[3]

[**628**] (xvii) 650   *[ab4]Anno Heraclii imperatoris sexto decimo, indictione quinta decima,[b] Eduuinus[c] precellentissimus rex Anglorum in Brytannia transhumbrane gentis ad aquilonem, predicante Paulino episcopo, quem misit de Cantia arciepiscopus Iustus, uerbum salutis cum sua gente suscepit. Anno autem undecimo regni sui, aduentus uero Anglorum in Brytanniam plus minus anno .ccxxx., hoc gessit. Ipse autem dedit Paulino sedem episcopatus Eboraci. Cui regi in auspicium uenture fidei regnique celestis terrena potestas creuit, totam enim Brytanniam,[5] preter Cantuariis tantum,[6] primus omnium Anglorum sibi subiecit. [7]Eo tempore, errorem Quartadecimanorum[d] in obseruatione pasce apud Scottos exortum Honorius papa per epistolam redarguit, sed et Iohannes, qui successori eius Seuerino successit, idem arguebat. Cum adhuc non esset electus in pontificatum pro eodem pasca eis scripsit, et pro Pelagiana heresi, que apud eos reuiuiscebat.[8]*

[**629**] (xviii) 651   [9]Westsaxonum reges[9] Cynegils et Cuichelm [9]suus filius[9] cum rege Merciorum Penda iuxta Cirenceastre pugnauere et post pace facta confirmataque discessere.[10]

---

[a] this annal starts under 627 CB, under 628 HL, under 627 and spreads over 628–35 (N)   *[b–b]* Anno . . . quinta decima] *written in larger and generously spaced-out letters* C   *[c]* in C gap with erasure at line-end after Ed of *Eduuinus, Eadwinus LP, Eaduuinus B   *[d]* .xiiii. annorum JW Mar.*

[1] *HE* ii. 9. Bede, followed by ASC, assigns these events to 626. For a possible misdating here, see above, p. 84 n. 1.
[2] ASC ABCE, like JW *Mercian Accounts* 14, date Penda's accession to 626 and assign him a 30-year reign while ABC give his age at accession as 50.
[3] Penda's genealogy in ASC A (as recovered from G) BCE differs from JW and from JW *Mercian Gen.* in the number of forebears and in the spelling of names.
[4] Marianus may have assigned this to 627; see above, p. 84 n. 2.
[5] Mar.

force that he wounded the king as well through the body of the slain warrior. On that same night of the Lord's Easter, the queen bore the king a daughter, who on Whit Sunday was the first Northumbrian to be baptized by Bishop Paulinus. She was called Eanflæd.[1] In his fiftieth year Penda gained control of the kingdom of the Mercians and held it thirty years.[2] He was the son of Pybba, son of Creoda, son of Cynewold, son of Cnebba, son of Icel, son of Eomær, son of Angengeat, son of Offa, son of Wermund, son of Wihtleng, son of Waga, son of Wothelgeat, son of Woden.[3]

[628] [4]In the sixteenth year of the Emperor Heraclius, in the fifteenth indiction, Edwin, the most glorious king of the Angles north of the Humber in Britain, received the word of salvation with his people by the preaching of Bishop Paulinus (whom Archbishop Justus sent from Kent). This happened in the eleventh year of his reign, about the 230th year after the arrival of the Angles in Britain. He himself gave Paulinus an episcopal see at York. The king's temporal power increased as earnest of the faith he was about to receive, and of the heavenly kingdom, for he was the first of all the Angles to bring under his sway all Britain,[5] except the people of Kent.[6] [7]At that time Pope Honorius refuted in a letter the error of the Quartodecimans on the observance of Easter which had arisen among the Irish, and John, who succeeded Honorius' successor, Severinus, also refuted the same error. Even before he was elected pope he wrote to them on the same question of Easter and on the Pelagian heresy which had revived among them.[8]

[629] [9]The kings of the West Saxons,[9] Cynegils and [9]his son.[9] Cwichelm,[9] fought with Penda, king of the Mercians, near Cirencester, then having made peace and confirmed it, they separated.[10]

---

[6] HE ii. 5. These three words were added by JW to Marianus, which was itself based on Bede, De temporum ratione, Chronicon AM 4591.

[7] Marianus assigned the following entry to 632, but in the manuscripts it followed closely on 627, and JW, perhaps influenced by Bede, may have decided to enter it in the same year as the previous entry (above, n. 4).

[8] Mar.   [9-9] Not in ASC.   [10] ASC ABCE (628).

[C³BP]
*ᵃ*Honorius *papa pallium* Paulino
misit, qui postmodum *Honorium
Iusti* successorem *in arciepiscop*-
atum *Cantuuariensem* consecrauit
in Lindissi prouincia.*ᵃ*¹

[632] (xxi) 654 *Eorpuuald,ᵇ fili*us *Reduualdi* regis, cuius pater
*Tytel cuius pater Wuffa, persuad*ente rege Eduuino, *superstitione idolorum relict*a, *fidem Christi*que *sacramenta cum sua susc*epit *prouincia.
Verum non multo* post *tempore occisus est a uiro gentili Ricberto
nomine.*²

[633] (xxii) 655 Gloriosus rex *Eduuine cum .xvii. annisᶜ Anglorum
simul et Brytonum genti preesset gloriosissime,* anno etatis sue *.xlviii.*
a pagano rege *Merciorum Penda, uiro strenuissimo,* et *Ceduuala, rege
Brytonum seuiore pagano, in campo Heaðfeld, conserto graui prelio,
est occisus die iduum Octobrium quarto. Turbatis rebus Norðanhymbrorum, Paulinus, assumpta secum regina* Eathelb*urga, rediit Cantiam
nauigio, et honorifice susceptus est ab Honorio archiepiscopo et rege
Eadbaldo,*³

[C³BP]
*ᵈ*et non multo post *Hrofensem
ecclesiam,* mortuo Romano,
suscep*it regendam.ᵈ*⁴

p. 259

[634] (xxiii) 656 *Rex Brytonum Ceaduuala* regem prius *Osricum*
regis *Eduuini* patruelem *cum toto* suo *exercitu deleuit, dein* regem
Eanfriðum, Eathelfriði regis filium, *ad se postulande pacis gratia
uenientem,* peremit. Quo perempto, *cum* | *paruo exercitu, sed fide
Christi munito,* frater suus Osuuald *superuen*it et *infand*um *Brytonum duc*em *cum imm*ensis *suis copiis, quibus* nil *resistere posse*

ᵃ⁻ᵃ Honorius . . . prouincia] *add. at line-end, running on to blank 630 C³, om. HL,
under 629, though runs on to 630 B, under 629 P*   *ᵇ* rex Orientalium Anglorum
interlin. B⁵   *ᶜ om. HL*   *ᵈ⁻ᵈ* et non . . . regendam] *add. at line-end, extending
into mg.* C³, *om. HL*

---

¹ *GP* i. 72 (p. 134). This implies that Paulinus received the pallium before he consecrated Archbishop Honorius, but Bede (*HE* ii. 17, 20, v. 24) suggests that he had

Pope Honorius sent the pallium to Paulinus, who afterwards, in the Lindsey province,
consecrated Honorius, successor of Justus, archbishop of
Canterbury.[1]

[632] Earpwald, son of King Rædwald, whose father was Tytel,
whose father was Wuffa, was persuaded by King Edwin to abandon the superstition of idols and, with his kingdom, received the
faith of Christ and the sacraments. But not long after he was
killed by a pagan called Ricberht.[2]

[633] On 12 October, when the glorious King Edwin had most
splendidly ruled both the Angles and the Britons for seventeen
years, he was killed (in his forty-eighth year) on Hatfield Plain
(where a major battle had been joined) by Penda, the pagan king
of the Mercians, a most vigorous man, and by Cadwallon, king of
the Britons, and crueller than a pagan. As matters in Northumbria
were thrown into confusion, Paulinus took Queen Æthelburg with
him, and returned to Kent by boat. He was honourably received
by Archbishop Honorius and King Eadbald,[3]

and not much later, on the
death of Romanus, he received
the government of the see of
Rochester.[4]

[634] Cadwallon, king of the Britons, first destroyed Osric, King
Edwin's cousin, and his entire army. Then he slew King Eanfrith,
King Æthelfrith's son, as he was coming to him to sue for peace.
Eanfrith was slain, but his brother Oswald, with a small army but
fortified with the faith of Christ, intervened and killed the wicked
leader of the Britons and his vast forces, which he boasted nothing

returned to Kent by the time the pallium had reached England. The location of the
consecration is presumably based on *HE* ii. 16, 18.
[2] *HE* ii. 15. JW's date comes from ASC. Plummer argued (*Bede*, ii. 196) that the
date should be 627 (after Easter) or 628.
[3] *HE* ii. 20. Bede describes Edwin's age differently ('cum esset annorum xl et viii')
nor does he say that Penda was king.
[4] *G.P* i. 72 (p. 134).

iactabat.[1] interfecit, et regni utriusque gubernacula suscepit, ac sequenti tempore *omnes nationes et prouincias Brytannie in* deditionem *accepit.*[2] *Eo tempore gens Occidentalium Saxonum, regnante Cinegislo* rege, *fidem Christi suscepit, predicante illis uerbum Dei*[a] *Birino episcopo.*[3]
Clodoueus filius Dagoberti rex Francorum uicesimus.[4]
[b]Sanctus Wilfridus nascitur.[b5]

[635] (xxiiii) 657 Rex *Osuuald misit ad maiores natu Scottorum petens ut sibi mitteretur antistes.* Cui pontifex missus est *Aidan*us[6] [c]per quem et per ipsum clarissimum et sanctissimum regem Oswaldum in prouincia Berniciorum primum fundatur ecclesia Christi et instituitur.[c7] *Euuangelizante* Birino, [d]ab Honorio papa predicandi gratia Angliam misso,[d] [e]in Westsaxonica *prouincia*[e] rex Cynegils *cum sua gente* credidit, quem de fonte baptismi *exeuntem* rex *uictoriosissim*us *suscep*it *Osuuald*us. A quibus regibus idem pontifex *ciuitatem Dorcic*c *ad faciendam inibi sedem episcopalem* accepit.[8]
Honorius papa obiit .iiii. idus Octobris et cessauit episcopatus anno .i., mensibus .vii., diebus .xvii.[9]

[636] (xxv) 658 *Eorpuualdi* regis Eastanglorum *frater*, Seabyrht,[10] *uir per omnia Christianissimus ac doctissimus, mox ubi regnare cepit, totam suam prouinciam fidei sacramento*rum *participem facere curauit. Cuius studiis faue*ns, Felix [f]*episcopus*, genere Burgundus,[11] *qui Sigeberto* Orientalium Anglorum regi[g] *in Gallia exulanti familiaris effectus, Angliam cum eodem post mortem Eorpwaldi uenit, et* East*anglorum episcopus* efficitur.[f12] *Illam ad fidem* Christi *perduxit*,

---

[a] om. HL   [b-b] Sanctus . . . nascitur] add. mg. near opening (end B) of 634 C (different hand, not like others) B¹?, at very end of annal P, penultimate sentence in annal before reference to Clovis HL   [c-c] per . . . instituitur] add. with signe de renvoi C³? [d-d] ab . . . misso] interlin. C³   [e-e] in Westsaxonica prouincia] om. B   [f-f] episcopus . . . efficitur] episcopus rewritten, rest is added at line-end and in mg. with signe de renvoi C³   [g] om. HL

[1] HE. iii. 1.   [2] HE iii. 6.
[3] HE iii. 7. The date of Birinus's mission is probably derived from ASC ABCEF.
[4] Norman Annals. AU, AG, ASN (633) record Clovis' accession. Clovis II 638-57.
[5] If Wilfrid died in 709 in his 76th year, this marginal addition gives the correct date of his birth.
[6] HE iii. 3. HE iii. 17 says that Aidan had completed 17 years as bishop when he died in 651.

could withstand,[1] and took control of both Northumbrian kingdoms and in the succeeding period received the submission of all
the nations and kingdoms in Britain.[2] At that time, in the reign of
King Cynegils, the West Saxons received the Christian faith
through the preaching of the word of God by Bishop Birinus.[3]

Clovis, son of Dagobert, was the twentieth king of the Franks.[4]
St Wilfrid was born.[5]

[635] King Oswald sent to the chief men of the Irish, asking them
to send him a bishop. Bishop Aidan was sent to him.[6] Through
Aidan and through the most glorious and holy King Oswald the
Church of Christ was founded and established in the kingdom of
the Bernicians.[7] Birinus, sent to England by Pope Honorius to
preach, spread the Gospel, in the kingdom of the West Saxons,
King Cynegils and his people believed, and the most victorious
King Oswald received him from the baptismal font. The same
bishop received from these kings the city of Dorchester that he
might establish there his episcopal seat.[8]

Pope Honorius died on 12 October, and the papacy was vacant
for one year, seven months, and seventeen days.[9]

[636] Sigeberht,[10] brother of Earpwald, king of the East Angles, a
man most thoroughly Christian and most learned, took pains from
the very outset of his reign to make his whole kingdom share in
the sacraments of the faith. Bishop Felix, a Burgundian by race,
supported his endeavours;[11] having become a friend of Sigeberht,
king of the East Angles, at that time an exile in Gaul, he came to
England with him after Earpwald's death and became bishop of
the East Angles.[12] He brought that kingdom to the Christian faith

[7] There are echoes here in this marginal addition of *HDE* i. 2 (i. 20), or of the end
of the *Vita Bedae* (*BHL* 1069), a copy of which was transcribed (probably by C[3]) in the
Worcester Passional, BL MS Cotton Nero E. I, Part ii, fo. 188[v]: 'ex quo per clarissi-
mos et sanctissimos regem et pontificem Oswaldum dico et Aidanum in prouincia Berniciorum primum fundata et ecclesia Christi et instituta . . .' Aidan would appear to
have been sent for in 634 as he had completed 17 years as bishop when he died.

[8] *HE* iii. 7. The date of Cynegils' baptism probably comes from ASC.

[9] Mar.

[10] The date for the accession of Sigeberht and the coming of Felix seems to be
derived from ASC, and, on the evidence of Bede's dates for the first three East Anglian
bishops, is too late (Plummer, *Bede* ii. 106).

[11] *HE* ii. 15.   [12] *GP* ii. 74 (p. 147).

*accept*aque *sede episcopatus in ciuitate Domm*uc *.xvii. ann*is *eidem* genti prefuit.[1] Eo tempore *de Hibernia uenit ad prouinciam Orientalium Anglorum uir sanctus nomine Furseus,* et *a rege prefato susceptus honorifice,* ibique predicans uerbum uite *multos incredulos ad Christum conuertit,* et postea *monasterium nobile constru*xit.[2] Interea *rex* idem, *relictis regni negotiis et cognato suo Ecgric*o *commendatis, monasterium quod sibi fecerat, intra*uit, *accept*aque *tonsura eterno* regi *multo tempore* deuote *mili*tauit. Sed dum paganus rex *Merciorum Penda aduersus* Eastanglos *in bell*um *proceder*et, *monasterio inuitus eru*itur *in certamen nolen*s ducitur, *uirgamque tantum in manu* tenens, *una cum rege Ecgric*o *occi*ditur, quibus in regnum successit *Anna filius Eni.*[3] Cuichelm rex,[a] regis Cynegilsi filius, in ciuitate Dorcicc a Birino episcopo baptizatur et eodem anno defungitur.[b4]

[637] (xxvi) 659 *Seuerinus*[5] *septuagesimus papa anno uno. Iudei in Hispania Christiani efficiuntur. Sisibutus*[6] *enim Gothorum gloriosissimus rex plurimas prouincias in Hispania, ⟨et⟩*[c] *militie Romane urbes sibi bellando subiecit ac Iudeos in suo regno ad fidem Christi conuertit. Seuerinus papa obiit .iiii. nonas Augusti. Iohannes*[7] *.lxxi. papa anno uno, mensibus .x.*[8]

[638] (xxvii) 660 *Heraclius Constantinopoli obiit.*
    Romanorum sexagesimus quintus regnauit Heraclonas[d9] *filius Heraclii annis duobus usque in annum sexcentesimum uicesimum nonum post passionem* Domini.[e10]

[639] (i) 661 *Theodorus*[11] *septuagesimus secundus papa annis sex, mensibusque .vi. Iohannes autem papa obiit .iiii. idus Octobris. Cirus Alexandrie, Sergius et Pirrus regie urbis episcopi, Acephalorum heresim instaurantes, unam operationem in Christo diuinitatis et humanitatis una uoluntate dogmatizant. E quibus Pirrus, his temporibus, sub Theodoro papa, Romam ueniens ex Affrica, ficta, ut post apparuit,*

---

[a] *interlin.* C[1]B[1], *om.* HL   [b] *long entry from Gesta Dagoberti (see App. B) on p. 261 below 628-36 B[1]?*   [c] *om.* JW   [d] *corrected from* Herodonas C[1]   [e] *om.* HL

---

[1] *GP* ii. 74 (p. 147).
[2] *HE* iii. 19. JW may have inferred this date for Fursey's arrival in East Anglia.
[3] *HE* iii. 18.
[4] ASC ABC describes Cwichelm as Cynegils's son under 648, not here. It does not mention Birinus.

and, after accepting the episcopal see in the city of *Dommoc*, he ruled that same people seventeen years.[1] At that time a holy man called Fursey came to the kingdom of the East Angles from Ireland and was received by the aforementioned king with honour. Preaching the word of life there, he converted many unbelievers to Christ and afterwards built a noble monastery.[2] Meanwhile, the same king set aside the affairs of the realm and commended them to his kinsman Ecgric. He entered a monastery he had founded for himself and, after receiving the tonsure, he strove devotedly for the Eternal King for a long time. But when Penda, the pagan king of the Mercians, was advancing to war against the East Angles, he was taken against his will from the monastery and led, unwilling, into battle, holding only a rod in his hand. He was killed together with King Ecgric. Anna, son of Eni, succeeded them in the kingdom.[3] King Cwichelm, son of King Cynegils, was baptized in the city of Dorchester by Bishop Birinus, and he died the same year.[4]

[**637**] Severinus,[5] the seventieth pope, reigned one year. The Jews in Spain were made Christian, for Sisebut,[6] the most glorious king of the Goths, subdued many provinces in Spain and the cities of the Byzantine army by war, and converted the Jews in his kingdom to the Christian faith. Pope Severinus died on 2 August. John,[7] the seventy-first pope, reigned one year and ten months.[8]

[**638**] Heraclius died at Constantinople.

The sixty-fifth emperor of the Romans, Heracleonas,[9] son of Heraclius, reigned two years to the 629th year after the Lord's Passion.[10]

[**639**] Theodore,[11] the seventy-second pope, reigned six years and six months. Pope John died on 12 October. Cyrus of Alexandria and Sergius and Pyrrhus, bishops of the imperial city, reviving the heresy of the Acephali, propounded the dogma of the single working in Christ of the divine and the human through the one will. Of this group Pyrrhus, coming to Rome from Africa at this time,

---

[5] Severinus 640.   [6] Sisebut 612–21.   [7] John IV 640–2.
[8] Mar.   [9] Heracleonas 641.   [10] Mar.
[11] Theodore I 642–9.

penitentia optulit eidem pape, presente cuncto clero et populo, libellum cum sua subscriptione in quo condempnarentur omnia que a se uel a decessoribus suis scripta uel acta sunt contra catholicam fidem. Vnde et benigne susceptus est ab eo quasi regie pontifex ciuitatis. Sed quia reuersus domum errorem repetiit, memoratus papa Theodorus, aduocatis cunctis sacerdotibus et clero in ecclesiam beati Petri apostoli, condempnauit eum sub uinculo anathematis.[1]

Birinus episcopus Cuthredum Cuichelmi regis filium in ciuitate Dorcicc baptizauit et eum[a] de fonte regenerationis suscepit.[2]

[640] (ii) 662 *His temporibus Ysidorus Hispaniensis episcopus clarus habetur.*[3]

*Eadbald rex Cantuariorum an*no *uicesimo* quinto *regni sui ex hac uita transiens regni gubernacula Erconber*h*to filio suo reliquit.* [b]*Hic primus*[b] *regum Anglorum in toto regno suo idola relinqui ac destrui, simul et ieiunium .xl. dierum obseruari precepit. Cuius filia Ercongota,* quam peperit ei sancta [c]*Sexburh,* regina exstitit *magnarum uirgo uirtutum.*[c][4]

Romanorum sexagesimus sextus Constantinus[5] *filius Heraclii regnauit mensibus sex quasi usque kalendas Nouembris in anno sexcentesimo uicesimo nono post passionem.*

Pirri successor Paulus non tantum uesana doctrina sicut predecessores eius, sed aperta persecutione catholicos cruciat. Apocrisiarios sancte Romane ecclesie qui ad eius correctionem missi fuerant, partim carceribus, partim exiliis, partim uerberibus afficiens, sed et altare eorum in domo Placidie sacratum in uenerabili oraculo sub|uertens diripuit, prohibens eos ibidem missas celebrare. Vnde et ipse sicut precessores[d] *eius ab apostolica sede iusta depositionis ultione dampnatur.*

p. 260

Romanorum sexagesimus septimus Constantinus,[6] *filius Constantini regnauit annis .xxviii. usque in annum sexcentesimum quinquagesimum septimum post passionem.*[7]

---

[a] *second stroke of* m *in* eum *over erasure* C[1]   [b-b] Hic primus] *over erasure* C[1]
[c-c] Sexburh . . . uirtutum] *slightly more compressed script, extending into mg.* C
[d] predecessores *from* precessores B

---

[1] Mar.
[2] ASC BCF call Cuthred king, and ABC describe Cuthred as Cwichelm's son under 648, not here. ASC F records only the fact of baptism.
[3] Mar.
[4] *HE* iii. 8, where Seaxburg is mentioned as the wife of Earconberht and mother of Earcongota.

during the reign of Pope Theodore, feigned penitence (as was afterwards evident), and in the presence of all the clergy and people offered the same pope a book with his own subscription in which was condemned everything that had been written or done against the Catholic faith by himself or by his predecessors. Hence he was received graciously as though the bishop of the imperial city. But because, when he returned home, he resumed his error, the already mentioned Pope Theodore, calling together all the priests and clergy in the church of the blessed Apostle Peter, laid on him the bonds of anathema.[1]

Bishop Birinus baptized Cuthred, son of King Cwichelm, in the city of Dorchester, and received him from the font of regeneration.[2]

[640] In these times the Spanish Bishop Isidore enjoyed great renown.[3]

Eadbald, king of the people of Kent, departing this life in the twenty-fifth year of his reign, left the government of the kingdom to his son Earconberht. Earconberht was the first of the English kings to order that the idols be abandoned and destroyed throughout his whole realm, and that the forty-day fast be observed. His daughter Earcongota, whom the saintly Queen Seaxburg bore him, was a virgin of great virtues.[4]

The sixty-sixth emperor of the Romans, Constantine[5] son of Heraclius, reigned six months up to 1 November in the 629th year after the Passion.

Paul, the successor of Pyrrhus, tormented the Catholics, not only like his predecessors with mad doctrine, but also with open persecution. He punished the *apocrisiarii* of the holy Roman church, who had been sent to reprove him, some with imprisonment, some with exile, others with flogging. He also destroyed their consecrated altar in the *Domus Placidiana*, overturning it in the revered sanctuary, and forbidding them to celebrate mass there. For that reason he also, like his predecessors, was condemned by the apostolic see to the well-deserved punishment of deposition.

Constans,[6] son of Constantine, reigned as the sixty-seventh emperor of the Romans for twenty-eight years, up to the 657th year after the Passion.[7]

---

[5] Constantine III 641.   [6] Constans II 641–68.   [7] Mar.

[641] (i) 663   *Hic deceptus est a Paulo sicut auus eius Heraclius a Sergio supradicto episcopo. Exposuit enim iste contra catholicam fidem nec unam nec duas uoluntates aut operationes in Christo diffiniens esse confitendas, quasi nil uelle uel operari credendus sit Christus.*[1]

[642] (ii) 666   *[a]*Nepos regis Eduuini, filius regis Æðelfriði, *rex Osuuald Christianissimus, peregrinis et pauperibus semper humilis benignus et largus, anno etatis sue .xxxviii.* regni autem nono, *commisso graui prelio, occisus est a* Penda *Merciorum rege pagano in loco Maserfeld nuncup*ato.[2] *Cuius frater Osuuiu iuuenis circiter .xxx. annorum,* breui post tempore in regnum illi successit et *per annos .xxviii. laboriosissime tenuit.*[3] Eodem anno Cenuualch, filius Cinigilsi regis, regimen Westsaxonici regni suscepit et .xxxi. annis*[b]* *[c]*tenuit, et Wintonie ecclesiam in qua sedes pontificalis est construxit.*[c]*[4]

[644] (iiii) 666   *Theodorus papa obiit .ii. idus Maii.*[5]

Paulinus, quondam Eboracensis sed tunc Hrofensis episcopus ciuitatis, postquam *.xviii. annos, menses duos, dies .xxi. episcopatum tenuit, .vi. iduum Octobrium die ad Dominum transiuit. [d]In cuius locum Honorius arciepiscopus,* Iusti successor, *Ithamar[e] ordinauit*

[HLP]	[C³BP]
*[f]*Ciclus solis incipit .iiii. concurrentibus bissextilibus.*[f]*	Hrofensi ecclesie *pontificem.[d]*[6]

[645] (v) 667   *Martinus*[7] *papa septuagesimus tertius annis sex, mensibus duobus.*[8]

---

[a] *this annal runs on to 643 CHLB, under 642–3 P*   *[b]* *anno JW*   *[c–c]* *tenuit . . .* *construxit] mg. starting at line-end C¹*   *[d–d]* *in cuius . . . pontificem] over erasure C³* *[e]* *anglus interlin. above* Ithamar *C³B¹P¹, om. HL*   *[f–f]* Ciclus . . . bissextilibus] *traces of these words in red below the rewriting of 644 n. c and the erasure at line-end C*

---

[1] Mar.

[2] *HE* iii. 6, 9, v. 24. The year of Oswald's death could have been inferred from iii. 9 or taken from v. 24 and confirmed by ASC A (against BCEF, which have 641).

[3] *HE* iii. 14. Osuiu died in 670 (*HE* iv. 5, v. 24, followed by JW) and his reign of 28 years could have begun in 642.

[4] JW's 642 for the accession of Cenwealh (unless this annal was meant to be divided and 643 was intended, see 642 n. a) agrees neither with the 643 of ASC A nor with the 641 of BCE (though F could be 642), and may have been calculated by subtracting the

[641] He was deceived by Paul, just as his grandfather Heraclius was by Sergius (the bishop mentioned earlier), for Paul's teaching was contrary to the Catholic faith and he decreed that neither one nor two wills nor energies are manifest in Christ—as if it were credible that Christ had neither will nor energy.[1]

[642] The most Christian king Oswald, nephew of King Edwin, son of King Æthelfrith, ever humble, gracious, and generous to strangers and the poor, was killed in his thirty-eighth year, the ninth of his reign, by Penda, the pagan king of the Mercians, in a fierce battle at a place called *Maserfelth*.[2] His brother, the young man Oswiu, aged about thirty, succeeded him in the kingdom after a short time, and held it with great exertion for twenty-eight years.[3] In the same year Cenwealh, son of King Cynegils, took up the governance of the West Saxon kingdom, and held it for thirty-one years, and built the church at Winchester, where the episcopal see is.[4]

[644] Pope Theodore died on 14 May.[5]

Paulinus, the former bishop of York, but at that time bishop of Rochester, passed to the Lord on 10 October after holding the office of bishop for eighteen years, two months, and twenty-one days. In his place Archbishop Honorius, successor of Justus, ordained Ithamar

The solar cycle begins with four concurrents in a bissextile year. to the episcopal see of Rochester.[6]

[645] Martin,[7] the seventy-third pope, reigned six years and two months.[8]

---

30 years assigned him under the record of his death in 672. The 31-years regnal length (here and in JW *West Saxon Accounts* 11, as against 30 years under 672) agrees with ASC ABCF (E's 21 years being probably erroneous). The building of Winchester is dated 641 in ASC E, 642 BCF and 643 A. ASC does not identify Cenwealh's father or describe Winchester as an episcopal see.

[5] Mar.

[6] *HE* iii. 14. The date of Paulinus's death is 644 in *HE* v. 24 and ASC AF, and 643 in BCE. The interlineated 'anglus' could have been taken from *GP* i. 72 (p. 135).

[7] Martin I 649–53.   [8] Mar.

Rex Westsaxonum *Cenuualh*, quia *Pende regis Merciorum sororem quam duxerat repudia*uit *bello petitus, ac regno ab illo priuatus, ad regem* East*anglorum Annam secessit.*[1] Hoc etiam anno *rex Osuuine aspectu uenustus, statura sublimis, affatu iocundus, moribus ciuilis, omnibus manu largus, reg*um *humill*imus, *amabilis omnibus, regis Eduuini* patruelis *Osrici fili*us in *Deirorum prouincia* regnare cepit et *.vii. annis* eidem *prefuit.*[2]

[646] (vi) 668   *[a]Ciclus .vii. decennouenalis incipit indictione .iiii.[a3]*
  Kenuualh rex apud Orientales Anglos a Felice pontifice baptizatus est.[4]

[647] vii (669)   *[b]Martinus papa propter predictam heresim congregauit Rome synodum .cv. episcoporum. [c]In qua synodo dampnauit sub anathemate Cirum, Sergium et Paulum hereticos prefatos episcopos.*[5]

[HL]	[C3BP]
Felix primus East*anglorum* episco*pus obiit, pro quo Honorius* archiepiscopus *Thomam diaconum eius ordinauit. [d]*Quo etiam *de hac uita subtracto, quin*to *sui episcopatus anno Bonifacium substituit eius loco.[d6]*	Felix Eastanglorum primus *episcopus in Dommuc sede* episcopali obiit. *Inde translatus, apud Sedam que est uilla iuxta stagnum, quod uolentibus ire in Heli quondam periculosum nauibus, nunc facta uia per palustre harundinetum transitur pedibus,* sepultus est. *Post*modum *corpus illius quesitum et repertum in Ramesiensi cenobio humatum est.*[7] Pro

[a–a] Ciclus . . . .iiii.] *om. though space left blank B, at end of 645 P*   *[b]* Martinus . . . ordinauit *(p. 100)] this annal is rewritten over erasure by C3 and starts under 646 at present as in B, starts under 647 Mar. and HL, Marianus sections under 646, English sections under 647 P   [c] 648 here (N)   [d–d] Quo . . . loco] add. at 647 n. a (p. 100) P*

[1] *HE* iii. 7 does not give the date of Cenwealh's expulsion, which is 645 in ASC AF and 644 in BCE.
[2] *HE* iii. 14. Oswine's accession would seem to have been 644 if his reign of seven years ended in 651.
[3] Mar.
[4] ASC. The baptism of Cenwealh is recorded under 646 in ASC AF and 645 in BCE. That Felix baptized Cenwealh is probably an inference peculiar to JW and to JW *West Saxon Accounts* 10.

Because Cenwealh, king of the West Saxons, repudiated his wife, the sister of Penda, the king of the Mercians, Penda attacked him and deprived him of his kingdom. He retreated to Anna, king of the East Angles.[1] Also in this year King Oswine, handsome in appearance, lofty of stature, pleasant in his address, courteous in his behaviour, dealing with a generous hand to all, the most humble of kings, beloved of all, son of Osric (a cousin of King Edwin), began to reign in the kingdom of Deira. He ruled it for seven years.[2]

[646] The seventh cycle of nineteen years begins in the fourth indiction.[3]

King Cenwealh was baptized in East Anglia by Bishop Felix.[4]

[647] Pope Martin assembled a synod of 105 bishops at Rome on account of the aforementioned heresy. At that synod he laid under anathema Cyrus, Sergius, and Paul, the aforementioned heretical bishops.[5]

Felix, the first bishop of the East Angles, died. Archbishop Honorius ordained the deacon Thomas in his place. Thomas too being taken from this life in the fifth year of his episcopate, Honorius substituted Boniface in his stead.[6]

Felix, the first bishop of the East Angles, died at the episcopal seat in *Dommoc*. He was translated thence and buried at Soham, a township next to the Fens, which was once dangerous for those wishing to go to Ely by ship. A road has now been made through the marshy tangle of reeds and it may be crossed on foot. Afterwards his body was sought, found, and buried in Ramsey Abbey.

[5] Mar.

[6] *HE* iii. 20. The year of Felix's death and of Thomas's succession could have been deduced from information in Bede.

quo *Honorius* archiepiscopus
Thomam diaconus eius ordi-
nauit.[a][1]

[648] (viii) 670 [2]Kenuualh rex de Eastanglia rediit in Westsaxoniam, et eodem anno non modicam ruris portionem[3] dedit
Cuthredo fratrueli suo Cuicchelmi regis filio.[4]

[649] (ix) 671 *Facta est sinodus prefata anno imperii Constantini*
.ix. mense Octobri, indictione septima.[5]

[650] (x) 672 *Post hec missus ab imperatore, Theodorus, exarchus*
tulit Martinum papam de ecclesia Constantiniana, perduxitque Con-
stantinopolim et inde religatur Cersona prouincie Sicilie [b]uel *Licie,*[b]
ibidemque .iiii. idus Nouembris obiit et multis uirtutum signis refulget.[6]

*Agilber*htus episcopus *natione Gallus, in prouincia* Westsaxonica a
rege Cenuualcho, defuncto iam Birino, *acce*pit *episcopa*tum et *eidem*
genti pontificali *iure annis prefuit multis.*[7]

[651] (xi) 673 *Eugenius*[8] *septuagesimus .iiii. papa annis duobus,*
mensibus decem.[9]

[c]⟨San⟩ctus *Cuthberhtus monasterium Mailro*nense *intrauit, suscep-*
tus a reuerentissimo Eata eiusdem ecclesie abbate.[c][10] Vir humilitatis
eximie, sanctitatisque non modice, Deirorum rex Osuuine, *comitis*
Hunuualdi sibi ut putabat *amicissimi prodit*us detectione, regni
sui anno .vii. *die kalendarum Septembrium .xiii.*, regis Osuuiu
iussione a *prefec*to suo *Atheluuin*o peremptus est, *detestanda omni-*
bus morte. Cui successit in regnum Oiðeluuald regis Osuualdi
filius. *Post occisionem regis* Osuuini *antistes Aidan* .ii. *kalend.*
*Septemb*rium ad celorum regna migrauit.[11] Cuius animam

---

[a] *see above, p. 98 n. b; 647 n. d (p. 98) add here* P   [b–b] uel Licie] *interlin.* C[1]B[1],
om. HL   [c–c] ⟨San⟩ctus . . . abbate] *add. mg. alongside 651* C[2]P[3]; B *incorporates at end*
of annal

---

[1] *GP* ii. 74 (p. 147).
[2] The year of Cenwealh's return, which is not given in ASC, could have been calculated by adding his 3-year exile in East Anglia (mentioned in *HE* iii. 7 and in ASC
under 658) to the year of his expulsion, 645 in ASC AF, though BCE give 644.
[3] 'non modicam ruris portionem' might reflect '.iii. þusendo londes' of ASC AE
(648) rather than the 'iii[m]. hida landes' of BC (647). ASC ABCE locates this land near
Ashdown. ASC ABC give the genealogy of Cenwealh.

Archbishop Honorius ordained the deacon Thomas in his stead.[1]

[648] [2]King Cenwealh returned from East Anglia to Wessex, and in the same year gave his nephew Cuthred, son of King Cwichelm, no small portion of land.[3,4]

[649] The aforementioned synod was held in October, in the seventh indiction in the ninth year of Constans' reign.[5]

[650] After this the exarch Theodore was sent by the emperor, took Pope Martin from the church of Constantine [St John Lateran], and led him to Constantinople, and then he was imprisoned in Cherson in the province of Sicily (or Lycia). There he died on 10 November and his fame shone forth in many miraculous signs.[6]

Bishop Agilbert, a Gaul by birth, received a bishopric in the West Saxon kingdom from King Cenwealh after the death of Birinus, and ruled that same people as bishop for many years.[7]

[651] Eugenius,[8] the seventy-fourth pope, reigned two years, ten months.[9]

St Cuthbert entered the monastery of Melrose and was received by the most reverend Eata, abbot of that church.[10] King Oswine of the Deirans, a man of remarkable humility and of no little holiness, was betrayed on the information provided by his gesith Hunwold, his dearest friend (as he thought), and was slain on 20 August, in the seventh year of his reign, at the command of King Oswiu, by his ealdorman Æthelwine, a death abominable to all. Oethelwald, son of King Oswald, succeeded him in his kingdom. On 31 August, after the murder of King Oswine, Bishop Aidan departed to the kingdom of heaven.[11] Cuthbert, a boy of fine

---

[4] ASC.   [5] Mar.   [6] Mar.

[7] HE iii. 7. The date could come from ASC, where AF agree with JW against BCE, which give 649.

[8] Eugenius I 654-7.   [9] Mar.

[10] HDE i. 3 (i. 22), from which the date 651 is derived, though it can be reconciled with the information provided by Bede, Vita Cuthberti, c. 4, mentioned in the last sentence of this annal.

[11] HE iii. 14. The length of Oswine's reign and the day of his death are from Bede, though ASC enters the deaths of Oswine and Aidan under 651 in ABC (F death of Aidan only) and under 650 in E. The succession of Oethelwald is in HE iii. 23.

puer bone indolis Cuthbertus uidit in *celum ferri ab angelis*,[1] quo
defuncto *Finan pro illo gradum episcopatus a Scottis ordinatus ac
missus accep*it.*ᵃᵇ*[2]

[652] (xii) 674   *Eugenius papa obiit .iiii. nonis Ianuarii.*[3]
                                    [C³BP]
                          ᶜDefuncto Thoma Eastanglorum
                          episcopo, successit Bonifacius,
                          genere Cantius.ᶜ[4]

[653] (xiii) 675   *Vitalianus*[5] *septuagesimus .v. papa.*[6]
   *Benedictus cognomento Biscop, regis Osuuiu minister, nobili stirpe
gentis Anglorum progenitus, domum cognatos* possessiones *patriam*
etatis sue anno .xxv. amore Christi *reliquit,* primo *Romam adiit* et
mox doctior rediit.[7] *Honorius* Doruuernensis archiepiscopus .ii.
kalend. Octob. ex hac luce migrauit. Cui post *annum et .vi. menses
Deusdedit,* ᵈ*sextus ab* Augustino, in regimen pontificatus successit,
et *ab Ithamaro Hrofensis ecclesie antist*ite *die .vii. kalendarum Aprili-*
p. 261   *um*ᵈ | ᵉ*ordinatus, annos .ix., menses .iiii. et duos dies ecclesiam rexit.*[8]
                                    [C³BP]
                          ᶠ*Esset id archiepiscopi Eboracensis*
                          solenne sed *hostili uiolentia*
                          Paulino pulso, et Cantiam
                          reuerso, nullus ei ibidem pontifi-
                          *cali iure iam successerat.*ᵉᶠ[9]
   Mediterranei Angli sub Peada principe, filio Pendan regis Merciorum,
fidem et sacramenta Christi *perceperunt.* Ipso principe primitus *a
Finano episcopo apud regem* Osuuium *in* Northymbria *cum omnibus*

ᵃ *incorporates 651 n. c (p. 100) here* B   ᵇ *Hoc tempore uisio sancti Fursei. Vide
(om.* P)] *add. mg. in small later 12th-c. hand alongside this annal* C, *add. mg. alongside
652–3* P³, *see App.* B *for Fursey addition in lower mgs. pp. 262–8 starting below 640* B². *C³
addition probably refers to the addition in* B *(see also 704 n. a).*   ᶜ⁻ᶜ *Defuncto . . .
Cantius] add. at line-end and with last three words in mg. linked by signe de renvoi* C³, *om.*
HL   ᵈ⁻ᵈ *sextus . . . Aprilium] written at bottom of page on supplementary unruled line*
C³   ᵉ⁻ᵉ *ordinatus . . . successerat] written over erasure* C³   ᶠ⁻ᶠ *Esset . . . suc-
cesserat] om.* HL

---

[1] These italicized words could have been taken from the rubric to c. 4 of Bede's *Vita
Cuthberti*, where, as in the *Anon. uita Cuthberti*, i. 5, this vision of Aidan's soul is
recorded.
[2] *HE* iii. 25.

qualities, saw Aidan's soul borne to heaven by angels.[1] After his death Finan, who had been ordained and sent by the Irish was preferred to the bishopric in his place.[2]

[652] Pope Eugenius died on 2 January.[3]

> On the death of Thomas, bishop of the East Angles, Boniface, a native of Kent, succeeded.[4]

[653] Vitalian[5] became the seventy-fifth pope.[6]

Benedict, surnamed Biscop, thegn of King Oswiu and by birth a nobleman of the English race, gave up his home, kinsmen, possessions, and country in his twenty-fifth year for the love of Christ and went, first, to Rome, and soon returned better instructed.[7] Honorius, archbishop of Canterbury, departed from this light on 30 September. After a year and six months Deusdedit succeeded him in the archbishopric as the sixth [inclusively] after Augustine, and was ordained by Ithamar, bishop of Rochester, on 26 March, and ruled the church for nine years, four months, and two days.[8]

> That consecration should have been performed by the archbishop of York, but when Paulinus had been driven out by the violence of the enemy and had returned to Kent no one succeeded him there as archbishop.[9]

The Middle Angles, under the leadership of Peada, son of Penda, king of the Mercians, received the faith and the sacraments of Christ. First their leader himself, with all who had come with him, was baptized by Bishop Finan in Northumbria at the court

---

[3] Mar.

[4] The information and date here could have been derived from *HE* iii. 20, though it is possible that the words 'genere Cantius' were derived from 'gente Cantuarita' in *GP* ii. 74 (p. 147). ASC ABC mention Cenwealh's battle at Bradford here.

[5] Vitalian I 657–62.   [6] Mar.

[7] Bede, *Hist. abbat.*, cc. 1–2. The date for Biscop's visit to Rome could have been inferred from Bede. The phrase 'etatis sue anno .xxv.' is more definite than is warranted by Bede's 'annos natus circiter .xx. et .v.'

[8] *HE* iii. 20.   [9] *GP* i. 72 (p. 135).

*qui secum uenerant, baptizat*o, postmodum uero eo, domum *reuers*o, ceteris de sua gente baptizatis a *presbite*ris *.iiii. Cedd, Adda, Betti et Diuma,* quos secum de prefata adduxerat prouincia.[1] *Eo tempore rex Orienta*lium *Saxon*um *Sigeber*ht, *qui post* Sæbertum[2] *cognomento Paruum, regnauit, in prouincia* Berniciorum fidem Christi per exortationem *regis Osuuiu cum ad eum ueniret* suscipiens, *a Finano* Norðhymbrorum *episcopo baptizatus est.* Quo *sui regni sedem repetente,* rex Osuuiu misit cum illo *uirum Dei Cedd* presbiterum ad *predica*ndum *uerbum* Eastsaxonicis, *ubi cum* ille *multam Domino ecclesiam congregasset* et *propter co*ll*oquium Finani episcopi domum* reuersus esset, *gradum episcopatus* ab eo *acc*epit, et in *prouinciam* reuersus *maior*i *auctoritate ceptum opus exple*uit.[3] Quadam uice *cum* ipse *Norðhymbrorum prouinciam exortandi gratia reuiseret, Deirorum* rex *Oiðeluuald regis, Osuualdi filius, postulauit eum possessionem terre aliquam a se ad construendum monasterium accipere.* Qui *regiis fauens uotis elegit sibi locum monasterii construendi* in loco qui *nunc Leastingaig* nuncupatur, et facto monasterio *religiosis moribus instituit.*[4] Interea regem Sigebertum, *instigante omnium bonorum inimico, sui interfecere propinqui,* quia *nimis ille suis parcere sole*bat *inimicis et factas ab eis iniurias mox obsecrantibus placida mente dimittere,* cui *successit in regnum Suiðelm, filius Sexbaldi.*[5]

[654] (xiiii) 676 *Constantinus princeps Vitaliano papa nuper ordinato misit beato Petro apostolo aurea euangelia, gemmis albis mire magnitudinis in circuitu ornata.*[6]

Anna rex Eastanglie a Penda *ᵃrege occiditur, cui frater suus Eathilhere in regnum successit. In loco qui dicitur Icanhoᵃ* monasterium construitur a sancto Botulfo.[7]

[655] (xv) 677 Perfidus rex Merciorum Penda, Sigeberti, Ecgrici, Anne, regum Eastanglorum necnon etiam Eduuini, Osuualdi

---

ᵃ⁻ᵃ rege . . . Icanho] *partly extending into mg. and partly over erasure* Cᵗ

---

[1] *HE* iii. 21. The date of this conversion (653 in ASC A(B)C, 652 in E) could have been inferred from *HE* iii. 21 and is dated in v. 24.

[2] 'Sæbertum' is an error for Sigeberht. This error is not found in JW *East Saxon Accounts* 6.

[3] *HE* iii. 24, on which the date ('eo tempore') for the reconversion of the East Saxons is based.

[4] *HE* iii. 23.

[5] *HE* iii. 22. The dates of Sigeberht's murder and of Swithhelm's succession are not

of King Oswiu: on his return home the rest of his people were baptized by four priests, Cedd, Adda, Betti, and Diuma, whom he had brought with him from the aforementioned province.[1] At that time Sigeberht, king of the East Saxons, who reigned after Sæberht,[2] called the Small, received the faith of Christ in the kingdom of the Bernicians at the urging of King Oswiu when he visited him, and was baptized by Finan, bishop of the Northumbrians. On Sigeberht's return to the seat of his kingdom, King Oswiu sent with him a man of God, the priest Cedd, to preach the Word to the East Saxons. There, when he had assembled a great church for the Lord, and had returned home to confer with Bishop Finan, he received the rank of bishop from him, and on his return to the kingdom completed the work he had begun with greater authority.[3] On one occasion, when he revisited the kingdom of the Northumbrians for encouragement, Oethelwald, king of Deira, son of King Oswald, asked Cedd to accept from him the grant of some land on which to build a monastery. Falling in with the royal wish, he chose a site for the construction of a monastery in a place now called Lastingham, and, when the monastery had been built, he established monastic observances.[4] Then King Sigeberht was killed by his own kinsmen at the instigation of the enemy of all good men because he was too much in the habit of sparing his enemies, peacefully pardoning the injuries they had done him as soon as they asked him. Swithhelm, son of Seaxbald, succeeded him in his kingdom.[5]

[654] When Pope Vitalian was newly ordained, the Emperor Constans sent to St Peter the Apostle a golden book of the gospels, adorned on the outside with white gems of amazing size.[6]

Anna, king of the East Angles, was killed by King Penda. His brother Æthelhere succeeded him to the kingdom. A monastery was built by St Botulf in a place called *Icanho*.[7]

[655] Penda, the treacherous king of the Mercians, slayer of Kings Sigeberht, Ecgric, and Anna of the East Angles, and also of Kings

known and JW may have inferred from Bede or might have intended 'interea' to suggest a time-lag of more than a few months.

[6] Mar.

[7] ASC A(B)C (654) E (653), but the identification of Penda as Anna's slayer and the succession of Anna's brother Æthelhere are derived from *HE* iii. 18, 24.

regum Norðanhymbrorum occisor, *.xxx. legionibu*s totidemque
nobillissimis ducibus^a ^b*instruct*us in Berniciam ad debellandum regem
Osuuium ascendit, cui ille *cum Alhfrido filio* unam tantum
legionem habens,^c *sed Christo duce confisus*, in loco qui dicitur Win-
uuidfelda¹ *occurrit.*^b *Inito certamine, fugati sunt et cesi pagani, duces
reg*um *.xxx. qui ad auxilium uenerant pene omnes interfecti, in quibus
Æthilhere, frater Anne regis eorundem, qui post eum regnauit, auctor
ipse belli, interemptus est*, cui in regnum frater suus Æðeluuoldus
successit. *Tum rex Osuuiu, pro collata sibi uictoria, .xii. possessi*ones
ad monasteria construenda et *filiam suam Ælfledam Deo optulit per-
petua ei uirginitate consecrandam*, que *monasterium quod* Heortesig
*nuncupatur, cui tunc Hild abbatissa prefuit, intrauit. Hoc bellum rex
Osuuiu in regione Loidis .xiii. regni sui anno, .xvii., die kalendarum
Decembrium, confecit, gentemque Merciorum ad fide*m *Christi*
conuertit, *sub quo primus in prouincia Merciorum et Lindisfarorum ac
Mediterraneorum Anglorum factus est episcopus Diuma* Scottus^d *cuius
supra* meminimus, *secundus Ceollah de genere Scottorum. Idem rex
.iii. annis* eidem *genti ceteris*que *australium prouinciarum populis prefuit, gentem*que *Pictorum regno Anglorum subiecit, et Pende regis filio
Peade suo cognato regnum australium Merciorum dedit.*²

[656] (xvi) 678   ^e*Peada rex sue coniugis proditione in ipso pascalis
festi tempore peremptus est multum nefarie.*³

[658] (xviii) 680   Kenuualh rex Westsaxonum cum Brytonibus
apud Peonnum pugnauit et eos Pedridan usque fugauit.⁴ Beata
*Hild abbatissa in loco qui dicitur Streoneshealh monasterium con-
stru*ere coepit, *in quo regis* Osuuiu *filia primo uite regularis discipula
deinde extitit magistra*, cuius mater Eanfleda regina in loco ubi rex
Osuuine filius uidelicet patruelis sui patris Osrici regis, peremptus

---

^a *written mg.* C¹   ^{b–b} instructus . . . occurrit] *probably rewritten over erasure* C
^c *written mg.* C¹   ^d *interlin.* C¹B¹, *om.* HLP   ^e Sequenti anno *interlin.* B⁵

---

¹ The site of the battle is mentioned under 654 in ASC E (Winwidfelda) and F
(Winwidfeldan). Bede has 'prope fluuium Winued'.
² *HE* iii. 24. This annal avoids the errors of ASC ABCE in speaking of Peada succeeding to the kingdom of the Mercians, and does not adopt EF's date of 654 for the
battle.
³ *HE* iii. 24. The death of Peada is entered under 656 in ASC EF and 657 in A(B)C.
JW may have inferred the date from Bede.

Edwin and Oswald, of the Northumbrians, went to Bernicia, when he had drawn up thirty legions under as many most renowned commanders to attack Oswiu. Oswiu and his son Alchfrith had only one legion, but, trusting in Christ their leader, they went to meet him in a place called *Winwædfeld*.[1] When battle was joined the pagans were put to flight and slain; almost all the kings' thirty commanders, who had come as auxiliaries, perished; among whom was killed Æthelhere, brother of their King Anna, and his successor in the same kingdom, himself the author of the war. His brother Æthelwald succeeded him in the kingdom. Then King Oswiu, for the victory he had been awarded, offered to God twelve estates for the construction of monasteries, and his daughter Ælfflæd, to be consecrated to Him in perpetual virginity. She entered the monastery called Hartlepool, then governed by Abbess Hild. King Oswiu ended this war in the area of Leeds on 15 November in the thirteenth year of his reign, and he converted the Mercians to the faith of Christ. Under him, the Irishman Diuma, whom we have mentioned before, was appointed the first bishop in the kingdom of the Mercians, of Lindsey, and of the Middle Angles. The second was Ceollach of Irish descent. The same king ruled that race and the other peoples of the southern kingdoms for three years, and subdued the Picts to the rule of the Angles, and gave the kingdom of the South Mercians to Penda's son Peada, his kinsman.[2]

[656] King Peada, betrayed by his own wife, was slain at the Easter feast itself, most wickedly.[3]

[658] Cenwealh, king of the West Saxons, fought the Britons at *Peonnan* and put them to flight as far as the Parret.[4] The blessed Abbess Hild began to build a monastery in a place called *Streonæshealch*, in which King Oswiu's daughter was first a learner, and then a teacher, of the life of the Rule. Her mother, Queen Eanflæd, built a monastery called Gilling in the place where King Oswine, the son of her father's cousin, King Osric, was unjustly

---

[4] ASC A(B)CE refer here to Cenwealh's exile in East Anglia, which JW had already mentioned under 645 and 648.

est iniuste, *monasteri*um *quod Ingetlingum dicitur* construxit, et *Trumhere Dei* uirum *occisi regis propinquu*m ibi abbatem constituit.[1]

[**659**] (xix[*a*]) 681 *Aduersus regem Osuuiu duces gentis Merciorum, Immin, Eaba et Eadberht, rebellauere, leuato in regem Wlfere filio Pendan adolescente quem occultum seruauere, sicque cum suo rege | Christo gaudebant seruire.*[2] *Idem rex habuit primum episcopum prefatum Trumhere,*

p. 262

$$[C^3BP]$$
[*b*]defuncto iam Ceollah presule,[*b*]

secundum Iaruman, tertium Ceaddan, .iiii. Winfridum.[3]

[**660**] (xx) 682 Rex Cenuualh Westsaxonicam *prouinciam in duas parrochias diui*sit et episcopo Wine *in ciuitate Wenta sedem episcopatus tribuit, unde Agilbertus* episcopus *grauiter offensus* in *Galliam rediit et episcopatu*m *Parisiace ciuitatis accep*it.[4] *Rex Ecfriđ*, Osuuiu regis filius, *Æđeldryđam Anne regis Orientalium Anglorum filiam* accepit coniugem.[5]
[*c*]Clotharius filius Clodouei.[*c*6]

[**661**] (xxi) 683 Cuthred, Cuiccelmi regis filius nepos uidelicet Cynegilsi regis et regum Cenuualh et Centuuini fratruelis, et Cenbryht subregulus, Ceaulini scilicet regis pronepos et pater Ceaduualle regis, obierunt.[7] Wlfere Merciorum rex prius Æscesdun deuastauit[8] et postmodum Wectam insulam cepit quam regi Australium Saxonum Ætheluuoldo,[*d*9] cuius patrinus exstitit, et Mauorum[*e*] *prouinciam in gente Occidentalium Saxonum* dedit. Finan

---

[*a*] .xviii. C   [*b–b*] defuncto . . . presule] *interlin.* C[3], *om.* HL   [*c–c*] Clotharius . . . Olod. *add. mg.* C (*different small hand, just possibly* C[3]), Clotharius filius Clodouei (Clodoueus H) rex Francorum .xxi. (*om.* L) HL, *see App.* B *for addition at line-end* B[1], Clotarius filius Clodouei rex Francorum *possibly over erasure* P.   [*d*] quia eum de baptismo excepit *add.* B[5]   [*e*] Meanuariorum HE iv. 13

---

[1] HE iii. 24. Bede's date for the construction of Whitby would seem to be 657 ('post biennium', sc. after Winwæd).
[2] Wulfhere's rebellion and accession, which is dated 657 by ASC A(B)C and 656 by EF, was three years after Winwæd according to Bede. As JW dates Winwæd 655, 659 is too late.
[3] HE iii. 24. Trumhere succeeded on Ceollach's resignation not on his death, and this interlineation may be an inference from GP iv. 172 (p. 307).

slain, and set up as abbot Trumhere, a man of God and a relative of the slain king.[1]

[659] The leaders of the Mercians, Immin, Eaba, and Eadberht, rebelled against King Oswiu, raised to the kingship Wulfhere, Penda's young son, whom they had kept hidden, and so they rejoiced in serving Christ with their king.[2] That king's first bishop
                    after the death of Bishop Ceol-
                    lach,
was the Trumhere mentioned above, his second Jaruman, his third Chad, and his fourth Winfrith.[3]

[660] King Cenwealh divided the West Saxon kingdom into two dioceses and awarded the episcopal seat in the city of Winchester to Bishop Wine, at which Bishop Agilbert, seriously offended, returned to Gaul and received the bishopric of the city of Paris.[4] King Ecgfrith, King Oswiu's son, married Æthelthryth, daughter of Anna, king of the East Angles.[5]

   Clothar, Clovis's son.[6]

[661] Cuthred, King Cwichelm's son (that is King Cynegils' grandson, and nephew of the kings Cenwealh and Centwine), and the under-king Cenberht (that is, the great-grandson of King Ceawlin and father of King Ceadwalla), died.[7] Wulfhere, king of the Mercians, first laid waste Ashdown,[8] and then seized the Isle of Wight, which he gave to Æthelwalh,[9] king of the South Saxons, to whom he was godfather, and the area of Meanware among the

---

[4] *HE* iii. 7. JW must have derived his date for the establishment of Wine and the withdrawal of Agilbert from ASC A(B)E 660, C (apparently 659), though he omits ASC's assignation of three years to the episcopacy of Wine.

[5] *HE* iv. 19 (17). The date for this marriage was probably calculated from information in *HE* and ASC.

[6] Norman Annals. *AU, ASN* (659), *AG* (654) all record the succession of Chlothar, *AG* naming two other joint successors. Chlothar III 657–73.

[7] The deaths of Cuthred and Cenberht are recorded by ASC A(B)CE after the battle of *Posentesbyrig*, which is omitted by JW. JW's description of Cenberht as 'subregulus' (against ASC's 'king') may reflect Cenwealh's position as chief king. The family relationships here accord with those described in ASC 641, 648, 676, and 685 and with genealogies, though they are not given under 661 in ASC.

[8] 'Æscesdun deuastauit' may reflect ASC BC 'on Æscesdune' or E 'of Æscesdune' against A 'oþ Æscesdune'.

[9] Æthelwalh is the name given by Bede and Stephanus, and JW's Æthelwold (here and in 685) comes from ASC ABCE.

episcopus Norðanhymbrorum obiit cui Colman *et ipse a Scottia missus, succe*ssit.*[a1]*

[C³BP]

[b]Defuncto Ithamar Hrofensi episcopo, *successit Damianus a Deusdedit archi*presule *constitutus.[b2]*

[663] (xxiii) 685   *[c]Constantinus post aliquot annos uenit Romam .v. die mensis Iulii, feria .iiii., indictione sexta. Tunc optulit dominico die super altare sancti Petri pallium auro textum, et* cum *toto exercitu cum cereis ecclesiam intrauit. Hoc uero factum est per indictionem sextam anno .xxiii. imperii* illius. *Postquam* uero *optulit pallium mansit in Roma diebus .xii. Inde indictione .vii. Siciliam ingressus est, in qua mansit usque ad indictionem duodecimam.[c3]*

[664] (xxiiii) 686   *Tricesimo* anno *episcopatus Scottorum quem gesserunt in prouincia* Norðanhymbrorum ac *.xxii. anno[d] regni Osuuiu regis,[4] mota questione* in eadem prouincia *de pasca uel tonsura uel aliis rebus ecclesiasticis, dispositum est ut in monasterio quod dicitur Streoneshalh cui tunc Hild abbatissa prefuit synodus fieri deberet. Venerunt* autem *illo reges Osuuiu* et Alhfrid filius eius qui regi Oiðeluualdo, regis Osuualdi filio, in regnum successit,[5] *episcop*us *Colman cum clericis suis, Ægilbertus* Westsaxonum episcopus *cum Agathone et Wilfrido presbiteris, Cedd Orientalium* Saxonum *episcopus, Hild abbatissa cum suis.* Qui multum inter se confligentes tandem *maiores una cum mediocribus, abdicata minus perfecta* Scottorum *institutione, ad ea que meliora cognouerant sese transferre festinabant.[6] Finito conflictu ac soluta* questione, *Agilbertus domum* regreditur, *Cedd, relictis Scottorum uestigiis, ad suam sedem rediit,[7] Colman unanimi intentione catholicorum superatus, ad suos* Scottiam *reuertitur.[8]*

[a-a] et . . . successit] *written over erasure* C¹   *[b-b]* Defuncto . . . constitutus] *add. over erasure and running into 662* C³, *runs into 662 B, om.* HL   *[c-c]* Constantinus . . . duodecimam] *under 656-62 (N)*   *[d]* anni H, *om.* L

---

[1] HE iv. 13, iii. 25. The year of Finan's death is probably inferred from the statement in *HE* iii. 26 that Colman had been bishop for three years before his departure after Whitby.

[2] GP i. 72 (p. 135). For a discussion of the inadequate evidence for the dates of the archiepiscopacy of Deusdedit and for the succession of Damian, see Harrison, *Framework*, pp. 93-4.

people of the West Saxons. Finan, bishop of the Northumbrians, died and Colman, himself sent by the Irish, succeeded him.[1]

> On the death of Ithamar, bishop of Rochester, Damian succeeded, being appointed by Archbishop Deusdedit.[2]

[663] After some years Constans came to Rome on Wednesday 5 July, in the sixth indiction. Then, on the Sunday, he presented on St Peter's altar a pallium woven with gold, and entered the church with his whole army bearing candles. This took place during the sixth indiction in the twenty-third year of his reign. He remained in Rome for twelve days after offering the pallium. Then, in the seventh indiction, he went to Sicily, where he remained until the twelfth indiction.[3]

[664] In the thirtieth year of the Irish episcopate exercised in the kingdom of the Northumbrians, and in the twenty-second year of King Oswiu's reign,[4] the question was raised in that kingdom concerning Easter, the tonsure, and other ecclesiastical matters, and it was decided that a synod should be held in the monastery called *Streonæshealch*, then ruled by Abbess Hild. To it came the kings Oswiu and Alchfrith (his son, who succeeded Oethelwald, King Oswald's son, to the kingdom);[5] Bishop Colman with his clergy; Agilbert, bishop of the West Saxons, with the priests Agatho and Wilfrid; Cedd, bishop of the East Saxons, and Abbess Hild with her followers. Great was their debate until, finally, all, great and small, abandoned the less perfect practices of the Irish and lost no time in transferring their allegiance to that which they had found to be better.[6] When the dispute was ended and the question solved, Agilbert returned home; Cedd, having abandoned the Irish practices, returned to his own see;[7] Colman, overcome by the unanimous determination of the Catholics, returned to his own people in the land of the Irish.[8] After his return home, Tuda

---

[3] Mar.   [4] *HE* iii. 26.

[5] JW clearly implies that Alchfrith, successor to Oethelwald, was king of Deira. Neither Bede nor Stephanus says so explicitly.

[6] *HE* iii. 25.   [7] *HE* iii. 26.   [8] *HE* iv. 1.

Quo *patriam reuerso, suscepit pro* eo *pontificatum Norðanhymbrorum Tuda, sed permodico tempore ecclesiam regens. Abbas monaster*ii *quod uocatur Mailros, Eata, uir reuerentissimus,* ^aqui Hrypensis monasterii fundator, rogatu regis Alhfridi, prius extitit, *abbatis iure Lindisfarnens*ibus *fratribus prepositus est,*[1] et beatum Cuthberhtum de Mailrosensi monasterio *ad insulam Lindisfarnensem transtulit.*[2] *Eodem anno facta e*st *eclypsis solis die* .iii. *mensis*^a *Maii hora* quasi .x. *diei.* Mox *subita pestilentie lues* secuta est, *qua sacerdos Domini Tuda de mundo raptus est.*[3] *Alhfrid rex*[4] *cum consilio atque consensu patris sui Osuuiu*[5] uenerabilem *presbiterum* et abbatem Hrypensis monasterii^b *Wilfridum ad regem Galliarum*[4] mittens *episcopum sibi rogauit ordinari cum esset circiter* .xxx. *annorum.*[5] *At ille misit eum ordinandum ad Agilbertum, qui, relicta Brytannia, Parisiace ciuitatis factus erat episcopus*[4] *cum quo et alii* .xi. *episcopi ad dedicationem antistitis conuenientes, multum honorifice ministerium impleuerunt.*[5] *Deusdedit,* .vi. ab Augustino archiepiscopus, *obiit* .ii. *iduum Iuliarum. Sed et Erconbert rex Cantuariorum eodem* anno *ac die defunctus, Ecgberto filio sedem regni reliquit.*[6] Wilfrido *adhuc in transmarinis partibus demorante*, consecratus est in episcopatum Eboraci a Wine ciuitatis Wentane presule, iussu regis Osuuiu, *monasterii quod Leastingaig* dicitur *abbas*, sancti pontificis *Ceddi* germanus, *Ceadda* uir sanctus.[7] *Deo dilecta mater* Bercinganensis monasterii Æthelburga *prima eiusdem cenobii abbatissa, mire sanctitatis uiri Erconuualdi futuri Lundonie ciuitatis episcopi germana,* .v. *iduum Octobrium* die *carnis ergastulo est educta. Cuius talem fuisse constat uitam ut nemo qui eam nouerit dubitare debeat quin ei de hac uita exeunti celestis patrie patuerit ingressus.*[8] Cui *successit in offici*um *abbatisse Deo* dilecta *famula Hil⟨d⟩ilið nomine.*[9] Paulo post Cedd

---

^{a-a} qui . . . mensis] *written over erasure and extending into mg.* C^a   ^b *in small letters at line-end* C

---

[1] *HE* iii. 26. That Alchfrith founded Ripon and that Eata was abbot could have been inferred from *HE* and from Bede's prose *Vita Cuthberti*, c. vii.

[2] *HE* iv. 27 (25). 'Et beatum . . . monasterio' (which may have been added during a rewriting by C², who contributed information and phrases from *HDE*), could have been derived from *HDE* i. 6 (i. 26), which itself relied on *HE* iv. 27.

[3] *HE* iii. 27. ASC A(B)CEF gives the year.   [4] *HE* iii. 28.   [5] *HE* v. 19.

[6] *HE* iv. 1. ASC A(B)CEF gives the year of Deusdedit's death.

[7] *HE* iii. 28. JW seems to have interpreted *HE* as indicating Chad's consecration in 664.

[8] *HE* iv. 8. Whereas JW's day for Æthelburg's death could have been taken from a calendar, the year is difficult to reconcile with the charter (S 1171 *BCS* 81) of Hodilred

received the episcopacy of the Northumbrians in his place, but
ruled the church for a very short time. The most reverend man
Eata, abbot of the monastery called Melrose, who had earlier
founded (at King Alchfrith's request) the monastery of Ripon, was
put in charge of the brethren at Lindisfarne as abbot,[1] and transferred the blessed Cuthbert from the monastery of Melrose to the
island of Lindisfarne.[2] In the same year there was a solar eclipse
on 3 May, at about 4 p.m. It was immediately followed by a sudden and disastrous plague, by which the Lord's priest Tuda was
taken from this world.[3] King Alchfrith,[4] on the advice and consent
of his father Oswiu,[5] sent Wilfrid, the venerable priest and abbot
of the monastery of Ripon, to the king of the people of Gaul,[4]
asking that he should be ordained his bishop. Wilfrid was then
about thirty years old.[5] And the king sent Wilfrid for ordination
to Agilbert, who, after leaving Britain, had become bishop of the
city of Paris.[4] Agilbert and eleven other bishops came to the episcopal consecration and performed the service with great
ceremony.[5] Deusdedit, the sixth archbishop after Augustine, died
on 14 July. Earconberht, king of the people of Kent, also died on
the same day in the same year, leaving his throne to his son Ecgberht.[6] As Wilfrid was still abroad, the holy man Chad, brother of
the holy bishop Cedd, and abbot of the monastery called Lastingham, was consecrated bishop of York by Wine, bishop of Winchester, at the command of King Oswiu.[7] Æthelburg, the beloved
of God, mother of the convent of Barking, first abbess of the same
convent, sister of that man of wonderful holiness, Eorcenwald, the
future bishop of London, was released from the prison of the flesh
on 11 October. It is agreed that her life was such that no one who
knew her should doubt that the door of the heavenly kingdom
stood open for her as she departed this life.[8] God's beloved servant, Hildilith by name, succeeded her in the office of abbess.[9]

(Oedelræd) to Hedilburg, abbess of a monastery called Beddanhaam (usually taken as
referring to Æthelburg of Barking), and which, if genuine, could be dated after c.680.
JW's reference to Hildilith, Æthelburg's successor, under 675 is from an addition based
mainly on GP, which refers to events both before and after 675.
[9] HE iv. 10. Though Hildilith was apparently still alive c.716 (when Eadburg, abbess
of Thanet, mentions her in a letter to Boniface (Die Briefe des heiligen Bonifatius und
Lullus, ed. M. Tangl (MGH Epp. sel. i, Berlin, 1916, repr. 1955), no. 15)), Bede's statement that she presided over the monastery until she was extremely old makes her succession as abbess in 664 just possible.

episcopus Orientalium Saxonum monasterium suum Leastingaig adiit *ibidem*que *corporis infirmitate tactus* .vii. kalendarum Nouembrium die obiit.[1] Rege Eastanglorum Atheluualdo defuncto, successit Aldulfus cuius mater Heresuitha, soror sancte Hilde abbatisse, quarum pater Hereric, cuius pater Eadfrith,[2] cuius pater Eduuine.[3] Boisilus sullimium uirtutum monachus, Mailronensis |

p. 263 cenobii prepositus, uir prophetico spiritu plenus, sacerdos Dei dilectus, letali morbo pressus, *perpetue lucis gaudi*a conscendit.[4] *Rex Orientalium Saxonum Sighe*re *cum sua parte populi ad apostasiam conuersus est, quod ubi rex* Merciorum *Wlfe*re *comperit, Iaruman episcopum, successo*rem *Trumhere, ad corrigendum errorem misit. Porro Sebbi socius et coheres regni eiusdem fidem perceptam cum suis omnibus seruauit.*[5]

[665] (xxv) 687 *Ciclus decennouenalis .viii. incipit indictione .viii.*[6]

Benedictus cognomento Biscop *tempore Vitaliani pape* secundo Romam adiit, et *post menses aliquot Lirinensem insulam* uenit, monachis se dedens attonsus est et *bienn*io sub abbatis regimine Deo regulari militauit tramite.[7]

[666] (xxvi) 688 *ᵃ*De sancto Aldelmo. Sanctus Aldelmus Melduni in ecclesia apostolorum Petri et Pauli abbas ordinatur*ᵇ* a Leutherio*ᵇ* Wessaxonum quarto episcopo.*ᵃ*[8]

[C³BP]
ᶜDe Licedfeld. *Licedfeld est uilla exigua in pago Stæffordensi*

ᵃ⁻ᵃ De sancto . . . episcopo] *mg. alongside 665–7 C³, incorporates at opening of 666 without heading* De sancto Aldelmo *HL, incorporates (without heading) and with 666 n. c at 668 n. e B, mg. alongside 666 P³*   *ᵇ⁻ᵇ* a Leutherio] a beato Leutherio *HL*

ᶜ De Licedfeld . . . opera noua (p. 116)] *mg. alongside 667–70 immediately below 666 n. a C³, om. HL, incorporated (without headings) at 668 n. e B, mg. alongside 666–7 P³*

---

[1] *HE* iii. 23. JW probably inferred the year of Cedd's death from Bede and possibly derived the day from a calendar.

[2] The statement that Hereric was the son of Eadfrith, which is also found in JW *Northum. Accounts* 6, is wrong, and probably rests on the rendering of the 'nepos' in Bede's description of Hild as 'filia nepotis Eduuini regis uocabulo Hererici' (*HE* iv. 23 (21)) as 'grandson' and not 'nephew.'

[3] The date of Aldwulf's accession is not precisely recorded by Bede or ASC but could have been calculated from Bede's statement that the council of Hatfield (Sept. 679) met in his seventeenth year.

[4] Bede, *Vita Cuthberti*, c. 8. JW's date for Boisil's death is a natural inference from Bede's words in this chapter 'morbo pestilentiae quo tunc plurimi per Brittaniam longe lateque deficiebant, correptus est'.

Shortly afterwards Cedd, bishop of the East Saxons, went to his own monastery of Lastingham, and there, stricken with physical weakness, he died on 26 October.[1] On the death of Æthelwald, king of the East Angles, Aldwulf succeeded. His mother was Hereswith, sister of the holy abbess Hild. Their father was Hereric, whose father was Eadfrith,[2] whose father was Edwin.[3] Boisil, a monk of the highest virtue, prior of the monastery of Melrose, a man full of the prophetic spirit, a priest beloved of God, was afflicted by a fatal illness, and ascended to the joys of the eternal light.[4] Sighere, king of the East Saxons, apostasized with his part of the people. When Wulfhere, king of the Mercians, learnt of this, he sent Bishop Jaruman, successor of Trumhere, to correct the error. But Sebbi, his companion and coheir in that kingdom, with his people, kept the faith he had received.[5]

[665] The eighth nineteen-year cycle begins in the eighth indiction.[6]

Benedict, surnamed Biscop, went to Rome a second time in the reign of Pope Vitalian and, after some months, went to the island of Lérins. He attached himself to the monks, received the tonsure, and for two years strove for God in the regular life under the authority of the abbot.[7]

[666] Concerning St Aldhelm. St Aldhelm was ordained abbot of Malmesbury in the church of the Apostles Peter and Paul by Leuthere, fourth bishop of the West Saxons.[8]

Concerning Lichfield. Lichfield is a small township in the

---

[5] *HE* iii. 20. JW's date for the East Saxon relapse into heathenism is probably inferred from Bede's 'eodem tempore' at the opening of this chapter, which refers to the sending of Wighard to Rome and from the association of the apostasy with the plague.

[6] Mar.

[7] Bede, *Hist. abbat.*, c. 2. JW's date for Biscop's second visit may have been based on the statements in Bede that Biscop made his return journey from Rome in the company of Theodore (newly consecrated in 668), after spending some months in Rome and two years in Lérins (*Hist. abbat.*, c. 3 and *HE* iv. 1).

[8] That Aldhelm was ordained abbot at Malmesbury by Leuthere is implied in *GP* v. 199 (p. 347), but *GP* v. 231 (p. 385) dates this supposed ordination to 674.

*longe a frequentia urbium,
nemorosa circa regio. Ibi sanctus
Ceadda sed*em habuit *et obiit.*[1]
De Legecestra. *Legecestra est
uilla antiqua in Mediterraneis
Anglis a Legra fluuio preter-
fluente sic uocata.*[2]
De Dorceceastra. *Doreecestra
est uilla in pago Oxenofordensi
exilis et infrequens, maiestas
tamen ecclesiarum magna seu
ueteri opera* ⟨seu⟩[a] *noua.*[b3]

Wine ciuitatis Wentane episcopus, a *rege* Cenuualcho de suo
presulatu *pulsus, ad regem Merciorum Wlfer*e sec*essit et ab eo
acquisita sede ciuitatis Lundonie, eius episcopus mansit usque ad ter-
minum uite sue.*[4]

[667] (xxvii) 689 *Reges Anglorum nobilissimi, Osuuiu prouincie
Norðanhymbrorum et Ecgberht Cantuuariorum, cum consensu sancte
ecclesie gentis Anglorum presbiterum nomine Wihardum, de clero Deusdedit* archi*episcopi, antistitem ordinandum Romam miserunt. Verum
ille Romam perueniens, priusquam consecrari in episcopatum posset,
morte prereptus est.*[5] *Ceadda* presul Eboracensis .iii. *annis ecclesiam
sublimiter*[c] re*xit, dehinc ad monasterii sui curam quod est in Leastin-
ga*ig *secessit, accipiente Wilfrido episcopatum totius Norðanhymbrorum
prouincie.*[6]

[C³BP]
[d]Berhtgils, qui et Bonifacius, .iii.
East Anglorum episcopus obiit
cui Bisi uir uenerandus
successit.[d7]

---

[a] *om C³BP*   [b] *see above, p, 114 n. c*   [c] *om. HL*   [d–d] Berhtgils . . . suc-
cessit] *add. at end of annal* C³, *om. HL*

---

[1] *GP* iv. 172 (p. 307).   [2] *GP* iv. 176 (p. 311).   [3] *GP* iv. 177 (p. 311).
[4] *HE* iii. 7. JW's date for Wine's expulsion from Wessex and acquisition of London
does not agree with the 663 implied by ASC. The evidence on which it is based is
difficult to assess.

district of Stafford, far from
the bustle of cities, surrounded
by wooded country. There St
Chad had his seat and died.[1]

Concerning Leicester. Leicester is an ancient township of
the Middle Angles, which is so
named from the river *Legra*
which flows through it.[2]

Concerning   Dorchester.
Dorchester is a small township
with few inhabitants in the
county of Oxford, but with
many very splendid churches
and old and new buildings.[3]

Wine, bishop of Winchester, was driven from his bishopric by
King Cenwealh, and withdrew to Wulfhere, king of the Mercians;
receiving from him the see of London, he remained its bishop
until the end of his life.[4]

[667] The most noble kings of the English, Oswiu of the kingdom
of the Northumbrians and Ecgberht of the people of Kent, with
the agreement of the holy church of the English people, sent a
priest called Wigheard, one of Archbishop Deusdedit's clerics, to
Rome for consecration as a bishop. But on his arrival at Rome he
was snatched away by death before he could be consecrated
bishop.[5] Chad, bishop of York, ruled the church gloriously for
three years, then he retired to the care of his own monastery Lastingham, and Wilfrid was made bishop of the whole kingdom of
the Northumbrians.[6]

Berhtgils, also known as Boniface, third bishop of the East
Angles, died. The venerable
man Bisi succeeded him.[7]

[5] *HE* iii. 29. When the two kings decided to choose a new archbishop is not stated
in *HE*: 667 is compatible with a Canterbury vacancy of 'non pauco tempore' (*HE* iv. 1)
whether Deusdedit died in 663 or 664.

[6] *HE* v. 19. JW, who wrongly recorded Chad's consecration under 664, here brings
his 3-year episcopacy to an end. It is likely that Chad was deposed in 669.

[7] This addition is incorrect, being contrary to *HE* iii. 20, iv. 5.

[668] (xxviii) 690 Biscop qui et Benedictus tertio Romam uenit. Quo *tempore erat Rome monachus Theodorus, Tharso Cilicie natus, seculari et ecclesiastica philosophia predit*us, *Grece et Latine* sufficienter *instructus, probus moribus, anno*rum *.lxvi.*[a]

[HL]	[C³B]
[b]Hunc *die .vii. kal.*	[c]Hunc *.vii. kal.*
Aprilium, dominica[b]	*Aprilium die dominica*

ordinatum archi*episcopum*, Biscopo, *quia* uir *sapien*s erat ac strenuus, papa Vitalianus *Brytanni*am perducendum simul et *abbat*em *commendauit Adrian*um.[1]

Constantinus imperator,[d] undecima *indictione, in Sicilia a suis in balneo occisus est quintodecimo die mensis Iulii, et non longe post Vitalianus papa obiit .vi. kalend. Februarii.*[ce]

Romanorum sexagesimus .viii. Constantinus[2] *filius Constantini superioris regis regnauit annis decem et septem usque in annum sexcentesimum septuagesimum .iiii. post passionem.*[3]

[669] (i) 691 *Adeodatus*[4] *septuagesimus .vi. papa post Petrum annis .iiii., mensibus duobus et obiit .vi. kal. Iulii.*[5]

Archiepiscopus Theodorus *die .vi. kalendarum Iuniarum, dominica,* Cantiam *uenit*[6] et Benedict*o,* qui et Biscop, *monasterium beati* [f]Petri apostoli abba*tis*[f] *iure regendum* dedit.[7] *Mox peragrata insula tota, locis opportunis episcopos ordina*uit et *ordinationem* Ceadde *denuo catholica ratione consummauit. In ciuitate etiam Hrofi, ubi defuncto Damiano episcopatus iamdiu cessauerat, Putta uirum ecclesiasticis disciplinis institutum ordinauit*[6] et non multo post *mortuo Iarumanno ac rege Wlfe*re *pet*ente et *rege Osuui*u *concedente iussit Ceadda*n *Merciorum simul et Lindisfarorum* pontificatum suscipere. *Ille iussis obsecundauit, magnaque uite perfectione susceptum* ministerium *administrare curauit. Cui* [g]*etiam rex*[g] Wlfe*re terram .l.*[h] *familiarum ad construendum monasterium in loco qui dicitur Ad Bearuwe donauit.*[8]

---

[a] *at line-end extending into mg. C³,* .lxvi. etatis *HLP*   [b–b] hunc die . . . dominica] hunc die .vii. kalendarum Aprilium die dominica *P*   [c–c] Hunc . . . Februarii] *written over erasure C³*   [d] om. HL   [e] 666 nn. a, c *incorporated here B*   [f–f] Petri . . . abbatis] *om., interlin. by 16th-c. hand and written in lower mg. with addition of* iu(re) *by C³ in C,* Petri apostoli extra murum *interlin. above* beati *B¹?, interlin. P³*   [g–g] etiam rex] rex etiam *HL*   [h] quinquaginta *interlin. above numeral* .l. *C¹*

[668] Biscop, also known as Benedict, visited Rome a third time. At that time there was at Rome a monk, Theodore, born at Tarsus in Cilicia, renowned for secular and ecclesiastical learning, well instructed in Greek and Latin, of upright conduct, aged sixty-six. Pope Vitalian ordained him archbishop on Sunday, 26 March, and entrusted Biscop, since he was a wise and energetic man, with taking him to Britain together with Abbot Hadrian.[1]

The Emperor Constans was killed in the bath by his own men in Sicily on 15 July, in the eleventh indiction, and Pope Vitalian died not long after on 27 January.

Constantine,[2] son of Constans, the former emperor, reigned as the sixty-eighth emperor of the Romans, for seventeen years up to the 674th year after the Passion.[3]

[669] Adeodatus,[4] the seventy-sixth pope after Peter, reigned four years, two months, and died on 26 June.[5]

Archbishop Theodore reached Kent on Sunday, 27 May,[6] and gave Benedict, also known as Biscop, the monastery of St Peter the Apostle to govern as abbot.[7] He then went through the whole island, and ordained bishops in suitable places, and reordained Chad according to Catholic practice. Furthermore, in the city of Rochester, where, after the death of Damian, the bishopric had long been vacant, he ordained Putta, a man well grounded in the teaching of the church,[6] and, not much later, on the death of Jaruman, he ordered, at King Wulfhere's request, and with King Oswiu's agreement, that Chad should receive the bishopric of the Mercians together with that of the people of Lindsey. Chad did as he was bid and with great holiness of life took pains to administer the charge he had received. In addition, King Wulfhere gave him fifty hides of land for the erection of a monastery in a place called Barrow.[8]

---

[1] *HE* iv. 1 and Bede, *Hist. abbat.*, c. 3. On the dating of Biscop's second and third visits to Rome see above, p. 115 n. 7
[2] Constantine IV 668-85.   [3] Mar.
[4] Adeodatus II 672-6.   [5] Mar.   [6] *HE* iv. 2.
[7] Bede, *Hist. abbat.*, c. 3.
[8] *HE* iv. 3. Stephanus (*Vita Wilfridi*, c. 14) asserted that when Wilfrid was at Ripon (667-9) he was often invited by Wulfhere to perform 'officia diuersa episcopalia'. This might be an argument for assigning the death of Jaruman to sometime between 667 and 669. Jaruman was alive when part of the East Saxon kingdom relapsed into heathenism (*HE* iii. 20), and there is no means of deciding between 667, 668, and 669 as the year of his death.

[670] (ii) 692   *Osuuiu rex Northanhymbrorum, pressus infirmitate, anno etatis sue quinquagesimo octauo die .xv. kalendarum Martiarum* mortem obiit et *Ecgfridum filium regni* *"heredem reliquit.*[a1] *Leutherium*, Agilberti Parisiace ciuitatis episcopi *nepotem*, rex Cenuualh et Occidentales Saxones *rogauerunt Theodorum, arciepiscopum Doruuernensis ecclesie, sibi antistitem consecrari. Qui consecratus* in Wenta *ciuitate, .vii. annis episcopatum solus gessit.*[2]

Sarraceni[b] *Siciliam inuadunt qui, preda nimia secum ablata, mox Alexandriam redeunt.*[3]

[671] (iii) 693   Auium strages facta est permaxima.[4] Venerabilis abbas Benedictus, qui et Biscop, *ubi duobus annis monasterio beati Petri apostoli* abbatis iure preesset archipresulis Theodori licentia *tertio de Britannia Romam* profectus est.[5] Cui in monasterii regimen successit Adrianus abbas cuius supra meminimus, *uir natione Afir, sacris litteris diligenter inbutus, Grece pariter et Latine lingue peritissimus.*[6]

[672] (iiii) 694   *'Ciclus solis incipit .iiii. concurrentibus bissextilibus.'* *Hic Constantinus princeps sextam synodum instituit.*[7]

Kenuualh rex Westsaxonum .xxx. anno regni sui defunctus est, cuius uxor Seaxburh regina secundum Anglicam cronicam uno post illum regnauit anno;[8] | secundum uero Bedam *subreguli regnum inter se diuisum annis circiter .x. tenuerunt.*[9] Regina Norðanhymbrorum *Ætheldryþa multum diu postulans regem* Ecgfridum *ut, relictis seculi curis, in monasterio regi Christo seruire permitteretur, ubi uix aliquando impetrauit, monasterium* sancte *Æbbe abbatisse, uidelicet sancti Osuualdi et Osuuiu regum germane ac Ecgfridi regis amite, intrauit* et *uelamen sanctimonialis habitus* ab

p. 264

---

a–a heredem reliquit] reliquit *H*, reliquit heredem *L*   *b second* r *interlin. C*[1]
c–c Ciclus . . . bissextilibus] *mg. with signe de renvoi C*[1], *after the sentence from Marianus HL, at end of 671 P*

---

[1] *HE* iv. 5. JW omits the genealogy of Oswiu, which is in ASC A(B)C.
[2] *HE* iii. 7. The date for the consecration of Leuthere (F also) and the statement that he held the see for 7 years are in ASC A(B)CE. JW has assumed that Bede's 'in ipsa ciuitate' means Winchester, but Bede's text could mean Canterbury.
[3] Mar.
[4] ASC A(B)CE.

[670] Oswiu, king of the Northumbrians, afflicted by illness, died on 15 February, in his fifty-eighth year, and left his son Ecgfrith heir to his kingdom.[1] King Cenwealh and the West Saxons requested Theodore, archbishop of Canterbury, to consecrate as their bishop Leuthere, nephew of Agilbert, bishop of Paris. When he was consecrated in the city of Winchester, he exercised the episcopal office alone for seven years.[2]

The Saracens invaded Sicily, carried off great booty, and then returned to Alexandria.[3]

[671] There was a very great mortality among the birds.[4] The venerable Abbot Benedict, also known as Biscop, having for two years governed the monastery of the blessed Apostle Peter with abbatial authority, set out a third time from Britain for Rome, with permission from Archbishop Theodore.[5] Abbot Hadrian, whom we mentioned above, succeeded him in the rule of the monastery. He was by birth an African, assiduously learned in sacred literature, and most skilful in Greek and Latin alike.[6]

[672] The solar cycle begins with four concurrents in a bissextile year. This Emperor Constantine organized a sixth synod.[7]

Cenwealh, king of the West Saxons, died in the thirtieth year of his reign. His wife, Queen Seaxburg, ruled for a year after him, according to the English chronicle,[8] but, according to Bede, under-kings held the realm, which they had divided among themselves, for about ten years.[9] Æthelthryth, queen of the Northumbrians, besought King Ecgfrith earnestly, and for a long time, that she might be permitted to leave secular concerns and serve Christ the king in a monastery. When she had in time with difficulty obtained this she entered the monastery of St Æbbe the abbess, the sister of the kings St Oswald and Oswiu, and the aunt of King Ecgfrith, and received the veil of the nun's habit from Bishop

---

[5] Bede, *Hist. abbat.*, cc. 3, 4. The date of Biscop's fourth visit to Rome (his third direct from Britain, that of 668 having been from Lérins) was presumably inferred from Bede. Biscop's dates as abbot of SS. Peter and Paul appear to be 669–71.

[6] *HE* iv. 1.

[7] Mar.

[8] ASC A(B)CEF. ASC A (643) BC (641) and JW *West Saxon Accounts* 11 (as well as JW annal 642) assign 31 years to Cenwealh's reign. Here JW's 30 years could be consistent with his dates for Cenwealh's accession (642) and death (672).

[9] *HE* iv. 12.

*antistite Wilfrido accep*it.[1] *Cum in* Merciorum *prouincia duobus annis ac dimidio* Ceadda episcopus *ecclesiam gloriosissime rexisset, languore corporis tactus, postquam obitum suum dominici corporis et sanguinis perceptione muniuit, .vi. die nonarum Martiarum eterna gaudia petiuit.* Qui dum e mundo transiret *Ecgbert pat*er *reuerentissim*us eius quondam *in Hibernia* condiscipulus *uidit animam Ceddi* episcopi *fratris ipsius cum angelorum agmin*ibus *de celo descendere, et assumpta secum anima eius ad celestia regna redire. In cuius locum ordinauit Theodorus Winfridum diacon*um eius, *cui ipse successerat antistitis.*[2] Roma Benedictus Biscop rediit, et *ingressus Brytanniam patriam gentem solumque in quo natus est* petit, *Ecgfridum transhumbrane* gentis *regem adiit,* qui *confestim terram .lxx. familiarum* ut construeret monasterium *ad ostium Wiri fluminis* illi dedit.[3]

[673] (v) 695   *Conus*[4] *papa .lxxvii.*[a] *anno .i. mensibus .vi.*[5]

*Rex Cantuuariorum Ecgb*ryht, *.ix.* regni sui anno, *mense Iulio, ob*iit *succedente in regnum fratre Hlothere quod ipse annos .xi. et menses .vii. tenuit.*[6] *Die .xxiiii. mensis Septembris indictione prima Theodorus Doruuernensis episcopus, in loco qui dicitur He*ortford, *episcoporum cogit concilium* in quo *Wilfrid Northanhymbrorum gentis episcopus per proprios legatarios* fuit. *Fuerunt et Putta Hrof*ensis *episcopus, Leutherius Occidentalium Saxonum episcopus, Winfrid prouincie Merciorum episcopus,* quibus affuit *Bisi Orientalium Anglorum* episcopus, *successor Bonefacii, cuius supra meminimus,*[7] *uir multe sanctitatis et religionis non* multo ante *a Theodoro ordina*tus, *quo adhuc superstite sed grauissima infirmitate ab administrando episcopatu prohibito, duo sunt pro illo, Aecci et Baduuine consecrati episcopi.*[b8] *In regione que uocatur Elge* beata Ætheldryþa *facta est abbatissa ubi*

---

[a] *.vii. interlin. C*[t]   [b] *685 n. d incorporated here B*

---

[1] iv. 19 (17). The date of Æthelfrith's entry into the monastery is not stated by Bede, but he does say that it took place 12 years after her marriage to Ecgfrith which JW has assigned to 660.

[2] HE iv. 3. JW infers the year of Chad's death from Bede's '2½ years' after his appointment, which JW has dated to 669.

[3] Bede, *Hist. abbat.* c. 4. The foundation of Wearmouth is dated 674 by Bede. JW probably inferred the date of Benedict's return from Rome from the statement that Biscop had intended to visit Cenwealh of Wessex but found him dead.

[4] Donus 676–8.   [5] Mar.

Wilfrid.[1] When Bishop Chad had ruled the church in the province of the Mercians most gloriously for two and a half years, he was stricken with physical weakness; having fortified himself for death by partaking of the Lord's body and blood, he sought eternal joy on 2 March. As he departed this world the most reverend father Ecgberht, once his fellow disciple in Ireland, saw the soul of his brother Bishop Cedd, with crowds of angels, descend from heaven, and return bearing Chad's soul with him to the heavenly kingdom. Theodore ordained in his place Winfrith, the deacon of the bishop he had himself succeeded.[2] Benedict Biscop returned from Rome, and on his arrival in Britain, his homeland, turned his steps to the people and the land where he was born. He approached Ecgfrith, king of the people beyond the Humber, and Ecgfrith at once gave him seventy hides to build a monastery at the mouth of the river Wear.[3]

[673] Donus,[4] the seventy-seventh pope, reigned for one year and six months.[5]

Ecgberht, king of the people of Kent, died in July, in the ninth year of his reign. His brother, Hlothhere, succeeded to the kingdom and held it eleven years and seven months.[6] On 24 September, in the first indiction, Theodore, bishop of Canterbury, summoned a council of bishops in a place called Hertford, at which Wilfrid, bishop of the Northumbrians, was represented by his own deputies. There, also, were Putta, bishop of Rochester, Leuthere, bishop of the West Saxons, and Winfrith, bishop of the Mercians. Present with them was Bisi, bishop of the East Angles, successor of Boniface (whom we mentioned earlier),[7] a man of great sanctity and religion, ordained not long before by Theodore and still alive but kept from carrying out his episcopal duties by a most serious illness. Two men, Æcce and Beaduwine, were consecrated bishops in his place.[8] In the region called Ely, where a monastery had been built, the blessed Æthelthryth was appointed

[6] In *HE* iv. 1, Bede had stated that Ecgberht's reign lasted 9 years. Like Bede, ASC dates his death to 673.

[7] Boniface has not been previously mentioned in the original annals, though C[3] named him in additions to 652 and 667.

[8] *HE* iv. 5. The proximity in Bede's text of the division of the East Anglian bishopric to the synod of Hertford probably led JW to date it to 673.

constructo monasterio uirginum Deo deuotarum mater uirgo et exemplis uite celestis esse cepit et monitis.[a1]

[674] (vi) 696 *Conus papa obiit .iii. idus Aprilis.*[2] [b]*Clodoveo*[3] *Dagoberti filio regni Francorum moderamina gubernante, abbas quidam ecclesie sancti Aniani, que est apud urbem Aurelianam, Leodebodus nomine, construxit monasterium in agro Floriacensi, colligensque ibi plures ad seruiendum Deo monachos, instituit illis abbatem nomine Mummolum. Qui diuina reuelatione premonitus, misit unum de suis monachis, Aiulfum nomine, ad montem Cassinum ut inde sibi deferret sanctissimi corpus Benedicti. Qui ueniens illo ibique pernoctans intempeste noctis silentio ipsum sancti Benedicti sepulchrum ita* c⟨e⟩litus[c] *uidit illustrari acsi densis lampadibus circumfunderetur. Mox reuerenter accessit, et effracto a latere sepulchro, illud exinaniuit, et quicquid ibi repperit, id est ossa sancte Scolastice uirginis sororis sue, in unius sportule sinu recondidit et Floriacum rediit.* [d]*Translatum est igitur uenerabile corpus* sancti *Benedicti a Cassino monte* Floriacum *anno incarnationis Domini .dclxxiiii.*[d] [e]*Computantur a transitu* sancti *Benedicti usque ad obitum pape Gregorii anni .lxviii. et ab obitu pape*[f] *Gregorii usque ad translationem* sancti *Benedicti anni .lxx.*[be4]

Æscuuine secundum Anglicam cronicam Occidentalium Saxonum suscepit regnum, qui fuit Cenfus, qui fuit Cenferð, qui fuit Cuthgils, qui fuit Ceoluulf, qui fuit Cynric, qui fuit Cerdic.[5]

Hibernia insula sanctorum sanctis et mirabilibus perplurimis sullimiter plena habetur.[6]

[g]Biscop *ad ostium Wiri fluminis indictione secunda.*[g7]

[a-a] uite . . . monitis] *written over erasure in text by 16th-c. hand, and in upper mg. by* C[3] C, *et doctrinis extitit* B   [b-b] Clodoueo . . . anni .lxx.] *mg. alongside 673-5* C[3], *incorporated at end of 674 (with order of last two sentences now reversed)* B, *incorporated at end of 673* P   [c] colitus C   [d-d] Translatum . . . dclxxiiii.] *in body of text after 674 n. e* B, *under Constantine IV (668-85)* G   [e-e] Computantur . . . anni .lxx.] *written twice: before 674 n. d in body of annal, and in lower mg. with a sign pointing to before 674 n. c (but this mg. addition has now been erased)* B   [f] om. HL   [g-g] Biscop . . . secunda] *added in compressed writing at end of annal* C[a]?

---

[1] HE iv. 19 (17). Not dated by Bede, this building of Ely is entered under 673 in ASC.

[2] Mar.

[3] Clovis II 638-57.

[4] Hugh of Fleury, pp. 153, 154, and 155. The name Leodebodus does not appear in the Cambridge Corpus MS of Hugh.

abbess, and became, by the examples and precepts of her heavenly life, a virgin mother of the virgins dedicated to God.[1]

[674] Pope Donus died on 11 April.[2] While Clovis,[3] son of Dagobert, was ruling the kingdom of the Franks, an abbot, Leudebod by name, of the church of Saint-Aignan, which is in the city of Orléans, built a monastery in the plain of Fleury, and there assembled many monks to serve God, appointing for them an abbot called Mummolus. He, forewarned by divine revelation, sent one of his monks, called Aigulf, to Monte Cassino to bring back to him thence the body of the most holy Benedict. He arrived there, spent the night there, and in the silent hours of the night saw the very tomb of St Benedict, so lit up from heaven as if it were surrounded by massed torches. He at once approached it reverently, and having broken into the tomb from the side, he emptied it, and put aside whatever else he found there namely the bones of the saint's sister, the virgin St Scholastica, inside a little bag, and returned to Fleury. Thus, therefore, the revered body of St Benedict was translated from Monte Cassino to Fleury in the 674th year of the Incarnation of Our Lord. Sixty-eight years are computed from the death of St Benedict to the death of Pope Gregory, and seventy years from the death of Pope Gregory to the translation of St Benedict.[4]

According to the English Chronicle, Æscwine received the kingdom of the West Saxons. He was the son of Cenfus, son of Cenferth, son of Cuthgils, son of Ceolwulf, son of Cynric, son of Cerdic.[5]

Ireland, isle of saints, was considered sublimely enriched with very many holy miracles.[6]

At the mouth of the river Wear, in the second indiction, Biscop.[7]

---

[5] ASC A(B)CE, E omitting the genealogy.

[6] Mar.

[7] Bede, *Hist. abbat.*, c. 4. This incomplete sentence (presumably on the foundation of Wearmouth) may have been added to remove any misunderstanding which might arise from the reference to King Ecgfrith's grant under 672.

126 CHRONICON IOHANNIS WIGORNENSIS [675

[675] (vii) 697 *Agatho*[1] *papa .lxxviii. annis .ii., mensibus .vii. et obiit .iiii. idus Ianuarii.*[2]

Wlfere rex Merciorum et Æscuuine rex Westsaxonum in loco qui dicitur Bydanheafd pugnauerunt.[3] Eodem etiam anno, ipse*ª* Wlfere, qui regum Merciorum primus fidem et lauacrum sancte regenerationis accepit, et in tota gente sua demoniorum culturam destruxit et penitus eradicauit,*ᵇ* Christique nomen ubique locorum regni sui predicare iussit, et multis in locis ecclesias edificauit, .xvii. anno ex quo regnauit ad uranica regna migrauit. Cuius regina sancta Eormengilda, que Cantuuariorum regis Erconberti sancteque Sexburge regine, Anne regis Orientalium Anglorum filie, sororis uidelicet sancte Ætheldryðe, exstitit filia, peperit ei *ᶜmagnarum uirginem uirtutum sanctam Wereburgam,ᶜ* que, patre defuncto, seculo renuntiauit et habitum sancte conuersationis susceptura genitricis matertere, sancte uidelicet Æðeldrythe, monasterium intrauit in quo*ᵈ* multa, Deo cooperante, miracula patrauit. Cuius sanctitatis famam cum suus patruus rex Æthelredus comperisset, eam quibusdam uirginum Deo deuotarum monasteriis abbatisse iure prefecit, cum quibus et in quibus regulariter uiuens, illisque in omnibus pie consulens, ad uite finem uero regi Christo militauit, ac in uno monasteriorum suorum quod Triccingaham dicitur e seculo migrauit, sicque ad complexum et nuptias sponsi celestis uirgo beata intrauit. Corpus autem illius ad monasterium cui est Heanbyrig uocabulum, ut ipsa uiuens precepit, est delatum et in illo honorifice tumulatum. Quod usque ad tempus quo gens pagana Danorum crudeli cede et tyrannica depopulatione Anglorum uastauerunt prouincias mansit incorruptum. *ᵉ*Fuerunt autem germani regis Wlferi Æthelredus qui post illum sceptra regni gubernauit, Peada, qui ut paucis prelibauimus, Australium Merciorum regnum habuit, Mereuuald, qui in occidentali plaga
p. 265 Merciorum regnum tenuit. | Cui regina sua sancta Eormenbeorga, regis Eormenredi filia, peperit tres filias, sanctam uidelicet Mildburgam, sanctam Mildrytham et sanctam Mildgitham, unumque filium Merefin eximie sanctitatis puerum.[4] *Offensus a*

ª interlin. Cᴵ   *ᵇ* eradificauit *from* edificauit Cᴵ   *ᶜ⁻ᶜ* magnarum . . . Wereburgam] *written over erasure* Cᴵ   *ᵈ* qua HL   *ᵉ this sentence starts on new line although previous half-line is blank* CB

---

[1] Agatho 678–81.   [2] Mar.

[675] Agatho,[1] the seventy-eighth pope, reigned two years and seven months, and died on 10 January.[2]

Wulfhere, king of the Mercians, and Æscwine, king of the West Saxons, fought in a place called *Biedanheafde*.[3] Moreover, in the same year, Wulfhere, who was the first of the kings of the Mercians to receive the faith and the baptism of holy regeneration, and destroyed and completely eradicated the cult of demons among his whole people, ordered the name of Christ to be preached everywhere in his kingdom, and built churches in many places, passed in the seventeenth year of his reign to the heavenly kingdom. His queen St Eormenhild, daughter of Earconberht, king of the people of Kent, and of the blessed Seaxburg (daughter of Anna, king of the East Angles, St Æthelthryth's sister), bore him a virgin of great virtue, St Werburg, who on the death of her father renounced the world to take the habit of the holy monastic life and entered the convent of her mother's aunt, namely of St Æthelthryth, where with God's help she performed many miracles. When her uncle King Æthelred learnt of her reputation for holiness, he set her as abbess over several monasteries of virgins devoted to God; living with them and among them according to the rule, and piously advising them in everything, she strove for Christ, the true king, until the end of her life. She departed this life in one of her monasteries called Threckingham, and so this blessed virgin entered the embrace of, and nuptials with, her heavenly spouse. Her body was borne, as she had ordered in her lifetime, to the monastery called Hanbury, and there buried with honour. There it remained incorrupt until the time when the pagan people of the Danes laid waste the regions of the English with cruel slaughter and savage devastation. These were the brothers of King Wulfhere: Æthelred, who ruled the kingdom with royal sway after him; Peada, who had the kingdom of the South Mercians, as we have indicated briefly; Merewalh, who held the kingdom in the western part of Mercia, whose queen, St Eormenburg, daughter of King Eormenred, bore him three daughters, namely St Mildburg, St Mildthryth, and St Mildgyth, and one son, Merefin, a boy of exceptional sanctity.[4] Archbishop

[3] The battle is entered under 675 in ASC ACE. F joins them in recording the death of Wulfhere.

[4] Some of the information concerning Wulfhere and the Mercian royal family is also found in JW *Mercian Gen.* and *Accounts* 7 as in *GR* i. 76 (i. 78).

*Winfrido Merciorum episcopo per meritum cuiusdam inobedientie Theodorus archiepiscopus eum de episcopatu deposuit, et in loco eius Saxulfum episcopum ordinauit, constructor*em *et abba*tem *monasterii quod dicitur* Burh *in regione Giruiorum. Depositus uero Winfrið ad monasterium suum* Bearuue *rediit, ibique in optima uitam conuersatione finiuit.*[1] *Tum etiam Orientalibus Saxonibus quibus eo tempore prefuerunt Sebb*e *et Sighere, in ciuitate Lundonia*

[C³BP]
ªdefuncto Ceddª

Erconwaldum *episcopum constituit, ubi predecessor eius* Wine *sedem episcopatus habuit.*[2] *Cuius uiri scilicet* Erconwaldi *et in episcopatu et ante episcopatum uita et conuersatio fertur fuisse sanctissima.*[3] *ᵇ*Hic *fecit duo monasterio, unum sibi,ᵇ ᶜalterum sorori. Suum* Certesie *dicitur, quod amminiculo* Frithewoldi *subreguli opulentia rerum et monachis impleuit; sororis cenobium appellatur* Berkingum*, ubi ipsa primum abbatissa constituitur. Post* Erconwaldum *fuit* Waldherus *et post istum* Incgualdus *ultimus quem* Beda *in* Hystoria Anglorum Lundoniensem *commemorat episcopum. Porro* Æthelburge, *ᵈsancti* Erconwaldi *sorori,ᵈ successit* Hildelith *ad quam sanctus* Aldelm*us scripsit librum de uirgini*tate. *Post* Hildeliðam *extitit* Wlfhild*is abbatissa* Eadgari regis tempore.*ᶜ*[4]

[676] (viii) 698 Agathonis *pape tempore indictione .iiii.ᵉ luna eclipsin pertulit die .xviii. mensis Iunii. Idem etiam papa rogatu Constantini Heraclii et Tiberii piissimorum principum, misit in regiam urbem legatos suos in quibus erat Iohannes, Romane ecclesie tunc diaconus, non longe post episcopus, pro adunatione facienda sanctarum Dei ecclesiarum. Qui benignissime suscepti a reuerentissimo fidei catholice defensore Constantino, iussi sunt, remissis disputationibus philosophicis, pacifico colloquio de fide uera perquirere, datis eis de bibliotheca Constantinopolitana cunctis antiquorum patrum, quos petebant, libellis.*

ª⁻ª Defuncto Cedd] *written in mg. with line through it* C³?, *om.* HL, defuncto Cedda P   *ᵇ⁻ᵇ* Hic . . . sibi] *written at line-end over erasure* C³   *ᶜ⁻ᶜ* alterum . . . tempore] *written mg. with signe de renvoi* C³   *ᵈ⁻ᵈ* sancti . . . sorori] sancti Erconwaldi H, *om.* L   *ᵉ* quinta *with* uel .iiii. *interlin.* (N)

---

[1] *HE* iv. 6; JW substitutes *Burh* for Bede's *Medeshamstede* and *Bearuue* for Bede's *Adbaruae*. Bede does not date Winfrith's deposition. Seaxwulf's see included Lindsey, and his appointment must have preceded the loss of that province to Northumbria in 674. He was in office in 676 when Putta of Rochester took refuge with him (*HE* iv. 12).

Theodore, displeased with Winfrith, bishop of the Mercians, because of some act of disobedience, deposed him from his episcopate, and ordained as bishop in his place Seaxwulf, the founder and abbot of the monastery called Peterborough in the territory of the *Gyrwe*. The deposed Winfrith returned to his own monastery of Barrow and there ended his life in the most pious fashion.[1] Then also, after the death of Cedd, he made Eorcenwald, bishop of the East Saxons (whom Sebbi and Sighere ruled at that time), in the city of London where his predecessor Wine had had his episcopal seat.[2] The life and conduct of this man, that is of Eorcenwald, both during and before his episcopacy, are said to have been most holy.[3] He built two monasteries, one for himself, the other for his sister. His own, which was called Chertsey, he filled with a wealth of possessions, and with monks in the reign of Frithuwald, the under-king. His sister's monastery was called Barking, and there she herself was first established as abbess. Waldhere followed Eorcenwald, and Ingwald followed Waldhere. Ingwald was the last whom Bede mentioned in the *English History* as bishop of London. But Hildelith, for whom St Aldhelm wrote his book *On virginity*, succeeded Æthelburg, sister of St Eorcenwald. After Hildelith, in the time of King Edgar, Wulfhild was abbess.[4]

[676] On 18 June, in the time of Pope Agatho, in the fourth indiction, a lunar eclipse occurred. Also, at the request of the most devout rulers, Constantine, Heraclius, and Tiberius, the same pope sent to the imperial city his legates, among whom was John, then a deacon of the Roman church, not long after a bishop, in order to reconcile God's holy churches. They were received most kindly by Constantine, the most revered defender of the Catholic faith, and ordered to dispense with philosophical disputations and seek the true faith in peaceful discussions; all the books of the ancient fathers which they requested were given them from the library of Constantinople. There were present 150 bishops under

---

[2] Bede links Eorcenwald's appointment to Winfrith's deposition by the words 'tum etiam': this may be the reason for JW's date.

[3] *HE* iv. 6.

[4] *GP* ii. 73 (p. 143). This addition in part repeats the information concerning Barking already given under 664.

Affuerunt autem et episcopi .cl., presidente Georgio patriarcha regie urbis et Antiochie Machario, et c⟨onvi⟩cti,[a] *sunt, qui unam uoluntatem et operationem astruebant in Christo, falsasse patrum catholicorum dicta perplurima. Finito autem conflictu, Georgius correctus est, Macharius uero cum suis sequacibus simul et precessoribus Ciro, Sergio, Honorio, Pirro, Paulo et Petro anathematizatus est, et in locum eius Theophanus abbas de Sicilia Antiochie episcopus est factus. Tantaque gratia legatos catholice pacis comitata est ut Iohannes Portuensis episcopus, qui unus ex illis erat, dominica octauarum pasce missas publicas in ecclesia sancte Sophie coram principe et patriarcha Latine celebraret. Hec est sexta synodus uniuersalis Constantinopoli celebrata, et Greco sermone conscripta, temporibus Agathonis pape, exequente ac residente piissimo principe Constantino intra palatium suum simulque legatis apostolice sedis et episcopis .cl. residentibus. Prima enim .i.*[b] *uniuersalis synodus in Nicea congregata est, contra Arrianum .cccxviii. patrum temporibus Siluestri pape sub Constantino magno. ii. Secunda in Constantinopoli .cl. patrum, contra Macedonium et Eudoxium, temporibus Damasi pape et Gratiani principis, quando Nectarius eidem urbi est ordinatus episcopus. iii. Tertia in Epheso ducentorum patrum, contra Nestorium auguste urbis episcopum sub Theodosio magno principe et papa Celestino. iiii. Quarta in Calcedone patrum .dcxxx., sub Leone papa temporibus Martiani. v. Quinta item in Constantinopoli, temporibus Vigilii pape sub Iustiniano principe contra Theodorum et omnes hereticos. vi. Sexta hec de qua in presenti diximus.*[1]

Benedictus Biscop cum Ceolfrido religioso monacho quarto Romam de Brytannia petit, *epistolam priuilegii* ab *Agathone papa cum licentia, consensu, desiderio, et hortatu regis Ecgfridi acceptam, qua monasterium* suum *tutum ac liberum perpetuo redderetur,* retulit.[2] *Accepit et Iohannem archicantor*em beati *Petri apostoli Britan*niam *perducendum, ut in monasterio suo cursum canendi per ann*um *edoceret.*[3] Æscuuine rex Westsaxonum moritur et Centuuine ei

[a] conuicti] *Mar., interlin. by 16th-c. hand* C, cuncti *CHLBP (N),* uicti *interlin.* L *(?early 13th-c. hand)*   [b] *space before and after* .i. C

[1] Mar.
[2] Bede, *Hist. abbat.,* c. 6. Pope Agatho was consecrated in June 678, and JW's error in dating Biscop's fifth visit to Rome (his fourth direct from Britain) to 676 was presumably caused by Marianus' incorrect dating of the pontificate of Agatho from 675 for three years and seven months.

the presidency of George, patriarch of the imperial city, and Macarios of Antioch, and those who ascribed to Christ one will and energy were proved to have misrepresented a very large number of the statements of the Catholic fathers. When the debate was finished George was corrected but Macarios, with his followers and predecessors, Cyrus, Sergius, Honorius, Pyrrhus, Paul, and Peter, were laid under anathema, and Theophanes, an abbot from Sicily, was made bishop of Antioch. Such favour attended the legates of the Catholic peace that John, bishop of Ostia, who was one of them, celebrated public masses in Latin on the Sunday of the octave of Easter in the church of St Sophia in the presence of the emperor and the patriarch. This was the sixth general council held at Constantinople and recorded in the Greek tongue in the time of Pope Agatho, accomplished and settled by the most pious Emperor Constantine in his own palace, together with the legates of the apostolic see and the 150 bishops. (1) The first general council, of 318 fathers, assembled at Nicaea against Arius in the time of Pope Silvester, under Constantine the Great. (2) The second, of 150 fathers, at Constantinople against Macedonius and Eudoxius in the time of Pope Damasus and the Emperor Gratian, when Nectarius was ordained bishop of the same city. (3) The third, of 200 fathers, at Ephesus, against Bishop Nestorius of the imperial city, at the time of the Emperor Theodosius the Great, and Pope Celestine. (4) The fourth, of 630 fathers, at Chalcedon, under Pope Leo, in the reign of Marcian. (5) The fifth, also at Constantinople, in the time of Pope Vigilius, under the Emperor Justinian, against Theodore and all heretics. (6) This sixth, about which we have here spoken.[1]

Benedict Biscop went to Rome from Britain a fourth time with the devout monk Ceolfrith. With the permission and consent, and at the request and urging, of King Ecgfrith, he brought back a letter of privilege received from Pope Agatho with which he secured for ever the security and liberty of his monastery.[2] He also took John, archcantor of St Peter the Apostle's, and brought him to Britain to teach the liturgical cursus throughout the year in his monastery.[3] Æscwine, king of the West Saxons, died, and Centwine, who was the son of Cynegils, son of Ceol, succeeded

---

[3] *HE* iv. 18 (16). John the archcantor's visit is incorrectly dated; JW must again have been misled by Marianus' incorrect dating of Agatho's pontificate.

succedit qui fuit filius Cynigisli filii Ceoli.[1] *Æthelred rex Merciorum Cantiam uasta*uit, *ciuitatem quoque Hrofi communi clade absum*psit.[2] *Quod ubi Putta eius episcopus comperiit ad Saxuulfum Merciorum* episcopum *diuertit, et, ab eo possessione cuiusdam ecclesie accepta, ibidem in pace uitam finiuit. Pro quo Theodorus Quiccelmum consecrauit episcopum, sed illo post non multum temporis pre inopia rerum ab episcopatu decedente, Gebmundum pro eo substituit antistitem.* Defuncto Westsaxonum episcopo Leutherio, *episcopatu Hæddi functus* est *pro illo in ciuitate Lundonia consecratus a Theodoro.*[3] *a*Sanctus Cuthberhtus *anachoretice contemplationis secreta petiit.*a[4]

[677] (ix) 699   *b*Leo[5] *septuagesimus nonus papa.*[6]

*Anno imperii regis Egcfridi .viii., apparuit mense Augusto stella come*tis.[7] *Quo etiam anno orta inter ipsum regem Egcfridum et reuerentissimum antistitem Wilfridum dissensione*bc | *pulsus est idem antistes a sede sui episcopatus, et duo in locum eius substituti episcopi, Bosa,* monachus reuerendus de monasterio Hild abbatisse, *qui Deirorum, et Eata,* uenerabilis abbas Mailronensis cenobii, *qui Berniciorum, prouinciam gubernaret. Hic in ciuitate Eboraci, ille in Hagustaldensi siue Lindisfarnensi ecclesia cathedram habens episcopalem, ambo de* monachorum collegio *in episcopatus gradum ascciti. Cum quibus et Eaðæd in prouinciam*d *Lindisfarorum quam nuperrime rex Ecgfrid, superato in bello et fugato Wlfere, optinuerat, ordinatur episcopus. Et hunc primum eadem prouincia proprium accepit presulem, secundum Ætheluuine, tertium Eadgarum, quartum Cyne*berhtum. *Habebat enim ante Eaðædum antistitem Saxuulfum, qui etiam Merciorum et Mediterraneorum Anglorum simul episcopus fuit, unde et expulsus de Lindissi in illarum prouinciarum regimine mansit. Ordinati sunt autem Eaðhæd, Bosa et Eata Eboraci ab archiepiscopo Theodoro.*[8] *Pulsus ergo ab episcopatu, Wilfrid Romamque iturus, ubi nauem conscendit, flante Fauonio, Fresiam est pulsus, ubi primus opus euangelicum cepit,*

p. 267

---

a–a Sanctus . . . petiit] *add. mg. with signe de renvoi* C[2]   b–b Leo . . . dissensione] *paler ink, but no trace of erasure* C   c dissensionem H, dissensione *corrected from* dissensionem L   d prouincia HL

---

[1] ASC A(B)CEF (marginal addition), the first three give the genealogy of Centwine.
[2] The date of Æthelred's invasion is in ASC and Bede.
[3] HE iv. 12. Hædde's succession is recorded in ASC A(B)CEF under this year.
[4] HDE i. 7 (i. 28) is probably the source both for the date of Cuthbert's withdrawal and for the italicized text though its first three words were derived from HE iv. 28.

him.[1] Æthelred, king of the Mercians, laid waste Kent.[2] He also destroyed the city of Rochester in the general devastation. When Putta its bishop learnt of it, he went to Seaxwulf, bishop of the Mercians, and, having received from him the grant of a church, he ended his life there in peace. In his place Theodore consecrated Cwichelm bishop, but as he laid aside the bishopric not much later for want of means, Theodore installed in his place the priest Gebmund. On the death of Leuthere, bishop of the West Saxons, Hædde performed the episcopal duties in his place and was consecrated by Theodore in London.[3] St Cuthbert sought the retreat of anchoritic contemplation.[4]

[677] Leo[5] was the seventy-ninth pope.[6]

In August, in the eighth year of the reign of King Ecgfrith, a comet appeared.[7] Also in that year, when dissension had arisen between King Ecgfrith himself and the most reverend Bishop Wilfrid, that same bishop was driven from his episcopal see, and in his place two bishops were substituted, Bosa, a reverend monk from Abbess Hild's monastery, to administer the province of the Deirans, and Eata, the venerable abbot of the monastery of Melrose, to govern that of the Bernicians. The former had his episcopal seat in the city of York, the latter in the church of Hexham or Lindisfarne. Both rose to the episcopal rank from the community of the monks. With them was Eadhæd as well, who was ordained bishop in the province of the people of Lindsey, which King Ecgfrith had gained very recently, after overcoming Wulfhere in battle and putting him to flight. He was the first bishop of its own that province had received; Æthelwine was the second, Edgar the third, Cyneberht the fourth. For, before Eadhæd, it had had Bishop Seaxwulf, who was also bishop of both the Mercians and the Middle Angles, and after his expulsion from Lindsey he remained in charge of those areas. Eadhæd, Bosa, and Eata were ordained by Archbishop Theodore at York.[8] Expelled, then, from his bishopric, Wilfrid set out for Rome, but on boarding ship he was driven by the west wind to Frisia, where he was

---

[5] Leo II 682–3.   [6] Mar.
[7] Why JW assigned the comet and the other events in this annal to 677, in the face of the 678 in Bede and in ASC, is not clear.
[8] *HE* iv. 12.

et *multa milia barbar*orum ad fidem conuertit *hiemem*que *ibi*dem *cum noua Dei ªplebe feliciter ex*egit.*ª*[1]

*ᵇ*Sanctus Audoenus episcopus obiit.[2] Sanctus Beda nascitur.*ᵇ*[3]

[678] (x) 700

[C³BP³]

*ᶜDe episcopis Herefordensibus.
Trans Sabrinam pene collimitatur
Walensibus ciuitas Hereford*um
*grandis. Huius a principio hi
fuerunt episcopi: Putta, Tirhtel,
Torhthere, Walhstod, Cutbert*us
*postea Cantuuariensis
archiepiscopu*s, *Podd*a, Esna.*ᶜ*[4]

[679] (xi) 701   Benedictus[5] *papa .lxxx. annis .iiii., mensibus .x. ᵈIste
ab ineunte etate in ecclesia militauit et paupertatis amator semper pro
Christo exstitit.*[6]

*Inter Ecgfrid*um regem Norðhymbrensium*ᵉ et Æthel*redum *regem
Merciorum conserto graui prelio iuxta fluuium Trenta, occisus est* rex
*Ælfuuin*e, *frater regis Ecgfridi,* cuius sororem *Osthryth*am rex
Æthelred habebat uxorem.[7] Wilfridus episcopus Fresiam reliquit,
Romam adiit, *ᶠet ubi Benedictiᶠ pap*e et *pluri*morum *episcop*orum
*iudicio absque crimine accusatus fuisse, episcopatu*que *inuentus est
dignus esse, Brytan*niam rediit, *prouinciam* Suðsaxonum Christo
credere fecit.[8] Beata uirgo Æðeldrytha Eliensis cenobii abbatissa

---

ª⁻ª plebe . . . exegit] *paler ink over ras. C', runs on to* 678 CB   *ᵇ⁻ᵇ* Sanctus . . .
nascitur] *add. in space left blank for end of* 677 C¹ *(though just possible that* Sanctus Beda
nascitur, *which is in a lighter ink, was added by* C²*), incorporated at end of* 677 *and running on to* 678 HB, *under* 678 L, *incorporated at end of* 677 P, Sanctus Beda nascitur
incorporated G   *ᶜ⁻ᶜ* De episcopis . . . Esna] *add. mg. alongside* 679 C³, *om.* HL,
add. (without heading) mg. alongside 676, *in a group with* 679 n. b *(p. 136), with signe de
renvoi for mg. addition, but none in text* P³   *ᵈ under* 680 *from here (N)*
ᵉ Northanhimbrorum H *(with* umbrensium *interlin.)* L   *ᶠ⁻ᶠ* et . . . Benedicti] *paler
ink, over erasure* C¹

---

[1] *HE* v. 19.
[2] Norman Annals. The *AU* and *ASN* record St Ouen's death under 677, and the
AG under 669.
[3] JW may have derived this incorrect date for Bede's birth either from *HDE* i. 8 (i.
29) or just possibly from the Marianus entry under 678, 'sanctus Beda presbiter . . .
clarus habetur'.

the first to begin the work of the gospel, and he converted many thousands of barbarians to the faith and passed the winter there happily with God's new people.[1]

St Ouen, the bishop, died.[2] St Bede was born.[3]

[678]

Concerning the bishops of Hereford. The great city of Hereford beyond the Severn almost borders on the Welsh territories. Its first bishops were as follows: Putta, Tyrhtel, Torhthere, Walhstod, Cuthberht, afterwards archbishop of Canterbury, Podda, and Esne.[4]

[679] Benedict,[5] the eightieth pope, reigned four years, ten months. He laboured in the church from his earliest years, and was always a lover of poverty for Christ.[6]

When a grievous battle between Ecgfrith, king of the Northumbrians, and Æthelred, king of the Mercians, had been joined near the river Trent, King Ælfwine, brother of King Ecgfrith, whose sister Osthryth was married to King Æthelred, was killed.[7] Bishop Wilfrid left Frisia, went to Rome, and there, by the judgement of Pope Benedict, and of many bishops, he was declared free of guilt, and found worthy of his bishopric. He returned to Britain, and brought the kingdom of the South Saxons to Christ.[8] The blessed virgin, Æthelthryth, abbess of the

---

[4] *GP* iv. 163 (pp. 298–9). There is an unexplained gap of three bishops between Podda and Esna.

[5] Benedict II 684–5.   [6] *Mar.*

[7] *HE* iv. 21 (19). Bede assigns this battle to the 9th year of King Ecgfrith, and ASC A(B)CE the death of Ælfwine (and ASC E the battle) to 679.

[8] *HE* v. 19. Wilfrid must have left Frisia in 678 or 679, but he cannot have left Rome until after the council of 27 Mar. 680, at which he was present (Stephanus, *Vita Wilfridi*, cc. 33, 53), and probably began his five years in Sussex in 681. Marianus' record of Benedict's accession in 679 may have caused JW to substitute Benedict for Agatho as the presiding pope.

.ix. die kalendarum Iuliarum*a* *in medio suorum rapta est ad Dominum cui soror eius Sexbur*h *in eius successit ministerium.*[1]

[C³BP³]

*b*Qualiter communi consilio regis
Æthelredi et Theodori
archiepiscopi in .v. episcopatus
sit Mercia diuisa. Merciorum
prouincia in quinque
parrochias diuisa, Bosel a
Theodoro archiepiscopo ad
Huuicciam presul ordinatur,
habens sedem presulatus in
ciuitate Wigorna, Cuthwinus ad
Licetfeldensem, Saxwlfus ad
Mediterraneam Angliam habens
episcopatus sedem in ciuitate
Leogora, ad Lindissim prouinciam
Ætheluuinus sedem presulatus
habens in Syddena, ad Suthangliam
Ætla habens sedem episcopatus in
Dorkeceastre.*b2*

[**680**] (xii) 702   *Anno .vi. regni Æthelredi reg*is *Merci*orum, *indictione .viii.*, *Theodor*us *archiepiscop*us *coetu*m episcoporum *doctorumque plurimorum colle*git *in loco qui* dicitur *Hæthfeld*, ut *cuius essent singuli fidei*[3] sciret sicut ei*c* Agatho papa per *Iohann*em *archicantor*em, qui *huic synodo intererat*, mandauerat.[4] Eiusdem regis tempore Merciorum prouincia in quinque parrochias est diuisa,[5] unde ad *prouinciam* Huuicciorum *Tatfrið*, *uir doctissimus de* Hild *abbatisse monasterio*, *delectus estd* antistes, sed *priusquam ordinari*

---

a feria .v. add. *G*   *b–b* Qualiter . . . Dorkeceastre] *mg. alongside 679–82 C³, om. HL, mg. alongside 678–79, grouped with 678 n. c P³   c interlin. C¹   d–d* electus est] est electus *HL*

---

[1] *HE* iv. 19 (17). ASC A(B)CEF assign Æthelthryth's death to 679, a date which cannot easily be reconciled with JW's 672 for her entry into St Æbba's monastery and with Bede's statement that she had spent a total of 8 years as a religious. The day of her death may have come from a calendar.

[2] For a discussion of the date of the division of the Mercian bishopric, see P. Sims-Williams, *Religion and Literature in Western England, 600–800* (Cambridge, 1990), pp. 87–91.

monastery of Ely, was taken to the Lord on 23 June in the midst of her people. Her sister Seaxburg succeeded her in her office.[1]

How, by the common agreement of King Æthelred and Archbishop Theodore, Mercia was divided into five bishoprics. The kingdom of the Mercians was divided into five bishoprics: Bosel was ordained bishop for the Hwicce by Archbishop Theodore, having his episcopal see in the city of Worcester; Cuthwine at Lichfield; Seaxwulf, ordained for Middle Anglia, had his episcopal see at Leicester; Æthelwine, appointed to the province of Lindsey, had his seat at *Syddena*; Ætla, appointed to South Anglia, had his episcopal seat at Dorchester.[2]

[**680**] In the sixth year of the reign of Æthelred, king of the Mercians, in the eighth indiction, Archbishop Theodore assembled in a place called Hatfield all the bishops and many of the learned that he might establish what each believed,[3] as Pope Agatho had commanded him through the archcantor John, who was present at this synod.[4] In the reign of the same king the province of the Mercians was divided into five dioceses,[5] and Tatfrith, a most learned man from Abbess Hild's monastery, was appointed bishop of the Hwicce, but before he could be ordained, he was snatched away by untimely death, for which reason the reverend man Bosel was ordained bishop of the same province not long after. The devout servant of Christ, Hild, abbess of the monastery called

---

[3] *HE* iv. 17 (15).
[4] *HE* iv. 18 (16). 680 is the date for the synod in ASC A(B)CEF and in *HE* v. 24. For its date in 679, see Poole, *Studies*, p. 49, and Harrison, *Framework*, pp. 41, 83.
[5] See discussion in Sims-Williams, *Religion and Literature*, pp. 87–91.

posset, morte immatura prereptus est, quapropter eidem prouincie uir reuerendus Bosel non multo post antistes ordinatus est. *Religiosa Christi famula Hild, monasterii quod Streoneshalh dicitur abbatissa, Hererici nepotis regis Eduuini filia, post multa que fecit in terris opera celestia ad percipienda uite celestis premia de terris ablata, cum esset annorum .lxvi., die .xv. calendarum Decembrium* de morte *transiuit* ad Dominum. Hec duo monasteria *Streoneshalh* scilicet et Hacanos construxit, in quibus *iustitie, pietatis, castimonie, ceterarumque uirtutum, sed maxime pacis et caritatis custodiam docuit.*[1] *In huius abbatisse monasterio* habitauit Cedmon ille famosus monachus, *qui diuinitus adiutus gratis canendi donum accepit.*[2] Oshere subregulus, *licentia prestantissimi regis Merciorum domini sui Æðelredi, terram .xxx. manentium in loco qui dicitur Rippel, Friðeuualdo monacho Winfridi episcopi,* cuius supra meminimus, dedit *ut ibidem ecclesiastice conuersationis normam exerc*eret.[3]

[681] (xiii) 703   Bone indolis puer Beda, *cum esset .vii. annorum,* suorum *cura propinquorum, reuerentissimo abbati* Biscopo *datus* est *educandus.*[4] *Post annos tres abscessionis Wilfridi, ad ecclesiam Hagustaldensem Tunber*htum, *remanente Eata ad Lindisfarnensem, et Trumuuine* ad terram *Pictorum, Theodor*us *archiepiscop*us *ordin*auit. *Eaðædum de Lindissi reuersum, eo quod Æthelred* rex *prouinciam recepisset, Rypensi ecclesie prefecit.*[5]

[682] (xiiii) 704   Kentuuine   rex   Westsaxonum   occidentales Brytones usque ad mare in ore gladii fugauit.[6] Reuerentissimus abbas Benedictus Biscop *presbiterum Eusteruuini* suum patruelem, sanctitate insignem, *de monasterio* suo *eligens abbatem eidem monasterio regendi iure prefecit.*[7] *Ecgf*rið rex *pro redemptione anime sue* etiam aliam *.xl. familiarum terram abbati Benedicto dona*uit, ubi missis monachis numero *uiginti duobus* et preposito abbate

---

[1] *HE* iv. 23 (21). 680 is the date for the death of Hild in *HE* and ASC. Probably it should be 679 on our reckoning. 680 is the date in the 19-year table in the JW MS C for Bosel, 'primus Huuicciorum episcopus'. The dates given for episcopal succession at Worcester in these tables will be noted only when they appear to conflict with the annals.

[2] *HE* iv. 24 (22).

[3] *S* 52 *BCS* 51. This spurious charter, from which the italicized words are taken, is in Hemming's cartulary.

[4] *HE* v. 24. The date for Bede's birth is reckoned as 674 in this annal, which

Streonæshealch, daughter of Hereric, nephew of King Edwin, after performing many heavenly deeds on earth, was taken from earth to receive the reward of heavenly life, when, on 17 November, in her sixty-sixth year, she passed from death to the Lord. She built two monasteries, namely *Streonæshealch* and Hackness, in which she taught the observance of justice, piety, chastity, and of the other virtues, but especially of peace and love.[1] In a monastery of this abbess there lived Cædmon, that renowned monk who received the gift of song by divine aid.[2] Oshere, the under-king, with the permission of his lord, Æthelred, the most distinguished king of the Mercians, gave thirty holdings in a place called Rippel to Frithuwald, a monk of Bishop Winfrith, whom we mentioned before, in order to establish regular ecclesiastical observance there.[3]

[**681**] When Bede, a boy of fine qualities, was seven he was given through the concern of his relatives to the most reverend Abbot Biscop to be educated.[4] Three years after the departure of Wilfrid, Archbishop Theodore ordained Tunberht to the church of Hexham, while Eata remained at Lindisfarne, and Trumwine in Pictish territory. He preferred Eadhæd (when he returned from Lindsey, because King Æthelred had regained the province) to the church of Ripon.[5]

[**682**] King Centwine of the West Saxons put the West Britons to flight as far as the sea with the edge of the sword.[6] The most reverend Abbot Benedict Biscop chose from his own monastery his cousin, the priest Eosterwine, renowned for his piety, and put him in charge of that same monastery as abbot.[7] King Ecgfrith, for the redemption of his soul, also gave forty hides of land to Abbot Benedict, on which, having sent there twenty-two monks under

cannot be reconciled with the information in the addition to 677. If Bede was in his 59th year in 731 (v. 24), then he must have been entrusted to Biscop in 679 or 680.
[5] *HE* iv. 12. The expulsion and departure of Wilfrid are here reckoned as 678 not 677 as stated in the annal for that year.
[6] This campaign is in ASC A(B)E (682) C (683) G (681).
[7] Bede, *Hist. abbat.*, c. 7. The date of Eosterwine's appointment (which JW probably inferred from *Hist. abbat.*, c. 8, where Bede says it occurred in the 9th year from the foundation of Wearmouth), is probably 682 or 683.

Ceolfrido, sui per omnia adiutore strenuissimo iussu regis monasterium beato Paulo apostolo in loco qui dicitur Giruum construxit.[1]

[684] (xvi) 706 *"Ciclus .ix. decennouenalis incipit indictione* xii.*[ab] Benedictus papa obiit .viii. idus Maii.*[2]

p. 268   *Ecgfrið rex Norðhymbrorum,* | *misso Hiberniam cum exercitu duce Berhto, uastauit misere gentem innoxiam.*[3] *Congregata synodo sub presentia regis Ecgfridi iuxta fluuium Alne in loco, qui dicitur Tuuiford, cui Theodorus archiepiscopus presidebat, Tunberhto ab episcopatu deposito, unanimo omnium consensu* ad episcopatum Hagustaldensis ecclesie Cuthberht eligitur, sed quia *ipse plus Lindisfarnensi ecclesie dilexit prefici, placuit ut, Eata reuerso ad Hagustaldensem, Cuðberht ecclesi*am *susciperet Lindisfarnensem.*[4] Benedictus Biscop *quinta uice de Brytannia Romam* petiit.[5]

[685] (xvii) 707 *Iohannes*[6] *.lxxxi. papa anno uno et mense uno et obiit .iiii. non. Augusti. Huius tempore regnauit Iustinianus*[7] *augustus mortuo patre in initio[c] mensis Septembris, indictione .xiii.*[8]

[C³BP³]

[d]Defuncto Bisi Orientalium Anglorum episcopo, duo rexerunt pontifices *prouinciam illam usque ad tempus Ecgberti regis Westsaxonum, quorum unus sedebat apud Dommuc alter apud Helmaham*: Beadwine et*[e]* Accce,*[f]* Nothbertus et Asculfus, Nothelacus*[g]* et Eardredus,*[h]* Athelferthus et Cuthwinus,

---

[a-a] Ciclus . . . indictione xii] *written in space for 683, but with sign pointing to 684 C, under 683 HL, under 683, but with line linking it to 684 B, under 683-4 P*   *[b] see App. B for mg. addition near 684 n. a B*[1]   *[c]* initio] *in interlin. C*[1]   *[d]* Defuncto . . . Alfrici p. 142)] *mg. alongside 684-6 with signe de renvoi C*[3], *om. HL, incorporates 673 n. b B, mg. with signe de renvoi P*[3]   *[e]* add. *to the left of mg. addition 685 n. d C*[3]   *[f] written over erasure C*[3], *Æcce B,* Acce P   *[g]* id est Heatholac *interlin. B*[1]   *[h] amends to* Heardredus *B*[1]

---

[1] *Anon. hist. abbat.*, c. 11. The foundation of Jarrow is said from the opening words of the section quoted here to have happened eight years after that of Wearmouth.

[2] *Mar.*

[3] *HE* iv. 26 (24), where the date of Berht's expedition is given.

Abbot Ceolfrith, his most vigorous helper in all things, at the king's command he built a monastery dedicated to St Paul the Apostle in the place called Jarrow.[1]

[684] The ninth cycle of nineteen years begins in the twelfth indiction. Pope Benedict died on 8 May.[2]

Ecgfrith, king of the Northumbrians, when he had sent his army to Ireland with his ealdorman Berht, wretchedly ravaged that innocent people.[3] Archbishop Theodore presided over a synod assembled in the presence of King Ecgfrith in a place called Twyford, near the river Aln. Tunberht was deposed from his bishopric and, by unanimous agreement, Cuthbert was elected to the episcopal see of Hexham but, because he preferred to govern the church of Lindisfarne, it was permitted that, when Eata returned to Hexham, Cuthbert should receive the church of Lindisfarne.[4] Benedict Biscop went to Rome from Britain for a fifth time.[5]

[685] John,[6] the eighty-first pope, reigned one year and one month, and died on 2 August. At this time the Emperor Justinian[7] reigned, his father having died at the beginning of September in the thirteenth indiction.[8]

On the death of Bisi, bishop of the East Angles, two bishops ruled that kingdom down to the time of Ecgberht, king of the West Saxons. The seat of one was at *Dommoc*, the other at Elmham. They were Beaduwine and Æcce, Nothberht and Æscwulf, Nothlac (Heathulac) and Heardred, Æthelfrith and Cuthwine, Eanfrith and

---

[4] *HE* iv. 28 (26), which dates the consecration of Cuthbert to Easter (26 Mar.) 685. Bede makes clear that the election took place at the beginning of winter 684/5 (*HE* iv. 28 (26) and *Vita Cuthberti*, c. 24).

[5] Bede, *Hist. abbat.*, c. 9. Bede says that Biscop made this sixth visit to Rome (fifth direct from Britain) 'not long' after the appointment of Ceolfrith and Eosterwine in 682. When Eosterwine died in 685 or 686, Biscop had not returned.

[6] John V 685-6.   [7] Justinian II 685-95.   [8] Mar.

Lanferth*ᵃ* ⟨et⟩*ᵇ* Aldbriht, Athewlf*ᶜ* ⟨et⟩*ᵇ* Ecglaf, Hunferth*ᵈ* ⟨et⟩*ᵇ* Ethred, Sigga*ᵉ* ⟨et⟩*ᵇ* Alhun*ᶠ*, Hunferth ⟨et⟩*ᵇ* Tidferth, Hunbriht ⟨et⟩*ᵇ* Wermund. Post quem Wilred. [1]*Tempore Ludecani regis Merciorum et Ecberti regis Westsaxonum,*[1] Hunberht et Wilred *fuerunt episcopi* Eastanglorum. *Sed eodem Ludecano et antecessore eius Burhredo incursante prouinciam, etiam episcopi* pre inopia *destituti sunt. Extinct*is *regibus, ex duobus unus episcopatus factus* est et *sedes* episcopalis *apud Helmaham* habitus est. *Fuerunt hi pontifices* Athulf qui [1]regis Edwii tempore[1] fuit, Ælfricus, duo Theodredi, Athelstanus, Algarus.*ᵍ* Hic de transitu Dunstani archiepiscopi uisionem uidit cui successit Alwinus,*ʰ* duo Alfrici.*ⁱʲ*[2]

*Lotheri rex Cantuuariorum in pugna Australium Saxonum uulneratus, .xii. ann*o *sui regn*i, *.viii. idus Februar*i*i,* *ᵏferia .ii.,ᵏ inter medendum est defunctus. Post* quem *Eadric, filius Ecgberti fratris sui, anno uno ac dimidio regnauit.*[3] Magna *pestilentie procella Brytanniam corripiens lata nece uastauit, in qua Deo dilectus abbas Eusteruuini per nonas Martii raptus est ad Dominum. Pro quo fratres cum consilio Ceolfridi abbatis, mire sanctitatis uirum, et scripturarum studiis abundanter instructum, Sigefridum, eiusdem monasterii diaconem, con-*

ᵃ Eanferth *B*   *ᵇ add.* et *B*⁵, *om. CP*   *ᶜ* Æthelfryth et Alfheard *interlin. and erased B*¹   *ᵈ* Alheard *interlin. B*⁵   *ᵉ* id est Sibba *interlin. B*¹   *ᶠ amended to* Ælfhun *B*¹   *ᵍ amended to* Alfgarus *B*¹   *ʰ amended to* Alfwinus *B*¹   *ⁱ see above, p. 140 n. d*   *ʲ* Ædnothus, Stigandus, Ægelmærus, Arfastus, Willelmus, Herbertus, Eouerardus *add.* here *B*⁴   *ᵏ⁻ᵏ* feria ii] *interlin. C*ⁱ, *mg. at appropriate point B*¹, *before* viii*ᵒ* idus Februarii *P*

---

[1]⁻[1] There is more than an echo of a phrase in the East Anglian *Epis.* lists.

[2] *GP* ii. 74 (pp. 147–50).

Aldberht, Æthelwulf and Ecglaf, Hunferth and Heardred, Sibba and Ælfhun, Hunferth and Tidferth, Hunberht and Wærmund, whom Wilred followed. [1]In the time of Ludecan, king of the Mercians, and of Ecgberht, king of the West Saxons,[1] Hunberht and Wilred were bishops of the East Angles, but on the invasion of the kingdom by that same Ludecan and his predecessor Burgred the bishoprics were also abandoned because of the lack of resources. When the kings had died, one bishopric was made from the two and the episcopal seat established at Elmham. These were the bishops: Athulf, [1]who was in King Eadwig's time;[1] Ælfric; two Theodreds; Æthelstan; and Ælfgar. The last saw the vision of the passing of Archbishop Dunstan and he was succeeded by Ælfwine and two Ælfrics.[2]

Hlothhere, king of the people of Kent, was wounded in a battle with the South Saxons on Monday, 6 February, in the twelfth year of his reign, and died during treatment. Eadric, son of his brother Ecgberht, reigned after him for one year and a half.[3] A great outbreak of plague struck Britain, causing widespread devastation and death, in which Abbot Eosterwine, beloved of God, was snatched away to the Lord on 7 March. In his place the brethren on the advice of Abbot Ceolfrith, appointed as abbot Sigefrith, deacon of that monastery and a man of wonderful sanctity, richly

---

[3] *HE* iv. 26 (24). ASC A(B)CEF agrees with Bede in giving the date for Hlothere's death as 685.

stituere abbatem.[1] [2]*Ecclesiasticorum donis commodorum* Biscop *loculple-tatus* et [3]*peregrina merce, ut semper, onustus*[3] Roma *rediit.*[2] *Ordinatio beati* Cuthberhti *in ipsa solennitate pascali completa est* Eboraci, *sub presentia regis* Ecgfridi, *ad consecrationem eius .vii. episcopis conueni-entibus, in quibus primatum tenebat* Theodorus *arciepiscopus.*[4] Ecgfrið *rex cum temere exercitum ad uastandam* Pictorum *prouinciam duxisset, anno etatis sue .xl. regni autem .xv. occisus est, die calendarum Iuniarum .xiii., sabbato.*[a] *Cui successit in regnum* Alhfrid *frater eius, uir in scripturis doctissimus.*[5] *Huius regni principio, defuncto* Eata [b]*episcopo* sanctissimo,[b] Iohannes *uir sanctus* Hagustaldensis *ecclesie presulatum suscepit.*[6] *Sanctissimus uir* Domini Trumuuine *episcopus de terra* Pictorum *cum suis recessit, et in* Streoneshalh *locum sibi mansionis elegit, ibique uitam non sibi solummodo sed et multis utilem plurimo annorum tempore duxit, ubi etiam defunctus,* celeste *regnum conscendit.*[7] Ceaduualla, *iuuenis strenuissimus de regio genere* Gewissorum, Ætheluualh *regem* Australium Saxonum *improuise cum exercitu superueniens interfecit, sed mox expulsus est a ducibus regis* Berhthuno *et* Æðelhuno *qui deinceps regnum prouincie tenuerunt.*[8] Centuuine rex Occidentalium Saxonum uita decedit, cui prefatus Ceaduualla in regnum succedit, qui fuit Cenbryht, qui fuit Ceadda, qui fuit Cutha, qui fuit Ceaulin, qui fuit Cynric, qui fuit Cerdic.[9]

Romanorum sexagesimus nonus Iustinianus minor *filius* Constantini *regnauit annis decem usque in annum sexcentesimum octogesimum quartum post passionem Domini.*[10]

[686] (i) 708   Conon[11] *octogesimus secundus papa anno uno, mensibus .xi.*[12]

---

[a] *interlin,* C¹H¹L¹B¹, *om.* P   [b–b] episcopo sanctissimo] *written over erasure* C, sanctissimo episcopo HL

---

[1] *Anon. hist. abbat.,* c. 13. The day ('per nonas Martii') seems to be derived from Bede, *Hist. abbat.,* c. 8; 685 is consistent with the statement that Eosterwine (elected abbot in 682) died in his fourth year, but not with his having lived in the monastery (founded 674) for 12 years.

[2–2] Bede, *Hist. abbat.,* c. 9.

[3–3] *Anon. hist. abbat.,* c. 15. For the date of Biscop's return from Rome, see above, p. 140 n. 5.

[4] *HE* iv. 28 (26). For the date of Cuthbert's consecration, see above, p. 140 n. 4.

[5] *HE* iv 26 (24); the error Alhfrid for Aldfrith is also found in JW *Northum. Gen.* and *Accounts* 5.   [6] *HE* v. 2.

versed in scriptural studies.[1] [2]Biscop returned from Rome, rich in suitable ecclesiastical gifts[2] and as always [3]laden with foreign wares.[3] The ordination of St Cuthbert was completed at York at the Easter feast itself, in the presence of King Ecgfrith. To his consecration came seven bishops, among whom Archbishop Theodore had precedence.[4] King Ecgfrith was killed on Saturday, 20 May, in his fortieth year, the fifteenth of his reign, when he rashly led his army out to lay waste Pictish territory. Aldfrith, his brother, succeeded him in his kingdom, a man most learned in the scriptures.[5] Eata, the most saintly bishop, died at the beginning of his reign, and the holy man John received the bishopric of Hexham.[6] The most holy man of God Bishop Trumwine withdrew from Pictish territory with his followers, and chose a place in *Streonæshealch* for his abode, and there he led a life, which was profitable not just for himself alone, but for many, for a period of many years. There also he died and ascended to the heavenly kingdom.[7] Cædwalla, a most vigorous man of the royal stock of the *Gewisse*, unexpectedly fell upon Æthelwalh, king of the South Saxons, with his army and slew him, but soon he was driven out by the king's ealdormen Berhthun and Æthelhun, who afterwards held the governance of the province.[8] Centwine, king of the West Saxons, departed this life. The aforementioned Cædwalla succeeded him in the kingdom. He was the son of Cenberht, son of Ceadda, son of Cutha, son of Ceawlin, son of Cynric, son of Cerdic.[9]

The sixty-ninth emperor of the Romans, Justinian the Younger, son of Constantine, reigned ten years to the 684th year after the Lord's Passion.[10]

[**686**] The eighty-second pope, Conon,[11] reigned one year, eleven months.[12]

---

[7] *HE* iv. 26 (24). The date for the accession of Aldfrith, of the election of Bishop John, and the withdrawal of Bishop Trumwine is inferred from Bede.

[8] *HE* iv. 15. This date is presumably inferred from Bede.

[9] The date of Cædwalla's accession comes from ASC A(B)CE, and the first three give the genealogy. ASC does not record Centwine's death.

[10] Mar.   [11] Conon 686–7.

[12] Mar.

Wilfridus episcopus *post longum exilium*[1] *sedem suam et episcopa-tum*[2] *Hagustaldensis ecclesie,*[1] *rege* Alcfrido*[a]* *inuitante, recepit.*[2] *Iohannes* uero, *defuncto Bosa, multe sanctitatis et humilitatis uiro,* episcopus *pro eo Eboraci substitu*itur.[1] *Ceaduualla rex Geuuissorum* duc*em* Suðsaxonum *Berthun*um occidit, *et prouincia*m illam *graui seruitio sub*egit.[3] Deinde idem ipse et frater suus Mul Cantiam depopulantur.[4] *Post hec rex ipse Ceaduualla cepit Vectam insulam, que eatenus erat tota idolatriae dedita,* et, *licet necdum in Christo regeneratus, quartam partem eius,* id est *.ccc. familia*s *Wilfrido epis-copo utendam pro Domino* optulit, *qua acce*pta *et Beruuino suo nepoti commenda*ta, *uerb*i ministros eidem insule destinauit.[5] *Duobus annis in episcopatu peractis,* uir Domini Cuthbertus episco-pus, *diuino admonitus oraculo insulam* Farne *repetiit.*[6] *Defuncto* Edrico Cantuariorum rege, *regnum illud* per *aliquod temporis spatium*[b] *reges dubii uel externi disperdidere.*[7]

[687] (ii) 709 *'Conon papa obiit die .xxi. mensis Septembris.'*[8]
Ceaduualle regis Westsaxonum fratrem Mul et .xii. milites eius flammis iniectos Cantuarienses atrociter in ipsa Cantia com-busserunt, unde rex Ceaduualla, ira commotus, rursum Cantiam deuastat.[9] *[d]Reuerentissimus* pater Cuthbertus, indictione *.xv.[d] [e].xiii. kalend. Aprilis,* feria *.iiii.,[e] [f]in insula Farne[f]* obiit, sed corpus illius ad insulam Lindisfarnensium relatu*m, in ecclesia* est tumulatum, cuius *episcopatum Wilfrid* Hagustaldensis episcopus *anno uno ser-ua*uit.[10] *Successit uiro Domini Cuthberto in exercenda uita solitaria,*

---

[a] Alchfrido *HL,* Alcfrido *corrected to* Alchfrido *B*[1]   *[b] interlin.* C[1]
[c–c] Conon . . . Septembris] *follows* 687 *n. b (p. 148) (N)*   *[d–d]* Reuerentissimus . . .
indictione *.xv.] paler ink over erasure* C[1]   *[e–e]* .xiii. kalend. . . . .iiii.] *written in mg.
near line-end and at beginning of line* C[1]   *[f–f]* in insula Farne] *paler ink over erasure
and starting in mg.* C[1]

---

[1] *HE* v. 3.
[2] *HE* v. 19. The first sentence is a conflation of passages from two chapters of *HE* concerning two episodes in Wilfrid's life separated by 20 years. Wilfrid recovered Hexham in 705 (as *HE* v. 3, 19 make clear) but JW's view that he received it in 686 is incorrect. JW *Epis. Lists* make Wilfrid its first bishop.
[3] *HE* iv. 15.
[4] ASC A(B)CEF (addition in F), which also record the attack on Wight.
[5] *HE* iv. 16 (14). The date of Cædwalla's attack on the South Saxons and his gift of

After a long exile, Bishop Wilfrid[1] received back his own see[2] and the bishopric of Hexham[1] at the invitation of King Aldfrith.[2] On the death of Bosa, a man of great sanctity and humility, John was appointed bishop of York to replace him.[1] Cædwalla, king of the *Gewisse*, slew Berhthun, ealdorman of the South Saxons, and reduced that province to grievous servitude.[3] Then he himself and his brother Mul ravaged Kent.[4] After that, King Cædwalla himself took the Isle of Wight, till then wholly given up to idolatry, and, although not yet reborn in Christ, he gave a quarter of it, that is 300 hides, to Bishop Wilfrid for the Lord's use. Wilfrid accepted it, and, having placed it in the charge of his nephew Beornwine, appointed ministers of the Word in the same island.[5] When he had completed two years in the episcopacy, Bishop Cuthbert, the man of God, warned by a divine oracle, returned to the island of Farne.[6] On the death of Eadric, king of the people of Kent, kings of doubtful legitimacy, or foreigners, wasted the kingdom for some time.[7]

[687] Pope Conon died on 21 September.[8]

The men of Kent cruelly cast Mul, brother of Cædwalla, king of the West Saxons, and twelve of his soldiers to the flames in Kent itself, and burnt them, at which Cædwalla, roused to anger, ravaged Kent again.[9] The most reverend father Cuthbert died on the island of Farne on Wednesday, 20 March, in the fifteenth indiction, but his body was borne to the island of Lindisfarne and buried in the church. Wilfrid, bishop of Hexham, took up Cuthbert's episcopal office for a year.[10] The venerable Oithelwald, whose life and merits were declared in the innumerable miracles

---

a quarter of the Isle of Wight was probably inferred from ASC and not derived from Bede.

[6] *HE* iv. 19 (17). Cuthbert's resignation as bishop and his return to Farne could be dated to 686 if the two years of his episcopate are reckoned from his election in 684. Bede, *Vita Cuthberti*, c. 27 says that Cuthbert retired to his island shortly after Christmas 686.

[7] *HE* iv. 26 (24). The year of Eadric's death is implied in Bede's statement that he reigned 1½ years after the death of Hlothhere (February 685).

[8] Mar.

[9] ASC A(B)CEF, where the equivalent of 'atrociter' and 'ira commotus' are not found.

[10] *HE* iv. 29 (27). On the erroneous description of Wilfrid as bishop of Hexham, see above, n. 2. The passages rewritten by C[2] are usually based on *HDE*.

uir uenerabilis Atheluuoldus *cuius meritum* et *uita qualis fuerit* innumera declarant*ᵃ* ab eo *patrata miracula.*¹

*ᵇSanctus Kilianus Scottus de Hibernia insula natus Wirzburgensis
episcopus clarus habetur.ᵇ²* |

p. 269 **[688]** (iii) 710 *Sergius*³ *octogesimus .iii. papa annis tredecim et mensibus .ix. Pippinus Ansgisi filii sancti Arnulfi filius regit Francos annis
.xxvii.*⁴

> *ᶜCulmen, opes, sobolem, pollentia regna, triumphos*
>   *Exuuias, proceres, moenia, castra, lares;*
> *Queque patrum uirtus, et que congesserat ipse,*
>   *Ceduual armipotens liquit amore Dei;*
> *Vt Petrum, sedemque Petri rex cerneret hospes,*
>   *Cuius fonte meras sumeret almus aquas,*
> *Splendificumque iubar radianti carperet haustu,*
>   *Ex quo uiuificus fulgor ubique fluit.ᶜ*

Abeunte Ceaduualla Romam suscepit imperium Ini de stirpe regia,ᵈ⁵
qui

[C³BP]
ᵉconsilio Aldelmi abbatisᵉ⁶
monasterium quod Glæstingebyrig*ᶠ* dicitur construxit.*ᵍ* Cuius
pater Cenred, cuius pater Ceoluuald, cuius pater Cutha, cuius
pater Cuthuuine, cuius pater Ceaulin.⁷

[C³BP³]
*ʰDe Glæstonia. Glæstonia est uilla
in Sumersetensi pago in quodam
recessu palustri posita. Ibi sepultus
est* Ine *in ecclesia sancti Petri
quam* ipse *a fundamentis*

ᵃ declarauit B, declarauerat *interlin.* B⁵   *ᵇ⁻ᵇ* Sanctus . . . habetur] *precedes 687 n.*
c (N)   *ᶜ⁻ᶜ* Culmen . . . fluit] *each verse indicated by a coloured initial, not by a new
line* C   *ᵈ* quod et .xxxvii. annos tenuit *interlin.* B⁵   *ᵉ⁻ᵉ* consilio . . . abbatis]
interlin. C³, *om.* HL   *ᶠ* Glæstingabyrig H, Glestingebyrig L, Glastingebyrig P
ᵍ see App. A for addition L, *add. mg. near 688* P⁵   *ʰ* De Glæstonia . . . actitarat
(p. 150)] *add. mg. alongside 688, followed by some erased words (of which the first three* et
primus abbas *are visible)* C³, *om.* HL, *added at end of 688* B, *add. mg. alongside 688 and
immediately above mg. addition 688 n. g* P³

---

¹ *HE* v. 1.   ² Mar.   ³ Sergius I 687–701.   ⁴ Mar.

he wrought, succeeded Cuthbert, the man of God, in the practice of the solitary life.[1]

St Kilian, born on the island of Ireland, and bishop of Würzburg, enjoyed great renown.[2]

[688] The eighty-third pope, Sergius,[3] reigned thirteen years and nine months. Pippin, son of Ansegisel, ruled the Franks for twenty-seven years.[4]

Sublimity, wealth, lineage, great realms, and triumphs,
The spoils of war, great thegns, walls, forts, and household gods:
Whatever his forefathers' fathers' valour or he himself amassed,
Cædwalla, strong in arms, for love of God abandoned,
That, pilgrim king, he might know Peter and Peter's chair,
Might drink pure waters from his reviving fount,
Draw in the splendid sheen in shining draughts
From which life-giving glory outward flows.

With Cædwalla's departure for Rome, Ine, a member of the royal family, received the kingdom[5] and,

on the advice of Abbot Aldhelm,[6]

built the monastery called Glastonbury. His father was Cenred, whose father was Ceolwald, whose father was Cutha, whose father was Cuthwine, whose father was Ceawlin.[7]

About Glastonbury. Glastonbury is a township in Somerset, set in a remote area of the marsh. There Ine is buried in the church of St Peter, which he himself built from the

[5] HE v. 7. The remainder of the epitaph whose first six lines are given here is under 689.
[6] This interlineation may be based on GP ii. 91 (p. 196).
[7] JW's version of ASC presumably included the sentence 'and he getimbrade bæt menster æt Glæstingabyrig' which occurs in ASC A (addition by hand 6: before c. 1001–1012×1013) and in G. The genealogy of Ine in JW's annal, which agrees with that in JW West Saxon Gen. and in ASC A (855) (B)CF (856), differs from that in ASC A(B)C in making Ceolwald's father Cutha instead of Cuthwine, though the preface to A has Cuthwulf in Cutha/Cuthwine's position.

construxerat. Eo etiam loci sanctus *Dunstanus prius solitariam
uitam monachus actitarat.*[a1]

Ordinatus est pro Cuthberto *Eadberht*us, *uir scientia scripturarum
diuinarum simul et preceptorum celestium obseruantia ac maxime elemosinarum operatione insignis.*[2] Benedictus Biscop et Sigefridus
abbates, [b]*diutina infirmitate lassati,*[3] *in lectum ambo sternuntur,*[b] *unde*
mox *inito cum fratribus consilio Benedictus*[4] *acciit abbatem
Ceolfridum, quem monasterio beati apostoli Pauli prefecerat*[3] *eum*que
*abbatem utriusque monasterii constituit, indictione prima, quarto iduum
Maiarum die. Eodem anno uenerabilis* ac Deo dilectus *abbas
Sigefridus*[4] *inductus in refrigerium sempiterne quietis, introiit*[c] *in*[d]
domum regni celestis, in holocaustis perpetue laudationis[5] *.xi. kalend.
Septembris*[4] sabbato.[e]

[C³BP]
[f]Defuncto Putta Herefordensi
episcopo, Tyrhtel successit.[fg6]

[689] (iiii) 711 *Iustinianus constituit pacem cum Sarracenis decennio
terra marique, sed et prouincia Affrica subiugata est Romano imperio,
que erat tenta a Sarracenis. Ipsa quoque Cartagine ab eis capta et
destructa.*[7]

Vitiorum uictor et uirtutum patrator egregius[8] Biscop *Benedictus
post longe caminum infirmitatis in qua Deo semper agere gratias solebat, .ii. idus Ianuarii requiem lucemque uite celestis adiit.*[9]
*Pontificatum agente Sergio, Ceaduualla Westsaxonum rex baptizatus
est die sancto sabbati pascalis.*

---

[a] see above, p. 148 n. h   [b–b] diutina . . . sternuntur] *paler ink, possibly over erasure* C¹   [c] introiuit LP   [d] om. H   [e] interlin. C¹B¹, om. HL incorpor.
before Septembris P   [f–f] Defuncto . . . successit] add. at line-end and running into
mg. C³, om. HL   [g] 688 n. h (p. 148) add. here B

---

[1] *GP* ii. 91 (p. 196). The puzzling reference to Ine's burial at Glastonbury seems
based on an entry referring to the burial of Bishop John of Wells 'in ecclesia sancti
Petri [at Wells], quam a fundamentis erexerat', which in WM's autograph *GP* witness
A (Oxford, Magdalen College MS 172) was originally misplaced under Glastonbury
after a sentence on Ine.

[2] *HE* iv. 29 (27), from which chapter the date has been inferred.

[3] Bede, *Hist. abbat.*, c. 13.   [4] *Anon. hist. abbat.*, cc. 15–17.

[5] Bede, *Hist. abbat.*, c. 14. From the two works he was using JW would not have
found it easy to assign to 688/9 or to 689/90 the election of Ceolfrith as abbot of

foundations. Also in that place
St Dunstan, as a monk, earlier
lived the solitary life.[1]

Eadberht was ordained in Cuthbert's place, a man learned in the
Holy Scriptures as well as renowned for his observance of the
divine commandments and especially for his almsgiving.[2] The
abbots Benedict Biscop and Sigefrith, worn out by long infirmity,[3]
both became bedridden, thereupon, Benedict, after consulting the
brethren,[4] summoned Abbot Ceolfrith, whom he had placed in
charge of the monastery of the blessed Apostle Paul,[3] and made
him abbot of both monasteries on 12 May, in the first indiction.
In the same year the venerable Abbot Sigefrith,[4] beloved of God,
admitted to the refreshment of eternal rest, entered into the
dwelling-place of the kingdom of heaven amid eternal praise[5] on
Saturday, 22 August.[4]

On the death of Putta, bishop
of Hereford, Tyrhtel suc-
ceeded.[6]

[689] Justinian made a ten-year peace with the Saracens by land
and sea, but the province of Africa, which had been subject to
Roman control, was held by the Saracens, and Carthage itself was
also captured by them and destroyed.[7]

Benedict Biscop, victorious over vices and an outstanding example of the virtues,[8] after the purification of a long illness in which
he was accustomed always to give thanks to God, went to rest and
the light of heavenly life on 12 January.[9] While Sergius was pope,
Cædwalla, king of the West Saxons, was baptized on Holy
Saturday at Easter.

Wearmouth as well as of Jarrow (12 May), the death of Sigefrith on 22 Aug. in the
same year, and that of Biscop on 12 Jan. following, for the evidence before him was
conflicting. As the anonymous life and Bede give Biscop 16 years as abbot and date
Wearmouth's foundation to 674, the date of his death should be 690. It is uncertain
whether 688-9 was the correct choice.

[6] JW's source for this date is not known. These are the first two Hereford bishops in
JW *Epis. Lists.*
[7] Mar.
[8] Bede, *Hist. abbat.*, c. 14.
[9] *Anon. hist. abbat.*, c. 17. For JW's date for Biscop's death see above, n. 5.

ᵃPercipiensque alacer rediuiue premia uite,
    Barbaricam rabiem, nomen et inde suum
Conuersus conuertit ouans: Petrumque uocari
    Sergius antistes iussit, ut ipse pater
Fonte renascentis, quem Christi gratia purgans
    Protinus albatum uexit in arce poli.
Mira fides regis, clementia maxima Christi,
    Cuius consilium nullus adire potest.
Hospes enim ueniens supremo ex orbe Britanni,
    Per uarias gentes, per freta, perque uias,
Vrbem Romuleam uidit, templumque uerendum
    Aspexit Petri mystica dona gerens.
Candidus inter oues Christi sociabilis ibit;
    Corpore nam tumulum, mente superna tenet.
Commutasse magis sceptrorum insignia credas,
    Quem regnum Christi promeruisse uides.ᵃ

Defunctus est autem sub *die .xii. kalendarum Maiiarum,* *ᵇferia .iii.,ᵇ* indictione .ii., *qui uixit annos minus .xxx.*[1]

[690] (v) 712 *Theodorus beate memorie archiepiscopus anno* etatis *sue .lxxxviii., episcopatus* autem *.xxii., defunctus est* die kalendarum Octobrium .xiii., *ᶜferia .ii.ᶜ*

    Scandens alma noue felix consortia uite,
      Ciuibus angelicis iunctus in arce poli.[2]

Archipresules Doruuernensis ecclesie hucusque Romani, postmodum extitere Anglici.[3]

[691] (vi) 713 *Sergius papa constituit ut tempore confractionis Domini corporis agnus Dei a clero cantaretur.*[4]
    Wilfridus Hagustaldensis episcopus, *denuo accusatus ab* Alhfrido *rege et plurimis episcopis, presulatu est pulsus,* qui mox ad regem Merciorum Æthelredum secessit, et ab eo *Mediterraneorum*

---

^{a–a} Percipiensque . . . uides] *each verse marked by a coloured initial, not a new line* C
^{b–b} feria .iii.] *interlin.* C¹B¹P³, *om.* HL   ^{c–c} feria .ii.] *interlin.* C¹B¹, *om.* HLP

---

[1] *HE* v. 7. The year of Cædwalla's baptism and death is given by Bede.
[2] *HE* v. 8. The year of Theodore's death is given by Bede. JW gives only the first and last lines of the epitaph.

Eagerly perceiving the rewards of life renewed
And changed, he shed barbarian ravings
And then, rejoicing, changed his own name; 'Peter'
Pope Sergius bade him be called, being father
To him who was reborn in the font; Christ's grace
Purified him and bore him at once, clad in white, to highest
   heaven.
Wonderful the king's faith, vaster Christ's mercy,
Whose purpose none can perceive.
Coming as a pilgrim from remotest Britain
Through many peoples, over sea and land,
The city of Romulus he saw and looked upon Peter's
Revered temple, in his hands mystical gifts.
He will go white among Christ's sheep.
The grave is for the body; he holds heaven in his heart.
You would believe that he has changed one realm for a greater,
Whom you see to have been rewarded with the kingdom of Christ.

He died on Tuesday, 20 April, in the second indiction, having
lived less than thirty years.[1]

[690] Archbishop Theodore of blessed memory died in his
eighty-eighth year, the twenty-second of his primacy, on Monday,
19 September.

> Happily attaining the reviving bonds of new life
> With angels joined in highest heaven.[2]

Up to now the archbishops of Canterbury had been Romans;
afterwards they were English.[3]

[691] Pope Sergius instituted the singing of the 'Agnus Dei' by
the clergy at the moment of the confraction of the Lord's body.[4]

   Wilfrid, bishop of Hexham, again accused by King Aldfrith and
by many bishops, was driven from his bishopric. He promptly
went to Æthelred, king of the Mercians, and received from him

---

[3] ASC A(B)C (690) EF (692) which all ignore Deusdedit in implying that there had
not been English archbishops before Theodore.
[4] Mar.

Anglorum episcopatum accepit.[1] *Quo tempore Bosel, antistes prouincie* Wicciorum, *tanta erat corporis infirmitate depressus, ut officium episcopatus* per *se implere non posset, propter quod omnium iudicio uir* singularis meriti ac sanctitatis eximie Oftfor, *qui in monasterio Hild abbatisse* presbiterii gradu diu functus est, sed tunc in supradicta prouincia *uerbum fidei predicauit, in episcopatum pro eo electus ac, iubente rege Æthelredo, per Wilfridum beate memorie antistitem ordinatus est episcopus,* quia *Theodorus archiepiscopus iam defunctus erat et necdum alius pro eo ordinatus episcopus.*[2] *Wihtred, filius Ecgberti* regis Cantuuariorum, *confortatus in regno religione simul et industria gentem suam ab extranea inuasione liberauit.* Cum quo rex Sueabheardus partem regni tenuit.[3]

[692] (vii) 714 *Iustinianus Sergium papam, quia erratice sue synodo, quam Constantinopoli fecerat, fauere et subscribere noluit, misso*
p. 270   *Zacharia prothospatario suo, iussit Constantinopolim deportari.* | *Sed preuenit militia Rauennate urbis uicinarumque partium iussa principis nefanda, et eundem Zachariam contumeliis et iniuriis ab urbe Roma pepulit.*[4]

Venerandus et cum omni honorificentia nominandus Ecgbertus, natione Anglus, *qui in Hibernia insula pro adipiscenda in celis patria uitam duxit peregrinam,* cum ad predicandum *in Germaniam uenire uellet nec ualeret, diuina sibi uoluntate obsistente,*[5] misit illo *in opus uerbi uiros sanctos et industrios, in quibus eximius Wilebrordus presbiteri gradu et merito prefulgebat,* quos *gratanter dux Francorum Pippinus* senior *suscepit et ad predicandum citeriorem Fresiam misit. Horum secuti exempla, duo presbiteri,* Heuualdi nominati, *de natione Anglorum, uenerunt ad prouinciam antiquorum Saxonum* ut ubi *aliquos predicando Christo acquirere⟨n⟩t*[a] sed ut *cognouerunt barbari quod essent alterius religionis,* illos *rapuerunt, et quinto nonarum Octobrium* martyrizauerunt.[6] *Willebrordus, data sibi a principe*

---

[a] acquiriret *C*, adquiriret *HB*

---

[1] *HE* v. 19, iv. 23. Bede dates Wilfrid's second expulsion 5 years after his return, which JW above dates 686. For the erroneous association of Wilfrid with the see of Hexham see above, p. 146 n. 2.

[2] *HE* iv. 23. The expulsion of Wilfrid in 691 and the vacancy at Canterbury 690-3 may have led JW to assign Oftfor's consecration to this year, particularly as he dates his death 692.

[3] *HE* iv. 26 (24). Swæfheard is mentioned in *HE* v. 8 as reigning with Wihtred in

the bishopric of the Middle Angles.[1] At that time Bishop Bosel of the province of the Hwicce was so stricken with bodily infirmity that he could not fulfil all his episcopal functions by himself, for which reason Oftfor was chosen by universal consent to fill his place in the bishopric. He was a man of exceptional merit and sanctity, and had for a long time acted as a priest in the monastery of the Abbess Hild, and then preached the word of faith in the abovementioned kingdom. At King Æthelred's command he was ordained bishop by Bishop Wilfrid of blessed memory, because Archbishop Theodore was already dead and no other had as yet been ordained bishop in his place.[2] Wihtred, son of Ecgberht, king of the people of Kent, was established in his kingdom, part of which King Swaæfheard shared with him. By his devotion and zeal he also freed his people from external invasion.[3]

[692] Justinian sent Zacharias his *protospatharios* with orders to deport Pope Sergius to Constantinople because he would not approve of, or subscribe to, the synod Justinian had improperly called at Constantinople. But the army of the city of Ravenna and the neighbouring areas frustrated the emperor's impious orders, and drove Zacharias from the city of Rome with contumely and insult.[4]

The venerable Ecgberht, whose name should be mentioned with all honour, an Englishman by birth, led a life of exile in Ireland that he might attain his homeland in Heaven. When he wished to go to Germany to preach, being unable to do so, since the divine will opposed it,[5] he sent there holy and active men, among whom Willibrord shone forth, outstanding as a priest and in virtue, and these men Pippin the Elder, ruler of the Franks, received with joy and sent to preach in nearer Frisia. Following their example, the two English priests called Hewald went to the province of the Old Saxons that they might win some for Christ with their preaching but, as the barbarians knew that they were of another religion, they seized them and martyred them on 3 October.[6] Willibrord,

---

Kent in 692. When recording Wihtred's death on 23 Apr. 725 (*HE* v. 23, quoted by JW under 725), Bede assigned him a reign of 34½ years, which would put his accession in the autumn of 690. *S* 15 *BCS* 86 would, however, date his accession to 691 (later than 17 July), ASC A(B)CEF assign it to 694, and give his genealogy there. Some discussion in Harrison, *Framework*, pp. 79–80, 142–6

[4] Mar.   [5] *HE* v. 9.   [6] *HE* v. 10.

Pippino *licentia predicandi*, iuit *Romam ut cum licentia Sergii pape euangelizandi opus iniret*, qui *cum sui uoti compos esset effectus, ad predicandum rediit.*[1] Bryhtuualdus, *qui erat abbas in monasterio quod iuxta ostium aquilonale fluminis*[a] *Genlade positum Raculfe* nominatur, *uir scientia scripturarum* imbutus, *sed et ecclesiasticis simul ac monasterialibus disciplinis summe instructus*, pro *Theodoro in episcopatum* est electus.[2] Defuncto Oftforo Wicciorum episcopo, sanctus Ecguuinus pro eo presulatum suscepit, et post annorum curricula paucorum licentia iuuamineque regis Æthelredi, monasterium quod Eouesham dicitur construere cepit.[3]

[693] (viii) 715 Brihtuualdus *ordinatus* est *a Goduuino metropolitano episcopo Galliarum .iii. die calendarum Iuliarum dominica, qui inter multos quos ordinauit antistites, etiam Gebmundo Hrofensis ecclesie presule defuncto, Tobiam pro illo consecrauit.*[4] Beda monachus *gradum diaconatus a Iohanne Eboracensi episcopo suscepit.*[5]

[694] (ix) 716 Cantuuarienses, facta pace cum Ine[b] Wessaxonum rege, .iii. milia .dccl. libras[6] illi[c] dedere, quia, ut prelibauimus,[7] Mul germanum suum combussere.[8]

[695] (x) 717 *Iustinianus* imperator *ob culpam perfidie regni gloria priuatus, exul in Pontem*[d] *secedit.*[9]
Beate *uirginis* Ætheldrythe *corpus*, post *.xvi. annos sepult*ure, cum ueste qua *inuolutum* est *incorruptum* reperitur.[10]
[e]*Romanorum septuagesimus Leo*[11] *regnauit annis tribus usque in annum sexcentesimum octogesimum septimum*[f] *post passionem.*[12]

[696] (i) (718) *Sergius papa in sacrario beati Petri apostoli capsam argenteam que in angulo obscurissimo diutissime iacuerat, et in ea*

---
[a] uel norðmuða *interlin.* B⁵?   [b] *in capitals over erasure* C¹   [c] *om.* HL
[d] Pontum *Mar.*   [e] capitula .lxx. *add. before* Romanorum L   [f] .viii. HL

---
[1] *HE* v. 11. The events grouped under this annal did not all take place in this year. JW has presumably dated Willibrord's mission to 692 because Bede's 'eo tempore' at the opening of *HE* v. 9 might suggest that it was contemporary with the election of Archbishop Berhtwald.
[2] *HE* v. 8. Bede gives the day of Berhtwald's election.
[3] For the probably later date of Oftfor's death, see P. Sims-Williams, 'Cuthswith, abbess of Inkberrow, and the Würzburg Jerome', *ASE* v (1976), 9 n. 1. The marginal

having been given permission to preach by the ruler, Pippin, went to Rome to obtain Pope Sergius' leave before embarking on his mission and having been granted his wish, returned to preach.[1] Berhtwald, who was the abbot of the monastery called Reculver, near the northern mouth of the River Yantlet, a man imbued with the study of the scriptures, but also most thoroughly versed in ecclesiastical and monastic matters, was elected to the episcopate to replace Theodore.[2] On the death of Oftfor, bishop of the Hwicce, St Ecgwine accepted the bishopric and, after the space of a few years, began to build the monastery called Evesham with the permission and assistance of King Æthelred.[3]

[693] Berhtwald was ordained by Godwin, metropolitan bishop of the people of Gaul, on Sunday, 29 June; among the many other bishops he consecrated, he ordained Tobias to fill the place of Gebmund, bishop of Rochester, on the latter's death.[4] The monk Bede received the rank of deacon from John, bishop of York.[5]

[694] The people of Kent, having made peace with Ine, king of the West Saxons, gave him 3,750 pounds[6] because, as we mentioned earlier,[7] they had burnt his brother Mul.[8]

[695] The Emperor Justinian was deprived of the glory of empire because he was guilty of perfidy, and was exiled to the Crimea.[9]

The body of the blessed virgin Æthelthryth, after sixteen years in the grave, was found incorrupt in the garment in which it was wrapped.[10]

Leo, the seventieth Roman emperor,[11] reigned three years to the 687th year after the Passion.[12]

[696] By divine revelation Pope Sergius found a silver reliquary, which had for a very long time lain in a very obscure corner of

entry in the 19-year table in the JW MS C, p. 60 gives 692 as the date for Oftfor's succession, and, apparently for his death.

[4] *HE* v. 8.
[5] *HE* v. 24. As under 681, the date of Bede's birth seems to be reckoned as 674.
[6] ASC ADEF read 30,000, which probably means 30,000 pence (Whitelock, *ASC*, p. 25 n. 2), BC read 30 pounds and G 30 men. The agreement between JW's sum and the 'triginta milibus auri mancis' of *GR* i. 35 (i. 34) was noted by Plummer (*Chronicle*, ii. 34).   [7] JW here refers to his annal 687.   [8] ASC.
[9] Mar.   [10] *HE* iv. 19 (17). Æthelthryth's death is entered above under 679.
[11] Leontius 695–8.   [12] Mar.

crucem diuersis ac pretiosissimis lapidibus adornatam, Domino reue-
lante, repperit. De qua tractis .iiii. petallis,ᵃ quibus gemme incluse
erant mire magnitudinis, portionem ligni salutiferi dominice crucis
interius repositam inspexit. Que ex tempore illo annis omnibus in basil-
ica que uocatur Constantiniana die exaltationis eius ab omni adoratur
*atque osculatur populo.*¹

Rogatu *Pippini* Francorum ducis, sanctus *Wilebrordus* de
Brytannia natus genere Anglus a *Sergio* papa *Fresonum genti die*
natalis beatissime *Cecilie* uirginis *archiepiscopus ordinatus est.*²

[697] (ii) 719 Sanctus Guthlacus *cum etatis sue ᵇuicesimum quar-*
*tum peregisset,ᵇ pompis abrenuntiansᶜ secularibus, relictis*que *suis*
omnibus, monasterium Hrypandumᵈ adiit, ibique ᵉsub abbatissa
*nomine Alfthrythaᶠ tonsuram et clericalem habitum suscepit.*³
Osthrytha regis Merciorum Æthelredi regina a Suthhymbrensibus
occiditur.ᵉ⁴

[698] (iii) 720 *Tiberius*⁵ *contra Leonem insurgens, regnum eius inua-*
*sit eumque quandiu ipse regnauit in eadem ciuitate in custodia tenuit.*⁶

Beati Cuthberti corpus, *transactis sepulture eius annis .xi.*⁷ *incor-*
ruptum quasi hora eadem defuncti, simul cum ueste qua tegebatur,
depositionis eiusdem die inuenitur, sicque de terra leuatur,⁸ *nouo*
*amictu inuolu*itur, *noua in theca recondit*ur et *supra pauimentum sanc-*
*tuarii p*onitur. *Nec mora, Deo dilectus antistes Eadberhtus morbo*
p. 271 *cor|reptus acerbo, non multo post, id est pridie nonas Maias, etiam*
ipse migrauit ad Dominum, cuius ᵍcorpus in sepulchro beati *Cuthberhti*
*ponentes, ap*posuerunt *desuper arcam, in qua incorrupta eiusdem patris*

ᵃ patellis *LP*   ᵇ⁻ᵇ uicesimum . . . peregisset] .xxiiii. peregisset annos *L*, .xxiiii.
annos peregisset *P*   ᶜ abrenuntiatis *Felix, Guthlac, ed. Colgrave,* abrenuntians *(pace
Colgrave) in the Worcester BL Cotton MS Nero E. I.*   ᵈ Hrypadun *Colgrave ed.,*
Hrypandun *(pace Colgrave) BL Cotton MS Nero E. I*   ᵉ⁻ᵉ sub . . . occiditur]
*closely written and extending into mg. on two lines, with some traces of erasure at the begin-
ning of these words Cᵗ*   ᶠ Alftrytha *HL,* Eldfrida *P,* Ælfthryth *Felix, Guthlac*
ᵍ corpus . . . Eadfridus *(p. 160)] written partly over erasure C²*

---

¹ Mar.
² *HE* v. 11 where 696 is given, but for the accepted date of 695, see Levison,
England and the Continent, p. 59.
³ Felix, *Vita Guthlaci,* cc. 19–20 (pp. 82, 84). The date for Guthlac's entry into
Repton was presumably calculated by subtracting 17 years (2 years at Repton, Felix,
Vita Guthlaci, cc. 23–4, and then 15 as a solitary, ibid., c. 1) from 714, ASC's date for

the sanctuary of the blessed Apostle Peter, and in it a cross adorned with a variety of very precious stones. When the four metal plates encrusted with gems of wondrous size were pulled out he saw a portion of the saving wood of the Lord's cross lying inside. From that time, it has been worshipped and kissed on the day of its exaltation every year by the whole people in the church called Constantinian.[1]

At the request of Pippin, ruler of the Franks, St Willibrord, an Englishman from Britain, was ordained archbishop of the Frisians by Pope Sergius on the feast-day of the most blessed virgin Cecilia.[2]

[697] St Guthlac, when he had completed his twenty-fourth year, renouncing worldly pomp, and, leaving all his possessions, entered Repton monastery, and there, under an abbess called Ælfthryth, he received the tonsure and the clerical habit.[3] Osthryth, queen of Æthelred, king of the Mercians, was murdered by the Southumbrians.[4]

[698] Tiberius,[5] rising against Leo, invaded his kingdom and held him prisoner as long as he himself reigned in the same city.[6]

The body of St Cuthbert, eleven years after its burial,[7] was found incorrupt as at the very hour of death, together with the garment in which it was wrapped on the day of its burial, and so it was raised from the earth,[8] wrapped in a new garment, laid in a new coffin, and placed on the floor of the sanctuary. At once Bishop Eadberht, beloved of God, was stricken with a grievous disease. Not much later, that is on 6 May, he also departed to the Lord. The monks laid his body in St Cuthbert's tomb, placing over it the chest in which they had laid the incorrupt limbs of the

his death. Felix's statement that Guthlac was in his 24th year on his entry into Repton seems incompatible with his statement that Æthelred was reigning at the time of his birth (673) since Bede (*HE* v. 24) dates the accession of Æthelred to 675.

[4] ASC DEF refer to the Southumbrians as the perpetrators of the crime, which is dated in *HE* v. 24.

[5] Tiberius III 698–705.   [6] Mar.

[7] *HE* iv. 30 (28) or Bede, *Vita Cuthberti*, c. 42.

[8] Marianus used Bede's *Chronicon*, AM 4652 from *De temporum ratione* for his extended entry on the translation of Cuthbert.

menbra locauerant.[1] Successit Eadberto in episcopatum uir Domini Eadfridus.*[a2]*

Romanorum .lxxi. regnauit Tiberius annis .vii. usque in annum .dcxciiii. post passionem Domini.[3]

[699] (i) 721   *Sinodus Aquilegie[b] facta ob imperitiam fidei quintum uniuersale concilium suscipere diffidit, donec salutaribus beati Sergii pape monitis instructa et ipsa huic cum ceteris Christi ecclesiis annuere consentit.[c4]*

Beatissimus uir Guthlacus *die kalendarum Septembrium .viii.* insulam *Cruland peruenit* ibique uitam anachoreticam ducere coepit.[5]

[700] (ii) 722   Ciclus solis incipit .iiii. concurrentibus bissextilibus.

[701] (iii) 723   *Sergius papa obiit .v. idus Septembris. Iohannes[6] papa octogesimus quartus annis[d] tribus et mensibus tribus.[e7]*

[703] (v) 725   *Ciclus decennouenalis .x. incipit indictione .i. Beda, in libro de temporibus, in anno quo eum condidit ita perhibet: 'si uis nosse quot sint anni ab incarnatione Domini iuxta Dionisium, scito quot fuerint indictionum ordines, utpote in presenti anno quinto Tiberii, quadraginta sex: hos multiplica per .xv., fiunt .dcxc., adde semper regulares .xii., quia quarta indictione secundum Dionisium natus est Dominus et indictionem anni illius cuiuscunque uolueris, utpote in presenti unam, fiunt septingenti tres. Isti sunt anni Domini iuxta Dionisium.' Hec Beda.[8]*

[704] (vi) 726   *Gisulfus,[9] dux gentis Longobardorum Beneuenti, Campaniam igne, gladio et captiuitate uastat; cunque non esset qui ei resisteret, apostolicus papa Iohannes qui Sergio successerat, missis ad eum sacerdotibus ac donariis perplurimis, uniuersos captiuos redemit,*

---

[a] see above, p. 158 n. g   [b] Aquileie HL   [c] see App. B for mg. addition with signe de renvoi B[1]   [d] extends on to line for 702 CB   [e] see App. B for addition at line-end extending into mg. B[1]

---

[1] *HE* iv. 30 (28) or Bede, *Vita Cuthberti,* cc. 42–3, or *HDE* i. 11 (i. 37). 'Nec mora' is found in *HE* and *HDE,* 'beati' in *Vita Cuthberti,* c. 43 and *HDE.* It is possible that the rewritten sections are based on *HDE.*

father himself.[1] Eadfrith, a man of God, succeeded Eadberht in the episcopacy.[2]

Tiberius, the seventy-first emperor of the Romans, reigned seven years, until the 694th year after the Lord's Passion.[3]

[699] A synod held at Aquileia put off, through ignorance of the faith, the acceptance of the fifth universal council until, instructed by the salutary counsels of the blessed Pope Sergius, it agreed, with Christ's other churches, to approve the fifth council.[4]

The most blessed man Guthlac arrived at the island of Crowland on 25 August, and there he began to lead the anchoritic life.[5]

[700] The solar cycle begins with four concurrents in a bissextile year.

[701] Pope Sergius died on 9 September. John,[6] the eighty-fourth pope, reigned three years and three months.[7]

[703] The tenth cycle of nineteen years begins in the first indiction. Bede, in his book *De Temporibus*, in the year in which he composed it, wrote thus: 'if you wish to know how many years there are, according to Dionysius, from the Lord's Incarnation, take the number of indiction-cycles, for example, in the present year, the fifth of Tiberius, 46; multiply this by 15 and it comes to 690: always add the constant number 12 because, our Lord was born in the fourth indiction, according to Dionysius, as well as the indiction of whichever year you want, 1 in the present year, making 703. These are the years of the Lord according to Dionysius.' Thus Bede.[8]

[704] Gisulf,[9] duke of the Lombards of Benevento, ravaged Campania with fire, the sword, and the taking of captives. Since there was none to resist him, the apostolic Pope John, who had succeeded Sergius, sent him priests and great sums of money, and

[2] This succession again could be based on *HDE* i. 11 (i. 37).
[3] Mar.   [4] Mar.
[5] Felix, *Vita Guthlaci*, c. 27 (p. 90). The year could have been calculated as is suggested above, p. 158 n. 3.
[6] John VI 701–5.   [7] Mar.   [8] Mar.
[9] Gisulf I 698–706.

hostesque domum redire fecit. Ipseque Iohannes papa obiit, indictione .iii. secundum gesta pontificum.[1]

*Æthelred*us *Merciorum* rex .*xxx.* anno regni sui *monachus factus, Cynredo* suo fratrueli *regnum dedit.*[a][2] Venerabilis monachus Beda per ministerium sancti *Iohannis* Eboracensis *episcopi, iubente Ceolfrido* suo *abbate, gradum presbiteratus suscepit.*[3]

[705] (vii) 727 *Iohannes*[4] *octogesimus quintus papa annis duobus, mensibus octo. Qui inter multa* [b]*opera illustria,*[b] *fecit oratorium sancte Dei genitrici opere pulcerrimo intra ecclesiam beati Petri apostoli.*[c] *Hereberhtus rex Longobardorum multas curtes et patrimonia Alpium Cottiarum que et quondam ad ius pertinebant apostolice sedis, sed, a Longobardis multo tempore fuerant ablata, restituit iuri eiusdem sedis et hanc donationem aureis scriptam litteris Romam direxit.*[d][5]

*Al*h*frið*[6] rex *Northanhymbrorum* [e]*in* Driffelda .xix. kalend. Ianuarii*i*[e][7] *defunctus est, anno regni sui .xx. necdum impleto. Cui succedens in imperium filius suus Osred, puer .viii. circiter annorum, regnauit annis .xi. Cuius regni principio antistes Occidentalium Saxonum Hædda celestem migrauit ad uitam. Quo defuncto episcopatus prouincie illius in duas parrochias diuisus est, una data Danieli, altera Aldel*mo *abba*ti *monasterii quod Maildul*fi *urbem nuncupant, ambo in rebus ecclesiasticis et in scientia scripturarum sufficienter instructi.*[8] [f]*Sanctus abbas*[g] *Aldelmus a beato Berhtuualdo*[h] *Dorubernensi archiepiscopo ordinatur episcopus.*[f][9] *Saxuulfus Merciorum episcopus uita quoque decessit.*[i][10]

---

[a] Tempore Kenredi. Vide, *later(?) 12th-c. hand add. in mg.* C, *om.* HL, *lower mg., pp. 276–81 below 705–8, introducing long HE addition (see App. B)* B[2], *though completed by another hand, tempore Kynredi incorporated in text* P; C[3]*'s addition probably refers to the long addition in* B (*also* 651 n. b)   [b-b] opera illu(stria)] *written mg. near beginning of line* C[1]   [c] 705 n. f *placed here* L   [d] 705 n. f *placed here* B   [e-e] *in* Driffelda . . . Ianuarii] *mg. near end and beginning of lines* C[1]   [f-f] Sanctus . . . episcopus] *mg. near opening of* 705 C[1], *incorporated at* 705 n. i H, *incorporated* 705 n. c L, *incorporated* 705 n. d B, *mg. alongside* 704 P[3], *under Tiberius III (698–705)* G   [g] *om.* HL   [h] Brihtuualdo H, Brihwoldo L   [i] 705 n. f *incorporated here* H

---

[1] Mar.
[2] Thirty-one years is apparently the period of rule in *HE*, though *HE* MS C (London, BL Cotton MS Tiberius C. II *teste* Plummer, *Bede*, i. 355) gives 30, and ASC 29. JW's 30th year (also JW *Mercian Accounts* 10) is consistent with his own date 675 for Æthelred's accession, and agrees with ASC's dates for accession and retirement. JW here and in *Mercian Accounts* 10 identifies Cenred as Æthelred's brother.

redeemed all the captives, and made the enemy return home. The same Pope John died in the third indiction, according to the *Liber Pontificalis*.[1]

Æthelred, king of the Mercians, became a monk in the thirtieth year of his reign, and gave the kingdom to his nephew Cenred.[2] The venerable monk Bede was ordained priest at the hands of St John, bishop of York, at the command of Ceolfrith, his abbot.[3]

[705] John,[4] the eighty-fifth pope, reigned two years and eight months. Among his many famous works he made the oratory of the holy Mother of God with the most beautiful workmanship inside the church of St Peter the Apostle. Aripert, king of the Lombards, restored to the control of the apostolic see many estates and endowments in the Cottian Alps that had formerly belonged to its jurisdiction, but had long before been seized by the Lombards, and he sent a deed of gift, written in letters of gold, to Rome.[5]

Aldfrith,[6] king of the Northumbrians, died at Driffield on 14 December,[7] during the twentieth year of his reign. His son Osred succeeded him to the throne as a boy about eight years old, and reigned eleven years. At the beginning of his reign Hædde, bishop of the West Saxons, departed to the heavenly life. After his death the bishopric of that kingdom was divided into two dioceses: one was given to Daniel, the other to Aldhelm, abbot of the monastery that is called the 'city of Maidulf' (Malmesbury). Both were thoroughly versed in ecclesiastical matters, and in the knowledge of the scriptures.[8] The holy abbot Aldhelm was ordained bishop by the blessed Berhtwald, archbishop of Canterbury.[9] Seaxwulf, bishop of the Mercians, also departed this life.[10]

---

[3] *HE* v. 24. As under 681 and 693 the date of Bede's birth is reckoned as 674.
[4] John VII 705–7.   [5] Mar.   [6] Same misspelling as above, p. 144 n. 5.
[7] Bede and ASC A(B)C give the year of Aldfrith's death, but ASC DE also state that he died on 14 Dec. in Driffield.
[8] *HE* v. 18.
[9] This marginal entry may be based on *GP* v. 223, 231, (pp. 376, 383), or inferred from *HE* v. 18.
[10] Seaxwulf died before Wilfrid, after his expulsion from Northumbria in 691, had been befriended by Æthelred (Stephanus, *Vita Wilfridi*, c. 44). JW's date and entry could be derived from ASC A(B)C.

[C³BP]

*ª*Post cuius decessum ¹prouincia
Merciorum   duos   episcopos
habuit, Headdan et Wilfridum,¹
Hæddan ad Licetfeld, Wilfridus
ad Leogeram. Sed illo *ui hostilitatis eiecto,*² mortuoque rege
Alhfrido ad pristini *sedem* episcopatus id est *Haugustaldum in
concordiam receptus* reuertitur.³
Hædda*ᵇ* uero *ambas* post rexit
parrochias et post eum Aldwine
qui et Wor.*ª²*

*Romanorum septuagesimus secundus regnauit Iustinianus*⁴ *secundus*ᶜ
*cum Tiberio filio suo annis sex usque in annum septingentesimum post
passionem.*

*ᵈHic auxilio Interpelli regis Wlgarorum*ᵉ *regnum recipiens, occidit
eos, qui se expulerunt patricios et Leonem, qui locum eius usurpauerat,
necnon et successorem eius Tiberium. Gallinicum autem patriarcham,
erutis oculis, misit Romam et dedit episcopatum Ciro, qui erat abbas in
Ponto eumque alebat exulem. Iohannes papa obiit .xv. kalend.
Nouembris.*⁵

[707] (ii) 729   *Sisinnius*⁶ *ᶠ.lxxxvi. papa mense .i.*ᵍ⁷

*Beda, .xxx. etatis sue anno, gradu presbiteratus accepto, libros suos
incepit facere, in quibus* componendis *.xxix. annis laborauit.*ᶠ⁸

[708] (iii) 730   *Constantinus*⁹ *octogesimus septimus papa annis .vii. et*
p. 272   *mense uno.* ʰ*Quem* | *Iustinianus, ad se uenire iubens, honorifice*

ª⁻ª Post . . . Wor] *written partly at line-end and partly in mg.* C³, *om.* HL
ᵇ Hedda *BP*   *ᶜ* secundo *(N)*   *ᵈ begins under 705 and continues under 706
CHLB, 706 begins here P (N)*   *ᵉ* Wlgariorum *HL*   *ᶠ⁻ᶠ* .lxxxvi. . . . laborauit]
written partly over erasure, partly in mg. C*ª*   *ᵍ* obiit octauo idus Nouembris *add.*
(N)   *ʰ under 707 (N)*

---

¹⁻¹ These words are shared with JW Mercian *Epis. Lists.*

² *GP* iv. 172 (p. 307). Though misdated by the erroneous 705 for Seaxwulf's death,
some of the information in this entry may be correct. When Wilfrid administered the
Middle Anglian see (Leicester), Headda could have been bishop of Mercia (Lichfield).
S 53 *BCS* 85, a charter dated 693, is witnessed by Wilfrid and Headda; the latter could
be the bishop of Lichfield if one assumes that the missing name among the episcopal

After his demise, [1]the province
of the Mercians had two bishops, Hædda and Wilfrid,[1]
Hædda at Lichfield, Wilfrid at
Leicester. But the latter was
expelled by hostile force,[2] and
on the death of King Aldfrith
he returned to the seat of his
former bishopric, namely
Hexham, and was received in
peace.[3] Headda ruled both dioceses, and after him Aldwine,
also known as Wor.[2]

Justinian II,[4] seventy-second emperor of the Romans, reigned
with Tiberius, his son, for six years up to the 700th year after the
Passion.

Justinian regained his empire with the aid of Tervel, king of the
Bulgars, and killed those nobles who had expelled him, and Leo
who had usurped his place, as well as his successor Tiberius. He
sent the patriarch Callinicus (after putting out his eyes) to Rome,
and gave the episcopacy to Cyrus, who was an abbot in Pontus,
and had sustained him in exile. Pope John died on 18 October.[5]

[707] Sisinnius,[6] the eighty-sixth pope, reigned one month,[7]

Bede, in his thirtieth year, after receiving the rank of priest,
began to write his books, in the composition of which he laboured
twenty-nine years.[8]

[708] Constantine,[9] the eighty-seventh pope, reigned seven years
and one month. Justinian requested his attendance and received

witnesses is Hædde of Winchester. The ejection of Wilfrid referred to could be that by
the synod of Austerfield, which deprived him of his possessions; and if the endorse-
ment on the spurious *S* 22 *BCS* 91 (which gives the names of the bishops present at
Clofesho in 716, and which shows Headda and Wor both present, is reliable), it is possible that Aldwine (Wor) was then bishop of Leicester and later between 716 and 731
ruled both Lichfield and Leicester.

 [3] *GP* iii, 110 (p. 245).   [4] Justinian II 705–11.   [5] Mar.
 [6] Sisinnius 708.   [7] Mar.
 [8] *HDE* i. 11 (i. 38). This addition agrees with the date for Bede's birth under 677,
but is at variance with the annal for 704 and the reckonings implied in 681, 693, and
704.
 [9] Constantine 708–15.

suscepit ac remisit ita ut eum die dominica missas sibi facere iubens communionem de manu eius acciperet, quem etiam prostratus in terra pro suis peccatis intercedere rogans, cuncta ecclesie priuilegia renouauit.[1]

Kynred rex *Merciorum* et *Offa* rex *Orientalium Saxonum, filius Sigheri regis,* eorundem re*l*ictis uxoribus, *agris, cognatis et patria, propter Christum et propter euangelium, Romam* ue*n*erunt, ibique *atton*si ac *monachi facti, ad limina apostolorum in precibus, ieiuniis et elemosinis usque ad[a] diem ultimum perman*serunt, sicque *ad uisionem beatorum apostolorum in celis diu desideratam peru*enerunt.[2] *Cum* quibus et sanctus Ecguuinus Huuicciorum episcopus rogatus, ab eis Romam uenit, et ut monasterium, [b]quod in territorio Wigornensi construxerat, ab improborum irruptione securius redderet, epistolam priuilegii a papa Constantino petiit et impetrauit.[b][3]

[709] (iiii) 731 [c]*Succ*essit Kynredo *in regnum Ceolred, filius Æthelredi* regis, *qui ante ipsum Kynredum idem regnum tenebat.*[4] Sanctus Aldelmus Westsaxonice prouincie antistes, *uir undecunque doctissimus,* migrauit ad Dominum, *pro* quo *pontificatum suscepit Forth*redus, *uir et ipse in scripturis sanctis multum eruditus.*[5]

> [d]*Wilfridus* sanctus[e] *meritis et nomine magnus*
> *Iactatus* multis *per tempora longa periclis,*
> *Quindecies ternos postquam egit episcopus annos*
> *Transiit, et gaudens celestia regna petiuit.*

Cuius corpus[f] *in primo suo monasterio quod* dicitur *Inhrypum, in ecclesia beati Petri apostoli* [g]est honorifice[g] *tumulatum.*[6] Quo defuncto, *Acca presbiter eius, uir strenuissimus, coram Deo et hominibus magnificus, cantor peritissimus, in litteris sanctis doctissimus,*

---

[a] *in HL*   [b–b] quod . . . impetrauit] *written in compressed hand and paler ink, possibly over erasure and running on to second line of* 709 C[1]*, runs on to* 709 *HLBP*   [c] *starts on second line of* 709, *but gap in line after last word* (impetrauit) *of* 708 *suggests new annal* C   [d] *verses indicated by coloured initials, not by new lines* C   [e] sanctis *HL*   [f] migrauit apud Vndalum iuxta fluuium quod dicitur Nen *interlin. B*[5]?   [g–g] est honorifice] honorifice est C

---

[1] Mar.
[2] *HE* v. 19. Of all versions of ASC, C alone places Cenred and Offa's journey to Rome in 708. ADE enter it under 709, as Bede does in *HE* v. 24, B's year being either 708 or 709.
[3] The earliest reference to the probably false tradition that Ecgwine accompa-

him honourably, permitting him to perform mass for him on Sunday, beseeching that he might take communion from his hand, and asking him, as he, Justinian, lay prostrate on the ground, to intercede for his sins. He renewed all the Church's privileges.[1]

Cenred, king of the Mercians, and Offa, king of the East Saxons, son of King Sighere, went to Rome, leaving wives, lands, kin, and country for Christ and the Gospel; they were tonsured and became monks there, at the shrine of the apostles, and they remained in prayer, fasting, and almsgiving to their last day. Thus they attained the vision of the blessed apostles in Heaven which they had long desired.[2] With them also St Ecgwine, bishop of the Hwicce, came to Rome at their request, and sought and obtained from Pope Constantine a letter of privileges, to protect the monastery which he had built in Worcestershire against the attack of evil men.[3]

[709] Ceolred succeeded Cenred to the kingdom. He was the son of King Æthelred, who had held that very kingdom before Cenred himself.[4] St Aldhelm, bishop of the West Saxon province, a man most learned in all fields, passed to the Lord, and Forthhere, a man also very learned in Holy Scripture, received his bishopric in his place.[5]

> St Wilfrid, great in merit and in name,
> Long tossed by many dangers,
> Departed, when forty-five years a bishop,
> And rejoicing sought the heavenly kingdom.

His body was ceremonially buried in the church of St Peter the Apostle, in his own first monastery, called Ripon.[6] After his death his priest, Acca, a most energetic man, glorious in the eyes of God and man, a most skilful singer, most learned in Holy Scripture,

---

nied the kings to Rome seems to be Byrhtferth's *Vita Ecgwini*. The privilege for Ecgwine's foundation of Evesham from Pope Constantine is a forgery (see J. Sayers, '"Original", cartulary and chronicle: the case of the abbey of Evesham; *Fälschungen im Mittelalter* (Schriften der MGH, xxxiii; Hanover, 1988), iv. 374–95.

[4] *HE*. v. 19; date from v. 24.

[5] *HE* v. 18. The date, not derived from Bede, is given as 709 in ASC ADEF, as 708 in C, and presumably as one of these two years in B. Aldhelm is more precisely identified as bishop of Sherborne in JW *Epis. Lists* and as bishop 'west of the wood' in ASC (B alone has 'be westan Selewuda').

[6] *HE* v. 19.

in catholice fidei confessione castissimus, in ecclesiastice institutionis regulis sollertissimus, ac Deo dilecti Bose Eboracensis episcopi quondam alumpnus, *Hagustaldensis ecclesie* presulatum *suscepit.*[1]

[710] (v) 732 *Berhtfrith*, regis Osredi *prefectus, cum Pictis pugnauit* et *uictor exstitit.*[2] *Geuuissorum* rex bellicosus Ine et Nun suus proximus cum Gerente Brytonum rege bellum gessere uictumque in fugam uertere.[3] *Reuerentissimus pater Adrianus*, monasterii beati Petri apostoli[a] *abbas, est defunctus et in* eodem *monasterio sepultus.* Cui *successit in regimine discipulus* suus *Albinus* qui *non minus Grec*e et *Latin*e *quam Angl*ice *lingue, que sibi* erat[b] *naturalis,* exstitit peritus.[4]

[C³BP]

^cDefuncto Tyrhtello Herefordie presule, successit Torhthere.^{c4}

[711] (vi) 733 Iustinianus *^dcum exercitum mitteret in Pontum, multum prohibente papa apostolico, ad comprehendendum Philippicum quem ibi reliquerat, conuersus omnis exercitus ad partem Philippici, fecit eum ibidem imperatorem. Reuersusque Constantinopolim pugnauit contra Iustinianum ad duodecimum ab urbe miliarium, et, uicto atque occiso Iustiniano, regnum suscepit Philippicus.*

Romanorum septuagesimus tertius regnauit Philippicus[6] *anno uno et mensibus sex usque in annum septingentesimum secundum post passionem Domini.*

^eHic eicit Cyrum de pontificatu, eumque ad gubernandum abbatis iure monasterium suum Pontum redire precepit.^e ^fIdem Constantino pape misit litteras praui dogmatis, quas ille cum apostolice sedis consilio respuit, et huius rei causa fecit picturas in porticu sancti Petri, que acta sex sanctarum synodorum uniuersalium continerent. Nam et huiusmodi picturas cum haberentur in urbe regia Philippicus iusserat

---

^a *om.* HLP   ^b *om.* HL   ^{c–c} Defuncto . . . Torhthere] *add. at end of annal* C³, *om.* HL   ^d *starts under 710 (N)*   ^{e–e} Hic . . . precepit] *this sentence runs on to 712 CHLB, 712 starts here* P *(N)*   ^f Idem . . . prolatum *(p. 170)] starts under 712, (in C not marked out from 711 by the distinguishing initial by which a new annal is usually announced)* CHLB

---

[1] *HE* v. 20. The date for Wilfrid's death and Acca's succession is in Bede.

[2] *HE* v. 24. JW follows ASC A (addition by hand 3) (B)CDEG (710) against Bede (711) in dating Berhtfrith's expedition, but lacks ASC DE's location of the battle ('betwux Hæfe and Cære') though (unlike ASC) he makes it clear that this was a Northumbrian victory as does HH *HA* iv c. 8 (Arnold p. 111).

most pure in his profession of the Catholic faith, most practised in the customs of the church, once a pupil of Bosa, bishop of York, the beloved of God, received the bishopric of Hexham.[1]

[710] Berhtfrith, ealdorman of King Osred, fought with the Picts and was victorious.[2] Ine, the warlike king of the *Gewisse*, and his kinsman Nun warred with Geraint, king of the Britons, defeated him and put him to flight.[3] The most reverend father Hadrian, abbot of the monastery of St Peter the Apostle, died and was buried in the same monastery. His pupil Albinus, who succeeded him in authority, was no less skilled in Greek and in Latin than he was in English, which was his mother tongue.[4]

> On the death of Tyrhtel, bishop of Hereford, Torhthere succeeded.[5]

[711] Against the strong objections of the apostolic pope, Justinian sent his army to Pontus to arrest Philippicus, whom he had left there. The whole army went over to Philippicus, made him emperor there, and, returning to Constantinople, fought Justinian twelve miles from the city; when Justinian had been defeated and slain, Philippicus took the throne.

Philippicus,[6] the seventy-third emperor of the Romans, reigned for a year and six months, up to the 702nd year after the Lord's Passion.

He expelled Cyrus from the bishopric and ordered him to return to Pontus to rule his monastery as abbot. He also sent letters to Pope Constantine of perverted teaching which the pope, on the advice of the apostolic see, rejected; because of this he had images made in the portico of St Peter's, depicting the acts of the six holy universal synods; for Philippicus had ordered similar

---

[3] JW agrees with ASC A (addition by hand 3) DE in describing Nun as Ine's 'proximus' and Geraint as 'king of the Britons', though ASC does not call Ine 'bellicosus' nor claim a victory. HH *HA* iv c. 8 (Arnold pp. 10–11) has Geraint being defeated.

[4] *HE* v. 20. The date of Hadrian's death is deduced from Bede's statement that it occurred in the year following Wilfrid's.

[5] Charters throw little light on this succession: Torhthere was among those who attested at the council of *Clofesho* in 716 (*S* 22 *BCS* 91); and Tyrhtel attests in 693 (*S* 53 *BCS* 85).

[6] Phillippicus 711–13.

auferri. Statuitque populus Romanus, ne heretici imperatoris nomen aut cartas uel figuram solidi susciperent, unde nec eius effigies in ecclesiam inducta est, nec nomen eius ad missam prolatum.ᵃ ᵇContra hunc Anastasius consurgens regno oculisque priuauit.ᵇ¹

[713] (ii) 735 Romanorum septuagesimus quartus regnauit Anastasius² annis tribus usque in annum septingentesimum tertium.

ᶜIste litteras Constantino pape Romam per Scolasticum patricium et exarchum Italie direxit, quibus se fautorem catholice fidei et sancti sixti concilii predicatorem esse dixit.³

[714] (i) 736 Anachorita probatissimus, Deique sacerdos fidelissimus delecte Christi uirginis Pegie germanus innumerabilium uirtutum, ᵈpatrator Guthlacus, ᵉindictione .xii.ᵉ .iiii. lumine festi pascalis, ᵉiii. idus Aprilis,ᵉ animamᵈ | ad gaudia perpetue emisit exultationis,⁴ cui Cissa qui diu paganis ritibus deditus erat sed post baptismum in Britannia ᶠperceperat successit.ᶠ⁵

p. 273

[715] (ii) 737 *Constantinus papa obiit .vi. idus Ianuarii. Gregorius⁶ papa octogesimus octauus annis decem et .vii., mensibus decem. Hic erat uir castus et sapiens, qui Bonifacium genere Anglumᵍ ordinauit episcopum sedi Mogontine per quem Germania uerbum salutis suscepit.ʰ Pippinus filius Ansgisi apud Gallias Francorum regnans obiit. Cui Karolus qui et maior domus filius eius in regnum successit per annos uiginti septem usque ad filios suos Karlomannum et Pippinum, primum imperatorem Francorum. Liutbrandus rex Longobardorum donationem patrimonii Alpium Cottiarum, quam Hereberctus rex fecerat, et ille repetierat, admonitione uenerabilis pape Gregorii, confirmauit.⁷ ⁱ⟨Q⟩uidam Petronax ciuis Brixiane urbis, diuino amore compunctus, Romam uenit indeque hortatu beati pape Gregorii montem Cassinum expetiit, ibique cum aliquibus simplicibus uiris habitare cepit. Et non multo post, suffragantibus sibi meritis eximii patris*

ᵃ see above, p. 168 n. f   ᵇ⁻ᵇ Contra . . . priuauit] *runs on to 713 CHL, 713 starts here (N)*   ᶜ *714 starts here (N)*   ᵈ⁻ᵈ patrator . . . animam] patrator indictione .xii., .iii. idus Aprilis Guthlacus .iiii. lumine festi paschalis animam P   ᵉ⁻ᵉ indictione .xii., .iii. idus Aprilis] *interlin.* C¹B¹ (*in* B *above* gaudie perpetue), *as shown in 714 n. c* P   ᶠ⁻ᶠ perceperat (*from* perceperit) successit *extends into mg. at line-end* C¹   ᵍ Hibernensem (N), Scottum *Mar.*   ʰ *715 n. i placed here HL*   ⁱ Quidam . . . cepit (p. 172)] *add. mg. alongside* 715–16 C³P³, *placed at* 715 n. h HL, *at end of annal B, under* Anastasius II (713–15) G

pictures, which existed in the royal city, to be removed. The Roman people resolved not to accept the name or documents or coin-images of a heretical emperor; in consequence, this likeness was not admitted in a church nor his name read out at mass. Anastasius rose against Philippicus and deprived him of his kingdom and his sight.[1]

[713] Anastasius,[2] the seventy-fourth emperor of the Romans, reigned three years, until the 703rd year.

He sent letters to Pope Constantine at Rome by way of Scholasticus, the patrician, exarch of Italy, in which he called himself a defender of the Catholic faith, and a supporter of the sixth holy synod.[3]

[714] The most approved anchorite Guthlac, a most faithful priest of God, brother of the virgin Pega, beloved of Christ, the performer of innumerable miracles, released his soul to the joys of eternal exultation on 11 April, on the fourth day of the Easter festival, in the twelfth indiction.[4] Cissa, who had long been devoted to pagan rites but later received baptism in Britain, succeeded him.[5]

[715] Pope Constantine died on 8 January. Pope Gregory,[6] the eighty-eighth pope, reigned seventeen years ten months. He was a man both upright and wise, who ordained the Englishman Boniface bishop of Mainz; through him Germany received the word of salvation. Pippin, son of Andegisel, and ruler of the Franks in Gaul, died. Charles, his son, who was also mayor of the palace, succeeded him as ruler for twenty-seven years to the time of his own sons, Carloman and Pippin, the first emperor of the Franks. Liutprand, king of the Lombards, admonished by the venerable Pope Gregory, confirmed the donation of the estates in the Cottian Alps which King Aripert had made, and had reclaimed.[7] One Petronax, a citizen of Brescia, pierced by divine love, went to Rome, and from there, at the urging of the blessed Pope Gregory, he made for Monte Cassino, and began to live

---

[1] Mar.   [2] Anastasius II 712–15.   [3] Mar.
[4] Felix, *Vita Guthlaci*, c. 50, (pp. 152, 158). On Guthlac's death see above, p. 158 n. 3.
[5] Felix, *Vita Guthlaci*, c. 48 (p. 148).   [6] Gregory II 715–31.
[7] Mar.

Benedicti multorum ibi monachorum ad se concurrentium pater effectus, reparatis habitaculis, regulariter uiuere cepit.[a1]

Ine rex Westsaxonum et Ceolred rex Merciorum in loco qui Wodnesberh dicitur pugnauerunt.[b2]

[716] (iii) 738   *Gregorius papa constituit ut in quadragesimali tempore ieiunium missarumque celebritas fieret, quod ante eum non erat.*[3]

⟨V⟩*ir domini Ecgbert*us, cuius supra meminimus, *Ienses monachos ad catholicum pasca et ecclesiasticam correxit tonsuram.*[4] *Osredo occiso, Cenred,* magnifici uiri Cuthuuini filius, *gubernacula regni Northanhymbrorum suscepit.*[5] Rex Merciorum Ceolred defungitur et Licethfeld sepelitur. Post quem Athelbaldus, consobrinus suus, filius uidelicet Aluueonis, patruelis scilicet patris sui regis Æthelredi, ut ei prophetico spiritu sanctus predixerat Guthlacus regnum nanciscitur.[6] Æthelredus, quondam rex Merciorum, post autem abbas Beardoniensis cenobii, quod ipse construxit e seculo migrauit et eterne felicitatis serenitatis ac lucis gaudia intrauit.[7] Magne uir sanctitatis et religionis Ceolfridus abbas *.vii. kalendarum Octobrium die, feria sexta,* apud *Lingonas Burgundiorum*[c] *ciuitatem*[8] peregrinus obiit et *in ecclesia sanctorum martyrum geminorum Speusipp*i *Eleusipp*i et *Meleusipp*i *sepultu*s est.[9] *Erat autem quando obiit* [d]*annorum .lxxiiii.*[d] *presbiterii gradu functus annis .xlvii. abbatis officium ministrans annis triginta quinque.*[10]

Romanorum septuagesimus quintus Theodosius[11] *regnauit anno uno usque in annum septingentesimum quintum post passionem Domini.*[e12]

---

[a] *see above, p. 170 n. i*   [b] *715 n. i placed here* B   [c] Burgundionum *JW*
[d-d] annorum .lxxiiii.] .lxxiiii. annorum HL   [e] *om. (N)*

---

[1] Hugh of Fleury, p. 161, who says that the translation occurred 110 years after the destruction of Cassino, which Mar. and JW assigned to 596.

[2] ASC. 'Wodnesberh' is closer to ASC DE's 'æt Wodnesbeorge' than to ABC's 'æt Woddesbeorge' (C originally 715, but carelessly altered to 710 by erasure of the Roman numeral .v., though 714 was almost certainly intended). Whitelock, *ASC* p. 26, accepts its identification with Adam's Grave in Alton Priors, Wilts. JW identifies the kingdoms of the two leaders.

[3] Mar.   [4] *HE* v. 24.

[5] *HE* v. 22. ASC DE say Osred was slain 'south of the border'. There is nothing in Bede or ASC to explain why Cuthwine is called 'magnificus'. JW's annal 729 (based on ASC 731) implies that Cenred was Cuthwine's grandson, not his son as this annal and JW *Northum. Gen.* and *Accounts* 17 say.

there with some ordinary men. Not much later, with the support of the merits of the outstanding father Benedict, he was made abbot of the many monks who had gathered about him there, and when the buildings had been repaired he began to live according to the rule.[1]

Ine, king of the West Saxons, and Ceolred, king of the Mercians, fought in the place '*Wodens Barrow*'.[2]

[716] Pope Gregory established that in the Lenten period there should be fasting and the celebration of masses, which had not been the case before him.[3]

Ecgberht, the man of God whom we mentioned earlier, corrected the monks of Iona to the Catholic Easter and the ecclesiastical tonsure.[4] When Osred was slain, Cenred, son of that splendid man Cuthwine, received the governance of the kingdom of the Northumbrians.[5] Ceolred, king of the Mercians, died and was buried at Lichfield. After him Æthelbald, his cousin, that is the son of Alweo, cousin of Ceolred's father Æthelred, as St Guthlac had foretold to him with prophetic inspiration,[6] received the kingdom. Æthelred, former king of the Mercians, and afterwards abbot of the monastery of Bardney, which he had built himself, left this world and entered into the joys of eternal happiness, peace, and light.[7] The very holy and religious abbot Ceolfrith died on his pilgrimage on Friday, 25 September, at Langres, a city in Burgundy,[8] in the church of the holy fellow-martyrs, Speusippus, Eleusippus, and Meleusippus.[9] He was seventy-four years old when he died, and had served in priest's orders for forty-seven years, exercising the office of abbot for thirty-five years.[10]

The seventy-fifth emperor of the Romans, Theodosius,[11] reigned one year, up to the 705th year after the Lord's Passion.[12]

---

[6] As well as recording Ceolred's (BC wrongly Ceolwold's) death and burial at Lichfield, ASC ADEF (716) C (716 from 717) B (716 or 717) give the length of Æthelbald's reign and full details of his genealogy (F confining its entry to Æthelbald's accession and the length of his reign). The reference to Guthlac's prophecy is based on Felix, *Vita Guthlaci*, c. 52.

[7] ASC. A–E (dates as for n. 6) simply record Æthelred's burial at Bardney; JW seems to have inferred from Bede and ASC that Æthelred was founder as well as abbot of Bardney and that he died in 716.

[8] *Anon. hist. abbat.*, c. 32.   [9] Ibid., c. 36.   [10] Bede, *Hist. abbat.*, c. 22.
[11] Theodosius III 715–17.   [12] Mar.

[717] (i) 739 *Anastasius cum classem in Alexandriam contra Sarracenos direxisset, exercitus de medio itinere reuertitur, et Theodosium imperatorem facit, coactumque eum in solio imperii confirmauit. Qui deinde apud Nicenam ciuitatem, graui prelio uicit Anastasium, in quo septem milia de exercitu* imperii *ceciderunt. Capto autem Anastasio, datoque sibi sacramento, clericum fieri ac presbiterum ordinari precepit. Theodosius uero ut regnauit cum esset catholicus, mox in regia urbe imaginem illam uenerandam in qua sancte sex synodi erant depicte, et a Philippico fuerat deiecta, pristino in loco erexit. Tiberis fluuius alueum suum egressus, multa Rome fecit exitia ita ut in uia Lata ad unam et semis staturam excresceret atque a porta sancti Petri usque ad pontem Muluuium aque descendentes se coniungerent. Mansit autem sic diebus .vii., donec agentibus letanias crebras ciuibus octauo demum die reuersus est.*[1]

Sanctus Ecguuinus tertius Wicciorum episcopus transiuit ad Dominum *a* indictione .xv., .iii. kalendarum Ianuariarum die, feria .v.,*a* pro quo Wilfridus, religionis uir eximie, electus, illo adhuc superstite, presulatum suscepit Wigornensis ecclesie.*b*[2]

Romanorum septuagesimus sextus regnauit Leo[3] *annis nouem et inde annis .xv. usque ad Pippinum primum Francorum imperatorem hoc est in annum .dccxxix. post passionem Domini.*[4]

[718] (i) 740 ʿKenred Northanhymbrorum rex moritur et Osric in regem eleuatur.*d*[5] Ingels, frater Ine regis Westsaxonum, uite modum fecit,[6] quorum sorores exstitere sancta Cuenburh et sancta Cuthburh, que monasterium uirginum Deo deuotarum in loco qui dicitur Winburnan construxit. Hanc autem Aldfriðᵉ rex Northanhymbrorum in coniugem habuit, sed ante finem sue uite conubio carnalis copule ambo [7]pro Dei amore[7] renuntiauere.*f*[8] |

a-a indictione .xv. *and* feria .v. *interlin. above date* C¹B¹P³   *b see App. B for addition at line-end extending into mg.* B¹   *c see App. B for addition in upper mg. with signe de renvoi* B¹   *d* leuatur HL   *e uel* Ferthe *interlin.* B⁵   *f see App. B for (i) a lower-mg. Frankish addition* B¹ *and (ii) a HE addition in lower mg. pp. 279–83 below 725–9* B². *Both these additions are accompanied by signes de renvoi, but there is only one sign at the end of 718 for the possible location of one or of both lower-mg. additions*

[1] Mar.
[2] JW is the earliest authority for the date of Ecgwine's death. It appears to be assigned to 716 in the JW MS C's 19-year table on p. 60. Ecgwine attended the council of *Clofesho* in July 716. The election of Wilfrid as his successor may be connected with

[717] When Anastasius sent his fleet to Alexandria against the Saracens, the force turned back in mid-voyage and made Theodosius emperor, and established him against his will on the imperial throne. He then defeated Anastasius in a crucial battle at the city of Nicaea in which 7,000 men of the imperial army were slain. When Anastasius had been captured and had sworn allegiance to him, he ordered that he be made a cleric and ordained a priest. Since Theodosius was a Catholic, as soon as he began his reign he erected in its original place in the imperial city the revered depiction of the six holy synods, which had been torn down by Philippicus. The river Tiber broke its banks and did great damage at Rome for, in the *Via Lata*, it rose to a height of one and a half feet, and its waters, as they poured down, spread from the door of St Peter's to the Milvian Bridge. It remained like this for seven days until it at last went down on the eighth day in response to the performance of many litanies by the citizens.[1]

St Ecgwine, third bishop of the Hwicce, passed to the Lord on Thursday, 30 December, in the fifteenth indiction. Wilfrid, a man of outstanding devotion, was chosen during Ecgwine's lifetime to fill his place, and received the church of Worcester.[2]

Leo,[3] the seventy-sixth emperor of the Romans, reigned nine years, and then fifteen, up to Pippin, first emperor of the Franks, that is the 729th year after our Lord's Passion.[4]

[718] Cenred, king of the Northumbrians, died, and Osric became king.[5] Ingild, brother of Ine, king of the West Saxons, came to the end of his life.[6] His sisters were St Cwenburg and St Cuthburg, who built the monastery of the virgins dedicated to God in the place called Wimborne. Aldfrith, king of the Northumbrians, married Cuthburg, but before the end of their lives both renounced their carnal union [7]for the love of God.[7,8]

---

the false assertion in Evesham's forged documents that, on Ecgwine's return from his alleged visit to Rome (709), he resigned his see and became abbot of Evesham (see Haddan and Stubbs, *Councils*, iii. 278-83).

[3] Leo III 717-41.   [4] Mar.

[5] ASC. The successions of Cenred and of Osric were recorded under 716 in ASC ADE, 716 (from 717), in C and either 716 or 717 in B, which makes the former reign 2 years and the latter 11. *HE* v. 23 refers to 725 as the seventh year of Osric.

[6] ASC ADE (716) C (717 from 718) B (717/718) F (718) call Ine's brother Ingild against Ingels here and in JW *West Saxon Gen.* and *Accounts* 16.

[7-7] Not in ASC.   [8] ASC.

[**719**] (ii) 741 *Sarraceni cum immenso exercitu Constantinopolim obsident, donec ciuibus multa orationum instantia ad Deum clamantibus, plurimi hostium frigore, fame* atque *pestilentia perierunt.*[a]1

[**721**] (iiii) 743 Daniel Wentane ciuitatis episcopus Romam iuit. Eodemque anno rex Ine clitonem Cyneuulfum occidit.[2] Sanctus Iohannes Eboracensis ecclesie episcopus, cum *pre maiore senectute minus episcopatui administrando sufficeret, ordinato* pro se *Wilfrido presbitero suo, secessit ad monasterium* suum, *quod dicitur In Silua Deirorum, ibique uitam in Deo digna conuersatione compl*ens celestia, [b]nonis Maii,[b] conscendit.[c]3 [d]Eadfridus Lindisfarnensis episcopus obiit cui *Mailrosensis abbas et presbiter Æthelwoldus successit.*[d]4

[**722**] (v) 744 *Ciclus decennouenalis .xi. incipit indictione .v.*[5]

Æthelburh regina castrum Tantun dictum penitus destruxit, quod prius rex Ine construxit, qui eodem anno[e] cum Australibus Saxonibus pugnauit.[6]

[**723**] (vi) 745 *Sarraceni pertesi obsidionis abscedunt. Qui inde regressi Wlgarorum gentem que est super Danubium bello aggrediuntur, ab hac quoque uicti refugiunt ac naues repetunt.*[7]

[**725**] (viii) 747 *Wih*tred *rex Cantuuariorum, filius Ecgberti, nono die kalendarum Maiarum obiit et regni quod per .xxxiiii. semis annos tenebat, filios .iii., Athilber*htum, *Eadbertum et Alricum* [f]reliquit heredes.[f]8 Rex Ine denuo cum Suthsaxonibus pugnans clitonem Aldbrihtum quem prius de Westsaxonia expulerat occidit.[g]9

---

[a] *runs over on to line for 720, which is now mostly blank, but with erasures with an opening initial C clearly visible* C   [b–b] nonis Maii] *interlin.* C[1]B[1]   [c] *written mg.* C[1] [d–d] Eadfridus . . . successit] *written over erasure* C[2], *mg. with signe de renvoi* H [e] Ine *interlin.* B[1]   [f–f] reliquit heredes *written in mg. at line-end* C[1]   [g] *written in mg. at line-end* C[1]

---

[1] Mar.

[2] ASC. Daniel's visit to Rome and the death (not in F) of Cynewulf are entered in ASC A(B)DEF (721) and C (720 from 721), DE calling Cynewulf 'the atheling'.

[3] *HE* v. 6. ASC DEF place John's death and (not F) burial at Beverley in this year, as Bede seems to do, but, as the exact date of his appointment is unknown, the day of his death could not be calculated from the precise length of his episcopacy given by ASC DEF. The day could have been taken from a calendar or from Folchard's *Life of John of Beverley* (*Historians of the Church of York*, i. 260).

[719] The Saracens besieged Constantinople with a vast army until, in response to the citizens' calling upon God with urgent and frequent prayers, many of the enemy perished of cold and hunger and disease.[1]

[721] Daniel, bishop of the city of Winchester, went to Rome. In the same year King Ine killed the atheling Cynewulf.[2] St John, bishop of York, being prevented by his great age from adequately running his bishopric, consecrated his priest Wilfrid in his place and retired to his monastery, which was called Beverley; there he rounded out his life in a manner honourable to God, and departed to Heaven on 7 May.[3] Eadfrith, bishop of Lindisfarne, died and Æthelwald, abbot of Melrose, and a priest, succeeded him.[4]

[722] The eleventh cycle of nineteen years begins in the fifth indiction.[5]

Queen Æthelburg completely destroyed the fort called Taunton, which King Ine had built earlier. He fought with the South Saxons in the same year.[6]

[723] The Saracens left, exhausted by the siege; on their return thence they made war on the Bulgarians, who are beyond the Danube. Defeated by them as well, they fled back to their ships.[7]

[725] Wihtred, king of the people of Kent, son of Ecgberht, died on 23rd April, leaving his three sons, Æthelberht, Eadberht, and Alric, heirs of the realm, which he had held for thirty-four and a half years.[8] King Ine, fighting again with the South Saxons, slew the atheling Eadberht, whom he had earlier driven out of Wessex.[9]

---

[4] HDE i. 12 (i. 39). C²'s 721 for Eadfrith's death may have been calculated from his own 698 for Eadfrith's accession and from the 22 years assigned his pontificate by HDE i. 11 (i. 37), but the date seems to be at variance with the possible dates for the pontificate of Eadfrith's successor Æthelwald. HDE i. 12, 13, 14, ii. 2 (i. 39, 41, 48) assigns 16 years to Æthelwald's pontificate, and implies that he died in 740, a date supported by Cont. Bede. JW had already in his original annal (based on ASC DE 737) assigned 738 to Æthelwald's death, and C² may have decided to leave the discrepancy unresolved.
[5] Mar.
[6] ASC. JW omits Eadberht's withdrawal into Surrey and Sussex recorded in ASC. Ine's expedition against the South Saxons is recorded in ASC A(B) (722) and C (721 from 722), not DE.
[7] Mar.   [8] HE v. 23.   [9] ASC. Ine's (second) war with the South Saxons is recorded in ASC DE. JW seems to be a little closer to DE, which describe Eadberht as atheling and say that he had previously been expelled by Ine.

Hoc anno Beda computator ^aminorem computi^a librum componit, ipso ita teste: 'si uis nosse per annos singulos quot sint epacte, sume annos Domini iuxta Dionisium quotquot fuerint, utputa in presenti octaua indictione .dccxxv., partire per decem et .ix., decies nouies triceni .dlxx., decies nouies octoni .cl. dipondius, remanent tres. Hos item multiplica per ^bdecem et .ix.^b Fiunt .xxxiii. Tolle .xxx.,^c remanent .iii., Iste sunt anno presenti.' Hec Beda.[1]

[726] (ix) 748 *Tobias Hrofensis ecclesie presul defunctus est* qui *ita Grecam cum Latina^d didicit linguam, ut tam notas ac familiares sibi eas quam natiuitatis sue* id est Anglice *loquelam haberet.*[2]

[HL]

^ePost quem episcopatus officium Alduulf, Berhtuualdo Doruuernensi archiepiscopo consecrante, suscepit.^{e2}

[C³BP]

*^f*Cui successit Aldulfus *in recensione Rofensium presulum apud Bedam extremus.* Cui successit Dunn, Eardulf, Deora, Wermund, Beornmod, Burhric, Alfstan, Goduuinus .ii., Siwardus *eo tempore episcopus quo Normanni uenerunt Angliam.*[f3]

[728] (xi) 750 Ciclus solis incipit .iiii. concurrentibus bissextilibus.

Relicto imperio ac Æthelhardo de prosapia Cerdici regis oriundo commendato rex *Ine ad limina beatorum apostolorum, Gregorio pontificatum agente, profectus est, cupiens in uicinia sanctorum locorum ad tempus peregrinari in terris, quo familiarius a sanctis recipi mereretur in celis.*[4] Eodem anno preliati sunt rex Æthelhardus et

---

^{a-a} minorem computi] morem computi *H*, compoti morem *L*   ^{b-b} decem et .ix.] decem *Mar.*, .xi. Bede, *De temporum ratione*, c. lii   ^c t (*for* triginta?) *interlin. above* .xxx. *C*[1]   ^d Latinam *HL*   ^{e-e} Post . . . suscepit] *written mg. alongside* 726 *P*[5]   ^{f-f} Cui . . . Angliam] *written over erasure running on to* 727 *C*³

---

[1] Mar.

[2] *HE* v. 23. ASC DEF (727) alone record the death of Bishop Tobias of Rochester. JW follows Bede's date.

In this year Bede the chronologer, composed his lesser book of computation, as he himself bears witness: 'If you want to know the epact for any year, take the years of the Lord according to Dionysius, whatever the number, for example 725 in the present eighth indiction; divide it by 19; 19 times 30 equals 570; 19 times 8 equals 152; the remainder is 3. Multiply them by nineteen. You have 33. Take away 30; the remainder is 3. That is the epact for the present year.' Thus Bede.[1]

[726] Tobias, bishop of the church of Rochester, died. He was so proficient in Greek and Latin that they were as well known and familiar to him as his mother tongue.[2]

After Tobias, Aldwulf became bishop, with Archbishop Berht-wald presiding at the consecration.[3]

Aldwulf succeeded him, the last, according to Bede, in the lists of the bishops of Rochester. Aldwulf was succeeded by Dunn, Eardwulf, Diora, Wærmund, Beornmod, Burgric, Ælfstan, Godwine II, and Siward, who was bishop at the time the Normans arrived in England.[3]

[728] The solar cycle begins with four concurrents in a bissextile year.

When King Ine had given up his kingdom and entrusted it to Æthelheard, a descendant of King Cerdic, he set out for the home of the blessed apostles, while Gregory enjoyed papal authority, desiring to make a pilgrimage in the neighbourhood of the holy places for a time on earth so that he might deserve to be received with greater friendship by the saints in heaven.[4] In the same year there was a battle between King Æthelheard and the atheling

---

[3] *GP* i. 72 (p. 136). Here, and in JW *Epis. Lists*, the gap of seven Rochester bishops between Beornmod and Burgric is retained, though JW (unlike WM) recognizes the two Godwines.

[4] *HE* v. 7. Plummer (*Chronicle*, ii. 39) pointed out that 'de prosapia Cerdici' is the equivalent of 'whose stock goes back to Cerdic' used of Æthelheard in the preface to ASC A. The date 728 is pecular to ASC A. 726 in ASC (B)CDE agrees better with Bede's statement that Ine had reigned 37 years when he abdicated.

Osuualdus clito filius Æthelbaldi, filii Cynebaldi, filii Cuthuuini, filii Ceauulini.[1]

[729] (xii) 751 *Mense Ianuario, comete due circa solem apparuere et duabus ferme septimanis perman*sere.[2] Quo anno sanctus *uir Domini* Ecgbertus, cuius sepe meminimus, ipso die *pasc*e quod *.viii. calendarum Maiarum die celebrabatur migrauit ad Dominum.*[3] *Et mox peracto pasca, hoc est .vii. idu*s Maïi, Osric rex Norðanhymbrorum uita decessit, *et fratrem Kynredi regis, qui ante se regnauerat, Ceoluulfum* heredem sibi fecit[4] ad quem *Beda famulus Christi presbiter* et monachus *hystoriam gentis Anglorum ecclesiasticam* scripsit.[5] Ceoluulfus exstitit filius Cuthe, qui fuit Cuthuuini, qui fuit Ecguualdi, qui fuit Aldhelmi, qui fuit Oce, qui fuit Ide, qui fuit Eoppe.[6]

[730] (xiii) 752 Osuualdus clito uir strenuissimus defunctus est.[7]

[731] (xiiii) 753 Brihtuualdus *archiepiscopus, longa consum*ptus *etate, die* quinto *iduum Ianuariarum* obiit.[8]
   Gregorius papa obiit .iii. idus Februarii.[9]
   Pro Brihtuualdo *Tatuuin*e, *presbiter monasterii quod uocatur Briudun de prouincia Merciorum, archiepiscopus consecratus est in* Doruuerni | *ciuitate a Daniele Wentano et Ingualdo Lundoniensi et Alduuino Licetfeldensi et Alduulfo Hrofensi antistitibus, die decima Iunii mensis, dominica, uir religione et prudentia insignis, sacris quoque litteris nobiliter instructus. Anno aduentus Anglorum in Brytan*niam *circiter ducentesimo octogesimo* secundo[10] *ecclesiis Cantuuariorum* Tatuuine *et Alduulf episcopi* prefuerunt. *Porro provincie Orientalium Saxonum Inguald episcopus, prouincie Orientalium Anglorum* Eadberht *et* Hadulac *episcopi, prouincie Occidentalium Saxonum Daniel et* Forðheri *episcopi, prouincie Merciorum*

p. 275

---

[1] ASC: A under 728, (B)CDF under 726, which all, like E, also give Æthelheard a 14-year reign. ASC ABC describe Oswald as atheling. EF omit the equivalent of the last sentence.
[2] *HE* v. 23.
[3] *HE* v. 22. ASC DE say that Ecgberht died at Iona, F describes him as 'of Iona'.
[4] *HE* v. 23. Osric's death is given under 731 in ASC A(B)C, under 729 in EF and under both dates in D.
[5] Preface to Ceolwulf.
[6] ASC. A(B)CD give the genealogy under 731. Leodwald is omitted here between Cuthwine and Ecgwald, but is found in JW *Northum. Gen.*

Oswald, son of Æthelbald, son of Cynebald, son of Cuthwine, son of Ceawlin.[1]

[729] In January two comets appeared near the sun and remained for about two weeks.[2] In this year Ecgberht, the holy man of God, whom we have often mentioned, departed to the Lord on Easter Day itself, which was celebrated on 24 April.[3] When Easter had barely passed, that is 9 May, Osric, king of the Northumbrians, departed this life, and made Ceolwulf, brother of King Cenred, who had reigned before him, his heir,[4] for whom Bede, the servant of Christ, priest, and monk, wrote the *Ecclesiastical History of the English People*.[5] Ceolwulf was son of Cutha, son of Cuthwine, son of Ecgwald, son of Aldhelm, son of Ocga, son of Ida, son of Eoppa.[6]

[730] The atheling Oswald, a most vigorous man, died.[7]

[731] Archbishop Berhtwald, worn out by advanced age, died on 9 January.[8]

Pope Gregory died on 11 February.[9]

Tatwine, a priest of the monastery called Breedon, in the kingdom of the Mercians, was consecrated archbishop in the city of Canterbury by the bishops Daniel of Winchester and Ingwald of London, Aldwine of Lichfield and Aldwulf of Rochester, on Sunday, 10 June. He was a man distinguished by his devotion and prudence, who was also excellently versed in Holy Scriptures. About 282 years[10] after the Angles came to Britain, Bishops Tatwine and Aldwulf ruled the churches of the Kentish people; Bishop Ingwald ruled the province of the East Saxons; Bishops Aldberht and Heathulac the province of the East Angles; Bishops Daniel and Forthhere the province of the West Saxons; Bishop Aldwine the province of the Mercians, and Bishop Walhstod those peoples who live beyond the River Severn to the west; Bishop

---

[7] ASC. ADEF.

[8] *HE* v. 23. The day (9 Jan.) of Berhtwald's death agrees with C-type manuscripts of *HE*, whereas ASC DEF follow an M-type text in giving 13 Jan.

[9] Mar.

[10] JW reckons the time passed since the coming of the English from his own date of 450. Bede gives about 285 years.

*Alduuine[a] episcopus, et eis populis qui ultra amnem Sabrinam ad occi-
dentem habitant Walhstod episcopus, prouincie Huicciorum Wilfrid*us
*episcopus, prouincie Lindisfarorum, Kyn*eber*ht prefuit, episcopatus
Vecte Insule ad Danielem pertinet, episcopum Wente ciuitatis.
Prouincia Australium Saxonum, iam aliquot annis absque [b]episcopo
manens,[b] ministerium sibi episcopale ab Occidentalium Saxonum antistite* quesiuit. *He omnes prouincie cetereque australes ad confinium
usque Humbre fluminis cum suis queque regibus Merciorum regi
Æthelbaldo subiecte* fuerunt. *At uero prouincie Northanhymbrorum
cui rex Ceoluulf prefuit, quattuor episcopi presulatum ten*uerunt:
*Wilfrid*us *in Eboracensi ecclesia, Ætheluuoldus in Lindisfarnensi,
Acca in Hagustaldensi, Pectelm*us *in ea que Candida Casa uocatur.
Brytones* magna *ex parte Anglorum seruitio mancipati* fuere.[1]

[732] (xv) 754   *Gregorius[2] octogesimus nonus papa annis .xi.[3]*

[733] (xvi) 755   *Eclypsis facta est solis .xviii. kalend. Septembris
circa horam diei tertiam ita ut pene totus orbis solis quasi nigerrimo et
horrendo[c] [d]situ [e]uel[d] scuto[e][4] uideretur esse coopertus.[5]*

*Sarraceni predicti cum nauibus alta peterent ingruente subita tem-
pestate plurimi ex ipsis mersi sunt et [f]necati. Plurime enim naues eorum
per littora fracte[f] iacebant. [g]Liutbrandus uero rex Longobardorum
audiens quod Sarraceni loca sancta corrumperent et quod depopulata
Sardinia etiam loca illa fedarent ubi ossa sancti Augustini episcopi
propter uastationem barbarorum olim translata et honorifice fuerant
condita, misit et dato pretio transtulit accepta Ticinis [h]id est Paueia[h]
ibidemque cum debito tanti patris honore recondidit.[6]*

[i]Hagustaldensis episcopus Acca presulatu pulsus est.[i][7]

---

   [a] Wor *interlin. by 12th-c. hand* C, qui et Wor *interlin.* B[1]   [b-b] episcopo manens]
over erasure C[1]   [c] horrido L   [d-d] situ uel *om.* LG   [e-e] uel scuto] *interlin.*
C[1]B[1]P[3], *om.* H, scuto L   [f-f] necati . . . fracte] *written in mg. at line-end and at
beginning of line* C[1]   [g] *734 starts here (N).*   [h-h] id est Paueia] *interlin.*
C[1]L[1]B[1]P[3] (N[2]?), Paueia *interlin.* H[1]   [i-i] Hagustaldensis . . . est] *compressed script
at end of annal with the distinguishing initial which usually marks the opening of an English
entry in an annal* C[1]

---

[1] *HE* v. 23. Bede gives Aldberct for JW's Eadberht as bishop of East Anglia.
Plummer (*Bede*, i. 350 n. 9) notes Ealdbercht in the second hand of *HE* MS C (BL
Cotton MS Tiberius C. II).

Wilfrid the province of the Hwicce, and Cyneberht the province of the people of Lindsey. The bishopric of the Isle of Wight belonged to Daniel, bishop of the city of Winchester. The province of the South Saxons, without a bishop for many years, sought episcopal ministrations from the bishop of the West Saxons. All these provinces and the others south of the River Humber, with all their kings, were subject to Æthelbald, king of the Mercians. But four bishops exercised the episcopal office in the kingdom of the Northumbrians, which King Ceolwulf ruled: Wilfrid at York, Æthelwald at Lindisfarne, Acca at Hexham, and Pehthelm in the place which is called *Candida Casa* (Whithorn). Most of the Britons were subject to English rule.[1]

[732] Gregory,[2] the eighty-ninth pope, reigned eleven years.[3]

[733] An eclipse of the sun occurred on 15 August, about the third hour of the day, so that almost the entire orb of the sun seemed to be covered with a very black and fearsome mould or shield.[4,5]

When many of the Saracens mentioned before went on the high seas in their ships, they were drowned and killed by the sudden onset of a storm. Many of their ships lay broken on the shore. Liutprand, king of the Lombards, heard that the Saracens were destroying holy places, and after laying Sardinia waste, were engaged in defiling those shrines where the bones of St Augustine the bishop had on account of barbarian ravages been formerly translated and honourably buried. He sent, and paid for, and translated the bones he had received in *Ticinum*, that is Pavia, and there they were reburied with the honour due to so great a father.[6]

Acca, bishop of Hexham, was expelled from his bishopric.[7]

[2] Gregory III 735-41.
[3] Mar.
[4] For the possible bearing of 'situ uel scuto' on the identification of JW's text of *HE*, see vol. i, Introduction.
[5] *Cont. Bede.*   [6] Mar.
[7] ASC DEF, without identifying his see. *Cont. Bede* gives a long vacancy by dating Acca's expulsion to 731 and the consecration of his successor to 735.

[734] (xvii) 756 *Luna sanguineo rubore perfusa quasi hora integra,
.ii. kalend. Februarii circa galli cantum, dehinc nigredine subsequente
ad lucem propriam* uisa est *reuersa.*[1] Doruuernensis archiepiscopus
Tatuuine .iii. kalend. Augusti de seculo migrauit[2] cui Nothelmus
ᵃecclesie Lundoniensis presbiterᵃ[3] in archiepiscopatus officium succes-
sit.ᵇ Sacerdos uenerabilis, monachus per omnia laudabilis, computator mirabilis, Beda sanctissimus secundum Anglicas cronicas
anno presenti, secundum uero suum discipulum Cuthberhtum qui
eius obitum descripsit sueque decessioni cum aliis quamplurimis
interfuit, anno sequenti ante Ascensionem dominicam, .iiii. feria,
id est .viii. kalend. Iunii, circa horam decimam, in magna mentis
deuotione et tranquillitate, ultimum e corpore spiritum efflauit,
sicque gaudens ad regna celestia migrauit. Hic sue gentis quam-
plurima gesta hucusque luculento descripsit sermone unumque
temporalis uite modumque terminauit hystorie. Nos uero, Deo
aspirante, ab eius uite felici exitu prout Anglicarum cronicarum
repperimus textu, fideliumque uirorum credibili relatu uel que nos
ipsi indubitata audiuimus, uel quedam que oculis asperimus,
amodo fideliter notata fidelium successorum relinquenda dignum
duximus memorie.[4]

[C³BP³]
ᶜ*Defuncto* Aldwino qui et Wor,
tres facti sunt episcopi in
Leogerensi *diocesi,* Wita
Licedfeld, Totta Leogeceastre,
Ætla Dorceastre.ᶜᵈ⁵

[735] (xviii) 757 Pectelmus Candide Case presul obiit, cui
Frithouualdus in pontificatus regimen successit.[6]

ᵃ⁻ᵃ ecclesie . . . presbiter] *mg. with signe de renvoi* C³   ᵇ *signe de renvoi indicates
insertion of 734 n. c here* P³   ᶜ⁻ᶜ Defuncto . . . Dorceastre] *add. mg. alongside 734*
C³, *om.* HL, *mg. alongside 731 with sign indicating insertion at 734 n. b* P³   ᵈ *see
App. B for added Epistola Cuthberti* B

---

[1] *Cont. Bede*
[2] The precise day of Tatwine's death (30 July) is also recorded in *HR* i. 33 (ii. 31).
[3] The preface to Ceolwulf in *HE* could have been the source of the italicized words,
but *GP* i. 3 (p. 8) is the more probable quarry.
[4] *Cont. Bede* gives 735 and ASC 734 for the death of Bede. The *Epistola Cuthberti*,
from which a few words seem to have been taken, assigns Bede's death to 'vii. kal. Iunii',
'ad diem ascensionis dominicae, id est .vii. kal. Iunii'. Ascension Day fell on 26 May in
735, though the hour of death ('a non hora') would indicate the evening before
and therefore 25 May, '.viii. kal. Iunii' as the day of his death.

[734] The moon was stained blood-red for almost a whole hour on 31 January, about cock-crow, then, after going black, was seen to return to its own light.[1] Tatwine, archbishop of Canterbury, departed this life on 30 July,[2] and Nothhelm, a priest of the church of London,[3] succeeded him as archbishop. The most holy Bede, a revered priest, a monk praiseworthy in every way, a marvellous computist, breathed forth his spirit from his body with great devotion and peace of mind and thus departed rejoicing for the heavenly kingdom, according to the English chronicles in the present year, but according to his disciple Cuthbert, who described his death, and was present, with many others, at his departure, it was in the following year, on the Wednesday before the Lord's Ascension, that is 25 May, about the tenth hour. He recorded many of the deeds of his own people down to that time in a splendid work, and ended at the one and the same time his earthly life and his history. With God's inspiration we have thought it fitting that, from the happy end of Bede's life, as we have found events in the text of the English chronicles and in trustworthy accounts of faithful men, and those things beyond doubt that we ourselves have heard, and some that we have seen with our own eyes, should henceforth remain faithfully recorded for the memory of our successors.[4]

> On the death of Aldwine, also known as Wor, three bishops were appointed in the diocese of Leicester: Hwita to Lichfield, Totta to Leicester, and Ætla to Dorchester.[5]

[735] Pehthelm, bishop of Whithorn, died. Frithuwald succeeded him to the episcopal authority.[6]

---

[5] GP iv. 172 (p. 307). Aldwine was certainly alive in 736 (S 89 BCS 154 dated 736, and S 1429 BCS 156 not earlier than 736) and HR i. 34 (ii. 32) assigns his death and the succession of Hwitta (Mercians) and Totta (Leicester) to 737. Ætla, bishop of Dorchester, who is mentioned by Bede (HE iv. 23 (21)) and is the only Mercian bishop of that see in JW Epis. Lists, must have been in office in the last quarter of the 7th c. WM gives Etherd (GP iv. 172 (p. 307)) or Edbedus (GP iv. 177 (p. 311)) as the Dorchester bishop.

[6] The consecration of Frithuwald is recorded (without reference to his see) in Cont. Bede, though the death of Pechthelm is not recorded elsewhere.

[736] (xix) 758 Nothelmus Doruuernensis archiepiscopus a Gregorio octogesimo nono papa pallium suscepit,[1]

[C³BP]

ᵃqui Australibus Saxonibus, *Wilfrido* cum *pace domum regresso,* Eadrihtum prefecit antistitem *cui successit* Eolla.*ᵃ²*

[737] (xx) 759 Episcopus Scireburnensis ecclesie Fortherus et Frithogitha Occidentalium Saxonum regina Romam perrexere.[3]

[738] (xxi) 760 *Gregorius papa predictus constituit in missa 'quorum*
p. 276   *sollennitas hodie' | et reliqua usque 'largitor admitte'.*[4]

Ceoluulfus, rex Northymbrorum, regni gubernaculo relicto, et Eadbrihto*ᵇ* patrueli suo, Eate scilicet filio, tradito, monachus efficitur.*ᶜ⁵* Atheluuoldus *ᵈ*Lindisfarnensis *ᵉ*et Acca Hagustaldensis presules morti debita persoluunt*ᵉ* et*ᶠ* Ætheluuoldo Cyneuulfus, Acce uero Frithobertus succedunt.*ᵈ⁶*

[741] (xxiiii) 763 *Ciclus decennouenalis .xii. incipit indictione .viii.ᵍ Leo imperator obiit. Constantinus[7] filius eius successit. Karolus, filius Pippini, qui et maior domus dictus, rex Francorum obiit.*[8]

Æthelhardus Westsaxonum rex obiit, cui propinquus suus Cuthredus in regnum successit,*ʰ* qui regem Merciorum Æthelbaldum frequenter bello lacessiuit.[9] Nothelmo Doruuernensi archiepiscopo .xvi. kalend. Nouembris defuncto, *ⁱ*Cuthbertus, qui quintus erat Herefordensis episcopus, arciepiscopatum suscepit*ⁱ*

ᵃ⁻ᵃ qui . . . Eolla] *add. at end of annal and running on to mg.* C³, *om.* HL   *ᵇ* et .xxi. annis regnauit *interlin.* B⁵   *ᶜ* et processu temporis Lindisfarnensis episcopus consecratur *add.* G   *ᵈ⁻ᵈ* Lindisfarnensis . . . succedunt] *runs on to* 739–40 CHB, *runs on to* 739 L, *under* 738 P   *ᵉ⁻ᵉ* et Acca . . . persoluunt] *written over erasure, extending into mg.* B¹   *ᶠ om.* B   *ᵍ* nona (N)   *ʰ* et .xvi. annis regnauit *interlin.* B⁵   *ⁱ⁻ⁱ* Cuthbertus . . . suscepit] *written over erasure at end and beginning of lines, and in left and right mgs.* C³

---

[1] ASC A–F. The name of the pope who sent the pallium could have been inferred from the election of Gregory II which is recorded under 732 by Marianus.
[2] *GP* ii. 96 (p. 205). Eolla died some years before 731 (*HE* v. 18, 23) and Eadberht was consecrated when Daniel was bishop of Winchester.
[3] ASC A–F. JW identifies the bishopric and kingdom.   [4] Mar.
[5] Eadberht's accession is given under 738 in all versions of ASC, but Ceolwulf's

[736] Nothhelm, archbishop of Canterbury, received the pallium from Gregory, the eighty-ninth pope.[1]

> When Wilfrid had returned home in peace, Nothhelm appointed Eadberht bishop of the South Saxons, and Eolla succeeded him.[2]

[737] Forthhere, bishop of Sherborne, and Frithugyth, queen of the West Saxons, went to Rome.[3]

[738] The aforementioned Pope Gregory inserted in the mass the words 'quorum solemnitas hodie', and so on, to 'largitor admitte'.[4]

Ceolwulf, king of the Northumbrians, abandoned the rule of his kingdom, having committed it to Eadberht, his cousin, that is the son of Eata, and became a monk.[5] Bishops Æthelwald of Lindisfarne and Acca of Hexham paid their mortal debt. Cynewulf succeeded Æthelwald, Frithoberht Acca.[6]

[741] The twelfth cycle of nineteen years begins in the eighth indiction. The emperor Leo died and his son Constantine[7] succeeded him. Charles, son of Pippin, also called mayor of the palace, died king of the Franks.[8]

Æthelheard, king of the West Saxons, died, and his kinsman Cuthred succeeded him on the throne, he who frequently attacked Æthelbald, king of the Mercians, in war.[9] On the death of Nothhelm, archbishop of Canterbury, on 17 October, Cuthbert, who was the fifth bishop of Hereford, received the archbishopric.

retirement to a monastery is found in ASC DEF and his entrusting of the kingdom to Eadberht, (who is described as the son of his paternal uncle) is found in ASC DE under 737 (also *Cont. Bede*). The relationship of Ceolwulf to Eadberht ('patrueli suo Eadbrihto, Eate filio') is found in JW *Northum. Gen.* and *Accounts* 20 and ASC.

  [6] ASC DEF record the deaths of Æthelwald and Acca and the consecration of Cynewulf (without identifying any sees) under 737. JW could have learnt that Frithoberht succeeded Acca from his own *Epis. Lists*, from *Cont. Bede* (Frithoberht's consecration 735) or ASC DEF (his death in 766 after 34 years), and, perhaps forgetting that Acca had been expelled in 733 (see above), he dated Frithoberht's consecration to the year of Acca's death, which is too late, for it is dated 735 by *Cont. Bede* and 8 Sept. 734 by *HR* i. 33 (ii. 31). Acca's death is assigned to 749 by *HR* i. 36 (ii. 32).

  [7] Constantine V 741-75.   [8] Mar.

  [9] ASC. A gives 741, (B) CDEF 740. Like F, JW does not record the length of Cuthred's reign. JW is like DEF in calling Æthelbald king of Mercia, and like DE in identifying Cuthred as Æthelheard's kinsman.

[C³BP]

*ᵃ*cui in episcopatum Herefordensem Podda successit.*ᵃ¹*

Mortuo quoque Hrofensi episcopo Alduulfo, Dunn consecratus est
pro eo.*ᵇ²*

*ᶜRomanorum septuagesimus septimus Pippinus³ filius Karoli
Francorum primus imperator annis uiginti septem usque in annum .dcc.
quinquagesimum quintum post passionem Domini.ᵈ⁴*

[C³BP³]

*ᵉ*De Karolo qui primus omnium
res ecclesiarum abstulit. Karolus
princeps, Pippini*ᶠ* regis pater,
qui primus inter omnes
Francorum reges ac principes res
ecclesiarum ab eis separauit
atque diuisit, pro hoc solo
maxime *ᵍ*eternaliter damnatus
est.*ᵍ* Nam sanctus Eucherius
Aurelianensium episcopus, qui in
monasterio sancti Trudonis
requiescit, in oratione positus ad
alterum seculum est raptus, et
inter cetera que Domino sibi
ostendente conspexit, uidit
ipsum Karolum in inferno inferiori torqueri. Cui interroganti ab
angelo responsum est ductore
quia sanctorum*ʰ* iudicatione,
qui futuro iudicio cum Domino

ᵃ⁻ᵃ cui . . . successit] *add. mg. directly below part of 741 n. i (p. 186) C³ om. HL,
incorporated at 741 n. e B*   *ᵇ 741 n. b incorporated here B*   *ᶜ* capitula .lxxvi.]
add. before Romanorum *L.*   *ᵈ rest of line had erasure, of which the first letter is a
capital D, and may represent the beginning of a first attempted addition of 741 n. e C*
ᵉ De Karolo . . . audierunt *(p. 190)] written mg. of p. 277 alongside 754–66, the mg. of
p. 276 adjoining the more appropriate position next to 741 having probably been already
used C³?, om. HL, incorporated (without rubric) B, add. (without rubric) lower mg. below*
*741 P³   ᶠ add. huius G   ᵍ⁻ᵍ*eternaliter damnatus est] est eternaliter dampnatus
ASN, est eternaliter perditus *MGH (reference and sigla above, p. 3)   ʰ add. est B*

---

¹ Cuthbert's appointment as archbishop of Canterbury and Dunn's as bishop of Rochester
are in ASC (with the dates shown above, p. 187 n. 9) though only F (in an interlineated

Podda succeeded him to the bishopric of Hereford.[1]

Aldwulf, bishop of Rochester, died also, and Dunn was consecrated in his place.[2]

Pippin,[3] son of Charles, seventy-seventh emperor of the Romans, the first of the Franks, reigned twenty-seven years, down to the 755th year after the Lord's Passion.[4]

Concerning Charles, who was the first to confiscate all the property of the church. The ruler Charles, father of King Pippin, who was the first of all the Frankish kings and rulers to part the churches from their property and to divide it, is damned totally and for eternity for this alone. For St Eucherius, bishop of Orléans, who lies at the monastery of St Trond, was, while kneeling in prayer, taken to the other world, and looking (among other things which the Lord revealed to him), saw Charles himself tormented in the lower depths of hell. To his inquiry his angel guide replied that because, by the judgement of all those saints (who will judge with the Lord at the judgement

---

entry not paralleled in *ADL*) refers specifically to the death of Nothhelm, and none mentions the death of Aldwulf. *Cont. Bede* and *HR* i. 35 (ii. 32) assign Nothhelm's death to 739; JW is the only chronicle source for the day of his death. The original reading of JW did not describe Cuthbert as the fifth bishop of Hereford. The revision probably shows the influence of *GP* iv. 162 (p. 298); it is questionable, since translations were not normal in the 7th and 8th centuries. JW's further addition (made at a later stage since it is not in MSS HL) that Podda succeeeded Cuthbert at Hereford could also be based on *GP* iv. 162 (p. 299), or, of course on JW *Epis. Lists. HR* i. 35 (ii. 32) and *Cont. Bede* date Aldwulf of Rochester's death 739, a date not necessarily in conflict with JW, who does not explicitly report Aldwulf's death in this year.

[2] ASC as above, p. 187 n. 9, p. 188 n. 1.   [3] Pippin III 741–68.   [4] Mar.

iudicabunt, quorumcunque res
abstulit et diuisit, ante illud[a]
iudicium anima et corpore sem-
piternis penis est deputatus, et
recipit simul cum suis peccatis
penas,   propter   ⟨peccata⟩[b]
omnium qui res suas et facultates in honore et amore Dei ad
sanctorum loca in luminaribus
diuini cultus et alimoniis seruo-
rum Christi ac pauperum pro
animarum suarum redemptione
tradiderunt. Qui in se reuersus
sanctum   Bonefacium   et
Fulradum, abbatem monasterii
sancti Dionisii et summum
capellanum regis Pippini, ad se
uocauit, eisque talia dicens iussit
ut ad sepulcrum illius irent et si
corpus eius ibidem non reperis-
sent ea que dicebat uera esse[c]
crederent.[d] Ipsi autem[e] pergentes
ad predictum monasterium, ubi
corpus ipsius Karoli humatum
fuerat, [f]sepulchrum eius[f] aperi-
entes, uisus est subito draco
exisse, et totum ipsum[g] sepulchrum inuentum est interius
denigratum ac si fuisset exus-
tum. Nos autem illos uidimus,
qui usque ad nostram etatem
durauerunt qui huic rei inter-
fuerunt, et nobis uiua uoce sunt
testati qui uiderunt et audierunt.[h1]

---

[a] illum *ASN*   [b] *om. JW ASN*   [c] *om. P*   [d] *om. and added in late 12th-
c. hand in outer mg.* C, *suprascript above* uera B¹, *incorporated* G, crederat *P*, concreder-
ent *MGH 1–6*   [e] *bis* G   [f-f] sepulchrum eius] sepulchrumque ipsius *ASN
MGH 7*, sepulchrumque illius *MGH 1–5*, sepulchrumque eius *MGH 8*   [g] illud
ASN MGH.   [h] *see above, p. 188 n. e*

to come), whose possessions he took and divided, he was condemned before that judgement, body and soul, to eternal punishment and receives, together with punishment for his own sins, punishment because of the sins of all who for the redemption of their souls gave their possessions and property for the honour and the love of God to the shrines of the saints, for lamps at holy worship, and for the giving of alms to the servants of Christ and to the poor. Eucherius, on his return, summoned St Boniface and Fuldrad, abbot of the monastery of St Denis and King Pippin's chief chaplain, reported this vision, and ordered them to go to Charles's tomb: if they did not find his body there, they were to believe that what he said was true. They went to the monastery already mentioned, where the body of that very Charles had been buried; when they opened his tomb, a dragon appeared to have suddenly departed, and the whole of his tomb was found to be blackened within, as if burnt out. We have seen those who survived to our own day who were present at this event, and testified to us with their own tongues to what they saw and heard.[1]

---

[1] The text has been compared with that in *ASN* (which lacks the rubric) though some variants from the textual tradition reported in *MGH Cap.* ii. 2, 432–3 have been shown. See discussion in *ASN*, pp. liv–lvi.

[742] (i) 764 *Gregorius papa obiit .iiii. kalend. Decemb., indictione .x. Zacharias*[1] *nonagesimus papa annis undecim.*[2]

[743] (ii) 765 Æthelbaldus Mercensium et Cuthredus Occidentalium Saxonum reges cum Brytonibus pugnauere.[3] Wilfrido Huuicciorum episcopo de hac uita subtracto, Milredus successit.[4] *Sanctus Bonifacius Mogontinus archiepiscopus clarus habetur.*[5] Vise sunt stelle quasi de celo cadere.[6]

[744] (iii) 766 *Sanctus Bonifacius Fuldam monasterium in solitudine Bochonia inchoauit.*[7] Wilfridus iunior Eboracensis ecclesie pontifex .iii. kalend. Maii hominem exiuit,[8] et Ecgbertus regis Ædberhti frater archiepiscopatus insigni sullimatur.[9] Daniel episcopus ciuitatis Wentane longa iam uenerabilis etate, sponte presulatu dimisso, in eadem ciuitate resedit et Hunfridus pro eo episcopatum suscepit.[10]

[C³BP³]

ªWillebrordus,ᵇ primus Traiectensium episcopus, de quo Beda memorat, migrauit ad Dominum, cui *in Frisia Bonifaciusᵇ* successit, *apud Traiectum* Banco *episcopo ordinato.ª*[11]

[745] (iiii) 767 *Karlomannus rex frater imperatoris ᶜsecundum consultum fratris regnum dimittensᶜ Romam uenit, et a Zacharia papa tonsuram accepit, deinde in monte Soracte apud ecclesiam sancti*

ª⁻ª Willebrordus . . . ordinato] *add. mg. alongside* 744–5 *C³, om.* HL, *add. mg. with sign indicating insertion at opening of annal* P³ ᵇ sanctus *interlin.* B¹ ᶜ⁻ᶜ secundum . . . dimittens] secundum (*possibly an error for* seculum) consultu fratris regnum dimittens (N), cum fratre tractat seculum dimittere *Mar.*

---

¹ Zacharias 741–52.   ² *Mar.*
³ ASC A–E. JW, like DE, identifies the kingdoms of the two English rulers.
⁴ JW alone records (here and in the 19-year tables on p. 61 of the JW MS C) the death of Wilfrid, bishop of Worcester, and the succession of Milred. It cannot be reconciled with the information in *HR* i. 40 (ii. 39) that a bishop 'in Wiccum' died in 745 nor with the attestation of a document which could be as late as 745 (*S* 98 *BCS* 171, Robertson, *Charters*, no. 1) by a Bishop Wilfrid and a Bishop Milred. There are

[742] Pope Gregory died on 28 November, in the tenth indiction. Zacharias,[1] the ninetieth pope, reigned eleven years.[2]

[743] King Æthelbald of the Mercians and King Cuthred of the West Saxons fought against the Britons.[3] When Wilfrid, bishop of the Hwicce, had departed this life, Milred succeeded him.[4]

St Boniface, archbishop of Mainz, enjoyed great renown.[5]

Stars were seen which seemed to fall from the sky.[6]

[744] St Boniface laid the foundations of the monastery of Fulda in the wilderness of *Buchonia*.[7]

Wilfrid the Younger, bishop of York, laid aside the flesh on 29 April,[8] and Ecgberht, brother of King Eadberht, was raised to archiepiscopal rank.[9] Daniel, bishop of Winchester, by then of venerable age, laid aside his bishopric of his own accord, and remained in the same city. Hunfrith received the bishopric in his place.[10]

Willibrord, the first bishop of Utrecht, of whom Bede speaks, departed to the Lord. Boniface succeeded him in Frisia; Banco was ordained bishop of Utrecht.[11]

[745] King Carloman, brother of the emperor, on the advice of his brother, gave up his kingdom, and went to Rome and received the tonsure from Pope Zacharias. Then he lived several years in God's

---

difficulties in Robertson's attempt to reconcile the conflicting evidence; it is possible that an error in the witness-list has crept in, and that JW's information is correct. JW does not equate this Wilfrid with Wilfrid II of York, whose death he records under 744.

[5] Mar.   [6] ASC DE (744). *HR* i. 40 (ii. 38) mentions 'ictus ignei in aere'.

[7] Mar.

[8] ASC DE mention the death of Wilfrid II (on 29 Apr.), and record a 30-year episcopate, *Cont. Bede* and *HR* i. 40 (ii. 39) give 745.

[9] This is probably a wrong inference as Ecgberht succeeeded Wilfrid II, not on his death, but on his retirement in 732 (*Cont. Bede*). For the evidence that Ecgberht was consecrated in 734, see Plummer, *Bede*, ii. 278, 378.

[10] ASC A-E, which do not here refer to Daniel's great age nor to his continued residence at Winchester.

[11] *GP* i. 6 (pp. 11–12), which does not specify the date of Willibrord's death (739). 'Banco' is the original reading in *GP*.

*Siluestri constructo monasterio, cum fratribus secum ad hoc uenientibus,
per aliquot annos Deo seruiens uixit, sed ob insolentiam Francorum
Romam uenientium, eumque ut dominum quondam suum uisitantium
ad monasterium sancti Benedicti in monte Cassino situm perrexit, ubi
postea regulariter uixit.*[1]

*ᵃDaniel,

[C³BP]

*ᵇqui dimisso presulatu Melduni,
quantum uixit, monachum exer-
ᶜuerat.ᵇ²*

anno .xliii. ex quo episcopatus officium suscepit post multiplices
caelestis militie agones

[HL]   [C³BP]

ad premia remunerationis per-   migrauit ad Dominum *ibidemque
petue transiuit.*[3]   *sepultus   asseueratur   qua*nuis
                                  *Wintonienses eum apud se haberi
                                  contendant.ᵃ²*

[746] (v) 768ᶜ Rex Eastsaxonum Selredus occiditur.[4]

[748] (vii) 770   [C³B¹P³]

                                  ᵈSeptembris mensis initio cele-
                                  brata est synodus *prope locum
                                  qui uocatur Clouesho, prese*nte
                                  *archiepiscopo Cuthberto, Rofensi
                                  antistite Dunno, Merciorum epis-
                                  copis Totta et Huuita,* Here-
                                  fordensi episcopo *Podda,
                                  Wicciorum Milredo, Occidental-
                                  ium ⟨Saxonum⟩ᵉ presulibus Hun-
                                  fertho et Herewaldo, Orientalium
                                  Anglorum Eardulfo, et Egulfo
                                  Orientalium Saxonum, Ald*wio
                                  Lindisse prouincie presule, *Sigga*

ᵃ⁻ᵃ Daniel . . . contendant] *written over erasure* C³   ᵇ⁻ᵇ qui . . . exercuerat] *om.*
HL   ᶜ 767 C   ᵈ Septembris . . . pontifice (p. 196)] *add. mg. alongside
747–53, with probably early modern sign pointing to 748* C³, *om.* HL, *mg. alongside 748–9*
B¹P³ *(with sign for 748* P³)   ᵉ *om. JW*

---

¹ Mar.   ² *GP* ii. 75 (p. 160).

service at the church of St Silvester at Mount Soracte, having built a monastery with some brethren who had come with him for this purpose, but because of the immoderation of the Franks who came to Rome and visited him as their former lord he went to the monastery of St Benedict at Monte Cassino, where he lived according to the Rule.[1]

Daniel,

who had laid aside his bishopric, for the rest of his life followed the monastic way of life at Malmesbury.[2]

and in the forty-third year from office, after many struggles for the

his acceptance of the episcopal heavenly army

passed over to the rewards of perpetual returns.[3]

departed to the Lord and was buried at Malmesbury, it is claimed, though the people of Winchester declare that he lies with them.[2]

[746] Selred, king of the East Saxons, was killed.[4]

[748]

At the beginning of September, a synod was held near a place called *Clofesho* at which were present Archbishop Cuthbert, Dunn, bishop of Rochester, Totta and Hwita, bishops of the Mercians, Podda, bishop of Hereford, Milred of the Hwicce, Hunfrith and Herewald, bishops of the West Saxons, Heardwulf of the East Angles, Ecgwulf of the East Saxons, Alwig, bishop of the province of Lindsey, and also

---

[3] JW's original reading was based on the information in ASC A–E concerning the death of Daniel. He has not been able to reconcile Daniel's 43 years as bishop with the date of 705 (based on Bede) for his election on Hædde's death.

[4] ASC. JW identifies the kingdom.

quoque   Australium   Saxonum
pontifice.[a1]

Grifo fugit in Saxoniam ob metum imperatoris.[2]

Kynricus Occidentalum Saxonum clito interficitur. Eadbirhtus rex Cantuariorum defungitur, suusque frater Æthelbertus in regnum constituitur.[3]

[749] (viii) 771   *Grifo iterum de Saxonia reuertitur.*[4]

[750] (ix) 772   *Pippinus   decreto   Zacharie   pape   a   Bonifacio Mogontino[b] archiepiscopo unguitur in imperatorem et ob id post papam secundus habetur episcopus Mogontinus.*[5]

Cuthredus rex Occidentalium Saxonum cum duce animosissimo pugnauit Æthelhuno.[6]

[751] (x) 773   Grifo   obiit.   Burchardus   primus   episcopus Wirziburg ordinatur qui sedit annis .xl.[7]

[752] (xi) 774   *Zacharias papa obiit idus Martii, indictione quinta. Stephanus[8] nonagesimus primus papa annis quinque mense uno.*[9]

Anno regni sui .xii. Cuthredus Westsaxonum et rex Merciorum Æthelbaldus iuxta Beorhtforda satis durum commisere prelium.[10]

[753] (xii) 775   *Stephanus papa cum predicto Carlomanno fratre regis monacho uenerunt ad Pippinum in Franciam, petentes defensionem contra Haistulfum regem Longobardorum.*[11] |

p. 277   Cuthredus rex denuo[12] cum Brytonibus pugnans [13]ex eis quam plurimos interfecit.[13,14]

[754] (xiii) 776   *Vnxit idem papa duos filios Pippini, Carlomannum et magnum Karolum imperatores .v. kalend. Augusti.*[15]

---

[a] *see above p. 194 n. d*   [b] Magontino *HL*

---

[1] *GP* i. 5 (p. 9). Discussion in Haddan and Stubbs, *Councils*, iii. 360.
[2] Mar.
[3] ASC ADE (under 748) C (747) B (under 747 or 748) record the death of Cynric and Eadberht of Kent; an addition to A (hand 8c) records the succession in Kent of Æthelberht son of Wihtred (both Eadberht and Æthelberht were sons of Wihtred). The statement that Eadberht died in 748 seems at variance with charter evidence (*S* 29 *BCS* 189, *S* 28 *BCS* 190, *S* 32 *BCS* 193) showing that Eadberht was still king in 761 and 762 (see *Handbook of British Chronology*, p. 14).

Sicgga (Sigeferth), bishop of the South Saxons.[1]

Grifo fled into Saxony for fear of the emperor.[2]

Cynric, the atheling of the West Saxons, was killed. Eadberht, king of the people of Kent, died, and his brother, Æthelberht, was set on the throne.[3]

[749] Grifo returned again from Saxony.[4]

[750] At Pope Zacharias' decree, Pippin was anointed emperor by Boniface, archbishop of Mainz, and on that account the bishop of Mainz was second in rank to the pope.[5]

Cuthred, king of the West Saxons, fought with the most vigorous ealdorman Æthelhun.[6]

[751] Grifo died. Burchard was ordained first bishop of Würzburg and he held the position for forty years.[7]

[752] Pope Zacharias died on 15 March in the fifth indiction. Stephen,[8] the ninety-first pope, reigned five years and one month.[9]

In the twelfth year of his reign Cuthred of the West Saxons and Æthelbald, king of the Mercians, fought a very fierce battle near *Beorhford*.[10]

[753] Pope Stephen went to Pippin in Francia with the aforementioned Carloman, the king's brother, to ask for protection against Aistulf, king of the Lombards.[11]

King Cuthred fought against the Britons again[12] and [13]slew very many of them.[13,14]

[754] The same pope anointed Pippin's two sons, Carloman and Charles the Great, emperors on 28 July.[15]

---

[4] Mar.   [5] Mar.
[6] ASC A-E, DE describing Cuthred as king of the West Saxons.
[7] Mar.   [8] Stephen II (III) 752–7.   [9] Mar.
[10] ASC A-E, DE being the only versions to name the kingdoms, though they add that Cuthred put Æthelbald to flight. ASC has no equivalent for 'satis durum'.
[11] Mar.   [12] No equivalent in ASC.   [13–13] Not in ASC.
[14] ASC A-E, DE again naming Cuthred's kingdom.
[15] Mar.

Cuthredus rex Westsaxonum obiit et suus propinquus Sigbertus filius Sigerici successit.[1] Defuncto Wentane ciuitatis presule Hunfertho, Cinehardus pro eo episcopatum suscepit. Dorubernia igne consumpta est.[2]

[755] (xiiii) 777   *Sanctus Bonifacius archiepiscopus predicans uerbum Dei in Fresia passus est cum aliis martyribus nonis Iunii.*[3]

[4]Kynewulfus de prosapia Cerdici regis oriundus, auxilium sibi ferentibus Westsaxonicis primatibus, regem illorum Sigebertum ob multitudinem suorum iniquorum factorum regno exterminauit et loco eius regnauit, unam tamen prouinciam que Hamtunscire dicitur eidem concessit, quam tandiu tenuit quoadusque ducem Cumbranum, qui ceteris diutius secum manserat iniuste peremisset. Postmodum uero ab ipso rege Cyneuulfo queritur, et in saltum qui lingua Anglorum Andred nominatur expellitur. Vbi dum diu moratur in uindictam necis prefati ducis a quodam subulco iuxta[a] Pryfetes flodan[5] lancea perforatur. Idem rex Cynewulfus Brytones sepissime preliis detriuit permaximis. [b]Rex Merciorum Æthelbaldus in Seccesuualde occiditur, corpusque eius Hreopedune deportatur ibidemque tumulatur. Cuius regnum Beornredus tyrannus[6] inuasit, et per modicum tempus in parua letitia et iocunditate tenens regnum cum uita perdidit. Quo mortuo, successit in regnum nepos patruelis Æthelbaldi[7] regis Merciorum Offa,[c] filius Thincgferthi, filii Eanuulfi, filii Osmodi,[d] filii Eope,[8] filii Pybbe, patris regis Pende.[9]

---

[a] *om. HL*   [b] *Rex Merciorum . . . Hemele (p. 200)] a red line (of indeterminate date, though the red ink seems very like that used for the Marianus years and rubrics) encloses this text and appears to transfer it to 756 n. c C; B appears to follow amended 755 of C in inserting this at 756 n. c*   [c] *qui .xxxix. annos regnum tenuit add. mg. B[5]*
[d] *-mun. interlin. above Osmodi B[1]*

---

[1] ASC A-F 754 (*recte* 756). F does not mention Sigeberht's succession; DE alone describe Cuthred as king of the West Saxons and Sigeberht as his kinsman. Sigeberht is identified as Sigeric's son only in JW and JW *West Saxon Accounts* 19, though the latter also describes Sigeric as 'subregulus'. These accounts and ASC ABCDE make Sigeberht king for 1 year.
[2] ASC A-F (F omits the burning of Canterbury). JW shares with ASC the same chronological dislocation from 756 to c.845, making dates in this period at least two years too early.

Cuthred, king of the West Saxons, died, and his kinsman, Sigeberht, son of Sigeric, succeeded him.[1] On the death of Hunfrith, bishop of Winchester, Cyneheard received the bishopric in his place. Canterbury was destroyed by fire.[2]

[755] St Boniface the archbishop, while preaching the word of God in Frisia, was slain with other martyrs on 5 June.[3]
[4]Cynewulf, of the lineage of King Cerdic, with the assistance of the West Saxon nobles, drove their King Sigeberht from the kingdom because of the great number of evil deeds he had committed, and Cynewulf reigned in his place. However, Cynewulf ceded him the one province called Hampshire, which he held until he unjustly slew the ealdorman Cumbra, who had remained with him longer than any of the others. After that he was hunted by King Cynewulf himself and driven into a wood which is called the Weald in the English tongue. When he had stayed there some time he was run through near the Privett's flood[5] with a spear by a certain swineherd in revenge for the death of the aforesaid ealdorman. That same Cynewulf weakened the Britons by very frequent great battles. Æthelbald, king of the Mercians, was killed at Seckington and his body was borne to Repton and buried there. The usurper[6] Beornred invaded his kingdom and held it for a short time with little joy or pleasure until he lost both kingdom and life. After his death there succeeded Offa, a nephew through his father of Æthelbald,[7] king of the Mercians, and son, that is, of Thingfrith, son of Eanwulf, son of Osmod, son of Eopa,[8] son of Pybba, father of King Penda.[9]

---

[3] Mar.
[4] Only the first few lines of the long West Saxon entry in 755 (*recte* 757) are entered here by JW, who assigns the account of the slaying of King Cynewulf by Cyneheard to 784. ASC F has an abbreviated annal. For the phrase 'de prosapia regis Cerdic', see above, p. 179 n. 4.
[5] 'æt Pryfetesflodan' in ASC A(B)C, 'æt Pryftesflodan' in DE.
[6] Not in ASC A-E, which record the succession of Beornred and Offa.
[7] No equivalent in ASC to 'nepos patruelis Æthelbaldi', which is not correct. JW *Mercian Accounts* 14 has 'patruelis Eanulfi nepos'.
[8] Eopa is presumably an error for Eawa.
[9] ASC ABC's genealogy ascends to Woden, DEF to Offa's father Thingfrith. JW does not have Æthelbald's regnal length nor the reference to Beornred's being put to flight which are in DE.

[C³BP]
*ᵃDefuncto Wita Licetfeldensi
presule, successit Hemele.ᵃᵇ¹*

[756] (xv) 778 Ciclus solis incipit .iiii. concurrentibus bissextilibus.ᶜ *Lull archiepiscopus post Bonifacium successit ᵈannis .xxxii.ᵈ²*

[757] (xvi) 779 *Organum primitus uenit in Franciam, missum a Constantino rege Grecorum Pippino imperatori. Stephanus papa obiit .v. kalend. Maii, cui successit germanus eius* Paulus.³

Eadberhtus, rex Norðhymbrensium, amore celestis patrie imperium reliquit, tonsuramque sancti Petri apostoli accepit, et filius suusᵉ Osuulfus regimen regni suscepit, et uno anno regnans .ix. kalend. Augusti⁴ a Northymbrensibus⁵ occiditur.⁶

[758] (xvii) 780 *Paulus nonagesimus secundus papa annis decem et mense uno.⁷*

Cuthberhtus Doruuernensis archiepiscopus .vii. kalend. Nouembris uite modum fecit.⁸ His temporibus Orientalibus Saxonibus Suithredus, Australibus Saxonibus Osmundus, Orientalibus Anglis Beorna, reges prefuerunt.⁹

ᵃ⁻ᵃ Defuncto . . . Hemele] *add. at line-end, partly over erasure* C³, *om.* HL, *treated as one with 755 n. b (p. 198) and therefore transferred to 756 n. c* B   ᵇ *see above, p. 198 n. b*   ᶜ *755 n. b (p. 198), 755 n. a (p. 200) incorporated here* B   ᵈ⁻ᵈ annis .xxxii.] -nis .xxxii. *presumably originally a runover on the last line of 755, now rewritten on same line to accommodate 755 n. a* C³   ᵉ *written in mg.* Cˡ

---

¹ The date for this succession is not recorded elsewhere. Hwita may have been in office in 749 (*S* 92 *BCS* 140), and Hemele by 757 (*S* 55 *BCS* 183).
² Mar.   ³ Mar. Paul I 757–67.
⁴ Both the abdication of Eadberht and the accession of Oswulf are entered under 758 in *Cont. Bede* and *HR* i. 42 (ii. 41), and the murder of Oswulf a year later in both. *HR* (like JW) gives the day (24 July). Of ASC DEF (which deal with this entry), E agrees with JW and *HR* in giving 24 July, D has 25 July, and F refers neither to Oswulf's 1-year reign nor to his murder.
⁵ For JW's 'a Northymbrensibus', ASC, *Cont. Bede* and *HR* i. 42 (ii. 41) have 'by his household' ('hiwan', 'ministri', 'familia').

On the death of Hwita, bishop
of Lichfield, Hemele suc-
ceeded.[1]

[756] The solar cycle begins with four concurrents in a bissextile
year. Archbishop Lul succeeded Boniface, and reigned for
thirty-two years.[2]

[757] An organ came to Francia for the first time, sent by
Constantine, king of the Greeks, to the emperor Pippin. Pope
Stephen died on 27 April; his brother Paul succeeded him.[3]

Eadberht, king of the Northumbrians, relinquished his realm for
the love of the heavenly kingdom and received the tonsure of St
Peter the Apostle. His son Oswulf received the government of the
kingdom and, after reigning a year, was killed on 24 July[4] by the
Northumbrians.[5,6]

[758] Paul, the ninety-second pope, reigned ten years and one
month.[7]

Cuthbert, archbishop of Canterbury, came to the end of his life
on 26 October.[8] In these times King Swithred ruled the East
Saxons, King Osmund the South Saxons, and King Beonna the
East Angles.[9]

---

[6] ASC DEF (F with omissions as above, n. 4).   [7] Mar.

[8] The chronological dislocation in this part of ASC A–F has led to Cuthbert's death
being assigned to 760, for which there is no independent evidence. ASC and *Cont. Bede*
date Cuthbert's consecration to 740; an addition to ASC F gives an 18-year episcopate,
which may indicate 758 as the year of his death (though see p. 202 nn. 2, 12). JW is
the only chronicle authority for the day of death.

[9] JW is the only source for this entry. Swithred appears in JW *East Saxon Accounts*
12; Osmund appears in charters (*Handbook of British Chronology*, pp. 20–1); Beorna
may be identical with the 'beanna' of Hunbeanna mentioned under 749 in *HR* i. 41 (ii.
39) and the Beonna on the coin in E. F. Keary, *Catalogue of English Coins in the British
Museum: Anglo-Saxon Series* (London, 1887), i. 83.

[759] (xviii) 781 *Pippinus imperator in Saxoniam ingreditur.*[1]
Breoguuinus post Cuthbertum die festiuitatis sancti Michaelis archiepiscopus ordinatur.[2] Moll Atheluuold regnum Northanhymbrorum suscepit.[3]

[760] (xix) 782 Ciclus decennouenalis .xiii. incipit indictione .xiii. *Pippinus in Wasconiam ingreditur.*[4]
Æthelbertus rex Cantuariorum obiit,[5] et Ceoluulfus, monachus religiosissimus, rex Nordhymbrorum quondam gloriosissimus, ad eterne lucis gaudia transiuit.[6]

[C³BP]
*"*Defuncto Hemele Licetfeldensi episcopo, successit Cuthfridus.*"*[7]

[761] (xx) 783 *Pippinus Italiam intrauit et bellum contra Haistulfum regem Longobardorum suscepit.*[8]
Hoc anno hiemps asperrima extitit[9] et Moll rex Norðhymbrensium .viii. idus Aug. iuxta Cliuum Eaduuini clitonem quendam nobilissimum Osuuinum occidit.[10]

[762] (xxi) 784 *Pippinus Haistulfum paucorum dierum obsidione apud Ticinum compulit et obsides dare, et recepta a Romanis oppida atque castella restituere et ut reddita non repeterentur sacramento fidem facere.*[11]
Sanctus[b] Breguuinus archiepiscopus ecclesie Cantuuariensis uite finem dedit .ix. kalend. Septembris.[c12]

---

a–a Defuncto . . . Cuthfridus] *add. at end of annal* C³, *om.* HL   *b* *interlin.* C¹B¹,
om. HLP (P mutilated)   *c* 763 n. a here HL

---

[1] Mar.
[2] Bregowine's consecration is entered under 759 (*recte* 761) in ASC, though neither its date nor the length of his episcopate (ASC F (addition) gives four years) can be determined with certainty. The first charter Bregowine witnesses (*S* 28 *BCS* 190) is dated 25 July 761 (for the most recent discussion see Scharer, pp. 120–4).
[3] ASC DEF record his regnal length and the loss (not in F) of his kingdom. *HR* i. 43 (ii. 41) has under this year 'Ethelwold qui et Moll dictus erat regnare incipit', and records his regnal length and his loss of the kingdom.
[4] Mar.
[5] If a genuine document lies behind the last known charter of Æthelberht, dated 762 (*S* 25 *BCS* 191), then there could be some confirmatory evidence for his death in this

[**759**] The Emperor Pippin invaded Saxony.[1]

Bregowine was ordained archbishop in succession to Cuthbert on the feast of St Michael.[2] Æthelwald Moll received the kingdom of the Northumbrians.[3]

[**760**] The thirteenth cycle of nineteen years begins in the thirteenth indiction. Pippin invaded Gascony.[4]

Æthelberht, king of the people of Kent, died,[5] and Ceolwulf, a most devout monk and before that a most glorious king of the Northumbrians, passed to the joys of eternal light.[6]

> On the death of Hemele, bishop of Lichfield, Cuthfrith succeeded.[7]

[**761**] Pippin entered Italy and embarked on a war with Aistulf, king of the Lombards.[8]

The winter was very bitter this year,[9] and Moll, king of the Northumbrians, killed a most noble atheling, Oswine, near 'Edwin's Cliff' on 6 August.[10]

[**762**] Pippin besieged Aistulf for a few days at Pavia and forced him to give hostages, and to restore the cities and fortresses taken from the Romans, and to pledge his word on oath not to attempt to regain what he had surrendered.[11]

St Bregowine, archbishop of Canterbury, came to the end of his life on 24 August.[12]

year reported by ASC A-F (760 *recte* 762). ASC A (addition by hand 8d) F (interlineation) say he was son of Wihtred.

[6] ASC DE give Ceolwulf's death under 760 (*recte* 762) though JW's description of him seems to be his own. See however HH *HA* iv c. 22 (Arnold p. 125). *HR* i. 44 (ii. 42) assigns Ceolwulf's death to 764.

[7] *HR* i. 45 (ii. 43) dates the death of Hemele and the succession of Cuthfrith to 765.

[8] Mar.

[9] ASC ADEF (761), (B)C (762), all *recte* 763. *HR* i. 43 (ii. 42) dates the hard winter 764; though some continental chronicles enter it under 763 and others 764, it is possible that *HR*'s date is too late.

[10] The killing of Oswine is entered under 761 in ASC DEF; the exact day is given in DE and *HR* i. 43 (ii. 41). The latter assigns the conflict to the third year of Moll's reign (761–2). JW alone describes Oswine as *clito nobilissimus*.

[11] Mar. [12] Independent evidence of Bregowine's survival to at least 764 could have been provided if the charter of Offa (*S* 105 *BCS* 195) issued in that year and witnessed by Bregowine were genuine (but see doubts expressed by Scharer, pp. 217–22). JW's day for his death (24 Aug.) differs from calendars' 26 Aug. F records his death.

[763] (xxii) 785 *ª*Cui successit Ianbrihtus*ᵇ* sancti Augustini abbas, et*ᵃᶜ* die purificationis sancte Marie in archiepiscopum leuatur,[1] eodemque anno Fritheuualdus Hwiternensis ecclesie antistes nonis Maii defungitur, pro quo Pechtuuinus .xvi. kalend. Aug. in regione que dicitur Ælfete consecratus episcopatu fungitur.[2]

[764] (xxiii) 786 Iaenberhtus archiepiscopus a papa Paulo Stephani pape sui precessoris germano pallium suscepit.[3]

[765] (xxiiii) 787 Moll regnum Northanhymbrorum dimisit et Alhredus filius Eanuuini successit,[4] qui fuit Byrnhom, qui fuit Bofa, qui fuit Bleacmon, qui fuit Earic, qui fuit Ide.[5]

[766] (xxv) 788 *Gordegangus Metensis episcopus corpora sanctorum Gorgonii et Nazarii a Roma in Franciam adduxit.*[6]
　　Ecgberhtus Eboracensis archiepiscopus .xiii. kalend. Decembris Eboraci obiit, cui successit Athelberhtus Coena.*ᵈ* Frithobertus
p. 278　Hagustaldensis | episcopus uita decessit, cui Alhmundus successit.[7]

[767] (xxvi*ᵉ*) 789 *Pippinus, finito Aquitanico bello contra Waifarium ducem Aquitanie quod continuis nouem annis gessit, Turonis causa orationis ad sanctum Martinum perrexit. ᶠInde egressus Parisius ad sanctum Dionisium uix perueniens, ibi morbo aque intercutis obiit .ix. kalend. Septembris ibique sepultus est.*[8]

ᵃ⁻ᵃ Cui . . . abbas et] *partly written over erasure, on opening line of 763 C³?, places at end of 762 HL (without* et)　*ᵇ* Iaenbryhtus *H*, Iaenbrihtus *L*　*ᶜ* Iaenberhtus *HL*, 763 *starts here HL*　*ᵈ* interlin. *C³?, om. HLP*, id est coena *interlin., and* Kene *also in mg. B¹*　*ᵉ* om. *C*　*ᶠ* 768 *starts here Mar.*

---

[1] The spelling *Ianbrihtus* and the information that he had been the abbot of St Augustine's (which are over an erasure in C, and are entered appropriately under 762 in HL) might suggest that the revision was based on *GP* ii. 7 (p. 15). Archbishop Jænberht's consecration 40 days after Christmas Day is entered in ASC A(B)C (763), DEF (762), BC calling him Eadbriht. F adds that he held office for 26 years. JW's Purification (2 Feb.) is 40 days after Christmas, though his 'leuatur' might possibly suggest election rather than consecration. A charter of Ecgberht of Kent of 765 (*S* 34 *BCS* 196, A. Campbell, *Charters of Rochester* (Anglo-Saxon Charters, i; Oxford, 1973), no. 7) witnessed by Jænberht suggests that he was in office by 765. In this case the alternatives of 765 and 766 for the date of his consecration mentioned by Plummer (*Chronicle*, ii. 49–50) should be resolved in favour of 765.
[2] ASC DE and (with less detail) F assign Frithuwald's death to 7 May and

[763] Jænberht, abbot of St Augustine's, succeeded him, and was preferred to the archbishopric on the day of the Purification of St Mary,[1] and in the same year Frithuwald, bishop of Whithorn, died on 7 May. Pehtwine was consecrated in his place on 17 July in the area called Elvet, and exercised the episcopal office.[2]

[764] Archbishop Jænberht received the pallium from Pope Paul, brother of Pope Stephen his predecessor.[3]

[765] Moll renounced the kingdom of the Northumbrians; he was succeeded by Alhred, son of Eanwine,[4] son of Byrnhom, son of Bofa, son of Blæcmon, son of Eadric, son of Ida.[5]

[766] Chrodegang, bishop of Metz, brought the bodies of the saints Gorgonius and Nazarius into Francia from Rome.[6]

Ecgberht, archbishop of York, died on 19 November at York. Æthelberht Coena succeeded him. Frithuberht, bishop of Hexham, departed this life, and Alhmund succeeded him.[7]

[767] When Pippin had brought to an end the Aquitanian war against Waifar, duke of Aquitaine, which he had waged for nine consecutive years, he went to Saint-Martin at Tours to pray. Then he left, and scarcely had he reached Saint-Denis at Paris than he died there of dropsy on 24 August, and there he was buried.[8]

Pehtwine's consecration on 17 July at Elvet to 762, *HR* i. 44 (ii. 42) gives 764. DE give the length of Frithuwald's episcopate.

[3] ASC A(B) (Eanbriht) C (Eadbriht) and F (interlineation) give 764, usually corrected to 766, for which there is no supporting evidence. JW identifies the pope.

[4] ASC DEF record the accession of Alhred; D says he reigned 9 years, E 8. *HR* i. 45 (ii. 43) records under 765 that Æthelwold (Moll) lost his kingdom and that Alhred, 'prosapia Idae regis exortus, ut quidam dicunt', succeeded to the kingdom.

[5] JW's genealogy is like JW *Northum. Gen.* save that his 'Earic' is there rendered Edric as in the Anglian genealogy in Cambridge, MS Corpus Christi College 183, fo. 65ᵛ (printed in D. N. Dumville, 'The Anglian collection of royal genealogies and regnal lists', *ASE*, v (1976), 32). Alhred in JW *Northum. Accounts* 22 is described as 'filius Eanuuini . . . trinepos regis Ide'. ASC has no genealogy.

[6] Mar.

[7] ASC DE and (with less detail) F have the material in this annal, DE adding the length of Ecgberht's and Frithuberht's episcopates. *HR* i. 45 (ii. 43) assigns the deaths of Archbishop Ecgberht and Bishop Frithuberht to 766, and their successors' ordination to 24 Apr. 767.

[8] Mar.

[768] (xxvii) 790 Paulus papa obiit.

Eximie religionis monachus Eadbrihtus, quondam rex Northanhymbrorum nobilissimus, .xiii. kalend. Septembris defunctus est ac in eadem porticu*a* in*b* qua frater suus Ecgbertus archiepiscopus iacet *c*tumulatus est.*cd*1

Romanorum septuagesimus octauus regnauit Karolus[2] *magnus filius Pippini annis quadraginta sex, mensibusque quattuor.*[3]

[C³BP]
*e*Defuncto Cuthfrido Licedfeldensi episcopo, successit Berhthunus.*e*4

[769] (i) 791 *Stephanus*[5] *nonagesimus tertius papa annis quattuor.*[6]

[770] (ii) 792 *Mortuo Pippino,*f *Franci generali conuentu totum regnum inter*g *filios eius Carolum et Carlomannum eque diuiserunt et Karolus partem patris eorum Pippini,* h*Carlomannus uero partem patrui eorum Carolomanni suscepit.*h7

[772] (iiii) 794 *Karlomannus autem post administratum biennio regnum in uilla Salmoniaco obiit .ii. non. Octobris, et Carolus totum regnum suscepit.* Stephanus papa obiit. *Adrianus*[8] *nonagesimus quartus papa annis uiginti tribus.*[9]

[C³BP]
i*Sigga Sealesiensis ecclesie presule defuncto, successit Alubrihtus.*ij10

[773] (v) 795 *Karolus, Hunoldo qui post mortem Waifari bellum sibi inferre conabatur fugato, et Aquitania subacta, rogatu Adriani pape, Italiam perrexit, et Desiderium Longobardorum regem longa*

---

a apud Eboracum *interlin. B*5   *b interlin. C*1   *c–c* tumulatus est] *extends into mg. C*1   *d* capitula lxxviii] *add. L*   *e–e* Defuncto . . . Berhthunus] *add. mg. C*3, *om. HL*   *f* rege .viii. kalend. Octob. *interlin. B*1   *g* inter duos *HL* *h–h* Carlomannus . . . suscepit] *runs on to 771 CB, starts at 771 H*   *i–i* Sigga . . . Alubrihtus] *add. at line-end C*3, *om. HL*   *j* 773 *n. b incorporated here B*

---

[1] ASC DEF record briefly the death of 'Eadberht Eating', D on 20 Aug. (like JW) and E on 19 Aug. *HR* i. 46 (ii. 44) records his death 'in clericatu'. ASC 738 may be the source of JW's statement concerning his burial-place, which is also in *HDE* ii. 3 (i. 49).

[768] Pope Paul died.

Eadberht, a monk of outstanding piety, formerly the most noble king of the Northumbrians, died on 20 August, and was buried in the very chapel in which his brother, Archbishop Ecgberht, lies.[1]

Charles the Great,[2] son of Pippin and the seventy-eighth emperor of the Romans, reigned forty-six years and four months.[3]

> On the death of Cuthfrith, bishop of Lichfield, Berhthun succeeded.[4]

[769] Stephen,[5] the ninety-third pope, reigned four years.[6]

[770] On the death of Pippin, the Franks at a general assembly divided the whole realm equally between his sons Charles and Carloman: Charles received the territory of their father Pippin while Carloman received that of their uncle Carloman.[7]

[772] Carloman, after administering the kingdom for two years, died in the township of Samoussy on 6 October, and Charles received the whole kingdom. Pope Stephen died. Hadrian,[8] the ninety-fourth pope, reigned twenty-three years.[9]

> On the death of Sicgga, bishop of Selsey, Aluberht succeeded.[10]

[773] When Charles had routed Hunuald, who tried to make war on him after the death of Waifar, and had subdued Aquitaine, he went to Italy at the invitation of Pope Hadrian and wore down

---

[2] Charlemagne 768–814.

[3] Mar.

[4] HR i. 45 (ii. 43) dates Cuthfrith's ordination to 765; the late writer Thomas of Chesterfield assigns him a pontificate of 3 (4 in London, BL Cotton MS Vespasian E. XVI) years (Anglia Sacra, i. 428).

[5] Stephen III (IV) 768–72.   [6] Mar.   [7] Mar.

[8] Hadrian I 772–95.   [9] Mar.

[10] Sicgga was consecrated bishop of Selsey in 733 (teste Cont. Bede) and was present at the council of Clofesho in 747 (Haddan and Stubbs, Councils, iii. 362). If, as has been suggested, part of the witness-list in S 108 BCS 208 (dated 772) is genuine, then Aluberht's successor Oswald was in office in that year. Little reliance can be placed on the two South Saxon charters which mention a bishop (or archbishop): S 48 BCS 198 dated 762 (probably for 765), and S 49 BCS 206 (dated 770).

obsidione fatigans in ditionem[a] suam suscepit, filiumque eius Adalgisum in quo omnes spem inclinabant ab Italia expulit, atque Italiam totam subegit, et omnia a Longobardorum regibus erepta tam Romanis quam Adriano pape restituit et tunc primum Romam sabbato sancto pasce uenit.[1]

[C³BP³]

[b]⟨*A*⟩*drianus papa Romam uenire Karolum* regem *ad defendendas res ecclesie postulauit. Karolus ergo Romam ueniens, Pauiam obsedit, ibique relicto exercitu, in sancta resurrectione* [c]*ab Adriano papa Rome honorifice susceptus est. Post sanctam uero resurrectionem reuersus*[c] *Papiam, cepit Desiderium regem. Deinde Romam reuersus,*[d] *constituit ibi synodum cum Adriano papa in patriarchio Laterani in ecclesia sancti Saluatoris. Que synodus celebrata est a .clvi.*[e] *religiosis episcopis et abbatibus. Adrianus autem papa cum uniuersa synodo tradiderunt Karolo ius et potestatem eligendi pontificem et ordinandi apostolicam sedem, dignitatem quoque* patriarchatus *ei concesserunt. Insuper arciepiscopos, episcopos* ⟨*per*⟩ *singulas prouincias ab eo inuestituram accipere* diffiniuit[f] *et, ut, nisi a rege laudetur et inuestiatur episcopus, a nemine consecraretur. Et quicunque contra hoc decretum* esset *anathematis uinculo eum innodauit* et, nisi*

[a] ed *interlin. above* ditionem *B*[1]   [b] Adrianus . . . precepit *(p. 210)] add. mg. alongside 766–83 C*³, *om. HL, incorporated at 772 n. j B, mg. alongside 768–73 P*³ [c-c] ab . . . reuersus] *over erasure at line-end and into mg. B*[1]   [d] ueniens *B* [e] .cliii. *MGH p. 826*   [f] definiunt *MGH p. 827, (reference below, p. 210 n. 1)*

---

[1] Mar.

Desiderius, king of the Lombards, with a long siege and received his submission. He expelled from Italy his son Adelchis, in whom all placed their hope, and subdued all Italy, and when he had stripped the Lombard kings of all their possessions he restored them to both the Romans and to Pope Hadrian and went to Rome for the first time on Holy Saturday.[1]

Pope Hadrian summoned Charles to come to Rome to defend the possessions of the church; Charles, on his way to Rome, besieged Pavia, left his army there, and was received with honour by Pope Hadrian at Rome on the day of the Resurrection. After the Holy Resurrection, he returned to Pavia, and captured King Desiderius. Then, on his return to Rome, he held, with Pope Hadrian, a synod in the church of the Holy Saviour in the Lateran Palace. This synod was attended by 156 devout bishops and abbots. Pope Hadrian, with the entire synod, entrusted to Charles the right and the power to choose the pope and order the apostolic see. They also granted him the patriarchal dignity. In addition, he decreed that archbishops and bishops in each province should be invested by him, and that no bishop be consecrated by anyone unless he was approved and invested by the king. And whoever opposed this decree he placed under the bonds of anathema and ordered that,

resipisceret, bona eius publicari
precepit.ᵃ¹

[774] (vi) 796 Rubicundi coloris signum in crucis modum in celo
apparuit post solis occasum. Merci et Cantuarienses apud
Ottanfordam preliati sunt. In prouincia Australium Saxonum uisi
sunt serpentes aspectu horribiles ualdeque mirabiles.² Festi pascalis tempore Norðhymbrenses regem suum Alhredum, Molli regis
successorem, Eboraco expulere, filiumque eiusdem regis Molli
Æthelbertum in regem leuauere.³

[775] (vii) 797 Huuicciorum episcopus Milredus obiit, cui in
pontificatus officium Wermundus successit.⁴

[776] (viii) 798 ᵇSubacta Italia, Saxonicum bellum biennio ante
Italicum inceptum repetitum est, et per .xxx. tres annos permansit.
Quorum Saxonum Karolus .x. milia hominum captiuorum cum
uxoribus et paruulis dispersit.⁵
ᶜPehtuuinus Candide Case presul .xiii. kalend. Octobris obiit.ᶜᵈ⁶

[778] (x) 800 ᵉKarolus Hispaniam subiecit et incolumi exercitu
reuertitur.ᵉ Domuit Brytones qui in occidente Gallie super litus reside-
bant.⁷
ᶠKyneuulfus ⁸rex Westsaxonum⁸ et Offa ⁸rex Merciorum⁸
propter Benesingtun graue gessere prelium, sed Offa, ⁸uictor existens,⁸ eandem uillam cepit et possedit.⁹ Huuicciorum episcopusᵍ

ᵃ see above, p. 208 n. b   ᵇ this annal ends under 777 C, starts under 775 and runs
on to 776 (N)   ᶜ⁻ᶜ Pehtuuinus . . . obiit] under 777, but could be run over from 776
C, under 777 B   ᵈ Conuersio Saxonum add. here B   ᵉ⁻ᵉ Karolus . . . reuerti-
tur] under 777 (N)   ᶠ 778 n. a incorporated here HL   ᵍ extends into mg. Cᴵ

---

¹ Decretum Spurium Hadriani papae, Ivo Carnotensis, Panormia, viii. 135 (MGH
Legum Sectio III, Concilia: Tomi II, pars i: Concilia Aevi Karolini, ed. A. Werminghoff
(Hanover, 1906), pp. 825–8).
² ASC A (773) B–F (all 774) record the red cross in the sky, the battle of Otford,
and the serpents in Sussex.
³ ASC DE record the expulsion of Alhred and DEF the setting-up of Moll's son as
king in Northumbria, giving him a reign of four years. He is named Æthelred in these

unless he recovered his senses,
his goods should be seized.[1]

[774] A red sign after the fashion of a cross appeared in the sky
after sunset. The Mercians and the men of Kent fought at Otford.
The most amazing serpents of terrifying appearance were seen in
the kingdom of the South Saxons.[2] At the time of the feast of
Easter, the Northumbrians expelled their king Alhred, successor of
King Moll, from York, and raised Æthelberht, son of that same
Moll, to the throne.[3]

[775] Milred, bishop of the Hwicce, died, and Wærmund succeeded him to the episcopal office.[4]

[776] When Italy had been subdued, the Saxon war, begun two
years before the Italian one, resumed and lasted for thirty-three
years. Of these Saxons Charles took 10,000 prisoners and dispersed them with their wives and chidren.[5]

Pehtwine, bishop of Whithorn, died on 19 September.[6]

[778] Charles conquered Spain, and returned with his army intact.
He conquered the Bretons who dwelt in western Gaul on the
coast.[7]

Cynewulf, [8]king of the West Saxons, [8]and Offa, [8]king of the
Mercians,[8] fought a major battle near Bensington, but Offa [8]was
victorious,[8] and took, and held the town.[9] Wermund, bishop of

---

chronicles, 'Æthelred qui et Æthelbert' in JW *Northum. Gen.* and *Accounts* 23, and
'Ethelberto qui et Adelredus dictus est' in WM, *GR* i. 72 (i. 74), and at the first reference to Ætheberht a MS of the third recension adds 'uel Adelredus' in the margin.
    [4] The death of Milred, but neither the name of the see nor the succession of
Wærmund, is entered under 772 (*recte* 774) in ASC A–F.
    [5] Mar.
    [6] ASC DEF record Pehtwine's death under 776, *HR* i. 49 (ii. 46) under 777 (DE
and *HR* giving the day); all give him an episcopacy of 14 years. JW dates his succession to 763 but it is just possible that he assigned his death to 777: the Marianus annal
for 776 runs over on to 777, where the death of Pehtwine immediately follows.
    [7] Mar.   [8-8] No equivalent in ASC.
    [9] ASC A–E under 777. 'Propter Benesingtun' may be a rendering of 'ymb
Benesingtun' (ABC).

Wermundus obiit et abbas Tilherus illi successit.[1] Athilbertus ad Candidam Casam .xvii. kalend. Iulii episcopus Eboraci ordinatur.[2] *ab*Athelberto a Northhymbrensibus*b* regno expulso, Alfuuoldus regnum Northanhymbrorum suscepit.*a*[3]

[779] (xi) 801 Ciclus decennouenalis .xiiii. incipit indictione secunda.

[780] (xii) 802 ʿHagustaldensis episcopus Alhmundus .vii. idus Septembris obiit, pro quo Tilbertus .vi. non. Octobris ordinatur et Higbaldus pro Cineuulfo apud Soccabyrig Lindisfarne episcopus consecratur. Rex Alfuuoldus, pro petendo pallio Eanbaldi, legatos Romam misit ad Adrianum papam.*c*[4]

*d*Karolus iterum in Saxoniam uenit et fames magna mortalitasque magna facta est in Francia. Sanctus Sturmi abbas primus Fuldensis obiit .xvi. kalend. Nouembris, cui successit Baogulfus.[5]

[781] (xiii) 803 Huicciorum presule Tilhero defuncto, Heathoredus pro illo functus est episcopatus officio.[6] Æthelberhtus Eboracensis archiepiscopus, Ecgberhti successor obiit. Cui Eanbaldus in archiepiscopatum successit,[7]

[C³BP]

*e*qui fuit discipulus Alhwini, magistri Karoli imperatoris.*e*[8]

---

a–a Athelberto . . . suscepit] *add. mg. with signe de renvoi* C¹, *incorporated at 778 n. e* HL, *at end of annal B, mg. alongside 777–8* P³   *b–b* Athelberto . . . Northhymbrensibus] Æthelberto a Northimbrensibus HL   *c–c* Hagustaldensis . . . papam] *add. mg. alongside 779–81 with signe de renvoi* C¹, *incorporated at end of 779* HLBP   *d* 781 *starts here (N)*   *e–e* qui . . . imperatoris] *written partly over erasure* C³, *om.* HL

---

[1] The death of Wærmund is recorded also in the 19-year cycle on p. 62 of JW MS C, which assigns the succession of Tilhere to 779. It is not prudent to use *S* 113 *BCS* 223 (which Tilhere attests) as evidence that he had succeeded by 777, as the date of this charter (778 but with indiction for 777) comes from a part of the document which cannot be accepted as genuine in its present form (Robinson, *Worcester*, pp. 24–5).

[2] ASC DEF enter Æthelberht's consecration as bishop of Whithorn under 777, in the year after Pehtwine's death (DE giving the day 15 June), and *HR* i. 49 (ii. 46) mentions his succession in the same annal (777) as Pehtwine's death. 15 June was a Sunday in 777, not 778.

[3] ASC DE record under 778 the expulsion of Æthelred, the accession of Ælfwald, the length of his reign, and the murder of three high-reeves, F giving only the succes-

the Hwicce, died, and Abbot Tilhere succeeded him.[1] Æthelberht
was ordained bishop of Whithorn at York on 15 June.[2] Æthelberht
was expelled from his kingdom by the Northumbrians, and
Ælfwald received the realm of the Northumbrians.[3]

[779] The fourteenth cycle of nineteen years begins in the second
indiction.

[780] Alhmund, bishop of Hexham, died on 7 September, and
Tilberht was ordained on 2 October in his place. Higbald was
consecrated bishop of Lindisfarne at Sockburn in Cynewulf's
place. King Ælfwald sent legates to Rome to Pope Hadrian to
request Eanbald's pallium.[4]

Charles went to Saxony again, and great famine and mortality
occurred in the Frankish kingdom. St Sturmi, the first abbot of
Fulda, died on 17 October, and Baogulf succeeded him.[5]

[781] On the death of Tilhere, bishop of the Hwicce, Heathured
exercised the episcopal office in his place.[6] Æthelberht, archbishop
of York, successor of Ecgberht, died. Eanbald succeeded him in
the archbishopric.[7]

> He had been the pupil of
> Alcuin, master of the Emperor
> Charles.[8]

---

sion of Ælfwald and the length of his reign. *HR* i. 48 (ii. 46) records the murder under
778 and the expulsion of Æthelred and Ælfwald's accession under 779. For the two
names Æthelberht and Æthelred see above, p. 210 n. 3.

[4] ASC DE and (less fully) F present the information in this annal, without mention-
ing Cynewulf, whose resignation they had recorded under 779, EF wrongly calling him
'Cynebald'. *HR* i. 50–1 (ii. 47) records the Hexham succession under 781 and, like
HDE ii. 4 (i. 50), Higbald's succession at Lindisfarne under 780. JW names the pope.

[5] Mar.

[6] The date for the death of Tilhere and the succession of Heathured, which does not
appear elsewhere, might be supported by *S* 116 *BCS* 236, dated 780, and witnessed by
Tilhere (though for doubts as to its genuineness see Scharer, pp. 247–9), and by *S*
1257 *BCS* 241 (transl. Whitelock, *EHD*, no. 77, pp. 505–7) which is Heathured's statement concerning business done at Brentford in 781. In MS C's 19-year table (p. 62)
the accession of Heathured is assigned to 782.

[7] The death of Archbishop Æthelberht and the succession of Eanbald are recorded
by ASC DEF under 779 and by *HR* i. 50 (ii. 47) under 780. *HR* says, and ASC DEF
imply, that Eanbald had been consecrated in Æthelberht's lifetime. JW identifies
Æthelberht as Ecgberht's successor.

[8] This addition may be based on *GP* iii. 112–13 (p. 246).

*ᵃKarolus Saxoniam capit.*ᵃ¹

ᵇSinodus apud Aclea celebratur et Cineuulfus Lindisfarnensis episcopus et Wereburh Ceolredi quondam regis Merciorum regina obierunt.ᵇ²

[C³BP³]
ᶜDefuncto Herewaldo Scireburnensis ecclesie presule, successit Æthelmodus, illique Denefridus, eique Wibertus.ᶜ³

[782] (xiiii) 804ᵈ *Karolus secundo Romam perrexit ibique baptizatus est filius eius Karlomannus, quem Adrianus papa, mutato nomine, uocauit Pippinum.*⁴

[783] (xv) 805 *Hiltigart regina obiit, tres filios Carolum, Pippinum et Ludouuicum Karolo relinquens, pro qua Karolus Fastradam sociauit in coniugium sibi.*⁵

[C³BP]
ᵉDefuncto Totta Leogorensi presule, Eadberht successit.ᵉ⁶ |

p. 279   [784] (xvi) 806 Ciclus solis incipit .iiii. concurrentibus bissextilibus.

Kyneuulfus, rex Occidentalium Saxonum,ᶠ clitonem Cinehardum, regis uidelicet Sigeberti germanum, suo de regno cum moliretur expellere, contigit illumᵍ uillam que Anglice Meretun dicitur causa mulieris cuiusdam cum paucis adisse. Quo cognito, suos clito conglobauit ilico, illoque festinus cum magno properauit gaudio. Quo cum uenisset, omesque alto sopori deditos inuenisset,

---

ᵃ⁻ᵃ Karolus . . . capit] *rewritten at line-end* C³   ᵇ⁻ᵇ Sinodus . . . obierunt] *add. mg. alongside 781–2 with signe de renvoi in mg. but that in text apparently erased* Cᵗ, *outer mg. alongside 774 (781 being in an inner column)* P³   ᶜ⁻ᶜ Defuncto . . . Wibertus] *add. mg. alongside 783, though traces of erasure at end of 782 might indicate an earlier attempt at insertion* C³, *om.* HL, *outer mg. alongside 774 (781 being in an inner column)* P³   ᵈ *erasure possibly after 800* C   ᵉ⁻ᵉ Defuncto . . . successit] *add. at end of annal* C³, *om.* HL   ᶠ qui .xxxvi. annos regnauit *add. mg.* B⁵   ᵍ ipsum regem *interlin. above deleted* illum B⁵?

---

¹ Mar.
² The synod of *Aclea* and the deaths of Bishop Cynewulf and Queen Werburg are

Charles took Saxony.[1]

A synod was held at *Aclea*, and Cynewulf, bishop of Lindisfarne, and Werburg, queen of Ceolred, formerly king of the Mercians, died.[2]

> On the death of Herewald, bishop of Sherborne, Æthelmod succeeded, and to him Denefrith, and to him Wigberht.[3]

[782] Charles went to Rome a second time, and there his son Carloman, whose name Pope Hadrian changed to Pippin, was baptized.[4]

[783] Queen Hildegar died, leaving three sons, Charles, Pippin, and Louis, and Charles took Fastrada as wife in her place.[5]

> On the death of Torhthelm, bishop of Leicester, Eadberht succeeded.[6]

[784] The solar cycle begins with four concurrents in a bissextile year.

When Cynewulf, king of the West Saxons, tried to expel the atheling Cyneheard, King Sigeberht's brother, from his kingdom, it so happened that he went to a township, which is called *Meretun* in English, with a few men to visit a woman. When the atheling learnt of this, he immediately assembled his own men, and hurried there with great joy. When he arrived there, and discovered them all given over to deep sleep, he ordered his men to surround closely the room in which the king lay sleeping. When the king became aware of this, he leapt from his bed, seized his

---

entered in *ASC* DEF (F omitting the queen's death) under 782, and the deaths of the bishop and queen in *HR* i. 53 (ii. 50) under 783.
    [3] The date of Herewald of Sherborne's death and the succession of Æthelmod, sometimes wrongly called Æthelmund, is not recorded elsewhere; 781 is too late for Æthelmod was in office in 774 (*teste* M. A. O'Donovan, *Charters of Sherborne* (Anglo-Saxon Charters, iii; London, 1988), p. 4, no. 2: *S* 263 *BCS* 224).
    [4] Mar.   [5] Mar.
    [6] This addition seems misdated: *HR* i. 44 (ii. 42) assigns Torhthelm's death and Eadberht's succession to 764.

cameram,[1] in qua rex dormiens iacebat, spissim circumuallare suis precipiebat. Quod rex ut comperit strato prosilit, arma arripit, ostium camere aperit, et pugnando se impugnantibus uiriliter resistit. Viso tandem clitone [2]in illum protinus irruit eumque oppido uulnerauit.[2] Cuius milites hoc uidentes simul omnes in regem insurrexere, uulneratumque interfecere. Exclamat mulier pre timore et dolore, impletque cameram flebili clamore. Accurrit paucitas militum, regem uidet occisum quem paulo ante reliquerat uiuum. Quapropter ire stimulis exagitata perplurimum, euaginatis macheris in eius interfectores magnum facit impetum. At illos clito allocutus blandissime, promittit cuique non modicum pecunie, promittit etiam uiuere, si ab inceptis uelint desistere. Illi uero promissa spernunt, ceptis insistunt, sed omnes, excepto uno Brytonico obside nimis uulnerato occidunt. Mane autem morte regis audita, dux ipsius Osricus sibi amicissimus et Wiferthus eius minister fidissimus cum omnibus, quos rex pridie domi reliquerat, citatim aduolarunt, sed fores cunctas seratas inuenerunt. Quas dum moliuntur effringere, ad eos clito accedens intrepide aurum argentum dignitates iuxta suum uelle spondet se eis daturum libenti animo si se regali sullimare uelint solio. Intimat etiam eis secum esse quamplurimos illis germanitate coniunctos qui nullo pacto se abicere, sed secum uelint mori et uiuere. At illi, spretis promissis, cognatos summopere rogitant ut abiecto suo domino incolumes ad se quantotius exeant. Quibus illi respondentes dixerunt: 'Quod nobis offertis sociis cum rege occisis prius optulimus uestris. Verum sicut illi nostre petitioni noluerunt acquiescere, ita et nos hac in re uestre nolumus obtemperare.' His auditis, illi propius accedunt, portas effringunt, sepes diruunt, et clitonem cum suis omnibus numero octoginta quattuor interficiunt, excepto solo dumtaxat ducis filiolo, oppido tamen uulnerato. Corpus prefati regis Wintoniam humandum deportatur, clitonis uero in monasterio quod Axanmynster dicitur tumulatur.[ab3]

---

[a] sign indicates insertion of 788 n. b here B   [b] see App. B for addition at line-end B[1]

---

[1] ASC ADEF 'bur', BC 'burh'.   [2-2] ASC A, not BC.
[3] ASC ADE (all 784) C (783) (B) (either 783 or 784) record the deaths of Cynewulf and Cyneheard and the succession of Brihtric; the date rightly corrected to 786, since Cynewulf was present at a meeting with papal legates in that year (*Alcuini Epistolae*, ed. E. Dümmler (*MGH Epp.* iv; Hanover, 1895), 3, transl. Whitelock, *EHD*, no. 191,

arms, opened the door of the room,[1] and put up a strong resistance by fighting his attackers. At length, when he saw the atheling, [2]he rushed at once upon him and wounded him severely.[2] The atheling's thegns, seeing this, rose all together against the king, whom they wounded and slew. The woman cried out in fear and grief, and filled the room with her tearful outcry. His few thegns ran up, and saw lying slain the king whom they had left alive a short time before. Wherefore, roused by stinging anger, they drew their swords and made a fierce attack on his slayers. But the atheling addressed them flatteringly, promised them each a fair sum of money, and also promised them their lives, if they would desist from what they had begun. But they spurned his offers, continued with their undertaking, and they all fell, except one seriously wounded British hostage. But, in the morning, when tidings of the king's death were heard, the ealdorman Osric, who was dearest to him, and Wigferth, his most loyal thegn, hastened there swiftly with all the men whom the king had left behind the day before, but they found all the gates barred. While they were trying to break them down, the atheling approached them boldly, promising that he would gladly give them gold, silver, and honours according to their desire if they would raise him to the royal throne. He also pointed out to them that there were many bound to him by kinship who would not abandon him on any condition but would live or die with him. But they, spurning his promises, requested his kinsmen earnestly the last time to abandon their lord and to go unharmed as soon as possible, to which they said in reply: 'What you offer us we formerly offered your comrades slain with the king, and just as they refused to accede to our request so we also will not submit to you in this matter.' When they heard this, they drew closer, broke down the gates, tore up the fences, and slew the atheling with all his eighty-four men, with the sole exception of the atheling's little son, and he was sorely wounded. The body of the aforementioned king was taken to Winchester for burial, but that of the atheling was buried in the monastery called Axminster.[3]

pp. 836-40). JW substitutes the narrative (slightly adjusted) entered under 755 in ASC taking from its 784 annal the number (84) slain with Cyneheard and omitting the succession of Brihtric. HH *HA* iv c. 24 (Arnold pp. 127-8) also puts the 755 material into its proper chronological place, and adds the 84 killed from 784.

[785] (xvii) 807 *Coniuratio Hardradi et orientalium. Karolus pergit Italiam. Qui matrem suam Berhtradam in basilica sancti Dionisii iuxta patrem humauit cum magna gloria.*[1]

In loco qui lingua Anglorum Cealchythe dicitur, litigiosa facta est synodus et iccirco modicam portionem sue parrochie archiepiscopus amisit Iainbertus. Defuncto Berhthuno Dorcestrensi[a] episcopo, Hygebrihtus ab Offa rege Merciorum in[b] episcopatum est electus et Ecgferthus [2]eiusdem regis natus[2] rex est consecratus.[3]

[786] (xviii) 808 *[d]Karolus tertio Romam perrexit et signum crucis [d]in uestibus hominum apparuit.[d] Lul archiepiscopus obiit .xvii. kalend. Nou. hora diei secunda. Richolfus sibi successit annis .xxvii. qui basilicam sanctissimi martyris Albani a fundamentis inchoauit, mirifico opere perfecit, interiusque ditauit. Sanguis e celo et terra profluxit.*[4]

[C³BP]

[e]Defuncto Podda Herefordensi episcopo, successit Ecca.[e5]

[787] (xviiii) 809 *Karolus a Roma pergit ad sanctum Benedictum et per Alamanniam uenit Bauuariam.*[6]

Filiam Offe regis Eadburgam duxit uxorem [7]Occidentalium Saxonum[7] rex Brihtricus. Cuius tempore Danici[8] pirate tribus cum nauibus Angliam adiere. Quorum aduentus dum regis preposito nuntiatus fuisset, eos cum paucis festinus adiit. Cunque penitus ignoraret qui essent uel unde uenissent, inuitos ad regiam minare uillam molitus est, sed mox ab eisdem occisus est. Hi primi fuerunt qui de Dania Angliam adierunt.[9]

---

[a] Licetfeld *interlin. by a later 12th-c. hand* C, Licenfeld *interlin* B¹   [b] uel ad *interlin.* C¹B¹   [c] *this annal is consolidated with previous annal under 785-6 (N)*   [d-d] in . . . apparuit] *written over erasure* C   [e-e] Defuncto . . . Ecca] *add. at line-end* C³, *om.* HL

---

[1] Mar.   [2-2] No equivalent in ASC.
[3] ASC A–F give the information in this annal under 785 (*recte* 787), though Berhthun's death is not mentioned. JW's slip, in assigning both Berhthun and Hygeberht to Dorchester and not Lichfield cannot be explained; it caused him to overlook Lichfield's elevation to an archbishopric. Hygeberht must have been elected as early as 779 since he must be the '. . .geberhtus electus presul' who attests *S* 114 *BCS* 230 in that year.
[4] Mar.

[785] Conspiracy of Hardrad and the Eastern Franks. Charles reached Italy. He buried his mother Berhtrada in the basilica of Saint-Denis next to his father with great pomp.[1]

In the place which is called Chelsea in English a disputatious synod was held, and because of it Archbishop Jænberht lost a small part of his diocese. On the death of Berhthun, bishop of Dorchester, Hygeberht was chosen by Offa, king of the Mercians, for the episcopacy, and Ecgfrith, [2]son of the same king,[2] was consecrated king.[3]

[786] Charles went to Rome for the third time and the sign of the cross appeared on his men's clothes. Archbishop Lul died on 16 October at the second hour of the day. Richulf succeeded him, and ruled twenty-seven years, and he began the church of the most holy martyr Alban from the foundations, finishing it with wonderful workmanship, and he enriched the interior. Blood flowed from heaven and earth.[4]

Acca succeeded on the death of
Podda, bishop of Hereford.[5]

[787] Charles went from Rome to St Benedict's and came to Bavaria by way of Alemannia.[6]

Brihtric, king [7]of the West Saxons,[7] married Eadburg, daughter of King Offa. In his time the Danish[8] pirates came to England in three ships. When their arrival was announced to the king's reeve, he hastily marched against them with a few men and, since he had no idea who they were or whence they had come, he endeavoured to drive them against their will to the royal township, but he was promptly killed by them. They were the first to come from Denmark to England.[9]

---

[5] This addition is misplaced. Acca was succeeded by Headda and Aldberht; since Aldberht was in office in 781 (S 1257 BCS 24, transl. Whitelock, EHD, no. 77, pp. 505–7) and possibly by 778 (S 113 BCS 223), Acca must have died before then. Acca witnesses S 265 BCS 327, (808 for 757×758) in the company of King Cynewulf (d. 757) and Archbishop Cuthbert (d. by 760), which shows that Podda died more than a quarter of a century before 786.

[6] Mar.   [7-7] No equivalent in ASC.

[8] ASC B–F have 'Norðmanna', D adding 'of Hæreðalande' and EF 'Hereðalande'.

[9] ASC A–F (F shorter) under 787 (recte 789).

[C³BP]

*a*Defuncto Higberto Licetfeldensi episcopo, successit Aldulfus.*a*1

[788] (xx) 810 Sinodus apud Pincanhale in Northymbria .iiii.
non. Septembris celebratur.²

[C³B¹? P³]

*b*Anni solares quinquies milleni
ab hora prima quarti diei saeculi
incepti, anno regni Karoli magni
Romanorum imperatoris uicesimo, hora uicesima quarta diei
kalendarum Aprilis tertii decimi
sunt expleti. Lustris complexi
millenis, mensibus solaribus sexagenis milibus, ebdomadibus
ducentenis sexagenis milibus ⟨oct-
ingentenis⟩ nonagenis ac binis,
diebus millenis milibus et octin-
gentis uicenis senis milibus et
ducentenis quinquagenis, horis
quadragies et ter millenis milibus
et octingentenis tricenis milibus,
punctis centies septuagies quinquies millenis milibus et trecentenis uicenis milibus, minutis
quadringenties tricies octies*c* millenis milibus et trecentenis
milibus, partibus sexcenties
quinquagies septies millenis
milibus et quadringentenis quinquagenis milibus, momentis
milies septingenties quinquagies
et ter millenis milibus et ducentenis milibus, ostentis bis milies
sexcenties uicies nouies millenis
milibus et octingentenis milibus,
atomis nongenties octuagies
octies milies millenis milibus

On the death of Hygeberht, bishop of Lichfield, Aldwulf succeeded.[1]

[788] A synod was held at *Pincanheale* in Northumbria on 2 September.[2]

Five thousand solar years have been completed since the first hour of the fourth day of the Creation, in the twenty-fourth hour of 20 March in the twentieth year of the reign of the Roman Emperor Charles the Great, that is 1,000 periods of five years, 60,000 solar months, 260,892 weeks, 1,826,250 days, 43,830,000 hours, 175,320,000 *puncta*, 438,300,000 *minuta*, 657,450,000 *partes*, 1,753,200,000

[a–a] Defuncto . . . Aldulfus] *add. at line-end* C³, *om. HL*   [b] Anni . . . milibus (p. 222)] *written in lower mg. p. 279* C¹, *om. HL, written lower mg. with sign pointing to insertion at 784 n. a* B¹?, *mg. alongside 786–9* P³   [c] decies *CBP*

---

[1] This addition is erroneous. Hygeberht attests a charter as archbishop in 799 (*S* 155 *BCS* 293). Though his successor Aldwulf was in office probably by 800/1 (*S* 106 *BCS* 201), a Hygeberht 'abbas' was still alive at the synod of 803 (*BCS* 312).
[2] ASC DEF enter the synod of *Pincanheale* under 788, DE dating it to 2 Sept.; *HR* i. 54 (ii. 51) dates it 2 Sept. 787. DE also record the death of Abbot Ealdberht (D adding 'of Ripon').

octingenties et quater millenis
milibus ac octingentenis milibus.*[a]*

[789] (xxi) 811   *Karolus Sclauos qui dicuntur Wlzi subegit.*[1]

Rex Northanhymbrorum Alfuuoldus a quodam uiro Sigan
nomine .ix. kalend. Octobris iniuste perimitur, et in ecclesia sancti
Petri Hagustalde sepelitur. In cuius loco occisionis sepius celitus
emissa lux apparuit immensa. Successit autem illi in regnum nepos
suus Osredus, regis Alhredi filius.[2]

[C³P³]

*b*Defuncto Kynehardo Wintonie
presule, *Æthelhardus ex abbate
Melduni* successit.*b3* |

p. 280   **[790] (xxii) 812**   *Basilica sancti Bonifacii Fuldense monasterium fundatur.*[c4]

Iainbertus Dorubernensis archiepiscopus .ii. idus Augusti
defunctus est,

[HLP]	[C³B]
in cuius locum Athelhardus abbas electus est.[5]	*d*cui successit Athelardus, .vii. Wintoniensis episcopus, ad quem scripsit epistolam *e*Albinus, uir undecunque doctissimus. Athelardo successerunt in presulatum Wintoniensem Egbald, Dudd, Cynebert, Alhmund, Wighein, Herefrið, Eadmund, Helmstan.*de6*

---

a see above, p. 220 n. b   *b–b Defuncto . . . successit] add. mg. alongside 788–9 C³,
om. HLB, mg. alongside 789 P³*   *c places 790 n. a (p. 224) here B*   *d–d cui . . .
Helmstan] rewritten over erasure and running on to 791–92 C³, runs on to 791–92 B
e–e Albinus . . . Helmstan] incorporated at opening of 792 P*

---

[1] Mar.
[2] ASC DEF (F much more briefly) record the killing of Ælfwald (without calling it
'iniuste'), his burial (not in F), the heavenly light which shone at the place of his

moments, 2,629,800,000 *ostenta*,
988,804,800,000 atoms.

[789] Charles subdued the Slavs who are called the Wilzi.[1]

Ælfwald, king of the Northumbrians, was unjustly slain by a certain man called Sicga on 23 September, and was buried in St Peter's church at Hexham. In the place where he was killed a great light of heavenly origin often appeared. His nephew Osred, son of King Alhred, succeeded him in the kingdom.[2]

On the death of Cyneheard, bishop of Winchester, Æthelheard from Malmesbury abbey succeeded.[3]

[790] The basilica of St Boniface was founded at the monastery of Fulda.[4]

Jænberht, archbishop of Canterbury, died on 12 August.

In his place abbot Æthelheard was chosen.[5]

Æthelheard, seventh bishop of Winchester, succeeded him, to whom Alcuin, a man most learned in all disciplines, wrote an epistle. To Æthelheard there succeeded in the bishopric of Winchester Ecgbald, Dudd, Cyneberht, Ealhmund, Wigthegn, Herefrith, Eadhun, and Helmstan.[6]

---

slaying, and the succession of Osred under 789; *HR* i. 54 (ii. 52) under 788. ASC also refers to a synod at *Aclea*.

[3] *GP* ii. 75 (p. 160). This addition is incorrectly placed. Cyneheard was appointed in 754 (*recte* 756; see 754 annal above) and Æthelweard's successor Ecgbald attests in 778 (*S* 264 *BCS* 225) and 781 (*S* 1257 *BCS* 241).

[4] Mar.

[5] ASC. A–F all enter Jænberht's death (though not the day) and Abbot Æthelheard's succession under 790 (*recte* 792), BC again name the former Eadberht.

[6] This addition is probably based on *GP* i. 8 (p. 17), ii. 75 (p. 160), in particular the incorrect identification of the archbishop of Canterbury with the seventh bishop of Winchester. For part of the addition's erroneous date see above, n. 3.

*a*Osredo*b* a Northymbrensibus regno expulso, Athelredus f*.c* A.*c* regnum recepit.*a1*

[791] (xxiii) 813
[HL]
dKarolus perrexit Pannoniam.d2
*e*Beaduulfus .xvi. kalend. Aug. Candide Case presul ordinatur.*e3*

[792] (xxiiii) 814
[HL]
fKarolus Auaros subigit et Hunorum regnum uastat.f4
*g*Osredus quem Norðhymbrenses regno expulerant capitur et .xviii. kalend. Oct. iniuste occiditur, et in monasterio ad ostium Tine fluminis sepelitur.*gh5*

[793] (xxv) 815 *Coniuratio Pippini contra patrem suum Karolum, qui consilio detecto tonsuratur et sociorum eius alii decollantur alii suspenduntur.*[6]

Gloriosissimus ac sanctissimus rex Orientalium Anglorum Ægelberhtus, uero regi Christo bonarum uirtutum merito acceptabilis, omnibus blando alloquio affabilis, Offe prepotentis regis Merciorum detestanda iussione sueque coniugis Cyneðrythe regine nefaria persuasione regno uitaque priuatus est capitis abscisione. Sed iniuste peremptus, terrisque exemptus, magno tripudio angelorum rex et martyr intrauit curiam spirituum beatorum.[7] Ordinatio Æthelhardi archiepiscopi *i*.xii. kalend. Aug.*i8*

---

a–a Osredo . . . recepit] *add. mg. with signe de renvoi* C*1*, *incorporated at* 790 *n. c* (*p. 222*) B   *b* Osredus B   *c–c* f. a. CLB (*erased*) P, frater Alfuuoldus H, filius Alfwoldi (*recte*) B*1*? (*mg., but letters written over at later date*)   *d–d* Karolus . . . Pannoniam] *written in uppermost mg. by* C*3*, *presumably indicating text to be erased to make way for* 791 *n. e, om.* B, *incorporated with* 792 *n. f following immediately* P   *e–e* Beaduulfus . . . ordinatur] *add. mg. alongside* 791 *with (B without) signe de renvoi* C*1*B*1*, *mg. alongside* 790 P*3*   *f–f* Karolus . . . uastat] *written in uppermost mg. by* C*3*, *presumably indicating text to be erased from* C *to make way for* 792 *n. g, om.* B, *incorporated immediately after* 791 *n. d and under* 791 P*3*   *g–g* Osredus . . . sepelitur] *add. mg. with signe de renvoi* C*1*, *mg. alongside* 790–1 P*3*   *h* 790 *n. d incorporated here* P   *i–i* .xii. kalend. Augusti] *interlin.* C*1*

---

[1] The expulsion of Osred and the restoration of Æthelred, son of Æthelwald, are recorded in ASC DEF and HR i. 55 (ii. 52) under 790.
[2] Mar.

When Osred had been driven from his kingdom by the Northumbrians, Æthelred, son of Æthelwald, received the kingdom.[1]

[791] Charles reached Pannonia.[2]
Beadwulf was ordained bishop of Whithorn on 17 July.[3]

[792]
Charles subdued the Avars and
laid waste the kingdom of the
Huns.[4]

Osred, whom the Northumbrians had driven from his kingdom, was captured and unjustly slain on 14 September, and was buried in the monastery at Tynemouth.[5]

[793] Pippin conspired against his father Charles. When his plot was discovered he was tonsured, and some of his associates beheaded, others hanged.[6]

The most glorious and most holy Æthelberht, king of the East Angles, pleasing to Christ by reason of his virtues, gracious to all with his agreeable speech, was robbed of his kingdom and his life by decapitation at the loathsome command of Offa, the very powerful king of the Mercians, and at the wicked urging of his [Offa's] wife, Queen Cynethryth. But the king and martyr, unrighteously slain, was taken from earth by a great band of angels and entered the courts of the blessed.[7] Æthelheard was ordained archbishop on 21 July.[8]

---

[3] ASC DEF record the consecration of Beadwulf (named Baldwulf) and name the officiating archbishop and bishop, and DE also give (like JW) the day of the consecration. *HR* i. 55 (ii. 53) records the consecration of Beadwulf under 790.

[4] Mar.

[5] ASC DE and *HR* i. 55 (ii. 54) record the day of the murder, and the burial, of Osred under this year. These also record the marriage of Æthelred to Ælfflæd. 'Iniuste' is not in ASC.

[6] Mar.

[7] ASC A–F record briefly under 792 (*recte* 794) the beheading of Æthelberht (without naming his kingdom) on Offa's orders. The story of his martyrdom appears in a *Passio Ethelberti*, printed by M. R. James, 'The lives of St. Ethelbert', *EHR* xxxii (1917), 236–44. There is verbal agreement in the brief record of the beheading here in *ASN* 794 and in JW *East Anglian Accounts* 14.

[8] The day of Æthelheard's consecration is not recorded elsewhere; it may be correct, since 21 July was a Sunday in 793. JW's apparent freedom from the chronological dislocation of ASC here contrasts with the misdating, 790 for 792, for Archbishop Jænberht's death and Æthelheard's election.

[794] (xxvi) 816 *Heresis Feliciana in synodo apud Franconofurt habita dampnatur. Fastrada regina^a de genere Germanorum obiit, et in monasterio sancti Albani ad aquilonalem plagam ante altare sancte Dei genitricis sepulta est, pro qua Karolus Liutgardam Alamannam duxit.*[1]

Rex Northymbrorum Æthelredus a suis interficitur ^b.iii. kalend. Maii.^b[2] Vnde Ceoluulfus Lindisfarnensis ecclesie episcopus et Ædboldus antistes de regno illo exierunt.[3] Eadberhtus qui et Pren super Cantuarios regnare coepit. Offe regi Merciorum defuncto ^c.iiii. kalend. Aug.^c[4] filius eius Ecgbertus^d in regni gloriam successit, et centum quadraginta .i. diebus regnauit eodemque anno uitam finiuit,[5] cui uir magnificus et sancta sobole felix Cenulfus[6] successit, qui in pace iustitia et pietate regni gubernacula rexit.[7]

[795] (xxvii) 817 *Adrianus papa obiit .vii. kalend. Ianuarii quem Karolus ut fratrem uel carissimum filium^e planxit.^f*[8]

[C³BP]
^gAlubrihto Sealesiensi episcopo defuncto, hi successerunt Bosa, Gislere, Totta, Pectun, Athelwlf, Bernegus.^g[9]

[796] (xxviii) 818 *Leo*[10] *nonagesimus quintus papa uiginti mensibus sex. ^hQuem Romani in letania maiori captum excecauerunt et radicitusⁱ linguam eius absciderunt.^j Qui in custodiam missus, noctu per murum*

---

^a *interlin.* C¹   ^{b–b} .iii. kalend. Maii] *interlin.* C¹, *date placed before previous three words* a suis interficitur HLBP   ^{c–c} .iiii. kalend. Augusti] *interlin.* C¹, *date placed before previous word* defuncto HLBP *(originally om., but added in mg.* P³*)* ^d Ecgferthus *interlin.* B⁵?   ^e *rewritten over erasure* C³   ^f *interlin. and rewritten at line end to make room for* 795 *n.* g C³   ^{g–g} Alubrihto . . . Bernegus] *written partly over erasure.* C³*, om.* HL   ^h Quem . . . Leone *(p. 228)*] *under* 797 *(N)* ⁱ *interlin.* C¹   ^j sed Deo iuuante uisum recepit et loquelam *add. mg.* B¹

---

[1] Mar.
[2] The murder of Æthelred by the Northumbrians is entered under 794 by ASC A–F and under 796 by *HR* i. 58 (ii. 57) though the latter does not say who was responsible. The day is 19 Apr. ('xiii kal. Maii') in ASC DE and 18 Apr. ('xiv kal. Maii') in *HR*; JW's 'iii kal. Maii' may be a misreading of his source.
[3] ASC A–F record the two bishops' departure, without identifying Ceolwulf's see. 'Lindisfarnensis ecclesie' is an error for Lindsey, which may have led to the mistaken causal link between the murder of the Northumbrian king and the departure of the two bishops.

[794] The heresy of Felix was condemned at a synod held at Frankfurt. Queen Fastrada, a German, died, and was buried in the monastery of St Alban on the north side in front of the altar of the Holy Mother of God. Charles married Liutgarda the Alemannian in her place.[1]

Æthelred, king of the Northumbrians, was killed by his own men on 29 April,[2] whereupon Ceolwulf, bishop of Lindisfarne, and Bishop Eadbald left that kingdom.[3] Eadberht, also known as Præn, began to rule the Kentish people. On the death of Offa, king of the Mercians, on 29 July,[4] his son Ecgberht succeeded to the honour of the kingdom and reigned 141 days and ended his life in the same year.[5] Cenwulf,[6] a splendid man and happy in his saintly offspring, succeeded him and he governed the kingdom in peace, justice, and piety.[7]

[795] Pope Hadrian died on 26 December, and Charles mourned him as though for a brother or a very dear son.[8]

> After the death of Aluberht, bishop of Selsey, there succeeded Bosa (Osal), Gislhere, Tota, Pectun (Wihthun), Æthelwulf, Beornheah.[9]

[796] Leo,[10] the ninety-fifth pope, reigned twenty years and six months. On the *Litania maior* [25 April], the Romans seized and blinded him, and cut out his tongue from the roots. He was put

---

[4] ASC A-F record the succession of Eadberht Præn and the death of Offa, but only DE, in the duplicate entry under 796, give the day (29 July as in JW) of Offa's death.

[5] JW calls Offa's son Ecgberht, JW *Mercian Accounts* 16 Ecgferthus, and JW *Mercian Gen.* and ASC (794) rightly Ecgfrith. That Offa's son reigned 141 days is in ASC 755.

[6] Cenwulf is first mentioned as already king in ASC under 796 not 794, though ASC ADEF (not BC) have the incorrect Ceolwulf.

[7] ASC.

[8] Mar.

[9] The addition may be based on *GP* ii. 96 (p. 205), with which it shares the errors Bosa for Osa and Pectun or Pehtun for Wihthun, and the reference to Bernegus. Aluberht's death could not have occurred as late as 795, for Gislhere was in office in 781 (*S* 1257 *BCS* 241), Tota in 786 (Dümmler, *Alcuini Epistolae*, no. 3) and Wihthtun in 789 (*S* 131 *BCS* 255), Campbell, *Charters of Rochester*, no. 13). (B)ernethus is added (probably by C³) to JW's Selsey *Epis. List*. He might be an error for Beornheah (*c*. 909, or 909×925–930×931).

[10] Leo III 795–816.

euasit, et ad legatos Karoli Viurundum abbatem et Witgisum*[a]*
Spolitanorum ducem ueniens, Spoletum ductus est et inde ad regem
Karolum in Saxoniam apud Paderbrunnam, presente Richolfo episcopo
Mogontino, peruenit, a quibus summo honore susceptus est. Karolus
unguitur in imperatorem a papa Leone.[b]1

Kenulfus rex Merciorum totam pene Cantiam deuastauit et
eorum regem Prenn cepit ʿligatumque in Merciam secum duxit.[2]

[C³BP]

*[d]*Defuncto Eadberto Leogerensi
episcopo, successit Vnwona.*[de]3*

[798] (xxx) 820   *Ciclus decennouenalis .xv. incipit indictione sexta.[f]*
Richolfus archiepiscopus consecratur .iiii. non. Martii, die dominico, in
monasterio beati Petri quod est Friteslar.[4]

Huicciorum episcopus Heathoredus obiit pro quo electus et consecratus est Deneberhtus.[5] *[g]*Corpus sancte Wihtburge uirginis filie
Anne regis Orientalium Anglorum, et sororis sanctarum uirginum
Sexburhge et Æthelburge ac Ætheldrythe, sine corruptione inuentum est, post annos fere .lv.*[h]* ex quo apud uillam que Dyrham
uocatur humatum est.*[g]6*

[799] (xxxi) 821   *Karolus legendi et psallendi disciplinam diligentis-*
sime emendauit.[7]

Dorubernensis archiepiscopus Æthelhardus et Cynebertus
Wentane ciuitatis pontifex Romam adierunt.[8]

---

[a] Winigisum *(N)*   *[b]* *see above, p. 226 n. h*   *[c]* *runs on to 797 here CB*
[d–d] Defuncto . . . Vnwona] *add. at line-end* C³, *om.* HL   *[e]* *798 n. g incorporated*
here B   *[f]* *798 n. g incorporated here HL*   *[g–g]* Corpus . . . est] *add. mg. along-*
side 798–99 C³, incorporated at 798 n. f HL, and at 796 n. e B, mg. alongside 796 P³,
under Charlemagne (800–14) G   *[h]* .lii. G

---

¹ Mar.
² This Kentish episode is described in similar terms in ASC under 796, though
ADEF erroneously call the Mercian king Ceoluulf. JW makes no mention of the
Merscware, who were laid waste with the people of Kent.
³ This addition is incorrect: Unwona, who was in office in 785 (*S* 123 *BCS* 247),
must have succeeded before that date and after 781, when Eadberht was still bishop of
Leicester (*S* 1257 *BCS* 241).
⁴ Mar.
⁵ The death of Bishop Heathured and the succession of Deneberht (which the 19-
year table in MS C, p. 63, dates 799), must be at least a year too early, for Heathured
attests a charter dated 799 (*S* 155 *BCS* 293, transl. Whitelock, *EHD*, no. 80, pp.
510–11). It is possible that the bishops whose names were attached to *S* 158 *BCS* 303

under guard but escaped over the wall by night, and going to Charles's legates, Abbot Wirund and Wintigis, duke of Spoleto, he was taken thence and brought to King Charles at Paderborn in Saxony, in the presence of Richulf, bishop of Mainz, by both of whom he was received with great honour. Charles was anointed emperor by Pope Leo.[1]

Cenwulf, king of the Mercians, laid waste almost the whole of Kent, and captured Præn, its king, and took him bound to Mercia with him.[2]

> On the death of Eadberht, bishop of Leicester, Unwona succeeded.[3]

[798] The fifteenth cycle of nineteen years begins in the sixth indiction. Archbishop Richulf was consecrated on Sunday, 4 March, in the monastery of the blessed Peter which is at Fritzlar.[4]

Heathured, bishop of the Hwicce, died, and Deneberht was elected and consecrated in his place.[5] The body of Wihtburg, the holy virgin, daughter of Anna, king of the East Angles, and sister of the holy virgins Seaxburg and Æthelburg and Æthelthryth, was found incorrupt almost fifty-five years after it was buried in the township called Dereham.[6]

[799] Charles most painstakingly reformed the rules for reading and singing the psalms.[7]

Æthelheard, archbishop of Canterbury, and Cyneberht, bishop of Winchester, went to Rome.[8]

(including Deneberht) were present when the dispute of which this is a late record was settled. According to *S* 1435 *BCS* 387 the dispute was in Cenwulf's 3rd year (799) not his 5th (801) as in *S* 158 *BCS* 303; in that case Deneberht had succeeded Heathured before the end of 799.

[6] This entry is found in ASC F (marginal addition 799), though without a mention of Wihtburg's father and sisters. She is not mentioned among Anna's daughters in JW *East Anglian Gen.* and *Accounts* 7. The *Liber Eliensis*, pp. 120-3, describes her translation from East Dereham to Ely and the tract on resting places of saints (*Die Heiligen Englands*, p. 21) mentions her resting place at Ely.

[7] Mar.

[8] ASC A-E 799 F 800 (from possibly 799) (*recte* 801), describing Cyneberht as bishop of the West Saxons.

[800] (xxxii) 822   *Karolus quarta uice Romam cum papa Leone per-git propter^a reparandum qui nimis turbatus erat ecclesie statum, ibique hiemem transegit.*[1]

Rex Occidentalium Saxonum Brihtricus obiit et Ecgbertus suc-cessit.[2] [3]Eodem uero die*^b*[3] quo rex Brihtricus uita decessit, contigit Merciorum ducem Æthelmundum de Mercia[4] cum suis exisse, uadumque quod lingua Anglorum Cymeresford[5] nominatur tran-sisse. Cuius aduentu cognito, Wiltoniensium dux Weolhstanus cum Wiltoniensibus ascendit contra eum. Commissoque graui pre-lio, multi ex his et ex illis ceciderunt, amboque duces occisi cor-ruerunt, uictoriam uero Wiltonienses habuerunt.[6] Alhmund filius Alhredi regis Norðhymbrorum occiditur.[7]

[801] (xxxiii) 823   *^cKarolus a Romanis Augustus appellatur.^c*[8]

[802] (xxxiiii) 824   *Amarmurmulus*[9] *rex Persarum elefantum et alia munera misit Karolo imperatori.*[10]

*^d*Weormundo Hrofensis ecclesie presule defuncto, Beornmodus consecratur pro eo.*^d*[11] *^e*Higbald Lindisfarnensis episcopus obiit, pro quo Ecbertus electus ab Eanbaldo Eboracensi archiepiscopo .iii. idus Iun. consecratur.*^e*[12]

[803] (xxxv) 825   *Karolus pontem quingentorum passuum longitudinis trans Hrenum Mogontiaco construxit: tanta est enim fluminis illius ibi latitudo.*[13]

---

^a *om. HL*   ^b *anno HL*   ^{c–c} Karolus . . . appellatur] *om. possibly erased to be replaced by mg. addition for which see 811 n. c B*   ^{d–d} Weormundo . . . pro eo] *placed after 802 n. e HL*   ^{e–e} Higbald . . . consecratur] *add. mg. alongside 802–3 C², incorporated before 802 n. d HL, mg. alongside 796 and immediately after 798 n. g and enclosed in same box P³*

---

[1] Mar.

[2] ASC A-E 800 (*recte* 802) add here the death of the ealdorman Wor.

[3–3] 'eodem uero die' translates 'þy ilcan dæge', which HH *HA* iv c. 28 (Arnold, p. 131) took to be not the day of Brihtric's death, but the day when Ecgberht, on his return from exile, was acknowledged as king. JW probably thought Ecgberht was in England when Brihtric died (see p. 254 n. 1).

[4] 'de Mercia' is presumably JW's rendering of ASC's 'of Hwiccium' (A-E).

[5] ASC has 'Cynemæresforda'.

[**800**] Charles went to Rome a fourth time with Pope Leo in order to put right the very troubled state of the church and there he passed the winter.[1]

Brihtric, king of the West Saxons, died and Ecgberht succeeded him.[2] [3]On the very day[3] that King Brihtric departed this life it happened that Æthelmund, ealdorman of the Mercians, left Mercia[4] with his army and crossed the ford which is called in English Kempsford.[5] When Weohstan, the ealdorman of the people of Wiltshire, learnt of his arrival, he went out against him with the men of Wiltshire. A fierce battle was joined, and many fell on either side, and both ealdormen were slain. The men of Wiltshire were victorious.[6] Alhmund, son of Alhred, king of the Northumbrians, was killed.[7]

[**801**] Charles was acclaimed Augustus by the Romans.[8]

[**802**] Amarmurmulus,[9] king of the Persians, sent an elephant and other gifts to the Emperor Charles.[10]

On the death of Wærmund, bishop of Rochester, Beornmod was consecrated in his place.[11] Higbald, bishop of Lindisfarne, died; Ecgberht was chosen in his place and consecrated by Eanbald, archbishop of York, on 11 June.[12]

[**803**] Charles built a bridge about half a mile across the Rhine at Mainz, for such is the width of that river there.[13]

---

[6] ASC A-F 800 (*recte* 802), F being abbreviated.

[7] *HR* i. 61 (ii. 63) has a fuller entry under 800 on Alhmund's death which is absent from ASC.

[8] Mar.

[9] Hārūn al-Rašīd, caliph, 786–809. 'Amarmurmulus' represents his title '*amīr al-mu'minīn*, 'Commander of the Faithful'.

[10] Mar.

[11] ASC A(B)C (original date) DEF 802 (*recte* 804), D (also 801), all without reference to Wærmund's death.

[12] Though Higbald's death (on 25 May) and Ecgberht's consecration are recorded in ASC DE (803), this addition by C[2] may be based on *HDE* ii. 5 (i. 52), which (unlike ASC DE) names Archbishop Eanbald as the consecrating bishop. It also (i. 50, 52) assigns 20 and 22 years to Higbald's pontificate, but appears to date his death to 802 (9 years after the Viking destruction of Lindisfarne). 11 June was a Sunday in 803 and therefore a probable day for Ecgberht's consecration, though it could have been a rush to assemble the archbishop of York and the bishops of Hexham and Whithorn in the 18 days after Higbald's death on 25 May. Perhaps 802 was the year of Higbald's death.

[13] Mar.

p. 280 Æthelhardus Dorubernensis archiepiscopus | ^{a}obiit cui Wlfredus successit.^{a1}

[804] (xxxvi) 826 *Leo papa uenit in Franciam.*^{2}
Wlfredus arciepiscopus a papa Leone pallium suscepit.^{3}

[805] (xxxvii) 827 *Ecclesia sancti Albani dedicatur hoc anno kalend. Dec., indictione .xiii., qui est* ^{b}*annus .xx. Richolfi post acceptum episcopatum, .viii. autem postquam episcopus est consecratus. Karolus, filius Karoli imperatoris, Boemias*^{c} *uastat,*

[HL]

^{d}*Lethonem regem eorum occidens.*^{d4}

Rex Cantuuariorum Cuthredus et Eabryhtus comes et Ceolburga abbatissa obierunt.^{5}

[C^{3}BP]

^{e}*Mortalitas maxima orta est in monasterio Fuldensi ita ut plurimi ipsorum monachorum morerentur.*^{e4}

^{f}Rex Cantuuariorum Cuthredus et Heabrihtus comes et Ceolburga, abbatissa de Beorclea,^{6} obierunt.^{bf5}

[807] (xxxviiii) 829 *Mortalitas maxima orta est in monasterio Fuldensi ita ut plurimi ipsorum monachorum morerentur.*^{7}

[808] (xl) 830 *Karolus religionem Christianam, qua ab infantia fuit imbutus, sanctissime* ^{g}*et* p̈issime docuit, *circa pauperes elemosina*s *deuotissimus* exercens.^{8}

[809] (xli) 831 ^{h}⟨C⟩orpus sancti Bartholomei de insula Lipparitana transuectum delatum est Beneuentum.^{h}

$^{a-a}$ obiit . . . successit] *written over erasure starting in mg.* C^t $^{b-b}$ annus . . . obierunt] *written over erasure and running on to 806–7* C^3, *a possibly preliminary guiding scribble in the upper mg. no longer legible* C, *runs on to 806–7* B ^{c} Boemios *HL* $^{d-d}$ Lethonem . . . occidens] *incorporated here but immediately before 805 n. e* P $^{e-e}$ Mortalitas . . . morerentur] *incorporated after 805 n. d* P $^{f-f}$ Rex . . . obierunt] *under 807* P ^{g} *runs on to 809* C, *808 runs on to 809* HLB, *808–10 run together* P $^{h-h}$ ⟨C⟩orpus . . . Beneuentum] *mg. alongside 809–10* C^t, *part of consolidated 808–10* P, *repeated at the end of 840 n. c* HL, *under Charlemagne (800–14)* G

Æthelheard, archbishop of Canterbury, died, and Wulfred succeeded him.[1]

[804] Pope Leo went to Francia.[2]
Archbishop Wulfred received the pallium from Pope Leo.[3]

[805] The church of St Alban was dedicated this year on 1 December in the thirteenth indiction, which was the twentieth year since Richulf received the bishopric, but the eighth after his consecration as bishop. Charles, son of the Emperor Charles, laid waste Bohemia

and killed their King Lech.[4]	A great mortality occurred in the monastery of Fulda, so that many of the monks died.[4]
Cuthred, king of the people of Kent, and Ealdorman Heahberht and Abbess Ceolburg died.[5]	Cuthred, king of the people of Kent, and Ealdorman Heahberht, and Abbess Ceolburg of Berkeley[6] died.[5]

[807]
A great mortality occurred in the monastery of Fulda so that many of the monks died.[7]

[808] Charles taught the Christian religion, in which he had been steeped from childhood, with great sanctity and piety, busying himself most devoutly with the giving of alms to the poor.[8]

[809] The body of St Bartholomew was conveyed from the island of Lipari and brought to Benevento.

[1] The death of Æthelheard and the consecration of Wulfred are in ASC A(B)C (original date) DEF (F over erasure) under 803 (recte 805). Like ASC DEF, JW does not mention the death of Abbot Forthred, recorded in A(B)C.
[2] Mar.
[3] Wulfred's receipt of the pallium is recorded in ASC A(B)C (original date) DEF under 804 (recte 806). JW identifies the pope who sent the pallium.
[4] Mar.
[5] The deaths of Cuthred, Heahberht, and Ceolburg are mentioned in ASC A(B)C (original date) DEF under 805 (C now 800; F omits Heahberht).
[6] S 1187 BCS 313 (transl. Whitelock, EHD, no. 81, pp. 512–13) seems to point to a connection between Ceolburg and the 'Berkeley people'.
[7] Mar.   [8] Mar.

[**810**] (xlii) 832   *Pippinus filius imperatoris Karoli*[a] *obiit. Maxima mortalitas boum totam pene uastauit Europam. Karolus imperator antequam obisset crebro febre quadriennio corripitur.*[1]

[**811**] (xliii) 833   *Karolus primogenitus imperatoris obiit. Ipse uero imperator Karolus anno quadragesimo tertio regni eius in Francia, in Italia autem trigesimo sexto, imperii undecimo, indictione quarta, thesauros et uestes, ceteraque omnia diuisit in tres partes. Quarum duas partes in unam et uiginti partes totidem metropolitanis ciuitatibus que in regno eius noscuntur partitus est, quarum nomina sunt hec: .i. Roma, .ii. Rauenna, .iii. Mediolanum, .iiii. Forum Iulii, .v. Grandus, .vi. Colonia, .vii. Mogontiacus, .viii. Iuuauum que et Salzburh, .ix. Treueris, .x. Senonis, .xi. Vesontio, .xii. Lugdunum, .xiii. Rotomagus, .xiiii. Remis, .xv. Arelato, .xvi. Vienna, .xvii. Darantasia, .xviii. Ebrodunum, .xix. Burdigala, .xx. Turonis, .xxi. Bituriges. Vnusquisque autem metropolitanus episcopus unam partem ecclesie sue et duas suffraganeis suis dare debuit. Tertia uero pars uel usque ad obitum eius uel usque dum usu cotidiano carere uellet mansit, ipsaque postremo quattuor diuisionibus secata*[b] *est. Prima pars addita est ad uiginti et unam supradictas. Altera cessit filiis et filiabus suis ac nepotibus. Tertia distributa est pauperibus. Quarta seruis et ancillis palatio famulantibus. Ad tertiam uero partem addita sunt uasa atque utensilia ex ere et ferro aliisque metallis cum armis et uestibus et omnis suppellex ad uarios usus ut sunt cortine, stragula, tapetia, filtra, coria, sagmata ut erogatio elemosine ad plures peruenire potuisset. Capellam id est ecclesiasticum ministerium quod per hereditatem sibi uenit integrum seruari decreuit, exceptis si qua ipse capelle eidem in uasis aut libris addidisset que qui uellet emeret. Horum ergo pretium atque librorum quorum magnam copiam in bibliotheca sua habuit pauperibus erogatur.*[c2]

[**812**] (xliiii) 834   [d]Ciclus solis incipit .iiii. concurrentibus bissextilibus.[d]

Wlfredus Doruuernensis archiepiscopus et Wibertus Scireburnensis ecclesie presul Romam perrexerunt.[3]

---

[a] *om. HL*   [b] *secuta HL*   [c] *see App. B for outer-mg. addition with signe de renvoi but without corresponding one for location in text; possibly intended for parallel annal in inner mg., 800 or 801 B*[1]   [d–d] Ciclus . . . bissextilibus] *om. HL*

---

[1] Mar.   [2] Mar.
[3] ASC A(B)C (original date) DE 812 F 814 (probably correct), in all of which Wigberht is called bishop of the West Saxons.

[810] Pippin, son of the Emperor Charles, died. A very severe murrain amongst the cattle devastated almost the whole of Europe. The Emperor Charles suffered for four years before he died from frequent attacks of fever.[1]

[811] Charles, the emperor's eldest son, died. The Emperor Charles himself divided his treasures and clothing fabrics and everything else into three parts in the forty-third year of his reign in Francia, the thirty-sixth in Italy, the eleventh of empire, in the fourth indiction. He divided two of these parts into twenty-one portions, one for each of the metropolitan cities recognized in his realm, whose names are as follows: (1) Rome, (2) Ravenna, (3) Milan, (4) Cividale del Friuli, (5) Grado, (6) Cologne, (7) Mainz, (8) *Juvavum*, also known as Salzburg, (9) Trier, (10) Sens, (11) Besançon, (12) Lyons, (13) Rouen, (14) Reims, (15) Arles, (16) Vienne, (17) Tarentaise, (18) Embrun, (19) Bordeaux, (20) Tours, (21) Bourges. Each and every metropolitan bishop was obliged to give one-third to his church and two-thirds to his suffragans. The third part he kept until his death or until he should wish to renounce daily necessities. Afterwards that same part was to be divided into four. The first was to be added to the twenty-one portions mentioned above; the second fell to his sons, daughters, and grandchildren; the third was to be distributed to the poor; the fourth to the male and female palace servants. To the third part were added the vessels and utensils of brass and iron and other metals, with the weapons and clothes and all the household equipment for various uses, such as the bed-curtains, coverlets, tapestries, felts, hides, and harnesses, so that the distribution of alms might reach more people. He decreed that the chapel, that is the ecclesiastical office which had come to him by inheritance, should be kept intact, except what he had contributed himself for that chapel in plate and books, which anyone who wished might buy. The money for them and for the books, of which he had a great number in his library, should be distributed to the poor.[2]

[812] The solar cycle begins with four concurrents in a bissextile year.

Wulfred, archbishop of Canterbury, and Wigberht, bishop of Sherborne, went to Rome.[3]

[813] (xlv) 835 *Pons, quem^a apud Mogontiacum per decem annos ⟨in⟩genti^b labore et opere mirabili de lignis Karolus rex construxit ita ut perpetuo durare posse uideretur, anno primo ante obitum suum ita tribus horis conflagrauit ut ne una quidem astula super aquam remaneret. Pontem autem ipsum Richolfus episcopus dicitur iussisse incendere propter latrocinia que noctibus in eo exercebantur, dum homines spoliati in flumen ipsum iacti necabantur, sed ⟨E⟩inhardus,^c qui uitam Karoli istius scripsit, hoc fortuitu refert contigisse. Richolfus episcopus obiit. Haistolfus post eum successit annis .xi. Karolus circa kalend. Nouembris habito generali conuentu, uocauit de Aquitania Ludouuicum filium suum, et die dominico cum post omnium consensum regem illum laudantium eum commonuisset, precepit ei ut propriis manibus de magno altari Aquisgrani coronam imperii capiti suo imponeret, ob recordationem paterne admonitionis, et, ita donatus magnis muneribus, Aquitaniam rediit. Imperator uero mense Ianuario post balneum febre corripitur. In qua cum septem dies laborasset, septimo die, accepto corpore et sanguine Domini ut confirmaret exitum suum, |*

p. 282 *laborauit ipso die et nocte sequenti. Sequenti uero die luce adueniente, sciens quid facturus erat manu dextera ut potuit signo sancte crucis totum corpus suum signauit, deindeque colligens pedes ac brachia super corpus extendens, clausisque^d oculis, hunc uersum psallens: 'in manus tuas Domine commendo spiritum meum', in senectute bona obiit .v. kalend. Feb., indictione septima, anno etatis sue septuagesimo secundo, incarnationis Domini secundum Dionisium octingentissimo^e tertio^f decimo. Ibique Aquisgrani eadem die in basilica Saluatoris sancteque Marie semper uirginis, quam ^gipse ex fundamento^g mirifico opere construxit, sepultus est.*[1]

Wlfredus archiepiscopus cum benedictione sancti ^hpape Leonis^h ad sui presulatus sedem reuertitur. Eodem anno Ecgbertus rex Wessaxonum occidentales Brytones ab orientali eorum termino usqueⁱ ad occidentalem deuastauit.[2]

^j*Romanorum septuagesimus nonus Ludouuicus*[3] *regnauit annis .xxvi., mensibusque undecim.*[4]

^a *interlin. C¹*   ^b *uiginti C, .xx. HP, et .xx. L, uiginti B, uiginti altered to* ingenti *(N)*   ^c Cinhardus *CLB,* Kynhardus *HP*   ^d que *interlin. C¹*   ^e gentissimo *of* octingentissimo *over erasure C¹*   ^f quarto *Mar.*   ^{g-g} ipse ex fundamento] *well spaced out over erasure at the beginning of line C¹*   ^{h-h} pape Leonis] *well spaced out over erasure C*   ⁱ *om. HL*   ^j *cap. .lxxix. add. here L*

---

[1] Mar. JW keeps the death of Charlemagne here with Marianus against ASC A–E (812, though C now shows 811) F (814 correctly).

[**813**] The wooden bridge which King Charles built at Mainz over a period of ten years with great toil and wonderful workmanship, so that it seemed that it could last for ever, burnt for three hours in the year before his death so that not one chip remained above the water. Bishop Richulf was said to have ordered the burning of the bridge because of the robberies which took place at night on it, when the men who were robbed were thrown into the river, but Einhard, who wrote the life of this Charles, says that it happened by chance. Bishop Richulf died. Aistulf succeeded him, and ruled for eleven years. Charles held a great assembly about 1 November, and summoned his son Louis from Aquitaine; on Sunday, when all had agreed to praise Louis as king, Charles admonished him, and then ordered him to place on his own head with his own hands the imperial crown from the great altar at Aachen that he might remember his father's warning. And so Louis returned to Aquitaine in receipt of great gifts. In January the emperor fell ill with a fever after bathing. He suffered from it for seven days; on the seventh day he received the body and blood of the Lord that he might gain strength for his passing and suffered that day and the following night. On the following day as the light dawned, knowing what he was about to do, he made the sign of the cross over his whole body with his right hand as best he could, then drew his feet together, stretched out his arms over his body, closed his eyes, and chanted this verse: 'Into thy hands, O Lord, I commend my spirit.' He died at a ripe old age on 28 January in the seventh indiction in the seventy-second year of his life, the 813th after the Incarnation of the Lord, according to Dionysius, and there at Aachen on the same day he was buried in the basilica of the Saviour and of St Mary, ever virgin, which he himself had built with wonderful workmanship from the foundations.[1]

Archbishop Wulfred returned to his episcopal see with the blessing of the holy Pope Leo. In the same year Ecgberht, king of the West Saxons, ravaged the western Britons from their eastern boundary to their western.[2]

Louis,[3] the seventy-ninth emperor of the Romans, reigned twenty-six years and eleven months.[4]

---

[2] Wulfred's return and Ecgberht's war against the 'west Britons' are entered under 813 in ASC A(B)C (original date) DE, and 815 (probably correct) in F.
[3] Louis I 814–40. [4] Mar.

[**814**] (i) 836   *Ludouuicus omnem iustitiam regni sui inquirens restaurat.*[1]

[**815**] (ii) 837   *Baogulfus abbas Fuldensis obiit .viii. idus Iulii, iussumque est ut omnes monachi cursum sancti[a] Benedicti cantarent.* Ratgerus [b]abbas successit Baogulfo[b] *annis quinque.*[2]

[**816**] (iii) 838   *Exercitus Ludouuici Sclauos superat et Leo papa obiit.*[3]
Anglorum scola Rome igne cremata est.[4]

[C³BP]
ᶜDefuncto   Wigberto   Scireburnensi   presule,   successit
Alhstanus.ᶜ[5]

[**817**] (iiii) 839   *Ciclus .xvi. decennouenalis incipit indictione decima. Stephanus*[6] *nonagesima sextus papa annis* tribus[d] *et mensibus septem. Iste obuia*uitᵉ *Ludouuico in magno campo Remensium susceptus sequenti die dominico coram omni populo unxit eum in imperatorem et coronam mire pulchritudinis, quam secum detulerat, imposuit capiti eius, aliamque coronam capiti Irmingarde regine, nominans*ᶠ *eam Augustam.* ᵍ*Qui postea donatus magnis muneribus, Romam rediit.*[7]

[**819**] (vi) 841   Stephanus papa *obiit.* ʰ*Monasterium sancti Bonifacii ad Fuldam dedicatur kalend. Nouembris.*ʰ[8]
Rex Merciorum sanctus Kenulfus post multa bona que in sua uita gessit opera, ad beatitudinem que in celis est transiuit perennem, filiumque suum sanctum Kenelmum septennem regni reliquit heredem. Sed paucis mensibus euolutis, germane sue Quendrythe insidiis, cuius seuam conscientiam dira cupido regnandi armarat, ausu crudelitatis ab Asceberto, nutritore suo

---

ᵃ beati *B*   ᵇ⁻ᵇ abbas . . . Baogulfo] ei successit *L*   ᶜ⁻ᶜ Defuncto . . . Alhstanus] *add. at line-end* C³, *om. HL*   ᵈ decem *(N)*   ᵉ obuiante *Mar.* ᶠ *at this point runs on to 818 C, 817 runs into 818 HB*   ᵍ *818 starts here (N)* ʰ⁻ʰ Monasterium . . . Nouembris *follows 820 n. d (N)*

---

[1] Mar.   [2] Mar.   [3] Mar.
[4] The burning of the English school at Rome is entered in ASC AC (original date) D (816) (B)E (815) F (817). As *LP* places the event under Paschal II (817–24), it is unlikely to have taken place before 817.

[814] Louis enquired into and reformed the entire administration of justice in his kingdom.[1]

[815] Baogulf, abbot of Fulda, died on 8 July, and the order was given for all monks to chant the office of St Benedict. Abbot Ratger succeeded Baogulf, and reigned five years.[2]

[816] Louis's army conquered the Slavs, and Pope Leo died.[3]
    The English school at Rome was burnt.[4]

>   On the death of Wigberht,
>   bishop of Sherborne, Ealhstan
>   succeeded.[5]

[817] The sixteenth cycle of nineteen years begins in the tenth indiction. Stephen,[6] the ninety-sixth pope, reigned three years and seven months. He went to meet Louis in the great plain at Reims and, having been received, on the following Sunday anointed him emperor in the presence of the whole people, and placed on his head a crown of amazing beauty which he had brought with him, and another crown on the head of Queen Ermengard, whom he proclaimed Augusta. Afterwards he returned to Rome in receipt of great gifts.[7]

[819] Pope Stephen died. The monastery of St Boniface at Fulda was dedicated on 1 November.[8]
    St Cenwulf, king of the Mercians, after a life devoted to good deeds, passed over to the eternal blessedness which is in heaven, and left his 7-year-old son St Kenelm heir of his realm. But when a few months had passed, by the treachery of his own sister Cwenthryth, whose cruel spirit had been roused by an awful lust for power, he was secretly done to death with cruel outrage by Æscberht, his most bloodthirsty tutor, in the shade of a thorn tree

[5] This is not recorded elsewhere, but might be correct, for ASC ADE (867) (B)C (868), recording Ealhstan's death, say that he held the see for 50 years. Wigberht was alive in July 816 when he attended the synod of Chelsea. An Ælfstan 'electus' attests S 283 BCS 377 (dated 924 for ?824), but the date of the charter is in doubt and the text includes later features.

[6] Stephen IV (V) 816–17.   [7] Mar.   [8] Mar.

cruentissimo, in uasta siluaque nemerosa sub arbore spinosa occulte traditur iugulo. Verum qui solo teste celo est iugulatus, celo teste per columpnam lucis postmodum est reuelatus. Absciditur caput Kenelmi natalis et innocentie candore lacteum unde lactea columba aureis pennis euolat in celum. Post cuius felix martyrium, Ceoluulfus regnum *ª*suscepit Merciorum.*ª¹* *ᵇ*Defuncto Ecgberto Lindisfarnensi episcopo, Heathoredus successit.*ᵇᶜ²*

[820] (vii) 842 *ᵈPascalis³ papa nonagesimus septimus.ᵈ Ratgerus abbas obiit .viii.ᵉ idus Dec. Euigil successit annis quinque. Ludouuicus imperator Brytanniam subegit, ducem eius Murcomannum occidens. Inde regrediens, Irmingardam reginam febricitantem inuenit que et paulo post obiit. ᶠLudowicus imperator in Ingelenheim uilla regia generale suum placitum habuit, et Iudith filiam Welfi ducis Bawarie reginam sibi sociauit.ᶠ⁴*

[821] (viii) 843 Rex Merciorum Ceoluulf regno expellitur et Beornuulfus in *ᵍ*regnum suscipitur.*ᵍʰ⁵*

[822] (ix) 844 *Ludouuicus imperator per exercitum suum orientales Sclauos uastat, duce eorum nomine Liduit fugato.⁶*

Duces robustissimi Burhelmus et Muca occiduntur et synodus in loco qui *ⁱ*dicitur Cloueshoo celebratur.⁷ Deneberhtus*ⁱ* Huuicciorum episcopus obiit, cui Heaberhtus successit.⁸

[823] (x) 845 *Ludouuicus imperator primogenito filioʲ suo Lothario, placito generali habito, filiam Hugonis comitis coniunxit.⁹*

ᵃ⁻ᵃ suscepit Merciorum *runs into mg. possibly rewritten* C²   *ᵇ⁻ᵇ* Defuncto . . . successit] *add. over some erasure* C²   *ᶜ* 840 n. f *follows here* B   *ᵈ⁻ᵈ* Pascalis . . . septimus] *precedes* 819 n. h *under* 818 *(see* 817 n. g) (N)   *ᵉ* .iiii. H   *ᶠ⁻ᶠ* Ludowicus . . . sociauit] *rewritten by* C²   *ᵍ⁻ᵍ* regnum suscipitur] regnum suscipit H, regno successit L, regnum successit P   *ʰ* -ur *sign erased* C   *ⁱ⁻ⁱ* dicitur . . . Deneberhtus] *signs of rewriting and erasure* C¹   *ʲ interlin.* B¹

---

¹ Cenwulf's death and Ceolwulf's accession are recorded without comment by ASC A(B)C (original date) DE under 819 (*recte* 821), F under 822. The intervening rule of Kenelm and the account of his death must have been derived from a *Passio Kenelmi*; see Rurik von Antropoff, *Die Entwicklung der Kenelm-Legende* (Bonn, 1965), pp. 188–9; and for possible verbal echoes pp. vi–ix.
² *HDE* ii. 5 (i. 52) gave Ecgberht an 18-year pontificate. Scribe C² in a previous addition had assigned 802 for Ecgberht's election and consecration. Here he may have

in a deserted wood. But he who was slain with heaven alone as
witness, was later revealed by heaven's witness through a column
of light. Kenelm's head was cut off, milk-white in the beauty and
innocence of birth, and from it a milky dove with golden wings
soared to heaven. After his happy martyrdom, Ceolwulf received
the kingdom of the Mercians.[1] On the death of Ecgberht, bishop
of Lindisfarne, Heathured succeeded.[2]

[820] Paschal[3] was the ninety-seventh pope. Abbot Ratger died on
6 December. Egil succeeded him, and ruled for five years. The
Emperor Louis conquered Brittany, killing the Breton leader
Morvan. On his return from there he found Queen Ermengard
with a fever, from which she soon died. The Emperor Louis held
his general assembly at Ingelheim, a royal township, and took as
his queen Judith, daughter of Welf, duke of Bavaria.[4]

[821] Ceolwulf, king of the Mercians, was driven from his kingdom, and Beornwulf was raised to the kingship.[5]

[822] The Emperor Louis laid waste the eastern Slavs with his
army, and put their leader, Ljudovit by name, to flight.[6]
   The most vigorous ealdormen Burghelm and Muca were killed,
and a synod was held in the place which is called Clofesho.[7]
Deneberht, bishop of the Hwicce, died, and Heahberht
succeeded.[8]

[823] The Emperor Louis held a general assembly at which he
married his eldest son Lothar to the daughter of Count Hugo.[9]

arrived at 819 as the year of his death, though if he became bishop in 803 (ASC), the
date of his death could be 821.
   [3] Paschal I 817–24.
   [4] Mar.
   [5] The expulsion of Ceolwulf (but not the accession of Beornwulf) is entered in ASC
A(B)C (original date) DE 821 (recte 823).
   [6] Mar.
   [7] The deaths of Burghelm and Muca and the synod of Clofesho are recorded by ASC
A(B)C (original date) DE 822 (recte 824).
   [8] This may be correctly dated though it is not recorded elsewhere. Deneberht seems
to have been living in 817 (S 182 BCS 359); Heahberht was in office in Sept. 822 (S
186 BCS 370).
   [9] Mar.

Brytones in loco qui dicitur Gafulford a Domnaniensibus cesi sunt.[1] Rex [2]Occidentalium Saxonum[2] Ecgbrihtus et rex Merciorum Beornuulfus in Ellandune,[3] [4]id est in monte Ealle,[4] pugnam iniere sed facta strage non modica Ecgbrihtus potitur uictoria. Vnde mox filium suum Atheuulfum et Ealhstanum [4]Scireburnensem episcopum[4] suumque ducem Wlfhardum cum magno exercitu Cantiam direxit. [4]Qui statim ut illo[a] uenerunt,[4] regem eiusdem prouincie

p. 283 Baldredum　　regno　　expulerunt.[5] Post　　hec　　Cantua | rienses, Suthregienses, Australes Saxones, Orientales Saxones,[b] sponte se regi dederunt Ecgbrihto ex cuius propinquorum manibus prius extorti, [4]extraneorum regum dicioni per aliquot annorum curricula inuiti sunt subacti.[4] Orientales Angli simul cum suo rege legatarios miserunt ad [4]regem Wessaxonum[4] Ecgbrihtum supplicantes ut patronus illis et fortis esset murus contra infestationem et impetum Mercensium. [4]Qui petitioni illorum adquieuit, et se libenter eos adiuturum in omnibus spopondit. Verum hec Beornuulfus rex Merciorum uilipendens exercitum collegit non modicum, illorumque fines hostiliter intrauit atque neci optimum quenque tradere festinauit.[4] Contra quem rex eorum cum suis ascendit, initoque prelio, illum [4]cum maxima parte sui exercitus[4] interfecit.[6] Cui propinquus Ludecan in regnum successit.[7]

[C³BP]

[c]Defuncto Aldulfo Licetfeldensi episcopo, successit Herewinus.[c][8]

[824] (xi) 846 *Ludouuicus imperator de placito generali Attinaco palatio Lotharium filium suum cum coniuge sua Irmingarda in Italiam direxit. Eugenius[9] nonagesimus octauus papa. Haistolfus episcopus Mogontinus obiit. [d]Otgarius successit. Qui cum ad Italiam ob discordiam filii ab imperatore cum aliis directus, Papiam uenisset, quidam clericus cum reliquiis sancti Seueri Rauenne urbis episcopi, necnon uxoris eius Vincentie, filieque eius Innocentie, quasi furto, abstulerat,*

---

[a] *interlin.* C¹ 　　[b] Anglos H, Angli L　　[c-c] Defuncto . . . Herewinus] *add. at line-end and running into mg.* C³, *om.* HL　　[d] *825 starts here (N)*

---

[1] ASC A(B)C (original date) DEF record the fight at Galford under 823 (*recte* 825).
[2-2] ASC DE only.　　[3] Wroughton.　　[4-4] No equivalent in ASC.
[5] ASC adds 'north across the Thames'.
[6] ASC A(B)C (original date) DEF (F briefer) under 823 (*recte* 825) agree in general with the differences shown.
[7] The accession of Ludeca is not recorded in ASC here though it is found in JW *Mercian Accounts* 19.

The Britons were slain by the men of Devon at a place called Galford.[1] Ecgberht, king [2]of the West Saxons,[2] and Beornwulf, king of the Mercians, joined battle at *Ellandun*,[3] [4]that is Mount Ealla,[4] but after great carnage had taken place, Ecgberht was victorious. From there he at once sent his son Æthelwulf, Ealhstan, [4]bishop of Sherborne,[4] and his ealdorman Wulfheard to Kent with a great army. [4]When they arrived there,[4] they at once expelled Baldred, king of that same province, from his realm.[5] After this the men of Kent and of Surrey, the South Saxons, and the East Saxons yielded of their own accord to Ecgberht. They had earlier been torn from the hands of his kinsmen, and, [4]against their will, made subject to the rule of foreign kings for a period of several years.[4] The East Angles sent ambassadors with their king to Ecgberht, [4]king of the West Saxons[4] asking him to be their protector and strong defence against the raids and attacks of the Mercians.[4] He acceded to their request, and promised that he would willingly help them in all matters. But Beornwulf, king of the Mercians, took no notice, assembled no small army, invaded their territory as an enemy, and hastened to slay any person of standing.[4] Their king went up with his own men against Beornwulf, and at the beginning of the battle killed him [5]and the greatest part of his army.[4,6] Beornwulf's kinsman Ludeca succeeded him to the realm.[7]

> On the death of Aldwulf, bishop of Lichfield, Herewine succeeded.[8]

[824] The Emperor Louis sent his son Lothar with his wife Ermengard to Italy after the general assembly at the palace at Attigny. Eugene[9] became the ninety-eighth pope. Haistolf, bishop of Mainz, died, and Otgar succeeded him. He was sent to Italy with others by the emperor on account of his son's disobedience; on Otgar's arrival in Pavia, a certain cleric came to him with relics of St Severus, bishop of Ravenna, and also of Severus' wife Vincentia and daughter Innocentia, which he had stolen, and

---

[8] This addition is incorrect, for there is enough reliable evidence to show that Herewine had succeeded Aldwulf before 823 (*S* 180 *BCS* 357, and *BCS* 358 both of 816, and possibly *S* 182 *BCS* 359 and *S* 181 *BCS* 360 of 817).

[9] Eugene II 824–7.

ad eundem Otgarium se contulit et ei quid egisset innotuit. Otgarius autem gaudens easdem reliquias suscepit et eas Mogontiacum secum adduxit atque in monasterio sancti Albani sanctam Vincentiam ad australem plagam, sanctam uero Innocentiam ad aquilonalem posuit, sanctum uero Seuerum iuxta altare sancti Albani, cuius postea reliquias ad Erfesfurt transtulit.[1]

[825] (xii) 847 *Ludouuicus imperator Britanniam uastat.*[2]

Rex Merciorum Ludecan sua militia coadunata ad ulciscendum predecessorem suum regem Beornuulfum in Orientalium Anglorum prouinciam mouit exercitum. Cui prouinciales illi cum rege suo festinato occurrerunt, consertoque graui prelio, illum et quinque duces eius exercitus cum aliis quampluribus occiderunt, reliquos uero fugauerunt. In regni autem gloriam ei Wiglaf successit.[3]

[826] (xiii) 848 *Eigil abbas Fuldensis obiit. Rabanus successit. Legati Wulgarorum imperatori munera portant.*[4]

[C³BP]
ᵃDefuncto Ecca Herefordensi episcopo, successit Ceadda.ᵃ[5]

[827] (xiiii) 849 *Valentinianus*[6] *nonagesimus nonus papa. ⟨Ludouicus⟩ᵇ in Ingelenheim Haroldumᶜ regem quondam Danorum de fonte baptismatis eleuauit, uxorem uero eius Iudith regina suscepit. Cui magnam partem Fresonum dedit et donis aliis ditatum cum legatis suis eum dimisit.*[7]

Sacrosancta nocte dominice natiuitatis facta est eclipsis lune, et eodem anno rex Occidentalium Saxonum Ecgbrihtus, expulso regno Wiglafo,[8] regnum Merciorum suo subiecit imperio. Deinde suam mouit expeditionem [9]ultra Humbre flumen.[9] Cui Norðhymbrenses in loco, qui Dore uocatur, occurrentes pacifice,

---

ᵃ⁻ᵃ Defuncto . . . Ceadda] *add. at end of 826 run over (on last line for 825) and running into mg.* C³, *om.* HL   ᵇ *om.* JW (N)   ᶜ Heroldum (N)

---

[1] Mar.   [2] Mar.
[3] ASC A-F record very briefly under 825 (*recte* 827) the death of Ludeca and five ealdormen and the succession of Wiglaf. Ludeca's invasion of East Anglia, which ASC does not mention, is recorded as taking place two years after his accession in JW *Mercian Accounts* 19 and *ASN*.
[4] Mar.

revealed to him what he had done. Otgar, rejoicing, received those same relics, and took them back with him to Mainz. He placed St Vincentia in the monastery of St Alban on the south side, St Innocentia on the north, and St Severus next to the altar of St Alban, whose relics he later translated to Erfurt.[1]

[825] The Emperor Louis laid waste Brittany.[2]

Ludeca, king of the Mercians, assembled his troops and marched his army into the province of the East Angles to avenge his predecessor King Beornwulf. The inhabitants of the province, led by their king, hastened to meet him; in a fierce battle they killed him and five of the leaders of his army with many others, and put the rest to flight. Wiglaf succeeded him to the regal dignity.[3]

[826] Egil, abbot of Fulda, died. Hrabanus succeeded him. The envoys of the Bulgarians brought gifts to the emperor.[4]

On the death of Acca, bishop of Hereford, Headda succeeded.[5]

[827] Valentinus[6] the ninety-ninth pope. Louis raised Harold, the former king of the Danes, from the baptismal font at Ingelheim, and Queen Judith received his wife. The emperor gave him a large area of Frisia, and sent him away enriched with other gifts in the company of his representatives.[7]

On the holy night of our Lord's nativity there was a lunar eclipse, and in the same year Ecgberht, king of the West Saxons, drove Wiglaf[8] from his kingdom, and subdued the kingdom of the Mercians to his rule. Then he moved his forces [9]beyond the river Humber.[9] The Northumbrians met him peacefully in a place called Dore, and offered him peace and humble submission, and

---

[5] As noted above p. 219 n. 5, Ceadda's successor was in office in 781 and both Acca and Headda (Headda in *Epis. Lists* in BL Cotton MS Vespasian B. VI) must have died before that date.

[6] Valentine 827.   [7] Mar.

[8] ASC A-F (827 *recte* 829) do not specifically mention Wiglaf's expulsion.

[9-9] 'ultra Humbre flumen' seems to be at variance with ASC A-F (827 *recte* 829) which state that Ecgberht led his army to Dore and the Northumbrians submitted, though it is worth noting that Roger of Wendover i. 277 suggests that the submission followed a West Saxon expedition into Northumbria.

ei concordiam humilemque subiectionem optulere, et sic ab inuicem diuisi sunt magna mentis alacritate.[1] Hic idem rex Ecgbrihtus octauus *quidem in regibus gentis Anglorum cunctis australibus eorum prouinciis, que Humbre fluuio et contiguis ei terminis sequestrantur a borealibus, imperauit. Nam primus imperium huiusmodi Ælle rex Australium Saxonum, ᵃsecundus Celin rex Occidentalium Saxonum,ᵃ qui lingua ipsorum Ceaulin uocabatur, tertius Æthilberhtus rex Cantuuariorum, quartus Reduuald rex Orientalium Anglorum, qui etiam uiuente Æthilberhto eidem sue genti ducatum prebebat, optinuit, quintus Eduuine rex Norðanhymbrorum gentis, id est eius, que ad borealem Humbre fluminis plagam inhabitat, maiore potentia cunctis qui Brytanniam incolunt, Anglorum pariter et Brytonum populis prefuit, preter Cantuariis tantum, necnon et Meuanias Brytonum insulas que inter Hiberniam et Brytaniam site sunt, Anglorum subiecitᵇ imperio. Sextus Oswald et ipse Norðhymbrorum rex Christianissimus hisdem finibus regnum tenuit, septimus Osuuiu frater eius equalibus pene terminis regnum nonnullo tempore cohercens, Pictorum quoque atque Scottorum gentes que septentrionales Brytannie fines tenent maxima ex parte perdomuit ac tributarias fecit.*[2] Octauus ut diximus exstitit rex Ecgbrihtus. Cuius ut fertur regni tempore ortus est beatus Suuithunus nobili parentum stirpe. Qui transactis annis puerilibus a sancto Helmstano presule Wintoniensis ecclesie sacris | est gradibus attitulatus. Cui etiam rex Ecgbrihtus filium suum commendauit Atheluulfum litteris sacris erudiendum.[3]

p. 284

[828] (xv) 850 *ᶜLudowicus imperator dirigens exercitum contra Sarracenos fugauit eos.*[4]

Rex Wiglaf regnum Merciorum recepit.[5] Heathoredo Lindisfarnensi episcopo defuncto, Ecgredus successit.[6] Ecgbertus

---

ᵃ⁻ᵃ secundus . . . Saxonum] *add. mg.* P³   ᵇ suscepit HL   ᶜ Ludowicus . . . Westsaxonum (*p. 248*)] *rewritten mostly over erasure.* C²

---

[1] ASC.   [2] HE. ii. 5. ASC A–F (827 *recte* 829) have a list of 'bretwaldas'.
[3] Faint echoes in the phrasing of the *Vita Suithuni* attributed to Goscelin, 'annis puerilibus in bono simplicitate . . . transactis . . . de gradu in gradum conscendens', should be noted (E. P. Sauvage, 'Vita Sancti Swithuni Wintoniensis episcopi, auctore Goscelino, monacho Sithiensi', *Analecta Bollandiana*, vii (1888), 375), but the reason for JW's date is not clear.

so they separated with great satisfaction.[1] This same Ecgberht was the eighth of those kings of the English to rule all their southern regions, which are separated from the north by the river Humber and the boundaries contiguous to it. For the first to gain such power was Ælle, king of the South Saxons; the second was Celin, king of the West Saxons, who in the language of his people, was called Ceawlin; the third Æthelberht, king of the people of Kent; the fourth Rædwald, king of the East Angles, who, even in the lifetime of that same Æthelberht, gained the military leadership for his own people. The fifth was Edwin, king of the Northumbrians, that is of the people who live on the north bank of the river Humber, who ruled with greater power all the peoples who inhabit Britain, both the English and the Britons, except the people of Kent, and in addition he made subject to English rule the Mevanian islands of the Britons, which lie between Britain and Ireland; the sixth was Oswald, also the most Christian king of the Northumbrians, who held the kingdom with the same boundaries; the seventh Oswiu, his brother, who maintained his kingdom for no little time with almost equal boundaries, and who also for the most part subdued, and made tributary, the Pictish and Scottish peoples who hold the northern parts of Britain.[2] As we have said, the eighth was King Ecgberht. During his reign, it is said, the blessed Swithhun was born of noble parents. When the years of his boyhood were over he was invested with holy orders by St Helmstan, bishop of Winchester. King Ecgberht entrusted to him his son Æthelwulf to be instructed in sacred letters.[3]

[828] The Emperor Louis sent his army against the Saracens, and put them to flight.[4]

King Wiglaf received the kingdom of the Mercians.[5] On the death of Heathured, bishop of Lindisfarne, Ecgred succeeded.[6]

---

[4] Mar.

[5] ASC A–F 828 (recte 830) record the restoration of Wiglaf and the death of Æthelwald, bishop of Lichfield, and (save for F) the subjection of the 'north Britons'.

[6] The death of Heathured of Lindisfarne is not in ASC; JW's addition was probably based on HDE. He began Heathured's pontificate in 819 and the 9 years assigned to his pontificate by HDE ii. 5 (i. 52) would have led JW to assign his death to 828. But if the death of Heathured's predecessor was in 821 (see above, p. 240 n. 2), then the date of Heathured's death must be 830. The statement in HDE ii. 5 (i. 52) that the pontificate of Ecgred began in the 22nd year of Eanred would give 830 or 832 depending on whether Eanred's reign began in 808 or 810.

rex Westsaxonum*ᵃ* in terram septentrionalium Brytonum exercitum duxit et eos licet inuitos suo domino subiugauit.¹

[C³BP³]

*ᵇ*Vbi uel quomodo Haugustald-
ensis episcopatus deficit. *Post
Æthilberhtum Hagustaldensem
episcopum Tilberhti successorem*, tres tantum Hagustaldenses
episcopi fuere: Heardredus,
Eanberhtus, Tidfrid. *Exercitus
enim Danorum uehemens, habita-
toribus extinctis uel effugatis,
habitaculorum tecta succendit, et
secreta celo exposuit. Nunc est
Hengsteldeham uilla* presulis
*Eboracensis.*² De Candida Casa.
*Candida Casa uocatur locus in
extremis Anglie iuxta Scottiam
finibus, ubi beatus Ni⟨ni⟩aᶜ confessor requiescit, natione Brytto, qui
primus ibidem Christi predica-
tionem euangelizauit. Nomen loco
ex opere inditum, quod ecclesiam
ibi ex lapide polito Brytonibus
miraculo fecerit. Ibi sub extremo
Bede tempore primus factus est
episcopus Pectelmus, qui multo
ante tempore in Westsaxonia com-
moratus sanctissimi Aldelmi discip-
ulatui interesse meruerat.* Ei
subsecuti sunt Frithewald,
Pehtwine, Æthelbriht, Beadulf,
Heathored. Post hunc *episcopatus
defec*it *quia extrema ora est*

ᵃ see above, p. 246 n. c   *ᵇ* Vbi . . . *oportuna (p. 250)] add. mg. alongside 827–36*
C³, *om.* HL, *incorporated (with rubrics in mg.) under 837 (see 836 n. c)* B, *outer mg.
alongside 827 (without rubric for the Hexham entry)* P³   *ᵇ* Nima CB (B *corrected to*
Ninia*)*

---

¹ ASC.   ² GP iii. 117 (p. 256).

Ecgberht, king of the West Saxons, led his army into the land of the North Britons, and subdued them, although unwilling, to his dominion.[1]

When and how the bishopric of Hexham came to an end. After Æthelberht, bishop of Hexham, Tilberht's successor, there were only three bishops of Hexham, Heardred, Eanberht and Tidferth, for the Danish troops in their ferocity burnt the roofs of the houses after slaying the inhabitants or putting them to flight, and exposed the interiors to the skies. Now Hexham is a township of the bishop of York.[2] Concerning Whithorn. Whithorn is the name of the place on the furthest borders of England, next to Scotland, where the blessed confessor Ninian lies. A Briton by race, he was the first to spread Christ's gospel by preaching. The place was so named from the construction, because he made a church there. It was of polished stone, marvellous to the Britons. There, near the end of Bede's time, Pehthelm was made first bishop; long before, he had stayed in Wessex, and had merited being a disciple of the most holy Aldhelm. His successors were Frithuwald, Pehtwine, Æthelberht, Beadwulf, and Heathured. After this man the bishopric came to an end because the furthest shores of

Anglorum et Scottorum uel
Pictorum depopulationi oportuna.[a1]

[829] (xvi) 851 *Ludouuicus imperator Wormaciam ueniens Karolo*
filio suo ex Iudith regina terram Alamannicam et Reticam partemque
Burgundie ⟨dedit⟩[b] coram filiis suis Lothario et Ludouuico et Pippino
indeque *hi tres germani indignati sunt. Corpora sanctorum Valentini et*
Genesii in Augeam insulam .vi.[c] idus Aprilis uenerunt.[2]
Dorubernensis archiepiscopus Wlfredus obiit.[3]

[830] (xvii) 852 Ceolnothus in gradum archiepiscopatus electus
et consecratus est.[4]

[831] (xviii) 853 *Gregorius[5] papa centesimus.*[6]
Ceolnothus archiepiscopus a Gregorio papa pallium suscepit.[7]
Ludouuicus imperator de Aquisgrani palatio uenit ad Compendium
ibique filius suus[d] Pippinus cum multis perfidis uenit ei obuiam uolens
eum de regno expellere, sed equiuocus imperatoris filius ⟨ei⟩[e] con-
tradixit. Dicebant autem illi perfidi Iudith reginam uiolatam esse a
quodam duce Bernhardo, qui erat de stirpe regali, mentientes omnia
sicque ui uelantes eam in monasterium miserunt, similiterque fratres
eiusdem regine Cuonradum et Ruodoluum tondentes eos. Quos omnes
imperator eodem anno in Nouiomaco castro super flumen Valum sito
cum ueritate superauit, reginamque obuiantem sibi ad Aquisgrani pre-
cepto Gregorii pape aliorumque episcoporum iusto iudicio suscepit.[8]

[832] (xix) 854 *Bernhardus dux in palatio Theodonis coram rege et*
duobus filiis eius Lothario et Ludouuico purificauit se de supradicto
stupro, cum nullus ausus esset pro hoc armis cum eo decertare.[9]
Danici[f] pirate inhiatores prede Sceapege depredati sunt.[10]

---

[a] see above, p. 248 n. b   [b] om. JW   [c] .v. Mar.   [d] eius (N)
[e] ei L, ei from eius P¹, eius CHB ?(N)   [f] -ci interlin. in Danici C¹, Paganici from
Danici B⁵

---

[1] *GP* iii. 118 (pp. 256–7). This marginal addition erroneously makes Heathured the
last bishop of Whithorn (in this agreeing with JW *Epis. Lists*, and going beyond *GP*'s
Whithorn list), and it may have been located here because the rewritten annal for 828
had recorded the death of Heathured of Lindisfarne.

[2] Mar.

[3] ASC A–F 829 (*recte* 832). F additionally (in mg.) records the election on 24 Apr.,
consecration on 9 June (a Sunday in 832), and death on 30 Aug. of an abbot named
Feologild.

the English and the Scots or
Picts are exposed to raids.[1]

[829] The Emperor Louis, coming to Worms, gave to Charles, his
son by Queen Judith, the land of Alemannia and *Rhaetia* and part
of Burgundy in the presence of his sons Lothar, Louis, and
Pippin. At this the three brothers were angry. The bodies of the
saints Valentine and Genesius came to Reichenau on 8 April.[2]
Wulfred, archbishop of Canterbury, died.[3]

[830] Ceolnoth was elected and consecrated archbishop.[4]

[831] Gregory[5] was the 100th pope.[6]
Archbishop Ceolnoth received the pallium from Pope Gregory.[7]
The Emperor Louis went from the palace at Aachen to
Compiègne, and there his son Pippin met him with many traitors,
wishing to drive him from his realm, but the emperor's son and
namesake spoke against him. However, the traitors alleged, quite
falsely, that Queen Judith had been ravished by a certain Count
Bernhard, who was of the royal blood, so, forcing her to take the
veil, they sent her to a convent and in a like fashion they tonsured
that same queen's brothers Conrad and Rudolf. All these enemies
the emperor overcame with truth at the fort of Nijmegen, situated
on the River Waal, and he received the queen, who met him at
Aachen, at the command of Pope Gregory, and by the equitable
judgement of the other bishops.[8]

[832] Count Bernhard cleared himself of the accusation mentioned
above in the palace of Thionville in the presence of the king and
his two sons Lothar and Louis, since no one had dared to chal-
lenge him in battle on this matter.[9]
The Danish pirates ravaged Sheppey, avid for booty.[10]

---

[4] ASC A-F 830 enter the election of Ceolnoth, and also (F 829) the death of an
'abbot Feologild'. Canterbury tradition (Gervase and later writers) records the election
of Ceolnoth on 29 June and his consecration on 27 Aug.; the latter was a Sunday in
831, but this seems an unlikely year, and 833 has been suggested as more probable
(Haddan and Stubbs, *Councils*, iii. 611 n. a; Brooks, *Canterbury*, p. 143).
[5] Gregory IV 827–44.
[6] Mar.   [7] ASC A-E 831, F 832. JW names the pope who gave the pallium.
[8] Mar.   [9] Mar.   [10] ASC A-E 832 (*recte* 835).

[**833**] (xx) 855   *Filii regis temptauerunt regnum patri auferre quod et perfecerunt ubi obuiauerunt ei cum Gregorio papa in campo magno qui est inter Argentinam et Basalam. Tunc separantes reginam ab eo, et mittentes eam*[a] *in Italiam in ciuitatem Dertunam, Pippinus in Aquitaniam, Ludouuicus in Bauuariam perrexit, Lotharius uero patrem ad Compendium palatium et inde Aquisgrani eum duxit et in custodia inclusit, ibi*que *celebrauit natale Domini patre adhuc incluso.*[1]

Rex Occidentalium Saxonum [b]Ecgbrihtus apud Carrum cum .xxxv. nauibus piratarum pugnauit sed strage magna facta, Dani potiti sunt uictoria.[2]

[**835**] (xxii) 857   *Post Epiphaniam uero, quia Ludouuicus cum patre contra eum erat, Lotharius compellit patrem secum ire ad Compendium. Quem cum multitudine secutus est Ludouuicus et cum prope esset fugit Lotharius. Ludouuicus uero patrem duxit ad sedem regalem Aquisgrani ibique pariter pasca celebrauerunt.*[3]

Dani multa cum classe in occidentalium Brytonum terram, [4]que Curualia [c]uel Cornubia[c4] uocatur, appulerunt, cum quibus Brytones foedus paciscuntur, et eos secum ducentes [4]fines regni Ecgbrihti regis depopulantur.[4] Quod ille audiens, festinanter copiam militum coadunauit, et in loco qui dicitur Hencgestes Dune, [4]id est mons Hencgesti,[4] cum eis certamen iniit. [4]Ex quibus multos trucidauit,[4] reliquos uero fugauit.[5]

[C³BP]
[d]Defuncto Unwona Legerecensi episcopo, successit Werenberhtus.[d6]

[**836**] (xxiii) 858   *Ciclus .xvii. decennouenalis incipit indictione .xiiii.*[7]

Ecgbertus rex Occidentalium Saxonum obiit. Quem Offa rex Merciorum et Brihtricus rex Wessaxonum antequam rex effectus esset de Anglia expulerunt.[8] Qui Franciam adiit, ibique per

---

[a] *om.* HL   [b] *runs on to 834 here* C, *833 runs over into 834* HB   [c–c] uel Cornubia] *interlin.* C¹L¹B¹P¹, *om.* H   [d–d] Defuncto . . . Werenberhtus] *add. at line-end* C³, *om.* HL

---

[1] Mar.
[2] ASC A–E 833 (*recte* 836), F 834. JW has 35 ships' companies as in ABC (25 in DEF). He does not mention the deaths of two bishops and two ealdormen recorded in ASC.
[3] Mar.   [4–4] No equivalent in ASC.

[833] The king's sons attempted to take the kingdom from their father, which they achieved when they met him with Pope Gregory in the great plain which lies between Strasburg and Basle. Then, separating the queen from him, and sending her into Italy to the city of Tortona, Pippin went to Aquitaine, Louis to Bavaria. Lothar took their father to the Compiègne palace, and then to Aachen, and kept him there under guard. There he celebrated Christmas with his father, who was still imprisoned.[1]

Ecgberht, king of the West Saxons, fought with thirty-five pirate ships at Carhampton, but after great slaughter the Danes were victorious.[2]

[835] After Epiphany Lothar, because Louis supported his father against him, forced his father to go with him to Compiègne. Louis followed him with a large force, and as he approached Lothar fled. Louis took his father to the royal seat at Aachen, and there they both celebrated Easter.[3]

The Danes landed with a great fleet in the land of the west Britons, [4]which is called Curvalia or Cornwall,[4] and the Britons made an agreement with them. The Danes took the Britons with them [4]and ravaged the lands of King Ecgberht's kingdom.[4] When he heard that, Ecgberht hastily assembled a large force and joined battle with them at a place called Hengest's Dune, [4]that is Hengest's Mount.[4] [4]He cut down many of them,[4] and put the rest to flight.[5]

> On the death of Unwona, bishop of Leicester, Wernberht succeeded.[6]

[836] The seventeenth cycle of nineteen years begins in the fourteenth indiction.[7]

Ecgberht, king of the West Saxons, died, whom Offa, king of the Mercians, and Brihtric, king of the West Saxons, drove from England before he was made king.[8] He went to France, and there

---

[5] ASC A–F 835 (recte 838) which do not identify the naval force as Danish.

[6] This addition is misplaced: Wernberht was in office in 803 when he attended the council of Clofesho.

[7] Mar.

[8] JW omits (like ASC DEF) the sentence saying that Brihtric helped Offa because he had married Offa's daughter.

triennium mansit. Inde Angliam rediit, et, mortuo Brihtrico, regni gubernacula, *"ut prelibauimus,"* suscepit.[1] Cuius post mortem filius suus Athulfus[2] in Wessaxonia regnare cepit, suumque filium Æthelstanum[3] Cantuariis, ⟨Eas⟩saxonibus,*[b4]* Suðregiis et Suðsaxonibus regem prefecit.[5]

[C³BP]
ᶜDefuncto Eanbaldo Eboracensi archipresule usque ad tempora regis Æthelstani hi successerunt: Wlfsius, Wigmundus, Wlfere, Athelbald, Rodewald, Wlfstanus. Post hunc Oscytel tempore regum Edredi, Edwii et Eadgari.ᶜ[6] |

[837] (xxiiii) 859 [HLP]
ᵈWulfhardus dux apud Hamtun cum .xxxiiii.[7] nauibus piratarum prelium gessit et ex eis multam stragem dedit, uictorque extitit nec multo post uita decessit.ᵈ

p. 285   ᵉIn regione que uocatur Port cum Danis prelium iniit dux Athelmus,[8] Dorcestrensibus auxilium sibi ferentibus, [9]eosque diu fugere[9] compulit, sed [10]tamen in ipsa fuga ab eis uulneratus[10] occubuit, Danicus uero miles uictoriam habuit.[11] Rege uero Athulfo regnante, sanctus Helmstanus episcopus uita decessit, cui iussu regis beatus Suithunus successit.[12]

ᵃ⁻ᵃ ut prelibauimus *om.* L   *ᵇ gap with erasure before* Saxonibus C, Saxonibus BP
ᶜ⁻ᶜ Defuncto . . . Eadgari] *add. over erasure and runs on to 837* C³, *om.* HL, *runs on to 837, where 828 n. b follows B, runs on to 837* P   *ᵈ⁻ᵈ* Wulfhardus . . . decessit] *immediately follows 836 n . c under 837* P   *ᵉ red initial usually marking new annal or section absent* C

---

[1] JW appears to place Ecgberht's return to England before the death of Brihtric. This sentence is not in ASC and could be interpreted in the same way as is suggested above p. 230 n. 3.
[2] Here and in 840 JW (as in JW *West Saxon Gen.* and *Accounts* 24) has Athulfus for Æthelwulf.
[3] ASC ABC (like JW) make Æthelstan the son of Æthelwulf, unlike DEF, which apparently makes him the son of Ecgberht.

he stayed three years. From there he returned to England, and, when Brihtric died, he received the government of the kingdom, as we said above.[1] After his death his son Æthelwulf[2] began to reign in Wessex, and he made his own son Æthelstan[3] king of the people of Kent, of the ⟨East⟩ Saxons,[4] of the people of Surrey, and of the South Saxons.[5]

From the death of Eanbald, archbishop of York, down to the time of King Æthelstan, these men succeeded: Wulfsige, Wigmund, Wulfhere, Æthelbald, Hrothweard, Wulfstan. After him followed Osketel in the time of the kings Eadred, Eadwig, and Edgar.[6]

[837] The ealdorman Wulfheard fought at Southampton against the pirates' crews of thirty-four ships.[7] He made a great slaughter there, and was victorious. Not long after he died.

The ealdorman Æthelhelm,[8] with the assistance of the men of Dorset, joined battle with the Danes in the area called Port, and [9]drove them in flight for a long time[9] but [10]at last, in that same rout, he fell, wounded[10] by them, and the Danish force was victorious.[11] In the reign of King Æthelwulf, the holy bishop Helmstan departed this life, and the blessed Swithhun succeeded him at the king's command.[12]

[4] ASC ABC have East Saxons, who are omitted in DEF.
[5] ASC A-F 836 (recte 839) which give also Ecgberht's regnal length.
[6] GP iii. 114–15 (p. 247). This was probably inserted here because the reviser thought that Wulfsige had died in 836. See discussion in R. Ray, 'Wulfsige and ninth-century Northumbrian chronology', Northern History, xxi (1985), 12–14.
[7] ASC ABDE 33 ships, C 34.
[8] Æthelm in ASC B, Æthelhelm in ACDE.
[9–9] This translates a sentence found in ASC ABC, not in DE.
[10–10] Not in ASC   [11] ASC A-E (837 recte 840).
[12] Swithhun probably became bishop in 852 (Haddan and Stubbs, Councils, iii. 634), Helmstan in 838 or 839 (O'Donovan, ii. 107) and it is possible that Helmstan's death has been erroneously entered under the year for his accession.

[838] (xxv) 860 *Pauto diaconus palatii lapsus est in Iudaismum.*[1]
Dux Herebrihtus *a*et *2*cum eo quamplures Merscuuariorum[2] a
Danis paganis occisi sunt, eodemque anno in Lindissi prouincia, in
Eastanglia et in Cantia ab eodem exercitu multi sunt interfecti.[3]
Wiglaf rex Merciorum uita decessit cui in regnum Beorhtuulfus
successit.*a*[4]

[839] (xxvi) 861 *bEclipsis solis facta est .iii. non. Maii inter
octauam et nonam horam in uigilia Ascensionis Domini.*[5]
In Lundonia et in Cuuentawic*c* in ciuitate quoque Hrofi, sepe-
dicti pagani quamplurimos dederunt neci.[6]

[840] (xxvii) 862 *d*Ciclus solis incipit .iiii. concurrentibus bissextilibus.*d* *Ludouuicus imperator, dum filium suum Ludouuicum trans
Hrenum persequeretur, morbo grauatus, naui per Moin flumen in
Hrenum deductus, uix in insulam Ingelenheim perueniens obiit ibi .xi.
kalend. Iunii et inde mense Martio asportatus in basilica sancti Arnulfi
sepelitur, statimque Lotharius Italia egressus imperium arrip⟨u⟩it.*e*[7]
Athulfus rex Occidentalium Saxonum apud Carrum cum .xxxv.
nauibus Danorum commisit prelium sed Saxones Danica uicit fortuna.[8]
*f*Quis composuit uersus 'Gloria laus' qui die Palmarum cantan-
tur? Temporibus Ludowici imperatoris floruit Theodulfus
Floriacensium abbas et Aurelianensium episcopus, qui cum insimulatus
multis criminibus apud imperatorem fuisset, Andegauis est exilio religa-
tus. Qui dum in custodia teneretur, contigit ut ibidem die Palmarum
ueniret iamdictus imperator. Et cum secus domum qua custodiebatur
idem T⟨heodulfus⟩ episcopus processio pertransiret facto silentio presente
imperatore illos pulcerrimos uersus, qui nunc usque per Galliam in
eadem solennitate psalluntur, a se editos per fenestram decantauit*

---

a–a et . . . successit] *compressed writing and paler ink* C[1]   *b* *starts towards line-end
leaving some space blank* C   *c* uel Cantawic *interlin.* B[5]?   *d–d* Ciclus . . . bis-
sextilibus] *add. mg.* C[1], *om.* HLP, *at end of 839* B   *e* arripit CB (N)
f Quis . . . composuit (p. 258)] *add. mg. p. 282, alongside 813–23* C[3], *omits rubric* HL,
incorporated 819 n. d without rubric B, *under Louis the Pious 814–40 and before the death
of Cenwulf (which was in 819 in JW)* G

---

[1] Mar.
[2–2] This seems to be JW's rendering of 'monige (men) mid him on Merscwarum' of
ASC ABC.
[3] ASC A–D (838 *recte* 841).

[**838**] Pauto, deacon of the palace, lapsed into Judaism.[1]

The ealdorman Hereberht and [2]with him very many men of (Romney) Marsh[2] were killed by the heathen Danes; in the same year many were killed by the same army in the province of Lindsey, in East Anglia, and in Kent.[3] Wiglaf, king of the Mercians, departed this life, and Brihtwulf succeeded him in the kingdom.[4]

[**839**] There was a solar eclipse on 5 May between the eighth and the ninth hour on the eve of the Lord's Ascension.[5]

In London and in Quentavic, also in the city of Rochester, the frequently mentioned heathen slew very many.[6]

[**840**] The solar cycle begins with four concurrents in a bissextile year. The Emperor Louis, while he was pursuing his son Louis across the Rhine, was afflicted by illness, was taken by ship along the River Main into the Rhine; scarcely had he reached the island of Ingelheim when he died there on 22 May. In March he was borne from there, and buried in the basilica of St Arnulf. Immediately Lothar came out of Italy, and took the imperial title.[7]

Æthelwulf, king of the West Saxons, joined battle at Carhampton with thirty-five Danish ships but Danish fortune conquered the Saxons.[8]

Who was the composer of the verses 'Gloria laus' which are sung on Palm Sunday? In the reign of the Emperor Louis lived Theodulf, abbot of Fleury and bishop of Orléans, who, having been falsely accused before the emperor of many crimes, was exiled to Angers. While he was being held in custody, it happened that the emperor already mentioned went there on Palm Sunday; and as the procession was passing by the house in which that same Bishop Theodulf was held, it fell silent and he chanted in the emperor's presence through the window the exquisite verses which he himself had composed and which are still chanted throughout

---

[4] The death of Wiglaf and the succession of Brihtwulf are not recorded elsewhere. JW *Mercian Accounts* 21 says that Wiglaf died in the 13th year of his reign, and, if Wiglaf succeeded in 825 (*recte* 827, see annal above), 838 (*recte* 840) will be the appropriate date for his death.
[5] Mar.   [6] ASC A–E (839 *recte* 842), C reads 'Canterbury' for 'Quentavic'.
[7] Mar.
[8] ASC ABDEF (840), C (841), to be corrected to 843 or 844 (Plummer, *Chronicle*, ii. 76). As under annal 836, *Athulfus* is the spelling of the West Saxon king.

quorum hoc est exordium: 'Gloria, laus et honor tibi sit rex Christe redemptor. Cui puerile decus prompsit Osanna pium.' Quibus imperator emollitus, mox eum a uinculis absolui precepit, et priori gratie redonauit. Sed dum ad sua reuertitur ueneno sicut ferunt extinguitur. Cui successit in episcopatum Ionas uir uenerabilis qui contra Claudium Taurinensem episcopum heresiarcham librum de adoranda^a edidit cruce. Dogmatizauit enim idem hereticus crucis dominice signum non oportere adorari; quod nisi adhibeatur frontibus nostris siue aquis quibus regeneramur aut crismati quo linimur aut sacrificio quo uegetamur, nihil rite perficitur. Sed ei memoratus episcopus Ionas satis lucide catholiceque illo suo respondit libello. Floruit etiam iisdem temporibus *uir quidam, Rabanus nomine, qui et ipse de laude crucis librum, diuersis scematibus decoratum, metrice composuit.*^{b1}

^c*Romanorum octogesimus Lotharius*² *regnauit annis quindecim.*^{d3}

[841] (i) 863 *Ludouuicus*⁴ *uero et Karolus*⁵ *paterno regno priuati, apud Fontaniacum fratrem Lotharium bello superant.*^{e6}

[842] (ii) 864 ^f*Tres supradicti fratres regnum Francorum inter se diuiserunt, Karolus occidentem tenet a Brytannico oceano usque ad Mosam fluuium.*⁷ Gregorius papa obiit.^{f8}

[843] (iii) 865

[C³BP]

^gDefuncto Herewino Licedfeldensi antistite, Oithelwald successit.^{g9}

[844] (iiii) 866 *Sergius*^{h10} *centesimus primus papa.* ^h*Ludouuicus suscepit orientem, id est omnem Germaniam usque Hreni fluenta et ali-*

---

^a ad (*sic*) adoranda *JW*   ^b *see above, p. 256 n. f*   ^c capitula .lxxx. (.lxxxi.*B*) add. *before* Romanorum *LB*   ^d *repeats 809 n. h here HL*   ^e Sanctus rex et martyr Eadmundus nascitur *add. at line-end extending into mg.* B⁵?   ^{f-f} Tres . . . obiit] *runs over into 843 JW*   ^{g-g} Defuncto . . . successit] *add. after end of 842 under 843, and run-over sign before* defuncto *might suggest intended for 843 C³, om. HL, under 842-3 BP*   ^h *erased initial S visible before* Sergius *C*   ⁱ *845 starts here* (*N*)

---

¹ Hugh of Fleury, pp. 180–1.   ² Lothar I 840–55.   ³ Mar.
⁴ Louis the German 840–76.
⁵ Charles the Bald, king 840–77, emperor 875–7.   ⁶ Mar.

Gaul on that solemn feast. This is the beginning: 'Glory, praise, and honour be thine, Christ, King and Redeemer, whose infant glory called forth the holy Hosannah.' Mollified by them, the emperor immediately ordered him to be released from his bonds, and restored him to the favour he had enjoyed before, but when he was returned to his own, he was, they say, poisoned. Jonas succeeded him to the bishopric. He was a revered man who wrote the book *On the Adoration of the Cross* against the heresiarch Claudius, bishop of Turin, for that same heretic taught as dogma that the sign of the Lord's Cross should not be adored; unless this is made on our foreheads or on those waters by which we are given new birth or with the chrism by which we are anointed or the sacrifice by which we gain strength, nothing is performed correctly. However, Bishop Jonas, already mentioned, answered him with great clarity and orthodoxy in his book. A certain man, Hrabanus by name, lived at the same time, and he also composed a book in praise of the Cross in verse adorned with various figures.[1]

Lothar,[2] the eightieth emperor of the Romans, reigned fifteen years.[3]

[841] Louis[4] and Charles,[5] deprived of their father's kingdom, overcame their brother Lothar in battle at Fontenoy.[6]

[842] The three aforesaid brothers divided the kingdom of the Franks among themselves. Charles held the west from the English Channel to the River Meuse.[7] Pope Gregory died.[8]

[843]   On the death of Herewine,
                            bishop of Lichfield, Æthelwald
                            succeeded.[9]

[844] Sergius[10] was the 101st pope. Louis received the east, that is, the whole of Germany as far as the River Rhine and some

---

[7] Mar.

[8] This is not in Marianus and may be an inference from the entry for 844, which names the next pope Sergius II. If so, it may be an argument for including the entry under 843.

[9] This addition is misplaced for Oithilwald (Æthelwald) died in 830 according to ASC (see above, p. 247 n. 5).

[10] Sergius II 844–7.

quas ciuitates trans Hrenum cum adiacentibus plagis propter copiam uini. ª Lotharius primogenitus et imperator medium inter utrosque tenuit regnum totam Prouinciam et omnia regna Italie cum ipsa Roma. Ab hoc Lothario regnum Lotharingorum hactenus dicitur.[1]

[845] (v) 867 Dux Eanulfus cum Sumersetunensibus[b] et Ealhstanus ²Scireburnensis ecclesie² episcopus et dux Osricus cum Dorcestrensibus ad ostium fluminis Pedridan cum Danico exercitu pugnantes, et ex eis non modicam stragem dantes, uictorie palmam sunt adepti.³ ʿDefuncto Ecgredo Lindisfarnensi episcopo, Eanbertus successit.ʿ⁴

[846] (vi) 868 *ᵈOtgarius episcopus Mogontinus obiit, Rabanus abbas Fuldensis successit.*⁵

[847] (vii) 869 *ᵉHatto successit abbas ad Fuldam.*⁶
Defuncto Huuiciorum episcopo Heaberhto, Alhhun successit.⁷

[849] (ix) 871 *Angulsaxonum rex Ælfred*us *in illa paga que nominatur Berrocscire*ᶠ *nascitur.*ᵍ⁸ *Cuius genealogia tali serie contexitur: Ælfred rex, filius Atheluulfi regis, qui fuit Ecgberhti, qui fuit Ealhmundi, qui fuit Eafe, qui fuit Eoppa, qui fuit Ingels.*ʰ *Ingels*ʰ *et Ine, ille famosus Occidentalium rex Saxonum, germani duo fuerunt. Qui Ine Romam perrexit, et ibi uitam presentem finiens honorifice, celestem patriam, cum Christo regnaturus, adiit. Qui fuerunt filii Coenred, qui fuit Ceoluuald, qui fuit Cutha, qui fuit Cuthuuine, qui fuit Ceaulin, qui fuit Cynric, qui fuit Creoda, qui fuit Cerdic, qui fuit Elesa,* ⁱ⁹*qui fuit Esla,*ⁱ⁹ *qui fuit Geuuis, a quo Brytones totam illam*

ᵃ *848 starts here (N)*   ᵇ Sumersetensibus *HL*, Sumersetuniensibus *P*
ᶜ⁻ᶜ Defuncto . . . successit] *add. line-end and running into mg.* C²   ᵈ *846-7 written in one block* C *(with some traces of erasure)* BP, *in* B *running on to the first line of 849, in* P *under a consolidated annal covering 846-9*   ᵉ *847 is consolidated with previous entry (see 846 n. d)* CBP   ᶠ in uilla regia que dicitur Wanating que pago taliter uocatur a Berroc silua ubi buxus habundantissime *add., as in Asser,* H, in uilla regia que uocata est Wanetinoge *add. lower mg. with signe de renvoi* B¹   ᵍ natus est *As*
ʰ Ingild *As*   ⁱ⁻ⁱ qui . . . Esla] *om. As*

---

¹ Mar.   ²⁻² No equivalent in ASC.   ³ ASC A-F (845). DEF have 'Earnwulf' (wrongly).
⁴ As Ecgred may have become bishop of Lindisfarne in 830 (see above p. 247 n. 6) and died in the 16th year of his episcopate and the 5th year of King Æthelred, 845-6

cities across the Rhine with the surrounding areas because of the great quantity of wine. Lothar, the first-born and the emperor, held the kingdom between the other two, the whole of Provence and all the Italian kingdoms, with Rome itself. From this Lothar the kingdom was thenceforth called Lotharingia.[1]

[845] The ealdorman Eanwulf with the men of Somerset, and Ealhstan, bishop [2]of Sherborne,[2] and the ealdorman Osric with the men of Dorset fought the Danish army at the river Parret, and after slaying no small number of them took the palm of victory.[3] On the death of Ecgred, bishop of Lindisfarne, Eanberht succeeded.[4]

[846] Otgar, bishop of Mainz, died, and Hrabanus, abbot of Fulda succeeded.[5]

[847] Hatto succeeded as abbot of Fulda.[6]

On the death of Heahberht, bishop of the Hwicce, Alhhun succeeded.[7]

[849] Alfred, king of the Anglo-Saxons, was born in that area called Berkshire,[8] and his genealogy stretches back in an unbroken line: King Alfred, son of King Æthelwulf, son of Ecgberht, son of Ealhmund, son of Eafa, son of Eoppa, son of Ingels. Ingels and Ine (that renowned king of the West Saxons) were two brothers. Ine went to Rome, and there, when ending his earthly life with honour, he went to his heavenly homeland to reign with Christ. They were the sons of Cenred, son of Ceolwald, son of Cutha, son of Cuthwine, son of Ceawlin, son of Cynric, son of Creoda, son of Cerdic, son of Elesa, [9]son of Esla,[9] son of Gewis (after whom the

---

(HDE ii. 5 (i. 53)), and since his successor Eanberht had completed 8 years rule by 854, the date of this addition by scribe C[2] could be correct. However it is impossible to reconcile with C[2]'s dating of Ecgred's succession to 828.

[5] Mar.   [6] Mar.

[7] For evidence that Alhhun was in office by 8 Nov. 845 and that his predecessor Heaberht was in office in 843 and 844, see O'Donovan, ii. 112. Even if this entry should be regarded as part of an extended 846 in MS C (it is so dated in the 19-year tables on p. 64), it may be wrong.

[8] Alfred's birthplace, Wantage, is omitted by JW, possibly through an oversight.

[9-9] These are apparent additions to the defective genealogy in As, possibly derived from ASC, or just possibly from JW's copy of Asser.

gentem Gewis nominant, qui fuit Wig, qui fuit Fræuuine, [1]qui fuit Freoðegar,[1] *qui fuit Brand, qui fuit Bealdeag, qui fuit Woden, qui fuit Frithouuald, qui fuit Frealaf, qui fuit Frithuwulf, qui fuit Fingolduulf,[2] qui fuit Geata, quem Getam iamdudum pagani pro deo uenerabantur, qui fuit Cætuua,[a] qui fuit Beauu, qui fuit Scelduuea, qui fuit Heremod, qui fuit Itermod, qui fuit Hathra, qui fuit Wala, qui fuit Beaduuig, qui fuit Sem,[b] qui fuit Noe, qui fuit Lamech, qui fuit Matusalem,* | *qui fuit Enoch,[c] qui fuit Malaleel, qui fuit Cainan, qui fuit Enos, qui fuit Seth, qui fuit Adam.[d3] Mater quoque eiusdem Osburh nominabatur, religiosa nimium femina, nobilis ingenio, nobilis et genere, que erat filia Oslac, famosi pincerne regis Aþelwulfi. Qui Oslac Gothus erat natione, ortus enim erat de Gothis et Iutis, de semine scilicet Stuf et Wihtgar, duorum fratrum et etiam comitum, qui, accepta potestate Vecte insule ab auunculo suo Cerdic rege et Cynric filio suo, consobrino eorum, paucos Brytones eiusdem insule accolas, quos in ea inuenire potuerunt, in loco qui dicitur Wihtgaraburh, occiderunt: ceteri enim accole eiusdem insule ante aut occisi erant aut exules aufugerant.[4]*

p. 286

[e]Kalendis Iunii[f] uigilia Pentecostes,[5] Berhtferthus filius regis Merciorum Beorhtuulfi suum cognatum iniuste peremit sanctum Wistanum. Hic itaque[g] nepos duorum extitit regum Merciorum, nam pater eius Wigmundus, Wiglaui regis filius, mater uero Ælfleda Ceoluulfi regis extitit filia. *Corpus autem illius ad monasterium tunc temporis famosum* quod *Reopedun* nominatur *delatum in mausoleo aui sui regis Wiglaui est tumulatum.* Sed illius martyrio celestia non defuere miracula, nam *de loco* in quo *innocenter* peremptus est *columpna lucis usque ad celum porrecta, omnibus eiusdem loci incolis per triginta dies conspicua stabat.[e6]*

---

[a] Cætuua *Ac Ao Au Aw*, Tætuua (*As*)   [b] Seth *HLBP* (*As*) *Ac Ao Au*, Sem *Aw HR i. 66 (ii. 69)*   [c] qui fuit Iared] *add. HB*[5] (*As*), *om. Ac Acott (teste Aw) Ao Au HR i. 66, ii. 69*   [d] primus homo *B*   [e-e] Kalendis . . . stabat] *add. mg. with signe de renvoi almost certainly pointing to end of 849 C*[1], *under 850 HL, under Lothar I (840–55) G*   [f-f] Kalendis Iunii] *om. HLBP*   [g] die kal. Iunii *interlin. B*[1]

[1-1] These are apparent additions to the defective genealogy in As, possibly derived from ASC, or just possibly from JW's copy of Asser.

[2] 'Fingolduulf' for 'Finn qui fuit Goduulf' is an error shared with Asser.

[3] Asser, c. 1.   [4] Id., c. 2.

[5] Pentecost was on 2 June 849, to which year Wigstan's death should be assigned.

849]   THE CHRONICLE OF JOHN OF WORCESTER   263

Britons named the whole of his people *Gewisse*), son of Wig, son of Freawine, [1]son of Freothegar,[1] son of Brand, son of Bældæg, son of Woden, son of Frithuwald, son of Frealaf, son of Frithuwulf, son of Fingoldwulf,[2] son of Geata—that Geta whom the heathens once venerated as a god—son of Tætwa, son of Beaw, son of Sceldwa, son of Heremod, son of Itermod, son of Hathra, son of Hwala, son of Bedwig, son of Shem, son of Noah, son of Lamech, son of Methuselah, son of Enoch, son of Mahaleel, son of Cainan, son of Enos, son of Seth, son of Adam.[3] His mother was called Osburg, a most devout woman, noble in character as well as noble by birth, who was the daughter of Oslac, King Æthelwulf's renowned cup-bearer. This Oslac was a Goth by race for he was descended from the Goths and the Jutes, that is from the line of Stuf and Wihtgar, two brothers, who were also ealdormen, and having received control of the Isle of Wight from their uncle King Cerdic, and from Cynric, his son and their cousin, killed the few British inhabitants of that island whom they could find on it at a place called *Wihtgarabyrig*, for the rest of the inhabitants of that island had either been killed before or had fled as exiles.[4]

On 1 June, on the eve of Whitsun,[5] Berhtferth, son of Berhtwulf, king of the Mercians, unjustly slew his kinsman St Wigstan. This man was the grandson of two kings of the Mercians, for his father was Wigmund, son of King Wiglaf, and his mother Ælfled was the daughter of King Ceolwulf. His body was borne to the monastery, at that time renowned, which was called Repton, and was laid in the mausoleum of his grandfather King Wiglaf. But divine miracles were not absent from his martyrdom, for, from the place where he was slain in his innocence, a column of light stretched up to heaven and remained visible for thirty days to all the inhabitants of that place.[6]

---

[6] A *Passio Wistani* was probably the source. The italicized words are found in the version in the mid-14th-c. BL MS Harl. 2523, fo. 140ᵛ. For discussion of the *Passio* manuscripts see D. W. Rollason. *The Search for St. Wigstan* (Leicester University, Vaughan Paper xxvii; Leicester, 1981), 7–10. The Wigstan matter is also found in JW *Mercian Accounts* 22.

[**850**] (x) 872   [C³BP]

*ᵃ*Defuncto Werenberto Legerensi presule, Rethhunus successit.*ᵃ¹*

[**851**] (xi) 873   *Irmingardis regina uxor Lotharii obiit, tres ei filios derelinquens, Lotharium, Ludouuicum et Carolum.*²

Ceorl, Domnanie comes, cum Domnaniis contra paganos pugnauit in loco, qui dicitur Wicganbeorh, et Christiani uictoriam habuerunt. Et ipso eodem anno primum hiemauerunt pagani in insula, que uocatur Sceapege,³ quod interpretatur insula ouium, que sita est in Tamesi flumine inter Eassæxum et Cantuarios, sed ad*ᵇ* Cantiam propior est quam Eassæxum, in qua monasterium optimum constructum est.⁴ Eodem quoque anno magnus paganorum exercitus cum trecentis quinquaginta nauibus in ostium Tamesis fluminis uenit et Doruberniam, id est Cantuuariorum ciuitatem, *ᶜet Lundoniam,*ᶜ⁵ que est sita in aquilonali*ᵈ* ripa Tamesis fluminis, in confinio Eastsæxum et Middelsæxum, sed tamen ad Eastsæxum illa ciuitas cum ueritate pertinet,*ᵉ* depopulati sunt, et Beorhtuulfum, Merciorum regem, cum omni exercitu suo, qui ad proeliandum contra illos uenerat, in fugam uerterunt.⁶ His ibi*ᶠ* ita gestis, idem*ᵍ* paganorum exercitus perrexit in Suðregiam,*ʰ* que paga sita est in meridiana Tamesis fluminis ripa ab occidentali parte Cantie. Et Apeluulfus*ⁱ* Wessaxonum*ʲ* rex, et filius suus Æþelbaldus cum omni exercitu in loco qui dicitur Aclea, id est in campulo quercus, diutissime pugnauerunt, ibique cum diu acerrime et animose ex utraque parte pugnatum esset, maxima pars pagane multitudinis funditus delata et occisa est, ita qualiter nunquam in aliqua regione in una die, ante nec post, ex eis occis⟨a⟩m*ᵏ* esse audiuimus, et Christiani uictoriam honorifice tenuerunt et loc⟨o⟩*ˡ* funeris dominati sunt.⁷ Eodem quoque anno Apelstan rex,*ᵐ* et Ealhere comes magnum

---

ᵃ⁻ᵃ Defuncto . . . successit] *add. in blank annal* C³, *om.* HL   ᵇ et HL
ᶜ⁻ᶜ et Lundoniam] (*As*) *Au Aw ASN, om. Ac Acott (teste Aw) Ao*   ᵈ aquilonali *Ac ASN,* aquilonari (*As*) *Aw Ao Au*   ᵉ fregerunt *interlin.* B⁵   ᶠ itaque *interlin. over deleted* ibi B⁵   ᵍ id est B, predictus *As ASN*   ʰ Suthrie (*As*) *Ac Au,* Suthriae *Aw,* Suthrye *Ao,* Suthrigie (*second* i *interlin.*) *ASN*   ⁱ *over erasure* C
ʲ Westsaxonum *HP,* Westsaxonum *L,* Occidentalium (⟨Occidentalium⟩ *As*) Saxonum (*As*) *Aw Ao Au ASN,* Saxonum *Ac Acott (teste Aw) HR* i. 66 (ii. 70)
ᵏ occisum *JW Ac Ao,* occisam (*As*) *Au Aw ASN*   ˡ loci *JW Ac ASN,* loco (*As*) *Aw Ao Au HR* i. 66 (ii. 70)   ᵐ rex *Ac Acott (teste Aw) Ao Au, om.* (*As*), rex filius Æthelwulfi regis *Aw,* rex filius Adheluulfi regis *ASN,* Cantuariorum *interlin.* B⁵

[850]   On the death of Wernberht,
                                    bishop of Leicester, Ræthhun
                                    succeeded.[1]

[851] Queen Ermengard, wife of Lothar, died, leaving him three
sons, Lothar, Louis, and Charles.[2]

Ceorl, ealdorman of Devon, with the men of Devon fought
against the heathen in a place called *Wicganbeorg*, and the
Christians were victorious. Also in that same year the heathen
wintered for the first time on the island which is called Sheppey[3]
(which means the island of the sheep), situated in the river
Thames between Essex and the men of Kent, but it is closer to
Kent than to Essex, and on it a splendid monastery has been
built.[4] Also in the same year a great heathen army with 350 ships
came into the mouth of the river Thames, and ravaged
Canterbury, the city of the men of Kent, and London[5] (which is
situated on the north bank of the river Thames on the borders
between Essex and Middlesex, though that city belongs really to
Essex), and they put to flight Berhtwulf, king of the Mercians,
with his whole army when he came to do battle with them.[6] After
these events, the heathen army advanced into Surrey, an area lying
on the south bank of the river Thames to the west of Kent.
Æthelwulf, king of the West Saxons, and his son Æthelbald
fought for a very long time with their whole army at a place called
Aclea (that is the field of the oak), and there the battle was fiercely
contested for a long time by both sides most fiercely and energetically; the greatest part of the heathen host was totally destroyed
and slain—so many that never have we heard of such a slaughter
made of them, before or since, in any region on a single day. The
Christians gained the victory with honour, and were masters of
the place of death.[7] Also in the same year King Æthelstan and the

---

[1] Ræthhun's presence at the synod of Chelsea of 816 demonstrates that he had succeeded Wernberht as bishop of Leicester much earlier (see O'Donovan, i. 43).
[2] Mar.
[3] Æthelweard (*The Chronicle of Æthelweard*, ed. A. Campbell (NMT, 1962) p. 32)
gives Sheppey, and ASC BC (853) DE (851) give Thanet as the place where the Danes
wintered.
[4] Asser, c. 3.
[5] London is not mentioned in the MS tradition of Asser. Its presence in both JW
and *ASN* might be evidence of a text not corrupted at this point; it could equally well
have been supplied from the context, or, a less likely possibility, borrowed from ASC
ABC.   [6] Asser, c. 4.   [7] Id., c. 5.

paganorum exercitum in Cantia, in loco, qui dicitur Sandwic, occiderunt, et ex nauibus eorum .ix. naues ceperunt,ᵃ ceteri per fugam elapsi sunt.[1]

[852] (xii) 874   Rex Merciorum Beorhtuulfus uita decessit, cui in regnum Burhredus successit.[2]

[853] (xiii) 875   *Leo*[3] *papa centesimus secundus post Petrum.*[4]

*Burhred*us, *rex Merciorum, per nuntios deprecatus est Apeluulfum, Occidentalium Saxonum regem, ut ei auxilium conferret, quo mediterraneos Brytones, qui inter Merciam et mare occidentale habitant, dominio suo subdere potuisset, qui contra eum immodice reluctabantur. Nec segnius Apeluulfus rex, legatione eius accepta, exercitum mouens, Brytanniam cum Burhredo rege adiit, statimque ut ingreditur gentem illam deuastans, dominio Burhredi subdit. Quo facto, domum reuertitur.*[5] *Eodem anno Apeluulfus rex prefatum filium suum Ælfredum, magno nobilium et etiam ignobilium numero constipatum, honorifice Romam transmisit. ᵇQuem Leo papa,ᵇ sui patris rogatu, oppido ordinans unxit in regem, et in filium adoptionis sibimet accipiens confirmauit.*[6] *Eodem quoque anno Ealhere comes cum Cantuariis, et Huda cum Suðregiis,ᶜ contra paganorum exercitum in insula, que Saxoniceᵈ dicitur Tenet, Britanniceᵉ Ruim, animose et acriter belligerauerunt, et primitus Christiani uictoriam habuerunt, prolongatoque diu prelio, ibidem ex utraque parte plurimi* occiderunt,ᶠ *et in aquam*ᵍ *mersi suffocati sunt: et comites illi ambo ibidem occubuerunt. Necnon et eodem anno rex Occidentalium Saxonum Apeluulfus post Pasca filiam suam*ʰ *Burhredo Merciorum regi, in uilla regia que dicitur Cippanham, nuptiis regaliter factis, ad reginam dedit.*[7]

ᵃ ceperunt (*As*) *Aw Ao Au ASN*, acceperunt *Ac Acott (teste Aw)*   ᵇ⁻ᵇ Quem Leo papa] Quo tempore dominus (dompnus *ASN*) Leo papa quartus (*om. Ac Acott (teste Aw)*) (*As*) *ASN*   ᶜ Suthriis (*As*) *Ac Aw Au ASN*, Suthreis *Ao*, Suthrigiis *HR i. 67* (*ii. 71*)   ᵈ in (*om. Ao*) Saxonica lingua (*As*), *om. ASN*   ᵉ Brittanico autem sermone *As*, *om. ASN*   ᶠ occiderunt *Ac*, ceciderunt (*As*) *Aw Ao Au ASN*   ᵍ aqua *As ASN*   ʰ Æthelswitham *mg. with signe de renvoi B*[5]

ealdorman Ealhhere slew a great heathen army in Kent, in the place called Sandwich, and captured nine of their ships; the rest escaped by flight.[1]

[852] Berhtwulf, king of the Mercians, departed this life. Burgred succeeded him in the kingdom.[2]

[853] Leo[3] was the 102nd pope after Peter.[4]

Burgred, king of the Mercians, through his envoys, besought Æthelwulf, king of the West Saxons, to help him subdue to his rule the inland Welsh who live between Mercia and the western sea, and who were resisting him very strongly. King Æthelwulf received his embassy, and mobilized his army rapidly. He approached Wales with King Burgred, and, as soon as he invaded it, ravaged that people, subduing them to Burgred's lordship. When that was done he returned home.[5] In the same year King Æthelwulf sent his son, the Alfred mentioned before, to Rome with pomp, accompanied by a large number of noble and common people. Pope Leo, at his father's request, arranged matters properly, anointed him king, and, receiving him himself as his godson, confirmed him.[6] Also in the same year, the ealdorman Ealhhere with the men of Kent and Huda, with those of Surrey, fought a spirited and fierce battle against the heathen army on the island which the Saxons call Thanet, the Britons *Ruim*, and at first the Christians were victorious. When the battle had lasted a long time many men fell on both sides, and, falling in the water, drowned. Both those ealdormen fell there. In the same year too, after Easter, Æthelwulf, king of the West Saxons, gave his daughter to Burgred, king of the Mercians, as queen, and the marriage ceremony was regally performed at the royal township which is called Chippenham.[7]

---

[1] Id., c. 6.

[2] The death of Berhtwulf and the succession of Burgred are not recorded elsewhere. ASC shows that Berhtwulf was alive in 851, and the succession of Burgred in 852 is attested, as Plummer (*Chronicle*, ii. 78) pointed out, by two charters (*S* 210 *BCS* 509 and *S* 214 *BCS* 524). The statement in JW *Mercian Accounts* 23 that Berhtwulf died in the 13th year of his reign cannot be reconciled with the record of his accession under JW 838.

[3] Leo IV 847–55.   [4] Mar.   [5] Asser, c. 7.   [6] Id., c. 8.
[7] Id., c. 9.

[854] (xiiii) 876 ᵃDefuncto Eanberto Lindisfarnensi episcopo, Eardulfus successit.ᵃ¹ |

p. 287

[855] (xv) 877 *Ciclus .xviii. decennouenalis incipit indictione .iii. Rabanus episcopus obiit. Karolus ei successit.* Lotharius imperator, con- uocatis primoribus regni, imperium inter filios suos diuisit. Ludouuico quidem Italiam tradidit eumque in imperatorem nomine suo appellari fecit. Lothario uero regnum quod ex suo nomine uocatum est concessit. Karolo autem iuniori Hessorum prouinciam mandauit. Qui ita dispo- nens seculum reliquit et in Prumia monasterioᵇ ueniens postquam habi- tum sancte conuersationis monachorum suscepit eodem anno .iii. kalend. Octobris obiit.²

³*Magnus paganorum exercitus tota hieme in prefata Sceapege insula hiemauerunt.*⁴ Eodem anno Apeluulfus rex decimam totius regni sui partem ab omni regali seruitio et tributo liberauit, et *in sempiterno grafio in cruce Christi, pro redemptione anime sue et antecessorum suo- rum, uni et trino Deo immolauit. Sicque magno cum honore Romam perrexit, filium*que *suum Ælfredum quem plus ceteris dilexit,ᶜ iterum in eandem uiam secum ducens, ibi anno integro remoratus est. Quo per- acto, ad patriam suam remeauit, afferens secum Iuðittam, Karoli, Francorum regis, filiam.*⁵ Interea tamen, Aðeluulfoᵈ rege ultra mare tantillo tempore immorante, quedam infamia contra morem omnium Christianorum in occidentali parte Selwudeᵉ orta est. Nam Æþelbald rex, et Ealhstan, Scireburnensis ecclesie episcopus, Eanwulf quoque Sumurtunensis page comes, coniurasse referuntur, ne unquam Apeluulf rex, a Roma reuertens, iterum in regno reciperetur. Quod inauditum omnibus seculis ante infortunium, episcopo et comiti solummodo per- plurimi reputant, ex quorum consilio hoc factum esse perhibetur. Multi quoque regaliᶠ solummodo insolentie deputant, quia et ille rex in hac re et in multis aliis peruersitatibus pertinax fuit, sicut quorundam hominum relatu audiuimus, quod et rei sequentis approbauit effectus. Nam redeunte eo a Roma, predictus filius regis Apeluulfi, cum omnibus

---

ᵃ⁻ᵃ Defuncto . . . successit] add. in blank annal C²   ᵇ monasteria HL
ᶜ diligebat As ASN   ᵈ Athulfo HL   ᵉ Selwuda As, Salouuda ASN
ᶠ Æthelbaldi add. mg. B⁵

---

¹ The succession of Eardwulf at Lindisfarne in 854 is recorded in *HR* i. 67 (ii. 71), in its later section, iii. 89 (ii. 101), and in *HDE* ii. 5. (i. 53). This entry was probably based (like C²'s other additions) on *HDE*.
² *Mar.*

[854] On the death of Eanberht, bishop of Lindisfarne, Eardwulf succeeded.[1]

[855] The eighteenth cycle of nineteen years begins in the third indiction. Bishop Hrabanus died. Charles succeeded him. The Emperor Lothar, having summoned the magnates of his realm, divided his empire among his sons. He gave Italy to Louis, and caused him to be called emperor in his own name. To Lothar he ceded the kingdom named after the emperor. To the younger Charles he gave the province of Hesse. When he had made these arrangements, he abandoned the world, and went to the monastery in Prüm; after receiving the habit of the holy monastic life, he died on 29 September in the same year.[2]

[3]The great heathen army passed the whole winter on the isle of Sheppey mentioned above.[4] In the same year King Æthelwulf released a tenth part of his whole kingdom from all royal service and tribute, and offered it to the Triune God as a perpetual gift signed with the cross of Christ, for the redemption of his soul and those of his predecessors. And so he went to Rome in great state and stayed a whole year there, taking again with him on that same journey his son Alfred, whom he loved more than any other son. When that mission was completed, he returned to his own country, taking with him Judith, daughter of Charles, king of the Franks.[5] Meanwhile, during King Æthelwulf's short stay abroad, a certain scandal, contrary to the practice of all Christians, occurred in the western part of Selwood. For King Æthelbald and Ealhstan, bishop of Sherborne, and also Eanwulf, ealdorman of Somerset, are said to have plotted that King Æthelwulf, on his return from Rome, should never be received again in his kingdom. This unfortunate matter, unheard-of in all previous times, is very widely blamed on the bishop and the ealdorman alone, on whose advice it was said to have been done. Many also hold royal arrogance alone responsible because that king was unyielding in this matter and in many other wrongful acts, as we have heard from the accounts of certain men, which the outcome of the following episode showed. On King Æthelwulf's return from Rome, his aforementioned son

---

[3] The events in this annal cover the period 855-8, if the flashback to Eadburg is excluded. In this, the example of ASC A-E and of Asser is followed, where the events of three years are grouped under 855 (ASC CF 856).
[4] Asser, c. 10.   [5] Id., c. 11.

suis consiliariis, immo insiliariis,*[a]*[1] *tantum facinus perpetrare* temptati
*sunt, ut regem a regno proprio repellerent: quod nec Deus ita fieri per-
misit, nec nobiles totius Saxonie consenserunt. Nam, ne irremedicabile,[b]
Saxonie periculum, belligerante patre et filio, quin immo tota cum
gente ambobus rebellante, atrocius et crudelius per dies singulos quasi
clades intestina augeretur, ineffabili patris clementia, omnium*que *astip-
ulatione nobilium, adunatum antea regnum inter patrem et filium
diuiditur, et orientales plage[c] patri, occidentales filio e contrario dep-
utantur. Vbi enim pater iusto iudicio regnare debuerat, illic iniquus et
pertinax filius regnabat, nam occidentalis pars Saxonie semper orientali
principalior est.*[2] *Adueniente igitur Atheluulfo rege a Roma, tota illa
gens, ut dignum erat, in aduentu senioris ita gauisa est, ut, si ille permitteret, pertinacem filium suum Apelbaldum cum omnibus suis consiliariis a totius regni sorte expellere uellent. Sed ille, ut diximus, nimia
clementia et prudenti consilio usus, ne, ad regni periculum perueniret,
ita fieri noluit: et Iuðittam Karoli regis filiam, quam a patre suo
acceperat, iuxta se in regali solio, sine aliqua suorum nobilium controuersia et odio, usque ad obitum uite sue, contra peruersam illius gentis consuetudinem, sedere imperauit. Gens nanque Occidentalium
Saxonum reginam iuxta regem sedere non patitur, nec etiam reginam
appellare,[d] sed regis coniugem, permittit.* [e]*Que controuersia, immo
infamia,[e] de quadam pertinaci et maliuola eiusdem gentis regina* [f]*orta
est,*[f] [g]maioribus nostris sic attestantibus.[g][3] *Fuit in Mercia moderno
tempore quidam strenuus rex, nomine Offa, cuius filiam, nomine
Eadburh, Brihtric, Occidentalium Saxonum rex* [h]ut prediximus,[h] *sibi
in coniugium accepit. Que mox*[i] *tyrannice uiuere, omnia odibilia Deo
et hominibus facere, quos posset ad regem accusare, et* sic[j] *uita aut
potestate per insidias priuare.* [k]*Et si a rege illud non posset impetrare,
ueneno eos* [l]coepit necare.[kl] *Hoc factum de adolescente quodam regi
dilectissimo habetur compertum, quem cum ad regem accusare non*

---

[a] insiliariis *ASN,* insidiariis *As*   [b] irremediabile *HL,* inremediabile *ASN,*
irremedicabile *As*   [c] uel page *interlin. B*   [d] appellare *Ac Aw Ao Au ASN,*
appellari *(As)*   [e-e] Que . . . infamia] quam controuersiam immo infamiam *As ASN*
[f-f] orta est] ortam fuisse *As ASN*   [g-g] maioribus . . . attestantibus] maiores illius
terræ perhibent *As,* maiores *ASN*   [h-h] ut prediximus *interlin.* C[1]   [i] confestim
As ASN   [j] ita aut *As,* ita ut aut *ASN*   [k-k] Et si . . . necacare] *written over
erasure and running into mg.* C[1]   [l-l] necabat *Aw Ao Au (As) ASN,* necabant *Ac*

---

[1] The reading 'insiliariis' (as in *ASN*) rather than 'insidiariis' could be the result of a
play on words.

with all his counsellors, or rather false advisers,[1] tried to perpetrate so great a crime as to drive out the king from his own realm, which God did not allow to be done and to which the nobles of all the Saxon realm did not agree. For, lest the danger to the Saxon land be irremediable with father and son warring—indeed, with the whole people in arms on both sides—the internecine strife should grow more wicked and cruel with every day, by the ineffable forbearance of the father and with the agreement of the nobles, the formerly united kingdom was divided between father and son; the eastern areas were allotted to the father, the western, to the son. For where the father should have ruled by just law, there the wicked and obdurate son ruled, for the western part of the Saxon land always took precedence over the eastern.[2] Therefore, with the arrival of King Æthelwulf from Rome his whole people, as was fitting, so rejoiced in the arrival of the elder king that, if he allowed, they were willing to drive out his obdurate son Æthelbald with all his counsellors from a share of the whole kingdom; but he, as we have said, with great clemency and by following prudent counsel, lest any danger should befall the kingdom, was not willing that this should be done. He ordered that Judith, the daughter of King Charles whom he had received from his father, should sit beside him on the royal throne until the end of his life, without any disagreement or ill-feeling on the part of his nobles, contrary to the wrongful customs of that people. For the West Saxons do not permit the queen to sit next to the king, or even allow her to be called the queen but only the king's wife. This dispute, indeed disgrace, began, on the testimony of our elders, with a certain obdurate and wicked queen of that same people.[3] In recent times there was in Mercia a certain vigorous king called Offa whose daughter, Eadburg by name, Brihtric, king of the West Saxons, as we have already said, took to wife. She soon began to behave tyrannically, to perpetrate all that was hateful to God and man, to denounce before the king whomever she could, and thus deprive them of life or authority by her plots, and if she could not carry this out through the king, she took to killing them with poison. That she did this became known in connection with a certain young man most dear to the king. Since she could not accuse him to the king, she killed him with poison. The

<hr>

[2] Asser, c. 12.   [3] Id., c. 13.

posset, ueneno eum necauit. De quo ueneno etiam prefatus rex Brihtric inscienter gustasse aliquid refertur, neque enim illa uenenum dare regi proposuerat sed puero, sed rex preoccupauit, inde ambo periere.[1] *Pro huiusmodi*[a] *regine malitia omnes accole illius terre coniurauerunt, ut nullum unquam regem super se regnare permitterent, qui reginam in regali solio iuxta se sedere imperare uellet.*[2] *Defuncto igitur Brihtrico rege, cum* regina[b] *inter Saxones diutius* esse[c] *non posset, ultra mare nauigans, cum innumerabilibus thesauris, Karolum illum*

p. 288 *famos⟨iss⟩imum*[d] | *Francorum regem, adiit. Ad quam, cum ante solarium multa regi* offerens[e] *dona staret, Karolus ait: 'Elige, Eadburh, quem uelis, me* aut *filium meum qui in isto solario stat mecum.' At illa, sine deliberatione stulte respondens ait: 'Si mihi electio conceditur, filium tuum in quantum te iunior est eligo.' Carolus* illi *respondens et* subridens[f] *ait: 'Si me eligeres, filium meum haberes, sed quia filium meum elegisti, nec me nec illum habebis.' Dedit* ei[g] *tamen unum magnum sanctimonialium monasterium in quo, deposito seculari*[h] *habitu, et sanctimonialium sumpto*[i] *indumento, perpaucis annis abbatisse fungebatur officio. Nam a* [j]*quodam* laico[j] *constuprata,*[k] *eiectaque*[l] *de monasterio, Karoli regis imperio, in paupertate et miseria loeto tenus uitam duxit.*[3] *Vixit ergo Apeluulfus rex duobus annis postquam* [m]*Roma* rediit,[m] *in quibus, inter alia multa presentis uite bona studia, cogitans de suo ad uniuersitatis uiam transitu, ne sui filii post patris obitum indebite inter se disceptarent, hereditariam scribere*[n] *imperauit epistolam, in qua et regni inter filios* [o]*Æðelbaldum et Æthelberhtum,*[o] *et proprie hereditatis inter filios et filiam et etiam propinquos, pecuniarum, que post se superessent, inter animam et filios et etiam nobiles suos, diuisionem ordinabiliter litteris mandare*[p] *procurauit. Pro utilitate nanque anime sue, quam a primeuo iuuentutis sue flore in omnibus procurare studuit, per omnem hereditariam terram suam semper in .x. manentibus unum pauperem, aut indigenam aut peregrinum, cibo, potu, uestimento, successoribus suis usque ad ultimum*[q] *diem iudicii post se pascere precepit: ita tamen, si illa terra hominibus et pecoribus*

---

[a] nimia namque illius *As ASN*   [b] illa *As ASN*   [c] fieri *Ac Aw Au (As) ASN,* fiere *Ao*   [d] famossimum *C*   [e] afferens *Ac Aw Ao (As) ASN,* adferens *Au*   [f] arridens *As ASN*   [g] illi *As ASN*   [h] secularis *HL*   [i] assumpto *As ASN*   [j-j] quodam laico] quodam suae propriae gentis homine *As ASN*   [k] constuprata *from* construpratra *C*   [l] que *interl.* *C*[1], deiecta *As ASN*   [m-m] Roma rediit] a Roma rediit *HL,* a Roma peruenit *As,* a Roma uenit *ASN*   [n] scribere *Ac Aw Ao Au ASN,* scribi *(As)*   [o-o] Æthelbaldum et Æthelberhtum] duos (duobus *Ac*) scilicet seniores *As ASN*   [p] mandare *Ac Ao Au ASN,* mandari *Aw (As)*   [q] ultimum *Ac Ao Au Aw ASN* ultimam *(As)*

aforesaid Brihtric is said to have tasted some of this poison unwittingly. The queen had not intended to give the poison to the king but to the youth, but the king took some first, whence they both died.[1] All the inhabitants of that country made a law, on account of the queen's evil deeds, that they would never allow any king to reign over them who wished to order the queen to sit next to him on the royal throne.[2] Therefore, on the death of King Brihtric, since the queen could no longer stay among the Saxons, she sailed across the sea with innumerable treasures and went to that most renowned king of the Franks, Charles. Charles said to her as she stood before the throne offering many gifts to the king: 'Choose, Eadburg, whom you want, me or my son who stands with me on this throne.' She, replying foolishly and without thought, said: 'If the choice is given to me I choose your son because he is younger than you.' Charles, smiling, said to her in reply: 'If you chose me you would have had my son, but, as you have chosen my son, you will have neither me nor him.' He gave her a great convent of nuns in which, after laying aside her secular garb, and taking the habit of the nuns, she performed the office of abbess for a very few years; for, debauched by some layman, she was expelled out of the monastery on King Charles's orders, and passed her life in poverty and distress until her death.[3] King Æthelwulf lived two years after his return from Rome, during which, among his many other meritorious concerns for the present life, considering his own departure after the way of all flesh, lest his sons after their father's death should dispute among themselves, he ordered that a testamentary letter be drawn up in which he took care to have set down in writing in due form the division of the kingdom between his sons, Æthelbald and Æthelberht, and of his own inheritance among his sons and daughter and also his kinsmen, and of the money which should remain after his death between his soul and his sons and also his nobles. For the welfare of his own soul, for which he had shown concern in all matters from the first flower of his youth, he ordered that from every ten hides throughout his inheritance one poor man, whether native or foreign, should be provided with food, drink, and clothing by his successors after him in perpetuity until the day of judgement, with

---

[1] Id., c. 14.   [2] Id., c. 13.   [3] Id., c. 15.

*habitaretur et deserta non esset. Rome quoque omni anno .ccc. man-
cusas denariorum portare precepit, que taliter ibi diuiderentur; scilicet
centum mancusas in honore^a sancti Petri, specialiter ad emendum
oleum, quo impleantur omnia luminaria illius apostolice ecclesie in uespera Pasce et equaliter in galli cantu, et .c. mancusas in honore^a sancti
Pauli apostoli, ^b eadem de causa,^b .c. quoque mancusas uniuersali pape
apostolico.*[1] *Defuncto autem illo ^c idibus Ianuarii^{c2} et apud
Wintoniam sepulto,*[3] *Æthelbald, filius eius, contra Dei interdictum et
Christianorum dignitatem, necnon et contra omnium paganorum consuetudinem, thorum patris sui ascendens, Iuðittam, Karoli Francorum
regis filiam, in matrimonium duxit, effrenisque duobus ac^d dimidio
annis Occidentalium Saxonum post patrem regni gubernacula
rexit.*[4] *Sanctissimus Deoque acceptus Ædmundus, ex antiquorum
Saxonum prosapia oriundus, fidei Christiane cultor ueracissimus,
omnibus blando eloquio affabilis, humilitatis gratia praecluis, egentibus
liberaliter dapsilis, pater clementissimus pupillis et uiduis, Eastengle
prouincie nactus est culmen regiminis.^{e5}*

^f Romanorum octogesimus primus Ludouuicus[6] *qui et Lotharius regnauit annis quindecim.*[7]

[857] (ii) 879

[C³BP]
^g Defuncto Ceadda Herefordensi
episcopo, Alderhtus successit.^{g8}

[858] (iii) 880   *Benedictus*[9] *centesimus tertius post Petrum.*[10]

    ^a honore *Ac Ao ASN JW note (vi) alongside West Saxon Gen,* honorem *Aw Au (As)
HR i. 68, (ii. 72; before* sancti Pauli *only)*   ^{b-b} eadem de causa] *JW note (vi)
alongside West Saxon Gen.,* eadem condicione *As ASN*   ^{c-c} idibus Ianuarii] *interlin.*
C¹H¹B¹, idibus Iunii *L*   ^d et *As ASN*   ^e *see App. B for addition and for separate annal for 856 B*   ^f capitula .lxxxi. *add. here L*   ^{g-g} Defuncto . . . succes-
sit] *add. in blank annal C³, om. HL*

_____

¹ Id., c. 16.
² The day of Æthelwulf's death, 13 Jan., is not recorded elsewhere. He married
Judith on 1 Oct. 856 (*Les Annales de Saint-Bertin*, ed. F. Grat, J. Viellard, and S.
Clemencet with introd. by L. Levillain (Paris, 1964), p. 73), and, after his return to
England, lived for 1 year according to Æthelweard, for 2 according to ASC and Asser
(c. 16). The *Annales Bertiniani* assign his death to 858; this date might with some
difficulty be reconciled (i) with Æthelweard's 1-year interval after his return to
England, (ii) with Asser's statement (c. 17) that Æthelbald, who died in 860 (c. 18),
reigned 2½ years after his father's death, and (iii) with S 328 BCS 496, which shows
Æthelbert, Æthelwulf's son and successor in Kent, as king in that kingdom in 858. S

this proviso, that the land should be occupied by men and beasts, and not be waste. Also, he ordered that each year 300 mancuses be taken to Rome, which should be divided thus: 100 mancuses in honour of St Peter, especially for the purchase of the oil with which all the lamps in that apostolic church might be filled on Easter Eve and likewise at cock-crow, and 100 mancuses in honour of St Paul the Apostle for the same purpose, and 100 mancuses for the universal apostolic pope.[1] He died on 13 January[2] and was buried at Winchester.[3] His son Æthelbald, in defiance of God's prohibition and Christian dignity, and even against all pagan custom, climbed into his father's wedding-bed, married Judith, daughter of Charles, king of the Franks, and held the government of the kingdom of the West Saxons without restraint for two and a half years after his father's death.[4] The most holy Edmund, accepted of God, born of the line of the ancient Saxons, the truest worshipper of the Christian faith, courteous to all with his pleasing speech, an outstanding example of the grace of humility, a generous entertainer of the needy, a most merciful protector of widows and orphans, rose to the pinnacle of government in the kingdom of the East Angles.[5]

Louis,[6] also known as Lothar, the eighty-first emperor of the Romans, reigned fifteen years.[7]

[857]   On the death of Headda, bishop of Hereford, Aldberht succeeded.[8]

[858] Benedict[9] was the 103rd pope after Peter.[10]

1196 BCS 497, however, might suggest that Æthelwulf was king in 859, and 13 Jan. 859 is a possible date for his death.
  [3] Winchester is the burial-place in ASC, in contrast to ASN, which gives Steyning.
  [4] Asser, c. 17.
  [5] Abbo of Fleury, Passio Sancti Eadmundi, cc. 3–4, Winterbottom, Lives, pp. 70, 71. Abbo does not date Edmund's accession, which is given as 855 in ASN. His death, recorded in ASC under 870 (as in JW), is said to have occurred in the 16th year of his reign in JW East Anglian Accounts 15, and in WM, GR i. 97 (i. 98).
  [6] Louis II emperor 855–75. Marianus confuses the Emperor Louis II with his brother King Lothar II of Lotharingia, who died in 869.
  [7] Mar.
  [8] This entry is misplaced since Headda and Aldberht were successive bishops of Hereford c. 755–90.
  [9] Benedict III 855–8.   [10] Mar.

[859] (iii) 881

[C³BP]

*ᵃDefuncto Oithelwaldo Licet-
feldensi pontifice, successit
Hunberhtus.ᵃ¹*

[860] (iiii) 882   *Meginradus heremita martyrizatur.²*

*ᵇRex Æthelbaldus defunctus estᵇ et in Scireburnan sepultus, et
Æðelberht, frater suus, Cantiam, Suðregiam, Suðseaxam quoque suo
dominio, ut iustum erat, subiunxit: in cuius diebus magnus paganorum
exercitus de mari adueniens, Wintoniam ciuitatem hostiliter inuadens
depopulatus est. Cui, cum ad naues cum ingenti preda reuerterentur,
Osric, Hamtunensium comes cum suis, et Atheluulf comes cum
Bearrocensibus, uiriliter obuiauerunt consertoque prelio pagani passim
trucidantur, et, cum diutius resistere non possent muliebriter fugam
arripiunt et Christiani loco funeris dominati sunt.³ Æthelberht itaque,
.v. annis regno pacifice et amabiliter atque honorabiliter gubernato,
cum magno suorum dolore uiam uniuersitatis adiit, et in Scireburnan
iuxta fratrem suum honorificeᶜ sepultus requiescit.⁴*

[C³BP]

*ᵈDefuncto Rethuno Legerecensiᵉ
episcopo, successit Aldredus.ᵈ⁵*

[861] (vi) 883   *Hatto abbas Fuldensis obiit. Thiodo post eum succes-
sit.⁶*

[862] (vii) 884   *ᶠSanctus transiuit Suuithunus et astra petiuit,*
                    [C³B]
indictione .x., .vi. nonis Iulii   Hic *margarita die ferme .c. annis*
feria .v.⁷   *latebat ingloria* cui in episcopatu

ᵃ⁻ᵃ Defuncto . . . Hunberhtus] *add. in blank annal* C³, *om.* HL   ᵇ⁻ᵇ Rex . . .
defunctus est] Æthelbald (Adhelbaldus *ASN*) Occidentalium Saxonum rex defunctus
est ⟨⟨rex defunctus est⟩ *(As)*⟩ A*w* Au *(As) ASN*, Aethelbald (Ethelbald *HR*) defunctus
est A*c* Ao *HR* i. *68 (ii. 72)*, Æthelbald A*cott (teste* A*w)*   ᶜ honorabiliter As *ASN*
ᵈ⁻ᵈ Defuncto . . . Aldredus] *add. at end of annal* C³, *om.* HL   ᵉ Legecestre *from*
Legerensi B   ᶠ Sanctus . . . Dunberhtus *(p. 278)] written over erasure* C³.

---

¹ This entry is misplaced, since Bishop Æthelwald's death is recorded in ASC under
828 (*recte* 830) and Hunberht must have succeeded soon afterwards.
² Mar.   ³ Asser, c. 18.   ⁴ Id, c. 19.
⁵ This entry is incorrect since Ealdred's successor Ceolred was certainly in office *c.*

[859]   On the death of Æthelwald,
                                          bishop of Lichfield, Hunberht
                                          succeeded.[1]

[860] Meginrad the hermit was martyred.[2]

   King Æthelbald died, and was buried at Sherborne and
Æthelberht his brother, as was right, added Kent, Surrey, and
Sussex also to his own kingdom. In his days a great heathen army,
arriving from the sea, attacked the city of Winchester, and laid it
waste. As they were returning to their ships with great booty,
Osric, ealdorman of Hampshire, with his men, and the ealdorman
Æthelwulf, with the men of Berkshire, waylaid them manfully;
battle was joined, and the heathen were cut down on all sides.
When they could no longer resist they womanishly took flight, and
the Christians were masters of the place of death.[3] And so
Æthelberht, when he had governed the realm in peace, affection,
and honour for five years, went the way of all flesh, to the great
grief of his people; he lies in an honourable tomb at Sherborne
beside his brother.[4]

                                          On the death of Ræthhun,
                                          bishop of Leicester, Ealdred
                                          succeeded.[5]

[861] Hatto, abbot of Fulda, died. Thiodo succeeded him.[6]

[862] St Swithhun passed away and sought the stars,
in   the   tenth   indiction,   Here the pearl lay ingloriously
Thursday, 2 July.[7]   concealed from the day for

843–4 (O'Donovan, i. 44–5). JW *Epis. Lists* say that Ceolred was bishop in the time of
Kings Alfred and Burgred.
   [6] Mar.
   [7] 2 July is the day given in the 9th-c. calendar Oxford, Bodl. MS Digby 63 (*English
Kalendars before A.D. 1100*, ed. F. Wormald (Henry Bradshaw Society, lxxii, London,
1934), i. 8) and Thursday is the right day of the week for 862 (O'Donovan, ii. 108).
JW's 862 is supported by Goscelin (E. P. Sauvage, *Analecta Bollandiana*, vii (1888),
382), though WM (in whom precise dates are rare) *GP* ii. 75 (p. 162), and *HR* iii. 91
(ii. 104), apparently deviating from its source (JW) give 863 and ASC F gives 861.
The latest possible charters attested by Swithhun are dated 862 (*S* 335 *BCS* 504, a
land-grant in Berkshire) and 863 (*S* 336 *BCS* 508, a land grant in Wiltshire). They
were issued by Æthelred as king (of the West Saxons). He succeeded Æthelbald as
king in 865, and the assumption that he was underking of the western area in his
brother's lifetime must be made if the charters are regarded as genuine.

successerunt   *Alfrithus,*   *Dun-*
bertus.[a1]

[863] (viii) 885
[b]Karolus ⟨Moguntinus⟩[c] episcopus
obiit. Liutbertus [d]post eum[d] suc-
cessit. Sanctus Nicolaus[2] papa
.ciiii.[b3]

p. 289

[864] (ix) 886 *Lotharius imperator, eo quod Thietbirgam reginam*
uxorem legitimam recusare | uellet, quam exosam habebat propter
Waldradam concubinam suam, quam cum adolescens erat, in domo
paterna nimio diligebat affectu, non parua res inde euenit. Fratres
enim regine hoc Nicolao pape Rome referunt. Vnde Nicolaus papa
Arsenium episcopum apocrisiarium suum et consiliarium uice sua in
Franciam anno isto direxit. Quo cum uenisset, conuocato episcoporum
conuentu, antequam protinus anathematis gladio feriretur, necessitate
constrictus[e] Lotharius uellet nollet, reginam in matrimonium recepit;
interposito iurisiurandi sacramento, ne eam a se separaret, neque ipsa
uiuente aliam super eam induceret. Sed postea proiecta regina, et
Waldrada pro ea inducta, sanctus papa Nicolaus in purificatione
sancte Marie Waldradam an⟨a⟩thematis[f] sententia ab omni consortio
sancte ecclesie excommunicauit.[4]

    Pagani hiemauerunt in insula Tenet, firmumque foedus cum
Cantuariis pepigerunt. Quibus Cantuarii pecuniam pro foedere seruan-
do[g] reddere promiserunt. Interea tamen, uulpino more pagani, noctu
clam castris erumpentes, [h]foedere dirupto,[i] et promissionem pecunie sper-
nentes (sciebant enim maiorem pecuniam se furtiua preda quam pace
adepturos), totam orientalem Cantie plagam depopulati sunt.[5]

---

    [a] see above, p. 276 n. f.   *[b-b] Karolus . . . ciiii.]* written in uppermost mg. presumably
indicating text to be erased C[3]   *[c] Moguntinus Mar.,* om. HLP (N)   *[d-d]* post
eum om. LP   *[e] contristus (N)*   *[f]* anethematis C   *[g]* seruato (seruuato
ASN) As ASN HR i. 69 (ii. 73)   *[h]* runs on to 865 here CHLB   *[i]* dirupto
ASN HR i. 69 (ii. 73), disrupto As

almost 100 years. Ealhferth and
Tunberht succeeded him in the
episcopate.[1]

[863] Bishop Charles of Mainz
died. Liutbert succeeded him.
St Nicholas,[2] the 104th pope.[3]

[864] There arose no small dispute on account of the Emperor
Lothar's wish to renounce his lawful wife, Queen Theuberga,
whom he considered hateful on account of his love for his mistress
Waldrada, with whom he had been besotted as a youth in his
father's house. The queen's brothers informed Pope Nicholas of it.
And so Pope Nicholas sent Bishop Arsenius, his *apocrisarius* and
counsellor, as his deputy, to Francia that year. When Arsenius had
arrived he summoned a synod of bishops and Lothar, before he
might be struck with the sword of anathema, was forced, whether
he wished it or not, to take back the queen as his wife after swearing an oath that he would not part from her during her lifetime,
nor bring in another woman in addition to her; but afterwards, he
drove out the queen, and then installed Waldrada in her place; the
holy Pope Nicholas excommunicated Waldrada at the Purification
of St Mary with the sentence of anathema from all association
with Holy Church.[4]

The heathen wintered on the island of Thanet and made a firm
treaty with the men of Kent. The men of Kent promised to pay
money that the treaty might be kept. Meanwhile, however, the
heathen, like foxes, burst out from their camp secretly at night,
broke the treaty, and, despising the promise of money—for they
knew they would take more money by secret looting than by
peace—they ravaged the whole eastern part of Kent.[5]

---

[1] *GP* ii. 75 (p. 162).   [2] Nicholas I 858–67.   [3] Mar.
[4] Mar.
[5] Asser, c. 20. The events are recorded in ASC ADEF (865), C and possibly B
(866). The evidence of Asser suggests 864; the difference between the two might be
reconciled by the evidence that the ASC year in the second half of the 9th c. began in
the autumn (Keynes–Lapidge, *Alfred*, p. 238).

[865] (x) 887

[C³BP]

*ᵃDefuncto Hunberto Licetfeld-
ensi episcopo, successit Cine-
ferth.ᵃ¹*

[866] (xi) 888 *Æthered, regis Æthelberhti frater, Occidentalium
Saxonum regni gubernaculaᵇ suscepit. Eodem anno magna paganorum
classis de Danubia² Britanniam aduenit, et in regno Orientalium
Anglorum,ᶜ quod Saxonice Eastengle dicitur, hiemauit, ibique ille
exercitus maxima ex parte equester factus est.³*

[867] (xii) 889 *Predictus paganorum exercitus de Orientalibus Anglis
ad Eboracum ciuitatem migrauit, que in aquilonali ripa
Humbreᵈ fluminis sita est.⁴ Eo tempore maxima inter Norðanhymbros
discordia diabolico instinctu orta fuerat, sicut semper populo, qui odium
incurrerit,ᵉ euenire solet. Nam Norðanhymbri eo tempore, ut diximus,
legitimum regem suum, Osbriht nomine, regno expulerant, et tirannum
quendam, Ælla nomine, non de regali prosapia progenitum, super regni
apicem constituerant. Sed, aduenientibus paganis, consilio diuino et
optimatum adminiculo, pro communi utilitate, discordia illa aliquantulum sedata, Osbyrht et Ælla, adunatis uiribus congregatoque exercitu,
Eboracum oppidum adeunt. Quibus aduenientibus, pagani confestim
fugam arripiunt, et intra urbis moenia se defendere procurant.ᶠ Quorum
fugam et pauorem Christiani cernentes, etiam intra urbis moenia eos
persequi, et murum frangere instituunt; quod et fecerunt. Non enim
tunc adhuc illa ciuitas firmos et stabilitos muros illis temporibus
habebat. Cunque Christiani murum, ut proposuerant, fregissent,
eorumque magna pars in ciuitatem simul cum paganis intrassent,ᵍ
pagani, dolore et necessitate compulsi, super eos atrociter irrumpunt,
cedunt, fugant, prosternunt, intus et extra. Illic maxima ex parte
omnes Northanhymbrensium coetiʰ occisis duobus regibus, deleti*

ᵃ⁻ᵃ Defuncto . . . Cineferth *written mg. alongside 865* C³, *placed under 865, but after
the end of 864, which had run over well into 865* B, *om.* HL   ᵇ gubernanacula C
ᶜ Anglorum *ASN HR i. 69, (ii. 73),* Saxonum *As*   ᵈ Humbrensis *As ASN*
ᵉ incurrerit Dei *As ASN*   ᶠ procurauit *H,* procurauerunt *LP*   ᵍ second n *in*
intrassent *interlin.* C¹, intrasset *As ASN*   ʰ coeti *Ac,* coetus *Aw (As),* capti *Acott
(teste Aw) Au ASN, om.* Ao

[865]

On the death of Hunberht, bishop of Lichfield, Cyneferth succeeded.[1]

[866] Æthelred, brother of Æthelberht, king of the West Saxons, received the government of the kingdom. In the same year a great heathen fleet came to Britain from the Danube,[2] and wintered in the kingdom of the East Angles which is called East Anglia in English, and there the greater part of that army was provided with horses.[3]

[867] The aforementioned heathen army moved from East Anglia to York, which is set on the north bank of the river Humber.[4] At that time great strife had arisen among the Northumbrians at the prompting of the devil, as always happens to a people which has incurred the wrath of God. For the Northumbrians at that time, as we have said, had driven from the realm their rightful king, Osberht by name, and had set at the head of the kingdom a usurper, one Ælle by name, not born of the royal line. But with the arrival of the pagans, by divine counsel, and with the aid of the nobles, that strife was allowed to die down somewhat for the common good. Osberht and Ælle united their forces, and assembled an army, and went to the city of York. On their arrival the heathen at once fled, and attended to their defences within the walls of the city. Perceiving their flight and their fear, the Christians determined to pursue them even within the city walls, and to break down the wall, and this was done. For in those times that city did not yet have strong, fortified walls. When the Christians, as they had intended, had broken down the wall, a large part of them entered the city along with the heathen. The heathen, driven by anger and necessity, attacked them viciously, slew, routed, and overthrew them within and without the city. There the greatest part of the whole Northumbrian army was

[1] The addition is misplaced as Cyneferth's successor, Tunberht, signs in 8 Nov. 845 (S 1194 BCS 448, O'Donovan, ii. 91). JW Epis. Lists speaks of Tunberht's episcopacy during the times of Kings Alfred and Burgred.
[2] On the erroneous 'de Danubia', see Stevenson, Asser, p. 217, Keynes–Lapidge, Alfred, p. 238.
[3] Asser, c. 21.
[4] Id., c. 26.

occubuerunt. Reliqui uero, qui euaserunt, pacem cum paganis pepigerunt.[1]

[HL]

[a]Eodem anno Ealhstan episcopus Scireburnensis ecclesie uiam uniuersitatis adiens postquam episcopatum per .l. annos honorabiliter rexerat in pace in Scireburnan sepultus est.[a2] [b]Ciclus solis incipit .iiii. concurrentibus bissextilibus.[b]

[C³BP]

[c]Defecerunt reges Norðanhymbrorum.[3] Alhstanus Scireburnensis episcopus .l. sui episcopatus anno obiit et Scireburne sepelitur.[4] Illi substituti sunt Heahmundus, Æthelhegus, Alsius, Asserus, qui librum Boetii de consolatione phylosophie planioribus uerbis elucidauit et iussu regis Ælfredi in Anglicum sermonem transtulit.[c5]

[868] (xiii) 890   *Cometis uisa est manifestissime hoc anno.*[6]

Venerabilis rex Ælfredus, secundarii tamen tunc ordine fretus, uxorem de Mercia, nobilem scilicet genere, filiam Æthelredi, Gainorum comitis, qui cognominabatur Mucil, subarrauit et duxit. Cuius femine mater Eadburh nominabatur, de regali genere Merciorum regis, uenerabilis scilicet femina et[d] per multos annos post obitum patris[e] *sui castissima uidua loeto tenus permansit.*[7] *Eodem anno predictus paganorum exercitus Norðanhymbros relinquens, in Merciam uenit, et Snotingaham, adiit, quod Brytannice Tigguocobauc interpretatur, Latine autem speluncarum domus, et in* illo[f] *loco eodem anno hiemauerunt. Quibus illic aduenientibus, confestim Burhred, Merciorum rex, omnes*que *gentis eiusdem optimates nuntios ad Æthered*um, *Occidentalium Saxonum regem, et* [g]ad *fratrem eius Alfred*um[g] *dirigunt, suppliciter obsecrantes ut* sibi[h] *auxiliarentur, quo possent contra prefatum pugnare exercitum. Quod et facile impetrauerunt. Nam illi*[i]

[a-a] Eodem . . . sepultus est] *scribbled traces in uppermost mg. indicating text to be erased* C³   [b-b] Ciclus . . . bissextilibus] *found at opening of 868 P, 868 possibly starts here* HL   [c-c] Defecerunt . . . transtulit] *written partly over erasure and running into mg.* C³   [d] et Ac Aw Ao Au, ⟨quæ⟩ *(As)*   [e] uiri *As*   [f] interlin. C¹, eodem *As* [g-g] ad . . . Alfredum] ad Alfredum fratrem eius *ASN*, Ælfred fratrem *As*   [h] illi illis *As ASN*   [i] om. *HL*

---

[1] ld., c. 27.   [2] ld. c. 28.
[3] This comment on the dying-out of the line of English kings in Northumbria, absent from ASC and Asser, is also found in JW *Northum. Accounts* 28 and in the

destroyed, and fell, their two kings slain. The rest who escaped made peace with the pagans.[1]

In the same year Ealhstan, bishop of Sherborne, went the way of all flesh after he had ruled with honour for fifty years. He was buried in peace at Sherborne.[2] The solar cycle begins, with four concurrents in a bissextile year.

The kings of Northumbria came to an end.[3] Ealhstan, bishop of Sherborne, died in the fiftieth year of his episcopacy and was buried at Sherborne.[4] To his place were appointed Heahmund, Æthelheah, Alfsige (Wulfsige?), Asser, who explained Boethius' book *Of the Consolation of Philosophy* in clearer words and at King Alfred's command translated it into the English tongue.[5]

[868] A comet was seen very clearly this year.[6]

The much-admired King Alfred, then, however, holding the rank of 'heir apparent', betrothed and married a wife from Mercia, a woman of noble birth, the daughter of Æthelred, (who was named Mucil), the ealdorman of the *Gaini*. The woman's mother was called Eadburg of the royal line of the king of the Mercians, a venerable woman who for many years after the death of her father and for the rest of her life lived as a most chaste widow.[7] In the same year the aforesaid heathen army, leaving Northumbria, came to Mercia, and reached Nottingham, which is called *Tig Guocobauc* in the language of the Britons, but in Latin the house of caves, and in that place they passed the winter that year. As soon as they had arrived, Burgred, king of the Mercians, and all the magnates of that same people immediately sent messengers to Æthelred, king of the West Saxons, and to his brother Alfred, humbly imploring them for assistance so that they could fight against the aforementioned army. This they obtained easily,

---

Chronicula, fo 71ᵛ. *HR* iii. 92 (ii. 106) adds, after copying verbatim much of JW 867: 'quibus peractis predicti pagani sub suo dominio regem Egbertum prefecerunt. Egbertus uero regnauit super Northumbros ultra Tine vi annis.'

[4] This sentence may be based on Asser, c. 28, which was originally in C (see above, *n. a*).

[5] *GP* ii. 80 (p. 177). Alsige appears as Alsius in *GP* and in the JW Sherborne *Epis. Lists*. He may be Wulfsige (879×889–(890×896)×900), who appears at this point.

[6] Mar.   [7] Asser, c. 29.

fratres, non segnius promissione, congregato ex omni parte sui immenso exercitu, Merciam adeunt, et usque ad Snotingaham, bellum unanimiter querentes, perueniunt. Cunque pagani, tuitione arcis muniti, p. 290 *bellum dare negarent, et Christianis frangere | ᵃmurum non suppetebatᵇ pace inter Mercios et paganos facta, duo illi fratres, Ætheredus ᶜrex et Ælfredusᶜ, cum suis cohortibus domum reuersi sunt.*[1] Oratorium sancti Andree apostoli Kemesege constructum et dedicatum est ab Alchuno Wigornensi presule.*ᵃ*[2]

[869] (xiiii) 891   *Sanctus Nicolaus papa obiit .viii. idus Decembris.*[3]
Prefatus paganorum exercitus iterum ad Norðanhymbros equitans, Eboracamᵈ ciuitatem adiit, ibique anno integro mansit.[4]

[870] (xv) 892   *Adrianus*[5] *centesimus quintus papa. Lotharius, audita morte Nicolai pape, misit ad papam Adrianum ut cum gratia eum susciperet. Cui rescripsit, ut si se immunem ab obiectis predictis sciret, ad appetendam sancti Petri benedictionem properaret; si culpabilem ut condigna remedia penitentie susciperet,ᵉ nichilominus sine dilatione ueniret. Qui cum Romam peruenisset ab Adriano papa honorifice susceptus est. Et cum a papa interrogaretur, si precepta sancti Nicolai, immo sanctiᶠ Petri, et iusiurandum dominici corporis obseruasset, respondit se ita obseruasse omnia ac si diuinitus essent precepta, quod etiam optimates et proceres sui attestati sunt. Cui papa: 'oportet te ergo,' inquit, 'O fili carissime corpus Christi nobiscum participare ut, per hanc participationem menbris Christi unde abscissus uidebaris inseri merearis.' Papa itaque, cantata missa, hora communicationis accipiens corpus Christi manibus suis, dixit Lothario: 'si innoxius es a predictis remissio sit tibi hec communicatio; sin autem nequaquam sumere presumas ne forte ᵍad iudicium etᵍ condempnationem tibi proueniat.' Rex autem captus mente obduratus pariter et obcecatus, absque retractione*

ᵃ⁻ᵃ murum . . . presule] *darker ink suggests possibly written over erasure* C   ᵇ suppetebat *Ac Ao Au Aw ASN,* suppeteret *(As)*   ᶜ⁻ᶜ rex et Ælfredus] et Ælfred *Aw* *(between square brackets) Ao (As),* om. *Ac Au*   ᵈ Eboracam *Ac ASN,* Eboracum *Aw* *Ao Au (As)*   ᵉ om. *HL*   ᶠ beati *Mar.*   ᵍ⁻ᵍ ad iudicium et] *H,* ad *L*

---

[1] Id. c. 30.
[2] The building of this oratory is not mentioned elsewhere. By a now lost charter (*BCS* 1853, *Hemming,* ii. 562, 581) said to have been dated 844, Bishop Alhhun granted to the cathedral church the minster of Kempsey with appurtenant land, and land at Bredon. Another lost document known only from the list of benefactors at the

for the brothers were not dilatory in the fulfilment of their promise, and went to Mercia with an immense army mustered from every area. They penetrated as far as Nottingham, all of one mind in seeking battle. When the heathen, protected by the defences of the fortress, would not give battle, and the Christians were not able to breach the wall, peace was made between the Mercians and the heathen. Those two brothers, King Æthelred and Alfred, returned home with their troops.[1] The oratory of St Andrew the Apostle was built at Kempsey, and dedicated by Alhhun, bishop of Worcester.[2]

[869] Pope St Nicholas died on 6 December.[3]

The aforementioned heathen army rode again to Northumbria, reached the city of York, and stayed there for a whole year.[4]

[870] Hadrian[5] was the 105th pope. When Lothar heard of the death of Pope Nicholas, he sent a request to Pope Hadrian that he might receive him favourably. The pope wrote back that if he knew he was free from the aforementioned charges he should hurry to receive St Peter's blessing; if guilty he should nevertheless come without delay to receive the due remedies of penance. When he came to Rome he was honourably received by Pope Hadrian, and when he was asked by the pope if he had observed the precepts of St Nicholas, or rather of St Peter, and the oath on the body of the Lord, he replied that he had thus observed everything as if the commands were of God, to which the nobles and courtiers bore witness. The pope said to him; 'You ought, therefore, O most beloved son, to partake of the body of Christ with us that through this sharing of the body of Christ you may deserve to be readmitted to that from which you were seen to have been cut off.' So, when the pope had sung the mass, at the hour of the communion, taking the body of Christ in his hands, he said to Lothar: 'If you are innocent of the aforementioned sins may this communion be your remission, but otherwise may you not presume to partake at all lest perchance it be brought forth to your judgement and condemnation.' However, the king, his mind in

beginning of the JW MS C (fo. 2ᵛ, printed Dugdale, *Monasticon*, i. 608, and to be reprinted and discussed in vol. i) was dated 847 and was a grant by the cathedral of the same minster and lands at Bredon to the bishop for two lives.
   [3] Mar.   [4] Asser, c. 31.   [5] Hadrian II 867–72.

*communicauit. Deinde papa sequacibus regis et fautoribus dixit singulis:
'si in adulterio predicto cum rege tuo non communicasti, hec communio
corporis Christi sit tibi in uitam eternam.' Nullus autem qui in hoc
scelere regi consensit et communicauit post annum uixit. Lotharius uero
imperator Roma egressus, morbo corripitur, et perueniens Placentiam
ciuitatem, obiit .vi. idus Augusti. Inde etiam et in populo mortalitas
maxima acta est. Cuius regnum Ludouuicus et Karolus senior fratres
eius in loco Marsana iuxta Mosam, una cum proceribus et optimatibus
suis, equis partibus inter se diuiserunt, Karolus ad Heristellium perrexit
cuius palatium ei acciderat.*[1]

Supra[a] *memoratus paganorum exercitus per Merciam in Orientales
Anglos transiuit, et ibi in loco qui dicitur Theodford, hiemauit.*[2]
Eodem anno sanctissimus ac gloriosissimus Orientalium Anglorum
rex Eadmundus, ut in sua legitur Passione, ab Inguaro rege pagan-
issimo, [b]indictione .ii., .xii. kalend. Decembris die dominico[b] martirizatus est.[c3] Quo etiam *anno Ceolnoth*us *Dorubern*ensis *archiepiscopus*
defunctus,[d] *in eadem ciuitate in pace sepultus est.*[4] [e]Cui uir reuerendus successit Ætheredus.[e5]

*Romanorum octogesimus secundus Luduuuicus filius Luduuuici uel
Lotharii regnauit annis iiii.*[6]

[871] (i) 893   *Luduuuicus ad Aquisgrani palatium rediuit.*[7]

*Exose memorie paganorum exercitus, Orientales Anglos deserens, reg-
numque*[f] *Occidentalium Saxonum adiens, uenit ad uillam regiam, que
dicitur Reading*um,[g] *in meridiana Tamesis fluminis ripa sitam, in illa
paga que dicitur Bearrocscire; tertioque aduentus sui die* duo[h8] *comites
eorum cum magna illius parte in predam equitauerunt, aliis uallum
inter duo flumina Tamesen*[i] *et Cynetan a dextra*[j] *parte eiusdem uille
regie facientibus. Quibus Atheluulf, Bearrocensis page comes, cum suis*

---

[a] s *of* supra *erased* C   [b–b] indictione . . . dominico] *interlin.* Cᵗ, *om. here but
partly included in addition 870 n. c* B   [c] *see App.* B *for addition* B   [d] uiam uniuersitatis adiit *As* ASN   [e–e] cui . . . Ætheredus] *possibly written over erasure* Cᵗ
[f] regnum HL   [g] Redingum HR i. *72 (ii. 77),* Rædigam Ac Aᵹ *(As),* Redigam Ao
Au, Redinga *from* Redingam ASN   [h] *om.* Ac Aᵹ Ao Au ASN, ⟨duo⟩ *(As)*
[i] Tamesan HL   [j] dextrali Au Aᵹ *(As)* ASN, dexterali Ac Ao

---

[1] Mar.   [2] Asser. c. 32.
[3] 20 Nov. is the day given by Abbo (*Passio Sancti Eadmundi,* c. 10, Winterbottom,
Lives, p. 79), whose *Passio* had already been used for annal 865. ASN (870) gives: 'xii
kal. Dec., indictione .iii., secunda feria.' If JW began his year in Sept. (like ASC, which
also gives 870), his Sunday and 2nd indiction would be correct for 869.
[4] Asser c. 4.

thrall, both obdurate and blind, took communion without retract-
ing. The pope said to each attendant and supporter of the king: 'If
you were not party with your king to the aforementioned adultery,
may this communion of the body of Christ be yours for eternal
life.' But no one who agreed to, and was party with, the king in
this crime lived beyond the year. When the Emperor Lothar left
Rome, he was struck by a disease, and, reaching the city of
Piacenza, he died on 8 August. Then, too, a very great mortality
occurred among the people. Louis and the elder Charles, his
brothers, with their nobles and magnates divided his kingdom
between them into equal shares in a place called Meersen by the
Meuse. Charles went to Herstal, where the palace had been
assigned to him.[1]

The aforementioned heathen army crossed through Mercia to
East Anglia and there passed the winter in a place called
Thetford.[2] In the same year the most holy and glorious Edmund,
king of the East Angles, was martyred by Inguar, a most heathen
king, on Sunday, 20 November, in the second indiction, as can be
read in his passion.[3] In this year also Ceolnoth, archbishop of
Canterbury, died, and was buried in peace in the same city.[4] The
revered Æthelred succeeded him.[5]

Louis, the eighty-second emperor of the Romans, son of the
Louis who was also known as Lothar, reigned four years.[6]

[871] Louis returned to the palace at Aachen.[7]

The heathen army of hateful memory, abandoning the East
Angles, entered the kingdom of the West Saxons and went to the
royal township which is called Reading (lying on the south bank of
the river Thames), in the area called Berkshire. On the third day
after their arrival, two[8] of their earls rode off, with a large section
of the army, to plunder, while the others put up a palisade
between the two rivers, the Thames and the Kennet, on the
right-hand [i.e. southern] side of that same royal residence.
Æthelwulf, ealdorman of Berkshire, met them with his men in a

---

[5] The succession of Æthelred, which is not in Asser, appears in additions to ASC AF.
[6] Mar. Under 855 (above, p. 275 n. 6), Marianus confused the emperor Louis II
(855–75) with his brother King Lothar II, and gave him a reign of 15 years. The
emperor is repeated here, and Lothar/Louis is given an imaginary son Louis, who is
allowed a 4-year rule, presumably to complete the 20-year imperial reign of Louis II.
[7] Mar
[8] The number of Danish earls is given in ASC, not in the other witnesses of Asser.

in loco qui Anglice*[a] Englafeld,* *[b]Latine angelorum campus[b] dicitur*
obuiauit, ubi[c] animose pugnatum[d] est ex utraque parte. Cunque ibi diu
utrique resisterent, altero paganorum comite occiso,[e] et maxima exerci-
tus parte deleta, ceterisque fuga elapsis, Christiani uictoriam accipi-
entes, loco funeris dominati sunt.[1] *His ita ibi gestis, post .iiii. dies*
Æthered rex et Ælfred, frater eius, adunatis uiribus congregatoque
exercitu, Rædingum adierunt. Cunque usque ad portam arcis peruenis-
sent, cedendo et prosternendo quoscunque de paganis extra arcem in-
uenissent, pagani non segnius certabant, lupino more, totis portis
erumpentes, totis uiribus bellum perquirunt. Ibique diu et atrociter ex
utraque parte dimicatum est: sed proh dolor, Christianis demum terga
uertentibus, pagani, uictoriam accipientes, loco funeris dominati sunt:
ibique Atheluulfus prefatus comes inter ceteros occubuit.[2] *Quo dolore et*
uerecundia Christiani commoti, iterum post .iiii. dies contra prefatum
exercitum in loco qui dicitur Æscesdun, quod Latine mons fraxini

p. 291 *| interpretatur, totis uiribus et plena uoluntate ad prelium prodeunt.*
Sed pagani, in duas se turmas diuidentes, equali[f] testudine[g] bellum
parant– habebant enim tunc duos reges multosque comites– concedentes
mediam partem exercitus duobus regibus et alteram omnibus comitibus.
Quod Christiani cernentes, et etiam ipsi exercitum in duas turmas
diuidentes, testudines non segnius construunt. Sed Ælfred citius et
promptius cum suis, ad locum proelii uenit:[h] nimirum erat enim tunc[i]
suus frater Æthered rex in tentorio in oratione positus, audiens missam,
*nimium*que *affirmans se inde non discessurum antequam sacerdos mis-*
sam finiret et diuinum pro humano nolle deserere seruitium, et ita fecit.
Que regis Christiani fides multum apud Deum*[j] ualuit sicut apertius*
declarabitur in sequentibus.[3] *Decreuerant ergo Christiani ut Æthered*
rex cum suis copiis contra duos paganos reges sumeret proelium. Ælfred
uero, suus frater, cum suis cohortibus contra omnes paganorum duces
belli sortem sumere debere sciret. Quibus ita firmiter ab utraque parte
dispositis, cum rex in oratione diutius moraretur et pagani parati
ad locum certaminis citius aduenissent. Ælfred, tunc secundarius, cum

---

[a] om. *As ASN*   *[b–b]* Latine . . . campus] om. *As ASN*   *[c]* et *As ASN*
[d] ibidem pugnatum *As ASN*   *[e]* cuius nomen erat Sidroc *interlin. B[5]*   *[f]* equali
Ac, equali lance ⟨⟨lance⟩ *(As)) Aw Au (As) ASN,* equali lancea *Ao*   *[g]* testudinis
Ac Ao, testudines *Aw Au (As) ASN*   *[h]* aduenit *As ASN*   *[i]* adhuc *As ASN*
[j] Deum *Ac Ao ASN,* Dominum *Aw Au (As)*

---

[1] Asser, c. 35. The 'right-hand side' is the Latin equivalent of a Welsh idiom, referring to something lying to the south.

place which is called Englefield in English—the field of the angels in Latin—and there both sides fought bitterly. Both sides held their ground there for a long time; then one of the pagan commanders was killed, and the greater part of the enemy army was destroyed. The rest escaped in flight; the Christians gained the victory, and were masters of the place of death.[1] Four days after these events had taken place there, King Æthelred and his brother Alfred, having assembled their men and mustered an army, went to Reading, and when they had arrived at the gate of the fortress, and had killed and brought low any of the heathen they found outside the fort, the heathen were not dilatory in fighting, but, like wolves, they rushed out through all the gates, seeking battle with all their might. And there both sides fought long and bitterly but, alas, when the Christians finally retreated, the heathen gained the victory and were masters of the place of death. There, among others, Æthelwulf the aforementioned ealdorman, fell.[2] The Christians, moved by that grief and shame, again marched to battle against the aforesaid heathen army four days later at a place called Ashdown, which means Mount Ash in Latin, with all their might and will. But the heathen, dividing themselves into two forces with equal shield-walls, prepared for battle, for they then had two kings and many earls, giving the central division of the army to the two kings and the other side to all the earls. When the Christians saw that, they also divided the army into two divisions, and did not hesitate to draw up shield-walls. But Alfred went to the battlefield more swiftly and rapidly with his men for his brother, King Æthelred, was then kneeling in prayer in his tent, hearing mass, and he declared firmly that he would not depart before the priest finished the mass, and that he would not abandon divine for human sacrifice, and thus he did. This faith of the Christian king was of great merit in the eyes of God, as will be shown more openly in what follows.[3] The Christians had decided that King Æthelred with his forces should join battle with the two pagan kings, but his brother Alfred should understand that, with his own divisions, he must undergo the fortunes of war against all the heathen earls. When matters had been thus firmly settled on both sides, the king lingered longer in prayer, and the heathen, already prepared, came to the place of battle more

[2] Id., c. 36.   [3] Id., c. 37.

diutius hostiles acies ferre non posset, nisi aut bello retrorsum cederet^a aut contra hostiles copias ante fratris aduentum in bellum prorumperet, demum uiriliter aprino^b more Christianas copias contra hostiles exercitus, ut ante proposuerant,^c quanuis rex adhuc non uenerat, dirigens, diuino fretus consilio et fultus adiutorio, testudine ordinabiliter condensata, confestim contra hostes uexilla mouet.[1] ^{d2-}Tandem rex Ætheredus, finitis quibus occupatus erat orationibus, aduenit, et, inuocato magno mundi principe, mox se certamini dedit.^{d2} *Sed ^ehoc in loco^e nescientibus intimandum est, quod ille locus certaminis belligerantibus inequalis erat, nam pagani editiorem locum preoccupauerant, Christiani ab inferiori loco aciem dirigebant. Erat quoque in eodem loco una^f spinosa arbor, breuis admodum, circa quam hostiles inter se acies, cum ingenti omnium clamore illi perperam agentes, isti pro uita et dilectis atque patria pugnaturi, hostiliter conueniunt. Cunque aliquandiu animose nimiumque atrociter hinc et inde utrique pugnarent, pagani diuino iudicio Christianorum impetum diutius non ferentes, maxima parte suorum^g occisa, opprobriosam fugam cepere: quo in loco alter de duobus paganorum regibus et .v. comites occisi occubuerunt, et multa milia illorum^h in eodem loco, et insuper per tota(m)^i campestrem Æscesdun latitudinem ubique dispersa et occisa corruerunt. Cecidit ergo illic Bagsecg rex, Sidroc senex comes, Sidroc iunior comes, Osbern comes, Fræna comes, Hareld comes et totus paganorum exercitus usque ad noctem et etiam usque ad diem sequentem, quousque ad arcem qui euaserant peruenerunt, in fugam uersus est.*[3] *His ibi ita^j gestis, iterum post .xiiii. dies Æthered rex una cum fratre Alfred*o, *adunatis uiribus contra paganos pugnaturus,^k Basengas adï*t.^l *Quibus hostiliter conuenientibus, et diu ^msimul certantibus,^m pagani ^nuictoria potiuntur.^n*[4] Rursus, duobus euolutis mensibus, rex Ætheredus et frater eius Alfredus cum paganis qui se in duas diuiserant turmas apud Meretun pugnantes, diu uictores existunt, aduersariis omnibus in fugam uersis, sed illis

---

^a cederet *Ao*, recederet *Ac Aw Au (As) ASN*   ^b a pristino *HL*   ^c proposuerant *Ac Aw Ao Au*, proposuerat *(As)*   ^{d-d} Tandem . . . dedit] *add. from JW As Au (As) ASN*   ^{e-e} hoc in loco] in hoc loco *HL*   ^f unica *As ASN*   ^g suarum copiarum *Ac Aw Au (As) ASN*   ^h paganae partis *As*, paganae gentis *ASN*   ^i totam *HL As ASN*, tota *CBP*   ^j ita *Ac Aw Ao Au ASN*, om. *(As)*   ^k pugnaturi *As ASN*   ^l adierunt *As ASN*   ^{m-m} simul certantibus] resistentibus *As ASN*   ^{n-n} uictoria potiuntur] uictoriam accipientes *As ASN*

---

[1] Id., c. 38.

[2-2] This sentence may be JW's addition to Asser (see Keynes–Lapidge, *Alfred*, p. 242).

swiftly. Alfred, then 'heir-apparent', when he could no longer withstand the enemy line unless he either retreated from the battle or advanced against the enemy troops before his brother's arrival at the battle, like a wild boar finally sent the Christian troops boldly forward against the enemy army as they had decided earlier, although the king had not yet come, encouraged by divine counsel, and sustained by His help. He closed the shield-wall in proper order and immediately advanced his standards against the enemy.[1] [2]Finally King Æthelred, having completed the prayers with which he was occupied, arrived, and having invoked the great Ruler of the world, at once entered the battle.[2] But it should be made clear at this point to those who do not know that that place of battle did not give the same advantages to all the warriors. For the heathen had already taken the higher ground, so the Christians directed their attack from below. Also in the same place there was a very small thorn-tree around which the close-packed opposing lines engaged with great clamour from all; on the one side strove those with a false cause, on the other those fighting for life, loved ones, and homeland. When both sides had fought with great ferocity and bitterness backwards and forwards, the heathen army could no longer withstand the Christians' attack, which was divinely supported. When most of them had been killed, they took to disgraceful flight. In that place one of the two heathen kings and five earls lay slain and many thousands of their men in that same place, and, in addition, everywhere throughout the whole broad plain of Ashdown they fell, scattered and slain. There fell King Bagsecg, Earl Sidroc the Elder, Earl Sidroc the Younger, Earl Osbern, Earl Fræna, Earl Harold, and the whole heathen army was driven in flight until nightfall and even until the following day, till they came to the stronghold from which they had set forth.[3] Fourteen days after these events had taken place, King Æthelred with his brother Alfred again united their forces to fight against the heathen, and went to Basing. When battle had been joined they strove together for a long time and the pagans were victorious.[4] Again, when two months had passed King Æthelred and his brother Alfred, fighting with the heathen, who had divided into two groups, at *Meretun*, were for a long time victorious, putting all their opponents to flight, but the English returned to

[3] Asser, c. 39.　　[4] Id., c. 40.

in proelium redeuntibus, multi ex his et ex illis corruunt, et
pagani uictoriam accipientes, loco funeris dominantur.[1] *Eodem
anno post pasca rex Ætheredus, regno .v. annis per multas tribulationes
strenue atque honorabiliter cum bona fama gubernato, uiam uniuersitatis adiens,* ª*.ix.* kal. Maiiª[2] *in Winburnan sepultus est,* ubi *aduentum
Domini primam*que *cum iustis resurrectionem expectat.*[3] Quo
defuncto, *supra memoratus Alfred*us, *qui usque ad id temporis uiuen-
tibus fratribus suis, fuerat secundarius, totius regni gubernacula, diuino
concedente nutu, cum summa omnium illius regni accolarum uoluntate,
confestim suscepit.*[4] Cius[b] *de infantilibus et puerilibus moribus hoc in
loco breuiter inserendum esse existim*amus.[c5] *Communi* itaque *et
ingenti patris sui et matris amore, supra omnes fratres suos, immo ab
omnibus, nimium dilig*ebatur,[d] *et in regio semper curto inseparabiliter
nutri*ebatur,[e] *accrescente* uero *infantili et puerili etate,* [f]*cunctis
fratribus forma decentior,[f] uultu, uerbis atque moribus gratiosior uidebatur: sed proh dolor, suorum parentum et nutritorum incuria, usque
ad duodecimum etatis annum illiteratus permansit. Saxonica* tamen[g]
poemata die noctuque sollers auditor, relatu[h] *aliorum sepissime audiens,
docibilis memoriter retinebat. In omni uenatoria arte incomparabilis
omnibus peritia et felicitate, sicut et in ceteris omnibus Dei donis,
fuit.*[6] *Cum ergo quodam*[i] *die mater sua sibi et fratribus suis quendam
Saxonicum* | *poematice artis librum, quem in manu habebat, osten-
deret, ait: Quisquis uestrum discere citius istum codicem* poterit,[j] *dabo
ei*[k] *illum. Qua uoce, immo diuina*[l] *inspiratione, instinctus* Alfredus[m] *et
pulchritudine principalis littere illius libri illectus, ita matri respondens
inquit: 'Verene dabis istum librum uni ex nobis, scilicet illi qui citissime
intelligere et recitare ante te possit?' Ad hec illa arridens: 'Dabo', infit,
'illi'. Tunc ille statim tollens librum de manu sua, magistrum adiit et
legit. Quo lecto, matri retulit et recitauit.*[7] *Post hec cursum diurnum
psalmos quosdam et orationes multas didicit:* [n]*que omnia in uno libro
congregat*a,[n] *in sinu suo die noctuque, orationis gratia, inter omnia*

p. 292

ª⁻ª ix kal. Maii] *interlin.* C¹B¹   [b] initium regni regis Ælfredi *add. mg.* P²
[c]existimo *As.*   [d] diligeretur *As.*   [e] nutriretur *As.*   [f⁻f] cunctis . . . decen-
tior] forma ceteris suis fratribus decentior *As*   [g] om. *As*   [h] relator *B*
[i] quadam *HL*   [j] possit *As*   [k] ei *HR i. 69 (ii. 74),* illi *As*   [l] om. *HL*
[m] om. *As*   [n⁻n] que . . . congregata] quos in uno libro congregatos *As*

---

[1] The battle of *Meretun*, omitted by Asser, is translated from ASC. JW's 'Meretun'
agrees with ASC AC 'Meretune' against B 'Merantune', D 'Meredune', E 'Mæredune'
and F 'Merendune'. In turning to ASC for this battle, JW omitted the reference to the
arrival of a Viking summer army, which is in the last sentence of Asser, c. 40, and

the battle and many fell on either side, and the pagans, who took the victory, were masters of the place of death.[1] After Easter in the same year, King Æthelred, after steering his kingdom through many tribulations for five years vigorously, honourably, and with good repute, went the way of all flesh on 23 April.[2] He was buried at Wimborne, where he awaits the Lord's coming and the first resurrection with the just.[3] On his death Alfred, referred to above, who had hitherto, while his brothers were alive, been 'heir-apparent', at once received the government of the whole kingdom with divine consent and with complete willingness on the part of all the inhabitants of his kingdom.[4] We think that a brief account of his infancy and boyhood should be inserted at this point.[5] He was greatly loved by his father and his mother alike, more than all his brothers, and indeed by absolutely everybody, and he was always brought up at the royal court, which he never left. As he passed through infancy and boyhood he appeared more handsome in appearance and more agreeable in manner, words, and behaviour than all his brothers, but, alas, through the negligence of his parents and teachers he remained ignorant of letters until his twelfth year. However, he was accustomed to hear Saxon poetry day and night, and, hearing it very frequently recited by others, he readily retained it in his memory. In every aspect of the art of hunting he excelled all in skill and success, just as he did in all God's other gifts.[6] When, therefore, one day his mother, showing him and his brothers a book of Saxon poetry which she had in her hand, said: 'To whichever of you can learn this book most quickly I shall give it', moved by these words, no, rather by divine inspiration and attracted by the beauty of the first letter of that book, Alfred spoke to this effect to his mother when he replied: 'Will you truly give that book to one of us, that is to him who can most speedily understand and recite it to you?' At this she smiled and said: 'I shall give it to him.' Then he, taking the book at once from her hand, went to his master and read it. When he had read it, he took it back to his mother and recited it.[7] After that he

[2] Though the day of Æthelred's death roughly agrees with ASC's 'after Easter' (15 Apr.), Stevenson's view (*Asser*, pp. 240–1) that JW has confused the day for Æthelred II's death with that for Æthelred I casts doubts on the value of this interlineation.
[3] Asser, c. 41.   [4] Id., c. 42.   [5] Id., c. 21.   [6] Id., c. 22.
[7] Id., c. 23.

which is mentioned in ASC (where in all versions save A it is described as arriving at Reading).

presentis uite curricula ubique circumducebat. Sed, proh dolor, quod maxime desiderabat, liberalem scilicet artem, desiderio suo non suppetebat, eo quod illo tempore grammatici[a] *in toto regno Occidentalium Saxonum non erant.*[1] *Cum* autem, *in primeuo iuuentutis sue flore, mentem suam in Dei mandatis stabilire uellet, seque a carnali desiderio abstinere non posse cerneret,* ne *offensam Dei incurreret,*[b] *si aliquid contrarium uoluntati illius perageret, sepissime, galli cantu et matutinis horis clam consurgens, ecclesias et reliquias sanctorum orandi causa uisitabat, ibique diu prostratus orabat, quo Deus omnipotens, propter suam misericordiam, mentem illius amore sue seruitutis per aliquam infirmitatem, quam posset sustinere, non tamen quo eum indignum*[c] *et inutilem in mundanis rebus faceret, corroboraret. Cunque hoc sepius magna mentis deuotione ageret, post aliquantulum interuallum fici dolorem Dei munere incurrit, in quo,*[d] *diu et egre per multos annos roborans*[e] *se, etiam de uita, desperabat. Sed quodam tempore, diuino nutu, cum Cornubiam uenandi causa adiret et ad quandam ecclesiam* [f]*orandi causa diuertisset, in qua sanctus*[f] *Gueriir requiescit, sanctus etiam Niot ibidem pausat*[2] *diu in oratione tacita prostratus* Dei[g] *misericordiam deprecabatur, quatinus pro sua immensa clementia stimulos presentis et infestantis infirmitatis aliqua qualicunque leuiori infirmitate mutaret, ea tamen conditione, ut corporaliter exterius illa infirmitas non appareret, ne despectus et inutilis esset. Oratione finita, ceptum iter arripuit, et non multo post tempore, ut in oratione deprecatus fuerat, se ab illo dolore medicatum esse diuinitus sensit, ita ut funditus eradicaretur. Sed, proh dolor, eo amoto, alius infestior in nuptiis eum arripuit, qui a uicesimo etatis sue anno usque ad quadragesimum quintum* [3]*et eo amplius*[3] *illum*[h] *die noctuque incessabiliter fatigauit.*[4] *Nati sunt ergo ei filii et filie de supradicta coniuge sua* Ealhsuuitha: [5]*Ægelflæd primogenita, post quam Eadward, deinde Æðelgeouu, postea Ælfðryð, deinde Ætheluuard natus est.*[5] *Æthelfled adueniente matrimonii tem-*

---

[a] lectores boni As   [b] incurrere As   [c] interlin. H[1]   [d] qua HL   [e] roborans Ac, laborans Aw Acott (teste Aw) Ao Au (As)   [f-f] orandi . . . sanctus] interlin. H[1]   [g] Domini As   [h] eum As

---

[1] Id., c. 24.

[2] The reasonable view that this reference to St Neot was not an interpolation in Asser has been argued most recently by Keynes–Lapidge, *Alfred*, pp. 254–5.

[3-3] 'et eo amplius' could be an inference of JW or taken from a revised version of Asser.

[4] Asser, c. 73 (74), which JW has curtailed and rearranged (see Stevenson, *Asser*, p. lvi, and vol. i, introduction, in this edition).

learnt the daily services, some psalms, and many prayers, all of
which he collected in one book which he kept with him everywhere, night and day, in his bosom that he might pray in the
midst of all the business of this present life. But, alas, what he
most desired, namely the liberal art (of Grammar), he could not
study because at that time there were no grammarians in the
whole of the kingdom of the West Saxons.[1] When, however, in
the first flower of his youth, he wished to fix his mind on God's
commands, he realized he could not abstain from fleshly lust. So
that he should not incur the wrath of God by performing anything
contrary to his will, he, very often rising secretly at cock-crow in
the morning, visited the churches and relics of the saints to pray,
and there, prostrate for a long time, he prayed that Almighty God
in his mercy would strengthen his mind by the love of his service
by means of any ailment that he might endure, but not one that
would make him unworthy and unfit for his worldly duties. When
he had done this many times with great devotion of mind, he
incurred, by God's gift, after an interval, the affliction of piles,
and in it he grew in strength long and painfully for many years,
even despairing of life. But by divine consent at a certain time
when he went to Cornwall to hunt, and had turned aside to pray
at a certain church in which St *Guerir* lay (and also St Neot lies
there),[2] he stopped a long time in silent prayer and prostrate,
besought God for his mercy until of his immense clemency he
changed the torment of the present distressing infirmity for
another, somewhat less severe, illness, but on the condition that
that affliction should not appear visibly on his body, lest he should
be despised and useless. When his prayer was ended, he continued
the journey he had begun, and, not much later, as he had begged
in prayer, he felt himself divinely cured of that affliction to such
an extent that it was totally destroyed. But, alas, when it was
removed, another more dangerous one took hold of him on his
wedding day and it tormented him incessantly night and day from
his twentieth year to his forty-fifth [3]and longer.[3,4] His wife, the
Ealhswith mentioned before, bore him sons and daughters:
[5]Æthelflæd was the first born and after her Edward, then
Æthelgifu, after her Ælfthryth, finally Æthelweard was born.[5]

[5–5] The children of this marriage are mentioned in a different order in JW *West
Saxon Accounts* 33.

pore, Atheredo[1] *Merciorum comiti matrimonio copulata est:*
Æthelgeofa monastice uite regulis, deuota Deo uirginitate, subiuncta et
consecrata, diuinum subiit seruitium: Ætheluuard, omnibus iunior lit-
terarie discipline, diuino consilio admirabilique regis prouidentia, ª*et*
omnesª *pene totius regionis* ᵇ*nobiles et etiam multi ignobiles,*ᵇ *sub dili-*
genti magistrorum cura, ᶜ*traditi* sunt,ᶜ *ut antequam aptas humanis art-*
ibus uires haberent, ᵈ*liberalibus* instituerentur *artibus.*ᵈ *Eaduuard et*
Ælfthryð semper in curto regio nutriti nonᵉ *sine liberali disciplina inter*
*cetera presentis uite studia, psalmos et Saxonicos libros, maxime*que
*Saxonica carmina, studiose didicere.*² ᶠ*At rex* Alfredus,ᶠ *inter bella et*
presentis uite frequentia impedimenta, necnon paganorum infestationes,
et cotidianas corporis infirmitates, regni gubernacula regere, omnem
uenandi artem agere, aurifices et artifices suos omnes, falconarios,
accipitrarios, canicularios quoque docere, edificia supra omnem antecces-
sorum suorum consuetudinem uenerabiliora et pretiosiora noua sua
machinatione facere, Saxonicos libros recitare, et maxime Saxonica
carmina memoriter discere, aliis imperare, solus assidue pro uiribus non
*desinebat: missam cotidie audire, psalmos quasdam*ᵍ *et orationes, horas*
diurnas et nocturnas celebrare et ecclesias nocturno tempore orandi
*causa clam suis*ʰ *adire solebat et frequentabat.* Elemosinarum dator
largissimus, omnium *affabilis*simus et *iocundis*simus, *ignotarum*
*rerum inuestigat*or *sollertis*simus. *Franci autem multi, Frisones, Galli,*
pagani, Brytones, Scotti et Armorici, sponte suo dominio subdiderant,
nobiles scilicet et ignobiles: quos omnes sicut propriam gentem secundum
suam dignitatem regebat, diligebat, honorabat, pecunia et potestate
*ditabat. Episcopos quoque suos omnem*que *ecclesiasticum ordinem,*
comites ac nobiles suos, ministeriales etiam et omnes familiares
ammirabili amore diligebat. Filios quoque eorum, qui in regali familia
nutriebantur, non minus propriis diligens, omnibus bonis moribus
p. 293   *instituere et litteris imbuere solus | die noctuque inter cetera non*
*desinebat.*³ *Cunque regnare prope quasi inuitus uno mense impleto*

ª⁻ª et omnes] cum omnibus *As*   ᵇ⁻ᵇ nobiles . . . ignobiles] nobilibus infantibus
et etiam multis (*om. Ac Ao*) ignobilibus (*As*)   ᶜ⁻ᶜ traditi sunt] traditus est *As*
ᵈ⁻ᵈ liberalibus . . . artibus] in liberalibus artibus studiosi et ingeniosi uiderentur *As*
ᵉ nec *As*   ᶠ⁻ᶠ At rex Alfredus] Interea tamen rex *As*   ᵍ quosdam *LP As*
ʰ suis *Ac*, a suis *Aw Ao Au (As)*

---

¹ The erroneous Eadred may have been Asser's reading and JW may have corrected
it.

When Æthelflæd reached marriageable age she was united by marriage with Æthelred,[1] ealdorman of the Mercians; Æthelgifu, subject and consecrated to the order of the monastic life, and having
vowed her virginity to God, entered His service. By divine counsel and the admirable foresight of the king, Æthelweard, the
youngest of all, and all the nobles of almost the whole region, and
even many who were not noble, were handed over to the discipline of letters under the diligent care of masters that, before they
had the strength for manly skills, they might be instructed in the
liberal arts. Edward and Ælfthryth, brought up in liberal studies
as well as the other concerns of this present life, and always at the
royal court, eagerly learnt the psalms and Saxon books, especially
Saxon songs.[2] But King Alfred, amidst the wars and the many
obstacles of this present life, as well as the heathen invasions and
the daily infirmities of the body, did not cease on his own for
want of strength to govern the realm unremittingly; to pursue
every form of hunting; to train all his goldsmiths and craftsmen
and also his falconers, hawkers, dog-handlers; to make treasures of
his own design which quite surpassed the manner of his predecessors, and were more admirable and more magnificent; to recite the
Saxon books and especially to commit to memory Saxon songs,
and to command others. He used to hear mass daily, to participate
in the reciting of certain psalms and prayers and the day and night
offices, and to go often to his churches at night to pray without
the knowledge of his followers. He was a most generous giver of
alms, the most courteous and cheerful of all men, the most skilful
investigator of unknown matters. Many Franks, Frisians, Gauls,
heathens, Britons, Scots, and Bretons offered him their submission
of their own accord, both nobles and commoners. He ruled, loved,
honoured, and enriched them all with wealth and power as if they
were his own people, as was suitable to his royal rank. And he
loved his own bishops and every rank of the clergy, his ealdormen
and nobles, also his thegns and all members of his household with
an admirable affection. Also the sons of those who were brought
up in the royal family he loved no less than his own, and did not
cease to instil into them his own all-virtuous habits and to instruct
them in letters, among other things, by day and night.[3] After the

[2] Asser, c. 74 (75).   [3] Id., c. 75 (76).

ceperat– nimirum enim non putabat ᵃin seᵃ diuino fultusᵇ auxilio tan-
tam paganorum posse solusᶜ sufferre austeritatem, quin etiam, uiuen-
tibus suis fratribus, cum magna multorum detrimenta sustinuisset–
contra uniuersum paganorum exercitum in monte qui dicitur Wiltun,
qui est meridiana ripa fluminis Guilou, de quo flumine tota illa paga
nominatur, cum paucis et nimium inequali numero acerrime belliger-
auit, et cum hinc inde utrique hostiliter et animose non parua diei
parte pugnarent, pagani ad integrum suum periculum cernentes, et
hostium infestationem diutius non ferentes, terga in fugam uerterunt.
Sed, proh dolor, ᵈper audaciam persequentium decipientes,ᵈ¹ iterum in
proelium prodeunt, et uictoriam capientes, loco funeris dominati sunt.
Nec hoc cuiquam mirabile uideatur, quod Christiani paruum in proelio
numerum habebant: erant enim Saxones maxima ex parte in uno anno
.uiii. contra paganos proeliis populariter attriti; ᵉin quibus .uiii. proeliisᵉ
unus rex paganorum et nouem duces cum innumeris cohortibus occisi
periere, exceptis cotidianis nocturnisque irruptionibus innumerabilibus
quasᶠ rex Alfredus et singuli duces illius gentis cum suis, etiamque per-
plures ministri regis contra paganos infatigabiliter exercebant. In quibus
frequentissimis irruptionibus quot milia ᵍpagane expeditionis occisa
perierunt, nisi soli Deo, incognitum est: exceptis his qui in octo predic-
tis preliis trucidati sunt.² Eodem quoque anno Saxones cum eisdemʰ
paganis, ea conditione ut ab eis discederent, pacem pepigerunt, quod et
impleuerunt.ᵍ³

[C³BP]
ⁱDefuncto Cinefertho Licetfeldensi episcopo, successit
Tunbrihtus.ⁱ⁴

[872] (ii) 894 *Adrianus papa obiit. Iohannes⁵ centesimus sextus*
papa.⁶
ʲDefuncto Huicciorum episcopo Alchuno, sancte Wigornensis
ecclesie nutritus, et uir *in diuin*is *scriptur*is doctissimus,

---

ᵃ⁻ᵃ in se] nisi *from* in se *B*, in se *Ac Aw Ao Au*, se nisi *(As)*   ᵇ fultus *Ac Ao Au*
ASN, fultum *Aw (As)*   ᶜ solus *Ac Ao Au Aw*, solum *(As)*   ᵈ⁻ᵈ per audaciam
. . . decipientes] peraudacitatem persequentium decipientes *As*, paucitatem persequentium despicientes *ASN*   ᵉ⁻ᵉ in . . . proeliis] *om. HL*   ᶠ quos *HL*
ᵍ⁻ᵍ pagane . . . impleuerunt] *darker ink, but not apparently over erasure C*   ʰ eisdem
Ao, iisdem *Aw Au (As)*, hisdem *Ac ASN*, isdem *HR i. 74, (ii. 81)*   ⁱ⁻ⁱ Defuncto
. . . Tunbrihtus] *add. mg. C³, om. HL. incorporated* 872 n. j *BP*   ʲ 871 n. i *incorpo-*
rated here BP

first month of a reign which he had undertaken almost reluc-
tantly—for he undoubtedly did not think that he alone could support such heathen ferocity unless aided by divine assistance, since
while his brothers were alive he had sustained severe losses of
many men—he fought very fiercely against the whole heathen
army on the hill which is called Wilton, which is on the south
bank of the river Wylye, from which river that whole district takes
its name, with few men, a much outnumbered force. When both
sides had fought fiercely and with spirit all over the field for much
of the day, the heathen, perceiving the extent of their danger and
that they could not withstand the enemy attack, turned and fled.
But alas, deceiving their overconfident pursuers,[1] they advanced
again into battle and, seizing the victory, were masters of the place
of death. Nor may this seem amazing to anyone because the
Christians had a small force at the battle, for the greatest part of
the Saxon people was exhausted by the eight battles against the
heathen in one year. In these eight battles one heathen king and
nine earls were slain and perished with innumerable soldiers.
These do not include the innumerable attacks on the heathen by
day and night which King Alfred and individual leaders of that
people with their own forces, and even many of the king's thegns,
made untiringly. How many thousands of the heathen invaders
were slain and died is not known in these countless skirmishes,
unless to God alone, not counting those who were cut down in the
eight battles already mentioned.[2] Also in the same year the Saxons
made peace with those same pagans on condition that they would
leave them, which they did.[3]

> On the death of Cyneferth,
> bishop of Lichfield, Tunberht
> succeeded.[4]

[872] Pope Hadrian died. John[5] was the 106th pope.[6]

On the death of Alhhun, bishop of the Hwicce, Wærferth, who
was brought up in the holy church of Worcester and was a man
most learned in Holy Scripture, was ordained bishop at Whitsun,

---

[1] Stevenson (*Asser*, pp. 241–2) and Keynes–Lapidge, *Alfred*, p. 243 prefer the reading of *ASN*, 'paucitatem persequentium despicientes' to that in the Cotton MS, 'peraudacitatem persequentium decipientes', but either is possible.
[2] Asser, c. 42.   [3] Id., c. 43.
[4] For this erroneous entry see above, p. 280 n. 1.
[5] John VIII 872–82.   [6] Mar.

Werefrithus, *ᵃ*.vii. idus Iunii die*ᵃ* Pentecostes ab Ætheredo Dorobernie archiepiscopo antistes est ordinatus.[1] *Qui imperio regis Ælfredi, libros Dialogorum beati pape Gregorii de Latinitate primus in Saxonicam linguam, elucubratim*ᵇ *et elegantissime* transtulit.*ᶜ* Hunc eundem et *ᵈprocessu temporisᵈ Plegimundum, genere Mercium, Dorubernensis ecclesie archiepiscopum, uenerabilem scilicet uirum, sapientia preditum, sacerdotes* quoque, *genere Mercios, Athelstan*um *et Weruulfum,* quam*ᵉ* optime litteris instructos, idem *rex ad se de Mercia* uocauit,*ᶠ multisque honoribus et potestatibus extulit,*[2] quo eum in desiderata, immo in discenda litterarum scientia adiuuarent. *Legatos* etiam *ultra mare ad Galliam direxit, indeque* sanctum*ᵍ Grimbaldum, sacerdotem et monachum, uenerabilem uirum, cantatorem*ʰ *optimum, ecclesiasticis disciplinis et in diuina scriptura eruditissimum, omnibusque bonis moribus ornatum; Iohannem quoque, eque presbiterum et monachum, acerrimi ingenii uirum,*[3] Asserum etiam *de occiduis ⁱet ultimisⁱ Britannie finibus, e monasterio sancti Deuuii* aduocaui.*ʲ*[4] *Quorum omnium doctrina et sapientia regis desiderium ita in dies crescebat et implebatur, ut in breui, librorum omnium notitiam* haber*et.*ᵏ[5] Prefatus exercitus paganorum Lundoniam *adiit, ibique hiemauit, cum quo Mercii pacem pepigerunt.*[6]

[C³BP]
*ˡ*Defuncto Aldberhto Herefordensi episcopo, successit Esne.*ˡ*[7]

[873] (iii) 895 *Ictu fulminis Wormatia comburitur. Luduuuico*ᵐ *imperatore*ⁿ *Romam uenien*te,*ᵒ ibique conuentum facien*te*ᵖ coram papa Iohanne, Adalgisus dux Beneuentanus, Grecorum persuasionibus corruptus, et contra Luduuuicum imperatorem manum eleuans, a senatu tirannus atque hostis rei publice proclamatur, bellumque contra eum*

ᵃ⁻ᵃ .vii. . . . die] *possibly written over erasure C*   *ᵇ* elucubratim *Ac Aw Ao Au,* elucabratim *(As)*   *ᶜ interpretatus est As*   *ᵈ⁻ᵈ* processu temporis] *interlin.* C¹, deinde *As*   *ᵉ* quos *L*   *ᶠ* aduocauerat *As*   *ᵍ* aduocauit *add. As* (aduocarit *Aw), cf.* 872 *n. k*   *ʰ* cantorem *HL*   *ⁱ⁻ⁱ* et ultimis] *interlin.* H¹   *ʲ om. As, though JW may have taken* aduocauit *from* 872 *n. g*   *ᵏ* habebat *As*   *ˡ⁻ˡ* Defuncto . . . Esne] *add. at end of annal* C³, *om.* C³, *om.*   *ᵐ* Luduuuico *from* Luduuuicus *C,* Luduuuicus *Mar.*   *ⁿ* imperatore *from* imperator *C,* imperator *Mar.*   *ᵒ* ueniente *from* ueniens C¹, ueniens *Mar.*   *ᵖ* faciente *from* faciens C¹, faciens *Mar.*

---

[1] This information is not recorded elsewhere. Alhhun's last signature of a charter is in 869 (*S* 214 *BCS* 524). 7 June was Whit Sunday in 873, which could have been the

7 June by Æthelred, archbishop of Canterbury.[1] In the reign of King Alfred he was the first to translate painstakingly and most judiciously the blessed Pope Gregory's book *The Dialogues*, from the Latin into the English language. The same king summoned to his presence from Mercia this very man and, in the process of time, Plegmund, a Mercian and archbishop of Canterbury, a venerable man, outstanding in his wisdom, and also the priests Æthelstan and Werwulf, by birth Mercian and excellently versed in letters. He endowed them with many honours and privileges[2] so that they might help him in his desire for, no rather his learning of, the knowledge of letters. He also sent messengers over the sea to Gaul and from there he obtained St Grimbald, priest and monk, a venerable man, an excellent chanter, most learned in church discipline and in Holy Scripture, and adorned by a virtuous way of life; and in addition John, also a priest and monk, and a man of the keenest intellect.[3] He also summoned Asser from the farthest western bounds of Britain, from the monastery of St David.[4] Thus the learning and wisdom of all these men fed and filled the king's desire from day to day so that in a short time he was acquainted with all books.[5] The aforementioned heathen army went to London and there wintered.[6]

> On the death of Aldberht, bishop of Hereford, Esne succeeded.[7]

[873] Worms was struck by lightning and burned down. When the Emperor Louis went to Rome, and there, at a council he held in the presence of Pope John, Adelchis, duke of Benevento (who had been corrupted by the blandishments of the Greeks, raising an army against the Emperor Louis), was proclaimed a usurper and

correct year for the consecration of Wærferth were it not for the lease (*S* 1278 *BCS* 533) dated 872, which he witnesses (O'Donovan, ii. 112). Wærferth's succession must have led JW to insert here under 872 those following passages of Asser, from c. 76 (77)–78 (79) dealing with Alfred's call to scholars.

[2] Asser, c. 76 (77).   [3] Id., c. 77 (78).

[4] Id., c. 78 (79). Although WM, *GP* ii. 80 (p. 177), speaks of 'Asserus ex sancti Deui euocatus', JW has probably adapted phrases at the beginning and end of Asser, c. 78 (79).

[5] Asser, c. 76 (77).   [6] Id. c. 44.

[7] This Hereford addition is inaccurate: both bishops lived in the 8th c. Documents dated 878 (*S* 128 *BCS* 254) and 879 (*S* 1430 *BCS* 256) show Ceolmund, the successor of Esne, already in office.

decernitur. Thiodo abbas Fuldensis obiit. Sigehart successit.[1]

Sepe memoratus exercitus Lundoniam deserens, in Northan-hymbrorum regionem perrexit, et ibi[a] *hiemauit, in paga que dicitur Lindesig, cum quo iterum Mercii pacem pepigerunt.*[2]

[C³BP]
[b]Defuncto Aldredo Legerensi pontifice, Ceolredus successit.[b3]

[874] (iiii) 896   *Ciclus decennouenalis .xix. incipit indictione .vii. Luduuuicus imperator obiit et Karolus senior rex Gallie Romam per-rexit.*[4]

[c]Supra memoratus[c] *exercitus Lindissi deserens, Merciam adiit, et hiemauit in loco qui dicitur Reopedun.*[d] *Burhredum quoque Merciorum regem regnum suum deserere et ultra mare exire Romamque adire contra uoluntatem suam coegit, anno .xxii. regni sui: qui, postquam Romam adierat, non diu uiuens, ibi defunctus est, et in scola Saxonum in ecclesia sancte Marie honorifice sepultus, aduentum Domini primamque* cum iustis resurrectionem expectat. Post cuius[e] expulsionem pagani[f] totum Merciorum regnum suo dominio subdiderunt, quod tamen miserabili conditione cuidam insipienti ministro, cuius[g] nomen erat Ceoluulf, eo pacto custodiendum commendauerunt, ut qualicunque die uellent [h]id sibi pacifice[h] assignaret. | Quibus in eadem conditione*

p. 294   *obsides dedit, et iurauit, nullo modo se uoluntati eorum contradicere uelle, sed obediens in omnibus esse.*[5]

Romanorum octogesimus tertius Karolus[6] *regnauit annis duobus.*[7]

[875] (i) 897   *Karolus ergo Romam perueniens, datis Iohanni pape et Romanis magnis muneribus, imperator factus est. Luduuuicus rex frater Karoli apud Franconfurt*[i] *palatium obiit .v. kalend. Sept., sepultusque est in monasterio sancti Nazarii Lorassam. Qui ex regina nomine Hemma tres filios habuit, id est Karlomannum, Arnulfi patrem, et Luduuuicum, Karolumque iuniorem postea imperatorem. Karolus ergo senior et imperator, audiens mortem fratris sui ad Aquisgrani palatium, et inde post paucos dies Coloniam est profectus. Carlomannus uero pri-*

---

[a] deinde *interlin. above deleted* ibi *B*[1]   *[b-b]* Defuncto . . . successit] *add. at end of annal C*[3]*, om.* HL   *[c-c]* Supra memoratus] *darker ink but no traces of erasure* C[1]   *[d]* *darker ink possibly over erasure* C[1]   *[e]* cuius *Ac ASN,* eius *(As)* A*w* Ao Au   *[f]* Dani pirati *H,* Dani parati *L*   *[g]* cui *L*   *[h-h]* id sibi pacifice] habere (nostre *Ac, where* hre *for* habere *was misread as* nre *for* nostre) iterum pacifice illis *As ASN*   *[i]* second n in Franconfurt *interlin.* C[1]

an enemy of the state by the senate, and war was declared against
him. Thiodo, abbot of Fulda, died. Sigehart succeeded him.[1]

The army often mentioned left London, and penetrated
Northumbrian territory, and there wintered in the area called
Lindsey. The Mercians again made peace with them.[2]

> On the death of Ealdred,
> bishop of Leicester, Ceolred
> succeeded.[3]

[874] The nineteenth cycle of nineteen years begins in the seventh
indiction. The Emperor Louis died and the elder Charles, the
king of Gaul, went to Rome.[4]

The army mentioned above left Lindsey, went to Mercia, and
wintered in a place called Repton. It also forced Burgred, king of
the Mercians, to abandon his kingdom, travel overseas, and go to
Rome against his will in the twenty-second year of his reign. He
did not live long after his arrival at Rome. He died there, and was
honourably buried in the Saxon school, in the church of St Mary,
and he awaits the coming of the Lord and the first resurrection
with the just. After driving him out, the pagans subdued the
whole of the kingdom of Mercia to their rule, and entrusted the
keeping of the kingdom, by a miserable arrangement, to a certain
stupid thegn whose name was Ceolwulf, on condition that he
would hand it over to them without resistance on whatever day
they might wish. He gave them hostages in pledge of this, and
swore that in no way would he willingly oppose their wishes, but
would be obedient in everything.[5]

Charles,[6] the eighty-third emperor of the Romans, reigned two
years.[7]

[875] Charles went to Rome, gave Pope John and the Romans
great gifts, and was made emperor. King Louis, Charles's brother,
died in the palace at Frankfurt on 28 August, and was buried in
the monastery of St Nazarius at Lorsch. He had three sons by his
queen, Emma by name: Carloman, father of Arnulf, and Louis,
and Charles the Younger, later emperor. Charles the Elder, the
emperor, hearing of his brother's death, set out for the palace at

---

[1] Mar.   [2] Asser, c. 45.
[3] This Leicester addition is inaccurate as Ceolred was in office 843–4 (see above, p.
276 n. 5).
[4] Mar.   [5] Asser, c. 46.   [6] Charles the Bald 875–7.   [7] Mar.

mogenitus Luduuuici fines Italie intrauit, quia Carolus senior inde recessit. Karolus autem frater eius in Alamannia morabatur. Porro Luduuuicus, qui ad obitum patris fuit, apud Franconfurt principalem sedem orientalis regni residebat. Qui quoque Karolum seniorem .viii. idus Octobris, in pago Moinense nomine ripuaria non longe ab Andrenato castello iuxta Renum, contra se pugnantem quinquaginta amplius milibus superauit. Deinde tres fratres in loco qui dicitur Sualifelt inter se regnum paternum diuiserunt. Carlomannus Bauuariam, Pannoniam, C⟨a⟩rinthiam^a et regna Sclauorum Beheimensium; Ludouuicus orientalem Franciam, Turingiam, Saxoniam, Fresiam, partemque regni Lotharii; Carolus Alamanniam et aliquas ciuitates regni Lotharii tenuit.[1]

Supra memoratus sepe exercitus Hreopedune deserens, in duas se diuisit turmas, cuius altera pars cum Halfdene in regionem Norðanhymbrorum perrexit, ibique hiemauit iuxta flumen quod dicitur Tine, et totam Norðanhymbrorum regionem suo subdidit dominio, necnon Pictos et Stratcluttenses depopulati sunt. Altera quoque pars cum Guðrum et Oscytel et Amund,^b tribus paganorum regibus, ad locum qui dicitur Grantegbrycge, peruenit, ibique hiemauit.[2] *Eodem anno Ælfred rex nauali proelio in mare contra sex^c[3] naues paganorum belligerauit, et unam ex eis cepit,^d ceteris per fugam elapsis.*[4]

[876] (ii) 898 *Karolus imperator Romam secundo profectus est, et ab urbe Roma in Bracham reuersus, Bosoni germano suo, Richildis regine, Irmingardam filiam Luduuuici imperatoris cum magna gloria uxorauit, deditque ei Prouinciam et, corona capiti eius imposita, regem eum iussit appellari, et inde euolutis paucis diebus Papiam ingreditur. In qua cum publicam rem disponeret, repente nuntiatum est ei Carlomannum cum ingenti armatorum multitudine Longobardorum regna intrasse. Qui mox pauore solutus, Ticinum Padumque pertransiit, summoque annisu in Gallias repedare contendit. Sed priusquam Alpium preminentia iuga angustaque itinera attingeret egritudine tunditur, de qua protinus .ii. non. Oct. obiit. Cuius corpus sui in feretro extra Italiam leuauerunt, sed ob intolerabilem fetorem eius compulsi sunt illud terre commendare.*

---

^a Corinthiam *JW*   ^b Anandus *ASN*, uel Anwed *interlin.* B[1]?   ^c .vii. B *ASN*
^d coepit *JW*

---

[1] Mar.   [2] Asser, c. 47.

Aachen and from there, after a few days, for Cologne. Carloman, Louis's eldest son, entered the land of Italy because Charles the Elder had departed thence. His brother Charles stayed in Alemannia; Louis, who was present at his father's death, stayed at Frankfurt, the main seat of the eastern kingdom. He also overcame Charles the Elder, who fought against him with more than 50,000 men on 8 October in the riverine area known as Main not far from Fort Andernach on the Rhine. Then the three brothers divided their father's kingdom among themselves at a place called Schwalefeldgau. Carloman held Bavaria, Pannonia, Carinthia, and the kingdoms of the Bohemian Slavs; Louis East Francia, Thuringia, Saxony, Frisia, and part of Lothar's kingdom; Charles held Alemannia, and some cities in Lothar's kingdom.[1]

The aforementioned army, leaving Repton, split into two divisions, of which one set out for the province of the Northumbrians with Healfdene and there wintered by the river called the Tyne. When they subdued the whole province of the Northumbrians to their rule, they also destroyed the Picts and the people of Strathclyde. The other division went to a place called Cambridge with Guthrum and Osketel and Anwend, three heathen kings, and wintered there.[2] In the same year King Alfred fought a battle at sea with six[3] heathen ships, and captured one of them. The others escaped by flight.[4]

[876] The Emperor Charles set out for Rome a second time, and, on his return from the city of Rome to *Bracha*, he married Ermengard, daughter of the Emperor Louis, to Boso (brother of his wife Queen Richildis), with great splendour, gave him Provence, and, placing the crown on his head, he ordered that he be called king. When a few days had passed, he went to Pavia. While he was there settling matters of state, he was informed suddenly that Carloman had entered the kingdoms of the Lombards with a great army. Charles at once, casting aside fear, crossed the Ticino and the Po, and strove with the utmost exertion to retreat into Gaul. But before he had reached the peaks and narrow passes of the Alps, he was stricken with an illness that led forthwith to his death on 6 October. His body was conveyed out of Italy in a litter, but had to be committed to the earth because of its

---

[3] Seven according to ASC and *ASN*.   [4] Asser, c. 48.

Post aliquantos autem annos, ossa eius translata sunt et Parisius in monasterio sancti Dionisii sepulta.[1]

Sepe memoratus paganorum exercitus noctu de Grantebrycge exiens, castellum quod dicitur Werham intrauit; ubi[a] *monasterium sanctimonialium inter duo flumina Flauu* [b]*et Terente*[b] *et in paga que Saxonice dicitur Þornsæta, tutissimo situ terrarum situm est nisi ab occidentali parte tantummodo, ubi contigua terra est. Cum quo exercitu Ælfred rex foedus firmiter* et *ea conditione, ut ab eo discederent, pepigit; cui ille exercitus electos obsides,*[2] *quantos* ipse[c] *nominauit, sine ulla controuersia dedit; necnon sacramentum in omnibus reliquiis, quibus ille rex maxime post Deum confidebat, iurauit, in quibus nec alicui genti prius iurare uoluit, se citissime de regno suo exiturum.*[d] *Sed more suo, solita fallacia utens, et obsides et iuramentum atque fidem promissam non* custodientes,[e] *nocte quadam, foedere dirupto,*[f] *omnes equites quos* rex[g] *habebat,* [h]*occidit.*[3] *Versusque inde*[hi] [j]alium *locum qui Saxonice*[k] *Exanceastre, Latine ciuitas* Exe *dicitur*, que[j] *in orientali ripa fluminis*[l] eiusdem *sita est, prope mare meridianum quod interluit Galliam Brytanniamque, inopinate* adiit.[m4] Quem, collecto exercitu, rex
p. 295 Alfredus est insecutus: sed quia ciuitatem iam | [n]intrauerat, illum assequi non poterat;[n] ueruntamen quot uel quantos uoluit obsides ab eis extorsit, firmumque cum eis foedus pepigit quod illi tempore non modico bene custodierunt, ibidemque hiemauerunt.[5] *Eodem anno* paganus *rex Halfdene Norðanhymbrorum regionem sibimet et suis diuisit, illam*que *cum suo exercitu coluit.*[6]

[o]Rollo cum suis Normanniam penetrauit, .xv. kalend. Decembris.[op7]

[a] quod *As* [b–b] ⟨et Terente⟩ (*As*) *Aw, om. Ac Acott (teste apparently Aw) Ao Au* [c] solus *As ASN* [d] exiturum *Ac*, exiturum esse (*As*) *Aw Ao Au ASN* [e] custodiens *from* custodientes *B*[1], custodiens *As ASN* [f] dirupto *ASN*, disrupto *As* [g] *om. As ASN* [h–h] occidit. Versusque inde] (*As*) *Ac Aw*, occidit uersusque mare *Ao*, occidentem versus *ASN* [i] in Domnaniam *interlin. above* inde *B*[5] [j–j] alium . . . que] ad (*om. Ao*) alium (*om. Ac Au Acott (teste Aw)*) locum qui dicitur Saxonice Exanceastre, Brittanice autem Cairuuisc, Latine quoque ciuitas autem (*om. Ac Ao Au Aw*) ⟨Exae, que⟩ (*As*) *Ao Ac Au Acott (teste Aw)*, ad locum qui dicitur anglice Exanceastra, que ciuitas *ASN* [k] Brittanice Cairuuisc (*as in As*) *interlin. above* qui Saxonice *B*[5] [l] Wisc id est Eaxa *interlin. above* fluminis *B*[5], fluminis Uuisc *As*, fluminis Exa *ASN* [m] direxit *As* [n–n] intrauerat . . . poterat] *darker ink in C*[1] [o–o] Rollo . . . Decembris] *ruled lines not visible so this could be over an erasure C* [p] *see App. B for addition B*

unbearable stench. After some years his bones were translated and buried in the monastery of Saint-Denis at Paris.[1]

The oft-mentioned heathen army, leaving Cambridge by night, entered the fortress called Wareham, where a convent of nuns is situated between two rivers, Frome and Tarrant, in a most secure position except on the western side alone, where it joins the mainland, in the area called Dorset in English. King Alfred made a firm treaty with the army on the condition that it should depart from him. The army gave as many hostages as he picked[2] without any disagreement, and swore an oath on all the relics in which the king had most faith (after God), on which they had not before been willing to swear for any nation, that they would leave his kingdom with all speed. But, as was their practice, using their habitual guile, they showed no regard for hostages, their oath, or their promised faith, and, having broken the treaty, one night they killed all the king's horsemen.[3] Then they turned away and without warning marched on another place, which is called Exeter in English, the city of the Exe in Latin, which is situated on the east bank of that same river, near the southern sea separating Gaul and Britain.[4] When he had gathered an army, King Alfred pursued them; but because they had already entered the city he could not follow them; however, he extorted from them as many hostages of whatever rank he wished, and he made a firm treaty with them which they kept very well for a time, and there they spent the winter.[5] In the same year the heathen King Healfdene shared out the province of the Northumbrians between himself and his men and settled there with his army.[6]

Rollo entered Normandy with his men on 17 November.[7]

---

[1] Mar.

[2] For Asser's reference to 'as many hostages as Alfred alone chose', see Keynes–Lapidge, *Alfred*, p. 245 n. 89.

[3] JW tries to make sense of Asser's difficult text by causing the Danes to kill Alfred's cavalry; see Stevenson (*Asser*, pp. 250–1), and Keynes–Lapidge, *Alfred*, p. 246 n. 91.

[4] Asser, c. 49.

[5] ASC A–E (877), where a loss of ships at Swanage is related, and BC do not give the reason for Alfred's failure to follow the Danes. JW presumably inserted this to make good an apparent gap in Asser.

[6] Asser, c. 50.

[7] Norman Annals. *AU, AG, ASN. AMSM* (875). This entry also appears in the 19-year table on p. 65 in the JW MS C. Cf. ASC E 876 (Latin) F (English).

Romanorum post Karolum regnauit filius eius Luduuuicus,[1] qui etiam appellabatur Balbus eo quod impeditioris erat eloquii, annis duobus.[2]

[877] (i) 899 Paganus exercitus, apud Werham cum classe relictus, Exancestre uenit, sed priusquam illo peruenisset, centum uiginti naues ex eis *ᵃmarina tempestateᵃ[3]* submerse sunt. Instante uero autumni tempore, paganorum apud Exanceastre pars resedit, pars Merciam adiit, cuius portionem aliquam Ceoluulfo (cui eamᵇ custodiendam, ut predictum est, commiserat) dedit, aliquam uero inter se distribuit.[4]

[878] (ii) 900 *Luduuuicus Balbus obiit tres filios relinquens, id est duos Luduuuicum et Carlomannum ex puella nomine Ansgrad, pro qua ipsa interdicta a Karolo patre suo quia sine consilio eius duxit eam, pater sibi uxorem Adelheid coniunxit, que, post mortem uiri, genuit filium nomine a⟨ui⟩,ᶜ id est Karolum.[5]*

Supra memoratus sepe exercitus Exeanceastreᵈ deserens, Cippanham, uillam regiam, que est sita in sinistrali parte Wiltunscire, adiit ibique hiemauit. Et multos eiusdem gentis ultra mare compulit hostiliter et penuria atque pauore nauigare, maximaque ex parte omnes regionis illius habitatores suo subdiderunt dominio.[6] Eodem tempore rex Alfredus, cum paucis suis nobilibus et etiam, cum quibusdam fasellis,ᵉ per siluestria et gronnosa Sumurtunensis page loca in magna tribulatione uitam inquietusᶠ ducebat. Nicil enim habebat quo uteretur, nisi quod a paganis uelᵍ etiam a Christianis, qui se paganorum subdiderant dominio, frequentibus irruptionibus aut clam aut etiam palam subtraheret.[7] Eodem anno frater Hinguari et Halfdene cum .xxiii. nauibus de Demeticaʰ regione, in qua hiemauerat, post multas ibi Christianorum strages factas, ad Domnaniam enauigauit, ibique a ministris regis cum mille ducentis infelici exitu perperam agens occisus

---

ᵃ⁻ᵃ marina tempestate] *interlin.* C¹   ᵇ *erasure before* eam C   ᶜ aui *Mar.*, ain *JW*   ᵈ *om.* H   ᵉ fasellis *Ac*, militibus et fasellis (*As*), militibus et uasallis (uasellis *Au*) *Aw Au ASN*, militibus uasellis *Ao*   ᶠ inquietam *As ASN*   ᵍ et *As ASN*   ʰ Demetia L

---

[1] Louis the Stammerer 877–9, who was not emperor.   [2] Mar.
[3] 'marina tempestate' might suggest that JW's version of ASC had 'micel yst' like ABE, and not 'micel myst' like CD.
[4] JW departs from ASC, principally by saying that part of the Danish army went to Mercia and part stayed at Exeter, in an attempt to accommodate Asser's statement (c.

After Charles his son Louis[1] reigned as emperor of the Romans for two years. He was also called the Stammerer because of his speech impediment.[2]

[877] The heathen army at Wareham left with its fleet and went to Exeter, but before it arrived there 120 of its ships were sunk by a storm at sea.[3] At the approach of autumn part of the heathen army settled again at Exeter while part went to Mercia. They had entrusted the safekeeping of part of that kingdom to Ceolwulf, as was mentioned before, while part they divided among themselves.[4]

[878] Louis the Stammerer died, leaving three sons, that is two, Louis and Carloman, by a girl called Ansgard—whom his father Charles banished because Louis married her without consulting him; in her stead his father married him to Adelheid, who, after the death of her husband, bore a son named after his grandfather, that is Charles.[5]

The army frequently mentioned before left Exeter, went to the royal township of Chippenham, which is situated in the left-hand [i.e. northern] area of Wiltshire, and there it wintered. Its hostile activity forced many of that people to cross the sea out of poverty and fear. They subdued all the inhabitants of the greatest part of that area to their rule.[6] At that time King Alfred was leading an anxious life in great tribulation with a few of his nobles, and even with some thegns among the woods and fens of Somerset. For he had nothing to live on except what he could take by frequent raids, secret or even open, from the pagans or even from the Christians who had submitted to pagan domination.[7] In the same year the brother of Inguar and Healfdene, after slaying many Christians, sailed with twenty-three ships from the area of Dyfed, where he had wintered, to Devon, and there in his wrongdoing he came to an unhappy end, slain with 1,200 men by the king's

---

52) that the Danes came to Chippenham from Exeter, which is not in ASC. For the view that Asser did not know ASC 877 and that the mangled c. 51 is an interpolation, see Keynes–Lapidge, *Alfred*, pp. 240–7.

[5] Mar.

[6] Asser, c. 51 (52). 'Left-hand side' is the Latin equivalent of a Welsh idiom, referring to something lying to the north.

[7] Id., c. 52 (53).

est ante arcem Cynuit; quia in eadem arce multi ministri regis cum suis se concluserant confugii causa. Verum^a *pagani cum arcem imparatam atque omnino immunitam nisi quod moenia nostro more erecta solummodo haberet, cernerent—non enim effringere moliebantur, quia ille locus situ terrarum tutissimus est ab omni parte, nisi ab orientali— obsidere eam c⟨o⟩eperunt, putantes homines illos manum cito daturos fame siti et obsessione coactos, quia nulla aqua illi arci^b contigua est. Quod non ita, ut putabant, euenit. Nam Christiani, antequam talem penuriam omnino subire paterentur, diuinitus instigati, multoque melius iudicantes aut mortem aut uictoriam mereri, diluculo super paganos ex improuiso irrumpunt, et a primo tempore^c hostes hostiliter cum rege suo maxima ex parte, paucis ad naues per fugam elapsis, prosternunt.*[1] *Eodem anno post Pasca Alfred rex cum paucis fecit arcem in loco qui dicitur Æthelingaeg, et de ipsa arce semper cum fasellis Sumurtunensibus paganos infatigabiliter debellauit.^d Iterumque in .vii.^e ebdomada post Pasca ad Petram Ecgbrihti, que est in orientali parte saltus qui dicitur Sealuudu, Latine autem silua magna, equitauit, ibique obuiauerunt illi omnes accole Sumurtunensis, Wiltunensis* et *Hamtunensis page, qui non ultra mare pro metu nauigauerant paganorum: uisoque rege, sicut dignum erat, quasi rediuiuum post tantas tribulationes recipientes, immenso repleti sunt gaudio, ibique castra metati sunt una nocte. Diluculo* uero *sequenti, rex inde castra commouens, uenit ad locum qui dicitur Ecglea,^f et ibi una nocte castra metatus est.*[2] *Inde sequenti* die^g *uexilla commouens, ad locum qui dicitur Ethandun, uenit, ubi^h contra paganorum exercitum uniuersum cum densa testudine atrociter belligerans, animoseque diu persistens diuino nutu, tandem uictoria potitus* est, *et paganos maxima cede prostrauit, fugientes* uero *usque ad arcem persecutus est, et omnia que extra arcem inuenit, homines scilicet equos et pecora, confestim cedens homines, subripuit, et ante portas arcis paganice cum omni exercitu suo uiriliter castra metatus est. Cunque ibi per .xiiii. dies moraretur,ⁱ pagani fame, frigore, timore et ad extremum desperatione perterriti, pacem ea conditione petierunt, ut rex nominatos obsides quantos uellet, ab eis*

---

^a Sed *As ASN*   ^b *interlin.* B¹   ^c uel aprino more *interlin.* B⁵   ^d rebellauit *As ASN*   ^e .iiii. *L*   ^f Æn- *interlin. above* Ec- *of* Ecglea B¹   ^g mane illucescente *As ASN*   ^h et *As ASN*   ⁱ remoraretur *As*, remorarentur *ASN*

---

[1] Id., c. 53 (54).   [2] Id., c. 54 (55).

thegns before the fortress of Countisbury, for many of the king's thegns had shut themselves in that same fortress, with their followers taking refuge there. But when the pagans perceived that the fortress was unprepared and entirely unfortified—except for the walls put up after our usual fashion, for they did not endeavour to take it by assault because that place is of all places the most secure, by virtue of its position, on all sides except the east—they began to besiege it, thinking that the defenders would soon surrender under compulsion from hunger, thirst, and the siege because there was no water close to that fortress. But matters did not turn out as they expected. The Christians, before they could bring themselves to undergo such hardship, divinely encouraged, and considering it much better to gain either death or victory, rushed out immediately and unexpectedly on the heathen at dawn, and, in their hostility, and straight away at the beginning laid low most of their enemies with their king. A few slipped away in flight to the ships.[1] In the same year, after Easter, King Alfred and a few men built a fortress in a place called Athelney, and from that same fortress continually and tirelessly with his thegns from Somerset fought the heathen. And again, in the seventh week after Easter, he rode to Ecgberth's Stone, which is in the eastern part of the wood which is called Selwood—in Latin the Great Wood— and there met him all the inhabitants of Somerset, Wiltshire, and Hampshire who had not sailed over the sea for fear of the heathen, and when they had seen the king, as was right, as if receiving one brought back to life after so many troubles, they were filled with great joy. There they encamped for one night. But at dawn on the following day the king moved camp from there, and came to a place called Iley, and there they made camp for one night.[2] Then on the following day he moved his standards, and came to a place called Edington where, battling bitterly with a packed shield-wall against the entire heathen army, and keeping this up fiercely for a long time, he was finally, by divine consent, victorious, and laid low the heathen with great slaughter. He pursued the fugitives right up to the fortress, and he seized everything he found outside it, men, horses, and cattle, and slew the men at once. He boldly set up camp before the gates of the pagan fortress with his whole army. When he had stayed there for fourteen days, the heathen, terrified and at the point of despair through hunger, cold, and fear, sought peace on the condition that

acciperet, | illeᵃ nullum eis daret, ita tamen qualiter nunquam cum aliquo pacem ante pepigerant. Quorum legatione audita, rex suatimᵇ misericordia motus, nominatos, quantos uoluit, obsides ab eis accepit. Quibus acceptis, pagani insuper iurauerunt se citissime de suo regno exituros, necnon Guthrum rex eorum Christianitatem subire et baptismum sub manu Alfredi regis accipere promisit. Que omnia ille et sui, ut promiserant, impleuerunt. Nam post ebdomadas .vii.ᶜ Guthrum, paganorum rex, cum .xxx. electissimis de exercitu suo uiris ad Alfredum regem prope Æthelingaege in loco qui dicitur Aalr, peruenit. Quem rex in filium adoptionis sibi suscipiens, de fonte sacr⟨o⟩ᵈ baptismatis elimauit.ᵉ¹ Cuius crismatis solutio .viii. die in uilla regia que dicitur Weadmor, fuit. Qui, postquam baptizatus fuit duodecim noctibus cum rege mansit. Cui rex cum suis omnibus multa et optima edificiaᶠ² largiter dedit.³

ᵍRomanorum octogesimus quintusʰ⁴ regnauit Karolus minor annis decem post primum introitum eius in Italiam.⁵

[879] (i) 901 *Karolus iunior filius Luduuuici Italiam primum intrauit, frater Karlomanni et Luduuuici.⁶*

ⁱPrefatusʲ paganorum exercitus de Cippanhamme, ut promiserat, consurgens, Cirenceastre adiit, que est in meridiana parte Huuicciorum, ibique per unum annum mansit.⁷ Eodem anno magnus paganorum exercitus de ultramarinis partibus nauigans in Tamensem fluuium uenit, adunatusque est superiori exercitui, sed tamen hiemauit in loco qui dicitur Fullanham, iuxta flumen Temense.⁸ Eodem anno eclypsis solis inter nonam et uesperam, sed propius ad nonam, facta est.⁹ ᵏDefuncto Dunberto Wintoniensi episcopo, successit Deneuulfus.¹⁰ Hic si fame creditur, ad multam etatem non solum

---

ᵃ ille *ASN,* et ille *HL As,* om. *B,* nec ullum *P*   ᵇ utens *add. mg. B⁵,* suatim utens (*As*) *Ac ASN,* sua ipsius *Ao Au Aw*   ᶜ om. *Ac Au Ao Aw,* tres (*As*) *ASN*
ᵈ sacro *As ASN,* sacri *JW*   ᵉ eliminauit *H,* elimauit *Ac,* eleuauit (*As*) *Aw Ao Au ASN*   ᶠ edificia *Ac Aw Ao Au ASN,* beneficia (*As*)   ᵍ capitula .lxxxv. *add. before* Romanorum *L*   ʰ quartus *(N)*   ⁱ incorporated 879 n. k here *LP*
ʲ predictus *HL*   ᵏ Defuncto . . . miraculo (p. 314)] *add. mg. adjoining* 879–82 *C³, incorporated at* 879 n. i *LP, incorporated at* 880 n. g *B*

---

¹ 'elimauit' and not 'eleuauit' is the reading in JW, *HR* iii. 97 (ii. 113), and the Asser witness *Ac.*; it is possible that this misreading was that of the Asser Cotton MS, deriving ultimately from a misunderstanding of 'eleuauit' as 'elimauit'.
² For the correctness of the word 'edificia' and its meaning as 'treasures', see Keynes–Lapidge, *Alfred,* pp. 249–50.

the king could receive from them as many chosen hostages as he wished, and that he gave them none. Never before had they made such a peace with anyone. When he had heard their proposal, the king was suddenly moved by pity, and took from them as many chosen hostages as he wanted. When he had taken them the heathen also swore that they would leave his realm with all speed, and Guthrum their king promised that he would become a Christian and receive baptism with King Alfred as sponsor. He and his men fulfilled all they had promised, for, seven weeks later, Guthrum, king of the heathen, went to King Alfred at a place called Aller, near Athelney, with thirty of the most distinguished men in his army. The king received Guthrum himself as his adopted son, and raised[1] him from the font of holy baptism. The unbinding of the chrism was held on the eighth day at the royal township called Wedmore. After his baptism he stayed twelve nights with the king. The king generously provided him and all his men with many of the best treasures.[2, 3]

Charles the Younger,[4] the eighty-fifth emperor of the Romans, reigned for ten years after his first entry into Italy.[5]

[879] Charles the Younger, son of Louis and brother of Carloman and Louis, entered Italy for the first time.[6]

The heathen army mentioned before left Chippenham, as promised, and went to Cirencester, which is in the southern part of the land of the Hwicce, and there it stayed for a year.[7] In the same year a great pagan army from beyond the sea sailed into the River Thames, and joined the former army; however it wintered in the place called Fulham, near the River Thames.[8] In the same year there was a solar eclipse between nones and vespers, but closer to nones.[9] On the death of Tunberht, bishop of Winchester, Denewulf succeeded.[10] He was, if common report is to be

---

[3] Asser, c. 55 (56).

[4] Charles the Fat 881–7. JW's numbering of Roman emperors, unlike Marianus', includes Louis the Stammerer and is consequently one ahead of Marianus from this point.

[5] Mar.   [6] Mar.   [7] Asser, c. 56 (57).   [8] Id., c. 57 (58).

[9] Id., c. 58 (59).

[10] The date for this marginal addition concerning Dunberht (i.e. Tunberht), bishop of Winchester and the succession of Denewulf is not given elsewhere. If no charter evidence conflicts with this date, there is, as O'Donovan, ii. 109 has pointed out, no satisfactory confirmatory charter evidence. Tunberht is omitted from JW Epis. Lists.

litterarum expers, sed etiam subulcus fuit. Eum rex Ælfredus, hostium uiolentie cedens, et in siluam profugus, casu sues pascentem offendit: cuius *comperto ingenio, litteris informandum tradidit* eximie*ᵃ* et postmodum *perfectius institutum crea*uit Wintonie presulem, *commentus rem dignam miraculo.*ᵇ¹

[880] (ii) 902 *Boso germanus Karoli senioris occupare regnum nitens a filiis Balbi fugatur.*²

*Sepeᶜ memoratus paganorum exercitus Cirenceastre deserens, ad Orientales Anglos ᵈperrexit, ipsamque regionem diuidens, c⟨o⟩epit inhabitare.*³ *Eodem anno exercitus paganorum qui in Fullanhamme hiemauerat, Brytannicam insulam deserens, iterumque ultra mare nauigans, ad Orientalem Franciam perrexit, et per unum annum in loco qui dicitur Gendi,ᵉ* id est Gent, *mansit.*⁴

[C³BP]

*ᶠÆlfredus rex Sceaftoni*am *quon-dam urb*em qui *modo est uicus* edificauit. *Ibi Ælfgiua regina Eadmundi qui fuit pronepos huius Ælfredi sanctimonialium monas-terium* construxit.*ᵈᶠᵍ⁵*

[881] (iii) 903 *Karlomannus maior rex Bauuarie pater Arnulfi obiit paralisi, sepultusque est in Bauuaria in uilla Odingas. Luduuuicas uero frater eius, possidens suum regnum, concessit Arnulfo Carinthiam quam ei pater prid⟨em⟩ʰ dedit.*⁶

*ⁱExercitus paganorum sepedictusⁱ⁷ in Franciam perrexit. Contra quem Franci pugnauerunt, finitoque proelio, pagani, equis inuentis, equites facti sunt.*⁸

ᵃ interlin. C³, om. HL   *ᵇ* see above, p. 312 n. k   *ᶜ* supra H   *ᵈ⁻ᵈ* perrexit . . . construxit] *partly rewritten over erasure and partly extending into mg.* C³   *ᵉ* Gendi (As) Ac Acott (teste Aw), Gaent Aw Au ASN, Gaynt Ao   *ᶠ⁻ᶠ* Ælfredus . . . construxit] om. HL   *ᵍ* 879 n. k *incorporated here* B   *ʰ* pridem *Mar*, pridem *from* pridie (N), pridie JW   *ⁱ⁻ⁱ* Exercitus . . . sepedictus] Praefatus exercitus superius As

---

¹ *GP* ii. 75 (p. 162).   ² Mar.   ³ Asser, c. 59 (60).
⁴ Id., c. 60 (61).

believed, not only illiterate but actually a swineherd into advanced age. King Alfred, giving way before the onslaught of the enemy, took refuge in the forest and came across him by chance when he was feeding his pigs. When Denewulf had revealed his ability the king handed him over to be instructed in letters, and afterwards, when he was well advanced in his studies, he made him bishop of Winchester, an idea worthy of wonderment.[1]

[880] Boso, brother of Charles the Elder, attempted to occupy the realm, and was put to flight by the sons of the Stammerer.[2]

The heathen army frequently mentioned left Cirencester, went to East Anglia and, dividing the area, began to settle there.[3] In the same year the heathen army, which had wintered at Fulham, left the island of Britain, and sailing again overseas, went to East Francia, and for a year stayed in a place called Gendi, that is Ghent.[4]

> King Alfred built Shaftesbury, once a town, now a village. There Ælfgifu, queen of Edmund, the great-grandson of this Alfred, built a convent for nuns.[5]

[881] Carloman the Elder, king of Bavaria, and father of Arnulf, died of palsy, and was buried in Bavaria in the township of Altötting, but Louis, his brother, taking possession of his kingdom, ceded to Arnulf Carinthia, which his father had formerly given him.[6]

The oft-mentioned[7] pagan army went to Francia. The Franks fought them, and when the battle was over, the heathen obtained horses and became a mounted army.[8]

---

[5] GP ii. 86 (p. 186), from which the date is derived. This might account for its insertion in the body of the text after erasure, where the other GP entries on this page in JW MS C (see above, p. 313 n. 4, and below, p. 317 n. 5) are placed in the margin.

[6] Mar.

[7] As Stevenson, Asser, p. 286 put it, 'superius' in Asser 'is a somewhat too literal rendering of the ufor' of ASC. JW chooses to interpret 'superius' differently from Asser.

[8] Asser, c. 61 (62).

[882] (iiii) 904 *Karolus iunior de Alamannia egressus Longobardorumque fines possidens in*ᵃ *paucis diebus totam Italiam accepit, Romamque perueniens a papa Iohanne et senatu fauorabiliter acceptus et cum magna gloria oleo consecrato unctus imperator creatur.*[1]

Prefatus exercitus paganorum *suas naues per flumen quod dicitur Mese sursum tanto longe in Franciam pertraxit,*ᵇ *ibique uno anno hiemauit.*[2] *Eodem anno rex Alfred*us *nauali proelio contra paganicas naues*ᶜ *in mare congressus est: ex quibus duas cepit, occisis omnibus qui in eis erant. Duarumque aliarum nauium duo principes, cum omnibus suis sociis, ualde proelio uulneribusque fatigati, depositis armis, curuo poplite, et supplicibus precibus, dederunt se regi.*[3]

[C³BP³]

ᵈ*De Æthelingæ. Æthelingea est non maris insula, sed stagnorum refusionibus et paludibus inaccessa, nauigio* solum*modo adi*tur. *Eius constructor fuit rex Ælfredus.*[4] Situs est idem locus *in Sumersetensi pago.*ᵈ[5]

[883] (v) 905 *Luduuuicus rex frater imperatoris obiit apud Franconfurt .xiii. kalend. Septembris, sepultusque est Lorassam ubi et pater eius.*[6]

Prefatus exercitus naues suas per flumen

[HL]

*quod dicitur Scald*ad, *contra flumen nauigans, ad monasterium quod dicitur Candath,*ᵉ *traxit, et ibi anno uno mansit.*[7]

[C³BP]

ᶠ*Scald*ad, *contra flumen, nauigans, ad monasterium sanctimonialium quod dicitur Candath,*ᵉ *traxit, ibique uno anno mansit.*[7]

ᵃ *in mg. near line* C¹   ᵇ protraxit L   ᶜ .iiii. *interlin.* B¹   ᵈ⁻ᵈ De . . . pago] *added mg. adjoining* 882–3 (directly below C³'s 879 n. k addition) C³, *om.* HL, *om. heading* B, *added mg. next to* 880, *possibly a more appropriate year* P³   ᵉ Cundoht Aw Ac Ao Au, Cundoth (As), Cundath *from* Candath B   ᶠ Scaldad . . . rediit (p. 318)] *written over erasure* C³

[882] Charles the Younger left Alemannia, occupied the land of the Lombards, and took all Italy within a few days. He went to Rome, and was favourably received by Pope John and the Senate and with great ceremony was anointed with the consecrated oil, and made emperor.[1]

The aforementioned heathen army drew its ships as far as possible up the river called the Meuse into Francia and wintered there that year.[2] In the same year King Alfred met the heathen ships at sea in a naval battle; he took two of them, and killed all who were on board. The two commanders of the other two ships and all their men, exhausted by the battle and their wounds, laid down their arms, and, on bended knee with prayers of supplication, yielded to the king.[3]

> Concerning Athelney. Athelney is not an island of the sea but, inaccessible because of the overflow of the marshes, it can be approached only by boat. King Alfred was its founder.[4] That place is situated in Somerset.[5]

[883] King Louis, brother of the emperor, died at Frankfurt on 20 August, and was buried at Lorsch, where his father also lies.[6]

The aforementioned army, sailing its ships up the river

which is called the Scheldt against the current, brought them to the monastery which is called Condé, and stayed there for a year.[7]

Scheldt against the current, drew them to the convent of nuns which is called Condé, and stayed there for a year.[7]

---

[1] Mar. [2] Asser, c. 62 (63). [3] Id., c. 63 (64).
[4] GP ii. 92 (p. 199).
[5] GP ii. 90 (p. 196). This marginal addition follows immediately the GP marginal addition under 879 (n. k), and could have been intended for addition there. The foundation of Athelney by Alfred has already been entered under 878, in a passage taken from Asser.
[6] Mar. [7] Asser, c. 64 (65).

*a*Assero Scireburnensi episcopo defuncto, successit Suithelmus qui regis Ælfredi elemosinam ad sanctum Thomam in Indiam detulit, indeque prospere rediit.*b1*

[884] (vi) 906 *Luduuuicus filius Balbi obiit apud* ⟨*sanctum*⟩*c Dionisium ubi et sepultus est. Cuius regnum frater eius Karlomannus tenuit. Marinus*2 *centesimus septimus papa.*3

Hic *scolam Saxonum in Roma morantium, pro amore et deprecatione Alfredi, Angulsaxonum regis, ab omni tributo et telone*d *benigne liberauit. Qui etiam multa dona predicto regi illa uice transmisit: inter que dedit* ei *non paruam illius sanctissime crucis partem, in qua Dominus noster Iesus Christus pro hominum salute pependit.*4 Memoratus exercitus paganorum Sunne fluminis ostium intrans, Embenum usque nauigauit, ibidemque uno anno mansit.*5 |

p. 297   [885] (vii) 907 Marinus papa obiit.6 *Agapitus*7 *centesimus octauus papa.*8

Paganorum *exercitus prefatus in duas* se*e turmas diuisit: una etenim in Orientalem Franciam perrexit, altera* uero turma *ad Brytanniam ueniens, Cantiam adiit, ciuitatemque, que Hrofeceaster Saxonice dicitur, in orientali ripa fluminis Meduueaq sitam, obsedit. Ante huius portam pagani castellum firmum subito fabricauerunt, nec tamen illam ciuitatem expugnare potuerunt, quia ciues illi se uiriliter defenderunt, quousque rex Alfred*us *cum magno exercitu adiutorium illis* collaturus*f superuenit. Et tunc pagani, relicta arce sua, omnibus*que *equis quos de Francia secum adduxerant, derelictis, maxima necnon captiuorum suorum parte dimissa,*g *adueniente subito rege, ad naues suas confestim confugiunt, Saxones* uero *derelictos a paganis captiuos et equos statim diripiunt. Pagani itaque, magna necessitate compulsi, eadem estate* rursus*h Franciam adierunt.*9 *Eodem anno Alfred,*

---

*a 884 begins here L   b see above, p. 316 n. f   c sanctum Mar. H, om. CLBP
d telonio (As) Aw, teloneo Ao Au, tolono Ac, theloneo ASN   e se (As) Ao ASN, om. Ac Aw Au   f conferens As, ASN   g pro arce dimissa Ac, in arce dimissa (As) Aw Ao Au ASN   h iterum As, ASN*

---

1 ASC BDEF 883, C 884 record that Sigehelm (not named by F), who seems to have been a layman (Stevenson, *Asser*, p. 290), took alms to Rome, and also to India ('Iudea' in BC) to SS Thomas and Bartholomew. WM, *GP* ii. 80 (p. 177), mistakenly identifies the ASC Sigehelm with a bishop of Sherborne of that name and makes him the immediate successor of Asser (O'Donovan, ii. 104–5). JW shares these mistakes

On the death of Asser, bishop of Sherborne, Swithhelm succeeded; he took King Alfred's alms to St Thomas in India,
whence he returned safely.[1]

[884] The Stammerer's son Louis died at Saint-Denis, and there
he was buried. His brother Carloman took his kingdom. Marinus[2]
was the 107th pope.[3]

He kindly freed the school for the Saxons staying in Rome from
all tribute and toll on account of the love, and at the request, of
Alfred, king of the Anglo-Saxons. He also sent many gifts to the
aforementioned king on that occasion, among which he gave him a
sizeable piece of that most holy Cross on which Our Lord Jesus
Christ hung for man's salvation.[4] The heathen army already mentioned entered the mouth of the River Somme, sailed as far as
Amiens, and stayed there for a year.[5]

[885] Pope Marinus died.[6] Agapitus[7] was the 108th pope.[8]

The aforementioned pagan army separated into two divisions:
one went to East Francia but the other division came to Britain,
arrived in Kent, and besieged the city which in English is called
Rochester, situated on the eastern bank of the River Medway. The
heathen quickly built a strong fortress in front of its entrance, but,
however, they could not take that city because the citizens
defended themselves vigorously until King Alfred could bring
them help, and arrived with a great army. Then the heathen, having left their defences and abandoned all the horses they had
brought with them from Francia, even released the greater part of
their prisoners, and fled to their ships in haste at the king's sudden arrival. The English immediately seized the prisoners and
horses abandoned by the enemy. So the heathen, driven by great
necessity, went to Francia again that summer.[9] In the same year

though he calls the bishop Suithelmus. JW *Epis. Lists* call this bishop Sigehelm and do
not make him the immediate successor of Asser. Æthelweard was Asser's successor.
  [2] Marinus I 882–4.   [3] Mar.   [4] Asser, c. 70 (71).
  [5] ASC. Asser omitted ASC A–E's annal for 884, accidentally according to
Keynes–Lapidge, *Alfred*, p. 251 n. 123.
  [6] Not in Marianus, but in Asser, c. 70 (71), 885 for 884, and ASC ADEF (885) (B)C
(886).
  [7] Not known at this date. An Agapitus follows Marinus in Marianus' list of popes.
This might be an error for Agapitus II (946–55), who follows Marinus II (942–6).
  [8] Mar.   [9] Asser, c. 65 (66).

Angulsaxonum rex, classem suam de Cantia plenam bellatoribus, in Orientales Anglos dirigens, predandi causa, transmisit. Cunque ad ostium Sture fluminis uenissent,ᵃ confestim .xvi.ᵇ¹ *naues paganorum, ad bellum parate, obuiauerunt eis, initoque nauali proelio hinc* et *inde acriter pugnantes, pagani omnes occisi, et omnes naues cum omni pecunia eorum capte sunt. Cunque inde uictrix regia classis* rediret,ᶜ² *pagani quiᵈ* ᵉ*Orientalem Anglorum regionemᵉ* inhabitabant,ᶠ *congregatis undecunque nauibus, eidem regie classi in ostio fluminisᵍ in mari obuiauerunt, consertoque nauali proelio, pagani uictoriam habuerunt.³ Regem Occidentalium Francorum Karlomannum, aprorum uenationem agentem, singulariʰ congressione horrendo dente* singularisⁱ *dilacerans* ferus, *miserabili funere percussit. Cuius frater Luduuuicus* ʲtertio *anno⁴* anteʲ *defunctus est, qui et ipse erat Francorum rex; ipsi etenim ambo filii Luduuuici regis Francorum erant. Qui supra memorato anno, quo eclypsis solis facta est, defunctus est. Ipse quoque Luduuuicus filius Karoli Francorum regis erat, cuius filiam Iuthittam Atheluulfus Occidentalium Saxonum rex, ad reginam sibi paterna uoluntate suscepit.⁵ Presentiᵏ quoque anno magnus paganorum exercitus de Germania in regionem Antiquorum Saxonum superuenit. Contra quos, adunatis uiribus, idemˡ Saxones et Frisones bisᵐ in uno anno uiriliter pugnauere. In quibus duobus bellis Christiani, diuina misericordia opitulante, uictoriam habuere.⁶ Eodem* insuperⁿ *anno Karolus, Alamannorum rex, Occidentalium Francorum regnum, et omnia regna, que sunt inter mare Terrenum illumque marinum sinum, qui inter Antiquos Saxones et Gallos adiacet, uoluntario omnium consensu accepit, absque Armoricano regno. Qui Karolusᵒ Luduuuici regis filius* erat;ᵖ *ipse uero Luduuuicus germanus* fuitᵛ *Karoli regis Francorum, patris Iuthitte predicte: qui duo germani fuerunt filii Luduuuici:* ʳLuduuuicus *uero ille filius Pippini.*ʳ⁷ *Eodem quoque anno*

ᵃ aduenissent *As*   ᵇ .xiii. *Ac*, tredecim *(As) Aw*, 13 *Ao Au*   ᶜ dormiret *As* ᵈ qui ad *(As) Aw Ao Au*, ad *Ac Acott (teste Aw)*   ᵉ⁻ᵉ Orientalem Anglorum regionem] *Ac Aw Ao Au*, Orientalium Anglorum regionem *(As)*   ᶠ habitabant *As*   ᵍ eodem die *interlin. B¹*   ʰ singulari *Ac Ao Aw Au ASN (interlineation) HR iii. 100 (ii. 117)*, singularis *(As)*   ⁱ *om. (As) Ac Acott (teste Aw) Ao Au*, aper *Aw ASN HR iii. 100 (ii. 117)*   ʲ⁻ʲ tertio . . . ante] superiori anno *As ASN*, precedenti anno *HR iii. 100 (ii. 117)*   ᵏ eodem *As*   ˡ idem *Ac Au*, iidem *(As) Ao Aw* ᵐ bis *(As)*, ibi *Ac Ao*, ibidem *Aw Au*   ⁿ quoque *As, om. ASN*   ᵒ *followed by erased* filius *C, add.* filius *Ac Au, add.* filius *add. here but omits it three words later Ao* ᵖ fuit *As ASN*   ᵠ *om. Ac Ao Au*, erat *(As) Aw ASN*   ʳ⁻ʳ Luduuuicus . . . Pippini] Lodwic vero filius Pipini *Ac*, Hlothuuic vero ille filius Caroli ⟨antiqui qui etiam fuit filius Pipini⟩ *(As)*, Hlothuuic vero ille filius Pipini siue Caroli *Acott (teste Aw)*, Hlothuuic (Lodouic *Ao* Hloduuicus *ASN* Ludouuicus *B*) vero ille filius Karoli magni ⟨qui *add. Ao*⟩ et antiqui atque sapientissime qui etiam fuit filius Pipini *Aw Ao Au ASN B* (Karoli . . . etiam fuit filius *om. through eyeskip and add. upper mg. with signe de renvoi B*)

Alfred, king of the Anglo-Saxons, directing his fleet filled with
warriors, sent it from Kent to East Anglia to loot. When he came
to the mouth of the river Stour, sixteen[1] pagan ships, ready for
battle, immediately encountered his, and a naval battle was joined
in which both sides fought fiercely to and fro. All the heathen
were slain, and all their ships with all their booty were captured.
When the victorious royal fleet returned[2] from there the heathen
who inhabited the land of East Anglia assembled ships from all
around, and met that same royal fleet at sea, at the mouth of the
river, and when the naval battle was joined the heathen took the
victory.[3] Carloman, king of the West Franks, while hunting boar,
was rent open by a single blow from one fearful tusk, which
struck him down in wretched death. His brother Louis had died
three years[4] earlier. He had also been king of the Franks, for they
were both sons of Louis, king of the Franks. He died in the year
mentioned above in which a solar eclipse occurred. That Louis
also was the son of Charles, king of the Franks, whose daughter
Judith Æthelwulf, king of the West Saxons, received as his queen
with her father's consent.[5] Also in the present year the great heathen army came from Germany into the land of the Old Saxons,
and the same Saxons and the Frisians joined forces and fought
fiercely against them twice in one year. In these two battles the
Christians, aided by divine mercy, were victorious.[6] Moreover, in
the same year Charles, king of the Alemannians, with the willing
agreement of all, received the kingdom of the West Franks and all
the   kingdoms,   except   that   of   Armorica,   between   the
Mediterranean and that bay of the sea which lies between the Old
Saxons and the Gauls. This Charles was also the son of King
Louis; that Louis was also brother of Charles, king of the Franks,
father of the aforementioned Judith. The two brothers were Louis'
sons, and Louis himself was the son of Pippin.[7] Also in that same

---

[1] Asser's 'xiii' could be a misreading of ASC's 'xvi'.

[2] For 'dormiret' in Asser as a scribal error for 'domum iret' or 'domum rediret', see
Stevenson, *Asser*, p. 291 and Keynes–Lapidge, *Alfred*, p. 252 n. 128.

[3] Asser, c. 66 (67).

[4] JW's 'tertio anno' may be the result of his wrongly identifying Louis, brother of
Carloman, with the king whose death is recorded in Marianus' annal for 883.

[5] Asser, c. 67 (68).   [6] Asser, c. 68 (69).

[7] Asser, c. 69 (70). Asser, as seen in the recorded MS tradition, and as followed by
JW, wrongly makes Louis the Pious the son of Pippin. *ASN*'s reading, which the JW
MS B gives in the margin, may be the original reading; see Keynes–Lapidge, *Alfred*,
pp. 253–4 n. 135.

paganorum exercitus qui in Orientalibus Anglis habitauit, pacem, quam cum Alfredo rege pepigerat, obprobriose fregit.[1]

[C³BP³]

*a*Post Esne Herefordensem episcopum hi in ordinem successerunt pontifices: Ceolmund, Vtel, Wlfheard, Beonna, Eadulf, Cuthuuulf, Mukel, Deorlaf, Kinemund, Eadgar, Tidhelm, Wlfhelm, Alfric, Athulf, Athelstan, Leouegar, Walter, Rotbertus, Gerardus, Reignelm, Gausfridus, Ricard. *Ornat sedem episcopalem rex et martyr Æthelbertus suis reliquiis apud Orientales Anglos natus. In diocesi presulatus cenobi*um est quod *Weneloch* dicitur ubi *fuit antiquissima sanctimonialium habitatio, ibique beatissima* uirgo *Mildburga soror sancte Mildrythe neptis Pende regis Merciorum ex filio uitam transegit* et requiescit. Sed *locum omnino desertum Rogeri*us *com*es *de Monte Gomerico monachis Cluniacensibus impleuit. Scrobbesbyriense* monasterium idem comes *constit*uit, *ibique mona*chos *ex Sagio locauit.*[a2]

[886] (viii) 908 *Carlomannus filius Balbi obiit et sepultus est apud sanctum Dionisium cum fratre et auo.*[3]

---

a–a Post . . . locauit] *add. mg. alongside* 885 C³, *om. HL, mg. alongside* 884–6 P³

---

[1] Asser, c. 71 (72).
[2] *GP* iv. 170–1 (pp. 305–6). It is not clear why scribe C³ placed these *GP* extracts at this point. The list of Hereford bishops could have been based on information in *GP*

year the heathen army which settled in East Anglia disgracefully broke the peace which they had made with King Alfred.[1]

These bishops succeeded Esne, bishop of Hereford, in this order: Ceolmund, Utel, Wulfheard, Beonna, Eadwulf, Cuthwulf, Mucel, Deorlaf, Cynemund, Edgar, Tidhelm, Wulfhelm, Ælfric, Æthelwulf, Æthelstan, Leofgar, Walter, Robert, Gerard, Reinhelm, Geoffrey, Richard. The king and martyr Æthelberht, a native of East Anglia, enhances the episcopal see with his relics. In the bishop's diocese is a convent called Wenlock, which was the most ancient establishment for nuns, and there the most blessed virgin Mildburg, sister of St Mildthryth, granddaughter of Penda, king of the Mercians, by his son, departed this life, and lies buried. Roger, count of Montgomery, filled the completely deserted place with Cluniac monks. The same count established the monastery at Shrewsbury, and placed monks from Séez there.[2]

[886] Carloman, son of the Stammerer, died, and was buried at Saint-Denis with his brother and grandfather.[3]

iv. 163 (pp. 299-304), where Ealdred is also omitted, though the spelling of the names is here closer to those in the original JW *Epis. Lists* (that is, up to 'Reignelmus') than to those in *GP*.
[3] Mar.

Memoratus sepe exercitus paganorum, *ᵃorientali Francia dere-licta,ᵃ¹ iterum in Occidentalium Francorum regionem uenit,* et *ᵇin* ostium *fluminis quod* Sequana *dicitur* intrans,*ᵇ contraque longe nauigans, Parisiam ciuitatem adiit, ibi*que hiemauit, quam *ciuitatem anno illo integro obsedit. Sed, Deo misericorditer fauente, munitionem irrumpere non potuit.² Eodem anno Alfred*us, *Angulsaxonum rex, post incendia urbium stragesque populorum, Lundoniam ciuitatem honorifice restaurauit et habitabilem fecit, quam* etiam *Ætheredo, Merciorum comiti seruandam commendauit. Ad quem regem omnes Angli* et *Saxones, qui prius ᶜubique dispersi fuerant, aut cum paganis sineᵈ³ captiuitate erant,* uenerunt*ᵉ et uoluntarie suo dominio se subdiderunt.ᶜ⁴*

[887]ᶠ (ix) 909   *ᵍAdrianus⁵ centesimus nonus papa.ᵍ Karolus imperator corpore et animo c(o)epit egrotare, et mense Nouembrio circa transitum sancti Martini Triburas uillam ueniens, conuentum conuocauit. Tunc cernentes optimates regni imperatorem non solum uiribus corporis sed etiam animi defecisse, Arnulfum Carlomanni filium, ultro in regnum attrahunt, et ab imperatore in triduo | ita deficiunt, ut cum illo uix aliquis remaneret, qui ei saltem officia humanitatis impenderet. Cibus tantum et potus ex Liutberti Mogontini episcopi sumptibus ei dabatur, cui supplicanti Arnulfus aliquantos in Alamannia fiscos concessit.⁶*

Predictus *ʰexercitus paganorum,ʰ ciuitatem Parisiam derelinquens incolumem, eo quod sibimet aliter proficere non poterat, classem suam contra* Sequanam*ⁱ longe remigando tam diu direxit, donec ad ostium fluminis quod Mæterne nominatur peruenisset. Tunc* Sequanam*ʲ deserentes, in ostium* fluminis *Meaterne diuertunt, contra quod diu ac longe nauigantes, demum non sine labore usque ad locum qui dicitur Caziei, id est uilla regia, peruenerunt. In quo loco anno integro hiemauerunt. Sequenti anno in ostium fluminis quod dicitur Iona, intrauerunt,* non

p. 298

ᵃ⁻ᵃ orientali . . . derelicta] regionem fugit *Ac*, regionem fugiens (*As*) *Aw Ao Au*   ᵇ⁻ᵇ in . . . intrans] naues suas intus in flumen quod Signe dicitur *Ac Acott (teste Aw)*, naues suas intrans in flumen quod Signe dicitur (*As*), naues suas dirigens in flumen quod Signe dicitur *Aw Ao Au*   ᶜ⁻ᶜ ubique . . . subdiderunt] *darker ink over erasure Cᵗ*   ᵈ sine *Ac Acott (teste Aw)*, sub (*As*) *Aw Ao Au ASN*   ᵉ converterunt (*As*), reverterunt *ASN*   ᶠ 887 *(from 877) C*   ᵍ⁻ᵍ Adrianus . . . papa] *placed at* 888 *n. d Mar.*   ʰ⁻ʰ exercitus paganorum] paganorum exercitus *HL As*   ⁱ Sigene *Ac*, Signe (*As*) *Aw Ao Au*   ʲ Sigonam *As*

¹ JW's 'orientali Francia derelicta' is needed to complete Asser's rendering of ASC 886.

The oft-mentioned heathen army, abandoning East Francia,[1] came again into the land of the West Franks. Entering the mouth of the river called the Seine, and sailing far upstream, they arrived at the city of Paris, and there they wintered, laying siege to the city for the entire year. But God in his mercy protected it, and they were unable to break through the fortifications.[2] In the same year, Alfred, king of the Anglo-Saxons, after the burning of the cities and the slaughter of people, rebuilt the city of London in grand style, and also entrusted its defence to Æthelred, ealdorman of Mercia. All the Angles and Saxons who had been scattered all over the country, or dwelt among the heathen though not in[3] captivity, came to the king and submitted to his rule of their own accord.[4]

[887] Hadrian[5] was the 109th pope. The emperor Charles began to sicken in body and mind, and in the month of November, near the feast of St Martin, he arrived at the town of Tribur, and called an assembly. Then, when the magnates of the realm perceived that the emperor had lost not only strength of body but also strength of mind, they brought Arnulf, Carloman's son, into the realm from outside and thus, within three days, they had abandoned the emperor to such an extent that scarcely anyone remained with him who would perform for him even the basic human services. He was given food and drink at the expense of Liutbert, bishop of Mainz, to whom at his request Arnulf granted some estates in Alemannia.[6]

The aforementioned pagan army, leaving the city of Paris unharmed because it could not do otherwise, rowed its fleet for a long time, and a long way up the Seine until it arrived at the mouth of the river called the Marne. Then, leaving the Seine, it turned into the mouth of the River Marne, up which it sailed long and far until at last, after great exertion, it arrived at a place called Chézy, that is 'royal township'. In that place they lay for a whole year. In the following year they entered the mouth of the river called the Yonne, doing great damage to the area, and there they

---

[2] Asser, c. 81 (82).
[3] Stevenson's 'sub' instead of 'sine' seems unlikely, see D. Whitelock, *The Genuine Asser* (Reading, 1968), p. 15.
[4] Asser, c. 82 (83).   [5] Hadrian III 884–5.   [6] Mar.

sine magno regionis dampno: et illic remorati sunt uno anno.[1] *Eodem anno Karolus, Francorum rex uiam uniuersitatis adiit; sed Arnulf, filius fratris sui, sexta, antequam defunctus esset, ebdomada, illum regno expulerat. Quo statim defuncto, quinque reges ordinati sunt, regnum*que in *ᵃquinque p*artes diuisum*ᵃ est: sed tamen principalis sedes regni ad Arnulf*um *iuste et merito prouenit, nisi solummodo quod in patruum suum indigne peccauit. Ceteri quattuor reges fidelitatem et obedientiam Arnulf*o, *sicut dignum erat, promiserunt: nullus enim illorum quattuor regum hereditarius illius regni erat in paterna parte, nisi solus Arnulf*us. *Quinque itaque reges confestim, Karolo moriente, ordinati sunt, sed imperium penes Arnulf*um *remansit. Talis ergo illius regni ᵇextitit diuisioᵇ: Earnulf orientales regiones Hreni fluminis, Hrothulfᶜ quoque internam partem regni, Oda occidentaleᵈ regnum, Beorngar et Witha Longobardiam, necnon et illas* partes,ᵉ *que in illa parte montis sunt. Nec tamen tanta et talia regna inter se pacifice seruauerunt. Nam bis pleno proelio inter se belligerauere, illaque regna persepe inuicem deuastauere, et unusquisque alterum de regno expul*ere.ᶠ[2] *Eodem quoque anno Athelelm*us, *Wiltoniensium comes, Alfredi regis et Saxonum elemosinam Romam* deportauit.ᵍ[3] *Quo* etiam *anno sepe memoratus Alfred*us, *Angulsaxonum rex, diuino instinctu legere et interpretariʰ simul uno eodemque* tempore*ⁱ primitus inchoauit*[4] in sancta uidelicet beati *Martini* Turonensis episcopi *sollennitate.*[5] *Erat itaque rex ille, quamuis in regia potestate constitutus, multis tribulationum clauis confossus: nam,* ut diximus, *a uigesimo etatis anno usque ad quadragesimum quintum,* et eo amplius,[6] *grauissima incogniti doloris infestatione incessanter fatiga*batur,ʲ *ita ut ne unius quidem hore securitatem habe*ret,ᵏ *quoˡ aut illam infirmitatem non sustineretᵐ aut sub illius formidine lugubriter constitutus non desperaret.ⁿ Preterea assiduis exterarum gentium infestationibus, quas sedulo terra marique sine ullius quieti temporis interuallo sustinebat, inquietabatur. Quid loquar de frequentibus contra paganos expeditionibus, deᵒ bellis, deᵒ incessabilibus regni gubernaculis, de ciuitatibus et urbibus*

ᵃ⁻ᵃ quinque . . . diuisum] quinque partibus concessum *Ac*, quinque partibus conscissum (*As*) *Aₚ Ao Au ASN*   ᵇ⁻ᵇ extitit diuisio] dinam (*from* diuisio fuit *conjectured in Stevenson, Asser, p. 72*) *Ac*, om. Acott (*teste Aₚ*), diuisio fuit (*As*) *Aₚ Ao Au ASN*   ᶜ Rodulf *HL*   ᵈ occidentalium *HL*   ᵉ regiones *As ASN*   ᶠ expulit *As ASN*   ᵍ duxit *As*   ʰ interpretari (*As*) *Au Aₚ*, interpretare *Ac Ao*   ⁱ die *As*   ʲ fatigatur *As*   ᵏ habeat *As*   ˡ quo *Ac Ao Au*, qua (*As*) *Aₚ*   ᵐ sustineat *As*   ⁿ desperet *As*   ᵒ⁻ᵒ et *As*

remained for a year.[1] In the same year, Charles, king of the Franks, went the way of all flesh, but Arnulf, his brother's son, had driven him from his realm six weeks before he died. As soon as he had died five kings were consecrated, and the empire divided into five parts, but the principal seat of the empire came to Arnulf, justly and deservedly (except for his unworthy offence against his uncle). The other four kings pledged Arnulf fealty and obedience, as was fitting, for none of those four kings was heir of that realm by hereditary right through his father except Arnulf alone. And so five kings were consecrated in haste on Charles's death, but imperial power remained with Arnulf. The division of the kingdom was as follows: Arnulf received the areas to the east of the River Rhine; Rudolf the inland part of the empire; Odo the western kingdom; Berengar and Guy Lombardy and also those areas which lie on the further side of the mountains. However, they did not hold kingdoms so great and of such importance peacefully among themselves, for twice they all fought each other in major battles, and they, in turn, very often laid waste those kingdoms and each drove the other from his kingdom.[2] Also in the same year Æthelhelm, ealdorman of Wiltshire, took the alms of King Alfred and the Saxons to Rome.[3] Also in that year the oft-mentioned Alfred, king of the Anglo-Saxons, by divine inspiration, first began to read and translate at one and the same time[4] on the holy feast of the blessed Bishop Martin of Tours.[5] Now that king, although established in his royal power, was pierced by the darts of many tribulations: as we have said, from the twentieth year of his life to the forty-fifth and beyond[6] he was incessantly wearied by very severe attacks of an unknown ailment so that he did not have a single hour of freedom during which he either did not endure that infirmity or, fixed by the mournful fear of it, did not despair. Besides, he was disturbed by the constant attacks of foreign peoples, which he sustained continually by land and sea without any peaceful interval. What shall I say about the constant campaigns against the heathen, about the wars, about the

---

[1] Asser, c. 83 (84). JW follows Asser in assigning to 887 movements of the Danish army which took place in 886–9; see Keynes–Lapidge, *Alfred*, pp. 266–7 n. 202.

[2] Asser, c. 84 (85). JW follows Asser and ASC in assigning to 887 events which took place in 887–9; see Keynes–Lapidge, *Alfred*, p. 267 n. 205.

[3] Asser, c. 85 (86).   [4] Id., c. 86 (87).   [5] Id., 87 (88).

[6] 'et eo amplius' may be JW's inference or taken from a later version of Asser (see above, p. 294 n. 3).

renouandis, et aliis, ubi nunquam ante fuerant, construendis? de edificiis aureis et argenteis incomparabiliter, illo edocente, fabricatis? de aulis et cambris regalibus, lapideis et ligneis suo iussu mirabiliter constructis? de uillis regalibus lapideis, antiqua positione mutatis,ᵃ et in decentioribus locis regali imperio decentissime constructis? Diuino sane *fultus adminiculo solus regni gubernaculum semel susceptum, titubare ac uacillare, quanuis inter ᵇ*fluctiuagas *ac multimodasᵇ presentis uite turbines, non sinebat.* Nam *assidue suos episcopos, comites, ac nobilissimos sibique dilectissimos ministros et prepositos suos, leniter docendo, hortando, imperando, ad ultimum inobedientes, post longam patientiam, acrius castigando, uulgarem stultitiam et pertinaciam omni modo abominando, ad suam uoluntatem, et ad communem totius regni utilitatem sapientissime* attrahebat.ᶜ ᵈ*At* siᵈ *inter regalia exortamenta, propter pigritiam populi, imperata non implerentur,ᵉ aut tarde incoepta, tempore necessitatis ad utilitatem exercentium minus finita non prouenirent, ut de castellis ab eo imperatis adhuc non inceptis loquar, aut nimium tarde inceptis ad perfectum finem non perductis, et hostiles copie terra marique irrumperent, tunc contradictores imper(i)aliumᶠ diffinitionum, sera penitentia attriti, regalia* seᵍ *precepta incuriose* despe|xisse doluereʰ *regalemque sapientiam collaudentes, quod ante refutauere totis uiribus implere* promisere.ⁱ¹ Inter cetera *que rex idem* gessit *bona, duo* construereʲ *imperauit monasteria: unum monachorum in loco qui* ᵏÆthelingaege *dicitur,ᵏ ubi diuersi generis* ˡmonachis *coad-unatis,¹² primitus Iohannem presbiterum et monachum, genere Ealdsaxonum, abbatem constituit.³ Aliud quoque monasterium iuxta orientalem portam Sceaftesbyrig, habitationi sanctimonialium habile, idem rex* edificareᵐ *imperauit, in quo propriam filiam Æthelgeofu, deuotam Deo uirginem, abbatissam constituit. Que duo monasteria terrarum possessionibus omnibusque diuitiis locupletatim ditauit.⁴ Ad hec etiam dimidiam partem omnium diuitiarum que annualiter ad eum cum*

p. 299

ᵃ mutatis *Aw (from JW)*, motatis *(As) Acott (teste Aw) Ac Ao Au*   ᵇ⁻ᵇ fluctiuagas ac multimodas *Ac Ao Au*, fluctiuagos ac multimodos *(As) Aw*   ᶜ usurpabat et annectebat *As*   ᵈ⁻ᵈ At si *(As) Ac*, Et si *Aw Ao Au*   ᵉ implentur *As*   ᶠ imperialium *As*   ᵍ *om. Ac Aw Ao Au*, se *(As) (from JW)*   ʰ dolent *As*   ⁱ promittunt *As*   ʲ construere *Ac Aw Ao Au ASN*, construi *(As)*   ᵏ⁻ᵏ Æthelingaege dicitur] dicitur Æthelingaeig (Æthelingaege *L*) *HL*   ˡ⁻ˡ monachis coadunatis] monachos undique congregauit et in eodem collocauit *As*, monachos in eodem monasterio congregare studuuit *ASN*   ᵐ edificare *Ao Aw Ac Au ASN*, edificari *(As)*

unceasing responsibilities of ruling the kingdom, about the restoration of towns and cities and the building of others where none had
been before; about treasures beyond compare adorned with gold
and silver made at his instruction; about royal halls and chambers,
wonderfully built at his command in wood or stone; about the
royal residences of stone, moved from their ancient position, and
built most fittingly at the royal command in more suitable places?
Borne up by divine assistance, he did not permit the rudder of the
kingdom, once he was in sole command, to sway or hesitate, even
among the multitudinous and wild tempests of this present life.
For by gently teaching, encouraging, commanding, and finally,
after showing great and long patience, punishing the disobedient
with some severity, and by denouncing every kind of popular stu-
pidity and obstinacy, he most assiduously and wisely drew his
bishops, ealdormen, and his most noble and beloved thegns and
reeves to his own will and the general advantage of the whole
kingdom. But if, amidst royal exhortations, some of his commands
were not fulfilled because of the sloth of the people, or were
tardily begun and in time of need were left unfinished—as I might
speak of the fortresses ordered by him but not then begun, or
begun too late, not brought to full completion—enemy troops
burst in by land and sea; then the opponents of the royal decrees,
in the attrition of late repentance, joined in praising the royal
commands and the royal wisdom which they had earlier resisted.
They grieved that they had heedlessly despised them, and resolved
to carry them out with all their might.[1] Among other benefits
which the same king conferred was the construction he ordered of
two monasteries, one for monks in a place which is called
Athelney, where monks of different nations were gathered,[2] and he
established as the first abbot John, a priest and monk of the Old
Saxon people.[3] The same king ordered the building of another
monastery near the east gate of Shaftesbury, one suitable for
a nunnery, in which he appointed as abbess his own daughter
Æthelgifu, a virgin dedicated to God. He endowed these
two monasteries lavishly with grants of land and rich
gifts of all kinds.[4] In addition he promised that he would
devoutly and faithfully give to God half of all the revenues
which customarily came to him every year by rightful acquisition,

---

[1] Asser, c. 90 (91).   [2] Id., c. 91 (92).   [3] Id. c. 93 (94).
[4] Id., c. 97 (98).

iustitia adquisite peruenire consueuerant, Deo deuote et fideliter se daturum spopondit, quod mentis alacritate *sapienter adimplere studuit.* Denique, *consilio diuinitus inuento omnium uniuscuiusque anni censuum successum bifarie primitus ministros suos diuidere equali lance imperauit.*[1] *His ita diuisis, partem primam* [a]*in* tres portiones[a] *sequestrari precepit,* quarum[b] *primam suis ministris nobilibus, qui in cultu*[c] *regio uicissim commorabantur in pluribus ministrantes ministeriis, annualiter largiebatur: in tribus nanque cohortibus prefati regis satellites prudentissime diuidebantur, ita ut prima c⟨o⟩hors*[d] *uno mense in cultu*[c] *regio die noctuque administrans commoraretur, menseque finito et alia cohorte adueniente, prima* [e]*domum redibat et ibi propriis*[e] *quis*[f] *necessitatibus studens, duobus commorabatur mensibus. Secunda itaque cohors mense peracto, adueniente tertia, domum redibat, ut ibi duobus commoraretur mensibus. Sed et illa, finito unius mensis ministerio, et adueniente prima cohorte, domum redibat ibidem duobus commoratura mensibus. Hoc ordine omni*[g] *uite* sue *tempore*[h] *talium uicissitudinum in regali cultu*[i] *rota*batur[j] *administratio.*[2] *Secundam* [k]uero partem[k] *operatoribus, quos ex multis gentibus collectos* [l]uel etiam[l] *comparatos propemodum innumerabiles habebat, in omni terreno edificio edoctos. Tertiam autem aduenis ex omni gente ad eum uenientibus,*[m] *longe propeque positis, et pecuniam ab illo exigentibus, etiam et non exigentibus, mirabili dispensatione hilariter impendebat.*[3] *Secundam* autem[n] *partem omnium diuitiarum suarum, que annualiter ad eum ex omni censu perueniebant* [o]*in quattuor equas* partes[o] *curiose suos ministros diuidere imperauit, ea condicione, ut prima pars pauperibus uniuscuiusque gentis, qui ad eum ueniebant, discretissime erogaretur. Secundam duobus monasteriis, que ipse fieri imperau*erat,[p] *et in his Deo seruientibus: tertiam scole quam ex multis gentis sue nobilibus et etiam pueris ignobilibus studiosissime congreg*arat:[q] *quartam circum finitimis in omni Saxonia et Mercia monasteriis, et etiam quibusdam annis per uices in Brytannia, Cornubia, Gallia, Armorica, Norðymbr*ia *et in Hibernia, ecclesiis, secundum possibilitatem suam distribuit.*[4] *His ita ab*

[a–a] in tres portiones] in tribus partibus *As* [b] cuius *As* [c] cultu *Ac*, culto *B*, curto (*As*) *Acott (teste Aw) Aw Ao Au* [d] choors *C* [e–e] domum . . . propriis] *possibly over erasure C* [f] suis *Ac Ao*, quivis (*As*) *Aw Au* [g] omnibus *As* [h] temporibus *As* [i] cultu *Ac Acott (teste Aw)*, curto (*As*) *Aw Ao Au* [j] rotatur *As* [k–k] uero partem] autem *As* [l–l] uel etiam] et etiam *Ao*, et (*As*) *Aw Au*, sed etiam *Ac* [m] advenientibus *As* [n] vero *As* [o–o] in . . . partes] in quattuor partibus equis (*As*) *Ac Ao*, in quattuor partibus *Aw Au* [p] imperauit *Ac*, imperauerat (*As*) *Ao Au Aw* [q] congregauerat *As*

and this he was assiduous in fulfilling wisely and willingly. And finally, when the divine plan had been revealed, he ordered firstly that his thegns should divide into two equal parts all his annual revenue.[1] When this division had been made he ordered the first part to be divided into three portions, of which the first was distributed yearly to his noble thegns who lived in turn at the royal court and served him in many functions. The aforementioned attendants of the king were most wisely divided into three groups so that the first group stayed one month, serving day and night at the royal court, and when the month was over, and the second group arrived, the first returned home, and there, attending to their own requirements, stayed for two months. And so the second group returned home on the completion of its month, and the arrival of the third group, and there it stayed for two months. That, too, having fulfilled its month of duty, returned home on the arrival of the first group, and stayed there for two months. The administration of the royal court was arranged on a rota in this order for the whole period of the king's life, passed as it was in such turns.[2] The second portion was for the almost innumerable craftsmen whom he had assembled and gathered from many peoples, and who were proficient in every earthly skill. The third he cheerfully dispensed with wonderful generosity to foreigners who came to him from every people living far or near and who asked him for money, and also to those who did not ask.[3] The second part of all the wealth which fell to him yearly from all his revenue he ordered his thegns to divide carefully into four equal portions so that the first might be distributed very judiciously to the poor of any race who came to him; the second to the two monasteries that he himself had commanded to be built, and to those serving God in them; the third to the school which he had most carefully assembled from many of the nobles of his own people and even from boys not of noble birth; the fourth he distributed to the neighbouring monasteries throughout Saxon territory and Mercia and even, in some years, to the churches in Wales, Cornwall, Gaul, Armorica, Northumbria, and Ireland in turn, according to his resources.[4] Thus these matters were arranged in an orderly

---

[1] Id., c. 98 (99).   [2] Id., c. 99 (100).   [3] Id., c. 100 (101).
[4] Id., c. 101 (102).

eo ordinabiliter^a dispositis dimidiam etiam partem seruitii mentis et cor-
poris, in quantum infirmitas, possibilitas atque suppetentia permitteret,
diurno scilicet ac nocturno tempore, totis uiribus se redditurum Deo
spopondit. Vnde *excogitare cepit, qua ratione promissum uoti sui*
tenorem loeto tenus incommutabiliter conseruare posset.[1] *Tandem in-*
*uento utili discreto*que *consilio,* sibi *ceram^b ^csufficienter offerrii,^c* et ad
denarios pensare^d in trutina^e *precepit, cunque tanta cera mensurata*
fuisset, que septuaginta duos denarios pensaret, sex candelas,
unamquanque equa lance, capellanis^f suis *inde facere* ^gmandauit;
ita^g *ut unaqueque candela .xii. uncias pollicis in se signatas in longitu-*
dine haberet. Itaque hac reperta ratione, sex ille candele per .xxiiii.
*horas die noctu*que^h *sine defectu coram multorum* sanctorumⁱ *reliquiis,*
*que semper ^j*cum eo^j *ubique comitabantur,* arde*bant.^k*[2] *Erat pretera*
rex idem *in exequendis iudiciis, sicut in ceteris aliis omnibus rebus, dis-*
cretissimus indagator. Nam omnia pene totius sue regionis iudicia, que
in absentia sua fiebant, sagaciter inuestigabat qualia fierent, iusta aut
etiam iniusta, aut si aliquam in illis iudiciis iniquitatem intelligere pos-
set, leniter illos ipsos iudices, aut per se ipsum aut per alios suos fideles
quoslibet interrogabat, quare tam nequiter iudicassent, utrum per igno-
rantiam aut propter aliam quamlibet maliuolentiam, id est, utrum pro
aliquorum amore, uel timore, aut odio, aut etiam pro alicuius pecunie
cupiditate. Denique si illi iudices profiterentur propterea se talia

p. 300
ita^l *iudicasse, eo quod nichil rectius de his rebus scire | poterant, tunc*
ille discrete ac *moderanter illorum imperitiam et insipientiam redar-*
guens, aiebat, ita inquiens: 'nimium admiror uestram hanc insolentiam
*eo quod, Dei dono et meo, sapientium ministerium et gradu*m^m
*usurpastis, sapientie autem studium operam*que *neglexistis. Quapropter*
aut terrenarum potestatum ministeria que habetis ilico dimittatis, aut
*sapientie studiis multo deuotius ⁿ*quam hactenus insistere, mando
studeatis.'ⁿ Quibus auditis uerbis, perterriti ac^o *ueluti pro maxima uin-*
dicta correcti comites et^p prepositi ad equitatis discende studium totis
uiribus se uertere nitebantur: ita ut mirum in modum illiteratos^q *ab*

^a ordinabiliter (*As*) *Ao*, ordinaliter *Ac Aw Au*   ^b ceram (*As*) *Aw*, coram *Ac*
Acott (teste Aw) Ao Au   ^{c—c} sufficienter offerri] i *in* offerri *possibly over erasure* C,
offere sufficienter *As*   ^d pensare *Ac Ao Au Aw* pensari (*As*)   ^e bilibri *As*
^f capellanos *As*   ^{g—g} mandauit ita] iussit (*As*) *Aw Ao Au*, ita *Ac*   ^h noctuque
Ao, nocteque (*As*) *Aw Ac Au*   ⁱ sanctis *As*   ^{j—j} cum eo *Ac*, eum (*As*) *Aw Ao*
Au   ^k ardentes (ardenter *Ao*) lucescebant *As*   ^l *om. HL*   ^m gradus *As*
ASN   ^{n—n} quam . . . studeatis] docere ut studeatis impero (*As*) *Aw Ao Au*, ut
studeatis impero *Ac*, de ceteris studeatis impero *ASN*   ^o *om. Ac Aw Ao Au ASN*,
ac (*As*) (*from JW*)   ^p ac *HL*   ^q illiteratos *Ac*, illiterati (*As*) *Ao Au Aw ASN*

fashion. Moreover, half of the endeavours of his mind and body, as far as illness, means, and opportunity permitted, he promised to render to God, day and night with all his might. Hence he began to consider how he might keep his sworn oath unchanged and unbroken until death.[1] At length, when he had taken useful and prudent counsel, he ordered a sufficient quantity of wax to be brought and weighed on the scales against the weight of pennies, and when the wax had been measured and weighed to the amount of seventy-two pennies, he ordered his chaplains to make six candles, each of equal length so that each candle was twelve inches long, and had these inches inscribed along its length. And so, when this method had been devised, those six candles burned through the twenty-four hours, day and night without fail, amidst the relics of the many saints which went everywhere with him.[2] The same king was a most discerning investigator of the execution of judgements, as he was of all other matters, for he wisely examined all the judgements of almost his entire kingdom which were given in his absence that he might discover whether they were just or unjust. If he could perceive any malpractice in these cases, he himself or some of his trusted officers gently questioned the judges themselves why they had judged so wrongly; whether they had done so through ignorance or from ill will of any sort, that is from love of other persons, or from fear, or hatred, or even greed for anyone's money. Then, if those judges confessed that they had passed such judgements because they were not better informed about these matters, he wisely and moderately rebuked them for their ignorance and foolishness, saying thus: 'I am amazed at this ignorance of yours, for you have usurped, by God's gift and mine, the office and rank of wise men, but you have neglected the study and pursuit of wisdom. Therefore, I command you to give up immediately the exercise of worldly authority which you have held, or to pursue the study of wisdom with greater assiduity than you have done hitherto.' Terrified at hearing these words, as if corrected by the most severe punishment, the ealdormen and reeves strove with all their might to devote themselves to the study of justice, so that in a wonderful way almost all the ealdormen, reeves, and thegns, illiterate from childhood, pursued

[1] Id., c. 102 (103).   [2] Id., c. 103 (104).

*infantia, comites pene omnes, prepositi ac ministri litteratorie arti stud-
erent, malentes insuetam disciplinam quam[a] laboriose discere, quam
potestatum ministeria dimittere.* Verum *si aliquis litteralibus studiis,
aut pro senio uel etiam pro nimia inusitati ingenii tarditate, proficere
non ualeret, suum, si haberet, filium aut etiam aliquem propinquum
suum, uel etiam, si aliter non* haberet,[b] *suum proprium hominem,
liberum uel seruum, quem ad lectionem longe ante promouerat, libros
ante se die* noctuque,[c] *quandocunque ullam haberet licentiam,
Saxonicos imperabat recitare.* Ipsi uero senes *nimium suspirantes,
intima mente dolebant, eo quod in iuuentute sua talibus studiis non
studuerant, felices arbitrantes huius temporis iuuenes, qui liberalibus
artibus feliciter erudiri poterant, se uero infelices existimantes, qui nec
hoc in iuuentute didicerant, nec etiam in senectute, quanuis inhianter
desiderarent, discere poterant.*[1]

Romanorum octogesimus sextus Arnulfus[2] *regnauit annis duodecim.*[3]

[888] (i) 910 *Arnulfus compositis in Francia feliciter rebus in
Bauuariam reuertitur. Karolus imperator obiit .ii. idus Iunii sepultusque est in Augia insula.*[d4]

[889] (ii) 911 *[e]Basilius*[5] *centesimus .x. papa.[e]* Liutbertus
⟨*Moguntinus*⟩[f] *episcopus obiit. Sunderoldus successit. Mortuo autem
Karolo, quedam pars populi Italici Berngarium, filium Eburhardi, qui
ducatum Foriiulianorum tenebat, regem sibi* constituit,[g] *quidam uero
Widonem filium Lantberti ducem Spolitanorum regia dignitate decer-
nunt subleuandum. Sed post multas strages inter eos factas, Wido uictor existens, Berngarium regno expulit.*[6]

Dux nobilis Beocca nomine Ælfredi regis et Wessaxonum elemosinam Romam detulit. Eodem anno soror regis Æthelsuuitha,
Burhredi regis Merciorum regina,[7] est defuncta et apud Ticinum
sepulta. Quo etiam anno dux Ætheluuoldus et Dorubernensis

---

[a] tam *LP*   [b] haberet *ASN*, habeat *As*   [c] noctuque *Ao*, nocteque (*As*) *Ac
Aw Au*, et nocte *ASN*   [d] 887 *n. g* here *Mar.*   [e-e] under 890 *Mar.*
[f] Moguntinus *Mar.*, om. *JW (N)*   [g] statuit *Mar.*

---

[1] Id., c. 105 (106).   [2] Arnulf, emperor 896-9.   [3] Mar.
[4] Mar. JW repeats, in this Marianus annal, the death of Charles the Fat, which he
had already recorded under 887 in an extract taken from Asser, c. 85 (86).

the art of letters, preferring to learn the unaccustomed discipline, with great pains, rather than lose the exercise of authority. But if anyone was unable to progress in the liberal arts, either from old age or from the excessive slowness of an untrained mind, the king ordered the man's son, if he had one, or some kinsman, or even, if he had no one else, one of his own men, free or bond, whom he had long before put to reading, to read books in English to him day or night, whenever he had any leisure. These elders grieved deeply in their hearts with many sighs because they had not applied themselves to such studies in their youth. They considered fortunate the youth of this time who had the good fortune to be learned in the liberal arts, and thought themselves unfortunate, who had not learnt in their youth, and could not in old age, even though they wished passionately to do so.[1]

Arnulf,[2] eighty-sixth emperor of the Romans, reigned twelve years.[3]

[888] Arnulf returned to Bavaria, having settled matters successfully in Francia. The Emperor Charles died on 12 June and was buried at Reichenau.[4]

[889] Basil[5] was the 110th pope. Bishop Liutbert of Mainz died. Sunderolt succeeded. On the death of Charles a part of the Italian people appointed as their king Berengar, son of Eberhard, who held the duchy of Friuli, but some decided that Guy, son of Lambert, duke of Spoleto, should be raised to the royal dignity. When great slaughter had taken place among them, Guy was victorious and expelled Berengar from the kingdom.[6]

The noble ealdorman, Beocca by name, carried to Rome the alms of King Alfred and the West Saxons. In the same year the king's sister Æthelswith, queen of Burgred, king of the Mercians,[7] died, and was buried at Pavia. Also in that year the ealdorman Æthelwald and Æthelred, archbishop of Canterbury, died in the

---

[5] Unknown. A Basil appears in the Marianus papal list after Hadrian I, and before Stephen V (VI).

[6] Mar.

[7] JW supplies the name of Æthelswith's husband, which is not in ASC, but lacks ASC F's statement (and DE's suggestion) that she was on her way to Rome.

archiepiscopus Ætheredus in uno mense obierunt, cui in archiepiscopatum successit Pleigmundus, litteris nobiliter instructus.[1]

[890] (iii) 912 *"Stephanus*[2] *centesimus undecimus papa.*[a] *Sanctus Edalricus Augustensis episcopus nascitur.*[3]

[891] (iiii) 913   Abbas Beornhelmus Ælfredi regis et Wessaxonum elemosinam Romam portauit. Guthrum rex Nordmannicus quem, [4]ut prefati sumus,[4,5] de sacro fonte rex suscipiens, Ælfredus nomen ei Æthelstan imposuit, hoc anno obiit.[b] Hic in Orientali Anglia cum suis habitauit, et prouinciam illam [4]post martirium sancti regis Eadmundi,[4] primitus incoluit et possedit. Eodem anno sepedictus exercitus paganorum Sequanam deserens, locum qui dicitur Santlaudan, inter Franciam et Armonicam situm, adiit; contra quos Brytones pugnauerunt, et eorum quibusdam in ore gladii peremptis, quibusdam uero in fugam uersis, et quodam in flumine mersis uictores exstiterunt.[6]

Sanctus Sunderodus archiepiscopus Mogontinus Wormatie a Nordmannis occiditur, sabbato, .vi. kalend. Iulii. [c]*Hatto episcopus successit annis uiginti et uno mensibus octo.*[7]

[892] (v) 914 Memoratus paganorum exercitus Occidentali Francia derelicta, Orientalem adiit. Sed priusquam illo classis eorum uenire posset, imperator Arnulfus cum Orientalibus Francis, Antiquis Saxonibus, Bauuariis contra [8]pedestrem exercitum[8] pugnam iniens, in fugam uertit. Tres Scottici uiri Duisblan, Mahbethu, Malinmumin, peregrinam ducere uitam pro Domino cupientes, assumpto secum unius ebdomade uiatico, occulte de Hibernia fugerunt, carabumque, qui coriis tantum ex duobus et dimidio factus erat, intrauerunt [9]mirumque in modum sine uelo et[9] armamentis, post .vii. dies in Cornubia applicuerunt, et postmodum regem Alfredum adierunt. Eodem anno Suuifneh doctor

---

[a–a] *under 893 Mar.*   [bc] *see App. B for addition B*   [c] *892 here (N)*

---

[1] ASC ADEF 888, (B)C 889, but Plegmund's election is only entered under 890 in F *ADL* (which mentions here neither Beocca's journey nor Æthelwald's death), in an addition by hand 7a to A, and in Latin at the end of 890 in E. It is not possible to determine whether he was chosen archbishop in 889 or 890 (O'Donovan, i. 31). The pallium list added to ASC A (hand 15 s. xi/xii) would, if reliable, favour a later date

one month. Plegmund, a man most nobly versed in letters, succeeded in the archbishopric.[1]

[890] Stephen[2] was the 111th pope. St Edalric, bishop of
Augsburg, was born.[3]

[891] Abbot Beornhelm took the alms of King Alfred and the
West Saxons to Rome. Guthrum, king of the Norsemen, whom,
[4]as we said above,[4,5] King Alfred received from the holy font, and
gave the name of Æthelstan, died this year. He lived in East
Anglia with his followers, and was first to settle and hold that area
[4]after the martyrdom of St Edmund the king.[4] In the same year
the oft-mentioned pagan army left the Seine, and reached the
place called St Lô, which lies between Francia and Brittany. The
Bretons fought them and, when they had slain them with the edge
of the sword, and put them to flight, drowning them in a certain
river, were victorious.[6]

St Sunderolt, archbishop of Mainz, was slain by the Norsemen
at Worms on Saturday, 26 June. Bishop Hatto succeeded him, and
reigned for twenty-one years and eight months.[7]

[892] The already mentioned pagan army, after leaving West
Francia, went east, but before their ships could arrive there,
Emperor Arnulf, with the East Franks, Old Saxons, and
Bavarians, fought against [8]the land army[8] and put it to flight.
Three Irishmen, Dubslaine, Macbethath and Maelinmuin, desiring
to lead the pilgrim life for the love of God, took with them provisions for a week, and fled secretly from Ireland. And they
embarked in a coracle made by only two and a half hides, and, [9]in
a miraculous fashion, without sails or oars,[9] landed in Cornwall
after seven days, and afterwards went to King Alfred. In the same
year Suibhne, the most skilful teacher of the Irish, died. In that

---

for Plegmund's election as Formosus (891–6) is said to have sent Plegmund the pallium.
  [2] Stephen V (VI) 885–91.   [3] Mar.
  [4-4] No equivalent in ASC.   [5] Annals 875 and 878 above.
  [6] ASC A(B)DEF 890, C 891.   [7] Mar.
  [8-8] JW's 'pedestrem exercitum', which is clearly not a translation of ASC's 'ræde-
here' is meant to distinguish the land forces from those in ships.
  [9-9] No equivalent in ASC.

p. 301   Scottorum peritissimus obiit. Quo etiam | anno stella que cometis
dicitur circa Rogationes uisa est.[1]

[C³BP]

*a*Defuncto   Suithelmo   Scireburnensi   episcopo,   successit
Æthelwardus.*a2*

[893] (vi) 915   *bCiclus decennouenalis .xx. incipit indictione .xi.b*
*cArnulfus rex cum ualida manu exercitus Longobardorum fines intrauit,
et usque Placentiam peruenit. Inde conuersus per Alpes
Appenninas,d Galliam intrauit et usque ad sanctum Mauricium peruenit. Sigehart abbas Fuldensis obiit. Huogi abbase successit.*[3]

Classicus et equestris paganorum exercitus Orientalem Franciam
deserens, Bononiam adiit, indeque simul cum suis equis .ccl.
nauibus[4] Cantiam transuectus, in ostio amnis Limene qui de *5*silua
magna*5* Andred nominata decurrit, applicuit.*f* A cuius ostio .iiii.
miliariis in eandem siluam naues suas sursum traxit, ubi quandam
arcem semistructam quam pauci inhabitabant uillani,[6] diruerunt,
aliamque sibi firmiorem in loco qui dicitur Apultreo construxerunt. Nec diu post Hæsten rex paganus cum .lxxx.
paronibus*g* ostium Tamensis fluminis intrans, munitionem sibi in
regia uilla que Middletun dicitur edificauit.[7]

[894] (vii) 916   *hFormosus8 papa centesimus duodecimus.*[9]

Pagani qui Norðhymbriam incoluere cum Alfredo rege pacem
firmam iuramentis stabiliere. Similiter et qui Eastangliam inhab-
itauere, datis insuper sex obsidibus, fecere. Sed foedere dirupto,
quotienscunque exercitus in Cantia residentes,[10] predandi causa de
suis munitionibus exiere, ipsi tunc aut cum illis perrexere aut per
se ubicunque potuere, predam egere. Quo cognito, rex Alfredus
partem exercitus secum assumens, partem ut solebat domi

a-a Defuncto . . . Æthelwardus] *added at line-end C³, om. HL*   *b-b* Ciclus . . .
.xi.] *added mg. H¹*   *c see App. B for mg. addition near opening of 893 B¹*
d Appeninas] Penninas *Vat. ms of Marianus*   *e om. HL*   *f see App. B for addition B*   *g* uel nauibus *interlin. B¹?*   *h 896 starts here (N)*

---

[1] ASC (B) CD 892, AF 891, but neither Arnulf's victory nor the comet is mentioned
in F, and for the comet's apparent inclusion under 892 in A, see Bately, *MS A*, p. 55.
[2] On Swithhelm see above, p. 318 n. 1. On Æthelweard as successor to Asser in or
after 909 or 910 see O'Donovan, ii. 104-5.
[3] Mar.

year also, a star which was called a comet, was seen about Rogationtide.[1]

On the death of Swithhelm, bishop of Sherborne, Æthelweard succeeded.[2]

[893] The twentieth cycle of nineteen years begins in the eleventh indiction. King Arnulf invaded the territory of the Lombards with a strong army, and penetrated as far as Piacenza. Then he turned round, crossed the Appennines, and invaded Gaul and went as far as Saint-Maurice. Sigihart, abbot of Fulda, died. Abbot Hugh succeeded.[3]

The heathen fleet and army left East Francia, went to Boulogne, and from there crossed to Kent together with their horses in 250 ships,[4] and landed at the mouth of the River Lympne, which flows from [5]the great wood[5] called Andred. From its mouth they dragged their ships uphill four miles into the same wood, and there they destroyed a half-built fort inhabited by a few peasants,[6] and they built another, stronger one in a place called Appledore. Not long after, the heathen king Hæsten entered the mouth of the River Thames with eighty ships, and built himself a fort in the royal township called Milton.[7]

[894] Formosus[8] was the 112th pope.[9]

The heathen who inhabited Northumbria made a firm peace with King Alfred on oath. Those who lived in East Anglia did likewise, and gave six hostages as well. But they broke the treaty and, as often as the army staying in Kent[10] left its fort to plunder, they themselves plundered either in its company or by themselves wherever they could. When he learnt of this King Alfred took part

---

[4] JW agrees with ASC AEF in the number of Danish ships, against BCD which give 200.

[5-5] 'silua magna' agrees with ASC AEF rather than with BCD ('miclan' not 'ilcan wudu').

[6] ASC AEF speak of 'fortress in the fen'.

[7] ASC AEF 892, (B)CD 893. JW's translation, which is shorter than, and not exactly like, any version of ASC, improves on ASC's recording of events by mentioning the first army's fortification at Appledore before that built at Milton by the second army under Hæsten.

[8] Formosus 891-6.   [9] Mar.

[10] Kent is not mentioned here in ASC. JW makes clear that these armies are those settled at Appledore and Milton (end of 893).

relinquens, nonnullos etiam presidii causa in castellis urbibusque constituens, Cantiam[1] festinato proficiscitur, et inter utrumque paganorum exercitum, [2]loco quidem situ naturali munito, utpote aquis plene circumfluentibus, undis admodum crispantibus, scopulis altis, silius undique se protelantibus,[2] castra metatus est, ita sane ut si aliquem campum prede uel proelii causa peterent, sine cunctatione cum illis certamen iniret. At illi, nunc pedestres nunc equestres turmatim latrocinando,[3] predam illis in partibus frequentabant, ubi regis exercitum abesse uidebant. Quibus tamen inopinantibus, non solum de regia expeditione, sed et de urbibus plerique singulis fere diebus ac noctibus cedem intentant, adeoque perturbant ut Cantiam relinquentes,[1] denuo predatum simul omnes sedibus exirent.[4] Nam in predam simul exierant dum illis in locis primitus habitare coeperant. Sed hac uice maiorem uberioremque predam ceperunt,[a] Tamensemque fluuium transire, Eassaxoniam adire, sicque classice manui quam premiserant cum preda obuiare decreuerunt. Verum ab exercitu regis preuenti, prelio cum eis iuxta Fearnham commisso, predaque simul erepta cum equis quos de transmarinis partibus adduxerant,[5] in fugam omnes uertuntur, Tamenseque fluuio sine uadis transito, in insulam quandam intra meatum Colne amnis sitam fugerunt, ubi tam diu obsidione cinguntur, donec regio exercitui et esca deficeret, et statutum tempus iam adueniret quo domum rediret, aliusque illo dirigeretur exercitus. Quo domum redeunte, et Alfredo rege cum sui exercitus medietate illo properante, pagani quia rex illorum oppido uulneratus erat, ideoque secum ducere ipsum non potuerunt, ibidem resederunt. Rex uero Alfredus nondum ad expugnandum hostem iter peregerat, et ecce, nunciatur ei paganos Norðhymbriam et Eastangliam incolentes ducentas quadraginta naues congregasse, et quosdam illorum australem Anglie plagam centum nauibus, quosdam uero septentrionalem plagam .xl. nauibus circumnauigasse, illos Exanceastram, istos arcem

---

[a] coeperunt JW

[1] Kent is not mentioned here in ASC. JW makes clear that these armies are those settled at Appledore and Milton (end of 893).

[2-2] JW locates Alfred's camp 'in a site affording him the protection of land and water' and expands ASC's ambiguous phrase, which probably located the camp near both to the forest fort and the river stronghold (Whitelock, ASC, p. 54 n. 12).

[3] ASC specifies the Weald as the area covered by these bands.

of his army with him, leaving part, as was his custom, at home—
he also placed a fair number in the forts and towns as garrisons—
and set out in haste for Kent.[1] He pitched camp between the two
heathen armies [2]in a natural stronghold completely surrounded by
streams with very rough waves and high, rocky banks, and by
woods extended all about,[2] so that if the enemy should take the
field for booty or for battle, he might join battle with them without delay. But they, robbing in bands, now on foot, now
mounted,[3] constantly plundered in those parts where they saw the
king had no military presence. However, many, not only from the
royal forces but also from the towns, attempted to slay them when
they were off-guard almost every day and night, and this so disturbed them that they left Kent,[1] plundered once more, and all
departed together from their bases.[4] They had all gone out
together when they first began to settle in those parts. But on this
occasion they took greater and richer booty, and they decided to
cross the River Thames, reach Essex, and thus, with their plunder, meet the fleet which they had sent on ahead. But they were
anticipated by the king's army, which joined battle with them near
Farnham, and seized the booty together with the horses, which
they had brought from abroad,[5] and put them to flight. They
crossed the River Thames without fords, and took refuge on an
island set in the channels of the River Colne. There they were
besieged on all sides until food supplies failed the royal army, and
the appointed hour for its return home, and for another army to
be sent there arrived. When the army was making for home, and
King Alfred was hurrying there with a section of his army, the
heathen remained there because their king had been gravely
wounded, and therefore they could not take him with them. But
King Alfred had not yet made his way to reduce the enemy,
when he was informed that the heathen inhabitants of
Northumbria and East Anglia had assembled 240 ships, and some
of them had sailed round the south coast of England in 100 ships,
and others round the north coast in 40 ships. The former besieged
Exeter, the latter, with no small force, a certain fortress in

[4] JW avoids ASC's statement that all the Danes left camp only twice, once before
Alfred's arrival in Kent, and once at the final abandonment.
[5] The reference to the horses brought from across the sea is found in ASC 892/893,
(JW 893) not under this annal.

quandam apud Domnaniam non modica manu obsedisse.[1] His
auditis, non hostium audacia in timorem sed de suis in obsidione
relictis rex uertitur in furorem.[2] Nec mora, omnem equitatum[3]
reducens, Exeanceastram adiit, paucis tamen ad debellandum
quem insequebatur hostem relictis. Ii Lundoniam usque pergentes
cum ciuibus et cum illis qui sibi ab occidentali Anglie plaga in
auxilium uenerant Beanflotam adueniunt. Illuc enim maximam
exercitus conductionem, que apud Apultreo resederat conuenisse,
regemque Hæsten cum suo exercitu de Middeltun aduenisse,
ibique munitionem sibi construxisse, sed tunc denuo in predam
audierant descendisse. Nam idem paulo ante, cum rege Alfredo
pace stabilita, obsides quamplures dederat, insuperque duos filios
lauacro salutari regenerandos, ut ipse rex petierat Alfredus, tra-
p. 302   diderat; quorum unum | ipse rex Alfredus, alterum de fonte sus-
cepit dux nobilissimus Ætheredus. Sed Beanflotam rex Hæsten
perueniens, facta citato munitione, mox fines regni compatris sui
Ætheredi deuastat.[4] Inito ergo cum paganis graui prelio, Christiani
prima congressione illos in fugam uertunt, opus exstructum
destruunt, queque reperiunt sumunt, mulieres cum filiis
Lundoniam secum ducunt, naues quasdam confringunt, quasdam
incendunt, quasdam Lundoniam uel ad ciuitatem Hrofi deducunt.
Vxorem quoque regis Hæsten cum duobus filiis, [5]priusquam ille
Beanflotam a preda rediret,[5] coeperunt et ad regem Alfredum per-
duxerunt. Quibus ille mali nil intulit, nam alter suus, ut diximus,
alter Ætheredi ducis erat filiolus, sed, pace denuo stabilita,
obsidibusque datis, roganti patri non solum uxorem et filios
uerum etiam non modicum pecunie reddidit, que denique [6]predic-
torum labore suorum sollicitatus,[6] postquam Exanceastram aduenerat, [6]pagani aduentu illius territi,[6] naues petunt. Sicque suas
sedes repetentes, prope ciuitatem que lingua Anglorum
Cissaceastre dicitur, in prouincia Australium Saxonum, predam
agunt, sed ab urbe inhabitantibus fugati, maximaque pars illorum uulnerati et cesi, quampluresque de nauibus eorum capte

---

[1] ASC A mentions two fleets, one attacking Exeter, the other attacking the north
coast of Devon, where the other versions with this annal imply that a fleet of about 100
divided into two before making these attacks. A gives 140 ships to the fleet against
JW's total 240, though JW mentions 140 specifically involved in these two attacks.
[2] JW alone speaks of Alfred's calm reaction and of his anger.
[3] JW makes Alfred's army mounted.
[4] In this account of the English attack on Benfleet, JW records these events in
chronological order.

Devon.[1] When he heard this the king was moved, not to fear by the boldness of the enemy, but to anger at his failure to relieve his own men conducting the siege.[2] Without delay he led back his entire mounted force,[3] and reached Exeter, having left a few men to attack the enemy whom he had been pursuing. These continued as far as London, and together with the citizens and with the men who had come as reinforcements from western England, marched to Benfleet. For they heard that the mighty mustering of the Viking army, which had settled at Appledore had assembled there, and that King Hæsten had come with his troops from Milton, and there had built himself a fortress, but that they had gone out again to plunder. The same king, a little before that, when peace was made with King Alfred, had given many hostages and, in addition, two sons to be reborn through the baptism of salvation, as King Alfred had himself requested. One of them King Alfred himself received from the font, the other the most noble ealdorman Æthelred. But King Hæsten, reaching Benfleet, and having hastily put up fortifications, at once ravaged the territory of the realm of his son's godfather, Æthelred.[4] Fierce battle was joined with the heathen; the Christians put them to flight at the first attack, destroyed the works they had erected, and seized whatever they found. They took the women and children to London, broke some ships, burnt others, and took yet others to London or to Rochester. They also seized the wife of King Hæsten with his two sons [5]before he returned to Benfleet from his looting,[5] and took them to King Alfred. He did them no harm, for one of them, as we have said, was his own godson, the other that of ealdorman Æthelred, but, when peace was made again and hostages given, he restored to the pleading father not only his wife and sons but also no small sum of money. Then, after Alfred, [6]concerned about the toils of his men, who were mentioned earlier,[6] had marched on to Exeter, [6]the heathen, terrified by his arrival,[6] returned to their ships. And so they went back to their own settlements near the city called in English Chichester in the province of the South Saxons, and began to plunder, but were put to flight by the inhabitants of the town; the greatest part of them were wounded or

---

[5-5] This is not in ASC and is an attempt to make the sequence of events clearer.
[6-6] No equivalent in ASC.

sunt.[1] Interea paganorum exercitus de Beamflote, ut diximus, a Christianis fugati, urbem que lingua Anglorum Sceobyrig in Eassaxonia sitam adeunt, firmamque sibi munitionem ibidem construunt. Quibus de Eastanglia et Norðhymbria sociatis paganorum quampluribus, [2]prius per Tamensis, postmodum per Sabrine fluminis ripas [2]predam agunt. Quorum nimiam infestationem duces nobilissimi, Ætheredus, Æthelmus, Athelnothus ceterique ministri regis, quos ipse presidii causa per munitiones, per oppida, per urbes, non solum in orientali plaga Pedredan sed etiam in occidentali plaga Sealuude, nec solum in australi, sed et in septentrionali plaga fluminis Tamensis constituerat, non ferentes, in hostem haud modicum congregant exercitum, Walensibus, [3]qui occidentalem Sabrine plagam inhabitant,[3] sibi in auxilium occurrentibus. Conglobati itaque in unum, hostem uadunt insecutum, quem apud Buttingtun in ripa Sabrine fluminis sitam comprehenderunt, et mox in quam fugerant munitionem ex utraque parte amnis obsidere coeperunt. Multis autem peractis ebdomadibus,[4] paganorum quidam fame moriuntur, quidam uero, equis iam comestis, munitione erumpentes, cum illis qui in orientali parte fluminis erant, prelium committunt. Sed [5]multis paganorum milibus cesis,[5] ceterisque omnibus in fugam uersis, Christiani loco dominantur funeris, in qua pugna Ordeah nobilissimus multique de ministris regis occisi sunt. Cunque pagani qui aufugerant Eassaxoniam reuersi, ad suas munitiones et ad naues uenissent, hieme iam incumbente magnum rursus de Eastanglia et[a] Northhymbria exercitum congregant; commendatisque uxoribus, pecunia, nauibusque suis in Eastanglia, relictisque munitionibus, sine intermissione iter agunt, et Ciuitatem Legionum, tunc temporis desertam, que Saxonice Legeceaster dicitur,[6] priusquam regis Alfredi et Atheredi subreguli exercitus qui illos insecutus est assequi poterant, intrant. Nonnullos tamen illorum comprehendentes interficiunt, pecudes et pecora que depredando ceperant excutiunt, biduo ciuitatem obsident, segetes partim igne comburunt, partim

[a] om. HL

[1] JW records, presumably for the sake of clarity, immediately after the Danish withdrawal from Exeter, their attack on Chichester, which ASC mentions in the next annal.
[2-2] JW's phrase renders a version of ASC which resembled AD rather than BC, perhaps nearest to A.
[3-3] No equivalent in ASC.

slain, and many of their ships were captured.[1] Meanwhile, the
pagan armies, put to flight from Benfleet, as we have said, by the
Christians, reached the city which is called Shoebury in the
English language, situated in Essex, and there they built themselves a strong fort. Reinforced by many of the heathen from East
Anglia and Northumbria, they plundered [2]along the banks of first
the River Thames, and then the Severn.[2] The most noble ealdormen Æthelred, Æthelhelm, Æthelnoth, and others of the king's
thegns, whom he himself set to defend the fortifications, towns,
and cities, not only on the eastern bank of the Parret, but also to
the west of Selwood, not only on the southern, but also on the
northern, bank of the River Thames, would not put up with these
excessive attacks, and assembled a great army against the enemy,
while the Welsh, [3]who lived on the western bank of the River
Severn,[3] hurried to their assistance. United in one body, they hastened to pursue the enemy, caught up with them at Buttington on
the bank of the River Severn, and at once laid siege, from both
banks of the river, to the fortress in which the heathen had taken
refuge. When many weeks had passed,[4] some of the heathen died
of hunger, but some, having by then eaten their horses, broke out
of the fortress, and joined battle with those who were on the east
bank of the river. But, [5]when many thousands of pagans had been
slain,[5] and all the others had been put to flight, the Christians
were masters of the place of death. In that battle the most noble
Ordheah and many of the king's thegns were killed. When the
retreating heathen who had fled to Essex reached their forts and
ships, at the onset of winter, they again assembled a great army
from East Anglia and Northumbria. Leaving their wives, wealth,
and ships in East Anglia, and abandoning their forts, they
marched without pause, and entered the City of the Legions, at
that time abandoned, which is called Chester in English,[6] before
the army which followed them of King Alfred and Æthelred the
underking could overtake them. However, they seized and slew
many of them, and recaptured the beasts and cattle which had
been pillaged. They besieged the city for two days, burnt part of
the crops, and gave part over to their horses. These are the deeds

---

[4] ASC makes clear at this point that Alfred was still engaged with the naval force.

[5-5] JW's phrase suggests that his version of ASC had a clause omitted by ASC A,
and found in BCD ('þara Deniscra þær wearð swiþe mycel geslegen' in B).

[6] ASC adds 'in the Wirral'.

sonipedibus distribuunt. Hec acta sunt post anni circulum, ex quo partibus de Gallicis ostium amnis Limene intrauerant.[1]

[895] (viii) 917   *Wido qui nomine imperatoris Italiam regebat obiit. Lantbertus filius eius regnum optinens, a papa sibi imponi diadema fecit.*[2]

Sepedictus paganorum exercitus quia unde uiuerent[a] non habebant, cuncta enim illis Christiani abstulerant, terram septentrionalium Brytonum petunt,[3] [4]quam longe lateque deuastantes[4] predam quam maximam secum educunt. Et quoniam propter Mercenses repedare per Merciam non audebant, prius per Norðhymbriam, deinde per Mediterraneam Angliam,[5] uxoribus nauibusque suis receptis in Eastanglia, modicam quandam insulam, Meresig dictam, et in orientali plaga Eassaxonie in mari sitam, adeunt. Eodem anno idem ipsi per fluuium Tamensem, et postmodum per amnem Ligean, suas naues sursum traxerunt, sibique munitionem prope ipsum amnem .xx. miliariis a Lundonia,[6] edificare ceperunt.[7]

[896] (ix) 918   Ciclus solis incipit [b]concurrentibus .iiii.[b] bissextilibus. *Synodus nonaginta sex episcoporum cum abbatibus probatisque multis clericis, qui residentes in monasterio Triburas contra plerosque seculares, | qui episcopalem auctoritatem minuere temptauerunt, plurima decreta super statum sancte ecclesie scripta roborauerunt. Arnulfus rex Wormatiam uenit, ibique obtimatibus omnibus regni sui sibi occurrentibus conuentum publicum celebrauit. In quo omnibus collaudantibus Zuendiboldum filium suum regno Hlotharii prefecit.*[8]

p. 303

Estatis tempore, magna pars ciuium Lundoniensium et de uicinis locis quamplures, munitionem quam sibi pagani edificarant destruere moliuntur, sed illis fortiter resistentibus, Christiani in fugam uertuntur, .iiii. que de ministris regis Ælfredi occiduntur.

---

[a] uiuerent *from* uiuerant C[t]   [b-b] concurrentibus .iiii.] .iiii. concurrentibus *HL*

---

[1] ASC (B)CD (894), A (893). The reference to Lympne is not here in ASC, but is in ASC AEF (892), (B)CD (893).

[2] Mar.

[3] JW's statement that the Christian population (of Cheshire) was responsible for the lack of food which forced the Danes to go to Wales makes apparently more sense than ASC, which could be interpreted as attributing it to the Danes' own plundering, though the devastation by the English in the previous year was the more likely cause.

of the heathen in the year after their coming from Gaul and entering the mouth of the River Lympne.[1]

[895] Guy, who ruled Italy in the name of the Emperor, died.
Lambert, his son, obtained his realm, and had the crown placed
on his head by the pope.[2]

The oft-mentioned heathen army, because it lacked the where-
withal to live (for everything had been taken from them by the
Christians) went to the land of the north Welsh,[3] [4]which they dev-
asted far and wide,[4] and took away great booty. Since they dared
not return through Mercia because of the Mercians, they went
first through Northumbria, then through Middle Anglia[5] and, having regained their wives and ships in East Anglia, to a certain
small island called Mersea, situated in the sea on the east coast of
Essex. In the same year they themselves dragged their ships up
the River Thames and afterwards up the River Lea, and began to
build themselves a fort near the same river and twenty miles from
London.[6,7]

[896] The solar cycle begins with four concurrents in a bissextile
year. A synod of ninety-six bishops with abbots and not a few
esteemed clerics assembled at the monastery of Tribur, and
confirmed numerous written decrees concerning the state of Holy
Church in opposition to many laymen who were attempting to
diminish episcopal authority. King Arnulf came to Worms, and
there all the nobles of his kingdom gathered before him, and he
called a solemn assembly, at which, to the applause of all, he set
his son Zwentibald over Lothar's realm.[8]

In the summer a great part of the citizens of London and many
from the surrounding areas strove to destroy the fortification
which the heathen had built for themselves, but they resisted
strongly, put the Christians to flight, and slew four of King

[4-4] Not in ASC.

[5] ASC does not mention 'mediterranea Anglia' and JW's reference to not daring to
go through Mercia explains ASC's statement that they went where the English army
could not reach them.

[6] The building of the fortress twenty miles from London took place in this year,
though ASC enters it under the next annal.

[7] ASC A (894) (B)CD (895). Here, and at the end of 896, JW does not have ASC's
refrain on the number of years which had passed since their arrival at Lympne.

[8] Mar.

Ipse autem rex, autumnali tempore non longe ab urbe castra mete-
tatus est ea de causa ne pagani messem prouincialibus ui auferrent.
Quadam uero dierum per ripas amnis rex equitans, considerauit
quonam in loco alueum illius obstrueret, ne Dani suas extrahere
naues possent. Nec mora, ex utraque amnis parte obstructuram
fieri mandat. Quod ubi paganis innotuit,[1] uxoribus in Eastanglia
denuo commendatis, nauibusque relictis, locum qui Quattbrycge
dicitur pedestres celeri fuga petunt, constructaque sibi munitione,
hiemem ibidem exigunt, quarum naues Lundonienses quasdam
Lundoniam uehunt, quasdam uero penitus confringunt.[2]

Arnulfus rex *secundo Italiam ingressus, Romam peruenit, et urbem
cum consensu Formosi pape ante Natale Domini armis cepit. Mater
autem Lantberti, que ad presidium a filio relicta fuerat, cum suis
latenter aufugit. Arnulfus uero urbem ingressus, cum magno honore a
Formoso papa susceptus, et ante confessionem sancti Petri unctus et
coronatus imperator creatur. Eodem autem anno Lantbertus nomine
imperatoris obiit, et Luduuuicus filius Bosonis fratris Karoli senioris, a
Longobardis inuitatus a Prouincia egressus Italiam intrauit.*[3]

[897] (x) 919 *Kindiboldus, qui et Zuendiboldus, hortatu Arnulfi
patris sui, Odonis comitis filiam nomine Odam post pasca uxorem
duxit.*[4]

Estiuo tempore paganorum exercitus qui apud Cwattbrycge[5]
hiemauerat pars quedam Eastangliam, pars quedam Norðhymbriam petit. Ex quibus nonnulli ibidem remanserunt, nonnulli
uero, nauibus acquisitis,[6] sepedictum flumen Sequanam adierunt.
O quam crebris uexationibus, quam grauibus laboribus, quam
duris modisque lamentabilibus non solum a Danis qui partes
Anglie tunc temporis occupauerant, uerum etiam ab his Satane
filiis tota uexata est Anglia.[7] Multo magis tamen per triennium et
animalium peste et hominum mortalitate nobiliorum maxime regis
ministrorum, qui per idem tempus defuncti sunt, uexabatur. In

---

[1] ASC A (originally 895) (B)CD (896), but neither C nor JW has the possibly confusing phrase. 'þærto gewicod hæfdon'.
[2] ASC A (originally 895) (B)CD (896). JW omits ASC's final sentence on the number of years which had passed since the first invasion into the Lympne.
[3] Mar.   [4] Mar.
[5] The location of the Danes' winter base is here provided by JW from the previous
annal.

Alfred's thegns. In the autumn the king himself was encamped not far from the city so that the heathen did not carry off the country people's harvest by force. But one day, when the king was riding along the bank of the river, he looked about for a place at which he might block the channel so that the Danes could not take their ships out. Without delay he ordered the river to be blocked on both sides. When the heathen perceived this,[1] they sent their wives into East Anglia again, abandoned their ships, and fled swiftly on foot to the place which is called Bridgnorth, and there, having put up fortifications for themselves, they passed the winter. The Londoners drew some of the Danish ships to London, but others they broke up completely.[2]

King Arnulf entered Italy a second time, reached Rome, and took the city by force before Christmas with the agreement of Pope Formosus. However, Lambert's mother, who had been left by her son to guard Rome, fled secretly with her own followers. Arnulf entered the city, and was received with great honour by Pope Formosus and was anointed, crowned, and made emperor before the tomb of St Peter. In the same year Lambert, the nominal emperor, died, and Louis, son of Boso the brother of Charles the Elder, came from Provence at the invitation of the Lombards, and entered Italy.[3]

[897] Kindibald, also known as Zwentibald, at the urging of his father Arnulf, married Count Otto's daughter, who was called Oda, after Easter.[4]

In the summer some of the heathen army, which had wintered at Bridgnorth,[5] went to East Anglia, others to Northumbria. Many of them remained there, but many, having acquired ships,[6] went to the oft-mentioned River Seine. O with what a host of tribulations, what heavy labours, in what cruel and grievous ways was all England harassed, not only by the Danes who at that time held part of England, but also by these sons of Satan![7] But England was much more distressed for three years by murrain among beasts and, most of all, by the mortality of men, in particular of the more noble of the king's thegns, who died in the same period.

---

[6] Those who acquired ships were described as 'feohlease' ('property/moneyless') in ASC.

[7] This lament is substituted for ASC's statement that the Danish army had not affected the English people very greatly.

quibus erat Suithulfus Hrofensis ecclesie presul, Ealheardus
Dorcecestrensis episcopus, Ceolmundus*^{a} dux Cantuuariorum,
Beorhtuulfus dux Orientalium Saxonum, Eadulfus in Suðsaxonia
regis minister,^{b} Beornuulfus Wintoniensium prepositus, Ecgulfus
strator regius[1] et quamplures alii, licet hi essent nobilissimi.[2]
Eodem anno exercitus paganorum in Eastanglia et Norðhymbria
residentium furtiuam predam circa ripas maris agentes, terram
Occidentalium Saxonum grauiter uexabant, maxime longis
celeribusque nauibus quas ipsi ante plures annos fabricarant,
aduersum quos bis longiores, altiores, celeriores minusque
nutantes, ex precepto regis Alfredi fabricantur naues, quarum uiolentia predicte hostium superari possent.[3] Quibus in mare missis,
mandat rex ut quos capere possent uiuos caperent, et quos uiuos
capere nequirent, occiderent.[4] Vnde actum est ut eodem anno .xx.
naues Danicorum piratarum caperentur, quorum quidam occiduntur ^{c}quidam uiui ad regem ducuntur et in patibulo suspenduntur.^{c5}

[C³BP]

^{d}Defuncto Scireburnensi episcopo Æthelwardo, cessauit episcopatus .vii. annis ui hostilitatis
cogente.^{d6}

[898] (xi) 920 ^{e}Bonifacius^7 centesimus .xiii. papa.^{e8} ^{f}Rollo primus
Normannorum dux cum exercitu suo Carnotensem ciuitatem
obsedit. Sed episcopus eiusdem urbis Waltelinus Ricardum
Burgundie ducem et Ebalum Pictauiensem comitem in suum
prouocans auxilium, tunicam sancte Marie in manibus ferens,
Rollonem ducem diuino nutu fugauit et ciuitatem liberauit.^{f9}
In Italia inter Luduuuicum filium Bosonis, et Berngarium multa

---

^{a} uel Ealh' interlin. B⁵? ^{b} þeng interlin. B⁵? $^{c-c}$ quidam . . . suspendun-
tur] written partly mg. and partly over erasure, and also scribbled in uppermost mg. presumably to indicate text to be inserted C³ $^{d-d}$ Defuncto . . . cogente] add. at end of
annal partly over erasure and extending slightly into mg. C³, om. HL $^{e-e}$ Bonifacius
. . . papa] 897 (N) $^{f-f}$ Rollo . . . liberauit] written mg. alongside 898 with signe de
renvoi C¹, incorporated 898 n. a HLB

---

[1] 'strator regis' is JW's rendering of 'cynges horsþegn'.
[2] ASC A had added Wulfred, ealdorman of Hampshire, to those who died in this
year.
[3] ASC refers to the practical and original design of the ships, built on neither the
Frisian nor the Danish pattern.

Among them were Swithwulf, bishop of the church of Rochester, Ealhheard, bishop of Dorchester, Ceolmund, ealdorman of the Kentish people, Brihtwulf, ealdorman of the East Saxons, Eadwulf, the king's thegn in Sussex, Beornwulf, town-reeve of Winchester, Ecgwulf, the king's marshal,[1] and many others, although these were the most noble.[2] In the same year the heathen army living in East Anglia and Northumbria secretly made raids around the sea coast, grievously harassing the land of the West Saxons, especially with their long, swift ships, which they had built many years before, against which, at King Alfred's command, ships were built twice as long, with a bigger draught, swifter, and less unsteady, by whose destructive force the afore-mentioned enemy ships might be overcome.[3] When they had been launched the king ordered that all those they could capture, they should take alive, and those they could not take alive, they should kill.[4] Whence it happened that, in the same year, twenty of the Danish pirates' ships were captured, some were killed and others were brought alive to the king, and hanged on the gibbet.[5]

On the death of Bishop Æthelweard of Sherborne, the episcopacy was forced by the violence of the enemy to remain vacant for seven years.[6]

[898] Boniface[7] was the 113th pope.[8] Rollo, first duke of the Normans, besieged the city of Chartres with his army, but Waltelin, bishop of that same city, called to his aid Richard, duke of Burgundy, and Ebalus, count of Poitiers, and, bearing the tunic of St Mary in his hands, put Rollo to flight by divine will, and freed the city.[9] In Italy many battles were fought between Louis, son of Boso, and Berengar, but at length Louis put Berengar to

[4] There is no obvious source in ASC for this royal command.

[5] JW's account of the naval operations of this year is much shorter than ASC's (A–D), omitting the fuller descriptions of Alfred's new ships, the details of the naval operations, and the names and numbers of the dead in the engagements. The original date for this annal in ASC A was apparently 896, though (B)CD assign it to 897.

[6] G.P. II. 80 (p. 177). This addition is erroneous since Æthelweard, Asser's successor, cannot have become bishop until 909 or 910 and the see was not vacant in the seven years following 897.

[7] Boniface VI 896.   [8] Mar.

[9] Norman Annals. *AR, AU, AG, AC, ASN.*

certamina gesta sunt. Sed tandem Luduuuicus fugans Berngarium Romam ingreditur ubi coronatus imperator nominatur. Stephanus[1] *papa .cxiiii. anno uno mensibus .iii.*[a2]

[899] (xii) 921   *Vngarii Italiam multum uastant. Arnulfus imperator obiit .iii. kalend. Decembris sepultusque est Odinga, ubi et pater eius iacet. Romanus*[3] *.cxv. papa mensibus .iiii.*

   Romanorum octogesimus septimus Luduuuicus[4] *regnauit annis duodecim.*[5]

[900] (i) 922   *Theodorus*[6] *centesimus sextus decimus papa.* [b]*Luduuuicum filium Arnulfi .ii. non. Februarii anno etatis sue septimo quem ex legitimo matrimonio | genuit Arnulfus, proceres et optimates regni regem super se constituunt et coronatum regiisque ornamentis indutum ad Foracheim congregati in unum in fastigium regni eleuant.* [c]*Iohannes*[7] *.cxvii. papa.*[8]

   Heahstanus[d] Lundonie episcopus obiit, cui successit Theodredus.[9] Eardulfus Lindisfarnensis presul[e] decessit, cui uir religiosus Cuthardus successit.[c10]

[901] (ii) 923   Famosus, bellicosus, uictoriosus, uiduarum, pupillorum, orphanorum, pauperumque prouisor studiosus, poetarum Saxonicorum peritissimus, sue genti carissimus, affabilis omnibus, liberalissimus, prudentia fortitudine iustitia temperantia preditus, in infirmitate quam assidue laborabat patientissimus, *in exequendis iudiciis indagator discretissimus,*[11] in seruitio Dei uigilantissimus et deuotissimus, Angulsaxonum rex Alfredus,[12] piissimi regis Athulfi filius, uiginti et nouem annis sexque mensibus regni sui peractis,[f] morte obiit,[g] [h]indictione quarta,[h] .v. kalend. Nouembris, [i]feria .iiii.[i13]

---

[a] *898 n. f incorporated here* HLB   [b] *899 starts here (N)*   [c–c] Iohannes . . . successit] *partly written over erasure, partly extending into mg.* C[2]   [d] Healhstanus HL   [e] *om.* HL   [f] *901 n. h incorporated here* HL   [g] *901 n. i incorporates here* HL   [h–h] indictione quarta] *interlin.* C[1], *incorporated at 901 n. f* HL   [i–i] feria .iiii.] *interlin.* C[1], *incorporated at 901 n. g* HL

---

[1] Stephen VI (VII) 896–7.   [2] Mar.
[3] Romanus 897.
[4] Louis the Child, king of the East Franks, not emperor, 900–11.
[5] Mar.   [6] Theodore II 897.   [7] John IX 898–900.   [8] Mar.

flight, and entered Rome where, after being crowned, he was called emperor. Stephen[1] reigned as the 114th pope for one year and three months.[2]

[899] The Hungarians severely devastated Italy. The Emperor Arnulf died on 29 November, and was buried at Altöttingen, where his father also lies. Romanus[3] the 115th pope reigned four months.

Louis,[4] the eighty-seventh emperor, reigned twelve years.[5]

[900] Theodore,[6] the 116th pope. The nobles and leading men of the kingdom set Louis, the son of Arnulf, whom he had fathered by a legitimate marriage, as king over them on 4 February, when he was seven years old. Assembled at Forcheim, they raised him, crowned and wearing the royal regalia, to the government of the kingdom. John[7] the 117th pope.[8]

Heahstan, bishop of London, died. Theodred succeeded him.[9] Eardwulf, bishop of Lindisfarne, died, and the religious man Cuthheard succeeded him.[10]

[901] Renowned, warlike, victorious, the zealous supporter of widows, wards, orphans, and the poor, most skilful of all Anglo-Saxon poets, most dear to his people, gracious to all, very generous, endowed with prudence, fortitude, justice, and temperance, most patient in the infirmity against which he strove unremittingly, most discrete in investigating the execution of judgements,[11] most watchful and devout in God's service,[12] Alfred, king of the Anglo-Saxons, son of the most devout Æthelwulf, died on Wednesday, 28 October, in the fourth indiction,[13] after a reign of

---

[9] The death of Heahstan is recorded in ASC A (897), (B)CD (898), but not the erroneous succession of Theodred. JW *Epis. Lists* have *Wufsius, Aethelwardus, Ealhstanus* between Heahstan and Theodred; JW may have confused Heahstan and Ealhstan in making Theodred succeed in this year (O'Donovan, ii. 97–8). ASC also records the death of Æthelm, ealdorman of Wiltshire.

[10] *HDE* ii. 16, (i. 72) assigns this to 899.

[11] Asser, c. 104, also annal 887 and JW *West Saxon Accounts* 32.

[12] This panegyric was possibly inspired by Asser, though there are some parallels in *ASN*. Some phrases are found in JW *West Saxon Accounts* 31–2.

[13] Alfred's death is recorded in ASC A (originally 900), (B) CDEF (901). The length of his reign is given as 28½ years in ASC, as 29½ years here, and as 29 years in JW *West Saxon Accounts* 35. The day is 26 Oct. in ASC against 28 Oct. here. The day of the week and the indiction, which are here interlineated, are correct for 901.

et Wintonie in Nouo Monasterio sepultus,[1] beate immortalitatis stolam, et resurrectionis gloriam cum iustis expectat. Huic filius successit Eadwardus, *cognomento Senior,*ᵃ litterarum cultu patre inferior, sed dignitate, potentia pariter et gloria superior, nam, ut in sequentibus clarebit, multo latius quam pater fines regni sui dilatauit, siquidem ciuitates et urbes multas edificauit, nonnullas uero destructas reedificauit, totam Eassaxoniam, Eastangliam, Norðhymbriam, pluresque etiam Mercie prouincias, quas Dani multo possederant tempore, manibus illorum extorsit, Merciam post obitum sue germane Ægelflede totam optinuit et possedit, Scottorum, Cumbrorum, Streatgleduualorum omnesque occidentalium Brytonum reges in deditionem accepit, reges et duces ab eo *ᵇprelio uicti cesique quamplurimi.[2] Ex muliere nobilissima Ecguuynna filium suum primogenitum Æthelstanum, *ᶜex regina autem sua Edgyua filios tres Edwinum, Eadmundum, Edredum, filiamque Deo deuotissimam uirginem, Eadburgam, tres insuper habuit filias,*ᵇ quarum unam Otto Romanorum imperator octogesimus nonus, alteram uero in coniugem habuit rex Occidentalium Francorum Karolus, cuius amitam, Karoli scilicet imperatoris filiam, uxorem duxit rex Occidentalium Saxonum Athulfus, tertiam autem filiam in uxorem habuit rex Northanhymbrorum Sihtricus.*ᶜ[3] Huius uidelicet regis Eaduuardi Senioris*ᵈ patruelis clito Atheluuoldus regiam uillam Tuueoxebeam nominatam, sine licentia regis primorumque eius, inuasit.[4] Alteram quoque Winburgam*ᵉ dictam inuasit, portis serisque obfirmauit, quo in loco, ut prefati sumus, sancta Cuthburga, Ini regis germana, Deo deuotarum uirginum construxit monasterium.[5] Qua re

---

ᵃ⁻ᵃ cognomento senior] *interlin,* Cˡ   ᵇ⁻ᵇ prelio . . . filias] *written partly over erasure and extending well into mgg.* Cˡ   ᶜ⁻ᶜ ex . . . Sihtricus] *see App. B for substituted text B*   ᵈ senioris] *interlin.* CˡBˡ, *om. HL*   ᵉ Winburnan *interlin. above deleted* Uuinburgam B

[1] Alfred's burial at Winchester is not recorded in ASC, since ASC F records the consecration of the New Minster under 903, it seems probable that (as WM, *GR* ii. 124 (i. 134), records) he was first buried in the Old Minster and moved to the New Minster by his son.

[2] The laudatory description of Edward is not in ASC; its resemblance to that in WM *GR* ii. 124. (i. 135) need not suggest that either used the work of the other.

twenty-nine years and six months. He was buried in the New
Minster at Winchester,[1] and awaits the garment of blessed immor-
tality and the glory of the resurrection with the just. His son,
Edward, surnamed the Elder, succeeded him, inferior to his father
in the practice of letters but his equal in dignity and power, and
his superior in glory, for, as will be made clear from what follows,
he enlarged the confines of his realm much more widely than his
father had, inasmuch as he built many cities and towns, indeed,
rebuilt some which had been destroyed; he wrested from Danish
hands the whole of Essex, East Anglia, Northumbria, and also
many areas of Mercia, which the Danes had long held; he took
and held all Mercia after the death of his sister Æthelflæd; he
received the submission of all the kings of the Scots, the
Cumbrians, the people of Strathclyde, and of the West Welsh
when he had conquered and slain many kings and leaders in battle.[2] He had his first-born son Æthelstan by the most noble
woman Ecgwynn, and by his queen Eadgifu three sons, Edwin,
Edmund, Eadred, and a daughter, Eadburg, a virgin most devoted
to God. He had, in addition, three daughters, of whom one married Otto, the eighty-ninth emperor of the Romans, the next was
wife to Charles, king of the West Franks, whose paternal aunt,
that is the daughter of the Emperor Charles, Æthelwulf, king of
the West Saxons, took to wife. Moreover, Sihtric, king of the
Northumbrians, married the third daughter.[3] The atheling
Æthelwald, his (King Edward the Elder's) cousin, attacked the
royal township called Twinham without permission of the king
and his magnates.[4] He also attacked another called Wimborne,
which he fortified with gates and bars, in which place, as we said
before, St Cuthburg, King Ine's sister, built a convent for virgins
dedicated to God.[5] When he learnt this, King Edward, having

---

[3] On Edward's family, see *Handbook of British Chronology*, pp. 24–5. The account
here is substantially the same as in JW *West Saxon Accounts* 35 (though there Egwynn,
the first wife is described as 'femina' not 'mulier') and is defective in omitting the second wife Ælflæd and five of her children. For the account in the JW MS B, see appendix B under 901, and for its relation to WM and Roger of Wendover see vol. i
Introduction.
[4] Edward's rebellious nephew is named Æthelwald by JW as in ASC C (BD
Æthelwold, A Æthelwald), but 'sine licentia' agrees with A against BCD.
[5] This identification of Cuthburg as the founder of Wimborne is JW's addition to
ASC here (see annal 718 above).

cognita, rex Eduuardus, collecto exercitu, in loco qui lingua
Anglorum Baddanbyrig dicitur prope Winburnan castra metatus
est. [1]Nec mora, clitoni rex mandat exire nequaquam differat.[1]
Negat ille, uelle se dicens *uitam uel mortem* ibidem manere.
[1]Sed hec frustra, nam regii multitudinem exercitus timens,[1] nocte
fugam iniit, Northhymbriam petit, [1]Danos exposcit ut non tam
ducem se quam commilitonem recipiant, unumque ex collegio suo
esse uelint,[1] quem in regia mox illi dignitate preficiunt sibi.[2]
[1]Conquestus uero rex talis fuge iniuriam,[1] quam citius suis mandat
illum insequi,[3] uerum ubi cognouit eum non posse comprehendi,
sanctimonialem quam absque sua et episcoporum licentia uxorem
duxerat, captam iubet ad suum monasterium Winburnan reduci.[4]
     Eodem anno *Kindiboldus rex filius Arnulfi occiditur.*[5]

[902] (iii) 924 *Stephanus comes, frater Walonis, cum in secessu resi-
dens aluum purgaret, sagitta per fenestram percutitur, inde eadem nocte
extinguitur.*[6]

[903] (iiii) 925 *Benedictus[7] centesimus .xviii. papa.*[8]
     Strenuissimus dux Athulfus, Ealhsuuithe regine, matris
regis[b] Eadwardi, *scilicet Senioris,* germanus, et uenerabilis abbas
de Scottia Virgilius obierunt. Sanctus etiam presbiter Grimbaldus,
magne uir sanctitatis, unusque magistrorum Alfredi regis, gaudia
scandit regni celestis.[9]

[904] (v) 926 *Focho Remorum episcopus a quodam satellite
Balduuini comitis, nomine Winnimaro, occiditur. Cui succedens
Heruicus cum multis aliis episcopis eundem Winimarum pro tanto
scelere perpetuo anathemate excommunicauit.*[10]
     Cantuuarienses cum multitudine Danicorum piratarum in loco
qui Holme dicitur pugnauerunt, et uictores exstiterunt. Multarum
p. 305   apparatu nauium | quas uel adquisierat uel quas de Eassaxonia

---

a–a uitam uel mortem] uiuum uel mortuum *LP*   *b* om. *P*   *c–c* scilicet
Senioris] *interlin. C¹, om. HL,* Senioris *interlin. B¹,* Senioris *P*

[1–1] No equivalent in ASC.
[2] ASC BCD agree with JW (against A) that the Northumbrian Danes made
Æthelwald their king.
[3] Edward's reaction to Æthelwald's escape is in ASC A.

mustered an army, pitched camp in a place which is called Badbury in the English tongue, near Wimborne. [1]The king at once ordered the atheling to leave without delay.[1] He refused, saying he wished to stay there dead or alive. [1]But this was idle talk for, fearing the size of the royal army,[1] he fled by night, headed for Northumbria, [1]begged the Danes to accept him not so much as military leader but as one of the comrades in arms, and be happy to make him a member of their *comitatus*.[1] They soon placed him over them with royal dignity.[2] But the king, [1]complaining of the damage caused by this flight,[1] ordered him to be pursued as quickly as possible,[3] but, when he knew he could not be taken, he ordered the nun whom he had married without the king's or the bishop's leave, and who had been captured, to be taken back to her convent at Wimborne.[4]

In the same year King Kindibald, Arnulf's son, was killed.[5]

[902] Count Stephen, Walo's brother, sitting in a privy, was struck, as he was relieving himself, by an arrow coming through the window, from which he died the same night.[6]

[903] Benedict[7] was elected 118th pope.[8]

The most vigorous ealdorman Æthelwulf, brother of Queen Ealhswith, mother of King Edward, that is the Elder, and Virgil, the venerable abbot from Scotland, died. The holy priest Grimbald, a man of great sanctity and one of King Alfred's tutors, ascended to the joys of the heavenly kingdom also.[9]

[904] Fulk, bishop of Reims, was killed by one of Count Baldwin's retainers, Winimar by name. Heriveus succeeded him, and, with many other bishops, excommunicated Winimar with perpetual anathema for so great a crime.[10]

The inhabitants of Kent fought with a host of Danish pirates at a place called Holme, and were victorious. The atheling

---

[4] The connection of the nun who married Æthelwald with Wimborne is not mentioned in ASC.

[5] Mar.   [6] Mar.   [7] Benedict IV 900–3.   [8] Mar.

[9] The three obits here are entered in ASC A (902) (B)CD (903), but the qualifiers 'strenuissimus', 'scilicet Senioris' (here as later), 'uenerabilis', and 'magne uir sanctitatis, unusque magistrorum Alfredi regis' are JW's.

[10] Mar.

contraxerat, clito Atheluuoldus in Angliam de transmarinis redit partibus.[1]

[905] (vi) 927   Eclipsis lune facta est.[2]

Luduuuicus filius Bosonis qui sortitus est nomen imperatoris Berngarium de Italia expellens totum illud possidet regnum. Qui de securitate presumens absoluto exercitu cum paucis Veronam ingressus est adhortante Adalhardo eiusdem ciuitatis episcopo. Quod cum ciues summa cum festinatione Berngario, qui tunc in Bauuaria exulabat, nuntiassent promittentes se portas ei aperire sic ille ueniens, Luduuuicum captum oculis regnoque priuauit regnumque Italie obtinuit. Leo[3] centesimus .xix. papa.[4]

[5]Magna prede portione promissa,[5] clito Atheluuoldus suadet Danis Eastangliam inhabitantibus secum predatum uadant in fines Merciorum. [5]Cui consentientes,[5] mox cum rege Eohrico[6] simul et Atheluuoldo Merciorum fines irrumpunt, predeque instantes, cuncta cedunt ferro, flamma cetera destruunt, tandemque Creccanfordam usque perueniunt, ubi Tamense fluuio transito et silua que Saxonice Bradene uocatur peragrata uillas circumcirca positas inuadunt, queque reperiunt diripiunt. Iamque prede ubertate ditati, domum aduolant leti,[7] [5]sed, frustra nanque rex inuictissimus[5] Eadwardus *a*scilicet Senior,*a* congregatam quam citius poterat expeditionem post eos mouens, terras illorum que inter terre limitem sancti regis Eadmundi et inter flumen Vsam site sunt deuastat,[8] qui a deuas⟨ta⟩tione*b* reuersurus, cunctum exercitum simul exire*c* mandat, cuius iussa spernentes Cantuuarienses, ibidem remanserunt, ad quos rex .vii. nuntios mittens ut exirent precepit. [5]Verum illi nil*d* hostilitatis formidantes, in quo ceperant securi permanserunt.[5]

---

a–a scilicet Senior] *interlin.* C[1], *om.* HL, Senior *interlin.* B[1], Senior P   *b* deuastione CBP (*changed to* deuastatione)   *c* procedere *interlin. above* exire B[5]
d superbe *interlin. above* nil B[5]

---

[1] ASC. In the annals 904–24 the two series of annals embodied in ASC, the West Saxon series or main chronicle (MC) and the Mercian Register (MR), are conflated; the year given in these notes with the acronym MC or MR is the accepted date. The battle of the Holme (MR 902) (not described as a Kentish victory) is entered in ASC (B)C (902), but not in D, and the return of the atheling Æthelwald (MC 902) in A (903), (B)CD (904). JW's 'quas uel adquisierat uel quas de Eassaxonia contraxerat' is a little closer to (B)CD, perhaps closest to D.
[2] The eclipse (MR 904) is entered in ASC BC (904).   [3] Leo V 903–4.
[4] Mar.   [5–5] Not in ASC.
[6] JW mentions King Eohric here, perhaps to introduce him before his death later in the annal.

Æthelwald returned to England from abroad with a fleet of many ships which he had either purchased or assembled from Essex.[1]

[905] A lunar eclipse took place.[2]

Louis, son of Boso, who received the title of emperor, expelled Berengar from Italy, and held the whole of that realm. Taking his security for granted, he disbanded his army, and entered Verona with a few men at the pressing invitation of Adalhard, bishop of that city. When the citizens, with the greatest haste, had informed Berengar, who was then in exile in Bavaria, of this, promising that they would open the doors to him, Berengar came on these terms, and, when he had captured Louis, deprived him both of sight and of kingdom, and seized the whole of Italy. Leo[3] was elected 119th pope.[4]

[5]With the promise of a great share in the booty[5] the atheling Æthelwald persuaded the Danish inhabitants of East Anglia to go on a raiding expedition with him inside Mercian borders. [5]As they agreed to this,[5] they presently, with King Eohric[6] as well as Æthelwald, broke through the Mercian borders, and, eager for booty, slew everything with the sword, destroyed the rest with fire, and finally reached Cricklade, where crossing the River Thames, and the wood which is called Braydon in English, they attacked townships established in the neighbourhood and destroyed whatever they found. Then, enriched with great quantities of booty, they joyfully[7] turned homewards, [5]but in vain, for the invincible[5] King Edward, that is, the Elder, bringing up the expeditionary forces which he had mustered as quickly as possible after them, laid waste their lands which lay between the boundaries of the holy King Edmund's land and the River Ouse.[8] He, as he was on the point of returning from the work of destruction, ordered the whole army to retire at once. The inhabitants of Kent, spurning his orders, remained there. The king sent seven messengers to them, ordering them to retire, [5]but they, having no fear of his enmity, remained unconcerned on the land they had captured.[5]

---

[7] Not in ASC.

[8] JW's 'inter terre limitem sancti regis Eadmundi et inter flumen Usam' is his rendering of ASC's 'the land between the Dikes and the Ouse (or the Wissey)', where he understands 'Wusan' as the Ouse and takes the boundaries of St Edmund's to be those of the kingdom of East Anglia. He omits the following phrase, 'as far north as the fens', in ASC.

Quo cognito, Dani festinato in unum conglobati repente super eos irruerunt, commissoque graui proelio, multi ex his et ex illis ceciderunt. Dux Sigulfus cum Sigbrihto filio, comes Sigelmus, regis minister Eaduuoldus, abbas Kenulfus, quamplures alii ex parte ceciderunt Cantuuariorum. Ex parte uero Danorum cecidit Eohric rex illorum, clito Atheluuoldus, quem sibi regem delegerant, multoque plures quam ex Anglis corruerunt, loco tamen funeris dominati sunt.[1] Religiosa Christi famula Ealhsuuiþa regina, mater regis Eaduuardi, uita decessit, que sanctimonialium monasterium Wintonie construxit.[a2]

[906] (vii) 928   Cometa stella uisa est.[3]
Cuonradus comes, pater Cuonradi iunioris, .iii. kalend. Martii bello occiditur, in loco qui dicitur Fritislar, ab Adalberto. Eodem anno mense Iulio, Luduuuicus rex conuentum generalem celebrauit apud Triburas uillam regiam, et in castro Terassa obsidione cinxit Adalbertum et decollauit .v. idus Septembris. Cristophorus[4] centesimus .xx. papa.[5]

Paganorum exercitus de Eastanglia et Norðhymbria inuictum esse regem Eaduuardum scientes, pacem cum eo faciunt in loco qui lingua Anglorum Yttingaford dicitur.[6]

[C³BP]
[b]Defuncto Kynefertho Licetfeldensi antistite, successit Tunbrihtus.[b7]

[907] (viii) 929   Bauuarii ab Vngariis interficiuntur. Sergius[8] centesimus .xxi. papa.[9]

---

[a] mg. addition alongside 905 (from GP) opening, 'Regis Pleigmundus . . . in sua amicitiam exciuit' was later erased C³ (see 909 n. b and n. 5)   [b–b] Defuncto . . . Tunbrihtus] added line-end C³, om. HL

---

[1] JW omits some of the names of those killed in the battle, Eadwold son of Acca, and, on the Danish side, Brihtsige, Ysopa, and Osketel. That the Danes had chosen Æthelwald as king agrees with ASC (B)CD against A, which does not regard him as king.
[2] In recording Ealhswith's death, ASC (MC 903 MR 902) neither describes nor identifies her and (like WM) does not say she founded Nunnaminster. The events of this annal (MC 903) are recorded in ASC A (904) (B) CD (905), JW's account being less economical of expression.

When the Danes learned of this, they grouped together in haste, and attacked them suddenly, and when battle was joined in earnest, many fell on both sides. The ealdorman Sigewulf, with his son Sigeberht, Sigehelm the ealdorman, Ealdwold, the king's thegn, Abbot Cenwulf, and very many others on the Kentish side fell. On the Danish side King Eohric, the atheling Æthelwald, whom they had chosen as their king, and very many more fell than were slain on the English side. However, the English were masters of the place of death.[1] Queen Ealhswith, Christ's devout follower, King Edward's mother, died. She built the convent for nuns at Winchester.[2]

[906] A comet was seen.[3]

Count Conrad, father of Conrad the Younger, was killed in battle by Adalbert on 27 February in the place which is called Fritzlar. In July of the same year King Louis held a general council at Tribur, the royal township, and besieged Adalbert on all sides in the fortress at Terassa, and beheaded him on 9 September. Christopher[4] was elected 120th pope.[5]

The heathen armies from East Anglia and Northumbria, knowing that King Edward was invincible, made peace with him at the place which is called Tiddingford in the English tongue.[6]

> After the death of Cyneferth, bishop of Lichfield, Tunberht succeeded.[7]

[907] The Bavarians were slain by the Hungarians. Sergius[8] was elected 121st pope.[9]

---

[3] The comet (MR 905) is entered under 905 in ASC BC in the separate MR batch of entries, and, at the opening of a consolidated MC–MR (905), in D, where it is precisely dated to 20 Oct.
[4] Christopher anti-pope 903-4.   [5] Mar.
[6] The peace of Yttingaford (MC 906) is recorded in ASC A (905), (B)CDE (906). These say that it took place 'as Edward decreed' (ABCD) or 'from necessity' (E), and make no reference to an 'inuictus' Edward. ASC ABCD (MC) record the reeve of Bath's death.
[7] This repeats the erroneous addition at the end of 871; see above, p. 281 n. 1.
[8] Sergius III 904-11.   [9] Mar.

[908] (ix) 930   *Vngarii Saxoniam et Tur⟨in⟩giam^a uastant.*[1]
Ciuitas que Karlegion Brytannice et Legeceaster dicitur
Saxonice, iussu Ætheredi ducis et Ægelflede restaurata est.[2]

[909] (x) 931   *Vngarii Alamanniam uastant.*[3]
Denulfus Wintoniensis presul obiit.[4]

> [C³BP]
> ^bCui successit Fristestanus qui
> ad Wintoniensem, Æthelstanus
> ad Cornubiensem, Werstanus ad
> Scireburnensem, Athelmus ad
> Wyllensem,   Eadulfus   ad
> Cridiensem, Bernethus Austra-
> libus Saxonibus, Kenulfus ad
> ciuitatem   Dorceceaster   a
> Pleigmundo Dorubernie archi-
> episcopo uno die Cantwarie
> ordinati   sunt   pontifices.
> *Æthelstanus* uero in *Wiltensi pago*
> *factus   episcopus   sedem   in*
> *Ramesberia habuit.*^b5

[910] (xi) 932   *Franci ab Vngariis aut occisi sunt uel fugati.*[6]
Mortuo Denulfo sanctus Friðestanus successit ei in episcopatum.[7] Sancti Osuualdi regis et martyris ossa de Bearthoneig
in Merciam translata sunt.[8] Rex inuictissimus Eadwardus,

---

^a Turgiam *JW*   ^b–b Cui . . . habuit] *mg. addition with signe de renvoi; some words
scribbled in uppermost mg. as guidance to revision; 905 n. a (p. 360) which partly over-
lapped with 909 n. b and 920 n. a had already been added in the mg. on this page but was
partially erased* C³ *(the mg. addition 905 n. a already on this page, but later erased, referred
to two of the consecrations), om.* HL

---

[1] Mar
[2] The fortification of Chester (MR 907) is recorded in ASC (B)C (907) in the separate batch of MR entries, though these do not provide its British name or attribute it
to the command of Æthelred and Æthelflæd.
[3] Mar.
[4] The death of Denewulf is recorded in ASC A (908) (B)CDF (909).
[5] *GP* ii. 80 (p. 178). The division of the West Saxon see was originally added alongside 905, to which year the alleged consecration of seven bishops in one day is assigned
in the Leofric Missal; whereas WM, *GR*, ii. 129 (i. 140–1) with which scribe C³ shares
many readings dates it 904. The marginal addition to 905, based largely on *GP* i. 13–14

[908] The Hungarians laid waste Saxony and Thuringia.[1]

At the command of the ealdorman Æthelred and of Æthelflæd, the city which is called Caerllion in British and Chester in English was restored.[2]

[909] The Hungarians laid waste Alemannia.[3]
Denewulf, bishop of Winchester, died.[4]

> Frithestan, who succeeded him to Winchester, Æthelstan to Cornwall, Wærstan to Sherborne, Athelm to Wells, Eadwulf to Crediton, Beornheah for the South Saxons, Cenwulf to the city of Dorchester were all ordained bishops on a single day by Plegmund, archbishop of Canterbury. But Æthelstan, who was ordained bishop in Wiltshire, had his see at Ramsbury.[5]

[910] The Franks were either slain or put to flight by the Hungarians.[6]

After the death of Denewulf, St Frithestan succeeded him in the bishopric.[7] The bones of St Oswald, king and martyr, were brought from Bardney to Mercia.[8] The invincible King Edward,

(pp. 20–1) was later erased (see above, p. 360 n. a) and its latter part added to 920 (see above, p. 382 n. a). Presumably Denewulf's death here led C[3] to assign the division to 909. Though he omits the reference to Pope Formosus (found in both the Leofric Missal and WM), with whom this division was associated from an early date, he is misled by WM into thinking that 'ad Cornubiensem' meant Cornwall and not Ramsbury, and, like him, he added a duplicate Æthelstan for Wiltshire or Ramsbury. The episcopal lists for Wessex (see vol. i) have neither the erroneous 'Cornubiensem' nor the duplicate Æthelstan. See discussion in Whitelock, Brett, and Brooke, *Councils* i, 165–9 (no. 35).

[6] Mar

[7] Frithestan's succession to Denewulf (which scribe C[3] repeated in his marginal addition to 909, see 909 n. b) is entered in ASC (MC 909) A (909) (B)CD (910) *ADL* (910). JW omits the reference in ASC to the death of Asser, perhaps because he had already erroneously assigned it to 883 (above, p. 318).

[8] The removal of Oswald's bones from Bardney (MR 909) is entered in ASC (B)C (909 MR batch of entries), D (906).

¹quia pactum quod secum Daniᵃ pepigerant, preuaricati sunt.¹ Wessaxonum et Merciorum exercitum in Norðhymbriam misit, qui cum illo uenissent, per .xl. ferme dies² eam deuastare non cessantes, quamplures Danorum occiderunt, multos etiam captos cum maxima preda secum reduxerunt, et reges ducesque eorum, uellent nollent, cum rege Eadwardo, ᵇscilicet Seniori,ᵇ pacem quam fregerant redintegrare compulerunt.³

[911] (xii) 933 ᶜLuduuuicus rex obiit et Cuonradus in regem eleuatur.ᶜ⁴

In prouincia Stæffordensi in loco qui dicitur Teotanhele, inter Anglos et Danos, insigne proelium actum est, | sed Angli potiti sunt uictoria.⁵ ⁶Eodem anno uictoriosus rex Eadwardus Senior,ᵈ centum naues coadunans, milites legit, naues conscendere iussit, sibique per terram iter facturo occurrere in Cantia precepit. Interea Danorum exercitus qui Norðhymbriam inhabitabant, foedere quod cum eo statuerant rursus dirupto, et omni rectitudine⁷ quam ipse suique primates eis obtulerant spreta, agros Merciorum ausu temerario depopulati sunt, estimantes sane maius robur in nauibus esse, et se quocunque uellent sine proelio ire posse. Quod ubi rex audiuit, exercitum Wessaxonum simul et Merciorum ad repellendos eos misit. Qui cum illos a depopulatione reuertentes, in campo qui lingua Anglorum Wodnesfeld dicitur comprehendissent,⁸ duos reges eorum Eouuils et Halfdene, fratr.ᶜ⁹ regis Hinguari comitesque duos, Ohter et Scurfa, nouemque proceres nobiliores multaque milia extinxerunt,

p. 306

_____

ᵃ pagani interlin. B⁵   ᵇ⁻ᵇ scilicet Seniori] interlin. Cⁱ, om. HLP, Seniori interlin. B¹
ᶜ⁻ᶜ Luduuicus . . . eleuatur] P incorporates here but repeats it at 911 n. a where HL have it   ᵈ interlin. CⁱB¹, om. HLP   ᵉ fr.] This could be fratrem or fratres CHLB, fratrem P

_____

¹⁻¹ Not in ASC.   ² ASC has 5 weeks not 40 days.
³ This northern expedition of Edward the Elder (MC 909) is in ASC A (909) (B)CD (910). The reference to the Danes' being forced to make peace is not here in ASC, but is implied in the opening words of its next annal.
⁴ Mar.
⁵ The battle of Tettenhall (MC and MR 910, but named only by MR), which JW locates in Staffordshire, occurs in ASC A(B)CDE (910) (B)CD (911) and again D (6 Aug. 909).
⁶ The rest of the annal, except for the building of the fortress of Bremesbyrig in the last sentence, translates the account of the campaign in MC 910 in ASC A (910) (B)CD (911).

[1]because the Danes violated the pact which they had made with him,[1] sent an army of West Saxons and Mercians into Northumbria. When they came there, they ravaged the country without ceasing for almost forty days,[2] killing very many Danes. They also brought back with them many captives, and very great booty, and the Danes' kings and nobles were compelled, willy-nilly, to restore the peace they had broken with King Edward, that is the Elder.[3]

[911] King Louis died, and Conrad was raised to the throne.[4]

In Staffordshire, in a place called Tettenhall, a famous battle took place between the English and the Danes, but the English were able to gain the victory.[5] [6]In the same year the victorious King Edward the Elder, assembling a hundred ships, chose soldiers, ordered them to embark, and commanded them to meet him in Kent, whither he would travel by land. Meanwhile the army of the Danes who had settled in Northumbria again broke the treaty which they had established with him, and, rejecting entirely the justice[7] which he and his leading men had offered them, laid waste the lands of Mercia with boldness and daring, thinking no doubt that his greater strength was at sea, and that they could go wherever they wished without a battle. When the king heard of this, he sent a combined army of West Saxons and Mercians to repel them. They, when they engaged the Danes in a field which is called Woden's field in English,[8] as they were returning from their work of destruction, slew two of their kings, Eowils and Healfdene, brother(s)[9] of King Inguar, and two earls, Ohter and Scurfa, and nine of the greater nobles and many thousands of the men, and when they had put the rest to flight they recaptured all

---

[7] 'omni rectitudine' suggests that JW's ASC was nearer to the 'riht' of BCD than the 'frið' of A.

[8] JW (like Æthelweard and *ASN*, but unlike ASC MC) names the site of this battle, which was the same as Tettenhall. His *Wodnesfeld* must have been in the versions used by Æthelweard (*Wednesfelda*) and *ASN* (*Wodnesfelda*). His duplication of the battle was probably shared by his source: ASC BC mention the battle twice (MR and MC), and D three times (MR, MC and once in agreement with E).

[9] As 'fr.' could be expanded to 'fratrem' or 'fratres', it is uncertain whether both Eowils and Healfdene were brothers of Inguar (Ivar), who, according to Æthelweard, was also killed in the battle. It is possible that this identification arose from annal ASC 878 (see above, p. 309) where Healfdene is described as brother of Inguar.

ceterisque fugatis omnem predam excusserunt.[1] Ægelfleda domina
Merciorum urbem Bremesbyrig construxit.[a2]
Romanorum octogesimus octauus Cuonradus[3] *regnauit annis .vii.*[4]

[912] (i) 934 *Ciclus decennouenalis .xxi. incipit indictione .xv. Hato*
episcopus ⟨Moguntinus⟩[b]*obiit. Herigerus successit.*[5]

Eximie uir probitatis dux et patricius dominus et subregulus
Merciorum, Ætheredus, post nonnulla que egerat bona, decessit.
Post cuius mortem uxor illius Ægelfleda, regis Alfredi filia, regnum Merciorum, exceptis Lundonia et Oxenoforda,[c] quas suus
germanus rex Eaduuardus sibi retinuit, haud breui tempore
strenuissime tenuit.[d6]

[913] (ii) 935 *Vngarii Alamanniam uastant et iuxta Ina flumen a*
Bauuariis et Alamannis grauiter feruntur.[e7]

Ægelfleda Merciorum domina .ii. nonas Maii [f]cum exercitu[f] ad
locum qui Sceargete dicitur uenit, ibidemque arcem munitam construxit. Dehinc [8]in occidentali plaga Sabrine fluminis,[8] in loco qui
Brycge dicitur, aliam edificauit.[9] [g]Circa festiuitatem sancti Martini,
iussu regis Eadwardi Senioris,[h] apud Heortfordam,[10] inter amnes
Memeran,[i11] Ficcean,[12] Lygean, in plaga septentrionali urbs conditur.[g13]

[914] (iii) 936 Post pasca exercitus paganorum de Norðanham-
tune et de Leogereceastre [14]in Oxenofordensi prouincia[14] predam
egerunt, et in regia uilla Hokernetune et in multis aliis uillis
quamplures occiderunt. Quibus domum reuersis, alius mox equi-
tatus paratur et [14]in prouinciam Heortfordensem[14] uersus Lygetun

---

[a] *incorporated* 911 *n. c here* HLP   [b] *om.* JW   [c] Oxeneferda HL   [d] *see*
App. B *for addition* B   [e] ceduntur *(N)*   [f-f] cum exercitu] *interlin.* C[1]. *om.*
HLP   [g-g] Circa . . . conditur] *om.* B   [h] *interlin.* C[1], *om.* HLP
[i] Meneran HL

---

[1] ASC BC names eight others as slain (ASC D two) against JW's 'nouem proceres'.
(A names none after King Eowils.) It is just possible that Ivar was the ninth or that JW
made two persons out of Osfrith Hlytta.
[2] This fortification (MR 910) is in the MR entries in ASC (B)C (910) D (909).
[3] Conrad I 911–19.   [4] Mar.   [5] Mar.
[6] Æthelred's death (though not the eulogy) and Edward's retention of London and
Oxford (and all the lands which belonged to them) come from MC 911 and are in ASC
A (911) (B)CD (912)—F 910 mentioning only the retention of London and Oxford—and

the booty.[1] Æthelflæd, lady of the Mercians, built the town of *Bremesbyrig*.[2]

Conrad,[3] eighty-eighth emperor of the Romans, reigned seven years.[4]

[912] The twenty-first cycle of nineteen years begins in the fifteenth indiction. Bishop Hatto of Mainz died. Heriger succeeded him.[5]

Æthelred, a man of outstanding probity, ealdorman and high nobleman, lord and underking of the Mercians, died after performing many good deeds. After his death his wife Æthelflæd, King Alfred's daughter, held the kingdom of the Mercians most vigorously, and for a considerable period of time, except London and Oxford, which her brother King Edward kept for himself.[6]

[913] The Hungarians laid waste Alemannia, but were severely beaten by the Bavarians and Alemannians near the River Inn.[7]

Æthelflæd, lady of the Mercians, came to a place called *Scergeate* on 6 May with an army, and there she built a fortress. Afterwards she built another [8]on the west bank of the river Severn,[8] in a place called Bridgnorth.[9] About the feast of St Martin a town was founded at the command of King Edward the Elder, at Hertford,[10] on the northern bank, between the rivers Meran,[11] Fisc,[12] and Lea.[13]

[914] After Easter the heathen army from Northampton and Leicester plundered [14]in Oxfordshire[14] and slew very many in the royal township of Hook Norton, and in many other townships. After their return home another troop on horseback was soon prepared, and sent [14]into Hertfordshire[14] in the direction of Luton,

the death of Æthelred is repeated in ASC MR (B)C (911). In none of these is reference made to Æthelflæd's control of the truncated Mercian territories.

[7] Mar.   [8–8] No equivalent in ASC.

[9] Æthelflæd's fortification of *Scergeate* (unidentified) and Bridgnorth (MR 912) is in ASC (B)C (912 MR batch of entries). JW's date of 6 May (against ASC's 'eve of the Invention of the Holy Cross' or 2 May) may be the result of misreading '.vi. non.' as '.ii. non.'

[10] Edward's building of the northern borough of Hertford (MC 912) is recorded in ASC A (912), (B)CD (913).

[11] Memeran agrees with the form in ASC AG and *ASN*. Cf. HH *HA* v c. 15 (Arnold, p. 155) 'Mimeran'.

[12] *Ficcean* must be a corruption of *Beneficcean* (ASC BC), Beneficcan (A) or *Beneficean* (D).   [13] ASC.   [14–14] No equivalent in ASC.

mittitur. Sed illis ad obsistendum prouinciales confluebant, et multis ex eis occisis ceterisque in fugam uersis, equos nonnullos et
arma illorum quamplura extorquebant, predamque quam ceperant
reducebant.[1] Relictis quibusdam ad edificationem urbis in australi
plaga Lygee amnis, rex Eadwardus Senior[a] post Rogationes cum
maiori parte exercitus Eassaxoniam profectus, in Mældune castra
posuit, ubi tamdiu moratus est donec apud Huuitham urbs
edificaretur et edificata firmaretur, cui magna pars populi, que sub
manibus paganorum erat, cum suis omnibus se dedebant.[2] Estatis
initio Ægelfleda Merciorum domina cum Mercensibus ad
Tommuueorðigina perrexit, [3]Deique auxilio[3] ipsam urbem restaurauit. Deinde Stæffordam tetendit et [3]in septentrionali plaga Souue
amnis[1] arcem construxit.[bc3,4]

[HL]

Hiems nimis magna et dura.[5]

[C³BP]

[d]Athelmo Wyllensi episcopo, in
archiepiscopatum Dorubernie
leuato, successit Wlfhelmus.[6]
[e]Beatus Audoenus translatus est
de Francia in Normanniam.[de7]

[915] (iiii) 937 *Vngarii totam Alamanniam igne et gladio cum
Turingia uastant, uenientes usque ad Fuldam. Anastasius[8] papa centesimus .xxii.*[9]

Defuncto Huuicciorum episcopo Werefertho, magne scientie et
sanctitatis uiro, Athelhunus [f]abbas de Beorclea[f] successit.[10] Estatis
initio Ægelfleda Merciorum domina urbem condidit, que

---

[a] *interlin.* C¹B¹, *om.* HLP   [b] *written mg. at line-end* C¹   [c] *see appendix B for*
addition in text B   [d–d] Athelmo . . . Normanniam] *written partly over erasure on two*
newly ruled lines squeezed into the space for one C³, *incorporated with two sentences reversed B*
[e–e] Beatus . . . Normanniam] *under Conrad I (911–19)* G   [f–f] abbas de Beorclea]
interlin. C³?, *om.* HL, de Beorclea G

---

[1] The raiding around Hook Norton and Luton is in ASC MC (913) A (913, altered
to 916 and then to 917) (B)CD (914) after the events in the next part of this annal (n.
2).
[2] Edward's activities at Maldon and Witham (MC 912) and the building of
fortifications on the south side of the Lea at Hertford are in ASC A (912, altered to
913) (B)CD (913).
[3] No equivalent in ASC.
[4] Æthelflæd's building of boroughs at Tamworth and Stafford (MR 913) is in ASC
(B)C (MR batch of entries) D (913), before Edward's building of the northern borough
of Hertford.

but the local people flocked to resist them, and when they had killed many of them they put the rest to flight, wresting many horses and a large number of weapons from them, and recapturing the booty they had seized.[1] King Edward the Elder, after Rogationtide, left some men to build a town on the south bank of the river Lea, and set out for Essex with the greater part of his army. He pitched camp in Maldon, and there he tarried until a town was built at Witham, and, when built, fortified. A large part of the population which was under heathen control submitted to him with all their property.[2] At the beginning of the summer Æthelflæd, lady of the Mercians, went to Tamworth with her Mercians, and, [3]with God's help,[3] restored that same town. Then she made for Stafford, and built a fortress [3]on the north bank of the River Sowe.[3,4]

The winter was exceedingly severe and hard.[5]	Wulfhelm succeeded Athelm, bishop of Wells, when he was elevated to the archbishopric of Canterbury.[6] The blessed Ouen was translated from Francia to Normandy.[7]

[915] The Hungarians lay waste the whole of Alemannia and Thuringia, with fire and sword, penetrating as far as Fulda. Anastasius[8] the 122nd pope.[9]

After the death of Bishop Wærferth of the Hwicce, a man of great learning and sanctity, Æthelhun, abbot of Berkeley, succeeded.[10] At the beginning of the summer Æthelflæd, lady of the

---

[5] Mar.
[6] The earliest reference to the death of Plegmund, which this notice of Athelm's translation from Wells to Canterbury as his successor implies, is in the early 12th-c. addition to ASC A (919, by scribe 9a, altered first to 922 and then to 923). If JW may have drawn on WM, *GP* i. 13 (p. 20), he could not have taken into account the 34 years WM assigns Plegmund's pontificate as JW begins Plegmund's pontificate in 889.
[7] Norman Annals. *AU, AG, AC, AMSM* (915).
[8] Anastasius III 911–13.   [9] Mar.
[10] There is no confirmatory evidence for the date of the succession (O'Donovan, ii, 113), though Æthelhun witnesses a Mercian charter (*S* 225 *BCS* 632) dated 878 for 915–16. The identification of Æthelhun as 'abbas de Beorclea', which is an interlineation (probably by scribe C³), may have been based on the grant of Ealdorman Æthelred to Berkeley in Hemming's Cartulary (*Hemming*, i. 103–6, ii. 556, *S* 218 *BCS* 551) which is attested by 'Æthelhun abbas', though the identification with the bishop may not be correct.

Eadesbyrig uocatur, et in fine autumni alteram que Wærewic nominatur.[1] [2]Pagani pirate, qui ferme ante .xix. annos, derelicta Brytannia, Gallicas adierant partes, de prouincia que Lyduuiccum dicitur, ducibus *cum duobus* Ohtero et Hroaldo, Angliam redeunt et, circumnauigata Wessaxonia et Cornubia, tandem Sabrine fluminis ostium ingrediuntur. Nec mora terras septentrionalium Brytonum inuadunt, et cuncta, que circa fluminis ripam reperiunt, pene diripiunt. Captum quoque, in campo Yrcenefeld nuncupato,[3] Brytonum episcopum Cymelgeac letantes non modicum ad naues deducunt secum, quem non multo post .xl. libris argenti | rex redemit Eadwardus Senior.*b* Nec diu, omnis exercitus nauibus exiliunt uersusque predictum campum depredationis causa iter arripiunt. Sed eis repente Herefordenses et Glauuornenses quamplures ex uicinis urbibus occurrunt, et cum eis proelium committunt. Dux hostium Hroaldus fraterque ducis alterius Ohteres magnaque pars exercitus interficiuntur, ceteri in fugam uertuntur, et a Christianis in quoddam sep⟨t⟩um coguntur ubi tamdiu obsidentur, quoad obsides ea conditione darentur, ut [4]quam citius[4] possent de regno regis Eadwardi exirent. Idem itaque rex, in australi plaga Sabrine fluminis a Cornubia ad ostium fluminis Auene, oportuna per loca suum diuiserat exercitum, ne pirate regiones illarum uastarent prouinciarum. Verum illi nocturno sub tempore in plaga orientali Weced, et rursus in loco qui Portlocon dicitur, [4]relictis in litore nauibus,[4] furtiuam agunt predam. Sed utraque uice cesi sunt omnes ab exercitu regis, preter illos qui ad naues turpiter[5] refugerant. Ii tamen clade oppressi quandam insulam que Reoric nominatur[6] petierunt, ubi tamdiu consederunt quousque plures illorum essent fame consumpti, unde necessitate compulsi prius ad Deomedum, deinde autumnali tempore ad Hiberniam nauigarunt. Post hec rex inuictissimus Eadwardus Senior*b* cum exercitu Buccingaham perrexit, ubi .xxx. diebus consedit, et ex

p. 307

---

a–a cum duobus *om.* HL   *b interlin.* C¹B¹, *om.* HLP

[1] The fortification of Eddisbury and Warwick (MR 914) is in ASC (B)C (913 MR batch of entries), D (Warwick only and without referring to Æthelflæd) 915. ASC has 'early' autumn for the foundation of Warwick.

[2] The rest of the annal is in ASC MC (914) A (914, altered to 917 and then to 918) (B)CD (915). JW identifies the invading army with that which left Berkshire for France in 897.

Mercians, founded a town called Eddisbury and, at the end of the autumn, another called Warwick.[1] [2]The heathen pirates, who had abandoned Britain almost nineteen years before and gone to Gaul, returned to England from the region known as Brittany under two earls, Ohter and Hroald, and, when they had sailed round Wessex and Cornwall, finally entered the mouth of the River Severn. Without delay they invaded the lands of the north Welsh, and completely destroyed everything they came across on the river bank. They also captured the Welsh bishop, Cyfeiliog, in the plain called Archenfield,[3] and with great joy took him to their ships with them. King Edward the Elder redeemed him not much later for forty pounds of silver. Not long after, the whole army disembarked and marched rapidly towards the plain aforementioned with the object of plundering, but suddenly men from Hereford and Gloucester, and many from the neighbouring towns, rushed upon them, and joined battle with them. Hroald, the enemy's leader, and the brother of the other earl, Ohter, and a large part of the army were slain. Others were put to flight, and were driven into an enclosure by the Christians where they were besieged for a long time until hostages were given, on condition that they would leave King Edward's realm [4]as quickly as possible.[4] And so that same king dispersed his army at suitable points to the southern shore of the River Severn, from Cornwall to the mouth of the River Avon, lest the pirates should lay waste areas of those provinces. But they plundered secretly by night the shore east of Watchet and again in a place called Porlock, [4]leaving their ships on the shore.[4] But on both occasions they were all cut down by the king's army, except for those who shamefully[5] took refuge in their ships. However, crushed by the disaster, they landed on a certain island called *Reoric*[6] where they stayed until most of them perished of hunger, whence, driven by necessity, they sailed first to Dyfed and then, in the autumn, to Ireland. After that, the most invincible King Edward the Elder went to Buckingham with his army, and there he encamped for thirty days and had fortifications

---

[3] 'in campo Yrcenefeld' is probably JW's mistranslation of 'Cameleac (ASC A, 'Camelgeac' BC, 'Camelgeeac' D) biscop (A, 'bisceop' BCD) on Ircingafelda' which means Cyfeiliog, bishop of Archenfield, Herefordshire (Plummer, *Chronicle*, ii, 127).
[4-4] No equivalent in ASC.   [5] Not in ASC.
[6] ASC had 'Bradan Relice' (A, i.e. River Flatholme) and 'Steapan Reolice' (BCD, i.e. Steepholme) as the island's name.

utraque parte amnis *a*uel fluminis*a* Vse[1] munitiones edificari fecit. Quam ob rem unus de Danorum ducibus Turkitellus et omnes nobiliores de Bedeforda multique de Norðhamtune coacti se dederunt regi.*b*[2] *c*Defuncto Cuthardo Lindisfarnensi episcopo, Tilredus successit.*c*[3]

[916] (v) 938   *Lando*[4] *d*papa* centesimus uicesimus tertius.*d*[5]

Rex inuictissimus Eadwardus Senior*e* ante festiuitatem sancti Martini Bedefordam adiit, et eam cum inhabitatoribus eius in deditionem accepit, ibidemque per [6].xxx. dies[6] moratus, urbem in australi plaga amnis Vse[7] condi precepit.[8] Ægelfleda Merciorum domina post Natiuitatem Domini duas urbes, Cyricbyrig uidelicet et Weadbyrig, et tertiam Runcofan *f*ante Natiuitatem edificauit.*fg*[9]

[917] (vi) 939   *Vngarii per Alamanniam in Alsatiam et usque ad fines regni Lotharii uenerunt. Iohannes*[10] *h*papa .cxxiiii.*h*[11] *ij*Obiit Rollo primus dux Normannorum,*j* cui successit Willelmus filius eius.*ij*[12]

Ante Natiuitatem Iohannis*k* baptiste rex inuictissimus Eadwardus Senior*l* Mældunam usque perrexit, ubi urbem reedificauit,[13] nec priusquam illam militum custodia muniret inde recessit. Eodem anno supra memoratus dux Turkitellus pace et iuuamine regis Eadwardi cum suis omnibus Gallicas adiit partes.[14] Venerabilis abbas Ecgbrihtus .vi. kalend. Iulii iniuste occiditur. Et post .iii. noctes Ægelfleda Merciorum domina in terram Brytonum ad expugnandam arcem apud Brycenanmere misit

---

a–a uel fluminis] *interlin. C'*, om. HL, id est fluminis *interlin. B'*   *b* Ædwardo *interlin. B'?*   *c–c* Defuncto . . . successit] *add. at line-end, extending into mg. C*[2]   *d–d* papa . . . tertius] .cxxiii. papa HL   *e interlin. C'B'*, om. HLP   *f–f* ante . . . edificauit] *mg. at line-end C'*   *g see App. B for addition B*   *h–h* papa .cxxiiii.] .cxxiiii. papa HL   *i–i* Obiit . . . eius] *add. mg. near opening of 917 C', add. at 917 n. a H*   *j–j* Obiit . . . Normannorum] Rollo primus dux Normannorum obiit HLBP   *k* sancti Iohannis LP   *l interlin. C'B'*, om. HLP

---

[1] River not identified in ASC.

[2] The building of two boroughs at Buckingham and the Danish submission (MC 914) are recorded as shown in ASC versions above (n. 1). JW's differences are 30 days for 4 weeks, the omission of 'before Martinmas' as the time when Edward's fortifications began, and the identification of the river as the Ouse.

[3] This addition was probably based on *HDE* ii. xvii (i. 74), who assigns 15 years to Cuthheard. Cuthheard succeeds in 900 according to JW.

put up on both sides of the stream (or river) Ouse.[1] Because of this, one of the Danish leaders, Thurketel, and all the greater nobles of Bedford, and many from Northampton, were forced to submit to the king.[2] On the death of Cuthheard, bishop of Lindisfarne, Tilred succeeded.[3]

[916] Lando[4] the 123rd pope.[5]

The most invincible King Edward the Elder went to Bedford before the feast of St Martin, and received the submission of the town with its inhabitants. And there he stayed [6]for thirty days,[6] ordering a town to be founded on the southern bank of the River Ouse.[7,8] Æthelflæd, lady of the Mercians, built two towns, namely Chirbury and *Weardbyrig*, after Christmas, and a third, Runcorn, before Christmas.[9]

[917] The Hungarians advanced through Alemannia into Alsace, and right up to the borders of Lothar's kingdom. John[10] 124th pope.[11] Rollo, the first duke of the Normans, died and his son William succeeded him.[12]

Before the Nativity of John the Baptist, the most invincible King Edward the Elder went as far as Maldon, where he rebuilt the town,[13] and he did not withdraw from there until he had strengthened it with a garrison. In the same year Earl Thurketel, mentioned above, went with all his men to Gallic territory in peace, and with the aid of King Edward.[14] The venerable Abbot Ecgberht was unjustly killed on 26 June, and, three nights later, Æthelflæd, lady of the Mercians, sent an army into Welsh territory to take the fortress at *Brecenanmere*, and when the fortress

---

[4] Lando 913-14.   [5] Mar.   [6-6] Four weeks in ASC.
[7] Not identified in ASC.
[8] Edward's activities at Bedford (MC 915) are in ASC A (915 altered to 918 and then to 919).
[9] Æthelflæd's building of three boroughs (MR 915) is in ASC (B)C (915 MR batch of entries). Both read 'Weardbyrig' and 'Rumcofan'.
[10] John X 914-28.   [11] Mar.
[12] Norman Annals. *AR, AU, AG, AC, AMSM.*
[13] ASC: 'getimbrede'. Compare 'restaurauit' for Tamworth under 914.
[14] Edward's visit to Maldon and the departure of Thurketel (MC 916) are in ASC A (916 altered to 919 and then to 920) G (920). Thurketel had been mentioned in annal 915.

exercitum qui, expugnata arce, uxorem regis Brytonum cum
.xxxiiii.[1] hominibus captiuos in Merciam adduxerunt.[a2]

[918] (vii) 940   Ex precepto regis Eadwardi Senioris,[b] ciuitas que
Toueceastre dicitur ante pasca, et altera post pasca circa
Rogationes apud Wiggingamere conditur. Post natiuitatem
Iohannis baptiste[3] pagani de Norðamtune et de Leogereceastre,[4]
statuta pace uiolata, Toueceastram adeunt quam per totum diem
impugnantes expugnare moliuntur, sed illis, qui intus erant sum-
mis uiribus resistentibus, sibique in auxilium uicinis accurrentibus,
omnes in fugam uertuntur. Deinde frequenter [5]in prouincia
Buccingamnensi[5] noctu super imparatos irruentes, non solum de
hominibus, sed et de iumentis predam agunt, multosque inter
Byrnuuda et Ægelesbyrig interficiunt. Eodem tempore paganorum
exercitus, qui Eastangliam et Huntadun inhabitabant, relicta munitione quam in Huntadune firmauerant, in loco qui dicitur
Temesforda firmiorem sibi construxere, arbitrantes sane terram
sibi ablatam inde se certamine recuperaturos esse.[6] Inde ad expugnandam Bedefordam prosiliunt, uerum aduentu illorum cognito,
urbem qui custodiunt ipsis in proelium occurrunt, congrediuntur,
hostes uincuntur, in fugam uertuntur, plurimi interficiuntur.
Paruo interiecto tempore rursus de Eastanglia, Eassaxonia[7] et de
Mercia pagani conglobati, urbem que Wingingamere dicitur adeunt et per totum fere diem impugnare non desinunt, sed qui intus
erant uiriliter illam defendebant, hostesque abigebant, qui rece-
dentes maximam secum predam reducunt.[8] Post hec ipso estatis
tempore, de proximis ciuitatibus et regionibus, que sub potestate
regis Eadwardi Senioris[b] erant, multus populus undecunque collec-
tus Temesfordam pergunt eamque obsident, impugnant, expug-
nant, incendunt, diruunt, regem[c] paganorum ducemque Togleas

---

[a] add. 917 n. i in lower mg. with signe de renvoi H   [b] interlin. C[1]B[1], om. HLP
[c] regemque H

---

[1] JW's 34 for 'feower and þritiga sume' could be correct (see Whitelock, *ASC*, p. 64
n. 7 and p. 15 n. 11).
[2] The killing of Abbot Ecgberht (with his companions), like Æthelflæd's expedition
into Wales (MR 916), are in ASC (B)C (916 MR batch of entries). These date the
death of the abbot to 16 June (the feast of St Ciriacus, that is SS Ciricus and Julitta)
and JW's '.vi. kal. Iulii' (26 June) could be a scribal error for '.xvi. kal. Iulii'.
[3] ASC's period is between Lammas (1 Aug.) and midsummer (24 June) against JW's
'after the nativity of John the Baptist' (24 June).

had fallen, they led back the Welsh king's wife and thirty-four men[1] to Mercia as captives.[2]

[918] At King Edward the Elder's command, the town that is called Towcester was founded before Easter, and another after Easter, about Rogationtide at *Wigingamere*. After the Nativity of John the Baptist[3] the heathen from Northampton and Leicester,[4] in violation of the peace settlement, arrived at Towcester, which they attacked for a whole day and strove to take, but those who were inside resisted them with all their might, and, with the neighbouring people rushing to their aid, all the heathen were put to flight. Then they made frequent attacks by night [5]in Buckinghamshire[5] on men unprepared, taking as booty not only men but also beasts, and they slew many between Bernwood and Aylesbury. At the same time the heathen army which lived in East Anglia and Huntingdon, having abandoned the fortifications which they had reinforced at Huntingdon, built themselves stronger ones in the place called Tempsford, clearly thinking that they would then regain by battle the land which had been taken from them.[6] From there they rushed out to attack Bedford, but, when their approach was known, those who guarded the town rushed into battle. They met, the enemy were defeated and put to flight, and very many were killed. After a short interval, the heathen again came together from East Anglia, Essex,[7] and Mercia, approached the town called *Wigingamere*, and did not stop attacking it for a whole day, but those who were inside defended it stoutly, and drove off the enemy, who took back very great booty as they retreated.[8] After this, during the summer, a multitude from the neighbouring towns and areas, which were in King Edward the Elder's control, assembled from all sides, and set out from there for Tempsford and besieged, attacked, took, burnt, and destroyed it, and they slew the heathen king and leader, Toglos, with his

[4] ASC adds here 'and north of these places' (Northampton and Leicester).

[5-5] Buckinghamshire is not in ASC and was probably inferred.

[6] 'recuperare' is presumably JW's rendering of 'geræcan' in ASC. JW seems to speak of 'strengthening' the fortress at Tempsford.

[7] Essex is not mentioned in ASC, though a duplicate East Anglia is deleted in A.

[8] JW makes the Danes take booty as they retreated, whereas ASC has them seize cattle round about during the siege of *Wigingamere*.

p. 308

cum filio suo, comite uidelicet Mannano, fratrem quoque illius omnesque se defendere | uolentes interficiunt, reliquos capiunt et queque reperiunt tollunt.[1] Exinde Danorum uires paulatim decrescebant, Anglorum uero in dies crescebant. Ægelfleda Merciorum domina ante kalend. Augusti Dorbeiam infringendo expugnauit ipsamque prouinciam optinuit, cuius ministri .iiii. de carioribus in porta urbis fortiter pugnantes occisi sunt.[2] Autumnali post hec tempore, de Cantia, Suðregia, Eassaxonia et de urbibus regionibusque in uicino positis, non parua multitudo populi in unum congregata,[a] unanimiter Coleceastram adiit, quam obsidione cingentes tamdiu impugnant donec expugnent. Omnes autem, exceptis paucis qui aufugerant, interficiunt et quicquid intus reperiunt diripiunt. Quod Dani Eastangliam incolentes grauiter ferentes suamque iniuriam ulcisci cupientes, cum piratis quos in auxilium sibi contraxerant, ad Mealdunam profecti sunt, et eam tamdiu obsidentes impugnabant, quoad Anglis de finitimis locis auxiliarii uenissent, quos cum Dani aduentare uidissent, ab urbis impugnatione recesserunt. Hoc uiso, Angli illos magno impetu persecuti, multa milia[3] et de piratis et ceteris prostrauerunt reliquos uero fugauerunt. Non multo post rex inuictissimus Eadwardus Senior[b] Wessaxonicam expeditionem ad Passanham duxit, et tamdiu ibi[c] consedit, donec urbs Toueceastre lapideo cingeretur muro. Vnde Danicus comes Turferthus,[4] quia regis diutius strenuitati resistere non ualebat, cum ciuibus et prouincialibus Norðamtunensibus, Danis et Anglis, regi se dedebat.[5] His gestis, rex domum rediit, aliumque exercitum ad Huntadun e uestigio misit, ut ciuitatem resarcirent et renouarent, et in ea custodes ponerent.[6] Quibus patratis, omnes[d] prouinciales illi [7]qui Danorum supererant crudelitati se manibus illorum euasisse gaudentes,[7] pacem et patrocinium regis petebant eique sui deditionem offerebant. Paucis uero interiectis diebus, Wessaxonico coadunato exercitu, ad Coleceastram rex abiit, et murum illius redintegrauit,

---

[a] congregati HL   [b] interlin. C¹B¹, om. HLP   [c] om. HL   [d] interlin. C¹

---

[1] JW's annal so far corresponds to the first part of the annal (MC 917), in ASC A (917 altered to 920 and then to 921) alone, and the sentence which follows was probably added to link MC and MR.
[2] Æthelflæd's capture of Derby (MR 917) is in ASC (B)C (MR batch of entries) and D (917).

son, that is the earl Manni, also his brother and all his men who
endeavoured to defend themselves.[1] They took the rest captive,
and plundered whatever they found. After that Danish strength
waned but that of the English increased from day to day.
Æthelflæd, lady of the Mercians, took Derby by assault before 1
August, and gained the same province. Four of her most valiant
thegns were killed fighting bravely at the town gate.[2] After this, in
the autumn, no small host collected from Kent, Surrey, Essex, and
the towns and regions in the vicinity, and, being of one mind,
went to Colchester, which they surrounded and besieged, and
attacked until they took it. They slew everyone, except a few who
fled, and plundered whatever they found inside. Because the
Danes inhabiting East Anglia bore this ill, and wished to avenge
their injury, they set out for Maldon with the pirates whose assistance they had hired, and attacked it, so besieging the town until
supporting forces came from the neighbouring places, at the sight
of whose approach the Danes withdrew from the attack on the
town. When they saw this the English pursued them, making a
great attack, laying low many thousands,[3] both pirates and the
others, and put the remainder to flight. Not long after, the most
invincible King Edward the Elder led a West Saxon expedition to
Passenham, and camped there until the town of Towcester was
encircled with a stone wall. Because of this, the Danish earl
Thurferth[4] yielded to the king with the citizens and country
people of Northampton, Danish and English, for he could no
longer resist the king's vigour.[5] When these things were completed
the king returned home, and straight away sent another army to
Huntingdon to repair and renew the city and place guards in it.[6]
After these things had been completed, all the country people
[7]who had survived the cruelty of the Danes, rejoicing at having
escaped from their hands,[7] sought the peace and protection of the
king, and offered him their submission. But when a few days had
passed the king mustered a West Saxon army, and left for
Colchester where he restored the wall, and manned it with paid

[3] ASC: 'hundreds'.   [4] ASC adds 'and the holds'.
[5] JW does not state that those of Northampton who submitted were 'as far north of
the Welland', and he refers, unlike ASC, to Danes and English.
[6] JW implies but does not say that Huntingdon was captured, and makes explicit the
intention of garrisoning the town.
[7-7] Apparent equivalent of ASC 'who had survived' ('eal þæt bær to lafe wæs').

uirosque in ea bellicosos cum stipendio posuit.[1] Interim de Eastanglia et Eassaxonia multi Anglorum qui ferme .xxx. annos[2] feritati[3] paganorum subiacebant, leto animo se regi subiciebant. Ad quem etiam Dani Eastangliam incolentes uenerunt, et se mari terraque nil quod regem offenderet penitus acturos sacramento firmauerunt. Venit et Danorum exercitus de Grantebrycgeie et illum in dominum et patronum delegit et hoc iuramentis, ut ipse uoluit roborauit.[4]

Huogi abbas Fuldensis obiit. Helmfrid successit. Cuonradus rex obiit .x. kalend. Ianuarii, sepultusque est in Fulda iuxta altare sancte crucis.[5]

[C³BP]
"Defuncto Werstano Scireburnensi episcopo, successit Athelbaldus."[a6]

Romanorum octogesimus .ix. Heinricus[7] regnauit annis decem et septem.[8]

[919] (i) 941 Ægelfleda Merciorum domina in principio anni cum auxilio Dei Leogereceastram pacifice adquisiuit, et exercitum Danorum qui ad illam pertinebat ferme totum in deditionem accepit. Cui etiam Dani, qui Eborace presidebant, quidam pacto, quidam iuramento, firmauerunt se ipsius uoluntati et consilio in omnibus consensuros.[9] Rex inuictissimus Eadwardus Senior, post Rogationes cum exercitu Stanfordam profectus est, firmamque in australi plaga amnis Welund[10] arcem muniuit, et non solum Danos qui in septentrionali plaga eiusdem amnis arcem tenebant, sed et omnes qui ad illam pertinebant, in deditionem accepit.[11] Dum hec aguntur soror illius Ægelfleda Merciorum domina insignis

---

a–a Defuncto . . . Athelbaldus] *add. at line-end* C³, *om.* HL

---

[1] Again, as at Huntingdon, JW makes clear that a garrison was established at Colchester, in this case 'cum stipendio'. He does not mention the date ('before Martinmas') of the expedition.

[2] 'Almost 30 years' could have been calculated, not from 878 (Plummer, *Chronicle*, ii. 129), but perhaps from 880, when, as JW puts it, the Danes divided up and began to inhabit East Anglia (in which case it should be amended to 'almost 40 years'), or from 886, when all the English who were not under Danish rule submitted to Alfred, and presumably all who did not submit were subject to the Danes. In both cases 'almost 30 years' would be inaccurate.

[3] No equivalent in ASC.

warriors.[1] Meanwhile many of the English from East Anglia and Essex, who had been subject to heathen harshness[3] for almost thirty years,[2] submitted to the king with a willing heart. Even the Danish inhabitants of East Anglia came to him, and confirmed by oath that they would do absolutely nothing by land and sea to offend the king. The Danish army from Cambridge also came and chose him as their lord and protector, and confirmed this with oaths, as he himself desired.[4]

Hugo, abbot of Fulda, died. Helmfrid succeeded him. King Conrad died on 23 December, and was buried at Fulda near the altar of the Holy Cross.[5]

On the death of Wærstan, bishop of Sherborne. Æthelbald succeeded.[6]

Henry,[7] eighty-ninth emperor of the Romans, reigned seventeen years.[8]

[919] At the beginning of the year Æthelflæd, lady of the Mercians, acquired Leicester peacefully, with God's help, and received the submission of almost the whole Danish army which was attached to the town. Moreover, the Danes who ruled York affirmed, some by treaty, some by oath, that they would be amenable to her wishes and advice in everything.[9] The most invincible King Edward the Elder set out with his army after Rogationtide for Stamford, and fortified the strong fortress on the south bank of the River Welland,[10] and received the submission not only of the Danes who held a fortress on the north bank of the same river, but also of those who belonged to it.[11] While these things were taking place his sister Æthelflæd, lady of the

---

[4] The latter part of this annal after MR 917 (above, p. 376, n. 2) corresponds to the second part of the annal (MC 917) in ASC A (917 altered to 920 and then to 921) G (921).

[5] Mar.

[6] It is not possible to verify the accuracy of this addition (O'Donovan, ii. 105).

[7] Henry I, king of the East Franks 919–36.   [8] Mar.

[9] The submission of Leicester and the promises of subjection by the Danes of York (MR 918) are in ASC (B)C (918 MR batch of entries), D (918). In this annal JW's sequence is MR MC MR MC.

[10] The river is not named in ASC.

[11] Edward's operations at Stamford (MC 918) are entered in ASC A (918 altered to 921 and then to 922) G (922).

prudentie et iustitie, uirtutisque eximie femina,[1] .viii. anno ex quo sola regnum Merciorum strenuo iustoque rexit moderamine,[2] .xix. kalend. Iul.[3] obiit, et unicam filiam suam Ælfwynnam ex Ætheredo subregulo susceptam, heredem regni reliquit,[4] cuius corpus Glauuornam delatum in ecclesia sancti Petri est honorifice tumulatum. Quod ut regi nunciatum est, Tomwurðigene mox properauit, eamque suo dominio subiugauit. Inde mouens exercitum, ad Snotingaham profectus est, captamque urbem resarcire iussit et in ea Anglos simul et Danos collocauit. Processu uero temporis prius Mercenses omnes et Danos Merciam inhabitantes, deinceps tres reges Brytonum, uidelicet Howel, Clyttwic et Iuthuual, cum suis populis in sui deditionem[a] optinuit.[5]

Helmfridus abbas Fuldensis obiit .viii. idus Dec. Haicho successit.[6]

[C³BP]
[b]Defuncto Athelstano Wiltuniensi episcopo successit Odo.[b7]

[920] (ii) 942 Autumnali tempore rex inuictissimus Eadwardus Senior[c] ad Thelauuale profectus est, ibidemque urbem construxit, et ad eius presidium quosque fortissimos de exercitu suo reliquit. | Misit etiam in Norðhymbriam Merciorum exercitum ut urbem Mameceaster restaurarent, et in ea fortes milites collocarent.[8] Post hec Ælfuuynne nepte sue potestatem regni Merciorum penitus ademit et in Wessaxoniam duci precepit.[9]

p. 309

---

[a] ditionem C   [b–b] Defuncto . . . Odo] *add. at line-end, though this is repeated at* p. 382 n. a C³, *om.* HL   [c] *interlin.* C¹B¹, *om.* HL

---

[1] As indicated above, p. 379 n. 9, the next part of the original annal (MR 918) comes from ASC (B)C (918 MR batch of entries), and D (918) though these lack JW's eulogistic words.

[2] ASC agrees with JW in giving Æthelflæd an 8–year rule, but JW's dates 912–19 agree with the length whereas ASC's 912–18 do not.

[3] The day of her death in ASC BCD (and in A which in its MC (918 altered to 921 and then to 922) version simply records her death) is '12 days before midsummer' (12 June) and D adds 'pridie Id. Iunii'. JW's '.xix. kal. Iulii' is the Ides of June (13 June) and is evidently a mistake.

[4] Ælfwynn is not mentioned in this annal in ASC, but could be an obvious inference from MR 919.

[5] As with the entry in 919 (above, p. 378 n. 11, Edward's occupation of Tamworth and Nottingham (MC 918) is in ASC A (918 altered to 921 and then to 922), though JW has rearranged the annal to consolidate the submissions of peoples (Mercian and Welsh) at its end.

Mercians, distinguished by her prudence and justice, a woman of outstanding virtue,[1] in the eighth year after that in which she began to rule on her own the kingdom of the Mercians with vigorous and just government,[2] died on the nineteenth day before the calends of July,[3] leaving Ælfwynn, her only daughter by Æthelred, the underking, as heiress to her kingdom.[4] Her body was borne to Gloucester and buried with honour in St Peter's church. When this was announced to the king he hurried at once to Tamworth, and subjugated it to his rule. Moving the army on from there, he set out for Nottingham, and, having taken the town, ordered it to be repaired and manned it with English as well as Danes. In due course he received the submission, first, of all the Mercians and the Danish inhabitants of Mercia, then of the three Welsh kings, namely Hywel, Clydog, and Idwal, with their people.[5]

Helmfrid, abbot of Fulda, died on 6 December. Haicho succeeded him.[6]

> When Æthelstan, bishop of Wilton died, Oda succeeded him.[7]

[920] In the autumn the most invincible King Edward the Elder set out for Thelwall, and there he built a town and left the stoutest men of his army to garrison it. He also sent a Mercian army into Northumbria to rebuild the town of Manchester and man it with stalwart soldiers.[8] After this he entirely deprived his niece Ælfwynn of rule in the kingdom of Mercia, and ordered her to be taken to Wessex.[9]

---

[6] Mar.

[7] Oda first appears in 927 (S 398 BCS 660), as O'Donovan, ii. 98–9 showed, though no charter before 930 (S 403 BCS 669) attested by him is entirely free from suspicion. Byrhtferth's *Vita Oswaldi* (*Historians of the Church of York*, i. 406) clearly implies that the same king (who must be Æthelstan) made Oda bishop of Wiltshire and later archbishop of Canterbury. He could not therefore have been bishop of Ramsbury before 924.

[8] The fortification of Thelwall and Manchester (MC 919) is in ASC A (919 altered to 922 and then to 923) G (923).

[9] Ælfwynn's removal to Wessex '3 weeks before Christmas' (MR 919) is in ASC (B)C (MR batch of entries), and D (919).

[C³BP]
*a*Defuncto Athelstano Wiltunensi
episcopo successit Odo. Hic*b*
Danice gentis oriundus erat, cuius
*parentes*c *regis Ælfredi tempore
Angliam infestauerant,* sed illis
*abeuntibus uel extinctis, Eadwardo
regi militans aliquandiu,* non
*multo post comam tonsus, clerica-
tum professus* est, *meritisque crescentibus, Wiltunensi   ecclesie
prelatus, Æthelstanum*   regis,
Eadwardi filium, *in sui amicitiam
exciu*it.*ad*1

[921] (iii) 943   Rex inuictissimus Eadwardus Senior ante natiuitatem Iohannis baptiste cum expeditione Snotingaham adiit, et in
australi ripa fluminis Trente urbem, contra urbem que in altera
ripa sita erat, edificauit et inter utramque firmum pontem fieri
mandauit.² Inde cum exercitu ad Beadecan Weallan³ profectus non
longe ab ea urbem construxit et in illa milites uiribus robustos
posuit. Eo tempore rex Scottorum cum tota gente sua, Reignoldus
rex Danorum cum Anglis et Danis Norðhymbriam incolentibus,⁴
rex etiam Streatcleduualorum cum suis, regem Eadwardum
Seniorem sibi in patrem et dominum elegerunt firmumque cum eo
foedus pepigerunt.⁵

[922] (iiii) 944   Clito Æthelwardus regis Eaduuardi Senioris*e* germanus .xvii. kalend. Nou. defunctus, Wintoniam defertur et
sepelitur.⁶ Huuicciorum episcopo Æthelhuno defuncto, Wilferthus
successit.*f*7

---

a-a Defuncto . . . exciuit] *add. at line-end and mostly in mg.: this had been part of a
later-erased marginal entry alongside 905 (p. 360 n. a) with scribbled guiding notes in the
uppermost mg. above these; note also the repetitive 919 n. b* C³, *om. HL*   *b* Hi CP
c occiso sancto Ædmundo *interlin.* B⁵   *d see App. B for addition B*   *e interlin.*
C¹B¹, *om. HL*   *f see App. B for addition B*

---

¹ *GP* i. 14 (p. 21). For this addition concerning Oda (which partly repeats the addition at the end of 919) see above, p. 381 n. 7.
² Edward's borough-building (MC 920) at Nottingham and Bakewell and the submission of the North Britons is in ASC A (920 altered to 923 and then to 924) G (924).

On the death of Æthelstan, bishop of Wilton, Oda succeeded. He was of Danish birth and his ancestors attacked England in the time of King Alfred, but on their departure or death he fought for some time for King Edward. Not much later he took the tonsure, professed himself a clerk, and, as his merits increased, was preferred to the see of Wilton and won the friendship of Æthelstan, son of king Edward.[1]

[921] The most invincible King Edward the Elder went to Nottingham with an army before the Nativity of John the Baptist, and built a town on the south bank of the River Trent, facing the town on the opposite bank of the river, and ordered that a strong bridge be made between the two.[2] From there he set out for Bakewell[3] with the army, and not far from there built a town, stationing stalwart soldiers in it, in strength. At that time the king of the Scots with his whole people, Ragnald, king of the Danes, with the English and Danish inhabitants of Northumbria,[4] and also the king of Strathclyde with his men, chose King Edward the Elder for their father and lord, and made a firm treaty with him.[5]

[922] The atheling Æthelweard, brother of King Edward the Elder, died on 16 October, was borne to Winchester, and was buried there.[6] After the death of Æthelhun, bishop of the Hwicce, Wilferth succeeded.[7]

[3] JW omits the reference to the Peak district in which Bakewell is situated.

[4] JW omits 'the sons of Eadulf' and 'Norsemen and others' among those who live in Northumbria and identifies Ragnald as king of the Danes.

[5] JW omits the MR (921) reference to the fortification of *Cledemutha* (ASC CD (921)) and the entries concerning Sihtric and Niall in EF (921), and Ragnald at York in DE (923) F (925).

[6] The death of Æthelweard is not in ASC. WM, *GR* ii. 130 (i. 141) says that he died 4 years before the death of Edward the Elder (dated by him 924), i.e. 920. Some discussion in Stevenson, *Asser*, p. 299.

[7] This entry may be accurate (O'Donovan, ii. 113).

[923] (v) 945   *Sanguis Domini uenit in Augiam^a .vi. idus Nouembris, qui de imagine Christi fluxit cum secundo in imagine sua a Iudeis priora pateretur.*[1]

[C³BP]
^bDefuncto Bernecho Sælesiensi episcopo, successit Kenredus.^bc2

[924] (vi) 946   Ciclus solis incipit .iiii. concurrentibus bissextilibus.

Inuictissimus rex Anglorum Eadwardus Senior[3] qui cunctis Brytanniam incolentibus, Anglorum, Scottorum, Cumbrorum, Danorum pariter et Brytonum populis gloriosissime prefuit,[4] post multas res egregie gestas, regni sui anno .xxiiii.,[5] in regia uilla que Fearndun nominatur,[6] indictione .xv.,[5] ex hac uita transiens, Athelstano filio regni gubernacula reliquit, cuius corpus Wintoniam delatum, in Nouo Monasterio regio more sepelitur.[7] Non multo post filius eius Alfuuardus apud Oxenofordam decessit, et sepultus est ubi et pater illius.[8] Athelstanus uero in Kingestone,^d id est regia uilla, in regem leuatur, et honorifice ab Athelmo Dorubernensi archiepiscopo consecratur:[9] cuius *temporibus oritur puer strenuus* Dunstanus *in Wessaxon*ie *finibus.*[10]

Haicho abbas Fuldensis obiit .iiii. kalend. Iunii, Hiltibertus successit. Vngarii totam Franciam, Alsatiam, Galliam, Alamanniamque igne et gladio uastant.[11]

[C³BP]
^eDefuncto Athelmo archiepiscopo, successit Wlhelmus, cui ad

---

^a *over erasure C*   ^b–b Defuncto . . . Kenredus] *at line-end extending into mg. C³, om. HL*   ^c *see App. B for addition B*   ^d Kingestone *from* Cingestune *C,* Kyngestune *H,* Kingestun *L,* Cingestune *BP*   ^e Defuncto . . . Bryhthelmus (*p. 386*)] *add. at line end and mostly in mg. C³, om. HL*

---

[1] Mar.

[2] This entry (calling Bishop Beornheah Bernechus) is inaccurate; he was the recipient of a grant from Æthelstan in 930 (*S* 403 *BCS* 669) and was succeeded by Wulfhun, though neither is mentioned in JW *Epis. Lists.* Cenred held office a century earlier (O'Donovan, ii. 101–2).

[3] The death of Edward is recorded in ASC (MC and MR 924, F 925). JW's account agrees most closely with that in ASC BCD (MR).

[4] ASC does not have the brief eulogy nor list of subject peoples, though under 924, F records the election of Edward over various peoples and princes.

[5] The year of the reign and the indiction (wrong as 924 was the 12th indiction) are not in ASC.

[923] On 8 November the Blood of the Lord came to Reichenau; it flowed from the image of Christ, who suffered again in His image as before He had suffered at the hands of the Jews.[1]

On the death of Beornheah, bishop of Selsey, Cenred succeeded.[2]

[924] The solar cycle begins with four concurrents in a bissextile year.

The most invincible king of the English, Edward the Elder,[3] who most gloriously held sway over all the inhabitants of Britain— English, Scots, Cumbrians, Danes, as well as the Welsh[4]—after performing many outstanding feats, departed this life in the twenty-fourth year of his reign, in the fifteenth indiction,[5] at the royal township called Farndon,[6] leaving the governance of the realm to his son Æthelstan. His body was borne to Winchester, and buried royally in the New Minster.[7] Not much later his son Ælfweard died at Oxford, and was buried where his father lies as well.[8] But Æthelstan was raised to the kingship at Kingston, which means royal township, and was consecrated with due honour by Athelm, archbishop of Canterbury.[9] In his time the energetic child Dunstan was born in West Saxon territory.[10]

Haicho, abbot of Fulda, died on 29 May, and Hiltibert succeeded him. The Hungarians laid waste all Francia, Alsace, Gaul, and Alemannia with fire and sword.[11]

When Archbishop Athelm died Wulfhelm succeeded, to whose

[6] The reference to Farndon is found in MR, not in MC. JW identifies it as a royal vill.

[7] ASC does not mention New Minster as the burial-place.

[8] The death of Ælfweard is in MR 924, and ASC BCD (924 MR batch). ASC D, but not BC, say that he died 16 days after Edward.

[9] The consecration of Æthelstan at Kingston is in ASC BCD (MR 924), but JW does not say that he was chosen king by the Mercians, and has no reference to his sister's marriage (which in D is said to have been to 'the son of the king of the Old Saxons'). That Archbishop Athelm consecrated Æthelstan is not in ASC but is supported by Adelard's *Vita Dunstani* (*Memorials Dunstan*, p. 56).

[10] *Vita Dunstani auctore B*, c. 3 (*Memorials Dunstan*, p. 6). Though post-Conquest writers understood this to mean that Dunstan was born in 925, JW's 'cuius temporibus' is more cautious (see Robinson, *Wells*, pp. 38–40).

[11] Mar.

Wyllensem ecclesiam successit
Ælfegus illique Wlfhelmus
illique Bryhthelmus.[a1]

[925] (vii) 947 Strenuus et gloriosus rex Anglorum Athelstanus
sororem suam[b] cum magno honore et gloria Northymbrorum regi
Sihtrico, Danica stirpe progenito, in matrimonium dedit.[c2]

[926] (viii) 948 [3]Ignei per totam Angliam uisi sunt radii in
septentrionali plaga celi. Nec multo post Northanhymbrorum rex
Sihtricus uita decessit, cuius regnum rex Æthelstanus, filio illius
Guthfertho, qui patri in regnum successerat, expulso, suo adiecit
imperio.[4] Omnes etiam reges totius Albionis, regem scilicet
Occidentalium Brytonum Huuual, dehinc regem Scottorum
Constantinum, regemque Wentorum Wuer, proelio uicit et
fugauit.[5] Aldredum quoque filium Eadulfi de regia urbe que lingua
Anglorum Bebbanbyrig nominatur expulit.[6] Ii omnes, ubi se
uiderunt non posse strenuitati illius resistere, pacem ab eo
petentes, in loco qui dicitur Eamotum .iiii. idus Iulii conuenerunt,
datoque sacramento,[d] firmum cum eo foedus pepigerunt.[7]
Herigerus episcopus Mogontinus[e] obiit kalendas Decembris.[f8]

[927] (ix) 949 *Hildibertus abbas Fuldensis successit. Post quem ad
Fuldam successit Hadamarus abbas.[gh9]*

[928] (x) 950 [i]Tilredus Lindisfarnensis episcopus obiit, cui
Wigredus successit.[i10]

---

[a] *see above p. 384 n. e*   [b] *add. Eadgytham B*   [c] *see App. B for addition in
lower mg. with signe de renvoi B[1]*   [d] *idolatrie renuntiantes interlin. B[5]*   [e] *om. HL*
[f] *runs over into 927 C*   [g] *runs on to 928 C, under 926 B*   [h] *see App. B for
addition B*   [i-i] *Tilredus . . . successit] added mg. alongside 928 C[2] (with same entry
scribbled by C[3] in uppermost mg., presumably as guide), under 927, continuing under 928 B,
after 929, under consolidated 927–32 P*

---

[1] That Wulfhelm probably succeeded Athelm in 926 and not 924 or 925 (ASC EF,
ADL (925) and addition by hand 8f to A (924 altered to 925)) is argued by Robinson,
Wells, p. 34, and O'Donovan, i. 32–3.
[2] The marriage of Æthelstan's sister to Sihtric is mentioned in ASC D (925), though
it could have been in the incomplete entry in BC (MR). Unlike D, JW mentions
Sihtric's Danish extraction (though he was a Norwegian), but does not say that the
occasion was a meeting between the two kings at Tamworth.
[3] This annal is in ASC D (926) with significant differences.

see at Wells Ælfheah suc-
ceeded, and to him Wulfhelm,
and to him Brihthelm.[1]

[925] The most vigorous and glorious Æthelstan, king of the
English, gave his sister in marriage with great ceremony and
splendour to King Sihtric of the Northumbrians, who was of
Danish stock.[2]

[926] [3]Fiery rays were seen throughout the whole of England in
the northern part of the sky. Not much later Sihtric, king of the
Northumbrians, departed this life, and King Æthelstan, having
expelled Sihtric's son, Guthfrith, who had succeeded his father as
king, added his kingdom to his dominion.[4] Also, he overcame in
battle and put to flight the kings of all Albion, namely Hywel,
king of the West Welsh, then Constantine, king of the Scots, and
Wer, king of the people of Gwent.[5] He also expelled Ealdred,
Eadwulf's son, from the royal town which is called Bamburgh in
the English tongue.[6] They all, when they saw they could not resist
his strength, sought peace with him. They met in a place called
Eamont on 12 July, and having sworn, made a firm treaty with
him.[7]

Heriger, bishop of Mainz, died on 1 December.[8]

[927] Hildibert succeeded as abbot of Fulda. Then Hadamar succeeded him as abbot at Fulda.[9]

[928] Tilred, bishop of Lindisfarne, died and Wigred succeeded
him.[10]

---

[4] The expulsion of Guthfrith is not mentioned by ASC D though EF refer to it
under 927 (without describing his parentage). He was Sihtric's brother, not his son.

[5] ASC D names Owain as king of the people of Gwent here, but does not speak of
Æthelstan's engaging these kings in battle and putting them to flight.

[6] The expulsion of Ealdred from Bamburgh is not mentioned in ASC D and may
possibly be a misunderstanding of 'from' in ASC in 'Ealdred Ealdulfing from
Bebbanbyrig'.

[7] ASC D refers to the renunciation of idolatry, presumably by the kings already
mentioned.

[8] Mar.   [9] Mar.

[10] Tilred's death and Wigred's succession are dated 925 in *HDE* ii. 18 (i. 75), but
since Tilred's accession is dated 915 by scribe C² (see above, p. 372 n. 3) and he was
bishop for 13 years and 4 months, JW here may have calculated afresh in an attempt to
resolve *HDE*'s contradictions.

[C³BP]

^aDefuncto Tunbryhto Licedfeld-
ensi presule, successit Ælle.^{ab1}

[929] (xi) 951   *Leo*² *.cxxv. papa.*³
Huuicciorum episcopo Wilfertho defuncto, successit
Cinewoldus.^{c4}

[930] (xii) 952   *Heinricus rex regem Obritorum et Nordmannorum
facit Christianos.*⁵

[931] (xiii) 953   Domnanie presul obiit Eadulfus, et in
Cridiantune est sepultus.⁶

[932] (xiiii) 954   Vir eximie sanctitatis Frithestanus Wintoniensis
episcopus, ordinato pro se in episcopatum uiro religioso
Byrnstano, Wintoniam resedit.⁷ ^dHic uir sanctus fuit. *Cotidie missam pro defunctorum requie cant*auit, noct*e cimiteria circu*iuit, *pro animarum salute psalmos* decantauit. *Quadam uice hoc* agens, dum
expletis omnibus subiungeret: 'requiescant in pace', subito *uoces quasi
exercitus infiniti e sepulchris audiuit respondentium: 'Amen'.*^{d8}

[933] (xv) 955   *Vngarii ab exercitu regis Heinrici occisi sunt, multique ex eis comprehensi sunt.*⁹
Sanctus Frithestanus obiit.¹⁰ |

310   **[934]** (xvi) 956   *Stephanus*¹¹ p. *.cxxvi. papa.*¹²
Strenuus rex Anglorum Athelstanus quia rex Scottorum
Constantinus foedus quod cum eo pepigerat dirupit, classica manu
perualida et equestri exercitu non modico ad Scottiam

---

^{a–a} Defuncto . . . Ælle] *add. mg. alongside 929, immediately below 928 n. i* C³, *om.
HL, under 928 B, under consolidated 927–32, immediately following 928 n. i* P   ^b *see
appendix B for addition B*   ^c *see App. B for addition B, 928 nn. i & a (p. 388)
follow immediately under consolidated 927–32* P   ^{d–d} Hic . . . Amen] *add. at line-end
and in mg.* C³

---

¹ 'Ælle (qui et Ælfwinus)' succeeds Tunberht in JW *Epis. Lists* with a gap in time
between the two apparently implied by the notes on them in the lists. For the evidence
that Tunberht was bishop in the middle of the 9th c. and that Ælle was bishop by 925,
and just possibly by 915, see O'Donovan, ii. 91, 95.
² Leo VI 928.
³ Mar.

When Tunberht, bishop of Lichfield, died, Ælle succeeded him.[1]

[929] Leo[2] the 125th pope.[3]

After the death of Wilferth, bishop of the Hwicce, Cenwald succeeded him.[4]

[930] King Henry made Christians of the king of the Obodritae, and the king of the Norsemen.[5]

[931] Eadwulf, bishop of Devon, died, and was buried at Crediton.[6]

[932] Frithestan, a man of exceptional sanctity, bishop of Winchester, when he had ordained the devout man Byrnstan to take his place in the bishopric, remained in Winchester.[7] He was a holy man. He sang mass every day for the repose of the dead. At night he walked about the graveyard, singing psalms for the deliverance of souls. He was doing this on one occasion, and when he added, after all had been completed, 'May they rest in peace', he suddenly heard voices, as if of an infinite host, from the graves, responding 'Amen'.[8]

[933] The Hungarians were slain by King Henry's army, and many of them were captured.[9]

St Frithestan died.[10]

[934] Stephen[11] the 126th pope.[12]

Since Constantine, king of the Scots, had broken the treaty he had made with him, Æthelstan, the vigorous king of the English, set out for Scotland with a very strong fleet and no small mounted

[4] There is no evidence against the date of this succession (O'Donovan, ii. 113). JW MS C's 19-year table on p. 66 dates Wilferth's death to 928.

[5] Mar. The Latin seems to make the Abodrites and the Norsemen subjects of the same king.

[6] Bishop Eadwulf attests as late as 934 (O'Donovan, i. 36).

[7] Byrnstan's consecration was recorded in ASC A (931 altered to, and then back from, 932). F (931), G (932) but JW adds that Frithestan remained in Winchester.

[8] *GP* ii. 75 (p. 163).   [9] Mar.

[10] ASC A (932 altered to, and then back from, 933); F enters Frithestan's death and Byrnstan's consecration under 931, G under 932.

[11] Stephen VII (VIII) 928–31.   [12] Mar.

proficiscitur, eamque maxima ex parte depopulatur.[1] Vnde ui compulsus[a] rex Constantinus filium suum obsidem cum dignis muneribus illi dedit, paceque redintegrata, rex in Wessaxoniam rediit.[2]
Eodem anno sanctus Byrnstanus Wintoniensis episcopus obiit.[b3]

[C³BP³]

ᶜWlfhelmo, Dorubernie arciepiscopo Athelmi successore,
defuncto, Odo *in primatum Cantie*
eligitur. *Sed ille qui nondum ami-*
cisset monachum constantius reniti,
ne morem maiorum ambitione sua
turbare uideretur. Nullum enim ad
id tempus nisi monachili scemate
indutum, ⟨archiepiscopum⟩ fuisse.
Sed cum regie uoluntati episcopo-
rum omnium assensus accederet,
tandem uir reuerentissimus,
propositi sui rigore edomito, tran-
sito mari, apud Floriacum
monachilia accepit, et, Angliam
rediens, in Cantuuariensi
arciepiscopatu magna *⟨familiari-*
tate⟩ apud Æthelstanum et *non*
imparis amicitie apud Eadmundum
et Edredum gratiam tenuit.[4]
Odoni successit in episcopatum
Wellensem Osulfus.*ᶜ5*

ᵃ erasure before compulsus *C*   *ᵇ erasure at blank line-end here C*
ᶜ⁻ᶜ Wlfhelmo . . . Osulfus] *added mg. alongside 934–9 C³, om. HL, outer mg. alongside*
938–40, but possibly meant for 934–5 in inner column P³

---

[1] ASC A (933 altered to, and then back from, 934) (B)CDEF (934). ASC does not
say that Constantine had provoked the war by violating the peace between him and
Æthelstan.
[2] That Constantine was forced to give a son as hostage seems JW's addition.
[3] ASC A (933 to, and then back from, 934) 'on All Saints' Day'.

force and ravaged a very large part of Scotland.[1] Whence, compelled by force, King Constantine gave him his son as a hostage, and worthy gifts, and when peace was restored, the king returned to Wessex.[2] In the same year St Byrnstan, bishop of Winchester, died.[3]

On the death of Athelm's successor, Wulfhelm, archbishop of Canterbury, Oda was elected to the primacy of Kent. But he, because he had not then taken the habit, resisted with greater constancy lest he should seem to overthrow the custom of his predecessors by his ambition, for up to that time there had been no archbishop who had not worn the monastic habit. But since the opinion of all the bishops was in accordance with the royal wish, that most reverend man at length, when the rigour of his resolution had been completely overcome, crossed the sea, and took monastic vows at Fleury, and on his return to England he enjoyed, as archbishop of Canterbury, great favour with Æthelstan, and with Edmund and Eadred, the gift of equal friendship.[4] Oswulf succeeded Oda in the bishopric of Wells.[5]

[4] *GP* i. 14, 15 (pp. 21, 22). For the view that Oda succeeded to Canterbury after 12 Feb. 941, see O'Donovan, i. 32–3.

[5] JW *Epis. Lists* agree with JW and WM, *GP* ii. 83 (p. 181), in ignoring Ælfric as Oda's immediate successor at Ramsbury, though JW seems alone responsible for the error of identifying the see as Wells.

[935] (xvii) 957   *Iohannes*[1] *.cxxvii. papa.*[2]
Religiosus monachus *Ælfegus, cognom*ento *Caluus,* beati Dunstani *propinquus,* suscepit episcopatum Wintoniensis ecclesie.[3]

[936] (xviii) 958   *Leo*[4] *.cxxviii. papa. Hildibertus episcopus ⟨Moguntinus⟩*[a] *obiit .ii. kalend. Iunii, cui Frithericus successit. Heinricus rex obiit .vi. non. Iulii, et Otto filius eius in regnum constituitur.*[b5]

[C¹? P]
[c]et rex Rodulfus defungitur.[c]
Romanorum nonagesimus *Otto*[6] *regnauit annis .xxxvi. et mensibus decem.*[7]
Huic rex Anglorum Æthelstanus unam sororem suam dedit in coniugem.[8]

[937] (i) 959   Hiberniensium multarumque insularum rex paganus Anlafus, a socero suo rege Scottorum Constantino incitatus, ostium Humbre fluminis ualida cum classe ingreditur.[9] Cui rex Athelstanus fraterque suus clito Eadmundus in loco qui dicitur Brunanburh cum exercitu occurrerunt, et prelio a diei principio in uesperum tracto, quinque regulos septemque duces, quos aduersarii sibi in auxilium conduxerant, interfecerunt, tantumque sanguinis quantum eatenus in Anglia nullo in bello fusum est fuderunt, et reges Anlafum et Constantinum ad naues fugere compellentes, magno reuersi sunt tripudio. Illi uero summam infelicitatem de interitu sui exercitus consecuti, cum paucis redeunt in sua.[10]

Monasteria sanctorum Galli et Bonefacii igne consumuntur. Vngarii per orientales Francos et Alamanniam multis ciuitatibus igne et gladio consumptis, iuxta Wormatiam Hreno transito usque ad mare oceanum regnum Gallie deuastauerunt et postmodum *per Italiam redierunt.*[d11]

---

[a] *om. JW (N)*   [b] *see App. B for addition B*   [c–c] et . . . defungitur] *interlin.* C¹?, *om.* HLB   [d] *erasure follows on rest of last line of* 937, *of which the first word of* 937 n. a (p. 394) *is visible, presumably indicating an attempted placing of that addition* C

---

[1] John XI 931–935×936.   [2] Mar.
[3] *Vita Dunstani auctore B,* c. 7 (*Memorials Dunstan,* p. 13). The succession of Ælfheah is entered in ASC A (934 altered to, and then back from, 935) F (935). For the view that Ælfheah was bishop-elect, but not yet consecrated in 935, see O'Donovan, ii. 111–12.
[4] Leo VII 936–9.   [5] Mar.   [6] Otto I 936–73.   [7] Mar.

[935] John[1] the 127th pope.[2]

The devout monk Ælfheah, surnamed the Bald, a kinsman of St Dunstan, received the bishopric of Winchester.[3]

[936] Leo[4] the 128th pope. Bishop Hildibert of Mainz died on 31 May, and Fritheric succeeded him. King Henry died on 2 July, and his son Otto was established as king.[5]

King Rudolf died.

Otto,[6] the ninetieth emperor of the Romans, reigned thirty-six years and ten months.[7]

Æthelstan, king of the English, gave him one of his sisters as wife.[8]

[937] The heathen king of the Irish and of many islands, Olaf, at the instigation of his father-in-law Constantine, king of the Scots, entered the mouth of the River Humber with a strong fleet.[9] King Æthelstan and his brother, the atheling Edmund, met him in a place called *Brunanburh* with their army, and when the battle had dragged on from dawn to dusk, they killed five underkings, and seven earls whom their adversaries had brought as allies, and more blood was shed than hitherto had been shed in any war in England. They forced the kings Olaf and Constantine to flee to their ships, and came home with great jubilation. But the kings, having experienced the depths of misfortune from the destruction of their army, returned to their own lands with few men.[10]

The monasteries of St Gall and St Boniface were consumed by fire. The Hungarians, after destroying many cities in eastern Francia and Alemannia with fire and sword, crossed the Rhine near Worms, laid waste the coastal area of Gaul to the sea, and afterwards returned through Italy.[11]

[8] The identification of Otto I as the husband of one of Æthelstan's sisters (already implied in 901 and ASC D under 924, see above, p. 385 n. 9) is JW's contribution to this annal.

[9] The description of Olaf's dominion and the statements that he was Constantine's son-in-law, that he was incited by the Scottish king, and that the fleet sailed up the Humber are peculiar to JW and are not in ASC. On this and on the identification of this Olaf as Guthfrith's (not Sihtric's) son, see Alfred P. Smyth, *Scandinavian York and Dublin: The History and Archaeology of Two Related Viking Kingdoms*, (2 vols., Dublin, 1975-9), ii. 43-4.

[10] JW gives the substance of the verse entry in ASC A (937 altered to, and then back from, 938) (B)CD (937) F (938 an even briefer annal) E (937) very brief.

[11] Mar.

[C³BP³]

ᵃMiddeltunensem ecclesiam fecit rex Athelstanus pro anima fratris sui Edwi⟨n⟩i, quem prauo corruptus consilio Anglia eiecit.[1] Simili pro causa *Micelenense cenobi*um construxit quod situm est *in Sumersetensi pago.*ᵃ²

[938] (ii) 960 *Otto a Bauuariis sibi resistentibus rediit. Frater autem eius Heinricus comprehensus est ab Eberhardo. Illo* uero *liberato, Eberhardum misit in exilium, atque iterum Bauuarios cum exercitu inuasit, omnesque sibi subdidit preter unum Arnulfi filium. Interim magna pars Vngariorum a Saxonibus occisa est.*ᵇ³

[939] (iii) 961 *Otto Lotheringiam intrauit usque ad Capri montem. ᶜInterea Luduuuicus rex Gallie inuasit Alsatiam. Tunc Otto reuersus uenit ad Brisacam et obsedit eam et Luduuuicus discessit. ᵈStephanus*[4] *centesimus .xxix. papa.*ᵈᵉ⁵

[940] (iiii) 962 Strenuus et gloriosus rex Anglorum Athelstanus .xvi. regni sui anno, indictione .xiiii., .vi. kalend. Nouembris, feria .iiii., apud Glauuornam uita decessit, et ad Maidulfi urbem delatus, honorifice est tumulatus, cui frater suus Eadmundus, .xviii. etatis sue anno, in regnum successit.ᶠ⁶

[941] (v) 963 Norðhymbrenses fidelitati quam magnifico regi Anglorum Eadmundo debebant, infidelitatem preferentes, regem Nordmannorumᵍ Anlafum sibi in regem elegerunt.[7] Eodem anno Alfredus Scireburnensis episcopus obiit.ʰ⁸

ᵃ⁻ᵃ Middeltunensem . . . pago] *add. mg. alongside 939–41 (mg. addition 934 n. c takes up much of top half of page, including space near 937)* C³, *om.* HL, *incorpor. at* 940 n. f B, *mg. next to* 937 P³   ᵇ *see App. B for addition B*   ᶜ *940–1 (N)*   ᵈ⁻ᵈ Stephanus . . . papa] *before* 939 n. c (N)   ᵉ *see App. B for addition B*   ᶠ *937 n. a incorporated here followed by addition printed in App. B*   ᵍ Ibernensium *interlin. over expunctuated* Nordmannorum B⁵   ʰ *see App. B for addition B*

---

[1] WM, *GP* ii. 85 (p. 186). There is no obvious reason for the attempted location of this addition at 937.
[2] This is probably based on WM, *GP* ii. 93, 90 (pp. 199, 196).
[3] Mar.   [4] Stephen VIII (IX) 939–42.   [5] Mar.

King Æthelstan built the church of Milton for the soul of his brother Edwin, whom he, corrupted by evil counsel, exiled from England.[1] For a like reason he built the monastery of Muchelney, which is situated in Somerset.[2]

[938] Otto returned from the Bavarians, who were opposing him. His brother Henry, however, was captured by Eberhard. But when he had been set free, Otto sent Eberhard into exile, and again attacked the Bavarians with an army, and subjected them all to himself except one, Arnulf's son. Meanwhile, a large number of Hungarians were killed by the Saxons.[3]

[939] Otto invaded Lotharingia as far as Chèvremont. Meanwhile, Louis, king of Gaul, invaded Alsace. Then Otto, turning back, came to Breisach, and besieged it, and Louis withdrew. Stephen[4] 129th pope.[5]

[940] The vigorous and glorious King Æthelstan died at Gloucester in the sixteenth year of his reign, on Wednesday, 27 October, in the fourteenth indiction. He was borne to the town of Malmesbury and buried honourably. His brother Edmund succeeded him as king in his eighteenth year.[6]

[941] The Northumbrians, preferring unfaithfulness to the fealty they owed the glorious Edmund, king of the English, chose Olaf, king of the Norsemen, as their king.[7] In the same year Alfred, bishop of Sherborne, died.[8]

---

[6] Æthelstan's death and Edmund's succession are given in ASC A (940 altered to, and then back from, 941) (B)CDEF (940). JW's '16th year' is probably an error for '15th' since ASC makes Æthelstan reign 14 years and 10 weeks, and the 14th indiction began on 24 Sept 940, but the feria agrees with 941. D alone mentions the place of Æthelstan's death; but his burial at Malmesbury is not in ASC.

[7] ASC D (941), which says that Olaf (who is not called king of the Northmen) was from Ireland. JW persistently calls Edmund 'magnificus'.

[8] The death of Alfred, bishop of Sherborne, is not recorded elsewhere. The Alfred who witnesses charters from 943 may be his namesake, the bishop of Selsey (O'Donovan, ii. 106).

[942] (vi) 964   *ᵃMarinus¹ papa centesimus .xxx. Huius pape tempore sanctus Vldaricus Romam uenit et ab eodem mortem episcopi sui audiens, simul etiam se episcopum futurum agnouit. Sed Hiltine post Adalberonem .xv. annis ecclesie Augustensi prefuit, moxque sanctus Vldaricus in episcopatum successit. Interim Eberhart dux occisus et Gisilbertus dux in Hreno submersus.²*

Magnificus rex Anglorum Eadmundus quinque ciuitates Lindicolinam, Snotingaham, Deorbeiam, Leogereceastram et Stanfordam manibus Danorum penitus extorsit, totamque

p. 311   Merciam | in sui potestatem redegit.³ Hic Dei seruo *Dunstano* summus et *eius consiliis gloriosus a quo diuersis honoribus sullimatus* Glæstonie, *in qua educatus est,* abbatis iure preficitur.⁴

*ᵇ*Willelmus dux Normannorum, filius Rollonis, .xvi. kalend. Ianuarii occiditur, cui successit Ricardus filius eius.*ᵇᶜ⁵*

[943] (vii) 965   Magnifico regi Eadmundo *cum sua regina* sancta *Ælgiua filium* peperisset *Eadgarum, sanctus* abbas *Dunstanus audiuit quasi in sullimi uoces psallentium atque dicentium: 'pax Anglorum ecclesie, exorti nunc pueri, nostri*que *Dunstani tempore'.⁶* Eodem anno idem rex Anlafum regem, cuius supra meminimus, de lauacro sancte regenerationis suscepit, regioque munere donauit, et paruo post tempore Reignoldum Norðanhymbrorum regem, dum ab episcopo confirmaretur, tenuit sibique in filium adoptauit.⁷

Otto dux obiit, cui Cuonradus successit.⁸

ᵃ *under 941, though annal ends under 942 (N)*   ᵇ⁻ᵇ Willelmus . . . eius] *add. at line-end, extending into mg. C¹*   ᶜ *see App. B for addition B*

---

¹ Marinus II 942–6.   ² Mar.

³ With a different eulogy, JW gives the substance of the verse annal in ASC A (942 altered to 941) BCD, but speaks of Mercia being freed from the Danes, and not (like ASC) of the Danes being freed from the Norsemen. ASC describes Mercia's boundaries.

⁴ *Vita Dunstani auctore Adelardo,* lectio 3 (*Memorials Dunstan,* p. 56). JW's date for Dunstan's appointment as abbot of Glastonbury may come from ASC A (addition by hand 7: s. xiᵉˣ) F (upper mg. without date), which speak of Glastonbury being entrusted to Dunstan. Adelard's 'et ipse beato Dunstano *summissus* et eius consiliis gloriosus' may lie behind the 'Dei seruo Dunstano *summus*' of JW.

⁵ Norman Annals. *AU, AG, AC, AMSM.*

[942] Marinus[1] the 130th pope. In this pope's time St Wuldaric came to Rome, and, hearing from him of the death of his bishop, at once realized that he also would be bishop. But Hiltine ruled the church of Augsburg for fifteen years after Adalbero, and St Wuldaric succeeded him immediately to the bishopric. Meanwhile Count Eberhard was killed, and Count Gilbert drowned in the Rhine.[2]

Edmund, the glorious king of the English, wrested completely out of Danish hands the five boroughs of Lincoln, Nottingham, Derby, Leicester, and Stamford, and brought all Mercia under his control.[3] He became most high and glorious through the counsels of God's servant Dunstan, whom, after advancing him to various honours, he put in charge of Glastonbury (where Dunstan was brought up), as abbot.[4]

William, duke of the Normans, son of Rollo, was killed on 17 December. His son Richard succeeded him.[5]

[943] When his queen, the saintly Ælfgifu, bore the glorious King Edmund a son, Edgar, St Dunstan the abbot heard, as it were on high, voices singing and saying: 'The peace of the English church shall fall in the time of this boy now born and of our Dunstan.'[6] In the same year the king received King Olaf, whom we have mentioned above, from the font of holy regeneration, and gave him a royal gift. A short time later, he presented Ragnald, king of the Northumbrians, on his confirmation by the bishop, and adopted him as his son.[7]

Count Otto died and Conrad succeeded him.[8]

---

[6] *Vita Dunstani auctore Adelardo*, lectio 3 (*Memorials Dunstan*, p. 56). The date of Edgar's birth could have been easily calculated from his age at accession.

[7] Apparently under 942 in ASC A-D, (though in BC the baptism starts on a new line). 'Regioque munere donauit' follows D's '7 he him cynelice gyfode', but much of D's annal concerning Olaf's capture of Tamworth and Edmund's siege of Leicester has been omitted. E's notice of the death of King Olaf (Guthfrith's son) in 942 is ignored, and JW follows all other versions of ASC in recognizing only one Olaf; this accounts for his characteristic addition here to ASC 'cuius supra meminimus'. See Smyth, *Scandinavian York and Dublin*, ii. 88–121 for the distinction between the Olaf (probably Guthfrith's son) chosen by the Northumbrians under 941 and his successor Olaf (Sihtric's son) who is mentioned here.

[8] Mar.

[C³BP]
*ᵃ*Defuncto Scireburnensi episcopo Athelbaldo, successit
Ælfredus.*ᵃᵇ¹*

[944] (viii) 966 *Otto rex in Lotheringiam cum exercitu exiuit omnes*que *suo subiugauit imperio, sed Metensis episcopus resistebat.*²

Magnificus rex Anglorum Eadmundus duos reges, Anlafum, regis uidelicet Sihtrici filium, et Reignoldum, Guthferthi filium, *ᶜ*de Norðhymbria expulit, eamque sue ditioni subegit.*ᶜ³ ᵈ*Wigredo Lindisfarnensi episcopo defuncto, Vhtredus successit, quo mortuo, Sexhelm loco eius ordinatur, sed paucis mensibus euolutis defungitur, pro quo Aldredus consecratur.*ᵈᵉ⁴*

[945] (ix) 967 Magnificus rex Anglorum Eadmundus terram Cumbrorum depopulatus est, illamque regi Scottorum Malculmo eo tenore dedit, ut terra marique sibi fidelis existeret.*ᶠ⁵*

[946] (x) 968 *Agapitus*⁶ *centesimus .xxxi. papa.*ᵍ⁷

Magnificus rex Anglorum Eadmundus, die festiuitatis sancti Augustini Anglorum doctoris,⁸ dum in regia uilla que Anglice Pucelecirce*ʰ*⁹ dicitur, suum dapiferum e manibus pessimi *cleptoris*ⁱ Leoue⁹ ne occideretur uellet eripere,¹⁰ quinque annis septemque mensibus regni sui peractis,¹¹ indictione .iiii., .vii. kalend. Iunii, feria .iii.,¹² ab eodem interficitur, et Glæstoniam delatus, a beato Dunstano abbate sepelitur.¹³ *Mox proximus heres Edredus, fratri*

ᵃ⁻ᵃ Defuncto . . . Ælfredus] *add. at line-end* C³, *om.* HL   *ᵇ see App. B for addition B*   *ᶜ⁻ᶜ* de . . . subegit] *rewritten at line-end* C²   *ᵈ⁻ᵈ* Wigredo . . . consecratur] *add. mg. but clearly for 944* C²   *ᵉ see App. B for addition B*   *ᶠ see App. B for (i) addition in text here, and (ii) addition in lower mg. with signe de renvoi* B⁴   *ᵍ see App. B for addition B*   *ʰ* Pucelencirce *interlin* B   *ⁱ* furis *interlin.* B

---

¹ This addition is wrong. Alfred's death had already been recorded in the original 941 annal (see above, p. 395 n. 8). JW *Epis. Lists* make clear that his immediate predecessor was Sigehelm.
² Mar.
³ ASC A–F (EF describe Olaf and Ragnald, not as kings, but 'of royal race', and do not name their fathers).
⁴ This information, added by scribe C², was based on *HDE* ii. 18, 19 (i. 76, 77), which gave Wigred a 17-year pontificate starting in 925 and therefore ending in 942. JW, who had calculated afresh the dates of the pontificates of Wigred's predecessor on the basis of other information in *HDE*, had Wigred succeed in 928 (above, p. 387 n. 10) and his entry here is internally consistent.

On the death of Æthelbald,
bishop of Sherborne, Alfred
succeeded him.[1]

[944] King Otto went forth with his army into Lotharingia and subjected all to his rule, but the bishop of Metz resisted him.[2]

The glorious King Edmund expelled Olaf, son of King Sihtric, and Ragnald, son of Guthfrith, from Northumbria, and subjected it to his rule.[3] On the death of Wigred, bishop of Lindisfarne, Uhtred succeeded. On his death, Seaxhelm was ordained in his place, but he died a few months later, and Ealdred was consecrated in his stead.[4]

[945] The glorious King Edmund laid waste the land of the Cumbrians, and gave it to Malcolm, king of the Scots, on condition of his being faithful to him, by land and sea.[5]

[946] Agapitus[6] the 131st pope.[7]

While the glorious Edmund, king of the English, was at the royal township called Pucklechurch in English,[9] in seeking to rescue his steward from the hands of Leofa,[9] a most wicked thief, lest he be killed,[10] was himself killed by the same man on the feast of St Augustine,[8] teacher of the English, on Tuesday, 26 May, in the fourth indiction,[12] having completed five years and seven months of his reign.[11] He was borne to Glastonbury, and buried by the abbot, St Dunstan.[13] Then the next heir, Eadred, succeed-

---

[5] ASC A-F, the grant to Malcolm being omitted by EF.

[6] Agapitus II 946–55.   [7] Mar.

[8] ASC A-D (946) EF (948) record Edmund's murder and A-D the day (26 May) on which it occurred.

[9] ASC D alone (though note erasure in A) names the assassin and the location of the crime. JW's description of Pucklechurch as 'regia uilla' (not in D) has the support of S 553 BCS 887.

[10] JW alone gives the occasion for Edmund's murder.

[11] ASC A-D give Edmund a reign of 6½ years, which may be calculated from the coronation, whereas JW may have reckoned from the time of Æthelstan's death, taken as 940 (Whitelock, ASC, p. 72 n. 4).

[12] The indiction, week-day, and Roman calendar date may be JW's correct calculation of St Augustine's Day in 946.

[13] The burial at Glastonbury by Abbot Dunstan is not in ASC; D, however, does mention Æthelflæd of Damerham as Edmund's wife at the time of his death, which is omitted by JW.

*succeden*s, *regnum naturale suscepit*,[1] et .xvii. kalend. Septembris, die dominica, in Kingestune[a] a sancto Odone Dorubernensi archiepiscopo [b]rex est[b] consecratus. Hic, ut suus germanus prius egit, totam Norðhymbriam in suum dominium redegit, et a Scottis ut sibi fideles essent iuramentum accepit.[c2]

[947] (xi) 969   *Heinricus frater regis Ottonis, proiectis armis, uenit ad eum.*[d3]

[948] (xii) 970   [C³BP⁵]
                                    ꞌDefuncto Kenredo Sælesiensi
                                    episcopo,   successit   Cuth-
                                    ardus.[ef4]

[949] (xiii) 971   Wlstanus Eboracensis archiepiscopus proceresque Norðhymbrenses omnes, in uilla que dicitur Taddenesscylf, egregio regi Anglorum Edredo fidelitatem iurauerunt, sed non illam diu tenuerunt, nam quendam Danica stirpe progenitum, Yrcum[g] nomine, super se regem leuauerunt.[5]

[950] (xiiii) 972   *Ciclus decennouenalis .xxiii. incipit indictione .viii.*[6]
Pro infidelitate Norðhymbrensium egregius rex Anglorum Edredus totam Norðhymbriam deuastat, in qua deuastatione monasterium quod dicitur In Hrypum, a sancto Wilfrido episcopo quondam constructum, igne est combustum. Redeunte uero domum rege, exercitus de Eboraca erumpens ciuitate, in loco qui dicitur Casterford, de extrema parte exercitus regis multam stragem dedit. Vnde rex nimis offensus, uoluit ilico redire et totam illam terram penitus delere, uerum hoc cognito Norðhymbrenses timore perterriti, Yrcum,[h] quem sibi regem prefecerant, abiecerunt, regis iniurias honoribus, detrimenta muneribus, expleuerunt, eiusque offensam pecunia non modica placauerunt.[7]

---

[a] Kingestone *from* Cingestune *C*, Kyngestune *H*, Kingestune *LP*, Cingestune *B*
[b–b] rex est] *om. H*   [c] *see App. B for addition B*   [d] regem Ludowicum *B⁵*?
[e–e] Defuncto . . . Cuthardus] *add. in blank annal C³, om. HL, mg. with signe de renvoi P⁵*   [f] *see App. A for addition in LP*   [g] Yricum *interlin. B⁵*   [h] Yricum *interlin. B⁵*

---

[1] *Vita Dunstani auctore B*, c. 19 (*Memorials Dunstan*, p. 29).
[2] Eadred's succession, the reduction of Northumbria to his rule, and the pledging of oaths by the Scots are in ASC EF (948), which do not refer to his coronation at

ing his brother, received the kingdom that was his birthright,[1] and on Sunday, 16 August, was consecrated king at Kingston by Oda, archbishop of Canterbury. As his brother had done before, he restored all Northumbria to his rule, and received from the Scots an oath of fealty to himself.[2]

[947] Henry, King Otto's brother, laid down his arms, and came to him.[3]

[948]   On the death of Cenred, bishop
                                         of   Selsey,   Guthheard   suc-
                                         ceeded.[4]

[949] Wulfstan, archbishop of York, and all the Northumbrian nobles swore fealty to Eadred, the illustrious king of the English, at the township called Tanshelf, but they did not keep their promise for long, for they raised a man of Danish stock, Eric by name, to be king over them.[5]

[950] The twenty-third cycle of nineteen years begins in the eighth indiction.[6]

Eadred, the illustrious king of the English, laid waste the whole of Northumbria because of the disloyalty of the Northumbrians. In this devastation the monastery called Ripon, formerly built by Bishop St Wilfrid, was burnt down. But as the king was returning home, the Danish army, sallying forth from the city of York, made a great slaughter of the rearguard of the king's fyrd in a place called Castleford. The king was greatly angered by this, and wanted to return at once and completely devastate the whole land, but when the Northumbrians learnt this they were terrified, deposed Eric, whom they had made their king, and made good the insult to the king with deference, the damage suffered with gifts, and appeased his displeasure with no small sum of money.[7]

Kingston by Archbishop Oda on 16 Aug. *S* 520 *BCS* 815 (transl. Whitelock, *EHD*, no. 105, pp. 551–2) proves that the coronation took place at Kingston in 946.
  [3] Mar.
  [4] As in the case of 923 (see above, p. 384 n. 2), this may be misplaced by over a century (O'Donovan, ii. 101–2).
  [5] ASC D (947). The election of Eric Bloodaxe is mentioned in D (948). Eadred is described as 'egregius' here and under 950 and 955, as 'inclitus' in 952. Osbern, *Vita Dunstani*, c. 22 (*Memorials Dunstan*, p. 94) calls him 'egregius'.
  [6] Mar.   [7] ASC D 948 (and more briefly 954).

[951] (xv) 973 *Per loca Gallie Germanieque plurimi et magni terre motus facti sunt.*[1]

Sanctus *Ælfegus* cognomento Caluus, *Wentanus episcopus, qui beatum Dunstanum*[a] *monachatus et presbiteratus gradu decorauit, huic uite modum fecit,*[2] cui Ælfsinus in episcopatum successit.[b3]

[952] (xvi) 974 Ciclus solis incipit .iiii. concurrentibus bissextilibus.

Inclitus rex Anglorum Edredus Eboracensem archiepiscopum Wlstanum in Iuthanbyrig artam posuit in custodiam, quia frequenter apud eum certis ex causis accusabatur. Iussit etiam ciues Theodfordenses quamplures occidere in ultionem abbatis Aldelmi iniuste ab eis occisi.[4]

[953] (xvii) 975 *Mogontia ciuitas ab Ottone rege obsessa est.*[5]

p. 312

*Æthelgar*us | *Chridionensis presul* .xxi. accepti episcopatus anno, *uitam in Christo fin*iuit, ibidemque sepultus est, *ᶜpro quo,ᶜ* beati Dunstani abbatis *consilio, uir uenerandus Ælfuuoldus* functus est presulatus officio.[d6]

[954] (xviii) 976 *Beatae memoriae domnus Frithericus, sancte Mogontiensis ecclesie archiepiscopus, .viii. kalend. Nouembris obiit. ᶜEodem uero anno ego Wilelmus, tante successionis indignus, loco eius cum consensu cleri et populi eiusdem sancte sedis, .xvi. kalend. Ianuarii sum electus in loco Aransteti, ipso die pace inter Ottonem regem et filium eius Liutolfum facta, et in die .ix. kalend. Ian. Mogontie ordinatus.'* Hec ait ipse Wilelmus episcopus filius Ottonis imperatoris.*[7]

Wlstano Eboracensi archiepiscopo a custodia soluto, episcopalis honor apud Dorceceastre restituitur.[8]

ᵃ gap with erased space before Dunstanum C   *ᵇ see App. B for addition B*
ᶜ⁻ᶜ pro quo *over erasure C*   *ᵈ see App. B for addition B*

---

[1] Mar.

[2] *Vita Dunstani auctore Adelardo*, lectio 4 (*Memorials Dunstan*, p. 56). The description 'cognomento Caluus' had already been used in 935, where it was taken from *Vita Dunstani auctore B*, c. 7 (*Memorials Dunstan*, p. 13).

[3] ASC A and *ADL* (interlineated) record Ælfheah of Winchester's death on St Gregory's Day (12 Mar.) 951, but do not mention Ælfsige's succession. King Eadred's grant of Pucklechurch to Glastonbury dated 950 (*S* 553 *BCS* 887) is witnessed by Bishop Ælfsige, but the year is apparently incorrect.

[4] ASC D, which does not have the word 'iniuste'.   [5] Mar.

[951] There were very many great earthquakes throughout the areas of Gaul and Germany.[1]

St Ælfheah, surnamed the Bald, bishop of Winchester, who honoured the blessed Dunstan with the orders of monk and priest, came at this point to the end of his life,[2] and Ælfsige succeeded him in the bishopric.[3]

[952] The solar cycle begins with four concurrents in a bissextile year.

Eadred, the illustrious king of the English, placed Wulfstan, archbishop of York, in strait custody at *Iudanbyrig* because he was frequently accused before him on certain charges. He also ordered that many of the citizens of Thetford be killed in revenge for Abbot Eadhelm, whom they had unjustly slain.[4]

[953] The city of Mainz was besieged by King Otto.[5]

Æthelgar, bishop of Crediton, ended his life in Christ in the twenty-first year of his tenure of the bishopric, and was buried there. On the advice of the blessed Abbot Dunstan, the venerable son Ælfwold filled the episcopal office in his place.[6]

[954] Master Fritheric of blessed memory, archbishop of the holy church of Mainz, died on 25 October. 'In the same year, I, William, unworthy of succeeding so great a man, was elected in his place with the consent of the clergy and people of the same holy see on 17 December at Arnstadt, on the very day that peace was made between King Otto and his son Liudolf, and was ordained on 24 December at Mainz.' Thus spoke Bishop William himself, son of the Emperor Otto.[7]

Wulfstan, archbishop of York, was released from custody, and his episcopal status was restored in Dorchester.[8]

---

[6] *Vita Dunstani auctore B*, c. 19 (*Memorials Dunstan*, pp. 29, 30). Charter evidence suggests 953 as a possible date for the succession at Crediton (O'Donovan, i. 37), but the length of Æthelgar's episcopate (21 years), while probably internally consistent with JW's date for Æthelgar's appointment in 931, is wrong, since he could not have succeeded before 934 (above, p. 389 n. 6). Æthelgar's burial at Crediton may be JW's reasonable inference.

[7] Mar.

[8] ASC D. 'Apud Dorceceastre' retains the ambiguity of D's 'on Dorceceastre', leaving open the question whether Wulfstan was given Dorchester or was restored to York at Dorchester. DEF also refer to the expulsion of Eric and the acceptance of Eadred by the Northumbrians, which JW probably thought had already been implied in 950.

[955] (xix) 977   Egregius *rex* Anglorum *Edredus* .x. anno regni sui *egrotauit et desperatus est, qui missa celeri legatione, confessionum suarum patrem,* beatum scilicet *Dunstanum* abbatem, *accersiuit. Quo festine ad palatium tendente et medium iam iter peragente, uox desuper clare sonuit, ipso audiente: 'Rex Edredus nunc in pace quiescit.' Ad hanc uocem equus cui insedit, pondus uocis angelice ferre non ualens, absque ulla sessoris lesione, cum interitu suo in terram corruit.* Regis autem corpus Wintoniam defertur et ab ipso abbate Dunstano in Veteri Monasterio *sepulture honestissime trad*itur.[1] Cuius fratruus clito Edwius, regis scilicet Eadmundi et sancte Ælfgiue regine filius, monarchiam imperii suscepit, et eodem anno in Cingestune[a] ab Odone Dorubernie archiepiscopo rex consecratus est.[2] Eodem anno Luduuuicus rex Occidentalium Francorum, filius Karoli regis et filie regis Anglorum Eadwardi Senioris, [b]obiit.[c3]

Liutolfus quoque *filius Ottonis imperatoris* et alterius filie eiusdem regis Eaduuardi[4] obiit, *et sepelitur[d] in choro monasterii sancti Albani Mogontie.[b5]*

[C³BP]
[e]Defuncto Ælle Licetfeldensi episcopo, hi usque ad tempora regis Willelmi successerunt: Algar, Kynsi, Wynsi, Alfeth, Godwine, Leofgar, Bryhtmar, Wlsius, Leofwinus.[e6]

[956] (xx) 978   Beatus *Dunstanus* abbas, a rege Anglorum Eduuio *pro iustitia as*scriptus, *mare transiit,* et ab *Arnulf*o *regie stirpis uir*o honorifice susceptus, in monasterio quod *Blandinium*[7] dicitur sub

---

[a] Kyngestune *H,* Kingestune *LP*   [b–b] obiit . . . Mogontie] *rewritten in compressed script over erasure to find space for 955 n. e* C³   [c] *see App. B for addition in mg. with first sentence by scribe and rest by a different hand* B   [d] sepultus est *HL*   [e–e] Defuncto . . . Leofwinus] *add. at line-end and mg.* C³, *om. HL*

---

[1] *Vita Dunstani auctore Adelardo,* lectio v (*Memorials Dunstan,* p. 58). The year of Eadred's death is 955 in ASC ADEF, 956 in BC, but AF also give its precise date (23 Nov.) and location (Frome). D agrees with JW in giving Eadred's burial place, without mentioning Dunstan.

[2] In ASC Eadwig's succession is in the same year as Eadred's death, but DF (partly in an addition), unlike JW and ABCE, speak of a succession divided between Eadwig

[955] Eadred, the illustrious king of the English, fell sick in the tenth year of his reign, and as his life was despaired of, he sent a swift embassy summoning his father confessor, namely the blessed Abbot Dunstan. As he was making his way in haste to the palace, and was in the middle of his journey, he heard a voice ringing out clearly from above: 'King Eadred rests in peace.' At this voice the horse on which he sat, unable to bear the burden of the angelic voice, crashed to the ground in death, without wounding its rider. However, the king's body was borne to Winchester and was buried by that same Abbot Dunstan most honourably in the Old Minster.[1] His nephew, the atheling Eadwig, the son of King Edmund and the blessed Queen Ælfgifu, received the rule of the realm, and in the same year was consecrated king at Kingston by Oda, archbishop of Canterbury.[2] In the same year, Louis, king of the West Franks, son of King Charles and of the daughter of the English King Edward the Elder, died.[3]

Liudolf, also, son of the Emperor Otto and of another daughter of that same Edward,[4] died, and was buried in the choir of the monastery of St Alban at Mainz.[5]

From the death of Ælle, bishop of Lichfield, until King William's time there succeeded: Wulfgar, Cynesige, Wynsige, Ælfheah, Godwine, Leofgar, Brihtmær, Wulfsige, and Leofwine.[6]

[956] The blessed Abbot Dunstan, when he was sentenced, on account of his righteousness, by Eadwig, king of the English, crossed the sea and was received honourably by Arnulf, a man of royal lineage, in the monastery called *Blandinium*,[7] and received

and his brother, whose mother D alone names. JW is the sole chronicle authority for locating Eadwig's consecration by Archbishop Oda at Kingston.

[3] The death of Louis d'Outremer, who died on 10 Sept. 954, is not in ASC.

[4] The identification of one of Edward the Elder's daughters as Otto's wife had already been made by JW in 901 and 936.

[5] Mar.

[6] This addition is certainly misplaced; see O'Donovan, ii. 94-5. Though this list could have been based on *GP* ii. 172 (p. 308), the spelling of its names are close to those in JW Lichfield *Epis. Lists*. Alfeth is presumably Ælfheah.

[7] St. Peter's, Ghent.

exilii sui tempore mansionem accepit.[1] Wlstanus Eboracensium archiepiscopus .vii. kalend. Ianuarii defunctus, in Vndalan tumulatur, cui uir reuerendus successit Oscytellus.[2]

Hadamarus Fuldensis abbas, qui monasterium Fuldense magnifico opere construxit, obiit. ªHatto filius sororisᵇ sue successit.ᶜ[3]

[957] (xxi) 979   *Iohannes*[4] *papa centesimus .xxxii. de regione* ᵈ*Vi⟨a⟩ Lata*ᵈ *ex Albrico patre principe Romano.*[5]

Rex Anglorum Edwius, *quoniam in commisso regimine insipienter egit,* a Mercensibus et Norðhymbrensibus contemptus relinquitur, et suus *german*us clito *Eadgar*us ab eis rex eligitur, sicque *res regum seiuncta est ut flumen Tame*nse *regnum disterminaret amborum.*[6] Mox rex Mercensium Eadgarus beatum Dunstanum abbatem *cum honore et gloria reuocauit.*[7] Excurso dehinc parui spatii tempore, *pastor Wigornensis ecclesie Coenwaldus, uir magne humilitatis et monastice professionis,* defungitur.[8] Pro quo *beatus* abbas *Dunstanus* ad episcopatum eligitur, et ab Odone ᵉ*Dorubernensi archiepiscopo*ᵉ consecratur, cui etiam anno sequenti rex Mercensium Eadgarus *Lundoniensem ecclesiam pio pastore uiduatam commisit regend*am.[9]

[C³BP]

ᶠBeatus   Dunstanus   Lundoniensem presulatum regens sanctum   Wlsinum   abbatem

---

ª *957 starts here (N)*   ᵇ sororis *interlin.* B¹   ᶜ *see App. B for addition B* ᵈ⁻ᵈ Via Lata] Violata *JW (N)*   ᵉ⁻ᵉ Dorubernensi archiepiscopo] archiepiscopo Dorobernensi *HL*   ᶠ Beatus . . . fecerat *(p. 408)] add. mg. next to last line of 957 and to 958; possible that this was meant for 958* C³, *om. HL*

---

¹ *Vita Dunstani auctore Adelardo,* lectio 6 (*Memorials Dunstan,* p. 59). The exile of Dunstan is in ASC A (Canterbury addition) (955), D (957). *Vita Dunstani auctore B,* c. 21 (*Memorials Dunstan,* pp. 32, 33) states that the quarrel between the king and Dunstan began at the coronation-feast and the persecution followed soon after. Dunstan must have withdrawn in 956, if not in 955.

² ASC D (957), giving the day as 16 Dec. and the place as Oundle. JW's '.vii. kal. Ian.' (26 Dec.) may have been an error for '.xvii. kal. Dec.' (16 Dec.), as Plummer suggests (*Chronicle,* ii. 150). The succession of Osketel is not in ASC D. ASC EF simply record the death of Wulfstan (with no further details) under 956.

³ Mar.   ⁴ John XII 955–64.   ⁵ Mar.

⁶ *Vita Dunstani auctore B,* c. 24 (*Memorials Dunstan,* pp. 35, 36). Edgar's succession to Mercia is in ASC (B)C (957). JW explicitly speaks of a Mercian revolt, and his inclusion of the Northumbrians among the rebels could be an inference from the dividing line between the two kingdoms.

shelter during his time of exile.[1] Wulfstan, archbishop of York, was buried at Oundle when he died on 26 December, and the revered man, Osketel, succeeded him.[2]

Hadamar, abbot of Fulda, who enhanced the monastic buildings at Fulda with splendid work, died. Hatto, his sister's son, succeeded him.[3]

[957] John[4] the 123rd pope. He was from the *Via Lata* district, and was the son of Alberic, a leading Roman figure.[5]

Eadwig, king of the English, since he behaved foolishly in the government entrusted to him, was abandoned by the Mercians and the Northumbrians with contempt, and his brother, the atheling Edgar, was chosen king by them, and the territory of the kings was divided so that the River Thames formed the boundary of both kingdoms.[6] Soon Edgar, king of the Mercians, recalled the blessed Abbot Dunstan with honour and glory.[7] When a short time had passed after that, Cenwald, pastor of the church of Worcester, a man of great humility and a professed monk, died.[8] The blessed Abbot Dunstan was elected to his bishopric in his place, and consecrated by Oda, archbishop of Canterbury. In the following year, Edgar, king of the Mercians, committed the rule of the London see, bereft of its pious shepherd, to him too.[9]

While the blessed Dunstan ruled the bishopric of London he appointed St Wulfsige abbot

---

[7] *Vita Dunstani auctore Adelardo*, lectio 7 (*Memorials Dunstan*, p. 60). ASC A (addition by hand 7, s. xi[ex]) F (both 959) alone record the recall of Dunstan.

[8] Cenwald, who attests charters of Eadwig in 957, attests for the last time (in the company of 'Dunstanus episcopus') a charter of Edgar (S 675 BCS 1042) in 958, presumably after the kingdom had been divided. Dunstan's episcopal rank in this charter could be explained by biographer B's statement, c. 25 (*Memorials Dunstan*, p. 36) that Dunstan was consecrated bishop without a see.

[9] *Vita Dunstani auctore B*, c. 25 (*Memorials Dunstan*, p. 37). Dunstan's successive appointments to Worcester and to London are mentioned in ASC A (addition by hand 7) F (959): Worcester and 'afterwards' London. The consecration by Oda is in Adelard, lectio 7 (*Memorials Dunstan*, p. 60) which does not share biographer B's view that he had been consecrated without a see. Dunstan attests a charter of Edgar (S 681 BCS 1051) in 959 as bishop of London. Dunstan could have been made bishop of Worcester in 958 and of London in 959, one year later than JW's dates.

constituit   *apud   Westmonas-*
terium, instructo ad .xii. mona-
chos   cenobiolo   in   loco   ubi
quondam   Mellitus   ecclesiam
sancto Petro fecerat.^{a1}

[958] (xxii) 980 Ælsius^b Dorsetensium episcopus obiit, cui
*Byrhthelm*us^c *uir mitis et modestus, humilis et benignus*² successit.
Sanctus ^dOdo Dorubernie arciepiscopus^d regem Wessaxonum
Eduuium et Ælfgiuam, uel quia, ut fertur, propinqua illius exstitit
uel quia illam *sub propria uxore adamauit* ab inuicem separauit.³
Eodem anno idem archipresul, *uir* quidem *clarus* ingenio *et uirtute
laudabilis* spiritu quoque prophetie pollens, *humanis excessit rebus,
angelorum   manibus   ad   Paradisum   deductus.*⁴ Huic successit
Wentanus episcopus Ælfsinus, et pro ipso ad episcopatum
Wintoniensis ecclesie ordinatus est Brihthelmus,

[C³BP]
^eWellensis episcopus .v.^{e5}

[959] (xxiii) 981 Ælfsinus Dorubernensis archiepiscopus, dum
Romam pro petendo *pallio tenderet, in Alpinis montibus gelu niu*eque
*obstri*ctus *def*ecit.⁶ Rex Wessaxonum Edwius, .iiii. annis regni sui
peractis defunctus, Wintonie in Nouo Monasterio est sepultus.⁷
Cuius regnum suus germanus rex Mercensium Eadgarus, ab omni

---

^a *see above p. 406 n. f*   ^b Alfsius *H, (erased capital)*lsi(*erasure, just possibly of*
-nus), *possibly* Ælfsinus, *a confusion with the first word in the next annal 959 L,* Ælfsius
from Ælsius *B*   ^c Brihthelmus *HL,* Brytelmus *B,* Brihtelmus *P*   ^{d-d} Odo . . .
arciepiscopus] *over erasure C*   ^{e-e} Wellensis . . . .v.] *add. at line-end* C³, *om. HL*

---

¹ *GP* ii. 81 (p. 178). Even if C³'s marginal addition should be assigned to 958, it is
still too early as Dunstan is unlikely to have appointed Wulfsige abbot until he had
become bishop of London (*Flete's History of Westminster Abbey,* ed. J. Armitage
Robinson (Cambridge, 1909), p. 79).

² *Vita Dunstani auctore B,* c. 26 (*Memorials Dunstan,* p. 38). JW's Ælsius (JW *Epis.
Lists* Alfsius) is presumably the Wulfsige of other lists who attests for the last time in
958 (*S* 650 *BCS* 1032). The election as archbishop of Canterbury of 'Byrhthelmus,
Dorsætensium praeuisorem', as the biographer B puts it, c. 26 (*Memorials Dunstan,*
p. 38), could explain JW's assigning him here to Sherborne as Wulfsige's successor,
though he is not known in any Sherborne list. It does not account for JW's date for
Wulfsige's death.

³ Alternative explanations for Oda's separation of Eadwig and Ælfgifu are found
under 958 in ASC D, and, undated, in Byrhtferth's *Vita Oswaldi,* i. 2 (*Historians of the
Church of York,* i. 402). The chapter divisions in this life are those of Lapidge's forth-
coming edition in *OMT.*

at Westminster, where he established a small monastery for twelve monks in the place where Mellitus had formerly built a church dedicated to St Peter.[1]

[958] Ælfsige, bishop of the people of Dorset, died and Brihthelm, a man gentle and modest, humble and kindly,[2] succeeded him. St Oda, archbishop of Canterbury, separated Eadwig, king of the West Saxons, and Ælfgifu, either because, as they say, she was Eadwig's relative, or because the king loved her adulterously as if she were his own wife.[3] In the same year the same archbishop, a man of wonderful intelligence and laudable virtue, who was also strong in the spirit of prophecy, departed from human concerns, and was led by the hands of angels to Paradise.[4] Ælfsige, bishop of Winchester, succeeded to his see and, in his place, there was ordained to the episcopacy of Winchester Brihthelm,

fifth bishop of Wells.[5]

[959] Ælfsige, archbishop of Canterbury, while he was making his way to Rome to receive the pallium, was trapped in the Alps by ice and snow and died.[6] Eadwig, king of the West Saxons, died after ruling for four years, and was buried in the New Minster at Winchester.[7] His brother Edgar, king of the Mercians, was chosen

---

[4] *Vita Dunstani auctore Osberno*, c. 32 (*Memorials Dunstan*, p. 107). ASC A (addition) F record the death of Oda under 961. He attests a charter of Eadwig for the last time in 958 (*S* 650 *BCS* 1032).

[5] Ælfsige's succession to Oda at Canterbury comes from B's biography, c. 26 (*Memorials Dunstan*, p. 37). Byrhthelm is not in JW *Epis. Lists*, though he is in two lists, Cambridge, Corpus Christi College MS 140, and the Winchester *Liber Vitae*, BL Cotton MS Titus D. XXVII. C³'s addition in the JW MS identifying Byrhthelm as bishop of Wells could have been based on *GP* ii. 90 (p. 194). See further above, p. 410 n. 6.

[6] *Vita Dunstani auctore B*, c. 26 (*Memorials Dunstan*, p. 38). The year of this journey is inferred by JW.

[7] Eadwig's death is recorded in ASC AF (958) (B)CDE (959). JW does not give the day, 1 Oct., which is in A. JW's statement about Eadwig's burial place, which is not recorded in ASC, is supported by New Minster tradition (*Liber Vitae*, cited by Plummer, *Chronicle*, ii. 151). The length of Eadwig's reign is presumably inferred.

Anglorum populo electus, anno etatis sue .xvi.,[1] aduentus uero
Anglorum in Brytanniam quingentesimo decimo,[a] trecentesimo
autem sexagesimo tertio ex quo sanctus Augustinus et socii eius |
p. 313   Angliam uenerunt, *suscepit diuisaque regna in unum copulauit.*[2]

[HL]

Brih*thelmus* Dorse*tensium*
episcopus ad patriarchatum
Cantuarie sedis deligitur.[b] Sed
quia *ad tantam rem minus* erat
idoneus iussus a rege Cantuuaria
discedit, atque ad relictam nuper
ecclesiam suam redit.[3] *Dehinc*
beatus *Dunstanus* [c]⟨ecclesie
Wigornensis episcopus ex
respectu diuino et sapientum⟩[c]

[C³BP]

Byrh*thelmus* [d]Sumorsetensium
episcopus ad archipresulatum[d]
Cantuuarie sedis deligitur.[b]
[d]Sed quia *ad tantam rem minus*
erat *idoneus* iudicio omnium *ad*
relictam nuper ecclesiam suam
rediit.[3] *Dehinc* beatus
Dunstanus,[4] *Athelmi archiepis-*
copi ex fratre nepos,[e] *Glæstonie*
abbas post Wicciorum et
Lundoniensium episcopus[5] *ex*
respectu diuino et sapientum[d]

consilio,[f4] *prime metropolis Anglorum primas et patriarcha institu-*
itur,[6] a quo et *ceteris sapientibus* ipse rex Anglorum Eadgarus *decen-*
ter instructus, passim improbos oppressit, rebelles sub asperitatis
*correctione redargu*it, *iustos et modestos dilexit, destructas Dei ecclesias*
*renouau*it et *ditauit,*[7] *abiectis ex cenobiis clericorum neniis,*[8] *ad laudem*

<hr/>

[a] *om. HL*   [b] *eligitur HR. iii. 111 (ii. 128)*   [c–c] ecclesie . . . sapientum]
these words are in HR iii. 111 (ii. 128) and were probably omitted by the exemplar of HL
[d–d] Sumorsetensium . . . archipresulatum *and* sed . . . sapi-] *written over erasure and
spilling into mg. (the revised text being scribbled, presumably to guide the revision, in the
.uppermost mg.) C³*   [e] *gap of two letters after* nepos *C³*   [f] *959 n. b to be incorporated here* P

<hr/>

[1] ASC BC say that Edgar was 16, not that he was in his 16th year.
[2] *Vita Dunstani auctore B*, c. 24 (*Memorials Dunstan*, p. 36).
[3] *Vita Dunstani auctore Osberno*, c. 32 (*Memorials Dunstan*, pp. 107–8).
[4] *Vita Dunstani auctore B*, c. 26 (*Memorials Dunstan*, p. 38).
[5] *GP* i. 18 (p. 26).
[6] *Vita Dunstani auctore Osberno*, c. 33 (*Memorials Dunstan*, p. 108). The biographers
of Dunstan leave in doubt whether Byrhthelm who was made archbishop and sent back
to his former see was appointed by Eadwig or Edgar. B mentions the death of Eadwig
before the appointment of Dunstan to Worcester and London, and of Ælfsige to
Canterbury, and perhaps implies that Byrhthelm was appointed and removed by Edgar.
Osbern places Dunstan's appointment to Worcester before Eadwig's death, but
definitely states that Edgar was king of all England when he made Dunstan bishop of
London, and seems to imply that both Ælfsige and Byrhthelm were appointed to
Canterbury when Edgar was sole king. JW, using both B and Osbern, records Ælfsige's
appointment before Eadwig's death, and the appointment of Byrhthelm after it. The

by all the English people in his sixteenth year,[1] and in the 510th after the arrival of the Angles in Britain, and in the 363rd from that in which St Augustine and his companions came to England. The divided realm he received he united.[2]

Brihthelm, bishop of Dorset, was chosen for the patriarchate of the see of Canterbury, but because he was not suited for so great a position, he left Canterbury at the king's command and soon returned to the church he had recently left.[3] Then the blessed Dunstan, ⟨bishop of the church of Worcester, from fear of the lord and⟩ by the counsel[4] ⟨of the witan,⟩	Brithelm, bishop of Somerset, was chosen for the archbishopric of Canterbury, but because he was, in the judgement of all, less suited for so great a position, he soon returned to his own see, which he had recently left.[3] Then the blessed Dunstan[4] (nephew of Archbishop Athelm through Athelm's brother), abbot of Glastonbury,[5] later bishop of the Hwicce and of London, from fear of the Lord and by the counsel of the witan,[4]

was appointed primate of the first metropolis of the English and patriarch.[6] By him and by other wise men, the English king, Edgar himself, was properly instructed: he destroyed the iniquitous everywhere; rebuked the rebellious with severe correction; loved the just and humble; restored and enriched God's destroyed churches,[7] and, when he had banished trivialities from the monasteries of the clerks,[8] he gathered hosts of monks and nuns to

evidence of charters suggests that both appointments were made in the lifetime of Eadwig (O'Donovan, i. 34). Under 958 JW recorded two Byrhthelms who coincidentally succeeded to bishoprics: the first followed Wulfsige at Sherborne; the second (called Brihthelm) replaced Ælfsige at Winchester. Under 959 he made the Sherborne Byrhthelm succeed at Canterbury. In a revision of both 958 and 959 (by C³), perhaps caused by the discovery, whether from episcopal lists (his own or someone else's) or from GP ii. 90 (p. 194), of a Byrhthelm at Wells, JW made inconsistent and confusing changes: under 958 he described the Brihthelm appointed to Winchester as having previously been the fifth bishop of Wells, but under 959 he made the Byrhthelm, who succeeded at Canterbury, also a Wells bishop. By these changes two Byrhthelms appear at Wells, one going to Winchester, the second to Canterbury. The Byrhthelm of London found in JW Epis. Lists does not find a place in the annals. Nor is it clear how JW discovered a Byrhthelm at Winchester. For the multitude of Byrhthelms see Robinson, Wells, pp. 62–6 and D. Whitelock, 'The appointment of Dunstan to Canterbury', Otium et Negotium, ed. F. Sandgren (Stockholm, 1973), pp. 232–47, and Brooks, Canterbury, pp. 233–40.

[7] Vita Dunstani auctore B, cc. 25, 26 (Memorials Dunstan, pp. 37, 38).

[8] Byrhtferth, Vita Oswaldi, iii. 10 (Historians of the Church of York, i. 425).

summi creatoris, monachorum et sanctimonialium *cateruas aggre-gauit*[1] et *plusquam .xl. monasteria cum* eis *constitui iussit, quos* omnes *ut fratres honorabat* et *ut filios karissimos diligebat,* admonens *per se pastores, quos ipsis preposuit, ut* illos regulariter *et irreprehensibiliter uiuere admonerent, quatenus Christo et sanctis* ªeius in omnibusª *plac-erent. Erat* itaque uir discretus, *mitis,* humilis, benignus, liberalis, *misericors, armipotens, bellicosus, iura regni bellica potestate regaliter protegens*: populum in obsequio principum, principes ad iustitiam imperiorum formauit, leges rectas instituit, regno tranquilissimo potitus est: neque bello alium lacessere, neque lacessitus inferre alii bellum necesse habuit; sed regni sui fines prudentia, fortitudine, iustitia, temperantia quoad uixit Deo auxiliante custodiuit; *et quo-niam iram ferocis leonis contra inimicos habuit, non solum insularum principes et tiranni* illum *pertimuerunt,* uerum *etiam reges plurimarum gentium, ipsius audientes* sapientiam et strenuitatem, quidam *timore atque terrore perculsi sunt,* quidam *uero pro sua* munificentia eum diligebant, honorabant, *magnificeque laudabant. Imperator* etiam primus Otto, qui suam amitam in coniugem habebat, *mira illi munera direxit* et cum eo *pactum firmissime pacis firmau*it.[2]

[C³BP]

ᵇ⟨R⟩egnante   *rege   Eadgar*o
Leofuuinus   qui   .viii.   extitit
Legerensis episcopus, *coniunxit episcopatus Lindisfarorum, qui nunc dicitur Lincoliensium, et Legcestrensium.*[3] Successit illi in episcopatum Ælnothus, illique Æscwius huius adminiculo sanctus Oswaldus Ramesense cenobium consecrauit, post hunc Ælfhelmus, Eadnothus, Athericus, Eadnothus, Vlf,

---

ª⁻ª eius in omnibus] in omnibus *H,* omnibus eius *L*   ᵇ Regnante . . . tempore *(p. 414)*] *written mg. alongside 959 C³, om. HL, outer mg. alongside 957 with sign pointing to 959 p. 410 n. fP³*

---

[1] *Vita Dunstani auctore B,* c. 25, 26 (*Memorials Dunstan,* pp. 37, 38).
[2] Byrhtferth, *Vita Oswaldi,* iii. 10, iv. 4 (*Historians of the Church of York,* i. 425–6, 435). JW seems to have identified the unnamed emperor with Otto I. JW's panegyric,

the worship of the most high Creator,[1] and ordered more than forty houses to be filled with them. He honoured them all as brothers and he loved them as very dear sons. He himself exhorted the pastors whom he had placed in authority over them, that they should urge them to live blamelessly according to the rule so that they might please Christ and his saints in everything. He was a man discerning, gentle, humble, kindly, generous, compassionate, strong in arms, warlike, royally defending the rights of his kingdom with military power. He taught this people to submit to their rulers, their rulers to rule justly; he instituted just laws; he kept the kingdom in complete peace. He needed neither to harm others with war nor, injured himself, to make war upon another, but, with God's help, he kept the confines of his realm with prudence, fortitude, justice, temperance, as long as he lived, and since he was like a fierce and angry lion towards his enemies, not only the rulers and tyrants of the islands feared him, but even the kings of many peoples, when they heard of his wisdom and vigour were, some of them, struck with fear and terror, but some loved, honoured, and praised him gloriously for his generosity. The Emperor Otto I, too, who had married his aunt, sent him wonderful gifts and established a very firm peace agreement with him.[2]

In the reign of King Edgar, Leofwine, who was the eighth bishop of Leicester, united the bishopric of Lindsey (which is now called Lincoln) and Leicester.[3] Ælfnoth succeeded him in the episcopacy, and was succeeded in turn by Æscwig, with whose support St Oswald consecrated Ramsey abbey, and after them Ælfhelm, Eadnoth, Æthelric, Eadnoth, Ulf and

based in part on the biographer B and Byrhtferth's *Vita Oswaldi*, does not seem to have contact with that in ASC DE (959) F (958).

[3] *GP* iv. 176 (p. 311). JW *Epis. Lists* state that Leofwine combined the dioceses of Leicester and Lindsey.

Wlfwius regis Eadwardi tempore.*a*1

[960] (xxiiii) 982   Sanctus Dunstanus *ad Romuleam urbem profectus,*2 indictione tertia, pallium a Iohanne papa suscepit, sicque *per pacis itinera ad patriam remeauit.*3 Paucis exinde mensibus interiectis, regalia petit limina, ianuam regie pietatis suggestione preceque pulsat humillima ut religiosum, mitem humilemque monachum, sui predecessoris Odonis fratruelem beatum Oswaldum, quem in timore diuino sanctisque uirtutum operibus uerissime probauerat excreuisse, promoueret ad pontificale decus Wigornensis ecclesie. Annuit rex Eadgarus quod sanctus petebat Dunstanus, et ab ipso inthronizatur ad summum sacerdotium beatus Oswaldus.4

[C³BP]

*b*Defuncto Guthardo Sælesiensi episcopo, successit Ælfredus.*bc*5

[961] (xxv) 983   *Otto rex unguitur in imperatorem ab Iohanne papa.*6

[C³? BP³]

*d*Cenobium in Domnania, quod Teauistok uocatur, iuxta Tav fluuuium* situm, *Ordgarus comes Domnaniensis pater Ælfthrythe uxoris regis Eadgari construxit.*d7

---

a see above, p. 412 n. b   *b–b* Defuncto . . . Ælfredus] add. at line end C³, om. HL
c see App. B for addition B   *d–d* Cenobium . . . construxit] add. mg. alongside
961–63 C³?, om. HL, outer mg. alongside 968, but possibly meant for annals 961–3 in inner column P³

---

1 Though based on the list in *GP* iv. 177 (p. 312), JW agrees with his own *Epis. Lists* (which are here abbreviated) in making Wulfwig succeed Ulf, who is omitted by *GP*. The reference to Bishop Æscwig's association with Oswald and Ramsey may come from the annal 991 or from its possible source, Byrhtferth's *Vita Oswaldi*, v. 11 (*Historians of the Church of York*, i. 463).
2 *Vita Dunstani auctore Osberno*, c. 33 (*Memorials Dunstan*, p. 108).

Wulfwig in King Edward's time.[1]

[960] St Dunstan set out for the city of Romulus[2] in the third indiction, received the pallium from Pope John, and so returned by peaceful stages to his own country.[3] Then, after a few months had passed, he sought the royal threshold, and knocked on the door of royal piety with the suggestion and most humble entreaty that he might promote to the episcopal glory of Worcester Oswald, a devout, gentle, and humble monk, the blessed nephew of his predecessor Oda, whom he had truly found increased greatly in the fear of the Lord, and in the holy works of virtue. King Edgar assented to St Dunstan's request, and the blessed Oswald was enthroned as bishop by the saint himself.[4]

On the death of Guthheard, bishop of Selsey, Alfred succeeded.[5]

[961] King Otto was anointed emperor by Pope John.[6]

The convent called Tavistock in Devon, located by the River Tavy, was built by Ordgar, ealdorman of Devon, and father of Ælfthryth, King Edgar's wife.[7]

---

[3] *Vita Dunstani auctore B*, c. 28 (*Memorials Dunstan*, p. 40). Neither the year of Dunstan's visit nor the name of the pope is recorded in the lives by B and by Osbern, and the visit is not recorded in ASC. John XII's privilege concerning the pallium (Whitelock, Brett, and Brooke, *Councils*, i, no. 25, pp. 88–92) is dated 'die .xi. kalendas Octobris, indictione .iv.' (i.e. 21 Sept. 960), and would seem to support JW's date, though Dunstan attests as archbishop in 959 (*S* 680 *BCS* 1051).

[4] Byrhtferth's *Vita Oswaldi*, iii. 5 (*Historians of the Church of York*, i. 420) attributes Oswald's promotion to the see of Worcester to the influence of Dunstan, but no year is given and ASC does not record this event. It may have been possible for Dunstan to consecrate Oswald late in the year of his visit to Rome, though Oswald does not attest as bishop until 961.

[5] C³'s addition is erroneous, for Guthheard was in office in 845 (*S* 1194 *BCS* 448) and Alfred, who was not his immediate successor, ceased to attest after 953 (O'Donovan, ii. 101, 102).

[6] Mar.

[7] *GP* ii. 95 (p. 202). *GP* does not date the foundation of Tavistock: though JW dates the death of the supposed founder Ordgar to 971, it is not clear why this marginal addition was placed here.

[962] (xxvi) 984   *Romanus rex Grecorum multum pius et laudabilis obiit. Nicaphorus¹ successit.*ᵃ²

[963] (xxvii) 985   Sanctus Ætheluuoldus uenerabilis abbasᵇ a beato Dunstano educatus, mortuo Brihthelmo, episcopatum Wintoniensis ecclesie suscepit, et eodem anno, iussu regis expulsis clericis, ᶜVetus Monasterium cum monachis instituit.ᶜ Hic nanque regem, cuius *eximius* erat *consiliarius, ad hoc maxime prouocauit ut clericos a monasteriis exp*elleret et monachos sanctimonialesque in eis collocari iuberet.ᵈ³

[964] (xxviii) 986   Rex Anglorum pacificus Eadgarus Ordgari ducis Domnanie filiam Ælförytham nomine, post mortem uiri sui Æthelwoldi, gloriosi ducis Orientalium Anglorum, in matrimonium accepit, ex qua duos filios Eadmundum et Ægelredum suscepit.⁴ Habuit etiam prius ex Ægelfleda Candida, ᵉcognomento Eneda,ᵉ Ordmæri ducis filia,ᶠ Eadwardum postea regem et martirem, et de sancta Wlfthrytha uirginem Deo deuotissimam Edgitham.⁵ Eodem anno rex idem monachos in Nouo Monasterio et in Middeltune collocauit, et illis Æthelgarum, istis Cinewardum abbates constituit.⁶

[965] (xxix) 987   ᵍIohannes⁷ papa centesimus tricesimus tertius.ᵍʰ⁸

[966] (xxx) 988   ⁱEberhardus comes obiit.ⁱʲ⁹

[967] (xxxi) 989   Rex Anglorum pacificus Eadgarus in monasterio Rumesige, quod auus suus rex Anglorum Eadwardus Senior con-

---

ᵃ see App. B for addition extending into mg. B   ᵇ abbas Abbendonensis ecclesie LP
ᶜ⁻ᶜ Vetus . . . instituit] see App. A for substituted text LP   ᵈ see App. A for addition
LP   ᵉ⁻ᵉ cognomento Eneda (Enede B)] interlin. CⁱHⁱLⁱBⁱ, at 964 n. f P
ᶠ 964 n. e add. here extending into mg. P³   ᵍ Iohannes . . . tertius] under 966 though
line for 965 is blank HL   ʰ see App. B for addition B   ⁱ⁻ⁱ Eberhardus . . .
obiit] under 967 HL   ʲ see App. B for addition B

---

¹ Nicephorus II 963–9.   ² Mar.
³ Byrhtferth, *Vita Oswaldi*, iii. 11 (*Historians of the Church of York*, i. 427). The phrase 'a beato Dunstano educatus' may have been derived from Adelard's *Vita Dunstani*, lectio 8 (*Memorials Dunstan*, p. 61) or from either Wulfstan's or Ælfric's *Vita Sancti Æthelwoldi* (Lapidge-Winterbottom, c. 9, p. 14; c. 5, p. 72 respectively). ASC AEF date Æthelwold's appointment to this year, but AE (later addition in Latin) F

[962] Romanus, the very devout and praiseworthy king of the Greeks, died. Nicephorus[1] succeeded him.[2]

[963] St Æthelwold, the venerable abbot brought up by the blessed Dunstan, was preferred to the bishopric of Winchester on the death of Brihthelm, and in the same year, at the king's command, established his monks at the Old Minster after the expulsion of the secular clergy. For he, who was the king's special counsellor, urged him most vigorously to expel the secular clergy from the monasteries, and to command that monks and nuns should be installed in them.[3]

[964] Edgar, the peaceable king of the English, took to wife the daughter of Ordgar, ealdorman of Devon, Ælfthryth by name, after the death of her husband Æthelwold, the glorious ealdorman of the East Angles, and by her he had two sons, Edmund and Æthelred.[4] He had previously also had, by Æthelflæd the Fair, called Eneda (the daughter of the ealdorman, Ordmær), Edward, afterwards king and martyr, and by St Wulfthryth Edith, a virgin most devoted to God.[5] In the same year this same king installed monks in the New Minster and in Milton, and appointed Æthelgar abbot of the former and Cyneweard abbot of the latter.[6]

[965] John[7] the 133rd pope.[8]

[966] Count Eberhard died.[9]

[967] Edgar, the peaceable king of the English, established nuns in the monastery of Romsey, which his grandfather, Edward the

record the expulsion of the clerks from the Old Minster (AF: 'and from the New Minster and Chertsey and Milton') under the following year.
[4] ASC DF (mg.) under 965 simply record Edgar's marriage to Ælfthryth, daughter of Ealdorman Ordgar. JW identifies Ordgar as earl of Devon, and mentions her first husband, and then her sons. Ælfthryth's first husband does not appear to attest after 962 (S 703 BCS 1082, S 700 BCS 1095). Unless S 725 BCS 1143 of 964 is genuine, she does not attest charters until late in Edgar's reign.
[5] JW West Saxon Accounts 43 names Edgar's first wife as Eneda 'femina generosissima', and describes Edward, Wulfthryth, and Edith as holy. The name Eneda is peculiar to JW.
[6] ASC AF (964) record these events as well as the expulsion of clerks from the Old Minster, the replacement of clerks by monks at Chertsey and at Milton Abbas, and the appointment of Ordbriht at Chertsey.
[7] John XIII 965-72.   [8] Mar.   [9] Mar.

struxerat, sanctimoniales collocauit, sanctamque Mærwynnam[a] super eas abbatissam constituit.[1] |

p. 314   **[968]** (xxxii) 990   *Otto filius imperatoris a Iohanne papa ante altare sancti Petri cum patre suo coronatus est. Wilelmus episcopus Mogontinus obiit .vi. non. Martii, et sepultus est ante altare sancti Stephani in monasterio sancti Albani in Mogontia.*[2]

Rex Anglorum pacificus Eadgarus, monachis in Exanceastra congregatis, uirum religiosum Sidemannum illis abbatis iure prefecit.[3]

Hatto abbas Fuldensis Wilelmo successit, ad Fuldam autem successit Werinherus abbas.[b4]

ᶜMortuo Aldredo Lindisfarnensi episcopo, successit Alsius.[c5]

[969] (xxxiii) 991   *Ciclus decennouenalis .xxiiii. incipit indictione .xii. ᵈNicaphorus rex Grecorum senex cum timuisset a filiis suis proici, uoluit eunuchizare eos. Tunc mater eorum regina, quia per nullum aliud ingenium filios liberare potuit, Iohanni suasit regem occidere et imperare. Iohannes itaque occulte cum funibus intrauit per fenestram in palatium, et, occiso rege, egressus imperauit.*[6]

Rex Anglorum pacificus Eadgarus sancto Dunstano Dorubernensis et beato Oswaldo Wigornensis et sancto Ætheluuoldo Wintoniensis ecclesie episcopis precepit ut, expulsis clericis in maioribus monasteriis per Merciam constructis, monachos collocarent. Vnde sanctus Oswaldus sui uoti compos effectus, clericos Wigornensis ecclesie monachilem habitum suscipere renuentes de monasterio[d] ᵉexpulit, consentientes uero hoc anno, ipso teste, monachizauit, eisque Ramesiensem cenobitam Wynsinum, magne religionis uirum, loco decani prefecit.[e7]

---

[a] Mearuuinam *H*, Mearwinnam *L*, Merwinnam *B*, Meruuinnam *P*   [b] *rewritten* C²?   ᶜ⁻ᶜ Mortuo . . . Alsius] *added at line-end* C²   ᵈ⁻ᵈ Nicaphorus . . . monasterio] *compressed script almost certainly over erasure* C¹   ᵉ⁻ᵉ expulit . . . prefecit] *spills over into mg. with signe de renvoi* C¹

---

[1] *GP* ii. 78 (p. 175) refers to Edgar's foundation of Romsey but its account seems independent of JW's and provides no date. JW's annal is repeated in *HR*, Hoveden, and Roger of Wendover. For Merewenna, see *Heads of Religious Houses*, p. 218.

[2] Mar.

[3] JW is the only source for this. See *Heads of Religious Houses*, p. 48 for Sideman's signature after 964.   [4] Mar.

[5] JW has presumably calculated this date from his source (*HDE* ii. 20 (i. 78)), which states that Ælfsige had been bishop for 22 years when he died in 990.

Elder, king of the English, had built, and appointed St Merewenna their abbess.[1]

[968] Otto, the emperor's son, was crowned by Pope John before the altar of St Peter with his father. William, bishop of Mainz, died on 2 March, and was buried before the altar of St Stephen in the monastery of St Alban in Mainz.[2]

Edgar, the peaceable king of the English, appointed the devout Sideman to rule the monks gathered at Exeter as abbot.[3]

Hatto, abbot of Fulda, succeeded William, and Abbot Werinher succeeded him at Fulda.[4]

On the death of Ealdred, bishop of Lindisfarne, Ælfsige succeeded.[5]

[969] The twenty-fourth cycle of nineteen years begins in the twelfth indiction. Nicephorus, king of the Greeks, fearing in his old age that he would be cast out by his sons, wished to have them castrated. Then the queen, their mother, because she could not free her sons by any other device, persuaded John to kill the king and rule. And so John secretly entered the palace through a window by means of ropes, and, when he had killed the king, he emerged as ruler.[6]

Edgar, the peaceable king of the English, ordered the bishops St Dunstan of Canterbury, the blessed Oswald of Worcester, and St Æthelwold of Winchester to expel the secular priests from the greater monasteries built throughout Mercia and install monks. Thence St Oswald, having achieved fulfilment of his wish, expelled from the monastery the secular clergy of Worcester, who refused to receive the monastic habit, but, on his own testimony, in this year, he made monks of those who agreed, and set over them as dean Wynsige, a monk from Ramsey, and a man of great piety.[7]

---

[6] Mar.

[7] Though the expulsion of monks from Mercia in general and from Worcester in particular could have been based on Byrhtferth's *Vita Oswaldi*, iv. 12 (*Historians of the Church of York*, i. 433–4), the role of Dunstan and the date could not (see Whitelock, Brett, and Brooke, *Councils*, i. 114–15). The date is given in the record of Wulfstan's synod of 1092 (see Whitelock, Brett, and Brooke, *Councils*, ii. 638). Wynsige (presumably the *Wynsinus* in Byrhtferth's life), a monk of Ramsey, a very recent foundation, could have gained some experience of the monastic life at the earlier foundation of Westbury. If S 1321 BCS 1243 is reliable, there may be confirmation of his holding office in 969. 'Ipso teste' may indicate access to a now lost source. For a sceptical view, see Julia Barrow, 'How the twelfth-century monks at Worcester perceived their past', *The Perception of the Past in Twelfth-century Europe*, ed. P. Magdalino (London, 1992), pp. 53–74.

[970] (xxxiiii) 992 *Hatto episcopus Mogontinus obiit .vi. kalend.*
*Mai⟨i⟩,ᵃ Rotbertus sibiᵇ successit.*¹

Sancteᶜ ac uenerabiles antistitis Suithuni reliquie, peractis a
sepultura eius centum et decem annis, indictione .xiii., idus Iulii,
feria .vi., sullate sunt de monumento a sancto Ætheluuoldo, uenerabili presule et ab Alfstano Glæstoniensis et Æthelgaro Noui
Monasterii abbatibus, et in basilica apostolorum Petri et Pauli
decentissime sunt recondite.² Eodem anno Osulfus Wiltoniensis
presul obiit, et in Wiltonia tumulatus est, pro quo uir uenerandus
ordinatus est Ælfgarus.ᵈ³

[C³BP]
ᵉDefuncto Ælfredo Sælesiensi
episcopo, successit Eadelmus.ᵉ⁴

[971] (xxxv) 993 Clito Eadmundus, regis Eadgari filius, obiit et
in monasterio Rumesige honorifice est sepultus.⁵ Eodem anno
Ælfegus Suðhamtunensium dux obiit, et Glæstonie tumulatus est.
Non multo post Ordgarus dux Domnanie, socer regis Eadgari,
decessit et in Exanceastre sepultus est.ᶠ⁶

[972] (xxxvi) 994 Rex Anglorum pacificus Eadgarus Noui
Monasterii ecclesiam, a patre suo rege Eadmundo inceptam, a se
uero perfectam, honorifice dedicare precepit.⁷ Eodem anno
Ælfuuoldus Domnanie presul .xix. episcopatus sui anno decessit et
in Cridiantune sepultus requiescit.

ᵃ Mai *CL*   ᵇ *om. HL*   ᶜ sancti *L*   ᵈ *over erasure* C³, abbas Alfstanus
HL, Alfgarus *P*   ᵉ⁻ᵉ Defuncto . . . Eadelmus] *add. at line-end* C³, *om. HL*
ᶠ *add. 972 n. b (p. 422) here* P

---

¹ Mar.
² JW's record of Swithhun's death in 862 does not accord with the passage of 110
years before his translation in this year. A rubric to *Narratio Metrica de Sancto
Swithuno Wulfstani Cantoris*, in *Frithegodi Monachi Breviloquium Vitae Beati Wilfredi et
Wulfstani Cantoris Narratio Metrica de Sancto Swithuno*, ed. A. Campbell (Zurich,
1971), p. 111 dates the translation to 15 July 971, 14th indiction, and the poem mentions the presence of Abbots Ælfstan and Æthelgar. The former is not in the lists of
Glastonbury abbots; Lapidge–Winterbottom, p. 28 n. 1 show that Lantfred's *Translatio
et Miracula* implicitly identifies the Ælfstan who was present at the translation as abbot
of the Old Minster.
³ This date is compatible with surviving charter evidence. C³'s probable substitution
of *Ælfgarus* for *Ælfstanus* was presumably to bring the succession into line with the
alteration, possibly based on *GP* ii. 83 (p. 181), made to the list of Ramsbury bishops
in JW *Epis. Lists*.

[970] Hatto, bishop of Mainz, died on 26 April. Robert succeeded him.[1]

The relics of the holy and venerable bishop Swithhun, when 110 years had passed after their burial, were raised from the tomb by the venerable bishop, St Æthelwold, and the abbots, Ælfstan of Glastonbury and Æthelgar of the New Minster, on Friday, 15 July, in the thirteenth indiction, and were reburied with all due ceremony in the basilica of the apostles Peter and Paul.[2] In the same year Oswulf, bishop of Wiltshire, died, and was buried at Wilton. In his place the venerable Ælfgar was ordained.[3]

On the death of Alfred, bishop
of Selsey, Eadhelm succeeded.[4]

[971] The atheling Edmund, son of King Edgar, died, and was buried honourably in the monastery of Romsey.[5] In the same year Ælfheah, ealdorman of the men of Southampton, died, and was buried at Glastonbury. Not much later Ordgar, ealdorman of Devon, King Edgar's father-in-law, died, and was buried at Exeter.[6]

[972] Edgar, the peaceable king of the English, ordered the church of the New Minster, begun by his father, King Edmund, but completed by himself, to be solemnly dedicated.[7] In the same year Ælfwold, bishop of Devon, died in the nineteenth year of his epis-copacy, and lies buried at Crediton.

[4] JW Epis. Lists make Eadhelm the immediate successor of Alfred, though it has been suggested that a Brihthelm (D. Whitelock, in Otium et Negotium, p. 235) preceded him. The date is wrong since Eadhelm attests in 963 (S 717 BCS 1101, S 714 BCS 1125).

[5] ASC A (971 now mostly erased) G (971) DE (970) record the death of Edmund, but his burial-place is in AG alone.

[6] Ealdorman Ælfheah's death and burial-place are not recorded elsewhere, but his will (D. Whitelock, Anglo-Saxon Wills (Cambridge, 1930), no. ix, pp. 22–3) supports JW's location of his burial. If S 784 BCS 1285 is correctly dated, he was alive in 972. No charter evidence conflicts with the date for his death, or with the burial-place of Ealdorman Ordgar, father of Edgar's third wife, Ælfthryth, which are not recorded elswhere.

[7] Edward the Elder's foundation of New Minster is known from other sources and both Wulfstan's and Ælfric's Vita Sancti Æthelwoldi (Lapidge–Winterbottom, c. 20, p. 36; c. 16, p. 76) record Æthelwold's expulsion thence of the clerks with King Edgar's approval, but neither Edmund's contribution nor the dedication of the church in 972 is recorded elsewhere.

[C³BP]

*ᵃCui Sidemannus successit.ᵃ¹
ᵇCridia est uillula Domnanie, que
dicitur Deuenescira, .xii. milibus
ab Exonia.ᵇ²*

Defuncto Eboracensi archiepiscopo Oskytello, suus propinquus
sanctus Oswaldus Wigornensis episcopus pro eo in archiepiscopatum eligitur.³

[973] (xxxvii) 995 *ᶜᵈStephanus⁴ papa .cxxxiiii.ᵈ⁵* a quo sanctus
Oswaldus pallium suscepit.⁶ *Otto imperator non. Mai⟨i⟩ᵉ obiit ᶠet
iacet in Maideburh.ᶠᵍ⁷*

Rex Anglorum pacificus Eadgarus *ʰanno etatis sue .xxx.,ʰ* indictione .i., .v. idus Mai⟨i⟩,ᵉ die Pentecostes, a beatis presulibus
Dunstano et Oswaldo et a ceteris totius Anglie antistitibus in ciuitate Acamanni benedicitur et cum maximo honore et gloria consecratur et in regem unguitur.⁸ Interiecto deinde tempore ille cum
ingenti classe, septentrionali Brytannia circumnauigata ad
Legionum Ciuitatem appulit, cui subreguli eius .viii., Kynath scilicet rex Scottorum, Malcolm rex Cumbrorum, Maccus plurimarum rex insularum, et alii .v., Dufnal, Siferth, Huuual, Iacob,
Iuchil, ut mandarat, occurrerunt et quod sibi fideles et terra et
mari cooperatores esse uellent, iurauerunt.⁹ Cum quibus die

---

*ᵃ⁻ᵃ cui . . . successit] interlin C, om. HL   ᵇ⁻ᵇ Cridia . . . Exonia] add. mg. along-
side 972 C³, om. HL, add. at 971 n. f P   ᶜ Stephanus . . . .vii. (p. 424)] whole
annal in compressed script over erasure C   ᵈ⁻ᵈ Stephanus . . . cxxxiiii] placed at 973
n. g (N)   ᵉ Mai CB   ᶠ⁻ᶠ et . . . Maideburh] mg. next to beginning of line Cᵗ
ᵍ places 973 n. d here (N)   ʰ⁻ʰ anno . . . xxx] etatis sue xxx anno HL*

---

¹ Ælfwold's death in the 19th year of his episcopate agrees with JW's record of his
accession in 953. Charters do not conflict with this succession, unless *S* 790 *BCS* 1292
of 973, which an Ælfwold attests without Sideman, is genuine.
² *GP* i. 94 (p. 200).
³ ASC (B)C (971) record the death of Archbishop Osketel on 31 Oct. after 20 years
as a bishop. Byrhtferth's *Vita Oswaldi*, iv. 5 (*Historians of the Church of York*, i. 435)
records without a date the appointment of Oswald. The *Epistola de archiepiscopis
Eboraci* (*Symeonis monachi opera*, i. 226) says that Osketel died in 970, that he was succeeded briefly by an Æthelwald who preferred a quieter life and retired, and that
Oswald was appointed in 971. Oswald 'Eboracensis aecclesie archiepiscopus' attests
Edgar's Barrow upon Humber grant to Bishop Æthelwold (*S* 782 *BCS* 1270) of 971,
though, unless there is a scribal error, he must have received the title before receiving
the pallium in the following year. ASC (B)C (971) has a longish entry on Osketel and
the translation of his body to Bedford.

Sideman succeeded him.[1] Crediton is a small township in *Dumnonia* (which is called Devonshire), twelve miles from Exeter.[2]

After the death of Osketel, archbishop of York, his kinsman St Oswald, bishop of Worcester, was elected to the archbishopric in his place.[3]

[973] Stephen[4] the 134th pope.[5] St Oswald received the pallium from him.[6] The Emperor Otto died on 7 May, and lies at Magdeburg.[7]

Edgar, the peaceable king of the English, was blessed, crowned with the utmost honour and glory, and anointed king in his thirtieth year at Pentecost, 11 May, in the first indiction, by the blessed bishops Dunstan and Oswald, and by the other bishops of the whole of England in the city of Bath.[8] Then, after an interval, he sailed round the north coast of Wales with a large fleet, and came to the city of Chester. Eight underkings, namely Kenneth, king of the Scots, Malcolm, king of the Cumbrians, Maccus, king of many islands, and five others, Dufnal, Siferth, Hywel, Iacob, and Iuchil, went to meet him, as he had commanded, and swore that they would be loyal to, and co-operate with, him by land and sea.[9]

---

[4] Stephen unknown here. Benedict VI (973–4) was pope.   [5] Mar.

[6] Oswald's visit to Rome is mentioned in Byrhtferth's *Vita Oswaldi*, iv. 5 (*Historians of the Church of York*, i. 435–6) without date. The *Epistola de archiepiscopis Eboraci* (*Symeonis monachi opera*, i. 226) assigns his visit to 972 and identifies the donor as Pope Benedict (i.e. Benedict VI, elected between Sept. 972 and Jan. 973). JW's erroneous Stephen arose from Marianus, but his year for Oswald's return from Rome could be correct.

[7] Mar.

[8] ASC A (973) (B)C (974) DEF (972) record the day and place of Edgar's coronation, ABCF sharing JW's name for Bath. 973 is the correct year since A(B)C (though (B)C give 974 as the year), say that it occurred 27 years before 1000, and DEF, while giving 972, say that Pentecost, the day of the coronation, was 11 May, which is correct for 973. The reference to Dunstan and Oswald could be based on Byrhtferth's *Vita Oswaldi*.

[9] ASC DE (972) record Edgar's naval visit to Chester where six kings met him and swore oaths to him, and Ælfric's *Life of St. Swithin* (*Ælfric's Lives of Saints*, ed. W. W. Skeat (Early English Text Society, lxxvi i. 468, transl. Whitelock, *EHD*, no. 239 (g), pp. 927–8) record the submission on a day of all the kings in this island, 'once eight kings in one day'. On the identification of all but two of these kings, who are also in WM, *GR* ii. 148 (i. 165), see Stenton, pp. 369–70.

quadam scapham ascendit, illisque ad remos locatis, ipse clauum gubernaculi arripiens, eam per cursum fluminis De perite gubernauit, omnique turba ducum et procerum, simili nauigio comitante, a palatio ad monasterium sancti Iohannis baptiste nauigauit. Vbi facta oratione, eadem pompa ad palatium remeauit. Quod dum intraret optimatibus fertur dixisse tunc demum quemque suorum successorum se gloriari posse regem Anglorum fore, cum tot regibus sibi obsequentibus potiretur pompa talium honorum.[1] Sumertunensis episcopus Brihthelmus obiit et in Wyllum humatus est, cui successit Middeltunensis*a* abbas Cinewardus.[2]

*Romanorum nonagesimus .i. Otto[3] regnauit annis decem, mensibus .vii.*b4

[974] (i) 996 Hoc anno terre motus per totam Angliam factus est maximus.[5]

*Ebergerius archiepiscopus Coloniensis obtulit in sempiternum Scottis monasterium sancti Martini in Colonia, quibus primus prefuit abbas Minborinus*c* Scottus.[6]*

[975] (ii) 997 Anglici orbis basileus, flos et decus antecessorum regum, pacificus rex Eadgarus non minus memorabilis Anglis quam Romulus Romanis, Cirus Persis, Alexander Macedonibus, Arsaces Parthis, Karolus magnus Francis, postquam cuncta regaliter consummauit, anno etatis sue .xxxii., regni autem illius in Mercia et | Norðhymbria .xix., ex quo uero per totam Angliam regnauit .xvi., indictione .iii., .viii. idus Iulii, feria .v., ex hac uita transiuit, filiumque suum Eadwardum et regni et morum heredem reliquit.[7] Corpus uero illius Glæstoniam delatum, regio more est tumulatum.[8] Is itaque dum uiueret .iii. milia .dc. robustas sibi congregauerat naues ex quibus, pascali emensa solennitate, omni anno mille .cc. in orientali, mille .cc. in occidentali, mille .cc. in

p. 315

[1] WM ibid. reads: 'Denique *fertur tunc demum posse successores* suos *gloriari se reges Anglorum* esse, cum tanta *honorum* praerogativa fruerentur.' The relationship between JW and WM is discussed in the introduction to vol. i.
[2] This is not recorded elsewhere. The charters cited by Robinson, *Wells*, p. 47 to suggest that Brihthelm was still in office in 974 are not free from suspicion. For this Brihthelm see above, p. 410 n. 6.
[3] Otto II 973-83.   [4] Mar.

With them, on a certain day, he boarded a skiff; having set them to the oars, and having taken the helm himself, he skilfully steered it through the course of the river Dee, and with a crowd of ealdormen and nobles following in a similar boat, sailed from the palace to the monastery of St John the Baptist, where, when he had prayed, he returned with the same pomp to the palace. As he was entering it he is reported to have declared to his nobles at length that each of his successors would be able to boast that he was king of the English, and would enjoy the pomp of such honour with so many kings at his command.[1] Brihthelm, bishop of Somerset, died, and was buried at Wells. Cyneweard, abbot of Milton, succeeded him.[2]

Otto,[3] the ninety-first emperor of the Romans, reigned ten years and seven months.[4]

[974] In this year a very severe earthquake occurred throughout the whole of England.[5]

Eberger, archbishop of Cologne, gave the Irish in perpetuity the monastery of St Martin of Cologne, where Minborin the Irishman first ruled as abbot.[6]

[975] The ruler of the English world, the flower and glory of preceding kings, the peaceable King Edgar, no less memorable to the English than Romulus to the Romans, Cyrus to the Persians, Alexander to the Macedonians, Arsaces to the Parthians, Charles the Great to the Franks, after accomplishing all things royally, departed this life on Thursday, 8 July, in the third indiction, in his thirty-second year, and in the nineteenth year of his reign in Mercia and Northumbria, and in the sixteenth from the time he ruled the whole of England, and he left his son Edward heir to both the kingdom and to his personal qualities.[7] His body was borne to Glastonbury, and buried in the royal fashion.[8] Now he had assembled during his lifetime 3,600 strong ships for his own use, from which, when the Easter feast was over, he used to assemble 1,200 on the east coasts of the island, 1,200 on the west,

---

[5] This earthquake is not recorded elsewhere.   [6] Mar.

[7] The day of Edgar's death is in ASC A (975 for 974) (B)CD (addition) and in Byrhtferth, *Vita Oswaldi*, iv. 11 (*Historians of the Church of York*, i. 443), and the year is not in doubt. JW presumably calculated the indiction, weekday, age, and regnal years.

[8] The king's burial at Glastonbury is not in other earlier sources, but is in WM, *GR* ii. 160 (i. 180).

septentrionali insule plaga coadunare, et ad occidentalem cum orientali classe, et illa remissa, ad borealem cum occidentali, ipsaque
remissa cum boreali ad orientalem classem remigare, eoque modo
totam insulam omni estate consueuerat circumnauigare, uiriliter
hoc agens ad defensionem contra exteros regni sui, et suum suorumque ad bellicos usus exercitium.[1] Hieme autem et uere, infra
regnum usquequaque per omnes prouincias Anglorum transire et
quomodo legum iura et suorum statuta decretorum a principibus
obseruarentur, neue pauperes a potentibus preiudicium passi
opprimerentur, diligenter solebat inuestigare. In uno fortitudini, in
altero iustitie studens, in utroque reipublice et regni utilitatibus
consulens. Hinc hostibus circumquaque timor, et omnium sibi
subditorum erga eum excreuerat amor.[2] *Cuius decessu totius regni
status est* per*turbatu*s, et *post tempus letitie quod* illius *tempore stabat
pacifice,* cepit *tribulatio undique aduenire.* Nam *princeps Merciorum
Ælfere* quampluresque regni primates, magnis *obceca*ti *muner*ibus,
*abbates cum monachi*s de monasteriis in quibus rex pacificus
Eadgarus eos locauerat *e*xpulerunt et *clerico*s *cum uxoribus suis*
intro*dux*erunt. Sed huic *uesani*e *uiri timorati,* dux Orientalium
Anglorum *Ætheluuin*us, Dei amicus, et suus germanus
*Ælfuuold*us,[a] et *Byrhtnothus comes, uir religiosus,* restiterunt, et *in
synodo constitut*i, se *nequaquam ferre posse* dixerunt, *ut monachi*
eicerentur de *regno, qui omnem* religionem *tenuerunt in regno.
Congregato* dein *exercitu,* monasteria Orientalium Anglorum maxima strenuitate defenderunt. Dum hec aguntur, de rege eligendo
magna inter regni primores oborta est dissensio, *quidam* nanque
regis filium Eaduuardum, quidam uero fratrem illius elegerunt
Ægelredum.[3] Quam ob causam archipresules Dunstanus et
Oswaldus cum coepiscopis, abbatibus, ducibusque quamplurimis in
unum conuenerunt et Eaduuardum, ut pater suus preceperat,
elegerunt, electum consecrauerunt, et in regem unxerunt.[4]

---

[a] Alfuuoldus *H*, Alfwoldus *L*

---

[1] Ibid. ii. 156 (i. 177–8): '*omni aestate, emensa* statim *Paschali* festivitate, naues per
omnia littora *coadunari* praecipiebat; *ad occidentalem* insulae partem *cum orientali classe,
et illa* remensa *cum occidentali ad borealem,* inde *cum boreali ad orientalem remigare* con-
suetus.'
[2] Ibid. ii. 156 (i. 178): '*hyeme et uere per omnes prouincias* equitando, judicia potentio-
rum exquirebat, uiolati juris seuerus ultor: *in* hoc *justitiae, in* illo *fortitudini studens; in
utroque reipublicae utilitatibus consulens*'.

and 1,200 on the north coasts of the island, and sail to the western fleet with the eastern, and, when he had sent that back, to the northern fleet with the western, and that sent back, with the northern fleet to the eastern, and in that way he used to circumnavigate the whole island every summer, acting thus vigorously for the defence of his kingdom against foreigners and to train for himself and his men in military exercises.[1] However, in winter and spring, he was accustomed to enquire diligently within his kingdom, travelling right through all the English provinces, about the manner in which the legal rights and the statutes he had promulgated were observed by the magnates, lest the poor should be crushed by the injustices they suffered from the powerful. By the first action concentrating on strength, by the second on justice, he sought the advantages of the state and kingdom in both. Hence the fear of his enemies on every side and the love of all those subject to him grew.[2] The state of the kingdom was thrown into confusion by his death, and after the period of rejoicing and peace which was maintained in his time, tribulation began to approach on all sides. For Ælfhere, ruler of the Mercians, and very many of the chief men of the kingdom, blinded by the prospect of gains, expelled the abbots and their monks from the monasteries in which the peaceable King Edgar had installed them, and introduced secular clerks with their wives. But the devout men Æthelwine, ealdorman of East Anglia, and God's friend, and his brother Ælfwold, and the Ealdorman Brihtnoth, a devout man, resisted this madness of fearful men, formed a council, and said that they could by no means permit the monks who preserved all the practices of religion in the kingdom to be cast out from the realm. Then they assembled an army, and defended the monasteries of East Anglia with the utmost vigour. While this was happening, a great dissension arose among the magnates of the realm about the election of a king, for some elected Edward, the king's son, but others Æthelred his brother.[3] Because of this the Archbishops Dunstan and Oswald assembled as many of their fellow bishops, abbots, and ealdormen as possible, and elected Edward, as his father had ordered, and having elected him, consecrated and anointed him king.[4]

---

[3] Byrhtferth, *Vita Oswaldi*, iv. 11–13, 17–18 (*Historians of the Church of York*, i. 443, 444, 445, 448, 449).

[4] Byrhtferth's *Vita Oswaldi* guided JW's account of the dissension after Edgar's death, which seems to owe little to ASC. For the relationship between JW and WM see the introduction to vol. i. Edward's succession is variously reported in ASC.

Cineuuardus*ᵃ* Sumertunensis episcopus obiit.[1] Cometis stella autumnali tempore uisa est.[2]

[976] (iii) 998 Fames ualida Angliam inuasit.[3] Quo anno uir magnificus dux Oslacus iniuste expellitur Anglia.[4]

$$[C^3BP]$$
*ᵇ*Defuncto Algaro Wiltunensi presule, successit *Ælfstanus* abbas*ᶜ* *monachus sancti* Athelwoldi *apud Abbendoniam*, illi substituitur Siricius.*ᵇ*[5]

[977] (iiii) 999 *Rotbertus Mogontinus episcopus obiit idus Ian. Willigisus sibi successit.*[6]

In Eastanglia*ᵈ* apud uillam que Cyrtling nominatur maxima synodus celebratur.[7] Deinc*ᵉ* apud Kalne regiam uillam dum alia celebraretur totius Anglie maiores natu, qui ibidem congregati fuerant, excepto sancto Dunstano, de solario corruerunt, quorum quidam mortui sunt quidam uero mortis periculum uix euaserunt.[8] Tertia apud Ambresbyrig sinodus celebrata est.[9] Domnanie presul Sidemannus obiit,*ᶠ*

$$[C^3?BP]$$
*ᵍ*cui Alfricus successit.*ᵍ*[10]

[978] (v) 1000 Rex Anglorum Eadwardus iussu nouerce sue Ælfthrythe regine, in loco qui Coruesgeate dicitur, *ʰ*a suis*ʰ* iniuste

---

ᵃ Kynehardus *HL*   *ᵇ⁻ᵇ* Defuncto . . . Siricius] *add. at line-end extending into mg.* *C*³, *om. HL*   *ᶜ interlin. C*³, *om. P*   *ᵈ over erasure. C*³?   *ᵉ* Dehinc *HL* *ᶠ see App. A for addition L*   *ᵍ⁻ᵍ* cui . . . successit] *add. at line-end extending into mg. C*³?, *om. HL*   *ʰ⁻ʰ* a suis] *om., though possibly erased L*

---

[1] ASC A (975 from 974) (B)C with day of Cyneweard's death but without identification of the see.
[2] ASC A-E, the first three poetically, the others more baldly.
[3] ASC A(B)DE (975); C (976).
[4] ASC A(B)DE (975) C (975 for 976), which have no equivalent to 'iniuste'.
[5] *GP* ii. 83 (p. 181). The original order in JW *Epis. Lists* was 'Ælfstanus, Alfgarus, and Siericus'. The position of the first two was reversed presumably in line with the order in *GP*, and this incorrect order is followed here, in 981, and in 970 (see 970 n. 3).

Cyneweard, bishop of Somerset, died.[1] A comet was seen in the autumn.[2]

[976] A great famine struck England.[3] In that year the glorious ealdorman Oslac was unjustly expelled from England.[4]

> Ælfgar, bishop of Wiltshire, died, and was succeeded by Abbot Ælfstan, a monk of St Æthelwold at Abingdon. Sigeric was appointed in his stead.[5]

[977] Robert, bishop of Mainz, died on 13 January. Willigisus succeeded him.[6]

A very great council was held in East Anglia at a township called Kirtlington.[7] Afterwards, while the nobles of all England were holding another council at the royal township of Calne, those who were gathered there, except St Dunstan, crashed down from an upper room and some died, while others barely escaped mortal danger.[8] A third council was held at Amesbury.[9] Sideman, bishop of *Dumnonia* died.

> Ælfric succeeded him.[10]

[978] Edward, king of the English, was unjustly murdered by his own men at the command of his stepmother, Queen Ælfthryth, at a place called Corfe, and was buried at Wareham without royal

---

[6] Mar.

[7] ASC (B)C (977, after Easter). Kirtlington in Oxfordshire is likely to have been a royal estate (see S 1497 BCS 812). C³'s East Anglia might suggest that the reviser had Kirtling in Cambridgeshire (which is close to the western bounds of East Anglia) in mind.

[8] ASC DEF (978). JW identifies Calne in Wiltshire as a royal vill.

[9] The third meeting at Amesbury, another royal vill in Wiltshire, is not recorded elsewhere.

[10] ASC (B)C have a fuller entry on Sideman's death, giving the day of his death (30 Apr.) at Kirtlington and recording his burial at Abingdon on the orders of King Edward and Archbishop Dunstan against his expressed wish to be buried at Crediton.

occiditur, et apud Werham non regio more sepelitur.[1] Cuius frater Ægelredus*a* *clito egregius, moribus elegans, pulcher uultu, decorus aspectu,* indictione .vi., die dominica, .xviii. kalend. Maii*b* post pascalem festiuitatem *a* sanctis archipresulibus *Dunstano et Osuualdo* et decem episcopis in Cingestune*c* *ad regni fastigium est consecratus.*[2] *d*Ælfuuoldus Dorsetensium episcopus obiit et in Scireburnan sepultus est.*d*[3]

[C³BP]
*e*Ælfuuoldo successit Æthelricus, illi Æthelsius, illi Bryhtwinus, illi Ælmarus, illi Bryhtwinus, illi Aluuoldus monachus Wintoniensis.*ef*[4]

Nubes per totam Angliam media nocte, nunc sanguinea, nunc ignea uisa est. Dehinc in radios diuersos et colores uarios mutata circa auroram disparuit.[5]

[979] (vi) 1001 *gDux* Merciorum*g* *Alfer*us *cum multitudine populi* Werham uenit, sanctumque *corpus* pretiosi regis et martiris Eaduuardi de tumulo *sulleuari precepit; quod dum* esset *nudatum, sanum* atque incolume *ab omni* clade *et contagione* est *inuen*tum, lotum deinde, *noui*sque *uestimentis indutum,*[6] ad Sceaftesbyrig est delatum et honorifice tumulatum.[7] |

p. 316   **[980]** (vii) 1002 Ciclus solis incipit .iiii. concurrentibus bissextilibus.

---

a Æthelredus *LP*   *b* Mai *CB*   *c* Kyngestune *H*, Kingestunæ *L*, Kingestune *P*   *d–d* Ælfuuoldus . . . sepultus est] *add. at 978 n. f P*   *e–e* Ælfuuoldo . . . Wintoniensis] *add. mg. alongside 978 C³, om. HL*   *f* 978 n. d placed here P   *g–g* Dux Merciorum] *written over erasure C*

---

[1] ASC AC (978) DEF (979). DEF give the day (18 Mar.) of his murder (C speaking of his 'martyrdom') and agree with JW in the location of both murder and burial. Byrhtferth's *Vita Oswaldi*, iv. 18 (*Historians of the Church of York*, i. 449) reference to Edward's harshness to his followers could conceivably account for JW's view of the murder being perpetrated 'a suis', though JW does not agree with Byrhtferth's identification of his murderers. Ælfthryth's role in the murder (which is neither in ASC nor in the earliest lives of Dunstan) goes back to an early 11th-c. account; see C. E. Fell, *Edward King and Martyr* (Leeds Texts and Monographs, NS, Leeds, 1971). pp. iii, xiv–xx.

[2] Byrhtferth, *Vita Oswaldi*, v. 4 (*Historians of the Church of York*, i. 455). ASC CDE (979) F (980) record the coronation of Æthelred at Kingston. Under 978, C had

rites.[1] His brother Æthelred, the illustrious atheling, elegant in his manners, handsome in visage, glorious in appearance, was consecrated to the most exalted position in the kingdom on Sunday, 14 April, in the sixth indiction, after the Easter feast by the blessed Archbishops Dunstan and Oswald and by ten bishops at Kingston.[2] Ælfwold, bishop of Dorset, died and was buried at Sherborne.[3]

> Æthelric succeeded Ælfwold, and was succeeded by Æthelsige, and he by Brihtwine, and he by Ælfmær, and he by Brihtwine, and he by Ælfwold, a monk of Winchester.[4]

A cloud, now bloody, now fiery, was seen in the middle of the night throughout England. It disappeared afterwards, about dawn, changing into scattered wisps of various colours.[5]

[979] Ælfhere, ealdorman of the Mercians, came to Wareham with a host of people, and ordered the holy body of the precious king and martyr Edward to be raised from the tomb. When it was laid bare it was found whole and sound, free from damage and corruption. Washed and clad in new garments,[6] it was borne to Shaftesbury, and honourably buried.[7]

[980] The solar cycle begins with four concurrents in a bissextile year.

---

already spoken of the succession of Æthelred and his consecration 'in the same year', but under 979, when it elaborates on the consecration, it gives the day ('a fortnight after Easter', i.e. 4 May) in 979 and the place. JW's 14 Apr. is two weeks after Easter in 978. C says that two archbishops and ten bishops were present. On the date of Æthelred's accession, see Whitelock, Brett, and Brooke, *Councils*, i. 183 n. 3.

[3] ASC C (978).

[4] This is inserted here because of the death of Ælfwold of Sherborne. It could be based on *GP* ii. 82 (p. 179), though the rendering of its names is closer to that in the JW Sherborne *Epis. Lists*.

[5] ASC C (979).

[6] Byrhtferth, *Vita Oswaldi*, iv. 19 (*Historians of the Church of York*, i. 450).

[7] ASC DEF (980) record the removal of Edward's body by Ealdorman Ælfhere from Wareham to Shaftesbury, which is also mentioned (without date) in the *Passio Edwardi* (C. E. Fell, *Edward King and Martyr*, p. 9.).

Æthelgarus Noui Monasterii uenerabilis abbas, *defuncto
Eadelmo,* .vi. nonis Maii, Seolisigensis ecclesie presulatum suscepit.[1] Eodem anno Suthamtonia a Danicis piratis deuastatur, et
eius ciues omnes fere uel occisi uel captiui sunt abducti. Nec
multo post Tenetland insulam idem deuastat[c] exercitus. Quo etiam
anno Ciuitatis Legionum prouincia a Noruuegenensibus piratis
deuastatur.[2]

[981] (viii) 1003   *Stephanus*[3] *papa .cxxxv.*[4]
Sancti Petroci confessoris monasterium in Cornubia deuastatum
est a piratis, qui anno preterito Suthamtoniam deuastarunt,[5] qui
deinde in Domnania et in ipsa Cornubia circa ripas maris
frequentes predas agebant. Alstanus[d] Wiltoniensis episcopus
defunctus, Abbandonie[e] sepelitur, pro quo Siricius[f] episcopatum
suscepit.[g6]
[HL]
Eximie uir religionis Wulstanus
Glæstoniensis decanus obiit.[6]

[982] (ix) 1004 Ad   prouinciam Dorsetensium tres   naues
piratarum applicuerunt et Portland deuastauerunt. Lundonia igne
cremata est. Suthamtunensium dux Æthelmarus et Suthsaxonum
dux Eduuinus decesserunt, et istius corpus Abbandonie, illius uero
Wintonie in Nouo Monasterio sepultum est. Hereluue
Sceaftesbyriensis et Wlfuuin Werhamnensis abbatisse de hac uita
transierunt. Eodem anno Romanorum imperator Otto secundus,
cum in partes Grecie deuenisset, Sarracenorum exercitum, terras
Christianorum depopulaturum, obuium habuit, cum quibus prelium iniit, cesisque multis ex his et illis, uictor extitit. Quo
domum reuertente, Otto, filius fratris sui Liutolfi, filii imperatoris
Ottonis primi et filie regis Anglorum Eaduuardi Senioris, obiit.[7]

[a–a] Æthelgarus Noui] *above these words an interlineation has been erased* C
[b–b] defuncto Eadelmo] *interlin.* C[3], *om.* HL   [c] deuastant CH   [d] Alfstanus
HLP   [e] *see App. A for addition* L   [f] *written over erasure* C[3], Wulgarus H
Wlgarus L   [g] *traces of erasure after* suscepit *with next line left blank* C

---

[1] ASC C does not give here the names of Æthelgar's monastery or of his predecessor at Selsey, but records the appointment of Æthelgar to New Minster under 964.
[2] ASC DE (981) confine their annal to the raid on Southampton by seven ships, but

Æthelgar, the venerable abbot of the New Minster, received the bishopric of Selsey on the death of Eadhelm on 2 May.[1] In the same year Southampton was ravaged by Danish pirates, and almost all its citizens were either slain or led away as captives. Not much later the same army laid waste the island of Thanet. In that year too the province of the city of Chester was laid waste by Norwegian pirates.[2]

[981] Stephen[3] 135th pope.[4]

The monastery of St Petroc the Confessor was laid waste by the pirates who had devastated Southampton the year before,[5] and who, after that, made frequent raids on the coasts of Devon and Cornwall itself. Ælfstan, bishop of Wiltshire, died, and was buried at Abingdon. Sigeric received the bishopric in his place.

Wulfstan, dean of Glastonbury,
a most devout man, died.[6]

[982] Three pirate ships landed in Dorset, and laid waste Portland. London was consumed by fire. Æthelmær, ealdorman of the men of Hampshire, and Edwin, ealdorman of the South Saxons, died. The body of the latter was buried at Abingdon, but that of the former at Winchester in the New Minster. The abbesses Herelufu of Shaftesbury and Wulfwyn of Wareham departed this life. In the same year the Roman Emperor Otto II, when he had entered Greek territory, encountered the Saracen army on the point of laying waste Christian lands he engaged in battle with them and after many of them had been slain on both sides had the victory. On his return home, Otto, son of his brother Liudolf (son of Emperor Otto I and of a daughter of Edward the Elder, king of the English), died.[7]

ASC C has all the English entries of this annal. JW's 'a Norwegenensibus piratis' may be an inexact translation of C's 'from norð scipherige'.
[3] Stephen unknown at this point. Benedict VII (974–83) was pope.   [4] Mar.
[5] The location of St Petroc's in Cornwall and the identification of the Danish invaders seem to be JW's contribution.
[6] ASC C. There are two differences of substance: JW originally recorded the death of Wulfstan of Glastonbury where ASC C gave the death of Womer, abbot of Ghent; and C[3], in line with the alterations under 970 and 976, substituted Sigeric for Wulfgar as Ælfstan's successor.
[7] ASC C. JW distinguishes between the two Ottos.

[983] (x) 1005 Dux Merciorum Alferus, regis Anglorum Eadgari propinquus, decessit, eiusque ducatum filius suus Alfricus suscepit.[1]

[984] (xi) 1006 Sanctus Ætheluuoldus Wintoniensis episcopus, indictione .ii., kalend. Augusti, e seculo migrauit, cui successit Bathonicus abbas Ælphegus. Hic in monasterio, cui Deorhyrste uocabulum est, religionis susceperat habitum.*[a2]*

Otto imperatur secundus obiit .vii. idus Dec., feria .ii., et iacet in Roma.

Romanorum nonagesimus secundus, *tertius Otto,*[3] *filius secundi Ottonis, regnauit annis decem et octo, mensibusque duobus.*[4]

[985] (i) 1007 *[b]*Venerabilis monachus Eduuinus Abbandunensi monasterio abbatis iure preficitur.*[b5]*

[C³BP]
*[c]*Kynewardo Wellensi episcopo defuncto, successit Sigarus.*[c6]*

[986] (ii) 1008 *Rex* Anglorum *Ægelredus propter quasdam dissensiones ciuitatem* Hrofi *obsedit, et* uisa *capiendi illam difficultate,* iratus discessit et terras sancti Andree apostoli deuastauit.[7] Dux Merciorum Alfricus, Ælferi ducis filius, Anglia expellitur.[8]

Minborinus abbas Scottus in monasterio sancti Martini in Colonia obiit .xv. kalend. Augusti, die dominica; *Kilianus sibi successit.*[9]

---

[a] see *App. A for addition* LP⁵ *(mg. alongside 984 P)*   *[b-b]* Venerabilis . . . preficitur] *om. and see App. A for substituted text* LP   *[c-c]* Kynewardo . . . Sigarus] *add. at line-end* C³, *om.* HL

---

[1] ASC CDE. JW identifies Ælfhere's ealdormanry, and adds (correctly) that Ælfhere was both *propinquus* of King Edgar and Ælfric's father, and omits the death of Pope Benedict (which is in ASC C), presumably because of conflict with Marianus entries concerning Popes Stephen (981) and Marinus (989). ASC A simply records Ælfhere's death.

[2] ASC ACDEF (984) all record the death of Æthelwold, AF naming his successor. C alone gives the day of his death, which is in other sources, e.g. Wulfstan's or Ælfric's *Vita Sancti Æthelwoldi* (Lapidge–Winterbottom, c. 41, p. 62; c. 26, p. 79). The succession of Edwin at Abingdon is included under this year in E, and under 985 in C. A records Ælfheah's other name Goduuine, and the date of his enthronement, but none refer to his previous history at Deerhurst and Bath. This information is found in WM *GP* ii. 76 (p. 169). Id. *De Antiquitate Glastonie Ecclesie,* c. 67 (in J. Scott, *The*

[983] Ælfhere, ealdorman of the Mercians, a kinsman of Edgar, king of the English, died, and his son Ælfric succeeded to his rank.[1]

[984] St Æthelwold, bishop of Winchester, departed this life on 1 August, in the second indiction, and Ælfheah, abbot of Bath, succeeded him. He had taken the religious habit in the monastery which is called Deerhurst.[2]

The Emperor Otto II died on Monday, 7 December, and lies in Rome.

Otto III,[3] son of Otto II, the ninety-second emperor of the Romans, reigned eighteen years and two months.[4]

[985] The venerable monk Edwin was preferred to the monastery of Abingdon as abbot.[5]

Sigar succeeded Cyneweard, bishop of Wells, when he died.[6]

[986] Æthelred, king of the English, besieged the city of Rochester because of certain dissensions, and, when he had perceived the difficulty of taking it, departed in anger, and laid waste the lands of St Andrew the Apostle.[7] Ælfric, ealdorman of the Mercians, son of the Ealdorman Ælfhere, was expelled from England.[8]

Minborin, the Irish abbot of the monastery of St Martin in Cologne, died on Sunday, 18 July, and Kilian succeeded him.[9]

Early History of Glastonbury: An Edition, Translation and Study of William of Malmesbury's De Antiquitate Glastonie Ecclesie (Woodbridge, 1981), p. 137) records his abbacy of Bath.

[3] Otto III 983–1002.   [4] Mar.   [5] ASC C (985) E (984).

[6] The death of Cyneweard, bishop of Wells, is entered under 975 in ASC A(B)C and JW. Sigar's first attested charter is S 834 K 621 of 979.

[7] Vita Dunstani auctore Osberno, c. 39 (Memorials Dunstan, p. 117). ASC C–F record Æthelred's devastation of Rochester, but to the notice taken probably from Osbern JW added information about the king's anger found in Sulcard of Westminster (B. W. Scholz, 'Sulcard, "Prologus de construccione Westmonasterii"', Traditio, xx (1964), 89).

[8] ASC CDE (985). JW, as in 983, identifies the ealdormanry and Ælfric's father.

[9] Mar.

[987] (iii) 1009 *ª*Hoc anno due retro seculis Anglorum genti incognite pestes, scilicet febris hominum et lues animalium, que Anglice scitta uocatur, Latine autem fluxus interraneorum dici potest, totam Angliam plurimum uexauerunt, et clade perualida tam homines afficiendo quam animalia penitus consumendo, per omnes fines Anglie inedicibiliter deseuierunt.*ª*[1]

[988] (iiii) 1010 *ᵇCiclus decennouenalis uigesimus quintus incipit indictione prima.*ᵇ[2]

Wecedport a Danicis piratis deuastatur, a quibus etiam satrapa Domnanie, Goda nomine, et *miles fortissimus Strenuuold*us *cum aliis nonnullis* perimuntur, sed tamen *ex illis plurior*ibus occisis,[3] Angli loco dominantur funeris. Beatus Dunstanus archiepiscopus indictione prima, *ᶜ*.xiiii. kalend.*ᵈ*

[HLP]	[C³B]
Iunii, sabbato, ex hac uita transiuit et superne ciuitatis sedem petiuit. Pro quo Athelgarus Seolisigensis episcopus archipresulatum suscepit, unoque anno tribusque mensibus tenuit.[4]	⟨Iunii⟩ obiit cui successit Æthelgarus[4] *primus in Nouo Monasterio abbas a beato Ætheluuoldo Wintonie factus, post Australium Saxonum* episcopus, *cuius sedes tunc erat apud Selesium,* illique successit *ᵈ*Ordbrihtus ad Selesiam.*ᶜᵉ*[5]

[989] (v) 1011 *ᶠMarinus*[6] *ᵍcentesimus tricesimus sextus papa.*ᶠᵍ[7]

[990] (vi) 1012

[HL(P)]	[C³B(P)]
*ʰ*Syricus Dorobernie archiepiscopus consecratur, Eduuinus	*ⁱʲ*Æthelgaro Dorubernie archiepiscopo successit

---

ª⁻ª Hoc . . . deseuierunt] *written in compressed script probably over erasure extending into both mgs.* C¹ *ᵇ⁻ᵇ* Ciclus . . . prima] *rubricated in mg. near opening of 988* C¹ *ᶜ⁻ᶜ* xiiii . . . Selesiam] *written over erasure* C³ *ᵈ* Iunii *interlin.* B¹ *ᵉ⁻ᵉ* Ordbrihtus ad Selesiam] *written over erasure and at line-end* B⁵? *ᶠ⁻ᶠ* Marinus . . . papa] *interlin.* L, *under 988* P *ᵍ⁻ᵍ* centesimus . . . papa] papa .cxxxvi. HL *ʰ* Syricus . . . successit *(p. 438)] misplaced at the end of 988, and before 989 n. f and 990 n. i, though a single signe de renvoi (without its twin) could suggest an abortive attempt to put the displacement right* P *ⁱ⁻ⁱ* Æthelgaro . . . induxit*(p. 438)] starts under 989* C³B, *starts under 988 after 989 n. f* P *ʲ⁻ʲ* Æthelgaro . . . successit *(p. 438)] written over erasure.* C³

[987] In this year two diseases unknown to the English people in earlier times, namely a fever in men and a plague in livestock, which is called *scitte* in English, but which can be called a flux of the bowels in Latin, afflicted all England very greatly and raged indescribably throughout English territory, visiting men with devastating slaughter as well as destroying almost all the beasts.[1]

[988] The twenty-fifth cycle of nineteen years begins in the first indiction.[2]

Watchet was laid waste by the Danish pirates, who slew an ealdorman of Devon, Goda by name, a very brave soldier, Strenwold, and many others; but since more of the Danes were killed,[3] the English were masters of the place of death. St Dunstan the archbishop, in the first indiction, on 29

May, a Saturday, left this life and sought the seat of the heavenly city. Æthelgar, bishop of Selsey, took over the archbishopric in his place, and held it for one year and three months.[4]	May died. His successor was Æthelgar,[4] who had been appointed the first abbot of the New Minster by the blessed Æthelwold of Winchester and was later bishop of the South Saxons, whose seat was then at Selsey. Ordbriht succeeded him at Selsey.[5]

[989] Marinus[6] the 136th pope.[7]

[990] Sigeric was consecrated archbishop of Canter-	Sigeric, bishop of Wiltshire, succeeded Æthelgar, archbishop

---

[1] ASC CDE (986). JW's description is much fuller than ASC's plain statement.

[2] Mar.

[3] Byrhtferth, *Vita Oswaldi*, v. 4 (*Historians of the Church of York*, i. 456). ASC CD (988) EF (987) record the devastation of Watchet, but JW identifies the assailants. The slaying of Goda is entered under 988 in versions C-F, but the name Strenwold, and his association with the campaign, are presumably derived from Byrhtferth; so too perhaps the fact of English victory.

[4] ASC C-F. JW's original wording on Dunstan's death is close to that in EF. The day of Dunstan's death is not in ASC and agrees with the information given by Adelard, lectio 11 (*Memorials Dunstan*, p. 66). JW identifies Æthelgar's see, which was identified in ASC 980.

[5] *GP* i. 20 (p. 32). C³'s additional note is correct as is the succession of Ordbriht to Selsey (see Keynes, *Diplomas*, p. 176).

[6] Presumably Marinus II 942-6.   [7] Mar.

Abbandunensis abbas obiit ^acui   Siricius,[1] *Wiltunensium episcopus*
Wulgarus successit.^{ab1}   *qui, clericis* a Cantuuaria *protur-*
batis, monachos induxit.^{c2}
^dDefuncto Alsio Lindisfarnensi presule, Aldhunus successit.^{de3} |

p. 317   **[991]** (vii) 1013 *Willigisus archiepiscopus Mogontinus dedicauit*
ecclesiam in Tur⟨in⟩lan,^f Wikkero comite rogante. Qui Wikkerus mox
eandem ecclesiam que etiam Dorlon nominatur cum omnibus que in
eadem marchia habuit, post obitum suum, sancto Martino et episcopo
Mogontino contradit.[4]

Eodem anno Gipesuuic Dani depopulati sunt, quorum duces
fuerunt Iustin et Guthmund filius Steitan,[5] cum quibus non multo
post strenuus dux Orientalium Saxonum Byrhtnothus iuxta
Mældunam proelium commisit, sed utrinque infinita multitudine
cesa, ipse dux occubuit, Danica uero^g fortuna uicit. Quo insuper
anno, Sirici Dorubernensis archiepiscopi et ducum Ætheluuardi et
Alfrici consilio,[6] Danis tributum quod erat decem milia librarum
primitus datum est, ut a crebris rapinis, cremationibus et
hominum occisionibus, quas circa ripas maris frequenter agebant,
desisterent pacemque firmam cum eis tenerent.[7] Sanctus
Osuualdus archiepiscopus monasterium Ramesege quod ipse et
Dei amicus dux Orientalium Anglorum Atheluuinus construxerunt, diuino adiutus auxilio et confortatus adminiculo

---

^{a–a} cui . . . successit] cui successit uir uenerabilis Wulgarus *L*   ^b *see above, p.*
436 n. h   ^c *see above, 436 n. i*   ^{d–d} Defuncto . . . successit] *incorporated twice,*
first before 989 n. f, and again after 990 n. i P   ^e *see above, p. 436 n. j*
^f Turmlan *JW*   ^g ibi *interlin. B*¹

---

[1] ASC C (990) E (989) have both the consecration of Sigeric and the Abingdon
entry, E reversing their order. ASC D (990) F (989) only record Sigeric's consecration,
F also adding his visit to Rome for the pallium. JW identifies the see and the abbey.
[2] *GP* i. 20 (p. 32). In MSS A (originally) BCE of *GP*, the italicized words describe
Ælfric, whom WM erroneously makes Æthelgar's immediate successor, and holds
responsible (like ASC F (995)) for the expulsion of clerks. The original reading of the
GP autograph MS A (Oxford, Magdalen College 172) was 'clericis a Cantuaria protur-
batis monachos induxit'. C³'s substitution of Sigeric for Ælfric was guided by JW's
original annal for 990.
[3] This addition is based on *HDE* ii. 20 (i. 78), and is consistent with that under 968.
[4] Mar.

bury. Edwin, abbot of Abingdon, died, and Wulfgar succeeded him.[1]

of Canterbury,[1] and he, when he had driven the secular clergy out of Kent, brought in monks.[2]

When Ælfsige, bishop of Lindisfarne, died, Aldhun succeeded him.[3]

[991] Willigis, archbishop of Mainz, dedicated a church in Turinlan at the request of Count Wigger. After his death this Wigger left the same church, which was also called Dorla, with all that he held in that march, to St Martin, and the bishop of Mainz.[4]

In the same year the Danes laid waste Ipswich under the leadership of Justin and Guthmund, son of Steitan.[5] Not much later the vigorous Brihtnoth, ealdorman of the East Saxons, joined battle with them near Maldon, but when an infinite host had been slain on either side, the ealdorman himself fell and Danish fortune triumphed. In addition, in that year, on the advice of Sigeric, archbishop of Canterbury, and of the ealdormen Æthelweard and Ælfric,[6] tribute amounting to 10,000 pounds was given to the Danes for the first time so that they might give up the numerous plunderings, burnings, and the slaughter of men which they frequently committed around the sea coast, and maintain a firm peace with them.[7] St Oswald the archbishop consecrated the abbey of Ramsey, which he and God's friend Æthelwine, ealdorman of East Anglia, had built with divine help, being supported by the

[5] ASC CDE record the Ipswich raid without mentioning the Scandinavian leaders. ASC A (993; for this date see Bately, *MS A* pp. lix-lxii, 79) records an Olaf who raided Folkestone, went on to Sandwich, and ravaged Ipswich before coming to Maldon.

[6] JW's account of the Maldon campaign is closer to ASC A than to CDE. ASC CDE do not report Ealdormen Æthelweard and Ælfric as joining Archbishop Sigeric in giving this advice. A later Canterbury addition to ASC A (993) speaks of Sigeric and Bishop Ælfheah of Winchester as advisers on making peace.

[7] ASC CDE. A (which had mentioned Olaf as the leader, see above, n. 5, but not the later payment of tribute) speaks of Æthelred acting as godfather at his baptism after the peace. The names of the Scandinavian leaders and of the English ealdormen (which are peculiar to JW) are found in the treaty between Æthelred and the Vikings (A. J. Robertson, *The Laws of the Kings of England from Edmund to Henry I* (Cambridge, 1925), pp. 56–63). ASC A does not mention tribute but speaks simply of peace being made after the Maldon campaign and of Æthelred acting as godfather at Olaf's baptism.

Æscwii Lincoliensis episcopi, .vi. idus Nou., feria .iii., conse-crauit.[1]

[992] (viii) 1014 *b*Sanctus Oswaldus archiepiscopus, indictione .v., .ii. kalend. Martii, feria secunda, transiens ex hac uita, regni celestis gaudia conscendit, et Wigorne in ecclesia sancte Marie quam ipse a fundamentis construxerat requiescit. Cui uenerabilis Medeshamstudensis abbas Aldulfus successit, pro quo Kenulfus abbatis iure fungitur. Nec diu post excessum beati Oswaldi egregie dux memorie Atheluuinus, Dei amicus, defunctus est,[2] qui fratribus suis Ætheluuoldo, Alfuuoldo et Ægelsino, licet iunior etate, illos tamen *mansuetudine, pietate, bonitate, et iustitia excellebat*, et, ut uir maxime honestatis et munditie, *Paradisi ciuibus, ut*i *credi libet, est allectus*, cuius corpus *maximo cum honore* Ramesegiam *delatu*m, a sancto Ælphego Wintoniensi episcopo est tumulatum.[3] Consilio iussuque regis Anglorum Ægelredi pro-cerumque suorum de tota Anglia robustiores Lundonie congregate sunt naues quas rex, [4]lectis instruens militibus,[4] illis Alfricum, [4]cuius supra meminimus,[4] et Thoredum duces, Ælfstanum Wiltoniensem[5] et Æscuuium episcopos prefecit, mandans ut, si quo modo possent, Danorum exercitum [6]in aliquo portu[6] circum-uallando comprehenderent. Verum dux Alfricus clanculo nuntium ad hostes mittens, hortatur [4]ut sibi consulerent, precauerent ne ab exercitu regis improuise circumuenirentur.[4] Ipse uero dux, exem-plum flagitii singulare, nocte que precessit diem quo cum Danis

---

a–a Æscwii Lincoliensis episcopi] *add. at line-end extending into mg.* C[1], *these words are in G, but not in* HR   *b* *see App. B for additions (i) in text, and (ii) in mg., with signe de renvoi* B[1]

---

[1] The account of the consecration of Ramsey seems to be connected with the description in Byrhtferth, *Vita Oswaldi*, v. 11, (*Historians of the Church of York*, i. 463, 469) of Oswald's visit to Ramsey shortly before his death. Ramsey tradition reports two consecrations, one on 8 Nov. 974 (*Chronicon abbatiae Rameseiensis*, ed. W. D. Macray (RS lxxxiii; London, 1886), p. 44), and, after a collapse of some buildings, a reconse-cration in the year (i.e. 991) before Oswald's death in the spring of 992 (ibid., pp. 85–101). The JW MS P has correctly changed the weekday from Tuesday to Sunday. According to Byrhtferth, *Vita Oswaldi*, v. 11 (*Historians of the Church of York*, i. 463), Bishop Æscwig of Dorchester was present on the occasion of Oswald's visit to Ramsey. *HR* omission of Æscwig at iii. 116 (ii. 134) may indicate that it used an early recension of JW.

[2] ASC CDE record these deaths and the successions at York, Worcester, and Peterborough, F simply the death of Oswald and the succession at York and Worcester. In the first three, the successions are separated from the deaths (with which

assistance of Æscwig, bishop of Lincoln, on Tuesday, 8 November.[1]

[992] St Oswald the archbishop departed this life on Monday, 29 February, in the fifth indiction, and ascended to the joys of heaven. He rests in the church of St Mary at Worcester, which he himself had raised from the foundations. Ealdwulf, the venerable abbot of Peterborough, succeeded him, and in his place Cenwulf exercised the abbatial office. Not long after the death of the blessed Oswald, Æthelwine, an ealdorman of glorious memory, and God's friend, died.[2] He, although younger in age than his brothers Æthelwold, Ælfwold, and Æthelsige, nevertheless outstripped them in meekness, piety, goodness, and justice, and, as a man of extreme honesty and purity, has now been admitted to the company in Paradise, as we are happy to believe. His body was borne to Ramsey with the utmost honour, and buried by St Ælfheah, bishop of Winchester.[3] On the advice and orders of Æthelred, king of the English, and of his nobles, stronger ships were assembled at London from all England, and these the king, [4]filling them with picked soldiers,[4] put under the command of the ealdormen Ælfric [4](whom we mentioned above)[4] and Thored, and the bishops Ælfstan of Wilton[5] and Æscwig, commanding that if they by any means could, they should take the Danish army [6]in any port[6] where they could blockade it. But the ealdorman Ælfric, secretly sending a messenger to the enemy, urged [4]them to take care they were not surrounded unexpectedly by the king's army.[4] Indeed, the ealdorman himself, an extraordinary example of shameful behaviour, on the night before the day when the English had determined to fight bravely against the Danes, fled secretly to

they are linked in JW) by the entry on national defensive preparations. JW added the burial of Oswald in the cathedral at Worcester, which he had founded, and the day of his death, which agrees with Byrhtferth, *Vita Oswaldi*, v. 20 (*Historians of the Church of York*, i. 472). As late as 995, Ealdwulf attests only as *electus* (S 885 K 688, S 886 K 692).

[3] Byrhtferth, *Vita Oswaldi*, iii. 14, v. 21 (*Historians of the Church of York*, i. 429, 475). The burial-places of Oswald and Æthelwine are in Byrhtferth, from whom JW also derived the information about Æthelwine's family, though unlike him, he names a fourth brother *Ægelsinus*.

[4–4] No equivalent in ASC.

[5] Ælfstan's see is not mentioned in ASC. JW's Ramsbury is wrong, for Ælfstan was bishop either of London or Rochester.

[6–6] ASC has 'ahwær utan'.

Angli statuerant fortiter dimicare, clam omnibus ad classem profugit Danicam, et cum eis mox fedam iniit fugam. Quod ubi cognouit classis regia, fugientes insequitur. Nec mora ex illis una tantum nauis capitur, omnique in ea multitudine cesa spoliatur, ceteris per fugam lapsis,[1] solum Lundonienses cum Orientalibus Anglis [2]fortuito casu[2] occurrerunt, commisoque prelio, multa milia Danorum occiderunt. Insuper etiam ducis Alfrici nauem, cum militibus et armis, ipso per fugam uix elapso, coeperunt, et uictores extiterunt.[3]

[993] (ix) 1015 [a]Hoc anno predictus exercitus Danorum Bebbanburh infregit, et omnia que in ea sunt reperta secum asportauit. Dehinc ad ostium Humbre fluminis cursum suum dirigens, in Lindesege et in Norðhymbria, multis uillis incensis hominibusque cesis, magnam predam cepit, contra quos prouinciales quamplures conglobati properanter ascenderunt, sed cum prelium essent commissuri, duces exercitus Frana uidelicet Frithogist et Goduuinus, [4]quia ex paterno genere Danici fuerunt, suis insidiantes,[4] auctores fuge primitus extiterunt. Eodem anno, iussu regis Ægelredi, excecatus est Algarus predicti ducis Alfrici filius.[5]

[994] (x) 1016 Anlafus rex Norreganorum[b6] et Suuein rex Danorum,[6] die natiuitatis sancte Marie .xciiii. trieribus Lundoniam aduehuntur, quam mox effringere et incendere conantur, sed Dei sueque genitricis Marie iuuamine non sine paruo detrimento sui exercitus a ciuibus repelluntur. Vnde, [7]furore simul et tristitia exasperati,[7] eadem die recesserunt inde et primitus | in Eassaxonia et Cantia circaque ripas maris deinde in Suthsaxonia, Suthamtunensique prouincia uillas incendunt, agros deuastant, et sine respectu sexus quamplures ferro et flamma absumunt, predamque ingentem agunt. Ad postremum uero, equos sibi rapientes, multasque per *prouincias debachando* discurrentes, ne *sexui quidem muliebri, uel innocue paruulorum* pepercerunt *etati, quin*

p. 318

---

[a] see App. B for mg. addition with signe de renvoi B[1]   [b] over erasure C

---

[1] That Ealdorman Ælfric with all his men fled to the Danish fleet and was pursued by the English is perhaps JW's inference from ASC.
[2–2] No equivalent in ASC.

the Danish fleet with all his men, and soon took shameful flight with them. When the royal fleet learned of this, it pursued those fleeing. Without delay one single ship was taken from amongst them, and was plundered when the whole host on board had been slain. The others escaped by flight.[1] [2]By a fortunate chance[2] the Londoners with the East Anglians encountered them and joined battle, slaying many thousands of Danes. In addition, they took the ealdorman Ælfric's ship, with men and arms, when he himself had with difficulty escaped, and they were victorious.[3]

[993] In this year the aforementioned Danish army broke into Bamburgh, and carried off with them everything they found there. Afterwards, directing their course towards the mouth of the River Humber, they took great booty in Lindsey and Northumbria, burning many townships, and slaying many men. A large number of the local inhabitants assembled and went against them in haste, but when they were on the point of joining battle, the army's leaders, Fræna, that is Frithugils, and Godwine, [4]because they were Danish on their father's side, betrayed their own people[4] and were the true initiators of the rout. In the same year, at the command of King Æthelred, Ælfgar, son of the aforementioned ealdorman Ælfric, was blinded.[5]

[994] Olaf, king of the Norwegians,[6] and Swein, king of the Danes[6] came to London at the Nativity of St Mary with ninety-four ships, and tried to break into and burn the city, but with the help of God and his mother Mary they were driven back by the citizens, not without some small damage to their armies. Hence, [7]enraged by both fury and sorrow,[7] they withdrew from there the same day, and, first in the coastal areas of Essex and Kent, then in Sussex and Hampshire, they burned townships, laid waste fields and, without respect of sex, destroyed very many with sword and flame, and took great booty. Finally, seizing horses for their own use, they rode madly about through many provinces, not sparing either women or innocent children, but they brutally

---

[3] The entry on the naval preparations and abortive expedition is in ASC C-F (F much shorter).
[4-4] No equivalent in ASC.
[5] ASC C-F (F is shorter). ASC name Fræna and Frithugils as two separate leaders.
[6] JW identifies the kingdoms of Olaf and Svein.   [7-7] Not in ASC.

uniuersos atrocitate ferina contraderent morti.[1] Tunc rex Ægelredus, procerum suorum consilio, ad eos legatos misit promittens tributum et stipendium ea conuentione illis se daturum ut a sua crudelitate omnino desisterent. Qui petitioni regis acquiescentes, ad suas regressi sunt naues, et sic ad Suthamtun totus congregatus exercitus ibidem hiemauerunt, quibus de tota Wessaxonia stipendium dabatur, de tota uero Anglia tributum, quod erat .xvi. milia librarum, dependebatur. Interea iussu regis Ægelredi, Wintoniensis[2] episcopus Alphegus, nobilisque dux Atheluuardus regem Anlafum adierunt, obsidibusque datis illum ad regiam uillam Andeafaran ubi rex manebat cum honore deduxerunt, quem rex honorifice suscepit, confirmari ab episcopo fecit, sibi in filium adoptauit, regioque munere donauit. Ille uero se non amplius ad Angliam cum exercitu uenturum, regi Ægelredo promisit, et ad naues postea rediit, estateque imminente ad patriam deuectus, sua promissa bene custodiuit.*ª3*

[995] (xi) 1017 Cometa uisa est.

[HL]	[C³BP]
Et Siricus Dorubernensis archiepiscopus obiit, et*ᵇ* Alfricus Wiltuniensium episcopus successit.*ᶜ4*	*ᵈ*Siricio*ᵉ* Dorubernie archiepiscopo successit Alfricus Wiltunensium episcopus illique successit ad Wiltuniam Brihtwoldus *ᶠ*monachus Glæstoniensis.*ᵈᶠ5*

*ᵍ*Lindisfarne id est*ʰ* dicitur insula a uulgo Haligealond apellatur. In mari sita est, maris recessus cotidie intrantibus siccum prebet iter. In hac insula sedes episcopales sunt Cuthberti et antecessorum eius, successorum quoque multo tempore. Ea uero tempestate quo Hinguar et Hubba Angliam uastauerunt, Eardulfus qui tunc

---

ª 995 *n. g incorporated here* B   *ᵇ* cui successit L   *ᶜ om.* L   *ᵈ⁻ᵈ* Siricio . . . Glæstoniensis] *written over erasure and running on to* 996 C³, *compressed writing at end of annal* B   *ᵉ* mortuo *interlin.* B¹   *ᶠ⁻ᶠ* monachus Glæstoniensis] *squeezed in at line-end and extending over numerals for* 995, *and meant to refer to* Brihtwoldus C³, *extending into mg.* B¹   *ᵍ* Lindisfarne . . . translata est *(p. 446)] add. mg. alongside* 994–1000 C²?, *incorporated at* 994 *n. a* B, *outer mg. alongside* 992–94 P³, *incorporated* 995 G   *ʰ long single stroke possibly standing for* id est *follows* Lindisfarne CHL, *erasure in space for one letter follows* B

---

[1] *HE* ii. 20.
[2] The see is identified by JW.

did to death absolutely all.[1] Then King Æthelred, on the advice of
his nobles, sent embassies to them, promising that he would give
them tribute and maintenance if they would give up their cruel
practices altogether. They fell in with the king's request, returned
to their ships, and so, assembling the whole army at Southampton,
they wintered there. The whole of Wessex gave them provisions,
but all England paid tribute amounting to 16,000 pounds.
Meanwhile, at King Æthelred's command, Ælfheah, bishop of
Winchester,[2] and the noble ealdorman Æthelweard approached
King Olaf and, when they had given him hostages, conducted him
ceremonially to the royal township of Andover where the king was
staying, and the king received him with honour, had him
confirmed by the bishop, adopted him as his son, and endowed
him with a royal gift. He promised King Æthelred that he would
not come to England again with an army, and then he returned to
his ships, and, as summer was drawing near, he sailed away to his
homeland, and was faithful to his word.[3]

[995] A comet was seen.

And Sigeric, archbishop of Canterbury, died, and Ælfric, bishop of Wiltshire, succeeded him.[4]	Ælfric, bishop of Wiltshire, succeeded Sigeric, archbishop of Canterbury, and Brihtwold, a monk of Glastonbury, succeeded him to the see of Wilton.[5]

Lindisfarne is said to be an island, and it is commonly called
Holy Island. It is set in the sea and everyday low tide permits
those approaching it to make a dry journey. The episcopal see of
Cuthbert and his predecessors, and also of his successors for a
long time, was on this island, but in the time when Inguar and
Hubba laid waste England Eardwulf, who was then bishop of the

---

[3] ASC CDEF (which has a shorter version). JW agrees with ASC with the exception
of the embellishment from Bede. That the departure of Olaf occurred in the following
year JW makes clear by 'estate imminente'.

[4] ASC C-F (995) record the comet and the death of Sigeric, F adding the succession
of Ælfric and (like JW) identifying his see. A (994) gives his death and the succession
at Canterbury, but does not refer to the comet. The day of Sigeric's death, 28 Oct., is
entered opposite 994 in the Easter tables in London, BL, Cotton MS Titus D. XXVII
(Keynes, Diplomas, p. 251 nn. 40–1).

[5] C³'s addition on Brihtwold's succession at Ramsbury, presumably based on WM,
GP ii. 83 (p. 182), is incorrect: Ælfric retained Ramsbury in plurality until his death in
1005.

episcopus erat Lindisfarnensis ecclesie cum his qui in ecclesia erant incorruptum sancti Cuthberhti corpus tollens, insulam reliquit propter barbarorum immanitatem, et per aliquot annos incertis sedibus cum sancti Cuthberhti corpore uagabatur donec in loco qui Cunegaceastre dicitur episcopalis cathedra esset locata, quod factum est tempore Ælfredi regis Anglorum. Post annorum curricula multorum, regnante Ægelredo rege Anglorum, corpus sanctum, sicut oraculo celesti premonstratum fuerat, in Dunhelmum perlatum est atque sedes episcopalis ibidem constituta. Iccirco sanctus Beda Lindisfarnensem ecclesiam ponit, ubi primitus sedes erat episcopalis, tempore nanque Bede nulla erat cognitio Dunhelmi. Anno uero ab incarnatione Domini nostri Iesu Christi nongentesimo nonagesimo quinto sedes episcopalis in Dunhelmum translata est.^{a1}

[996] (xii) 1018
[HL]
^{b}Alfricus Dorobernie archiepiscopus consecratur.^{bc2}

[997] (xiii) 1019 Danorum exercitus, ^{3}qui remanserat^3 in Anglia, circumnauigata Westsaxonia, ostium Sabrine fluminis intrauit, et nunc septentrionalem Brytanniam, nunc Cornubiam, nunc in Domnania,^{d} Wecedport deuastauit, uillisque quamplurimis incensis, multas hominum strages dedit. Deinde, Penuuithstort regirato, in ostium fluminis Tamere, ^{3}Domnaniam et Cornubiam sequestrantis,^{3} deuectus, ^{3}nauibus prosiliuit, nulloque prohibente,^{3} usque ad Lydefordam suum incendium continuauit, et cedes hominum reiterauit. Ad hec etiam Ordulfi Domnanie primatis monasterium, quod Teauistoce nominatur, combussit, ingentique preda onustus, ad naues repedauit, ^{3}eodemque in loco hiemauit.^{3,4}

[C^{3}BP]
^{e}Defuncto Sigaro Wellensi episcopo, successit Alwinus.^{e5}

---

^{a} see above, p. 444 n. g $^{b-b}$ Alfricus . . . consecratur] initial Æ visible through erasure of this entry C ^{c} see App. B for addition B ^{d} Domnaniam HL $^{e-e}$ Defuncto . . . Alwinus] add. at line-end C^3, om. HL

church of Lindisfarne, left the island with those of his church because of the cruelty of the barbarians, bearing the incorrupt body of St Cuthbert, and for many years he wandered about among insecure settlements with St Cuthbert's body until the episcopal see could be established in a place called Chester-le-Street, which occurred in the time of Alfred, king of the English. After the course of many years, in the reign of Æthelred, king of the English, the holy body, just as had been revealed by the heavenly oracle, was borne into Durham and the episcopal see established there. St Bede located the church at Lindisfarne, where the episcopal see was at first, since in his time Durham was not known. But in the 995th year from the incarnation of Our Lord Jesus Christ the bishop's seat was translated to Durham.[1]

[996] Ælfric was consecrated
       archbishop of Canter-
       bury.[2]

[997] The Danish army [3]which had remained[3] in England sailed around Wessex, entered the mouth of the River Severn, and, now in north Wales, now in Cornwall, now Devon, laid waste Watchet, burning many townships, and slaying many men. Then, when they had sailed round Land's End, they sailed into the mouth of the river Tamar, [3]which separates Devon from Cornwall, disembarked and, with no opposition,[3] continued their burning as far as Lydford, and repeated the massacre. In addition, they also burned the monastery of Ordwulf, ealdorman of Devon, which is called Tavistock, and, laden with great booty, returned to their ships. [3]They wintered in the same place.[3,4]

On the death of Sigar, bishop of Wells, Ælfwine succeeded.[5]

---

[1] C²?'s marginal addition on the see of Cuthbert and the wanderings of his remains is presumably based on the longer account in *HDE* iii. 1 (i. 78–80), but verbal borrowings are hard to find.
[2] ASC CDE which add the place of the consecration, Christ Church, F adding (995) the place of election.
[3-3] No equivalent in ASC.   [4] ASC CDE 997. JW identifies Ordwulf's office.
[5] C³'s addition concerning Wells appears to be correct; see Robinson, *Wells*, p. 48, Keynes, *Diplomas*, Table 3.

[998] (xiiii) 1020   *Agapitus*[1] *centesimus .xxxvii. papa.*[2]

Memoratus paganorum exercitus ostium fluminis quod Frome dicitur appulsus, Dorsetaniam maxima ex parte deuastauit. Dein frequenter Insulam Vectam adiit, [3]sepe Dorsætaniam repetiit, moreque solito prede institit et quotienscunque[3] in Vecta iacuit de Suthsaxonia et de Suthamtunensi prouincia sibi uictum accepit. Aduersus tantam tempestatem multotiens congregatus est exercitus, sed quotiens prelium essent commissuri, Angli, aut insidiis aut aliquo infortunio impediti, terga uerterunt et hostibus uictoriam dederunt.[4]

[C³BP]

[a]Domnanie presule Ælfrico defuncto, successit Alwoldus, illique alter Alwoldus.[a][5]

[999] (xv) 1021 Sepedictus exercitus paganorum ostium Tamensis fluminis ingressus, per flumen Meodeuueage Roueceastram aduehitur, [6]eamque paucis diebus obsidione cinxit.[6] Ad quos repellendos conglobati Cantuuarienses, asperum cum eis prelium ineunt, sed [7]multi⟨s⟩[b] ex his et illis cesis,[7] Dani loco dominantur funeris.[8] Hinc equites effecti, occidentalem Cantie plagam ferme totam sunt demoliti. Qua re cognita, rex Anglorum Agelredus, suorum primatum consilio, et classem et pedestrem congregauit exercitum. Verum dum parate essent naues, [9]duces exercitus[9] de die in diem moram ceptis innectentes, populum[10] grauiter uexabant. Ad ultimum uero nec classica nec pedestris manus quicquam [11]communis utilitatis[11] agebat preter populi laborem, pecunie perditionem, hostium incitationem.[12]

[a–a] Domnanie . . . Alwoldus] *add. at line-end C³, om. HL*   [b] multi *CHBP*

---

[1] Presumably Agapitus II 946–55.   [2] Mar.
[3–3] No equivalent in ASC.
[4] ASC CDE, which insert the comment on English ineffectiveness between the Danish military activities in Dorset and Wight.
[5] Ælfwold of Crediton witnesses from 987 (*S* 863, P. H. Sawyer, *Charters of Burton Abbey* (Anglo-Saxon Charters, ii; Oxford, 1979), no. 25, pp. 41–2) to 1011 (*S* 923, Sawyer, *Charters of Burton*, no. 33, pp. 64–5). The only evidence for two bishops of the same name in this period, apart from this entry, is in JW *Epis. Lists*.
[6–6] No equivalent in ASC C–F for this phrase, which makes clear that Rochester was besieged.

[998] Agapitus[1] the 137th pope.[2]

The aforementioned heathen army landed at the mouth of the river which is called Frome, and laid waste most of Dorset. Then they made frequent landings on the Isle of Wight, [3]returning often to Dorset, and after their usual custom were eager for booty and, as often[3] as they landed on the Isle of Wight they took their provisions from Sussex and Hampshire. Against so great a disaster an army was many times mustered, but as often as battle was joined the English, hampered by treachery or by some other misfortune, turned their backs, and yielded the victory to the enemy.[4]

> On the death of Ælfric, bishop
> of Devon, Ælfwold succeeded,
> and to him another Ælfwold.[5]

[999] The oft-mentioned pagan army entered the mouth of the river Thames, went up the Medway to Rochester [6]and, in a few days, besieged it on all sides.[6] The men of Kent gathered to repel them, fought bitterly with them but, when [7]many had been slain on both sides,[7] the Danes gained the mastery of the place of death.[8] From this point they became horsemen, and almost destroyed the whole of western Kent. When he learned of this, Æthelred, king of the English, on the advice of his chief men, assembled a fleet and an army of footsoldiers. But when the ships were ready, the [9]leaders of the army[9] delayed setting out from day to day, severely annoying the people,[10] and in the end neither the naval nor the land forces achieved anything [11]of general benefit,[11] but caused the labour of the people, the loss of money and the encouragement of the enemy.[12]

[7–7] No equivalent in ASC, which speaks of the Kentish levy turning and fleeing.

[8] ASC E explains that the Danish victory was caused by the inadequate support provided.

[9–9] 'Duces exercitus' suggests closeness to ASC C 'ylcodan þa deman' against D 'ilkede man' and E 'elkede man'.

[10] ASC: 'wretched people on the ships'.   [11–11] No equivalent in ASC.

[12] ASC C–E. JW slightly compresses the latter part of the annal on the ineffectiveness of English military activity. His 'nec classica nec pedestris manus' could suggest agreement with C, which refers to sea and land activity, against E, which refers to 'scipfyrding' only, and D, which refers explicitly to neither.

[1000] (xvi) 1022 Danorum classis prefata hoc anno Nortmanniam petit.[1] Rex Agelredus terram Cumbrorum fere totam depopulatus est. Hic sue classi mandauit ut, circumnauigata
septentrionali Bryttannia,[2] in loco constituto sibi occurreret, [3]sed
ui uentorum prepedita[3] non potuit, | insulam tamen que Monege
dicitur deuastauit.[4]

p. 319

[1001] (xvii) 1023 [a]Inuentio corporis sancti Iuonis archiepiscopi.[a][5] Memoratus paganorum exercitus de Normannia[b]
Angliam reuectus, ostium fluminis Eaxe ingreditur, et mox ad
expugnandam urbem Exanceastram egreditur. Sed dum murum
illius destruere moliretur a ciuibus urbem uiriliter defendentibus
repellitur. Vnde [6]nimis exasperatus, [6]solito uillas succendendo,
agros depopulando, homines cedendo,[6] per Domnaniam[6] uagatur.
Quare Domnanienses et Sumerseatunenses in unum congregati in
loco qui dicitur Penho certamen cum eis ineunt, sed Angli [6]pro
militum paucitate[6] Danorum multitudinem non ferentes, fugam
capessunt, illi uero multa strage facta uictores existunt. Deinde
adeptis caballis, per totam fere Domnaniam peiora prioribus, mala
gesserunt, ingentique preda capta, naues repetierunt. Inde ad
Vectam Insulam cursum direxerunt et modo in ea, [6]modo in
Suthamtonia, modo in Dorseatania, [6]nullo obsistente, diu solite
prede institerunt,[c] et in homines ferro et in uillas igne sunt in tantum grassati ut cum illis nec classica manus nauali nec pedestris
exercitus certare auderet prelio terrestri. Iccirco et regi non parua
mestitia et populo indicibilis inerat tristitia.[7]

[1002] (xviii) 1024 *Otto tertius imperator obiit .x. kalend. Feb.,
sepultusque est Aquis.*[8]

[a–a] Inuentio . . . archiepiscopi] *add. mg. near last line of 1000 and first of 1001 C³?,
mg. alongside opening of 1001 P³, under 1001 G*   [b] Normannia *from* Nordmannia C,
Nordmannia P   [c] insisterunt H, insistentes L

---

[1] ASC CDE place this at the end of the annal and have 'summer' for JW's 'year'.
[2] ASC CDE speak of the fleet going round Chester.
[3–3] No reason is given in ASC for the failure of the fleet to meet the king at the
appointed time.
[4] ASC CDE.
[5] Goscelin, *Vita Sancti Ivonis* (*PL* clv. 86) gives this date for the alleged

[**1000**] The aforementioned Danish army went to Normandy this year.[1] King Æthelred laid waste almost all Cumbria. He commanded his fleet, when it had sailed around northern Britain,[2] to meet him at a place agreed but, [3]hindered by the force of the winds,[3] it could not. However, it laid waste the island called Man.[4]

[**1001**] The Invention of the body of St Ives the archbishop.[5] The aforementioned heathen army, on its return to England from Normandy, entered the mouth of the river Exe, and soon went out to attack Exeter. But, while striving to destroy the walls, they were driven off by the citizens' vigorous defence of the city. [6]Roused to extreme fury[6] by this, they roamed [6]through Devon[6] burning townships, laying waste fields, slaughtering men as usual. Therefore, the inhabitants of Devon and Somerset, having assembled at a place called Pinhoe, joined battle with them, but the English, unable to withstand the multitude of Danes [6]because of their own lack of soldiers,[6] took to flight. The Danes, indeed, emerged victorious after great slaughter. Then, when they had taken mounts, they committed crimes even worse than their earlier ones throughout almost the whole of Devon and, having taken great booty, returned to their ships. From there they turned their course to the Isle of Wight and now here, [6]now in Hampshire, now in Dorset,[6] they for a long time continued with their usual plundering with no opposition. They fell so violently upon men with the sword and upon townships with fire that neither the fleet at sea nor the footsoldiers on land dared contest with them in battle. And from this arose no small grief for the king and indescribable sorrow for the people.[7]

[**1002**] The Emperor Otto III died on 23 January; he was buried at Aachen.[8]

discovery by the monks of Ramsey of the remains of the Persian archbishop Ivo or St Ives.

   [6–6] These may be inferences of JW's.

   [7] ASC C–F are close to JW's account; A is different though it describes the same campaign. In the last sentence, ASC's comment on the general demoralization is specifically related to king and people by JW, and its statement that the Danes never ceased from their evil-doing is omitted.

   [8] Mar.

Rex Anglorum Agelredus, habito consilio cum regni sui primatibus, utile duxit a Danis dextras accipere, illisque ut a malis cessar-
ent stipendium dare, et placabile tributum soluere.¹ Huius rei
gratia dux Leofsius ad eos est transmissus, qui cum uenisset
stipendium et tributum ut acciperent flagitauit. Illi uero legationem eius libenter amplectentes, petitis adquieuerunt, et pro
tenenda pace quantum tributi sibi dependeretur statuerunt. Nec
diu post .xxiiii. milia librarum illis persoluebantur. Interea idem
dux Leofsius*ᵃ* nobilem uirum Eafic summum regis prepositum
occidit, unde rex, ira succensus, patria illum expulit.² Eodem anno
Emmam, Saxonice Ælfgiuam uocatam, ducis Nortmannorum primi
Ricardi filiam, rex Ægelredus duxit uxorem.³ Aldulfus archipresul
Eboracensis, coepiscopis, abbatibus, presbiteris, monachis, religiosis quoque uiris aggregatis, sancti Oswaldi archipresulis ossa, anno
regis Anglorum Ægelredi .xxv., indictione .xv., .xvii. kalend. Maii,
feria .iiii., e tumulo leuauit et in scrinio quod parauerat honorifice
locauit.⁴ Et non multo post, id est, .ii. non. Maias,⁵ ipse defunctus
in ecclesia sancte Marie Wigorne est sepultus, cui successit abbas
Wlstanus.⁶ Quo etiam anno rex Ægelredus omnes Danos Angliam
incolentes, maiores et minores utriusque sexus occidere iussit, quia
illum*ᵇ* suosque primates uita regnoque priuare et totius Anglie
dominium sue ditioni conati sunt subdere.⁷

*ᶜRomanorum nonagesimus .iii.ᶜ Heinricus⁸ regnauit annis .xxii. Qui
die dominico .vii. idus Iunii electione populi laudatus in regem,ᵈ ipso
die ab archiepiscopo Mogontino Willigiso ante altare sancti Martini
consecratus et coronatus est.⁹*

ᵃ Leofsinus *HL*   ᵇ in die festiuitate sancti Britii *interlin. B¹?*
ᶜ⁻ᶜ (R)omanorum nonagesimus .iii.] *written over erasure C*   ᵈ rege *(N)*, regem
Mar.

---

¹ JW renders 'gafol gyldan' by 'stipendium . . . et tributum', but this could be
because ASC distinguishes 'metsunge' from 'gafol' later in the annal.
² ASC C-F have the same details of this truce, the killing of Æfic (not in F), and
the banishment of Leofsige (not in F), the royal 'ira succensus' being presumably reasonable inference.
³ ASC C-F speak of the queen, Richard's daughter, coming to England in the
spring, F naming her as Ymma (Ælfgiva interlineated) here and as Ælfgifu Emma
under 1017. JW explicitly refers to the marriage. She signs as Ælfgifu in 1004 (*S* 909
K 709, trans. Whitelock, *EHD*, no. 127, pp. 590–2).
⁴ Not in ASC. The translation is described in much greater detail by Eadmer in his
Miracula Sancti Oswaldi (*Historians of the Church of York*, ii. 45–6) and both he and
WM (*GP* iii. 115 (p. 250)) imply that it took place in 1003–4, but 1002 is correct, for

Æthelred, king of the English, having taken counsel with the leading men of his kingdom, considered it expedient to accept pledges from the Danes, and to give them provisions so that they would cease from evil-doing, and to pay them tribute by way of appeasement.[1] The ealdorman Leofsige was sent to them concerning this matter, and he, when he came, urged them to accept the maintenance and tribute. They gladly embraced his mission, agreed to his requests, and established the amount of tribute they should be paid for keeping the peace. Not long after this 24,000 pounds were paid to them. Meanwhile, that same ealdorman Leofsige slew the noble man Æfic, the king's high reeve, whereby the king, inflamed with anger, banished him from the country.[2] In the same year, King Æthelred married Emma, called Ælfgifu in English, daughter of Richard I, duke of the Normans.[3] Ealdwulf archbishop of York, in the presence of his fellow bishops, abbots, priests, monks, and pious laymen, raised the bones of St Oswald the archbishop from the tomb on Wednesday, 15 April, in the twenty-fifth year of Æthelred, king of the English, in the fifteenth indiction, and placed them ceremonially in the shrine he had prepared.[4] Not much later, that is on 6 May,[5] he himself died, and was buried in the church of St Mary, Worcester. Abbot Wulfstan succeeded him.[6] In that same year too, King Æthelred ordered all Danish settlers, greater and less, and of either sex, to be killed because they tried to deprive him and his leading men of life and rule, and to subdue the whole kingdom to their sway.[7]

Henry,[8] ninety-third emperor of the Romans, reigned twenty-two years. Acclaimed king by the election of the people on Sunday, 7 June, he was consecrated, and crowned on that very day by Willigis, archbishop of Mainz, before the altar of St Martin.[9]

Archbishop Ealdwulf, who was present at the translation, died in the summer of that year.

[5] ASC C-F only speak of Ealdwulf's death in the summer (not in F) without any more details. An 11th-c. Worcester calendar, Oxford, Bodleian MS Hatton 113, assigns 4 June ('ii Non. Jun.') as the day of his death, and it is possible that JW's 6 May ('ii Non Mai.') is a slip. ASC does not name Ealdwulf's successor.

[6] There is evidence that Wulfstan was bishop of London at the time of his promotion to York (see D. Whitelock, 'A note on the career of Wulfstan the Homilist', EHR, lii (1942), 460–5) and JW's 'abbas' seems misleading.

[7] ASC C-F (1002) give the precise date (St Brice's Day, 13 Nov.) of this massacre and speak of 'Deniscan men' as the intended victims.

[8] Henry II 1002–24.   [9] Mar.

[**1003**] (i) 1025   *Octauianus*[1] *.cxxxviii. papa.*[2]

Hoc anno rex Danorum Suuein per insilium, incuriam et traditionem Nortmannici comitis Hugonis, quem regina Emma Domnanie prefecit, ciuitatem Execeastram infregit, spoliauit, murum ab orientali usque ad occidentalem portam destruxit, et cum ingenti preda naues repetiit.[3] Post hec autem, cum Wiltoniensem prouinciam deuastaret, fortis exercitus de Suthhamtunensi et Wiltunensi prouinciis congregatus, uiriliter et constanter aduersus hostes pugnaturus ascendit. Sed cum tam prope essent exercitus ut alter alterum uidere quiuisset, Alfricus dux supra memoratus, qui loco ducis Anglis tunc extitit, antiquas artes statim prodidit et, simulata infirmitate, uomere cepit dicens se magnam infirmitatem incurrisse,[4] et ob hoc cum hostibus dimicare nequiuisse. Cuius inertiam et timiditatem ut uidit exercitus, a suis inimicis sine pugna diuertit mestissimus,[4] unde dictum est in antiquo prouerbio: tremiscente duce in prelio, ceteri omnes preliatores efficuntur pauidiores. Suuein autem uidens Anglorum inconstantiam, ad ciuitatem Wiltoniam suum duxit exercitum eamque deuastauit et incendit. Simili quoque modo Searebyriam consumpsit et post suas naues repetiit.[5]

Kilianus abbas Scottorum sancti Martini, ipseque Scottus, obiit .xix. kalend. Ianuarii. Helias Scottus post eum successit.[6]

[**1004**] (ii) 1026   Rex Danorum Suuein cum sua classe Northuuic aduectus, illam deuastauit | et incendit. Tunc magne strenuitatis dux Eastanglorum Vlfketel,[7] quia ex improuiso uenit nec contra eum spatium congregandi exercitum habuit, cum maioribus Eastanglie habito consilio, pacem cum eo pepigit. Verum ille, dirupto foedere, tertia post hec ebdomada cum copiis suis latenter e nauibus prosiliens, Theodfordam inuasit, deuastauit, nocte una in ea mansit, diluculo incendit. Quo cognito, dux Vlfketel quibusdam de prouincialibus mandauit ut hostium naues confringerent. At illi [8]uel non audebant uel[8] iussa perficere negligebant. Ipse uero

---

[1] Misplaced and repeated John XII 955–64.
[2] Mar.
[3] ASC CDEF (1003) refer to the sack of Exeter 'on account of the French ceorl Hugh, whom the queen had appointed as her reeve'. JW is fuller about the sack, and gives Hugh the rank of count and authority over Devon.
[4-4] ASC simply says: 'thus he betrayed the people whom he should have led'.
[5] ASC CDEF (F briefer). Here JW seems very close to ASC.

[1003] Octavian[1] the 138th pope.[2]

In this year through the evil counsel, negligence, and treachery of the Norman Earl Hugh, whom Queen Emma had put in command of Devon, Swein, king of the Danes, broke into the city of Exeter, despoiled it, destroyed the wall from the east gate to the west, and returned to his ships with great booty.[3] After this, however, while he was plundering Wiltshire, a strong army from Hampshire and Wiltshire assembled, and came to fight vigorously and unflinchingly against the enemy. But when the armies were close enough to see one another, Ælfric, the ealdorman already referred to, who was then in command of the English, at once revealed his old tricks and, feigning illness, began to vomit, saying that he had fallen seriously ill [4]and therefore could not fight with the enemy. When the army saw his inactivity and cowardice, they turned away from their enemies in deepest grief, without battle.[4] As it is said in the old proverb: 'A leader who trembles in battle makes all the other fighters more fearful.' Swein, seeing the irresolution of the English, led his army to the city of Wilton, and plundered and burned it. In a like manner he destroyed Salisbury as well and then returned to his ships.[5]

Kilian, abbot of St Martin's of the Irish, and himself an Irishman, died on 14 December. Helias, an Irishman, succeeded him.[6]

[1004] Swein, king of the Danes, landed with his fleet at Norwich, and pillaged and burnt it. Then, when Ulfketel, ealdorman of East Anglia[7] and a man of great vigour, had taken counsel with the nobles of East Anglia, he made peace with Swein because he had come unexpectedly, and he, Ulfketel, had no time to muster an army. But Swein broke the treaty in the third week after this: secretly emerging from his ships with his troops he attacked Thetford, pillaged it, spent one night in it, and burnt it at dawn. When Ealdorman Ulfketel heard of this, he ordered some of the people of the region to break up the enemy's ships but they [8]either did not dare or[8] did not bother to carry out his orders. But

---

[6] Mar.
[7] Ulfketel is not described as ealdorman in ASC or in the charters; see Keynes, *Diplomas*, p. 208 n. 199.
[8–8] No equivalent in ASC.

interim quam citius potuit clam suum congregans exercitum aduersus hostes audacter ascendit. Quibus[a] ad naues repedantibus, [1]non equa manu militum[1] illis occurrit, durissimumque cum eis prelium commisit, multisque ex his et ex illis cesis, nobiliores quique de Eastanglia corruerunt, Dani uero uix euaserunt, sed si uires Eastanglorum iam adessent, nullo modo naues suas repeterent, ut enim ipsi testati sunt, durius et asperius bellum in Anglia nunquam experti sunt quam illis dux Vlfketel intulerat.[2]

[1005] (iii) 1027   Hoc anno dira magnaque fames Angliam inuasit, quapropter rex Danorum Suuein Denemarciam reuertitur, post non longum tempus reuersurus.[3]

[C³BP]
[b]Aluuino Wellensi episcopo defuncto, successit Liuingus[c] [d]qui et Alstanus.[bd4]

[1006] (iiii) 1028   Alfricus Dorubernensis archiepiscopus obiit,[e] cui Wintoniensis episcopus Alphegus successit, et pro illo Kenulfus, [f]Burgensis abbas,[f] episcopatum suscepit.[5] Rex Ægelredus Wlfgeatum Leouece filium, quem pene omnibus plus dilexerat, propter iniusta iudicia et superba que gesserat opera, possessionibus omnique honore priuauit.[6] Dolosus et perfidus Edricus Streona dolum aduersus nobilem ducem Ælfhelmum cogitans apud Scrobbesbyrig magnum ei parauit conuiuium ad quod, cum inuitatus uenisset, suscepit eum Edricus quasi suus familiaris amicus. Sed insidiis preparatis, .iii. uel .iiii. die conuiuii illum secum uenatum in siluam duxit, ubi cunctis circa uenationem

---

[a] Thedfordia interlin. B[5]   [b–b] Aluuino . . . Alstanus] add. at line-end C³, om. HL   [c] Alstanus Liuingus B   [d–d] qui et Alstanus] interlin. above Liuingus C³, Aldstanus interlin. above Liuingus B¹, et East Anglia add. P   [e] see App. A for addition LP[5] (mg. with signe de renvoi P)   [f–f] Burgensis abbas] interlin. C¹, om. HL

[1–1] No equivalent in ASC.

[2] ASC C–F (F much shorter). JW rearranges the annal slightly here, perhaps for greater clarity. E omits the equivalent text after 'testati sunt'.

[3] ASC C–F, where Swein is not mentioned, and JW has nothing corresponding to ASC's rhetorical phrase describing the famine as being unprecedented.

[4] The pontificate of Ælfwine, who succeeded in 997 (above, p. 447 n. 5), must have been brief since his successor Lyfing attests in 998 (S 815 K 701, Keynes, Diplomas, Table 3). C³ interlineates 'qui et Æthelstanus' above Lyfing in JW Epis. Lists. The interlineations here, under 1013 and in JW Epis. Lists correspond to WM, GP i. 21 (p. 33)

in the meantime, he himself secretly mustered an army with all possible speed, and went boldly against the enemy. [1]With a band of soldiers not the equal of theirs,[1] he met them as they were returning to their ships, and engaged them in a most grievous battle, and many were slain on both sides, and all the greater men from East Anglia fell. The Danes escaped, but only just. But if the East Anglians had been in full force the Danes would certainly not have returned to their ships for, as they themselves attested, they had never experienced a harder or bitterer battle in England than that which the Ealdorman Ulfketel fought against them.[2]

[1005] In this year a great and terrible famine struck England, for which reason Swein, king of the Danes, returned to Denmark. He was to return not long after.[3]

> After the death of Ælfwine, bishop of Wells, Lyfing, also known as Ælfstan, succeeded him.[4]

[1006] Ælfric, archbishop of Canterbury, died; he was succeeded by Ælfheah, bishop of Winchester, in whose place Cenwulf, abbot of Peterborough, received the bishopric.[5] King Æthelred stripped Wulfgeat, son of Leofeca, whom he had loved more than almost all others, of his possessions and of every dignity because of the unjust judgements and arrogant deeds he had perpetrated.[6] The crafty and treacherous Eadric Streona, plotting to deceive the noble ealdorman Ælfhelm, prepared a great feast for him at Shrewsbury at which, when he came as a guest, Eadric greeted him as if he were an intimate friend. But on the third or fourth day of the feast, when an ambush had been prepared, he took him with him into the wood to hunt. When all were busy with the

'Liuingus qui et Ethelstanus', and ii. 90 (p. 194), 'Liuingus qui et Elstan'. ASC D 1019 refers to Archbishop Ælfstan, who was called Lyfing.

[5] ASC A (1005) C–F (1006) record the death of Archbishop Ælfric, to which the succession (A: consecration) of Ælfheah is added by ASC ACDEF (1006). JW identifies Ælfheah's see as Winchester and presumably infers Cenwulf's succession from the record of his death entered later in the annal and in ASC C–F. ASC EF refer to Brihtwold's succession to the bishopric of Ramsbury which is entered by C[3] under 995. The interlineated 'Burgensis abbas' may be derived from GP ii. 76 (p. 170).

[6] ASC CDE simply record the confiscation of Wulfgeat's property. On Wulfgeat and JW, see Keynes, Diplomas, pp. 192–3, 210–11,

occupatis, quidam Scrobbesbyriensis carnifex Goduuinus Porthund, id est oppidi canis, quem multo ante donis magnis multisque promissionibus pro patrando facinore excecauerat Edricus, ex insidiis subito prosiluit et ducem Ælfhelmum nefarie peremit.[1] Paruo interiecto tempore, filii eius Wlfheagus et Vfegetus, iussu regis Ægelredi apud Cocham ubi ipse tunc degebat cecati sunt.[2] Kenulfus Wintoniensis episcopus obiit cui Atheluuoldus successit.[3] Mense dehinc Iulio[4] Danorum classis[5] innumera Angliam aduecta, portum Sandicum subiit, et cede et incendio obuia queque consumens, [6]modo in Cantia, modo in Suthsaxonia[6] maximam predam egit. Ob hoc rex Ægelredus de Mercia et Wessaxonia exercitum congregauit et cum eis fortiter dimicare statuit. Sed illi cum eo palam confligere nullatenus uoluerunt, uerum nunc in his, nunc in illis locis, rapinas frequentes exercuerunt, et mox ad naues solito repedabant, eoque modo per totum autumnum Anglorum uexabant exercitum.[7] Quo domum redeunte, nam hiemps imminebat, illi cum enormi preda Vectam Insulam adiere, et ibidem usque ad Natiuitatem Domini mansere. Qua adueniente, quia rex tunc temporis in Scrobbesbyriensi prouincia morabatur, per Suthhamtunensem prouinciam ad Bearrucscire uenerunt, et Readingum, Walingafordam, Ceolesegiam uicosque quamplures combusserunt.[8] Inde mouentes, Eascesdune transito, Cuuicelmeslauue[a] adierunt. Vnde per aliam uiam reuertentes, iuxta Kenetan incolas loci paratos ad prelium offenderunt statimque cum eis commiserunt, illosque fugauerunt, et postmodum cum preda quam ceperant ad naues repedarunt.[9]

[1007] (v) 1029 *Ciclus decennouenalis .xxvi. incipit indictione quinta.*[10]

---

[a] *gap between* Cuui *and* cel. C.

---

[1] ASC C–F simply record the killing of Ealdorman Ælfhelm without involving Eadric Streona in the crime. Hemming is apparently the first to call Eadric 'Streona id est adquisitor' (*Hemming*, i. 280). JW consistently uses this pejorative term to describe Eadric.

[2] ASC C–F again simply record the blinding of Wulfheah and Ufegeat, but do not identify them as Ælfhelm's sons, though D. Whitelock, *Anglo-Saxon Wills*, p. 153 seems to provide supporting evidence. Cookham was a royal residence.

[3] The names of Cenwulf's see and his successor are not given by ASC C–F when they record his death.

dorman Ælfhelm.[1] After a short space of time his sons, Wulfheah and Ufegeat, were blinded, at King Æthelred's command, at Cookham, where he himself was then staying.[2] Cenwulf, bishop of Winchester, died. Æthelwold succeeded him.[3] Then in July[4] an immense Danish fleet[5] came to England and entered the port of Sandwich; the Danes destroyed whatever they came across with fire and slaughter, and [6]now in Kent, now in Sussex[6] they took very great booty. For this reason King Æthelred mustered an army from Mercia and Wessex, and resolved to fight fiercely against them. But the Danes were far from willing to fight a pitched battle. They pillaged constantly, now here, now there, and soon returned to their ships, as was their custom, and in that way they harassed the army of the English all autumn.[7] On their homeward journey, for winter was approaching, they landed on the Isle of Wight with their enormous booty, and stayed there until Christmas. When Christmas came, as the king was at that time staying in Shropshire, they came through Hampshire to Berkshire, and burned Reading, Wallingford, Cholsey, and very many villages.[8] Moving on from there, they crossed Ashdown, and came to Cuckamsley Knob. Returning from there by another road, they met, near the Kennet, the local inhabitants, ready for battle, and attacked them on the spot, and put them to flight and afterwards returned to their ships with the booty they had taken.[9]

[1007] The twenty-sixth cycle of nineteen years begins in the fifth indiction.[10]

In this year Æthelred, king of the English, on the advice of his leading men, despatched envoys to the Danes under orders to inform them that he was willing to give them provisions and tribute on condition that they desisted from plundering and kept a

---

[4] ASC CDE say the fleet came after 'midsummer'.

[5] Only ASC E describes the fleet as Danish (F 'Danish army').

[6-6] No equivalent in ASC.   [7] ASC puts this differently.

[8] That the raid into Berkshire took place during or because of Æthelred's withdrawal to Shropshire (which is mentioned at a later point in ASC) could be inferred from ASC.

[9] ASC C-F (F much shorter). Apart from the omission of the important information that the Danes were bought off, JW's account of warfare in 1006 is considerably abbreviated.

[10] Mar.

Hoc anno rex Anglorum Ægelredus, cum consilio primatum suorum nuntios ad Danos legans, eis nuntiare mandauit quod sumptus et tributum eo tenore illis dare uellet ut a rapinis desisterent et pacem cum eo firmam tenerent. Cuius postulationi consenserunt et ex eo tempore de tota Anglia sumptus illis dabatur et tributum, quod erat .xxxvi. milia librarum, persoluebatur.[1] Quo etiam anno *rex Edricum* supra memoratum, Ægelrici *ᵃuel Leofuuiniᵃ* filium,[2] *hominem humili quidem genere, sed cui lingua diuitias ac nobilitatem comparauerat, callentem ingenio, suauem eloquio, et qui omnes id temporis mortales tum inuidia atque perfidia, tum superbia et crudelitate superauerat,*[3] Merciorum constituit ducem.[4] Cuius fratres extiterunt Brihtricus, Ælfricus,ᵇ Goda, Ægeluuinus, Ægeluuardus, Agelmarus, pater Wulnothi, patris Westsaxonum ducis Goduuini.[5]

[1008] (vi) 1030 Ciclus solis incipit .iiii. concurrentibus bissextilibus.

p. 321   Rex Anglorum Agelredus de trecentis et decem cassatis unam trierem, de nouem uero loricam et cassidem fieri, et per totam | Angliam naues intente precepit fabricari.[6] Quibus paratis, electos in eis milites cum alimentis posuit, et ut ab exterorum irruptionibus fines regni sui defenderent illas ad Sandicum portum congregauit.[7] Eo tempore uel paulo ante *frater* perfidi ducis Edrici Streone Brihtricus, [8]homo *lubricus*, ambitiosus et *superbus*,[8,9] apud regem iniuste[10] accusauit Suthsaxonicum ministrum Wlnothum[11] qui, [8]ne caperetur,[8] mox fugam iniit, et, .xx. nauibus adquisitis, circa ripas maris rapinas frequentes exercuit. Vbi autem regie

---

ᵃ⁻ᵃ uel Leofuuini. *interlin*] CᵗHᵗLᵗBᵗ, *om.* P   ᵇ *large space blank after* Ælfricus CHLB, *no blank space* P.

[1] These two sentences bring together the decision taken 'after the Christmas season' to buy peace from the Danes (ASC C–F 1006) and the payment of tribute under 1007 (C–F). CD have 36,000 pounds, EF 30,000.
[2] JW is the only source for the information concerning Eadric's father.
[3] Osbern, *Vita Elphegi* in *Anglia Sacra*, ii. 132, and the fuller text in BL Cotton MS Nero C. VII, fo. 52ʳᵃ. Note Osbern's 'et nobilitatem'.
[4] ASC C–F (1006) simply record Eadric's appointment as ealdorman of the Mercians.
[5] ASC C–F (1009) describe Brihtric as Eadric's brother, but JW is the only chronicle source for his other brothers, though there is supporting charter evidence (see Keynes, *Diplomas*, pp. 211–13). The main objection to JW's identification of Æthelmær as the father of Wulfnoth, father of Godwine, is that the father of Godwine was known

In this year Æthelred, king of the English, on the advice of his leading men, despatched envoys to the Danes under orders to inform them that he was willing to give them provisions and tribute on condition that they desisted from plundering and kept a stable peace with him. They agreed to his request, and from that time provisions were given to them by the whole of England and tribute amounting to 36,000 pounds was paid.[1] In that year also the king made the Eadric mentioned above (son of Æthelric that is Leofwine),[2] ealdorman of the Mercians.[4] He was indeed a man of low birth but his tongue had won for him riches and rank; ready of wit, smooth of speech, he surpassed all men of that time, both in malice and treachery and in arrogance and cruelty.[3] His brothers were Brihtric, Ælfric Goda, Æthelwine, Æthelweard, and Æthelmær, father of Wulfnoth, father of Godwine, ealdorman of the West Saxons.[5]

[1008] The solar cycle begins with four concurrents in a bissextile year.

Æthelred, king of the English, ordered ships to be built energetically all over England: one ship to be supplied from 310 hides, a breast-plate from nine.[6] When they had been prepared he filled them with picked soldiers and provisions, and assembled them at the port of Sandwich that they might defend the boundaries of his kingdom against foreign invaders.[7] At that time, or a little earlier, a brother of the treacherous ealdorman, Eadric Streona, Brihtric, [8]a slippery man, ambitious and arrogant,[8,9] unjustly[10] accused before the king Wulfnoth,[11] the ealdorman of the South Saxons, and he at once took flight [8]to avoid capture,[8] and, having acquired twenty ships, made frequent raids along the coast. When,

---

as Wulfnoth 'Cild' the South Saxon (ASC F 1009) and that ASC C–F (1009) would seem to make it clear that Wulfnoth Cild was not Eadric's nephew.

[6] ASC C–F (see Plummer, *Chronicle*, ii. 186–7, Whitelock, *ASC*, p. 88 n. 6 for the confusing readings of DE for 310 hides). Each corselet and helmet is to be raised from eight, not nine, hides in ASC.

[7] ASC C–F (1009). The naval assembly (presumably linked to the tax) is placed under 1008 by JW, who does not have ASC's remark on the ineffectiveness of this and other previous naval assemblies.

[8–8] No equivalent in ASC.

[9] Osbern, *Vita Elphegi* in *Anglia Sacra*, ii. 132, BL Cotton MS Nero C. VII, fo. 52ra.

[10] Not in ASC.

[11] ASC C–F (1009) call Wulfnoth 'Cild' but not 'minister', and all, save C, identify him as South Saxon.

classi nuntiatum est quod si quis uellet illum facile capere posset,
.lxxx. trieribus assumptis, ad persequendum illum Brihtricus profectus est. Sed cum diu prospere nauigasset, subito ualidissima
tempestas oborta naues diuerberauit, conquassauit, et in aridam
proiecit, quas Wlnothus non multo post exussit. Ea re cognita, rex
cum ducibus et proceribus domum rediit, classis uero iussu*a* illius
Lundoniam adiit, sicque totius populi maximus labor periit.[1]

[1009] (vii) 1031   *Leo*[2] *.cxxxix. papa.*[3]
Danicus comes Turkillus sua cum classe ad Angliam uenit.[4]
Exinde mense Augusto alia classis Danorum innumerabilis, cui
preerant duces Hemmingus et Eglafus, ad Tenetland insulam
applicuit, et predicte classi sine dilatione se iunxit.[5] Deinde ambe
Sandicum portum subeunt et, e nauibus prosilientes, ciuitatem
Cantuariam hostiliter adeunt, eamque effringere ceperunt. A
quibus mox ciues Cantuuarienses cum Orientalibus Cantuuariis
dextras petentes acceperunt, et eis .iii. milia libras pro firma pace
dederunt. Illi autem naues repetentes, ad Vectam Insulam cursum
direxerunt, dein in Suthsaxonia et Suthhamtunensi prouincia circa
ripas maris,[6] uti consueuerant, frequenter predam egerunt, et uillas
quamplures incenderunt. Quocirca rex Ægelredus de tota Anglia
exercitum congregauit [7]et per prouincias mari uicinas aduersus
illorum irruptiones locauit,[7] sed illi pro hoc non destiterunt quin
pro situ ubique locorum rapinas agerent. Quadam igitur uice, dum
illi solito longius a mari predatum descenderent, et onerati preda
redirent uiam, qua suas ad naues reuersuri erant, rex preoccupauit,
multis armatorum milibus instructus, et [7]ut totus erat exercitus
mori uel uincere paratus.[7] [8]At perfidus dux Edricus Streona, gener

---

a praedicta *interlin. B*[5]

---

[1] ASC CDEF (F much shorter) (1009), where the Brihtric episode, which began at
roughly the same time as the naval assembly, ends 'after Lammas' with the arrival of
Thorkell's army. Apart from transferring the annal to 1008, JW's account is close to
ASC save for some minor differences, which include omitting the final lament on the
ineffectiveness of past and present naval preparations.

[2] Misplaced Leo VIII 963–5.

[3] Mar.

[4] ASC CDEF (F much abbreviated) record, with the differences shown, the events
in this annal. Only C names Thorkell.

[5] The arrival of the second army is peculiar to JW. For the possibility that
Hemming was Thorkell the Tall's younger brother, and that Eglaf was the 'Eglaf dux'

however, it was announced to the royal fleet that if anyone wished to capture him he could easily do so, Brihtric took eighty ships, and set out in pursuit of him. But when he had sailed uneventfully for a long time a very violent storm suddenly blew up, and struck the ships, shattered them, and cast them up on dry land. Wulfnoth set them on fire not much later. When the king learned this he returned home with his ealdormen and nobles, but the fleet went to London at his command. And thus the extremely great labour of an entire nation came to nothing.[1]

[1009] Leo[2] the 139th pope.[3]

The Danish earl Thorkell came to England with his fleet[4] and afterwards, in August, another immense fleet of the Danes, under the command of Hemming and Eilaf, put in at the Isle of Thanet, and without delay joined the fleet aforementioned.[5] Both then entered the port of Sandwich, and the men, swarming down from the ships, marched with hostile intent on the city of Canterbury, and began to storm it. The citizens of Canterbury with the men of East Kent soon sought, and made an agreement with them and gave them 3,000 pounds for a secure peace. They, however, returning to their ships, steered a course for the Isle of Wight, then they pillaged frequently in Sussex and Hampshire around the coast,[6] as was their practice, and burned very many townships. For this reason King Æthelred mustered an army from the whole of England [7]and disposed it throughout the coastal districts to meet their incursions,[7] but they did not give up for all that but plundered at every possible place. On one occasion, therefore, when they had gone further from the sea for plunder than was customary, and returned weighed down with booty, the king, furnished with many thousands of armed men ready for battle, [7]and this army to a man prepared to conquer or die,[7] blocked the road by which they were to return to their ships. [8]But the treacherous

---

who attests diplomas in the earliest part of Cnut's reign, see *Encomium Emmae*, pp. 73, 86, 87, 90, and Keynes, *Diplomas*, p. 220. 'After Lammas' is ASC's date for Thorkell's arrival.

[6] JW may have added 'circa ripas maris' to locate the provinces ravaged by the Danes, and this could have led to the omission of Berkshire, which is mentioned in ASC.

[7–7] Not in ASC.

[8] In place of this sentence ASC here simply records the customary obstruction of Eadric.

eius, habuit enim in coniugio filiam eius Edgitham, et insidiis et perplexis orationibus ne prelium inirent, sed ea uice suos hostes abire permitterent, modis omnibus allaborauit, suasit et persuasit et a manibus Anglorum Danos, ut patrie proditor, eripuit et abire permisit.[1] Illi uero ab eis diuertentes, magno cum gaudio ad suas regressi sunt naues.[2] Post hec, emensa sancti Martini festiuitate, in Cantiam deuecti, in Tamensi flumine hiemalem stationem elegerunt, et sumptus de Eassaxonia aliisque prouinciis utrique ripe fluminis uicinis sibi rapuerunt. Sepe etiam ciuitatem Lundoniam aggressi, expugnare moliti sunt, sed a ciuibus non sine paruo suorum detrimento repulsi sunt.[3]

[C³BP]
*a*Defuncto Osbrihto Sæliensi episcopo, successit Ælmarus.*a*[4]

[1010] (viii) 1032 *Brun episcopus martyrizatus est.*[5]

[6]Memoratus Danorum exercitus, mense Ianuario, nauibus exilientes per saltum qui dicitur Ciltern Oxenofordam adeunt, eamque deuastantes incendunt, et sic in utraque parte Tamensis fluminis in reuertendo predam agunt. Quibus cum nuntiatum fuisset, exercitum aduersus illos Lundonie congregatum et cum eis prelium commissurum, [7]pars exercitus per septentrionalem ripam gradientis in loco qui dicitur Stane transiuit, et, in unum collecti,[7] predeque ubertate ditati, [8]per Suthregiam ad suas repedarunt naues,[8] quas tempore quadragesimali, dum consisterent in Cantia, refecerunt.[9] Post Pasca Eastangliam aduecti, et propter Gipesuuic nauibus egressi ad locum qui Ringmere dicitur,[10] ubi ducem Vlfketelum cognouere cum exercitu consedisse, perrexerunt, et

---

a-a Defuncto . . . Ælmarus] add. *at line-end and partly over erasure* C³, *om.* HL

---

[1] In place of this sentence ASC here simply records the customary obstruction of Eadric.
[2] This seems an inference from ASC.
[3] ASC
[4] For the evidence that Ordbriht of Selsey attests diplomas in 1007, and his successor Ælfmær in 1011, and that Selsey may have been vacant in 1009, see Keynes, *Diplomas*, p. 264.
[5] Mar.
[6] ASC CDEF (F much shorter) (1009 and 1010). The last passage in ASC 1009 referring to events after Christmas was assigned to 1010 by JW, who, with the differences shown, covers the events recorded in ASC.

ealdorman Eadric Streona, his son-in-law, for he had married his
daughter Edith, laboured by all means, by wiles and baffling arguments, that they should not join battle but permit their enemy, on
that occasion, to depart, and so as a traitor to his country he urged
and persuaded and snatched the Danes from the hands of the
English and allowed them to get away.[1] They, turning from the
English, with great joy returned to their ships.[2] After this, when
the feast of St Martin had passed they sailed to Kent, selected a
winter station on the River Thames, and seized provisions for
themselves from Essex and other neighbouring counties on either
bank of the river. Also, they often attacked the city of London,
endeavoured to storm it, but they were driven back by the citizens
with no small damage to their men.[3]

> After the death of Ordbriht,
> bishop of Selsey, Ælfmær suc-
> ceeded.[4]

[1010] Bishop Bruno was martyred.[5]

[6]In the month of January, the army of the Danes already mentioned disembarking from their ships, approached Oxford through
the pass called Chiltern, and, laying the city waste, they burnt it.
And thus they looted on either side of the River Thames on their
return. When they were informed that an army had been mustered
against them at London and would do battle against them, [7]the
section of the army which was going along the north bank crossed
the river at a place called Staines and, reunited,[7] and enriched
with booty in abundance, [8]they returned through Surrey to their
ships[8] which they refitted in Lent while they were stationed in
Kent.[9] After Easter they sailed to East Anglia, and, disembarking
from their ships near Ipswich, they went on to a place called
Ringmere,[10] where they knew that the ealdorman Ulfketel was
encamped with his army, and they fought a fierce battle with him

---

[7–7] ASC does not speak of only part of the army crossing at Staines, and of the
subsequent consolidation of the Danish forces.

[8–8] Not in ASC.

[9] ASC says the campaign lasted all winter, but that 'ðone Lencten' the Danes
repaired their ships.

[10] The site of the battle, which is not mentioned in ASC, seems confirmed by the
Old Norse poems' reference to fighting at Ringmere Heath (M. Ashdown, *English and
Norse Documents Relating to the Reign of Ethelred the Unready* (Cambridge, 1930), pp.
159–67, trans. Whitelock, *EHD*, nos. 12–14, pp. 332–5).

durum cum eo prelium .iii. non. Maii[1] commiserunt. Sed cum
pugna uehemens esset, Eastangli terga uertere, quodam Danico
ministro Turkytelo, Myrenheafod *a2*id est eque caput*a2* cognomento, fugam primitus incipiente, uerum Grantebrycgenses
uiriliter pugnantes diu restiterunt, uicti demum fugerunt. In eo
prelio gener regis Æthelstanus, nobilis minister Osuuius cum filio,
Wlfricus Leofuuini filius, Eaduuius Æfici*b* prefati[3] germanus et
multi alii nobiles ministri, populusque innumerabilis corruerunt.
Dani uero loco funeris dominati, [4]Eastangliam optinuerunt et
equites effecti[4] tribus mensibus per totam prouinciam discurrere,
predas agere, uillas cremare, homines et animalia non cessabant
trucidare, in paludibus etiam id idem per omnia fecerunt. Exin
Theodfordam et Grantebrycge deuastantes cremauerunt. His
gestis, [5]pedites nauibus deuecti, equites uero equis subuecti[5]
Tamensem fluuium repetierunt. Paucis diebus interiectis, iterum
depredaturi exierunt, et recto tramite ad Oxenofordensem prouinciam tetenderunt, eamque primitus deinde Buccingamnensem,
Bedefordensem, Heortfordensem prouincias uillasque cremando,
homines et animalia trucidando depopulati sunt, et post ad naues
suas cum ingenti preda regressi sunt.[6] Post hec, circa festiuitatem
sancti Andree apostoli, Northamtuniam et in circuitu eius quan-
p. 322   tum uolebant igni tradiderunt | et, inde Tamensem fluuium
transeuntes, Wessaxoniam adierunt, et, Caningamersce [7]maiorique
parte Wiltoniensis prouincie[7] cremata solito more, cum preda
magna suas ad naues circa Natiuitatem Domini reuersi sunt.[8]

[**1011**] (ix) 1033   *Willigisus episcopus Mogontinus obiit feria .vi., .vii.*
kalend. Martii. Erchanbaldus abbas Fuldensis successit ei.[9]

[10]Æstanglia,*c* Eastsaxonia, Middelsaxonia, Heortfordensi,
Buccingahamnensi, Oxenofordensi, Bedefordensi, Grantebrycgensi

---

a–a id . . . caput] *interlin.* C[1]L[1]B[1]P[3], *om.* H   *b* Alfrici H, Ælfrici L
c ⟨Æ⟩stanglia B

---

[1] JW's day (5 May) for the battle seems confirmed (against ASC's 18 May) by the
Ely calendar, Cambridge, Trinity College MS o. 2. 1, which assigns the death of Oswig
to that day (B. Dickins, 'The day of Brihtnoth's death and other obits from a
twelfth-century Ely kalendar', *Leeds Studies in English*, vi (1937), 14–24).
[2–2] Not in ASC.
[3] JW's 'aforementioned' suggests that he identifies this Æfic with the high-reeve who
was murdered in 1002.

on 5 May.[1] But when the battle was heated the East Anglians fled, a certain Danish thegn, Thurketel, surnamed *Myrenheafod*, [2]that is Mare's head,[2] being the first to take flight, but the men of Cambridge, fighting manfully, stood firm for a long time. At last they fled, defeated. In that battle fell Æthelstan, the king's son-in-law, the noble thegn Oswig with his son, Wulfric, son of Leofwine, Eadwig, brother of the aforementioned[3] Æfic, and many other noble thegns and innumerable common people. The Danes, having gained the mastery in that place of death, [4]won East Anglia, and, taking to horseback,[4] did not cease for three months, to scour the whole province, plundering, burning townships, slaughtering man and beast. In the fens, too, they did just the same in every detail. Then they plundered and burned Thetford and Cambridge. When they had done this, they returned to the River Thames, [5]those on foot by ship but the riders on their horses.[5] After an interval of a few days they set out again to plunder, and, heading for Oxfordshire by a direct route, they laid waste first that province, then Buckinghamshire, Bedfordshire, Hertfordshire, burning townships, slaughtering man and beast, and afterwards they went back to their ships with immense booty.[6] After this, about the feast of St Andrew the Apostle, they burned Northampton and as much of the surrounding area as they wished to, and then, crossing the River Thames, they approached Wessex, and, after burning Cannings Marsh [7]and the greater part of Wiltshire[7] in their usual manner, returned to their ships about the nativity of Our Lord with great booty.[8]

[1011] Willigis, bishop of Mainz, died on Friday, 23 February. Erkenbald, abbot of Fulda, succeeded him.[9]

[10]When East Anglia, Essex, Middlesex, Hertfordshire, Buckinghamshire, Oxfordshire, Bedfordshire, Cambridgeshire, also

---

[4–4] ASC DEF (no reference to horses in F) not C.

[5–5] Perhaps a rendering of ASC's 'the mounted men rode towards the ships'.

[6] JW adds Hertfordshire to the shires ravaged by the Danish army ('Bedfordshire' is his rendering of 'and so along the Ouse until they reached Bedford'), and omits ASC's final 'as far as Tempsford'. The long passage which follows in ASC lamenting English ineffectiveness and indecisiveness is not in JW.

[7–7] This appears to be an addition to ASC's 'Cannings Marsh'.

[8] ASC.   [9] Mar.

[10] ASC C–F (F much shorter) has the events in this annal, though there are many differences, particularly in the account of the Danish capture of Canterbury, where JW uses Osbern.

prouinciis, medietate quoque Huntedunensis prouincie, magnaque
parte Northamtunensis pagi, in australi uero plaga Tamensis
fluminis, Cantia, Suthregia, Suthsaxonia, Suthamtunensi,
Wiltoniensi, Barrucscirensi prouinciis,[1] a memorato Danorum
exercitu ferro flammaque demolitis, rex Anglorum Ægelredus et
regni sui primates ad illos miserunt legatos pacem ab eis petentes
et ut a depopulatione desisterent, stipendium et tributum eis
promittentes. Quibus auditis, ut rei probauit exitus, non sine dolo
et simulatione oblatis consenserunt.[2] Licet enim eis affluenter sumptus pararetur, et ad sua uota tributum penderetur non tamen destiterunt, quin turmatim per prouincias ubiuis discurrentes, uillas
deuastarent, rebus suis miseros quosdam spoliarent, quosdam uero
necarent. Ad ultimum, inter Natiuitatem sancte Marie et sancti
Michaelis festiuitatem, Cantuuariam circumuallantes obsederunt.
Vicesimo autem obsidionis die per insidias Ælmari archidiaconi,[3]
quem sanctus Alphegus ne morti traderetur prius eripuit, [4]pars
ciuitatis incenditur,[4] *exercitus ingreditur*, urbs capitur. *Alii ferro
iugula*ntur, *alii flammis comsum*untur, *plure*s quoque de *muris pre-
cipites da*ntur, *nonnulli per uerenda suspensi deficiunt, matrone*
crinibus *per plateas ciuitatis distracte*, demum *flammis iniecte, moriuntur. Paruuli a matrim uberibus a*uulsi *aut lanceis excipi*untur *aut
superacto* carro *minutatim conter*untur.[5] Interea archipresul
Alphegus capitur, uincitur, tenetur et uariis modis afficitur.
Almarus abbas monasterii sancti Augustini[6] abire permittitur.
Capiuntur Goduuinus, Hrofensis[6] episcopus, Leofruna abbatissa
monasterii sancte Mildrythe,[6] Alfredus[7] regis prepositus, monachi
quoque et clerici, populusue utriusque sexus innumerabilis. [8]Exin
ecclesia Christi spoliata comburitur,[8] grex monachilis et turba uir-
ilis sed muliebris nec infantilis decimatur, [8]nouem trucidantur,
decimus uite reseruatur. Quattuor monachis et .dccc. uiris decima-
torum summa perficitur.[8] Populo ceso, urbe spoliata et tota cremata, archipresul Alphegus *uinctus extrahitur*, impellitur, grauiter
sauciatur, *ad classem ducitur*, post in *carcerem* retruditur, *ibique*

---

[1] JW omits the Hastings district from the list of regions ravaged by the Danes, possibly because he knew it as a place, and not as a district.
[2] Again JW omits ASC's reference to the dilatory and ineffective policy of the
English, and he imputes deliberate deception to the Danes.
[3] ASC does not call Ælfmær 'archdeacon'.
[4-4] This information is derived from *Vita Elphegi*, not from ASC.
[5] Osbern, *Vita Elphegi*, in *Anglia Sacra*, ii. 135; BL Cotton MS Nero C. VII, fo. 53ᵛ.

half of Huntingdonshire and a great part of Northamptonshire, and, south of the River Thames, Kent, Surrey, Sussex, Hampshire, Wiltshire, and Berkshire[1] had been destroyed by the aforementioned Danish army with fire and sword, Æthelred, king of the English, and the leading men of his kingdom sent his envoys to them to sue for peace, and to promise them maintenance and tribute to give up their marauding. When they had heard them, they accepted the offers, not without guile and deceit, as the outcome of the matter showed,[2] for, although ample provisions were prepared for them and the tribute paid in accordance with their wishes, yet they did not desist, but scoured the country everywhere in bands, and plundered townships, despoiling some wretches of their possessions, even killing others. Finally, between the nativity of St Mary and the feast of St Michael, they surrounded and besieged Canterbury. However, on the twentieth day of the siege, through the treachery of the archdeacon[3] Ælfmaer, whom St Ælfheah had earlier sent away so that he should not be killed, [4]part of the city was burnt,[4] the army entered, and the city fell. Some were slain by sword, others were consumed by fire, many were cast headlong from their walls, no small number perished from being hung up by their testicles. Matrons, dragged through the streets of the city by their hair were thrown at last into the flames to die. Infants, torn from their mothers' breasts, were either cut to pieces with spears or ground to bits under cartwheels.[5] Meanwhile, Archbishop Ælfheah was taken, bound, held prisoner, and afflicted in various ways. Ælfmær, abbot of St Augustine's[6] was allowed to depart. Godwine, bishop of Rochester,[6] Leofrun, abbess of St Mildred's convent,[6] Alfred,[7] the king's reeve, monks and canons also, and innumerable people of either sex were taken prisoner. [8]Then Christ Church was pillaged and burnt.[8] The band of monks and the crowd of men, but not the women and children, were grouped in tens. [8]Nine out of every ten were slain, the tenth left alive. The total slain reached four from the monks and 800 of the men.[8] When they had slain the people, sacked the city and burned the lot, they brought out Archbishop Ælfheah in fetters and seriously wounded, and,

---

[6] The identifications of the see of Godwine, and of the houses of Ælfmær and Leofrun (ASC EF wrongly Leofwine) are JW's.

[7] ASC calls the reeve Ælfweard.

[8]-[8] This information could have come from Osbern (*Anglia Sacra*, ii. 136).

*septem mens*ibus affligitur.[1] *Interea ira Dei in homicidiam populum deseui*ens, ex eis *duo mili*a *per diros internorum cruciatus prostra*uit, *ceter*i *quoque simili* modo *percuss*i, *a fideli*bus *common*entur *ut pontifici satisfaciant,* sed *differunt. Preualuit interim clades et nunc* denos, *nunc uicen*os, *nunc plur*es *absump*sit.[2]

[1012] (x) 1034 [3]Perfidus dux Edricus Streona et omnes Anglie primates utriusque ordinis ante Pasca Lundonie congregati sunt et ibi tamdiu morati sunt quousque tributum Danis promissum, quod erat .xlviii. milia librarum,[4] persolueretur. *Interea sacrosancto dominice requiei sabbato* arcipresuli Alphego a Danis *propon*itur *conditio, ut si uita ac libertate uelit potiri,* .iii. milia librarum *persoluat.*[5] Illo nolente, necem eius usque ad aliud sabbatum protelant. Quo adueniente, aduersus illum exarserunt ira magna, et quia uino nimis inebriati fuerant et quia prohibuerat ne quis pro sua redemptione quicquam eis daret, proinde *de carcere ducitur, ad* eorum *concilium* pertrahitur. Mox illi *e sedibus prosiliunt, auersis securibus* illum *deiciunt, lapidibus,* ossibus, bouinis capitibus *obruunt.*[6] Ad ultimum quidam Thrum[7] nomine, *quem* confirmarat pridie, *impia motus pietate, securim capiti illius infixit, qui statim* in Domino .xiii. kalend. Maii obdormiuit et *uictorem spiritum cum triumpho ad celum dir*exit.[6] Cuius corpus die sequenti Lundoniam defertur, a ciuibus honorifice suscipitur, et ab episcopis Eadnotho Lindicolinensi[8] et Alfhuno Lundoniensi[8] in ecclesia sancti Pauli sepelitur. Post hec, tributo soluto, et pace iuramentis firmata, Danica classis ut prius erat congregata, longe lateque dispergitur. Sed cum rege .xlv. naues remansere eique fidelitatem iurauere, et aduersus exteros Angliam se defensuros eo tenore promisere ut eis uictum tegimenque preberet.[9]

---

[1] The seven-month period in gaol is specified in Osbern, *Vita Elphegi* (*Anglia Sacra,* ii. 137) though it could have been inferred from ASC.

[2] Osbern, *Vita Elphegi,* in *Anglia Sacra,* ii. 136–7; BL Cotton MS Nero C. VII, fo. 54[r–v].

[3] ASC CDEF record the events in this annal with the differences shown.

[4] ASC CD 48,000 pounds; EF 8,000 pounds.

[5] Osbern, *Vita Elphegi,* in *Anglia Sacra,* ii. 137–8; BL Cotton MS Nero C. VII, fo. 55[rb], where the sum (which is not specified in ASC) is 'sexaginta argenti talenta persoluat singulis talentis quinquaginta librarum pondere appensis', that is 3,000 pounds.

driving him on, took him to the fleet. Then he was cast into prison again and there tormented for seven months.[1] Meanwhile, the wrath of God, raging against that people because of the slaughter, laid low 2,000 of them with cruel gripings. The rest, struck down in a similar fashion, were advised by the faithful to make satisfaction to the archbishop but they put it off. Meanwhile, the scourge prevailed, and carried them off, now in tens, now twenties, now more.[2]

[1012] [3]The treacherous ealdorman, Eadric Streona, and all the leading Englishmen of both orders assembled at London before Easter, and stayed there until the tribute of 48,000 pounds[4] promised to the Danes was paid. Meanwhile, on Holy Saturday, when Our Lord rested in the grave, this condition was proposed to Archbishop Ælfheah by the Danes: that if he wished to enjoy life and liberty he should pay 3,000 pounds.[5] At his refusal, they put off his death to the next Saturday. When that came they burnt with great anger against him, and because they were extremely drunk with wine, and because he had forbidden anyone to give them anything for his ransom, he was accordingly brought from prison and dragged to their council. They at once sprang down from their seats, tossed aside their battle-axes, and threw him down, overwhelming him with stones, bones, and ox-skulls.[6] Finally one man, Thrum[7] by name, whom Ælfheah had confirmed the day before, moved by impious piety, split his head with his battle-axe. Ælfheah at once fell asleep in the Lord on 19 April, and sent up his victorious spirit in triumph to heaven.[6] His body was borne to London the following day, received with honour by the citizens, and buried by Bishops Eadnoth of Lincoln[8] and Ælfhun of London[8] in St Paul's church. After this, with the tribute paid and peace confirmed by oaths, the Danish fleet, which before had kept together, was dispersed far and wide. But forty-five ships remained with the king, swore fealty to him, and promised that they would defend England against invaders on condition that he would supply them with food and clothing.[9]

---

[6] Osbern, *Vita Elphegi*, in *Anglia Sacra*, ii. 139–41; BL Cotton MS Nero C. VII, fos. 56ᵛ–57ʳ. Much of the circumstantial detail (dates of the ultimatum, the drunkenness of the Danes, etc.) is from ASC, not from Osbern.

[7] JW seems to be the earliest source for the executioner's name.

[8] JW identifies the sees of the two bishops.   [9] ASC.

[**1013**] (xi) 1035 ¹Liuingus, *qui et Athelstanus,² Wyllensis episcopus .ix.,* archipresulatum Dorubernie suscepit. Mense Iulio rex
Danorum Suanus cum ualida classe ad Sandicum portum est
appulsus, ³ibique paucis diebus³ moratus discessit, et, Eastanglia
circumnauigata, ostium Humbre fluminis intrauit, de quo in
flumen Trentam intrauit, et Geagnesburh nauigauit ubi ³et castra
posuit,³ cui sine cunctatione comes Vhtredus et Northymbrenses
et Lin|disienses primitus, deinde Fifburgenses, mox etiam omnis
populus qui habitabat in septentrionali plaga Weatlingastrete, ³id
est strata quam filii Weatle regis ab orientali mari usque ad occidentale per Angliam strauerunt,³ deditionem optulerunt, et, pace
cum illo stabilita, obsidibusque datis, fidelitatem ei iurauerunt,
quibus precepit ut equos et alimenta suo exercitui pararent. His
impletis, et classe cum obsidibus Canuto filio suo commendata,
⁴sibi lectos auxiliarios de deditis sumens,⁴ ⁵aduersus australes
Mercios⁵ expeditionem mouit et, pertransita Weatlingastreta, suis
edictum posuit, ⁶uidelicet ut agros deuastarent, uillas cremarent,
ecclesias spoliarent, quicquid masculini sexus in manus ueniret
sine respectu misericordie iugularent, feminas ad suam libidinem
explendam reseruarent, et omnia que possent mala peragerent.
Quibus ita facientibus, et rabie ferina debachantibus,⁶ uenit
Oxenofordam et illam citius quam putauit optinuit, obsidibusque
acceptis, festinato Wintoniam properauit. Quo cum uenisset,
crudelitatis eius magnitudine ciues Wintonienses perterriti, pacem
cum eo sine mora fecerunt, et obsides, quos uel quot expetiit,
dederunt. Quibus acceptis, uersus Lundoniam⁷ mouit exercitum,
de quo multi in Tamensi fluuio summersi interierunt, quia nunquam pontem neque uadum querere uoluerunt. Cunque
Lundoniam uenisset, multis modis illam ³uel dolo capere uel ui
expugnare conatus est,³ sed rex Anglorum Ægelredus cum ciuibus
et iuuamine Danici comitis Turkilli sepe memorati, qui secum
tunc temporis intus erat, muros urbis uiriliter defendit et illum

⁻ qui . . . .ix.] *interlin.* C³, *om. HL*, qui et Æelstanus Willensis episcopus .ix. *incorporated* P

¹ ASC C-F (F much briefer) 1013 have the substance of this annal with the
differences shown.
² For WM *GP* as a possible source for 'qui et Æthelstanus', see above, p. 456 n. 4.
His position in the Wells bishops was probably derived from *GP* or from JW *Epis.
Lists.*

[**1013**] [1] Lyfing, also known as Æthelstan,[2] ninth bishop of Wells, was preferred to the archbishopric of Canterbury. In July, Swein, king of the Danes, came to the port of Sandwich with a strong fleet; [3]after staying there a few days,[3] he departed and, having sailed round East Anglia, entered the mouth of the River Humber, from whence he entered the River Trent, and sailed to Gainsborough, [3]where he encamped.[3] Without delay, Earl Uhtred and the Northumbrians and the men of Lindsey first, then the people of the Five Boroughs, and soon afterwards all the people also who live north of Watling Street —[3]that is the high road which the sons of King Weatla laid across England from the eastern to the western sea[3]— capitulated, and when peace had been established with Swein and hostages given swore fealty to him; he ordered them to prepare horses and provisions for his army. When these things were done, and he had entrusted the fleet with the hostages to his son Cnut, [4]taking auxiliaries chosen from these peoples subject to him,[4] he mounted [5]an expedition against the south Mercians,[5] and, after crossing Watling Street, gave orders to his men [6]to lay waste fields, burn townships, plunder churches, slay any member of the male sex who came into their hands without any thought of pity, keep the women for the satisfaction of their lust, and do all the evil they could. While they were doing this, behaving with the bacchanalian fury of wild beasts,[6] Swein came to Oxford and took it more quickly than he had expected. He took hostages, and moved on in haste to Winchester. When he arrived there, the citizens of Winchester, terrified by his extreme cruelty, made peace with him without delay, and gave him as many hostages of his own choice as he demanded. When he had received them, he moved his army towards London.[7] Many of his men perished, drowned in the River Thames, because they never bothered to look for a bridge or ford. And when he came to London he tried by many methods [3]either to take it by stratagem or to attack it with force[3] but Æthelred, king of the English, with the citizens and with the aid of the Danish earl Thorkell often mentioned, who was at that time inside with him, resolutely defended the walls of the city, and drove him off. When he was

---

[3–3] No equivalent in ASC.   [4–4] No exact equivalent in ASC.
[5–5] ASC has 'southwards' here.
[6–6] This passage stands for ASC's 'greatest damage that any army could do'.
[7] ASC: 'eastwards to London'.

abegit. Qui repulsus, primo Walingafordam dein Bathan,[1] [2]obuia
queque more solito rapiendo et demoliendo,[2] adiit, ibique exercitum suum refrigerando consedit. Tunc uenit ad eum Athelmarus
Domnanie[3] comes, et cum eo occidentales ministri et, pace cum
illo facta, obsides illi dederunt. [4]Quibus omnibus ad uelle
peractis,[4] ad suam classem reuersus, ab omni Anglorum populo
rex, [2]si iure queat rex uocari, qui fere cuncta tirannice faciebat,[2] et
appellabatur, et habebatur. Ciues etiam Lundonienses obsides illi
miserunt et pacem cum eo fecerunt, [5]metuebant enim furorem
illius in tantum super se exardescere, ut, omnibus suis rebus
ablatis, uel oculos illorum erui, uel manus uel pedes detruncari,[5]
iuberet. Quod cum uidisset, rex Ægelredus reginam Emmam, [a6]id
est Algiuam,[a6] Nortmanniam ad suum fratrem, secundum
Ricardum Nortmannorum comitem, et filios suos Eaduuardum et
Alfredum cum magistro illorum Ælfhuno, Lundoniensi[3] episcopo,
et Alsium Medeshamstudensem abbatem nauiter misit.[b7] Ipse uero
cum Danica classe, que in Tamensi iacebat in loco qui Greneuuic
nominatur, aliquantisper mansit, et post ad Vectam Insulam
deuectus, Natiuitatem Domini in illa celebrauit. Qua peracta,
Nortmanniam deuehitur, et a Ricardo comite honorifice
suscipitur.[8] Interea Suanus tirannus[9] sue classi sumptus affluenter
parari et tributum fere importabile solui precepit, similiter per
omnia comes Turkillus classi que apud Greneuuic iacebat solui
mandauit. Et super hec omnia uterque illorum quotienscunque eis
libuerat, predas egerunt et multa mala fecerunt.[10]

[C³BP]

[c]Post Liuingum extitit Wyllensis episcopus Æthelwinus
*Euesham*nensis *abbas, postea*

[a–a] id est Algiuam] *interlin. C¹B¹, om. HLP*   [b] *see App. B for mg. addition with*
signe de renvoi B (not scribe)   [c] *Post . . . Saxonicus (p. 476)] add. at line-end,*
extending into mg. C³, om. HL

---

[1] ASC has 'so west across the Thames to Bath' (F 'so to Bath').
[2–2] No equivalent in ASC.   [3] Place not specified in ASC.
[4–4] Perhaps nearer to ASC DE's 'he eall þus gefaren hæfde' rather than C, which
omits 'eall'.
[5–5] This stands for what ASC calls 'the Londoners' fears that he would destroy
them'.

driven off he went first to Wallingford, then to Bath,[1] [2]destroying and plundering whatever he came across according to his normal practice,[2] and there he rested his army to refresh his men. Then, Æthelmær, ealdorman of Devon,[3] came to him and with him the western thegns, and, having made peace with him, gave him hostages. [4]When everything had been executed as he desired[4] he returned to his fleet, and by all the people of the English he was called, and acknowledged as, king, [2]if he could rightfully be called king who did almost everything tyranically.[2] Even the citizens of London sent him hostages and made peace with him, [5]for they feared his fury would be inflamed to such an extent against them that, when he had confiscated all their property, he would order their eyes to be torn out or their hands or feet cut off.[5] When he saw that, King Æthelred sent Queen Emma, [6]that is Ælfgifu,[6] to Normandy to her brother, Richard II, duke of the Normans, and his sons Edward and Alfred, with their master Ælfhun, bishop of London,[3] and Ælfsige, abbot of Peterborough, by sea,[7] but he himself stayed for a while with the Danish fleet which lay in the Thames at a place called Greenwich, and he later sailed to the Isle of Wight where he celebrated Christmas. When that was over he sailed to Normandy and was received with honour by Duke Richard.[8] Meanwhile, the tyrant[9] Swein ordered lavish provisions to be prepared for his fleet and an almost insupportable tribute to be paid. The Earl Thorkell commanded that the fleet which lay at Greenwich should receive the same treatment in all respects. And in addition to all this, both of them plundered and committed many crimes whenever they wished.[10]

> Æthelwine, abbot of Evesham, became bishop of Wells after Lyfing, then he was ejected,

---

[6-6] ASC F alone names Æthelred's queen (interlined 'Ælfgive Ymma').

[7] The journeys to Normandy of the queen and the athelings might appear to be made separately in ASC. ASC makes Abbot Ælfsige of Peterborough accompany the queen, and JW's 'magister' of Bishop Ælfhun presumably renders 'he hi bewitan sceolde'.

[8] Æthelred's movements from the Thames to the Isle of Wight and the sending of Emma to Normandy are placed at the end of the annal in ASC, after Swein's and Thorkell's demands for tribute and provisions.

[9] Not so described in ASC.

[10] ASC's comment on the ineffectiveness of the English response to Danish ravaging is omitted by JW.

eiectus, cui successit Bryht-
uuinus sed ille *iterum reuersus et
Brihwinus eiectus, itemque*
Atheluuino *eiecto*, Bryhtuuinus
reuersus, Merewit, qui et
Bryhwi, Dudeca Saxonicus.[a1]

[1014] (xii) 1036 Suanus tirannus post innumerabilia et crudelia
mala, que uel in Anglia uel in aliis terris gesserat, ad cumulum sue
dampnationis ex oppido ubi corpus pretiosi martyris Eadmundi
incorruptum requiescit, quod nemo prius audebat facere ex quo id
oppidum datum fuerat memorati sancti ecclesie, grande tributum
ausus est exigere, quod si cito non penderetur se procul dubio
ipsum oppidum cum oppidanis crematurum ipsius martiris ecclesiam funditus euersurum, clericos uariis modis cruciaturum minatus est sepissime. Insuper frequenter ipsi martyri multis modis
detrahere, et illum nil sanctitatis habere, fuit ausus dicere, at quia
modum sue malitie noluit ponere, ultio diuina non permisit blas-
phemum diutius uiuere. Denique imminente [b]uespera diei,[b] qua in
generali placito, quod apud Geagnesburh tenuerat hec eadem
minitans reiterauit, cum Danorum cuneis circumuallatus esset den-
sissimis, sanctum Eadmundum ex aduerso uenientem solus uidit
armatum. Quem cum uidisset, expauit et nimio cum clamore
uociferari cepit: 'Succurrite', inquiens, 'commilitiones, succurrite,
ecce sanctus Eadmundus me uenit occidere,' et, hec dicendo,
acriter a sancto confossus cuspide de emissario cui insederat
decidit, et usque ad noctis crepusculum magno cruciatus tormento,
.iii. non. Februarii, miserabili morte uitam finiuit.[c] Quo mortuo,
filium eius Canutum sibi regem constituit classica manus
Danorum.[2] At maiores natu totius Anglie[3] ad regem Agelredum
pari consensu nuntios festinanter misere, dicentes se nullum plus

---

[a] *see above, p. 474 n. c*   [b–b] uespera diei] uespera diei Purificationis sancte Marie
add. B   [c] *see App. B for addition B*

---

[1] *GP* ii. 90 (p. 194). Æthelwine, abbot of Evesham, attests as bishop from 1018 (if *S*
951 *K* 728, transl. Whitelock, *EHD*, no. 131, pp. 597–9 is reliable) to 1022 (*S* 958 *K*
734). The confused succession at Wells is discussed by Robinson, *Wells*, pp. 50, 52, 68,
where it is judged to have been caused by JW *Epis. Lists*.
[2] ASC C–F record the death of Swein on 2 Feb. (by implication at Gainsborough),
and the election of Cnut as king. JW's description of Swein as a tyrant and of his
cruelty are consistent with his earlier remarks, but Swein's threats to Bury

and Bryhtwine succeeded him,
but he returned again, and
Bryhtwine was expelled, and
when Æthelwine was again
expelled Bryhtwine returned.
Then came Merehwit, who was
also called Byrwi, ⟨and⟩ Duduc
the Saxon.[1]

[1014] After many cruel atrocities, which he perpetrated both in
England and in other lands, the tyrant Swein filled up the measure of his damnation by daring to demand enormous tribute from
the town where the incorrupt body of the precious martyr
Edmund lay, a thing no one had dared to do before since that
town had been given to the church of the aforementioned saint.
He very frequently threatened that if it were not speedily paid he
would destroy utterly the martyr's church, and he would torture
the clergy in various ways. In addition, he frequently disparaged
the martyr himself in many ways—he dared to say that he had no
sanctity—and, because there were no bounds to his malice, divine
vengeance did not allow the blasphemer to live any longer. At last,
when the evening was approaching of the day on which, at the
general assembly which he held at Gainsborough, he repeated the
same threats, at a time when he was surrounded by Danish troops
crowded together, he alone saw St Edmund, armed coming
towards him. When he had seen him, he was terrified and began
to shout very noisily, saying: 'Help, fellow-warriors, help! St
Edmund is coming to kill me!' And while he was saying this he
was run through fiercely by the saint with a spear, and he fell
from the stallion on which he sat, and, tormented with great pain
until twilight, he ended his life with a wretched death on 3
February. After his death the men of the Danish fleet made his
son Cnut king.[2] But the leading men of all England,[3] by general
agreement, sent messengers in haste to King Æthelred, saying that

and the apparition of St Edmund come from another source, possibly, as Plummer,
Chronicle, ii. 192 suggested, a *Passion of St Edmund*. The work that Hermann of Bury
found difficult to understand when he used it *c.* 1100 (*Memorials St. Edmunds*, i. 328) is
a possibility.
[3] 'Totius Anglie' could correspond to ASC CF's 'all the councillors who were in
England' rather than DE's 'all the councillors'.

amare uel amaturos esse quam suum naturalem dominum, si ipse
uel rectius gubernare uel mitius eos tractare uellet quam prius

p. 324   tractarat. | Quibus auditis, Eaduuardum filium suum cum legatis
suis ad eos dirigens, maiores minoresque gentis sue amicabiliter
salutauit, promittens se illis mitem deuotumque dominum futurum, in omnibus eorum uoluntati consensurum, consiliis acquietu-
rum, et quicquid sibi uel suis ab illis probrose et dedecorose
dictum uel contrarie factum fuerat placido animo condonaturum,
si omnes unanimiter et sine perfidia illum recipere uellent in regnum. Ad hec cuncti benigne responderunt. Dein amicitia plenaria
ex utraque parte et uerbis et pacto confirmatur. Ad hec principes
se non amplius Danicum regem admissuros in Angliam unanimiter
spoponderunt. His gestis, ab Anglis in Normanniam mittitur, rex
festinato Quadregesimali tempore reducitur, et ab omnibus honorabiliter excipitur. Interea[1] Canuto et Lindisiensibus conuenit ut
caballis exercitui sui paratis, predatum simul descenderent. Sed
antequam essent parati, uenit illo rex Ægelredus cum exercitu
ualido, et [2]Canuto cum classica manu expulso,[2] Lindesegiam totam
depopulans flammisque consumens, omnes incolas quos poterat
occidit. Ille uero fuge presidio celeriter arrepto, uersus austrum
cursum dirigens, breui Sandicum ad portum est appulsus, et
obsides qui de tota Anglia patri suo dati fuerant in terram exposuit, illorumque manibus truncatis, auribus[3] amputatis, naribus
precisis, abire permisit et deinceps profectus est Denemarciam,
anno sequenti reuersurus.[4] Super hec omnia mala rex Ægelredus
classi, que apud Greneuuic iacuit, tributum quod erat .xxx. milia
librarum[5] pendi mandauit. Mare litus egreditur .iii. kalend. Oct.,
et in Anglia uillas quamplurimas innumerabilemque populi multitudinem summersit.[6]

[1015] (xiii) 1037 [7]Hoc anno, cum apud Oxenofordam magnum
haberetur placitum, perfidus dux Edricus Streona digniores et
potentiores ministros ex Seouenburhgensibus, Sigeferthum et
Morkerum [8]filios Earngrimi,[8] in cameram suam dolo suscepit, et

---

[1] ASC refers to Cnut remaining with his army at Gainsborough until Easter.

[2–2] ASC has 'Cnut put out to sea with the fleet'.

[3] ASC EF do not mention 'ears'.

[4] ASC does not mention here Cnut's return to Denmark, which is mentioned in
Encomium Emmae, p. 141.

[5] ASC's figure is 21,000 pounds (not in F).

there was no lord they loved, or would love, more than their natural lord, if he would either govern more justly or treat them with
more kindness than he had treated them with before. When
Æthelred heard this, he sent his son Edward to them, with his
legates: he greeted his people, great and small, amicably; promising that he would be a gentle and loving lord, would be ruled by
them in everything, would fall in with their advice, and would
pardon with an unruffled spirit whatever shameful and disgraceful
things had been said to him or to his by them, or done against his
wishes, if all, unanimously and without treachery, would receive
him back into the kingdom. To this everyone replied favourably.
The complete accord on both sides was confirmed by word and
covenant. At this the leading men promised unanimously that they
would not allow the Danish king into England. This done, the
English sent to Normandy, the king was bought back in haste in
Lent, and was honourably received by all. Meanwhile,[1] Cnut and
the men of Lindsey agreed that, when horses had been made
ready for the army, they would go off raiding together. But before
they had been prepared, King Æthelred arrived there with a
strong army, and [2]when he had expelled Cnut and his fleet,[2] he
killed all the inhabitants he could, ravaging and plundering the
whole of Lindsey. But Cnut, who had hastily taken refuge in
flight, steered a course towards the south, and in a short time
arrived at the port of Sandwich. The hostages who had been given
to his father from the whole of England he turned out on to the
land, and, having cut off their hands and their ears,[3] and slit their
nostrils, he allowed them to depart. He then set out for Denmark,
only to return the next year.[4] In addition to all these disasters
King Æthelred ordered that a tribute of 30,000 pounds[5] be paid to
the fleet lying at Greenwich. There was a tidal wave on 29
September which submerged very many townships and innumerable people in England.[6]

[1015] [7]In this year, when the great council was held at Oxford,
the treacherous ealdorman, Eadric Streona, with evil intent
received the more worthy and more powerful thegns of the Seven
Boroughs, Sigeferth and Morkar, [8]the sons of Earngrim,[8] in his

---

[6] ASC C–F (F much shorter) with differences shown.
[7] ASC C–F record the events in this annal with the differences shown.
[8-8] ASC does not mention the father of Sigeferth and Morkar.

occulte illos ibi necare iussit. Quorum facultates rex Ægelredus accepit, et derelictam Sigeferthi, Aldgitham,[1] ad Maidulfi urbem[a] deduci precepit. Que cum ibi custodiretur, uenit illuc Eadmundus clito et, contra uoluntatem sui patris, illam sibi uxorem accepit, et [2]inter Assumptionem et Natiuitatem sancte Marie[2] profectus ad Fifburhgingos,[3] terram Sigeferthi et Morkeri inuasit ac populum illarum sibi subiugauit. Eodem tempore Canutus, rex Danorum,[4] cum magna classe ad Sandicum portum uenit, et, mox Cantia circumnauigata, ostium Frome fluminis introiuit, et in Dorsetania et Sumerseatania,[b] Wiltoniensique prouincia magnam predam egit. Tunc quia rex Agelredus apud Cossham egrotauit, Eadmundus clito filius eius [5]ex[c] sua parte,[5] et dux [6]insidiis et dolo plenus[6] Edricus Streona in sua,[d] magnum congregauerunt exercitum, sed cum in unum conuenirent, modis omnibus insidias clitoni dux tetendit, [7]illumque dolo perimere temptauit.[7] Quibus cognitis mox ab inuicem discesserunt et locum suis inimicis dederunt. Non diu post idem dux de regia classe .xl. naues, [6]Danicis militibus instructas,[6] sibi allexit et Canutum adiens, ipsius dominio se mancipauit. Idem Wessaxones datis obsidibus fecerunt et post exercitui caballos parauerunt.[8]

[C³BP]

[e]Defuncto Ætheluuoldo Wintoniensi episcopo, successit Ælsius eique Ælfwinus.[e9]

[1016] (xiiii) 1038   [10]Rex Danorum Canutus et perfidus dux Edricus Streona cum multo equitatu,[11] amnem Tamensim in loco qui Cricgelade dicitur transeuntes, ante Epiphaniam Domini Merciam hostiliter intrauerunt, et multas uillas in Weariuuicana prouincia populantes incenderunt, ac omnes quos inuenerant occiderunt. Quod ut audiuit clito Eadmundus, [12]cognomine Ferreum Latus,[12] exercitum festinato congregauit, sed cum

---

[a] om. HL, id est Malmasberiam interlin. B (late 13th-c. hand)   [b] Sumersetonia HL (from Sumertonia), Sumerseatania BP   [c] uel in interlin. C¹B¹   [d] contra Cnutum interlin. B⁵   [e–e] Defuncto . . . Ælfwinus] add. at line-end C³, om. HL

---

[1] ASC does not name Sigeferth's widow.
[2–2] ASC has 'before the nativity of St Mary'.
[3] ASC has 'from the west' (omitted by F), 'north to the Five Boroughs'.
[4] Not in ASC.   [5–5] ASC (not F) has 'in the north'.
[6–6] Not in ASC.   [7–7] Goes beyond ASC's statement of treachery.

chamber, and ordered them to be slain secretly there. King
Æthelred took possession of their property, and ordered Aldgyth,[1]
Sigeferth's widow, to be taken to the city of Malmesbury. While
she was confined there, the atheling Edmund came thither, and,
against his father's wish, took her to wife, and [2]between the
Assumption and the Nativity of St Mary[2] he set out for the Five
Boroughs,[3] invaded Sigeferth and Morkar's territory, and subdued
the people of those lands to himself. At the same time Cnut, king
of the Danes,[4] came to the port of Sandwich with a great fleet,
and soon, having sailed around Kent, entered the mouth of the
River Frome, and took great booty in Dorset and Somerset and
Wiltshire. Then, because King Æthelred lay ill at Cosham, the
atheling Edmund his son, [5]on his part,[5] and Eadric Streona, the
ealdorman [6]full of plots and deceit,[6] on his, mustered a great
army, but when they joined forces, the ealdorman laid all sorts of
traps for the atheling [7]and tried to destroy him with guile.[7] When
this came to light they separated at once and gave way to their
enemies. Not long after the same ealdorman chose for himself
forty ships [6]manned by Danish soldiers,[6] from the royal fleet, and,
approaching Cnut, placed himself at his service. The West Saxons
did the same, giving hostages, and afterwards providing horses for
the army.[8]

> On the death of Æthelwold,
> bishop of Winchester, Ælfsige
> succeeded, and after him
> Ælfwine.[9]

[1016] [10]Cnut, king of the Danes, and the treacherous Eadric
Streona crossed the River Thames in the place called Cricklade
with a large group of horsemen,[11] entered Mercia with hostile
intent before the Lord's Epiphany, and plundered and burned
many townships in Warwickshire, killing all they came across.
When he heard this the atheling Edmund, [12]surnamed Ironside,[12]

---

[8] ASC.

[9] Æthelwold attests for the last time in 1012 (*S* 929, Sawyer, *Charters of Burton*, no.
36, pp. 70–1), and Ælfsige seems to have been in office by 1013 (*S* 931 *K* 1308).

[10] ASC C–F (F very selective, omitting most of the annal before Æthelred's death
and all the battles save those of Aylesford and Ashingdon) with the differences shown.

[11] ASC EF (referring to Cnut's forces) add 'of 160 ships'.

[12–12] Not in ASC here or elsewhere.

congregatus esset ¹cum Wessaxonicis et Danis nolebant congredi
Mercenses¹ ᵃnisi cum illis essent rex Agelredus et ciues
Lundonienses,ᵃ quapropter expeditione dimissa unusquisque redit
in sua. Festiuitate uero transacta, iterum Eadmundus clito
maiorem congregauit exercitum.² Quo congregato nuntios
Lundoniam misit rogans patrem suum ut cum omnibus quos
habere poterat sibi quam citius posset occurreret, qui multis pug-
natoribus coadunatis, illi festinanter occurrit.³ Sed cum exercitus
in unum conuenissent,⁴ intimatum est regi quod nisi precaueret
sibi, quidam ex suis auxiliariis essent illum tradituri. Iccirco mox
exercitu dimisso, Lundoniam rediit, clito uero in Northymbriam
iuit, unde putabant nonnulli quod adhuc aduersus Canutum congregare maiorem uellet exercitum, sed sicut Canutus et Edricus ex
una parte, ita ille et Vhtredus Northymbrorum comes prouincias
sunt populatiᵇ nonnullas, nam prius Stæffordensem, deinde
Scrobbesbyriensem et Legece|strensem⁵ prouincias deuastauere
quia aduersus Danorum exercitum ad pugnam exire noluere.⁶
Interea Canutus et Edricus Streona primitus Buccingahamnensem,
Bedefordensem, Huntadunensem, Northamtunensem, Lindicolin-
ensem, Snotingahamnensem prouincias, dein Northhymbriam
depopulantur.⁷ Quo cognito, clito Eadmundus, populatione
dimissa, ad patrem suum Lundoniam properauit.⁸ Comes uero
Vhtredus domum festinanterᶜ rediit, et necessitate compulsus, ad
Canutum cum omnibus Northymbrensibus se contulit, et obsides
ei dedit, et tamen eius iussu uel permissu, a Turebrando nobili et
Danico uiro est peremptus, et cum eo Turketelus Neauaneᵈ filius.⁹
Quo patrato, Canutus Egricum pro Vhtredo comitem posuit, et
post alacer uersus austrum per aliam uiam regressus,¹⁰ ante pas-

p. 325

ᵃ⁻ᵃ nisi . . . Lundonienses] nisi cum eis essent et ciues Lundonienses et rex
Agelredus L   ᵇ gap before populati H, depopulati LP (de add. P³)   ᶜ om. HL
ᵈ uel Nafenan interlin. B⁵

---

¹⁻¹ JW's apparent equivalent for 'nothing would satisfy them' in ASC CDE.
² JW makes clear that Edmund assembled this second army, but makes no reference
to the full penalty for non-attendance.
³ 'citius' and 'festinanter' have no equivalent in ASC.
⁴ JW has not the brief comment on the ineffectiveness, as before, of this military
assembly.
⁵ JW misunderstands 'Legceastre' as 'Leicestershire'.
⁶ JW does not imply (like ASC CDE) that Edmund and Uhtred would both assemble an army against Cnut, but he does make clear that both jointly ravaged various

hastily mustered an army but, when it had assembled, [1]the Mercians refused to attack the West Saxons and the Danes[1] unless King Æthelred and the Londoners were with them. For this reason the troops were disbanded, and each man returned home. But when the feast had been observed the atheling Edmund again mustered an even greater army,[2] and when it had assembled he sent messengers to London to ask his father to meet him as quickly as possible with all the men he could get. The king assembled many fighters, and quickly came to meet him,[3] but when the armies were joined,[4] the king was warned that unless he was very careful some of his auxiliaries would betray him. Therefore the army was soon disbanded, and he returned to London, but the atheling went to Northumbria, so that many thought that he wished to muster a still greater army against Cnut, but just like Cnut and Eadric on the one hand, so he and Uhtred, earl of the Northumbrians, on the other, ravaged many provinces: for first they laid waste Staffordshire, then Shropshire and Leicestershire,[5] because they would not go into battle against the Danish army.[6] Meanwhile, Cnut and Eadric Streona ravaged first Buckinghamshire, Bedfordshire, Huntingdonshire, Northamptonshire, Lincolnshire, Nottinghamshire and then Northumbria.[7] When he learnt of this the atheling Edmund gave up his work of devastation, and hurried to his father at London.[8] But Earl Uhtred returned home in haste and, driven by necessity, went to Cnut with all the Northumbrians, and gave him hostages. Yet, at Cnut's command, or with his assent, he, with Thurketel, son of Neafena, was murdered by Thurbrand, a Danish noble.[9] When that had been perpetrated, Cnut replaced Uhtred with Earl Eric, and afterwards went briskly back to the south by another route,[10] and returned to his

provinces. He states (as ASC does not) that the unwillingness of the inhabitants of these provinces to fight the Danes was the main reason for the ravaging.

   [7] ASC does not explicitly state that Eadric acted jointly with Cnut in these devastations, and, in describing the progress of destruction, adds 'along the Fens to Stamford' after Northamptonshire (which is not in E) and 'towards York' after Northumbria.

   [8] ASC places Edmund's departure to London after Uhtred's return to Northumbria, his murder, and his replacement by Eric (F omitting the Uhtred episodes). In placing Edmund's departure after Uhtred's death, JW necessarily assigns 'populatione dimissa' to Edmund, not Uhtred.

   [9] ASC C says that Uhtred was murdered on Eadric's advice. JW's 'eius iussu uel permissu' is nearer to DE. ASC does not mention Thurbrand, who is named as the assassin in Durham material: De obsessione Dunelmi, c. 5 (Symeonis monachi opera, i. 218), and the account of the earls of Northumbria incorporated in HR iii. 159 (ii. 197).

   [10] ASC adds 'keeping to the west.'

calem festiuitatem suas cum omni exercitu naues repetiit. Eo tempore rex Anglorum Ægelredus, .xiiii. indictione, .ix. kalend. Maii, feria .ii., Lundonie defunctus est, post magnos labores et multas uite sue tribulationes.[1] Quas super illum uenturas, regalis *consecrationis sue die, post impositam coronam*, prophetico spiritu, sanctus ei *predix*erat *Dunstanus*: '*Quoniam*', inquit, '*aspirasti ad regnum per mortem fratris tui, quem occidit mater tua,*[2] *propterea audi uerbum Domini. Hec dicit Dominus:*[3] "*non deficiet gladius de domo tua, seuiens in te omnibus diebus uite tue*", *interficiens de semine tuo, quousque regnum tuum transferatur in regnum alienum cuius ritum et linguam gens cui presides non nouit: nec expiabitur nisi longa uindicta peccatum tuum et peccatum matris tue et peccatum uirorum qui interfuere consilio eius nequam.*'[2] [4]Corpus autem illius in ecclesia sancti Pauli apostoli honorifice sepultum est. Cuius post mortem episcopi, abbates, duces et quique nobiliores Anglie in unum congregati, pari consensu, in dominum et regem sibi Canutum elegere, et, ad eum in Suthamtoniam uenientes, omnemque progeniem regis Agelredi coram illo abnegando repudiantes, pacem cum eo composuere, et fidelitatem illi iurauere, quibus et ille iurauit quod et secundum Deum et secundum seculum fidelis esse uellet eis dominus.[4] At ciues Lundonienses et pars nobilium qui eo tempore consistebant Lundonie clitonem Eadmundum unanimi consensu in regem leuauere. Qui solii regalis sullimatus culmine intrepidus [5]Westsaxoniam adiit sine cunctatione, et ab omni populo magna susceptus gratulatione, sue ditioni subegit eam citissime.[5] Quibus auditis, multi Anglorum populi magna cum festinatione illi se dederunt uoluntarie.[6] Canutus autem interim cum tota sua classe circa Rogationes Lundoniam deuehitur,[7] quo cum uenissent in australi parte Tamensis[8] magnam scrobem foderunt et naues suas in occidentalem plagam pontis traxerunt, dein urbem alta lataque fossa et obsidione cingentes, ingressum et egressum cunctis intercluserunt, ac eam frequenter expugnare moliti sunt, sed a ciuibus illis uiriliter resistentibus procul a moenibus repelluntur.

---

[1] ASC DE say 'after great toil and difficulties of his life'. JW as usual contributes the indiction and weekday.

[2] Osbern, *Vita Dunstani*, in *Memorials Dunstan*, pp. 114–15.

[3] WM, *Vita Dunstani*, ibid., p. 309.   [4]–[4] Not in ASC.

[5]–[5] In ASC this is placed later and retrospectively after the Danish siege of London. JW describes the submission to Edmund as being with 'great joy'.

ships with his entire army before Easter. At that time, on Monday, 23 April, in the fourteenth indiction, Æthelred, king of the English, died, after the great toils and many tribulations of his life.[1] These St Dunstan had prophetically announced would come upon him when he, on the day of his coronation, had placed the crown upon his head: 'Because,' he said, 'you obtained the kingdom through the death of your brother, whom your mother killed;[2] hear therefore the word of the Lord. Thus saith the Lord,[3] "The sword shall not depart from thine house, raging against thee all the days of thy life", slaying those of your seed until your kingdom is given to an alien power whose customs and tongue the people you rule do not know; and your sin and your mother's sin and the sin of the men who committed murder at the wicked woman's advice will not be expiated except by long-continued punishment.'[2] [4]His body was honourably buried in the church of St Paul the Apostle. After his death, the bishops, abbots, ealdormen and all the nobles of England, assembled together and, by general agreement, elected Cnut as their lord and king, and, coming to him at Southampton, renounced and repudiated in his presence all the descendants of King Æthelred and made peace with him and swore fealty to him, and he swore to them that he would be a faithful lord to them, both in religious and in secular matters.[4] But the London citizens and those of the nobles who were at that time at London by unanimous agreement raised the atheling to the throne. He, raised to the height of royal dignity, [5]undauntedly approached Wessex without delay and was received with great joy by the whole population, whom he very swiftly subjected to his rule.[5] When they heard this many of the English hastily yielded to him voluntarily.[6] Meanwhile, however, Cnut sailed to London with his whole fleet,[7] about Rogationtide, and when they had arrived there they dug a great trench on the south side of the Thames,[8] and dragged their ships to the west side of the bridge, then, encircling the city with a ditch deep and wide, they besieged it. They cut off all ingress and egress, and made frequent attempts to storm it, but they were driven back far from the

---

[6] JW apparently extends the geographical range of those who submitted to Edmund, extending 'from all the people' (possibly in Wessex) to 'multi Anglorum populi'.

[7] In ASC (not F) the reference to Cnut's naval visit to London is placed before Edmund's departure to Wessex.

[8] ASC C-F specify Greenwich for the south side of the Thames.

¹Quapropter, obsidione ad tempus dimissa, exercitusque parte ad
naues custodiendas relicta, in Westsaxoniam abierunt propere, et
regi Eadmundo Ferreo Lateri spatium congregandi exercitum non
dedere. Quibus tamen ille cum exercitu, quem in tantillo spatio
congregarat, Dei fretus auxilio, audacter in Dorsetania occurrit et
in loco, qui Peonnum uocatur, iuxta Gillingaham, cum eis congressus, uicit*ᵃ* et eos in fugam uertit.¹ Post hec, media estate
transacta, denuo maiori quam prius exercitu congregato, fortiter
confligere statuit cum Canuto cui occurrit ²in Huuiccia² in loco
qui Scearstan nominatur. Vbi *exercitum pro loco* et *copiis instruit,*
optimum quenque in primam aciem subducit, ceterum exercitum in sub-
sidiis locat unumquenque nominans appellat, hortatur, rogat, ut mem-
inerint se pro patria, pro liberis, pro coniugibus, *atque suis* domibus
certare, et optimis sermonibus *militum animos accendebat,* deinde
tubicines canere et *cohor*tes *paulatim incedere iube*t. *Idem facit*
hostium exercitus. Vbi *eo uentum est* ubi ab illis *preliu*m *committi pos-*
*set, maximo clamore cum infestis signis o*ccurrunt, lanceis et *gladiis*
pugna *geritur, maxima ui certatur. Interea* rex Eadmundus Ferreum
Latus *in prima acie comminus acriter insta*bat, *omnia prouide*bat, *mul-*
*tum ipse pugna*bat, *sepe hostem feri*bat, *strenui militis et boni impera-*
*toris officia simul exequebatur.*³ Sed quia Edricus Streona dux
perfidissimus et Almarus dilectus, Algarusque filius Meauues,⁴ qui
ei auxilio esse debuerant, ²cum Suthamtoniensibus et
Wiltoniensibus prouincialibus,² innumeraque populi multitudine in
parte Danorum fuerant, eius exercitus nimis erat defatigatus ᵇuel
laborabat.ᵇ Attamen primo die belli, lune scilicet die,ᶜ tam durum
tamque cruentum extitit prelium ut uterque exercitus pre lassitu-
dine diutius non ualens pugnare, sole iam occidente, ab inuicem
sit digressus spontanea uoluntate. ⁵Sed postera die rex Danos pro-
tereret omnes si perfidi ducis Edrici Streone non essent insidie.
Siquidem cum pugna uehemens esset et Anglos fortiores esse

ᵃ die .v. iduum Iunii *add. B*   ᵇ⁻ᵇ uel laborabat] *interlin. C¹B¹, om. HLP*
ᶜ .vii. Kalendarum Iulii *interlin. B¹*

---

¹⁻¹ ASC (not F) simply records here Edmund fighting against the Danish army at
Penselwood near Gillingham.
²⁻² Not in ASC.   ³ Sallust, *Catiline,* lix. 1–lx. 4.
⁴ Ælfgar, son of Meaw, is not mentioned in ASC. On him see Keynes, *Diplomas,* p.
227 n. 265.

walls by the citizens' vigorous resistance. [1]Wherefore, abandoning the siege for the time, and leaving part of the army to guard the ships, they went to Wessex in haste, and did not give King Edmund Ironside time to muster an army. However, with the army which he had gathered in so short a time he, trusting in God's help, went boldly to meet them in Dorset, and in a place called Penselwood, near Gillingham, he gave them battle, won, and put them to flight.[1] After this, when midsummer had passed, and he had mustered an army, one greater than before, he determined to fight vigorously against Cnut, whom he encountered [2]in *Hwiccia*[2] at a place called Sherston. When he drew up his army according to the terrain and the forces he had, he moved the best soldiers into the front line, placed the rest of the army in reserve, and addressing each man by name, exhorted and entreated them to remember that they strove for their country, children, wives and homes, and with these most inspiring words he fired the soldiers' spirits. Then he ordered the trumpets to sound, and the troops to advance gradually. The enemy army did the same. When they arrived at the place where they could join battle they rushed together with their hostile standards and with a great shout. They fought with spear and lance, striving with all their might. Meanwhile, King Edmund Ironside made his presence felt in fierce hand-to-hand fighting in the front line. He took thought for everything; he himself fought hard, often smote the enemy; he performed at once the duties of a hardy soldier and of an able general.[3] But, because Eadric Streona, the most treacherous ealdorman, and Ælfmær Darling, and Ælfgar, son of Meaw,[4] who ought to have been supporting him [2]with the men of Hampshire and Wiltshire[2] and with an innumerable mass of people, were on the Danish side his army was quite exhausted and quite overstretched. However, on the first day of battle, that is on Monday, so harsh and cruel was the conflict that both armies were unable for weariness to fight any longer, and they left the place at sunset of their own accord. [5]But on the following day, the king would have crushed all the Danes if it had not been for the wiles of Eadric Streona, the treacherous ealdorman; for, when the battle was at its height and he observed that the English were stronger,

[5] The accounts of Sherston and Eadric's ruse are not in ASC, though the latter is in WM, *GR* ii. 180 (i. 215), and (at the battle of Ashingdon) in HH *HA* vi c. 13 (Arnold, p. 184). ASC gives no indication of the duration of the battle of Sherston.

p. 326 cerneret, cuiusdam uiri regi Eadmundo facie capillisque simillimi, Osmeari nomine, capite amputato et in altum | leuato, exclamat, Anglos frustra pugnare dicens: 'uos Dorsetenses, Domnani, Wiltonienses, amisso capite precipites fugite, en domini uestri caput, Eadmundi basilei, hic teneo manibus, cedite quantotius.' Quod ubi Angli accepere, magis atrocitate rei quam fide nuntii terrentur, unde factum est ut inconstantiores quique paulum a fuga abessent, sed ilico quod rex uiueret comperto, animos tollebant et in Danos acrius incedebant, ex illisque multos prostrabant summis certantes uiribus usque ad crepusculum noctis, qua adueniente ut pridie digressi sunt spontanee. At ubi plerunque noctis processit, Canutus e castris suos abire silentio iussit, et uersus Lundoniam iter arripiens, ad naues repedauit ac non multo post Lundoniam reobsedit.[1] Vbi autem dies aduenit et rex Eadmundus Ferreum Latus Danos fugisse comperit, maiorem congregaturus exercitum in Westsaxoniam reuertitur.[2] Cuius strenuitatem uidens sororius eius perfidus dux Edricus ut naturalem dominum requisiuit illum, et, pace cum eo redintegrata, se fidelem ei permansurum iurauit.[3] Itaque exercitu uice tertia congregato, Lundonienses ciues ab obsidione rex liberauit,[4] Danos ad suas naues fugauit. Post biduum Tamensim[a] in loco qui Brentford nominatur transfretauit cum Danis tertio[5] prelium commisit et fugatis eis uictor extitit. Ea uice multi Anglorum populi, dum incautius flumen transirent, demerguntur. Exinde rex numerosiorem congregaturus exercitum in Westsaxoniam properat. Dani uero Lundoniam repetunt, obsidione illam cingunt, et omni ex parte oppugnant, sed, Deo iuuante, nil omnino proficiunt. Ob quam rem cum sua classe recedentes inde, amnem qui Areuue dicitur intrant, et nauibus exilientes, predatum in Merciam pergunt, obuios quosque cedunt, more solito uillas incendunt, predam agunt, post ad naues redeunt, pedestres in flumen quod Meodeuueage nuncupatur, nauibus deuehuntur,

---

[a] Tamensi *HL*

---

[1] Cnut's departure by night after the battle of Sherston is not in ASC.

[2] Edmund's return to Wessex is not in ASC.

[3] ASC records Eadric's submission to Edmund after, not, as here, before the campaign in Kent. Against Plummer's view (*Chronicle*, ii. 197) that JW simply misunderstood the chronicle, there is the evidence of *Encomium Emmae*, p. 24, in support of JW's sequence of events.

he cut off the head of a certain man called Osmear, very like King Edmund in face and hair, and raising it aloft he shouted, saying that the English fought in vain: 'You men of Dorset, Devon, Wiltshire, flee in haste, for you have lost your leader. Look, I hold here in my hands the head of your lord, King Edmund. Flee as fast as you can.' When the English perceived this they were appalled, more by the horror at the action than by any trust in the announcer, whence it happened that the waverers were on the verge of flight; but as soon as they realized that the king was alive their spirits rose, and they attacked the Danes the more fiercely, and they slew many of them, striving with all their might until dusk. When that arrived, as on the previous day, they separated voluntarily. But when the night was far advanced Cnut ordered his men to leave the camp silently and, going back to London, returned to his ships again, and not much later he besieged London again.[1] However, when day came, and King Edmund Ironside perceived that the Danes had fled, he returned at once to Wessex to raise a larger army.[2] The treacherous ealdorman Eadric, his brother-in-law, seeing his vigour, turned to him again as his natural lord, and, when peace with him had been restored, swore he would remain faithful to him.[3] And so, having mustered an army for the third time, the king freed the citizens of London from the siege,[4] and sent the Danes in flight back to their ships. Two days later he crossed the Thames at a place called Brentford, joined battle with the Danes for a third time,[5] and, having put them to flight, was the victor. On that occasion many of the English were drowned when they crossed the river incautiously. From there the king hurried into Wessex to assemble a more numerous army. But the Danes returned to London, besieged it all around, and assaulted it on every side, but with God's help they were totally unsuccessful. For that reason they withdrew from there with their fleet, entered the river which is called the Orwell, and, disembarking, plundered Mercia. They slew those they met, burned townships, according to their usual practice, took booty, then went back to their ships. The footsoldiers travelled by ship into the river called the Medway, but the horsemen

[4] ASC C speaks of Edmund keeping north of the Thames and going through Clayhanger *en route* to London.

[5] Not in ASC, though it had spoken earlier (unlike JW) of Edmund assembling an army for the third time.

equestres uero uiuam predam per terram minant.[1] Interea rex
Eadmundus Ferreum Latus exercitum fortem de tota Anglia
quarto congregauit, et, [2]in loco ubi prius Tamensi fluuio trans-
meato,[2] in Cantiam citus intrauit, ac iuxta Ottafordam[3] cum Danis
pugnam iniit, at illi non ferentes impetum eius terga uerterunt et
cum suis equis in Sceapege fugerunt. Ex quibus tamen omnes
quos comprehendere potuit occidit, et, ni perfidus dux Edricus
Streona*a* suis insidiis et insiliis eum apud Eagelesford ne suos
persequeretur hostes retineret, eo die plena potiretur uictoria.[4]
[5]Quo in Westsaxoniam reuerso,[5] Canutus suas copias in
Eastsaxoniam traiecit, et iterum predandi causa Merciam repetiit,
et peiora prioribus exercitum facere iussit. Illi autem satis impigre
iussa peragunt, et omnibus qui in manus uenerant obtruncatis, uillis quamplurimis incensis, agris depopulatis, prede ubertate ditati,
ad naues repedant festini.[6] Quos rex Anglorum Eadmundus
Ferreum Latus cum exercitu quem de tota Anglia contraxerat
insecutus, in monte, qui Assandun, [5]id est mons asini,[5] nominatur,
abeuntes est consecutus. Ibi festine *triplicibus subsidiis aciem instruit,
dein singulas turmas circumiens, monet atque obtestatur uti memores
pristine uirtutis* atque *uictorie sese regnumque suum a* Danorum *auari-
tia defendant cum* iis *certamen fore quos antea uicerunt.* Interea
Canutus *paulatim in equum locum suos deducit.* At contra rex
Eadmundus *aciem sicuti instruxerat* uelociter mouet, *et repente signo
dato* Danos *inuadit.*[7] Summa ui utrinque dimicatur, ex his et illis
multi cadunt. Verum perfidus dux Edricus Streona, uidens
Danorum aciem inclinatam et Anglos habituros uictoriam, [5]ut
prius Canuto promiserat,[5] cum Magesetensibus et exercitus parte
cui preerat fugam capessit, et dominum suum regem Eadmundum
et Anglorum exercitum dolis circumuenit, et Danis uictoriam suis
insidiis dedit. Occisus est in ea pugna Alfricus dux, Goduuinus
dux,[8] Vlfketelus Eastanglorum dux, Atheluuardus dux, filius ducis

---

a *om. HL*

[1] ASC speaks of the ships and herds being driven to the Medway.
[2-2] ASC identifies the place as Brentford which JW had already mentioned.
[3] The battle of Otford is not mentioned in ASC.
[4] JW explicitly links Eadric's meeting Edmund at Aylesford with the Danes' escape.
ASC simply records the presumed acceptance of Eadric's submission and adds the
aside (which is not in JW) that it was extremely foolish.
[5-5] Not in ASC.

drove their plundered beasts by land.[1] Meanwhile, King Edmund Ironside, for the fourth time, mustered a strong army from the whole of England, and, [2]crossing the River Thames in the same place as before,[2] he entered Kent swiftly, and near Otford[3] he joined battle with the Danes, but they, not enduring his attack, turned their backs, and fled with their horses into Sheppey. However, he slew all of them that he could catch, and, had not the treacherous ealdorman Eadric Streona with his wiles and the evil counsel that he should not pursue his enemies, held him back at Aylesford, he would have gained total victory that day.[4] [5]When he had returned to Wessex,[5] Cnut sent his forces over into Essex, and again returned to Mercia for the purpose of pillaging, and he ordered his army to perpetrate greater crimes than before. They carried out his orders energetically, and when they had cut down all who fell into their hands they burnt a large number of townships, laid waste the fields, and, grown rich with abundant spoil, swiftly returned to their ships again.[6] Edmund Ironside, king of the English, pursued them with an army drawn from all England, and overtook them, as they were going back, at Mount Ashingdon, [5]which means Ass's Hill.[5] There he hastily drew up his battle line with three lines of reserves, then, going round each troop, he exhorted, and adjured them to defend themselves and his kingdom from Danish greed, remembering their former courage and victory, and that the struggle would be with men whom they had beaten before. Meanwhile, Cnut led his men slowly to level ground. But, on the other hand, King Edmund moved his battle line swiftly in the order in which he had drawn it up, and suddenly gave the signal, and attacked the Danes.[7] Both sides fought with all their might, many fell on either side. But the treacherous ealdorman Eadric Streona, seeing the Danish battle line waver and that the English would win the victory, took flight, [5]as he had earlier promised Cnut,[5] with the *Magonsæte* and the section of the army under his command. He deceived his lord King Edmund and the English army with his tricks, and gave the Danes the victory with his stratagems. Slain in that battle were Ælfric the ealdorman, Godwine the ealdorman,[8] Ulfketel, ealdorman of the East

---

[6] ASC simply describes the Danes as destroying everything in their path.

[7] Sallust, *Jugurtha*, xlix. 2–l. 3. ASC says that this was the fifth engagement between the rival armies.

[8] ASC C describes Godwine as ealdorman of Lindsey.

Eastanglorum Atheluuini Dei amici,[1] totusque fere globus nobili-
tatis Anglorum qui nullo in bello maius unquam uulnus quam ibi
acceperunt. Eadnothus, [2]quoque Lindicolinensis episcopus,
Ramesigensis quondam prepositus,[2] et Wulsius abbas,[3] *qui ad
exorandum Deum pro milite bellum agente conuenerant,*[4] interfecti
sunt.[a] Interiectis post hec paucis diebus, cum rex Eadmundus
Ferreum Latus cum Canuto uellet adhuc congredi,[5] perfidus dux
Edricus et quidam alii id nullo modo sinebant fieri, sed illi consilium dabant ut pace facta cum Canuto regnum diuideret. Quorum
suggestionibus, licet inuitus, ad postremum cum consentiret,
recurrentibus internuntiis et obsidibus ad inuicem datis,[6] ambo
reges ad locum qui Deorhyrst[7] nominatur in unum conuenerunt;
Eadmundus cum suis in occidentali ripa Sabrine, Canutus uero in
orientali cum suis consedit. Dein uterque rex in insulam que
Olanege[8] appellatur et est in ipsius fluminis medio sita, trabariis
aduehitur, ubi pace, amicitia, fraternitate et pacto et sacramentis
p. 327   confirmata | regnum diuiditur. Westsaxoniam, Eastangliam,
Eastsaxoniam cum Lundonia[b] Canuto[c] regni[d] Eadmundo remansit.[9]
Dein armis et uestibus mutuatis, tributoque quod classice manui
penderetur statuto, ab inuicem discesserunt. Dani tamen cum
preda quam diripuerant suas ad naues redierunt, cum quibus
pacem dato pretio ciues Lundonienses fecerunt, et eos secum
hiemare permiserunt. Post hec rex Eadmundus Ferreum Latus,[e]
circa festiuitatem sancti Andree apostoli, .xv. indictione, decessit[f]
Lundonie,[g] sed cum auo suo rege pacifico Eadgaro sepultus est
Gleastonie.[10] Cuius post mortem rex Canutus omnes episcopos et

---

[a] et hoc bellum factum est die festiuitatis sancti Luce euangeliste *add. interlin.* B[1]
[b] Lundoniam HL   [c] *rewritten by* C[3]? *followed by about three-quarters of a line left
blank* C, *om. but with over a line left blank* HL, *om. and no blank space* BP
[d] corona (coronam H) tamen regni HLBP, coronam regni G   [e] nocte sequentis
diei festiuitatis sancti Andree *add. over erasure* B[1]   [f] *om.* B   [g] perimitur dolo
Eadrici Streone perfidissimi *add. in part over erasure, and extending into mg.* B[1]

---

[1] JW identifies Æthelwine as ealdorman of East Anglia and 'Dei amicus'.
[2-2] Not in ASC. Eadnoth had been abbot of Ramsey (*Heads of Religious Houses*, p.
61).
[3] JW normally identifies sees and houses of ecclesiastics, but his omission of Ramsey
here could be due to his earlier added identification of Eadnoth as formerly a *prepositus*
of that house.
[4] *HE* ii. 2.
[5] Edmund's intention of resuming the struggle, which is not in ASC, could have
been inferred by JW.
[6] ASC D omits the reference to the exchange of hostages.

Anglians, Æthelweard the ealdorman, son of Æthelwine (the friend of God,[1] ealdorman of the East Anglians), and almost all the nobility of England, who had received no greater loss in any battle than they received there. Also Eadnoth, [2]bishop of Lincoln, formerly prior of Ramsey,[2] and Abbot Wulfsige,[3] who had come to pray to God for the soldiers fighting the battle,[4] were killed. A few days after this, while King Edmund Ironside still wished to fight Cnut,[5] the treacherous ealdorman Eadric Streona and certain others would by no means permit that to take place, but counselled him to make peace with Cnut and divide the kingdom. To their suggestions, although unwilling, he finally agreed, and messengers were sent back and forth, and, when each in turn had given hostages,[6] both kings met at a place called Deerhurst.[7] Edmund was stationed with his men on the west bank of the River Severn, and Cnut on the east with his. Then each king went in fishing boats to the island called Alney,[8] situated in the middle of the river, where, when peace, friendship, and brotherhood had been confirmed by both covenant and oaths, the kingdom was divided. Wessex, East Anglia, Essex with London to Cnut, to Edmund remained the realm.[9] Then, having exchanged arms and garments and established the tribute that should be paid to the fleet, they both left. However, the Danes returned to their ships with the plunder they had seized and the citizens of London made peace with them by paying the price and allowed them to spend the winter with them. After this King Edmund Ironside died at London in the fifteenth indiction about the time of the feast of St Andrew the Apostle, but he was buried at Glastonbury with his grandfather, the peacable King Edgar.[10] After his death King

---

[7] The first, or preliminary, meeting at Deerhurst with each party on either bank of the Severn is not in ASC, though Gloucestershire had been specified earlier as the area where Edmund was and to which Cnut had gone.

[8] ASC D adds 'by Deerhurst'.

[9] ASC assigns Wessex to Edmund and Mercia (D 'to the north part') to Cnut. JW's source must have been corrupt at this point. Roger of Wendover, i. 459 seems to preserve a rendering of this division: 'diuiditur itaque regnum, Eadmundo dictante, inter duos, ita ut corona totius regni regi remaneat Eadmundo; cedunt ergo in usus eius totam Angliam ad australem plagam Thamesis fluminis, cum Est-Sexia et Est-Anglia ciuitate Lundoniarum, quae caput est regni; Cnutone etiam aquilonales partes Angliae obtinet.'

[10] The place of Edmund's death is not mentioned in ASC, but it might be confirmed by Hermann, De miraculis S. Edmundi (Memorials St Edmunds, i. 39)). JW omits the death of Wulfgar, abbot of Abingdon, and the succession of Æthelsige, which are in ASC CE.

duces necnon et principes cunctosque optimates gentis Anglie
Lundonie congregari iussit. Qui, cum uenissent ante eum, quasi
nesciens, interrogauit eos sagacissime qui fuerunt testes inter eum
et Eadmundum, quando conuentionem amicitie et diuisionem
regni inter ipsos gesserunt, qualiter ipse et Eadmundus de
fratribus et filiis eiusdem inter se locuti fuissent: utrum fratribus
et filiis eius liceret in regno Occidentalium Saxonum post patrem
eorum regnare, si Eadmundus moreretur uiuente illo. At illi
coeperunt dicere se proculdubio scire quod rex Eadmundus
fratribus suis nullam portionem regni sui, nec se spirante neque
moriente, commendasset; dixeruntque hoc se nosse, Eadmundum
regem uelle Canutum adiutorem et protectorem esse filiorum eius
donec regnandi etatem habuissent. Verum illi, testante Deo, fal-
sum perhibuerunt testimonium et fraudulenter mentiti sunt, esti-
mantes illum sibi et mitiorem esse propter mendacium eorum et se
ab eo pretium sumere magnum. Ex quibus falsis testibus quidam
non post multum tempus ab eodem rege interfecti sunt. Tunc rex
Canutus, post supradictam interrogationem, conatus est a prefatis
optimatibus fidelia iuramenta recipere. At ipsi iurauerunt illi quod
eum regem sibi eligere uellent, eique humiliter obedire et suo
exercitui uectigalia dare. Et accepto pignore de manu sua nuda,
cum iuramentis a principibus Danorum, fratres et filios Eadmundi
omnino despexerunt eosque reges esse negauerunt. Vnus autem ex
ipsis prefatis clitonibus erat Eaduuius, egregius ac reuerentissimus
regis Eadmundi germanus quem ibidem cum consilio pessimo
exulem esse debere constituerunt. Et cum audisset Canutus rex
adulationem supradictorum et despectionem quam fecerunt in
Eaduuium gaudens introiuit in cameram suam, uocansque ad se
perfidum ducem Edricum sciscitatur*a* ab eo quomodo decipere
ualuisset Eaduuium ut mortis subiret periculum. Qui respondens,
dixit se scire quendam uirum alium, Atheluuardum nomine, qui se
facilius eum in mortem tradere quiuisset, cum quo colloquium
habere posset illique nimiam mercedem promittere. Cognito autem
uiri nomine, uocauit eum rex ad se astutissime dicens: 'sic et sic
allocutus est me dux Edricus, dicens te posse seducere Eaduuium
clitonem ut occidatur, modo adquiesce consiliis nostris et potieris
omni honore et dignitate patrum tuorum, et quere mihi caput eius

---

a sciscisabatur *HL*

Cnut ordered all the bishops and ealdormen and chief men and all
the nobles of the English people to assemble at London. When
they had come before him he asked them very shrewdly, as if he
did not know, who were the witnesses of what had been agreed
between him and Edmund when they made the covenant of
friendship and the division of the kingdom, how he and Edmund
had spoken between themselves about the latter's brothers and
sons: whether his brothers and sons should be permitted to reign
in the kingdom of the West Saxons after the death of their father,
if Edmund should die during his, Cnut's, lifetime. And they
began to say that they knew beyond doubt that King Edmund had
not entrusted any portion of the kingdom to his brothers, either in
life or in death; they said this they did know, that Edmund wished
Cnut to be the guardian and protector of his sons until they were
old enough to rule. They, indeed, as God is a witness, gave false
testimony, and deceitfully lied, thinking that he would be more
gracious to them because of their lies, and they would receive
from him handsome payment. Certain of these false witnesses
were killed by that same king not long after. Then King Cnut,
after the aforementioned interrogation, sought to take oaths of
fealty from the aforesaid nobles; and they swore to him that they
were willing to elect him king, and obey him humbly, and make
payments for his army. And when a pledge from his bare hand
had been received together with oaths from the Danish leaders,
they repudiated Edmund's sons and brothers altogether and
declared them not to be kings. Moreover, one of the aforementioned princes was Eadwig, the excellent and most revered brother
of King Edmund, for whom there, by most evil counsel, they
decreed exile. And when King Cnut had heard the cringing
flattery of those mentioned above, and the despite done to Eadwig,
he entered rejoicing into his chamber, and, calling to him the
treacherous ealdorman Eadric, asked him how he might entrap
Eadwig so that his life should be in danger. He, in reply, said he
knew another man, called Æthelweard, who could more easily
bring him to his death, with whom he could discuss the matter
with the promise of a great reward. However, when he knew the
man's name the king summoned him, saying most cunningly:
'Eadric the ealdorman has spoken thus, saying that you can entrap
the atheling Eadwig so that he may be slain. Only agree with our
plans, and you will receive all the honour and dignity of your

et eris michi carior fratre germano.' Ille uero dicebat se uelle eum
querere ut interficeretur si ullo modo ualuisset. Verumtamen nondum illum necare uolebat sed propter excusationem hoc promittebat; erat enim ille ex nobilissimo genere Anglorum ortus.[1]

[C³? B]

ᵃReuerendus uir Leofsius
Thornegiensis abbas suscepit
episcopatum Wigornensis eccle-
sie.ᵃ²

[C³?]

ᵇ⟨F⟩uit quidam comes in partibus Alamannie diues et prepotens, habens filium
Heremannum nomine. Hic cum
in puerili esset etate, quadam
die cum coequeuisᶜ suis
intrauitᵈ nemus, quo ambie-
batur castrum patris sui
ludendi gratia. Vbi dum irent,
ecce ursus patris eius ex
improuiso superueniens, omnes
qui cum eo uenerant fugere
compulit, eumque quoniam
postremus omnibus erat,
ungulis apprehensum, quia
morsibus nequiuit, brachiis et
ungulis durissime comprimens
debilitauit et nisi citius serui
patris eius, aliorum clamore
puerorum excitati, concurris-
sent, exanimem eum reddidis-
set. Fugato itaque urso,
Heremannus puer semiuiuus in

ᵃ⁻ᵃ Reuerendus . . . ecclesie] *mg. alongside 1017 C³?, om. HLP, incorporated at 1017*
n. d. (p. 504) B ᵇ ⟨F⟩uit . . . insinuabat (p. 502)] *add. mg. of pp. 325–7 alongside*
1016 C³?, om. HLBP; found in Cambridge, Corpus Christi College MS III (= Camb.)
ᶜ *coequeuis C³, coequis Camb.* ᵈ *intrauit Camb., intinuit C³*

---

[1] Cnut's succession is simply recorded in ASC CDE (1017), and JW's account of the
preliminary discussion (which justified both Cnut's claim to succeed and the disin-

fathers, and get me his head and you will be dearer to me than my own brother.' The man indeed said he wished to seek out Eadwig that he might be killed if it was at all possible. However, he promised this, not because he wished to kill Eadwig but as a pretence, for Eadwig was born of the most noble of English families.[1]

The reverend man Leofsige, abbot of Thorney, accepted the bishopric of Worcester.[2]

There was a rich and powerful count of Alemannia, who had a son called Hermann. In his boyhood he went into the woods which surrounded his father's castle with others of his own age to play. While they were there, his father's bear came upon them unexpectedly, forced all who had come with Hermann to flee, and seized him with his claws as he was the last of them all. Crushing the boy cruelly with his arms and claws, since he could not use his teeth, he maimed him, and, if his father's servants, alerted by the cries of the other boys, had not run swiftly up, would have killed him. When the bear had been chased away, the boy Hermann was carried half-alive into the castle. The prolonged attention of doctors had partially healed the flesh which the bear had mauled, but could by no means restore the

heritance of Edmund's brothers), and of the attempt to have Eadwig murdered, are not in ASC, and 'read more like saga' (Whitelock, *ASC*, p. 97 n. 3).

[2] Leofsige's grant as bishop to his thegn Godwine (*S* 1388 *K* 724) is dated 1016. This addition could have been intended for 1017.

castellum defertur, ubi diuturna
medicorum cura[a] carnes quidem eius quas ursus conquassauerat qualitercunque sanate
sunt, sed usus manuum et
pedum nullatenus redintegrari
potuit. Vnde pater et mater
eius grauiter afflicti definierunt
a Deo querundum quod
humanum prestare nequibat
auxilium, et circumferentes
eum per ecclesias longe lateque
constitutas, diuinam pro sani-
tate eius misericordiam inten-
tissime flagitabant, sed puero in
eodem statu manente nihil
proficere potuerunt. Vnde
magis afflicti, Romam ad
imploranda beatorum apostolorum patrocinia pro miserabili
filii sui debilitate profecti sunt.
Vbi cum in uigiliis, orationibus
et ieiuniis tres noctes ducerent
insomnes, tertia nocte, patre et
matre uigilantibus, puer
obdormiuit, et ecce uir clarus
uenerando habitu in somnis,[b] ei
astitit, eumque blando sermone
sciscitatus est utrum mallet plenam corporis habere sospitatem
an sapientiam. Cui dum puer
diuino monitus instinctu sapientiam magis quam corporis
sanitatem se uelle respondisset,
uir qui astabat: 'quoniam', ait,
'quod melius est elegisti,
noueris te sapientiorem cunctis
qui in Romano consistunt
imperio futurum, adeo ut nullus tibi in scientia possit

use of his hands and feet. His father and mother, gravely distressed by this, decided to seek from God what human help could not provide, and, carrying him round the churches established far and wide, they most earnestly sought divine mercy for his health, but, as the boy remained in the same condition, they could achieve nothing. All the more distressed by this, they set out for Rome to implore the protection of the blessed apostles for their wretched son in his infirmity. There, when passing three sleepless nights in vigils, prayers, and fasting, on the third night, while his father and mother kept watch, the boy fell asleep, and, behold, the shining figure of a man of venerable appearance stood by him in a dream, and asked him agreeably whether he would prefer complete health of body or wisdom. Prompted by divine inspiration, the boy replied to the man that he desired wisdom rather than health of body. The man said: 'You have chosen the better part. You will find that you will be so much wiser than all who dwell in the Roman empire that no one will be your equal in knowledge.'

---

^a *Camb., C mg. (blank space in text with erasure)*   ^b insomnis *Camb.* insoni *C*

equari.' His dictis, ab oculis eius euanuit. Ipse uero quasi de graui somno euigilans, cuncta que in somnis uiderat et audierat patri et matri retulit. Quibus auditis, intellexerunt non esse Dei uoluntatem ut sanitatem quam amiserat puer reciperet. Factoque mane domum reuersi sunt, habitoque consilio cum amicis suis, sepe-dictum puerum in ecclesia beatissime Dei genitricis sem-perque uirginis Marie, que apud Augustam Vindelicam habetur, liberalibus studiis tra-diderunt imbuendum. Et quo-niam ut diximus officio manuum et pedum omnimodis destitutus erat, cotidie a min-istris ad hoc deputatis ad scolas delatus, ante pedes scolastici ponebatur. Vnde miranda res accidit ut non solum omnes, qui ad studium liberalium artium[a] ante eum non modico tempore confluxerant, in breui superaret, uerum etiam ipsos quibus commendatus erat mag-istros sapientia sibi diuinitus inspirata transcenderet. Hic musice artis peritissimus ad laudem Dei plures cantus composuit, quos cum discipulis suis propter dissonantiam et

---

[a] liberalium artium *Camb.*, artium liberalium C

Having said these things, he vanished from the boy's sight. But Hermann, as one waking from a deep slumber, told his father and mother everything that he had seen and heard in his dream. When they had heard his account, they realized that it was not God's will that the boy should regain the health he had lost. When morning came, they returned home, and having taken counsel with friends, they entrusted the oft-mentioned boy to the church, which is at Augsburg, of Mary, most blessed Mother of God and eternal Virgin, to be instructed in the liberal arts. And being, as we have said, entirely without the use of his hands and feet, he was carried to school each day by servants deputed to do so, and laid at the feet of the master. Whence the wonderful situation arose that he quickly surpassed not only those who had gathered to study the liberal arts a short while before him, but he outstripped even the very masters to whom he had been entrusted, with his divinely inspired wisdom. Extraordinarily skilled in the art of music, he composed many songs in God's praise, which, wishing, in view of the dissonance and harshness of his voice, so to utter them that his

raucedinem uocis ut intelligere
possent proferre uellet,^a usu
monocordi   magis   diatonici
quam   chromatici   uel   enar-
monici prout poterat insinuabat.^{b1}

[1017] (xv) 1039   *Benedictus*² *centesimus quadragesimus papa.*³

⁴Hoc anno rex Canutus totius Anglie suscepit imperium idque
in quattuor partes diuisit: Westsaxoniam sibi, Eastangliam Turkillo
comiti, Merciam Edrico duci, Northymbriam Yrco^c comiti. Foedus
etiam cum principibus et omni populo ipse et illi cum ipso per-
cusserunt, et amicitiam firmam inter se iuramentis stabilierunt,
omnesque ueteres inimicitias postponentes sedauerunt.⁵ Dein consilio perfidi ducis Edrici, rex Canutus clitonem Eaduuium, regis
Eadmundi germanum, et Eduuium qui ^drex appellabatur rustico-
rum,^d exlegauit.⁶ Verum sequenti tempore cum rege pacificatus est
Eduuius.⁷ Eaduuius uero clito, deceptus illorum insidiis, quos
eotenus amicissimos habuit, iussu et petitione regis Canuti, eodem
anno innocenter occiditur.⁸ Dedit etiam consilium Edricus ut cli-
tunculos Eaduuardum et Eadmundum, regis Eadmundi filios,
necaret.⁹ Sed quia magnum dedecus sibi uidebatur ut in Anglia
perimerentur, paruo elapso tempore, ad regem Suuanorum occi-
dendos misit. Qui, licet foedus esset | inter eos, precibus illius
nullatenus adquiescere uoluit, sed illos ad regem Vngariorum,
Salomonem nomine,¹⁰ misit nutriendos uiteque reseruandos.
Quorum unus, scilicet Eadmundus, processu temporis ibidem
uitam finiuit, Eaduuardus uero Agatham filiam germani impera-

p. 328

---

^a uellet *Camb.*, posset *C*   ^b *see above, p. 496, n. b*   ^c Yrico *from* Yrco *B*
^{d–d} rex . . . rusticorum] rex appellabatur rex rusticorum *H*, appellabatur rex rusticorum
L

---

¹ This Augsburg legend is printed in J. Handschin 'Hermannus Contractus-
Legenden—nur Legenden?', *Zeitschrift für deutsches Altertum und deutsche Literatur*, lxxii
(1935), 1–8 at p. 2 from a 12th-c. Bath MS, Cambridge, Corpus Christi College 111.
pp. 47–8.
² Misplaced Benedict V 964.
³ Mar.
⁴ ASC C–F have the bare bones of this annal, which is much fuller in JW.
⁵ There is nothing corresponding to this sentence in ASC.

pupils might understand them,
he communicated as best he
might by the use of a mono-
chord,   diatonic   rather   than
chromatic or enharmonic.[1]

[**1017**] Benedict[2] 140th pope.[3]

[4]In this year King Cnut undertook the government of the whole
of England, and he divided it into four parts: Wessex for himself,
East Anglia for Earl Thorkell, Mercia for Eadric the ealdorman,
Northumbria for Earl Eric. He also concluded a treaty with the
nobles and the whole people, and they with him, and they
confirmed a firm friendship between them with oaths, and laid
aside, and set at rest all their own animosities.[5] Then, on the
advice of the treacherous Ealdorman Eadric, King Cnut outlawed
the atheling Eadwig, brother of King Edmund, and Eadwig, who
was called king of the Ceorls.[6] This Eadwig indeed made peace
with the king at a later date,[7] but the atheling Eadwig, deceived
by the wiles of those whom he held until then as his closest
friends, was, for all his innocence, killed at the command and
behest of King Cnut in that same year.[8] Eadric also advised him
to kill the little athelings, Edward and Edmund, sons of King
Edmund,[9] but because it would seem as a great disgrace to him if
they perished in England, when a short time had passed, he sent
them to the king of Sweden to be killed. He, although there was a
treaty between them, would in no wise comply with his entreaties,
but sent them to the king of Hungary, Solomon by name,[10] to be
reared and kept alive. One of them, namely Edmund, with the
passage of time, ended his life there. But Edward received Agatha,

[6] In ASC the killing of Eadric (without specifying Cnut's reasons) and other
Englishmen precedes the exile of the atheling (omitted by F) and (in DE under 1017,
in C under 1020) of Eadwig, king of the Ceorls, which is not attributed to Eadric's
advice.
[7] ASC C (1020) DE (1017) do not record Eadwig's subsequent reconciliation with
Cnut.
[8] The killing of the atheling on Cnut's orders is recorded by ASC C alone.
[9] ASC D (1057) alone records the banishment of one son (Edward) of Edmund
Ironside, and says that he married Agatha, a kinsman of the emperor and begat a noble
family. JW's account of the fate of the exiles is much fuller than D's. WM, *GR* ii. 180
(i. 218) mentions two sons, Eadwig and Edward, and regards Edward as the younger.
[10] Not Solomon (1063–74) but Stephen (1000–38).

toris Heinrici[1] in matrimonium accepit, ex qua Margaretam
Scottorum reginam, et Cristinam sanctimonialem uirginem, et clitonem Eadgarum suscepit. Mense Iulio rex Canutus derelictam
regis Ægelredi reginam Alfgiuam, *scilicet Emmam,* in coniugium
accepit,[2] ac in Natiuitate Domini, cum esset Lundonie perfidum
ducem Edricum in palatio iussit occidere quia timebat insidiis ab
eo aliquando circumueniri sicut domini sui priores Ægelredus et
Eadmundus, *scilicet Ferreum Latus,* frequenter sunt circumuenti,
et corpus illius super murum ciuitatis proici ac insepultum precepit
dimitti, cum quo dux Nortmannus, filius Leofuuini ducis, frater
scilicet Leofrici comitis,[3] et Atheluuardus, filius Agelmari ducis,[4]
et Brihtricus, filius Alphegi, Domnanienses satrape, sine culpa[5]
interfecti sunt.[6] Leofricum pro Nortmanno suo germano rex constituit ducem, et eum postmodum ualde carum habuit.[d7]

[1018] (xvi) 1040   [8]Hoc anno de tota Anglia .lxxii. milia et de
Lundonia .x. milia .d. libre[9] exercitui Danorum sunt persolute, et
cum rege Canuto .xl. naues remansere, cetere uero Denemarciam
sunt reuecte. Angli et Dani apud Oxenofordam de lege regis
Eadgari tenenda concordes sunt effecti.[10]

[1019] (xvii) 1041   Hoc anno rex Anglorum et Danorum Canutus
Denemarciam adiit, et ibi per totam hiemem mansit.[11]

[C³BP]
*Defuncto   Ælmaro   Sæliensi
episcopo,   successit   Æthelricus.*[e12]

<hr>

a-a scilicet Emmam] *interlin.* C¹B¹, Emmam *interlin. by a later 13th-c. hand* H, *om.*
LP   *b-b* scilicet . . . Latus] *interlin.* C¹B¹, *om.* HLP   *c* greatan *interlin.* B⁵
d add. 1016 n. a (p. 496) here B, *see App. A for addition* L   *e-e* Defuncto . . .
Æthelricus] *add. at line-end* C³, *om.* HL

<hr>

[1] Whereas ASC D (1057) does not name the emperor whose kinswoman Agatha was,
WM, ibid. describes Agatha as sister of the queen. The evidence is considered in G.
Ronay, *The Lost King of England* (Woodbridge, 1971), pp. 109-21. Perhaps 'germani' is
a slip for 'germane', so that Agatha was niece to Henry II and his sister Gisela, queen
of Hungary. WM will then have conflated two generations (possibly Agatha, like
Gisela, bore the same name as her mother).
[2] ASC C-F record the fetching of Æthelred's widow (not named) to be Cnut's wife,
before 1 Aug. F names her Ælgife in English, Emma in French.
[3] ASC does not call Northman an ealdorman nor say that he was the brother of
Leofric.

daughter of the Emperor Henry's brother.[1] in marriage, by whom he begot Margaret, queen of the Scots, and Christina, a nun, and the atheling Edgar. In July King Cnut married Ælfgifu, that is Emma King Æthelred's widow,[2] and at Christmas, when he was at London, he ordered the treacherous Ealdorman Eadric to be killed in the palace because he feared that some day he would be entrapped by Eadric's treachery, just as Eadric's former lords Æthelred and Edmund, that is Ironside, were frequently deceived, and he ordered his body to be thrown over the city wall, and left unburied. Ealdorman Northman, son of Earl Leofwine, that is brother of Leofric the ealdorman,[3] and Æthelweard, son of Æthelmær the ealdorman,[4] and Brihtric, son of Ælfheah, governor of Devon, were killed with him,[6] [5]although blameless.[5] The king made Leofric ealdorman in place of his brother Northman, and afterwards held him in great affection.[7]

[1018] [8]In this year the Danish army was paid 72,000 pounds, and 10,500 pounds[9] from London, and forty ships stayed with King Cnut, but the others sailed back to Denmark. English and Danes came to an agreement at Oxford about keeping King Edgar's law.[10]

[1019] In this year Cnut, king of the English and the Danes, went to Denmark, and stayed there the whole winter.[11]

> On the death of Ælfmær, bishop of Selsey, Æthelric succeeded.[12]

---

[4] ASC calls Æthelmær 'the Stout' not an ealdorman.

[5-5] This is not in ASC.

[6] ASC CDE, in recording the killing of these Englishmen before the exile of the atheling, give neither the place nor the date, nor record Cnut's reasons nor say that Eadric's body was thrown over the city wall. F (recording only Eadric's death) speaks of his being 'very rightly' killed at London. Hemming (i. 281) speaks of Eadric 'extra murum Lundonie ignominiae projectus' and being left unburied. *Encomium Emmae*, pp. 30–2, confirms Cnut's distrust of Eadric's record of treachery.

[7] ASC does not record Leofric's appointment in Northman's place.

[8] ASC C–F.

[9] ASC CD gives 10,500 pounds, EF wrongly 11,000.

[10] ASC D has 'according to Edgar's law'.

[11] ASC C–F. D adds that Cnut went to Denmark with nine ships.

[12] Ælfmaer, whom JW records succeeding under 1009, appears to have been alive later, if he is the bishop of that name who attests charters in 1023 (*S* 960 *K* 739) and 1031 (*S* 963 *K* 744), though the last charter is attested by Earl Hákon, who was drowned in 1030 (see below).

[1020] (xviii) 1042 *Benedictus papa, presente Heinrico imperatore et Richardo Fuldensi abbate, in eodem cenobio publicam missam cantauit in Natale sanctorum Philippi et Iacobi.*[1]

Canutus rex Angliam rediit, et in pascali festiuitate apud Cirenceastram magnum concilium habuit, et Atheluuardum ducem exlegauit.[2] Liuingus, Dorubernie archiepiscopus, uita decessit, cui Athelnothus, qui bonus appellabatur, nobilis uiri Ægelmari filius, successit.[a][3] Eodem anno ecclesia quam rex Canutus et comes Turkillus in monte qui Assandun dicitur construxerant, illis presentibus, a Wlstano Eboracensi archiepiscopo et multis aliis episcopis cum magno honore et gloria dedicata est.[4] *[b]Defuncto Aldhuno Lindisfarnensi episcopo, tribus pene annis ecclesia pastorali destituebatur solacio. Facto in unum conuentu,* cum de episcopi electione *tractaretur,* religiosus *presbyter quidam Eadmundus* nomine *superuenit* et *ioco* dixit: '*Cur me episcopum non eligitis?*' Cuius *iocum non iocose* accepere qui aderant, sed elegerunt illum, et *triduano* indicto *ieiunio,* sancti Cuthberti uelle super hoc querebant. *Celebrante presbytero* missam *ad caput ipsius sancti, in medio canone, quasi de* eiusdem *patris sepulchro, uox audita* est *que tribus uicibus Eadmundum episcopum nominauit.[b5]*

[1021] (xix) 1043 *Erconbaldus episcopus Mogontinus obiit .xvi. kalend. Septembris,* cui *[c]Aribo successit.*[6]

Canutus rex Anglorum et Danorum ante festiuitatem sancti Martini Turkillum sepedictum comitem cum uxore sua Edgitha expulit Anglia.[7] Algarus Orientalium Anglorum episcopus obiit cui Aluuinus successit.[8]

---

[a] *see App. B for addition B*   [b–b] Defuncto . . . nominauit] *add. mg. alongside 1021–5 C*[2]*?, mg. alongside 1029–31 P*[3]   [c] *1022 starts here (N)*

---

[1] Mar.
[2] ASC C–F (F omits the Cirencester meeting and the exile of Æthelweard). C adds that Eadwig, king of the Ceorls, was also outlawed.
[3] ASC CEF (1020) D (1019) for the death of Archbishop Lyfing, though DEF also have the succession of Æthelnoth in 1020, D giving the day (13 Nov) of his consecration. Æthelnoth is called 'se goda' by CD under 1038 but not here. JW alone names the father of the new archbishop. ASC DEF describe the latter as monk and dean of Christ Church, Canterbury.

[1020] Pope Benedict sang mass in public in the monastery of Fulda on the feast of the nativity of SS Philip and James in the presence of the Emperor Henry and Richard, abbot of the same monastery.[1]

King Cnut returned to England and held a great assembly at Cirencester on Easter Day, and outlawed Æthelweard the ealdorman.[2] Lyfing, archbishop of Canterbury, departed this life, to whom succeeded Æthelnoth, called 'the Good', son of the noble man Æthelmær.[3] In the same year the church which King Cnut and Earl Thorkell had built on the hill called Ashingdon was dedicated in their presence by Wulfstan, archbishop of York, and by many other bishops with great ceremony and magnificence.[4] After the death of Aldhun, bishop of Lindisfarne, that church was destitute of the solace of a pastor for almost three years. At an assembly of the chapter, when the election of a bishop was discussed, a certain devout priest, Edmund by name, came forward and said in jest: 'Why do you not elect me bishop?' Those present took his jest seriously, and elected him, and having proclaimed a three-day fast, they enquired St Cuthbert's will in this matter. While the priest was celebrating mass at the head of that very saint, mid-way through the canon a voice was heard, as if from the said father's tomb, which three times named Edmund bishop.[5]

[1021] Erkenbald, bishop of Mainz, died on 17 August and was succeeded by Aribo.[6]

Cnut, king of the English and of the Danes, expelled the oft-mentioned Thorkell with his wife Edith from England before the feast of St Martin.[7] Ælfgar, bishop of East Anglia, died, and Ælfwine succeeded him.[8]

---

[4] ASC CDF. JW's description of Cnut and Thorkell as co-founders could be inference. He does not have F's reference to Ashingdon being given to a priest, Stigand.

[5] *HDE* iii. 6 (i. 85–6). As *HDE* ii. 20 (i. 78) states that Aldhun succeeded in 990 and held the see for 29 years, he must have died in 1018–19.

[6] Mar.

[7] ASC C-F record Thorkell's expulsion, CDE 'at Martinmas'. None mention Thorkell's wife Edith.

[8] ASC D records the death of Ælfgar, 'the charitable bishop' (on Christmas Day), without naming either his see or his successor.

[**1022**] (xx) 1044 Æthelnothus Dorubernie archiepiscopus Romam iuit, quem Benedictus papa magno cum honore suscepit et pallium illi dedit.[1]

[**1023**] (xxi) 1045 *Eclipsis solis hora nona, uerno tempore.*[2]
   Corpus sancti Alphegi martiris de Lundonia Doruberniam est translatum.[3] Wlstanus Eboracensium archiepiscopus Eboraci, .v. kalend. Iunii, feria .iii., defungitur, sed corpus eius Heli defertur et ibi sepelitur, cui successit Alfricus, *a*4scilicet Puttuc,*a* Wintoniensis prepositus.[4,5]

[**1024**] (xxii) 1046 *Benedictus papa obiit. Iohannes*[6] *centesimus .xli. papa. Heinricus pius obiit, .ii. idus Iulii,* feria .iii., *et sepultus est in Babonis monte* *b*id est Babenberh.*b*
   Romanorum nonagesimus .iiii. Cuonradus[7] *regnauit annis quindecim.*[8]

[**1025**] (i) 1047 *c*Eadmundus uir religiosus Lindisfarnensem epis-copatum suscepit.*c*9

[**1026**] (ii) 1048 *Ciclus decennouenalis .xxvii. incipit indictione nona.*[10]
   Ælfricus Eboracensis archiepiscopus Romam iuit, et a Iohanne papa pallium suscepit.[11] Obiit Ricardus secundus dux Normannorum, cui successit Ricardus .iii., qui eodem anno mor-tuus est, cui Rotbertus frater eius successit.*c*12

---

a–a scilicet Puttuc] *interlin. C*[1], Puttoc *H,* id est Puttunc *interlin. L*[1], id est Puttuc *interlin. B*[1], *om. P*   *b–b* id est Babenberh] *interlin, C*[1]*B*[1] *(N*[2]*?), om. HL*
c–c Eadmundus . . . suscepit] *add. in blank annal C*[2]

---

[1] ASC C–F record Archbishop Æthelnoth's visit to Rome to receive the pallium, DEF at some length. JW agrees with DEF's account of the reception by Pope Benedict, but omits the remainder, including the puzzling papal consecration (in D) of Æthelnoth (see Whitelock, Brett, and Brooke, *Councils,* i. 448–9). He also omits Abbot Leofwine's visit to Rome, which is in EF, as well as Cnut's visit to the Isle of Wight (which is in CDE).
[2] Mar.
[3] ASC C–F record this translation, D very fully, C attributing it to Cnut, EF to Archbishop Æthelnoth ('with Cnut's full permission' D). C also mentions Cnut's return to England and reconciliation with Thorkell.
[4–4] Not in ASC.

[**1022**] Æthelnoth, archbishop of Canterbury, went to Rome; Pope Benedict received him with great honour, and gave him the pallium.[1]

[**1023**] There was a solar eclipse at the ninth hour in the spring.[2]

The body of St Ælfheah the martyr was translated from London to Canterbury.[3] Wulfstan, archbishop of York, died on Tuesday, 28 May, but his body was borne to Ely and buried there. Ælfric, [4]that is Puttoc, prior of Winchester,[4] succeeded him.[5]

[**1024**] Pope Benedict died. John[6] the 141st pope. Henry the Pious died on Tuesday, 14 July, and was buried at Mount Babo, that is Bamberg.

Conrad,[7] the ninety-fourth emperor of the Romans, reigned fifteen years.[8]

[**1025**] The religious man Edmund received the bishopric of Lindisfarne.[9]

[**1026**] The twenty-seventh cycle of nineteen years begins in the ninth indiction.[10]

Ælfric, archbishop of York, went to Rome to receive the pallium from Pope John.[11] Richard II, duke of the Normans, died. Richard III, who died in the same year, succeeded him, and his brother Robert succeeded him.[12]

---

[5] ASC EF record the facts of Wulfstan's death and Ælfric's succession (and consecration by Archbishop Æthelnoth in F). The day of his death is confirmed in the Ely calendar, Cambridge, Trinity College MS 0. 2. 1 (B. Dickins, *Leeds Studies in English*, vi (1937), 15, 17) and his burial at Ely is recorded in the *Liber Eliensis*, ii. 87 (pp. 155-7).

[6] John XIX 1024-32.   [7] Conrad II 1024-39.   [8] Mar.

[9] JW's marginal addition under 1020-1 had referred to a 3-year vacancy after Aldhun's death, which might be assigned to 1018/19. JW's date is internally consistent with Edmund's death in 1048, if, as *HDE* stated he was bishop for 23 years. Discussion in J. Cooper, 'The dates of the bishops of Durham in the first half of the eleventh century', *Durham University Journal*, LX (1968), 131-7. ASC EF (1025 *recte* 1026) gives an account of Cnut's war in Denmark.

[10] Mar.

[11] ASC D, in recording Ælfric's visit to Rome, gives the exact day on which the pallium was bestowed.

[12] Norman Annals. *AU, AG, AC, AMSM*.

[**1027**] (iii) 1049 Cum regi Anglorum et Danorum Canuto intimatum fuisset quod Norregani regem suum Olauum propter eius simplicitatem et mansuetudinem, equitatem et religiositatem, nimis uilipenderent, multum auri et argenti quibusdam illorum misit, multis rogans petitionibus ut illo spreto et abiecto, deditionem illi facerent ac illum super se regnare permitterent, qui cum ea que miserat auiditate magna suscepissent ei remandari iusserunt ad illum suscipiendum se paratos fore quandocunque uellet uenire.[1] |

[**1028**] (iiii) 1050 Canutus rex Anglorum et Danorum .l. nauibus magnis Norregam deuectus, Olauum regem de illa expulit sibique eam subiugauit.[2]

Eodem *anno natus est Marianus,[a] Hiberniensis[b] probabilis Scottus, cuius studio et labore hec cronica precellens est de diuersis libris coadunata.*[3]

[**1029**] (v) 1051 Canutus rex Anglorum, Danorum et Norreganorum ad Angliam rediit, et post festiuitatem sancti Martini Danicum comitem Hacun, qui nobilem matronam Gunnildam, sororis sue et Wyrtgeorni regis Winidorum filiam, in matrimonio habuit, quasi legationis causa in exilium misit. Timebat enim ab illo uel uita priuari uel regno expelli.[4]

[**1030**] (vi) 1052 *Predictus comes Hacun in mari periit.*[5] Quidam tamen dicunt eum fuisse occisum in Orcada insula.[6] Sanctus Olauus rex et martyr, Haroldi regis Norreganorum filius, in Norrega iniuste perimitur a Norreganis.[cd7]

---

[a] *om.* HL   [b] Hiberniensis *from* Hibernensis C[1]L[1], Hibernensis *(N)*
[c-c] Predictus . . . Norreganis] *compressed writing though probably not over erasure* C[1]
[d] *see App. A for addition* L

---

[1] The bribery by Cnut of disaffected Norwegians before the conquest of Norway is not in ASC, but is supported by Sighvat the Skald (Whitelock, *EHD*, no. 18, pp. 339–40).
[2] ASC C-F. DEF say that Cnut came from England. C does not mention Olaf's expulsion.
[3] Mar.

[**1027**] When Cnut, king of the English and of the Danes, was informed that the Norwegians greatly despised Olaf their king because of his simplicity and mildness, justice and piety, he sent some of them much gold and silver, beseeching them, when they had rejected and cast out Olaf, to surrender to him, and permit him to reign over them. Accepting his gifts with great avidity, they sent word to him in reply that they were prepared to receive him whenever he wished to come.[1]

[**1028**] Cnut, king of the English and of the Danes, sailed to Norway with fifty great ships, and expelled King Olaf from that country and subjugated it to himself.[2]

In the same year Marianus of Ireland, the worthy Scot, was born, by whose zeal and labour this outstanding chronicle was compiled from various books.[3]

[**1029**] Cnut, king of the English, the Danes, and the Norwegians, returned to England and, after the feast of St Martin sent the Danish earl Hákon, who had married the noble lady Gunnhild, his sister's daughter by Wyrtgeorn, king of the Wends, into exile as if he were sending him on an embassy, for Cnut feared that he would be deprived of life or expelled from his kingdom by Hákon.[4]

[**1030**] The aforementioned Earl Hákon was drowned[5] in the sea. Some, however, said he was killed in the Orkneys.[6] St Olaf, king and martyr, the son of Harold, king of the Norwegians, was unjustly slain by the Norwegians.[7]

---

[4] ASC DEF simply record the return of Cnut (without naming his kingdoms) to England; JW is the sole authority for the rest of the annal. Campbell (*Encomium Emmae*, p. 85) has cast doubt on the statement that Gunnhild was Hákon's wife since Scandinavian sources say that Hákon was drowned while returning from a visit to England to fetch his bride. In fact JW does not say that she accompanied him on the pretended embassy. Under 1044 JW records Gunnhild's sons by her subsequent marriage to an earl named Harold. Campbell has also doubted whether Hákon could have been distrusted by Cnut (as JW says), since Scandinavian sources say he had had him made viceroy (ibid., p. 72).

[5] ASC C records 'brave' Hákon's death at sea, but after the killing of King Olaf.

[6] Theodricus, *Ágrip af Noregs konunga sögum*, places Hákon's shipwreck in the Pentland Firth (*Encomium Emmae*, p. 71).

[7] ASC CDE. 'Iniuste' is JW's contribution.

[1031] (vii) 1053 ¹Canutus rex Anglorum, Danorum et Norreganorum de Denemarcia magno cum honore Romam iuit, et
sancto Petro apostolorum principi ingentia dona in auro et argento
aliisque rebus pretiosis optulit, et a Iohanne papa ut scolam
Anglorum ab omni tributo et telone liberaret impetrauit. Et in
eundo et redeundo, largas pauperibus elemosinas erogauit, ac multas per uiam clausuras ubi thelon a peregrinis extorquebatur,
ingenti pretio dato, dissipauit.² Hic etiam ante sepulchrum apostolorum, sue uite morumque emendationem Deo deuouit. Vnde et
epistolam memorie dignam per uirum prudentissimum Liuingum,
tunc Tauestokensis ecclesie abbatem post uero mox eodem anno in
Cridiatunensis ecclesie pontificatu Eadnothi, successorem qui sibi
comes itineris extitit, aliosque suos legatos Angliam misit, dum
ipse Roma rediens per uiam quam ierat, Denemarciam priusquam
Angliam peteret, cuius epistole textum hic subscribere dignum
duximus.³

Canutus, rex totius Anglie et Denemarcie et Norreganorum⁴ et
partis Suanorum, Athelnotho metropolitano et Alfrico Eboracensi
archiepiscopo omnibusque episcopis et primatibus, et toti genti
Anglorum, tam nobilibus quam plebeiis, salutem.

1. ᵃNotifico uobis me nouiter isse Romam, oratumᵇ pro redemptione peccaminum meorum et pro salute regnorum quique meo
subiacent regimini populorum.

2. Hanc quidem profectionem Deo iam olim deuoueram, sed pro
negotiis regni et causis impedientibus huc usque perficere non
poteram.

3. Nunc autem ipsi Deo meo omnipotenti ualde humiliter gratias ago, qui mihi concessit in uita mea sanctos apostolos suos,
Petrum et Paulum, et omne sanctuarium, quod infra urbem

ᵃ the division into paragraphs is not in JW but conforms with that in Whitelock, Brett,
and Brooke, Councils, i, no. 65, pp. 508–13   ᵇ orare HL

---

¹ ASC DEF simply record Cnut's visit to Rome, his return to England, and subsequent visit to Scotland to receive the king of Scot's submission. WM GR ii. 182 (i.
221–4) records these visits, but, like JW, gives the text of the letter. The most recent
edition and discussion of the difficulties of dating the visit to 1031 and not to 1027, are
in Whitelock, Brett, and Brooke, Councils, i, no. 65, pp. 506–13.
² WM says that Cnut spent some days in Rome redeeming his sins by gifts to the
churches. JW alone records Cnut's other actions (on his journey and return to
Denmark), the freeing of the English school from tribute and toll, and the large gifts of

[1031] [1]Cnut, king of the English, the Danes, and the Norwegians, went from Denmark to Rome with great state and offered to St Peter, prince of the apostles, great gifts of gold and silver and other precious objects, and obtained from Pope John the concession that the English school should be free of all tribute and toll. On both the outward and the return journeys he gave generous alms to the poor, and at great price he abolished the many barriers along the way where tolls were extorted from pilgrims.[2] He also swore to God before the sepulchre of the apostles to amend his life and ways, and from there he sent to England an epistle worth remembering delivered by the hand of that most prudent man Lyfing, then abbot of Tavistock but soon after, in the same year, successor to the episcopacy at Crediton of Eadnoth (who was his travelling companion), and by the hands of other ambassadors. He himself returned from Rome by the route he took out, visiting Denmark before England. We considered the text of his letter worthy of being subjoined.[3]

Cnut, king of all England and Denmark and the Norwegians[4] and part of the Swedes, to the metropolitan Æthelnoth and Ælfric, archbishop of York, and to all the bishops and leading men and to all the English people, both nobles and ceorls, greetings.

1. I inform you that I have recently gone to Rome, and have prayed for the redemption of my sins, and for the safety of the kingdoms whose people are subject to my rule.

2. I had vowed to God to make this journey long ago now, but I could not accomplish it earlier because of the affairs of the kingdom and other sources of obstruction.

3. Now, however, I most humbly thank my Almighty God, who has suffered me, in my lifetime, to visit His holy apostles, Peter and Paul, and every sanctuary which I could find within the City

alms to the poor, both on the way to Rome and on the return, none of which could have been inferred from the letter.

[3] WM also refers to Lyfing's bringing the letter back, and his imminent appointment to the bishopric of Crediton. He was granted land as bishop of Crediton in 1026 (S 962 K 743), which may be wrongly dated if Lyfing was appointed in 1027 or 1031. He attests as bishop in 1031 (S 963 K 744) in the company of Earl Hákon, who was apparently drowned in 1030.

[4] If the visit was in 1027, 'et Norreganorum' is an insertion unless for reasons unknown Cnut used the title before the conquest of the kingdom.

Romam aut extra addiscere potui expetere, et secundum desiderium meum presentialiter uenerari et adorare.

4. Ob id ergo maxime hoc patraui, quia a sapientibus didici sanctum Petrum apostolum magnam potestatem a Deo accepisse ligandi atque soluendi, clauigerumque esse celestis regni, et ideo specialius eius patrocinium apud Deum diligenter expetere ualde utile duxi.

5. Sit autem uobis notum, quia magna congregatio nobilium in ipsa pascali solennitate[1] ibi cum domno[a] papa Iohanne et imperatore Cuonrado erat, scilicet omnes principes gentium a monte Gargano usque ad istud proximum mare, qui omnes me et honorifice suscepere et donis pretiosis honorauere; maxime autem ab imperatore donis uariis et muneribus pretiosis honoratus sum, tam in uasis aureis et argenteis, quam in palliis et uestibus ualde pretiosis.

6. Locutus sum igitur cum ipso imperatore et domno papa et principibus, qui ibi erant, de necessitatibus totius populi uniuersi regni mei, tam Anglorum quam Danorum, ut eis concederetur lex equior et pax securior in uia Romam adeundi, et ne tot clausuris per uiam artentur, et propter thelon iniustum fatigentur; annuitque postulatis imperator, et Rodbertus[b2] rex qui maxime ipsarum clausurarum dominatur, cunctique principes edictisque firmauerunt, ut homines mei, tam mercatores quam alii orandi causa uiatores, absque omni angaria clausurarum et theloneariorum, firmaque pace et iusta lege securi, Romam eant et redeant.

7. Conquestus sum iterum coram domno papa, et mihi ualde displicere causabar, quod mei archiepiscopi in tantum angariabantur immensitate pecuniarum, que ab eis expetebatur, dum pro pallio accipiendo secundum[c] morem apostolicam sedem expeterent; decretumque est,[d] ne id deinceps fiat.

8. Cuncta enim que a domno papa et ab ipso imperatore et [e]a rege Rodberto[2] ceterisque[e] principibus, per quorum terras nobis transitus est ad Romam, pro mee gentis utilitate postulabam,

---

[a] donno *CLB*   [b] -bertus *over erasure* C^3?, Rodulfus *HL*   [c] secundo *CBP* (*altered to* secundum P^3)   [d] om. *HL*   [e-e] a rege . . . ceterisque] Rodbertus *over ras.* C^3?, a rege Rodulfo ceterisque *HL*

---

[1] Conrad's coronation, for which this assembly must have gathered, took place on Easter Day (26 Mar.) 1027, and provides the strongest internal evidence for dating the visit and letter to that year.

of Rome or outside it and, according to my desire, to worship and adore in person.

4. The most particular reason why I performed this was that I learnt from the wise that St Peter the Apostle received from God the great power of binding and loosing, and bears the keys of the kingdom of heaven, and thus more especially I considered it very profitable to seek diligently his special advocacy with God.

5. Be it known to you that a great crowd of nobles was there at the very Easter celebration with the lord Pope John and the Emperor Conrad,[1] to wit all the princes of the peoples from Mount Garganus to the nearest sea, who all both received me with honour and honoured me with precious gifts. However, I was honoured most by the emperor with various gifts and priceless presents, both in gold and silver vessels and in cloaks and extremely precious garments.

6. Therefore I spoke with the emperor himself and the lord pope and the princes who were there about the needs of all the people of my entire realm, both English and Danes, that a juster law and securer peace might be granted to them on the road to Rome, and that they should not be straitened by so many barriers along the road, and harassed by unjust tolls; and the emperor agreed, and likewise King Robert,[2] who governs most of these same toll-gates. And all the princes confirmed by edicts that my people, both merchants and the others who travel to make their devotions, might go to Rome and return without being afflicted by barriers and toll-collectors, in firm peace and secure in a just law.

7. Again I complained in the lord pope's presence and expressed my grave displeasure that my archbishops were so greatly straitened by the vast sum of money which was required of them when they travelled to the apostolic see according to custom to receive the pallium; and it was decreed that this should not henceforth occur.

8. For everything which I requested from the lord pope and the emperor himself and King Robert[2] and the other princes through whose lands our road to Rome lay, for the advantage of my

---

[2] 'Rodbertus' is an error which must have displaced the correct 'Rodulfus', WM's reading and HL's.

libentissime annuerunt, et concessa sacramento etiam firmauerunt | sub testimonio quattuor archiepiscoporum et .xx. episcoporum, et innumere multitudinis ducum et nobilium, qui ibi aderant.

9. Quapropter Deo omnipotenti gratias magnificas reddo, quia omnia que desideraueram, prout mente decreueram, prospere perfeci,[a] uotisque meis ad uelle satisfeci.

10. Nunc itaque notum sit omnibus uobis, quia ipsi Deo omnipotenti supplex deuoui uitam meam amodo in omnibus iustificare, et regna mihi subdita populosque iuste et pie regere, equumque iudicium per omnes obseruare. Et si quid per mee iuuentutis intemperantiam aut negligentiam hactenus preter id quod iustum erat actum est, totum, Deo auxiliante, deinceps dispono emendare.

11. Iccirco obtestor et precipio meis consiliariis, quibus regni consilia credidi, ne ullo modo aut propter meum timorem aut alicuius potentis persone fauorem aliquam iniustitiam amodo consentiant uel patiantur pullulare in omni regno meo.

12. Precipio etiam omnibus uicecomitibus[1] et prepositis uniuersi regni mei, sicut meam amicitiam aut suam salutem habere uolunt, ut nulli homini, nec diuiti nec pauperi, uim iniustam inferant, sed omnibus, tam nobilibus quam ignobilibus, et diuitibus et pauperibus, sit fas iusta lege potiundi, a qua nec propter fauorem regiam, aut alicuius potentis personam, nec propter mihi congregandam pecuniam, ullo modo deuietur, quia nulla mihi necessitas est, ut iniqua exactione mihi pecunia congregetur.

13. Ego itaque, quod uobis notum fieri uolo, eadem uia qua exiui regrediens, Danemarciam eo, pacem et firmum pactum omnium Danorum consilio cum eis gentibus et populis compositurus, qui nos et regno et uita priuare, si eis possibile esset, uolebant; sed non poterant, Deo scilicet uirtutem eorum destruente, qui nos sua benigna pietate in regno et honore conseruet, omniumque inimicorum nostrorum potentiam et fortitudinem deinceps dissipet et adnichilet.

14. Composita denique pace cum gentibus que in circuitu nostro sunt, dispositoque et pacato omni regno nostro hic in oriente, ita ut a nulla parte bellum aut inimicitias aliquorum timere habeamus,

---

[a] per *interlin. in* perfeci *C*[1]

---

[1] 'Vicecomes' suggests that this is a post-Conquest Latin translation.

people, they most freely granted, and withal confirmed these con-
cessions by oath, witnessed by four archbishops and twenty bishops and an innumerable multitude of dukes and nobles present
there.

9. Wherefore, I give great thanks to Almighty God because
everything I desired, as far as I had conceived it in my mind, I
have successfully carried out, and I have fulfilled my vows completely.

10. And so be it known to you all now that, because I have
humbly vowed to Almighty God himself to lead my life henceforth justly in all things, and to rule justly and devoutly the kingdoms and peoples subject to me, and to observe equitable justice
in all matters, if anything has been done hitherto other than what
was just and through the intemperance of my youth, or through
my negligence, I intend henceforth, with God's help, to amend it
entirely.

11. Therefore I adjure and command my councillors whose
advice concerning the kingdom I have trusted that they do not
henceforth in any way, either from fear of me or favour of some
powerful person, consent to any injustice or suffer it to flourish in
all my kingdom.

12. Also I command all the sheriffs[1] and reeves of my entire
kingdom, if they desire my regard or their own safety, that they
use no unjust compulsion on any man, rich or poor, but that
impartial justice may be enjoyed by all, noble and common, rich
and poor. Let there be no deviation from this, either because of
royal favour or because of any influential person, or for the purpose of amassing money for me, for I have no need of money
accumulated by iniquitous exaction.

13. So I, as I wish to be made known to you, returning by the
same route that I took out, am going to Denmark to arrange peace
and a firm treaty, with the counsel of all the Danes, with those
races and peoples who would have deprived us of life and rule if
they could, but they could not, God destroying their strength.
May he preserve us by his bounteous compassion in rule and honour and henceforth scatter and bring to nothing the power and
might of all our enemies!

14. And finally, when peace has been arranged with the surrounding peoples and all our kingdom here in the east has been
properly ordered and pacified so that we have no war to fear on

quam citius hac estate apparatum nauigii procurare potero, Angliam uenire dispono.

15. Hanc autem epistolam iccirco premisi, ut de mea prosperitate omnis populus regni mei letificetur, quia, ut uos ipsi scitis, nunquam memet ipsum nec meum laborem abstinui, nec adhuc abstinebo, impendere pro omnis populi mei necessaria utilitate.

16. Nunc igitur precipio et obtestor omnes meos episcopos et regni prepositos per fidem quam Deo et mihi debetis, quatinus faciatis ut, antequam ego Angliam ueniam, omnia debita que Deo secundum legem antiquam debemus, sint persoluta, scilicet elemosine pro aratris et decime animalium ipsius anni procreatorum et denarii quos Rome ad sanctum Petrum debemus, siue ex urbibus siue ex uillis, et mediante Augusto decime frugum, et in festiuitate sancti Martini primitie seminum ad ecclesiam sub cuius parrochia quisque deget,^{a} que Anglice ciricsceatt^b nominantur.

17. Hec et his similia si, dum uenero, non erunt^c persoluta, regia exactione secundum leges in quem culpa cadit, districte absque uenia comparabit. Valete.

Aribo Mogontinus episcopus obiit .viii. idus Apr. Sanctus Bardo successit annis uiginti, baculum die sancto Pentecostes accipiens.^{d1}

[1032] (viii) 1054 ^{e}Ecclesia sancti Eadmundi regis et martiris hoc anno dedicata est.^{2}

[1033] (ix) 1055 Magne religionis et modestie uir, Leofsius Huuicciorum episcopus, in episcopali uilla Kemesegia, .xiiii. kalend. Septembris, feria .iii., obiit, et, ut credi fas est, ad celica regna migrauit, cuius corpus in ecclesia sancte Marie Wigorne tumulatur honorifice. In cuius sedem Persorensis abbas Brihteagus filius uidelicet sororis Wlstani Eboracensis archiepiscopi leuatus est.^{3}

---

^{a} *om. H, degit L* ^{b} *circesceat H, circesceatt L, cirricsceant P* ^{c} *fuerint L,* fuerint *interlin. P*^{3} ^{d} *see App. B for addition in mg. near opening of 1031 B (probably* B^1) ^{e} *see App. B for different 1032 B*

---

^{1} Mar.
^{2} Not recorded in ASC, where EF record a damaging appearance of wildfire and a second episcopal succession at Winchester. On the authenticity of *S* 980 *K* 735, a charter of Cnut (1021 × 1023) to Bury St Edmunds, see Harmer, *Writs*, pp. 433–4, C. R. Hart, *The Early Charters of Eastern England* (Leicester, 1966), no. 86.

any side or the hostility of individuals, I intend to come to England as early this summer as I can attend to the equipping of a fleet.

15. I have sent this letter on ahead in order that all the people of my kingdom may rejoice in my success, for as you yourselves know, I have never spared either myself or my labour to provide needful services for the whole people.

16. Now therefore, I command and adjure all my bishops and the reeves of the kingdom, by the faith you owe to God and to me, in so far as you may do, that, before I come to England, all those dues which we owe to God according to ancient law are set-tled, such as the alms for the ploughs and the tithes on livestock born in the same year, and the pence which we owe to St Peter at Rome, either from the cities or from the townships; and in mid-August the tithe of fruits, and on the feast of St Martin the first fruits of the grain to the church in the parish where one lives, which are called church scot in English.

17. If, when I come, these and others like them have not been paid the royal dues shall be exacted according to the laws appro-priate to the crime strictly and without remission from him who is at fault. Farewell.

Aribo, bishop of Mainz, died on 6 April. St Bardo succeeded him and reigned for twenty years, receiving the crozier on the holy day of Pentecost.[1]

[1032] The church of St Edmund, king and martyr, was dedicated this year.[2]

[1033] Leofsige, a very devout and humble man, bishop of the Hwicce, died in the episcopal township of Kempsey on Tuesday, 19 August, and, as we may trust, passed to the kingdom of heaven. His body was buried with honour in the church of St Mary of Worcester. To his see the abbot of Pershore, Brihtheah, son, that is, of the sister of Wulfstan, archbishop of York, was preferred.[3]

---

[3] ASC D records Bishop Leofsige's death, his burial at Worcester, and the succes-sion of Brihtheah. The precise day (19 Aug.) and place (Kempsey) of Leofsige's death, and the information that Brihtheah was abbot of Pershore and nephew of Archbishop Wulfstan, are JW's contributions. Plummer (*Chronicle*, ii. 208) noted that 19 Aug. was a Sunday, not a Tuesday, in 1033. ASC EF record the death and burial-place of Merehwit, bishop of Wells.

[1034] (x) 1056 Eathericus Lindicolinensis episcopus defungitur, et in monasterio Ramesige[a] sepelitur, cui successit Eadnothus.[1] Malcolm rex Scottorum obiit.[2]

[1035] (xi) 1057 Canutus rex Anglorum ante suum obitum super Norreganos regem constituit Suanum,[3] qui suus et Northamtunensis Alfgiue, filie uidelicet Alfhelmi ducis et nobilis matrone Wlfrune, dicebatur filius, quem tamen nonnulli asserebant non regis et eiusdem Alfgiue filium extitisse, sed eandem Ælfgiuam ex rege filium habere uoluisse sed nequiuisse, et iccirco recenter natum infantem cuiusdam presbitere sibi afferri iussisse, regemque omnino credulum fecisse, se filium illi | iam peperisse.[4] Super Danos etiam suum et Alfgiue regine filium Heardecanutum regem constituit.[5] Et postea hoc anno, .ii. idus Nouembris, feria .iiii., apud Sceaftesbyriam uita decessit, sed Wintonie in Veteri Monasterio satis honorifice sepelitur.[6] Quo tumulato, regina Alfgiua ibidem resedit.[7] Haroldus uero dixit[b] se filium esse Canuti regis et Northamtunensis Alfgiue, licet id uerum esset minime. Dicunt enim nonnulli filium cuiusdam sutoris illum fuisse, sed Alfgiuam eodem modo de illo fecisse quo de Suano fertur egisse. Nos uero, quia res in dubio agitur, de neutrorum genitura quid certi sciuimus definire.[8] Is tamen, adepta regia dignitate, misit Wintoniam suos constipatores celerrime et gazarum opumque quas rex Canutus Alfgiue reliquerat regine maiorem melioremque partem ademit illi tirannice,[9] spoliatamque dimisit ibidem ut coeperat residere, atque, consentientibus quam plurimis maioribus natu Anglie, quasi iustus heres coepit regnare, non tamen ita potenter ut Canutus quia iustior heres expectabatur Heardecanutus. Vnde breui post tempore regnum sorte diuiditur Anglie, et Haroldo pars septentrionalis, Heardecanuto prouenit

p. 331

---

[a] Rumesige *C*, Ramesie *P*   [b] *interlin. C*¹

[1] ASC CDE record the death of Æthelric, and CD his burial at Ramsey. JW identifies the see anachronistically and names his successor.
[2] ASC D records Malcolm's death.
[3] Cnut's setting up of Swein as ruler of Norway (not in ASC) is borne out by Scandinavian sources (see *Encomium Emmae*, p. 72).
[4] The details concerning Swein's parentage and the story of the fraud practised by Ælfgifu are peculiar to JW.
[5] This appointment is not mentioned in ASC, though it could have been inferred.

[1034] Æthelric, bishop of Lincoln, died, and was buried in the abbey of Ramsey. Eadnoth succeeded him.[1] Malcolm, king of the Scots, died.[2]

[1035] Before his death, Cnut, king of the English, made Swein king over the Norwegians.[3] He was said to be his son by Ælfgifu of Northampton, that is the daughter of Ælfhelm the ealdorman and the noble lady Wulfrun. However, several asserted that he was not the son of the king and that same Ælfgifu, but that Ælfgifu wanted to have a son by the king, and could not, and therefore ordered the new-born child of some priest's concubine to be brought to her, and made the king fully believe that she had just borne him a son.[4] Also, he set up as king over the Danes Hardacnut, his son by Queen Ælfgifu.[5] And later in this year, on Wednesday, 12 November, he departed this life at Shaftesbury, but was buried with due honour at Winchester in the Old Minster.[6] After his burial Queen Ælfgifu settled there.[7] But Harold claimed to be the son of King Cnut by Ælfgifu of Northampton, but that is quite untrue, for some say that he was the son of a certain cobbler, but that Ælfgifu had acted in the same way with him as she is said to have done with Swein. But, because the matter concerned is open to doubt, we have been unable to make a firm statement about the parentage of either.[8] Harold, however, having seized the royal dignity, sent his personal attendants to Winchester with great speed, and tyranically deprived Ælfgifu of the bigger and better part of the treasures and riches which King Cnut had left her,[9] and left her, despoiled, where she had just settled. With the consent of many of the nobles of England he began to reign as if the rightful heir, not, however, as powerfully as Cnut because Hardacnut, the heir with the stronger claim, was awaited. Whence, after a short time the kingdom of England was divided by lot, and the northern part fell to Harold,

[6] ASC C-F record Cnut's death at Shaftesbury and his burial at Winchester, EF giving the length of his reign. CD give the precise date (12 Nov.) and EF specify the Old Minster as the burial-place.

[7] Ælfgifu's residence at Winchester is stated in ASC CD, and implied in E.

[8] Doubts about Harold's parentage were expressed in ASC. D alone calls Ælfgifu 'of Northampton', but JW further identifies Harold's father as a shoemaker, and records the deception practised on Cnut.

[9] ASC CD record this seizure.

australis.[1] Obiit Rotbertus dux Nortmannorum, cui successit Willelmus bastard filius eius in puerili etate.[2]

ᵃBrun Wirziburgensis episcopus obiit.ᵃ[3]

[**1036**] (xii) 1058 Ciclus solis incipit .iiii. concurrentibus bissextilibus. *Piligrinus episcopus Coloniensis, instigatus quorundam inuidorum monachorum, de monasterio sancti Pantaleonis uerbis, qui Heliam abbatem Scottorum, qui illis quoque prefuit, propter districtionem suam et alios Scottos, quos secum habuit, odio habebant. Prefatus episcopus minatus est eidem Helie quod postquam de curte regia uenisset,ᵇ nullum Scottum neque ipsum ibi dimisisset. Tunc Helias et alii Scotti responderunt: 'Si Christus in nobis uere est peregrinus non reuertetur uiuus ad Coloniam episcopus Piligrinus.' Ita quoque Dominus effecit, et Helias duo monasteria rexit.[4]*

[5]Innocentes clitones Alfredus et Eaduuardus,[6] Athelredi quondam regis Anglorum filii de Normannia,ᶜ [7]ubi cum Ricardo auunculo suo manserant tempore longo, multis Normannicisᵈ militibus secum assumptis,[7] in Angliam [7]paucis transuecti nauibus[7] ad sue matris colloquium, que morabatur Wintonie, uenere. Quod indigne grauiterque ferebant potentes nonnulli quia, licet iniustum esset, Haroldo multo deuotiores extitere quam illis, maxime ut fertur comes Goduuinus.[8] Hic quidem Alfredum, cum uersus Lundoniam ad regis Haroldi colloquium ut mandarat properaret, retinuit, et artam in custodia posuit. Sociorum uero illius quosdam disturbauit, quosdam catenauit, et postea cecauit. Nonnullos cute capitis abstracta cruciauit, et, manibus ac pedibus amputatis, multauit, multos etiam uendere iussit, et, mortibus uariis ac miserabilibus, apud Gyldefordam sexcentos uiros occidit. Sed illorum nunc animas in paradiso creditur gaudere cum sanctis, quorum

---

ᵃ⁻ᵃ Brun . . . obiit] *om. H*   ᵇ uenisset *LP* (*from* uenissent *P*), uenissent *CHB*
ᶜ Normannia *from* Nortmannia *C*   ᵈ Normannicis *from* Nortmannicis *C*

---

[1] In recording this seizure of treasure ASC CD show Harold acting with authority, but E speaks of his acting as regent, not as king, and (though EF end their annal with the statement that in spite of his parentage he became fully king) JW's account might reflect this uncertainty. The council at Oxford, where Harold was offered a protector's role, and the divisions among the leading men about the succession, reported in ASC EF, are not in JW. The division of England is not spelt out in ASC.
[2] Norman Annals *AU, AG, AC, AMSM.*   [3] Mar.
[4] Mar.

the southern to Hardacnut.[1] Robert, duke of the Normans, died. William the Bastard, his son, succeeded him in his boyhood.[2]

Brun, bishop of Würzburg, died.[3]

[1036] The solar cycle begins with four concurrents in a bissextile year. Pilgrim, bishop of Cologne, was stirred up by the words of envious monks from the monastery of St Pantaleon who hated Elias, who was abbot of the Irish, and who also ruled over them, because of his strictness and because of the other Irish whom he had with him. The aforesaid bishop threatened the same Elias that, when he had returned from the royal court, he would allow no Irishman there, not even Elias himself. Then Elias and the other Irish answered: 'If Christ is truly with us, Bishop Pilgrim will not come back alive to Cologne.' This indeed the Lord brought about, and Elias ruled the two monasteries.[4]

[5]The innocent athelings, Alfred and Edward,[6] sons of Æthelred, formerly king of the English, came from Normandy, [7]where they had for a long time stayed with their uncle Richard. They brought with them many Norman knights[7] and, [7]when they had crossed over with a few ships[7] to England, went to hold discussions with their mother, who was living at Winchester. This many of the leading men seriously and undeservedly resented because, although it was unjust, they were much more devoted to Harold than to the princes, especially, they say, Earl Godwine.[8] He detained Alfred when he was hastening towards London to confer with King Harold as he had commanded, and placed him in strait custody. Indeed, he dispersed some of his companions, some of whom he put in chains and afterwards blinded. He tortured several by scalping and punished them by cutting off their hands and their feet; he also ordered many to be sold, and he put 600 men to various pitiable deaths at Guildford. But it is to be believed that the souls of those whose blameless bodies were so cruelly destroyed on

[5] The events in this annal are recorded in ASC CD, but there are important differences.

[6] Neither ASC nor the *Encomium Emmae* mentions Edward's accompanying his brother. Norman sources record a military expedition which precedes Alfred's visit, and does not seem to be linked to it.

[7-7] No equivalent in ASC.

[8] The hostility of Godwine and others to Alfred's visit to his mother is in ASC C (D speaking only in general of 'those with much power in the land').

corpora tam crudeliter sine culpa perempta sunt in aruis.[1] Quo audito, regina Alfgiua filium suum Eaduuardum qui secum remansit maxima cum festinatione Normanniam[a] remisit.[2] Deinde Goduuini et quorundam aliorum iussione, ad insulam Elig clito Alfredus strictissime uinctus ducitur, sed ut ad[b] terram nauis applicuit in ipsa, mox eruti sunt oculi eius cruentissime, et sic ad monasterium ductus, monachis traditur custodiendus. Vbi breui post tempore, de hac migrauit luce, et in australi porticu in occidentali parte ecclesie corpus eius sepelitur debito cum honore, anima uero paradisiaca fruitur amenitate.[3]

[1037] (xiii) 1059 [4]Haroldus rex Merciorum et Northymbrorum,[5] ut per totam regnaret Angliam, a principibus et omni populo rex eligitur. Heardecanutus uero, quia in Denemarcia moras innexuit et [6]ad Angliam, ut[c] rogabatur, uenire distulit,[6] penitus abicitur. Cuius mater Alfgiua, [d6]scilicet Emma,[d6] Anglorum quondam regina hiemis initio sine misericordia expellitur Anglia. Que rate mox parata in Flandriam[7] transuehitur, et a nobili comite Balduuino cum honore suscipitur. Is ut talem uirum decuit, quandiu necessitas poposcerat ei necessaria gratanter ministrare curauit. Eodem anno paulo ante magne [e]religionis uir,[e] Auicus, Eoueshamnensis decanus, obiit.[8]

Piligrinus episcopus obiit, .viii. kalend. Sept., feria .v., et Herimannus successit .xx. annis. Sanctus Bardo archiepiscopus, presente Cuonrado imperatore, indictione .v., quarto die idus Nou., feria quinta, dedicauit monasterium sancti Martini Mogontiensis[f] archiepiscopatus in honorem sancti Martini episcopi et confessoris.[9] |

---

[a] Normanniam *from* Nortmanniam *C*   [b] *om. HL*   [c] *om. HL*   [d-d] scilicet Emma] *interlin. C*[1], *om. HLP*, id est Emme *interlin. B*[1]   [e-e] religionis uir] uir religionis *HL*   [f] Mogontiensis *(N)*, Mogotiensis *CBP*

---

[1] ASC CD record Alfred's arrest by Godwine (who is not named by D), and his companions' torture and murder, but do not say where these events took place. The *Encomium Emmae* records Godwine's supposed oath to Alfred, Godwine's diversion of Alfred from London to Guildford, and the butchery by Harold's men at Guildford. Norman sources also agree with the *Encomium Emmae* in saying that the companions were handed over to Harold for execution. JW alone speaks of Harold's commanding that Alfred be brought to London. ASC is not specific about the numbers slain, though the *Encomium Emmae* says they were large.

earth now rejoice in paradise with the saints.[1] When she heard this, Queen Ælfgifu sent her son Edward, who remained with her, back to Normandy in great haste.[2] Then, at the command of Godwine and certain others, the atheling Alfred was led most tightly bound to the Isle of Ely, but as soon as the ship touched land his eyes were most bloodily plucked out, and he was led thus to the monastery, and handed over to the custody of the monks. When, shortly afterwards, he departed this light, his body was buried with due honour in the south chapel at the west end of the church, but his soul enjoys the loveliness of paradise.[3]

[**1037**] [4]Harold, king of the Mercians and the Northumbrians,[5] was elected by the leaders and the whole people to rule all England as king, but Hardacnut, since he wasted his time in Denmark, and [6]delayed coming to England as he was invited,[6] was completely deposed. His mother, Ælfgifu, [6]that is Emma,[6] formerly queen of the English, was driven out of England without pity at the beginning of winter. As soon as a vessel had been prepared she sailed to Flanders[7] and was received with honour by the noble Count Baldwin. He, as was fitting for such a man, took care, as long as necessity demanded, to furnish her freely with what she needed. A little earlier in the same year Æfic, dean of Evesham, and a very devout man, died.[8]

Bishop Pilgrim died on Tuesday, 25 August, and Hermann succeeded him, and ruled for twenty years. St Bardo the archbishop, in the presence of the Emperor Conrad, consecrated the monastery of St Martin in the archbishopric of Mainz in honour of St Martin, bishop and confessor, on Thursday, 10 November, in the fifth indiction.[9]

---

[2] As already stated in 1036 (above, p. 523, n. 6, Edward's visit to England (and therefore his return to Normandy) are mentioned neither in ASC nor in the *Encomium Emmae*.

[3] ASC CD record the taking of Alfred to Ely, his blinding, and his death and burial. The *Encomium Emmae* says Alfred was dead when entrusted to the monks.

[4] ASC CD record, like JW, though with the differences shown, the acceptance of Harold as king of all England, the expulsion of Emma, her reception by Baldwin of Flanders, and the death of Æfic of Evesham. EF record only Emma's expulsion and exile in Bruges.

[5] The description of Harold's share of the kingdom is not in ASC, but is consistent with JW's record of the division of the kingdom under 1035 (see above, p. 522 n. 1).

[6-6] No exact equivalent in ASC.   [7] ASC has Bruges, not Flanders.

[8] ASC   [9] Mar.

[**1038**] (xiiii) 1060 Æthelnothus Dorubernensis archiepiscopus *ª*.iiii. kalend. Nouembris*ª* uita decessit,[1] cuius obitus die .vii. Æthelricus Suthsaxonie presul obiit. Petierat enim a Deo ne post mortem dilectissimi sui patris Athelnothi in hac luce diu uiueret,[2] cui Grymkytel in episcopatum, Æthelnotho uero regis capellanus Edsius[3] in archiepiscopatum successit. Decessit etiam eodem anno Alfricus Eastanglorum episcopus, et Huuicciorum episcopus Brihteagus .xiii. kalend. Ianuarii, feria .iiii., uitam finiuit, cuius*ᵇ* episcopatum Liuingo Cridiatunensi antistiti rex dedit Haroldus.[4] Pro Alfrico uero *Stigandus*, regis capellanus est constitutus, *sed postmodum eiectus, et Grymkytel*

[HL]	[C³BP]
pro eo est *electus*;	*ᶜSuthsaxonum episcopusᶜ ᵈpro auroᵈ* est electus:

habuitque *duas* parrochias tunc, *Australium Saxonum et Orientalium Anglorum*.[5] Sed iterum Stigandus receptus et Grymketel est eiectus,

[C³BP]

*ᵉ*et Stigandus quidem *Australium Saxonum* episcopatum tenuit, *et fratri* suo *Ægelmaro Orientalium Anglorum* presulatum *acqui*siuit. *Minimumque id animositati sue ratus, Wintoniensem et Cantuuariensem thronos ascendit, uix egreque exoratus, ut Australibus Saxonibus*

ª⁻ª .iiii. kalend. Nouembris] *interlin. C*¹   *ᵇ* cui *CHBP*   *ᶜ⁻ᶜ* Suthsaxonum episcopus] *interlin. C³*   *ᵈ⁻ᵈ* pro auro] *over erasure C³*   *ᵉ* et Stigandus . . . Theodfordum (p. 528)] add. at line-end and in mg. with signe de renvoi C³, written on small inserted leaf between fos. 101 and 102 with signe de renvoi H, om. L*

---

[1] ASC C-F all record Archbishop Æthelnoth's death, EF giving the precise day (1 Nov.). London BL Cotton MS Nero C. IX, fos. 14ʳ, 20ʳ gives '.v. kalend. Nou.' (28 Oct.) against JW's 29 Oct.

[2] The death of Bishop Æthelric is in ASC C-F, but D alone states that he prayed not to live long after Æthelnoth's death and died within seven days.

[3] ASC F alone describes Eadsige as 'king's priest'.

[4] The bishop of East Anglia's death is recorded by ASC CEF, the bishop of Worcester's by C-F. The succession at Canterbury, Sussex, and Worcester (not at East Anglia) is given by EF. CD (not E) give the day of Brihtheah's death (20 Dec.). JW alone identifies the new bishop of Worcester, Lyfing, as bishop of Crediton.

[1038] Æthelnoth, archbishop of Canterbury, departed this life on 29 October.[1] Seven days after his death Æthelric, bishop of Sussex, died; for he had besought God that he should not live in this light long after the death of his most beloved father Æthelnoth.[2] Grimketel succeeded him in the bishopric, but the king's chaplain,[3] Eadsige, was preferred to Æthelnoth's archbishopric. In the same year Ælfric, bishop of East Anglia, died also, and Brihtheah, bishop of the Hwicce, ended his life on Wednesday, 20 December. His bishopric King Harold gave to Lyfing, bishop of Crediton.[4] Stigand, the king's chaplain, was appointed in Ælfric's place, but was afterwards ejected and Grimketel

was elected in his place.

was elected bishop of Sussex for gold.

Then he had two dioceses, of the South Saxons and the East Angles.[5] But Stigand was again appointed, and Grimketel ejected,

and Stigand held the bishopric of the South Saxons, and acquired the bishopric of the East Angles for his brother, Æthelmær. Thinking that very little for one of his ambition, he ascended the thrones of Winchester and Canterbury; it was with much difficulty and great reluctance that he was persuaded to let the South Saxons have a bishop of their

[5] For some of the confusion in this entry, see R. R. Darlington, 'Ecclesiastical reform in the late Old English period', *EHR*, li (1936), pp. 385-428 at 400 n. 3. JW ignores the immediate succession of Ælfric by his namesake, who survived to 1042 or 1043 (Harmer, *Writs*, no. 8, pp. 153-4), and who is in the WM and JW *Epis. Lists* for East Anglia. As ASC did not record the death of a second Ælfric, but did record the succession of Stigand to Elmham under 1043 (C), his departure in the same year (C), and his restoration in 1044 (E only), JW may have decided to assign Stigand's succession at Elmham to this year, as well as its temporary administration by Grimketel during Stigand's temporary loss of it (which is not in ASC but is confirmed by a writ of Edward the Confessor concerning the rights of Bury St Edmunds addressed to Bishop Grimketel and the Suffolk thegns, Harmer, *Writs*, no. 10, p. 155). The same account occurs in JW *Epis. Lists* (with which WM, *GP* ii. 74, (p. 150) shares some words). C³ substituted 'pro auro' for 'pro eo', the reading attested by the JW MSS *HL*. Stigand was never bishop of Selsey.

proprius^a ordinaretur episcopus. Post Ægelmarum^b fuit Helmanensis episcopus Arfastus, qui ne^c nihil fecisse uideretur, ut sunt Normanni fame in futurum studiosissimi, episcopatum de Helmaham transtulit ad Theodfordum.^{d1}

[1039] (xv) 1061   *^eCuonradus imperator obiit, .ii. idus Ianuarii ^fferia .iiii.,^f et sepultus est in Spira. Ricardus abbas Fuldensis obiit .xiii. kalend. Aug. Sigeuuart successit.²*

³Quo anno hiemps⁴ extitit durissima. Brihtmarus Licedfeldensis episcopus obiit, cui Wlsius successit.⁵ Eduuinum, Leofrici comitis germanum, et nobiles regis ministros Turkillum et Ælfgeatum, filium Eatsii,⁶ multosque cum eis uiros occiderunt Walenses. Heardecanutus ⁷rex Danorum⁷ Flandriam⁸ deuectus, ad matrem suam ⁷Alfgiuam, ^gscilicet Emmam,^g⁷ uenit.

Romanorum nonagesimus .v. Heinricus⁹ filius Cuonradi imperatoris regnauit annis decem et septem.¹⁰

[1040] (i) 1062   Haroldus rex Anglorum obiit Lundonie et in Westmonasterio sepelitur.¹¹ Quo sepulto, proceres ferme totius Anglie legatos ad Heardecanutum Brycge, ubi cum matre sua morabatur, mittentes, et se bene facere putantes, rogauerunt illum ut Angliam ueniret et sceptra regni susciperet.¹² Qui nauibus .lx.¹³ paratis, et ¹⁴Danicis militibus instructis,¹⁴ ante mediam estatem Angliam aduehitur, et gaudenter ab omnibus suscipitur regnique solio mox sullimatur, sed sui imperii tempore nil egit dignum

---

^a prius H   ^b Agelmarus H   ^c om. H   ^d see above, p. 526 n. e ^e reverses order of first two sentences (N)   ^{f-f} darker ink C¹   ^{g-g} scilicet Emmam] interlin. C¹, om. HL, id est Emme interlin. B¹, id est Emmam interlin. P³

---

¹ *GP* ii. 74 (p. 150). Æthelmær did not become bishop of Elmham until Stigand's translation to Winchester in 1047.
² Mar.
³ ASC C alone records the events here with the differences shown.
⁴ JW has 'hiemps' for ASC's 'wind'.
⁵ ASC does not name Brihtmær's successor.
⁶ ASC does not name Ælfgeat's father. Under 1052 JW reports these deaths as occurring in an ambush.
⁷⁻⁷ Not in ASC.   ⁸ ASC has Bruges for Flanders.

own ordained. After Æthelmær, Herfast was bishop of
Elmham, and he, lest he should
appear to have done nothing—
for Normans are most eager for
lasting fame—translated the
seat of the bishopric from
Elmham to Thetford.[1]

[1039] The Emperor Conrad died on Wednesday, 12 January, and
was buried at Speyer. Richard, abbot of Fulda, died on 20 July.
Sigward succeeded him.[2]

[3]In that year the winter[4] was very harsh. Brihtmær, bishop of
Lichfield, died, and Wulfsige succeeded him.[5] The Welsh killed
Edwin, Earl Leofric's brother, and the king's noble thegns,
Thorkell and Ælfgeat, son of Eadsige,[6] and with them, many men.
Hardacnut, [7]king of the Danes,[7] sailed to Flanders,[8] and visited
his mother [7]Ælfgifu or Emma.[7]

Henry,[9] the ninety-fifth emperor of the Romans, son of
Emperor Conrad, reigned for seventeen years.[10]

[1040] Harold, king of the English, died at London, and was
buried at Westminster.[11] After his funeral the leading men from
almost all England sent ambassadors to Hardacnut at Bruges,
where he was staying with his mother, and, thinking they were
doing the right thing, asked him to come to England and receive
the sceptre of the realm.[12] He prepared sixty[13] ships, [14]which he
manned with Danish troops[14] and came to England before midsummer, and was joyfully received by all, and was at once raised
to the throne of the kingdom, but during the period of his rule

[9] Henry III 1039–56.   [10] Mar.
[11] ASC A (addition by Hand 9: s. xii[1], post 1115?) CD (1040) EF (1039) record
Harold's death, and E gives its location (Oxford against JW's London) and date, his
burial place (as does F) and the length of his reign. A also records the visit of
Archbishop Eadsige to Rome.
[12] This invitation to Hardacnut at Bruges, and the implied questioning of its wisdom, are in ASC CD, though JW, in addition, repeats the information given under
1039 that Emma was staying there.
[13] ASC CD, not EF.
[14–14] Not in ASC.

potestati regie.[1] [2]Nam mox ut regnare cepit, iniuriarum quas uel
sibi uel sue genitrici suus antecessor fecerat rex Haroldus, qui
frater suus putabatur, non immemor, Alfricum Eboracensem
archiepiscopum, Goduuinum comitem, Styr maiorem domus,
Edricum dispensatorem, Thrond suum carnificem et alios magne
dignitatis uiros Lundoniam misit, et ipsius Haroldi corpus effodere
et in gronnam proicere iussit. Quod cum proiectum fuisset, id
extrahere et in flumen Tamense mandauit proicere. Breui autem
post tempore, a quodam captum est piscatore, et ad Danos allatum
sub festinatione, in cimiterio, quod habuerunt Lundonie, sepultum
est ab ipsis cum honore.[2] Quibus actis, octo marcas unicuique sue
classis remigi, et [3]duodecim unicuique gubernatori[3] de tota Anglia
precipit dependi, tributum uidelicet tam graue ut uix aliquis id
posset persoluere, quapropter omnibus qui prius aduentum eius
desiderabant magnopere factus est exosus summopere.[4] [5]Ad hec
etiam pro nece sui fratris Alfredi aduersus Goduuinum comitem et
Wigornensem episcopum Liuingum, accusantibus illos Alfrico
Eboracensi archipresule[a] et quibusdam aliis, exarsit ira magna.
Iccirco episcopatum Wigornensem Liuingo abstulit, et Alfrico
dedit, sed sequenti anno ablatum Alfrico, Liuingo secum
pacificato benigne reddidit. Goduuinus autem regi pro sua amicitia
dedit trierem fabrefactam, [b]caput uel rostrum[b] deauratum haben-
tem, armamentis optimis instructam, decoris armis electisque
octoginta militibus decoratam, quorum unusquisque habebat duas
in suis brachiis aureas armillas, sedecim uncias pendentes, loricam
trilicem indutam, in capite cassidem ex parte deauratam, gladium
deauratis capulis renibus accinctum, Danicam securim auro argen-
toque redimitam in sinistro humero pendentem, in manu sinistra
clipeum cuius umbo clauique erant deaurati, in dextra lanceam
que lingua Anglorum ategar appellatur. Insuper etiam non sui con-
silii nec sue uoluntatis fuisse quod frater eius cecatus fuisset, sed
dominum suum regem Haroldum illum facere quod fecit iussisse,

---

[a] archiepiscopo *HL*   [b–b] caput uel rostrum] uel rostrum *interlin. after* caput
C[1]B[1]P[3], uel rostrum *om. H*, uel caput *interlin. above* rostrum *L[1]*

---

[1] ASC EF record Hardacnut's arrival at Sandwich 'seven days before midsummer'.
The reference to his unworthiness as ruler is in CD only.
[2–2] Only in ASC CD which are much briefer, simply recording the throwing of
Harold's body, after it had been exhumed, into the fen.
[3–3] Not in ASC.

did nothing worthy of royal power.[1] [2]For as soon as he began to rule, remembering the injuries which his predecessor King Harold, who was considered his brother, had perpetrated against both him and his mother, he sent Ælfric, archbishop of York, Earl Godwine, Stor, master of his household, Eadric his steward, Thrond his executioner and other men of great rank to London, and ordered them to dig up Harold's body and throw it into a marsh. When it had been thrown there, he ordered it to be pulled out, and thrown into the River Thames. However, a short time later, it was taken by a certain fisherman, borne in haste to the Danes, and was honourably buried by them in the cemetery they had in London.[2] When these things were done, he ordered eight marks to be paid to each oarsman of his fleet, and [3]twelve to each steersman[3] from the whole of England. That is tribute so heavy that scarcely anyone could pay it, wherefore to all who had greatly desired his coming, he became supremely hateful.[4] [5]Furthermore he burnt with great anger because of his brother Alfred's death against Earl Godwine and Lyfing, bishop of Worcester, who were accused of responsibility for it by Ælfric, archbishop of York, and certain others. Therefore he took the bishopric of Worcester from Lyfing, and gave it to Ælfric, but the following year he took it from Ælfric and graciously restored it to Lyfing, having made peace with him. However, Godwine, to regain his friendship, gave the king a skilfully made galley, with a gilded prow or beak, furnished with the best tackle, well equipped with suitable arms and eighty picked soldiers. Each one of them had two golden armlets on his arms, weighing sixteen ounces, was clad in a triple mail corselet, with a part-gilded helmet on his head, was girt about the loins with a sword with gilded hilts; a Danish axe bound with gold and silver hung from his left shoulder; in his left hand was a shield with gilded boss and studs, in his right a spear called an *ætgar* in English. In addition, he also swore to the king, with the ealdormen of almost all England and the greater thegns, that it had not been by his advice or at his wish that his brother was

---

[4] The tax and its burdensomeness are in ASC C-F, and the reaction of those who had originally invited Hardacnut in ASC CD, though there these precede the exhumation of Harold's body. E distinguishes a presumably regular tax for the maintenance of 16 ships collected as in Cnut's time from that raised by Hardacnut for 62 ships. E mentions the rise in the price of wheat.

[5] The remainder of the annal is not in ASC. There are echoes of JW's description of Godwin's ship in *GR* ii. 188 (i. 299).

cum totius fere Anglie principibus et ministris dignioribus regi iurauit.[1]

[1041] (ii) 1063 Hoc anno rex Anglorum Heardecanutus suos huscarlas misit per omnes regni sui prouincias ad exigendum quod indixerat*a* tributum, ex quibus duos, Feader scilicet et Turstan, Wigornenses prouinciales cum ciuibus, seditione exorta, in cuius-

P. 333 dam turris Wigornensis mo|nasterii solario quo celandi causa confugerant .iiii. nonas Maii, feria .ii., peremerunt. Vnde rex, ira commotus, ob ultionem necis illorum, Thuri Mediterraneorum, Leofricum Merciorum, Goduuinum Westsaxonum, Siuuardum Northymbrorum, Roni Magesetensium et ceteros totius Anglie comites, omnesque ferme suos huscarlas cum magno exercitu, Alfrico adhuc *b*Wigornensem pontificatum*b* tenente, illo misit mandans ut omnes uiros si possent occiderent, ciuitatem depredatam incenderent, totamque prouinciam deuastarent. Qui die ueniente .ii. iduum Nouembrium, et ciuitatem et prouinciam deuastare coeperunt, idque per .iiii. dies agere non cessauerunt, sed paucos uel e ciuibus uel prouincialibus ceperunt aut occiderunt, quia precognito aduentu eorum, prouinciales quoque locorum fugerant, ciuium uero multitudo in quandam modicam insulam in medio Sabrine fluminis sitam, que Beuerege nuncupatur, confugerant, et, munitione facta, tamdiu se uiriliter aduersus suos inimicos defenderant, quoad, pace recuperata, libere domum licuerit eis redire. Quinta igitur *c*die ciuitate*c* cremata, unusquisque magna cum preda rediit in sua et regis statim quieuit ira.[2] Non multo post Eaduuardus, Agelredi quondam regis Anglorum natus, de Normannia,*d* ubi multis exulabat annis, uenit Angliam, et, a fratre suo Heardecanuto rege susceptus honorifice, in curia sua mansit.[3]

[1042] (iii) 1064 Rex Anglorum Heardecanutus, dum in conuiuio, in quo Osgodus Clapa, magne uir potentie, filiam suam

---

a dixerat *HL*   *b-b* Wigornensem pontificatum] pontificatum Wigornensem *HL*
c-c die ciuitate] *darker ink possibly over erasure* C¹   *d* Normannia *from* Nortmannia
C, Nortmannia *P*

---

[1] See above, p. 531 n. 5.
[2] ASC CD (1041) refer simply to the retaliatory ravaging of Worcestershire on account of the slaying of two unnamed housecarls, who were in Worcester to exact the

blinded, but that his lord King Harold had ordered him to do what he did.[1]

[1041] In this year Hardacnut, king of the English, sent his house-carls through all the provinces of his kingdom to extort the tribute he had imposed. Two of them, Feader and Thurstan, were slain on Monday, 4 May, by the country people of Worcestershire and the townspeople, in an upper room in one of the towers of Worcester monastery to which they had fled to hide when a dis-turbance had broken out. The king was enraged by this and to avenge their deaths, he sent there Thored of the Midlanders, Leofric of the Mercians, Godwine of the West Saxons, Siward of the Northumbrians, Hrani of the *Magonsæte*, and all the other English ealdormen and almost all his housecarls with a great army, while Ælfric was still bishop of Worcester, ordering them to slay all the men if they could, to plunder and burn the city, and to lay waste the whole area. Arriving on 12 November, they began to lay waste both the city and the countryside, and did not stop doing that for four days, but they took or killed few of the townsfolk or the country people because, having received advance notice of their arrival, the country people had fled in all directions, and a great number of the townspeople had taken refuge on a small island called Bevere situated in the middle of the River Severn, and fortified it, and defended themselves so strongly against their enemies that when peace had been restored they were allowed to return home freely. On the fifth day, accordingly, when the city had been burnt, and all returned home with great booty, the king's anger was straightway slaked.[2] Not much later Edward, son of Æthelred, former king of the English, came to England from Normandy where he had spent many years as an exile, and as he was honourably received by his brother, King Hardacnut, he stayed at his court.[3]

[1042] While at a feast at a place called Lambeth, at which Osgod Clapa, a very powerful man, married his daughter Gytha with

tax mentioned under 1040 (CD). ASC EF (1040) give the precise amounts raised by the two taxes (the army tax and the tax for 32 ships); the rest is distinctive to JW.

[3] ASC CD (1041) EF (1040) refer to Edward's return to England, all stressing his kinship with Hardacnut, but CD mention also the betrayal of Earl Eadwulf of Northumbria, and D the consecration of Archbishop Æthelric.

Gytham, Danico et prepotenti uiro. *"Touio Prudan cognomento,*[a] in loco qui dicitur Lamhythe magna cum letitia tradebat nuptui,[b] letus, sospes et hilaris, cum sponsa predicta et quibusdam uiris bibens staret, repente inter bibendum miserabili casu ad terram corruit et sic mutus permanens, .vi. idus Iunii, feria .iii., expirauit, et, Wintoniam delatus, iuxta patrem suum regem Canutum est tumulatus.[1] Cuius frater Eaduuardus, annitentibus maxime comite Goduuino et Wigornensi presule Liuingo, Lundonie leuatur in regem, cuius pater Agelredus, cuius pater Eadgarus, cuius pater Eadmundus, cuius pater Eaduuardus Senior, cuius pater Alfredus.[2]

[c]*Helias Scottus abbas obiit .ii. idus Apr., uir prudens et religiosus, et ideo monasterium sancti Pantaleonis* [d]*cum suo, id est sancti Martini, sibi commissum est regendum. Ipse optimum missalem librum monachi Franci, sine licentia, in commune scriptum in monasterio sancti Pantaleonis*[d] *igne consumpsit, ne alius quid sine licentia facere auderet.* [e]*Cui successit Maiolus Scottus, uir sanctus.*[cef3]

[1043] (iiii) 1065 Eadwardus, ab archipresulibus Edsio Dorubernensi et Alfrico Eboracensi, aliisque ferme totius Anglie presulibus, prima die Pasce, unguitur in regem Wintonie.[4] Eodem anno .xiiii. diebus ante festiuitatem sancti Andree apostoli, festinato rex cum comitibus Leofrico, Goduuino et Siwardo de ciuitate Glauuorna Wintoniam uenit improuise et, ut illi consilium ei dederant, sue genitrici quicquid in auro, argento, gemmis, lapidibus, aliisue rebus pretiosum habuerat, abstulit, uel quia priusquam rex esset effectus uel post minus quam uolebat illi dederat, et ei ualde dura extiterat, uerumtamen sufficienter ei ministrari necessaria precepit, et illam ibidem quiete manere iussit.[5]

[a–a] Touio . . . cognomento] nomine . . . (*long dash through blank space*) . . . Canuto *over erasure* B[1]   [b] nuptii HL   [c–c] Helias . . . sanctus] *darker ink* C[1]   [d–d] cum . . . Pantaleonis] *om., but add. in mg. with signe de renvoi* P[5]   [e–e] cui . . . sanctus] *om.* HL   [f] *see App. B for addition in mg. with signe de renvoi in mg. but none corresponding in text B (hand not found elsewhere)*

---

[1] ASC ACD (1042) EF (1041) all record Hardacnut's death, and EF its exact date as well as the places of death and burial and length of reign. Though CD say he died 'as he was standing at his drink', JW alone records the occasion.

[2] Although ASC CD (1042) EF (1041) record the acknowledgement of Edward as king ('as was his natural right' in CD), EF says this happened at London. JW alone makes Godwine and Bishop Lyfing chiefly responsible for it, and Edward's genealogy seems his contribution at this point. EF go on to record a very bad year for crops and cattle, and E the death of Abbot Ælfsige and the succession of Arnwig at Peterborough.

great joy to Tofi, surnamed the Proud, a Dane and a man of influence, Hardacnut, king of the English, merry, in good health, and in great heart, was standing drinking with the aforementioned bride and certain men when he suddenly crashed to the ground in a wretched fall while drinking. He remained speechless until his death on Tuesday, 8 June. He was carried to Winchester, and buried next to his father, King Cnut.[1] At London, mainly by the exertions of Earl Godwine and Lyfing, bishop of Worcester, his brother Edward ascended the throne, whose father was Æthelred, whose father was Edgar, whose father was Edmund, whose father was Edward the Elder, whose father was Alfred.[2]

Elias, the Irish abbot, a prudent and devout man, died on 12 April. To his rule, because of his qualities, the monastery of St Pantaleon as well as his own, that is St Martin's, was committed. He himself destroyed by fire the excellent missal which a Frankish monk had written without permission in a current hand in the monastery of St Pantaleon, lest anyone else should dare to make one without leave. The holy man, Maiol, an Irishman, succeeded him.[3]

[1043] Edward was anointed king at Winchester by Eadsige, archbishop of Canterbury, and by Ælfric of York and by almost all the other English bishops on the first day of Easter.[4] In the same year, fourteen days before the feast of St Andrew the Apostle, the king came unexpectedly to Winchester with Earls Leofric, Godwine, and Siward, and, as they counselled him, took from his mother whatever gold, silver, gems, stones, or other precious objects she had, because, both before he became king and after, she had given him less than he wanted, and had been extremely harsh to him. However, he commanded that an adequate supply of necessities be ministered to her, and ordered her to live there quietly.[5]

[3] Mar.

[4] ASC ACD (1043) EF (1042) record the consecration of Edward at Westminster (A does not name the place), CEF alone referring to Archbishop Eadsige's officiating and giving general advice. JW adds Archbishop Ælfric and 'other bishops' to those who took part.

[5] JW's account of the despoiling of Emma is closer to ASC D (1043) than to C (1043) E (1042) in giving the precise date, in describing Edward (acting on advice) as journeying from Gloucester in the company of those named earlier, and coming upon Emma unexpectedly, and in saying that Emma was allowed to stay on at Winchester. In describing the spoil, CEF refer to land being seized. CEF refer to Stigand's consecration as bishop of Elmham, and C to his deposition.

Animchadus Scottus monachus et inclusus in Fulda obiit,[a] *super cuius sepulchrum uisa sunt lumina et psalmodia audita est. Super cuius sepulchrum Marianus, huius cronice auctor, decem annis ad pedes eius stans inclusus missam cantauit, qui etiam hec*[b] *de supradicto Animchado retulit. 'Ipse,' inquit, 'cum Hibernia esset in insula que Keltra dicitur, quadam die, fratribus quibusdam aduenientibus, cum licentia senioris sui nomine Cortram, caritatem eis fecit. Cunque quidam post cibum essent egressi, illi qui remanserant ad ignem se calefacientes consederunt atque bibere ab eo petierunt, quo nolente sine licentia, coegerunt illum. Tandem consensit, prius tamen ex eo potu seniori suo quasi benedictionem misit.* ᶜ*Crastino autem ab eo interrogatus, unde sibi illum potum misisset, omnia que gesta erant retulit, moxque propter hanc tantum culpam eum senior de Hibernia exire iussit,*ᶜ *quod ille humiliter adimpleuit, sicque Fuldam ueniens, sancte uiuendo inclusus, ut predixi, obiit. Hoc autem michi retulit Tigernah, senior meus, cum quandam culpam paruam coram eo fecissem. Me quoque audiente in Fuldam incluso, quidam religiosissimus eiusdem cenobii monachus nomine Willelmus* P. 334   *supradictum | Animchadum iam sepultum rogauit ut se benediceret, atque sicut postea mihi confirmauit eadem nocte per uisum uidit Animchadum in sepulchro suo stantem, nimio fulgore nitentem, et extensa manu se benedicentem totamque ipsam noctem etiam, ego mellifluo plenam odore duxi.' Hec ait Marianus.*[1]

[C³BP³]

[d] De Dorsetania. *In Dorsetensi pago sunt abbatie Cerneliensis, Middeltunensis uirorum, Sceaftoniensis feminarum.* In quo pago olim colebatur deus Helit sed predicans ibidem uerbum Dei sanctus *Augustinus, uidit mentis oculo diuinam adesse presentiam,* hilarisque factus *ait: 'Cerno Deum qui nobis suam retribuet*

---

[a] .iii. kalend. Februarii] *add. Mar., add. mg. with signe de renvoi* B¹   [b] *gap follows* hec C   ᶜ⁻ᶜ Crastino . . . iussit] *om., but add. mg. with signe de renvoi* P⁵   [d] De Dorsetania . . . instituit (p. 540)] *add. mg. alongside end of 1043–8* C³, *om.* HL, *first two (Dorset and Wiltshire) sections in outer mg. alongside 1043–4, third (Berkshire) in inner mg. alongside 1047 (headings om.)* P³

Anmchad, the Irish monk and anchorite, died at Fulda, above whose tomb lights were seen, and psalmody heard. Marianus, author of this chronicle, who lived as an anchorite at his feet for ten years, sang the mass over his sepulchre. He also recounted this anecdote about Anmchad mentioned above. 'When he was in Ireland on *Inis-Celtra*, one day he prepared refreshments for some brothers who arrived, with the permission of his superior, Corcoran by name. And when some had eaten and gone out, those who remained sat together warming themselves at the fire and asked him for something to drink. He was unwilling to provide it without permission but they pressed him. In the end he agreed. First, however, he sent some of the drink to his superior as if for a blessing. The next day, however, when he asked him why he had sent him that drink, he related all that had been done, and his superior ordered him to leave Ireland at once for such a fault. This he humbly obeyed, and so he came to Fulda, lived devoutly as a holy anchorite and, as I said before, died. This indeed my superior, Tigernach, told me when I had committed some small fault in his presence. Also, in my hearing while I was enclosed in Fulda, a certain most devout monk of the same monastery, called William, asked the aforesaid Anmchad, already in his grave, to bless him, and, as he declared afterwards to me, that same night he saw with his own eyes Anmchad standing on his tomb, shining with great splendour, and blessing him with his outstretched hand, and I also found the same night was filled with the most delicious odour.' These are the words of Marianus.[1]

Concerning Dorset. In Dorset there are the abbeys of Cerne and Milton for monks, Shaftesbury for nuns. In that region the god Helit was formerly worshipped but St Augustine, preaching the word of God there, saw, in his mind's eye, that the divine presence was there and, rejoicing, said: 'I perceive the God who will restore to us His

_____
[1] Mar.

gratiam.' Euentus, uel potius uer-
bum, Cerneliensi *loco indidit*
uocabulum ut uocaretur Cernel,
ex duobus uerbis Ebraico et
Latino, quod Hel deus dicatur
Ebraice. Ibi succedentibus annis,
Edwoldus, frater Eadmundi regis
et martyris, uitam heremiticam
solo pane et aqua triuit. Post
uero *religiose actam uitam*
magna sanctitatis opinione ibi-
dem se*pelitur.* Cui succedens
*Ægelward*us *homo prediu*es *ceno-*
bium eo in *loco sancto Petro con-*
*stru*xit.[1]

De Wilsetania. *In Wilt*unensi
pago sunt cenobia, Malmesberie
uirorum, Wiltonie et Ambresberie
feminarum.[2] *Malmesberie* monasterium *quidam Meldum, qui alio*
nomine uocatur Maidulf, natione
Scottus, professione monachus
fecerat.[3] *Wiltunense cenobium*
beata Eadgitha, filia regis
Eadgari, dulcibus exuuiis ornat.
Ambresberie Ælfthrytha sancti
*Eadwardi interfectr*ix, *causa*
penitentie fecit.[2] De Barr⟨o⟩cia.
In Berrukensi pago sunt monaste-
ria duo Abbandoniense et
*Radingense. Abbandoni*am *Cissa*
pater Ine fundauit.[4] *Rading*e
quondam fuit cenobium sanctimo-
nialium quod *rex Heinricus pro*
indicta sibi penitentia restaurare
intendens, duo alia olim diruta

[1] *GP* ii. 84 (pp. 184–5). These seem to be part of a block of *GP* monastic entries added in the margin on pp. 334–6 of the JW MS C, with no clear reason for their insertion in particular annals.
[2] *GP* ii. 87 (p. 188).

grace.' The incident, or rather the word, gave the place Cerne its name, derived from two words, Hebrew and Latin, as God is called *Hel* in Hebrew. There in later years Eadwold, brother of Edmund, king and martyr, lived as a hermit on bread and water alone. Indeed, after he had led a devout life with a great reputation for sanctity he was buried there. Æthelweard, a very rich man, succeeded him, and built a monastery dedicated to St Peter in that place.[1]

Concerning Wiltshire. In Wiltshire there are the religious houses, Malmesbury for monks and Wilton and Amesbury for nuns.[2] One Meldum, also known as Maidulf, an Irishman by race, by profession a monk, founded the monastery of Malmesbury.[3] The blessed Edith, daughter of King Edgar, adorned the convent of Wilton with sweet spoils. Ælfthryth, St Edward's murderess, built Amesbury as her penance.[2] Concerning Berkshire. In Berkshire there are two monasteries, Abingdon and Reading. Cissa, Ine's father, founded Abingdon.[4] Reading was formerly a convent of nuns to which King Henry, intending to restore it as part of the

[3] *GP* iv. 188 (pp. 333-4).   [4] *GP* ii. 88 (p. 191).

Lefminstre et Celsi adiunxit et
monachos instituit.*a1*

[**1044**] (v) 1066 *Benedictus*[2] *papa centesimus .xlii. Hic cum papatiam suam emisset, Heinricus *b*imperator perrexit Romam et pro eo Clementem constituit papam, quia ex ore sancti Petri emptor et uenditor gratie spiritualis cum Simone Mago sunt anathematizati.*[3]

*c*Aluuardus*d* Lundoniensis presul, qui et ante episcopatum et in episcopatu abbatis iure Eoueshamnensi cenobio prefuit, cum pontificatum administrare pro sua infirmitate minus sufficeret, Eoueshammi residere uoluit, sed fratres loci illius id omnino consentire noluerunt. Quapropter, ablatis ex maxima parte libris et ornamentis que ipse eidem contulerat loco, et quedam, ut fertur, qui alii contulerant, ad monasterium Ramesege secessit, et omnia que attulit sancto contulit Benedicto, ibique resedit, et hoc anno, .viii. kalend. Aug., feria .iiii., defungitur, ibidemque sepelitur.[4] In generali concilio quod eodem tempore celebratum est Lundonie, religiosus Eoueshamnensis monachus Wlmarus, qui et Manni, ut abbatis iure suo monasterio preesset eligitur, et, .iiii. idus Augusti, feria .vi., ordinatur.[5] Eodem anno nobilis matrona Gunnilda, regis Wurtgeorni et sororis Canuti regis filia et comitum Hacuni, et post Haroldi morte uiduata, cum duobus filiis Hemmingo et Turkillo expellitur de Anglia, que Flandriam deuecta in loco qui Brycge dicitur aliquandiu resedit, et sic Danemarciam adiit.[6] Capellanus regis Stigandus presulatum Eastanglie suscepit.[7]

---

a see above, p. 536 n. d   *b* frequent changes of ink at this point on p. 334 (annals 1044–8) C.   *c* see App. A for addition before Aluuardus L   *d* Aluuardus from Aluuordus C, Ælfwardus H, Alfwordus L, Aluuordus B, Alwordus P

---

[1] *GP* ii. 89 (p. 193).   [2] Benedict IX 1045.   [3] Mar.
[4] ASC D (1045 *recte* 1044) alone records the death of Bishop Ælfweard on 25 July, which was, as JW says, a Wednesday in 1044. D also says that he had been both abbot and benefactor of Evesham and that he went to Ramsey and died there. JW makes explicit his retention of the abbacy during his episcopate and relates his retirement as bishop through illness, his admission to Ramsey after he had been refused entry at Evesham, and his transfer of books and ornaments from Evesham to Ramsey. The accounts of this episode in *Chronicon abbatiae de Evesham*, ed. W. D. Macray (RS xxix; London, 1863), p. 85, and *Chronicon abbatiae Rameseiensis*, ed. W. D. Macray (RS lxxxiii; London, 1886), pp. 157–8, are similar to JW's, though the Ramsey chronicle says Ælfweard was suffering from leprosy. Macray (*Chron. abb. de Evesham*, p. 85) dates Ælfweard's death to 27 July on the evidence of London BL Cotton MS Vespasian B. XV, fo. 17[v], but ASC D and JW's 25 July should be preferred to this later source.

penance publicly enjoined him, joined two others, Leominster and Cholsey, which were already decayed, and installed monks.[1]

[1044] Benedict[2] the 142nd pope. Since this man had bought his papacy, the Emperor Henry went to Rome, and made Clement pope in his stead because, in the words of St Peter, the buyer and seller of spiritual grace are anathematized with Simon Magus.[3]

Ælfweard, bishop of London, who both before and during his episcopate ruled the monastery of Evesham as abbot, wanted to live at Evesham when, because of his infirmity, he lacked sufficient strength to administer the episcopate, but the brothers there would by no means agree to this. Wherefore, he took away most of the books and the ornaments which he had donated himself to the place, and some, so they say, which others had contributed, and withdrew to the monastery of Ramsey, and everything which he took he offered to St Benedict, and there he settled, and in this year, on Wednesday, 25 July, there he died, and was buried.[4] At the general synod which was held at London the devout monk of Evesham, Wulfmær, also known as Mannig, was elected to rule his monastery as abbot, and on Friday, 10 August, he was ordained.[5] In the same year the noble lady Gunnhild, the daughter of King Wyrtgeorn, and the sister of King Cnut, the widow of Earl Hákon, and after his death of Earl Harold, was banished from England with her two sons, Hemming and Thorkell. Conveyed to Flanders, she stayed in the place called Bruges for some time, and thus went to Denmark.[6] The king's chaplain Stigand obtained the bishopric of East Anglia.[7]

[5] ASC D 1045 (recte 1044) records Manni's election and consecration on 10 Aug. as abbot of Evesham. JW contributes his other name (Wulmarus), the occasion (a council at London) of this election, and the weekday, which is correct for 1044. See Heads of Religious Houses, p. 47.

[6] ASC D 1045 (recte 1044) records the exile and wanderings of Gunnhild (described as Cnut's kinswoman), but does not name her parents and her two husbands, some of which information JW had already given under 1029. See Encomium Emmae, p. 84.

[7] ASC E 1043 (recte 1044) records Stigand's receiving the bishopric (of East Anglia) to which he had already been consecrated the previous year (C 1043 E 1042 recte 1043) only to be deprived of it soon afterwards (C 1043). C (1044) E (1043 recte 1044) also record the resignation of Archbishop Eadsige, the nomination of his successor, the famine, the naval exercise to Sandwich by Edward, Edward's marriage to Edith (C only), and the succession of Æthelstan to the abbacy of Abingdon.

[**1045**] (vi) 1067   *Ciclus decennouenalis .xxviii. incipit indictione tertia decima.*[1]

Brihtuuoldus Wiltoniensis episcopus obiit, cui regis capellanus Herimannus de Lotharingia oriundus successit.[2] Quo anno rex Anglorum Eadwardus ad Sandicum portum congregauit classem preualidam contra Magnum Norreganorum regem, Angliam adire disponentem, sed bellum a Suano rege Danorum illi illatum iter impediuit.[3]

[**1046**] (vii) 1068   *Clemens*[4] *papa .cxliii.*[5]

Liuingus Huuicciorum, Domnanie et Cornubie presul, .x. kalend. Aprilis, die dominica, obiit.[6] Cuius post decessum, regis cancellario Leofrico Brytonico mox Cridiatunensis et Cornubiensis datus est presulatus,[7] et Aldredus, qui primo monachus Wintoniensis, post abbas Teauistokensis extitit, Huuicciorum pontificatum suscepit.[8] Osgodus Clapa expellitur Anglia.[9] Magnus Norreganorum rex, sancti Olaui regis filius, fugato rege Danorum Suano, sibi Danemarciam subiugat.[10]

[**1047**] (viii) 1069   *Clemens papa obiit .vii. idus Oct. Poppo,*[11] *qui et Damasus, papa centesimus .xliiii. Nix in occidente tanta cecidit ut siluas quoque frangeret*[12] quo etiam anno hyemps extitit durissima.[13]

Grymkytelus Suthsaxonie presul obiit, cui regis capellanus Heca successit.[14] Decessit quoque Aluuinus Wintoniensis episcopus, in

---

[1] Mar.

[2] ASC C–F (F 1044 altered to 1046?) all record the death of Bishop Brihtwold, C with the day, DF naming the see, and EF giving the length of his episcopacy. All name his successor Hereman, CEF calling him Edward's priest, C making clear he was appointed by the king. JW alone names his country of origin.

[3] Though ASC CD mention the assembly of a large fleet at Sandwich, D alone says that this was to meet the anticipated invasion by Magnus of Norway, which was prevented by his war with Swein of Denmark. E records here the marriage of Edward and Edith and the consecration of Wulfric, abbot of St Augustine's.

[4] Clement II 1046–7.

[5] Mar.

[6] ASC C (1045) D (1047) E (1044 *recte* 1046) F (1046 from 1045?) all record the death of Bishop Lyfing. D agrees with JW on the day (23 Mar., a Sunday in 1046), while C gives 20 Mar. (under 1045 as C ends its year on 24 Mar.). D names all three of Lyfing's bishoprics, C none, E Devonshire and F Exeter. D describes him as 'eloquent'.

[7] ASC C (1045) D (1047 *recte* 1046) E (1044 *recte* 1046) F (1046 from 1045) mention Leofric's succession (D to Devon and Cornwall, E to Devonshire, F to Exeter), and CEF describe him as Edward's priest. JW's 'cancellarius regis' and 'Brytonicus' are

[1045] The twenty-eighth cycle of nineteen years begins in the thirteenth indiction.[1]

Brihtwold, bishop of Wilton, died, whom the king's chaplain, Hereman, a native of Lotharingia, succeeded.[2] In that year Edward, king of the English, assembled a very strong fleet at the port of Sandwich against Magnus, king of the Norwegians, who was intending to invade England, but the war made upon him by Swein, king of the Danes, prevented him from undertaking the journey.[3]

[1046] Clement[4] the 143rd pope.[5]

Lyfing, bishop of the Hwicce, of Devon and of Cornwall, died on Sunday, 23 March.[6] After his death the bishopric of Crediton and Cornwall was soon given to the king's chancellor,[7] Leofric the Welshman, and Ealdred, who had been first a monk of Winchester and was afterwards abbot of Tavistock, received the bishopric of the Hwicce.[8] Osgod Clapa was driven out of England.[9] Magnus, king of the Norwegians, son of the king, St Olaf, having put Swein, king of the Danes, to flight, subdued Denmark to himself.[10]

[1047] Pope Clement died on 9 October. Poppo,[11] also known as Damasus, the 144th pope. So much snow fell in the west that it broke even the woods;[12] in this year, too, the winter was very bitter.[13]

Grimketel, bishop of Sussex, died, whom the king's chaplain Heca succeeded.[14] Ælfwine, bishop of Winchester, also died, to

peculiar to him, and WM *GP* ii. 94 (p. 201) says he was brought up and educated in Lotharingia.

[8] ASC D (1047 *recte* 1046) alone mentions Ealdred's succession to Worcester, but not that he had been a monk at Winchester—which *GP* iii. 115 (p. 251) also claims— and abbot of Tavistock. An 'Ealdred episcopus' attests a grant of 1044 (*S* 1004 *K* 772). As *Heads of Religious Houses*, p. 73 suggests, he may have acted as Lyfing's coadjutor.

[9] ASC C (1046) D (1047 *recte* 1046) E (1044 *recte* 1046) F (1046 from 1044?) record Osgod's expulsion, D calling him the 'staller'.

[10] ASC D (1047 *recte* 1046) alone records the conquest by Magnus though JW identifies him and mentions the flight of Swein.

[11] Damasus II 1048.   [12] Mar.

[13] ASC C (1046) describes the winter after Candlemas 1046. D assigns it to 1048 (*recte* 1047).

[14] ASC C (1047) D (1048 *recte* 1047) E (1045 *recte* 1047) F (1047 from 1046). C also gives the burial-place of Grimketel as Christ Church. Heca is described as Edward's priest in CEF, C making clear that the king appointed him.

cuius sedem presul Eastanglie sullimatur Stigandus.[1] Suanus rex
Danorum suos legatos misit ad Eadwardum regem Anglorum, et
rogauit ut sibi classem mitteret contra Magnum regem
Norreganorum. Tunc comes Goduuinus consilium regi dedit, ut
saltem quinquaginta naues militibus instructas ei mitteret, sed quia
Leofrico comiti et omni populo id non uidebatur consilium, nullam ei mittere uoluit.[2] Post hec Magnus rex Norreganorum,
[3]classe multa et ualida constipatus,[3] cum Suano prelium commisit,
et, multis milibus utrinque occisis, illum de Danemarcia expulit, et
post in illa etiam regnauit, atque tributum sibi non modicum pen-
dere Danos coegit, ac non multo post obiit.[a4]

[1048] (ix) 1070 *Poppo papa obiit.*[5]

Suanus Danemarciam recepit et Haroldus Haruager, Siuuardi
regis Norreganorum filius, et ex parte matris frater sancti Olaui,
patruus scilicet Magni regis, Norregam repetiit breuique post tempore suos nuntios ad regem Eaduuardum misit, et pacem amiciti-
amque illi optulit et recepit.[6] [b]Ad quem etiam rex Danorum
Suanus legatos mittens, rogauit ut ei nauale mitteret adiutorium,[b]
sed licet comes Goduuinus uoluisset ut saltem .l. naues illi mitter-
entur, Leofricus comes omnisque populus uno ore contradixerunt.[7] Terre motus, kalend. Maii, die dominica, extitit magnus
Wigorne, Wic, Deorbegia et multis aliis locis. Mortalitas hominum
et animalium multas occupauit Anglie prouincias, et ignis aereus,
uulgo dictus siluaticus in Deorbegensi [c]prouincia et quibusdam
aliis prouinciis uillas et segetes multas ustulauit.[c8] | [d]Eadmundus
Lindisfarnensis episcopus Glaorne obiit, sed a suis deportatus

p. 335

---

[a] *see App. B for addition at line-end B*[1]   [b–b] Ad . . . adiutorium] *compressed writing C*[1]   [c–c] prouincia . . . ustulauit] *written on extra line at bottom of page C*[2]
[d] Eadmundus . . . substituitur *(p. 546)] written on last line of 1048, partly over erasure
and extending into mg. C*[2]

---

[1] ASC C (1047) D (1048 *recte* 1047) E (1045 *recte* 1047) F (1046) all record this
death and succession, CE giving the day of Ælfwine's death, C stressing the king's role
in Stigand's appointment, EF calling Stigand 'bishop in the north'.
[2] ASC D (1048 *recte* 1047) also covers this episode saying that Swein, 'asking for
help suggested that 50 ships should be sent, but that it seemed foolish to all, and that
it was hindered because Magnus had a great naval force'. In contrast, JW says that
Godwine advised sending the 50 ships and that Leofric was among those who opposed
the scheme, and makes no reference at this point to Magnus' navy.
[3–3] ASC D gives the size of the navy as an impediment to the despatch of an English
force.

whose see Stigand, bishop of East Anglia, was translated.[1] Swein, king of the Danes, sent his legates to Edward, king of the English, and asked him to send a fleet against Magnus, king of the Norwegians. Earl Godwine advised the king that he might safely send him at least fifty ships with their complement of soldiers but, because that did not seem advisable to Earl Leofric and all the people, he refused to send him any.[2] After this Magnus, king of the Norwegians, [3]with a very great fleet heavily manned,[3] joined battle with Swein, and, when many thousands had been killed on both sides, expelled him from Denmark, and then reigned over that country and forced the Danes to pay him no little tribute. Not long after he died.[4]

[1048] Pope Poppo died.[5]

Swein retook Denmark, and Harold Fairhair, son of Siward, king of the Norwegians, and, on his mother's side, brother of St Olaf (he was also King Magnus's paternal uncle), returned to Norway and a short time after sent his envoys to King Edward, desiring of him, and obtaining, peace and friendship.[6] Swein, king of the Danes, sent envoys to Edward, asking him to send naval assistance, but although Earl Godwine was willing for at least fifty ships to be sent, Earl Leofric and all the people with one voice opposed it.[7] A great earthquake occurred on Sunday, 1 May, at Worcester, Droitwich, Derby, and many other places.[8] Sudden death for man and beast swept many regions of England, and fire in the air, commonly called wildfire, burnt many townships and cornfields in Derbyshire and several other regions.[8] Edmund, bishop of Lindisfarne, died at Gloucester, but was taken away by

[4] ASC D (1048 recte 1047). CE have information not in D or JW: the death of Abbot Athelstan at Abingdon in C, the stay of Swein at Bruges in E (also in F).
[5] Mar.
[6] ASC D (1049 recte 1048) alone records Swein's recovery of Denmark, the acceptance by the Norwegians of Magnus' paternal uncle Harold, and his approaches to England. JW gives Harold's parentage though he is wrong in calling Harold 'Hârfager' and Siward king of Norway.
[7] ASC D (1049 recte 1048) records Swein's unsuccessful appeal for assistance from Edward (50 ships at least), which appears to repeat the request of 1047. Here JW sticks closer to D though, as under 1047, he mentions Godwine as supporting, and Leofric as opposing Swein's request.
[8] ASC C (1048) D (1049 recte 1048) record the earthquake, and D the pestilence, which C had mentioned under 1047. D is closest to JW in naming the day of the earthquake and the three places affected. The south-east raid in C (1048) E (1046 recte 1048) F (1048) is not in JW.

Dunholmi sepelitur, cui successit Edredus, sed illo diuina ultione percusso in eius locum Ægelricus, Burgensis monachus substituitur.*ᵃ¹*

[C³B]

ᵇIn Oxenofordensi ciuitate fuit antiquitus monasterium sanctimonialium in qua requiescit Fritheswitha uirgo sanctissima. Que sponsi celestis amore terreno despecto *sponso, statuit monasterium.* Quod *tempore regis Ægelredi Danis neci adiudicati*s et *in illud confugi*entibus cum illis *flammis absumpt*um est, *sed* non multo post ab eodem rege *restitutum. Nostro tempore datus est ille locus a Rogerio Sælesberiensi episcopo* cuidam *Wimundo canonico,* ⟨*qui*⟩ *multos, ibi canonicos regulariter uicturos Deo exhibuit. Pagus* Hertfordensisᶜ *continet abbatiam sancti Albani* martyris. Cuius *corpus* sanctissimum *quod diu in terrae* latuerat *puluere iacuerat, rex Offa scrinio collocatum erexit in lumen basilica pulcerrimi operis et monachorum numerositate honorauit. In Huntendunensi pago* sunt Enulfesburhᵈ *Ramesia et* Crulandᵉ *ᶠin pago Lincoliensi.ᶠ Burh olim Medeshamstede dic*itur, *sed postquam Kenulfus abbas*

ᵃ *see above, p. 544 n. d, see App. A for addition LP⁵ (lower mg. with signe de renvoi P⁵)*
ᵇ *In Oxenofordensi . . . Northamtunensi (p. 548)] add. mg. on most of p. 335, probably would have taken up whole mg. had not top three lines already been occupied by spill over of 1048 n. d. No sign of intended point of insertion; may be regarded as part of block mg. addition 1043 n. a, which occupies all mg. of p. 334 C³, om. HLP*   ᶜ *Hertfor over erasure* C   ᵈ *C (rewriting a little later than C³), B, Burch GP*   ᵉ *et Berdennig] add. interlin. Bˣ*   ᶠ⁻ᶠ *in . . . Lincoliensi] hand which contributed 1048 nn. d (above) and a (p. 548) add. to left of 1048 n. b C*

his own people, and buried at Durham. Eadred succeeded him but he was struck down by divine vengeance. Æthelric, a monk of Peterborough, was appointed in his stead.[1]

In the city of Oxford there was from ancient times a convent of nuns in which lay the remains of Frideswide the most holy virgin. She founded the monastery from love of her heavenly husband, having spurned an earthly one. In the time of King Æthelred it was consumed by flames when the Danes had been sentenced to death and had taken refuge in it with them, but not long after it was restored by the same king. In our time the place was given by Roger, bishop of Salisbury, to one Wimund, a canon, who supported many canons there living for God according to Rule. Hertfordshire contains the abbey of St Alban the martyr. His most holy body, which had long lain hidden in the earth, had fallen to dust, which King Offa placed in a shrine and raised to the light, honouring it with a basilica of the most beautiful work and a host of monks. In Huntingdonshire are St Neots and Ramsey, and in Lincolnshire Crowland. Peterborough was formerly

---

[1] As noted above, p. 509 n. 9, the date for Bishop Edmund's death here is internally consistent with a 23-year episcopate, and the addition could be based on *HDE* iii. 6, 9 (i, 86, 91). See J. Cooper, *Durham University Journal*, lx (1968), 131–7.

locum muro cinxit a similitudine urbis
Burh uocatus est, *ᵃ*et est in pago
Northamtunensi.*ᵇᵃ1*

[1049] (x) 1071 *Leo² papa .cxlv. Iste est Leo qui nouum cantum de*
*sancto Gregorio papa fecit.*³

⁴Heinricus imperator innumerabilem congregauit exercitum contra ⁵Flandrensium comitem⁵ Balduuinum, maxime eo quod apud
Neomagum suum palatium combusisset atque fregisset pulcherri-
mum.⁶ In qua expeditione fuit Leo papa et de multis terris nobiles
et magnifici uiri quamplurimi. Suanus etiam rex Danorum, ut
imperator illi mandarat, cum sua classe ibi affuit, et ea uice
fidelitatem imperatori iurauit.⁷ Misit quoque ad regem Anglorum
Eaduuardum et rogauit illum, ne Balduuinum permitteret effugere
si uellet ad mare fugere. Iccirco cum magna classe rexᶜ Sandicum
portum adiit, et ibi tamdiu mansit quoad imperator de Balduuino
omnia que uoluit habuisset. ⁸Interea Suanus comes, Goduuini
comitis et Gythe filius,⁹ qui relicta prius Anglia eo quod Edgiuam
Leonensis monasterii abbatissam quam corruperat, in matrimonium habere non licuerit,¹⁰ Danemarciam adierat nauibus .viii.
rediit, dicens cum simulatione se cum rege fideliter amodo
remansurum.¹¹ Cui Beorn comes, filius auunculi sui Danici comitis
Vlfi filii Spraclingi filii Vrsi, ac frater Suani Danorum regis,¹²
promisit se a rege impetraturum ut suus ei comitatus redderetur.¹³
Pacificato itaque cum imperatore Balduuino comite, comites

ᵃ⁻ᵃ et . . . Northamtunensi] *hand which contributed 1048 nn. d and f (p. 546) add. at*
end of 1048 n. b C   *ᵇ see above, p. 546 n. b*   *ᶜ* ad *add.* H

---

¹ *GP* iv. 178–80 (pp. 315–17). These marginal additions could have been part of a
block on monasteries added by C³, starting above p. 538 n. 1.
² Leo IX 1049–54.   ³ Mar.
⁴ Plummer, *Chronicle,* ii. 229–31 has set out in tabular form the divergences (up to
the invasion from Ireland) between JW's account and those of ASC C (1049) D (1050
recte 1049) E (1046 *recte* 1049); F's very abbreviated entry under 1048 deals with the
Reims council, the Swein episode, and episcopal succession at Dorchester- on-Thames.
In general JW's account of the war between Henry III and Baldwin, count of Flanders,
with which the annal opens is similar to those in CD.
⁵⁻⁵ ASC CD: 'of Bruges'.
⁶ ASC CD refer also to other injuries done by Baldwin.
⁷ JW is the only source for Swein's role in this war.
⁸ JW's narrative of the return of Swein, the eldest son of Earl Godwine, his murder
of Earl Beorn, and expulsion, and the doings of Osgod Clapa is closest to D and furthest from E, though in some particulars nearer to C than to D. JW's peculiarities are
noted.

called Medeshamstead, but after
Abbot Kenulf had surrounded the
place with a wall, it was called
Burh from its similarity to a town.
It is situated in the district of
Northampton.[1]

[**1049**] Leo[2] the 145th pope. He was the Leo who composed the
new hymn in honour of the holy Pope Gregory.[3]

[4]The Emperor Henry assembled an innumerable army against
Baldwin [5]count of Flanders,[5] above all because he had burnt and
destroyed his most beautiful palace at Nýmegen.[6] In that expedition there took part Pope Leo and the nobles and very many great
men from many lands. Swein, king of the Danes, was also present
with his fleet at the emperor's command, and on that occasion
swore fealty to him.[7] The emperor also sent to Edward, king of
the English, as well, and asked him not to allow Baldwin to escape
if he should retreat to the sea. The king therefore went to the port
of Sandwich with a great fleet, and there he remained until the
emperor had extracted from Baldwin all he wanted. [8]Meanwhile,
Earl Swein, son of Earl Godwine and Gytha,[9] who had left
England earlier because he was not permitted to marry Eadgifu,
abbess of the convent at Leominster, whom he had seduced,[10]
went to Denmark, and returned with eight ships, saying dishon-
estly that he would henceforth remain faithful to the king.[11] Earl
Beorn, son of Swein's maternal uncle, the Danish Earl Ulf, son of
Spracling, son of Urse, and brother of Swein, king of the Danes,[12]
promised to procure from the king the restoration of his earldom,[13] and so, when peace had been restored between Count
Baldwin and the emperor, Earls Godwine and Beorn sailed, with

[9] JW alone gives Swein's parentage.
[10] ASC C (1046) had mentioned this abduction, but JW gives the victim's name. D
(1050 *recte* 1049) says he had disgraced himself in Denmark. Hemming (i. 275–6) refers
to Swein's seizing some Shropshire estates in revenge for Bishop Lyfing's condemnation of his abduction of the abbess of Leominster and 'suo per totius anni curriculum
conjugio sociauit'.
[11] ASC E (1046 *recte* 1049) mentions Swein's arrival with 7 ships at Bosham, though ASC C
(1049) D (1050, *recte* 1049) make it clear (later in the annal) that Swein had ships at Bosham.
[12] ASC D (1050 *recte* 1049) and E (1046 *recte* 1049) describe Beorn respectively as
the son of Swein's uncle and as Cnut's nephew, but JW gives more information.
[13] JW agrees with ASC D in making Beorn promise to assist Swein in his plea for
reinstatement, whereas C records Swein's request for Beorn's support. JW's 'comitatus'
as the object of Swein's return is different from C ('lands to support himself on'), D
('submission') or E ('every honour that he had previously held').

Goduuinus et Beorn .xlii. nauibus Peuenesea regis licentia[1] sunt deuecti, reliquam uero classis partem domum iussit redire, paucis secum nauibus ibi retentis. Cui cum nuntiatum fuisset, quod Osgodus Clapa cum .xxix. nauibus[2] in Vlpe iaceret, [3]de nauibus quas remisit quot potuit reuocauit.[3] Osgodus autem, uxore sua quam apud Brycge commiserat recepta, sex nauibus Danemarciam rediit,[4] alie uero Eastsaxoniam[5] adeuntes, preda circa promunctorium Eadulfi rapta non modica, redibant. Verum eas in redeundo seua corripuit tempestas, omnesque summersit, exceptis duabus que in transmarinis partibus capte sunt, occisis omnibus qui in illis erant.[6] [7]Dum hec agebantur, Suanus comes Peuenesea uenit, et consobrinum suum Beorn comitem cum dolo rogauit, ut ad Sandicum portum secum iret, et ut illi promiserat eum cum rege pacificaret, qui fisus in consanguinitate, tribus tantum sociis assumptis cum illo, proficisci coepit. At ille ad Bosanham, ubi naues eius erant, eum duxit, et in nauim introductum duris mox loris uinciri iussit, ac secum tamdiu habuit donec ad ostium Derte ueniret, ubi illo occiso et in altam fossam proiecto terraque obruto.[7] Dimiserunt illum sex naues, quarum duas paulo post ceperunt Heastingenses, et occisis qui fuerunt in eis, naues ad Sanduuic conducentes regi optulerunt.[8] Suanus uero ad Flandriam duabus fugiens nauibus, ibi mansit quoad Wigornensis episcopus Aldredus illum reduceret,[a] et cum rege pacificaret.[b9] [10]Eodem anno, [11]mense Augusto,[11] Hybernienses pirate .xxxvi. nauibus ostium intrantes Sabrine, [12]in loco qui dicitur Wylesceaxan,[12] appulerunt, et cum adiutorio Griffini regis australium Brytonum[13] circa loca illa predam agentes nonnulla mala

---

[a] uel -xit] *interlin. above* -ceret C^1B^1,   [b] uel -uit *interlin. above* -ret C^1B^1

---

[1] JW alone makes clear that the king gave permission, though E might have suggested this.

[2] ASC C 29 and D 39 ships.   [3-3] Closest to ASC D.

[4] JW's statement that Osgod, accompanied by his wife at Bruges, sailed for Denmark with 6 ships is at variance with ASC CD, which says that Osgod placed his wife at Bruges and returned (to an unnamed destination) with 6 ships. Whitelock, *ASC*, p. 113, says there could have been a misunderstanding of the Old English.

[5] JW does not share ASC D's mistake of 'Sussex' for 'Essex'.

[6] ASC D alone mentions the storm which 4 (not 2) ships escaped.

[7-7] Again closest to ASC D. JW does not mention the subsequent translation (in CDE) of Beorn's body to Winchester.

[8] Two differences from ASC D. In D the men of Hastings capture two of Swein's ships before, not after, the murder of Beorn. Though D's text leaves some room for

the king's permission,[1] in forty-two ships to Pevensey. The king kept a few ships there with him, ordering the rest of the fleet to return home. When he learned that Osgod Clapa lay at Wulpe with twenty-nine ships,[2] [3]he recalled as many as he could of the ships he had sent back.[3] However, Osgod, having taken back his wife, whom he had left at Bruges, returned to Denmark[4] with six ships but the others went to Essex[5] whence they returned after taking no little booty near Eadulf's promontory [the Naze]. But on their return a cruel storm caught them, and drowned all except two which were captured across the seas, and all who were in them were killed.[6] [7]While these things were happening Earl Swein came to Pevensey, and cunningly asked his cousin, Earl Beorn, to go with him to the port of Sandwich and, as he had promised, to make Swein's peace with the king. He, trusting in his kinship, set out with him, taking only three companions. But Swein led him to Bosham where his ships lay and, when he had brought him aboard, ordered him to be bound at once with cruel bonds, and he held him until he came to Dartmouth where he killed him, and threw him into a deep ditch, and covered his body with earth.[7] Six ships deserted him. The men of Hastings captured two of them a little while later and, after killing those on board, took the ships to Sandwich, and offered them to the king.[8] Swein then fled to Flanders with two ships, and stayed there until Ealdred, bishop of Worcester, called him back, and he made peace with the king.[9] [10]In the same year, [11]in the month of August,[11] Irish pirates with thirty-six ships, entering the mouth of the Severn, landed [12]at a place called Welsh Axe,[12] and, with the aid of Gruffydd [ap Rhydderch] king of the South Welsh,[13] plundered in that area and did considerable

doubt whether the total of 8 for Swein's ships includes the 2 captured by the men of Hastings, JW, apparently by a rearrangement of the text, makes the total clearly 8 (as in C), of which 2 were captured by the men of Hastings, and 2 (as in CD) stayed with him.

[9] Swein's visit to Bruges and his stay there are in ASC CE, which also say under 1050 that his outlawry was reversed. JW alone explicitly mentions 2 ships going with him, and the reconciliation with Edward effected by Bishop Ealdred.

[10] The war between the English and the South Welsh and allies from Ireland is in ASC D, but JW is fuller and different as shown below.

[11-11] Not in ASC.

[12-12] JW seems to be mistranslating a phrase such as ASC D's 'comon upp on Wylisce Axa'.

[13] Gruffydd is named as the Welsh king in ASC D, though JW's 'Southern Welsh' identifies him as Gruffydd ap Rhydderch, king of Deheubarth c. 1044–55.

fecerunt. Dein coniunctis uiribus, rex et ipsi [1]pariter flumen quod
Weage nominatur transeuntes Dymedham incenderunt[1] et omnes
quos ibi reperiebant peremerunt. Contra quos Wigornensis episcopus Aldredus et pauci de prouincialibus Glauuornensibus ac
Herefordensibus[2] festinanter ascenderunt, sed Walenses quos
secum habuerant eisque fidelitatem promiserant ad regem
Griffinum clanculo nuntium miserunt, rogantes ut quam citius
posset super Anglos irrueret,[3] qui mox et cum suis et piratis
Hiberniensibus aduolauit, et diluculo super Anglos irruens, multos
ex illis occidit, ceteris per fugam lapsis.[4] Eadnothus Dorcestrensis
episcopus obiit,[5] cui regis capellanus Vlf, genere Nortmannus, successit.[6] Osuuius abbas Thornegensis, et Wlnothus, abbas
Westmonasterii, decesserunt.[7] [a]Decessit quoque Siuuardus Edsii
Dorubernensis archiepiscopi corepiscopus, et Abbandonie est
tumulatus.[a8] Quo etiam anno sanctus papa Leo, rogatu eximie religionis abbatis Herimari in Franciam uenit, habens in comitatu suo
prefectum et digniores quosque Romulee urbis, et sancti Remigii
Francorum apostoli monasterium, Remis constitutum, maximo
cum honore dedicauit, et postmodum in ipsa urbe magnam synodum archiepiscoporum, episcoporum et abbatum sex diebus celebrauit, in qua fuit Aluuinus, Ramesigensis abbas, et abbas
monasterii sancti Augustini, a rege Anglorum Eadwardo illo
directi.[9] |

[1050] (xi) 1072 *Rex Scottie[b] Machethad[c] Rome argentum spar-
gendo distribuit.*[10]
   [11]Edsius, Dorubernensis archiepiscopus, obiit, cui Rotbertus,
[d12]monachus Gemmeticensis,[d12] Lundoniensis episcopus, genere
Nortmannus,[13] successit. Spearhafocus, abbas Abbandunensis,
Lundonie presulatum suscepit, sed antequam esset consecratus

[a-a] Decessit . . . tumulatus] *om. and see App. A for the substituted reading LP[5] (mg.
alongside 1050-1 P)*   [b] Scottorum *HL*   [c] Macbethad *Mar.*
[d-d] monachus Gemmeticensis] *interlin. C[3]?, om. HLP,* monachus *in mg. and*
Gemmeticensis *interlin. B[1]*

[1-1] No equivalent in ASC.
[2] ASC D does not identify the bishopric or the people that resisted.
[3] That some Welshmen were with the English and betrayed them is peculiar to JW.
[4] ASC D says this happened on 29 July, which is earlier than JW's August for the
arrival of the pirate ships.

damage. Then, having joined forces, the king and ¹they crossed the river called the Wye together, burnt *Dymedham*,¹ and slew all whom they found there. Against them Bishop Ealdred of Worcester and a few men from Gloucestershire and Herefordshire² rose in haste, but the Welsh whom they had taken with them, and who had promised their loyalty, secretly sent King Gruffydd a messenger, asking him to fall upon the English as soon as possible.³ He soon rushed up, both with his own men and with the Irish pirates, and fell upon the English at dawn, killing many of them; the rest escaped by flight.⁴ Eadnoth, bishop of Dorchester,⁵ died, and the king's chaplain, Ulf, a Norman by birth, succeeded him.⁶ Oswig, abbot of Thorney, and Wulfnoth, abbot of Westminster, died,⁷ and also Siward, coadjutor bishop of Archbishop Eadsige of Canterbury, died, and was buried at Abingdon.⁸ In that year also the holy Pope Leo, at the request of the Abbot Herimar, an exceptionally devout man, came to France with his household, the prefect, and certain nobles of the city of Rome, and with great ceremony dedicated the monastery, built at Reims, of Saint-Rémy, apostle of the Franks, and afterwards held a synod of archbishops, bishops, and abbots which continued for six days in that very city. Ælfwine, abbot of Ramsey, and the abbot of the monastery of St Augustine were present, sent there by Edward, king of the English.⁹

[1050] Macbeth, king of Scotland, distributed alms lavishly at Rome.¹⁰

¹¹Eadsige, archbishop of Canterbury, died and Robert, ¹²monk of Jumièges,¹² bishop of London and a Norman by birth,¹³ succeeded him. Sparrowhawk, abbot of Abingdon, accepted the bishopric of London, but was ejected ¹²by King Edward¹² before he

---

⁵ ASC CD 'bishop to Oxfordshire', EF 'bishop to the north', *ADL* 'episcopus aqui⟨lo⟩narium Saxonum'.

⁶ If ASC C concurs with JW in describing Ulf as Edward's priest, it does not call him a Norman. ASC C judges the appointment bad, and D hints at shameful reasons for this judgement.

⁷ The deaths of Oswig and Wulfnoth are recorded in ASC CD.

⁸ This is in ASC D, though not JW's description of Siward's function.

⁹ This is in ASC D, but that Leo's visit was at the invitation of Herimar, abbot of Saint-Rémy of Reims, is peculiar to JW. DEF record the attendance of the abbots of Ramsey (named by JW) and St Augustine's, to which EF (which mention the synod at the opening of their annal) add Bishop Dudoc of Wells to those sent by Edward.

¹⁰ Mar.   ¹¹ ASC D is closest to this paragraph with the differences shown.
¹²⁻¹² Not in ASC.   ¹³ 'Frenchman' in ASC D.

¹a rege Eadwardo¹ est eiectus.^a Heremannus, Wiltunensis² episco-
pus, et Aldredus, Wigornensis² antistes, Romam ierunt.³

[C³B]

^bIn Burh uirgines eximie Kyneþrytha et Kyneswitha, Pende regis filie, requiescunt. Quarum sodalitatem ornat rex sanctus Oswaldus, cuius ibi brachium haberi dicunt^c neruis, cute, carne integrum. Ramesiensis ecclesie edificator fuit sanctus Oswaldus, Eboracensis archiepiscopus, cooperante Ægelwino quodam ⟨Orientalium⟩ Anglorum comite. Felix ibi Orientalium Anglorum episcopus primus de Saba^d uilla^e iussu comitis asportatus iacet. Duo etiam germani Æthelredus ac Æthelbertus, quos filios patrui sui Ecgbertus, rex Cantuuariorum in suum regnum adolescere metuens aliquandiu circa se habitos, tandem ab aule frequentia remouit, contuitum suum eis inuidens. Accessit malignitati regie funestus minister, nomine Thunur, quod tonitruum sonat, qui eos cotidianis deceptos basiis, inter amplexus ipsos pugione confodit. Interempti scrobi profunde immerguntur.

---

^a see App. A for addition LP⁵ (added mg. alongside 1050–1 P⁵) ^b In Burh . . . teneri (p. 556)] add. mg. whole p. 336, presumably continuation of mg. additions on pp. 334, 335, 1043 n. d, 1048 n. b, with no indication of intended point of insertion C³, om. HLP ^c et uerum est interlin. for insertion after dicunt B¹ ^d Saham B
^e uilla regia interlin. B¹

---

^{1–1} Not in ASC. ² See identified by JW.
³ The precise date of Eadsige's death (ASC C 1050 E 1047 F 1049), the disbandment of the fleet (C 1049 and 1050 E 1047), the return of Swein (C 1050 E 1047), the

was consecrated. Hereman, bishop of Wilton,[2] and Ealdred, bishop of Worcester,[2] went to Rome.[3]

The glorious virgins Cynethryth and Cyneswith, daughters of King Penda, rest at Peterborough. The holy King Oswald, whose arm they say is kept there whole, in tendons, skin, and flesh, adorns the foundation. St Oswald, archbishop of York, was the builder of the church at Ramsey, with the assistance of Æthelwine, a certain ealdorman of the East Angles. There Felix lies: he was the first bishop of the East Angles, and was translated from the township of Soham at the command of the ealdorman. There also are the two brothers, Æthelred and Æthelberht, whom (as sons of his paternal uncle), Ecgberht, king of the people of Kent, fearing that their growth into adults would threaten his kingdom, after keeping them about him for some time sent them away from court, refusing them his presence. The sinister thegn, called Thunur, that is Thunderclap, pandered to the royal malice. Having deceived them with daily kisses, he buried his dagger in them in the very act of embracing them. The slain brothers were

appointment of Bishop Rothulf as abbot of Abingdon (C 1050 E 1048), and the attendance of English ecclesiastics at two papal councils (E 1047 F 1049) are not recorded by JW.

Quos *comes prouincie* prefatus
Ægelwinus postmodum *Rames-*
iam pro*duxit. Iacet* etiam *ibi*
sanctus *Iuo Persarum episcopus.*[1]
Cruland est una insularum iacen-
tium in illo tractu orientalium
stagnorum que a meditullio terre
orientia, et per .c. et eo amplius
milia fluentia, in mare cum mul-
tis et magnis fluminibus impetu
suo precipitantur. Ibi sanctus
Gutlacus requiescit. *Sanctus*
quoque *Neotus, quondam* sancti
Erconwaldi episcopi *discipulus*
pausat. *Waltheofus* quoque
comes filius Siuuardi Norðhym-
brorum comitis ibi *sepultus*
habetur. Qui *a Willelmo rege*
innocenter occisus est. *Prior*
uero *loci* illius *narrauit miraculis*
se commotum nobile corpus comitis eiusdem *ab omni labe* diu
post occisionem *contrectasse,*
caput reliquo corpori compagina-
tum, rubra tantum quasi linea
signum cedis ostentante, uidisse et
ideo pro sancto teneri.*a*[2]

[**1051**] (xii) 1073 Ælfricus, Eboracensis arciepiscopus, Suthuue-
alle defunctus, Medeshamstyde, *b*id est Burh,*b* sepelitur, cui
regis capellanus Kinsigius successit.[3] Rex Eaduuardus absoluit
Anglos a graui uectigali tricesimo octauo anno ex quo pater suus

---

a *see above, p. 554 n. b*   *b–b* id est Burh] *interlin. C*[1]*B*[1]*, om. HLP*

[1] *GP.* iv. 180–1 (pp. 317–19).
[2] *GP* iv. 182 (pp. 321–2). These are the last of the batch of marginal entries from *GP* on pp. 334–6 in the JW MS C (see above, pp. 538–9 nn. 1–4, p. 540 n. 1 and p. 548 n. 1).

cast into a deep ditch. The aforementioned Æthelwine, ealdorman of the province, later translated them to Ramsey. St Ives, bishop of the Persians, also lies there.[1] Crowland is one of the islands lying in that area of the eastern fens, which rising from the inland area, and flowing more than a hundred miles, pour into the sea under their own impetus with many great rivers. There St Guthlac rests. St Neot also, formerly a disciple of St Eorcenwald the bishop, lies ... Also Earl Waltheof, son of Siward, earl of the Northumbrians, is buried there. He was slain for all his innocence by King William. But the prior of that place related that he had handled the earl's noble body miraculously freed from all corruption long after the murder: he had seen the head attached to the rest of the body with, as it were, a red line as the sole sign of the killing, and so he was considered a saint.[2]

[1051] Ælfric, archbishop of York, died at Southwell, and was buried at Medeshamstead, that is Peterborough. Cynesige, the king's chaplain, succeeded him.[3] King Edward released the English from the heavy tax in the thirty-eighth year after his

[3] ASC C (1050) D (1052 *recte* 1051) E (1047) record the death of Archbishop Ælfric, CE giving the day (22 Jan., C, 29 Oct. E) and burial at Peterborough, D saying he was 'very venerable and wise'. JW contributes the place of death and the name and office of his successor.

rex Agelredus primitus id Danicis solidariis solui mandarat.[1] [2]Post hec [3]mense Septembri Bononiensis comes,[3] Eustatius Senior,[a] qui sororem Eadwardi regis Godam nomine[4] in coniugium habuerat, [5]paucis Doruuerniam applicuit nauibus,[5] in qua milites eius cum stolide et insipienter sibi hospitia quererent, unum e ciuibus peremerunt. Quod uidens eius conciuis ulciscitur illum, occiso milite uno.[6] Ob quam rem comes et sui nimis irati, [7]uiros et mulieres quamplures armis interfecerunt, pueros et infantes suorum pedibus equorum contriuerunt.[7] Sed ubi ciues ad obsistendum concurrere uiderunt, turpem[8] fugam ineuntes, uix euaserunt, septem[b] ex sociis illorum peremptis,[9] et ad regem Eadwardum, qui tunc temporis Glauuorne morabatur, fugerunt.   [10]Talia geri in suo comitatu comes Goduuinus grauiter ferens nimiaque commotus ira, de toto suo comitatu, scilicet de Cantia, Suthsaxonia et Westsaxonia, et filius eius primogenitus Suanus de suo, id est de Oxnafordensi, Glauuornensi, Herefordensi, Sumerseatunensi, Barrucscirensi prouinciis, alterque filius Haroldus de suo comitatu, uidelicet de Eastsaxonia, Eastanglia, Huntedunensi et Grantebrycgensi prouinciis,[11] innumerabilem congregauerunt exercitum, [12]quod regem Eaduuardum non latuit.[12] [13]Iccirco nuntiis ad Leofricum Mercensium et Siuuardum Northymbrorum comites festinato missis, rogauit ut, ad se, [12]in magno periculo constitutum,[12] cum omnibus quos habere poterant uenire accelerarent. Illi autem primo cum paucis uenerunt, sed ubi cognouerunt quomodo se habuit res, per suos comitatus [12]celeres miserunt ueredarios,[12] et magnum congregauerunt exercitum. Similiter et Rodulfus comes, [14]Gode sororis Eadwardi regis filius,[14] de suo comitatu quot

---

[a] interlin. C¹H¹B¹P³   [b] .x. et octo interlin. B⁵

[1] ASC D (1052 recte 1051) alone records the abolition of the heregeld in the 39th (JW 38th) year after it was first levied by Æthelred. JW does not have D's comments on the oppressiveness of this tax.

[2] The account of the arrival of Count Eustace at Dover (JW has Canterbury) and the incident in which his followers were involved is closer to ASC D (1052 recte 1051) with the differences shown than to E (1048) F (1050, brief, dependent on E). It is not in C.

[3-3] Not in ASC.   [4] JW contributes the name of Edward's sister.

[5-5] No reference to ships in ASC.

[6] JW probably translated D's 'geferan' in the singular, see Whitelock, ASC, p. 117 n. 4.

[7-7] ASC D talks simply 'of great damage' being 'done on either side with horses and weapons'.

father, King Æthelred, first ordered that it should be paid to the Danish mercenaries.[1] [2]After this, [3]in the month of September,[3] Eustace the Elder, [3]count of Boulogne,[3] who had married King Edward's sister, Goda by name,[4] landed [5]with a few ships at Canterbury,[5] where, when his soldiers stupidly and crassly sought lodgings, they killed one of the townsmen. When a fellow towns-man of the victim saw that he avenged him by killing a soldier.[6] On that account the count and his men, greatly enraged, [7]slew many men and women with their swords and crushed their chil-dren and babies beneath their horses' hooves.[7] But when they saw the citizens flocking together to withstand them they turned to shameful[8] flight, and barely escaped; seven of their companions were slain.[9] They fled to King Edward, who at that time was stay-ing at Gloucester. [10]Earl Godwine, taking it hard that such events should happen in his earldom, was moved to very great anger, and mustered an innumerable army from his whole earldom, that is Kent, Sussex, and Wessex, and his eldest son Swein from his, that is Oxfordshire, Gloucestershire, Herefordshire, Somerset, and Berkshire, and his other son, Harold from his earldom, that is from Essex, East Anglia, Huntingdonshire, and Cambridgeshire;[11] [12]this did not remain secret from King Edward.[12] [13]Messengers were on that account sent in haste to the Earls Leofric of the Mercians and Siward of the Northumbrians, whom the king asked to hasten to him, [12]placed as he was in great danger,[12] with all those they could muster. However, they came at first with only a few men, but when they learnt of the state of events, [12]they sent swift couriers[12] through their earldoms and gathered a great army. Likewise Earl Ralph, [14]son of King Edward's sister Goda,[14] assembled as many as he could from his earldom. Meanwhile,

---

[8] 'turpem' is JW's addition.

[9] ASC D mentions the 7 followers of Count Eustace immediately after 'geferan' (above, n. 6).

[10] JW's account of the remaining events in 1051 is much closer to ASC D in attitude and detail (with differences shown) than to either EF, which are favourable to Godwine, or to C, which simply records the exile of the family.

[11] The listing of the shires in the earldoms of Godwine, Swein, and Harold is not in ASC.

[12]-[12] Possible inference from ASC.

[13] The king's appeal to Leofric and Siward, their arrival with a small force, their subsequent summons of a larger force, and the support of Earl Ralph are placed in ASC D after, not before, Godwine's demands for the surrender of the Frenchmen.

[14]-[14] Identified by JW.

potuit congregauit. Interea Goduuinus et filii eius cum suis exercitibus post natiuitatem sancte Marie[1] in Glauuornensem prouinciam uenientes, in loco qui dicitur Langetreo, castra metati sunt, et legatis Glauuornam ad regem directis, comitem Eustatium et socios eius insuper et Nortmannos, et Bononienses, qui castellum in Doruuernie cliuo tenuerunt,[2] sub denuntiatione belli reposcebant. Ob id autem ad tempus rex perterritus, et in angore magno constitutus, quid ageret ignorabat penitus.[3] Sed ubi exercitum comitum Leofrici, *Siuuardi et*[a] Rodulfi aduentare comperit,[4] [5]se nullatenus Eustatium aliosque requisitos traditurum constanter respondit. Quo audito, uacui redeunt legati.[5] Quibus abeuntibus, exercitus Glauuornam intrauit, ita inflammatus[6] et concordi animo ad pugnam paratus ut statim, si rex permitteret, cum exercitu Goduuini pugnam inire uellet. At quia de tota Anglia quique meliores in sua et illorum parte erant coadunati, comiti Leofrico et quibusdam aliis magnum uidebatur insilium, ut ipsi cum suis compatriotis bellum inirent,[7] sed obsidibus ad inuicem datis, rex et Goduuinus die constituto ad placitandum Lundoniam conuenirent. Probato consilio et nuntiis intercurrentibus, obsidibus datis et acceptis, dux in Westsaxoniam rediit.[8] Rex uero de tota Mercia et Northymbria copiosiorem exercitum congregauit, et secum Lundoniam duxit.[9] Goduuinus autem et filii eius ad Suthuueorce uenere cum magna Westsaxonum multitudine, sed quia suus ab eo paulatim defluxerat exercitus,[10] placitum inire cum rege non audebat, uerum nocte superuenienti fugam iniit. Quare mane facto, rex in suo concilio et omnis exercitus unanimi consensu illum et quinque filios eius exules fore decreuerunt. Qui mox cum coniuge sua Gytha,[11] et Tosti cum uxore sua Iuthitta, filia uidelicet Balduuini Flandrensium comitis,[11] ac duo alii eius filii,[b] Suanus et Gyrth | ad Thornege ubi nauis eis parata fuerat uenerunt, in

p. 337

---

a–a Siuuardi et] et Syuuardi *H*, et Siwardi *L*   *b* om. *CHB, interlin. L¹P¹*

---

[1] ASC D dates this assembly before, not after, the nativity of Mary. E speaks of the king assembling followers near to this feast.

[2] Where ASC D speaks of 'Eustace's men', and of the 'Frenchmen who were in the castle', JW identifies the first as 'socios eius insuper et Nortmannos', and the second apparently as 'Bononienses'. ASC E refers to the ill deeds of the foreigners who had built a castle in Herefordshire, which is not explicitly mentioned in D.

[3] The king's troubled reactions and uncertainty are not in ASC D.

[4] ASC D adds 'though it was late'.

[5–5] Not formally expressed in ASC.   [6] Not in ASC.

Godwine and his sons, entering Gloucestershire after the feast of the nativity of St Mary,[1] encamped in a place called Langtree, and sent envoys to the king at Gloucester, demanding on threat of war Count Eustace and his associates as well as both the Normans and the men of Boulogne who held the castle on the cliff at Canterbury.[2] The king, terrified for a time, and in great anguish, did not know at all what to do.[3] But when he observed the approach of the army of Earls Leofric, Siward, and Ralph,[4] [5]he replied firmly that he would by no means hand over Eustace and the others demanded. The messengers returned empty-handed when they heard this.[5] As they were leaving, the army entered Gloucester, so inflamed[6] and prepared to a man for battle that, if the king permitted, they were willing to engage Godwine's army in battle immediately. But, as, from all England, all men of standing were on one side or on the other, it appeared to Earl Leofric and to certain others a great folly that they should embark on a war with their compatriots.[7] So, when hostages had been given by both parties, the king and Godwine agreed to meet at London on an appointed day to plead their cases. The plan was approved, and, with messengers toing and froing, and hostages given and received, the earl returned to Wessex.[8] But the king mustered a more numerous army from all Mercia and Northumbria, and led it with him to London.[9] However, Godwine and his sons came to Southwark with a great host of West Saxons, but, because his army gradually seeped away from him,[10] he dared not go to the parley with the king, but took to flight when night fell. Wherefore, when morning came, the king in council, with the unanimous consent of the whole army, sentenced him and his five sons to exile. Godwine, with his wife Gytha,[11] and Tostig with his wife Judith, the daughter of Baldwin, count of Flanders[11] and two of his other sons, Swein and Gyrth, thereupon went to Thorney, where a ship

[7] ASC D does not specifically mention Leofric among those counselling against civil war.

[8] ASC D does not specify Godwine's return to Wessex, which could have been inferred.

[9] ASC D speaks of 'the folk in all this northern province, in Siward's earldom and Leofric's and elsewhere being ordered' to go to London.

[10] At this point ASC D states that the thegns of Harold were transferred to the king's allegiance and Swein outlawed.

[11] ASC D does not name the wives of Godwine and Tostig, and describes Judith as a 'kinswoman' of Baldwin.

quam tantum auri et argenti, aliarumque rerum pretiosarum quam illa portare potuit, festinanter imponentes,[1] eamque citatim conscendentes, ad Flandrensium comitem Balduuinum cursum direxerunt. Porro Haroldus et Leofuuinus filii eius Brycstouuam adeuntes, nauem, quam frater illorum Suanus sibi parauerat, conscenderunt,[2] et in Hiberniam transuecti sunt. Reginam uero Edgitham rex, [3]propter iram quam aduersus patrem suum Goduuinum habuerat,[3] repudiauit et [3]cum una pedissequa[3] ad Huuereuueallam eam [3]sine honore[3] misit, et abbatisse custodiendam commendauit. His gestis, Nortmannicus comes Willelmus cum multitudine Nortmannorum Angliam uenit, quem rex Eaduuardus et socios eius honorifice suscepit, et magnis multisque donatum muneribus ad Nortmanniam remisit.[4] Eodem anno Wilelmus, regis capellanus, Lundoniensem episcopatum, qui Spearhafoco prius datus fuerat, suscepit.*[5]

Sanctus Bardo episcopus Mogontinus obiit ⟨.iiii.⟩[b] idus Iunii. [c]Liupoldus ei successit.[6]

[C²B]

[d]*Ecclesiam Lindisfarnensem Ægelrico presule regente, res inusitate facta terribili exemplo ministris altaris iram Dei ostendit imminere, si ad sacrosanctum mysterium* incesti *presumant accedere. Quidam presbiter non longe ab urbe[e] ecclesiam habe*bat, *sed, cum uxori copulatus esset, indignam sacerdotis officio uitam ducebat. Quadam die multi, tam nobiles, quam priuati, primo mane ad ipsum locum placitaturi conuenerunt, sed ante placitum ut*

---

[a] *see App. A for addition (mg. alongside 1051–2 P⁵) LP⁵*   [b] .vi. *JW*   [c] *1052 starts here (N)*   [d] Ecclesiam . . . custodiuit *(p. 566)] add. mg. whole of p. 337, alongside 1051–2 C², om. HLP*   [e] urbem *C*

---

[1] In ASC D the remark that Godwine's ship was stocked with treasure is placed after the departure to Ireland of Harold and Leofwine.
[2] ASC D records that Bishop Ealdred was sent to interrupt the departing bands of

had been prepared for them. Into her they hastily put as much gold and silver and precious things as she could carry,[1] and, quickly boarding her, they steered a course for Baldwin, count of Flanders. But his sons, Harold and Leofwine, arriving at Bristol, boarded the ship which their brother Swein had prepared for himself,[2] and crossed to Ireland. But the king repudiated Queen Edith [3]because of his anger with her father Godwine,[3] and sent her [3]without ceremony[3] to Wherwell [3]with one waiting-woman,[3] and committed her to the custody of the abbess. When these things had been done, the Norman duke William came to England with a host of Normans. King Edward received him and his companions with honour, and sent him back to Normandy in receipt of many great gifts.[4] In the same year William, the king's chaplain, received the bishopric of London, which had earlier been given to Sparrowhawk.[5]

St Bardo, bishop of Mainz, died on 10 June and Liutpold succeeded him.[6]

At the church of Lindisfarne, under the rule of Bishop Æthelric, an extraordinary event took place and showed by a terrible example how God's anger hovers over priests of the altar if they presume to approach the consecrated mystery when unchaste. A certain priest had a church not far from the city, but since he had espoused a wife he led a life unworthy of the priestly office. Early in the morning, on a certain day, many, both nobles and ordinary citizens, gathered at that place for law pleadings, but before the hearing they

Harold and Leofwine, and notes the difficulties these two faced in their flight to Ireland.
   [3-3] Not in ASC.   [4] ASC D alone records Duke William's visit.
   [5] The appointment of the king's chaplain, William, as bishop of London is in ASC D (1051) E (1048 *recte* 1051) F (1050).
   [6] Mar.

presbiter eis missam celebraret rogauerunt. At ille, qui ipsa nocte cum uxore dormierat, ad sacrum officium accedere formidabat. Itaque negauit se id facturum. Illis autem semel, bis, terque rogantibus, sibi missam celebrari, presbiter nimis ex utraque parte angustabatur, hinc uerecundia, inde timore. Vicit tamen humana uerecundia diuinum timorem. Itaque missam celebrauit. Hora qua sacrosancta mysteria sumere deberet in calicem introspexit, et ecce particulam dominici corporis, que iuxta morem missa fuerat in calicem, ita cum sanguine in teterrimam speciem commutatam uidit, ut, sicut postea fatebatur, magis in calice picis colorem quam panis et uini conspexit. *Ilico reatum intelligens presbiter pallere, et, quasi iam tunc flammis ultricibus tradendus cepit* primum *pauere. Multum*que *anxius erat quid de hoc quod in calice uiderat facere deberet. Exhorrebat illud uelut suam mortem sumere. Volebat in terram effundere, sed quoniam consecratum erat id metuebat* agere[a]. *Reputans ergo quoniam quicquid*

---

[a] agere *bis* C

asked the priest to celebrate mass. But he, who had that very night slept with his wife, feared to perform the sacred office and so he refused to do it. However, on their asking him once, twice, and thrice to celebrate mass for them, the priest was extremely distressed for two reasons, on the one through shame, and the other through fear. However, human shame conquered the fear of God and so he celebrated mass. In the moment in which he was due to receive the holy mysteries, he looked into the chalice, and lo, he saw the portion of the Lord's Body, that according to custom was placed in the chalice changed along with the Blood into the most loathsome sight, so that, as he later confessed, he saw in the chalice the colour of pitch rather than of bread and wine. Understanding his guilt, the priest began to turn pale and to fear at first that he was at that very moment to be handed over to the avenging flames. And he was very anxious about what he should do concerning that which he saw in the chalice. He shuddered to take it as if it were his own death. He wished to pour it out on the ground, but since it had been consecrated he feared to do so. Considering, therefore, that

facerent, omnipotentis iudicium effugere non ualeret, magno cum tremore ac formidine illud sumpsit, sed tante amaritudinis fuit, ut nil ad gustandum amarius esse potuisset. Vix missa peracta, confestim equum ascendens ad episcopum festinauit, rem ex ordine retulit. Cui indicta penitentia, precepit, ut sinceram deinceps et castam uitam Deo *offerre studeret. Quod* ille *promisit, et promissum* quoad uixit *caste uiuendo custodiuit.*[a][1]

[1052] (xiii) 1074   *Marianus chronographus seculum reliquit.*[2]

Ælgiua Imme, coniunx regum Agelredi et Canuti, .ii. nonas Martii Wintonie obiit, et ibi sepulta est.[3] Eodem anno Walensium rex Griffinus magnam partem Herefordensis prouincie depopulatus est, contra quem prouinciales illi et de castello quamplures Nortmanni ascenderunt, sed multis ex illis occisis, ille uictoriam habuit et secum predam magnam abduxit. Hec pugna facta est eodem die quo ante .xiii. annos fratrem comitis Leofrici Eduuinum Walenses per insidias interfecerunt.[4] [5]Paruo post hec tempore, Haroldus comes et frater eius Leofuuinus,[6] de Hibernia redeuntes, et ostium Sabrine nauibus multis intrantes, in confinio Sumerseatanie et Dorsetanie applicuerunt, et illis in partibus uillas ac agros depredati sunt multos. Aduersus quos et de Domnania et Sumersetania quamplures congregati ascenderunt, sed eos uicit Haroldus, cesis ex illis plusquam triginta nobilibus ministris cum aliis multis. Dein ad naues cum preda rediit, et mox

---

[a] see above, p. 562 n. d

[1] *HDE* iii. 10 (i. 93-4)   [2] Mar.
[3] ASC C (1051, 14 Mar.) D (1052, 6 Mar.) E (1052) record the death of Emma (EF giving her two names), and C her burial at the Old Minster, Winchester. Her obit, added in the late 11th c. to the Winchester calendar, BL Cotton MS Titus D. XXVII (W. De Gray Birch, *Liber Vitae: Register and Martyrology of New Minster and Hyde Abbey, Winchester* (Hampshire Record Society, v; London, 1892), p. 270) gives 6 Mar.
[4] ASC D (1052) records the Welsh invasion, adding that Gruffydd (ap Llywelyn) came near to Leominster. Here and under 1039, JW identifies Edwin as the brother of Earl Leofric.

whatever he did he could not flee the judgement of the Almighty, he partook with great trembling and fear, but it was of such bitterness that nothing could be bitterer to taste. Scarcely was mass completed than, mounting his horse at once, he hurried to the bishop, and recounted the affair without a pause. Having prescribed a penance, he enjoined upon him to strive from then on to offer to God a sincere and chaste life. That he promised, and he kept the promise by living chaste as long as he lived.[1]

[1052] Marianus the chronographer retired from the world.[2]

Ælfgifu Emma, wife of Kings Æthelred and Cnut, died on 6 March at Winchester, and was buried there.[3] In the same year Gruffydd [ap Llywelyn] king of the Welsh, ravaged a great part of Herefordshire. The people of that area and very many Normans from the castle rose against him but, when he had killed many of them, he had the victory, and took great booty away with him. This battle took place on the same day as that when, thirteen years earlier, the Welsh killed Edwin, brother of Earl Leofric, in an ambush.[4] [5]Shortly after this, Earl Harold and his brother Leofwine,[6] returning from Ireland, and entering the mouth of the Severn with many ships, landed on the borders of Somerset and Dorset, and plundered many townships and fields in those parts. Very many from both Devon and Somerset, having assembled, rose against them, but Earl Harold defeated them, having slain of them more than thirty noble thegns with many others. Then he returned to his ships with booty and presently sailed round Land's

---

[5] ASC CDE (1052) F (1051) record the return of Godwine and his sons, EF's account having a different version from CD, which differ from each other but slightly. JW is different from E, and seems closer to C than to D, though containing matter which is in neither, as is shown below.

[6] ASC CD do not mention Leofwine.

Penuuithsteort circumnauigauit. Tunc rex Eaduuardus .xl. naues,
alimentis electisque militibus instructas, ad Sandicum portum festinato misit,[1] et eos aduentum Goduuini comitis[2] opperiri et
obseruare iussit. Sed tamen, ignorantibus omnibus, ille [3]cum paucis nauibus[3] reuersus, in Cantia applicuit, et, missis latenter nuntiis, primitus Cantuarienses, dein Suthsaxones,[4] Eastsaxones,[5]
Suthregienses et omnes butsecarlas de Heastinga, et ubique circa
ripas maris aliosque nonnullos in adiutorium sui allexit. Hi omnes
uno ore aut uiuere aut mori cum eo se paratos fore sibi
promiserunt. Quod ubi regie classi que ad Sandicum portum iacebat innotuit, illum insecuntur, uerum ipse fugiens euasit et [6]quo in
loco potuit se occultauit.[6] Illi uero ad Sandicum portum sunt
reuecti et inde Lundoniam sunt reuersi. Hoc cognito, comes
Goduuinus ad Vectam Insulam reuehitur, et circa ripas maris
tamdiu uagabatur, donec ad illum filii eius Haroldus et
Leofuuinus[7] sua cum classe uenirent, sed [8]ex quo in unum conuenerant[8] a depredatione ac populatione desistebant, uictum tamen
exercitui suo cum res exposceret sumebant. Circa ripas autem
maris et ubicunque locorum, omnes, quos poterant sibi in adiutorium allicientes, et butsecarlas omnes, quos obuios inuenerant
secum legentes, uersus Sandicum portum cursum direxerunt.[9]
Quo cum uenissent, regi Eaduuardo, [10]tunc temporis Lundonie
demoranti,[10] illorum aduentus nuntiatur, qui nuntiis propere missis omnibus qui a se non defecerant mandauit, ut in adiutorium
sui uenire maturarent. At illi nimis tardantes ad tempus non
uenerunt. Interea cum sua classe Goduuinus comes aduersus cursum Tamensis deuectus die exaltationis sancte crucis, feria
secunda,[11] ad Suthuueorce uenit, et ibi tamdiu expectauit, quoad
maris accessus [a]uel estus[a] ueniret. Interim[b] [12]quosdam per[c] inter-
nuntios quosdam per se[12] ciues Lundonienses, [12]quos uariis pollic-
itationibus prius illexerat,[12] conuenit, et ut omnes fere que uolebat
omnino uellent effecit. Inde rebus omnibus dispositis et ordinatis,

[a-a] uel estus] interlin. C'H'L'B', om. P   [b] small erasure after Interim C
[c] interlin. C'

[1] Where ASC C states that the ships had been on the watch for several weeks, D
simply records their assembly.
[2] ASC CD record Godwine's location at Bruges in the winter.
[3-3] Apparently JW's contribution.   [4] ASC C alone mentions Sussex.
[5] ASC C has 'all the east province' in place of Essex and before Sussex.
[6-6] ASC C not D.   [7] ASC CD do not mention Leofwine.

End. Then King Edward, having equipped forty ships with provisions and picked soldiers, sent them in haste to the port of Sandwich,[1] and ordered them to await the arrival of Earl Godwine,[2] and to keep watch. However, unknown to all, the earl turned back [3]with a few ships,[3] landed in Kent, and, having secretly sent messengers, drew to his support first the people of Kent, then the South Saxons,[4] the East Saxons,[5] and the men of Surrey and all the seamen from Hastings and everywhere around the coast, and many others. They all, with one voice, promised him that they were prepared to live or die with him. When that was made known to the royal fleet which lay at the port of Sandwich it pursued him, but he escaped by flight, and [6]took cover where he could.[6] But the fleet sailed back to the port of Sandwich, and from there returned to London. When he learnt this, Earl Godwine sailed back to the Isle of Wight, and for a long time drifted about the coast until his sons, Harold and Leofwine,[7] joined him with their fleet. But, [8]from the time they joined forces,[8] they desisted from looting and destruction; nevertheless they took provision for their troops when it was necessary. Drawing to their support all those they could around the coast and in many other places, and collecting all the seamen they met, they directed their course towards the port of Sandwich.[9] When they had reached it, their arrival was announced to King Edward, [10]at that time staying at London.[10] He sent messengers in haste to all who had not defected from him, ordering them to hasten to his aid. But they were too slow, and did not come in time. Meanwhile, Earl Godwine, having sailed his fleet up the Thames against the current, came to Southwark on Monday,[11] the day of the exaltation of the Holy Cross, and waited there until the incoming or flood-tide should arrive. In the interval, he met the London citizens, [12]some through mediators, some in person, whom he had previously bound himself to with promises of one sort and another,[12] and succeeded in bringing almost everybody into agreement with his desires. When everything had been arranged and ordered, they

---

[8-8] ASC C not D.

[9] ASC CD assign to Godwine an overwhelming force.

[10-10] Possibly inferred from ASC.

[11] The day of Godwine's arrival is not mentioned at this point in ASC CD, though C gives it in that later part of the annal which is absent from D, describing it as on the 'Monday after St Mary'.

[12-12] Not in ASC CD.

reumate adueniente, festinanter anchoras sustulerunt ac, [1]nullo in
ponte obsistente,[1] per australem fluminis crepidinem sursum
nauigauerunt. Venit et pedestris exercitus ac se per oram fluuii
ordinatim disponens, spissam terribilemque fecit testudinem. Dein
classis se [2]uersus aquilonalem ripam[2] uertit quasi regis classem cir-

p. 338   cundare uellet, habebat enim et rex | classem ac numerosum
pedestrem exercitum. Sed quia ibi et cum rege et cum Goduuino
erant perpauci qui fortitudinis aliquid haberent nisi tantum Angli
pugnare aduersus suos propinquos ac compatriotas pene omnes
abhorrebant.[3] Vnde sapientiores quique ex utraque parte inter
regem et ducem pacem redintegrantes, [4]exercitum ab armis
discedere iusserunt.[4] [1]Mane autem facto,[1] concilium rex habuit
pristinumque honorem pleniter reddidit Goduuino et uxori sue,
filiisque omnibus excepto Suano,[5] ille enim ductus penitentia, eo
quod, ut prelibauimus, consobrinum suum Beorn occiderat, de
Flandria nudis pedibus Ierusalem iam adierat, indeque rediens
inualitudine ex nimio frigore contracta, mortuus est in Liccia.[6]
Filiam quoque ducis Edgitham reginam digniter rex recepit ac
pristine dignitati restituit. Facta igitur concordia paceque firmata,
omni populo rectam legem promiserunt; et omnes Nortmannos qui
leges iniquas adinuenerant, et iniusta iudicia iudicauerant multaque regi insilia aduersus Anglos dederant, exlegauerunt. Paucos
tamen, scilicet Rotbertum diaconem, et generum eius Ricardum
filium Scrob, Alfredum regis stratorem, Anfridum cognomento
Ceocesfot, et quosdam alios quos plus ceteris rex dilexerat, eique
et omni populo fideles extiterant, in Anglia remanere
permiserunt.[7] Porro Rotbertus, Dorubernie archiepiscopus, et
Lundonie presul Willelmus et Vlf, Lindicolinensis antistes, cum
suis Nortmannis uix euadentes mare transierunt.[8] [9]Sed Wilelmus
propter suam bonitatem paruo post tempore reuocatus, in suum
episcopatum recipitur.[9]

[1-1] Not in ASC CD.   [2-2] ASC C not D.

[3] ASC CD refer here to the potential danger of exposing England to outside invasion.

[4-4] JW's addition.

[5] Swein is not specifically excepted in ASC, though C places his pilgrimage to
Jerusalem in that later part of the annal which is not in ASC D.

hastily weighed anchor as the tide rose and, [1]with no resistance at the bridge,[1] sailed up river along the south bank. The footsoldiers arrived as well, and, drawn up in order along the bank of the river, they made a dense and terrible formation. Then the fleet turned [2]towards the north bank of the river[2] as if it would surround the king's fleet, for the king had both a fleet and a large army on foot. But, because there were, both with the king and with Godwine, very few men of spirit who were not English, almost all were most loath to fight their kinsmen and fellow countrymen.[3] For this reason the wiser on both sides restored peace between the king and the earl, and [4]they ordered the armies to lay down their weapons.[4] However, [1]when morning came,[1] the king took counsel, and fully restored their former honours to Godwine and his wife and to all their sons, except Swein,[5] for he, moved by penitence because, as we have mentioned before, he had killed his cousin Beorn, went from Flanders to Jerusalem barefoot, and on his return from there fell ill from the excessive cold and died in Lycia.[6] The king also took back Queen Edith, the earl's daughter, with honour and restored her to her former dignity. Therefore, when concord was made, and peace established, they promised a just law to the whole people, and outlawed all the Normans who had devised evil laws and pronounced unjust judgements and given the king much bad counsel, to the prejudice of the English. However, they permitted a few, like Robert the deacon and his son-in-law Richard, son of Scrob, Alfred, keeper of the king's horse, and Anfrith, surnamed *Ceocesfot*, and certain others whom the king loved more than the rest, and who were loyal to him and to the whole people, to remain in England.[7] But Robert, archbishop of Canterbury, and William, bishop of London, and Ulf, bishop of Lincoln, with their Normans, barely escaping, crossed the sea.[8] [9]But William, because of his goodness, was recalled after a short time, and restored to his bishopric.[9]

---

[6] Swein's pilgrimage and death (dated Michaelmas) are in ASC C alone. JW is alone in giving the reason for the pilgrimage (as expiation for the murder of Beorn), and in stating that he went barefoot and died from the extreme cold in Lycia.

[7] ASC does not name the Frenchmen allowed to remain in England.

[8] JW identifies the sees of William and Ulf.

[9–9] Not in ASC.

[C³BP]

ᵃStigandus, qui quondam dimisso Anglorum Orientalium episcopatu, sullimiorem gradum meditatus Wintoniensem inuaserat, innocentis regis Eadwardi *simplicitatem circumueniens,* uiuente Rotberto, Cantuuariensem *archiepiscopatum optinuit.ᵃ¹*

²Osbernus uero cognomento Pentecost et socius eius Hugo sua reddiderunt castella, et comitis Leofrici licentia per suum comitatum Scottiam adeuntes, a rege Scottorum Macbeotha*ᵇ* suscepti sunt.² Eodem anno in nocte festiuitatis sancti Thome apostoli tantus tamque uehemens extitit uentus ut multas ecclesias domusque dirueret, et innumerabiles arbores frangeret uel radicitus erueret.³

[1053] (xiiii) 1075 Griffini regis australium Walensium frater, Res nomine, propter frequentes predas quas egit in loco qui Bulendum dicitur, iussu regis Eaduuardi occiditur, et Glauuornam caput eius ad regem in uigilia Epiphanie Domini est allatum.⁴ ⁵Eodem anno, dum secunda pascalis festiuitatis celebraretur feria, Wintonie Goduuino comiti, solito regi ad mensam assidenti, suprema euenit calamitas, graui etenim morbo ex improuiso percussus, mutus in ipsa sede declinauit. Quod filii eius, comes Haroldus, Tosti et Gyrth uidentes, illum in regis cameram portabant⁶ sperantes eum post modicum de infirmitate conualescere, sed ille, expers uirium, quinta post hec feria, miserabili cruciatu uita decessit, et in Veteri Monasterio sepultus est, cuius ducatum suscepit filius eius Haroldus, et eius comitatus datus est Algaro, Leofrici comitis filio.⁷ ⁸Mense Octobri,⁹ Wlsius, Licetfeldensis

---

ᵃ⁻ᵃ Stigandus . . . optinuit] *add. mg. with signe de renvoi* C³, *om.* HL   ᵇ Macheotha *HL*

---

¹ *GP* i. 23 (p. 35).   ²⁻² Not in ASC.
³ ASC C (1052) D (1053 *recte* 1052) mention the gale on 21 Dec., C saying that it did great damage, and D that there was also a great wind all through Christmas.
⁴ ASC C (1052) D (1053) record the killing of Rhys, but D alone identifies him as the Welsh king's brother, and relates the bringing of his head to Gloucester on 5 Jan. JW specifies the 'south' Welsh king (Gruffydd ap Rhydderch), explicitly says that Edward ordered the execution, and gives its location.
⁵ ASC A (1053: hand 9: s. xii¹-post 1115?) simply records the death of Godwine, but

Stigand, who had formerly given up the bishopric of the East Angles, purposing a higher elevation, appropriated Winchester and, deceiving the innocent simplicity of King Edward, obtained the archbishopric of Canterbury in Robert's lifetime.[1]

[2]But Osbern, nicknamed Pentecost, and his comrade Hugo surrendered their castles, and, approaching Scotland through Earl Leofric's territory, with his permission, were received by Macbeth, king of the Scots.[2] In the same year, on the night of the feast of St Thomas the Apostle, there was so great and so fierce a wind that it destroyed many churches and houses, and broke down innumerable trees, or tore them up by the roots.[3]

[1053] On account of his frequent raids, the brother of Gruffydd, king of the South Welsh, Rhys by name, was killed at a place called Bullington on the order of King Edward, and his head was brought to the king at Gloucester on the eve of the Epiphany.[4] [5]In the same year, while Easter Monday was being celebrated at Winchester, the ultimate calamity befell Earl Godwine as he sat in his usual place at the king's table; struck down by a sudden and unexpected illness, he collapsed silent in his very chair. Seeing this, his sons Earls Harold, Tostig, and Gyrth carried him into the king's chamber,[6] hoping that he would recover a little later from the infirmity, but deprived of his strength, he departed this life the following Thursday in wretched pain and was buried in the Old Minster. His son Harold received his earldom, and Harold's earldom was given to Ælfgar, son of Earl Leofric.[7] [8]In the month

CDEF (1053) record his death and the succession to his earldom (JW being closest to C), C placing it (like JW) before, and D after, the deaths of bishops and abbots, which are not recorded here in E.

[6] ASC C mentions the presence of Harold and Tostig, but not their carrying (with Gyrth) their dying father.

[7] ASC does not give Ælfgar's parentage, but CE record Godwine's burial at the Old Minster.

[8] JW's passage concerning the death and succession of prelates is closer to that in ASC D (1053) than to that in C (1052), even though as noted above, under n. 5, it is closer to C's account of the death of Godwine.

[9] ASC D says slightly differently 'before All Souls' Day' 'in the same month'.

episcopus, et abbates Goduuinus Wincelcumbensis et Ageluuardus Glæstoniensis decesserunt. Wlsio Leofuuinus, Couentrensis abbas,[2] et Ægeluuardo Ægelnothus, eiusdem monasterii monachus,[3] successerunt. Aldredus uero, Wigornensis episcopus, abbatiam Wincelcumbensem tamdiu in manu sua tenuit, donec Godricum, regis capellani Godmanni filium, abbatem constitueret,[4] Alfricus, germanus Odde comitis, apud Deorhyrste .xi. kalend. Ianuarii obiit, sed in monasterio Persorensi est tumulatus.[5]

Aed clericus barbosus in Hibernia, uir famosissimus et mire religionis fuit, qui clericorum, puellarum et laicorum magnam scolam habebat, puellasque more clericorum tondebat, propter quod etiam de Hibernia proiectus est.[6]

[**1054**] (xv) 1076   *ᵃLeo papa obiit .xvi. kalend. Maii.ᵃ[7]*
[8]Strenuus dux Norðhymbrorum[9] Siuuardus, [10]iussu regis,[10] et [11]equestri exercitu et classe ualida[11] Scotiam adiit et cum rege Scottorum Macbeotha[12] prelium commisit ac multis milibus Scottorum et [10]Normannis omnibus,[10] quorum supra fecimus mentionem,ᵇ[13] occisis, illum fugauit, et Malcolmum regis Cumbrorum filium, ut rex iusserat, regem constituit.[14] In eo tamen prelio suus filius et multi Anglorum et Danorum ceciderunt.[15] Eodem anno festiuitate sancti Kenelmi martiris Aldredus, Wigornensis episcopus, Godricum abbatem Wincelcumbe constituit.[16] Dein magnis cum xeniis regis fungitur legatione ad imperatorem, a quo simul et ab Herimanno Coloniensi archipresule magno susceptus honore, ibidem per integrum annum mansit, et regis ex parte imperatori suggessit ut,

---

ᵃ⁻ᵃ Leo . . . Maii] *mg.* H.   ᵇ t *in* mentionem *erased and interlin.* Cᵗ

---

[1] ASC D says slightly differently 'before All Souls' Day' 'in the same month'.
[2] This identification is in ASC C not D.
[3] The succession of Æthelnoth is not in ASC C, but in D.
[4] ASC D speaks of Ealdred's succession to Winchcombe, but JW speaks of his temporary retention of the abbacy and adds the details of Godric's succession.
[5] ASC D alone, which does not give the day of Ælfric's death.   [6] Mar.
[7] Mar.   [8] The account of this war is in ASC CD.
[9] Identified by JW.   [10]-[10] Not in ASC.   [11]-[11] ASC D.
[12] Macbeth is named in ASC D.

of October.[1] Wulfsige, bishop of Lichfield, and the Abbots
Godwine of Winchcombe and Æthelweard of Glastonbury died.
Wulfsige was succeeded by Leofwine, abbot of Coventry,[2] and
Æthelweard by Æthelnoth, a monk of the same monastery.[3] But
Ealdred, bishop of Worcester, kept the abbey of Winchcombe in
his own hands until he appointed Godric, the king's chaplain, son
of Godeman, as abbot.[4] Ælfric, brother of Earl Odda, died at
Deerhurst on 22 December, and was buried in the monastery at
Pershore.[5]

Áed, a bearded clerk in Ireland, was a most famous man and
extraordinarily devout. He had a great school of clerks, girls, and
laymen, and he tonsured the girls like clerks, for which indeed he
was expelled from Ireland.[6]

[1054] Pope Leo died on 16 April.[7]

[8]Siward, the vigorous earl of the Northumbrians,[9] [10]at the
king's command,[10] went to Scotland [11]with a mounted force and a
powerful fleet[11] and joined battle with Macbeth,[12] king of the
Scots, and when many thousands of Scots and [10]all the
Normans,[10] whom we mentioned above,[13] had been killed, he put
them to flight and, as the king commanded, he set up Malcolm,
son of the king of the Cumbrians, as king.[14] However, in that battle his own son and many of the English and the Danes fell.[15] In
the same year, on the feast of St Kenelm the martyr, Ealdred,
bishop of Worcester, appointed Godric abbot of Winchcombe.[16]
Then, with great gifts from the king, he performed the office of
ambassador to the emperor, by whom, and by Hermann, archbishop of Cologne, he was received with great honour. There he
stayed a whole year, and proposed to the emperor, on the king's
behalf, that, an embassy should be sent to Hungary in order to

---

[13] See above, the penultimate sentence in 1052.

[14] The setting up of Malcolm at Edward's command is not in ASC. WM, *GR* ii. 196
(i. 137) states that Edward ordered both Siward's invasion and the setting up of
Malcolm 'filius regis Cumbrorum'. See A. O. Anderson, *Early Sources of Scottish
History* (Edinburgh, 1922), i. 593–4, Freeman, *NC* ii. App. FF.

[15] Closest to ASC C, which says that Siward's son was among those killed. D names
two of the slain, gives the day of the battle, and does not mention Danes among the
dead.

[16] The consecration of Godric, whose succession has already been indicated above,
n. 4, is not mentioned elsewhere.

legatis Vngariam missis, inde fratruelem suum Eaduuardum, regis uidelicet Eadmundi Ferrei Lateris filium, reduceret Angliamque uenire faceret.*¹ |

[1055] (xvi) 1077 *Victor² papa centesimus .xlvi.*³

Siwardus, dux Northanymbrorum,⁴ Eboraci decessit et in monasterio Galmanho, quod ipse construxerat, sepultus est. Cuius ducatus Tostio, Haroldi ducis germano, datus est.⁵ ⁶Non multo post, rex Eaduuardus, habito Lundonie concilio,⁷ Algarum comitem, filium Leofrici comitis, ⁸sine culpa⁸ exlegauit. Qui mox Hiberniam petiit, et decem et octo piraticis nauibus adquisitis, rediit, et Griffinum regem Walensium adiit, eumque petiuit ut contra regem Eaduuardum sibi esset in auxilium.⁹ Ille statim de toto regno suo copiosum exercitum congregans, Algaro precepit ut loco constituto sibi et exercitui cum suis copiis occurreret, quibus in unum conuenientibus fines Anglorum depopulaturi, Herefordensem prouinciam intrauerunt.¹⁰ Contra quos timidus¹¹ dux Rauulfus, regis Eaduuardi sororis filius,¹² exercitum congregans, et duobus miliariis¹³ a ciuitate Hereforda .ix. kalend. Nouembris¹⁴ illis occurrens, Anglos contra morem in equis pugnare iussit, sed cum prelium essent commissuri comes cum suis Francis et Normannis fugam primitus capessit.¹⁵ Quod uidentes Angli, ducem suum fugiendo secuntur, quos aduersarii fere omnes insecuti .cccc. uel quingentos uiros ex eis peremerunt, multosque uulnerauerunt.¹⁶ Dein uictoria potiti, rex Griffinus et comes Algarus Herefordam intrauerunt, et .vii. canonicis qui ualuas principalis basilice defenderant occisis,¹⁷ ac monasterio, quod uerus Dei Christicola antistes Æthelstanus construxerat, cum omnibus ornamentis et reliquiis

---

ª see App. B for addition at line-end B¹

¹ ASC CD both record Bishop Ealdred's visit to Germany, D specifying the place, duration, the reason for the visit and the entertainment by both emperor and archbishop of Cologne. JW names the archbishop and the presents he bore and is specific about the king's business. ASC CD mentions the death of Osgod Clapa and the consecration of Evesham.

² Victor II 1055–6.   ³ Mar.   ⁴ Identified by JW.

⁵ ASC (C)DEF record the death of Siward, CD the location of his death at York and burial in the minster at Galmanho (which they say he had dedicated to God and His saints, (Olaf, D)), and DEF the appointment of his successor.

⁶ ASC C-F all record the exile of Ælfgar, and CDE the Welsh war, E's account being brief.

⁷ ASC C alone gives the location of the council, E stating that it occurred 'a week before mid-Lent'.

escort back from there the king's nephew Edward, that is the son of King Edmund Ironside, and bring him to England.[1]

[**1055**] Victor[2] the 146th pope.[3]

Siward, earl of the Northumbrians,[4] died at York, and was buried in the minster at Galmanho which he himself had built. His earldom was given to Tostig, Earl Harold's brother.[5] [6]Not much later, King Edward, having taken council at London,[7] outlawed [8]the guiltless[8] Earl Ælfgar, son of Earl Leofric. He soon went to Ireland, and returned when he had acquired eighteen pirate ships and approached Gruffydd, king of the Welsh, to request his help against King Edward.[9] Gruffydd at once assembled a large army from his whole realm, and commanded Ælfgar to hurry to meet him and his force with his own troops at the place appointed; having joined forces they entered Herefordshire with the intention of laying waste the English borders.[10] Against them the timorous[11] Earl Ralph, son of King Edward's sister,[12] mustered an army, and meeting them on 24 October[14] two miles[13] from the city of Hereford, he ordered the English, contrary to custom, to fight on horseback, but when they were about to join battle, the earl with his French and Normans was the first to take flight.[15] The English, seeing this, followed their commander in flight. Almost the whole of the enemy army pursued them, and slew 400 or 500 of them and wounded many.[16] Then, having gained the victory, King Gruffydd and Earl Ælfgar entered Hereford, slew the seven canons who had held the doors of the main basilica,[17] burnt the minster which Æthelstan, God's truly Christian bishop, had built with all the ornaments and the relics

[8-8] Closest to ASC C ('without any guilt'), and closer to D ('without having committed any crime') than to E which has Ælfgar admit his treachery. On Ælfgar and the Welsh, see K. L. Maund, *Ireland, Wales and England in the Eleventh Century* (Woodbridge, 1991), pp. 129–38.

[9] Closest to ASC C in mentioning 18 ships and in naming the Welsh king at this point.

[10] JW is here expanding ASC C.   [11] 'timidus' is JW's adjective here and later.

[12] Earl Ralph's parentage is JW's addition.   [13] This distance is JW's.

[14] This date is given towards the end of the annal in ASC CD, after the successful English retaliation.

[15] ASC C says simply that the English fled because they were on horseback, and mentions neither the presence of Frenchmen nor their flight, which precipitated that of the English.

[16] ASC C gives the numbers as 400–500 (without referring to the wounded), but it also says that none of the enemy was killed.

[17] ASC D alone refers to priests killed inside the minster.

¹sancti Agelberti regis et martiris aliorumque sanctorum,¹ combusto, et nonnullis e ciuibus necatis, multisque captiuitatis, ciuitate etiam spoliata et cremata, prede ubertate ditati redierunt. ²Quod ubi regi innotuit, de tota mox Anglia exercitum congregari iussit, cui Glauuorne congregato strenuum ducem Haroldum prefecit, qui deuote iussis obtemperans, Griffinum et Algarum impigre insequitur ac fines Walanorum audacter ingressus, ultra Straddele castra metatus est, sed illi, quia uirum fortem et bellicosum ipsum sciebant, cum eo committere bellum non audentes, in Suthuualiam fugerunt. Quo comperto, maiorem exercitus partem ibi dimisit, mandans eis ut suis aduersariis, si res exposceret, uiriliter resisterent. Cum cetera uero multitudine Herefordam rediens, uallo lato et alto illam cincxit, portis et seris muniuit.³ Interea legatis intercurrentibus, Griffinus, Algarus et Haroldus et qui cum illis fuerant in loco, qui Byligesleagea dicitur, conuenerunt, et, pace data et accepta, firmam amicitiam inter se pacti sunt. Quibus patratis, classis Algari comitis Legeceastram deuecta, stipendium quod eisᵃ promiserat ibi expectauit. Ipse uero ad regem uenit, et ab eo suum comitatum recepit.⁴ Eo tempore religiosus uir Tremerin, Walonicus antistes, decessit. Hic multo tempore uicarius Athelstani Herefordensis presulis extitit, postquam ipse ministerium episcopale per se implere nequiuit, erat enim per annos tredecim oculorum lumine priuatus.⁵ Herimannus, Wiltonie prouincie presul, offensus quia ei sedem episcopalem transferre de uilla que Reamnesbiri dicitur ad abbatiam Mealmesbyriensem rex nollet concedere, episcopatum dimisit, marique transfretato, apud sanctum Bertinum monachicum habitum suscepit, ibique in ipso monasterio .iii. annis mansit.⁶

[1056] (xvii) 1078 Magne uir sanctitatis Herefordensis episcopus Athelstanus .iiii. idus Feb. in episcopali uilla que uocatur

ᵃ interlin. Cᵗ

¹⁻¹ Not identified in ASC.
² ASC C gives an account of the king and Earl Harold's retaliatory action, but JW is fuller, and much of the first sentence (e.g. the royal order, the reference to the Straddle) seems to be JW's own contribution.
³ ASC C does not make it clear that the ditch was built round Hereford rather than Gloucester.
⁴ ASC C says that Ælfgar was reinstated and then given all that had been taken

[1]of St Æthelberht, king and martyr, and of other saints,[1] killed many citizens, took many captives, despoiled and burnt the city, and returned enriched with a lavish quantity of booty. [2]When the king was informed of this, he ordered an army to be mustered directly from the whole of England. It assembled at Gloucester, and the king put the vigorous Earl Harold in charge of it. Zealously obeying his orders, Harold energetically pursued Gruffydd and Ælfgar, and boldly invaded the Welsh borders. He encamped beyond Straddle, but they, because they knew him to be a strong and warlike man, not daring to embark on war with him, fled into South Wales. When this was known, he dismissed the greater part of his army there, ordering the men to resist the enemy vigorously, if occasion should demand. On returning to Hereford with the rest of the host, he encircled it with a broad and deep ditch, and fortified it with gates and bars.[3] Meanwhile, envoys were exchanged, and Gruffydd, Ælfgar, and Harold and those who were with him met at a place called Billingsley, and when peace had been given and received, they established a firm friendship among them. When these matters had been accomplished, Earl Ælfgar's fleet sailed away to Chester, and there awaited the payment he had promised. But he himself went back to the king, who restored his earldom to him.[4] At that time, the devout man Tremerig, a Welsh bishop, died. He was for a long time the deputy of Æthelstan, bishop of Hereford, when he could not fulfil the episcopal office by himself, for he was without sight for thirteen years.[5] Hereman, bishop of Wiltshire, displeased because the king would not allow him to move the episcopal seat from the township called Ramsbury to Malmesbury abbey, laid aside his bishopric, and crossed the sea to take the monastic habit at Saint-Bertin, and there, in that very monastery, he remained for three years.[6]

[1056] Æthelstan, bishop of Hereford and a man of great sanctity, died on 10 February in the episcopal township called Bosbury. His

from him, and places this before the reference to Ælfgar's fleet. CD give here the day of the slaughter (24 Oct.).

[5] ASC CD record the death of Tremerig, Bishop Æthelstan's deputy during his infirmity, which is not described.

[6] JW's information concerning Hereman in this annal and in 1058 may be correct. WM *GP* ii. 83, v. 264 (pp. 182–3, 420) also deals with Hereman's attempt to establish himself at Malmesbury during a vacancy, but his chronology is confused. JW's *Epis. Lists* mention Hereman's uniting of the sees of Ramsbury and Sherborne.

Bosanbyrig decessit. Cuius corpus Herefordam delatum in ecclesia, quam ipse a fundamentis construxerat, est tumulatum.¹ Cui Leouegarus ducis Haroldi capellanus successit, qui eodem anno .xvi. kalend. Iul. a Griffino Walanorum rege in loco qui Clastbyrig uocatur, cum clericis suis et uicecomite Agelnotho et multis aliis, occisus est. Mansit autem in episcopatu undecim septimanis et .iiii. diebus.² Quo perempto, Aldredo Wigornensi presuli, donec antistes constitueretur, commissus est episcopatus Herefordensis.³ Post hec idem episcopus et comites Leofricus ac Haroldus cum rege Eadwardo Walanorum regem Griffinum pacificauerunt.⁴

Herimannus Coloniensis episcopus obiit. Anno successit. Marianus, peregrinus factus pro celesti patria, uenit Coloniam ibique in monasterio Scottorum sancti Martini, quinta feria, kalend. Aug., monachus factus est.⁵

⟨E⟩cclesiarum^a amator, pauperum recreator, uiduarum et pupillorum defensor, oppressorum subuentor, uirginitatis custos, comes Ægeluuinus ᵇid est Oddaᵇ ab Aldredo Wigornensi episcopo ante suum obitum monachizatus .ii. kalend. Sept. apud Deorhyrste decessit, sed in monasterio Persorensi honorifice sepultus quiescit.⁶

p. 340 Dunholmensis episcopus, Agelricus, | episcopatu sponte relicto, ad monasterium suum quod dicitur Burh, ubi nutritus et monachus est factus, secessit ibique annis .xii. deguit, cui eiusdem monasterii monachus frater ipsius Ageluuinus in episcopatum successit.⁷

Imperator Heinricus .iii. non. Octobris obiit et sepultus est Spira ubi et pater eius.

Romanorum nonagesimus .vi. Heinricus⁸ filiusᶜ superioris Heinrici regnauit annis .l.ᵈ⁹

ᵃ Ex *erased before* -cclesiarum C   ᵇ⁻ᵇ id est Odda] *interlin.* C¹B¹H¹, Odda *interlin.* L¹P³?   ᶜ eius *add.* HL   ᵈ decem *Mar.*

---

¹ ASC (C)D record Æthelstan's death and his burial at Hereford, but JW alone gives the place of death, and repeats that Æthelstan had been responsible for the building of Hereford cathedral.
² ASC CD record these facts about Leofgar, though JW alone names the battle site. JW omits references to Leofgar's characteristics, and to the evil consequences (as expressed in C) of the battle in which he and others died.
³ JW's statement is more precise than ASC CD's plain statement of Ealdred's succession.

body was taken to Hereford, and buried in the church which he himself had constructed from the foundations.[1] To him Leofgar, Earl Harold's chaplain, succeeded, and he was killed in the same year on 16 June by Gruffydd [ap Llywelyn], king of the Welsh, in a place called Glasbury, with his clerks and Ælfnoth the sheriff and many others. He held the bishopric for eleven weeks and four days.[2] When he was killed, the bishopric of Hereford was committed to the care of Ealdred, bishop of Worcester, until a bishop might be appointed.[3] After this, the same bishop and the Earls Leofric and Harold, with King Edward, made peace with Gruffydd, king of the Welsh.[4]

Hermann, bishop of Cologne, died, and Anno succeeded him. Marianus, having become a pilgrim for the sake of the heavenly kingdom, came to Cologne, and there in the Irish monastery of St Martin, on Thursday, 1 August, became a monk.[5]

The lover of churches, succourer of the poor, defender of widows and orphans, helper of the oppressed, guardian of virgins, Earl Æthelwine, that is Odda, was made a monk by Ealdred, bishop of Worcester, before his death. He died on 31 August at Deerhurst, but he rests, honourably buried, at Pershore.[6] Æthelric, bishop of Durham, having freely given up his bishopric, retired to his monastery called Peterborough, where he was brought up, and took monastic vows, and there he lived twelve years. A monk of the same monastery, his own brother Æthelwine, succeeded him in the bishopric.[7]

The Emperor Henry died on 5 October, and was buried at Speyer, where his father also lies.

Henry,[8] ninety-sixth emperor of the Romans, son of the above mentioned Henry, reigned fifty years.[9]

---

[4] ASC C alone records the peace, adding that Gruffydd became Edward's under king.
[5] Mar.
[6] ASC CD record the death of Earl Odda, its day, and the place of burial, D commenting on his qualities, though neither JW's epithets nor the place of death nor the role of Ealdred in making him a monk occur in ASC.
[7] The retirement of Æthelric to Peterborough, and the succession of his brother, Æthelwine, is at the opening, not the end, of ASC D (1056). The presence of Æthelric in Peterborough is again mentioned in ASC DE under 1069. The other facts about Æthelric and his brother's monastic life at Peterborough are not in ASC.
[8] Henry IV 1056–1106.   [9] Mar.

[**1057**] (i) 1079   *Victor papa obiit .v. kalend. Aug.*[1]

[2]Clito Eaduuardus, regis Eadmundi Ferrei Lateris[3] filius, ut ei mandarat suus patruus rex Eaduuardus de Hungaria quo multo ante, ut prediximus,[4] in exilium missus fuerat, Angliam uenit. Decreuerat enim rex illum post se regni heredem constituere,[5] sed ex quo uenit paruo post tempore uita decessit Lundonie.[6] [7]Excellentis uir memorie laudabilis comes Leofricus, ducis Leofuuini filius, in propria uilla que dicitur Bromleaga, .ii. kalend. Septembris in bona decessit senectute, et Couentreo sepultus est honorifice. Quod monasterium inter cetera bona que in sua uita gessit opera, ipse et uxor eius, Dei cultrix, sancteque Marie semper uirginis amatrix deuota, nobilis comitissa Godgiua, de suo patrimonio a fundamentis construxerunt, et id terris sufficienter locupletauerunt ornamentis uariis adeo ditauerunt ut in Anglia tanta copia auri, argenti, gemmarum, lapidumque pretiosorum in nullo inueniretur monasterio, quanta tunc temporis habebatur in illo. Leonense etiam et Wonlocanense cenobium sanctique Iohannis baptiste ac sancte Wereburge uirginis monasteria in Legeceastra sita, et ecclesiam, quam Lindicolinensis presul Eadnothus[8] [a]in loco famoso qui sancte Marie Stou Anglice,[a] Latine uero sancte Marie locus, appellatur, ⟨construxit⟩,[b] pretiosis ditauerunt ornamentis. Wigornense quoque monasterium terris et Eoueshamnense edificiis, ornamentis uariis terrisque locupletauerunt. Huius itaque comitis sapientia quandiu uixit regibus omnique Anglorum populo multum profecit, cuius ducatum filius suus Algarus suscepit. Heca presul Australium Saxonum obiit, pro quo Ægelricus, Christi ecclesie monachus Cantuuariensis, eligitur.[9] Rodulfus supradictus comes .xii. kalend. Ianuarii decessit, et in abbatia que Burh uocatur tumulatus est.[10]

[a-a] in . . . Anglice] *compressed writing* C   [b] *om.* JW

[1] Mar.
[2] ASC DE record the atheling's return to England, and JW is closer to D than to the relatively brief E. In the first sentence JW makes clear that King Edward had requested his nephew's return.
[3] 'Ironside' is the title given in ASC D, and almost invariably elsewhere in JW.
[4] ASC D puts here the earlier history of Edward, which JW had placed under 1017.
[5] ASC does not record the king's intention.
[6] ASC E says he was buried in St Paul's Minster, but the place of death is not recorded by DE. JW does not have D's reflections on the fate of the atheling.

[**1057**] Pope Victor died on 28 July.[1]

[2]The atheling Edward, son of King Edward Ironside,[3] came as his uncle King Edward had ordered to England from Hungary where, as we have said,[4] he had been sent into exile long before, for the king had decided that he should be established as his heir[5] and successor to the realm. But a short time after his arrival he departed this life at London.[6] [7]Earl Leofric, that praiseworthy man of excellent memory, son of Earl Leofwine, died at a good old age in his township called Bromley on 31 August, and was honourably buried at Coventry. Among the other good works which he performed during his life, he and his wife, the noble Countess Godgifu, a worshipper of God and devout lover of St Mary ever-virgin, built the monastery there from the foundations out of their own patrimony, and endowed it adequately with lands and made it so rich in various ornaments that in no monastery in England might be found the abundance of gold, silver, gems and precious stones that was at that time in its possession. They enriched with precious ornaments the monasteries of Leominster and Wenlock too, and the monasteries at Chester of St John the Baptist and of St Werburg the virgin, and the church which Bishop Eadnoth[8] of Lincoln founded in the famous place which is called Stow St Mary in English, and in Latin of the place of St Mary. They also endowed the monastery at Worcester with lands, and that at Evesham with buildings, various ornaments, and lands. The wisdom of this earl during his lifetime was of great advantage to the kings and all the people of the English. His son Ælfgar received his earldom. Heca, bishop of the South Saxons, died. In his place Æthelric, a monk of Christ Church, Canterbury, was elected.[9] The above mentioned Earl Ralph died on 21 December and was buried in the abbey called Peterborough.[10]

---

[7] ASC DE record the death of Earl Leofric, and the succession of Ælfgar, D giving the day (30 Sept.), his burial-place, and a brief eulogistic sentence. All the other information in JW is peculiar to him. HH *HA* vi. c. 24 (Arnold p. 195) mentions the foundation of Coventry, Stow 'and many other churches.' *S* 1478 *K* 956 (Whitelock, Brett, and Brooke, *Councils*, no. 73, pp. 538–43) records the endowment of Stow by Leofric and Godgifu.

[8] Possibly Eadnoth I of Dorchester 1009–16.

[9] ASC D (1057) E (1058) record Heca's death and the succession of Æthelric, whom E, like JW, describes as a monk of Christ Church, Canterbury. E says that Stigand consecrated Æthelric.

[10] ASC D records the day of Earl Ralph's death, and his burial at Peterborough.

[1058] (ii) 1080 *Stephanus,*[1] *ᵃabbas de monte Cassino,ᵃ papa .cxlvii. Paderbrunna ciuitas cum duobus monasteriis, id est episcopatus et monachorum, feria sexta ante Palmas, igne consumitur. In monasterio autem monachorum erat monachus, nomine Paternus, Scottus, multisque annis inclusus, qui etiam ipsum prenuntiabat incendium, qui pro cupiditate martirii nullo modo exiuit, sed in clausula sua combustus est, et per hunc ignem transiuit in refrigerium. De cuius etiam sepulchro quedam bona narrantur. 'Ipsis uero statim diebus, feria secunda post octauas pasce, ⟨exiens⟩ᵇ de Colonia, causa claudendi, cum abbate Fuldensi ad Fuldam super mattam supra quam combustus est, ego oraui.' Hec ait Marianus Scottus inclusus.*[2]

Algarus, [3]Merciorum[3] comes, a rege Eaduuardo [3]secundo[3] exlegatus est, sed regis Walanorum Griffini iuuamine et Norreganice classis adminiculo, que ad illum uenerat ex improuiso, cito per uim suum comitatum recuperauit.[4]

Stephanus papa obiit ᶜ.iii. kalend. Aprilis.ᶜ[5]

Benedictus[6] successit, qui Stigando Dorubernie archiepiscopo pallium misit. Agelricus Suthsaxonum presul ordinatur et ᵈabbas Siuuardusᵈ consecratur episcopus ad Hrofensem ecclesiam.[7] Aldredus, Wigornensis episcopus, ecclesiam, quam in ciuitate Glauuorna a fundamentis construxit, in honore principis apostolorum Petri honorificeᵉ dedicauit, et postea regis licentia Wilstanum, Wigornensem monachum, a se ordinatum abbatem constituit ibidem.[8] Dein presulatu Wiltoniensis ecclesie, qui sibi ad regendum commissus fuerat dimisso, et Herimanno cuius supra meminimus reddito, mare transiit, et per Vngariam profectus est Ierosolimam, quod nullus archiepiscoporum uel episcoporum Anglie eatenus dinoscitur fecisse.[9]

ᵃ⁻ᵃ abbas . . . Cassino] *interlin. C*ᴵ*, om. LBP*   ᵇ *om. JW*   ᶜ⁻ᶜ .iii. kalend. Aprilis] *interlin. C*ᴵ   ᵈ⁻ᵈ abbas Siuuardus] *darker ink over erasure C*ᴵ   ᵉ *darker ink C*ᴵ

---

[1] Stephen IX (X) 1057–8.   [2] Mar.   [3–3] Not in ASC.
[4] ASC D records Ælfgar's expulsion, and his return with Welsh assistance. The arrival of a Norwegian fleet, recorded in D, is explicitly linked to Ælfgar's return by JW. JW makes clear that Ælfgar recovered his earldom, but has nothing corresponding to D's remark on the tediousness of relating how the return was managed.

[**1058**] Stephen,[1] abbot of Monte Cassino, the 147th pope. The city of Paderborn (with its two monasteries, the bishop's and the monks') was consumed by fire, on the Friday before Palm Sunday. However, in the monks' monastery there was a monk called Paternus, an Irishman who had been an anchorite for many years, and who had even predicted that very fire. He, from a passionate desire for martyrdom, would by no means leave but was burnt in his cell, and through this fire passed over into consolation. Much that is good is told about his tomb, 'for, immediately, during those very days, on the Monday after the octave of Easter, as I was leaving Cologne for Fulda for the purpose of becoming a monk, I prayed with the abbot of Fulda on the mat on which Paternus was burnt.' These were the words of Marianus, the Irish anchorite.[2]

Ælfgar, earl [3]of the Mercians,[3] was outlawed by King Edward [3]a second time,[3] but with the help of Gruffydd [ap Llywelyn], king of the Welsh, and the support of the Norwegian fleet, which joined him unexpectedly, he quickly recovered his earldom by force.[4]

Pope Stephen died on 30 March.[5]

Benedict[6] succeeded, who sent the pallium to Stigand, archbishop of Canterbury. Æthelric was ordained bishop of the South Saxons, and Abbot Siward was consecrated bishop of Rochester.[7] Ealdred, bishop of Worcester, dedicated the church of Gloucester, which he built from the foundations, with great ceremony in honour of Peter, the prince of the apostles, and afterwards he established there as abbot, by royal licence, Wulfstan, whom he had ordained as a monk of Worcester.[8] Then, having resigned the bishopric of Wiltshire, which had been committed to his rule, and restored it to the Hereman whom we mentioned above, he crossed the sea and set out through Hungary for Jerusalem, which no English archbishop or bishop was known to have done up to then.[9]

---

[5] Mar.   [6] Benedict X (anti-pope) 1058–9.

[7] ASC DE record Stigand's reception of the pallium, and the consecration (E: by Stigand) of the bishops of Selsey and Rochester.

[8] ASC D records Ealdred's foundation and consecration of St Peter's, Gloucester, but not the appointment of Wulfstan as abbot there.

[9] ASC D mentions Ealdred's pilgrimage to Jerusalem, and his offering of a gold chalice there, but neither the return to England of Hereman of Ramsbury nor the route via Hungary taken by Ealdred.

[1059] (iii) 1081 Nicolaus,[1] ciuitatis Florentie episcopus, papa eligitur, et Benedictus eicitur.[2]

Marianus inclusus cum Sigifrido Fuldensi abbate iuxta corpus sancti Kiliani in Wirziburh consecratus est presbiter, sabbato medie quadragesime, .iii. idus Martii, et feria sexta post Ascensionem Domini, pridie idus Maii, inclusus est in Fulda per annos decem. Liupoldus episcopus Mogontinus obiit .vii. idus Dec. Sigifridus ei successit.[3]

[1060] (iiii) 1082 Heinricus, rex Francorum, obiit cui filius eius
p. 341   primogenitus Philippus successit.[4] | Wyllensis episcopus Duduc obiit, cui successit Gisa, regis capellanus, ambo de Lotharingia oriundi.[5] Eboracensium archiepiscopus Kinsius .xi. kalend. Ian. Eboraci obiit, cuius corpus ad monasterium quod Burh dicitur delatum honorifice est tumulatum, pro quo Wigornensis episcopus Aldredus ad archiepiscopatum in Natiuitate Domini eligitur.[6] Et Herefordensis presulatus, qui ei propter suam industriam fuerat commissus, capellano Edgithe regine Waltero Lotharingo est datus.[7]

Sigifridus abbas Fuldensis, dominica die, Natalis Domini de Fulda ad regiam curtem exiens baculum Mogontiensis[a] archiepiscopatus accepit in Epiphania Domini, pape Nicholai legato, qui non longe post papa effectus est Alexandro, hoc idem annuente. Widratus decanus Fuldensis abbas successit.[8]

[1061] (v) 1083 [b]Aldredus, Eboracensis archiepiscopus, cum Tostio comite Romam iuit, et a Nicolao papa pallium suscepit.[c9]

[HL]	[C³BP]
[d]*Maiolus, abbas Scottorum, Colonie obiit, Foilanus post eum*	Vbi etiam Gisa Wellensis et Walterus Herefordensis ab ipso

---

[a] Mogontiensis *HL (N)*, Mogotiensis *CBP*   [b] Aldredus . . . successit *(p. 588)] most seems written over erasure C³*   [c] *1061 n. d assigned here by signe de renvoi P⁵*   [d] Maiolus . . . successit *(p. 588)] mg. with signe de renvoi pointing to 1061 n. c P⁵*

---

[1] Nicholas II 1058–61.
[2] ASC DE, D having in addition a Peterborough entry.   [3] Mar.
[4] ASC DE record the death of King Henry I, and E the succession of Philip.
[5] ASC D (1060) E (1061) record the succession of Gisa to Duduc at Wells, though neither describes them as Lotharingians nor Gisa as king's chaplain.

[**1059**] Nicholas,[1] bishop of the city of Florence, was elected pope, and Benedict was deposed.[2]

Marianus, the anchorite, with Sigifrid, abbot of Fulda, was ordained priest on the Saturday in mid-Lent, 13 March, near the remains of St Kilian in Würzburg, and on the Friday after the Lord's Ascension, 14 May, was enclosed at Fulda for ten years. Liutpold, bishop of Mainz, died on 7 December. Sigifrid succeeded him.[3]

[**1060**] Henry, king of the Franks, died, and his eldest son Philip succeeded him.[4] Duduc, bishop of Wells, died, and was succeeded by Gisa, the king's chaplain. Both were from Lotharingia.[5] Cynesige, archbishop of York, died on 22 December at York; his body was borne to the monastery called Peterborough and honourably interred. Ealdred, bishop of Worcester, was elected to the archbishopric at Christmas in his place,[6] and the bishopric of Hereford, which had been entrusted to him because of his diligence, was given to Walter of Lotharingia, Queen Edith's chaplain.[7]

Sigifrid, abbot of Fulda, setting out from Fulda on Christmas Day for the royal court, accepted the crozier of the archbishopric of Mainz at Epiphany with the approval of Pope Nicholas' legate, who not long after became Pope Alexander. Widrat, dean of Fulda, succeeded Sigifrid as abbot.[8]

[**1061**] Ealdred, archbishop of York, went to Rome with Earl Tostig, and received the pallium from Pope Nicholas.[9]

Maiol, abbot of the Irish, died   There also Gisa of Wells and at Cologne. Foillán succeeded   Walter of Hereford were

---

[6] ASC DE record the Archbishop Cynesige's death on 2 Dec., and Ealdred's succession. Neither gives the place of death (though D gives the final-resting place) nor the day of Ealdred's appointment.

[7] ASC DE record Walter's succession to Hereford, but neither refers to Ealdred's administration of the bishopric nor identify Walter as a Lotharingian and as Queen Edith's chaplain.

[8] Mar.

[9] ASC D records Ealdred's visit to Rome for the pallium, which also refers to Tostig and his wife's visit to Rome, and the hardship suffered by bishop and earl. This episode appears in *Vita Wulfstani*, pp. 16–17.

successit.ᵃ   Nicolaus papa obiit.
Alexander papa¹ .cxlix.²

papa episcopi ordinati sunt.
Vsque ad Iohannem succes-
sorem istius Gyse *omnes* episcopi Wyllensis ecclesie *sedes*
suas Wellis habuerunt in ecclesia
sancti Andree apostoli.³
    Nicolaus   papa   obiit.
Alexander¹ successit.ᵇ²

[1062] (vi) 1084 ⁴Wlstanus, uir uenerandus, pontifex Wigornensi
ecclesie preficitur. Hic Deo amabilis regione Merciorum in prouincia Wareuuicensi parentibus religiosis oriundus, patre uidelicet
Eatstano, matre uero Wlfgeoua nomine, in nobili autem monasterio quod Burh nominatur litteris et ecclesiasticis officiis optime
extitit imbutus. Qui ambo scilicet parentes eius in tantum religioni
studebant ut longe ante finem uite castitatem professi, se ab
inuicem separantes, sub sancte conuersationis habitu uitam con-
summare gauderent. Quorum exemplo ipse adolescens incitatus,
matreᶜ id maxime persuadente, seculum reliquit atque in eodem
Wigornensi monasterio quo et ante pater Deo seruierat,
monachicum habitum et ordinem a uenerabili Brihteago eiusdem
ecclesie episcopo suscepit, a quo etiam in gradum tam diaconatus,
quam presbiteratus, ordinatus est. Statimque in ipso initio arduam
et omni religiositate plenam uitam arripiens, in uigiliis, ieiuniis,
orationibus, omnique uirtutum genere subito admirandus apparuit.
Hinc, ob morum disciplinam, primo magister et custos infantum
aliquandiu constituitur, deinde ob sollertiam ecclesiastici officii,
cantor simul et thesaurarius ecclesie ex precepto seniorum efficitur.
Nactus uero occasionem liberius Deo seruiendi ex commissa sibi
custodia ecclesie, totum se contemplatiue uite dedit, die noctuque
in ea aut orationi aut diuine lectioni insistens bidui triduique ieiunio assidue corpus macerans, sacris uigiliis in tantum deditus ut
non modo noctem sed etiam persepe diem ᵈcum nocteᵈ aliquando,
quod a nobis uix crederetur si non ab ipsius ore hoc audissemus,
.iiii. dies cum noctibus absque somno transigens, fere exsiccato

---

ᵃ *see above, p. 586 n. d*   ᵇ *see above, p. 586 n. b*   ᶜ *apparently an addition*
over erasure Cᴵ   ᵈ⁻ᵈ cum nocte] *spread out over erasure.* Cᴵ

---

¹ Alexander II 1061–73.   ² Mar.   ³ *GP* ii. 90 (p. 194).

him. Pope Nicholas died. Alexander[1] the 149th pope.[2]

consecrated bishops by the pope himself. Up to the time of John, successor of this Gisa, all bishops of Wells had their seat at Wells in the church of St Andrew the Apostle.[3]

Pope Nicholas died. Alexander[1] succeeded him.[2]

[1062] [4]Wulfstan, that venerable man, was preferred to the see of Worcester. He, beloved of God, was born in Warwickshire, in the province of Mercia, to devout parents, namely a father called Æthelstan and a mother called Wulfgifu. He was placed in the noble monastery called Peterborough, and given the best education in letters and ecclesiastical offices. His parents were both so zealous in religion that, long before the end of their lives, they took vows of chastity, and lived apart from one another, and rejoiced in perfecting their lives in the customs of the holy monastic life. Wulfstan, fired by their example and particularly by his mother's persuasion, abandoned the world in his youth, and, in the same monastery at Worcester where his father too before him had served God, he took the monastic habit and order from the venerable Brihtheah, bishop of that same church, who also ordained him deacon and priest. At once, from the very beginning, he eagerly embraced the demanding and strict life with complete dedication. He at once seemed astonishing in vigils, fastings, prayer and in every kind of virtue. Hence, on account of his disciplined conduct, he first served for some time as the master and guardian of the novices, then, because of his expertise in the ecclesiastical office, he was made precentor and sacristan of the church at the bidding of his superiors. But, having obtained the opportunity to serve God more freely through being entrusted with the custody of the church, he gave himself up wholly to a life of contemplation, applying himself day and night to that, or to prayer, or to sacred reading, mortifying his body assiduously with two- and three-day fasts, and so given to pious vigils lasting not only a night but even, very often, a day and a night, passing four days and nights without sleep—which would scarcely have been believed by us if we had not heard this from his own mouth—

---

[4] ASC does not refer to Wulfstan's appointment. That JW derived this from Coleman's Life was shown by Darlington in *Vita Wulfstani*, pp. xi–xvi.

cerebro periculum incurreret nisi sopore prelibato nature satisfacere maturaret. Denique et cum ui nature dormire compelleretur, non lecto aut lectisterniis menbra ad soporem fouebat, sed super aliquod scamnum ecclesie, libro in quo orabat siue legebat caput sustentans, paulisper se reclinabat. Post aliquod autem tempus, defuncto Ageluuino priore monasterii, ipse uir reuerendus prior et pater congregationis ab Aldredo episcopo ponitur, quod officium ualde laudabiliter adimplens, prioris conuersationis austeritatem minime reliquit, immo, ut ceteris exemplum bene uiuendi daret, multipliciter adauxit. Deinde post aliquot annorum curricula, electo ad archiepiscopatum Eboracensis ecclesie ipso Aldredo Wigornensis ecclesie episcopo, fit unanimis consensio tam cleri quam etiam totius plebis in eius electione, rege uidelicet annuente ut quem sibi uellent presulem eligerent. Contigit nanque eo tempore et legatos sedis apostolice eius electioni interesse, Armenfredum scilicet Sedunensem episcopum et alium, qui a domno papa Alexandro pro responsis ecclesiasticis ad regem Anglorum Eaduuardum missi, regio precepto Wigorne per totam fere quadragesimam degebant, expectantes responsum sue legationis usque ad curiam regalem proximi pasce. Hi uidentes dum ibi morabantur eius laudabilem conuersationem, in eius electione non tantum consentiebant, immo, tam clerum, quam plebem, maxime ad hoc instigabant, suaque auctoritate eius electionem firmabant. Illo uero obstinacissime renuente, seque | indignum acclamante, et cum sacramento etiam affirmante se multo libentius decollationi, quam tam alte ordinationi succumbere uelle. Cum sepe et frequenter a pluribus uiris religiosis et uenerabilibus personis super his circumuentus, ad consentiendum minime persuaderi posset[a] tandem a uiro Dei Wlsio incluso, qui tunc plus[b] .xl. annis solitariam uitam egisse noscebatur, acriter pro inobedientia et obstinacia correptus, diuino etiam oraculo territus, consentire cum maximo cordis dolore compulsus est atque die decollationis sancti Iohannis baptiste electione canonice confirmata, et episcopatu suscepto, dominico die, quo natiuitas sancte Marie ab ecclesia celebrabatur consecratus, uita et uirtutibus clarus Wigornensis ecclesie presul effulsit. Consecratus est igitur episcopus a uenerando Aldredo, Eboracensium archiepiscopo, eo quod Stigando Dorubernie archiepiscopo officium episcopale tunc a domno[c]

p. 342

[a] non *erased before* posset C, non posset H   [b] plusquam *interlin.* B[1]
[c] donno CB

almost endangering his parched brain if he did not hasten to satisfy nature with a taste of sleep. At last, when he was compelled
by the force of nature to sleep, he did not pamper his members
with a bed or coverings but lay down briefly on any of the church
benches, supporting his head on the book which he used for
prayer or reading. After some time, when Æthelwine, the prior of
the monastery had died, the reverend man was made prior and
father of the convent by Bishop Ealdred, which office he filled
most laudably, not giving up the austerity of his earlier way of life
but, that he might, by living well, give an example to others,
increasing it many times over. Then, after the lapse of some years,
when Ealdred, bishop of Worcester, was elected to the archbishopric of York, there was unanimous agreement among both clergy
and all the laity as well on electing Wulfstan, for the king had
given permission for them to elect the bishop they wanted. And so
it happened at that time that the legates of the apostolic see were
present at the election, namely Ermenfrid, bishop of Sion, and
another who had been sent by the lord Pope Alexander to obtain
some answers on ecclesiastical matters to Edward, king of the
English, and at the king's command they spent almost the whole
of Lent, until the royal court of the approaching Easter, at
Worcester, waiting for his reply on the subject of their mission.
While they stayed there they saw Wulfstan's praiseworthy mode of
life, and did not so much consent to his election as enthusiastically
urge both clergy and laity on to it, confirming his election by their
authority. But he most obstinately refused, proclaiming himself
unworthy and even affirming on oath that he would much rather
yield to decapitation than to so high an ordination. When he could
not be moved at all to agree on these matters, surrounded often
and repeatedly as he was by a host of devout men and venerable
persons, he was at last forced to consent, with great and most
heartfelt grief, by a recluse, Wulsi, a man of God, who was then
known to have led the solitary life for more than forty years and
who fiercely reproved him for disobedience and obstinacy, and by
the fear inspired by a divine oracle. On the day of the beheading
of St John the Baptist, the election was confirmed canonically, and
the bishopric received, and on the Sunday on which the nativity
of St Mary was celebrated by the church he was consecrated
bishop by the worshipful Ealdred, archbishop of York, because
Stigand, archbishop of Canterbury, was then forbidden to exercise

apostolico interdictum erat, quia, Rodberto*ᵃ* archiepiscopo uiuente, archiepiscopatum suscipere presumpsit, canonica tamen professione ᵇprefato Dorubernensi archiepiscopo Stigando non suo ordinatori Aldredo facta.*ᵇ*¹ Insuper et ipse Eboracensis arciepiscopus eius ordinator coram rege et regni optimatibus, ipso Stigando factitante, propter subsequentium calumnias, profiteri iussus est se nullum ius ecclesiastice seu secularis subiectionis super eum deinceps uelle clamare, nec propter quod ab eo consecratus est nec quia ante consecrationem eius monachus factus est.² Facta est autem hec illius ordinatio anno etatis sue plus quinquagesimo, regni uero regis Eaduuardi anno .xx., indictione .xv.

[1063] (vii) 1085   ³Strenuus dux Westsaxonum Haroldus, ⁴iussu regis Eaduuardi,⁴ post Natiuitatem Domini equitatu⁵ non multo secum assumpto de Glauuorna, ⁴ubi rex tunc morabatur,⁴ ad Rudelan ⁴multa cum festinatione⁴ profectus est, ut regem Walanorum Griffinum, ⁴propter frequentes depopulationes, quas in Anglorum finibus agebat, ac uerecundias, quas domino suo regi Eaduuardo sepe faciebat,⁴ occideret.⁶ At ille eius aduentu precognitio fugam cum suis iniit, nauem ascendit, et uix euasit.⁷ Haroldus uero ut eum fugisse comperit palatium incendere et naues eius cum armamentis comburere iussit, eodemque die rediit.⁸ Sed circa rogationes de Bryccstouue classica manu profectus, magna ex parte terram Walanorum circumnauigabat, cui frater suus comes Tostius, ⁴ut rex mandarat,⁴ cum equestri occurrit exercitu et uiribus simul iunctis, regionem illam depopulari coeperunt. Vnde Walani coacti, datis obsidibus, se dederunt et se tributum illi daturos promiserunt regemque suum Griffinum exlegantes abiecerunt.⁹

ᵃ written over erasure C   ᵇ⁻ᵇ Prefato . . . facta] compressed writing possibly over erasure Cˣ

¹ That Wulfstan made a profession of obedience to Stigand is contrary to Wulfstan's own statement in his profession to Lanfranc (*Vita Wulfstani*, p. 190).
² There is reason to doubt Ealdred's formal renunciation.
³ JW's account, though close to D, differs in the particulars shown.
⁴⁻⁴ Not in ASC.
⁵ The sense implies a land force though this is not explicitly stated in ASC.

his episcopal office by the apostolic lord as he had presumed to accept the archbishopric while Archbishop Robert was alive. However, the canonical profession was made to the aforementioned Stigand, archbishop of Canterbury, himself, not to Ealdred, his ordainer.[1] In addition, at the instigation of Stigand, the archbishop of York himself, his ordainer, was ordered, in the presence of the king and nobles of the realm, in order to forestall false claims made by his successors, to swear that he would not in the future claim any submission, ecclesiastical or secular, of him either because he was consecrated by him or because, before his consecration, he had been his monk.[2] His ordination was, however, performed when he was more than fifty years old, in the twentieth year of King Edward's reign, in the fifteenth indiction.

[1063] [3]After Christmas, [4]at the command of King Edward,[4] Harold, the vigorous earl of the West Saxons, took a small troop of horsemen[5] from Gloucester, [4]where the king was then staying,[4] and set out for Rhuddlan [4]in great haste[4] to kill Gruffydd [ap Llywelyn], king of the Welsh, [4]because of the frequent and destructive raids which he often made within the English borders and the disgrace which he often brought upon his lord King Edward.[4,6] But Gruffydd, having learned in advance of his approach, took flight with his men, embarked on a ship, and just managed to escape.[7] On learning of his flight, Harold ordered his palace to be burnt and his ships set on fire with their tackle, and turned back the same day.[8] But about Rogationtide he set out from Bristol with a naval force, and sailed around a great part of Wales. His brother Earl Tostig met him with mounted troops, [4]as the king commanded,[4] and they at once joined forces, and began to lay waste that region. By that the Welsh were coerced, and gave hostages. They surrendered, and promised that they would pay him tribute, and they deposed and outlawed their King Gruffydd.[9]

---

[6] The reasons and aim behind Harold's expedition to Rhuddlan are presumably inferred by JW.
[7] ASC D simply says that Gruffydd was put to flight.
[8] These actions follow Gruffydd's flight in ASC.
[9] ASC E records the Welsh giving hostages and surrendering, but like D refers to their slaying of Gruffydd (the much more elaborate D identifying those whom Edward appointed).

[1064] (viii) 1086 *Cyclus magnus paschalis* hic *incipit indictione .ii.ᵃ Multi diuites et pauperes cum Mogontino archiepiscopo, Traiectensi quoque necnon Babenbergensi atque Radisponensi episcopis, post transitum sancti Martini, plus .vii. milibus hominum Ierusalem perrexerunt. Vbi autem episcopi sedebant, ad dorsa eorum pallia pendebant, uasis quoque aureis seu argenteis cibus potusque inferebantur. Arabite uero fama pecunie congregati, multos eorum in parasceue occiderunt. Qui autem euadere potuerunt in quoddamᵇ uacuum castellum nomine Curuasalim fugerunt. Quod claudentes lapidibus et fustibus defendebant se contra iacula Arabitarum querentium pecuniam eorum auferre, uel uitam cum pecunia. Tunc unus optimus miles nullo periculo uictus quin sepulchrum Domini uideret, foras exiit. Arabite uero statim eum comprehendentes, resupinum in terram in modum crucis distenderunt et manus ac pedes eius clauis transfigentes in terram, ab imo uentris usque ad guttur dissecantes eum omnia uiscera eius scrutati sunt. Postremo cum eum menbratim diuisissent, dux ipsorum primum lapidem super eum misit, deinde omnes. Tunc sociis illius de castello hec omnia intuentibus dixerunt: 'Vos ita eritis nisi omnem pecuniam uestram nobis tradideritis.' Christianis itaque promittentibus, dux Arabitarum ingressus est castellum ad eos et sedecim alii cum gladiis. Qui dux cum uidisset adhuc cum tanta gloria episcopos sedere, cernens episcopum Babenbergensem, nomine Guntherum, ceteros magnitudine seu pulcritudine corporis precellentem, putauit illum dominum esse Christianorum, et sicut mos est gentilibus reos tenere, misit corrigiam in collum episcopi* p. 343 *et ait: | 'Tu et ista omnia tua mea erunt.' Episcopus uero per interpretem ait illi: 'Quid mihi facies?' Ille dixit: 'Istum pulchrum sanguinem gutturis tui sugam et suspendam te ante castellum sicut canem.' Tunc episcopus, apprehenso capite eius, uno colapho elisit ducem in terram, alii autem omnes ligati sunt. Quo comperto, hi qui foris erant super castellum irruerunt, sed illi qui ligati erant, suspensi in muro contra eos, prohibuerunt illos sue salutis causa. Ipsi uero latrones propter pecuniam quam prius Christianis tulerunt rixati, inuicem se magna ex parte peremerunt. Interea dux de Ramala, rogatus a Christianis qui euadere poterant, secundo die pasce cum ualida manu aduenit, Arabitasque fugauit. Deinde accipiens .d. aureos a Christianis, cum duce Arabitarum inimico regis Sarracenorum domini sui, perduxit eos Ierusalem et inde ad nauim. Ita autem omnis multitudo Christianorum*

ᵃ *1065 starts here* Mar.	ᵇ *over ras.* C

[1064] The great paschal cycle begins here in the second indiction. A host of more than 7,000 men, rich and poor, with the archbishop of Mainz and the bishops of Utrecht, Bamberg, and Ratisbon as well, set out for Jerusalem after Martinmas. However, when the bishops made a halt, they draped their palls over their backs, and were served food and drink in vessels of gold and silver. But the Arabs who gathered at the report of their wealth killed many of them on Good Friday. However those who managed to escape fled into a certain empty fort called Kafr Salīm, which they barricaded and defended themselves with stones and staves against the darts of the Arabs who sought to take their money, and with their money, their lives. Then one excellent soldier, allowing no danger to stand in the way of his seeing the Lord's sepulchre, went out. But the Arabs at once seized him and, laying him flat on the ground, stretched him out in the form of a cross, and fastening his hands and feet with nails to the earth, and cutting him open from the base of the stomach to the throat, they exposed all his entrails. Finally when they had dismembered him, their leader cast the first stone upon him, then they all did. Then they said to his companions who watched all this from the fort: 'This will be your lot unless you hand over to us all your money.' As the Christians promised to do so, the Arab leader and sixteen others with swords entered the fort. When the leader saw the bishops sitting in such great state, perceiving that the bishop of Bamberg, Gunther by name, who excelled the others in size and in physical beauty, he thought he must be the lord of the Christians and, as is the pagan custom for holding criminals, he placed a thong around the bishop's neck and said; 'You and all your property shall be mine.' But the bishop through an interpreter said to him: 'What will you do to me?' He said: 'I shall suck this beautiful blood from your throat and hang you in front of the fort like a dog.' Then the bishop seized him by his head, and with one blow smashed the leader on to the ground; and all the others were bound. When this was made known, those who were outside attacked the fort, but those who had been bound were hung on the walls facing them, and forbade them to do so from concern for their own safety. But those robbers quarrelled about the money which they had taken, from the Christians; most of them died at one another's hands. Meanwhile, the prince of Ramleh, at the request of those Christians who had managed to

consumpta est ut uix de septem uel amplius milibus duo milia sint reuersa.[1]

Rex Walanorum Griffinus non. Aug. a suis interficitur, et caput eius caputque nauis ipsius cum ornatura comiti Haroldo mittitur, que mox ille regi detulit Eaduuardo. Quibus gestis, suis fratribus Blethgento et Rithuualano rex terram Walanorum dedit, cui et Haroldo comiti fidelitatem illi iurauerunt, et ad imperium illorum mari terraque se fore paratos, ac omnia que prius de terra illa regibus anterioribus fuerant pensa, obedienter se pensuros spoponderunt.[2]

[1065] (ix) 1087 Reuerendus[a] uir Ageluuinus, Dunholmensis episcopus sancti Osuuini regis quondam Berniciorum[3] ossa in monasterio quod iuxta ostium Tine fluminis situm est de tumulo leuauit, transactis a sepultura eius .cccc. et .xv. annis, et in scrinio cum magno honore locauit.[4] [5]Strenuus dux Westsaxonum Haroldus in terram Walanorum, in loco qui Portascith nominatur, mense Iulio magnum edificari iussit edificium et multa que pertinent ad esum et potum illuc[b] congregari mandauit, ut dominus suus rex Eaduuardus illic aliquandiu uenationis causa degere posset. Sed Cradoc, filius [6]regis Suthuuallanorum[6] Griffini, [6]quem ante paucos annos Griffinus rex Northuualanorum occiderat,[6] eiusque regnum inuaserat, cum omnibus quos habere poterat die festiuitatis sancti Bartholomei apostoli illuc uenit, et operarios fere cunctos cum illis qui eis preerant peremit, et omnia bona que ibi congregata fuerant abstulit. [7]Dein post festiuitatem sancti Michaelis archangeli .v. non. Octobris. feria .ii., Northymbrenses ministri Gamelbearn, Dunstanus, filius Athelnethes, Glonieorn, filius Heardulfi, cum .cc. militibus Eboracum uenerunt, et pro

---

[a] *possibly over erasure C; see App. B for addition before* Reverendus B   [b] *some traces of erasure C*

---

[1] Mar.

[2] JW is closer to ASC D (1063) than to the briefer E (1063).

[3] Oswine was king of Deira.

[4] JW's account of the alleged discovery and translation of Oswine's bones seems supported by Roger of Wendover, i. 504–7, and by the 12th-c. *Vita Oswini* (*Miscellanea Biographica*, Surtees Society 2 (1838)), pp. 11–13. *HR* ii. 260–1 (under 1121), and *HDE* iv. 4 (i. 124), give the impression that they had not been translated by the late 11th c.

[5] Although ASC CD largely agree in their account of the Welsh episode as set out in the following two sentences, JW does not mention D's enigmatic professed ignorance of the first prompting of Gruffydd's first attack on Portskewet.

escape, came with a strong force on the second day of Easter, and put the Arabs to flight. Then, on receipt of 500 gold coins from the Christians, he took them to Jerusalem, with an Arab chief who was at odds with the Saracen emir, his lord, and from there to their ships. The large number of Christians was so diminished that of the 7,000 or more, barely 2,000 returned.[1]

Gruffydd, king of the Welsh, was killed by his own men on 5 August, and his head and the prow of his ship with its ornaments were sent to Earl Harold, who at once sent them to King Edward. When these things had taken place, the king gave Wales to Gruffydd's brothers, Bleddyn and Rhiwallon, and they swore fealty to him and to Earl Harold, and promised that they would obey their command by land and sea, and that everything which had previously been paid to former kings by that country they would obediently pay.[2]

[1065] The revered man, Æthelwine, bishop of Durham, raised the bones of St Oswine, once king of the Bernicians,[3] from the tomb in the monastery situated at the mouth of the River Tyne 415 years after their burial, and placed them with great honour in a shrine.[4] [5]Harold, the vigorous earl of the West Saxons, ordered a great building to be erected in Wales, in a place called Portskewet, in July, and he commanded that large supplies of food and drink should be gathered there so that his lord, King Edward, could stay there sometimes for the chase. But Caradog, son of Gruffydd, [6]king of the South Welsh (Gruffydd, king of the North Welsh, had killed him a few years earlier[6] and invaded his kingdom), went there on the feast-day of St Bartholomew the Apostle with all the men he could raise, and slew virtually all the workmen with their overseers, and took away all the goods which had been stockpiled there. [7]Then, after the feast of St Michael the Archangel, on Monday, 3 October, the Northumbrian thegns, Gamelbearn, Dunstan, son of Æthelnoth, and Glonieorn, son of Heardwulf,

---

[6-6] Not in ASC.

[7] JW's account of the uprising in the north is much fuller than ASC CD (1065) E (1064), which say that after Michaelmas (C), soon after 24 Aug. (D), the thegns of Yorkshire (C), the thegns in Yorkshire and Northumberland (D), the men of Northumbria (E) went to York, killed Tostig's housecarls (C), bodyguard and all they could get at, English and Danish (DE); outlawed Tostig (DE); seized his weapons (DE) and his treasure (CDE). C gives some general reasons for the uprising, but is not very specific.

execranda nece nobilium Northymbrensium ministrorum
Gospatrici, quem regina Edgitha, germani sui Tostii causa, in
curia regis .iiii. nocte dominice Natiuitatis per insidias occidi iussit, et Gamelis, filii Orm, ac Vlfi, filii Dolfini, quos anno precedenti Eboraci in camera sua *sub pacis federe per insidias comes
Tostius* occidere precepit, necnon* pro immensitate tributi quod
de tota Northymbria iniuste acceperat, eodem die primitus illius
Danicos huscarlas Amundum et Reauensuartum de fuga retractos
extra ciuitatis muros ac die sequenti plusquam .cc. uiros ex curial-
ibus illius in boreali parte Humbre fluminis peremerunt. Erarium
quoque ipsius fregerunt ac omnibus que illius fuerant ablatis,
recesserunt. ¹Omnis dehinc fere comitatus illius in unum congregati, Haroldo Westsaxonum duci et aliis quos rex Tostii rogatu
pro pace redintegranda ad eos miserat in Northamtonia occurre-
runt.² Vbi prius et post apud Oxnefordam,ᶜ die festiuitatis apostolorum Simonis et Iude,³ dum Haroldus et alii quamplures
comitem Tostium cum eis pacificare uellent,⁴ ⁵omnes unanimi
consensu contradixerunt, ac eum cum omnibus qui legem iniquam
statuere illum incitauerunt, exlegauerunt.⁵ Et post festiuitatem
Omnium Sanctorum,⁶ cum adiutorio comitis Eduuini, de Anglia
Tostium expulerunt,⁷ qui mox cum uxore sua Balduuinum
Flandrensium comitem adiit, et apud sanctum Audomarum
hiemem exegit.⁸ Post hec rex Eaduuardus paulatim egrotare cepit.
In Natiuitate uero Domini curiam suam ut potuit Lundonie
tenuit,⁹ et ecclesiam quam ipse a fundamentis construxerat die
sanctorum Innocentium in honore sancti Petri apostolorum principis cum magna gloria dedicari fecit.ᵈ¹⁰

[1066] (x) 1088 ᵉAnglorum decus, pacificus rex Eaduuardus,
Athelredi regis filius, postquam .xxiii. annis, mensibus .vi., et

ᵃ⁻ᵃ sub . . . Tostius] *compressed writing, some of which is possibly over erasure* Cᵗ
ᵇ non *interlin. above* nec Cᵗ   ᶜ *over erasure* C   ᵈ *see Appendix A for addition* L
ᵉ *JW omits Mar. entry, see App. B for addition* B

¹ ASC CDE record the events leading to Tostig's departure to Flanders but there
are differences, and JW's account is closer to C than to DE.
² The steps leading to the meeting at Northampton (which DE may imply went on
to the eve of St Simon and St Jude, 27 Oct.) are not explained in the same way in
ASC, which in DE is much fuller. JW omits all reference to Morkar as the elected earl
of Mercia.
³ The meeting at Oxford and its date are mentioned in ASC C.

came with 200 soldiers to York, and, on account of the disgraceful death of the noble Northumbrian thegns Gospatric (whom Queen Edith, on account of her brother Tostig, had ordered to be killed in the king's court on the fourth night of Christmas by treachery), Gamel, son of Orm, and Ulf, son of Dolfin (whose murders Earl Tostig had treacherously ordered the preceding year at York in his own chamber, under cover of a peace-treaty), and also of the huge tribute which Tostig had unjustly levied on the whole of Northumbria, they, on that same day, slew first his Danish house-carls, Amund and Reavenswart, hauled back from flight, beyond the city walls, and on the following day more than 200 men from his court, on the north side of the River Humber. They also broke open his treasury, and, having taken away all his goods, they withdrew. [1]After that, almost all the men of his earldom united to meet Harold, earl of the West Saxons, and others whom the king at Tostig's request had sent to them to restore peace, at Northampton.[2] There first, and later at Oxford, on the day of the feast of the apostles Simon and Jude,[3] while Harold and very many others wished to make peace between Earl Tostig and them,[4] [5]all unanimously spoke against it and they outlawed him and all who had encouraged him to establish his iniquitous rule.[5] And after the feast of All Saints,[6] with the aid of Earl Edwin, they drove Tostig out of England;[7] he and his wife then approached Count Baldwin of Flanders, and spent the winter at Saint-Omer.[8] After this, King Edward began to weaken by degrees but at Christmas he held his court, as best he could, at London,[9] and had the church which he himself raised from the foundations consecrated in honour of St Peter, the Prince of the Apostles, with great splendour on the day of the Holy Innocents.[10]

[1066] The glory of the English, the peacable King Edward, son of King Æthelred, after governing the Anglo-Saxons for twenty-three

[4] Harold's wish for reconciliation is mentioned in ASC C.
[5–5] Closer to ASC C than to DE, particularly in the outlawry of Tostig by the Northerners.
[6] This date (1 Nov.) is not in ASC.
[7] The reference to Edwin's help here is peculiar to JW.
[8] ASC C alone mentions Saint-Omer.
[9] ASC does not refer to Edward's illness nor to his holding a court at London, although it records his going to Westminster at Christmas.
[10] ASC CD (1065) E (1066) record the consecration of Westminster (28 Dec.) before giving details of Edward's death and burial and CD conclude with a verse panegyric.

p. 344 .xxvii. diebus potestate regia prefuit Anglisaxonibus, | indictione
.iiii., Epiphanie Domini uigilia, feria .v., mortem obiit Lundonie,
et in crastino sepultus regio more, ab omnibus qui tunc affuere
non sine lacrimis plangebatur amarissime.[1] Quo tumulato, subregulus Haroldus, Goduuini ducis filius, quem rex ante suam deces-
sionem regni successorem elegerat, a totius Anglie primatibus ad
regale culmen electus die eodem ab Aldredo Eboracensi archiepiscopo in regem est honorifice consecratus.[2] Qui mox ut regni
gubernacula susceperat, leges iniquas destruere, equas cepit con-
dere, ecclesiarum ac monasteriorum patronus fieri, episcopos,
abbates, monachos, clericos colere simul ac uenerari, pium,
humilem, affabilemque se bonis omnibus exhibere, malefactores
exosos habere, nam ducibus, satrapis, uicecomitibus et suis in
commune precepit ministris fures, raptores, regni disturbatores
comprehendere, et pro patrie defensione ipsemet terra marique
desudare.[3] Eodem anno .viii. kalend. Maii, stella cometis non
solum in Anglia, sed etiam, ut fertur, per totum mundum uisa,
per .vii. dies splendore nimio fulgebat.[4] [5]Non multo post, comes
Tostius [6]de Flandria[6] rediens, ad Vectam Insulam applicuit, et
postquam insulanos sibi tributum et stipendium soluere coegerat,
discessit et circa ripas maris donec ad Sandicum portum ueniret,
predas exercuit. Quo cognito, rex Haroldus, qui tunc Lundonie
morabatur, classem non modicam et equestrem exercitum congregari precepit, ipse uero Sandicum portum adire parabat.[7] Quod
dum Tostio nuntiatum fuisset, de butsecarlis quosdam uolentes
quosdam nolentes secum assumens recessit, et cursum ad
Lindesegiam direxit,[8] in qua uillas quamplures incendit, multosque
homines neci tradidit. His cognitis, dux Merciorum Eduuinus et
Northymbrorum comes Morkarus cum exercitu aduolant, illumque
de regione ipsa extrudunt. Ille autem inde discendens, regem
Scottorum Malcolmum adiit et cum eo per totam estatem mansit.

---

[1] The days of Edward's death and burial (5 and 6 Jan.) are in ASC CD (1065) E
(1066), though JW does not specifically mention Westminster as the burial place.
[2] That Harold was Edward's choice seems implied by the verses in ASC CD (1065)
and by E (1066), though JW seems the only chronicle source for the statement that
Ealdred consecrated him king.
[3] This eulogy seems JW's, and contrasts with the staccato sentence with which the
annal for 1065 ASC CD ends.
[4] ASC CD.
[5] In general, JW's account of 1066 is closer to ASC C than to DE, as is exemplified
by his account of Tostig's movements (from Flanders to Scotland via the Isle of Wight,

years, six months, and twenty-seven days, in the fourth indiction, on Thursday, the eve of Epiphany, met his death at London, and was royally buried the next day, most bitterly lamented, not without tears by all who were present.[1] When he was entombed, the underking, Harold, son of Earl Godwine, whom the king had chosen before his demise as successor to the kingdom, was elected by the primates of all England to the dignity of kingship, and was consecrated king with due ceremony by Ealdred, archbishop of York, on the same day.[2] He soon, when he had undertaken the government of the realm, destroyed iniquitous laws, and set about establishing just ones; becoming patron of churches and monasteries, cultivating and venerating at the same time bishops, abbots, monks, and clerks; showing himself pious, humble and affable to all good men; detesting malefactors, for he ordered the earls, ealdormen, sheriffs, and his own officers generally to seize thieves, robbers, and disturbers of the realm, and to exert themselves by land and sea for the defence of their country.[3] In that same year, on 24 April, a comet was seen, not only in England but also, so they say, throughout the whole world, blazing for seven days in great splendour.[4] [5]Not much later, Earl Tostig, returning [6]from Flanders;[6] landed on the Isle of Wight, and having forced the islanders to pay tribute and maintenance, departed and raided the coast as far as the port of Sandwich. When King Harold, who was then staying at London, learnt this, he ordered a large fleet and a force of cavalry to be assembled, and he himself prepared to go to the port of Sandwich.[7] When this was reported to Tostig, he retreated, taking some of the seamen with him, whether they wished to go or not, and steered his course towards Lindsey,[8] where he burnt many townships, and did to death many men. When he learnt this, Edwin, earl of the Mercians, and Morkar, earl of the Northumbrians, hurried up with an army, and expelled him from that region. Retreating thence, he went to Malcolm,

Sandwich, and Lindsey), and of the reactions of King Harold and of the earls Edwin and Morkar to them, E not mentioning these movements of Tostig and D being much briefer.

[6-6] ASC CD 'from overseas'; E no equivalent.

[7] At this point ASC C says that the fleet and army (larger than any previously assembled) had been assembled to meet the threat from Normandy.

[8] ASC C speaks of his going north to an unnamed place and ravaging in Lindsey.

[1]Interea rex Haroldus ad Sandicum portum uenit, ibique classem suam expectauit. Que cum fuisset congregata Vectam insulam adiit, et quia Nortmannorum comes Willelmus, Eaduuardi regis consobrinus, in Angliam cum exercitu uenire parabat, tota estate et autumno aduentum illius obseruabat, ad hec etiam pedestrem exercitum locis opportunis circa ripas maris locabat. Adueniente itaque Natiuitate sancte Marie, uictu deficiente, et classicus et pedestris exercitus domum rediit. [2]Quibus gestis, cum classica manu perualida, scilicet plus .d.[a] magnis nauibus,[3] Haroldus Haruagra rex Norreganorum, frater sancti regis Olaui,[4] in ostio Tine fluminis improuise applicuit. Ad quem comes Tostius, ut prius condixerant, sua cum classe uenit, et citato cursu ostium Humbre fluminis intrauerunt, et sic aduersus cursum Vse fluminis nauigantes, in loco qui Richale dicitur[5] applicuerunt. Quod ubi regi Haroldo innotuit, uersus Northymbriam expeditionem propere mouit. Sed priusquam rex illuc ueniret, duo germani comites uidelicet Eduuinus et Morkarus cum ingenti exercitu in uigilia sancti Mathei apostoli, feria .iiii., in boreali ripa Vse fluminis[6] iuxta Eboracum cum Norreganis prelium commisere et in primo belli impetu uiriliter pugnantes, multos prostrauere. At postquam diu certatum est, Angli Norreganorum impetum non sufferentes, haud sine paruo detrimento suorum terga dedere, multoque plures ex illis in fluuio demersi fuere quam in acie cecidere. Norregani uero loco dominantur funeris et, obsidibus .cl. de Eboraca sumptis, ad naues repedarunt, relictis in ea de suis .cl. obsidibus.[7] [8]Verum quinto post hunc die, id est .vii. kalend. Octobris, feria secunda,[9] rex Anglorum Haroldus, multis milibus pugnatorum armis bellicis instructorum, Eboracum ueniens, et Norreganis in loco, qui Stanfordbrycge dicitur, occurrens, in ore gladii regem

---

[a] quingentis *interlin.* C[1]

---

[1] Again the account of Harold's preparations and the dismissal of the fleet are closest to ASC C, which describes William as Edward's kinsman.

[2] The account of Harold Hardrada is again closer to ASC C than to DE.

[3] While ASC DE speak of 300 ships, C is defective at this point.

[4] Although JW confuses Hardrada with Fairhair (like Marianus and ASC D), his identification of the Norwegian king as brother of St Olaf is correct.

[5] The approach through the Humber and the landing-place are not mentioned in ASC.

[6] The site of the battle is not named in ASC, and JW's 'in boreali ripa Vse fluminis' is more precise than C's 'andlang Usan'.

king of the Scots, and remained the whole summer with him. [1]Meanwhile, King Harold came to the port of Sandwich and there he awaited his fleet. When it had been drawn up, he went to the Isle of Wight and, because William, duke of the Normans, cousin of King Edward, was preparing to come to England with an army, he watched all summer and autumn for his arrival, against which he also placed his infantry at strategic places around the coast. And so, with the approach of the nativity of St Mary, as food was running out, both the fleet and the infantry returned home. [2]When these things had been done, Harold Fairhair, king of the Norwegians, brother of St Olaf the king,[4] landed unexpectedly at the mouth of the River Tyne with an extremely strong fleet; that is more than 500 great ships.[3] Earl Tostig joined him with his fleet as he had previously promised, and on a swift course they entered the mouth of the River Humber; sailing thus up the River Ouse, they landed at a place called Ricall.[5] When King Harold learnt of this, he speedily undertook an expedition to Northumbria. But before the king arrived there, the two brother earls, Edwin and Morkar, with a great army joined battle with the Norwegians on the north bank of the River Ouse,[6] near York, on Wednesday, the eve of St Matthew the Apostle's day, and fighting manfully in the first thrust of the battle, they laid many low. But after the struggle had continued for a long time, the English were unable to withstand the Norwegian attack. Not without some small loss they turned to flee, and many more of them were drowned in the river than had fallen in battle. But the Norwegians gained the mastery in that place of death and, having taken 150 hostages from York, they returned to their own ships, having left in York 150 hostages of their own.[7] [8]But on the fifth day after this, that is on Monday,[9] 25 September, Harold, king of the English, with many thousands of well-armed fighting men, marched to York and met the Norwegians at a place called Stamford Bridge. He put to the sword King Harold and Earl Tostig and the greater part of their

[7] Again the account of Fulford is closest to ASC C, though JW alone gives the number of hostages surrendered to the victors, and records leaving 150 of their men as hostages when they went to their ships.

[8] JW's account of Harold Godwineson's march to the north and of the victory at Stamford Bridge has points of resemblance with D rather than C. The advantage of surprise of Harold's unexpected arrival is not mentioned in JW.

[9] The day of the battle is implied in ASC CD, and D, like JW, speaks of the five days' interval between Fulford and Stamford Bridge.

Haroldum comitemque Tostium cum maiori parte sui exercitus occidit, ac plenam uictoriam, licet acerrime repugnatum fuisset, habuit. Filium autem eius Olauum et comitem de Orcada insula, Paulum nomine,[1] [2]qui ad naues custodiendas cum exercitus parte fuerant dimissi, acceptis prius ab eis obsidibus[2] et sacramentis, cum .xx. nauibus[3] et reliquiis exercitus in patriam redire libere permisit. Interea dum hec agerentur [2]et rex omnes suos inimicos autumaret detritos fuisse,[2] nuntiatum est ei Willelmum comitem gentis Normannice [4]cum innumera multitudine equitum, fundibalariorum, sagittariorum, peditumque aduenisse, utpote qui de tota Gallia sibi fortes auxiliarios conduxerat,[4] et in loco qui Pefnesea[5] dicitur suam classem, appulisse. | Vnde rex statim uersus Lundoniam suum mouit exercitum magna cum festinatione, et licet de tota Anglia fortiores quosque preliis in duobus bene sciret iam cecidisse, mediamque partem sui exercitus nondum conuenisse,[6] quam citius tamen potuit in Suthsaxonia suis hostibus occurrere non formidauit, et nouem miliariis ab Heastinga,[7] ubi sibi castellum firmauerant priusquam tertia pars sui exercitus ordinaretur [a].xi. kalend. Nouembris,[a] sabbato,[8] cum eis prelium commisit. Sed [2]quia arto in loco constituti fuerant Angli, de acie se multi subtraxere[2] et cum eo perpauci constantes corde remansere. [2]Ab hora tamen diei tertia usque noctis crepusculum[2] suis aduersariis restitit fortissime et se ipsum pugnando tam fortiter defendit et tam strenue ut uix ab hostili interimi posset agmine. At postquam ex his et illis quamplurimi corruere, heu, ipsemet cecidit crepusculi tempore. Comites etiam Gyrth et Leofuuinus fratres illius cecidere, et fere nobiliores totius Anglie, Willelmus uero comes cum suis Heastingam rediit.[9] Regnauit autem Haroldus mensibus [b]nouem et diebus totidem.[b] Cuius morte audita, comites Eduuinus et Morkarus, [2]qui se cum suis certamini substraxere,[2] Lundoniam uenere et [2]sororem suam Aldgitham reginam sumptam ad ciuitatem Legionum misere.[2] Aldredus autem

[a-a] .xi. kalend. Nouembris] .ii. idus Octobris *interlin. C (scratchy hand of ? mid-12th c.)*, .ii. idus Octobris *BP*   [b-b] nouem . . . totidem] decem et illa die qua occubuit *substituted at later date C*, et ille die qua occubuit *B*, nouem et illa die qua occubuit *P*

---

[1] These are mentioned in ASC D, though the earl of Orkney is not named.
[2-2] Not in ASC.   [3] ASC D 24 ships.
[4-4] William's forces are not identified in this way in ASC.
[5] ASC D gives Pevensey on 28 Sept., E Hastings on 29 Sept.

army, and after a most bitter battle gained total victory. However, he permitted Harold's son Olaf, and the earl of Orkney, Paul by name,[1] [2]who had been sent off to guard the ships with part of the army, after first taking hostages and oaths from them,[2] to return freely to their own land with twenty ships[3] and the remainder of the army. While these things were happening, and [2]the king supposed all his enemies had been destroyed,[2] he was informed that William, duke of the Normans, had landed his fleet at a place called Pevensey,[5] [4]with an innumerable multitude of knights, slingers, archers and foot-soldiers, for he had brought strong auxiliaries from the whole of Gaul with him.[4] Whereupon the king at once moved his army to London in great haste, and although he knew that all the more powerful men from the whole of England had already fallen in two battles, and that half of his army had not yet assembled,[6] yet he did not fear to go to meet his enemies in Sussex with all possible speed, and nine miles from Hastings,[7] where they had earlier built a fortress for themselves, before a third of his army had been drawn up, on Saturday,[8] 22 October, he joined battle with the Normans. [2]But because the English were drawn up in a narrow place many slipped away from the battle-line,[2] and very few of a constant heart remained with him. [2]However, from the third hour of daylight until dusk[2] he resisted his enemies most stoutly, and defended himself by fighting so strongly and so vigorously that he could scarcely be slain by the enemy line. But afterwards, when very many had fallen on both sides, he himself fell, alas, at dusk. Earls Gyrth and Leofwine, his brothers, also fell, and the more noble of almost all England, but Duke William returned to Hastings with his own men.[9] Harold reigned nine months and as many days. When they heard of his death, Earls Edwin and Morkar, [2]who had slipped away from the battle with their men,[2] came to London and [2]took their sister Queen Edith and sent her to the city of Chester.[2] However, Ealdred,

---

[6] That Harold was taken by surprise is recorded by ASC D, but not his move to London and the quickly assembled army.

[7] The distance of the battle site from Hastings is not in ASC.

[8] ASC D has 14 Oct. (the day interlineated in the JW MS C), which fell on a Saturday in 1066.

[9] ASC DE both mention the men slain, but only D records William's return to Hastings.

Eboracensis archiepiscopus et idem comites cum ciuibus Lundoniensibus et butsecarlis[1] clitonem Eadgarum, Eadmundi regis Ferrei Lateris nepotem, in regem leuare uoluere et cum eo se pugnam inituros promisere. Sed dum ad pugnam descendere multi se parauere, comites suum auxilium ab eis retraxere, et cum suo exercitu domum rediere.[2] Interea comes Willelmus Suthsaxoniam, Cantiam, Suthamtunensem prouinciam, Suthregiam, Middelsaxoniam, Heortfordensem prouinciam deuastabat et uillas cremare hominesque interficere non cessabat donec ad uillam que Beorhchamstede[a] nominatur ueniret.[3] Vbi Aldredus[b] archiepiscopus, Wlstanus Wigornensis episcopus, Walterus Herefordensis episcopus, clito Eadgarus,[b] comites Eduuinus et Morkarus et de Lundonia quique nobiliores cum multis aliis ad eum uenerunt et datis obsidibus, illi deditionem fecerunt, fidelitatemque iurauerunt, cum quibus et ipse foedus pepigit, et nichilominus exercitui suo uillas cremare et rapinas agere permisit.[4] Appropinquante igitur dominice Natiuitatis festiuitate, cum omni exercitu Lundoniam, ut ibi in regem sullimaretur, adiit, et, [5]quia Stigandus primas totius Anglie ab apostolico papa calumniatus est pallium non suscepisse canonice,[5] ipsa Natiuitatis die, que illo anno feria .ii. euenit, ab Aldredo Eboracensium archiepiscopo in Westmonasterio consecratus est honorifice, prius, ut idem archipresul ab eo exigebat, ante altare sancti Petri apostoli coram clero et populo iureiurando promittens se uelle sanctas Dei ecclesias ac rectores illarum defendere necnon et cunctum populum sibi subiectum iuste et regali prouidentia regere, rectam legem statuere et tenere, rapinas iniustaque iudicia penitus interdicere.[c6]

---

[a] stede *interlin.* C (*?mid-12th c.*), Beorcham *HL*, Beorchanstede *B*, Beorchamstede *P*
[b] *erasure* C   [c] *see App. B for addition B*

---

[1] Not mentioned in ASC D.
[2] The proposed choice of Edgar the atheling is in ASC DE, but JW's reference to the earls' withdrawal of their support is not explicitly spelt out there.

archbishop of York, and those earls, with the citizens of London and the seamen,[1] wished to raise to the throne the atheling Edgar, grandson of King Edmund Ironside, and promised to enter battle with Duke William. But while they prepared to go down into battle, the earls withdrew their support from them, and returned home with their army.[2] Meanwhile, Duke William laid waste Sussex, Kent, Hampshire, Middlesex, and Hertfordshire, and did not cease from burning townships and slaying men until he came to the township called Berkhamsted.[3] There Archbishop Ealdred, Wulfstan, bishop of Worcester, Walter, bishop of Hereford, the atheling Edgar, Earls Edwin and Morkar, and the more noble citizens of London, with many others, came to meet him, and having given hostages, made him their submission, and swore fealty to him. He himself made a treaty with them, but none the less he permitted his army to burn and plunder townships.[4] Therefore, as the Christmas feast was approaching, he came to London with his whole army that he might be raised to the throne there. [5]Because Stigand, the primate of all England, was accused by the apostolic pope of not having received the pallium canonically,[5] William was consecrated with due ceremony by Ealdred, archbishop of York, on Christmas Day itself, which in that year fell on a Monday, at Westminster, first swearing, as the same archbishop required of him, on oath before the altar of St Peter the Apostle, in the presence of clergy and people, that he would defend the holy churches of God and their rulers too, and would govern the whole people subject to him justly, and by royal provision would establish and maintain right law, and totally forbid rapine and unjust judgements.[6]

[3] Although ASC D mentions the ravaging and its terminal point at Berkhamsted, JW is specific about the counties destroyed.

[4] ASC D, though JW adds the names of the bishops of Worcester and Hereford among those who submitted.

[5-5] Not in ASC.

[6] The account of William's coronation and of the promises exacted is closest to ASC D.

APPENDIX A

ABINGDON ADDITIONS IN LONDON, LAMBETH PALACE MS 42 (WITNESS L) AND CAMBRIDGE, CORPUS COLLEGE MS 92 (WITNESS P)

L is the base text, and P's variants are shown in the critical apparatus. Identified sources are printed in italics. In the case of one of these sources, the Abingdon Chronicle, the printed edition is imperfect, and recourse has also been made to one of the two manuscripts of the Chronicle, London, BL Cotton MS Claudius C. IX, which is given the siglum A.

Anglo-Saxon Æ/æ are printed as they appear in the manuscript and ę has been printed as e.

⟨ ⟩ indicates an editorial addition to the base MS.

688 n. g (add. L, add. mg. near 688 P[5])

et ⟨Ine⟩ monasterium quod dicitur Abbendona, quod prius uir nobilis Cissa et rex Ceadwala inceperunt, perfecit.

948 n. f (divisions into paragraphs as in L; text is also in P)

Incliti regis Edredi tempore, uir Domini Æthelwoldus, qui in monasterio Gleastoniensi in monachico habitu sub abbate Dunstano Domino Iesu Christo deuote seruiebat, *cupiens ampliori scripturarum scientia doceri, decreuit ultra marinas adire partes, sed regina Eadgifa, mater regis memorati, preuenit eius conamina, dans consilium regi ne talem uirum sineret egredi de regno suo; insuper asserens tantam in eo fuisse Dei sapientiam, que et sibi et aliis sufficere posset, quamuis ad aliene patrie fines ob hanc causam minime tenderet. Quibus auditis, delectatus rex magnam circa Dei famulum cepit habere dilectionem, placuitque ei suadente matre sua, dare sancto uiro quendam locum uocabulo Abbandoniam in quo modicum antiquitus monasteriolum habebatur, sed erat tunc neglectum ac destitutum, uilibus edificiis consistens, et .xl. tantum mansas possidens, reliquam uero prefati loci terram, que centum cassatorum lustris hinc inde giratur, regali dominio subiectam rex ipse posside-bat.*[1] *Quis autem antiquorum*[a] *illius primum institutor fuerit, monimento*

---

[a] antiquorum autem P

---

[1] Wulfstan, *Vita S. Æthelwoldi*, cc. 10–11 (Lapidge–Winterbottom, *Life*, pp. 18–20).

ueterum accepimus, quod Cissa rex Heano cuidam religiose uite uiro ac abbati simulque sorori eiusdem Cille nomine, locum ad omnipotentis ⟨Dei⟩ cultum construendi cenobii dedit, quod Abbandun antiquitus appellatur. *Collatis ad hoc regio munere plurimis beneficiis et possessionibus ob uite necessarium inibi fore degentium, uerum non multo post, antequam insisteretur designato operi, rex ipse* obiit. Rex autem *Ine primo donationes* supradictas *irritas* fieri *decreuit, deinde facti penitens, de suis etiam easdem longe uberius auxit,*[1] adeo ut .ccl. cassatorum descriptionem sub anno incarnationis dominice .dcxcix. regali edicto sanciret, predicto abbate Heano regimen loci tenente. Horum posteriori tempore testamentum principum Æthelbaldus rex sue quoque auctoritatis collatione ratum esse constituit sub Danielis antistitis et Cumani eiusdem loci abbatis attestatione.

Succedentibus nonnullis postea annis, Kenulfo rege[2] ius regium optinente, Rethunus quidam officio episcopali functus abbatis locum in Abbandonia est adeptus. Qua tempestate idem cenobium tam grauibus implicabatur regis officialiumque eius exactionibus, ut maximum suarum rerum illic commanentibus fieret tedium. Siquidem rex ipse solito conuiuia sibi requirere et homines quos solidarios dicimus ibi subdiurnandos consueuerat commendare. Officialium autem uenatorum et falconariorum regis quisque pro posse possessiones ecclesie uexabant. Vnus uir ille unum inuenit remedium, precio cum precibus obuius ire. *Centum itaque et .xx. libras* necnon *et .c. manentes ad regalem uillam,* que *Suthun* dicitur, eo tenore regi optulit; quatinus omni post tempore in Abbandonia et in uniuersis eius possessionibus libertas predictarum inquietudinum fieret. Cuius uoluntati rex in omnibus assensum prebuit. Quod decretum anno regni sui .xxv. ab incarnatione uero dominica .dcccxxi. sancitum est. His ita peractis, antistes ille Romam adiit; sanctum papam Leonem Petri apostoli uice tunc agentem repperit; qui eius itineris causam audiens, benigne ut requirebat Abbendonensi loci libertatem apostolica auctoritate sanciuit, regique Kenulfo et ceteris in Anglia potentibus litteras dirigens hortatus est eos ad reuerentiam cultumque eiusdem loci. Que postquam ille patrauit in summa quiete quoad uixit cenobium illud gubernauit. Post cuius discessum quid huic loci contigerit usque ad gloriosi principis Æthelstani imperium quia nusquam certi quicquam addiscere potui, suo meus stilus caruit officio. Rege Æthe⟨l⟩stano regnante et Abbendonensi cenobio presidente Cinatho abbate uillas que ab incolis Swinford et Sanford uocantur, et Dumeltum in Gloecestre comitatu sitam largitus est, anno ab incarnatione dominica .dccccxxxi. *Nec multo post rex ipse* obiit. *Post obitum* uero eius *ad tantam est solitudinem redactum, ut omnibus sibi adiacentibus possessionibus regio subactis dominio, a monachis omnino destitueretur. Cuius infortunii malum quibus ex causis acciderit, nil ueri ad meam*

---

[1] *Chronicon de Abingdon* i. 1, 9 (A, fo. 102ʳ).　　[2] *Chronicon de Abingdon* i. 21 A, fo. 103ᵛ).

*peruenit noticiam. Verumtamen testamentorum libri possessiones ecclesie conti-
nentium, reseruati sunt Dei prouidentia. A tempore autem Ine regis, sub quo
cenobium primo constructum est, ad hanc eius desolationem, .cc. et .xl. reuolu-
tio annorum fuisse reputatur.*[1]

Factumque est, consentiente Dunstano abbate, secundum[a] *regis uoluntatem, ut
uir Dei Æthelwoldus prenotati loci susciperet curam, quatinus in eo monachos
ordinaret regulariter Deo seruientes. Venit ergo seruus Dei ad locum sibi commissum. Congregauitque sibi in breui spacio gregem monachorum, quibus ipse
abbas, iubente rege, ordinatus est. Dedit etiam rex possessionem regalem, quam
in Abandonia possederat, hoc est centum cassatos, cum optimis edificiis, abbati et
fratribus ad augmentum cotidiani uictus, et de regio thesauro suo multum eos in
pecuniis iuuit; sed mater eius largius solatia munerum eis direxit.*

*Venit ergo rex quadam die ad monasterium ut edificiorum structuram per se
ipsum ordinaret: mensusque est omnia fundamenta propria manu, quemad-
modum muros erigere decreuerat, rogauitque eum abbas in hospitio cum suis
prandere. Annuit rex ilico; et contigit adesse sibi non paucos optimatum suorum uenientes ex gente Northanhinbrorum, qui omnes cum rege adierunt
conuiuium. Letatusque est rex, et iussit abunde propinare hospitibus ydromel-
lum. Quid multa? Hauserunt ministri liquorem tota die ad omnem sufficientiam
conuiuantibus; sed nequiuit ipse liquor exhauriri de uase, nisi ad mensuram
palmi, gaudentibus Northanhimbris et uesperi cum letitia recedentibus.*[2]

*Operariorum prouidere alimenta Ælfstanus monachus precepto abbatis
curam acceperat.*[3] *Accidit namque quadam die, dum abbas more solito pera-
graret monasterium, ut aspiceret illum fratrem stantem iuxta feruens caldarium
in quo uictualia preparabat artificibus et intrans uidit omnia uasa mundissima
ac pauimentum scopatum. Coxit enim carnes cotidie solus et operariis minis-
trabat focum accendens et aquam apportans et uasa denuo emundans. Dixitque
ei sanctus Æthelwoldus: 'O mi frater si talis miles Christi es, qualem te
ostendis, mitte manum tuam in bullientem aquam, et unum frustum de imis
mihi impiger attrahe'. Quod sine mora fecit, non sentiens calorem feruentis
aque. Quo uiso abbas iussit deponi frustum, et nemini hoc indicare uiuenti.*[4]
*Qui cum postea ob uite meritum pontificatus culmen apud Wiltonam adeptus
fuisset, adueniente sui ab hac uita euocatione Abbandoniam deportatus atque
sepultus est anno ab incarnatione Christi .dccccLxxx.*

*Erat et puer in eodem monasterio pure innocentie studii, nomine Ædmerus,
quem abbas ac fratres*[5] *nimium diligebant. In tali itaque etate et gratia*

---

[a] ad P

---

[1] *Chronicon de Abingdon* i. 21, 90 (A, fos. 103ᵛ, 110ᵛ).   [2] Wulfstan, *Vita S.
Æthelwoldi*, cc. 11–12 (Lapidge–Winterbottom, *Life*, pp. 20–4).   [3] *Chronicon de
Abingdon* i. 128 (A, fo. 111ᵛ).   [4] Wulfstan, *Vita S. Æthelwoldi*, c. 14
(Lapidge–Winterbottom, *Life*, pp. 26–8).   [5] *Chronicon de Abingdon* i. 128 (A, fo.
111ᵛ).

constitutus, infirmitate correptus, peruenit ad uite ultima. Cunque exitus horam prestolaretur, subito in extasi factus, celesti se interesse curie atque ibi matrem Dei Mariam residere conspicatur. Ante eam itaque hic adolescens adducitur, atque ab eadem an cum assistentibus sibi amodo remanere an in uita adhuc mortali degere uelit, affabili ut semper est uultu sciscitatur. Ille nil tristitie, nil indigentie his, quos intendebat, adesse considerans, malle se illic dixit quam alias, si mereretur iam associari. Cuius delectioni cum effectus fore promitteretur; inter uisionis illius gaudia ad se reuersus, abbati suo que uiderat queque audierat pandit. Et ut uera esse que narrarat*a* probarentur; spiritus eius a corpore exiens mox illius, quam acceperat, promissionis in sanctorum cetu compos efficitur.

⟨V⟩t*b* *districtioris autem uite tramitem cum e diuersis Anglie partibus, uiri Dei Æthelwoldi audita sanctitate, plurimi differenti more legendi canendique instituti ad eum conuenirent atque reciperentur uolens eos in ecclesia consona Deo uoce iubilare, ex Corbiensi cenobio, quod in Francia situm est, ecclesiastica ea tempestate disciplina* famosum *uiros accersiit sollertissimos*, ut illos *in legendo psallendoque sui imitarentur.*[1]

Ad beati quoque Benedicti cenobium Floriacum de suis monachis unum, Osgarum nomine, transmisit, normam uiuendi, prout illic mos erat, discere, ac inde domum reuersum socios horum que didicerat participes efficere. Quibus rebus factum est ut qui nouitii in ecclesiastico instituebantur discipulatu, breui aliis in Anglia perfectiores doctioresque predicarentur. Sanctus etiam Æthelwoldus trium regum sibi inuicem in regno succedentium dum regimen abbatie gereret, simul et archiepiscoporum, antistitum, abbatum primatuumque regni confirmatione ac auctoritate tria priuilegia de loci libertate acquisiuit canonica ac regali descriptione roborata. *Ea tempestate non habebantur monachi in gente Anglorum, nisi tantum qui in Glestonia morabantur et Abbandonia.*[2] Quantum uero ipsa fratrum collectio profecerit, regnum Anglie quamdiu constiterit testabitur, in cuius multis regionibus a patre Æthelwoldo cenobia fundata celeberrima, ac de eius monachorum numero Abbendonie electi abbates cum monachis et illic sunt directi. Quorum ista sunt uocabula: Heli, Burch, Torni. In quibus huius hominis quanta fuerit probitas, miranda est cum solus tot ecclesias in Anglia construxerit tum quod tales discipulos habuerit ut quidam archiepiscopi, nonnulli episcopi, plures uero abbates ac monasteriorum fundatores fierent. Ante uero quam ipse uir sanctus ad episcopatum eligeretur, *ditatus est locus*, quem regebat, scilicet Abbendonensis *sexcentis et eo amplius cassatis, insuper et eterne libertatis*

---

a narrat P   *b* Ad P

[1] *Chronicon de Abingdon* i. 129 (A, fo. 112r).
[2] Wulfstan, *Vita S. Æthelwoldi* c. 18 (Lapidge–Winterbottom, *Life*, p. 32).

suffultus priuilegiis, diuina simul et regia auctoritate conscriptis, que laminis aureis sigillati inibi usque hodie conseruantur.[1]

963 n. c (add. LP).

clericis monachis Abbendonensibus Vetus Monasterium instituit.

963 n. d (add. LP)

⟨V⟩ice*[a]* uero sancti Æthelwoldi*[b] Abbendonie abbas constituitur Osgarus eius-dem* monasterii *monachus. Sed quia ecclesiam Abbendonensem ante susceptum episcopatum dedicandam reliquerat, post sui consecrationem et ipsam una cum beato Dunstano et aliis nonnullis coepiscopis suis in honore Dei genitricis* Marie *consecrauit .v. kal. Ian.*[2]

977 n. f (add. L)

cuius corpus Abbandoniam defertur et in porticu sancti Pauli apostoli illic decenter humatur.[3]

981 n. c (add. L)

sicut ipse optauerat honorifice.[4]

984 n. a (add. L, mg. alongside 984 P[5]).

Domnus etiam Osgarus abbas Abbendonie per idem tempus diem clausit ultimum.[5]

985 n. b (add. LP)

Venerabilis . . . preficitur] *om. and following substituted*: Erat tunc maior domus regie *Ælfricus quidam prepotens fratrem habens Edwinum institutione monachum. Hic apud regem precio exegit ut* his*[c] frater eius Abbendonie abbas preficeretur.*[6] Quod et factum est.

1006 n. e (add. L, mg. P[5], *signe de renvoi* in P)

et sepultus est Abbendonie unde monachus extiterat sed regnante Kanuto rege ad sedem suam translatus.[7]

---

[a] ⟨V⟩ice *L*   *[b]* Ætheluuoldi *P*   *[c]* hic *P*

---

[1] Wulfstan, *Vita S. Æthelwoldi*, c. 21 (Lapidge–Winterbottom, *Life*, p. 36).
[2] *Chronicon de Abingdon* i. 348–9 (A, fo. 120ᵛ).
[3] *Chronicon de Abingdon* i. 356 (A, fo. 123ᵛ).
[4] Printed in Thorpe i. 146.   [5] Printed in Thorpe i. 147.
[6] *Chronicon de Abingdon* i. 357 (A, fo. 123ᵛ). In this annal the text has been com-pared with that in the MS as the printed text is inaccurate.
[7] Partly printed in Thorpe i. 158.

1017 n. d (p. 504) (add. L)

Pius pastor Abbendonie Wulgarus obiit anno .xxviii. ex quo illum diuina pietas eidem ecclesie prefecit. Cuius *abbatis industria uigilante* necnon et *Dei miseri*cordia *protegente, inter tam dissidentes in Anglia motus, cenobium Abbendonense a Danorum deuastatione permansit immune; cum dextra leuaque hostium incursio passim loca uniuersa subrueret, aut si beniuolentior fieret maximo sese pretio habitatores eorum redimere sineret. Cui in pastoralitate domnus Adelwinus successit.* Quem rex Kanutus pro laudabilis uite merito secretorum suorum conscium efficiens a noxiis sese retrahere ac recta appetere eius suasionibus studebat. Hinc et cenobium Abbendonense a rege diligitur et muneribus eius cumulatur, nam inter alia sua donaria capsam *de argento et auro* parari *fecit* in qua sancti *Vincentii leuite et martiris reliquie* col*locarentur.*[1]

1030 n. d (add. L)

Venerabilis abbas Abbendonie Adelwinus obiit. Cui ex hac *uita decedenti Siwardus ex Glestoniensi cenobio monachus* successit, *tam secularium quam ecclesiasticarum uigore admodum* fultus.[2]

1044 n. c (add. *L*)

Hoc anno *Cantuariensis metropoli*tanus *archiepiscopus Edsius accitum Siwardum abbatem* Abbendonie, *quem prudentia plurimum uigere nouerat, regis consensu et regni primorum pontificatus decorauit apice, ac patriarchatus sui uice ipsum fungi instituit. Nam ipse priuatus uti uolebat, quia egritudine laborabat. Abbendonensi autem ecclesie Æthelstanus eiusdem loci sacrista abbas constitutus est.*[3]

1048 n. a (add. LP, lower mg. with *signe de renvoi* P[5])

Vir Domini *Æthelstanus*[a] *abbas* Abbendonie obiit cui successit quidam *de monasterio sancti Eadmundi* monachus in auri argentique fabricio operator mirificus *nomine Sperafoc.*[b4]

1049 n. a (p. 552) (add. LP, mg. alongside 1050–1 P[5])

Decessit . . . tumulatus] *om. and the following substituted* sed et archiepiscopi uices moderans Siwardus egritudine correptus Abbendoniam a Cantia eger defertur et duobus illic mensibus lecto detentus ab hac uita educitur atque ibidem sepelitur.[5]

[a] Alfstanus P   [b] Sperafoch P

[1] *Chronicon de Abingdon* i. 432–3 (A, fo. 128ᵛ).
[2] *Chronicon de Abingdon* i. 434 (A, fo. 129ʳ).
[3] *Chronicon de Abingdon* i. 451 (A, fo. 130ʳ⁻ᵛ).
[4] *Chronicon de Abingdon* i. 462 (A, fo. 131ᵛ).
[5] Printed in Thorpe i. 203.

1050 n. a (add. LP, mg. alongside 1051–2 P⁵)

Venerat per hos dies ad regem quidam de Norwegia gente episcopus uocabulo Rodulfus regi propinquus. His^a Abbendonensibus^b abbatis iure preficitur.[1]

1051 n. a (p. 562) (add. LP, mg. alongside 1051–2 P⁵)

Rodulfus episcopus et abbas Abbendonensis ecclesie obiit cui successit Ordricus eiusdem monasterii monacus.[2]

1065 n. f (add. L)

Abbas Abbendonie *Ordricus postquam domum sibi commissam honorifice gubernasset et a memoria principum apostolorum ad sua remeasset diutina coctus egritudine diem sortitur ultimum. Ealdredus uero in eodem monasterio prepositure officium exhibens abbatie dominatum post illum adipiscitur.*[3]

---

^a Is P   ^b Abbandoniensibus P

---

[1] Printed in Thorpe i. 204.   [2] Printed in Thorpe i. 207.
[3] *Chronicon de Abingdon* i. 482 (A, fo. 135ʳ).

APPENDIX B

ADDITIONS IN OXFORD, BODLEIAN MS 297
(WITNESS B)

Introduction

There are substantial additions in B both in the text and in the margins. In the body of the chronicle text, B's interpolations and substituted readings include: the annals from Flodoard for 920 to 966; some Bury material (1014, 1020, 1032 and 1065); matter shared with the Annals of St Neots (e.g. the *Epistola Cuthberti* under 734, details about St Edmund under 855, 856, and 870, the *Visio Rollonis* under 876, the death of Guthrum under 891, additions to the Anglo-Saxon Chronicle under 893 and 912); and some single items such as details about Edward the Elder's family (901), the legend of the Seven Sleepers (1066) and a few Norman annals (916, 992, and 996). These are considerable additions, and the only one of these to duplicate existing annals is the addition under 912, which is shared with the Annals of St Neots. This deals with Edward's building of defences at Hertford and Witham, which had already been described in John's annals for 913 and 914.

The main scribe B[1] also added in the margin further annals from sources already used in the body of the text. Thus Flodoard, already drawn upon for the tenth century in the text, contributed the marginal annal for 955, and the Norman Annals contributed additional marginal entries, such as 701 or 784, which were sometimes shared with the Annals of St Neots. These marginal additions from the Norman Annals were used to plug gaps left by the Worcester chronicle (e.g. in Merovingian history under 620, 660 or 717, or later Norman events under 786, 1047, or 1054). Conversely, these annals were not used for Carolingian history where the existing annals from Marianus were usually fuller than the Norman.[1] B[1] may also have added in the margin the extract from the *Gesta Dagoberti* (636). The second main scribe, B[2], added in the margins extensive extracts from Bede's *Historia Ecclesiastica*

---

[1] An exception is the marginal addition (which erroneously adjoins 811) of the Norman annal on the coronation of Charlemagne which is fuller than the already entered annal of Marianus under 801.

(which are also found in the Annals of St Neots), and another scribe, B[4], a Bury document (945).[1]

The overlap between the additions in B and the Annals of St Neots has long been recognized, and has recently been examined by David Dumville.[2] The text of B's additions, whether incorporated or marginal, is extremely close to the Annals of St Neots. Witness, for instance, the already mentioned shared annal for 912, the many Norman Annals (mostly marginal in B) also in the Annals of St Neots (here very occasionally also marginal), the shared description 'ducem Nordmannorum' in the annal for 912, which is not in the Norman Annals, the incorporated *Visio Rollonis*, the *Epistola Cuthberti*, the lengthy extracts from Bede (all marginal in B), and, very tellingly, the description of the size of the Weald added to the annal for 893. In one of these shared texts, Abbo's *Passio S. Edmundi*, the Annals of St Neots' much fuller use of the *Passio* rules out their borrowing here from B. In the case of the Norman Annals, B and the Annals of St Neots sometimes act independently of each other, since the Annals of St Neots use them when they are not in B and vice versa. There are more significant differences between the two. B numbers one Merovingian king (in this conforming to the practice of the John of Worcester manuscript C), where the Annals of St Neots do not. B adds information to Norman annals shared with the Annals of St Neots (e.g. 720 where the added information does not seem to come from a Norman annal, and 914 where it does). In most of the other shared passages (e.g. *Epistola Cuthberti de obitu Bedae*, and *Visio Rollonis*) the two are very close, but B's omission in the Bedan marginal addition for 718 (705 in the Annals of St Neots, see 718 n. f) of seven words (which take up almost exactly one line in the Annals manuscript) makes the Annals of St Neots' derivation from B in this case extremely improbable and the reverse derivation very likely. B therefore probably borrowed most of its shared sources from the Annals, and the Annals of St Neots were therefore completed before the John of Worcester MS C came to Bury.

There remain two other textual links between the Annals of St Neots and B which may be conveniently considered here, though, as they are not additions, they are not printed in this appendix. First the *Visio Eucherii* under 741. This is incorporated in the text of the Annals of St Neots, of B, and in the John *chronicula* G. B's exemplar, C (which may

---

[1] For all the scribes of B see above, pp. liif., and for the attributions see below in this appendix. Different and slightly later scribes were responsible for the interesting entry on Eadric of Laxfield (1013) and for the Ramsey addition (1042).

[2] *ASN*, pp. lxf. It can be noted here that the text of Flodoard used in B belongs to the family which included the preliminary annal for 877 on the death of Charles the Bald, which appears in the Annals of St Neots (see *ASN*,, pp. liiif.). B's text of Flodoard is particularly close to witness Paris, Bibl. Nat. MS lat. 9768 in Lauer's edition.

have started to add it at the end of its annal 741), placed it in the margins adjoining annals 754–66, the margin next to 741 probably being already occupied (see 741 nn. *d*, *e* on p. 188). The critical apparatus printed above for the John of Worcester annal 741 (nn. *g*, on p. 188, *a*, *f*, *g* on p. 190) suggests that the versions in the Annals of St Neots and in CBG were independent of each other. B may have been guided by the Annals of St Neots' assignation of this entry to 741 (as David Dumville suggests), but not by its version of the *Visio*.[1] Second, the annals for 651, 731, 794, and 827 in the Annals of St Neots which are found almost word for word in the preliminary sections of the chronicle of John of Worcester.[2] Three are East Anglian: 651, Ecgric's unwilling participation in battle against Penda, and the succession of Anna; 794, Offa's execution of Æthelberht, which are both in the *East Anglian Accounts* 5–6, and 14; and 827, the slaying of Ludeca by the East Anglians, which is in the *Mercian Accounts* 19. The fourth is Northumbrian: 731, Ceolwulf's bizarre supposed elevation to the episcopacy of Lindisfarne, which is among some marginal notes written around the Deiran genealogical tree in John of Worcester. As was noted above, the episcopal lists could be used to date the composition of these accounts and notes in the John of Worcester preliminary sections to before 1114–15.[3] It is certainly possible for the Annals of St Neots here at least to have borrowed these details from the MS C during its postulated stay at Bury. It was, however, noted above that the East Saxon and East Anglian elements shared between these accounts and William of Malmesbury's *Gesta Regum* could either have been derived from a common source, or have been taken by William from Worcester before C had been written.[4] If, as has been suggested at the end of the last paragraph, the Annals of St Neots were written before C's arrival in Bury, then these four annals must have been taken from a source common to Bury and Worcester, or, have been derived from an earlier independent circulation of the preliminary sections of the Worcester chronicle.[5] In summary, these four annals in the Annals of St Neots were probably taken from a common source or from an earlier circulated John of Worcester preliminary text; the *Visio Eucherii* in both the Annals of St Neots and B were independent of each other; and most, if not all, of those additions in the main chronicle in B which were also found in the Annals of St Neots were taken from that manuscript.

[1] *ASN*, p. lvi n. 93.
[2] *ASN*, pp. lx f. The preliminary sections will be printed in vol. 1.
[3] See above, pp. xxxiv f.
[4] See above, pp. lxxvi.
[5] For the possibly earlier existence of these preliminary sections, see Brett, 'John of Worcester', p. 115 n. 4, and see above, pp. lxxiv–lxxvi.

Note on the principles of the edition of this appendix

Identified sources are shown in italics, and the source of an addition indicated in the historical footnotes. As the relationship of B to *ASN* is of importance, *ASN* readings are often shown in the critical apparatus, and, in the case of the *Epistola Cuthberti* (incorporated by B under 734), the text has been compared with that in *ASN* although published editions of the letter exist.

Anglo-Saxon Æ and æ are printed as they appear in the MS, and ę is rendered as e.

Additions or substituted readings

620 n. j (B[1] add. mg. near 620–1 on p. 260)

Dagobertus rex Francorum .xix.[1]

636 n. b (lower mg. p. 261, possibly by scribe B[1])

Beatus Audoenus scribit de Dagoberto rege ita dicens: '*post gloriosam* et diutinam *regni administrationem,* .xxxiiii.,[a] *postquam regnum sortitus fuerat, anno. .xiiii.* uero *kal. Febr.,* apud *Spinogil*um *uillam humanis rebus exemptus est*[2] et *cum ingenti populorum dolore atque frequentia in basilicam beatissimorum martirum* [b]Dyonisii *et sociorum eius,*[b] quam ipse fundauerat, *translatus, et, iuxta eorum tumulum, in dextro latere honore merito* conditus.[3] *Legationem tum forte, illustris defensor Pictauensis ecclesie, Ansoaldus, in partes Sicilie agebat. Ea peracta, cum nauali reuerteretur subsidio, applicuit ad quam*dam *breuem insulam, in qua reuerentissimus quidam senex, cui erat nomen Iohannes, solitariam ducebat uitam. Ad quem, mare commeantium, ut orationis eius fulcirentur* auxilio, *plurimi uentitabant. Ad hanc ergo insulam tanti uiri meritis redimitam, appulsus diuino nutu, Ansoaldus, dum de celestibus gaudiis cum eo sermocinaretur, interrogat senex unde uel cur uenisset. Igitur cognito de Galliis qua de causa missus fuisset, rogat senex ut Dagoberti regis Francorum sibi mores studiumque exponat. Quod cum ille diligenter fecisset, senex addidit, quod dum quadam die, utpote iam fractus etate et fatigatus uigiliis, quieti paululum indulsisset, accessisse ad se uirum quendam canitie*

---

[a] .xvi. *Gesta Dagoberti*   [b-b] Dyonisii . . . eius] *in mg. with signe de renvoi*

---

[1] Norman Annals. *AU, AG, ASN.* None say that Dagobert was the nineteenth king of the Franks.

[2] *Gesta Dagoberti I Regis Francorum,* c. 42 (*MGH SrM,* ed. B. Krusch, ii. 419–21).

[3] *Gesta Dagoberti,* c. 42 (p. 421).

uenerandum seque expergefactum admonuisse, quatinus propere surgeret, et pro Dagoberti regis Francorum anima Domini *clementiam exoraret, eo quod ipso die spiritum ex*halasset. *Quod dum facere maturaret apparuisse sibi haud procul in pelago teterrimos spiritus, uinctum regem Dagobertum in lembo per spatium maris agitantes, atque ad uulcania loca, inflictis insuper uerberibus trahentes, ipsumque Dagobertum beat*issimos *Dyonisium et Mauritium martyres et sanctissimum Martinum confessorem ad sui liberationem continuis uocibus flagitantem. Nec mora intonuisse celum, fulminaque per procellas disiecta, interque ea repente apparuisse praecellentissimos uiros, niueis comptos uestibus, seque tremefactum ex eis quaesisse, quinam essent; illosque respondisse quos Dagobertus in adiutorium uoc*arat *Dyonisium scilicet et Mauricium ac Martinum esse, ut eum ereptum in sinu Habrahe collocarent. Itaque hostes humani generis insequentes, animam, quam uerberibus minisque uexabant, ereptam ad ethera secum leuasse, canentes: "Beatus quem elegisti et assumsisti Domine inhabitabit in atriis tuis. Replebimur in bonis ⟨domus⟩ tuae, sanctum est templum tuum, mirabile in equitate".* Nec mirum *quoniam idem rex, cum et alias longe lateque ecclesias, tum precipue horum copiosissime locupletauit. Vnde et eorum post mortem flagitabat auxilium quos pre ceteris* dum uixit se *dilexisse meminerat'.*[2]

651 n. c (lower mgg. pp. 262–8 by B[2])

⟨*V*⟩*bi quadam infirmitate corporis arreptus, angelica meruit uisione perfrui, in qua admonitus est cepto Verbi ministerio sedulus insistere, uigiliisque consuetis et orationibus indefessus incumbere; eo quod certus sibi exitus, sed incerta eiusdem exitus esset hora futura, dicente Domino: 'Vigilate itaque, quia nescitis diem neque horam'. Qua uisione confirmatus, curauit locum monasterii, quem a prefato rege Sige*berch*to acceperat, uelocissime construere, ac regularibus instituere disciplinis. Erat autem monasterium siluarum et maris uicinitate amenum, constructum in castro quodam, quod lingua Anglorum Cnobheresbur*h, *id est urbs Cnobheri, uocatur: quod deinde rex prouincie illius Anna ac nobiles quique augustioribus edificiis ac donariis adornarunt. Erat autem uir iste de nobilissimo genere Scottorum, sed longe animo quam carne nobilior. Ab ipso tempore pueritiae suae curam non modicam lectionibus sacris* p. 263 *simul et monasticis exhibebat disciplinis, et, quod maxime sanctos | decet, cuncta, que agenda didicerat, sollicitus agere curabat. Quid multa? Procedente tempore et ipse sibi monasterium, in quo liberius celestibus studiis uacaret, construxit; ubi correptus infirmitate, sicut libellus de uita eius conscriptus sufficienter edocet, raptus est e corpore;*[a] *exutus, angelicorum agminum et*

---

[a] *eight words from* HE *are omitted here and in* ASN

---

[1] *Gesta Dagoberti,* c. 44 (p. 421).

aspectus intueri, et laudes beatas meruit audire. Referre autem *ᵃsolitus erat,ᵃ* quiaᵇ *aperte eos inter alia resonare audiret: 'ibunt sancti de uirtute in uirtutem'; et iterum: 'uidebitur Deus deorum in Syon.'* Qui reductus in corpore, et die tertia rursum eductus, uidit non solum maiora beatorum gaudia, sed et maxima malignorum spirituum certamina, qui crebris accusationibus inprobi iter illi celeste intercludere contendebant*ur; nec tamen, protegentibus eum angelis, quicquam proficiebant. De quibus omnibus siqui plenius scire uult (id est, quanta fraudis solertia demones et actus eius, et uerba superflua, et ipsas etiam cogitationes quasi in libro descriptas replicauerint; que ab angelis sanctis, que a uiris iustis sibi inter angelos apparentibus | leta uel tristia cognouerit),* p. 264 *legat ipsum libellum uite eius, et multum ex illo, ut reor, profectus spiritalis accipi*at. *In quibus tamen unum est, quod et nos in ᶜhoc locoᶜ ponere multis commodum duximus. Cum ergo in altum esset elatus, iussus est ab angelis, qui eum ducebant, respicere in mundum. At ille oculos in inferiora deflectens, uidit quasi uallem tenebrosam su*ptus *se in imo positam. Vidit et quattuor ignes in aere non multo ab inuicem spatio distantes. Et interrogans angelos, qui essent* hïi *ignes, audiuit hos esse ignes, qui mundum succendentes essent consumpturi. Vnum mendacii, cum hoc, quod in baptismo abrenuntiare nos Satane et omnibus operibus eius promisimus, minime implemus; alterum cupiditatis, cum mundi diuitias amori celestium preponimius; tercium dissensionis, cum animos proximorum etiam in superuacuis rebus offendere non formidamus; quartum impietatis* fraus*ᵈ cum infirmiores spoliare et eis fraudem facere pro nichilo ducimus. Crescentes uero paulatim ignes usque ad inuicem sese extenderunt, atque in inmensam adunati sunt flammam. Cumque a*ppropinquassent, per*timescens ille dicit angelo: 'Domine, ecce ignis mihi a*ppropinquat.' *At ille: 'Quod non incendisti,' inquit, 'non ardebit in te; nam etsi terribilis iste ac grandis esse rogus uidetur, tamen iuxta | merita operum singulos examinat;* p. 265 *quia uniuscuiusque cupiditas in hoc igne*ᵉ *ardebit. Sicut enim quis ardet in corpore per inlicitam uoluptatem, ita solutus corpore ardebit per debitam poenam.' Tunc uidit unum de tribus angelis, qui sibi in tota utraque uisione ductores adfuerunt, precedentem ignes flamme diuidere, et duos ab utroque latere circumuolantes* et *ab ignium se periculo defendere. Vidit autem et demones per ignem uolantes incendia bellorum contra iustos struere. Sequuuntur aduersum*ᶠ *ipsum accusationes malignorum, defensiones spirituum bonorum, copiosior celestium agminum (uisio; sed)ᵍ et uirorum de sua natione* Scottorum,*ʰ quos olim sacerdot*ali *gradu non ignobiliter potitos fama iam uulgante, conpererat; a quibus non pauca, que ⁱuel sibiⁱ uel ipsi uel omnibus qui audire uellent, mul-*

ᵃ⁻ᵃ solitus erat *ASN,* erat solitus *HE*   ᵇ quia *ASN,* quod *HE*   ᶜ⁻ᶜ hoc loco *ASN,* hac historia *HE*   ᵈ fraus *interlin. ASN.*   ᵉ igne *ASN,* igni *HE* ᶠ aduersum *ASN,* aduersus *HE*   ᵍ *erasure here*   ʰ Scottorum *ASN,* sanctorum *HE*   ⁱ⁻ⁱ uel sibi *ASN*

tum salubria essent, audiuit. Qui cum uerba finissent, et cum angelicis spir-
itibus ipsi quoque ad celos redirent, remanserunt cum beato Furseo tres angeli,
de quibus diximus, qui eum ad corpus referrent. Cumque prefato igni maximo
adpropiarent, diuisit quidem angelus, sicut prius, ignem flamme. Sed uir Dei
ad patefactam usque inter flammas ianuam peruenit, arripientes inmundi spiri-
tus unum de eis, quos in ignibus torrebant, iactauerunt in eum, et contingentes
humerum maxillamque eius incenderunt; cognouitque hominem, et quod[a] *ues-*

p. 266 *timentum eius morientis acceperit, | ad memoriam reduxit. Quem angelus*
sanctus statim apprehendens in ignem reiecit. Dicebatque hostis malignus:
'Nolite repellere, quem ante suscepistis; nam sicut bona eius peccatoris suscepis-
tis, ita et de penis eius participes esse debetis.' Contradicens angelus: 'Non,'
inquit, 'propter auaritiam, sed propter saluandam eius animam suscepit'; ces-
sauitque ignis. Et conuersus ad eum angelus: 'Quod incendisti,' inquit, 'hoc
arsit in te. Si enim huius uiri in peccatis suis mortui pecuniam non accepisses,
nec pena eius in te arderet.' Et plura locutus, quid erga salutem eorum, qui ad
mortem peniterent, esset agendum, salubri sermone docuit. Qui postmodum in
corpore restitutus, omni uitae suae tempore signum incendii, quod in anima
pertulit, uisibile cunctis in humero maxillaque portauit; mirumque in modum,
quod[b] anima in occulto passa sit, caro palam premonstrabat. Curabat autem
semper, sicut et antea facere consueuerat,[c] omnibus opus uirtutum et exemplis
ostendere, et predicare sermonibus. Ordinem autem uisionum suarum illis
solummodo, qui propter desiderium compunctionis interrogabant, exponere uole-

p. 267 *bat. Superest adhuc frater quidam senior | monasterii nostri, qui narrare solet*
dixisse sibi quendam multum ueracem ac religiosum hominem, quod ipsum
Furseum uiderit in prouincia Orientalium Anglorum, illasque uisiones ex ipsius
ore audierit; adiciens, quia tempus hiemis fuerit acerrimum et glacie constric-
tum, cum sedens in tenui ueste uir ita inter dicendum, propter magnitudinem
memorati timoris uel suauitatis, quasi medie estatis caumate sudauerit. Cum
ergo, ut ad superiora redeamus, multis annis in Scotia uerbum Dei omnibus
annuntians, tumultus irruentium turbarum non facile ferret, relictis omnibus,
que habere uidebatur, ab ipsa quoque insula patria discessit; et paucis cum
fratribus per Brittones in prouinciam Anglorum deuenit, ibique predicans uer-
bum Dei, ut diximus,[d] monasterii negotiis alienare, reliquit monasterii et ani-
marum curam fratri suo Fullano et presbiteris Gobbano et Dicullo, et ipse ab
omnibus mundi rebus liber in anchoretica conuersatione uitam finire disposuit.
Habuit alterum fratrem uocabulo Vltanum, qui de monasterii probatione diu-
turna ad heremiticam peruenerat uitam. Hunc ergo solus petens, annum totum
cum eo in continentia et orationibus, in cotidianis manuum uixit laboribus.
Dein turbatam incursione gentilium prouinciam uidens, et monasteriis quoque

p. 268 *periculum imminere preuidens, dimissis ordinate omnibus nauigauit | Galliam,*
ibique a rege Francorum Lodowico uel patricio Erconuualdo honorifice suscep-

---

[a] quod *ASN*, quia *HE*   [b] quod *ASN*, quid *HE*   [c] consueuerat *ASN*, consuerat
HE   [d] *fifteen words omitted here and in ASN (from* monasterium *to* monasterii*)*

tus, monasterium construxit in loco Latiniaco nominato, ac non multo post infirmitate correptus diem clausit ultimum. Cuius corpus idem Erconwaldus patricius accipiens, seruauit in porticu quodam ecclesie, quem[a] in uilla sua, cui nomen est Parrona,[b] faciebat, donec ipsa ecclesia dedicaretur. Quod dum post dies .xxvi.[c] esset factum, et corpus ipsum de porticu ablatum prope altare esset recondendum, inuentum est ita inlesum, ac si eadem hora de hac luce fuisset egressus. Sed et post annos .iiii., constructa domuncula cultiore receptui corporis eiusdem, ad orientem altaris, adhuc sine macula corruptionis inuentum, ibidem digno cum honore translatum est; ubi merita illius multis sepe constant Deo operante claruisse uirtutibus. Hec et de corporis eius incorruptione breuiter attigimus, ut, quanta esset uiri sublimitas, legentibus notius existeret. Que cuncta in libello eius sufficientius, sed et de aliis commilitionibus ipsius, quisque legeret,[d] inueniet. Hec Beda.[1]

660 n. c (B[1] add. at line-end on p. 265)

Mortuo Clodoueo rege Francorum, regnauit Clotharius filius eius.[2]

684 n. b (B[1] add. mg. near 684 n. a on p. 265)

Mortuo Childerico rege Francorum, regnauit Theodericus.[3]

699 n. c (B[1] add. mg. with *signe de renuoi* on p. 275)

Rex Francorum Theodericus obiit, successit Chlodoueus secundus.[4]

701 n. e (B[1] add. at line-end and extends into mg. on p. 275)

Clodoueus obiit, successit Childebertus frater eius.[5]

704 n. a (B[2] add. lower mgs. pp. 276–8)

Fuit autem temporibus huius[e] Kenredi regis, fratris scilicet sancte Werburge uirginis, uir in laico habitu atque officio militari positus; sed quantum pro industria exteriori regi placens, tantum pro interna suimet neglegentia displicens. Ammonebat illum sedulo rex, ut confiteretur, et emendaret, ac relinqueret scelera sua, priusquam subito mortis superuentu tempus omne penitendi et emendandi perderet. Verum ille, frequenter licet admonitus, spernebat uerba salutis, seseque tempore sequente penitentiam acturum esse promittebat. Hec

---

[a] quem *ASN*, quam *HE*   [b] Parrona *ASN*, Perrona *HE*   [c] .xxvi. *ASN*, .xxvii. *HE*   [d] legeret *ASN*, legerit *HE*   [e] *add. ASN*

---

[1] *HE* iii. 19. *ASN* has this under 651.
[2] Norman Annals. *AU* (659), *AG* (654; refers also to the accession of two other sons) and *ASN* (654; accession only).
[3] Norman Annals. *AG*, *AU* and *ASN* (all 682).
[4] Norman Annals. *AU*, *AG* and *ASN* (all 698). *ASN* records only the accession.
[5] Norman Annals. *AU*, *AG* and *ASN* (all 700). *ASN* records only the accession.

inter tactus infirmitate, decidit in lectum, atque acri cepit dolore torqueri. Ad quem ingressus rex, diligebat enim eum multum, hortabatur, ut uel tunc, antequam moreretur, penitentiam ageret commissorum. At ille respondit, non se tunc uelle confiteri peccata sua, sed cum ab infirmitate sua[a] *resurgeret; ne exprobrarent sibi sodales, quod timore mortis faceret ea, que sospes facere nolebat;[b] fortiter quidem, ut sibi uidebatur, locutus, sed miserabiliter, ut post patuit, demonica fraude seductus. Cumque morbo ingrauescente, denuo ad eum uisitandum ac docendum rex intraret, clamabat statim miserabili uoce: 'Quid*

p. 277 *uis modo? Quid huc uenisti? Non enim[c] aliquid utilitatis aut salutis potes | ultra conferre.' At ille: 'Noli,' inquit, 'ita loqui, uide ut sanum sapias.' 'Non,' inquit, 'insanio, sed pessimam mihi* conscientiam[d] *certus pre oculis habeo.' 'Et quid,' inquit, 'hoc est?' 'Paulo ante,' inquit, 'intrauerunt domum hanc duo pulcherrimi iuuenes, et residerunt circa me, unus ad caput, et unus ad pedes; protulitque unus libellum perpulchrum, sed uehementer modicum, ac mihi ad legendum dedit; in quo omnia, que umquam bona feceram, intuens scripta repperi, et hec erant nimium pauca et modica. Receperunt codicem, neque aliquid mihi dicebant. Tum subito superuenit exercitus malignorum et horridorum uultu spirituum, domumque hanc et exterius obsedit, et intus maxima ex parte residens impleuit. Tum[e] ille, qui et obscuritate tenebrose faciei, et primatu sedis maior esse uidebatur eorum, proferens codicem horride[f] uisionis, et magnitudinis enormis, et ponderis pene inportabilis, iussit uni ex satellibus[g] suis mihi ad legendum deferre. Quem cum legissem, inuenio omnia scelera, non solum que opere uel uerbo, sed etiam que tenuissima cogitatione peccaui, manifestissime in eo tetricis esse descripta litteris. Dicebatque ad illos, qui mihi adsederant,[h] uiros albatos et preclaros: "Quid hic sedetis, scientes certissime, quia noster est iste?" Responderunt: "Verum dicitis: accipite et in cumultum dampnationis uestre*

p. 278 *ducite." Quo dicto statim disparuerunt; surgentesque | duo nequissimi spiritus, habentes in manibus* 'furcas ignitas,'[i] *percusserunt me, unus in capite et alius in pede: qui uidelicet modo cum magno tormento inrepunt* [j]mea uiscera[j] *in interiora corporis mei, moxque ut ad se inuicem perueniunt, moriar, et paratis ad rapiendum me demonibus in inferni claustra pertrahar.' Sic loquebatur miser desperans, et non multo post defunctus, penitentiam, quam ad breue tempus cum fructu uenie facere supersedit, in eternum sine fructu penis subditus facit. De quo constat quia, sicut beatus papa Gregorius de quibusdam scribit, non pro se ista, cui non profuere, sed pro aliis uiderit, qui eius interitum cognoscentes differre tempus penitentie, dum uacat,[k] timerent, ne inprouiso mortis articulo preuenti inpenitentes perirent. Quod autem codices diuersos per bonos siue malos spiritus sibi uidit offerri, ob id superna dispensatione factum*

---

[a] sua *interlin.* B, ASN   [b] nolebat ASN, noluerat HE   [c] enim ASN, enim mihi HE   [d] conscientiam ASN, scientiam HE   [e] Tum ASN, Tunc HE [f] horride ASN, horrendae HE   [g] satellibus ASN, satellitibus HE   [h] adsederant *from* assederant   [i-i] furcas ignitas (ignitas *interlin.*) ASN, uomeres HE [j-j] mea uiscera ASN   [k] uacat *from* uocat

est, ut meminerimus facta et cogitationes nostras non in uentum diffluere, sed ad examen summi Iudicis cuncta seruari; et siue per amicos angelos in fine nobis ostendenda sunt,[a] *siue per hostes. Quod uero prius candidum codicem protulerunt angeli, deinde atrum daemones; illi perpar⟨uum⟩,[b] isti enormem; animaduertendum est quod in prima etate bona aliqua fecit, que tamen uniuersa praue agendo iuuenis obnubilauit. Qui se e contrario errores pueritie corrigere in ad*olescentia,[c] *ac bene faciendo a Dei oculis abscondere curasset, posset eorum numero sociari, de quibus ait psalmus: 'Beati, quorum remissae sunt iniquitates, et quorum tecta sunt peccata.'* Hec Beda.[1]

717 n. b (B[1] add. at line-end and extends into mg. on p. 278)

Obiit Childebertus rex Francorum, successit Dagobertus.[2]

718 n. c (B[1] add. upper mg. with *signe de renvoi* on p. 279)

Karolus filius Pippini maior domus fit.[3]

718? n. f (i) (B[1] add. lower mg. with *signe de renvoi* for mg. addition but no clear guide to its location in text, on p. 279)

Mortuo Dagoberto secundo, Franci Danielem clericum in regem leuauerunt, atque Chilpericum nuncupant[4] contra quem Karolus in pugnam iniit atque in fugam uictor compulit.

718 n. f (ii) (B[2] add. lower mgs. pp. 279–83 with *signe de renvoi* possibly pointing to Aldfrith).

⟨Tem⟩pore huius Aldfridi regis Nordanhymbrorum *erat* quidam[d] *pater familias in regione que uocatur Incuneningum, religiosam cum domu sua gerens uitam; qui infirmitate corporis tactus, et hec crescente per dies, ad extrema perductus, primo tempore noctis defunctus est; sed diluculo reuiuescens, ac repente residens, omnes, qui corpori flentes adsederant, timore inmenso perculsos in fugam conuertit; uxor tantum, que amplius amabat, quamuis multum tremens et pauida remansit. Quam ille consolatus: 'Noli,' inquit, 'timere, quia iam uere* resurrexi[e] *a morte, qua tenebar, et apud homines sum* [f]uiuere iterum[f] *permissus; non tamen ea mihi, qua ante consueueram,[g] conuersatione, sed multum dissimili ex hoc tempore uiuendum est.' Statimque surgens,* | *abiit ad*   p. 280

---

[a] *interlin. ASN*   [b] *perparinum B*   [c] *adolescentia from* adolescientie *B*
[d] *ASN*   [e] resurrexi *ASN,* surrexi *HE*   [f-f] uiuere iterum *ASN,* iterum uiuere
HE   [g] consueueram *ASN,* consueram *HE*

---

[1] *HE* v. 13. *ASN* has this under 704.
[2] Norman Annals. *AU, AG* and *ASN* (all 716). *ASN* records only the accession, and an interlineation makes Dagobert the second of that name.
[3] Norman Annals. *AU* (717). *ASN* has a fuller entry.
[4] Norman Annals. *AU, AG* and *ASN* (all 720). *ASN* alone gives Daniel's new name as king. It is not clear that *B*'s marginal addition should be linked to 718.

uillule oratorium, et usque ad diem in oratione persistens, mox omnem, quam possiderat,[a] substantiam in tres diuisit portiones, e quibus unam coniugi, alteram filiis tradidit, tertiam sibi ipse retentans, statim pauperibus distribuit. Nec multo post seculi curis absolutus ad monasterium Mailros, quod Tuuidi fluminis circumplexu[b] maxima ex parte clauditur, peruenit; acceptaque tonsura, locum secrete mansionis, qua⟨m⟩[c] preuiderat abbas, intrauit; et ibi usque ad diem mortis in tanta mentis et corporis contricione durauit, ut multa illum, que alios laterent, uel horenda uel desideranda uidisse, etiamsi lingua sileret, uita loqueretur. Narrauit autem hoc modo, quod uiderat: 'Lucidus,' inquiens, 'aspectu et clarus erat indumento, qui me ducebat. Incedabamus autem tacentes, ut uidebatur mihi, contra ortum solis solstitiale⟨m⟩; cumque ambularemus, deuenimus ad uallem multe latitudinis ac profunditatis, infinite autem longitudinis; que ad leuam nobis sita, unum latus flammis feruentibus nimium terribile, alterum furenti grandine ac frigore niuium omnia perflante atque uerrente non minus intollerabile preferebat. Vtrumque autem erat animabus hominum plenum, que uicissim hinc[d] inde uidebantur quasi tempestatis impetu iactari. Cum enim uim feruoris inmensi tolerare non possent, prosiliebant misere in medium[e] flammarum inextinguibilium. Cumque hac infelici uicissitudine longe lateque, prout aspicere poteram, sine ulla quietis intercapedine innumerabilis spirituum deformium multitudo torqueretur, cogitare cepi, quod hic fortasse esset infernus, de cuius tormentis intolerabilibus narrare[f] sepius audiui. Respondit cogitationi mee ductor, qui me precedebat: "Non hoc," inquiens, "ut[g] suspiceris; non enim hic infernus est ille, quem putas." At cum me hoc spectaculo tam horrendo perterritum paulatim in ulteriora pro | duceret, uidi subito ante nos obscurari incipere loca, et tenebris omnia repleri. Quas cum intraremus, in tantum paulisper condensate sunt, ut nichil praeter ipsas aspicerem, excepta dumtaxat specie et ueste eius, qui me ducebat. Et cum progrederemur "sola sub nocte per umbras", ecce subito apparent ante nos crebri flammarum tetrarum globi, ascendentes quasi de pu⟨teo⟩[h] magno, rursumque decidentes in eundem. Quo cum perductus essem, repente ductor meus disparuit, ac me solum in medio tenebrarum et horride uisionis reliquid. At cum idem globi ignium sine intermissione modo alta peterent, modo ima baratri repeterent, cerno omnia que ascendebant, fastigia flammarum plena esse spiritibus hominum,[i] nunc ad sullimiora proicerentur, nunc retractis ignium uaporibus relaberentur in profundum.[j] Sed et fetor incomparabilis cum eisdem uaporibus ebulliens omnia illa [k]loca tenebrarum[k] replebat. Et cum diutius ibi pauidus consisterem, utpote incertus, quid agerem, quo uerterem gressum, qui me finis maneret; audio subito[l] post terga sonitum inmanissimi ⟨f⟩letus[m] ac miserrimi,

[a] possiderat *ASN*, possederat *HE*   [b] circumplexu *ASN*, circumflexu *HE*
[c] qua *ASN*   [d] hinc *ASN*, huc *HE*   [e] *fifteen words from HE om. through eyeskip B*   [f] narrare *ASN*, narrari *HE*   [g] ut *ASN*   [h] *erasure here B*
[i] *six words from HE om. B*   [j] profundum *ASN*, profunda *HE*   [k-k] loca tenebrarum *ASN*, tenebrarum loca *HE*   [l] subito *ASN*, subitum *HE*
[m] priletus *B*

*simul et chachinnum crepitantem quasi uulgi indocti captis hostibus insultantis.
Vt autem sonitus idem clarior redditus ad me usque peruenit, considero turbam
malignorum spirituum, quecumque^a animas hominum merentes heiulantesque,
ipsa multum exultans et chachinnans, medias illas trahebat in tenebras;* | *e* p. 282
*quibus uidelicet hominibus, ut dinoscere potui, quidam erat adtonsus ut clericus,
quidam laicus, quedam femina. Trahentes autem eos maligni spiritus descen-
derunt in medium baratri illius ardentis; factumque est, ut cum longius subeun-
tibus eis, fletum hominum et risum demoniorum clare discernere nequirem,
sonum tamen adhuc promiscuum in auribus haberem. Interea ascenderent
quidam spirituum obscurorum de abysso illa flamiuoma, et adcurrentes circum-
dederunt me, atque oculis flammantibus, et de ore ac naribus ignem putidum
efflantes angebant; forcipibus quoque igneis, quos tenebant in manibus, minita-
bantur me comprehendere, nec tamen me ullatenus contingere* potuerunt,^b
tametsi terrere presumebant. Qui cum undiqueuersum hostibus ^c*conclusus et
cecitate tenebrarum,^c huc illucque oculos circumferrem, si forte aliunde,^d quid
auxilii, quo saluarer, adueniret, apparuit retro uia, qua ueneram, quasi fulgor
stelle micantis inter tenebras, qui paulatim crescens, et ad me ocius festinans,
ubi adpropinquauit, dispersi sunt at aufugerunt omnes, qui me forcipibus rapere
querebant spiritus infesti. Ille autem, qui adueniens eos fugauit, erat ipse, qui
me ante ducebat; qui mox conuersus ad dextrum iter, quasi contra ortum solis
solsticialem^e brumalem me ducere cepit.* | *Nec mora, exemptum tenebris in* p. 283
*auras serene lucis eduxit; cumque me in luce aperta duceret, uidi ante nos
murum permaximum, cuius neque longitudini hinc uel inde, neque altitudini
ullus esse terminus uideretur. Cepi autem mirari, quare ad murum accedere-
mus, cum in eo nullam ianuam, uel fenestram, uel ascensum alicubi con-
spicerem. Cum ergo peruenissemus ad murum, statim nescio quo ordine fuimus
in summitate eius. Et ecce ibi campus erat latissimus ac letissimus, tantaque
fraglantia^f uernantium flosculorum plenus, ut omnem mox fetorem tenebrosi
fornacis, qui me peruaserat, effugaret admirandi huius suauitatis odoris. Tanta
autem lux cuncta ea loca perfuderat, ut omnis splendor diei siue solis meridiani radiis uideretur esse preclarior.* ^g*Erant* namque^g *in hoc campo innumera
hominum albatorum conuenticula, sedesque plurime agminum letantium.
Cumque inter choros felicium incolarum medios me duceret, cogitare cepi, quod*
^h*fortasse hoc^h esset regnum celorum, de quo predicari sepius audiui. Respondit
ille cogitatui meo: "Non," inquiens, "non hoc est regnum celorum quod autu-
mas." Cumque procedentes transsissemus et has beatorum mansiones spirituum,
aspicio ante nos multo maiorem luminis gratiam quam prius; in qua etiam
uocem cantantium dulcissimam audiui; sed et odoris fraglantia^f miri tanta de
loco effundebatur, ut is, quem antea degustans quasi maximum rebar, iam per-*

---

^a quecumque *ASN*, quae quinque *HE*   ^b interlin. *ASN*   ^{c-c} conclusus . . .
tenebrarum] *ASN*, et caecitate tenebrarum conclusus *HE*   ^d aliunde *ASN*, ali-
cunde *HE*   ^e interlin. *ASN*   ^f fraglantia *ASN*, flagrantia *HE*   ^{g-g} erant
namque *ASN*, erantque *HE*   ^{h-h} fortasse hoc *ASN*, hoc fortasse *HE*

modicus mihi odor uideretur; sicut etiam lux illa campi florentis eximia in comparatione.[1]

734 n. d (pp. 281–2)

Incipit epilogium de obitu beati atque eximii doctoris Bede qui Giruuinensis monasterii presbyter extitit doctorque precipuus. Dilectissimo in Christo collectori Cuthuuino Cuthbertus condiscipulus in Deo eternam salutem.

Munusculum quod misisti multum libenter accepi, multumque gratanter litteras tue deuote eruditionis legi, in quibus quod maxime desiderabam, missas uidelicet et orationes sacrosanctas pro Deo dilecto patre ac nostro magistro Beda a uobis diligenter celebrari repperi. Vnde delectat magis pro eius caritate quantum fruor ingenio paucis sermonibus dicere quo ordine migraret e seculo, cum etiam hoc te desiderasse et poposcere intellexi. Grauatus quidem est infirmitate maxima creberrimi anhelitus, sine dolore tamen, ante diem resurrectionis dominice, *"*id est fere duabus ebdomadibus; et sic postea letus et gaudens gratiasque agens omnipotenti Deo omni die et nocte, immo horis omnibus, usque ad diem ascensionis dominice,*ab* id est .vii. kal. Iunii uitam ducebat, et nobis suis discipulis cotidie lectiones dabat, et quicquid reliquum erat diei in psalmorum decantatione occupabat. Totam quoque noctem in letitia et gratiarum actione peruigil ducebat, nisi tantum modicus somnus impediret; euigilans autem statim consueta repetiuit, et expansis manibus Deo gratias agere non desinit. O uere beatus uir! Canebat sententiam beati Pauli apostoli, 'Horrendum est incidere in manus Dei uiuentis,' et multa alia de sancta scriptura. Et in nostra quoque lingua, hoc est anglica, ut erat doctissimus in nostris carminibus, dixit:

> For tham nedfere   neni wyrtheth
> thances snotera   thonne him thearf sy
> to gehicgenne   er his heonen gange
> hwet his gaste   godes othe yueles
> efter deathe heonon   demed weorthe.

Cantabat etiam antiphonas secundum nostram consuetudinem et sui, quarum una est, 'O rex glorie, Domine uirtutum, qui triumphator hodie super omnes celos ascendisti, ne derelinquas nos orphanos, sed mitte promissum patris in nos, spiritum ueritatis. Alleluia.' Et cum uenisset ad illud uerbum, 'ne derelinquas nos orphanos,' prorupit in lacrimas et multum fleuit. Et post horam cepit repetere que inchoauerat. Et nos hec

a–a id est . . . dominice] *repeats at 734 n. b*   *b* *734 n. a repeated here and struck through*

[1] HE v. 12. *ASN* has this under 705, the appropriate lower mg. in MS B being taken up with the addition to 704.

audientes luximus cum illo; altera uice legimus, altera plorauimus, immo semper cum fletu legimus. In tali leticia quinquagesimales dies usque ad diem prefatum deduximus, et ille multum gaudebat, Deoque gratias agebat quia sic meruisset infirmari. Referebat et sepe dicebat, 'Flagellat Deus omnem filium quem recipit', et multa alia de sancta scriptura, sententiam quoque sancti Ambrosii, 'Non sic uixi ut me pudeat inter uos uiuere; sed nec mori timeo, quia bonum Deum habemus'. In istis autem diebus duo opuscula multum memoria digna, exceptis lectionibus quas accepimus ab eo et cantu psalmorum, facere studebat, euangelium sancti*a* Iohannis in nostram linguam ad utilitatem ecclesie conuertit, et de libris rotarum Ysidori episcopi excerptiones quasdam, dicens, 'Nolo ut discipuli mei mendatium legant, et in hoc post obitum meum sine fructu laborent.' Cum uenisset autem .iii. feria ante ascensionem Domini, cepit uehementius egrotare in anhelitu, et modicus tumor in pedibus apparuit; totum autem illum dicebat et hilariter dictabat, et nonnumquam inter alia dixit, 'Discite cum festinatione; nescio quandiu subsistam, et si post modicum tollat me Factor meus.' Nobis autem uidebatur quod suum exitum bene sciret. Et sic noctem in gratiarum actione peruigil duxit, et | mane   p. 282 illucescente, id est .iiii. feria, precepit diligenter scribi que ceperamus, et hoc facto usque ad .iii. horam ambulauimus deinde cum reliquiis sanctorum, ut consuetudo illius diei poscebat. Vnus uero erat ex nobis cum illo qui dixit illi, 'Adhuc, magister dilectissime, capitulum unum deest. Videturne tibi difficile plus te interrogari?' At ille, 'Facile', inquit, 'est. Accipe tuum calamum et tempera, et festinanter scribe.' Et ille hoc fecit. Ad nonam autem horam dixit mihi, 'Quedam pretiosa in mea capsella habeo, id est piperem oraria et incensa. Sed curre uelociter, et presbiteros nostri monasterii adduc ad me, ut et ego munuscula, qualia Deus donauit, illis distribuam. Diuites autem in hoc seculo aurum, argentum, et alia queque preciosa dare student; ego autem cum multa caritate et gaudio fratribus meis dabo quod Deus dederat.' Et allocutus est unumquemque, monens et obsecrans pro eo missas et orationes diligenter facere. Quod illi libenter spoponderunt. Lugebant autem et flebant omnes, maxime quod dixerat quia amplius faciem eius in hoc seculo non essent uisuri. Gaudebant autem quia dixit, 'Tempus est ut reuertar ad eum qui me fecit, qui me creauit, qui me ex nichilo formauit. Multum tempus uixi; bene michi pius*b* Iudex uitam meam preuidit. Tempus resolutionis mee instat, quia cupio dissolui et esse cum Christo.' Sic et alia multa locutus in leticia, diem usque ad uesperum duxit. Et prefatus puer dixit, 'Adhuc una sententia, magister dilecte, non est descripta.' At ille, 'Scribe', inquit, 'cito.' Post modicum dixit puer, 'Modo sententia descripta est.' At ille, 'Bene,' inquit, 'ueritatem dixisti. Consummatum est. Accipe meum caput in manus tuas, quia multum me delectat sedere ex aduerso loco sancto

---

a sci⟨licet⟩ sancti *ASN*   *b* prius *B and ASN*

meo, in quo orare solebam, ut et ego sedens patrem meum inuocare possim.' Et sic in pauimento sue casule, decantans 'Gloria Patri et Filio et Spiritui Sancto', cum Spiritum Sanctum nominasset, spiritum e corpore exalauit ultimum, ac sic regna migrauit ad celestia. Omnes autem qui uidere beati patris obitum, nunquam se uidisse ullum alium in tam*a* magna deuotione atque tranquillitate uitam finisse dicebant quia, sicut audisti, quousque anima in corpore fuit. 'Gloria Patri' et alia quedam spiritalia, expansis manibus, Deo uiuo et uero gratias agere non cessabat. Scito autem, frater karissime, quod multa narrare possem, de eo, sed breuitatem sermonis ineruditio lingue facit.[1]

784 n. b (B[1] add. at line-end)

Witichingis cum sociis in Atiniaco baptizati sunt.[2]

811? n. c (B[1] add. outer mg. p. 289 with *signe de renvoi* for mg. addition but no clear guide to its location in text; it is likely that this was meant for an annal in the inner margin, probably 801 which has an account of the same event by Marianus on which this addition expands)

Karolus rex imperator factus est, et a Romanis appellatus est augustus, qui illos qui Leonem papam dehonestauerunt, morte damnauit, sed precibus sanct⟨i⟩*b* pape morte indulta, exilio retrusit. Ipse enim papa Leo imperatorem eum sacrauerat.[3]

855 n. e on p. 274 (p. 298)

.viii. kal. Ian., id est die natalis Domini anno etatis sue .xiiii.[4]

856 n. e on p. 274 for 855 (p. 298)

Hunberhtus antistes hoc anno unxit oleo consecrauitque in regem Ædmundum gloriosissimum cum magno gaudio et honore maximo in uilla regia que dicitur Buran,*c* quia tunc temporis regalis fiscus*d* erat, anno etatis sue .xv., sexta feria, luna .xxiiii., die natalis Domini.[5]

---

a vitam B and ASN   *b* sancte B and ASN   *c* Burna with uel Buran *added by scribe ASN*   *d* sedes with uel fiscus *added by scribe ASN*

[1] This is Cuthbert's *Epistola de obitu Bedae* (*HE*, pp. 502–3). As variants from Mynors's printed text in *HE* are so numerous, the text has here been compared with that in *ASN*.
[2] Norman Annals. *AU*, *AG* and *ASN* (all 783 and all refer to the grant of land to the Vikings), *AC* (784).
[3] Norman Annals. *AU* and *ASN* (both 800), *AG* (798).
[4] *ASN*.   [5] *ASN*.

870 n. c on p. 286 (p. 299)

after martirizatus est *add.* die .xii. kalendarum Decemb., indictione .iii., secunda feria, luna .xxii., anno etatis sue .xxix., anno uero regni sui .xv.,[a] et anno etiam imperii Karoli .xv., anno Atheredi regis Occidentalium Saxonum .v. sancto rege sic martirizato, eheu proh dolor, pagani nimium gloriantes,[b] totam illam regionem suo dominio subdiderunt, eo quod omnes fortiores et nobiliores eiusdem gentis una cum sancto rege, siue ante beatum regem, crudeliter occubuerunt.[1]

876 n. p (p. 306)

Idem Normannorum dux Rollo, cum in antiqua Brytannia siue Anglia hiemaret militaribus fretus copiis, quadam nocte fruitur uisione mox future certitudinis. Visum est enim sibi dormienti, supra se et exercitum suum subito exsurrexisse examen apum, suoque stridore auolare uersus occidentem per maris medium, terramque petentes insidere gregatim in frondibus diuersarum arborum, moxque omnem circa regionem quasi aduenientibus congratulantem, aspersam coloribus uariorum florum. Euigilans itaque industrius dux, secum primo uisionem tractat, eiusque significantiam sapienter ad requiem cursus sui suorumque in eisdem partibus, ubi apes uiderat requieuisse, coniectat. Pulchreque in hanc spem confortatur, quod tota illa regio subitis floribus induebatur. Erat enim hoc quasi quedam diuine pietatis euocatio[c] ut ex Dei munere adepta terra illa mox in Christi floreret[d] titulo, uariisque uirtutum floribus in uera religione sua suorumque ornaretur successio. Aduocatis ergo suis, strenuus dux edocet somnium, illucque totius classis iubet parari cursum. Aspirat quoque prospere diuina miseratio, tum necessario uenti spiraculo,[e] tum maris et celi habitu iocundissimo subeunt Sequane hostium, optatoque cursu perueniunt ad ipsam metropolim Rothomagum, fiuntque rebellantium internities, dedentium uero se et eorum societati confauentium defensio et requies. Amore ergo pacis, potissimum autem prelii tedio, allecto Francorum rege, impellenteque hinc gratia illinc uiolentia, facta est tota regio illa ducis suorumque Normannorum dominica, ut eam scilicet suis usibus possiderent et in regis Francorum fidelitate eam sibi recognoscerent et deseruirent. Suscepta itaque tota monarchia illa, redit inclitus dux Rothomagum, destructum eius releuat murum, reparat propugnacula, fossaque et turribus eius ambit menia. Interea frequentius accersito ad colloquium suum eius archiepiscopo Francone, uenerabilis uite uiro, diuine religionis instruitur documentis,[f] et super talibus

---

[a] .xv. *from* .xvi. *B*, .xvi. *ASN*   [b] gloriantes *from* gloriantis   [c] euocatio *from* euacatio   [d] florerent *B and ASN*   [e] spiraeulo *ASN*   [f] documento *ASN*

---

[1] *ASN*.

paulatim cepit delectari, interius inspirante Spiritu Sancto. Abluitur tandem, eodem pontificante, diuine regenerationis sacramento in agnitionem Dei, eiusque exemplo omnis exercitus eius eodem modo Christo regeneratus in albis candescit fidei. Insistit deinde Christiane fidei amator gloriosus dux in combustis ecclesiis et monasteriis reparandis in Christi honore, sanctorumque corporibus referendis que sua suorumque hostili sublata*a* fuerant formidine, relataque ad sua ampliori relocauit cultu et reuerentia: summo enim studio usus est et diligentia circa sanctorum reliquias deuotius recondendas, adhibitis in eorum famulitio clericis uel monachis, prout didicerat quosque fuisse in singulis sanctorum locis. Terras etiam, non solum eas que ex antiquo eis adiacebant, uerum plures superaddidit, ut eos intercessores haberet apud Deum, qui eos sibi sanctificauit. Omnibus itaque recte curatis, uerus Christicola, ut pius pater, omnibus pene prefuit.[1]

891 n. b (p. 313)

Mortuus est itaque anno .xiiii. postquam baptismum suscepit mausoleatusque in uilla que uocatur Headleaga apud Orientales Anglos.[2]

893 n. c (p. 313: B[1] add, near opening in mg., which is mutilated)

Initium regis Karoli puer. Huius miles Hagano. Capta est ⟨ci⟩uitas Ebroacensis a Nordman⟨nis⟩ sed episcopus, Sebar nomine, Deo auctore euasit.[3]

893 n. f (p. 314)

que silua habet spatium in longitudine ab oriente in occidente⟨m⟩ miliaria .cxx. et eo amplius et in latitudine .xxx.[4]

901 n. c (p. 317)

After Ex muliere nobilissima Ecguuynna filium suum Æthelstanum *add.* suscepit. Cui regina sua Alfleda, filia Ethelmi comitis, duos filios peperit, scilicet Ethelwardum et Eaduuinum, peperitque ei filias .vi., ex quibus Eadfleda sanctimonialis femina cum sorore Ethelhilda apud Wiltunam requiescit. Cetere*b* uero .iiii., id est Eadgyua, Eadhilda, sancta Eadgytha, Ealfgifa, quarum unam in coniugem habuit Otto imperator Romanorum, id est Eadgyuam, alteram Karolus rex Occidentalium Francorum, id est Eadhildam, terciam Sihtricus rex Northanymbrorum, id est sanctam

---

a ablata *ASN*   *b* cetere *from* ceteri

---

[1] *ASN.*   [2] *ASN* (890).
[3] Norman Annals. *AG, AU, ASN,* (893). *AC* (893; last sentence only).
[4] *ASN* (892). This description comes ultimately from *ASC*, but it is a telling instance of *B*'s dependence on *ASN*.

Eadgytham, que apud Tamuuordam requiescit, quartam Hugo, filius Rodberti ducis, id est Ealfgifam; regina uero sua Eadgyua duos filios ei peperit, uidelicet Eadmundum et Edredum, et sanctam Eadburgam que apud Wintoniam requiescit.[1]

912 n. d (pp. 319–20)

Eodem anno Eaduuardus rex iussit edificare urbem aquilonalem apud Heortfordam, inter flumina que nuncupata sunt Memeran et Beneficeam et Lygeam, circa festiuitatem sancti Martini. Circa quoque festiuitatem sancti Iohannis baptiste precepit construere urbem apud Wittham. Item ipso anno apud Heortfordam in australi parte Lygean fluminis. Hoc etiam anno baptizauit Franco archiepiscopus Rotomagensis Rollonem ducem Nordmannorum.[2]

914 n. c (p. 320)

Facta est pax inter Karolum regem Francorum et Rollonem ducem Nordmannorum, deditque Karolus ei filiam suam nomine Gislam, de qua nullum filium habuit.[3]

916 n. g (p. 321)

Mortua Gisla accepit Rollo Popam uxorem filiam comitis Widonis Siluanectensis, de qua genuit Willelmum.[4]

920 n. d (p. 323)

Hoc etiam anno *pene omnes Francie comites regem suum Karolum apud urbem Suessonicam, quia Haganonem consiliarium suum, quem de mediocribus potentem fecerat, dimittere nolebat, reliquerunt. Herueus autem, Remorum archiepiscopus, accipiens regem cum omnes eum deseruissent, duxit eum ad hospitia sua in uilla que dicitur Carca*siria. *In crastinum uero uenerunt in Crustu*acum, *Remensis episcopi uillam, ibique manserunt donec uenirent Remis. Sicque deduxit eum per .vii. fere menses, usque quo illi suos principes eumque suo restitueret regno. Remis, ad monasterium sancti Petri, ad portam quedam puella aduenerat, nomine Osanna, de pago Vozinsi, carnem non comedens,*

---

[1] This substituted account of Edward's wives and children, like B's marginal addition under 925 concerning Edith and her apostasizing husband Sihtric, is close to that in Roger of Wendover (i. 368–9). Wendover does not mention here Edith's burial at Tamworth, though this is in Hugh Candidus' list of saints' resting-places, and Goscelin of Saint-Bertin implies that the Edith, who was Edgar the Peacable's sister, founded Tamworth (A. Wilmart, 'La légende de Ste Edith en prose et en vers par le moine Goscelin', *Analecta Bollandiana*, lvi (1938), 54).

[2] *ASN*. Parts of the last sentence are in *AG*, *ABM* (both 912), *AU* (911), *AC* (913).

[3] Norman Annals. *AU*, *AMSM*, and *ASN* (all 914), *AR* (?) and *AG* (both 912), *AC* (913). *ASN* does not refer to the marriage.

[4] Norman Annals. *AG* (912), *AC* (913), *AMSM* (916), *AU* (917).

neque panem ab annis iam duobus edere ualens, cui multe uisiones ostendebantur. Hec in ipsis diebus, ebdomada plena iacuit immota, et sanguinem cum omni admiratione sudauit, ita ut frons eius tota et facies usque ad collum operiretur sanguine, in qua uita uel tantum calor remanserant alitu etiam tenuissime spirante. Tunc quoque multa se uidisse perhibuit, ex quibus aliqua dixit; plurima que uiderat se dicere non audere professa est. [Flodoard]

922 n. f (p. 323)

Karolus cum Hereberto et Haganone clam Laudunum egressus, ob Hagananis amorem. Dux *Rotbertus super Axonam tentoria* sua *fixit. Karolus* rex, *abnegato sibi introitu Lauduni, resedit super fluuium Saram, et Rotbertus castra metatus est super Aleam. Et cum cotidie, copiis Rotberti crescentibus, decrescerent Karoli, clam tandem secedens cum Haganone trans Mosam proficiscitur. Franci Rotbertum seniorem eligunt, ipsique sese committunt. Rotbertus itaque rex*[a] *Remis, apud sanctum Remigium, ab episcopis et primatibus regni constituitur. Herueus, Remorum archiepiscopus, obiit tertia die post consecrationem Rotberti regis, scilicet sexto non. Iulii, quarto die ante .xxii. sui episcopatus expleret annum. Cui successit in episcopatum Seaulfus qui tunc urbis eiusdem ministerio fungebatur archidiaconatus.* [Flodoard]

923 n. c (pp. 323–4)

Karolus rex *cum suis Lothariensibus inducias, quas nuper a Rotberto rege acceperat, infringentibus Mosam transiens, ad Attiniacum uenit, et antequam Rotbertus* rex *suos fideles adunare potuisset, super Axonam inspirate, ubi Rotbertum sub urbe Suessonica sedere compererat, adiit. Et in crastinum, die dominica, hora iam sexta preterita, Francis dehinc illa die prelium non sperantibus, plurimis quoque prandentibus,* rex *Karolus Axonam transiit, et super Rotbertum cum armatis Lothariensibus uenit. Rotbertus uero* rex *armatis his qui* cum *eo erant, contra processit. Commissoque prelio, multis ex utraque parte cadentibus, Rotbertus quoque rex lanceis perfossus cecidit. Hi tamen, qui erant ex parte Rotberti* regis, *Hugo scilicet, filius ipsius, et Herebertus comes cum ceteris uictoria potiti* sunt. *Karolum* regem *cum suis Lothariensibus in fugam uerterunt, sed ob mortem regis sui Rotberti, eos persequi destiterunt, campum uero obtinuerunt, spoliaque ab eis, direpta sunt. Karolus* rex *mox ad Herebertum comitem* et ad *Seaulfum archiepiscopum, ceterosque regni primates multis legationibus* mittens *ut ad se reuertantur. Quod illi rennuentes, pro Rodulfo filio Ricardi genero Rotberti regis in Burgundiam transmiserunt, qui otius cum multa suorum manu illis occurrit. Auditoque Franci quod Karolus* rex *ad se uenire Nordmannos mandasset, ne illi coniungerentur, inter Karolum et Nordmannos super Isram fluuium cum Rodulfo medii resederunt. Tuncque, Karolo trans Mosam refugiente, Rodulfum cuncti eligunt. Rodulfus, filius Ricardi, rex apud urbem Suessonicam* in monasterio sancti Medardi *constitu-*

---

[a] *interlin.*

itur, et Herebertus comes Bernardum, consobrinum suum, cum aliis legatis
ad Karolum regem *dirigit, qui ab eisdem sacramentis persuasus, ad*
Herebertum cum paucis proficiscitur, quique eum in castello suo super
Somnam, apud sanctum Quintinum, suscepit, indeque his qui cum eo uenerant
remissis, Karolum regem *in quandam munitionem suam, que uocatur castellum*
Theoderici, super Maternam fluuium, deduci fecit, ibique illum, subministratis
uictui necessariis, sub custodia detenuit, et sic ipse Rodulfum regem in
Burgundiam prosecutus est. [Flodoard]

925 n. c (B¹ add. lower mg. p. 324 with *signe de renvoi* and slightly mutilated)

Qui propter amorem sancte uirginis, cultur⟨am⟩ paganorum deriliquit et
sanctum baptismum suscepit, sed non multo post ⟨sanct⟩am uirginem
repudiauit, ac religionem sancte Christianitatis abiecit, idolorumque culturam restaurauit. Ipse itaque demum ut apostata male periit. Sanct⟨a⟩
uirgo namque reuersa est ad Merciam regionem, haud longe ab urbe regia
que uocata est Tamuurda, ibique in loco, qui dicitur Pollesuuorda, in
uigiliis et orationibus et elemosiniis et crebris ieiuniis persistens usque ad
diem ultimum. Transit autem uirgo sancta post aliquot annos die iduum
Iuliarum; sepulta est ibidem ubi usque hodie signa atque miracula plura
choruscat.¹

927 n. h (p. 325)

Hugo, filius Rotberti, filiam Eaduuardi regis Anglorum, sororem coniugis
Karoli, duxit uxorem. [Flodoard, 926]

928 n. b (p. 325)

Herebertus, comes Remis, cum Karolo uenit, indeque litteras mittit Romam
Iohanni pape, significans ei de restitutione et honore Karoli, ut ille sibi etiam
sub excommunicationis interminatione mandauerat se pro uiribus decertare.
[Flodoard]

929 n. c (p. 325)

Karolus quoque rex apud Peronam obiit. [Flodoard]

936 n. b (p. 325)

Sub eisdem fere diebus, rex Rodulfus defungitur, sepeliturque Senonis, apud
sanctam Columbam, cuius ecclesia factione quorumdam paulo ante fuerat
incensa. Britones a transmarinis regionibus, Athelstani regis presidio,

---

¹ See above p. 633 n. 1. Wendover's annal for 925 (i. 385) states that Edith, wife to
Sihtric, rests at Pollesberia (corrected in the margin to Polesworth), and an Edith rests
at Polesworth in the late Anglo-Saxon text of saints' resting-places (*Die Heiligen*
Englands, p. 13). See discussion in C. Hohler, 'St Osyth and Aylesbury', *Records of*
Buckinghamshire, xviii (1966–70), 61–72 at p. 72.

reuertentes terram suam repetunt. Hugo comes trans mare mittit pro accersiendo ad apicem regni suscipiendo Ludouuico, Karoli filio, quem rex Athelstanus auunculus ipsius, accepto prius iureiurando a Francorum legatis, in Franciam cum quibusdam episcopis et aliis fidelibus suis dirigit, cui Hugo et ceteri Francorum proceres obuiam profecti, mox nauim egresso, in ipsis littoreis harenis, apud Bononiam sese committunt, ut erat utrimque depactum. Indeque ab ipsis Laudunum deductus, ac regali benedictione ditatus, ungitur atque coronatur a domno Artaldo archiepiscopo, presentibus regni principibus cum episcopis .xx. et amplius. [Flodoard]

938 n. b (p. 326)

Hugo princeps, filius Rotberti, sorore⟨m⟩ Ottonis regis Transrenensis, filiam Heinrici, ducit uxorem. [Flodoard]

939 n. e (p. 326)

Lotharienses Ottonem suum regem deserunt et ad Ludouuicum regem uenerunt. Qui eos recipere distulit, ob amicitia⟨m⟩ que inter eos, legatis ipsius Ottonis et Arnulfo comite mediante, depacta erat. Castellum Herluini maritimum[a] quod uocatur Monasteriolum, comes Arnulfus tradente quodam proditore cepit, et uxorem ipsius Herluini trans mare, cum filiis, ad Adalstanum regem mittit. Nec longum post collecta Nordmannorum non modica manu, Herluuinus castrum pugnando recepit et ex militibus Arnulfi, quos intus inuenit, nonnullos interemit, quosdam uero, propter uxorem recipiendam, reseruauit. Lotharienses iterum ueniunt ad regem Ludouuicum et proceres ipsius regni. Gislebertus scilicet dux, et Otto, Isaac atque Theodericus comites se regi committunt. Gislebertus dux Lothariensium trans Renum profectus predatum, Saxonibus sed dum reuertitur insequentibus, in Renum fertur dissiluisse cum equo ui enecatus undarum postea repperiri non potuit, ut fertur. Quidam tamen ferunt quod a piscatoribus sit repertus et humatus atque propter spoliorum ipsius ornamenta celatus. Ludouuicus rex, in regnum Lothariense regressus, relictam Gisleberti Gerbergam ducit uxorem, Ottonis scilicet regis[b] sororem. [Flodoard]

940 n. f (p. 326)

Rex Ludouuicus abiit obuiam Willelmo, princip⟨i⟩[c] Nordmannorum, qui uenit ad eum in pago Ambianensi et se illi commisit. At ille dedit ei terram quam pater eius Karolus Nordmannis concesserat, indeque contra Hugonem perrexit. [Flodoard]

941 n. h (p. 327)

Ludouuico regi filius nascitur. [Flodoard]

---

[a] maritimum *from* miritimum   [b] regis *from* reges   [c] princip *from* principe

942 n. c (p. 327)

⟨L⟩udouuicus rex Ottoni regi obuiam proficiscitur, et amicabiliter se mutuo suscipientes amicitiam suam firmant conditionibus, multumque de pace inter regem Ludouuicum et Hugonem laborans Otto, Hugonem tandem ad eundem regem conuertit. Herebertus etiam pariter cum equiuoco filio suo homo ipsius regis Ludouuici efficitur. Domnus Odo uenerabilis abbas, multorum restaurator monasteriorum sancteque regule reparator, Turonis obiit, et sepultus est apud sanctum Iulianum. [Flodoard]

943 n. b (p. 327)

Arnulfus comes Willelmum, Nordmannorum principem ad colloquium euocatum dolo perimi fecit. Rex Ludouuicus Ricardo filio ipsius Willelmi natum de concubina Britanna, nomine Sprouua, terram Nordmannorum dedit, et quidam principes ipsius se regi committunt, quidam uero Hugoni duci. Heribertus comes obiit, quem sepelierunt apud sanctum Quintinum filii ipsius. Ludouuicus Rodomum repetens, Turmodum Nordmannum. qui, ad idolatriam gentilemque ritum reuersus, ad hec etiam filium Willelmi aliosque cogebat regique insidiabatur, simulque cum Setrico rege pagano congressus, cum eis interimit. Et Herluino Rodomum committens, reuertitur ad Compendium. Herluuinus, cum Arnulfo congressus uictoriaque potitus, eum quoque, qui Willelmum, Nordmannorum principem, interemerat, occidit. Et amputatas manus ipsius, Rodomum transmisit. Hugo dux filiam regis ex lauachro sancto suscepit, et rex eidem[a] ducatum Francie delegauit omnemque Burgundiam ipsius ditioni subiecit. Idem uero Hugo Arnulfum cum rege pacificauit, cui rex infessus erat ob necem Willelmi. [Flodoard]

944 n. e (p. 327)

Ludouuicus rex, pace facta inter Herluuinum et Arnulfum, castrum Ambianensium eidem Herluuino dedit. [Flodoard]

945 n. f (i) (addition in text, pp. 327–8)

Dum rex Ludouuicus moraretur Rodomi, Haigroldus Nordmannus, qui Baiocis preerat, mandat ei, quod ad eum uenturus esset condicto tempore uel loco, si rex ad illum locum accederet. Veniente denique rege cum paucis ad locum denominatum, Haigroldus cum multitudine Nordmannorum armatus aduenerat, inuadensque sotios regis, pene cunctos interemit. Rex solus fugam iniit, prosequente se Normanno quodam sibi fideli. Cum quo Rodomum ueniens, comprehensus est ab aliis Normannis, quos sibi fideles esse putabat et sub custodia detentus. Hugone duce de regis ereptione laborante, Nordmanni filios ipsius regis dari sibi obsides querunt, nec aliter regem se dimmissuros asserunt. Mittitur ad reginam pro pueris. Illa minorem mittens, maiorem fatetur se non esse missuram. Datur igitur minor, et ut rex dimittatur, Wido Suessorum

---

[a] eidem *from* iidem

episcopus sese obsidem tradit. Dimissus itaque rex a Nordmannis, suscipitur ab Hugone principe, quique committens eum Tetbaldo, cuidam suorum, proficiscitur Othoni regi obuiam. Qui rex, nolens loqui cum eo, mittit ad eum Conradum ducem Lothariensium. [Flodoard]

945 n. f (ii) (B⁴ addition in lower mg; pp. 327–31)

Hoc etiam anno rex Eadmundus dedit hoc priuilegium sancto Ædmundo regi et martyri.*ᵃ*

⟨I⟩n nomine sancte Trinitatis. Quamuis decreta pontificum et uerba sacerdotum uelut fundamenta montium in districtis ligaminibus fixa sint, tamen plerumque tempestates et turbines secularium rerum etiam religio sancte Dei ecclesie maculis reproborum dissipatur ac rumpitur. Iccirco incertum futurorum temporum statum prouidentes posteris succedentibus; profuturum esse decreuimus, ut ea que communi tractu salubri consilio definiuntur sertis litterulis roborata confirmentur. Quapropter ego Eadmundus rex Anglorum terrarumque gentium in circuitu persistentium gubernator et rector ad memoriam reuoco gesta antecessorum meorum, qui terrenis opibus ecclesias sanctorum ditauerunt; quorum exempla imitatus,*ᵇ* ad monasterium quod situm est in loco qui dicitur Badericesuuyrthe, in quo sanctus Ædmundus rex et martyr quiescit cor-

p. 328

pore, | terramque circa illum locum esse uidetur libenter tribuo et eternaliter persistat, eatenus ut illam eiusdem monasterii familia possideat atque suis posteribus*ᶜ* eadem dictione derelinquat. Sit autem predicta terra libera ab omni mundiali obstaculo, cum omnibus que olim ad ipsum locum pertinere dinoscuntur tam in magnis quam in modicis rebus campis, pascuis, pratis, siluis. Et non reddat aliquid debitum, nisi ad necessitatem familie eiusdem ecclesie. Si quis autem propria temeritate uiolenter inuadere presumpserit nostram prenotatam donationem, sciat se procul dubio ante tribunal districti*ᵈ* iudicis titubantem tremebundumque rationem redditurum. nisi prius hic digna satisfactione emendare maluerit. Istis terminibus predicta terra circumgyrata esse uidetur.

This synden tha landgemæro. the Ædmund kyng gebocade into sancte

p. 329

Ædmunde. thonne is thær ærest suth be eahte treouuan. and thonne | up be Ealhmundes treouuan. and suua forth to Osulfes lea. and suua forth on gerichte be manige hyllan. and thanan up to Hamar lunda. and suua forth to fouuer hogas. and suua æfter them uuege to Litlantune. and thonan ofer tha ea æfter tham uuege to Bertunedene. and suua on gerihte east*ᵉ* to Holegate.*ᶠ* and suua forth an furlang be eastten Bromleaga, and thonan suth to niuuan tune meaduue. ⟨Fa⟩cta est hec prefata donatio, anno ab incarnatione Domini nostri Iesu Christi, .dccccxlii., indictione .iii.

ᵃ erasure follows *ᵇ imitatus from imitatur* *ᶜ sic MS* *ᵈ districti from districtis* *ᵉ over erasure* *ᶠ erased letter before a in Holegate*

⟨E⟩go Ædmundus rex Anglorum prefatam donationem cum sigillo sancte crucis*a* indeclinabiliter confirmaui.

⟨E⟩go sancta*b* Elfgyua regina*c* firmiter confirmaui et corroboraui. | p. 330

⟨E⟩go sanctus*b* Odo Dorobernensis ecclesie archiepiscopus eiusdem regis principatum et beniuolentiam cum sigillo sancte crucis*a* conclusi.

⟨E⟩go Theodred Lundonienis ecclesie episcopus corroboraui.

⟨E⟩go Ælfheah Wintoniensis ecclesie episcopus testitudinem sancte crucis*a* subscripsi et confirmaui.

⟨E⟩go Kenuuald episcopus predictum donum consensi.

⟨A⟩thelm dux.

⟨Æ⟩dmund miles.

⟨Æ⟩lfgar miles.

⟨E⟩go Ælfric episcopus consignaui.

⟨Æ⟩thelstan dux.

⟨W⟩ulfric miles.

⟨W⟩ihtgar miles.

⟨E⟩go Ælfred episcopus confirmaui.

⟨Æ⟩lfgar dux.

⟨Æ⟩lfstan miles.

⟨Æ⟩lfred miles.

⟨E⟩go Burhric episcopus consensi.

⟨Æ⟩thelwold dux. | p. 331

⟨Æ⟩lfheah miles.

⟨Æ⟩thelgeard miles.

⟨E⟩go Æthelgar episcopus roboraui.

⟨E⟩alhhelm dux.

⟨Æ⟩thered miles.

⟨Æ⟩thelsige miles.

⟨E⟩go Æthelwold episcopus consignaui.

⟨A⟩thelmund dux.

⟨Æ⟩lfsige miles.[1]

946 n. g (p. 328)

Eadmundus Anglorum rex legatos ad Hugonem principem pro restitutione Ludouuici regis dirigit, et idem princeps proinde conuentus publicos cum nepotibus suis aliisque regni primatibus agit. [Flodoard]

946 n. c (p. 328)

Eodem anno *uxor regis Ottonis,* nomine Eadgyua, *soror ipsius* Edredi et *Eadmundi, decessit. Hugo, dux Francorum, ascito secum Hugo*ne *Nigro, filio*

---

a a cross interlin.   *b* interlin.   *c* erasure follows

---

[1] *S* 507 BCS 808. Printed in *Memorials St Edmund's,* i. 340–1.

Ricardi, ceterisque regni primatibus Ludouuicum regem, qui fere per annum sub custodia detinebatur apud Tetbaldum comitem, in regnum restituit, recepto Lauduno castro, quod regina Gerberga tenebat, et eidem Tetbaldo commisso. Qui dux Hugo, renouans regi Ludouuico regium honorem uel nomen, ei sese cum ceteris regni committit primoribus. [Flodoard]

951 n. b (pp. 328–9)

Ludouuicus rex Aquitaniam cum exercitu petiit. Sed, antequam eandem ingrederetur prouinciam, Karolus Constantinus, Vienne princeps, et Stephanus Auernorum presul ad eum uenientes, sui efficiuntur. Gerberga, ᵃid est Eadhilda,ᵃ *regina, mater Ludouuici regis, egressa Lauduno, conducentibus se quibusdam tam Hereberti quam Adalberti, fratris ipsius, hominibus, ad Heribertum proficiscitur, qui suscipiens eam, ducit in coniugem. Vnde rex Ludouuicus iratus, abbatiam sancte Marie, quam ipsa Lauduni tenebat, recepit, et Gerberge uxori sue dedit. Otto rex Italiam adiit, ad cuius aduentum Berengario, Langobardorum rege, ab urbe Papia fugiente, ipse Otto eandem ingreditur urbem, uxorem quoque Lotharii regis defuncti, filii Hugonis, sororem Conradi, regis Iurensis, sibi coniugem ducit.* [Flodoard]

953 n. d (p. 329)

Exoritur interea inter Ottonem regem et Liudulfum, filium eius, quem ei peperit Ædgyua regina, *Conradum quoque ducem et quosdam regni ipsius primates discordia. Nato siquidem regi filio ex moderna coniuge, ferebatur eidem puero rex regnum suum promittere, quod olim, prius quam Italiam peteret, Liudolfo delegauerat, et magnates suos eidem promittere fidelitatem iureiurando fecerat. Rex igitur Conradum a ducatu Lothariensium remouet, et Conradus querebat ut regem caperet. Quo comperto, caute se agere cepit, de interitu uero Conradi querere. Cepit Conradus autem oppida sua munire.* [Flodoard]

955 n. c (add. mg. p. 329 with *signe de renvoi*: B¹ starts the addition but another scribe continues)

mausoleatusque est ⟨Ludouuicus⟩ *honorifice apud sanctum Remigium. Hlotharius puer filius Hloduici regis apud sanctum Remigium rex consecratur ab Artaldo archiepiscopo, fauente Hugone principe, ac Brunone archiepiscopo ceterisque presulibus ac proceribus Francie atque Aquitaniae. Dantur quoque ab ipso Hugoni Burgundia et Aquitania.* [Flodoard: 954]

956 n. c (p. 330)

Hugo princeps obiit. [Flodoard]

ᵃ⁻ᵃ id est Eadhilda] *interlin.*

960 n. c (p. 331)

Richardus filius Willelmi, Nordmannorum princeps, filiam Hugonis trans Sequanam quondam principis duxit uxorem. Otto et Hugo filii Hugonis, mediante auunculo ipsorum Brunone episcopo, ad regem Lotharium ueniunt ac sui efficiuntur. Quorum Hugonem rex ducem constituit, addito illi pago Pictauensi ad terram quam pater ipsius tenuerat, concessa Ottoni Burgundia. [Flodoard]

962 n. a (p. 331)

Otto rex Romam pacifice adiit et amabiliter exceptus, atque honore illic imperiali sublimatus est. Quod Berengarius, Italie rex, indigne ferens, regiones, quas regere debebat, incendere atque uastare cepit. [Flodoard]

965 n. h (p. 331)

Otto imperator ab urbe Roma regrediens, Coloniam uenit. Ibique Gerbergam reginam, sororem suam, cum filiis Lothario rege Karoloque puero ad se uenientem excepit, et cum eis aliisque multis proceribus placitum magnum habuit. [Flodoard]

966 n. j (p. 331)

Lotharius rex uxorem accepit Emmam, filiam regis quondam Italici. [Flodoard]

992 n. b (i) (in text p. 335)

Obiit Hlotharius rex Francorum in quo progenies Karoli magni a regno funditus destituitur. Filii enim regis Hlatharii capiuntur, et Hugo magnus, filius Hugonis, Rotberti ducis filii, in regem eleuatur.[1]

992 n. b (ii) (B¹ add. mg. p. 335)

Mater ipsius Hugonis regis et mater regis Lotharii sorores erant, scilicet Ottonis imperatoris et Brunonis qui et Leonis pape.[2]

993 n. a (B¹ add. mg. on p. 336)

Hugo rex Francorum obiit. Regnauit Rotbertus rex filius eius pro eo.[3]

996 n. b (p. 337)

Obiit Ricardus primus dux Nortmannorum filius Willelmi, cui succedit Ricardus .ii. filius eius.[4]

---

[1] Norman Annals. *AG* and *AC* (both 992) and *AMSM* (972).
[2] This information could have been deduced from earlier entries.
[3] Norman Annals. *AMSM, AG, AU* (all 993), and the *AC* (995) simply record Duke Robert's accession.
[4] Norman Annals. *AC, AG* (both 996).

1013 n. b (written by hand which does not appear elsewhere in blank left column on p. 344)

Edrico domino Laxfeldie et totum honorem Eye cum*a* septies .xx. militibus casato,*b* qui regis Æþelredi consanguineus duobus annis*c* in Normannia eidem ministrauit usque ad mortem regis Æþelredi. Post cuius mortem, reducta regina in Angliam feliciter, ut decebat, et cum pompis; regali consilio magnatum totius Anglie coniuncta est regi Cnutoni et iterum coronata apud Westmonasterium presentibus et assistentibus archiepiscopis Cantuariensi et Eboracensi eorumque suffrageneis, filiis suis, Ælfredo et Ædwardo in Normannia moram facientibus cum patre immo patruo suo duce Ricardo et salutare domini expectantibus, donec aquilonali grandine quod uineam Domini Sabaoth in Anglia conquassauerat, in temporem mutata uirtutes flores denuo pullularent, et Oliue trunco iam pene marcido, ramus non degener per Dei gratiam insequeretur.[1]

1014 n. c (p. 345)

ut autem gloriosi regis et martyris Eadmundi de tyranno uictoria longe lateque claresceret: omnipotens Dominus hoc operari dignatus est sua ineffabilli clementia. *Si quidem in prouincia* *d*que *lingua Anglorum Æstsexe dicitur*d* *egrotus quidam*e* *tanto* *f*languore percussus*f* *iacebat, ut nullo membrorum suorum officio, ne lingue quidem, uteretur. Triduoque in agonia protracto, morti finitimus cunctus spem uite denegabat. Cuius cum quadam nocte parentes et uicini circumstantes exitum prestolarentur, recuperata uirtute in sensum se erigens, uoce gratulabunda dixit, 'Hac nocte et hac hora, sancti Eadmundi lancea transuerberatus rex Suein oppetiit'.*g* Quod cum dixisset*h* in lectulo recubans*i* ultimum flatum emisit, atque morte sua, tyranni mortem indubitanter asseuerauit.*[2]*

a de *interlin.* above cum   *b* eidem regine ministrante *interlin.*   *c* et eo amplius] *interlin.*   *d–d* que . . . dicitur] Orientalium Saxonum *Miracula* P, Anglorum que Esexe dicitur *Miracula* T (*for sigla see below, n. 2*)   *e* nomine Wlmerus nobili genere preclarus *add. in mg.*   *f–f* percussus *Miracula* P, perculsus languore *Miracula* T   *g* interiit *Miracula* P, occubuit *Miracula* T   *h* perdixisset *Miracula* P, dixisset *Miracula* T   *i* recubans *Miracula* P, recumbans *Miracula* T

---

[1] Campbell in *Encomium Emmae*, p. xliv n. 4 refers to 'Roger of Wendover's unsupported story (ed. Coxe, i. 448) that Eadric Streona went abroad with Emma, and remained with her two years'.

[2] *Miracula S. Eadmundi*. This extract retains some readings dropped by Samson's postulated version of the *Miracula*, whilst introducing readings either identical with, or close to, Samson's, as analysed and published by R. M. Thomson, 'Two versions of a saint's life from St Edmund's Abbey', *Revue bénédictine*, lxxxiv (1974), 385–408 at p. 404. The versions are in New York, Morgan Library MS M. 736 (*siglum* P) and London, BL Cotton MS Tiberius A. VIII (*siglum* T). The sick man is not identified in the Bury traditions, though a sick *uillanus* named Wulmar benefits from a miracle in Hermann's *De miraculis sancti Eadmundi* (*Memorials St Edmund's*, i. 80–3).

1020 n. a (p. 350)

Eodem etiam anno indictione .iii., Canutus rex Anglorum aliarumque gentium plurimarum, cum consilio et decreto archiepiscoporum, episcoporum, et optimatum suorum, maxime uero Ælfgyue, ^aid est Emme,^a regine sue et Alfuuini presulis Orientalium Anglorum,^b et Turkilli comitis, constituit monachos in monasterio quod Badriceswrde uocatur, in quo sanctissimus rex et martyr Eadmundus incorrupto corpore diem expectat beate resurrectionis. Prefecitque eis patrem et abbatem nomine Wium, uirum scilicet humilem, modestum, mansuetum et pium, presbiteros uero, qui inibi inordinate uiuebant aut in eodem loco ad religionis culmen erexit, aut datis aliis rebus de quibus habundantius solito uictum et uestitum haberent in alia loca mutauit.[1]

1031 n. d on p. 518 (B[1] near the opening of 1031 on p. 351)

Obiit Rodbertus rex Francie. Successit Heinricus filius eius.[2] Eodem anno obiit Gunnordis comitissa mater Ricardi secundi ducis Normannorum.[3]

1032 n. e (pp. 353-4)

^cIndictione xv,^c constructam basilicam apud Bedrichesuurtham beate memorie Dorobernensis archipresul Ægelnothus consecrauit in honore Christi et sancte Marie sanctique Eadmundi regis et martyris die .xv. kalend. Nouembris. Ipso tempore, sed et ante aliquot annos, id est anno .mxxviii. ^dsecundum Dionysium,^d indictione .xi., benignissimus rex Canutus concessit sanctissimo regi et martyri Eadmundo hoc priuilegium. In nomine poliarchis Iesu Christi saluatoris mundi totiusque creature creatoris, cuius diuino dominatui queque dominationes debito seruitio subnixe deseruiunt, cuius etiam omnipotentatui uniuersi potentatus obsecundari examussim^e preproperant, quia bonitas eius bonitatis est incomprehensibilis, et miseratio interminabilis, dapsilitas bonitatis ineffabilis, longanimitas quoque super prauorum nequitias quantitatis prolixitate cuiuslibet longior, qui cottidianis admonitionibus religiosam conuersationem ducentes monet, ut pie sectando iusticie culturam non eam deserendo linquant, quin potius perseuerabili instantia in eius cultura ut permaneant^f paterno^g affectu hortatur, qui nichilominus eadem affectione mandat pecccatoribus ut resipiscant, a suis iniquitatibus conuer-

---

^{a–a} id est Emme] *interlin.*   ^b *blank space follows*   ^{c–c} Indictione .xv.] *written below Dionysian year without indication of point of insertion*   ^{d–d} secundum Dionysium] *interlin.*   ^e id est diligentissime *add.* B[5]   ^f permaneant *from* permanent   ^g paterno *from* paterna

---

[1] Printed in *Memorials St Edmund's*, i. 341–2.
[2] Norman Annals. *AC, AMSM, AU,* (all 1031) and *AG* (1035).
[3] Norman Annals. *AC* and *AU.*

tentes, quia eorum execratur mortem. Eius amoris stimulo et fide suffultus cuius largiflua miseratione ego Cnut rex totius Albionis insule aliarumque nationum plurimarum in cathedra regali promotus, cum consilio et decreto archiepiscoporum, episcoporum, abbatum, comitum, aliorumque omnium meorum fidelium, elegi sanciendum atque perpeti stabilimento ab omnibus confirmandum, ut monasterium quod Badricesuurde nuncupatur sit per omne euum monachorum gregibus deputatum ad inhabitandum, et ab omni dominatione omnium episcopo-

P. 354   rum comitatus illius funditus liberum, ut in eo Domino seruientes[a] | monachi sine ulla inquietudine pro statu regni Dominum preualeant precari. Placuit etiam mihi hanc optionis electionem roborare priuilegio isto, in quo indere precepi libertatis donum, quod iam olim Eadmundus rex Occidentalium Saxonum largitus est suo equiuoco, pro nanciscenda eius gratia et mercede eterna, scilicet Eadmundo regi et martyri, quod bone ⟨uoluntatis⟩ uoto augere cupimus, quatinus eius promereri precibus merear portionem eius beatitudinis post huius cursum uite.

Tali libertate concedo fundo frui illi, in quo idem sanctus pausat, ut quotiens populus uniuersus persoluit censum Danis, uel ad naues seu ad arma, persoluant inhabitantes in ipso fundo eadem, ad usus quos elegerint fratres illius loci. Sitque nobis remedio hoc, mihi quippe, eque regine mee Ælfgeue, [b]id est Emme,[b] ac filiis nostris, omnibusque qui pridem ei hoc contulerunt.

Huic libertati concedo additamentum, scilicet maritimos pisces qui mihi contigere debeant annualiter per thelonei lucrum, et piscationem quam Vlfkytel habuit in Wylla, et omnia iura quarumcumque causarum in uillis que monasterio adiacent, et que adiciende sunt per gratiam Dei. Dedi quoque regine mee assensum, concedens ei pro sua elemosina dare .iiii. milia anguillarum cum muneribus que pertinent ad illas pro annuali censu in uilla que cognominatur Lakyngehythe. Si quislibet, quod absit, istam libertatem quoquolibet conatu nititur seruitutis iugo subigere, uel praua intentione transmutare, ut rursus clericos in eo collocet loco, sit addictus captiuitati eterne, carens sempiterna libertate, et mancipatus seruitio diaboli, eiusque consortio sit inextricabilibus habenis constrictus, nisi satisfatio eius erratui subueniat, quod prorsus optamus.

+ Ego Cnut rex gentis Anglorum aliarumque nationum nichilominus hoc priuilegium iussi componere, et compositum cum signo dominice crucis confirmando impressi.

+ Ego Ealfgyua [b]id est Emme[b] regina omni alacritate mentis hoc confirmaui.

+ Ego Ailnothus Cantuariensis archiepiscopus corroboraui.

+ Ego Wlstanus archiepiscopus Eboracensis consensi.

+ Ego Goduuinus episcopus confirmaui.

---

[a] seruientes *from* seruientis   [b-b] id est Emme] *interlin.*

+ Ego Ælfuuinus episcopus assensum dedi.
+ Ego Ealfsinus episcopus Wintoniensis*a* consignaui.
+ Ego Eathericus episcopus conclusi.
+ Ego Ealfuuinus episcopus roboraui.
+ Ego Brihtuuoldus episcopus*a* confirmaui.

+ Ego Yric dux.	+ Ego Goduuinus dux.
+ Ego Vlf dux.	+ Ego Eglaf dux.
+ Ego Hacun dux.	+ Ego Leofuuinus dux.
+ Ego Godricus dux.	+ Ego Leofricus abbas.
+ Ego Ealfuuardus abbas.	+ Ego Eathelstanus abbas.
+ Ego Ealfsinus abbas.	+ Ego Leofuuinus abbas.
+ Ego Wlfredus abbas.	+ Ego Oskytelus abbas.
+ Ego Oslacus miles.	+ Ego Thoredus miles.
+ Ego Turhkyllus miles.	+ Ego Thrym miles.
+ Ego Brother miles.	+ Ego Ealfricus miles.
+ Ego Ealfuuinus miles.	+ Ego Ealfuuius miles.
+ Ego Ealfricus.	+ Ego Leofsinus.
+ Ego Ealfricus.	+ Ego Leofricus.

+ Ego Thurkyllus Eastanglorum comes libenter consilium dedi.[1]

1042 n. f (p. 358 with margin mutilated)

[V]enerabilis abbas Ramesiensis ⟨ecc⟩lesie Æthelstanus in uigilia sancti Mi[ch]aelis archangeli infra ecclesiam [per] uespertinalem sinaxim, a quodam [ ] alienigena absque culpa cum [mar]tello perfossus, occisus est, et Alf⟨wi⟩nus prepositus eiusdem loci dono Ædwar[di] regis ei in abbatiam successit.[2]

1047 n. a (B[1] at line-end on p. 359)

Bellum apud Uallium Dunas.[3]

1054 n. a (B[1] at line-end on p. 365)

Bellum apud Mare Mortuum.[4]

a interlin.

---

[1] S 980 K 735. Printed in *Memorials St Edmund's*, i. 342–4.
[2] This addition is based on information available to the author of the Ramsey Chronicle.
[3] Norman Annals. This battle is recorded in *AU*, *AG* (both 1047), *AC* (1046), and *AMSM* (1048).
[4] Norman Annals. This battle is recorded in *AU*, *AG*, *AC* and *AMSM*.

1065 n. a on p. 596 (pp. 370–2)

Leofstanus abbas decessit .xvii. kalend. Augusti die saturni. Successit ei
uir uenerandus abbas Balduuinus, genere Gallus, natus scilicet apud
Carnotum, nutritus ac monachus professus in nobile monasterio sancti
Dionisii, rexitque ecclesiam sancti Eadmundi annis .xxxii., mensibus .v.
Iste preclarus uir tam uita religiosa quam insigni doctrina idem monasterium, a Domino Iesu Christo et a rege Anglorum Eadwardo Ætheldredi
filio sibi canonice et catholice creditum ut uerus Christianus fideliter rexit,
de bono in melius strenue prouexit et terris atque maximis possessionibus
copiosissime augmentauit. Gloriosus rex Willelmus, qui primus ex
Normannorum gente prudentia sua et fortitudine totam Angliam suo
p. 371 sub|iugauit imperio, hanc licentiam et facultatem eidem Balduuino con-
tulit, ut quocunque modo posset terras ecclesie sancti Eadmundi adiceret
uel pecunia eas a uicinis suis redimendo, uel dono ipsorum proprio et
spontanea eorum uoluntate adquirendo. Vnde factum est ut plures liberos
homines quos sokemannos uocamus et illorum homagia adquireret, et
eorum adquisitione monasterium suum locupletaret. Cum autem his atque
aliis modis infinitis honor per eum creuisset ecclesie, creuit in quibusdam
et exarsit insatiabilis fames auaritie, ita ut eundem locum inuaderent, et
suo eum dominio subiugare temptarent. Extitit malicie huius exactor et
princeps quidam Erfastus Tedfordensis episcopus, qui propter cupiditatem
possessionum, apud sanctum Dei Eadmundum sibi constituere uolebat
episcopatum. Orta uero tali de causa inter episcopum et abbatem graui
contentione et graui controuersia, domnus Baldewinus abbas consilio et
auxilio famosissimi regis Willelmi Romam profectus est, domnumque
Alexandrum papam secundum in sede beati Petri principantem inuenit. A
quo benigne et diligenter susceptus, maximo honori et uenerationi habitus,
insigne priuilegium ad gloriam et laudem beati regis et martyris Eadmundi
optinuit, cuius premunitione eandem ecclesiam usque ad finem seculi in
maxima libertate Deo protegente collocauit. Fuit autem cum domino papa
conuersans aliquantis diebus, donec eum ad ordinem presbiterii promoueret, et quibusdam dignitatibus ultra quosdam abbates honorifice
insigniret. Dedit ei uirgam pastoralem et anulum, curamque illi delegauit
animarum. Altare preterea quoddam ex porphiritico lapide pretiosum, et
in honore beate Dei genitricis et sanctissimi regis Eadmundi solenniter ab
ipso consecratum, cum maxima dulcedine et dulci deuotione abbati
Baldewino dominus papa dedit, eique in hec uerba denuntiauit, dicens: si
totum regnum Anglorum aliqua excommunicationis causa a diuino cessaret
officio, quandiu altare istud integrum et illibatum custodire poteritis, nunquam a sacris missarum solenniis pro aliqua prohibitione nisi dominus
papa hoc nominatim interdixerit cessabitis. Et, ut in priuilegio subsequenti
patebit, ex auctoritate Dei et beati Petri apostolorum principis et sanctorum canonum sanciuit et confirmauit ut idem locus sub abbatis regimine

in perpetuum ordini monastico deseruiat, neque aliqua ecclesiastica aut secularis persona eundem in sedem episcopalem conuertat. Priuilegium uero ita incipit. Alexander episcopus seruus seruorum Dei dilecto in Christo filio Baldoguino abbati monasterii sancti Eadmundi quod Badricesuurde nuncupatur in Anglia constituti, eiusque successoribus in perpetuum. Quanquam sedes apostolica uniuersalis mater et omnium ecclesiarum princeps uniuersas ecclesias communi iure et dispositione contineat, plereque tamen inueniuntur, que in singulare patrocinium sancte Romane ecclesie commendari, ac proprie eius iuri applicari ac summitti cupiunt, quatinus singulari prouidentia et caritate sue matris amplexe, usquequaque liberiores et munitiores existant, et ad exercenda diuine seruitutis obsequia, inde tranquillitatis, et presidii munitiones accipiant, unde magisterium sacre traditionis expectant. Si igitur in eadem apostolica sede presidenti hec sollicitudo et cura singularis incumbit, ut ex ipsa consideratione regiminis omnibus tam in defensione et corroboratione diligentiam, quam in spiritali speculatione et doctrina uigilantiam, quantum Deo auxiliante preualet, circumferre debeat, ualde congruit, ut si quando ea que ad honorem et utilitatem ecclesiarum Dei pertinent ab eo postulantur benigna donatione concedat et ad sinum matris, id est, sancte Romane ecclesie domicilium proprie commendationis deuotione fluentes, egregia benignitate affectuque custodiendi suscipiat. Nos itaque, dilectissime fili Baldoguine, in apostolatus administratione non nostris meritis sed diuina locati gratia, equitatem tue postulationis et commisse tibi congregationis necnon karissimi filii | nostri Guillelmi regis benigna interpellationis uota attendentes, uidelicet ut predictum monasterium sancti Eadmundi, cui diuina dispositione preesse dinosceris, in tutelam et defensionem sancte Romane ecclesie susciperemus eiusque statum et attinentia bona apostolici priuilegii firmamento muniremus. Cum omni beniuolentia et caritate uobis concedendum esse peruidimus. Quapropter in hac presenti sanctionis nostre pagina, salua quidem in omnibus huius sancte sedis reuerentia, concedimus et confirmamus tibi tuisque successoribus prefatum monasterium cum omnibus que nunc sibi iure pertinent, aut in futurum Deo annuente ibi conferenda sint, ut sine omni molestia et inquietudine illud in uestra gubernatione teneatis, statuentes et apostolica auctoritate corroborantes, ut idem monasterium in hoc statu et monastico ordine perpetua stabilitate permaneat, nec aliqua potestas secularis aut ecclesiastica eundem uenerabilem locum ad episcopalem sedem mutare possit aut debeat, et quecunque donationes rerum aut libertatis eidem monasterio regiis statutis et preceptis tradite sint aut in posterum pro Dei nomine conferende, ex nostra apostolica confirmatione rate illibateque permaneant, salua apostolice sedis reuerentia. Igitur ad honorem Dei et utilitatem predicti monasterii cupientes hanc nostram constitutionem sempiterna stabilitate teneri, sancimus et apostolica auctoritate firmamus, ut nullus rex, dux, comes,

p. 392

episcopus, abbas seu aliqua persona secularis aut ecclesiastica iam sepe fatum monasterium uel fratres ibi Deo seruientes inquietare presumat, nec aliquid eorum que nunc iure habet aut in futurum Deo concedente adquisierit cuiuscunque modi sint, ab eo alienare aut inuadendo diripere, nec aliqua occasione uexare aut sine licentia abbatis tenere audeat. Si quis autem temerario ausu hec nostra statuta contaminare presumpserit aut infringere, anathematis laqueo se innodatum, et iudicio superni iudicis plectendum esse cognoscat. Qui uero pie deuotionis intuitu huius nostre sanctionis custos et obseruator extiterit, et bona sua ad amplificationem eiusdem monasterii contulit, aut conferre studuerit, apostolice benedictionis gratiam consequatur et eterne retributionis gloria repleatur. Bene ualete. Deus nostrum refugium et uirtus; magnus Dominus noster et magna uirtus eius. Datum Lateranis .vi. kalend. Nouembris, per manus Petri sancte Romane ecclesie presbiteri cardinalis ac bibliothecarii, anno .xi. pontificatus domni Alexandri secundi pape, anno uidelicet dominice incarnationis millesimo septuagesimo primo, indictione septima.[1]

1066 n. e on p. 598 (pp. 373–5)

Quamuis Eaduuardus rex secularibus curis multum esset occupatus abiect⸢is⸣ tamen plerumque noxiis honoribus, diuinorum studiorum erat indagator feruidus. Vnde rex regum multa ei archana reuelauit, et nonnulla de futuris sicut seniorum relatione didicimus insinuauit. Nam quondam apud Westmonasterium in die pasce dum regalem curiam regali more tenuisset et peractis diuini cultus misteriis diademate redimitus regiam ᵃcum regaliᵃ tripudio repetisset, dominici corporis et sanguinis sacramento saciatus ad prandium resedit, ibique diuinitus supra se ductus, mira et relatu digna uidere promeruit. Cunctis enim qui ad mensam regis sedebant silentibus et auide post quadragesimale ieiunium commedentibus, rex subito uocem suam in risu exaltauit nimiumque, aperte ridens, omnium commedentium oculos ad se prouocauit. Mirantibus itaque cunctis quod sine causa ut putabant risisset, nemo tamen ausus fuit palam interrogare cur hoc euenisset. Peracto autem prandio cum iam in conclaui intrasset et diadema ut moris est deposuisset, Haroldus dux cum duobus proceribus quorum unus erat presul alter abbas, secreto dixit ei. 'Rem insolitam, domine rex, hodie uidimus, unde nos omnes ualde mirati sumus.' Cumque rex interrogasset quid fuit hoc, respondit: 'Nunquam te tam aperte ridentem sine causa, sicut hodie uidimus.' At ille ait: 'Mira uidi, ideoque non sine causa risi.' Tunc illi tres proceres tantum uirum de

---

ᵃ⁻ᵃ cum regali] *mg. with signe de renvoi; the corrector may have overlooked the insertion of* curiam, *which presumably preceded* cum regali

---

[1] Printed in *Memorials St Edmund's*, i. 343–7, and in *The Pinchbeck Register*, ed. Francis Hervey (2 vols., Brighton 1925), i. 3–4.

uanitate non estimantes taliter risisse, ceperunt suppliciter illum rogare, ut occasionem tante leticie dignaretur illis intimare. Cumque multis precibus ab illis coactus fuisset, ait, 'Plusquam ducenti anni sunt ex quo septem dormientes in spelunca in monte Celio apud Ephesum super dextrum latus quieuerunt, sed nunc postquam epulari cepimus super sinistrum latus conuersi sunt, et super illud usque ad septuaginta .iiii. annos iacebunt. Hec nimirum conuersio, dirum omen portendit mortalibus. Nam ea que Dominus in euangelio minatur in his .lxxiiii. annis multis modis perficientur, nam surget gens contra gentem et regnum aduersus regnum, et terre motus magni erunt per loca et pestilentie et fames | terroresque de celo, et signa magna erunt. Bella et oppressiones gentium, genus humanum incomparabiliter torquebunt, et multorum regnorum mutationes erunt. Gentiles in Christianos insurgent, et nichilominus Christiani paganos Christi uirtute conterent.' Hec itaque audientes obstupuerunt, et qui septem dormientes fuerint percunctati sunt. Quibus rex ait, 'Temporibus Decii imperatoris .vii. nobiles uiri apud Ephesum comprehensi sunt, et pro Christi nomine plurima tormenta perpessi sunt. Tandem in speluncam sub monte Celio ingressi sunt, ibique iussu perfidi cesaris imperiales ministri ostium spelunce magnis lapidibus obstruxerunt, et sancti testes Christi .cclxxii. annis quasi una nocte sine metu et angore obdormierunt, et adhuc ibidem requiescunt. Nomina uero eorum si scire uultis, hec sunt, Maximianus, Malchus, Martinianus, Dionisius, Iohannes, Serapion et Constantinus.' Deinde retulit eis formas eorum et qualitates, acsi eius semper fuissent sodales. His auditis prefati proceres cum admiratione a rege recesserunt, et mox .iii. legatos unusquisque ordinis sui ad indagandam ueritatem preparare decreuerunt. Haroldus enim dux militem, episcopus clericum, et abbas monachum cum regiis muneribus et litteris sigillo regis Eadwardi signatis direxerunt Manicheti Constantinopolitano imperatori, poscentes ut regis Eaduuardi nuntiis iuberet .vii. dormientes ostendi. Maniches autem imperator legatos cum muneribus de tam longe uenientes benigne suscepit, et deduci eos ad episcopum Ephesiorum fecit, eique ut Anglicis peregrinis predictos dormientes monstraret precepit. At ille per omnia iussis imperatoris obediuit. Nam causam cur Greciam appetissent libenter audiuit, cum clero et populo ad speluncam eos adduxit, et deuote cum aromatibus introduxit, ibique sanctos dormientes eis cum summa reuerentia ostendit. Anglici uero legati ut speluncam ingressi sunt, omnia indicia de sanctis dormientibus que rex Eaduuardus in Anglia retulerat inuenerunt et oblatis muneribus Deo gratias agentes leti ad propria regressi sunt. Episcopus autem Ephesiorum et omnes indigene qui hoc audierunt uehementer admirantes Deum laudauerunt, qui regi ad mensam residenti Lundonie liquido enucleauerit, quid in abdito Celionensis[a] spelunce erga sanctos suos operatus fuerit, et

p. 374

---

[a] Celionensis *from* Celiensis

per transmarinos Saxones Ephesiis qualiter se haberent sui contubernales nescientibus propalauerit. Subsequenti tempore uaticinium regis Eaduuardi terrigene ueris celeriter experti sunt. Nam eodem ut opinor anno Henricus Francorum rex, militia et bonitate laudabilis, potione accepta et male seruata obiit, eique Philippus puer filius suus sub tutela Balduini Flandrensium satrape in regno successit. Circa hec tempora Henricus Cononis filius bonus imperator Romanorum obiit, et Henricus filius eius patre tam seculari quam spirituali probitate ualde inferior successit, cuius tempore multas perturbationes grauissimas ecclesia Dei et Romanus orbis per ipsum pertulit. In his .vii. annis .iii. pape Victor et Stephanus ac Nicholaus defuncti sunt, et apostolicam sedem uicissitudine tali contristauerunt. Non nostri propositi est describere quantas tribulationes Greci perpessi sunt, dum post mortem Manichetis, Diogenes et Michalis et Butinacius et Alexius de imperiali*a* sede uicissim sese precipitauerunt, et multum sanguinis proprio*b* uel alieno mucrone in factione talium pro fauore partis amice effuderunt. Agareni et Arabes et Turci ac Commagene alieque barbare gentes Christo resistente⟨s⟩ in Christianos surrexerunt, et Syriam Liciamque aliaque regna sibi uicina depopulati sunt, ecclesias destruxerunt, iniuriisque multis Christicolas oppresserunt. Vesania nempe huiusmodi per annos .xl. paga|ni contra Christianos debachati sunt, donec Vrbano papa instigante occidentales Christiani arma sumpserunt, relictis opibus et fundis cum caris pignoribus peregre profecti sunt, et Niceam et Antiochiam ipsamque Ierusalem, primitiue ecclesie sedem aliasque multas urbes et oppida ceperunt, ac innumera gentilium agmina subueniente Deo diuersis in locis diuersisque modis strauerunt. Quid de Anglia dicam? Quid posteris referam? Ve tibi est Anglia que olim sancta prole fulsisti Anglicam, sed nunc pro peccatis ualde gemis anxia. Naturalem regem tuum perdidisti, et alienigene bello cum ingenti tuorum sanguine fuso succubuisti. Filii tui miserabiliter in te occisi sunt, et consiliarii principesque tui uincti seu necati uel exhereditati sunt. Sicut in his prouinciis, quas ex uicinitate nouimus, multa bellorum et famis ac pestilentie aliorumque malorum aduersa euenisse describimus, sic sine dubio in aliis regionibus quas pro longinquitate minus nouimus, iuxta prophetiam eius contigisse pro certo scimus.[1] *Rex* noster *Eaduuardus ante natalis sui diem Deo est electus, unde ad regnum non tam ab hominibus quam diuinitus est consecratus. Cuius consecrationis dignitatem sancta conseru-*

a imperiali *from* imperiale   *b* proprio *from* propria

---

[1] Published and discussed as representing the earliest version of Edward's vision of the Seven Sleepers in F. Barlow, 'The *Vita Ædwardi* (Book II); the Seven Sleepers: some further evidence and reflections', *Speculum*, xl (1965), 385–97. See also *The Life of King Edward*, ed. F. Barlow, 2nd ed. (OMT, 1992), pp. 102–10.

ans castimonia, omnem uitam agebat Deo dicatam in uera innocentia. Quam Deus in holocaustum acceptionis approbans, ex affectu intimo eum fecit carum hominibus, et uenerabilem cum supernis ciuibus. Nam sicut bonis et idoneis uiris contestificantibus comperimus, his in hac corruptibili uita signis glorificauit eum Deus.[2] *Quidam cecus somnio suasum sibi astipulabatur quia si ex aqua qua rex manus abluisset ceca eius facies lauaretur, et cecitatem pelleret,*[3] *et uisionem reuelatum dixit quod ex aqua ablutionis eius cecitati sue proueniret medela, facie lota cecitas euanescit. Assertorque permanet in* presens uel qualiter sibi irruerint tenebre et qualiter cesserint pulse, oppitulante beato Eadwardo rege.*[a]*[4]

1066 n. c on p. 606 (377–9)

Regnante autem Eadwardo quem ex sorore Ricardi secundi *comitis Nortmannorum, Imma nomine, rex Anglorum Ægelredus filium susceperat, monasteriorum que usque id temporis destructioni supererant, plurima destructio facta est. Qua tempestate Goduuinus Cantie comes magnus per Angliam terra marique habebatur. Hic orto inter regem et illum graui discidio* [b]*propter* Eustachium Bononiensem comitem, ut prelibauimus,[b] *exul ab Anglia cum suis omnibus fore iudicatus est. Iuit itaque ad comitem Balduuinum in Flandriam, et Haroldus filius eius in Hiberniam. Hinc, matre regis Imma defuncta, Godwinus et Haroldus in Angliam reuersi sunt, numerosis uterque nauibus et ualida militum manu uallatus. Quod multi principum regis agnoscentes, et bellum hinc inde moueri horrescentes, ut pax utrinque fieret institerunt. At rex, Goduuini uersutias suspectui habens, restitit, nec paci adquiescere uoluit, nisi primo quibus sibi securitas pararetur obsides haberet. Wlnothus itaque filius Goduuini et Hacun filius Suani filii sui obsides dantur, ac in Normanniam Willelmo comiti, filio scilicet Roberti filii Ricardi fratris matris sue, custodiendi destinantur. Quibus gestis, Goduuinus mala morte post breue tempus interiit, et Haroldus filius eius commitatum Cantie patri succedens obtinuit. Is, elapso modico tempore, licentiam petiuit a rege Normanniam ire et fratrem suum atque nepotem qui obsides tenebantur liberare, liberatos reducere. Cui rex, 'hoc', inquit, 'non fiet per me. Verumtamen, ne uidear te uelle impedire, permitto ut eas quo uis ac experiare quid possis. Presentio tamen te in nichil aliud tendere nisi in detrimentum totius Anglici regni et opprobrium tui. Nec enim ita noui comitem mentis expertem, ut eos aliquatenus uelit concedere tibi, si non prescierit in hoc magnum proficuum sui.' Ascendit itaque Haroldus nauem, suo* magis[c] *quam regis consilio credens, cum*

---

[a] *an erased note follows (presumably referring to the misplaced addition printed below as 1066 n. g):* hic debet scriberi quod scribit in subsequenti folio ? regis Edwardi [b-b] propter . . . prelibauimus] *add. in mg. with signe de renvoi* [c] *interlin.*

---

[2] ibid., pp. 90–2.
[3] ibid., p. 94.   [4] ibid., p. 96.

*ditioribus et honestioribus hominibus suis, auro et argento uesteque pretiosa
nobiliter instructis. Mare turbulentum nauigantes exterritat et nauem undarum
cumulus uehementer exagitat. Eiecta tandem cum omnibus que ferebat in
Pontium fluuium qui Maia uocatur, a domino terre illius pro ritu loci captiuitati addicitur, et homines in ea consistentes diligentiori custodie mancipantur.
Constrictus igitur Haroldus, quemlibet ex uulgo promissa mercede illectum clam*

p. 378   *ad comitem Normannie dirigit, | exponere illi quid sibi contigerit. At ille festi-
nato per nuncios mandat domino Pontiui Haroldum cum suis ab omni calumnia
liberum sibi quantotius mitti si pristina amicitia sua amodo uellet ex more
potiri. Sed cum ille hominem dimittere nollet, iterum in mandato accepit, se
necessario Haroldum missurum alioquin certissime sciret Willelmum Normannie
ducem armatum pro eo Pontiuum iturum. Mittit igitur uirum cum sociis, primo
tamen eis que meliora detulerant simul ablatis. Hinc ad Willelmum Haroldus
ueniens, honorifice suscipitur. Et audito cur patriam exierit, bene quidem rem
processuram, si in ipso non remaneret, Willelmus respondit. Tenuit ergo uirum
aliquot diebus circa se, et in mora illa more prudentis aperuit ei quod habebat
in mente. Dicebat itaque regem Eadwardum quando secum iuuene olim iuuenis[a]
in Normannia demoraretur, sibi interposita fide sua pollicitum fuisse quia si rex
Anglie foret, ius regni in illum iure hereditario post se transferret. Et subdens
ait: 'Tu quoque si mihi te in hoc ipso adminiculaturum spoponderis, et insuper
castellum Dofris cum puteo aque ad opus meum te facturum, sororemque tuam
quam uni de principibus meis dem in uxorem te ad me tempore quo nobis conue-
niet destinaturum, necne filiam meam te in coniugem accepturum fore promis-
eris, tunc et modo nepotem tuum, et cum in Angliam regnaturus uenero,
fratrem tuum incolumem recipies. In quo regno si aliquando tuo fauore fuero
confirmatus, spondeo quia omne quod a me tibi rationabiliter concedi petieris,
obtinebis.' Sensit Haroldus in his periculum undique, nec intellexit qua
euaderet, nisi in omnibus istis uoluntati Willelmi adquiesceret. Adquieuit itaque.
At ille, ut omnia rata manerent, prolatis sanctorum reliquiis ad hoc Haroldum
perduxit, quatinus super illas iurando testaretur, se cuncta que conuenerant
inter eos opere completurum, nisi communi mortalibus sorte presenti uite pre-
riperetur. His ita gestis, Haroldus, adepto nepote, in patriam suam reuersus est.
Vbi uero quid acciderit, quid egerit regi percunctanti narrauit, 'Nonne dixi
tibi', ait, 'me Willelmum nosse et in illo itinere tuo plurima mala huic regno
contingere posse?' In breui post hec obiit Eadwardus, [b]Anglorum decus,[b] et
iuxta quod ipse ante mortem statuerat in regnum ei successit Haroldus. Dein
uenit nuncius in Angliam a prefato Willelmo directus, expetens sororem
Haroldi, iuxta quod conuenerat Willelmo et illi. Alia etiam que uiolato sacramento seruata non erant, calumniatus est. Ad que Haroldus hoc modo fertur
respondisse: 'soror mea, quam iuxta condictum expetis, mortua est, quod si corpus eius quale nunc est uult comes habere, mittam, ne iudicer sacramentum uio-
lasse quod feci. Castellum Dofris et in eo puteum aque, licet nesciam cui, ut*

---

[a] *iuuenis from* iuuenes   [b-b] Anglorum decus] *mg. without signe de renvoi*

nobis conuenit, expleui. Regnum quod necdum fuit *meum, quo iure potui dare uel promittere? Si de filia sua quam debui in uxorem, ut asserit, ducere agit, super regnum Anglie mulierem extraneam, inconsultis principibus, me nec debere nec sine grandi iniuria posse adducere nouerit.' Reuersus nuncius, responsa retulit domino suo. Quibus ille auditis, iterum ei amica familiaritate mandauit, quatinus aliis omissis, seruata fidei sponsione saltem filiam suam uxorem duceret alioquin se promissam regni successionem armis sibi uendicaturum*[a]* procul dubio sciret. At ipse nec illud quidem se facere uelle, nec hoc formidare respondit. Vnde Willelmus indignatus, magna spe uincendi belli ex hac Haroldi iniusticia est animatus. Parata igitur classe, Angliam petit *[b]*usque huc*[b]* consertoque graui prelio, Haroldus in acie cecidit et Willelmus uictor regnum obtinuit. De quo prelio testantur adhuc Franci qui interfuerunt quoniam, licet uarius casus hinc inde extiterit, tamen tanta strages ac fuga Normannorum fuit, ut uictoria qua potiti sunt uere et absque dubio soli miraculo Dei ascribenda sit, qui puniendo per hanc iniquum periurii scelus Haroldi, ostendit se non Deum esse uolentem iniquitatem. Rex itaque factus Willelmus, quid in principes Anglorum qui tante cladi superesse poterant fecerit, dicere cum nichil prosit, omitto.* Quid enim prodesset si nec unum in toto regno de illis dicerem pristina potestate uti permissum, sed omnes aut in grauem paupertatis erumnam | detrusos, aut exhered⟨it⟩atos patria pulsos, aut oculis effosis uel ceteris amputatis membris opprobrium hominum factos, aut certe miserrime afflictos uita priuatos? Simili modo utilitate carere existimo dicere quid in minorem populum non solum ab eo sed etiam a suis actum sit, cum id dictu sciamus difficile, et ob inmanem crudelitatem fortassis incredible. *Vsus ergo atque leges quas patres sui et ipse in Normannia habere solebant in Anglia seruare uolens, de huiusmodi personis episcopos, abbates et alios principes per totam terram instituit de quibus indignum iudicaretur si per omnia suis legibus, postposita omni alia consideratione, non obedirent, et si ullus eorum pro qua uis terreni honoris potentia caput contra eum leuare auderet, scientibus cunctis unde qui ad quid assumpti fuerint. Cuncta ergo diuina simul et humana eius nutum expectabant. Non ergo pati uolebat quemquam in omni dominatione sua constitutum Romane urbis pontificem pro apostolico nisi se iubente recipere, aut eius litteras si primitus sibi ostense non fuissent illo pacto suscipere. Primatem quoque regni sui archiepiscopum dico Cantuariensem seu Dorobernensem, si coacto generali episcoporum concilio praesideret non sinebat quicquam statuere aut prohibere, nisi que sue uoluntati accommoda, et a se primo essent ordinata. Nulli nichilominus episcoporum suorum concessum iri permittebat, ut aliquem* nominatum uirum de ipsorum parochia, *siue incestu siue adulterio, siue aliquo capitali crimine denotatum publice nisi eius precepto* argueret *aut excommunicaret ut ulla ecclesiastica* lege *constringeret.*[1]

p. 379

---

[a] uendicaturum *from* uindicaturum   *[b–b]* usque huc] *interlin.*

---

[1] *Eadmeri historia novorum in Anglia*, ed. M. Rule (RS lxxxi; London, 1884), pp. 5–10.

INDEX OF MANUSCRIPTS CITED

INDEX OF CHARTERS CITED

CONCORDANCE

Thorpe, i	This edition	Thorpe, i	This edition
85	290–2	137	406–8
86	292	138	408–10
87	292–4	139	412–14
88	294–6	140	414–16
89	296–8	141	416–20
90	298–300	142	420–2
91	300–2	143	422–4
92	302–6	144	424–6
93	306	145	426–30
94	306–8	146	430–2
95	308–10	147	432–4
96	310–12	148	434–8
97	312–14	149	438–40
98	314–18	150	440–2
99	318	151	442–4
100	318–20	152	444–6
101	320–4	153	446–8
102	324–6	154	448–50
103	326–8	155	450–2
104	328–30	156	452–4
105	330	157	454–6
106	330–2	158	456–8
107	332–4	159	458–60
108	334–6	160	460–2
109	336–8	161	462–4
110	338–40	162	464–6
111	340–2	163	466–8
112	342–4	164	468–70
113	344	165	470
114	344–8	166	470–2
115	348–50	167	472–4
116	350–4	168	474–6
117	354	169	476–8
118	354–8	170	478–80
119	358–60	171	480–2
120	360–4	172	482–4
121	364–6	173	484
122	366–8	174	484–6
123	368–70	175	486–8
124	370–2	176	488–90
125	372–4	177	490
126	374–6	178	490–2
127	376–8	179	492–4
128	378–80	180	494–6
129	380–2	181	502–4
130	382–6	182	504
131	386–8	183	506–8
132	388–94	184	508–10
133	394–6	185	510–12
134	398–400	186	512–14
135	400–2	187	514–16
136	402–6	188	516–18

Thorpe, i	This edition	Thorpe, i	This edition
189	518–20	210	570–2
190	520	211	572–4
191	520–2	212	574–6
192	522–6	213	576–8
193	526–8	214	578–80
194	528–30	215	580–2
195	530–2	216	582–4
196	532–4	217	584–6
197	534–6	218	586–8
198	536–40	219	588–90
199	540–2	220	590
200	542–4	221	590–2
201	544–8	222	592–6
202	548–50	223	596–8
203	550–2	224	598–600
204	552–8	225	600–2
205	558–60	226	602–4
206	560–2	227	604
207	562–6	228	604–6
208	566–8	229	606
209	568–70		

GENERAL INDEX

Hwita, bishop of Lichfield 184-5, 194-5, 200-1
Hygeberht, archbishop of Lichfield 218-19, 220-1
Hypatius, consul 26-7
Hywel Dda, Welsh prince 380-1, 386-7
Hywel, underking, probably son of Idwal 422-3

Iacob, underking, probably Iago ab Idwal, king of Gwynedd 422-3
Iago ab Idwal, see Iacob
Icanho, monastery at 104-5
Icel, Penda's forebear 86-7
Ida, king of Bernicia 54-5, 68-9
  Ceolwulf's forebear 180-1
  father of Eadric 204-5
Idwal, Welsh prince 380-1
Illus, consul 20-1
Immin, Mercian leader 108-9
Incuneningum, see Cunningham
Ine, West Saxon king, son of Cenred 148-9
  and Glastonbury 148-9, 150 n.
  people of Kent make peace with 156-7
  wars with Geraint 168-9
  fights Ceolred at 'Woden's Barrow' 172-3
  kills the atheling Cynewulf 176-7
  had built fort at Taunton 176-7
  fights the South Saxons twice 176-7
  kills the atheling Eadberht 176-7
  resigns kingdom and goes to Rome 178-9, 260-1
  Alfred's forebear 260-1
  and Abingdon 610
Ingels, see Ingild
Ingild:
  Alfred's forebear 260-1
  brother of Ine 174-5
Inguar, Danish king 286-7, 444-5
  brother of Healfdene 308-9, 364-5
Ingui, Ida's forebear 54-5
Ingwald, bishop of London 128-9
Inis-Celtra 536-7
Inn, river 366-7
Innocent II, pope xxxv, lii
Innocent III, pope liv
Inportunus, Flavius, consul 28-9
interpolations:
  in JW MSS LP 609-15
  in JW MS B 619-53
Iohannes, consul (456) 8-9

Iohannes, consul (467) 14-15
Iohannes Gibbus, consul 24-5
Iohannes Scytha, consul 24-5
Iona, monastery of 62-3, 172-3
Ipswich, laid waste by the Danes 438-9
Ireland:
  enriched with miracles 124-5
  invaded by Northumbrians 140-1
Irish, pirates 550-3
Isaac, count of Cambrai 636
Isidore, bishop of Seville 94-5
Itermod, Alfred's forebear 262-3
Ithamar, bishop of Rochester 96-7, 102-3, 110-11
Iuchil, underking 422-3
Iudanbyrig 402-3
Ives, St 74-5
  discovery of his body 450-1
  rests at Crowland 556-7

Jænberht, archbishop of Canterbury, abbot of St Augustine's 204-5, 212-13
  loses jurisdiction over Lichfield 218-19
Jaruman, bishop of the Mercians xxv, xliii, xlviii, lv, lxi, 108-9, 118-19
  sent to the East Saxons 114-15
Jerusalem:
  captured by the Persians 78-9
  pilgrimages to 570-1, 584-5, 597-9
Jews, in Spain, become Christian 92-3
Jocelin de Bohun, bishop of Salisbury xliii, lv
Jocelin of Brakelond liii
Jocelin of Wells, bishop of Bath lv
John, first abbot of Athelney, an Old Saxon 300-1, 326-7
John, the archcantor 130-1, 136-7
John, bishop of Hexham 144-5
  bishop of York 146-7
  his ordinations as bishop 156-7, 162-3, 176-7
  retires and dies 176-7
John I, bishop of Rochester xxiv, xxxvii, xlvii, lx
John I, emperor 418-19
John, a holy man in Sicily 619
John, monk at St Andrew's on the Caelian Hill 70-1
John I, pope 32-3, 34-5
John II, pope 36-7, 48-9
John III, pope 60-1, 62-3, 64-5
John IV, pope 86-7, 92-3

Pybba:
  Offa's forebear 198–9
  Penda's forebear 86–7
Pyrrhus, bishop of Constantinople 92–5, 130–1

Quentavic 256–7

Rædwald, king of East Anglia 82–3, 246–7
  father of Earpwald 88–9
Ræthhun, bishop of Leicester 264–5, 276–7
Ragnald, king of the Danes 382–3
Ragnald, king of Northumbria 396–7, 398–9
Ralph, earl, son of Goda 558–9, 576–7, 582–3
Ralph of Burgundy, king of the West Franks 634–5
Ralph d'Escures, archbishop of Canterbury, bishop of Rochester xxiii, xxiv
Ralph Luffa, bishop of Chichester xxiv
Ramleh, Arab prince of 594–7
Ramsbury, bishops of, see Æthelstan, Oda, Oswulf, Ælfgar (for Wulfgar?), Ælfstanus, Sigeric, Ælfric, Brihtwold, Hereman
Ramsey:
  monastery of 438–9, 546–7, 554–5
  Bishop Ælfweard retires to 540–1
  burial place 98–9, 440–1, 520–1
  relics at 554–7
  Wynsige monk of 418–19
  abbots of, see Æthelstan, Ælfwine
Rannulf Flambard, bishop of Durham xxvi, xxxviii, xliii, lvi, lxii
Ratger, abbot of Fulda 238–9, 240–1
Ratisbon, bishop of 594–5
Ravenna:
  and Theoderic 22–3, 24–5, 34–5
  army of, frustrates Justinian II 154–5
  metropolitan see of 234–5
Reading:
  and the Danes 288–9, 458–9
  burnt by the Danes 458–9
  monastery at 538–41
Reavenswart, Tostig's Danish housecarl 598–9
Reccared, king of the Visigoths 64–5
Reculver, monastery of 156–7
Redemptus, bishop of Ferentis 64–5

Reichenau:
  bodies of SS Valentine and Genesius come to 250–1
  the Blood of Christ flows from His image at 384–5
Reims:
  metropolitan see of 234–5
  archbishops of, see Fulk, Heriveus, Seulf, Artaud
  monastery of Saint-Rémy 552–3, 635, 640
  abbots of Saint-Rémy, see Herimar
Reinhelm, bishop of Hereford xxv, 322–3
Remigius, St, bishop of Reims 16–17, 18–19
Reoric, island shelter 370–1
Repton:
  monastery of 158–9, 198–9
  mausoleum of King Wigmund 262–3
  Danes winter in 304–5
Rethun, abbot of Abingdon 610
Rhaetia 4 n., 250–1
Rhigyfarch 13 n., 53 n.
Rhine, river 256–7, 636
Rhiwallon, brother of Gruffyyd 596–7
Rhuddlan, Harold sets out for 592–3
Rhys, brother of Gruffydd ap Rhydderch 572–3
Ricberht, slayer of Earpwald 88–9
Riccall 602–3
Richard, abbot of Fulda 506–7, 528–9
Richard (the Justiciar), here called duke of Burgundy 350–1
Richard I, duke of Normandy 396–7, 641
Richard II, duke of Normandy 474–5, 508–9, 641
Richard III, duke of Normandy 508–9
Richard, son of Scrob 570–1
Richard de Belmeis I, bishop of London xxiv, xlii
Richard de Capella, bishop of Hereford xxv, xliii, xlviii, lv, 322–3
Richard of Dover, archbishop of Canterbury xxxvi, liv, lviii
Richulf, archbishop of Mainz 218–19, 228–9, 236–7
Ricimer, consul, patrician and emperor-maker 12–13, 14–15
Ringmere, battle at 464–7
Ripon:
  monastery 112–13, 166–7, 400–1
  bishop of, see Eadhæd

De Antiquitate Glastonie Ecclesie of
434 n.
William of Sainte-Mère-Eglise, bishop of
London liv
William Turbe, bishop of Norwich
xxxvii, lx
William Warelwast, bishop of Exeter xxv,
xxxvii, xliii, xlviii, lv, lxi
Willibrord, preaches in Frisia 154–5,
156–7, 158–9, 192–3
Willigis, archbishop of Mainz 438–9,
452–3, 466–7
Wilred, bishop of Dunwich 142–3
Wilton:
battle at 298–9
plundered and burnt by Swein 454–5
convent at, Edith, a nun at 538–9
burial place 420–1, 632
bishops of, see Ramsbury, bishops of
Wiltshire:
men of, resist Mercians 230–1
army from, fights Swein 454–5
ravaged by the Danes 466–9
monasteries in 538–9
Wilzi 222–3
Wimborne, monastery of 174–5, 354–5,
356–7
Winchcombe, abbots of, see Godwine,
Godric
Winchester:
citizens of, buy peace from Swein
472–3
church built at 96–7
Edward the Confessor anointed at
534–5
Godwine dies at 572–3
New Minster at: early construction
420–1; monks installed at 416–17;
burial place 382–3, 384–5, 408–9,
432–3; Æthelgar, abbot of 436–7
Old Minster at: monks installed at
416–17; burial place 404–5, 520–1,
534–5, 566–7, 572–3; relics of St
Swithhun translated 420–1
bishops of, see Wine, Leuthere, Hædde,
Daniel, Hunfrith, Cyneheard,
Æthelheard, Ecgbald, Dudd,
Cyneberht, Ealhmund, Wigthegn,
Herefrith, Eadhun, Helmstan,
Swithhun, Ealhferth, Tunberht,
Denewulf, Frithestan, Byrnstan,
Ælfheah I, Ælfsige, Brihthelm,
Æthelwold I, Ælfheah II, Cenwulf,

Æthelwold II, Ælfwine, Stigand,
William Giffard, Henry of Blois,
Peter des Roches
Winchester, city of, citizens buy peace
from Swein 472–3
Wine, bishop of Winchester 109–10,
112–13, 116–17
Winfrith, bishop of Lichfield 122–3,
128–9
wind, in 1052 572–3
Winimar, Count Baldwin's retainer 356–7
winter, harsh:
in 914 368–9
in 1039 528–9
in 1046 542–3
Wintigis, duke of Spoleto 228–9
Winwædfeld, battle at 106–7
Wipped, Kentish warrior 14–15
Wippidesfleote, battle at 14–15
Wirund, abbot, Charlemagne's legate
228–9
Witham 368–9
Witta 4–5
Wlencing, son of Cissa 18–19
Woden:
Ælle's forebear 60–1
Alfred's forebear 262–3
Cerdic's forebear 54–5
Hengest's forebear 4–5
Ida's forebear 54–5
Penda's forebear 86–7
'Woden's Barrow' battle at 172–3
Woden's field, battle of (see also
Tettenhall) 364–5
Wodensbeorh, battle at 70–1
Womer, abbot of Ghent 433 n.
Wor, see Aldwine
Worcester:
cathedral of, conversion of clerks to
monks 418–19
burial place 452–3, 518–19
monastery at, endowed 582–3
revolt at, against Hardacnut's tax
532–5
bishops of, see Tatfrith, Bosel, Oftfor,
Ecgwine, Wilfrid, Milred,
Wærmund, Tilhere, Heathured,
Deneberht, Heahberht, Alhhun,
Wærferth, Æthelhun, Wilferth,
Cenwald, Dunstan, Oswald,
Ealdwulf, Leofsige, Brihtheah,
Lyfing, Ealdred, Wulfstan II,
Theulf,